Contemporary Literary Criticism

Guide to Thomson Gale Literary Criticism Series

For criticism on	Consult these Thomson Gale series
Authors now living or who died after December 31, 1999	*CONTEMPORARY LITERARY CRITICISM (CLC)*
Authors who died between 1900 and 1999	*TWENTIETH-CENTURY LITERARY CRITICISM (TCLC)*
Authors who died between 1800 and 1899	*NINETEENTH-CENTURY LITERATURE CRITICISM (NCLC)*
Authors who died between 1400 and 1799	*LITERATURE CRITICISM FROM 1400 TO 1800 (LC)* *SHAKESPEAREAN CRITICISM (SC)*
Authors who died before 1400	*CLASSICAL AND MEDIEVAL LITERATURE CRITICISM (CMLC)*
Authors of books for children and young adults	*CHILDREN'S LITERATURE REVIEW (CLR)*
Dramatists	*DRAMA CRITICISM (DC)*
Poets	*POETRY CRITICISM (PC)*
Short story writers	*SHORT STORY CRITICISM (SSC)*
Literary topics and movements	*HARLEM RENAISSANCE: A GALE CRITICAL COMPANION (HR)* *THE BEAT GENERATION: A GALE CRITICAL COMPANION (BG)* *FEMINISM IN LITERATURE: A GALE CRITICAL COMPANION (FL)* *GOTHIC LITERATURE: A GALE CRITICAL COMPANION (GL)*
Asian American writers of the last two hundred years	*ASIAN AMERICAN LITERATURE (AAL)*
Black writers of the past two hundred years	*BLACK LITERATURE CRITICISM (BLC)* *BLACK LITERATURE CRITICISM SUPPLEMENT (BLCS)*
Hispanic writers of the late nineteenth and twentieth centuries	*HISPANIC LITERATURE CRITICISM (HLC)* *HISPANIC LITERATURE CRITICISM SUPPLEMENT (HLCS)*
Native North American writers and orators of the eighteenth, nineteenth, and twentieth centuries	*NATIVE NORTH AMERICAN LITERATURE (NNAL)*
Major authors from the Renaissance to the present	*WORLD LITERATURE CRITICISM, 1500 TO THE PRESENT (WLC)* *WORLD LITERATURE CRITICISM SUPPLEMENT (WLCS)*

ISSN 0091-3421

Volume 221

Contemporary Literary Criticism

Criticism of the Works
of Today's Novelists, Poets, Playwrights,
Short Story Writers, Scriptwriters, and
Other Creative Writers

Jeffrey W. Hunter
PROJECT EDITOR

Detroit • New York • San Francisco • New Haven, Conn. • Waterville, Maine • London • Munich

Contemporary Literary Criticism, Vol. 221

Project Editor
Jeffrey W. Hunter, Kathy D. Darrow

Editorial
Jessica Bomarito, Gabrielle Bussey, Jelena O. Krstović, Michelle Lee, Thomas J. Schoenberg, Noah Schusterbauer, Lawrence J. Trudeau, Russel Whitaker

Data Capture
Frances Monroe, Gwen Tucker

Indexing Services
Factiva®, a Dow Jones and Reuters Company

Rights and Acquisitions
Jackie Jones, Ron Montgomery, Shalice Shah-Caldwell

Imaging and Multimedia
Dean Dauphinais, Leitha Etheridge-Sims, Lezlie Light, Mike Logusz, Dan Newell, Christine O'Bryan, Kelly A. Quin, Denay Wilding, Robyn Young

Composition and Electronic Prepress
Gary Oudersluys

Manufacturing
Rhonda Dover

Associate Product Manager
Marc Cormier

LIBRARY OF CONGRESS CATALOG CARD NUMBER 76-46132

ISBN 0-7876-7991-7
ISSN 0091-3421

Printed in the United States of America
10 9 8 7 6 5 4 3 2 1

Contents

Preface

Named "one of the twenty-five most distinguished reference titles published during the past twenty-five years" by *Reference Quarterly,* the *Contemporary Literary Criticism* (*CLC*) series provides readers with critical commentary and general information on more than 2,000 authors now living or who died after December 31, 1999. Volumes published from 1973 through 1999 include authors who died after December 31, 1959. Previous to the publication of the first volume of *CLC* in 1973, there was no ongoing digest monitoring scholarly and popular sources of critical opinion and explication of modern literature. *CLC,* therefore, has fulfilled an essential need, particularly since the complexity and variety of contemporary literature makes the function of criticism especially important to today's reader.

Scope of the Series

CLC provides significant passages from published criticism of works by creative writers. Since many of the authors covered in *CLC* inspire continual critical commentary, writers are often represented in more than one volume. There is, of course, no duplication of reprinted criticism.

Authors are selected for inclusion for a variety of reasons, among them the publication or dramatic production of a critically acclaimed new work, the reception of a major literary award, revival of interest in past writings, or the adaptation of a literary work to film or television.

Attention is also given to several other groups of writers—authors of considerable public interest—about whose work criticism is often difficult to locate. These include mystery and science fiction writers, literary and social critics, foreign authors, and authors who represent particular ethnic groups.

Each *CLC* volume contains individual essays and reviews taken from hundreds of book review periodicals, general magazines, scholarly journals, monographs, and books. Entries include critical evaluations spanning from the beginning of an author's career to the most current commentary. Interviews, feature articles, and other published writings that offer insight into the author's works are also presented. Students, teachers, librarians, and researchers will find that the general critical and biographical material in *CLC* provides them with vital information required to write a term paper, analyze a poem, or lead a book discussion group. In addition, complete bibliographical citations note the original source and all of the information necessary for a term paper footnote or bibliography.

Organization of the Book

A *CLC* entry consists of the following elements:

- The **Author Heading** cites the name under which the author most commonly wrote, followed by birth and death dates. Also located here are any name variations under which an author wrote, including transliterated forms for authors whose native languages use nonroman alphabets. If the author wrote consistently under a pseudonym, the pseudonym will be listed in the author heading and the author's actual name given in parenthesis on the first line of the biographical and critical information. Uncertain birth or death dates are indicated by question marks. Single-work entries are preceded by a heading that consists of the most common form of the title in English translation (if applicable) and the original date of composition.

- A **Portrait of the Author** is included when available.

- The **Introduction** contains background information that introduces the reader to the author, work, or topic that is the subject of the entry.

- The list of **Principal Works** is ordered chronologically by date of first publication and lists the most important works by the author. The genre and publication date of each work is given. In the case of foreign authors whose works have been translated into English, the English-language version of the title follows in brackets. Unless otherwise indicated, dramas are dated by first performance, not first publication.

- Reprinted **Criticism** is arranged chronologically in each entry to provide a useful perspective on changes in critical evaluation over time. The critic's name and the date of composition or publication of the critical work are given at the beginning of each piece of criticism. Unsigned criticism is preceded by the title of the source in which it appeared. All titles by the author featured in the text are printed in boldface type. Footnotes are reprinted at the end of each essay or excerpt. In the case of excerpted criticism, only those footnotes that pertain to the excerpted texts are included.

- A complete **Bibliographical Citation** of the original essay or book precedes each piece of criticism. Source citations in the Literary Criticism Series follow University of Chicago Press style, as outlined in *The Chicago Manual of Style,* 15th ed. (Chicago: The University of Chicago Press, 2003).

- Critical essays are prefaced by brief **Annotations** explicating each piece.

- Whenever possible, a recent **Author Interview** accompanies each entry.

- An annotated bibliography of **Further Reading** appears at the end of each entry and suggests resources for additional study. In some cases, significant essays for which the editors could not obtain reprint rights are included here. Boxed material following the further reading list provides references to other biographical and critical sources on the author in series published by Thomson Gale.

Indexes

A **Cumulative Author Index** lists all of the authors that appear in a wide variety of reference sources published by Thomson Gale, including *CLC*. A complete list of these sources is found facing the first page of the Author Index. The index also includes birth and death dates and cross references between pseudonyms and actual names.

A **Cumulative Nationality Index** lists all authors featured in *CLC* by nationality, followed by the number of the *CLC* volume in which their entry appears.

A **Cumulative Topic Index** lists the literary themes and topics treated in the series as well as in other Literature Criticism series.

An alphabetical **Title Index** accompanies each volume of *CLC*. Listings of titles by authors covered in the given volume are followed by the author's name and the corresponding page numbers where the titles are discussed. English translations of foreign titles and variations of titles are cross-referenced to the title under which a work was originally published. Titles of novels, dramas, films, nonfiction books, and poetry, short story, or essay collections are printed in italics, while individual poems, short stories, and essays are printed in roman type within quotation marks.

In response to numerous suggestions from librarians, Thomson Gale also produces an annual cumulative title index that alphabetically lists all titles reviewed in *CLC* and is available to all customers. Additional copies of this index are available upon request. Librarians and patrons will welcome this separate index; it saves shelf space, is easy to use, and is recyclable upon receipt of the next edition.

Citing *Contemporary Literary Criticism*

When citing criticism reprinted in the Literary Criticism Series, students should provide complete bibliographic information so that the cited essay can be located in the original print or electronic source. Students who quote directly from reprinted criticism may use any accepted bibliographic format, such as University of Chicago Press style or Modern Language Association (MLA) style. Both the MLA and the University of Chicago formats are acceptable and recognized as being the current standards for citations. It is important, however, to choose one format for all citations; do not mix the two formats within a list of citations.

The examples below follow recommendations for preparing a bibliography set forth in *The Chicago Manual of Style,* 15th ed. (Chicago: The University of Chicago Press, 2003); the first example pertains to material drawn from periodicals, the second to material reprinted from books:

Miller, Mae. "Patterns of Nature and Confluence in Eudora Welty's *The Optimist's Daughter."* *Southern Quarterly: A Journal of the Arts in the South* 35, no. 1 (fall 1996): 55-61. Reprinted in *Contemporary Literary Criticism.* Vol. 220, edited by Jeffrey W. Hunter, 304-09. Detroit: Thomson Gale, 2006.

Aronoff, Myron J. "Learning to Live with Ambiguity: Balancing Ethical and Political Imperatives." In *The Spy Novels of John le Carré: Balancing Ethics and Politics,* 201-14. New York: St. Martin's Press, 1999. Reprinted in *Contemporary Literary Criticism.* Vol. 220, edited by Jeffrey W. Hunter, 84-92. Detroit: Thomson Gale, 2006.

The examples below follow recommendations for preparing a works cited list set forth in the *MLA Handbook for Writers of Research Papers,* 5th ed. (New York: The Modern Language Association of America, 1999); the first example pertains to material drawn from periodicals, the second to material reprinted from books:

Miller, Mae. "Patterns of Nature and Confluence in Eudora Welty's *The Optimist's Daughter."* *Southern Quarterly: A Journal of the Arts in the South* 35.1 (fall 1996): 55-61. Reprinted in *Contemporary Literary Criticism.* Ed. Jeffrey W. Hunter. Vol. 220. Detroit: Thomson Gale, 2006. 304-09.

Aronoff, Myron J. "Learning to Live with Ambiguity: Balancing Ethical and Political Imperatives." *The Spy Novels of John le Carré: Balancing Ethics and Politics,* New York: St. Martin's Press, 1999. 201-14. Reprinted in *Contemporary Literary Criticism.* Ed. Jeffrey W. Hunter. Vol. 220. Detroit: Thomson Gale, 2006. 84-92.

Suggestions are Welcome

Readers who wish to suggest new features, topics, or authors to appear in future volumes, or who have other suggestions or comments are cordially invited to call, write, or fax the Associate Product Manager:

Associate Product Manager, Literary Criticism Series
Thomson Gale
27500 Drake Road
Farmington Hills, MI 48331-3535
1-800-347-4253 (GALE)
Fax: 248-699-8983

Acknowledgments

The editors wish to thank the copyright holders of the criticism included in this volume and the permissions managers of many book and magazine publishing companies for assisting us in securing reproduction rights. Following is a list of the copyright holders who have granted us permission to reproduce material in this volume of *CLC*. Every effort has been made to trace copyright, but if omissions have been made, please let us know.

COPYRIGHTED MATERIAL IN *CLC*, VOLUME 221, WAS REPRODUCED FROM THE FOLLOWING PERIODICALS:

The American Poetry Review, v. 31, March-April, 2002 for "Invisible Green V" by Donald Revell; v. 33, March-April, 2004 for "Across the Millennium: The Persistence of John Ashbery" by Fred Moramarco; v. 34, May-June, 2005 for "The Poet as Art Critic" by John Yau. All reproduced by permission of the authors.—*Arizona Quarterly*, v. 59, spring, 2003 for "Ashbery, O'Hara, and the Neo-Avant-Garde Manifesto" by Mark Silverberg. Copyright © 2003 by the Regents of the University of Arizona. Reproduced by permission of the publisher and the author.—*College Literature*, v. 27, fall, 2000. Copyright © 2000 by West Chester University. Reproduced by permission.—*Contemporary Literature*, v. 37, spring, 1996; v. 42, winter, 2001; v. 43, winter, 2002; v. 43, summer, 2002. Copyright © 1996, 2001, 2002 by the Board of Regents of the University of Wisconsin System. All reproduced by permission.—*Contemporary Review*, v. 280, January, 2002. Copyright © 2002 *Contemporary Review*. Reproduced by the permission of Contemporary Review Ltd.—*Cross Currents*, v. 47, summer, 1997. Copyright © 1997 by Cross Currents Inc. Reproduced by permission.—*The Georgia Review*, v. 45, summer, 1991. Copyright © 1991 by The University of Georgia. Reproduced by permission.—*History of European Ideas*, v. 20, 1995. Copyright © 1995 Elsevier Science Ltd. Reprinted with permission from Elsevier.—*The Hudson Review*, v. 50, spring, 1997; v. 55, summer, 2002. All reproduced by permission.—*The Kenyon Review*, v. 13, winter, 1991 for "Creation and the Courtesy of Reading" by Ronald A. Sharp. Copyright © 1991 by *The Kenyon Review*. Reproduced by permission of the author.—*Modern Age*, v. 36, winter, 1994; v. 42, spring, 2000; v. 47, winter, 2005. All reproduced by permission.—*The New Criterion*, v. 22, January, 2004 for "The Steiner School" by Paul Dean. Copyright © 2004 Foundation for Cultural Review. Reproduced by permission of the author.—*The New Republic*, v. 215, September 30, 1996. Copyright © 1996 by The New Republic, Inc. Reproduced by permission of The New Republic.—*New Statesman*, v. 14, March 19, 2001; v. 16, December 8, 2003. Copyright © 2001, 2003 New Statesman, Ltd. All reproduced by permission.—*19th-Century Music*, v. 18, fall, 1994 for "Men with a Past: Music and the 'Anxiety of Influence,'" by Lloyd Whitesell. Copyright © 1994 by the Regents of the University of California. All rights reserved. Republished with permission of The Regents of the University of California, conveyed through Copyright Clearance Center, Inc., and the author.—*P. N. Review*, v. ld, March-April, 1991. Copyright © Poetry Nation Review 1991. All rights reserved. Reproduced by permission of Carcanet Press Limited.—*Parnassus: Poetry in Review*, v. 28, 2005 for "Power Games" by Adam Kirsch. Copyright © 2005 Poetry in Review Foundation, NY. Reproduced by permission of the author.—*Raritan*, v. 21, fall, 2001. Copyright © 2001 by *Raritan: A Quarterly Review*. Reproduced by permission.—*Religion & Literature*, v. 22, summer-autumn, 1990; v. 28, spring, 1996. All reproduced by permission of the University of Notre Dame.—*Salmagundi*, v. 132, fall, 2001 for "Charms and Afflictions" by Calvin Bedient; summer-fall, 2002 for "A Refusal to Mourn the Fate of the Muses" by Robert Boyers. All reproduced by permission of the authors.—*Shakespeare Quarterly*, v. 54, spring, 2003. Copyright © 2003 The Johns Hopkins University Press. Reproduced by permission.—*Southern Humanities Review*, v. 36, fall, 2002 for a review of "Grammars of Creation" by Gene Fendt. Copyright 2002 by Auburn University. Reproduced by permission of the author.—*Southwest Review*, v. 87, 2002. Copyright © 2002 Southern Methodist University. All rights reserved. Reproduced by permission.—*The Spectator*, v. 279, September 6, 1997; v. 286, March 31, 2001. Copyright © 1997, 2001 by *The Spectator*. All reproduced by permission of *The Spectator*.—*Studies in Short Fiction*, v. 31, fall, 1994. Copyright © 1994 by *Studies in Short Fiction*. Reproduced by permission.—*Studies in the Novel*, v. 34, winter, 2002. Copyright © 2002 by North Texas State University. Reproduced by permission.—*Style*, v. 38, spring, 2004. Copyright © Style, 2004. All rights reserved. Reproduced by permission of the publisher.—*Theology Today*, v. 47, January, 1991 for "The Startling Testimony of George Steiner" by Frank Burch Brown; v. 59, July, 2002 for a review of George Steiner's *Grammars of Creation* by Carver T. Yu. All reproduced by permission of the publisher and authors.—*University of Toronto Quarterly*, v. 73, summer, 2004. Copyright © 2004 by University of Toronto Press. Reproduced by permission of University of Toronto Press Incorporated.—*Victorian Poetry*, v. 41, summer, 2003 for "War of the Winds: Shelley, Hardy, and Harold Bloom," by Martin Bidney. Copyright © West Virginia University, 2003. Reproduced by permission of the author.—*The Virginia Quarterly Review*, v. 80, spring, 2004. Copyright 2004, by *The Virginia Quarterly Review*, The University of Virginia. Reproduced by permission of the publisher.—*The Wallace Stevens Journal*, v. 26, fall, 2002. Copyright © 2002 The Wal-

Thomson Gale Literature Product Advisory Board

The members of the Thomson Gale Literature Product Advisory Board—reference librarians from public and academic library systems—represent a cross-section of our customer base and offer a variety of informed perspectives on both the presentation and content of our literature products. Advisory board members assess and define such quality issues as the relevance, currency, and usefulness of the author coverage, critical content, and literary topics included in our series; evaluate the layout, presentation, and general quality of our printed volumes; provide feedback on the criteria used for selecting authors and topics covered in our series; provide suggestions for potential enhancements to our series; identify any gaps in our coverage of authors or literary topics, recommending authors or topics for inclusion; analyze the appropriateness of our content and presentation for various user audiences, such as high school students, undergraduates, graduate students, librarians, and educators; and offer feedback on any proposed changes/enhancements to our series. We wish to thank the following advisors for their advice throughout the year.

John Ashbery

1927-

(Full name John Lawrence Ashbery; also wrote under the pseudonym Jonas Berry) American poet, critic, playwright, essayist, and novelist.

The following entry presents criticism of Ashbery's works through 2005. For further discussion of his life and career, see *CLC*, Volumes 2, 3, 4, 6, 9, 13, 15, 25, 41, 77, and 125.

INTRODUCTION

Ashbery is considered a prominent voice in postwar American poetry. Frequently cited as the foremost representative of the 1950s New York School of poets, Ashbery has explored the complex and elusive relationship between language, perception, time, and artistic expression throughout his oeuvre. His signature style of verse is marked by random associations, conversational speech, rhetorical equivocation, and sudden moments of lyrical intensity. Though Ashbery's fixation with the powers of abstraction and identification inherent in language is sometimes characterized as impenetrable, the casual, even humorous, inflection of Ashbery's poetry continues to draw attention to the challenging discourse underlying his work.

BIOGRAPHICAL INFORMATION

Ashbery was born in Rochester, New York, and raised in Sodus, a small town near Lake Ontario. The eldest son of Chester Frederick, a fruit farmer, and Helen Ashbery, a biology teacher, he showed an early interest in the arts, taking painting classes until age fifteen. At age thirteen Ashbery suffered the death of his brother, four years his junior, to leukemia. In 1943, soon after disclosing his homosexuality to his mother, Ashbery left home for Deerfield Academy, where his first poems were published in the school journal. He was accepted at Harvard University in 1945, and befriended poets Frank O'Hara and Kenneth Koch while serving on the editorial board of the *Harvard Advocate*. After earning his B.A. in 1949, Ashbery moved to New York City to pursue a master's degree in French literature from Columbia University, which he received in 1951. During his stay in New York, Ashbery became involved in the postwar arts scene, socializing and collaborating with a group of avant-garde intellectuals—including O'Hara, Koch, poet James Schuyler, and painters Larry Rivers and Jane Freilicher—which became known as the New York School. His first, limited-edition volume of poetry, *Turandot*, was published in 1953, featuring illustrations by Freilicher. While working as a copyeditor for McGraw-Hill and Oxford University Press, Ashbery began publishing dramas, which he later collected in *Three Plays* (1978). His second volume of verse, *Some Trees* (1956), was selected by poet W. H. Auden as the winner of the Yale Series of Younger Poets competition. He briefly taught elementary French at New York University, but soon left for Paris upon receiving two Fulbright scholarships.

Ashbery spent the subsequent decade in France, contributing poetry and art criticism to the *New York Herald Tribune* and *Art International,* and working as an editor for *Locus Solus* and *Art and Literature.* His next collection, *The Tennis Court Oath,* was published in 1962, winning the Harriet Monroe Poetry Award. After returning to New York in 1965, Ashbery began working as the executive editor of *ARTnews,* as an art critic for both *New York* and *Newsweek,* and as a poetry editor for the *Partisan Review.* From 1974 to 1990 he served as co-director of the M.F.A. program in creative writing at Brooklyn College, City University of New York and accepted a post as the Charles P. Stevenson, Jr. Professor of Language and Literature at Bard College in 1990. Ashbery was honored with the Robert Frost Medal from the Poetry Society of America in 1995 and the Gold Medal for Poetry from the American Academy of Arts and Letters in 1997. In 2001 he was awarded the prestigious Signet Society Medal for Achievement in the Arts from Harvard University as well as the Wallace Stevens Award from the Academy of American Poets. Ashbery was designated the State Poet of New York from 2001 to 2003, and the order of France's Légion d'Honneur was conferred upon him in 2002.

MAJOR WORKS

Although a disjointed, surrealistic compositional style and an informal tone are characteristic of all of his collections, Ashbery's early verse is most closely associated with the New York School of poetry. Such works as *Some Trees, Rivers and Mountains* (1966), and *The Double Dream of Spring* (1970) reflect the influence of the visual arts on his writing and incorporate avant-garde techniques generally linked to abstract expressionism. For example, "Europe" and "The Skaters," two poems from early in Ashbery's career, each consist of rearranged passages from early twentieth-century children's books. While the concept for these poems is modeled after the collage method prevalent in avant-garde painting and plastic arts, Ashbery's choice of source material reflects his preoccupation with popular culture and marginal, disparaged, or overtly commercial literature. Comprised entirely of prose poetry, *Three Poems* (1972) marks Ashbery's shift toward a more accessible, contemplative writing style. The overall tone of the volume is casual, yet urgent, as Ashbery's meditations on the nature of language and writing call upon history, philosophy, religion, and mundane observation to illuminate the larger systems and organizational principles at work in the world.

Winner of the Pulitzer Prize, National Book Award, and National Book Critics Circle Award, *Self-Portrait in a Convex Mirror* (1975) is widely considered Ashbery's masterpiece. The lengthy title poem, inspired by a painting of the sixteenth-century artist Francesco Parmigianino, explores the difficulties of assigning a specific form to the complex state of consciousness from which artistic creation springs. The author's concerns with mainstream culture, stylistic experimentation, and creative writing are apparent in *Houseboat Days* (1977). Representative poems from this collection include "And *Ut Pictura Poesis* Is Her Name," which ponders the relationship between poetry and painting, and "Daffy Duck in Hollywood," which depicts a fractured version of modern American society. Ashbery demonstrated a new poetic format in "Litany," from *As We Know* (1979). Written in parallel columns that cover sixty pages, "Litany" provides a simultaneous discussion of Ashbery's belief in both the limitations and endless potential of the written word. *Flow Chart* (1991) is a pastiche of personal memory, literary allusion, extraneous fragments of daily experience, and internal dialogue. Written over the course of six months, in six sections, this book-length poem focuses primarily on the ability of language to either hinder or forge interpersonal connections. *Girls on the Run,* (1999), another book-length poem, is based upon a children's story written by "outsider" artist and recluse Henry Darger. The work's fractured syntax, bizarre imagery, and tone of mock-innocence hearken back to Ashbery's early poems.

A sense of buoyancy mixed with solemnity pervades Ashbery's other collections of the last decade, most notably *Wakefulness* (1998), *Chinese Whispers* (2002), and *Where Shall I Wander* (2005). The poems in these recent volumes exhibit a contented, humorous attitude toward aging and express an understated acceptance of mortality, incorporating rare autobiographical elements. "The History of My Life," from *Your Name Here* (2000), for instance, begins by mentioning the death of a younger brother, an event which draws comparisons to Ashbery's own experiences. Ashbery's myriad critical essays and reviews have been collected throughout his career. *Reported Sightings* (1989) contains art criticism dating back to his years in France, *Other Traditions* (2000) was originally delivered as a series of lectures on the study of minor poets, and *Selected Prose* (2004) assembles a number of essays on literature and the visual arts.

CRITICAL RECEPTION

Ashbery is revered as one of the leading poets of his generation and a powerful influence in contemporary American letters. Though some critics initially accused him of intentional obscurity and ostentation, Ashbery's challenging and idiosyncratic verse has met with increasingly high praise over the past five decades. Moreover, the overwhelming critical success and widespread scholarly acceptance of both *Self-Portrait in a Convex Mirror* and subsequent collections has prompted a critical reevaluation of Ashbery's earlier, more experimental poems. Specifically, scholars have examined the influence of the Parisian arts scene on the construction of *The Tennis Court Oath,* and have affirmed the diversity of the New York School by juxtaposing the avant-garde aesthetic of Ashbery with that of Frank O'Hara. Additionally, Ashbery's primary poetic influence has been a source of debate, with some critics viewing him as the successor to Wallace Stevens, and others underscoring his indebtedness to W. H. Auden. Recent studies have focused on the importance of humor and camp in Ashbery's poetry, and his recurring concern with the representational qualities of language is likened to the metaphysical philosophy of Martin Heidegger. Other critical analyses have examined his art criticism as a guide to understanding his verse. Reviewers have lauded Ashbery's steady proliferation of work since *Wakefulness,* finding the poet's playful use of cliché an intriguing counterpoint to the otherwise elegiac sense of summation surrounding his later volumes.

PRINCIPAL WORKS

Turandot: And Other Poems (poetry) 1953
Some Trees (poetry) 1956
The Tennis Court Oath: A Book of Poems (poetry) 1962
Rivers and Mountains (poetry) 1966
Selected Poems (poetry) 1967
A Nest of Ninnies [with James Schuyler] (novel) 1969
The Double Dream of Spring (poetry) 1970
Three Poems (poetry) 1972

CRITICISM

Peter Nicholls (essay date 2000)

SOURCE: Nicholls, Peter. "John Ashbery and Language Poetry." In *Poetry and the Sense of Panic: Critical Essays on Elizabeth Bishop and John Ashbery,* edited by Lionel Kelly, pp. 155-67. Amsterdam: Rodopi, 2000.

[*In the following essay, Nicholls concentrates on the experimental poems in* The Tennis Court Oath, *and addresses the critical debate over the alleged superiority of Ashbery's later, more lyrical style.*]

The connection between John Ashbery and the Language poets is important for several reasons. In the first place, the way in which we read Ashbery perhaps more than any other contemporary American poet situates us, defines our position in relation to an artistic practice which, it seems to me, is ever more divided against itself. To put this another way, consider the following proposition from a well-known essay by Joseph Epstein published in the magazine *Commentary* in 1988. Epstein begins with a daunting question: "Who killed Poetry?" he asks. His answer is as follows:

Institutional, linguistic, historical factors have also doubtless exerted their influence in pushing poetry into the dark corner it now inhabits. Yet nearly every explanation of the situation of poetry in our time . . . seems to let the poets themselves off the hook.[1]

Poets, it seems, don't write what people want to read, and even though more and more work is being produced, with creative writing programmes ever in the ascendant, poetry in America has been driven into a "dark corner". It is possible, though, to read this situation very differently, as does Language poet Ron Silliman in his afterword to a recently published anthology of contemporary poetry: "[W]e in North America", claims Silliman, "are living in a poetic renaissance unparalleled in our history".[2] Poetry, it seems, is either dead or exuberantly alive, and this quite staggering difference in view typifies a widening rift in American literary culture, a rift of disagreement which turns less on whether a particular poem is any good or not, but on whether it actually deserves to be called a poem at all.

A brief quotation from Language poet Charles Bernstein puts a finger on the problem. This is from his poem-essay called "Artifice of Absorption"; Bernstein is considering Helen Vendler's introduction to *The Harvard Book of Contemporary American Poetry*:

. . . perhaps the most irritating thing about Vendler's manner of argument is that it is always referring to what "all" poems do, making it impossible for her to even consider that some poems may come into being just because they don't do what some other poems have done. Vendler says she hopes readers will be provoked by some of the anthologized poems to say— "Heavens, I recognize the place, I know it!" I would hope readers might be provoked to say of *some* poems, "Hell, I don't recognize the place or the time of the 'I' in this sentence. I don't know it."[3]

The flashpoint of disagreement is an exemplary one: for Vendler, a great poem restores the world to us as something new yet familiar—"It insists," she says, "on a spooling, a form of repetition, the reinscribing of a groove, the returning upon an orbit already traced."[4] For Bernstein, however, that looping back upon an experience already lived produces only a kind of epistemological deadlock. For him, the linguistic world of the poem is a radically disjunctive one where the subject may easily misrecognize itself and others. In Vendler's view, poets "attempt that accuracy—of perception, of style"; Bernstein comments, "& what does accuracy have to do with it anyway?" This rejection of the residual mimeticism Bernstein finds in Vendler's position indicates a fundamental divergence or, indeed, an unbridgeable difference in aesthetic thinking. For the writing Bernstein represents—a writing which is "language—centered", deploying strategies of "diminished reference"—this writing spurns the allegedly second-order experience of "re-cognition" and accepts nothing but itself by which to measure its own "accuracy". One cannot but be impressed by the distance which separates Vendler and Bernstein; it is unlikely, one might think, that their bookshelves contain many of the same contemporary poets.

It is here that Ashbery's work occupies a pivotal position, for with the partial exception of Wallace Stevens he is the one recent poet to be admired on both sides of the poetry divide. Not that he is admired in exactly the same way, of course, for, as is well-known, it is precisely the part of Ashbery's work that so upset Harold Bloom which has exerted a lasting appeal for many of the Language poets. This is the Ashbery of the 1962 volume *The Tennis Court Oath,* notable in Helen Vendler's view for its "wilful flashiness and sentimentality".[5] Of course, it helps if Bloom and Vendler are so negative about these poems—as Geoff Ward puts it in *Statutes of Liberty,* "if Harold Bloom dislikes them so intensely, there must be something in them".[6] As presumably there must, since the poets who have admired them—poets like Bruce Andrews, Barrett Watten and Susan Howe—are something more than the "rabblement of poetasters" Bloom intemperately described as the book's main audience. What is striking is the consensus amongst these writers about the central importance of *The Tennis Court Oath.* Bruce Andrews, for example, writes to Lyn Hejinian in 1978 that "(It is his most important book, even if Ashbery is now too scared or heedless to recognize it) . . .",[7] and in a piece called "Misrepresentation (A Text for *The Tennis Court Oath* of John Ashbery)", Andrews declares that the volume "poses for us a radical questioning of established forms, yet at the same time, and so appropriately in its own form, it explores the implications of that questioning—not as an idea, but as an experience and a *reading*".[8] Susan Howe has similarly testified to the volume's importance to her development,[9] and Barrett Watten has written in some detail about the general impact of *The Tennis Court Oath* and its particular relevance to the work of Clark Coolidge.[10] Perhaps not surprisingly, this way of seeing Ashbery's career in terms of an early radicalism later sold short reappears in the work of some of the pro-Language critics. Jerome McGann, for example, sees Ashbery's work after 1972 as a falling away from innovation and a growing cultivation of what he calls "suburban and personal interests".[11]

In what follows I shall be less concerned with this representation of Ashbery's later career than with the significance of *The Tennis Court Oath* as an apparently pivotal text. For with the benefit of some critical hindsight it is easy to see how various features of this volume might provide a forceful example for poets like Bruce Andrews. While, as John Shoptaw observes, the poems are not uniformly disruptive,[12] the work is marked by a mordantly humorous management of genre,

voice and context. The most striking poems from this point of view are those which set the pronominal self adrift in a kaleidoscopic whirl of tones and idioms. (The technique, of course, would become a recurring feature of Ashbery's work, though the aggressive abruptness of the self's mutations in *The Tennis Court Oath* would be eased into the more sinuous mutations of the extended period in many of the later volumes.) Ashbery has often commented on this aspect of his writing—for example: "I find it very easy to move from one person in the sense of a pronoun to another and this again helps to produce a kind of polyphony in my poetry. . . ."[13] Pronouns are thus envisaged as merely linguistic items rather than distinct positionalities, and this dissolution of the self in writing would have important reverberations for younger poets. In the interview from which I have quoted, for example, Ashbery goes on to remark "a loosening of syntactical connections that allows experience to happen rather than to make sense".

It is not just a case, then, of fractioning the self into different "voices", but of defining subjectivity as a process which unfolds as the poem, ostensibly without an end in view. Compare this comment by Rae Armantrout, one of the most interesting of the Language poets:

> The pronouns are fairly arbitrary in my poetry. I would imagine this is so for many other writers as well. Like the characters in dreams, pronouns are aspects of oneself. I may choose a pronoun for the tone it creates. For instance, using *you* can make a poem sound either seductive or confrontational. I provide *little* context for these pronouns partly because I am not necessarily trying to establish them as solid identities, separate from myself. I'm interested in the multiplicity, and also the duplicity, of inner voices . . . the ideation is the process of forming ideas—that is more than one. Thinking may be mainly sensing relations. I can connect ideation in this way with my interest in internal voices.[14]

Armantrout's way of linking multiplicity with duplicity has a curious relevance to the work I am considering here. It is as if, for Ashbery, the force of the lyric convention and the range of its "authentic" voices are so powerful that the poet is compelled to take evasive action. In the first place, the poems are radically decontextualised; the more detail we are given, the less securely situated the language seems to be (as Bruce Andrews observes, "a welter of adjectives has not added up to an external world").[15] Yet while there is an obvious fascination with forms of concealment and hiding in the poems—Ashbery constantly conjures with clues which have dropped out of detective stories—the question remains as to what was there to be hidden in the first place. If there is, as he says in the much later *Self-Portrait* [*Self-Portrait in a Convex Mirror*], "no point of view / like the 'I' in a novel",[16] we can begin to see how the Language poets might have found hints of their own view, that (in Barrett Watten's words) "inner speech is social", and that "there is a substrate in which 'language' itself speaks, not just is spoken by a speaker".[17] In *The Tennis Court Oath,* Ashbery clearly taps one vein of the tradition running through Dada and Surrealism for which, once more in Watten's words, "language and psyche (are) a kind of vast reservoir for collage".[18] It is the *principle* of collage which is important here, rather than the materials themselves. In what is in one sense almost a parody of Poundian modernism, Ashbery tends to choose trivial, often banal texts on which to work. John Shoptaw's account of the poem **"Europe"** and its debt to *Beryl of the By-plane,* for example, tells us much about Ashbery's methods of composition but it does not really help us to understand the poem any better. Indeed, the customary use here of ellipsis (the "leaving out business"[19]) and the pseudo-declarative sentence not only block immediate under-standing but assert its impossibility, even its undesir-ability.

This is a poetry of "how it feels, not what it means", as Ashbery puts it in the later *Houseboat Days,*[20] a poetry in which "thought" is not something to be articulated but rather something that is encountered in the making of the poem ("I always begin at zero", says Ashbery, "and discover my thought by writing"; compare Lyn Hejinian's related observation, that "where one once sought a vocabulary for ideas, now one seeks ideas for vocabularies"[21]). It is this aspect of *The Tennis Court Oath* which now seems so prescient, so indicative of things to come. For this reordering of priorities denies us the forms of identification we assume from conven-tional lyric at the same time as it also blocks the sort of hermeneutic impulse encouraged by *The Cantos* or *The Maximus Poems.* Take the first stanza of **"Leaving the Atocha Station"**, a celebrated or, depending on how you look at it, infamous example of Ashbery's new style:

> The arctic honey blabbed over the report causing dark-
> ness
> And pulling us our of there experiencing it
> he meanwhile . . . And the fried bats they sell there
> dropping from sticks, so that the menace of your
> prayer folds . . .
> Other people . . .   flash
> the garden are you boning
> and defunct covering . . .   Blind dog expressed
> royalties . . .
> comfort of your perfect tar grams nuclear world bank
> tulip
> Favourable to   near the night pin
> loading formaldehyde.   the table torn from you
> Suddenly   and we are close
> Mouthing the root   when you think
> generator   homes enjoy leered[22]

Ellipses and typographical spaces produce moments where sense simply fails, and in that failure we are meant to discover both pleasure and a certain eerie

foreboding of incompletion. For poems like this (to adapt what Charles Bernstein has said of Clark Coolidge) "refuse . . . the syntactic ideality of the complete sentence, in which each part of speech oper-ates in its definable place so that a grammatic paradigm is superimposed on the actual unfolding of the semantic strings".[23] If there is something a little too cute about some of Ashbery's periphrastic moves here—"tar grams" for "cigarettes", for instance—any attempt to transcode the lines confronts us with an unrelenting banality (as in Shoptaw's gloss for the "blind dog" lines: "While reading the newspaper . . . and smoking . . . we watched the seeing eye dog dig up a tulip garden for a buried bone"[24]). It is the rapidity of the transitions—often, as for the Language poets, a result of suppressing transitive verbs in favour of passive constructions and unhooked participles—which would make this volume so significant for later experimental writers. As Andrews observes, in *The Tennis Court Oath* "the construction is not a shawl, enveloping & smoothing the shifts, as in later work, but is at the heart of our experiencing these shifts at all—the jagged kaleidoscope of melancholia and expiration".[25]

One way of describing this effect is to say that syntax has somehow become absolute (or "total", to use Bar-rett Watten's word). To put it another way, the poem has set its face against what Andrews calls "communica-tive competence" and in doing so has repudiated any notion of linguistic "transparency".[26] It is here perhaps that we can see Ashbery's relation to a particular ver-sion of Surrealism. What is at issue is less the poetics of dream imagery than a sense of the anti-referentiality of some Surrealist language. This is Surrealism as, for example, William Carlos Williams had understood it in the thirties: "Surrealism does not lie. It is the single truth. It is an epidemic. It is. It is just words".[27] That view of Surrealism not as a poetics of the inner life but as a practice of *writing* is the one which helps us to understand how "Surrealism" could become a sort of portmanteau word for an alternative non-image based poetics in America running from Gertrude Stein to the Language writers ("It is simple," wrote Williams, "There is no symbolism, no evocation of an image").[28]

There is plenty of straightforwardly Surrealist imagery in Ashbery's poems, of course ("the spoon of your head", and so on,[29] the kind of thing exploited by the more "orthodox" of Breton's American followers such as Kenneth Patchen and Charles Henri Ford). Yet the line of development in which we might situate Ashbery is actually closer to what has frequently been called "literary Cubism", a tendency best represented by one of his favourite poets, Pierre Reverdy. It was Reverdy, of course, who gave Breton the original definition of the Surrealist image as "a pure creation of the mind. It cannot be born from a comparison but from a juxtaposi-tion of two more or less distant realities".[30] But where

Reverdy differed from Breton was in the latter's refusal of any conscious "juxtaposition": "In my opinion", wrote Breton, "it is erroneous to claim that 'the mind has grasped the relationship' of two realities in the presence of each other. First of all, it has seized nothing consciously".[31] The difference in emphasis is finely caught in Kenneth Rexroth's account of Reverdy's work:

> Poetry such as this attempts not just a new syntax of the word. Its revolution is aimed at the syntax of the mind itself. Its restructuring of experience is purposive, not dreamlike, and hence it possesses an uncanniness fundamentally different in kind from the most haunted utterances of the Surrealist or Symbolist unconscious.[32]

The "restructuring" of which Rexroth speaks is primarily a praxis of writing, not of recollection; and it is here that we can begin to discern a sort of faultline which separates the canonical works of Anglo-American modernism—*The Waste Land, The Cantos, Paterson, A*—from what Rexroth calls "literary cubism". In the great modernist works, says Rexroth:

> . . . as in Apollinaire's "Zone", the elements, the primary data of the poetic construction, are narrative or at least informative wholes. In verse such as Reverdy's, they are simple, sensory, emotional or primary informative objects capable of little or no further reduction. Eliot works in *The Waste Land* with fragmented and recombined arguments; Pierre Reverdy with dismembered propositions from which subject, operator and object have been wrenched free and re-structured into an invisible or subliminal discourse which owes its cogency to its own strict, complex and secret logic.[33]

So in place of the unconscious as an absent scene to be represented we have this "secret logic" which, for Ashbery, entails a constant movement between "meaningfulness" and "randomness", as he puts it.[34] The terms Rexroth uses here—"dismembered", "wrenched"—point up the violence which shadows this act of poetic "reduction", a violence which in *The Tennis Court Oath* attends both the literary echo and the twisted references to "ordinary" speech. What results is a certain linguistic *opacity*, which is rather different from the referential *difficulty* or "the eternal dead weight of symbolism and allegory" which Ashbery finds in Eliot, Pound, Yeats and Joyce.[35] As Bernstein suggests in another context, we are witnessing a "shift of attention from the rhetorical effect (the thing said/depicted) to the rhetoricity",[36] by which he seems to mean that the primary focus of our reading now proves to be the prosodic intersection of different registers and idioms. And with this goes an emphasis on reading as a productive act—the reader not now working to restore a context to the poem on the page, to reconstitute fragmented propositions and bits of knowledge, but engaged rather in what Lyn Hejinian calls a "generative" as opposed to a "directive" reading: "Reader and writer engage in a collaboration from

which ideas and meanings are permitted to evolve".[37] This is not just some sort of free play, however, at least not in theory, for the Language poets are intensely interested in the ways in which readers interpret messages whose context they cannot assume.[38] In such cases, a powerful self-consciousness is developed, one paralleling that of the writer. As syntax departs increasingly from the normative structures of everyday exchange, so the breakdown of simple, extrapolable "meaning" yields a proliferation of social frames or contexts, often triggered at the level of the individual word. In Bernstein's words, "Meaning is no where *bound* to the orbit of purpose, intention, or utility",[39] and when it escapes it reveals language as an endlessly rich but common environment.

It is here that we can begin to approach the limits of Ashbery's interest for the Language poets, for as Christopher Beach observes, Ashbery "does not appear to be deeply committed to a fundamental critique of language itself or of its operations within a social or ideological context".[40] Nonetheless, Ashbery's experiments in *The Tennis Court Oath* surely implied a sort of negative knowledge of social discourse which had a significant impact on early Language poetry. I am thinking particularly of some of the more extreme effects here, effects which create what is a now familiar packing or jamming of the poetic line (as in the passage which so dismayed Bloom in **"Leaving the Atocha Station"**: "for that we turn around / experiencing it is not to go into / the epileptic prank forcing bar. To borrow out onto tide-exposed fells / over her morsel", etc.[41]). Ashbery's lines might be said to produce, in Bernstein's phrase, a deliberate "viscosity of thought"[42] which requires us to consider not only the obtrusive materiality of words, but also the tendency they have to swerve away from the paths of normal communication. Take, for example, Ashbery's use of what Shoptaw calls "crypt words", by which he means "both a puzzle, something encoded, and a burial plot, something hidden, forgotten, or simply covered over":[43] For instance, "it all came / gushing down on me", where the crypt word is "crashing", or "emotions / The crushed paper heaps", where "crushed hopes" gives the encrypted echo; or, in **"Leaving the Atocha Station"**, "establishing the vultural over / rural area cough pollution", where the crypt word is presumably "cultural" ("culture vulture"?). Shoptaw's idea of a cryptonymic reading (drawn from the psychoanalytic theory of Nicolas Abraham and Maria Torok) is suggestive, though not pursued in sufficient detail to make it fully convincing. Indeed, one might wonder whether the very idea of a readability, at which cryptonomy aims, is misplaced in relation to *The Tennis Court Oath,* for when the apparently effaced word is restored, what we acknowledge is not exactly a repression—whose would it be?—but rather the jarring proximity of "poetic" to everyday language.

Ashbery, of course, would continue to be fascinated by the intricacies of everyday language, by its cliches and platitudes, yet this fascination would increasingly produce a play of tones and voices caught up within the paradoxically monological order of a reflective language. I generalise too much, perhaps, yet one can see how the measured movements of a poem like **"Self-Portrait in a Convex Mirror"** might disappoint admirers of *The Tennis Court Oath.* For their part, the Language writers have variously—very variously, as Douglas Messerli's recent anthology demonstrates[44]—pursued forms of linguistic opacity in the conviction that this is the way to avoid the commonplace imaginary of expressive conventions and to confront instead the determining forces of language. It is important to grasp the political locatedness of this endeavour, for Language writing had its origins in the Vietnam period, as Lyn Hejinian has observed. When questioned in interview about the collectivity of writers associated with Language, she explained that "We discovered each other in the intense aftermath of the Vietnam war era, having had intense experience of institutions and disguised rationality. And by some coincidence, we all individually had begun to consider language itself as an institution of sorts, determining reasons, and we had individually begun to explore the implications of that".[45] What that exploration has often entailed are extreme forms of self-reflexivity in language use, forms which exceed lyric self-interrogation. Barrett Watten, for example, writes of one of Steve Benson's performances that:

> the performer acts out a continually reflexive encounter with his language, trying to hear what it is saying and respond verbally at all points. The total self-involvement can only undermine its own authority; the other is rendered intact, but it is simultaneously the speaking subject that is the other. Benson's work casts the shadows of lyrical self-consciousness in Ashbery and O'Hara into the light of public discourse.[46]

For many of the Language writers, that move toward "public discourse" has been the crucial one, and while many of their most powerful devices may have been learned from Ashbery and O'Hara, their push toward extreme forms of opacity has been intended to open an ethical dimension of writing more expanded than anything attempted in the lyric mode, however ironized. I want to conclude with some problematic, though characteristic, propositions from Charles Bernstein. To support his view that "Language is the commonness in being", Bernstein proposes that:

> The move from purely descriptive, outward directive, writing toward writing centered on its wordness, its physicality, its haecceity (thisness) is, in its impulse, an investigation of human self-sameness, of the place of our connection: in the world, in the word, in ourselves.[47]

Note how Bernstein takes linguistic opacity not simply as a means by which to enact or embody certain forms of mental process. For him, to grasp the "wordness" of writing, as he puts it, is also to understand language as "the place of our connection". If poetic language is "political", then, it is apparently because it can make a certain practice of reading the basis of an ethical relation which has been exiled from the conventional category of the aesthetic—this is, though, an "ethics" in almost the Levinasian sense, a recognition of the claims of others rather than a body of moral rules and values. We can now begin to see how far poets like Bernstein have travelled from the disruptive moment of *The Tennis Court Oath* at the same time as making its necessity absolute. For any kind of "clarity" or "transparency" is now taken to signal a lapse into conventional formalism. This is what Bernstein has to say about George Oppen, a poet whose major work, we remember, was appearing around the time of *The Tennis Court Oath* and who, more persistently than Ashbery, tried to construct a "social" poetics. Bernstein suggests that while Oppen manages to understand language as "the place of our connection", for him the temptation often still remains to speak *about* that connection. Bernstein notes acutely that Oppen's:

> often claimed commitment to clarity, however qualified annuls a number of possibilities inherent in his technique . . . That is, he tends, at times, to fall back onto "clarity" as a self-justifying means of achieving resolution through scenic motifs, statement, or parable in poems that might, given his compositional techniques, outstrip such controlling impulses.[48]

Bernstein's observation invites us—rightly, I think—to read Oppen's work as a sort of hinge between modernism and Language poetry. In each case, he implies, a certain opacity in the writing directs attention away from self-expression toward language as the medium of social connection. Ashbery's work has moved in a different direction, though the experimental vein of *The Tennis Court Oath* seems to have gestured toward this horizon. We might think that Ashbery's refusal of linguistic opacity was wise; or we might think that it led him to then produce affecting but ultimately comfortable work. Either way, the development of the devices of *The Tennis Court Oath* in Language poetry leave us to confront one of the major paradoxes of contemporary American writing: namely that its pursuit of a "commonness" in language has become wedded to forms of often intractable linguistic opacity. Does that, finally, relegate poetry to Epstein's "dark corner", or does it testify to Silliman's unparalleled "poetic renaissance"? The question is not one to be too hastily resolved, though Ashbery's work seems—tantalisingly and magisterially—to countenance both possibilities.

Notes

1. Joseph Epstein, "Who Killed Poetry?", in *Commentary,* 86.2 (August 1988), 17.

2. Ron Silliman, "The Practice of Art", in Dennis Barone and Peter Ganick, eds. *The Art of Practice: Forty-Five Contemporary Poets,* Elmwood, 1994,

377. This volume is intended as a kind of supplement to two earlier path-breaking anthologies, Ron Silliman's *In the American Tree,* Orono, 1986, and Douglas Messerli's *"Language" Poetries: An Anthology,* New York, 1987. In his afterword to *The Art of Practice,* Silliman projects yet another wave of contemporary writing, giving a long list of younger poets deserving of consideration.

3. Charles Bernstein, *A Poetics,* Cambridge, MA, 1992, 42.

4. Helen Vendler, "Introduction" to *The Harvard Book Of Contemporary American Poetry,* Cambridge, MA, 1985, 2.

5. Helen Vendler, "Understanding Ashbery", in Harold Bloom, ed. *Modern Critical Views: John Ashbery,* New York, 1985, 180. For Bloom's dismissal of *The Tennis Court Oath,* see his "The Charity of Hard Moments", *ibid.,* 52. As noted in John Shoptaw, *On the Outside Looking Out: John Ashbery's Poetry,* Cambridge, MA, 1994, 125, the other influential text for the Language writers has been Ashbery's *Three Poems.*

6. Geoff Ward, *Statutes of Liberty: The New York School of Poets,* London, 1993, 110.

7. Bruce Andrews, letter to Lyn Hejinian, in The Lyn Hejinian Papers, Mandeville Department of Special Collections, University of California at San Diego, Box 1, Folder 6, May 27, 1978.

8. Bruce Andrews, "Misrepresentation (A Text for *The Tennis Court Oath* of John Ashbery)", in Ron Silliman ed. *In The American Tree,* Orono, 1986, 522.

9. Shoptaw, 42.

10. Barrett Watten, *Total Syntax,* Carbondale and Edwardsvile, 1985, 90-91. See also George Hartley, *Textual Poetics and the Language Poets,* Boomington and Indianapolis, 1989, 23.

11. Jerome McGann, "Contemporary Poetry, Alternate Routes", *Critical Inquiry,* XIII, Spring, 1987, 627. See also Andrew Ross, "The New Sentence and the Commodity Form: Recent American Writing", in Cary Nelson and Lawrence Grossberg, eds *Marxism and the Interpretation of Culture,* London, 1988, 370. For a critique of this view of Ashbery's development, see Vernon Shetley, *After the Death of Poetry: Poet and Audience in Contemporary America,* Durham NC and London, 1983, 144-48.

12. Shoptaw, *On the Outside Looking Out,* 44. "Only a third of the volume's poems aggressively disrupt grammar, syntax, punctuation and physical layout. The rest are written in an 'intermediate' style and some (ten or so) would not be out of pace in *Some Trees.*"

13. Interview with Ashbery in 1972 quoted in Marjorie Perloff, *Poetic License: Essays on Modernist and Postmodernist Lyric,* Evanston, 1990, 280.

14. Interview in Manuel Brito, *A Suite of Poetic Voices: Interviews with Contemporary American Poets,* Santa Brigida, 1992, 19-20.

15. Bruce Andrews, "Misrepresentation: (A Text for *The Tennis Court Oath* of John Ashbery)", 525.

16. John Ashbery, *Self-Portrait in a Convex Mirror,* Manchester, 1977, 56.

17. Manuel Brito, "An Interview with Barrett Watten", in Ron Smith, ed. *Aerial 8: Barrett Watten,* Washington, DC, 1995, 27, 29.

18. Barrett Watten, *Total Syntax,* 40.

19. John Ashbery, "The Skaters" in *Rivers and Mountains,* New York, 1977, 144.

20. John Ashbery, "Saying It to Keep It from Happening", in *Houseboat Days,* Harmondsworth, 1978, 29.

21. Ashbery quoted in Shoptaw, *On the Outside Looking Out,* 6. Lyn Hejinian, "If Written is Writing", in Bruce Andrews and Charles Bernstein, eds *The L=A=N=G=U=A=G=E Book,* Carbondale and Edwardsville, 1984, 29.

22. John Ashbery, *The Tennis Court Oath,* Middletown, 1982, 33.

23. Charles Bernstein, *A Poetics,* 60.

24. Shoptaw, *On the Outside Looking Out,* 44.

25. Bruce Andrews, "Misrepresentation: (A Text for *The Tennis Court Oath* of John Ashbery)", 522-23.

26. *ibid.,* 521

27. *A Novelette* (1932) in William Carlos Williams, *Imaginations,* New York, 1971, 281.

28. *ibid.,* 299.

29. John Ashbery, *The Tennis Court Oath,* 28.

30. Quoted in André Breton, *Manifesto of Surrealism* (1924), in Richard Seaver and Helen R. Lane, trans. *André Breton: Manifestoes of Surrealism,* Ann Arbor, 1972, 20.

31. Breton, *ibid.,* 36-37.

32. Kenneth Rexroth, "Introduction" to trans. *Pierre Reverdy: Selected Poems,* New York, 1969, vii.

33. *ibid.,* vi-vii.

34. Interview with Ashbery (1974) quoted in Helen Vendler, 'Understanding Ashbery', 185: "In the last few years I have been attempting to keep meaningfulness up to the pace of randomness . . . but I really think that meaningfulness can't get along without randomness and that they somehow have to be brought together".

35. John Ashbery, "Reverdy en Amérique", *Mercure de France,* 344 (January/April 1962), 111, (my translation).

36. Charles Bernstein, *A Poetics*, 79.

37. Lyn Hejinian, "The Rejection of Closure", in Bob Perelman, ed. *Writing/Talks,* Carbondale and Edwardsville, 1985, 272.

38. See for example Manuel Brito, "An Interview with Barrett Watten", 38, on "quoted cultural conundra that, taken as far out of context as possible, work to lay bare the prior assumptions of communication . . . as the possibility of poetic speech".

39. Charles Bernstein, *A Poetics,* 13.

40. Christopher Beach, *ABC of Influence: Ezra Pound and the Remaking of American Poetic Tradition,* Berkeley, Los Angeles, 1992, 240.

41. See Bloom's account ("The Charity of Hard Moments", 52) of his "outrage and disbelief" when confronted by this poem.

42. Charles Bernstein, *Content's Dread: Essays 1975-1984,* Los Angeles, 1986, 67.

43. Shoptaw, *On the Outside Looking Out,* 7.

44. See Douglas Messerli, ed. *From the Other Side of the Century: A New American Poetry 1960-1990,* Los Angeles, 1994.

45. Lyn Hejinian, interview with Tyrus Miller, *Paper Air,* 4, 2 (1989), 34. Cf. Hejinian, interview in Brito, ed. *A Suite of Poetic Voices,* 84: "A major component of my poetics, or let's say of my poetic impulse, is a result of that war and the meaning of its never being named".

46. Barrett Watten, *Total Syntax,* 113-14.

47. Charles Bernstein, *Content's Dream,* 32. See also *ibid.,* 20, ". . . political writing becomes disoriented when it views itself as description and not discourse; as not being *in* the world but *about* the world".

48. Charles Bernstein, "Hinge/Picture", *Ironwood,* 26 (Fall 1985), 241.

Nick Lolordo (essay date winter 2001)

SOURCE: Lolordo, Nick. "Charting the Flow: Positioning John Ashbery." *Contemporary Literature* 42, no. 4 (winter 2001): 750-74.

[*In the following essay, Lolordo views* Flow Chart *as a synthesis of modernist and avant-garde verse, citing the influences of T. S. Eliot and Wallace Stevens on the poem.*]

Recent literary history tells us that there are two John Ashberys. These figures correspond to the two traditions of contemporary American poetry, traditions alive in polemic now for some forty years. Donald Allen's

1960 *The New American Poetry* presented various recent groups of poets as a postwar American avant-garde, "the true continuers of the modern movement in American poetry" unified by "a total rejection of all those qualities typical of academic verse" (xi). Allen's avant-garde anthology was revised and reissued in 1982 as *The Postmoderns: The New American Poetry Revised.* The title marks a shift in categories: while the earlier rejection of academic verse might be read as signaling a claim that modernism in its full range of radical energy remained open—as the almost-religious fervor of the phrase "true continuers" suggests—by 1982 a new term, "postmodernism," had been added to the polemical lexicon; and with this change came a shift in emphasis, from a synchronic picture of the contemporary moment in poetry to a periodizing, historical view. The concept of postmodernism has tended, unsurprisingly, to do work more polemical than analytical in debates over canons of post-World War II American poetry. In his introduction to the 1994 *Postmodern American Poetry: A Norton Anthology,* Paul Hoover asserts that postmodernism is today's avant-garde and defines it in terms of opposition to vaguely described "mainstream" or "centrist" values; the value of the term "postmodern" for him seems to lie (paradoxically?) in evoking both a new dominant mode and a new openness of practice—a marginal dominant.[1] But a rhetoric of conflict traceable to Allen remains in use. Indeed, as Alan Golding has recently argued, the mid-1990s saw a return of the 1960s "anthology wars": "editors are once again unapologetically using terms like 'avant-garde,' 'center,' 'mainstream,' and so on" ("New, Newer, and Newest American Poetries" 339). (Allen's anthology was reissued in 1999.)

An influential genealogy of the two traditions was provided by Marjorie Perloff in *The Poetics of Indeterminacy* (1981): "what we loosely call 'Modernism' in Anglo-American poetry is really made up of two separate though often interwoven strands: the Symbolist mode that Lowell inherited from Eliot and Baudelaire and, beyond them, from the great Romantic poets, and the 'anti-Symbolist' mode of indeterminacy or 'undecidability,' of literalness and free play . . . that goes from Rimbaud to Stein, Pound, and Williams by way of Cubist, Dada, and early Surrealist art" (vii). Ashbery's polemical value becomes apparent when Perloff says that she chooses to refer to her subject, the tradition of "indeterminacy," as "the other tradition," remarking, "I take the phrase from the title of a poem by John Ashbery" (vii). But Perloff is hardly alone in making claims about Ashbery. His ubiquity in recent anthologies is unequaled; he seems to lean and loaf at his ease, surveying the terrain on either side of the fence.[2]

American poetry, in these debates, takes the form of a wishbone; and the wish fulfillment of critics on both sides demands that Ashbery be part of *their* piece. In the one tradition (which I will call the high modernist tradition), *Self-Portrait in a Convex Mirror* is the key book: it swept the Pulitzer Prize, the National Book Award, and the National Book Critics Circle Award in 1975, and its title poem, which unfolds with greater discursive consistency than anything else in Ashbery's oeuvre, is Ashbery's most-discussed work. Harold Bloom and Helen Vendler have been the most influential champions of this Ashbery. Bloom's Ashbery stands as the major poet of our day; Bloom writes, in *Figures of Capable Imagination,* of "the 'central' kind of poet he is fated to become, in the line of Emerson, Whitman, Stevens" (206). Vendler's "comes from Wordsworth, Keats, Tennyson, Stevens, Eliot; his poems are about love, or time, or age" (qtd. in Schultz, *Tribe* 3). The positions of Vendler and Bloom are in certain respects directly opposed; while the latter asserts that Ashbery "is at his best . . . when he dares to write most directly in the idiom of Stevens" (*Figures* 172), the former feels that "when he echoes [Stevens and Eliot] most compliantly, he is least himself." But both take Ashbery as a major poet, best read in a temporal line of succession descending from his predecessors.

The "other" line on Ashbery is very different: many poets and critics associated with or sympathetic to Language poetry praise his second book, 1962's *The Tennis Court Oath,* but are skeptical of the much-laureled later work (or at least of those providing the garland).[3] Hank Lazer refers to "the domestication and acceptance of John Ashbery's experimental poetry as a kind of strategic tokenism" (19). At moments like this, it is unclear whether Ashbery is being viewed as a victim of, or complicit in, this acceptance. Charles Bernstein is more explicit when he remarks that Ashbery's unwillingness to produce an oppositional poetics is "a great disappointment" for our letters (157); the self-conscious echo of William Carlos Williams's famous remark about T. S. Eliot clearly if discreetly alludes to Ashbery's sins of omission.[4] One aspect of Ashbery's project has been to transcribe the protean moods of the atomic self; and this tendency has been taken to correspond with the socioeconomic fact of Ashbery's post-1976 ascendancy to major or even "greatest American poet" status. Bob Perelman is unusually specific (and scathing) when he describes Ashbery's constant preoccupation as "the casual truth of an unfettered personal existence bathetically circumscribed by metaphysical constraints" (123). Whatever its stance toward the centrality and self-sufficiency of the personal (a matter I will take up), Ashbery's poetry has typically appeared too easily recuperable by what writers associated with Language poetry see as the post-Romantic vocabulary of mainstream poetry criticism.

Established in the 1970s and 1980s, these positions have become firmly entrenched. Marjorie Perloff's "Normalizing John Ashbery" marks a recent flare-up of conflict. I quote its opening sentences: "Has success spoiled John Ashbery? By no means, as I shall suggest below, if we are talking about such recent volumes as *Can You Hear, Bird?* (1995). But the current discourse *on* Ashbery's work is something else again." Perloff asserts that a number of critics are engaged in the process to which her title refers, by means of reading Ashbery as having "all along written under the sign of Eliot or Stevens." In her account, these narratives of ancestry or influence are polemical: the goal of normalizing critics is to reestablish modernism as hegemonic, "the movement from which no later twentieth-century poet (not even Ashbery) can actually deviate," by denying that there is "a genuine *difference* between modernist and postmodernist poetics." She goes on to develop her argument through a critique of two recent "normalizing" accounts of Ashbery by James Longenbach and Vernon Shetley: the former makes the mistake of preferring Ashbery's atypically unified poems rather than fully confronting his "difficulty" (Perloff's quotation marks), hence neglecting the extent to which he makes it new, while the latter acknowledges Ashberian novelty only in modernist terms, as in referring to the poetry's "moments of fragmentation and opacity" (132) as an index of "the frustrations of the poet's situation."[5]

Perloff's criticisms are by no means without merit. Longenbach is right to criticize strategic uses of a "weak modernism" to prove postmodern points. But the presumably "strong" modernism implied by his choice of persistent modernists is partisan to the extent of making any claims to capaciousness seem doubtful, deriving as it does from an ultra-academic high modernism in which Eliot is exalted as *fons et origo* while figures as different as Charles Olson, Robert Duncan, and Melvin Tolson are ignored (I list these poets merely as among those figures whose engagement with the questions posed by modernism seems most visible). Longenbach writes chapters on Elizabeth Bishop, Robert Lowell, Randall Jarrell, Amy Clampitt, Richard Wilbur, Richard Howard, Jorie Graham, and Ashbery—clearly the only one of his chosen few, whatever their merits, who might serve as a representative of the "other" tradition. His argument that the strongest American poetry has remained within the horizon of modernism would be far better served by a more various selection of poets. By the same token, however, Perloff's decision to leave unchallenged the conflation of modernism with this formally conservative canon (with one, so to speak, of her own "two traditions") unnecessarily weakens the larger, literary-historical claims of her polemic.[6] To account for that aspect of Ashbery's work which remains in contact with modernist poetics need not involve assenting to narratives such as Longenbach's. Merely to oppose Ashbery's production to New Critical paradigms, as does Shetley, is not to offer a full account of his notorious "difficulty"—and yet such readerly difficulty remains one of the strongest lines of continuity between the ambitions of *both* strands of modernism and recent radical poetics, most obviously those of language-centered poetries. Such a line may be traced without conceding that Ashbery writes in the tradition of a hegemonic modernism.

Ultimately, I would argue, Ashbery is a recalcitrant poet-champion for anyone to enlist, more likely to provide what he once called "the shield of a greeting" (**"Self-Portrait in a Convex Mirror"**) than the impenetrable shield most useful when riding into polemical combat. At the present moment, Ashbery appears to have been to the second half of the twentieth century what Eliot was to the first: the most universally acknowledged of poets writing in English. (The crucial difference between the two—visible in the differing extent and range of their respective influences—is that unlike Eliot, Ashbery did not invent a critical apparatus which would compel agreement on the *nature* of his achievement.) In the remainder of this essay, I want to read Ashbery as he positions himself in relation to the debates I have outlined thus far, taking 1991's book-length **Flow Chart** as my exemplary text.[7] The poem is both the most daily, most environmental of Ashbery's works and the most historical: it constantly contextualizes the momentary, by positioning the act of writing within different schemes of time (phenomenological, personal-autobiographical, historical) and space (central, marginal, peripheral). Hal Foster has suggested that formal or high modernism plots its trajectory along the temporal or diachronic axis of literary history, while avant-gardist or postmodern work seeks to break with the past and to widen the space of art by a synchronic expansion onto the space of life (xi). Ashbery's poem is engaged in both these activities: it looks back at poetic tradition while absorbing more and more discourses into its present practice. Ashbery positions himself both in the present tense of writing (the moment of writing in "open form" that puts him in recognizable continuity with radical contemporary practice) and within literary history (by means of an allusiveness that puts his poem in a problematic contact with ideas of high modernism, specifically those of Eliot and the New Criticism). I will trace this dual conversation in the poem by following its metaphors of centrality and marginality, which form a strand of language at once phenomenological and sociological, consisting of images that evoke some central point and those that figure edges, margins, peripheries. These images present space and time as both perceptual categories and categories of literary-historical discourse. In **Flow Chart,** Ashbery "ask[s] the diagram" (3)—asks us and himself—where and when reading and writing take place.[8] His answer involves both the open present of contemporary radical or postmodern practice and the still-present past that we call modernism.

* * *

The author of **Flow Chart** begins, traditionally enough, in the middle of things, facing the ongoing difficulty of writing at the present time:

> Still in the published city but not yet
> overtaken by a new form of despair, I ask
> the diagram: is it the foretaste of pain
> it might easily be?

The fragile present tense is poised between the moment of completion or publication—a kind of fixity, even death ("Still in the published city")—and a "new form of despair." Thus the poem opens on an edge, poised between the dangers of poetic history and a modernist imperative to innovate which might itself be only more poetic history, a temporally paradoxical predicament: the new pursues, seeking to overtake from the past. This edge is the poem's present—a state of still/not yet that is defined, held responsible by ideas of past and future and yet resists them. The act of invocation becomes an unanswered question. And the equally double titular metaphor develops a potential internal tension. A flow chart is "a diagram of the movement or actions of things or persons engaged in a complex activity." The idea of poem as flow chart implies a complicated attitude toward representation and its temporality: does a flow chart create its subject, map it belatedly, or predict an idealized version of events? It might be said—to borrow Adorno's aphoristic verdict on modern art—that a flow chart is "as abstract as the real relations among men" (31): it is a realistic presentation of events that are themselves fundamentally abstract, processes that cannot literally be seen. The poem returns over and over again to a sense of processes within processes: "We know life is so busy, / but a larger activity shrouds it, and this is something / we can never feel" (3). In this sense, the "chart" aspect of the poem, its mapping of internal and external movements, is inherently inadequate to the complexity of the "flow." Ashbery's oscillation between figures of flux and flow places the poem in this liminal position: it is the flow and the diagram, just as we flow through the poem and inevitably chart our progress through the complex activity of reading it.

The "published city" is of course also the city of authorial identity—the city inhabited not by people, nor by writers, but by "authors" (those constructions Foucault analyzes under the category of the "author function"). Aware that his papers were going straight to the Houghton Library to be catalogued, Ashbery charted his flow by noting the date of each typed manuscript page "for scholars to come" (Shoptaw 303). And the poem acknowledges its author's social position in other ways:

> What right have you to consider yourself anything but
> an enormously eccentric though
> not too egocentric character, whose sins of omission
> haven't omitted much,

whose personal-pronoun lapses may indeed have
   contributed to augmenting the hardship
silently resented among the working classes? If I
   thought that for a minute I'd . . .

                                   (150; Ashbery's ellipses)

By referring to "personal-pronoun lapses," the voice of
accusation gestures both at self-critique and at criticism.
Noting such an errant use of pronouns, particularly of
the lyric "I," a kind of errancy that couldn't exactly be
called "egocentric," has long been a prominent feature
of Ashbery criticism. Noting political "sins of omission" (as in the strictures of Bernstein and Perelman)
has been another such feature. Thus anticipated—forcibly pinned into the first person, the very one he'd rather
"lapse" away from—"Ashbery"'s reply sputters out into
ellipses. Equally revealing is the metaphorics of centrality that trail, as it were incidentally, through the accuser's language. The two terms ("eccentric" and
"egocentric") are potentially opposites, and the opposition is revealing; the eccentric "character" of **Flow
Chart** is not centered within the "I" or ego but stands
outside this center, is etymologically speaking *ekken-
tros,* outside the center. This is not to argue that Ashbery is claiming a marginal identity. His question is different: what would it mean for poetry—and for the act
of writing poetry—to have or want a central position?

Early in the poem Ashbery considers an adversarial
model of history and the individual agent's place in it:

                                   if an execu-
   tive
can teeter on his perch all day long from dawn to
   dusk, a wren
can say to him, why don't you go on an organized
   outing, stop
fooling yourself, this world-situation isn't nonsense
   though *real politik* may not be
the accurate term for it either, so why explode like a
   timebomb that was set long ago
and may no longer be operable? But you see so many
of us are like that bird, that man I mean, that for but a
   few can life resonate with
anything like serious implications. So many were hung
   out to dry, or, more accurately, to rot.
And these marginalia—what other word is there for
   them?—are the substance of the text,
by not being allowed to fit in. One can proceed like a
   ghost
along corridors and find that doors are closed to one,
   and then
what good is being invisible?

                                                           (37)

The play of metaphor here is characteristic. Consider
the relationship of those who were hung out to rot and
the figure of the "marginalia": the ghost of "vehicle"
and "tenor" remain, but not only are relations of priority impossible to determine, the two are living separated
yet related existences within the text. One may have

produced the other, in the writing process, but this
doesn't prevent the other sense of the word from suddenly emerging into prominence. "So many" of us, Ashbery tells us, are marginalized, a group of ghostly
outsiders to whom doors remain closed, occupying a
corridor. (A related, more socially specified space appears earlier on the same page: "the narrow, closetlike
conundrum / of their own / slender existences.") But
this social meaning coexists with the textual reference
the same passage enacts. The text gestures at the
particular quality of "so many" of its own lines, the
consequence of their "not being allowed to fit in." If we
take seriously for a moment the possibility that marginalia form "the substance of the text," the formal
consequences are radical. Such a work would stand as a
response to another, absent form that could never be
known through these secondary notations, deriving its
own notion of form from the discourse it is parasitic
upon. In this sense, the poem itself is marginal—written
in the margins of other ongoing processes. ("We know
life is so busy, / but a larger activity shrouds it, and this
is something / we can never feel, except occasionally,
in small signs" [3].) And these two readings can be
brought together. The poem portrays its reader as a
producer of marginalia, one who is refused access to
any central chamber of symbolic depth. There are no
penetralia. Readers are kept outside, on the surface of
the text—"doors are closed"—*creating* meaning rather
than reading *through* to meaning.

At other moments, metaphors of position refer specifically to the discourses of literary history and evaluation:

                         It seems I was reading some-
   thing;
I have forgotten the sense of it or what the small
role of the central poem made me want to feel. No
   matter.
The words, distant now, and mitred, glint. Yet not one
ever escapes the forest of agony and pleasure that
   keeps them
in a solution that has become permanent through
   inertia. The force
of meaning never extrudes. And the insects,
of course, don't mind.

                                                           (3-4)

Once established as canonical—positioned as a "central
poem"—a text can harden into an alien, senseless literary monument—a fairy-tale location in the timeless
"forest of agony and pleasure," where nothing ever
changes. Ashbery's poem works very differently from
this "central" poem of stasis. If meaning is to be found,
it must be provisional meaning, that obtained within a
process of reading that continues rather than leaving
texts as read, as monuments. This process must be as if
eternal, for upon completion, linguistic inertia seals up
meaning like an insect in amber. Here my metaphor

points to the "insects" in order to get at the poem's own sliding style of signification. This moment is easy to take as a typically sudden and flippant switch of discursive registers—which, of course, it is. But the "solution that has become permanent through inertia" provides an implicit metaphor: the words are as if sealed in amber, linking them to the "insects" of the next line. The contingency of this reading is the very point; it suggests a practice in which the writer looks very like a reader of his own text: he rereads his own writing as it drifts toward the metaphorical (as it always will), then takes up the key term of the implied metaphor (words are insects) to start a new stream of language. It is this continual slippage, a quest that slides, placing reader and writer together, on edge, rather than locating or penetrating to some "center," that characterizes the poem's production of meaning.

The "central poem" alludes to a characteristic Stevensian image. In "A Primitive Like an Orb," the complexity and distance of such a hypothesized "central poem," like some medieval proof of God's existence, merely confirms Stevens's faith in its certainty: "The central poem is the poem of the whole, / The poem of the composition of the whole" (442). Ultimately this "central poem" is transformed into a personage, "A giant on the horizon. . . . At the center on the horizon, concentrum, grave / And prodigious person, patron of origins," and in the lyric's final stanza, Stevens affirms the part-whole relations of traditional poetics of representation: "Each one, his fated eccentricity, / As a part, but part, but tenacious particle, / Of . . . the total / Of letters" (443). These individual moments of "eccentricity" somehow all add up to a "concentrum": this coinage shows the strain, forging a substantive from an entirely relative adjective, "concentric," which denotes the state of sharing a center.[9] By contrast, Ashbery's sense of a shared marginality renders it impossible to find a solid or central position, a fixed ground for judgment. His "I" lacks this perspective; it is part of a "we" who are "other" to the idea of a dominant discourse. Centrality itself, as Charles Bernstein puts it, is "the power of the dominant margin" (188); all centers are relative, or projections from the viewpoint of (other) margins, fictions supported by power. Nor should social marginality be converted by a neat reversal into a site for claims about the transcendental power of poetry. Rather, the marginality of all particular positions must be acknowledged: the marginal voice / marginal poem may *contain* multitudes but declines to *represent* a whole or a central figure that could stand for this whole.

But this skeptical refusal is only one aspect of *Flow Chart*'s complex engagement with literary tradition. The seemingly endless unfurling variety of Ashbery's diction incorporates that most traditional (and traditionally high modernist) of devices, allusion; and Ashbery's own allusiveness enacts a covert engagement with the central figure of high modernism, T. S. Eliot. Consider again Ashbery's explanation of our marginality ("But you see so many / of us are like that bird, that man I mean. . . . So many were hung out to dry, or more accurately, to rot"). The passage echoes *The Waste Land,* in which the speaker, both shocked and judging, looks from the outside at a Dantean circulation of commuters: "A crowd flowed over London Bridge, so many, / I had not thought death had undone so many." The borrowed repetition highlights the difference in perspective between Eliot's stance and Ashbery's. The published city, as I have already suggested, is in part the city of literary tradition, and in this sense, the presence of allusion in Ashbery's poem becomes problematic: such a device is typically read as itself implying the notion of continuity, of poetry as an internally organized tradition (Hollander), rather than as a concept of intertextuality that emphasizes the interpermeability of discourses and levels distinctions between them.

These two stances have, of course, long been aligned with modern and postmodern views of literary relations. By way of illustrating this contrast, I will return briefly to the argument of Perloff's "Normalizing John Ashbery." The thrust of the essay, as I've already suggested, is to argue against reading Ashbery in either a personal or a symptomatic relationship to any continuous history of poetry since modernism. This effort is supported in the latter part of the piece by a reading of a recent Ashbery lyric (**"A Day at the Gate,"** the first poem in *Can You Hear, Bird?*), which takes up a distinction Perloff had first made in *The Poetics of Indeterminacy,* between modern and postmodern modes of allusion and citation:

> In Eliot's case, we know (or can find out) where the citations come from; we can assess the degree of irony in the poet's use of Nerval's "Le Prince d'Aquitaine à la tour abolie" or in "The Game of Chess"'s version of Ovid's tale of Philomela. But in Ashbery's poetry, it is usually impossible to identify the citation, and, even when we do, such identification doesn't necessarily help us to understand the poem. . . .
>
> . . . Indeed, in Ashbery, almost everything *sounds* like a citation, sounds like something we've heard before or read somewhere—but where? And that is of course one of the main features of Ashbery's poetic: living at a moment when one's language is so wholly permeated by the discourses that endlessly impinge on it, a Keatsian image complex, or even an Eliotic distinction between citation and invention . . . is felt to be no longer possible.

This account of the Ashbery style is persuasive, and to a significant extent I'm in agreement with it—as, I suspect, would be Ashbery. I suspect this because he often provides self-reflexive stylistic analysis in the course of his poetry, in *Flow Chart* doing so by the classically "modernist" device of allusive quotation: "'Whatever things men are doing shall germ / the motley subject of my page.' And that shall leave a great deal after it / in the way of trails" (105). The passage seems straightforward enough. Ashbery's borrowed verse says what Perloff's prose says, although it says it by implying a relation between cited and invented discourse, whereby one comments wryly on the other, performing, as it were, the impinging. The actual source of Ashbery's quotation is one William Gifford's 1817 translation of Juvenal's first Satire:

> Whatever passions have the soul possest,
> Whatever wild desires inflamed the breast,
> Joy, Sorrow, Fear, Love, Hatred, Transport, Rage,
> Shall form the motley subject of my page.
>
> (137)

The distinction between citation and invention now looks even more frail. Perloff's sense that Ashbery's allusions are not Eliot's little nuggets of cultural capital, the exegesis of which will provide crucial interpretive aid, seems entirely accurate. The quoted phrase stands not as a meaningful allusion to poetic history—as if to say, "we should pay more attention to Gifford"—but as a concrete instance of the point. Ashbery's passage as a whole suggests, After all, writing is a kind of doing, and one of the things men do is produce translations of Juvenal, the majority of which, like other deeds, are soon forgotten. "[I]t is usually impossible to identify the citation, and, even when we do, such identification doesn't necessarily help us to understand the poem."[10]

This account of the Ashbery poetic maps perfectly onto Fredric Jameson's well-known distinction between modernist and postmodern literary style. (Jameson, in passing, includes Ashbery in a list of the most important "postmodernist" artists.) Jameson regards the notion of stylistic originality or uniqueness as definitively modernist; postmodern conditions are marked by the "disappearance of the individual subject" and "its formal consequence, the increasing unavailability of the personal style." The possibility of a dominant speech norm imposed by the ruling classes is replaced by "a neutral and reified media speech . . . which itself then becomes but one more idiolect among many." Correspondingly, the unique, "fingerprint" style is replaced by the practice of blank pastiche—a kind of play without satirical intentions or even discernible authorial affect on what Jameson calls "a field of stylistic and discursive heterogeneity without a norm" (16-17).

But no consensus exists on the nature of Ashbery's style. Jameson's very definition of *modernist* style has also been invoked to praise Ashbery's poetic diction. The modernist claim implies that Ashbery's ability to transmute the debased metals of various contemporary discourses into the gold of a genuine poetic style identifies him as a major poet. A review cited on the back cover of the poem's first paperback edition is represen-

tative: "This is what real achievement in a contemporary poet consists of," asserts John Bayley; "he has laid down guidelines and made his mark on the language of the tribe." What Bayley and many critics like him have remarked is the Ashbery style, which we recognize in his work. The style is seemingly paradoxical: answering Jameson's criteria of postmodernism perfectly, it yet successfully projects an effect of powerful originality.

The paradox itself, I would argue, is hardly novel; an early formulation of it occurs in a discussion of *Ulysses* by T. S. Eliot. Writing on recent English prose in *Vanity Fair,* Eliot observed that in the new novel, Joyce had achieved "a very singular and perhaps unique literary distinction: the distinction of having, not in a negative but in a very positive sense, no style at all. I mean that every sentence Mr. Joyce writes is peculiarly and absolutely his own; that his work is not a pastiche; but that nevertheless, it has none of the marks by which a 'style' may be distinguished." What we would come to call postmodern pastiche had, then, already been noted by Eliot—in an essay written just after *The Waste Land*—as an innovation productive of new possibilities for modern writing, a style which attacked and destroyed "style" itself. The debate, then, remains inside the terms imagined by modernism. On the one hand, a passage like Ashbery's discussion of the "marginalia" is obviously a tour de force of "stylistic and discursive heterogeneity without a norm"; on the other, it's "vintage Ashbery": the style proves assimilable to either paradigm.

To escape this dichotomy, I turn to Ashbery's own position on the question of modernist style, one that can best be seen through his reading of Eliot. In a 1962 exhibition-catalogue essay, **"The New Realists,"** Ashbery remarks dismissively, "Today it is possible not to speak in metaphors, whereas in the 1920s a poet such as Eliot couldn't evoke a gasworks without feeling obliged to call the whole history of human thought into play" (*Reported Sightings* 82). But if familiarity had bred contempt, or simply boredom with Eliot's "dull canal," Eliot's *method* remained of interest to Ashbery twenty years later (writing about R. B. Kitaj in *Art in America*):

> Faced with an altered reality, Eliot reacts as though in a stupor. Despite all his craft and scholarship, *The Waste Land* achieves its effect as a collage of hallucinatory, random fragments, "shored against my ruin." Their contiguity is all their meaning, and it is implied that from now on meaning will take into account the randomness and discontinuity of modern experience, that indeed meaning cannot be truthfully defined as anything else.
>
> (*Reported Sightings* 301-2)

This invocation of randomness must be seen as an aggressively anti-high modernist reading of Eliot's poem. The modernist reading of Ashberian style carries with it the implication that the poet has a duty toward the language itself, the ultimate subject of all poetry: the poet's individual style reinvigorates the collective language. (Bayley's judgment evokes a constellation of modernist dicta: "Little Gidding"—"Since our concern was speech, and speech impelled us / To purify the dialect of the tribe"—or Eliot's source, Mallarme's dictum that the poet must *"Donner un sens plus pur aux mots de la tribu"* [from "Le Tombeau d'Edgar Poe"].) In this account, any difficulties into which poetic language might be forced—difficulties that included the problem of citation—were to be taken as the necessary consequence of the poet's efforts to maintain the language. As early as 1921, Eliot had famously observed,

> [I]t appears likely that poets in our civilization, as it exists at present, must be *difficult*. Our civilization comprehends great variety and complexity, and this variety and complexity, playing upon a refined sensibility, must produce various and complex results. The poet must become more and more comprehensive, more allusive, more indirect, in order to force, to dislocate if necessary, language into his meaning.

> (*Selected Essays* 248)

He was thus positioned to fulfill his own prophecy with the appearance of *The Waste Land* a year later. The poet of Eliot's remark is both passive and active: an instrument sensitive to the winds of change, he is also a masterful figure capable when necessary of doing violence to language against its will. In Ashbery's revisionary account, this agent becomes a patient; the "randomness" and "discontinuity" of modern life assert themselves against the poet's will: *they* are what is meaningful.

Ashbery, then, provides what could be called a symptomatic reading of Eliot's poem. Moreover, his allusions to *The Waste Land* in ***Flow Chart*** suggest the possibility of a similar reading, both of *The Waste Land* and of the values of high modernism. At various points in Ashbery's poem, we find such allusions, inflected variously. A self-mocking question: "I sat / naked and disconsolate at a corner of a crevice, hat in hand, fishing, / for who can tell what God intends for us next?" (121); a weary inquiry: "what else is there to do, except sweep the floor / with automatic hand" (62); a surreal episode: "Another day we read the thunder its own prepared statement. / The effect was stupefying" (153); a vatic pronouncement: "I will show you fear in a handful of specialists" (201).

"I will show you fear in a handful of specialists." The sentence protrudes with epigrammatic sharpness from the poem's undergrowth:

> The truly vitiated look haggard and mean,
> whether they be socially

acceptable or no, and still the perquisite authority
hasn't been distilled;
it is everyone's, for everyone to see. I will show you
fear in a handful of specialists. Furthermore
the burliest male is but as a handmaiden to the
suspicion of his own history:
he's got it right, OK?

The phrase serves to conflate the poem that has chilled the blood of American poets since William Carlos Williams with the ideology and the body of literary professionals associated with the promotion of high modernism (the latter, it would seem, characterized as "burly" men haunted—and metaphorically feminized—by an internalized, self-policing suspicion). Changing a single word, Ashbery dusts off the line and redeploys it as a critique.

The identity of the specialist was one that Eliot self-consciously assumed, as did, later, various of the New Critics. F. R. Leavis's attack on English scorn for the "specialist" and John Crowe Ransom's manifesto "Criticism, Inc." shared an adversary that Eliot had identified as early as 1918: the amateur spirit in literary analysis. Responding to a *Times Literary Supplement* attack on the "easy difficulty" of professionalism in 1918, Eliot observed in *The Egoist* that "An attitude which might find voice in words like these is behind all of British slackness for a hundred years and more: the dislike of the specialist." It's often been noted that the burden of this criticism was an extended campaign against the Victorians, conducted on the terrain of literary language.[11] An engagement especially pertinent to my purposes was Eliot's attack on Swinburne. Along this line he wrote two early essays, "Swinburne as Poet" and "Swinburne as Critic," both of which were reprinted in *The Sacred Wood*. In the former essay, Eliot damns with high praise; told that "[o]nly a man of genius could dwell so exclusively and consistently among words as Swinburne" (150), we might nevertheless sense that such a world of words is not the healthiest of dwelling places; and this fear is quickly confirmed by the ominous remark that in Swinburne's verse, "language, uprooted, has adapted itself to an independent life of atmospheric nourishment"—whereas "[l]anguage in a healthy state presents the object" (149). Such a rootless language must be understood as in opposition to "the language of the tribe": Swinburne's concern was never with "speech"; and this, for Eliot, is what separates Victorian frivolity from high-modernist seriousness. Swinburne's failure is one not of genius but of professionalism; and here Eliot's indictments overlap. In the latter essay, we find that Swinburne is ultimately "an appreciator and not a critic" (19)—not, that is to say, a specialist.

I dwell on Swinburne here because he makes an important (if covert) appearance in Ashbery's ***Flow Chart***. Near its conclusion, ***Flow Chart*** coalesces into the twelve twelve-lined stanzas of a double sestina. To introduce the sestina, Ashbery offers his readers an unusually explicit extended passage, one of the more extended metapoetic discussions in *Flow Chart*:

> Look guys. In the interests of not disturb-
> ing my fragile ecological balance
> I can tell you a story about something. The expression
>   will be just right, for it will be adjusted
> to the demands of the form, and the form itself shall
>   be timeless though
> hitherto unsuspected. It will take us down to about
>   now,
> though a few beautiful archaisms will be allowed to
>   flutter in it—"complaint,"
> for one.
>
> (185)

Ashbery's terse opening remark, "Look guys," is perhaps the poem's single most succinct example of a gleefully antipurist attitude toward "the language." The sestina form is indeed "timeless though hitherto unsuspected," and archaisms can indeed be found (though not "complaint," which functions as a kind of unusable clue). The first two lines of Ashbery's super-sestina make a self-conscious gesture at poetics: "We're interested in the language, that you call breath, / if breath is what we are to become, and we think it is, the southpaw said" (186). Ashbery's "concern" is "speech," to return to Eliot's words of "Little Gidding"—but consider his purposes. The heroic gesture of the poet is defined in terms of an ambition that is recognizably modernist, as the production of a "timeless yet hitherto unsuspected" form. Yet it is at the same time to be borrowed from the (flagrantly inappropriate) artifice of Swinburne, and hence content is to be adjusted to form, rather than vice versa. The form signifies variously: a part of Ashbery's own tradition of tour de force fixed forms, it steals its twelve end words from Swinburne's "The Complaint of Lisa" (itself no "major poem" but part of an "other" tradition). Ashbery simply typed these words down the right margin of his page and then wrote toward them.[12] The most artificial forms of language, as well as the most natural, are part of the ecology of poetry. And the sestina, of course, is a doubly allusive form. Its internal repetition of material, as each stanza's final line is echoed and revised by the first line of the following stanza, enacts a kind of revisionary allusion. Moreover these particular end-words have been used before. Demonstrating his care for the poetic environment, Ashbery creates a world of borrowed (or stolen) words, making it new by recycling.[13] Swinburne's words in Ashbery's margins, Ashbery's words in the margins of the "text" of literature—a marginal tradition of revisionary commentary begins to appear.

* * *

Ashbery's poem, I have argued, frees the reader into an active marginality, one maker of meanings among many,

while at the same time positioning writing as a marginal practice. Its concluding line directs the reader back out into the world by pointing to an openness that the poem cannot fully contain: "It's open: the bridge, that way." Yet I want to suggest that for all its revisionary gestures toward modernist ambition, *Flow Chart* finally remains ambivalent about the particular value claims of contemporary radical poetics. The contemporary consensus tells us that an avant-garde or postmodern poem will question and problematize, disrupting certainties and emphasizing differences—will precisely not seek, as did the modern work, to "compel conviction." But the question remains: how will such poetic critique further a re-imagination of social relations? The poem often thematizes claims that are recognizably those of contemporary radical poetics and concludes, I think, that poetic intervention can only affect the ground for discursive exchange. I quote Lyn Hejinian on "openness": "The 'open text,' by definition, is open to the world and particularly to the reader. It invites participation, rejects the authority of the writer over the reader and thus, by analogy, the authority implicit in other . . . hierarchies" (134). Ashbery's own sense of the language allows the possibility of a relationship that exists outside the discourse of linguistic mastery to continually reemerge:

> What we are to each other is both less urgent and
>   more
> perturbing, having no discernible root, no raison
>   d'être, or else flowing
> backward into an origin like the primordial soup it's
>   so easy to pin
> anything on, like a carnation to one's lapel. So it
>   seems we must
> stay in an uneasy relationship, not quite fitting
> together, not precisely friends or lovers though
>   certainly not enemies, if
> the buoyancy of the spongy terrain on which we exist
>   is to be experienced
> as an ichor, not a commentary on all that is missing
>   from the reflection
> in the mirror. *Did I say that? Can this be me?*
>
> (10)

The slide of language here from metaphorical to literal, and the consequent undermining of the idiom ("to pin anything on"), mimics the sponginess of the linguistic terrain we inhabit—our shared linguistic conventions. No argument from a concept of origins (reversing the flow) will ease this tension. Instead, we have an "uneasy" present-tense pragmatics; and it is this "not quite fitting" / "together" (our collective marginality, to read the line break strongly) that will preserve us. Rather than an object to be maintained by the poet, language is the very ground on which all our relations are conducted. At the same time, to experience this ground as an "ichor" is to experience it as a foreign substance that is yet within us, preserving the surprise, the otherness of language and the nonidentity of our words and selves: *"Did I say that? Can this be me?"*

The alternative of a "commentary on all that is missing," another lament on our internal division, another evocation of lyrical pathos, might yet be avoided.

And yet this freedom is both problem and solution in Ashbery's poem: the reader of the "open" text is not always properly grateful: "And if I told you / this was your life, not some short story for a contest, how would you react? / Chances are you'd tell me to buzz off and continue writing" (81). The infinite form here, "writing," allows for a fruitful ambiguity, one that points to the poem's general conditions as established by Ashbery's off-the-rack pronouns. Either "you" or "I," in this case, can prove to have been doing the writing—but the problem remains. In the end, the notion of freeing the reader into writing gets presented as desirable and impossible—at best, as a process that must be repeated over and over again. Readers are or can be writers and vice versa, but the two, traditional roles remain, however ridiculous—as, in the introduction to the double sestina, Ashbery reminds us:

> not that you
> don't
> already love him enough, more than any writer
> deserves. He won't thank you for it.
> But you won't mind that either, since his literature
> will have performed its duty
> by setting you gently down in a new place and then
> speeding off before
> you have a chance to thank it. We've got to find a
> new name for him. "Writer" seems
> totally inadequate; yet it is writing, you read it before
> you knew it. And besides,
> if it weren't, it wouldn't have done the unexpected
> and by doing so proved that it was quite
> the thing to do, and if it happened all right for you,
> but wasn't the way you
> thought it was going to be, why still
> that is called fulfilling part of the bargain. And by do-
> ing so
> he has erased your eternal debt to him. You are free.
> You can go now.
>
> (185-86)

The passage is a fabulously delicate send-up of those two legendary figures, Author and Reader, and of now equally famous revisionary ideas about their relationship. The parodic element begins with the subtly false note of Ashbery's sly reference to "his literature." A secondary meaning, unobtrusively detonated in the midst of these ambitious claims, deflates the writer, leaving just another salesman or zealot, the kind who might wonder if you'd be interested in some "literature." And the writer "fulfills" the bargain, it should be noted, and so erases our debt to him—not vice versa, as might be expected. In providing this surprising yet pleasurable textual experience, this yet-to-be renamed figure replaces the old notion of the "writer," that guide on whom we always relied for meaning: the process

described and parodied here is that which Barthes so grandly prophesied in "The Death of the Author," the effort toward "suppressing the author in the interests of writing (which is, as will be seen, to restore the place of the reader)" (143). But in Ashbery's scenario, our freedom quickly becomes the marvelously ambiguous freedom to "go." Have we—returning to Barthes's language—been born as readers, freed from the oppressive mythic regime of the Author to make meaning on our own, or have we, like students, been dismissed from text?

Claims of marginalization and disavowals of dominance have become so prevalent in poetry circles as to evoke a reversal of the famous image: the poetry world is a circle at whose circumference is everyone, its center no one. The relation between eccentricity and centrality in Ashbery's poem is a fraught one. Ashbery's use of Swinburne is hardly a parallel to Eliot's use of the "metaphysical" poets; Ashbery's allusions have no such canonizing ambitions. (His 1990-91 Norton Lectures at Harvard—concerning T. L. Beddoes, Raymond Roussel, John Wheelwright, Laura Riding—were entitled **"An Other Tradition."** The revisionary indefinite article should be noted.)[14] What I wish to suggest is that Ashbery's own self-positioning cannot be understood without acknowledging his "reading" of high-modern ambition. The insistently eccentric Ashbery has been installed as our "central" poet—but he tries to remain a moving target, struggling to create a revised context, a modernity without mastery. Ashbery includes both Eliot and Swinburne, central and marginal figures, in his own world of borrowed words, a world in which the notion of a break is desirable, bewildering, painful. The opening lines of *Flow Chart* place him in the only sense in which he can be truly "placed," in his habitual fragile present tense, at the center of the present, at the edge of modernism, writing: "Still in the published city but not yet / overtaken by a new form of despair." As the poem concludes, he is again in suspension, unable to travel the route he writes that leads to somewhere outside the space of the poem. The poet points, like some fixed star directing the (traffic) flow: "It's open, the bridge: that way."

Notes

1. Hoover's use of the indefinite article is a nicely "postmodern" touch; but given the established power of Norton in determining teaching canons at the university level, until "Postmodern Poetry: Another *Norton* Anthology" appears, the gesture might also seem somewhat disingenuous.

2. Ashbery appears in *The Norton Anthology of Modern Poetry, Postmodern American Poetry: A Norton Anthology*, Helen Vendler's *Harvard Book of Contemporary American Poetry*, Harold Bloom's recent *The Best of the Best American Poetry, 1988-1997*, Dou-

glas Messerli's *From the Other Side of the Century,* Eliot Weinberger's *American Poetry since 1950: Innovators and Outsiders,* and J. D. McClatchy's *The Vintage Book of Contemporary American Poetry*—to list merely a few influential anthologies which make overt claims at defining the shape of contemporary writing. Alan Golding has recently discovered that Ashbery was the last poet *cut* from Donald Hall, Robert Pack, and Louis Simpson's *The New Poets of England and America*; his presence therein would have made him the only poet enlisted by both sides in the original "anthology wars" (see "*The New American Poetry,* Revisited, Again").

3. Bruce Andrews's 1980 "Misrepresentation" ("a text for *The Tennis Court Oath* of John Ashbery") treats Ashbery's early volume as embodying "a relativism grounded in practices, in the round of language, which demands *responsiveness* from us and not simply *decipherment*" (521).

4. In his autobiography, Williams called *The Waste Land* "the great catastrophe to our letters. . . . Our work staggered to a halt for a moment under the blast of Eliot's genius which gave the poem back to the academics" (146).

5. Shetley in a sense disqualifies himself by the mistaken observation—which Perloff catches—that Ashbery did not appear in Donald Allen's *The New American Poetry,* the first anthology that tried to describe the sense of a difference in American poetry since the Second World War.

6. A stronger version of modernism is provided by Charles Bernstein's analysis of modern American poetry, in which Bernstein locates the avant-garde as an impulse active within a broadened and radicalized body of modernist work (as opposed to the more narrowly defined New Critical modernist canon): the avant-garde and modernism are "fractions of the same dialectical movement" (*Poetics* 102), a movement which, for Bernstein, remains active.

7. Susan M. Schultz has recently located a sustained and ambivalent engagement with Harold Bloom's critical championing in several of Ashbery's works, most notably *Flow Chart.* While I agree with Schultz's argument that the poem "obsessively engages" (36) with the idea of tradition while remaining irreverent toward it, I am not entirely convinced by the specifics of her claim that the poem's use of the verb "bloom" in particular passages marks an engagement with and critique of Bloom's theories. (A Bloomian account of criticism might regard Schultz's move as revisionary, in that the possibility of such a tactic had already been demonstrated—to very different ends—by Bloom himself: the epigraph to his *Wallace Stevens: The Poems of Our Climate* cites these lines from Stevens's "From the Packet of Anacharsis": "And the circles quicken and crystal colors come / And flare and Bloom with his vast ac-

cumulation / Stands and regards and repeats the primitive lines.")

8. Such a stance has a number of precursors (if not necessarily a "tradition"): consider David Antin's argument in "What It Means to Be Avant-garde," where Antin remarks, "i want to occupy the present" (121), or Gertrude Stein's theory and practice of writing in the present tense. *Flow Chart* contains at least one Stein joke: "one is doomed, / repeating oneself, never to repeat oneself, you know what I mean?" (7).

9. One could of course trace this stance back to Emerson—to the tradition of poetry variously invoked by Americanist scholarship and the work of Harold Bloom. Emerson's poet "is representative. He stands among partial men for the complete man, and apprises us not of his wealth, but of the commonwealth. . . . He is a sovereign, and stands on the center" (223). This representativeness might be contrasted with the "misrepresentative poetics" that John Shoptaw, in his superb study, attributes to Ashbery. Shoptaw argues that in Ashbery's work the appropriateness of part-whole relations, the possibility of such synecdochic representation, is constantly questioned, but "his misrepresentations do not as a consequence rule out meaning, expression and representation; they renovate them" (3). Within this tradition, misrepresentation becomes a fundamentally political strategy—which is not to say that it can be linked to any political *position*; rather, it intervenes by misrepresentative revision of the various discourses surrounding the poet's production.

10. Gifford might have been impossible to track without the aid of the English Poetry CD-ROM; but once found, the pathos of the minor writer becomes part of the larger pathos of temporality itself. The (overly?) earnest reader who traces the line gains not edification but the peculiarly Ashberian pleasure of a certain melancholy: Gifford is long buried, his trail gone cold.

11. The best account of Eliot's anti-Victorian position I know is Louis Menand's *Discovering Modernism.*

12. A page of the manuscript is reproduced in Shoptaw (320).

13. I allude, of course, to T. S. Eliot's famous distinction in "Philip Massinger": "One of the surest tests is the way in which a poet borrows. Immature poets imitate; mature poets steal" (*Sacred Wood* 125).

14. These lectures have since been published under a vaguer title, *Other Traditions.*

Works Cited

Adorno, Theodor. *Aesthetic Theory.* Trans. Robert Hullot-Kentor. Minneapolis: U of Minnesota P, 1997.

Allen, Donald, ed. *The New American Poetry.* New York: Grove, 1960.

Allen, Donald, and George F. Butterick, eds. *The Postmoderns: The New American Poetry Revised.* New York: Grove, 1982.

Andrews, Bruce. "Misrepresentation." *In the American Tree.* Ed. Ron Silliman. Orono, ME: National Poetry Foundation, 1986. 520-29.

Antin, David. "What It Means to Be Avant-garde." *Artifice and Indeterminacy: An Anthology of New Poetics.* Ed. Christopher Beach. Tuscaloosa: U of Alabama P, 1998. 109-29.

Ashbery, John. *Can You Hear, Bird?* New York: Farrar, 1995.

———. *Flow Chart.* New York: Knopf, 1991.

———. *Other Traditions.* Cambridge, MA: Harvard UP, 2000.

———. *Reported Sightings: Art Chronicles, 1957-1987.* Ed. David Bergman. New York: Knopf, 1989.

———. *Self-Portrait in a Convex Mirror.* New York: Viking, 1975.

———. *The Tennis Court Oath.* Middletown, CT: Wesleyan UP, 1962.

Barthes, Roland. *Image, Music, Text.* Trans. Stephen Heath. New York: Hill, 1977.

Bernstein, Charles. *A Poetics.* Cambridge, MA: Harvard UP, 1992.

Bloom, Harold, ed. *The Best of the Best American Poetry, 1988-1997.* New York: Scribner, 1998.

———. *Figures of Capable Imagination.* New York: Seabury, 1976.

———. *Wallace Stevens: The Poems of Our Climate.* Ithaca, NY: Cornell UP, 1977.

Eliot, T. S. *Complete Poems and Plays.* New York: Harcourt, 1971.

———. "Contemporary English Prose." *Vanity Fair* July 1923: 51.

———. "The Metaphysical Poets." *Selected Essays.* New York: Harcourt, 1932. 241-50.

———. "Professional, or . . ." *Egoist* Apr. 1918: 61.

———. *The Sacred Wood.* London: Methuen, 1960.

Ellmann, Richard, and Robert O'Clair, eds. *The Norton Anthology of Modern Poetry.* New York: Norton, 1988.

Emerson, Ralph Waldo. "The Poet." *The Essays of Ralph Waldo Emerson.* Cambridge, MA: Belknap-Harvard UP, 1979. 221-42.

"Flow chart." *The Concise Oxford Dictionary of Current English.* 8th ed. 1990.

Foster, Hal. *The Return of the Real.* Cambridge, MA: MIT P, 1996.

Foucault, Michel. *Aesthetics, Method and Epistemology.* Ed. James D. Faubion. Trans. Robert Hurley et al. New York: New, 1998.

Gifford, William. *The Satires of Decimus Junius Juvenalis, and of Aulus Persius Flaccus, Translated into English Verse.* 2 vols. London: W. Bulmer, 1817.

Golding, Alan. "*The New American Poetry* Revisited, Again." *Contemporary Literature* 39 (1998): 180-211.

———. "New, Newer, and Newest American Poetries." *The Recovery of the Public World: Essays on Poetics in Honour of Robin Blaser.* Ed. Charles Watts and Edward Byrne. Burnaby, BC: Talonbooks, 1999. 339-50.

Hejinian, Lyn. "The Rejection of Closure." *Poetics Journal* 4 (1984): 134-43.

Hollander, John. *The Figure of Echo.* Berkeley: U of California P, 1981.

Hoover, Paul, ed. *Postmodern American Poetry: A Norton Anthology.* New York: Norton, 1994.

Jameson, Fredric. *Postmodernism, or, The Cultural Logic of Late Capitalism.* Durham, NC: Duke UP, 1991.

Lazer, Hank. *Opposing Poetries: Issues and Institutions.* Vol. 1. Evanston, IL: Northwestern UP, 1996. 2 vols.

Leavis, F. R. "English Poetry of the 18th Century." *Scrutiny* June 1936: 13-31.

Longenbach, James. *Modern Poetry after Modernism.* New York: Oxford UP, 1997.

McClatchy, J. D., ed. *The Vintage Book of Contemporary American Poetry.* New York: Vintage, 1990.

Menand, Louis. *Discovering Modernism: T. S. Eliot and His Context.* New York: Oxford UP, 1987.

Messerli, Douglas, ed. *From the Other Side of the Century: A New American Poetry, 1960-1990.* Los Angeles: Sun & Moon, 1994.

Perelman, Bob. "Three Case Histories: Ross's 'Failure of Modernism.'" *Poetics Journal* Sept. 1987: 118-25.

Perloff, Marjorie. "Normalizing John Ashbery." *Jacket* Jan. 1998. <http://www.jacket.zip.com.au/jacket02/perloff02.html>.

———. *The Poetics of Indeterminacy.* 1981. Evanston, IL: Northwestern UP, 1999.

Ransom, John Crowe. *The World's Body.* New York: Scribner's, 1938.

Schultz, Susan M. "'Returning to Bloom': John Ashbery's Critique of Harold Bloom." *Contemporary Literature* 37 (1996): 24-48.

————, ed. *The Tribe of John: Ashbery and Contemporary Poetry.* Tuscaloosa, AL: U of Alabama P, 1995.

Shetley, Vernon. *After the Death of Poetry: Poetry and Audience in Contemporary America.* Durham, NC: Duke UP, 1993.

Shoptaw, John. *On the Outside Looking Out.* Cambridge, MA: Harvard UP, 1994.

Stevens, Wallace. *The Collected Poems of Wallace Stevens.* New York: Knopf, 1954.

Vendler, Helen, ed. *The Harvard Book of Contemporary American Poetry.* Cambridge, MA: Belknap-Harvard UP, 1985.

Weinberger, Eliot, ed. *American Poetry since 1950: Innovators and Outsiders.* New York: Marsilio, 1993.

Williams, William Carlos. *Autobiography.* New York: Random, 1951.

James Gibbons (review date fall 2001)

SOURCE: Gibbons, James. "Eccentric Visions: Ashbery's *Other Traditions.*" *Raritan* 21, no. 2 (fall 2001): 146-61.

[*In the following review, Gibbons lauds Ashbery's celebration of minor poets in* Other Traditions, *highlighting the chapter on John Wheelwright's life and work.*]

What is minor poetry? In the opening remarks of his Charles Eliot Norton lectures delivered at Harvard in 1989 and 1990, John Ashbery regards the question, rightly, as an invitation to frivolity. It's not asked much these days, for reasons that probably have more to do with the fate of reading than the nature of the question. As for frivolity, Ashbery cites the example of Auden, who in his introduction to *Nineteenth-Century British Minor Poets* (1966) proposed that a major poet satisfies "about three and a half" of five conditions concerning output, range, originality, technical skill, and evolution of style and treatment. The minor poets are those who fail the test. Granting his usual archness, Auden might well have been serious, but only to the extent that such criteria confirmed rather than displaced his intuited sense of value among poets. He writes, "I know perfectly well that Shelley is a major poet, and [William] Barnes a minor one," and so do we, so why can't we leave it at that?

Ashbery's Norton lectures, touched up and published last year under the title *Other Traditions,* suggest that the question of minor poetry is still worth asking, if only as a point of departure. The book provides a survey of Ashbery's taste for poets who are peripheral for most readers but of central importance to him. By way of introduction, he claims with somewhat unconvincing modesty that he could add little "of value to the critical literature concerning the certifiably major poets whom I feel as influences," a group that includes Stevens, Stein, Bishop, and Auden. Instead, he asks us to consider six poets of a different order: the Englishmen John Clare and Thomas Lovell Beddoes, the French writer Raymond Roussel, and three American moderns, John Wheelwright, Laura Riding, and David Schubert. These poets are cherished for being "certifiably," and more than merely, "minor": Ashbery contends that he values Schubert's slender oeuvre more than the poems of Pound or Eliot, and he has made substantial claims for John Wheelwright for decades. The poets of *Other Traditions* are eccentric, erratic, quirky, sometimes mad, but they are not, for Ashbery at least, second-rate.

These lectures might be taken as a rejoinder to Eliot's remark, in "Tradition and the Individual Talent," that "no poet, no artist of any art, has his complete meaning alone." Ashbery's six poets are tangential to *any* tradition, and not only the "canonical" one (always a vaguer notion than it seems, in any case). The "other" traditions, it turns out, aren't really traditions at all, since these poets are all lonely figures whose works, as Ashbery writes of Beddoes's "Death's Jest Book," have a "stupefying originality." Originality, that is, without issue. Raymond Roussel's writing is distinct "from the rest of literature . . . almost as though it had a different molecular structure"; John Wheelwright's strain of improbably visionary protest poetry defies imitation; Laura Riding's imperious perversity in refusing to allow her work to be reprinted guaranteed its limited if not quite negligible influence. Madness claimed Clare and Schubert. Because these poets do not take center stage, Ashbery can read them in isolation, which, given the peculiarities of each, is the most profitable and perhaps the only way to read them.

The eccentricities of the poets in *Other Traditions* provide more than just the seasoning of novelty and particularity. Ashbery isn't interested in those secondary figures whose poems are so often numbingly representative of their own era, defining the ground that sets off the major poets in high relief. None of Ashbery's poets are "minor" in this way; they are all too odd for that. He likes poems that seem ragged and fractured even in their diction: David Schubert's lines are "sharpened" by their "slight skewings"; the works of Roussel and Wheelwright are characterized by radical shifts of focus that Ashbery likens to the effects of Cubist paintings. As for larger formal structures, Ashbery regards the failure to realize fully achieved forms as an accomplishment of sorts, particularly when he discusses the two nineteenth-century figures, Clare and Beddoes, whose works anticipate later developments in poetry. Clare's "sonnets haven't the shapeliness of real sonnets, his longer poems the graceful expansiveness of the odes of William Collins he so admired, but to our ears they capture the rhythms of nature, its vagaries and messiness, in a way that even Keats never did." Ashbery values Clare for his refusal to let the countryside of his native Northhamptonshire stand for anything but what it is, without relying on the mediating concepts favored by the preceding generation of Romantic poets. "We are far from emotion recollected in tranquility or even the gently shaping music of Keats's grasshopper sonnet. Clare's poems are dispatches from the front," Ashbery writes. This is Clare's "seeming modernity." The ornately decadent verse of Thomas Lovell Beddoes, the subject of the second lecture, seems as far as possible from Clare's visionary sincerity (and Ashbery notes that the two poets represent opposing tendencies in his own work), but perhaps they aren't so different after all: Beddoes's fractured poems also anticipate modernism, and "Eliot's and subsequent fragmentations in poetry have shown us how to deal with fragments: by leaving them as they are, at most intuiting a meaning from their proximity to each other, but in general leaving it at that."

Ashbery's taste for fragmentary poems attracts him to works that resist interpretation, poems whose difficulty often edges toward opacity. At times he comes off as a connoisseur of the esoteric, or at the very least as a reader incapable of frustration. But not all forms of bewilderment are identical, and one of Ashbery's virtues as a critic is the patience he brings to poems that don't give up their secrets easily, if at all. Ashbery's refusal to rush to judgment about a poem, his pleasure in holding manifold possibilities of meaning in suspension, results in a kind of focused reticence that allows him to remain alert to a range of effects and to convincingly show that these poets are worth a second look—or perhaps a first look. Ashbery wants to make the seemingly paradoxical case that these six poets are marginal *and* essential, and for the most part he succeeds.

It's a case that he makes almost in spite of himself. Ashbery's appointment to the Norton chair appears to have surprised him, and he is reluctant to make sweeping critical generalizations about even these "certifiably minor" figures. He tells us that his judgments can't be separated from his career as a poet, and if his readings seem bound to his working needs, well, perhaps this was why he was awarded the Norton chair in the first place. He speculates that the committee that named him to the lectureship might have expected an explanation of his own "hermetic" poems, since "there seems to be a feeling in the academic world that there's something interesting about my poetry, though little agreement as to its ultimate worth and considerable confusion about what, if anything, it means." If this were the case, the committee, by his own admission, is bound to be disappointed. For Ashbery, as we'll see, explaining poetry is

the same as explaining it away, and poets, at any rate, are notoriously faulty guides to their own work. At the beginning of the first lecture, he recalls a workshop hosted by Richard Howard in which Howard's students, mystified by Ashbery's work, were freshly baffled when he tried to answer their questions about it. "They wanted the key to your poetry," Howard later told him, "but you presented them with a new set of locks." Ashbery doesn't want to seem willfully obscure or coy or haughty about the import of his work, but he insists that the poetry is its own explanation. Nevertheless, he keeps hinting that the lectures may leave some clues for those who care to look, perhaps because of some nervousness about their coherence as a whole. In the lecture on Laura Riding, the fifth of the series, he claims that he "chose the writers under discussion partly because I like them and partly because I felt they would shed some light on my own writing for those who feel the need of it. So far, I agree, not much of the latter has happened, but perhaps by the end it will have, if only by default."

This sort of diffidence is found throughout *Other Traditions,* which seems at first glance a genial but merely personal tour of Ashbery's avowedly off-center sensibility, and one that will be of interest only for those devoted to him as a poet, admittedly a substantial group. But *Other Traditions* is more than simply a gloss on the poetry "for those who feel the need of it" (and whether the lectures succeed in illuminating Ashbery's poems "if only by default" is an open question). Rather startlingly, given the affable and nearly defensive tenor of some of his observations, Ashbery asks whether there is something minor poetry "can do for us when major poetry can merely wring its hands," and tells us that he often returns to his minor poets when he needs to be reminded "what poetry is." There are several ways his claim for these poets can be taken. In its weakest sense, it is simply a comment on his working methods, since each of these poets, with the exception of Roussel, have set him to work on new poems (in his phrase, they have provided him with "a poetic jump-start for times when the batteries have run down"). Why these poets in particular? Ashbery shrugs his shoulders; his preferences seem arbitrary and mysterious in their origin. "One can't choose one's influences, they choose you," he writes. "If that means I too am off-center, so be it: I am only telling it as it happened, not as it should have happened."

For Ashbery, the distance between "as it happened" and "as it should have happened" is what separates the experience of private reading, with its missteps, grasping intuitions, and random endearments, from the retrospective consensus of literary history. Although he has been reading these poets for years, he has not been able to dispel the aura of oddness that first attracted him to their works. Nor, it seems, would he want to. Their poems remain as peculiar as ever; repeated reading does not lead to mastery but to a state of lucid familiarity, which is not quite the same as comprehension or interpretive certainty. This sort of reading experience is hardly confined to Ashbery's six poets, of course, and one way to distinguish major writers is by the inexhaustibility of interpretations that can be brought to bear on their works. But even the most difficult and demanding of poems, if it has been written by a major poet, has been integrated into narratives of literary history and can be read on terms other than simply those of the poem itself. Or, to go further, even if we limit ourselves to "the poem itself," the way we read it tends to be informed, if not overdetermined, by the accumulation of criticism and influence. This must be what Ashbery means when he claims, in his fifth lecture, that reading the work of the poets in *Other Traditions* "isn't quite as simple as it is with a poet such as, say, John Keats, where one can simply take down a book from a shelf, open it, and begin reading and enjoying it. With each of them, some previous adjustment or tuning is required." Keats, presumably, doesn't require such adjustment because it has already been made, since Keats's poetry has helped to define what we expect when we read a poem.

Apart from his personal enthusiasms, then, Ashbery is making a larger claim for these seemingly peripheral figures. It is, I think, that the poets in *Other Traditions,* precisely because of their idiosyncrasies, restore poetry to its fundamental strangeness. Their poems demand to be read on their own terms. He speculates that were Beddoes's verse dramas to be staged, "they would require a specially trained audience," and the same might be said of the other poets he takes up. These poets give us unexplored alternatives: if John Wheelwright's work, as Ashbery claims, is "as pregnant with options for the future of poetry as anything Pound or Eliot produced," we have to take this on faith, since no one, except perhaps Ashbery himself, has tried to realize these options. The poems remain isolated artifacts, "pure" in the sense that they resist assimilation into the story of a movement or era except in the broadest terms. In short, for Ashbery's minor figures as for his own poetry, the poem is its own explanation.

Ashbery's sense of the poem's autonomy leads him to reject the guidance offered by the poets themselves. Considering Laura Riding, whose fanatical theorizing culminated in a smug and vigilant renunciation of poetry, Ashbery writes:

> Her poetry, hedged about with caveats of every sort in the form of admonitory prefaces and postscripts, presents us with something like a minefield; one reads it always with a sensation of sirens and flashing red lights in the background. What then are we to do with a body of poetry whose author warns us that we have very little chance of understanding it, and who believes that poetry itself is a lie? Why, misread it, of course, if it seems to merit reading, as hers so obviously does.

Riding's case is so extreme that misreading her is inevitable, but Ashbery's views here typify his attitude toward any attempt to paraphrase or decipher the work of the poets in *Other Traditions.* Noting that admirers of Roussel have sought "some hidden, alchemical key for decoding the work," Ashbery insists that this sort of approach risks "diluting the very glamour that brings readers to that work in the first place." And, he might have added, brings them back to that work again and again. Ashbery wants to illuminate these poets without demystifying them, preserving the "glamour" that retains something of the excitement and uncertainty of a first reading. This skirts dangerously close to critical impressionism, but Ashbery is able to provide real insight into the works of these poets, which he has been reading since at least the 1950s, while keeping their mystique intact.

The lecture on John Wheelwright is the strongest chapter of *Other Traditions,* the essay in which Ashbery's biographical commentary is fused most seamlessly with his discussion of individual poems. Although a small but varied group of poets, ranging from Kenneth Rexroth to John Hollander, have expressed their admiration for Wheelwright's poetry over the years, Ashbery has been the most persistent and enthusiastic advocate. Writing in the *New York Times Book Review* in 1979, he called Wheelwright's *Collected Poems* "one of the hundred most important works of Western civilization since World War II"; thirteen years earlier, eulogizing Frank O'Hara, he had written that O'Hara's death had been "the biggest secret loss to American poetry since John Wheelwright was killed by a car in Boston in 1940." I'd like to spend the remainder of this essay discussing Ashbery's treatment of Wheelwright and his work, in part because Wheelwright remains a relatively little known figure, but primarily because Wheelwright epitomizes the sort of poet who Ashbery feels is far too important to be ignored, yet remains stubbornly, intractably marginal.

Wheelwright's value as a poet depends on the quality of his poems, but his life is important too, as are the lives of the five other poets in *Other Traditions.* I've noted that the eccentricities of the poems that Ashbery discusses are not incidental to his estimation of their worth, and neither are the oddities of these poets' lives. In each of the lectures, Ashbery includes a biographical sketch of the poet, which need not be taken as anything more than a courtesy to his audience (who might recall something of the lives of Clare or Riding, but can hardly be expected to know much about the others). And yet these biographies, extreme even by the standards of poets' lives, suggest a pattern of attraction. There is the case of Laura Riding, whose erotic entanglement with Robert Graves and the Irish poet Geoffrey Phibbs led her to leap from the third-story window of the house she shared with Graves on the island of Mallorca; this was but one—and not the final—act in a life of outrageous histrionics. Writing the verse novel *La Doublure*, the nineteen-year-old Raymond Roussel experienced, by his own account, a monomaniacal "sensation of universal glory" that caused him to believe he was the equal of Dante and Shakespeare: "I felt what the aging Victor Hugo felt at seventy, what Napoleon felt in 1811, what Tannhäuser dreamed at the Venusberg: I felt glory." The madness of Clare and Schubert has already been mentioned. Without a doubt, Ashbery is drawn to these sorts of personalities: we might recall that his **Girls on the Run** (1999) was inspired by the works of Henry Darger, the Chicago recluse whose illustrated epic of child heroines pitted against their enslavers in cosmic warfare has made him, posthumously, the world's most renowned outsider artist.

These biographies make for some fascinating storytelling—and are certainly more interesting than a résumé of prizes and university appointments—but they serve a larger purpose by confirming that the difficulties and quirks of the poems are not the result of willful obscurity. These poets write the way they do because of needs that have something to do with their "disordered affective lives" (a phrase Ashbery uses to describe Clare and Beddoes but that could be applied with equal aptness to Roussel, Wheelwright, Riding, and Schubert). Ashbery is too astute to marry the biographical cause to the poetic effect with specificity; in fact, a good share of the lecture on Schubert argues against a critic who reads the poems too literally as a gloss on the life. The personalities of the poets are, nonetheless, important because they guarantee, as it were, the authenticity of the odd features of the work. This seems especially important for the three Americans who came of age during the 1920s and 1930s, since, as anyone who has browsed the little magazines of the time will recognize, there were plenty of poets writing during these decades whose difficulties are merely the borrowed clothes of modernism. The lives of the poets in **Other Traditions** suggest that the idiosyncratic gestures of each poet are the expression of an evolved sensibility, however mannered, and represent more than the superficial appropriation of fashionable trends.

Wheelwright's life, though by no means the strangest of those featured in **Other Traditions,** makes the eccentricities of his poems seem inevitable. Wheelwright had a large circle of acquaintances, as is evident from the dedications that accompany most of his poems, and those who remember him have left behind anecdotes of his peculiarities. Matthew Josephson remembers Wheelwright's taste for sharply creased suits and bowler hats even when taking summer hikes in the country and recalls that he carried fourteen pairs of shoes with him while traveling in Europe in the 1920s. He was known to burrow beneath a rug and crawl on all fours across a room in the middle of fashionable Boston parties.

Descended from two of New England's original and most prosperous families, Wheelwright spent his childhood like a character out of a James novel, living in what he later called "the most splendid garden of Massachusetts," an enormous estate north of Boston that had been bought when Wheelwright's great-great-grandfather was the richest merchant in New England. He later became a passionately committed Marxist but never entirely disavowed his birthright of inherited privilege, which at any rate became increasingly symbolic after the family's fortune began to seep away in the wake of his father's suicide in 1912. Not surprisingly, given his background, he was sent in 1916 to Harvard, where he hoped to begin his education for the Anglican priesthood. There he became involved with a literary circle of students that included e. e. Cummings, Malcolm Cowley, and John Dos Passos (as well as the Blake scholar and forgettable poet S. Foster Damon, who would become his brother-in-law and remain a close friend for the rest of his life). He was expelled shortly before he was scheduled to graduate either because of pranks or irregular class attendance. After spending two years in Europe, he returned to Boston and made an abortive attempt at a career as an architect, his father's profession. (Ashbery discusses one of Wheelwright's most moving poems, "Father," that begins with a description of the bridge across the Charles designed by the elder Wheelwright and ends by asking "my first friend, Father" to "come home, dead man, who made your mind my home.") By the early 1930s he had fully embraced socialism and became involved in the founding of Harvard's John Reed Club and the Vanguard Verse project, which sponsored a correspondence course in poetry and published the little magazine *Poems for a Dime*; he even ran for public office on the Socialist Party ticket. In the meantime, the family's "splendid garden" had been parceled into lots and sold, and Wheelwright's already modest allowance evaporated when his brother's investments collapsed in the first years of the Depression. But neither his reduced means nor his Marxism kept Wheelwright from playing the dandy: he sported his trademark raccoon coat and Molacca cane even as he took to preaching revolution from a soapbox during rallies in Boston's South End. He was killed by a drunk driver shortly after his collection *Political Self-Portrait* was published in 1940, an accident that seems all the more tragic to Ashbery since Wheelwright was, in his estimation, "at the height of his creative powers" and "at last poised for recognition as one of the leading American poets of his time."

Wheelwright's poems never moved far from the religious preoccupations that propel the exploratory thrusts and chaotic vigor of his early poetry, and as a result his work bears little relation to the poems of social protest that were spun out by the yard by "committed" poets during the 1930s. And, it must be said, he was far more gifted than the poets who shared his political sympathies at the time. He could write poems with intricately formal effects, though his use of traditional verse forms such as the sonnet was unorthodox and innovative, anticipating the unconventional sonnets of Berryman and Edwin Denby. He had a fine ear and could duplicate the weary speech of a New England fisherman (in "State of Maine") or mock the idiom of political sloganeering (in "Masque with Clowns") with an ease that rivals that of Dos Passos or Kenneth Fearing. Passages of ferocious social satire are scattered throughout the poems. When he chose, Wheelwright could write strange and brittle lyrics such as "Why Must You Know?" with its indelible closing quatrain, "One who turns to earth again / finds solace in its weight; and deep / hears the blood forever keep / the silence between drops of rain." Lyric writing, rarely sustained for very long in Wheelwright's work, is but one of several modes that make up the ever changing texture of the poetry. It is precisely this collagelike texture that appeals to Ashbery. Discussing the opening sonnet of the book-length sequence *Mirrors of Venus,* he charts how the poem moves from the "disarmingly folksy tone that could be out of the *Saturday Evening Post*" to end in an entirely different register. Later, in the lecture on David Schubert, he writes that "the typical Schubert poem has the appearance of something smashed, not too painstakingly put back together, and finally contemplated with remorse and amusement." Ashbery likes poems built out of incongruous fragments: instead of Williams's smooth-running machines made of words, these are rough-hewn contraptions that have some of the charm (if none of the artlessness) of naive art.

Readers new to Wheelwright's work who have less tolerance for his disorienting shifts of tone may find his poems impenetrable at first and may be reluctant to return to them. Well aware that Wheelwright is a tough sell, Ashbery acknowledges the poetry's difficulty from the start but stresses that Wheelwright's "conviction is contagious." This may seem an odd quality to emphasize in light of Ashbery's subsequent remark that "in his person as well as in his writing, Wheelwright was literally a set of walking contradictions," but it is precisely Wheelwright's "conviction" that gives his contradictory gestures the appearance and weight of necessity. Wheelwright's reluctance or inability to resolve his conflicting tendencies yields the "positive results of failure in his work." Works of art thrive on contradictions, of course, and rarely efface all traces of opposing tensions. But even in the self-consciously fragmentary works of modernism there are usually movements toward resolution, transitions that mute the dissonance of antithetical techniques and themes. This isn't the case with Wheelwright's poetry, and Ashbery is right to emphasize his "inborn tendency to elide transitions." Although Ashbery claims (without much elaboration) that Wheelwright's late works dispel these antithetical

pressures, it is clear that what interests him most about Wheelwright's poems is the "fertile short-circuiting, the result of many tensions pulling in opposite directions, that is the air his poetry breathes."

These terms recall Ashbery's praise of the painter R. B. Kitaj, whose greatness, according to an essay published in *Art in America* in 1982, results from "the spirit of genuine contradiction, fertile in its implications, [that] thrives in the work, though not in the discussions of it between Kitaj and his critics." The "discussions" concerned Kitaj's statements about the centrality of the human figure in art and his insistence that his paintings and drawings, despite their eclectic range of allusion, are meant for a mass audience. Ashbery stresses that Kitaj's works are more nuanced and conflicted than his more programmatic remarks would lead one to expect; Kitaj's "exemplary" contradictions give his paintings their force and vitality. Along the same lines, Wheelwright's poetry belies and even undermines his doctrinaire tendencies, the didactic side that comes out in the schematic (though hardly clear) commentary that accompanies the poems. As in the case of Riding, the poems are better than his explanations would have you believe.

That said, the quality of Wheelwright's work is uneven. Many of the more ponderous poems wear down the reader because of their dependence on symbols and archetypes steeped in the darkness of Wheelwright's personal cosmology. He was proud of his heterodox Puritan ancestors, particularly the John Wheelwright who was banished from Boston after supporting Anne Hutchinson in the Antinomian Controversy, and he inherited their disputatious temperament and dogmatic sense of righteousness. His work is pervaded by a sermonizing impulse that, at best, gives his knotty rhetoric a ceremonial grandeur. In its most taxing passages, the poetry reads like some remote doctrinal quarrel among the voices in Wheelwright's head, each with its own cryptic logic and angry fire. This gets exhausting (Ashbery cites a critic of the early poetry who wrote, hyperbolically but not without a measure of accuracy, that it "leaves the mind in a state bordering on collapse"), but to get anywhere with Wheelwright's work, one has to read all of it. His poems do not anthologize well (when they are anthologized at all), particularly the long poems that are all but impossible to excerpt meaningfully. The three books (excepting pamphlets and broadsides) published in Wheelwright's lifetime, *Rock and Shell: Poems 1923-1933* (1933), *Mirrors of Venus: A Novel in Sonnets* (1938), and *Political Self-Portrait* (1940), contain interrelated poems, and even Wheelwright's seemingly self-contained lyrics suffer when read by themselves. A lyric from *Rock and Shell,* entitled "Would You Think?," gives a sense of Wheelwright's abilities and the limitations of reading his poems in isolation:

Does the sound or the silence make
music? When no ripples pass
over watery trees; like painted glass
lying beneath a quiet lake;
    would you think the real forest lay
    only in the reflected
    trees, which are protected
    by non-existence from the air of day?
Our blood gives voice to earth and shell.
They speak but in refracted sounds.
The silence of the dead resounds,
But what they say we cannot tell.
    Only echoes of what they taught
    are heard by living ears.
    The tongue tells what it hears
    and drowns the silence which the dead besought.
The questioning, circumambient light
the answering, luminiferous doubt
listen, and whisper it about
until the mocking stars turn bright.
    Tardy flowers have bloomed long
    but they have long been dead.
    Now on the ice, like lead
    hailstones drop loud, with a rattlesnake's song.

The poem moves from its opening question to a scene so generalized that it appears to be hypothetical: an image reflected on frozen water offers itself as an emblem of a Platonic "real forest" protected from the threat of "the air of day." The mere suggestion of the otherworldly "real forest" leads to impenetrable thickets. The poem's speaker tries to clarify the relationship between sound, silence, and music—which are separated by distances akin to those that divide the living and the dead—but can only blur his distinctions. In characteristic Wheelwright fashion, every proposition the speaker makes is qualified, if not rescinded, by what follows. But by the end of the poem the scene reveals itself as not merely an enabling premise for speculation but an actual setting, subject to time. In one of the sonnets in *Mirrors of Venus,* Wheelwright claims to "unthink the nonsense of Shelley's 'If Winter comes, can Spring be far behind?'—a mere treadmill, and no path to heaven." The wintry landscape of "Would You Think?" promises death rather than redemption in the cycle of the seasons; the unnamed menace of the "air of day" is brought forth in a shower of hail. Whether the "rattlesnake's song" is an act of compensation or scorn is one of the poem's unresolved ambiguities.

"Would You Think?" becomes less opaque—or at least achieves a fuller, more suggestive opacity—when read beside other poems in *Rock and Shell.* It appears to have been written as a companion piece to the previous poem, "Why Must You Know?," in which the sound of a frozen bird falling on a patch of snow prompts a dialogue about the violence of being (the air is figured as a bird of prey) and the longing for nonexistence. (Wheelwright tells us in a note that one of the two figures in "Why Must You Know?" speaks throughout "Would You Think?," but this isn't much help since the note also raises the possibility that the speakers may be the product of a single mind.) The pairing of "questioning, circumambient light" and "answering, luminiferous doubt," baffling when the poem is read by itself, recalls the "Argument" to "Forty Days," a long poem about Saint Thomas, which opens with the statement, "The risen Christ came to show not questioning but doubt to the Apostles as the arena of faith." The repetition of terms links the Platonic speculation of "Would You Think?" to the skeptically refashioned Christianity that characterizes Wheelwright's most ambitious work.

This helps, but how much? It's not that "Forty Days" or any of the other poems in *Rock and Shell* make "Would You Think?" more transparent. But Wheelwright's tendency to return to a circumscribed if by no means small set of terms, images, idiosyncrasies of phrasing, and oppositions allows one to make headway with the poems in spite of their difficulties and suggestive incoherence. For all that Wheelwright comes across as a poet of ideas, struggling through the orthodoxies of Christianity and Marxism in order to create a revolutionary credo of his own, what endures in his work is the record of a mind whose relationship to its own thought is constantly in flux. The best way to read Wheelwright's poetry is to track its recurring images and figures as they take on new and often opposed inflections. In the poem that Ashbery calls Wheelwright's greatest work, "Train Ride," the poet returns repeatedly to the slogan of the German socialist Karl Liebknecht, "Always the enemy is the foe at home," as he spins out his variations on Liebknecht's theme. The quotation orders the unfolding movement of "Train Ride" but is itself a part of the poem's motion, its meaning altered with each repetition. Although such characteristic shifts and dislocations of meaning can appear within the space of a line or two, these local transformations usually resonate with larger trajectories in Wheelwright's work as a whole.

Wheelwright's poems are filled with ideas and abstractions that are incessantly fragmented by their contact with reality. As such they require a special kind of reading, and Ashbery may be as close to an ideal reader as Wheelwright's work will ever get. Which brings us back to the question of influence on Ashbery's own poetry. Setting aside Wheelwright's radical politics, there are strong affinities between the two poets. Wheelwright's example, more than any of the other poets in *Other Traditions* (with the possible exception of Riding), clarifies Ashbery's intention in his own poetry, stated at the outset of the first lecture, "of somehow turning these [thought] processes into poetic objects, a position perhaps kin to Dr. Williams's 'No ideas but in things,' with the caveat that, for me, ideas are also things."

Williams, of course, is a major poet, but after reading *Other Traditions* the distinction between "major" and "minor," though real, seems more irrelevant than ever. Ashbery's lectures celebrate the imagination's efforts to understand the particularity of experience without recourse to the false transcendence of purely abstract thought. Even more so than Williams's famous dictum, Ashbery's observations on poetry in *Other Traditions* recall the late poems of Stevens, the gorgeous final lyrics such as "The Course of a Particular" and "Not Ideas about the Thing but the Thing Itself." "Ariel was glad he had written his poems," he writes in "The Planet on the Table," because they bore "Some lineament or character, / Some affluence, if only half-perceived, / In the poverty of their words, / Of the planet of which they were part." Ashbery's lectures have increased our sense of poetry's affluence from unlikely sources, and for that we should be grateful.

Calvin Bedient (review date fall 2001)

SOURCE: Bedient, Calvin. "Charms and Afflictions." *Salmagundi* 132 (fall 2001): 186-94.

[*In the following review, Bedient admires the "painstaking, generous deliberations of Ashbery's clear and balanced intellect" in* Other Traditions, *and characterizes* Your Name Here *as lackluster and verbose, contrasting both works with the poetry and criticism of William Logan.*]

After all these years, John Ashbery still has it out for simplicity, harmony, and being forgotten. Especially the last: *your name here, or else.* Although his poems assume that one + everything is already an impossible mathematics, they don't like to say it any more than they like to say it. Lately, in fact, he has been publishing so many fat volumes that he might be piling up sandbags against the anticipated flood of oblivion.

It's the recent flood of his ink that has me worried. But, of course, the excesses in what has become one of the longest codas in recent memory—his spectacularly spoiled sentiments, his increasingly glaring, bewildering sense of humor—hardly matter. His name, Ashbery, with its built-in trope of having it both ways: ruin and fruition, is already written into the history of poetry. In a sense, it was always already written there; as the poet who created the reverse side of Whitman, who drowned modernism in disappointment, he was as inevitable as he is unique. He's arguably the major American poet of the last forty years. Forget *that.*

In his Charles Eliot Norton lectures, delivered at Harvard ten years ago but only recently ballasted with end notes, he befriends six minor poets whose eccentricity compares with his own and who (almost for that reason) must not be forgotten. One way to recommend yourself

to Ashbery is to be wrongly afflicted with neglect, both because your work needs some tolerance and because it didn't help that you went crazy, committed suicide, died early of a disease or an accident, or like Laura Riding shot your Pegasus after riding him ruthlessly toward "An empty whole, a whole emptiness" ("The Signs of Knowledge"). This poet turns away from the splashy, overvisited, dahlia talents ("I myself value Schubert more than Pound and Eliot," and he means David, not Franz, Schubert) and lingers, instead, before relatively unmolested yuccas with their "cadaverous bloom" (Wallace Stevens). He even calls the work of John Clare, Thomas Lovell Beddoes, Raymond Roussel, John Wheelwright, Riding, and Schubert *other traditions,* as if each alone were a tradition—a magnificence of status even a Pound or an Eliot could not sustain. He wonders aloud if he too wishes "to be given 'special treatment,'" or is it just that he likes "writing that isn't simple, where there is more than at first meets the eye." But even ten years ago he had already had plenty of special treatment (how much is enough?), and without the inconvenience of having to die first. And can he really be saying that Eliot and Pound are simple?

What makes this brilliantly peculiar major poet a friend to brilliantly peculiar minor poets may be a touching case of survivor's guilt. But for the grace of W. H. Auden—who on the recommendation of a friend called back the manuscript of *Some Trees,* which had not passed the initial screening test for the Yale Younger Poets award—there goes another David Schubert, if even so much. From Auden's *The Sea and the Mirror* Ashbery quotes Caliban's remark to his master that "we might very well not have been attending a production of yours this evening, had not some other and maybe— who can tell?—brighter talent married a barmaid or turned religious," etc. Should not those of lucky prominence remember the others? Ashbery says in his new poem **"Hang-Up Call"**—the title is his trope for personal existence—"Now give me my pants and money and let me go back and join the others. They're crying, you know."

"We believe in what survives," he notes in a lecture. In fact, the six poets had been surviving in a minor-minor way before his intervention, and he quotes dutifully and helpfully from the scholarship. So his quarrel is perhaps not so much with oblivion as with the neglect of High Eccentricity.

Adopting Ashbery's guess that his lectures might "shed some light" on his own work "for those who feel the need of it," what does one find? On the one hand, in Clare, Beddoes, and Roussel, there are anticipations of the poetics of open form that Ashbery himself has occasionally licked like sherbert. Clare, he writes wonderfully, "often starts up for no reason, like a beetle thrashing around in a weed patch, and stops as suddenly." But of course anything comparable in Ashbery's own work (and there isn't much) is already self-lit and on stage; it's sophisticated artistry. And after each of his flow-chart book-length poems, he returns to his favorite form, the traditional lyric (still traditional, no matter how many scrims of strangeness are hanged before it). Hence Ashbery's praise of and attention to short, stringent formal triumphs in lectures—for instance, Clare's "I Am," Beddoes's "Dream-Pedlary," Wheelwright's "Why Must You Know?," Schubert's "The Visitor," and Riding's—but I'm not persuaded by his choices from the work of this humorlessly hectoring poet; I recommend "Dear Possible." Though his new book hardly sustains the fact, he loves form for form's sake, almost as much as he loves mad little fits of splendor in modest contexts.

There is a much better reason to read *Other Traditions* than to look for what points toward Ashbery's own poetry, maps to which have already been supplied in spades by Ashbery's interviews and by his critics. More to be valued, I suggest, are the painstaking, generous deliberations of Ashbery's clear and balanced intellect and his numerous fine discriminations between each poet's good and not so good work.

With regard to his own recent books the not so good has dominated. The reader's expectation of more masterpieces from him may well sit down on the wayside and turn to that sillier thing, hope. Ashbery's work, from having been "a steely glitter chasing shadows like a pack / of hounds," as he put it in *Flow Chart* (1991), has become garrulous and desultory. (*Flow Chart* itself is so.)

Certainly, there are still passages in *Your Name Here* that electrify, that are strange new things in the world, such as, from **"Last Legs,"**

> My nephew—you remember him—
> tongue along a dusty fence.
> And I the day's coordinates.
> That's what an impression I am

—but much of the poetry relaxes into a patter whose intention to amuse fails to percolate: "This is *my* day! Anybody doesn't realize it / is a goddamn chameleon or a yes man!" (**"Lemurs and Pharisees"**). Chuckling to itself, it asks to be indulged: "The Sheriff of Heck is coming over, and you know what that means." Or else Ashbery now wants to have a good time in poetry. Where "Once it was all grace in the lifting. Awkward, yes, and not a little disconcerting" (**"The Water Inspector"**), often the new work is glibly cynical: "Life is a carnival, / I think. Besides, it's elsewhere" (**"Slumberer"**).

We glimpse the greatly charming Ashbery again in the following moment in **"Short-Term Memory"**:

> What about your immortal soul?
> I may have lost it, just this once, but other chapters
> will arrive, bright as a child's watercolor,
> and you'd want to be around me.

Strong, too, are parts of **"Crowd Conditions," "Enjoys Watching Foreign Films," "Strange Cinema," "Has to be Somewhere," "Vintage Masquerade," "And Again, March is Almost Here," "Slumberer," "Onion Skin," "This Room,"** and **"The History of My Life."** But even the good poems are given to slumps. Ashbery's apparent low opinion of himself, of us, of life, naturally makes it hard for him to rise above the Heck level. As for escaping oblivion, who really deserves to do so? **"The History of My Life,"** the one poem in *Your Name Here* that walks a straight plank, minus blindfolded caperings, raises the question:

> Once upon a time there were two brothers.
> Then there was only one: myself.
>
> I grew up fast, before learning to drive,
> even. There was I: a stinking adult.
>
> I thought of developing interests
> someone might take an interest in. No soap.
>
> I became very weepy for what had seemed
> like the pleasant early years. As I aged
>
> increasingly, I also grew more charitable
> with regard to my thoughts and ideas,
>
> thinking them at least as good as the next man's.
> Then a great devouring cloud
>
> came and loitered on the horizon, drinking
> it up for what seemed like months or years.

With that cloud soaking up the horizon (the antithesis of the six-day Lord-bearing cloud in Exodus), it hardly matters who survives and who doesn't. But, no, it *must*. The work must justify the life. Art is forgiveness through style and form—that kind of "grace"—if not a forgetting in the content. Nonetheless, Ashbery's poems are now likely to cut themselves into funny paper hats and it's all over but the sad little party. His work implies that it is time to be charitable toward it all, with an apologetic laugh. So, often stanza follows stanza without necessity, "like a barber adding an extra plop of lather / to a stupefied customer's face" (**"Heartache"**).

* * *

As a poet, William Logan is as confident and serious as Ashbery is jittery and apologetic. The antithesis lies deep: where for Ashbery a subject is a crisis—how circumscribe it? identify it? tolerate it?—Logan goes up to one as if it were simply there, like a house, an event, and sternly confronts it. He sets up before it his powers of observation and judgment, and not least his determination to take a formal stand and to display, in the snap and grace of his craft, an indomitable will to remain self-possessed, intact. Notable among his confreres in this regard are the English poets Michael Hofmann and James Fenton.

Logan stands off the subject, and stands apart from it even as he takes it on. Just how it reaches him, if it does, is not always apparent. The impression of his own poise and singleness is the thing. Those who prize self-possession as the highest quality in poetry will instantly take to his work. Of its kind, it is solidly made and pure.

Though Logan's fifth book of poems, *Night Battle,* is often good in very much the way that, among others, Robert Lowell, Philip Larkin, Elizabeth Bishop, and Geoffrey Hill have already been good, there is much to admire if one adopts while reading them the poems' own terms of ambition and measure. Logan's work has what he hopes to find in others' poetry: intelligence, knowledge, a tone distanced from "psychological concerns," serious insights, and the decencies and superior air (but not airs) of form. Often his lines are taut and vivid, as in "Long Island Sins":

> At 91, coldcocked on Demerol,
> Grandmother basks among the hyacinths,
> lost to the stale, sweet pall of Jacksonville,
> the lazy river and its hoodlum boats.

Like James Fenton (whom Logan admires) and Frederick Seidel, not to go back to Lowell, Logan makes quatrains fist up: the formal equivalent of machismo brooding within the tradition.

Unlike Lowell and Seidel, Logan lacks the rack and benefits of a commanding obsession, of a question addressed to existence or a passionate objection against it—lacks the ultimate note of necessity. His insights are usually familiar. Consider these lines in "The Livery of Byzantium": "the banded owl calls down / dominion on the pathways of the mouse. / More light! More light!" The manner and words (and not just Goethe's dying cry) re-echo in the marble halls of "the tradition" (something of Shakespeare, for starters). And the intimation, evoked in an old-fashioned high style, is, after all, a commonplace, if one of the great ones of literature: death (an owly darkness) terrorizes life. And although Logan occasionally refers to religious concepts, his poems neither confirm belief nor open it up as an abyssal question. "And then the rain— / the corrugated tin

erupted like sin" is powerful evocation, but in a poem by Lowell or Geoffrey Hill, the concern with errancy itself would have rendered secondary the rained-on tin, made it the illustration rather than, as here, the focus.

Even when he doesn't address it openly, Logan feels a nostalgia for purity. It dominates my favorite among these poems, "Paradise." I'll begin with the fourth stanza:

> The British goddess lies beneath the shed
> in a frieze of worm—not a Paradise,
> still less what Paradise would become:
>
> weedy, mean, trivial,
> the flint knapping up through the winter ground.
> In the bleakest marches,
>
> Romans never passed a night
> without a pitched camp of rampart and ditch.
> Your house still overlooks a prospect
>
> of benevolent brick facades,
> each concealing its private signature of garden.
> Not much changes. Not much in us changes
>
> here, beyond the material end of Paradise.

These lines have the substance, and not just the accents, of seriousness. The language is direct as a thumb pressed against the jugular. The thought snaps along electrically, you cannot stop it. Here is the real thing.

In his criticism, too, Logan is in some ways Ashbery's opposite. Ashbery is not quick to judge or at least to condemn; Logan, famously, is quick to do both. His opinions are frank, sometimes blunt, and come forward at once.

Logan is a fiery critic (though less so in *Reputations of the Tongue: On Poets and Poetry,* the most recent collection of reviews and essays, than before) partly because he has a commanding, almost unforgiving sense of what poetry is and should be. It's true that as you read through this new collection, it's hard to locate the center and shape of that sense. But its force is felt as Logan displays again and again his acute sense of how underachieving the poets are whose work comes before him. It is the same sense that history has displayed toward the hundreds and thousands of poets in each generation. Logan has the ambition of being as smart about contemporary poetry as history itself will be. His severe scrutinies are not as charming—or as charmingly wicked—as Randall Jarrell's (and of all critics Logan most resembles Jarrell; his manner is a nephew of the master's): usually, but not always, the bubbles are missing from the champagne. But there is much stimulation in their sharp-edged, decided intelligence and their frequent hum of gyroscopic precision. They turn a book of poems every which way to the light, albeit a jack light. And there is force, fluidity, and trajectory in their phrasing.

Not the least of Logan's qualities and merits as a critic is his undauntedness. His mind seems dressed in a natural armor (the metal of a good conscience?), which makes it fearless. Unlike most critics, Logan brushes the tissue paper of reputation aside to see what is really in the box. (And it doesn't help, so it appears, to be a long-standing friend of his, like Geoffrey Hill, even if Logan rivals Yale in admiring him. You could be a Milton and still get it from Logan, so long as you hadn't yet died. Because in that case you might learn something about the plaguing mixture of strengths and limitations in what you're doing.) Logan doesn't hold tea parties for older reputations; instead, he conducts trials. Here he is on Adrienne Rich: "Adrienne Rich was a poet before she became a polemicist. . . . It is not the politics I object to but the banality of their expression, the rhythm that becomes a rant." On James Tate: "He shares with Ashbery a sublime self-indulgence. . . . Ashbery, at least on occasion, toys with large and important concerns; but Tate usually settles for the hollow laugh or frivolous act (a better poet would know how to make his frivolity pointed.) . . . Tate is proud of his carelessness, of his unwillingness to favor the Imagination in a kingdom ruled by Fancy." On Robert Creeley: "In Creeley we never get a memorable image, a thing seen precisely, a sentence carried as far as thinking will take it. He has eliminated most of the texture of verse, of the pleasurable massing of words. . . . Nothing replaces this loss of the frivolity of beauty except the quiet squalor of sentiment."

Logan likes best (until the next surprising judgment) art that responds "*to* tradition . . . *within* tradition." By tradition he seems to mean the English measure (it is strategic to echo William Carlos Williams here). But there are other traditions, if not, a la Ashbery, one per poet. What does "within" mean in Logan's formula for correctness? It sounds like a fold, a pale, the city walls. Logan favors poets (such as Amy Clampitt, J. D. McClatchy, and Gjertrud Schnackenberg) who keep a formal distance without altogether sacrificing warmth ("the world is at times more deeply entered through an isolation from it"). He can be as severe on a "chilly formal manner" and rinky-tink neo-formalism as on the weak generation of fields of meaning in some avant-garde poems (of Michael Palmer's work he says, "My complaint is not that this poetry raises a challenge, but that it is not challenging enough"). Such preferences are matters of temperament—basically unarguable. My own bias tells me that for some time now "the tradition" has been overfull of itself and in danger of becom-

ing stuffed. Ashbery knows the feeling—Ashbery whose sensibility, Logan too killingly says, is "utterly fraudulent." Logan is the critic as the Man of Taste, to whom the man attuned to primordial indeterminacy, in the distinction Giorgio Agamben makes in *The Man Without Content,* draws a blank.

Aidan Wasley (essay date winter 2002)

SOURCE: Wasley, Aidan. "The 'Gay Apprentice': Ashbery, Auden, and a Portrait of the Artist as a Young Critic." *Contemporary Literature* 43, no. 4 (winter 2002): 667-708.

[*In the following essay, Wasley examines the influence of W. H. Auden's* The Sea and the Mirror *on Ashbery, and illustrates a generally unrecognized didactic aspect of Ashbery's poetry.*]

It is a well-rehearsed episode in the history of postwar American poetry that W. H. Auden selected John Ashbery for the Yale Younger Poets Prize in 1956, inaugurating the younger writer's public career as the most honored and influential American poet of his generation. What is less well known by readers and critics, however, is that Ashbery had chosen Auden more than a decade earlier. While critical accounts of Ashbery's poetics have often, and justifiably, emphasized his connections to Wallace Stevens, Ashbery himself claims Auden as his most significant poetic model. "Auden . . . was the first big influence on my work, more so than Stevens," he has said ("Art" 37), contra Harold Bloom, his earliest and most influential critical champion, who has famously placed Ashbery in the lineage of what he calls the "American sublime" of Emerson, Whitman, and Stevens. "Auden was the most important because he came first," Ashbery has continued to remind interviewers (Interview with the author [1989]).[1] Indeed, on one occasion, when asked about the importance of Auden to his own poetry, Ashbery responded with a chuckle and his best imitation of one of his friend Bloom's characteristic oracular pronouncements: "Once, when I pointed out to him that he sort of ignored Auden's effect on me, Harold told me, 'Nonsense, darling. You only *think* you were influenced by Auden. But it's Stevens who made you who you are'" (Interview with the author [1997]).

In the following pages, I want to challenge Bloom's and other common critical presumptions about Ashbery by taking Ashbery's claims about his own poetics seriously, prompted by a few basic questions: What are we to make of the disparity between how Ashbery sees himself and how he is seen? What is the responsibility of critics toward authorial claims of self-knowledge and intention? Is there something to be learned by *listening* to this poet and his poems, rather than reading through or against them? What does it mean to read Ashbery as a self-conscious inheritor of Auden's civic tradition, rather than heir to the various romantic traditions— from Wordsworth to Whitman to the high modernisms of Stevens or Eliot—with which he is customarily linked? Is there an understanding of poetic influence itself that can accommodate Ashbery's acknowledgment of Auden's role in the development of his poetry that doesn't reduce either to trivial allusion- or echo-identification, or to competing claims of supposed poetic priority and authenticity? In the end, my goal is less to reject prior understandings of Ashbery than to augment and complicate them, and to suggest that in doing so, we discover an Ashbery who is even richer—both more familiar and more strange, more conventional and more radical—than we may have seen.

This other Ashbery traces his beginnings to 1944, when he was seventeen and, upon the suggestion of a family friend who taught poetry at the nearby University of Rochester, started reading Auden intensely. "She was the only person I knew who'd read any poetry and she told me I should read a lot of Auden's poetry," Ashbery recalls, "So I did and I found myself seeming to understand it and became mad about it" (Interview with the author [1997]). A year later, in an essay entitled **"Recent Tendencies in Poetry,"** written for his high school English class and preserved on a few tattered notebook pages in Harvard's Houghton Library, the precocious poet-to-be singled out Auden as one of the two most important young poets (alongside Stephen Spender) since Eliot, whose "poems are complex because they must spring from a mind which has been made complex by its double-existence—its social responsibility and its inward enigma."

Ashbery's enthusiasm for Auden's poetry, and his attention to its dualistic tension between "social responsibility" and "inward enigma," continued during his years at Harvard, even as he was being introduced by teachers like F. O. Matthiessen to the more recondite mysteries of Stevens's work and was honing his craft in the company of friends and fellow Harvard poets Frank O'Hara and Kenneth Koch and the artist Edward Gorey. Auden's impact on the young poet is clearly evident in early poems like **"The Painter,"** written in the summer of his junior year in 1948, whose form finds its origin in Auden's sestinas "Have a Good Time" and "Paysage Moralisé," and whose subject, an iconoclastic artist thrown by his audience into the sea, recalls the Icarus of "Musée des Beaux Arts."[2] **"Illustration,"** written a year later, about a novice who jumps from a building to her death, also echoes the protagonist of "The Second Temptation" of "The Quest" sonnet sequence from *The Double Man,* who leaps from a university tower "And plunged into the college quad, and broke" (*Collected Poems* 288).[3] The "reticent" lovers whose "accents seem their own defense" in **"Some Trees"**—written during Ashbery's senior year, and the title poem of the volume

to which Auden would award the Yale Younger Poets Prize seven years later—also bears an unmistakable Auden stamp, as John Shoptaw has suggested (24), in its echoes of his anxious lovers, "Always afraid to say more than it meant."[4] In many of these early poems, we find Audenesque figures torn between the claims of society and the "inward enigmas" of their own private art and desires.

But the lasting significance of this youthful engagement with Auden's work finds its most compelling articulation not in an early poem but in a piece of literary criticism Ashbery wrote at the same time, his Harvard undergraduate senior honors thesis, written in 1949 and entitled **"The Poetic Medium of W. H. Auden."** As an undergraduate analysis of Auden's English and early American career, this fascinating document, also in the Harvard archives and for the most part unstudied by Ashbery's critics, demonstrates considerable sophistication in Ashbery's early skills as a sympathetic reader of another poet's work. But it is as a record of Ashbery's own nascent poetics that it offers the greatest interest and insight. If, as Ashbery would later observe, "Poets when they write about other artists always tend to write about themselves" (*Reported Sightings* 106), then Ashbery's account of Auden's poetic medium provides his readers with a singular perspective on the development of his own work. In what amounts to a poetic manifesto—a rare thing in the career of the famously evasive poet he would become—the undergraduate Ashbery offers the initial formulation of ideas and themes that would come to seem, over the course of his career, characteristic of his own poetics.

Looking at Ashbery as a young critic accomplishes a paradoxical double task: First, it shows us in embryo the Ashbery familiar to us from his later poetry and suggests ways in which his practice as a critic contributed to the formation of his poetic identity. But it also shows us a newly unfamiliar Ashbery, an Audenesque Ashbery whose attentions are directed outward at the world and not in toward the self, and who sees poetry as exerting a moral influence on that world. Through his poetical and critical engagement with his first and most important influence, we can also hear and trace Ashbery's Audenesque notion about the unanxious relation between a poet and his precursors, as well as his thoughts on the relation between poetry and consciousness.

But perhaps most importantly, in his reading of Auden we can see Ashbery developing a conception of poetry as what the elder poet calls "embodied love" (*Collected Poems* 272), a notion that is crucial, I want to argue, for an understanding of Ashbery's poetic ambitions. Like Auden, Ashbery sees poetry as concerned with the ethical relations between private people and construes the relationship between poet and reader as a romantic, even erotic one, founded on a desire for contact, communication, and community. For both poets, poetry serves as an expression of longing in the face of loss, and as a space of hopeful exchange in a world of alienation and isolation. It is in this space of exchange between himself and Auden that we see the young Ashbery taking the first steps in the direction of the poet he will become—a poet whose own poems reach out hopefully to the reader, like a lover yearning for an ideal partner, even as those poems both acknowledge and enact the difficulty, if not impossibility, of that ambition. The difficulty of an Ashbery poem, with all its evasions, revisions, and misrepresentations, is the same difficulty shared by Auden poems like "The Orators" or, as we will see, "Caliban's Address to the Audience" from *The Sea and the Mirror*: it is the difficulty of the wounded, and therefore guarded, lover whose desire for the beloved manifests itself in a reticence that is also a challenge. The poet's withdrawal demands a pursuit, and the true lover / reader is the one who takes up the challenge, who senses the rewards amid the defensive misdirections, who is willing to work to understand him and, in so doing, reach that place of true contact and communion. With the promise that the labors will be worthwhile, the speaker of an Ashbery poem asks the reader to *work* at it, thereby simultaneously proving the reader's love while earning his. And as we will see, and as Ashbery addresses in his essay, this idea of his poetry as "embodied love" might also prove to have intriguing consequences for how Ashbery's readers and critics— those willing to do the hard work of listening to him, and of attending to his glinting, deceptive surfaces— construe their relation to the poet and his work.

Interestingly, Ashbery's undergraduate response to Auden's work also marks, to a certain extent, the high point of Auden's influence on him. Ashbery has said on a number of occasions that he stopped reading Auden seriously after *The Sea and the Mirror*—the primary critical focus of Ashbery's essay—as Auden's poetry turned increasingly domestic, conservative, and prosaic, in keeping with his developing religious, cultural, and aesthetic perspective. But this early engagement with Auden has an impact that will echo through his entire career. In many ways, the Ashbery we know was formed in response to the Auden of the decade between 1939 and 1949, the years when Auden was redefining himself as an American poet and when Ashbery was reading— and writing through—him most intensely. Reading the young Ashbery reading Auden, we see a self-portrait of the future artist, reflected in the elder poet's mirror.

Indeed, the very first lines of Ashbery's essay set the terms for this future Ashbery and begin the argument for seeing the Ashbery we know as a product of his engagement with the example of Auden. Ashbery opens his study with a declaration of critical and poetic independence reflecting the bravado of a confident twenty-two-year-old undergraduate, but significant in its implications for his later work:

> It is often said that we read so-called "intellectual" poetry for its style rather than its content; anthologists and instructors assure us that Pope's *Essay on Man* contains not a single fresh idea; that its saving feature is the vigor and grace with which it expresses old ones. Such a false division between form and content presupposes two boxes, one of which contains old, hashed-over ideas which everyone assimilated years ago, and from which the poet takes whatever he needs to "stuff" his poem; and the other, brand-new, unthought of ideas, to which the philosopher resorts when seeking inspiration. But there are no new ideas, any more than there are any old ones; there are merely old and new ways of looking at the world. Every new poem is a fresh discovery, and Pope stands acquitted on the charge of commonplace subject matter; "what oft was thought but n'er so well expressed" might as well be what n'er was thought for those who, but for the poet, might have understood the idea but not to have been able to apply it within their realm of experience.

In the space of this single introductory paragraph, we see, *ab ovo,* notions of poetics that will find expression throughout Ashbery's own mature poetry and reflect his Audenesque inheritance. Beginning with an attack on what would become one of his favorite targets, literary critics, Ashbery styles himself as a brash iconoclast, not unlike the painter of his sestina, by setting up the "anthologists and instructors" of his Harvard classes as the straw men for a defense of poetry that acknowledges the power to be gained from belatedness and bases its claims for poetry's value on its capacity to help people apply poetic truth "within the realm of their own experience." This claim, which is echoed in the final line of the thirty-two-page essay in which Ashbery stakes Auden's importance on his achievement in having "brought innumerable people closer to the world in which they live," signals Ashbery's inheritance of an Audenesque notion of poetry's place in the world. Like the newly American Auden of "In Memory of W. B. Yeats," written soon after the poet's arrival in the United States in 1939, the young Ashbery asserts poetry's power not to "make something happen," but to be a "way of happening" in which the experience of reading the poem serves as what Auden elsewhere called a "rehearsal for living" ("Writing," *English Auden* 311), offering the reader access to ideas he "might have understood but not . . . been able to apply." Poetry, for the young poet—as it was for Auden—is essentially didactic, if not in content then in effect.

And this is not simply the idealistic position of the unsophisticated twenty-two-year-old budding poet, later to be abandoned as he matured into the famously jaded, postmodern ironist familiar to us from our own "anthologists and instructors." Thirty years later, the now-established Ashbery was still reaffirming his claim as an inheritor of Auden's post-emigration vision of poetry's power to effect change, telling an interviewer:

> [T]here's a celebrated line from Auden: "poetry makes nothing happen." It doesn't, but its value is precisely the fact that it doesn't, because that's the way it *does* make things happen. The pleasure that you get, if you love poetry, is a pleasure that's going to cause you to act, it forces you back into life. Poetry is in fact—I was just reading a quotation from Hazlitt—not a branch of literature, but life itself. So that an intense poetic experience for me causes me to want to, you know, go out and be with people, perhaps join a political demonstration, which I have done and did during the Vietnam war. . . . I did this somewhat dubiously because I felt that poetry makes nothing happen, nevertheless, here was a case where I felt that even though this is true, maybe people will, by the nature of my non-political poetry, be persuaded to become more *people.* I mean a person will become more of a person and will therefore do these not only politically helpful and constructive things, but things that will make him more aware of his own life and the people around him and will influence his actions on a number of levels, not just one.

("John Ashbery" [Sommer] 307-8)

In the history of Ashbery's critical reception, little attention has been paid to this aspect of his poetics, namely its insistence that the experience of reading his poetry ought to—and indeed, does—have a didactic, constructive, even moral effect on the reader.[5] He is more often seen, under Bloom's guidance, as a figure of "triumphant solipsism" (*Map* 9), lost in the discursive drama of himself: "Like his master, Stevens, Ashbery is essentially a ruminative poet, turning a few subjects over and over, knowing always that what counts is the mythology of the self, blotched out beyond unblotching," says Bloom (*John Ashbery* 7). Or he is proposed as a disengaged representative of late capitalism, whose "intractable" poetics, as Mutlu Konuk Blasing summarizes it, "confirms the opinion that poetry does not make any difference, unless, perhaps, it markets difference" (152).[6] Ashbery's insistence that poetry is "not a branch of literature, but life itself" and can make the reader "more aware of his own life and the people around him and will influence his actions on a number of levels" argues strongly against his many critics who find in Ashbery the paradigm for a contemporary poetics of detachment, fragmentation, and Stevensian philosophical solipsism.[7] Ashbery is less the Stevensian man on the postmodern dump than, as we will see, an Audenesque love poet with a vision of poetry's constructive, moral power as "a way of happening." For Ashbery, the knowledge of the world's difficulty, and its expression in his difficult poetry, is not the verdict to which we surrender in existential despair, but the inhospitable terrain in which we, self-aware, continue to strive, and act, and hope, even in the face of probable failure. Like his mentor Auden, who saw in poetry

the power to "make a vineyard of the curse," Ashbery sees his poetry as an act of hopeful cultivation: amid the decay of the dump or the stony rubbish of the wasteland, the poet can still bring forth life.

* * *

In that first paragraph of his honors thesis, and throughout the rest of the essay, Ashbery sets forth a number of Audenesque notions that would come to define his own poetics. Perhaps the most pronounced of those features that would later become familiar to his readers is what Auden called, in a critique of Romantic poets, an "awareness of the dialectic" (*Double Man* 118). Ashbery announces himself immediately as a writer distinguished by a relentlessly dialectical perspective. From his initial observations about "intellectual" poetry, whose ironizing quotation marks imply a dubiousness about its presumed antithetical relation to its "emotional" opposite, to his remarks about the "false divisions" between style and content, between new ideas and old ones, and between poet and philosopher, the young poet-critic's opening flourish bursts with dialectical pairings. And in each case, these pairs are shown to be more complexly related than a simple antinomy: "There are no new ideas, any more than there are any old ones; there are merely old and new ways of looking at the world."

As every reader of Ashbery's poetry soon discovers, his is a poetics defined by its dialectical vision.[8] As Ashbery himself asks in his double-columned poem **"Litany,"** calling attention to the interplay between the competing voices of the opposing lines of verse, "Who can elicit these possible, / Rubbery spirals? . . . Antithesis chirping / To antithesis" (*As We Know* 8). Like the Auden of *The Double Man* (whose "tedious dialectical obscurity" Ashbery chastises, but assimilates, later in the thesis), and the doubly conscious Auden of Ashbery's high school essay, divided between "social responsibility and inward enigma," Ashbery refuses to take sides, continually seeking what Auden, in "New Year Letter," calls "the gift of double-focus" (220). For the young Ashbery, as it would be for the older, the challenge of seeing the world truthfully is the challenge of seeing it from contending perspectives and trying to make sense of, and live within, each: "a kind of fence-sitting / Raised to the level of an aesthetic ideal," as he would wryly put it in **"Soonest Mended"** (*Double Dream* [*The Double Dream of Spring*] 18). With these introductory remarks, Ashbery embarks on his reading of Auden—and, in a very real sense, the "new way of looking at the world" that would manifest itself in his poems—armed with that old dialectical "gift," inherited from Auden himself.[9]

For Ashbery, as for Auden, the ultimate space of dialectic in human experience, and therefore in poetry, is the tense dialectic of *eros,* as lovers continuously seek or resist the stability of their union. In one section of Ashbery's essay, we see him staging the poetic transmission of this idea, in a scenario full of erotic implication—between younger and elder poet, between poet and his reader, and even between poet and his critics. While devoting most of his critical attention to *The Sea and the Mirror*, Ashbery reserves his highest praise for one portion in particular, Caliban's address to the audience, calling it "probably the most brilliant writing Auden has ever done." Ashbery has acknowledged in interviews the formal influence of this poem's Jamesian prose upon his own work, in particular his prose **Three Poems,** but the significance and utility for Ashbery of "Caliban to the Audience" extends beyond his later adoption of its form. Ashbery's choice of emphasis in his analysis is telling, as he focuses special attention on Caliban's remarks not to the audience but to the "strange young man" who has come to the performance "not to be entertained but to learn" (*Collected Poems* 430). To this figure of the younger artist, the "gay apprentice in the magical art who may have chosen this specimen of the prestidigitatory genus to study this evening in the hope of grasping more clearly just how the artistic contraption works, of observing some fresh detail in the complex process by which the heady wine of amusement is distilled from the grape of composition" (430), the worldly Caliban recounts the history of his own artistic career, including his tempestuous relationship with Ariel, his doppelgänger and muse. This relationship, in Caliban's account of it and in Ashbery's pointed summary of it, reaches a crisis when Ariel, the imaginative spirit upon whom Caliban the artist had depended for his art, the bodiless inspiration who could be summoned and dismissed at will, suddenly insists on his own freedom, identity, and corporeality:

> Striding up to Him in fury, you glare into His unblinking eyes and stop dead, transfixed with horror at seeing reflected there, not what you had always expected to see . . . but a gibbering fist-clenched creature with which you are all too unfamiliar, for this is the first time indeed that you have met the only subject that you have, who is not a dream amenable to magic but the all too solid flesh you must acknowledge as your own.

(433)

Throughout Caliban's address to the young artist, Auden characterizes this multifaceted dialectical artistic relation—between Caliban and Ariel, between the artist and his muse, between body and spirit, between the self and its alienated other, between himself and the "gay apprentice"—as being an explicitly romantic, and erotic, one: "at last you have come face to face with me, and are appalled to learn how far I am from being, in any sense, your dish" (433). Caliban details the stormy nature of this imaginatively fraught romance, including the charged and angry nights spent "wrestl[ing] through long dark hours," and the drunken days spent "jump-

[ing] stark naked from bed to bed" (434), as the fractious duo repeatedly spurn, then return to one another. That Auden has in mind a specifically homoerotic—and therefore culturally risky—model of relations is made clear by Caliban's ironic observation, "Such genuine escapades, though, might have disturbed the master at his meditations and even involved him in trouble with the police" (434). But the pair, like an old couple whose wild-oats-sowing days are behind them, eventually settle down into something resembling domestic harmony, or at least nonconflict:

> From now on we shall have, as we both know only too well, no company but each other's, and if I have had, as I consider, a good deal to put up with from you, I must own that, after all, I am not just the person I would have chosen for a life companion myself; so the only chance, which in any case is slim enough, of my getting a tolerably new master and you a tolerably new man, lies in our both learning, if possible and as soon as possible, to forgive and forget the past, and to keep our respective hopes for the future within moderate, very moderate limits.

(435)

In portraying the relation between the artist and his muse as not unlike his own turbulent yet domesticated partnership with Chester Kallman, Auden offers a humble but powerful metaphor for his vision of the dialectical nature of poetic art, governed by the "hidden law" of love. For Auden, as for Ashbery, the relation between the poet and his muse, like the relation between the poet and his reader, is a manifestly difficult, tension-filled one: poetry, like love, is hard, repetitive work and requires significant amounts of patience, forbearance, acceptance, and trust to make it work, however imperfectly. The question implicit in this difficulty is whether we, as readers, are willing to commit, as it were, to the demands of this relationship.

Ashbery, in his essay, opts not to comment explicitly on Auden's homoerotic construction of his poetics, or on the possible implications of Auden's term for the student artist as the "gay apprentice," even though, as Shoptaw has pointed out, "Ashbery remembers first hearing the word 'gay' as 'homosexual' at Harvard in 1946" (356n5) and had used the word suggestively in his own undergraduate poems (21-22). This omission—apart from making perfect sense in the less-liberal environment of 1949 Harvard—would be, for Shoptaw, further evidence of what he has helpfully termed Ashbery's "misrepresentative poetics" (3), in which Ashbery's rhetoric of evasion simultaneously masks and enacts its "homotextual" perspective (4).[10] But it also suggests Ashbery's ambition to reach out, not just past the limits of self, but past the limits of gender as well, toward a vision of civil, equal relations built on individual, often intimate and private, mutual acknowledgment. Ashbery, who has resisted being read as a "gay poet," assimilates

Auden's notion of the erotics of poetic relation—itself formed in the context of, if not in response to, Auden's own homosexuality—and responds to its vision of homoerotic relations as a trope for all hopeful human relations. Ashbery's poetic love, like Auden's, while emerging from a homoerotic context, reaches out to any and all who might respond.[11]

Ashbery expands on the pathos and difficulty inherent in this dialectic, and emphasizes his rejection of the absolutist's insistence on an either / or choice, in his essay's comments on Caliban's closing remarks, in which Ashbery discusses (citing the poet-critic Henry Reed's own reading of Auden) "the two false paths" his reality-seeking audience might take: "The one is an attempt to discover a world of false childhood, a world of looking to others for comfort, a world conceived as free and without responsibility . . . ; the other a state of false adulthood which achieves a state of disregarding the separate existence, a world likewise free and irresponsible." Ashbery's "solution"—and Auden's—to overcoming these equally tempting, solipsistic falsehoods is a self-aware recognition of one's "very moderate limits," an acknowledgment of mutual dependence, and a confession of love:

> The only solution is seeing ourselves as we are—actors in a *completely unconvincing and unbeautiful drama,* "the greatest grandest opera rendered by a very provincial touring company indeed" (Caliban's detailed description of it is magnificently adequate). Only by realizing how "indescribably inexcusably awful" it has been, by seeing ourselves as we truly are, can we succeed in gaining the "full bloom of the unbothered state," the "sounded note" of the "restored relation." Last of all, Ariel's song comes as the "sounded note," begging Caliban to "Weep no more but pity me . . . helplessly in love with you" and reassuring him that "I will sing if you will cry. . . . *I*'"
>
> [emphasis Ashbery's]

This scene, of the conflicted traveler facing the choice of forking paths and seeking a "solution" that will resolve them, reappears throughout Ashbery's poems, including **"The System,"** one of Ashbery's Caliban-influenced *Three Poems*:

> That's the way it goes. For many weeks you have been exploring what seemed to be a profitable way of doing. You discovered that there was a fork in the road, so first you followed what seemed to be the less promising, or at any rate the more obvious, of the two branches until you felt you had a good idea of where it led. Then you returned to investigate the more tangled way, and for a time its intricacies seemed to promise a more complex and therefore a more practical goal for you, one that could be picked up in any number of ways so that all its faces or applications could be thoroughly scrutinized. And in so doing you began to realize that the two branches were joined together again, farther ahead; that this place of joining was

indeed the end, and that it was the very place you set out from, whose intolerable mixture of reality and fantasy had started you on the road which has now come full circle. It has been an absorbing puzzle, but in the end all the pieces fit together like a ghost story that turns out to have a perfectly rational explanation. Nothing remains but to begin living with this discovery, that is, without the hope mentioned above. Even this is not so easy, for the reduced mode or scope must itself be nourished by a form of hope, or hope that doesn't take itself seriously.

> (90)

Here, the traveler's "solution" lies—as it does for Caliban—neither in choosing one path as "more practical" than the other, nor in successfully achieving some grand, transcendent synthesis of the two. Rather, resolution comes from complete self-awareness, total consciousness of the "intolerable mixture of reality and fantasy" that compels the artist to "set out" in the first place. The two paths are not options to be chosen between but are in fact part of the same road: "this place of joining was indeed the end, and . . . the very place you set out from." The "end"—the "purpose"—of Ashbery's poetry is to reach this "place of joining," and the pathos-filled "solution" for achieving this end is the painful recognition that we are always already there without knowing it and are destined to go on not knowing it. Poetry's purpose is to communicate, however inadequately, that knowledge, that instantaneous self-awareness, so that we can try to "begin living with this discovery."

It is a melancholy knowledge, "how indescribably inexcusably awful" our fate is, in Caliban's words, to keep seeking that which we already have but can never grasp, yet from this knowledge comes, as Ashbery puts it in **"The New Spirit,"** the first of his prose poems, "a strange kind of happiness within the limitations" (*Three Poems* 27). This happiness is achieved, says Ashbery, only by "seeing ourselves as we truly are," a phrase he repeats twice in his essay and a third time, with a slight variation, in the first line of *Some Trees*'s first poem, "We see us as we truly behave." Our journey must be, as Ashbery significantly describes Auden's poem, an "epic of self-consciousness." Only by seeing ourselves as "actors in a completely unconvincing and unbeautiful drama," as travelers through an "intolerable mixture of reality and fantasy," can we succeed in reaching that "place of joining," or, as Ashbery paraphrases Auden, "in gaining the 'full bloom of the unbothered state,' the 'sounded note' of the 'restored relation.'" That "sounded note" is the note of love, the "restored relation" where both understanding and consolation are found. Ariel's love song to Caliban, "Weep no more but pity me . . . helplessly in love with you," and their mutual acknowledgment of their dependence—"I will sing if you will cry . . . *I*'"—signals that ideal moment of self-knowledge which comes, paradoxically, through an awareness of otherness. As Auden defines it in *The Orators,* which Ashbery has called one of his favorite poems, "awareness of difference—love" ("Journal of an Airman," *English Auden* 75).

This awareness is everywhere to be found in Ashbery's own poetry. He is, as surprisingly few of his critics have observed, in every sense an Audenesque "love poet."[12] From the brief early lyric **"Some Trees,"** whose trees tell the reticent lovers that "soon / We may touch, love, explain," to grander projects like **"A Wave,"** which figures love itself as the "giant wave" that propels the poem, it is easy to claim, as Ashbery does of his long poem **"Fragment,"** "Like maybe all of my poems, it's a love poem" ("Craft" [Bloom and Losada] 93). Ashbery has even teasingly offered his critics a foundational biographical moment that places the origins of his poetic ambitions in a specifically erotic context, telling one interviewer that, as a boy, "I fell deeply in love with a girl who was in [my art] class but who wouldn't have anything to do with me. So I went to this weekly class knowing that I would see this girl, and somehow this being involved with art may have something to do with my poetry" ("Art" 35). Ashbery's intriguing placement of the erotic origins of his poetic career at a moment of heterosexual desire both subtly disputes his critics' attempts to read him as a "gay poet" and reinforces his (and Auden's) notion that poetry, like love, is the expression of the yearning for connection between people, regardless of sex. For Auden, love is both the genesis and the end, the conception and the consummation of poetry, and, as is made clear in poem after poem, Ashbery shares Auden's notion that the fundamental dialectic at the heart of poetry is the dialectic of love. Indeed, the last lines of **"A Wave"** offer a rewriting of Caliban's account of his final domestic arrangement with Ariel, in which the artist / muse partners—who are also the aspects of the divided self, the artist and his audience, the poet and his "gay apprentice"—settle into a stable, loving relationship grounded in their own differences: "And so each of us has to remain alone, conscious of each other / Until the day when war absolves us of our differences. We'll / Stay in touch. So they have it, all the time. But all was strange" (*Wave* 89).

To be in love, as Roland Barthes has suggested, is to desire affirmation (1).[13] The continuous dialectical voices in Ashbery's poems are continually seeking affirmation, from one "erotic double" to another: "Thank you. You are a very pleasant person. / Thank you. You are too" (*As We Know* 82). The double columns of **"Litany"** enact this erotic dialectic as one column first affirms, then dismisses the other—"It was nice of you to love me / But I must be thinking about getting back" (44-45)—while its partner plaintively looks for support, as in the poem's final lines, which pointedly ask, "would you / Try?" (68). Ashbery has described the two

columns as "like two people whom I am in love with simultaneously" ("Art" 50), setting up a love triangle between the poet and the dual voices of his poem. Ashbery becomes Caliban's figure of the "master," while the squabbling yet dependent columns again re-create the roles of Caliban and Ariel, the dialectical constituents of his poetic identity.

In "As I Walked Out One Evening," Auden famously depicts a solitary lover singing "Under an arch of the railway" of his eternal devotion, claiming "Love has no ending" and that his love will last "till the ocean / Is folded and hung up to dry / And the seven stars go squawking / Like geese about the sky" (*Collected Poems* 133). His love, the amorous singer asserts, is "The Flower of the Ages, / And the first love of the world." But "all the clocks in the city," Time's stern representatives, correct the young lover, telling him, "O let not Time deceive you, / You cannot conquer Time." Love, they tell him, at least in the real world of "crooked neighbor[s]" with "crooked heart[s]," is never eternal except in mutability. Worldly love is a fickle, changeable, confusing thing, and in the war between Love and Time, Time always wins. In **"Thank You for Not Cooperating,"** Ashbery updates Auden's singing lover: "Two lovers are singing / Separately, from the same rooftop: '*Leave your change behind,* / Leave your clothes, and go. It is time now. / It was time before too, but now it is really time'" (*Wave* 12). The single lover has become two, not "under an arch of the railway" but up on "the same rooftop." These are lovers who have already learned the lesson of the clocks. They are singing together, but "separately," and they know that what defines their relationship is "change." In fact, the only way to "leave [their] change behind" is to part, and rather than trying to conquer time, they welcome its decision: "It is time now."

In Ashbery's poems, the lovers already know that their love is doomed by time, but they go on loving anyway. Ashbery's lovers, like the "human" and "faithless" lovers of Auden's early poems, begin with the knowledge that love is mortal and always moving: "It's they can tell you how love came and went / And how it keeps coming and going, ever disconcerting, / Even through the topiary trash of the present, / Its undoing, and smiles and seems to recognize no one" (*Wave* 82). Love doesn't conquer time but actually shares some of its properties: "Love is different. / It moves, or grows, at the same rate / As time does, yet within time" (*As We Know* 56). In Ashbery, love "moves" and "grows" and, like time, is inescapable.

In **"Late Echo,"** Ashbery develops this idea of love's "difference":

> Alone with our madness and favorite flower
> We see that there really is nothing left to write about.

Or rather, it is necessary to write about the same old
  things
In the same way, repeating the same things over and
  over
For love to continue and be gradually different.

(As We Know 88)

Ashbery here defines love by its cyclicality, its repetitiveness. Paradoxically, in order for "love to continue and be gradually different," the lovers must repeat "the same things over and over." In **"A Love Poem,"** he makes the same point, as the lovers write "notes to each other, always repeated, always the same" (101). In the quotidian context of a romantic relationship, this makes sense, as we can recognize the aspect of repetitiveness that goes into a relationship of any duration while also recognizing that to a certain extent it is the very stability of doing these "same old things / In the same way" that allows that "love to continue." As with Caliban and Ariel, domestic harmony often comes at the expense of "difference." But in terms of poetry, this definition of love has other implications.

In both **"Late Echo"** and **"A Love Poem,"** Ashbery equates love with the act of writing itself: the poet must "write about the same old things" for "love to continue and be gradually different." Under the guise of a domestic love-lyric, Ashbery is making a startlingly bold—and Audenesque—claim: for love to survive, we need poetry. Poetry, which, as we recall from Ashbery's introduction to his thesis, repeats the "same old" truths of our existence ("There are no new ideas, any more than there are any old ones; there are merely old and new ways of looking at the world"), is "necessary"—using Auden's own abstracted term for the inescapability and obligations of love—to the world of human relations. In **"And *Ut Pictura Poesis* Is Her Name,"** Ashbery writes,

Something
Ought to be written about how this affects
You when you write poetry:
The extreme austerity of an almost empty mind
Colliding with the lush, Rousseau-like foliage of its
  desire to communicate
Something between breaths, if only for the sake
Of others and their desire to understand you and desert
  you
For other centers of communication, so that under-
  standing
May begin, and in doing so be undone.

(Houseboat Days 45-46)

Ashbery here reverses the formula from **"Late Echo,"** and follows the example of Auden's Caliban, in describing poetry in the language of a romantic relationship. Poetry is defined as an economy of "desire": the poet's "desire to communicate something . . . for the sake of others" and others' "desire to understand . . . and desert

[him] / For other centers of communication," or other poets. The relation between poet and audience is figured here, as in Caliban's address, as an erotic one. Poet and reader "desire" one another, and "desire to understand" one another, but the relationship, like any romantic relationship, is likely a doomed one. With time, they will "desert" each other. But with this separation comes a kind of "understanding." For Ashbery, "understanding" is what Auden in "New Year Letter" calls "a process in a process / Within a field that never closes" (*Collected Poems* 208), an endless cycle of setting out and coming home, of seeking and abandonment, whose meaning comes through repetition, not resolution. "Understanding" is the dialectical process itself, always seeking and never finding, yet worth continuing nonetheless. Love, too, works this way—"coming and going, ever disconcerting, / Even through the topiary trash of the present, / Its undoing, and smiles and seems to recognize no one"—yet is somehow "necessary."

Both poetry and love seek "understanding," and both are subject to time and the frustrations and contingencies of existence. As Ashbery puts it in **"A Wave,"** "What were the interruptions that / Led us here and then shanghaied us if not sincere attempts to / Understand and so desire another person" (*Wave* 83). In Ashbery's terms, to "desire another person" is to "attempt to understand" them. "Desire" and "understanding" are, for Ashbery, the same thing. Poetry and love are unified in their shared ambition, and their shared pathos. As he puts it in **"Litany,"** "The essence of it is that all love / Is imitative, creative, and that we can't hear it" (*As We Know* 66). Ashbery's poems, then, are love songs: "imitative, creative" songs of "desire" and "understanding" to himself, to lovers, to the reader, to the world. The pathos and anxiety of the poet—and the lover—is that these songs of himself will go unheard, that there will be no Ariel to echo his Caliban cry of *"I."* The title of one of Ashbery's books is *Can You Hear, Bird?* and this—with an implied emphasis on "hear"—is Ashbery's continual question, and plaint, to his readers: "Can you *hear*—as opposed to talk over, or project onto—me?" For readers of Ashbery, looking for hidden significances and latencies, or observing the fragmentations and evasions, is, in some sense, the easy part—it's the simple listening that is difficult. It's hard work, but Ashbery asks us, "would you / Try?" It's an earned intimacy that, while it may become familiar, never becomes any easier—like love, like life. And if poetry is love, and if to read a poet is to love and be loved in return, then, in the history of Ashbery's poetic affairs, Auden stands as his first, never-to-be-forgotten romance.

* * *

In Ashbery's undergraduate essay we see the young poet achieving what Auden calls, in his own essay on the importance of Thomas Hardy to the development of his poetics, a "literary transference," as the young artist identifies and assimilates aspects of his mentor that will help him become the poet he wants to be. The bond between the "gay apprentice" and the elder artist is figured as a relationship of love as well as a relationship of convenience and utility, and the aspiring poet suggests that these two kinds of association need not be mutually exclusive. The young Ashbery *uses* Auden to become the future Ashbery—a poet who, in welcoming the difficult world into his consciousness and reflecting it in his poetry, hopes in some way to transform it.

Auden's range of discursive reference, from science to popular songs, suggested to Ashbery a kind of cultural democratization that would prove useful in his own poetry. He cites at length and with approval a 1935 *Poetry* review that contrasts Auden favorably with Eliot and declares, "Allusiveness in Auden . . . tends to be on a lower, more generally comprehensible plane," which offers "the opportunity to catch poetry in the act of returning from the remote realms of symbolist subtlety to the workaday world of proletarian experience, refreshed with new powers." Ashbery adds his own encomium:

> No other poet at this time, I feel, has a comparable medium for expressing the ideas which are common to most modern poets. Eliot, it is true, did much of the ground work for Auden. But his poetry as a whole, though it introduced the idea that the everyday world is part of the province of poetry, remains allusive and refined, lacking in the immediacy and concreteness which Auden gives to all he touches.

He concludes with a peroration on Auden's poetic pluralism and utility:

> His poetry is, as Hindemith describes his own music, "for use"; its beauty as poetry functional, though surpassing whatever "pure" poetry we have today. He has absorbed certain common techniques of thought (the cataloging, the characterizing by denoting an unusual quality) and rhythms (those of the cabaret, the birthday card, the political broadsheet) which are very much a part of our life, using them to convey ideas which matter very much to us. If he is not a great poet, a decision which must be made by time, he has brought innumerable people closer to the world in which they live.

For Ashbery, the poet whose own range of allusiveness stretches from the Marvell of **"Picture of Little JA in a Prospect of Flowers"** to the Popeye of **"Farm Implements and Rutabagas in a Landscape,"** Auden served as the crucial link between "the remote realms of symbolist subtlety" and the "poetry of the everyday world" that he wanted to write. Auden consolidated and synthesized Eliot's innovations in allusion and the incorporation of the demotic into poetry, "using them to convey ideas which matter very much to us" and making them available "for use." Poetry, as he will later say, "is not a branch of literature but life itself" and can be a vehicle to carry people back more forcefully and engagedly into that life.

Evidence of Ashbery making *use* of Auden's poetry to articulate his own poetics is everywhere to be found in his undergraduate essay. Ashbery's notion of the "crypt word," which Shoptaw has shown to be a defining feature of Ashbery's poetics, finds its first expression in his analysis of the first lines of *The Sea and the Mirror*, in which the Stage Manager sets the dramatic mood in expectation of the night's performance: "The aged catch their breath, / For the nonchalant couple go / Waltzing across the tightrope / As if there were no death / Or hope of falling down" (*Collected Poems* 403). Comparing Auden's use of the metaphor of the tightrope walker with its less effective use by a minor contemporary poet named (felicitously enough) Walker Gibson, Ashbery remarks on Auden's provocative and productive substitution of an unexpected word in the formula of a cliché: "In his poem he has made this 'hope of falling down' a happening as ordinary as the 'fear of falling down.'" This was a lesson the young poet would take to heart, making a habit throughout his own work of revealing the hidden freight carried by words in familiar combinations, from this "mooring of starting out" of his own career to the "mourning forbidding valediction" (*Hotel* [*Hotel Lautréamont*] 114) of his later books.

Ashbery also tellingly observes Auden's penchant for list-making: "Instead of a traditional presentation and examination of an object, its illumination through metaphor and simile, Auden gives us lists of objects interesting and significant without description; which are, indeed, often only named, and then draws or allows to be drawn the poetic conclusion." Identifying this mode as "a special kind of poetry which Auden has created," he goes on to theorize its relevance to the contemporary moment:

> Such a poetic theory seems peculiarly of our time. In the first place, when we think of the ubiquity of the list, the sheet of tabulations, in almost every category of modern life; in science, business, even in popular poetry—think of the numerous popular songs in which the beloved is designated by lists of desirable objects ("You're a Paris hat, a month in the country, a hot fudge sundae," etc.) it is not surprising that a poet so completely contemporary as Auden should have absorbed the process. Secondly, our age seems to be characterized as well by a rapid drawing of conclusions from certain particulars—one thinks of scientists, technicians, and even our present-day conversation, which, in growing more sophisticated has tended to make a code of all that can be observed easily or rather easily, and is able to adduce particulars immediately when a name, a quality is mentioned.

From early poems like **"Popular Songs"** (the second poem in *Some Trees*), whose disjointed romance narrative ("He continued to consult her for her beauty" [22]) is spiked with evocative song titles like "The Gardens of the Moon," to later works like **"Daffy Duck in Hollywood,"** with its "mint-condition can / Of Rumford's Baking Powder, a celluloid earring, Speedy / Gonzales, the latest from Helen Topping Miller's fertile / Escritoire, a sheaf of suggestive pix on greige, deckle-edged / Stock" (**Houseboat Days** 31), Ashbery's work repeatedly enacts Auden's "poetic theory" of lists. In **"And *Ut Pictura Poesis* Is Her Name,"** Ashbery explicitly addresses this theory, asking "Now, / About what to put in your poem-painting: / Flowers are always nice, particularly delphinium. / Names of boys you once knew and their sleds, / Skyrockets are good—do they still exist?" (**Houseboat Days** 45), and in **The Vermont Notebook** he writes a book of lists, consisting almost entirely of obscurely defined catalogs, like "Front porches, back porches, side porches, door jambs, window sills, lintels, cornices, gambrel roofs, dormers, front steps, clapboards, trees, magnolia, scenery, Mc-Donald's, Carrol's, Kinney Shoe Stores" (25). If this is a "special kind of poetry which Auden has created," then it is a kind Ashbery has made his own.

Elsewhere in his essay, Ashbery relates this idea of Auden's poetic inclusiveness, accumulativeness, and utility specifically to the question of poetic "influence" itself. In a discussion of Auden's play *Paid on Both Sides,* which takes its inspiration from Auden's beloved Icelandic sagas, Ashbery observes:

> It is rather futile to talk about "influences" in *Paid on Both Sides,* as it would be to discuss influences on Joyce in the "Oxen of the Sun" (hospital) episode in *Ulysses.* A literary influence usually implies an unconscious or semi-conscious assimilation of authors which slowly alters a writer's style into something new. Auden, like Joyce, has gone out of his way to imitate many styles, and if, in doing so, he has finally achieved stylistic detachment, he has reached that state fully conscious of the direction in which he was traveling. At any rate, the many styles which occur throughout the early *Poems* and throughout the individual poems themselves are drawn from many sources: besides the saga language, we find technical and scientific terms, contemporary *argot,* Shakespearean rhetoric, satires on occasional, "family" verse, and the clumsy meter and rhyming of the political broadside, all jostling each other, yet in most cases seeming to form a unified and satisfactory whole. It is our task to discover how and with what justification, what purpose, the poet has used these sources.

Here Ashbery articulates a notion of literary influence that eschews the "unconscious or semi-conscious assimilation of authors" in favor of a process, achieved through "stylistic detachment," by which the poet "imitates" and chooses from a variety of sources—literary and otherwise—"fully conscious of the direction in which he is traveling." Auden's formal and discursive diversity, and the "unified and satisfactory whole" he makes of those chosen "influences," demonstrates for

Ashbery a "functional" way of incorporating both the tradition and the world around him into a poetry that represents the whole vocabulary of conscious experience yet still reflects a shaping, "purposeful," self-aware intellect. This model of poetic influence and originality corresponds closely with Auden's own formulation of the relation between the tradition and the individual talent: "Originality," in modernity, says Auden in his essay "The Poet and the City," "no longer means a slight modification in the style of one's immediate predecessors; it means a capacity to find in any work of any date or place a clue to finding one's authentic voice. The burden of choice and selection is put squarely upon the shoulders of each individual poet and it is a heavy one" (*Dyer's Hand* 80). In the pursuit of his own originality, Ashbery chooses the assimilation of Auden's example as a means of finding his own "authentic voice."

In his essay's first paragraph (quoted earlier), Ashbery had laid the groundwork for this Audenesque conception of poetic originality in his assertion that it is the new poet's rearticulation of old ideas, and his ability to make those ideas new again, that constitutes his special contribution to the tradition, not his invention of "brand-new unthought of ideas." All poets, says Ashbery, "stand acquitted on the charge of commonplace subject matter" simply because their unique selection, absorption, and expression of what they inherit from the past necessarily gives it a new spin. It is the new poet's particular sensibility, and his skill in seeing old sights with new eyes, that makes "every new poem a fresh discovery." Even as an apprentice poet, Ashbery is already demonstrating an unanxious relation to the poetic past, less worried about his belatedness and the necessity for "making it new" than cheerfully confident that his singular "way of looking at the world," his individual talent, will, in a sense, do the job for him. Much like Eliot's famous poet-as-shred-of-platinum, whose mind transmutes his environment into poetry without being affected by that change, the young Ashbery asserts the poet's ability to transform the world he inherits—including the poetic tradition—through the prism of his own consciousness, without having to struggle against that world.[14] Readers of Ashbery will encounter this idea again and again in poems and interviews: "A poem for me is very much a question of the relation between elements that are sort of given to one, or which one chooses arbitrarily when one starts to write a poem and which don't require other justification" ("Craft" [Osti] 87).

Ashbery's approach to experience, including his experience of past poets, is a radically open, welcoming one, rather than combative, anxious, and agonistic. "I never consciously felt that I had to destroy the poets I was being influenced by," Ashbery has argued, engaging the famous theory of influence propounded by his friend

Bloom: "When I discovered them in my work I was happy to welcome them. It was nice that they dropped by. Of course, unconsciously who knows what I may have been up to. *Harold* obviously does . . ." (Interview with the author [1997]). In this jocular corrective to Bloom's ideas about the Freudian struggle between a poet and his influences, as in his early assertion of the poet's unanxious acknowledgment of his own belatedness, Ashbery raises a crucial question about the relation of his poetry to prevailing theories of the development of poetic identity, as well as other, larger questions about poetry criticism in general. Ashbery's authorial assertion of Auden's importance to his work, and Bloom's blithe dismissal of it, suggest a significant rift between Ashbery's own notion of his poetics and its critical reception. It is a truism that, as Auden himself points out in his essay "Reading," "The critical opinions of a writer should always be taken with a large grain of salt" (*Dyer's Hand* 9), especially since, as "anthologists and instructors" from Cleanth Brooks and Robert Penn Warren to Bloom have argued, questions of authorial intent are entirely ancillary—if not actively opposed—to the disinterested business of literary criticism. Yet Ashbery's protest, in the context of his own work, merits examination.[15]

Ashbery calls *The Sea and the Mirror* an "epic of self-consciousness," and it is this total exploration of consciousness that yields, he says, Auden's "finest writing to date." Taking issue with one of Auden's earliest academic critics, the "somewhat misguided" Francis Scarfe, who describes Auden's "style which is no style," Ashbery offers his reading of Auden's "style":

> As Mr. Scarfe's explanation of what his term means is not helpful, may I submit that perhaps he means to refer [to] the *consciousness* of Auden's poetry? For a style is, after all, an unnamable quality; it is only *recognized* by authors, who agree that it will develop only if left alone. Now the vast, hygenic self-consciousness of Auden, which is aware beforehand of exactly the impression a word or phrase will create, and is always darting ahead of us, clearing up new mysteries before we have arrived at them, could never be expected to have created a style which is an article, useless and decorative, to be left around to clutter up the meaning of a poem. If there were such a thing in his poetry, he would have written a poem analyzing it and pointing it out to us. What I mean is that "the style which is no style" (though I am thinking primarily of *The Sea and the Mirror*, and I realize Mr. Scarfe is discussing earlier poetry) is a style in which clarity, transparency, wit, verbal decoration, and imagery are all superbly functional, so much as to be invisible.

Ashbery defines "style" as "consciousness" itself, emphasizing that while it can be "recognized," it cannot be named, much as he had defined "poetry" earlier in the essay as "a perceived relation between things; we can recognize it and point out examples of it, but can never satisfactorily describe it." Poetry for Ashbery *is*

consciousness, and Auden's "vast, hygenic self-consciousness" produces, for him, a poetry whose representation of the active, "darting" mind is so complete—so "functional"—that it renders the deliberation of its own making "invisible." It is a consciousness so supremely self-aware that it achieves what Ashbery a few lines later calls the "paradox" of expressing an "unconscious quality . . . in which a small uncertainty, a not-being-sure-exactly-what-is-happening, enters." Distinguishing Auden's achievement in *The Sea and the Mirror* from his earlier poems, which "always give one an intelligent man's impressions of pity or terror, but never the deep dark emotion itself," Ashbery identifies Auden's magisterial poem—a text, significantly, comprised of self-conscious imitations of other poems, forms, and literary styles, from Shakespearean soliloquies and songs to villanelles to Jamesian prose—as a new kind of poetry, simultaneously familiar yet original, conscious yet apparently unpremeditated, intellectual yet emotional: "In *The Sea and the Mirror,* by a strange twist, we are presented with such a spectacle, more moving than intuition, and yet not really planned—that of an artist seeking truth. So this poem, by its very lucidity and penetration achieves the unconscious which we find in the greatest poetry—our view of the poet himself, the unsatisfied voyager." It is a spectacle—poet as "unsatisfied voyager"—with which many of Ashbery's own readers will be familiar.

Ashbery's is a poetry deeply concerned with the representation of consciousness, and with the troubled question of authorial intent. From the daydreaming scribe of **"The Instruction Manual"** to "The unsatisfactoriness, the frowns and squinting, the itching and scratching as you listen without taking in what is being said to you, or only in part, so that you cannot piece the argument together" (*Three Poems* 79) of longer, meanderingly discursive, self-descriptive poems like **"The System,"** Ashbery's work continually construes itself as reflecting the conscious mind responding to the complex and conflicting stimuli around it. "It's a kind of mimesis of how experience comes to me," is how he has described it to more than one interviewer ("John Ashbery" [Sommer] 305; "Craft" [Osti] 87). His poems also repeatedly address the poet's capacity to say what he wants to say, "unimportant but meant," as he puts it in **"Self-Portrait in a Convex Mirror"** (*Self-Portrait* [*Self-Portrait in a Convex Mirror*] 70). His poems often begin with avowals of intention: "They are preparing to begin again" (**"The Task,"** *Double Dream* 13); "You can't say it that way any more" (**"And *Ut Pictura Poesis*"** [**"And *Ut Pictura Poesis* Is Her Name"**], *Houseboat Days* 45); "And they have to get it right" (**"A Love Poem,"** *As We Know* 101); "This movie deals with the epidemic of the way we live now" (**"This Configuration,"** *As We Know* 109); "This poem is concerned with language on a very plain level" (**"Paradoxes and Oxymorons,"** *Shadow Train* 3);

"The conception is interesting: to see, as though reflected / In streaming windowpanes, the look of others through / Their own eyes" (**"Wet Casements,"** *Houseboat Days* 28). **"The New Spirit"** begins with the self-conscious rumination, "I thought that if I could put it all down, that would be one way. And next the thought came to me that to leave all out would be another, and truer, way" (*Three Poems* 3), and **"Self-Portrait"** [**"Self-Portrait in a Convex Mirror"**] takes as its ambition "As Parmigianino did it," "To take his own portrait, looking at himself for that purpose / In a convex mirror" (*Self-Portrait* 68). Ashbery's poet is both reacting to what he finds around him and acting consciously upon it—trying, as he puts it in **"Grand Galop,"** to "write poetry / Using what Wyatt and Surrey left around, / Took up and put down again / Like so much gorgeous raw material" (*Self-Portrait* 19). Ashbery's poetics is not one of simple passive receptivity. His response to the world is active and engaged, formulating that response in particular, conscious aesthetic decisions: "There are a lot of echoes in my work of not just forms but of language and of conventions of the poetry of the past which I feel very close to in certain ways. I don't want simply to repeat this language but to stretch or expand it, much in the same way, I guess, as Stravinsky did in his neoclassical music where he used music by Pergolesi and Tchaikovsky, transforming it" ("John Ashbery" [Labrie] 32).

For Ashbery, the mystery surrounding poetic intention results from the clash between "The extreme austerity of an almost empty mind / Colliding with the lush Rousseau-like foliage of its desire to communicate" (**"And *Ut Pictura Poesis*," *Houseboat Days*** 45). The poet becomes for him a figure of pathos precisely because his ambitions are so often thwarted, not by the unconscious but by his own consciousness and by the circumstances of the poem's composition:

> It is the principle that makes works of art so unlike
> What the artist intended. Often he finds
> He has omitted the thing he started out to say
> In the first place. Seduced by flowers,
> Explicit pleasures, he blames himself (though
> Secretly satisfied with the result), imagining
> He had a say in the matter and exercised
> An option of which he was hardly conscious,
> Unaware that necessity circumvents such resolutions
> So as to create something new
> For itself, that there is no other way,
> That the history of creation proceeds according to
> Stringent laws, and that things
> Do get done in this way, but never the things
> We set out to accomplish and wanted so desperately
> To see come into being.

> **("Self-Portrait,"** *Self-Portrait* 80)

"Seduced by flowers, / Explicit pleasures," the poet's distractible consciousness betrays his own intentions, but it is this very betrayal that results in "something

new." The poet, says Ashbery, customarily consoles and deludes himself by attributing this unexpected bounty to talents he did not even know he possessed, "imagining / He had a say in the matter and exercised / An option of which he was hardly conscious." That is, the poet typically identifies his inspiration—his muse—with the unconscious, claiming credit for his surprising originality through forces that are beyond his conscious control, yet unmistakably within him. But Ashbery debunks this comforting myth, asserting that it is the Audenesque notion of "necessity," not the unconscious, that calls the shots. For the American Auden that Ashbery would have been reading as an undergraduate, "necessity" is the most crucial of words and concepts. In poem after poem in the 1940s, including "New Year Letter" and the "Quest" sonnets, Auden construed himself as being on a quest for "necessity" or "the necessary"—the eternally elusive condition where what we need from the world is perfectly balanced by what we owe it, what he elsewhere calls "the hidden law" and in other places simply "Love."[16] Here, "necessity" is Ashbery's word for the interdependence between the poet's demand for inspirational stimuli and the world's demand for the "new" art it needs. Ashbery yields authorial control not to the unconscious but to his environment, to time, to the world around him. The powers of history, the requirements of culture, the demands of the moment, one's poetic influences—these are the forces impinging on the poet's consciousness and driving him toward "something new," not some mystical but ego-satisfying trope of unknown, inner capabilities engaged in psychic agon. As he puts it in another poem,

> Although I mean it, and project the meaning
> As hard as I can into its brushed-metal surface,
> It cannot, in this deteriorating climate, pick up
> Where I leave off.

> **("The Ice-Cream Wars,"** *Houseboat Days* 60)

For Ashbery, it is "this deteriorating climate"—the difficult but knowable world outside him, not the unknowable world within—that changes the course of the poem, resulting in "something new" but "never the things we set out to accomplish."[17]

Ashbery's poetry is also, in a literal sense, all about surfaces. "[Y]our eyes proclaim / That everything is surface. The surface is what's there / And nothing can exist except what's there," as he puts it in **"Self-Portrait"**:

> And just as there are no words for the surface, that is,
> No words to say what it really is, that it is not
> Superficial but a visible core, then there is
> No way out of the problem of pathos vs. experience.

> (*Self-Portrait* 70)

The surface, for Ashbery, is "necessity," that liminal, evasive space where dialectic ("pathos vs. experience") gets resolved, that paradoxical point where two things truly touch, but if that point were ever to be apprehended, it would vanish, as a bubble bursts or "balloon pops" (70) at the approach of an inquisitive finger. To reach that surface—that moment of true resolution, true contact, true understanding, true love—is what the poet continually, and frustratingly, quests for, "emblematic / Of life and how you cannot isolate a note of it" (*Houseboat Days* 69). But "the surface is what's there / And nothing can exist except what's there," he says: even as we seek to inhabit that surface, to fully perceive and experience it, the pathos of our plight ("the pity of it smarts" [69]) is that we are already uncomprehendingly living in it, in the "bubble-chamber" (72) of the instantaneous, ungraspable present:

> These windows on the past enable us to see enough to stay on an even keel in the razor's-edge present which is really a no-time, continual straying over the border into the positive past and the negative future whose movements alone define it. Unfortunately we have to live in it. We are appalled at this. Because its no-time, no-space dimensions offer us no signposts, nothing to be guided by.

> **("The System," *Three Poems* 102)**

The poet's goal—through his poems' mimesis of a consciousness trying to analyze, understand, and respond constructively to its predicament in the "no-time, no-space dimensions" of instantaneous existence—is to offer us those missing signposts, to suggest some guidance, enabling its readers, as the young Ashbery says of Auden, "to apply it within the realm of their experience."

So if Ashbery's poetics is manifestly *about* the "surface" of the consciousness responding to its surroundings—rather than the presumably "deeper" unconscious, buried somewhere beneath the skin of awareness—and if "the surface isn't the surface but the visible core," perhaps it's time his critics took the surface seriously. That is, rather than privileging Freudian concepts of sublimated conflict in defiance of his poetry's own notion of itself and its ambition, or reading his poems as mere transcripts of what one critic calls the "aim to communicate without communicating anything of substance" (Blasing 154), critics should pay attention to the activity of consciousness that the poems themselves set out to reflect: a consciousness which is actively responsive to the world, making sense of it by making self-aware—albeit continually frustrated—choices of order, form, and intention. Instead of drafting Ashbery into a high romantic critical program that sees the solitary, contending ego as its central trope, or reducing him to a deconstructive collagist, we can gain new insight into Ashbery by trying to see him as he sees himself, as a self in context, an identity questing for stability rather than dominance, a lover seeking contact and understanding, an intellect assimilating and welcoming and ordering

the riotous world around him. As Ashbery puts it in, again, **"Self-Portrait,"**

> Each person
> Has one big theory to explain the universe
> But it doesn't tell the whole story
> And in the end it is what is outside him
> That matters, to him and especially to us
> Who have been given no help whatever
> In decoding our own man-size quotient and must rely
> On second-hand knowledge.
>
>   (81-82)

"It is what is outside" the poet, and his efforts to "decode" and pass on to his readers what little he can—his "own man-sized quotient" of "second-hand knowledge"—"that matters," not some grand formula—Freudian, deconstructive, ideological, or otherwise—"to explain the universe."

This idea of reclaiming Ashbery from the "one big theory" has, paradoxically, a number of polemical implications. First, in its privileging of responsive dialectic over fixed cultural or ideological absolutes, it reasserts the importance of the post-1939 Auden's non-ideological example to Ashbery's work (and to his generation of poets in general). Second, in its emphasis on Ashbery's constructive assimilation of experience and his "desire to communicate" that experience, it argues for Ashbery as a poet seeking to engage the world rather than deconstruct it. Third, in suggesting the value of Ashbery's own articulation of his poetic process, it proposes him as an example of a new poetics that acknowledges choice, craft, and consciousness over anxiety and agon. And fourth, in challenging one-sided critical constructs of Ashbery's project, it figures the relationship between criticism and the poetry it takes as its subject as a fundamentally dialectical one. This last theme—of criticism's problematic links with its sources—is one to which Ashbery has often addressed himself, and it is with a discussion of this question, in dialogue with Ashbery's own inaugural effort at literary criticism, that I want to conclude.

"We see us as we truly behave" is the first line of the first poem of Ashbery's first book, and we might be tempted to read it—with an assertive emphasis on that initial "we"—as a proleptic authorial admonition to his future critics. "The critics always get everything wrong," he has said, citing one of his "favorite lines" from Vaslav Nijinsky's journal: "Criticism is death" ("John Ashbery" [Sommer] 295; "John Ashbery" [Gangel] 14). Ashbery's most sustained explicit engagement with the role of criticism comes midway through 1979's **"Litany,"** when one of the voices embarks on a lengthy, and uncharacteristically prosaic, consideration of the function of criticism at the present time:

> Just one minute of contemporary existence
> Has so much to offer, but who

Can evaluate it, formulate
The appropriate apothegm, show us
In a few well-chosen words of wisdom
Exactly what is taking place all about us?
Not critics, certainly, though that is precisely
What they are supposed to be doing, yet how
Often have you read any criticism
Of our society and all the people and things in it
That really makes sense, to us as human beings?

(As We Know 32)

Ashbery, by 1979 the subject of considerable criticism himself, much of it unappreciative, in the wake of *Self-Portrait in a Convex Mirror*'s sweep of the major literary prizes three years earlier, strikes back at his critics and finds *them* wanting.[18] He continues, mocking his own impulse to sermonize, in what Auden self-critically designates in his own work "the preacher's loose immodest tone" (204), the theatrically elevated voice of the call-and-response litanist:

It behooves
Our critics to make the poets more aware of
What they're doing, so that poets in turn
Can stand back and be enchanted by it
And in this way make room for the general public
To crowd around and be enchanted by it too,
And then, hopefully, make some sense of their lives,
Bring order back into the disorderly house
Of their drab existences.

The job of critics, admonishes the preacherly Ashbery, is not to impose their own theoretical structures upon the poem but to engage it on its own terms, to participate fully in it, and, in a sense, yield themselves to it. Criticism can be constructive—in the sense of active collaboration in a shared project—but only if it enters the poetry as an attentive companion. The poem, not the critic, is the host, to reverse J. Hillis Miller's famous—and contemporaneous—formulation.[19]

The experience of inhabiting the poem should be a didactic one, for both critic and "the general public": a true poem should teach us how to read it, and thereby teach us—if only in small, "man-sized quotients"—how better to live. Only when the critic has engaged in the poem's life-affirming dialectic will he be able to offer insight of value to the poet, enabling him to write new poems that will help his readers "make some sense of their lives." The mocking, deflationary tone of the description of his readers' "drab existences"—as if he were quoting some ironic version of himself as the arrogant *artiste,* intent on enlightening the masses—serves to underscore the feeling of frustration provoking this ambition, as Ashbery acknowledged in an interview conducted around the time of **"Litany"'**s composition:

I really don't know what to think when I read criticism, either favorable or unfavorable. In most cases, even when it's sympathetic and understanding, it's a

sort of parallel adventure to the poetry. It never gives me the feeling that I'll know how to do it the next time I sit down to write, which is my principal concern. I'm not putting down critics, but they don't help the poetry to get its work done.

("John Ashbery" [Gangel] 14)

The only solution, he concludes, is to take the matter into his own hands:

Therefore a new school of criticism must be developed.
First of all, the new
Criticism should take into account that it is we
Who made it, and therefore
Not be too eager to criticize us: we
Could do that for ourselves, and have done so.
Nor
Should it take itself as a fitting subject
For critical analysis, since it knows
Itself only through us, and us
Only through being part of ourselves, the bark
Of the tree of our intellect.

Ashbery's notional school for critics recalls Auden's similarly proscriptive criterion for useful criticism:

What is the function of a critic? So far as I am concerned, he can do me one or more of the following services:

1) Introduce me to authors or works of which I was hitherto unaware.

2) Convince me that I have undervalued an author or a work because I had not read them carefully enough.

3) Show me relations between works of different ages and cultures which I could never have seen for myself because I do not know enough and never shall.

4) Give a "reading" of a work which increases my understanding of it.

5) Throw light upon the process of artistic "Making."

6) Throw light upon the relation of art to life, to science, economics, ethics, religion, etc.

("Reading," *Dyer's Hand* 8-9)

For Ashbery, as for Auden, the function of criticism is to help poetry "to get its work done," and critics can do that only by joining with the poet in his project of "Making," such that new light can be shed "upon the relation of art to life." Ashbery's objection to contemporary criticism is both personal ("they shouldn't be so eager to criticize us"), perhaps reflecting bruised feelings, and professional ("nor should it take itself as a fitting subject for critical analysis"). Rather than being an isolated "parallel adventure" to poetry, criticism should be a dialectical partner with it, like the twin columns of **"Litany,"** each engaging, commenting, and reflecting on the other, each driving the other forward in a shared, hopeful endeavor of describing life and "all the people and things in it" in a way "that really makes sense, to us as human beings." Again, those final three words of **"Litany"**—the last standing alone on its line—suggest this wished-for sense of constructive collaboration, as one column calls hopefully across to the other, "would you / Try?" As I've already suggested, the impulse to "try"—to understand, to communicate, to make contact, to love—is at the heart of Ashbery's poetics, as is the notion that he can't, or doesn't want to, do it alone.

Ashbery's critics are supposed to do what poets aim to do: "show us / In a few well-chosen words of wisdom / Exactly what is taking place all about us." That is, Ashbery's ideal critics are, in fact, not critics at all, but poets, in a Wordsworthian redefinition of "poet," suggesting the capacity for understanding that potentially exists in everyone. Ashbery's attack on criticism amounts to a defense of poetry as a superior form of criticism in itself. Ashbery has argued as much outside the margins of his poems:

> It seems to me that poetry is already criticism and that it's criticizing something that one doesn't know about, some unknown situation. Criticism of poetry is at a further remove. The poem has already said it all in the only way that it can be said. Paraphrases merely get in the way. The poem should be read again.
>
>   ("John Ashbery" [Murphy] 40)

What we know as literary criticism, the self-centered criticism of "big ideas" that has been inflicted upon his work, Ashbery agrees with Nijinsky, is "death." True criticism, on the other hand—that is, poetry—is "life itself."

As a student critic, Ashbery was already addressing the notion that poets and critics share, in Auden's words, "a common, noble and civilising task." He was also taking seriously the idea that poetry itself is the truest form of criticism, as demonstrated in the intimate relation between his analysis of Auden's work and his own developing poetic practice. In the first poem in *The Sea and the Mirror,* the "Stage Manager" addresses "the Critics," asking "[W]ho in his own backyard / Has not opened his heart to the smiling / Secret he cannot quote?" (*Collected Poems* 403). Early on in his critique of Auden's work, Ashbery suggests a similar sense of the unsatisfactoriness of critical language for the kind of perception available only through poetry: "Clearly there is but one kind of poetry (though its subject matter be limitless) which we cannot define by any other word, and which we are continually forced to think of as a nameless ichor, a kind of perceived relation between things; we can recognize it and point out examples of it, but can never satisfactorily describe it." As critic, Ashbery attempts to describe Auden's work, but as a young poet, and throughout the rest of his career, we can see him applying the "criticism" that he learned from Auden's poetry to his own.

Ashbery remarks upon Auden's "overwhelming (and utterly praiseworthy) tendency to give the abstract 'a local habitation and a name'" and cites as an example a few lines from *The Sea and the Mirror*: "Historic deeds, drop their hauteur and speak of shabby childhoods / When all they longed for was to join in the gang of doubts / Who so tormented them." One need only look as far as the earliest poem in **Some Trees, "The Painter,"** to see Ashbery exploring this idea, and building upon it. The Painter paints "the sea's portrait," expecting "his subject / To rush up the sand, and, seizing a brush, / Plaster its own portrait on the canvas" (65). Ashbery depicts the artist in his poem, as he depicts Auden in his essay, as concerned with personifying abstractions, of painting the "sea's portrait." In the poem's next canvas, however, we see Ashbery taking Auden's idea and reversing it, as the Painter chooses "his wife for a new subject, / Making her vast, like ruined buildings." Here Ashbery's artist experiments with art's capacity to abstract the personal, as the wife's individuality is distilled into pure "vastness." In the poem's climax, art and artist come together in a synthesis of the personal and abstract, as the artist paints a "self-portrait," "leaving the canvas / Perfectly white" (66). The Painter's audience, outraged and confused by the artist's visionary self-abstraction, responds—as Ashbery's real critics often have—with savage condemnation: "They tossed him, the portrait, from the tallest of the buildings; / And the sea devoured the canvas and the brush / As if his subject had decided to remain a prayer."[20] The artist and his portrait become one, and both plunge into the "angry and large" sea, martyred by the critical mob.

Of *The Sea and the Mirror,* Ashbery observes in his essay, "the theme, announced by the title, is the venerable one of the inevitableness of life (the sea) and art (the mirror)," and he calls the rebellious figure of Antonio "the personification of the sea, 'The life', from which poetry, as long as it seeks to describe, to resolve it, will always be excluded." While Prospero surrenders his books "To the silent dissolution of the sea" (*Collected Poems* 404), choosing his life over his art, Ashbery's artist refuses to choose one over the other—arguing, again, that art, and specifically poetry, "is life itself"— and achieves a kind of perfection in that very "dissolution." **"The Painter,"** then, works as a triple fable for Ashbery's career: first, as an early metaphor for Ashbery's ambition to create an art in which the dialectics of poet and poem, life and art, achieve a kind of transcendent synthesis; second, as a parable of the younger artist assimilating the example of the older and then developing from it a new, original perspective; and last, as the initial salvo in Ashbery's ongoing—and sometimes overtly self-defensive—war with criticism.[21]

"The conception," says Ashbery in **"Wet Casements,"** "is interesting": to see "the look of others through /

Their own eyes" (**Houseboat Days** 28). This is Ashbery's vision of criticism—and, as we have seen, his own critical practice—and it is a vision that may bear some sympathetic scrutiny on the part of those whose profession it is to read and explain his work. If poetry is in fact criticism, rather than imposing an external rubric or theory upon the work, perhaps we can derive a fruitful critical approach from within the work itself. This is not, of course, to argue for some naive conception of authorial infallibility, or even truthfulness, since as Shoptaw has convincingly shown, misrepresentativeness is one of the hallmarks of Ashbery's poetic mode.[22] Nor is it a rearguard attempt to reduce the scope of criticism to boundaries set by the authors themselves. Rather, it is to suggest a way of reading Ashbery—and indeed other writers, including Auden—that recognizes the poem's power to instruct and its ambition to embrace its reader and the world. By taking the poems themselves as a model for criticism—a model that places itself in context, that welcomes contingency and influence, that emphasizes the act of consciousness, that looks outward to the consequences of its insight, that espouses collaboration over contention, that *"tries"*—we can gain a new, and perhaps surprising, perspective on Ashbery's work and indeed on recent literary history.

If Ashbery's work is truly "postmodern," as it is often described, this is not, I would argue, because it exhibits characteristics, or "symptoms," that conform to the multiple "big theories" that have come to stand behind that word. What makes Ashbery "postmodern" is not his demonstration of various contemporary critical figurations, from ironic fragmentation, to the deaths of the metanarrative and the author, to psychoanalytic tropes of belatedness.[23] Rather, if we look at the poetry rather than the intervening theories, we find an art that is genuinely "postmodernist" in its active revision of its American modernist predecessors. Ashbery's work, in its optative, socially constructive mood, moves past the poetics of despair, isolation, solipsism, unreclaimable fragmentation, frustrated romanticism, and cultural conservatism of Eliot, Pound, and Stevens. In its claims for poetry's didactic force, its positive dialectics, and its humane pluralism, Ashbery's poetry articulates a mode of perceiving that gives a new—and specifically poetic and literary historical—meaning to the term "postmodern." Ashbery isn't shoring fragments against his ruin, or even playing resignedly with the shards on the dump. Instead, he's trying to build a shelter out of those fragments, give to the welter of our moment—in a phrase Ashbery applies to Auden's own poetics—"a local habitation and a name," and welcome us inside. And his great teacher in this project—the "Old Master" to his "gay apprentice"—was Auden.

Selections from the John Ashbery Papers are quoted with the permission of Houghton Library, Harvard University.

Notes

1. Ashbery repeats this assertion in his Charles Eliot Norton lectures, noting that among the "certifiably major poets whom I feel as influences"—including Stevens, Marianne Moore, Gertrude Stein, Elizabeth Bishop, William Carlos Williams, Boris Pasternak, and Osip Mandelstam—he considers Auden, "chronologically the first and therefore the most important influence" (*Other Traditions* 4).

2. For the dates of specific poems, and for its overview of Ashbery's career, I am indebted to John Shoptaw's crucial *On the Outside Looking Out: John Ashbery's Poetry.*

3. Lynn Keller reads both "The Painter" and "Illustration" as being in dialogue with Stevens, although she acknowledges "Auden's strong influence . . . in *Some Trees.*" See Keller 18, 22, 271n.

4. Interestingly, Marjorie Perloff places another poem from Ashbery's first book, "Two Scenes" (which includes the obviously Audenesque lines "A fine rain anoints the canal machinery. / This is perhaps a day of general honesty / Without example in the world's history" [21]), within an Audenesque lineage without acknowledging that she is doing so: "In its fidelity to 'a way of happening' rather than to 'what happens,' 'Two Scenes' anticipates Ashbery's later work" ("'Fragments'" 77).

5. Willard Spiegelman offers a brief but helpful discussion of Ashbery's "didactic voice" and "pedagogic 'tone,'" calling him "a teacher in search of a subject" (251-54).

6. Blasing's relation of Ashbery to Fredric Jameson's notion of the integration of aesthetic production into commodity production (112), and to what she deems the characteristically postmodern "passive stance of 'waiting'" (115), also seems apposite here. For other "postmodern" constructions of Ashbery, see Perloff, *Poetics*; and Conte.

7. David Herd's useful recent book, *John Ashbery and American Poetry,* makes some suggestive remarks along these lines, observing, "Understanding of Ashbery has . . . been ill served by theoretical readings of the poetry" (14), and concluding that Ashbery "aims to make communication possible in a liberal-democratic society" (19).

8. As Shoptaw, among many critics, puts it, "The emphasis in Ashbery's work is always upon the movement or rhythm between poles rather than upon the bipolar opposites themselves" (91). For another discussion of Ashbery's "negative dialectics" as manifested in his prose poems, see Monte 181-226.

9. There is a connection between what I, following others, am calling Ashbery's "dialectic" (and Auden's) and Mikhail Bakhtin's notion of dialogism, with its suggestion of an utterance's ambition for a listening subject. For a discussion of Bakhtin's relation to Ashbery's "desire to reach beyond the 'I,' the speaking or writing self," see Murphy 51.

10. The illustrator and writer Edward Gorey, who was a college friend of Ashbery's and Frank O'Hara's roommate (it was at one of Gorey's parties that Ashbery and O'Hara first met), in one of his early illustrated books depicts—in something of a non sequitur, given the fanciful nature of the rest of the narrative—a rather chilling vignette of a writhing figure being set afire atop the statue of John Harvard by a young, torch-wielding mob, illustrating this limerick: "Some Harvard men, stalwart and hairy, / Drank up several bottles of sherry; / In the Yard around three / They were shrieking with glee: / 'Come on out, we are burning a fairy'" (25). Donald Hall, another Harvard classmate, presents a more benign view of Harvard in the late 1940s in his recollections of O'Hara: "Being gay was relatively open, even light, in the Harvard of those years. One of Frank's givens was that *everybody* was gay, either in or out of the closet" (qtd. in Lehman 53).

11. For two readings of Ashbery that place his work specifically within a poetics of homosexuality, see Imbriglio and Vincent.

12. Charles Altieri has written significantly on Ashbery as "love poet" but does so principally within the context of generic definitions of "love lyrics" and makes little comment on the erotic basis of Ashbery's poetics. James McCorkle has also remarked on "Eros and its function of making" in Ashbery's work and relates it to Ashbery's polyvocality, arguing, "The lyric, in Ashbery's poetics, becomes choral, in that a range of voices give voice(s) to the survival of the community. No longer the domain of the self-sufficient self, the lyric reveals the self's reliance upon others" (111).

13. Barthes's title, *A Lover's Discourse: Fragments,* and his account of his project—to present a portrait of the loving "I" which "offers the reader a discursive site: the site of someone speaking within himself, *amorously,* confronting the other (the loved object), who does not speak"—make an admirable description of Ashbery's own poetics. Another reading of Ashbery might productively trace Barthes's various "fragments" of erotic discourse—"absence," "to understand," "body," "embrace," "identification," "unbearable," "magic," "silence," "waking," "remembrance," "truth"—through their continual appearance in Ashbery's work.

14. For a persuasive reading of Ashbery's Eliotic inheritance, and a complementary analysis of Ashbery's notion of his relation to the poetic tradition, see Longenbach.

15. For an account of Ashbery's ongoing response to Bloom's critical construction of his work, see Schultz, "'Returning to Bloom.'"

16. For the definitive discussion of the importance of this concept to Auden's work, see Greenberg.

17. For an Ashberian fable about the ways authorial intent is overmastered by both the demands of the text and the world outside the text, see Ashbery's play *The Compromise,* in which the characters of a melodrama, Pirandello-like, take over the action from the smug yet indecisive figure of the "Author," who wants his play to remain unfinished in order to imitate "the very uncertainty of life, where things are seldom carried through to a conclusion, let alone a satisfactory one." At the "conclusion" of the play, all the characters walk out, leaving the Author to protest, "Where are you going? Stop! . . . I haven't finished . . . You can't desert me! . . . What are you doing to me?" The Author's folly, the audience is told by the comic stock-figure of a wise old Indian chief, is that he tried to impose his own inner vision of existence upon the intractable realities of the world outside him. As the Author falls asleep onstage, the Indian chief intones a prayer: "Now, spirit of the great raven, descend on your unhappy son. For of all of us, he suffers the most and knows the least . . . Give him, for a while, the sleep you hold in your dusky sable plumes. And perhaps when he awakens the world and the people in it will be more the way he thinks they ought to be" (*Three Plays* 118-19).

18. For a contextualization of "Litany" within the culture of deconstructive criticism in the late 1970s, see Shoptaw 234-35.

19. In my articulation of these ideas, I have found helpful Martin Kevorkian's reading of Ashbery's dialectical relation to his critics, including the argument that Ashbery's poems assimilate, engage, and preempt specific literary theoretical responses to his work, among them Miller's host-parasite paradigm.

20. In the introduction to *Beyond Amazement,* David Lehman offers a synopsis of the history of Ashbery's negative critical reception (21-23). Among the more notorious assaults has been that of Charles Molesworth, who calls Ashbery's aesthetic "a flirtation with nihilism, the fag end of an autotelic art that apotheosizes symbolism's elevation of style over content" (165).

21. This poem may also point to a particular moment in the divergence of Auden and Ashbery's poetic projects. In the Painter's heroic martyrdom to the idea that art and life are inseparable, and its implicit rejection of Prospero's—and Auden's—decision to privilege life over art, we can perhaps see the seeds of Ashbery's disaffection with the direction in which Auden's later poetry would take him.

22. The strength of Shoptaw's approach, from this polemical perspective, is that it takes its cues from the poetry itself. The poems insistently teach us to

look for that thing outside the poem—the crypt word, the homosocial context, in Shoptaw's analysis—and the critic, alert to this lesson, engages the poetry on its own "misrepresentative" terms.

23. Keller's description is characteristic: of contemporary poets, Ashbery "may well be the most thoroughly and obviously postmodern—most concerned with indeterminacy, with process, and most determined to embody his ideas about the radical uncertainties of language and experience in the diction and movement of his poems" (13-14). Perloff anticipates, and preemptively rejects, the argument for reading Ashbery as something other than a poet whose chief aim is to embody radical indeterminacy, in her 1998 response to Longenbach's *Modern Poetry after Modernism* and Vernon Shetley's *After the Death of Poetry: Poet and Audience in Contemporary America*. These critics, says Perloff, in trying to reclaim Ashbery from the "breakthrough narratives" of postmodernism, and in particular by tracing his poetic roots back to Eliot, are engaged in an effort to "normalize" Ashbery, thereby rendering him, according to Perloff, insufficiently progressive and interesting ("Normalizing John Ashbery").

Works Cited

Altieri, Charles. "Ashbery as Love Poet." Schultz, *Tribe* 26-37.

Ashbery, John. "The Art of Poetry XXXIII: John Ashbery." Interview with Peter Stitt. *Paris Review* 90 (Winter 1983): 30-59.

———. *As We Know.* New York: Penguin, 1979.

———. "Craft Interview with John Ashbery." With Janet Bloom and Robert Losada. *Poet's Craft: Interviews from "The New York Quarterly."* Ed. William Packard. New York: Paragon, 1987. 79-97.

———. "The Craft of John Ashbery." Interview with Louis Osti. *Confrontations* 9.3 (1974): 84-96.

———. *The Double Dream of Spring.* New York: Ecco, 1976.

———. *Hotel Lautréamont.* New York: Knopf, 1992.

———. *Houseboat Days.* New York: Viking, 1977.

———. Interview with the author. March 1989.

———. Interview with the author. 13 May 1997.

———. "John Ashbery." Interview with Sue Gangel. *American Poetry Observed: Poets on Their Work.* Ed. Joe David Bellamy. Urbana: U of Illinois P, 1988. 9-20.

———. "John Ashbery: An Interview by Ross Labrie." *American Poetry Review* May-June 1984: 29-33.

———. "John Ashbery: An Interview in Warsaw." With Piotr Sommer. *Code of Signals: Recent Writings in Poetics.* Ed. Michael Palmer. Berkeley, CA: North Atlantic, 1983. 294-314.

———. "John Ashbery." Interview with John Murphy. *Poetry Review* 75.2 (1985): 20-25.

———. *Other Traditions.* Cambridge, MA: Harvard UP, 2000.

———. "The Poetic Medium of W. H. Auden." Senior Essay, Harvard U., 1949. John Ashbery Papers, AM-6, Houghton Library, Harvard University.

———. "Recent Tendencies in Poetry." 1945. John Ashbery Papers, AM-6, Houghton Library, Harvard University.

———. *Reported Sightings: Art Chronicles, 1957-1987.* Ed. David Bergman. Cambridge, MA: Harvard UP, 1989.

———. *Self-Portrait in a Convex Mirror.* 1972. New York: Penguin, 1976.

———. *Shadow Train.* 1980. New York: Viking, 1981.

———. *Some Trees.* New Haven, CT: Yale UP, 1956.

———. *Three Plays.* Manchester, Eng.: Carcanet, 1988.

———. *Three Poems.* New York: Ecco, 1989.

———. *The Vermont Notebook.* Los Angeles: Black Sparrow, 1975.

———. *A Wave.* New York: Viking, 1984.

Auden, W. H. *Collected Poems.* Ed. Edward Mendelson. New York: Vintage, 1991.

———. *The Double Man.* New York: Random, 1941.

———. *The Dyer's Hand.* New York: Vintage, 1989.

———. *The English Auden: Poems, Essays and Dramatic Writings, 1927-1939.* Ed. Edward Mendelson. 1977. London: Faber, 1986.

———. *New Year Letter.* London: Faber, 1941.

Barthes, Roland. *A Lover's Discourse: Fragments.* Trans. Richard Howard. New York: Noonday, 1978.

Blasing, Mutlu Konuk. *Politics and Form in Postmodern Poetry: O'Hara, Bishop, Ashbery, and Merrill.* New York: Cambridge UP, 1995.

Bloom, Harold. *A Map of Misreading.* New York: Oxford UP, 1975.

———, ed. *John Ashbery.* Modern Critical Views. New York: Chelsea, 1985.

Conte, Joseph M. *Unending Design: The Forms of Postmodern Poetry.* Ithaca, NY: Cornell UP, 1991.

Gorey, Edward. *Amphigorey.* New York: Putnam, 1972.

Greenberg, Herbert. *Quest for the Necessary: W. H. Auden and the Dilemma of Divided Consciousness.* Cambridge, MA: Harvard UP, 1969.

Herd, David. *John Ashbery and American Poetry.* New York: Palgrave, 2000.

Imbriglio, Catherine. "'Our Days Put on Such Reticence': The Rhetoric of the Closet in John Ashbery's *Some Trees.*" *Contemporary Literature* 36 (1995): 249-88.

Keller, Lynn. *Re-making It New: Contemporary American Poetry and the Modernist Tradition.* New York: Cambridge UP, 1987.

Kevorkian, Martin. "John Ashbery's *Flow Chart*: John Ashbery and The Theorists on John Ashbery against The Critics against John Ashbery." *New Literary History* 25 (1994): 459-76.

Lehman, David, ed. *Beyond Amazement: New Essays on John Ashbery.* Ithaca, NY: Cornell UP, 1980.

———. *The Last Avant-Garde: The Making of the New York School of Poets.* New York: Doubleday, 1998.

Longenbach, James. *Modern Poetry after Modernism.* New York: Oxford UP, 1997.

McCorkle, James. "Nimbus of Sensations: Eros and Reverie in the Poetry of John Ashbery and Ann Lauterbach." Schultz, *Tribe* 101-25.

Molesworth, Charles. *The Fierce Embrace: A Study of Contemporary American Poetry.* Columbia: U of Missouri P, 1979.

Monte, Steven. *Invisible Fences: Prose Poetry as a Genre in French and American Literature.* Lincoln: U of Nebraska P, 2000.

Murphy, Margueritte S. "John Ashbery's *Three Poems*: Heteroglossia in the American Prose Poem." *American Poetry* 7.2 (1990): 50-63.

Perloff, Marjorie. "'Fragments of a Buried Life': John Ashbery's Dream Songs." Lehman, *Beyond Amazement* 66-86.

———. "Normalizing John Ashbery." *Jacket* 2 Jan. 1998. <http://jacketmagazine.com>.

———. *The Poetics of Indeterminacy: Rimbaud to Cage.* Princeton, NJ: Princeton UP, 1981.

Schultz, Susan M. "'Returning to Bloom': John Ashbery's Critique of Harold Bloom." *Contemporary Literature* 37 (1996): 24-48.

———, ed. *The Tribe of John: Ashbery and Contemporary Poetry.* Tuscaloosa: U of Alabama P, 1995.

Shetley, Vernon. *After the Death of Poetry: Poet and Audience in Contemporary America.* Durham, NC: Duke UP, 1993.

Shoptaw, John. *On the Outside Looking Out: John Ashbery's Poetry.* Cambridge, MA: Harvard UP, 1994.

Spiegelman, Willard. *The Didactic Muse: Scenes of Instruction in Contemporary Amerian Poetry.* Princeton, NJ: Princeton UP, 1989.

Vincent, John. "Reports of Looting and Insane Buggery behind Altars: John Ashbery's Queer Poetics." *Twentieth Century Literature* 44.2 (Summer 1998): 155-75.

Donald Revell (essay date March/April 2002)

SOURCE: Revell, Donald. "Invisible Green V." *American Poetry Review* 31, no. 2 (March/April 2002): 23-4.

[*In the following essay, Revell asserts that Ashbery's poetry embodies a peaceful vision of America reminiscent of Thomas Jefferson.*]

> Methinks my own soul must be a bright invisible green.
>
> —Henry David Thoreau, *A Week on the Concord and Merrimack Rivers,* 193

A bliss began to happen somewhere. There was America. There was need of America, of an ecstasy whose earth would remain unstolen by a soul. Are we Americans? I ask because I believe all poets everywhere to be Americans in the necessity and abandoned stewardship of bliss. A poem's ambition rests with earth. ("Language is fossil poetry," said Emerson, remember? Buried or exposed, the fossil rests. A poem rests. Only poetry, the ambition of the earth itself, rives on.) And so, in the just governments our poetry conceives, geography is peace, and geography is the guardian of joys. We are (were) Americans only so long as our poems show(ed) non-aggressive expansions of this peace. Manifest Destiny unconfines not nations but rivers and mountains. And the rivers and mountains in their turn more tenderly confine us to grander scales of joy. Thoreau walked a very long time to test the mercy of geography, and he found its limits beyond all measurement, and serene.

> I trust that we shall be more imaginative, that our thoughts will be clearer, fresher, and more ethereal, as our sky—our understanding more comprehensive and broader, like our plains—our intellect generally on a grander scale, like our thunder and lightning, our rivers and mountains and forests—and our hearts shall even correspond in breadth and depth and grandeur to our inland seas. Perchance there will appear to the traveler something, he knows not what, of *laeta* and *glabra,* of joyous and serene, in our very faces. Else to what end does the world go on, and why was America discovered?
>
> —"Walking," 238

Whenever it is discovered (and the discovery involves poetry), America finds itself increased by new surroundings. Geography works its wild, wild peace from the outside in. The work is poetry. The poem, non-aggressive even so far as the end of the world, resounds and rests.

And even before Thoreau went walking, a founding father, Jefferson, described a dynamic peace at work in the confines of his native country. His *Notes on the State of Virginia* declare the sweet dependency of Vision upon geography, declaring also the ways in which geography really acts to rile and then to rest our views. A great passage from "Query IV. A Notice of its Mountains" shows these actions plain.

> The passage of the Potomac through the Blue Ridge is, perhaps, one of the most stupendous scenes in nature. You stand on a very high point of land. On your right comes up the Shenandoah, having ranged along the foot of the mountain an hundred miles to seek a vent. On your left approaches the Potomac, in quest of a passage also. In the moment of their junction, they rush together against the mountain, rend it asunder, and pass off to the sea. The first glance of this scene hurries our senses into the opinion, that this earth has been created in time, that the mountains were formed first, that the rivers began to flow afterwards, that in this place particularly, they have been dammed up by the Blue Ridge of mountains, and have formed an ocean which filled the whole valley; that continuing to rise they have at length broken over at this spot, and have torn the mountain down from its summit to its base. The piles of rock on each hand, but particularly on the Shenandoah, the evident marks of their disrupture and avulsion from their beds by the most powerful agents of nature, corroborate the impression. But the distant finishing which nature has given to the picture, is of a very different character. It is a true contrast to the foreground. It is as placid and delightful as that is wild and tremendous. For the mountain being cloven asunder, she presents to your eye, through the cleft, a small catch of smooth blue horizon, at an infinite distance in the plain country, inviting you, as it were, from the riot and tumult roaring around, to pass through the breach and participate of the calm below. Here the eye ultimately composes itself; and that way, too, the road happens actually to lead.
>
> —182

Jefferson, the figure and fact of a poet here, is seen to "stand." It is the Shenandoah that "comes up" to him, itself already having widely "ranged." And as the Shenandoah "seek(s)," so the Potomac "quest(s)." The waters work, and Jefferson is exalted stilly in his place. His very senses are hurried by force of earth and not by any effort of his own. They arrive in good and easy time to see "the distant finishing which nature has given to the picture." Geography's self-evident imagination composes a wild peace in which Jefferson may safely praise and in whose dynamic confines of "riot and tumult" he safely moves. He passes through. The peace keeps him. Great masses and massive forces invite his eye to "calm." Here is ecstasy *in* place and *of* it. Here is exaltation freely given, an expansion of soul involving neither force of will nor act of aggression. Elisa New, in her beautiful study *The Line's Eye* rightly finds an *ars poetica*, a *pax poetica* here.

This paragraph from "Query IV" makes human will a function of natural fullness, differentiated from that fullness in experience but not strictly in essence. The river's importunities resolve in the smooth sky their movement reflects, and the overall design of the scene makes present urgency, or will, a temporary state that the broadness of experience cycles back into its profounder depths. What Jefferson reveals is an expansive containment, like the Psalmist's image of a cup running over.

—77

Will dissolves into the wider authority of World. Likewise, human force is obviated by "natural fullness." What New so wisely calls "expansive containment" describes as well a model of American ecstasy, a method of American poetic peace. All transpires by grace and under the guardianship of real geography. On a free Earth, "perception. . . . perception finds a sweet socket of its relatedness" (New 78). Vision leads the harmless eye to Visionary peace, right here, right now. America at peace is the only real America.

I am writing in early October 2001, and a terrible violence has seized the American eye. Imaginations make wars in Central Asia and mad menaces at home. And so I'm looking for America. I want to find a contemporary eye for peace and a practice of Vision characterized by what Denise Levertov once called (in "Life at War") "the quickness, the sureness, / the deep intelligence living at peace would have." Jefferson gives me the Model and models a Way. And thanks to Elisa New's sweet notion of "expansive containment," I have a test for these in poetry, the place I want to matter. Because it must be an American place, one will of course mean many. I'll choose John Ashbery.

The experimental insouciance of Ashbery's poetry has often distracted readers, myself included, from its fundamental simplicity. Ashbery's is a quiet voice sounded inside worlds it knows and shows to be majestically prolific. Action rests with those worlds, and all his authority derives from the limits they expand within his sight. Thus is Ashbery a true Jeffersonian, and so have his geographies ever described American landscapes of real peace. In **"Soonest Mended,"** his first explicit declaration of dependence, Ashbery made his purpose plain.

> To step free at last, miniscule on the gigantic plateau—
> This was our ambition: to be small and clear and free.
>
> —*The Double Dream of Spring,* 17

Freedom rests in an enormous surround. Good poems evidence a clarity of purpose, backgrounded on a grand and moving scale by Earth whose purpose is our home. Like Jefferson, Ashbery finds himself at sites of revelation, there to find forces much greater but guardian to his own. As the future president was borne up, the latter-day poet is "borne on."

The clarity of the rules dawned on you for the first
time.
They were the players, and we who had struggled at
the game
Were merely spectators, though subject to its vicis-
situdes
And moving with it out of the tearful stadium, borne
on shoulders, at last.
Night after night this message returns, repeated
In the flickering bulbs of the sky, raised past us, taken
away from us,
Yet ours over and over until the end that is past truth,
The being of our sentences, in the climate that fostered
them,
Not ours to own, like a book, but to be with, and
sometimes
To be without, alone and desperate.
But the fantasy makes it ours, a kind of fence-sitting
Raised to the level of an esthetic ideal.

—18

To the spectator are all spectacles displayed. Sentences
of a wild climate, translated onto human scale, become
calm, "a kind of fence-sitting / Raised to the level of an
esthetic ideal." Call it the impassive passive, a continental peace. Nothing in this place is "ours to own," and
yet the mercy of geography underwrites imagination,
and imagination "makes it ours." Once again, Earth's
purpose is our home.

It has been Ashbery's genius almost effortlessly to map
the liberal expanse of nature's sovereignty—i.e. the
imagination—upon which human fantasy conducts its
peaceful play. Leveled, poetry is raised. (This is
democracy in action.) Earth and the poetry of earth
show equal justice in expanse and containment.

And you see, both of us were right, though nothing
Has somehow come to nothing; the avatars
Of our conforming to the rules and living
Around the home have made—well, in a sense, "good
citizens" of us,
Brushing the teeth and all that, and learning to accept
The charity of the hard moments as they are doled
out,
For this is action, this not being sure, this careless
Preparing, sowing the seeds crooked in the furrow,
Making ready to forget, and always coming back
To the mooring of starting out, that day so long ago.

—19

I think of William Blake's Clod of Clay: "I ponder, and
I cannot ponder; yet I live and love." Thus early in a
masterly career, John Ashbery ordered the broad way of
human limits towards its brightest flow. Uncertainty
moves within a certain sequence, and the arts of
peace—"Preparing, sowing the seeds crooked in the
furrow"—prove the mystery of that sequence even as
they master, by "making ready to forget," the limits it
secures.

In peacetime, sequence is both dynamic and secure, a
motive force for trust. And it was via trust that Ashbery

entered the major phase of his writing life, continuing
still. Trust dispenses with sorrow. It ends the conflicts
memory, usually in the form of aggressively misremem-
bered claims, sustains against our better natures. In
"The New Spirit," Ashbery finds a quiet name for Elisa
New's "expansive containment." Too, he entitles
Thomas Jefferson's "small catch of smooth blue
horizon." It is happiness.

Are you sad about something today? On days like this
the old flanking motion almost seems to be possible
again. Certainly the whiff of nostalgia in the air is more
than a hint, a glaring proof that the old irregular way of
doing is not only some piece of furniture of the memory
but is ours, if we had the initiative to use it. I have lost
mine. It has been replaced by a strange kind of happiness within the limitations. The way is narrow but it is
not hard, it seems almost to propel or push one along.
One gets the narrowness into one's seeing, which also
seems an inducement to moving forward into what one
has already caught a glimpse of and which quickly
becomes vision, in the visionary sense, except that in
place of the panorama that used to be our customary
setting and which we never made much use of, a
limited but infinitely free space has established itself,
useful as everyday life but transfigured so that its signs
of wear no longer appear as a reproach but as indications of how beautiful a thing must have been to have
been so much prized, and its noble aspect which must
have been irksome before has now become interesting,
you are fascinated and keep on studying it. We have
broken through into the consequences of the grey, sag-
ging flesh that was our due, and it is surface enchantment, healing to the eye and to the touch.

—*Three Poems,* 27

As Jefferson was hurried, so is Ashbery "propel(led)"
and "push(ed)." "Glimpse," contained but moving
forward—the dynamic sequence!—"quickly becomes
vision." And Vision establishes its further peace. In "a
limited but infinitely free space" limitation is no
reproach. Earth suffices and then more than suffices as
it goes about its daily task of transfiguration. Rivers
rend mountains asunder. Our irksome, misremembering
will to power is quieted where quiet is ennobled. Vision
enchants this surface world even as it heals the eye.
And what the eye goes on to see is peace.

Ashbery describes this spectacular event of quietude in
a later poem, **"On the Towpath"** from *Houseboat Days.*

If the thirst would subside just for awhile
It would be a little bit, enough.
This has happened.
The insipid chiming of the seconds
Has given way to an arc of silence
So old it had never ceased to exist
On the roofs of buildings, in the sky.

—22

As the will subsides, the world proves wide. Where the
myth of man-as-measure ends, "an arc of silence" roofs
a peaceful earth. Under rigor of the spectacle, earth
shows more than wide enough.

The question has been asked
As though an immense natural bridge had been
Strung across the landscape to any point you wanted.
The ellipse is as aimless as that,
Stretching invisibly into the future so as to reappear
In our present.

—23

Of the Natural Bridge in Virginia, Jefferson wrote "If the view from the top be painful and intolerable, that from below is delightful in an equal extreme" (186). Such radical humility is a delighted extreme, one that **"On the Towpath"** finds in native motion, presenting the future to a present which remains at rest. Geography commands dynamic trust. As our Jeffersonian poet avers, the command is peace.

Ashbery has kept faith with earth's commands and keeps it still. Delighted trust in expansive containment has left his poetry open, at all levels of discourse, to the dynamics of peace. Limit is not poverty where limits, in their providence, provide abundant distances. In Ashbery's newest book, *Your Name Here,* such tender nearness of expanse resounds with special clarity in **"Nobody Is Going Anywhere."**

I don't understand why you object
to any of this. Personally I am above suspicion.
I live in a crawlup where the mice are rotted,
where midnight tunes absolve the bricklayers
and the ceiling abounds in God's sense.

Something more three-dimensional must be breathed
into action.

—98

Here, forces of faith—"I am above suspicion"—and the dynamic work of peace—"where midnight tunes absolve the bricklayers"—breathe life and magic into seeming deprivation. And so deprivation suddenly "abounds." The poet finds "God's sense," creation's sense, at the limits of his own. And then the limits move. This is the truly magical realism of environment. Its prospects are peace. Its products are an effortless affirmation.

The porch is loaded, a question-mark
swings like an earring at the base of your cheek:
stubborn, anxious plain. Air and ice,
those unrelenting fatheads, seem always to be saying,
"This is where we will be living from now on."

In the courtyard a plane tree glistens.

The ship is already far from here, like a ghost ship.

The core of the sermon is always distance, landscape
waiting to be considered, maybe loved a little
eventually. And I do, I do.

—Ibid.

A glistening plane tree rebukes the "unrelenting fatheads." Everything remains in place, but nothing is still, nothing is captive. Distance, the visible motive of eye and earth, brings new landscapes always nearer. And landscapes are the peace when eye weds earth. "And I do, I do." So much trust, so much time and forbearance are invested in the bold, bold word "eventually." And this investment is the most considered and considerable work of Ashbery's art.

It is October 15, 2001. We have stopped taking the newspaper, and this morning my son complained that he was missing the news. I thought of the bombs falling somewhere in his little name, and I opened the windowshade. I pointed to the red sunrise reflected on the near Spring Mountains and said "There's the news." And I prayed to believe my words myself. In *Self-Portrait in a Convex Mirror,* John Ashbery offered a poem called **"The One Thing that Can Save America."** Its final lines remain an anthem of forbearance and a timely forecast of the prospects for peace.

Its truth is timeless, but its time has still
Not arrived, telling of danger, and the mostly limited
Steps that can be taken against danger
Now and in the future, in cool yards,
In quiet small houses in the country,
Our country, in fenced areas, in cool shady streets.

—45

Everything abides the world's time, and its truth is coming on—eventually. For now, there are limits to mend, and in the future, limits too. Our country's peace must find and follow them. Then superabundant energies of peace will fill them to overflowing. Everything rides on this eventual earth. As my dear wife Claudia Keelan has avowed in her poem "Day Book," the American soul is "attached / & adventing." We are here, and something is under way here. If this is America, it must be peace. The rivers and mountains and a glistening plane tree all insist: it must be peace.

Works Cited

Ashbery, John. *The Double Dream of Spring.* New York: E. P. Dutton, 1970.

———. *Three Poems.* New York: Viking Press, 1972.

———. *Self-Portrait in a Convex Mirror.* New York: Viking Press, 1975.

———. *Houseboat Days.* New York: Viking Press, 1977.

———. *Your Name Here.* New York: Farrar, Straus & Giroux, 2000.

Jefferson, Thomas. *The Life and Selected Writings of Thomas Jefferson.* Edited by Adrienne Koch and William Peden. New York: Random House, 1993.

Keelan, Claudia. "Day Book." In *Gare du Nord* 2 (1999): 4.

Levertov, Denise. *Poems 1968-1972.* New York: New Directions, 1987.

New, Elisa. *The Line's Eye.* Cambridge: Harvard University Press, 1998.

Thoreau, Henry David. *Collected Essays and Poems.* New York: Literary Classics of the United States, 2001.

———. *Henry David Thoreau.* Edited by Robert Sayre. New York: Literary Classics of the United States, 1985.

Mark Silverberg (essay date summer 2002)

SOURCE: Silverberg, Mark. "Laughter and Uncertainty: John Ashbery's Low-Key Camp." *Contemporary Literature* 43, no. 2 (summer 2002): 285-316.

[*In the following essay, Silverberg analyzes the "double-edged," ambiguous quality of Ashbery's humor as exemplified by the poem "Variations, Calypso and Fugue on a Theme by Ella Wheeler Wilcox," in which, he maintains, Ashbery challenged conventional notions of serious and light poetry.*]

"Amusement," wrote poet Frank O'Hara and painter Larry Rivers in their New York school mock-manifesto "How to Proceed in the Arts," "is the dawn of Genius" (98). The New York school poets, a group that includes O'Hara and John Ashbery as two of its defining members, was one of the first American movements to make humor a consistent part of its aesthetic. Although most readers of John Ashbery recognize that humor is essential to his work, surprisingly little has been written on the topic. Ashbery is undoubtedly among the most discussed postwar poets. We have essays on Ashbery as a Romantic (Harold Bloom) and as a post-Romantic poet (Frank Lepkowski), as a deconstructionist (Steve Connor), a love poet (Charles Altieri), a philosopher (Altieri again), a surrealist (Susan McCabe and others), and a New York school artist (Geoff Ward, David Lehman). We have essays on the painterly Ashbery, the musical Ashbery, "The Prophetic Ashbery" (Douglas Crase) and on Ashbery as an ephemeral "metaphysical subject" (John Koethe). However, among all these essays—over two hundred entries listed by the *MLA* under the poet's name over the past twenty years—there is but one article, from 1984, on "The Comic Thrust of Ashbery's Poetry" (this by Thomas A. Fink, published in *Twentieth Century Literature*).

While many critics recognize the playful and parodic elements of Ashbery's unusual forms, Fink seems to be the only writer to focus specifically on the question of comedy. Unfortunately, the critic's essay gives little theoretical attention to Ashbery's humor and instead spends most of its thirteen pages explaining the jokes in nearly a dozen, briefly discussed poems:

> **"Crazy Weather"** makes an absurdly hackneyed conversational phrase the point of departure for a powerful lyric. . . . The poet breathes zany new life into a lump of banality [talk of the weather] by ignoring its figural status and by taking it as a literal (surreal) truth. Since the weather often serves as a scapegoat for people's inner dissatisfactions and as a topic for discussion for those who have nothing to say to each other, the extended personification proves comically apt: the weather can be viewed as a loud drunk or madman whose erratic behavior is a source of annoyance.
>
> (6)

After needlessly detailing the ways Ashbery creates humor by attacking "excessive generalization" and "rigid attitudes" (4), Fink concludes that since his humor is so broad, "[t]he comic dimension of Ashbery's poetry cannot usefully be placed in any convenient literary category" (13). Could this be the reason so little is written on the topic? Probably not, since Ashbery's ability to escape bounds of classification is legendary and has never discouraged critics from discussing other aspects of his aesthetic. I suspect that the difficulty of categorizing Ashbery's humor is related to a more basic and troubling difficulty: that of knowing when or even *if* his poems are supposed to be funny. In poem after poem, readers are faced with a slightly uncomfortable, undecidable humor:

> A great plane flew across the sun,
> and the girls ran along the ground.
> The sun shone on Mr. McPlaster's face, it was green
>   like an elephant's.
>
> Let's get out of here, Judy said.
> They're getting closer, I can't stand it.
> But you know, our fashions are in fashion
> only briefly, then they go out
> and stay that way for a long time. Then they come
>   back in
> for a while. Then, in maybe a million years, they go
>   out of fashion
> and stay there.
> Laure and Tidbit agreed,
> with the proviso that after that everyone would
>   become fashion
> again for a few hours. Write it now, Tidbit said,
> before they get back. And, quivering, I took the pen.
>
> (*Girls on the Run* 3)

This ambiguous "quivering" (in anticipation, anxiety, or amusement?) is a classic Ashbery pose. It is a mannerism of laughter and uncertainty which leaves readers quite unsure about how to take it—or if, in fact, the reader is "being taken," as the phrase goes. Such gestures can be usefully defined in terms of camp (from the French *se camper,* to posture or flaunt), which, as

Susan Sontag notes in the first theoretical treatment of the phenomenon, is related to "the love of the exaggerated, the 'off,' of things-being-what-they-are-not" (279). This sense of uncertainty, the hesitant doubleness of so many of Ashbery's poems, is central not only to the poet's unique humor but more broadly to his complex, camp-inflected sensibility. While Fink argues that "the most salient aspect of [Ashbery's] humor" is its propensity "to 'ask' *not* to be taken seriously" (1), I believe that Ashbery demands something more difficult. He asks to be taken seriously *and* humorously, sincerely *and* facetiously, at the same time. His poetry is "alive to a double sense in which some things can be taken" (281), as Sontag says of camp, and it is this double-edged quality that makes Ashbery's humor both so effective and so elusive.

While Frank O'Hara's vocal, out, dressed-up poetry has long been understood as camp, Ashbery's reticent, dressed-down humor has too often been ignored or misunderstood. This essay will focus on Ashbery's low-key camp as a crucial part of his overall aesthetic. It begins by looking generally at the poet's unstable humor and the difficulties it raises for categorizing his poetry. One of Ashbery's central preoccupations, in fact, is to confound the process of categorization through camp. By willfully mixing and confusing such value-laden categories as serious and humorous, high and low, avant-garde and kitsch, Ashbery raises questions about traditional notions of poetic value. By treating so-called light verse seriously, for example, Ashbery asks readers to rethink not only the specific work he quotes but more broadly the very categorizations of light and serious. The second half of this essay looks specifically at this process by reading one of Ashbery's oddest poems and queerest associations—that with the queen of nineteenth-century light verse, Ella Wheeler Wilcox. While Wilcox would be dismissed by many sophisticated readers as the epitome of bad taste and/or bad verse, through the lens of Ashbery's **"Variations, Calypso and Fugue on a Theme of Ella Wheeler Wilcox,"** we can begin to see Wilcox's value as a consummate and complicated example of camp. For Ashbery, and undoubtedly many other readers, Wilcox's writing is "good" precisely because it is so "bad." Its value, in other words, has to do in part with its ability to disturb the very categories of poetic value—the distinction between good and bad, high and low, light and serious verse.

LAUGHTER AND INDETERMINACY

While John Ashbery's New York school colleagues such as Frank O'Hara and Kenneth Koch give us poems that are deliberately funny, Ashbery's tone is more difficult to place. With their reticence, their ironies, their rapid and easy variance from philosophical musing to surrealistic non sequitur, Ashbery's poems present a constantly unstable tone. Harold Bloom helped establish the poet's academic reputation by assuring us that we are reading high Romanticism, but many readers of Ashbery since that time have felt equally sure that they are reading low comedy—or at least a bit of both. Ashbery's shifting tone prevents readers from knowing whether he is singing true songs of praise (in "Whitmanian expansiveness," according to Bloom [172]), or whether his tongue is firmly planted in his cheek. Here, for example, are some typically problematic lines from **"Soonest Mended,"** which Bloom reads as a "representative poem" of Ashbery's Romantic inheritance, a poem "astonishingly poignant and wise" (174):

> Barely tolerated, living on the margin
> In our technological society, we were always having
>   to be rescued
> On the brink of destruction, like heroines in *Orlando
>   Furioso*
> Before it was time to start all over again.
> . . . .
> And then there always came a time when
> Happy Hooligan in his rusted green automobile
> Came plowing down the course, just to make sure
>   everything was O.K.,
> Only by that time we were in another chapter and
>   confused
> About how to receive this latest piece of information.
> *Was* it information? . . .
> . . . .
> And you see, both of us were right, though nothing
> Has somehow come to nothing; the avatars
> Of our conforming to the rules and living
> Around the home have made—well, in a sense, "good
>   citizens" of us,
> Brushing the teeth and all that, and learning to accept
> The charity of hard moments as they are doled out,
> For this is action, this not being sure, this careless
> Preparing, sowing the seeds crooked in the furrow,
> Making ready to forget, and always coming back
> To the mooring of starting out, that day so long ago.
>
> (*Mooring* [*The Mooring of Starting Out*] 231-33)

I have trouble seeing this poem, as Bloom suggests, as an "evenly distributed rumination" which proclaims "the wisdom of a wiser passivity" (168). Instead, it seems to be a poem of instability and imbalance, with its sudden appearances (from Ariosto to Happy Hooligan); its balancing act of "daily quandary" (231) and epistemological crisis; its half-parodic, self-reflexive turns; its platitudes, mixed clichés ("nothing has come to nothing"), contradictions ("careless preparing," "making ready to forget"), uncertainties ("—well, in a sense"), and mock certainties (that "good citizenship" should be defined by teeth brushing). Like most of Ashbery's work, this is a precarious poem whose gestures of lyrical closure in tone ("that day so long ago") are undercut by the indeterminacy of its content.

Rather than the more straightforward hilarity and absurdity of Koch, or the campy exuberance of O'Hara, Ashbery's particular brand of humor comes precisely from the sense of imbalance his poems produce in readers. The sudden surprise, the unusual juxtaposition, the deformed cliché—in general, the sense of bemused bewilderment that Ashbery provokes—is the essential ingredient of his humor. His readers are observing the performance of a clever fool who follows his own arcane and amusing rules of composition: stumbling forward, falling behind, advancing always by digression. And at the same time readers are excitedly anticipating the moment when the rug will be pulled out from under them. I suspect that most readers who delight in Ashbery want to be fooled and bewildered, and that they keep returning to his work because he continually finds new, more sophisticated or more silly, ways of perplexing them.

This imbalance which produces uncertainty, anticipation, or laughter has been commented on (both approvingly and disapprovingly) by many critics. Daniel Hoffman in the *Harvard Guide to Contemporary American Writing* provides a perfect example of the negative reaction, calling such indeterminacy "solipsistic aestheticism" (496). He condemns Ashbery's work for being "detached from external reality" (553) and "purposely lacking in logic" (555). On the positive side, such imbalance has been famously defined by Marjorie Perloff as part of Ashbery's provocative "indeterminacy," which produces the sense that "disclosure of some special meaning seems perpetually imminent" (11). In general, this imbalance is related to Ashbery's "difficulty"—the sense that his poems, and the "subjects" they ostensibly represent, are inevitably blurry, shadowy, or distorted (as in the famous convex mirror). Ashbery's statements seem perpetually conditional, his lines perpetually open to revision. Indeed the "revising voice" (which may be either uncertain or mock-authoritative) is one of Ashbery's most familiar tones:

> This, thus, is a portion of the subject of this poem
> Which is in the form of falling snow:
> That is, the individual flakes are not essential to the
>   importance of the whole's becoming so much of a
>   truism
> That their importance is again called in question, to be
>   denied further out, and again and again like this.
> Hence, neither the importance of the individual flake,
> Nor the importance of the whole impression of the
>   storm, if it has any, is what it is,
> But the rhythm of the series of repeated jumps, from
>   abstract into positive and back to a slightly less
>   diluted abstract.

> Mild effects are the result.

> **("The Skaters,"** *Mooring* 199)

The particular "mild effects" of this revision *ad infinitum* will vary depending on the reader. Some, such as Hoffman, will be annoyed at this "aimless noodling that fatigues and exasperates the reader" (559), while others will be intrigued or amused by Ashbery's puzzling.

These latter readers likely enjoy being tripped up by uncertainties such as those presented in the passage above (What *is* the subject of this poem? What is the relationship between part and whole, flake and storm?). Those who "get" the humor here, or who believe there is humor to get (with Ashbery, the question is always open), are likely laughing at the simultaneity of the poet's and reader's attempts to find sense in his gratuitous snowstorm of meanings. What we see here, as so often in Ashbery, is not meaning-as-an-end (a solution or answer) but meaning-as-a-means (a process, a way among many). It is this process—of meaning as search rather than end—that is encoded in Ashbery's self-revising lines which thus have the knack of being simultaneously bewildering and illuminating.

Ashbery's knowing uncertainties are reminiscent of the self-conscious camp of Oscar Wilde, in which assertions seem to be always bracketed by invisible quotation marks that warn us not to take them "too seriously." As with the best instances of camp, there is a doubleness to many of Ashbery's gestures, especially his endings, which seem to offer traditional moments of lyrical closure, but whose slight oddness or offness forecloses on a completely un-ironic reading. Given this frequent doubleness, our best strategy might be to take Ashbery seriously—but not too seriously. Readers need to understand that in this poetry the "trick" is just as good as the real thing—or perhaps that the trick *is* the real thing:

> Yes, friends, these clouds pulled along on invisible
>   ropes
> Are, as you have guessed, merely stage machinery,
> And the funny thing is it knows we know
> About it and still wants us to go on believing
> In what it so unskillfully imitates, and wants
> To be loved not for that but for itself[.]

> **("The Wrong Kind of Insurance,"** *Selected Poems*
>   238-39)

This duplicity in Ashbery helps explain why Bloom is not entirely wrong in reading the poet as a traditional Romantic heir. Half the time the poet's gestures seem to point in just this direction. Of course, the other half of the time Ashbery seems to parody or camp up the very Romantic ideals Bloom finds so central to his aesthetic. And the real problem, or the real humor, in Ashbery is that these are not in fact divided halves, but simultaneous moments.

A good example of this doubleness occurs with one of Ashbery's seemingly simplest, most anthologized poems, **"The Instruction Manual"** (from *Some Trees*, 1956). This poem has often been taken as a sincere representation of Romantic transport (à la Keats's "Ode to a Nightingale," Wordsworth's "Tintern Abbey," or Coleridge's "Frost at Midnight"), where the speaker and his readers are carried "from the mundane and often tedious realities of our daily lives to this exotic, marvelous world, brimming over with a vitality that is clearly absent in the world of instruction manuals" (Moramarco 448). Fred Moramarco argues that Ashbery's goal in this poem is to show us "that literature and art can provide these moments of revitalization for us, and although we must always return to the real world, our esthetic encounters impinge upon our sensibilities and leave us altered" (448). David Lehman also offers a similarly straightforward, unironic reading. For Lehman, Ashbery is "at heart a romantic poet, who conceives of the Imagination as a realm apart from experience, or reality, or time" (*Last Avant-Garde* 30). Thus the speaker's transport to Guadalajara is "a parable of the imagination with its power to fulfill desire and supply any lack" (29). What both Lehman and Moramarco fail to notice, however, is that the descriptive details of the poem, far from being "rich" and "vitalized" (Moramarco 448), are in fact utterly prosaic, banal, and uninspired:

> Around stand the flower girls, handing out rose- and
> lemon-colored flowers,
> Each attractive in her rose-and-blue striped dress (Oh!
> such shades of rose and blue),
> And nearby is the little white booth where women in
> green serve you green and yellow fruit.
> The couples are parading; everyone is in a holiday
> mood.
> First, leading the parade, is a dapper fellow
> Clothed in deep blue. On his head sits a white hat
> And he wears a mustache, which has been trimmed
> for the occasion.
> His dear one, his wife, is young and pretty; her shawl
> is rose, pink, and white.
> Her slippers are patent leather, in the American
> fashion,
> And she carries a fan, for she is modest, and does not
> want the crowd to see her face too often.
> But everybody is so busy with his wife or loved one
> I doubt that they would notice the mustachioed man's
> wife.
>
> (*Mooring* 8-9)

Such shades of rose and blue indeed. The poem goes on in this monotonous, hackneyed way for three pages. It more closely resembles a high school "What I did for my summer holiday" composition than it does Keats or Coleridge—which, appropriately, is what one might expect from the writer of an "instruction manual on the uses of a new metal" (5). Far from being charged with imaginative power and redemptive significance, these details are so packed with Ashbery's deadpan wit that they constitute not a Romantic transport, but rather a mimicry of such transport.[1] The little flower girls, the white-hatted man and his "dear" wife, along with all the quaintly trite scenes of "young love, married love, and the love of an aged mother for her son" (10), are the products of a writer who intends to be serious but whose corny innocence is absolutely absurd:

> But I have lost sight of the young fellow with the
> toothpick.
> Wait—there he is—on the other side of the bandstand,
> Secluded from his friends, in earnest talk with a young
> girl
> Of fourteen or fifteen. I try to hear what they are say-
> ing
> But it seems they are just mumbling something—shy
> words of love, probably.
> She is slightly taller than he, and looks quietly down
> into his sincere eyes.
> She is wearing white. The breeze ruffles her long fine
> black hair against her olive cheek.
> Obviously she is in love. The boy, the young boy with
> the toothpick, he is in love too . . .
>
> (*Mooring* 9)

Such "aw shucks" scenes are perfect examples of what Susan Sontag calls "naïve, or pure, Camp," whose "essential element is seriousness, a seriousness that fails" (283). In **"The Instruction Manual,"** Ashbery consciously employs what might otherwise be read as naive camp. His portrait of "exotic" Guadalajara, with the band playing schlock-romantic *Scheherazade* by Rimsky-Korsakov," while "everyone is in a holiday mood," is so bad it's good.

While there seems to be this duplicity to Ashbery's poem, in a way Lehman and Moramarco and undoubtedly countless other readers are correct. **"The Instruction Manual"** is Ashbery's most anthologized poem not because of its subtle irony but because people have enjoyed it as "a version of the Greater Romantic Lyric" (Perloff 264), with its focus on reverie, daydream, and sentimental exoticism. What is uniquely Ashberian is the fact that the work can be read as both ironic and straight. There is a part of Ashbery that quite authentically enjoys and freely indulges in "bad" sentimental verse, both his own and that of others. How, if not as an example of "good" "bad" verse, are we to take a poem like **"Some Words,"** which Ashbery translated from the French of notorious poet-boxer-showman Arthur Cravan and included in both *The Double Dream of Spring* (1975) and his *Selected Poems* (1985):

> Each hour has its color and forever gives place
> Leaving less than yon bird of itself a trace.
> In vain does memory attempt to store away
> The scent of its colors in a single bouquet
> Memory can but shift cold ashes around
> When the depths of time it endeavors to sound.
>
> (*Mooring* 274)

How, again, should we take a poem such as **"Into the Dusk-Charged Air,"** whose Romantic-sounding title is followed by five monotonous pages describing the flowing of various rivers:

> The dark Saône flows silently.
> And the Volga is long and wide

As it flows across the brownish land. The Ebro
Is blue, and slow. The Shannon flows
Swiftly between its banks. The Mississippi
Is one of the world's longest rivers, like the Amazon.
It has the Missouri for a tributary.
The Harlem flows amid factories
And buildings. The Nelson is in Canada,
Flowing. Through hard banks the Dubawnt
Forces its way. . . .

(*Mooring* 173-74)

Ashbery seems to be keenly interested in tediousness here, in seeing how far he can push dull poetry and what kind of response it will elicit. A final example, and another species of bad poetry, is from **"Variations, Calypso and Fugue on a Theme of Ella Wheeler Wilcox,"** a poem which plays on the work of one of the most famous "bad" writers of the last century:

So my youth was spent, underneath the trees
I always moved around with perfect ease

I voyaged to Paris at the age of ten
And met many prominent literary men

Gazing at the Alps was quite a sight
I felt the tears flow forth with all their might

A climb to the Acropolis meant a lot to me
I had read the Greek philosophers you see

(*Mooring* 239)

One way of reading such moments of patently bad or mundane writing (and more like them) is by invoking the discourse of camp, which Sontag calls "a mode of seduction—one which employs . . . gestures full of duplicity, with a witty meaning for cognoscenti and another, more impersonal, for outsiders" (281). This is to suggest that there is considerably more at stake in Ashbery's deployment of bad verse than there is in the lines of the high school sophomore who might also have written the above-quoted couplets. Ashbery's entertaining flirtations with schlock have consequences which become clear only when we consider the aesthetic ideology behind this particular project.

Ashbery's sponsorship of bad taste (which is closely related to his delight in the cliché and the hackneyed phrase) is a key ingredient both of his humor and of an aesthetic philosophy that calls into question the distinctions between good and bad, or high and low, art. Along with New York school colleagues such as Koch, O'Hara, James Schuyler, and Barbara Guest, Ashbery set out to cross what Andreas Huyssen has called "the Great Divide" of modernism (which strictly categorizes works into elite and mass modes), by mixing and confusing the classical and the popular, avant-garde and kitsch.[2]

Against the elitist aesthetic politics of an Ezra Pound or Clement Greenberg (whose influential 1939 essay "Avant-Garde and Kitsch" argues the absolute incommensurability of these two kinds of artistic production), Ashbery and his colleagues insisted that the distinctions between high and low—and coincidentally good and bad—were illusory or, more to the point, that they were categories of cultural power and control that sought to direct the artistic market through exclusion.[3] As Kenneth Koch put it, the distinction between high and low art is "like the difference between being attracted to someone at court or in a bowling alley." There is, in fact, no difference, Koch argues, since each can be a significant experience and "along the way one may say something memorable" ("Interview" 192). An important part of the New York school project was to free American taste from elitist assumptions reinforced by the academic bent of fifties poetry, with T. S. Eliot as "the Great Dictator / Of literature." This phrase is from Koch's "Seasons on Earth," a poem that humorously describes the strictly regulated artistic marketplace of the 1950s:

It was the time, it was the nineteen fifties,
When Eisenhower was President, I think,
And the Cold War, like *Samson Agonistes,*
Went roughly on, and we were at the brink.
No time for Whitsuntides or Corpus Christis—
Dread drafted all with its atomic clink.
The Waste Land gave the time's most accurate data,
It seemed, and Eliot was the Great Dictator
Of literature. One hardly dared to wink
Or fool around in any way in poems,
and Critics poured out awful jereboams
To *irony, ambiguity,* and *tension*—
And other things I do not wish to mention.

(*Rainway* 310)

The poetry of Ashbery and his colleagues attempts to escape the solemnity of the time not (as is sometimes supposed) by *inverting* but instead *opening* standards of taste to embrace popular culture. It does this by promoting the value of such genres as pulp fiction, comic books, and Hollywood movies which Greenberg and other cultural critics such as Dwight Macdonald so condemned.[4]

This equal embrace of high and low can be seen in the way that Ashbery's most successful poems are as likely to feature pop-cultural figures such as Popeye and Daffy Duck as avant-garde exemplars such as Parmigianino or de Chirico. And, more importantly, signature poems such as **"Daffy Duck in Hollywood"** or **"Self-Portrait in a Convex Mirror"** succeed precisely to the extent that they are able to synthesize the philosophical and the facetious into one seamless product. Of course the unity or seamlessness of these poems is based on the kind of comic duplicity I have been describing all along—that is, on their ability to be simultaneously silly and suggestive:

Something strange is creeping across me.
La Celestina has only to warble the first few bars

Of "I Thought about You" or something mellow from
Amadigi di Gaula for everything—a mint-condition
    can
Of Runford's Baking Powder, a celluloid earring,
    Speedy
Gonzales, the latest from Helen Topping Miller's
    fertile
Escritoire, a sheaf of suggestive pix on greige, deckle-
    edged
Stock—to come clattering through the rainbow trellis
Where Pistachio Avenue rams the 2300 block of
    Highland
Fling Terrace. He promised he'd get me out of this
    one,
That mean old cartoonist, but just look what he's
Done to me now! I scarce dare approach me mug's at-
    tenuated
Reflection in yon hubcap, so jaundiced, so *déconfit*
Are its lineaments—fun, no doubt, for some quack
    phrenologist's
Fern-clogged waiting room, but hardly what you'd
    call
Companionable.

("Daffy Duck in Hollywood," *Selected Poems* 227)

"Daffy Duck in Hollywood," which finds its source in
Chuck Jones's mischievous 1953 cartoon "Duck
Amuck" (Shetley 125), elevates into the realm of
philosophical reflection Daffy's comic predicament of a
character subject to the rapidly changing whims of a
maniacal cartoonist-creator. What begins as a madcap
romp ("Where Pistachio Avenue rams the 2300 block of
Highland / Fling Terrace") through various scenes and
roles (from "the Fudds' garage" to the river Lethe; from
the Princesse de Clèves to "Walt, Blossom, and little
Skeezix") ends as a meditation on the relationship
between language and experience:

Not what we see but how we see it matters; all's
Alike, the same, and we greet him who announces
The change as we would greet the change itself.
All life is but a figment; conversely, the tiny
tome that slips from your hand is not perhaps the
Missing link in this invisible picnic whose leverage
Shrouds our sense of it. Therefore bivouac we
On this great, blond highway, unimpeded by
Veiled scruples, worn conundrums. Morning is
Impermanent.

(229-30)

An important part of this dexterous performance is Ashbery's ability to keep both levels of discourse in play—
since both the humor and the intellectual interest of the
poem are generated by the simultaneity and odd congru-
ity of the "high" and the "low."

As I've suggested, Ashbery's enjoyment and deployment of the quackery of Daffy Duck, or outpourings of
Helen Topping Miller's or Ella Wheeler Wilcox's
"fertile escritoire," have a provocative doubleness which
functions both as a source of entertainment and a source
of meaning. On the one hand, Ashbery employs authors
such as Miller or Wilcox for their comedic value as
exemplars of naive camp (of art that's so bad it's good).
On the other hand, the poet is interested in putatively
"bad" writing because such work raises important questions about taste and value, and about how we make
distinctions between high and low or serious and light
verse. **"Variations, Calypso and Fugue on a Theme
by Ella Wheeler Wilcox"** (from *The Double Dream of
Spring,* 1970) encapsulates many aspects of Ashbery's
double-edged humor—its combinations of parody and
homage, irony and emulation, laughing *at* and laughing
with. In this poem Ashbery both parodies and honestly
performs a Wilcoxian brand of "bad" poetry, ultimately
presenting her light-verse aesthetic not as an object of
ridicule but as a significant artistic position.

SHADES OF ELLA WHEELER WILCOX

Ella Wheeler Wilcox is perhaps the most famous "bad"
poet of the past century. Adored and voraciously
purchased by countless readers who admired her for
such famous platitudes as "Laugh, and the world laughs
with you; / weep, and you weep alone," and "It is easy
enough to be pleasant, when life flows by like a song,"
Wilcox was, according to the *London Times* obituary
(October 31, 1919), "the most popular poet of either
sex and of any age, read by thousands who never open
Shakespeare."

Wilcox has always been seen as a poet for the middle
class and of the middle way. "She believed," wrote
Smart Set editor Charles Towne in 1926, "that she was
an evangelist who spoke in rhyme to her immense audience" (94). Her first book, *Drops of Water* (1872), was
a collection of lilting, conservative temperance poems.
This was followed by *Shells* (1873), a volume of cheer-
ful religious and moral verses, and *Maurine* (1876), a
sentimental poetic narrative. Her real fame came,
however, in 1883 when her *Poems of Passion* was
rejected by a Chicago publisher as immoral. The
publisher's literary as well as moral sense might have
been inflamed by references to the "Impassioned tide
that sweeps through throbbing veins" and the "convulsive rapture of a kiss." The volume was snapped up by
a more commercially minded publisher who recognized
the value of sensation and sold more than sixty thousand
copies in its first two years, scandalizing and titillating
readers with verses like the following:[5]

Love, when we met, 'twas like two planets meeting.
    Strange chaos followed; body, soul, and heart
Seemed shaken, thrilled, and startled by that greeting,
    Old ties, old dreams, old aims, all torn apart[.]
            . . . . .
My being trembled to its very centre
    At that first kiss. Cold Reason stood aside
With folded arms to let a grand Love enter
    In my Soul's secret chamber to abide.

> Its great High Priest, my first Love and my last,
> There on its altar I consumed my past.
>
> ("Surrender," *Poetical Works* 61-62)

Wilcox, who became known as the Poetess of Passion, went on to produce over forty more best-selling volumes which were either ignored or belittled by the literary establishment of the day. "One may be allowed to guess," one critic wrote of her readers in 1899, "that those admirers are found pretty exclusively among men who have dealt in lumber or pork with but little time for literature" (Brown 184).⁶ Regardless of such criticism, Wilcox earnestly and steadfastly continued her work, maintaining, as she put it in her famous manifesto poem, that "heart, not art" was the essential ingredient for poetry: "Though critics may bow to art, and I am its own true lover, / It is not art, but heart, which wins the wide world over" ("Art and Heart," *Poetical Works* 52). Wilcox's appeal grew steadily, particularly through the syndicated column of prose, poetry, and advice she wrote for various yellow-sheet newspapers. Eventually, Wilcox took up the rather odd dual role of Poetess of Passion and Domestic Bard. In this second guise, she presented herself as a matron of common sense, offering optimistic adages for the weary at heart:

> There is nothing, I hold, in the way of work
> That a human being may not achieve
> If he does not falter, or shrink or shirk,
> And more than all, if he will *believe*.
>
> ("Limitless," *Poetical Works* 121)

In the end, Wilcox's astounding popular success may give us reason to agree with her biographer's assessment that she was "not a minor poet, but a bad major one" (Ballou 98). What seems significant about her verse today is how hard it tries to be good: how excessive and passionate and dedicated is her failure. In other words, Wilcox has become a perfect example of what Sontag calls "pure" or "naïve" camp. Her verse is best when it is at its worst, and it is exactly this confusion or reversal of categories of taste and value, this messing with accepted standards, that John Ashbery may have found so attractive in Wilcox's work. It takes a poet with Ashbery's devious sense of humor to appreciate the remarkable success of Wilcox's failing verse.

Ashbery's **"Variations, Calypso and Fugue on a Theme by Ella Wheeler Wilcox"** can be read as a kind of low-key drag performance in which the poet fondly performs and exaggerates the gestures of the original—its excess and cliché, its enchantment with emotion, sentiment, and "personal growth." As with the drag queens who imitate Bette Davis, Judy Garland, Marlene Dietrich, and other powerful women, Ashbery's performance is meant not to ridicule Wilcox but to enjoy her—though on slightly different terms from her own. Furthermore, Ashbery's poem offers the flamboyant

gestures of the original, its "passionate" mixture of Art and Heart, as a new, camp-inflected set of artistic standards. These are standards which move beyond (or rather between) the strictly regulated positions of the two poetic camps of the 1950s—frequently pitted against one another as in the famous "anthology wars" of the decade. These wars were waged between formalist "academic" forces (as presented in Donald Hall, Robert Pack, and Louis Simpson's 1957 anthology *The New Poets of England and America*) and experimentalist, "oppositional" challengers (represented in Donald Allen's rival anthology of 1960, *The New American Poetry*). Wilcox's light-verse aesthetic might be appealing to Ashbery given the unusual fact that it represents a position that is intolerable both to formalists (who would see her work as trite, unsophisticated, a mockery of formal strictures) and to avant-gardists (who would judge her popular verse as degenerate, pandering to the masses, the epitome of kitsch). Such a position, beyond the preachy rivalries of the day, is exactly the place where Ashbery imagines truly vital new art will be created. In his 1968 lecture **"The Invisible Avant-Garde,"** Ashbery ponders the possibility of an artistic space "between the extremes of Levittown and Haight-Ashbury" (393) and comes to the conclusion that such a space can be found only by adopting an attitude "which neither accepts nor rejects acceptance but is independent of it" (394). Wilcox's blithe disregard for the rules and standards of art thus makes her, ironically enough, a good example of the kind of "outsider" artist that Ashbery has long favored.

As its title suggests, Ashbery's composition / performance is divided into three stages. The "variations" section opens with the final quatrain from Wilcox's poem "Wishing," which includes such philosophical reflections as these:

> Do you wish the world were wiser?
>   Well, suppose you make a start,
> By accumulating wisdom
>   In the scrapbook of your heart[.]
> . . . .
> Do you wish the world were happy?
>   Then remember day by day
> Just to scatter seeds of kindness
>   As you pass along the way,
> For the pleasures of the many
>   May be ofttimes traced to one,
> As the hand that plants an acorn
>   Shelters armies from the sun.
>
> (*Poems of Power* 18)

Taking Wilcox's shade image as the impetus for his performance, Ashbery spins it out, in the scrapbook of his (he)art, to absurd lengths:

> And in places where the annual rainfall is .0071 inches
> What a pleasure to lie under the tree, to sit, stand, and
>   get up under the tree!
> *Im wunderschönen Monat Mai*

The feeling is of never wanting to leave the tree,
Of predominantly peace and relaxation.
Do you step out from under the shade a moment,
It is only to return with renewed expectation, of
    expectation fulfilled.

(*Mooring* 238)

Ashbery's scrapbook is a collage of all kinds of language—from cliché and comic banality to quotations that might have been lifted from *The Waste Land*. While Wilcox's art is based on the soothing power of the cliché to comfort readers looking for easily swallowed truths, Ashbery uses but varies these clichés, twisting them into less comfortable forms:

Yes, the world goes 'round a good deal faster
When there are highlights on the lips, unspoken and
    true words in the heart,
And the hand keeps brushing away a strand of chestnut
    hair, only to have it fall back into place again.
But all good things must come to an end, and so one
    must move forward
Into the space left by one's conclusions. Is this grow-
    ing old?
Well, it is a good experience, to divest oneself of
    some tested ideals, some old standbys,
And even finding nothing to put in their place is a
    good experience,
Preparing one, as it does, for the consternation that is
    to come.

(238)

Readers accept the familiar homily that "all good things must come to an end" (this is exactly the kind of pacifying cliché Wilcox might have used in her advice column), but what does it mean to "move forward into the space left by one's conclusions"? How does one apply this lesson (if lesson it is)? Likewise, we might fairly easily understand why it is worthwhile "to divest oneself of some . . . old standbys," but what would it mean to put nothing in their place? And how would this prepare one "for the consternation that is to come"? What consternation?

The cliché is a kind of shorthand for experience that ultimately short-circuits experience, putting custom and routine in its place. Ashbery's deformed clichés, on the other hand, renew the unique, unpredictable, troubling messiness of experience. In Ashbery's work the cliché is problematized by phrases that sound quite reasonable but in fact make no sense at all ("Yes, the world goes 'round a good deal faster / When there are highlights on the lips, unspoken and true words in the heart, / And the hand keeps brushing away a strand of chestnut hair"). By simultaneously exaggerating and diverging from Wilcox, Ashbery reinvigorates the cliché, making it more difficult and seductive in a new (less comforting, more indeterminate) way. He moves readers from "the feeling . . . of predominantly peace and relaxation," at the beginning of the "variations" section, to

the sense "That the tree should shrivel in 120-degree heat, the acorns / Lie around on the worn earth like eyeballs, and the lead soldiers shrug and slink off" at the end (239).

In the next, "calypso," section of the poem, Ashbery employs bad verse couplets as a way of performing and transforming Wilcox's view of the connection between poetry and personal growth. Throughout the poem, but in this section in particular, he plays with the cliché that poetry must be an expression of "heart" and emotion:

Gazing at the Alps was quite a sight
I felt the tears flow forth with all their might

A climb to the Acropolis meant a lot to me
I had read the Greek philosophers you see

In the Colosseum I thought my heart would burst
Thinking of all the victims who had been there first

On Mount Ararat's side I began to grow
Remembering the Flood there, so long ago

(*Mooring* 239)

Later in the poem we come across Ashbery's sly version of Wilcox's famous elevation of heart over art:

This age-old truth I to thee impart
Act according to the dictates of your art

Because if you don't no one else is going to
And that person isn't likely to be you.

(240)

As Ashbery's poem of noble travels and thoughtful morals ("Thinking of all the victims . . . Remembering the Flood") progresses, it becomes stranger, less moral, and more surreal—less heartful and more artful:

On the banks of the Ganges I stood in mud
And watched the water light up like blood

The Great Wall of China is really a thrill
It cleaves through the air like a silver pill

(239)

While Wilcox invited her readers to dream of Christian simplicities ("Keep Love and Sympathy and Faith alone in your Soul and you can Defeat Time"), Ashbery's "calypso" section advises us to "trust in the dream that will never come true / 'Cause that is the scheme that is best for you / And the gleam that is the most suitable too" (240). Once again the deformed cliché revives the palpable oddness of experience—the gleam of the dream that will never come true.

The longest section of the poem, the prose collages which make up the "fugue," are fugal in two ways. First, as the musical derivation of the word suggests, this section is a polyphonic orchestration of voices and themes. The second, psychiatric, derivation of the word helps highlight the obscured theme that organizes this section. According to the *Oxford English Dictionary*, a fugue is "a dissociative reaction to shock or emotional stress . . . during which all awareness of personal identity is lost." This meandering section of the poem is subtly organized by images and indications of fugue, forgetfulness, and some unmentionable "incident" (also alluded to as "these things" and "such issues") which may occasion this fugal condition.

> In the morning you forget what the punishment was. Probably it was something like eating a pretzel or going into the back yard. Still, you can't tell. These things could be a lot clearer without hurting anybody. But it does not follow that such issues will produce the most dynamic capital gains for you. . . .
>
> . . . .
>
> . . . No one ever referred to the incident again. The case was officially closed. Maybe there were choruses of silent gratitude. . . . The point is no ear ever heard them. Thus, the incident, to call it by one of its names— choice, conduct, absent-minded frown might be others—came to be not only as though it had never happened, but as though it never *could* have happened. Sealed into the wall of all that season's coming on. And thus, for a mere handful of people—roustabouts and degenerates, most of them—it became the only true version.
>
> (241)

"These [unmentionable] things" which "could be a lot clearer without hurting anybody"—this "choice," "conduct," or covered-up crime ("the case was officially closed")—point to what John Shoptaw calls the "homo-textual" level of Ashbery's poetry:[7]

> Many pleasures may be ofttimes traced to one illicit experience. This impossible theme was first announced in **"Fragment"** ("the incident is officially closed"). In the discourse of the criminal justice system ("incident," "officially closed," "roustabouts and degenerates") the roustabout poet orchestrates his prosecutors. "For a mere handful of people" this criminalized, obliterated response to stimuli is not dismissed as an unspeakable aberration but trusted as the homosexual scheme of existence.
>
> (Shoptaw 110)

The curious behaviors of this last section—its shifting perspectives, voices, tones, and scenes; its vaguely introduced characters (Peter and Christine, Mother and Alan, Professor Hertz); and its obscure transitional couplets ("pink purple and blue / The way you used to do," "The crystal haze / For days and days")—will be familiar to readers of Ashbery. One way of explaining this dissociative, fugal style (a style which gives the impression of identity dispersal, as if each part is a lost, unconnected unit) is suggested by theorists like Shoptaw

and Thomas E. Yingling. In *Hart Crane and the Homosexual Text,* Yingling argues that evasion and disguise have long been central to the thematics and stylistics of texts by gay men. He proposes that while gay men have historically had access to the means and codes of literary production because they were men, they have, nevertheless, been unable to exploit them because "those codes denied validity to their experience as homosexuals" (25). Gay authors have thus been "empowered to speak, but unable to say" (26). Yingling argues that until recently "the homosexual has been almost literally unable to speak of itself coherently except in a vocabulary of remorse" (26). This inability to speak from, or of, a coherent identity is one useful way of explaining the dissociation of so many of Ashbery's poems.

The language of allusion without direct reference, which speaks incessantly but never says ("There is something to all this, that will not elude us: / Growing up under the shade of friendly trees, with our brothers all around" **["Variations"** **["Variations, Calypso and Fugue on a Theme by Ella Wheeler Wilcox"**] 238]), may be another quality Ashbery picked up on and found intriguing in Wilcox's poetry. While Wilcox's poems were censored and condemned in proper Victorian fashion for indecorous sexual enthusiasm, what remains unnamed by the poet and her critics is the issue of *to whom* these passionate poems seem to be directed. In all the commentary I've found, everyone carefully skirts the fact that many of these fervent laments were written by a woman to another woman:

> She touches my cheek, and I quiver—
>   I tremble with exquisite pains;
> She sighs—like an overcharged river
>   My blood rushes on through my veins;
> She smiles—and in mad-tiger fashion,
>   As a she-tiger fondles her own,
> I clasp her with fierceness and passion,
>   And kiss her with shudder and groan.
>
> ("Delilah," *Poetical Works* 24)

Many of Wilcox's poems, like Ashbery's, point toward some oblique, unmentionable incident, secret, or "crime":

> Sometimes I think there is not space or room
> In all the earth for such a love as mine,
> And it soars up to breathe in realms divine.
>
> ("Individuality," *Poetical Works* 7)

> Once in the world's first prime,
>   When nothing lived or stirred,
> Nothing but new-born Time,
>   Nor was there even a bird—
> The Silence spoke to a Star,
>   But I do not dare repeat
> What it said to its love afar:
>   It was too sweet, too sweet.

. . . .
For the great white star had heard
    Her silent lover's speech;
It needed no passionate word
    To pledge them each to each.
O lady fair and far,
    Hear, oh, hear, and apply!
Thou the beautiful star—
    The voiceless Silence, I.

("Love Song," *Poetical Works* 25-26)

Of course Wilcox is generally far less oblique and subtle, both more innocent and more public than Ashbery:

I know, in the way that sins are reckoned,
    This thought is a sin of the deepest dye
But I know, too, if an angel beckoned,
    Standing close by the Throne on High,
And you, adown by the gates infernal,
    Should open your loving arms and smile,
I would turn my back on things supernal,
    To lie on your breast a little while.

("Ad Finem," *Poetical Works* 11)

Her poems are also dramatically self-censoring, with a confessional tone that leaves readers completely unsure about how to take them:

In the midnight of darkness and terror,
    When I would grope nearer to God,
With my back to a record of error
    And the highway of sin I have trod,
There come to me shapes I would banish—
    The shapes of deeds I have done;
And I pray and I plead till they vanish—
    All vanish and leave me, save one.

("Delilah," *Poetical Works* 24)

The obvious way of destigmatizing these poems is to suggest that Wilcox was writing in the voice of a (male) persona. Strangely, the poet seems not to have ever made this suggestion. Reviewers dutifully skirted the issue of sexual orientation and instead condemned the morality of talking about sex at all in poetry—never mind what kind of sex. Even her biographer, twenty years after Wilcox's death, sidesteps the problem of the "offending" poems:

The poems that had caused this minor revolution were, some of them, lovely in their lilt, overbrimming with an authentic freshness of emotion. She had never sought the "word" for which Hart Crane committed suicide. But, within her natural frame, she could have saved herself, if she had matured in it, the doom of that smile at the mere mention of her name, which among the real lowbrows indicated all by itself a brushing denunciation, and among the highbrows, among the policemen of letters, amounted to a literary criticism which needed no further annotation.

(Ballou 95)

Ella Wheeler Wilcox's actual sexual desires will probably remain unknown and are not really what is at stake here. What *is* of interest is the way Wilcox starts to symbolize a kind of doubleness—whether in the goodness of her bad poetry, or in the irony of the woman who was both the disreputable Poetess of Passion and a revered advice columnist and matron of morality. One of the ways Ashbery uses Wilcox, particularly in the last section of his poem, is to introduce the topic of sexuality, to talk about and around desire, without specifically naming names—and on this account, Ashbery and Wilcox may have more in common than he realized:

Oh, you who read some song that I have sung—
What know you of the soul from whence it sprung?

Dost dream the poet ever speaks aloud
His secret thought unto the listening crowd?
    . . . . .

Our songs are shells, cast out by waves of thought;
Here, take them at your pleasure; but think not

You've seen beneath the surface of the waves,
Where lie our shipwrecks, and our coral caves.

("Introductory Verses," *Poetical Works* v)

It is quite possible that Ashbery has no idea about the *Poems of Passion* scandal and is interested in Wilcox solely based on the camp potential of so much of her verse. Nonetheless, many queer theorists would argue that it is important not to separate style from content but to read camp style as an exhibitive register of desire.

* * *

To appreciate Ashbery's humor, we have to understand its doubleness and be willing to live with uncertainty about when, why, or if we should be laughing. Much of this uncertainty arises from Ashbery's violations of poetry's rules of decorum in the late 1950s and early 1960s. As Vernon Shetley argues in *After the Death of Poetry,* Ashbery's infamous "difficulty" is tied to "this decision not to write the sort of poem Lowell was writing, not to produce within the paradigms offered by the New Criticism" (104). Shetley provides a detailed analysis of the ways in which Ashbery violates these rules, but he neglects to focus much attention on a key ideological idea behind them: that is, Greenberg's separations of the spheres of avant-garde and kitsch, high and low art. Ashbery foils readerly expectations not only by destabilizing such anticipated constants as speaker, situation, time frame, logic, pronoun reference, syntax, and sentence structure—in general, expectations about unified structure—but also by violating rules about what should and shouldn't count as poetry. He does this in many ways: by applying mundane, instruction-manual language to a poem of putative

Romantic transport; by investing Daffy Duck with the same weight as Milton's Satan or Shakespeare's Hamlet; by taking as inspiration the overwrought outpourings of Ella Wheeler Wilcox. What's tricky about these gestures (and many more like them) is determining where to draw the line between the parodic and the nonparodic. And what's especially daunting is that in many cases the line can't be drawn. In poems such as **"Daffy Duck in Hollywood"** and **"Variations,"** we need to take Ashbery both seriously and ironically at once.

Such uncertainty and doubleness is productive in two ways. First, it helps produce that quizzical, bemused laughter that Ashbery inspires in so many readers. As well, the uncertainty of Ashbery's humor is also productive of an important intellectual challenge regarding artistic value. It tacitly poses questions about what's good and what's bad in art and why. Ella Wheeler Wilcox helps illustrate Ashbery's duplicitous project in several ways. While her work is easily dismissed both on the "right" (from a formalist perspective) and on the "left" (from an avant-garde sensibility), Ashbery, ever in search of a position between right and left, finds a way to recuperate it as a genuine instance of camp. As with most camp, both Wilcox's and Ashbery's verse works through what one queer theorist calls an "aggressive passivity" that doesn't challenge so much as ignore the rules (Bergman 106-7).[8] Rather than accept a formalist or experimentalist position, Wilcox plays by her own rules:

> And it is not the poet's song, though sweeter than
>   sweet bells chiming,
> Which thrills us through and through, but the heart
>   which beats under the rhyming.
>
> And therefore I say again, though I am art's own true
>   lover,
> That it is not art, but heart, which wins the wide world
>   over.
>
>   ("Art and Heart," *Poetical Works* 53)

When critics advised the poet, as they often did, to write less and more thoughtfully, to stretch herself beyond cliché and rhyme, she answered in what could be the only appropriate way for her:

> And quite out of date, too, is rhythmical metre;
> The critics declare it an insult to art.
>   But oh! the sweet swing of it, oh! the clear ring
> of it,
>   Oh, the great pulse of it, right from the heart,
> Art or no art.
>
>   (qtd. in Lewis 52)

The risk involved in choosing her own way, art or no art, is certainly something Ashbery would have appreciated. In the 1950s, Ashbery and his colleagues were taking a similar risk by disregarding the standards of their day, particularly the formalist insistence on craft and control.[9] At a time when American poetry was still governed by "the men with their eyes on the myth / And the Missus and the midterms," as Kenneth Koch put it ("Fresh Air," *Rainway* 73), Ashbery and the New York school poets reintroduced the value of excess à la Whitman or Stevens (or, for that matter, Wilcox, though she was never mentioned). While Wilcox naively diverged from the expectations put on professional (but not amateur) artists, Ashbery consciously diverges from these expectations, playing the role of the gifted amateur. The humor of his poems often comes from this consciously chosen irresponsibility. After an era in which the New Critics insisted that every word in every poem needed to be carefully selected and justified, the New York school revived the value of humor and excess, the joys (à la Wilcox) of extravagance and waste.

Wilcox's poetry is campy, after all, not only in its corny innocence but also in its extravagance. Like the best camp performers, Wilcox is nothing if not excessive. The maudlin theatricality of her poetry was matched by her melodramatic personality and appearance. According to commentators, Wilcox strove all her life (from her early years as the country girl with the "inspired pen" to her final days as yellow journalism's domestic bard) to be the center of attention (Baird 607). Syndicated poetry and advice columnist, spiritualist and theosophist, war matron and popular moralist, Ella Wheeler Wilcox was as extravagant in her own way as Oscar Wilde was in his.[10] At a time when poets were beginning to make their work more precise and imagistic, to rid it of excesses, "to use absolutely no word that did not contribute to the presentation," as F. S. Flint demanded in the rules of "Imagisme" (199), Wilcox was writing the same gleefully long-winded and light-headed sentimental poems. Ezra Pound's ultimatum that "It is better to present one Image in a lifetime than to produce voluminous works" (201) is absolutely ridiculed by Wilcox's forty-plus volumes, the tens of thousands of poems she "dashed off" (these are her words) during her lifetime.[11] Of course Ashbery, too, is famous for his lack of restraint, as evidenced by the extravagance of **"Variations"** itself—not to mention the sprawling, immoderate long poems that appear in almost every Ashbery volume. We can easily see why the author of preposterous sestinas such as **"Crone Rhapsody"** and **"Farm Implements and Rutabagas in Landscape,"** an absurdist novel of manners like *A Nest of Ninnies,* a parodic play like *The Compromise* (based on a silent Rin Tin Tin feature), and so many poems that are constantly flirting—more or less delicately—with the boundaries of farce might find an oddly congenial precursor in Ella Wheeler Wilcox.

Finally, both Wilcox and Ashbery are funny, and yet we're never quite sure when, or whether or not, they're supposed to be. But this uncertainty, the doubleness with which their work can be taken, is an essential part of their aesthetic and their humor. Charles Towne has a wonderful anecdote in *Adventures in Editing* (1926) where he describes an unfortunate printer's error in setting up a Wilcox poem—which now, from a certain perspective, looks like a marvelous case of poetic justice or insight. The poem in question began with what Towne calls "one of her most cosmic lines, typical of her style" (97). The line was supposed to read,

> *My soul is a lighthouse keeper.*

However, the printer accidentally set up the line to read,

> *My soul is a light housekeeper.*

That both these lines now seem equally valid, equally funny, and equally "good" says something important about the singular, eccentric quality of Wilcox's verse. And this eccentricity and doubleness is a quality that John Ashbery has long exploited to produce a not dissimilar, oddly funny indeterminacy.

Notes

1. Both Perloff and Geoff Ward move toward this interpretation of "The Instruction Manual," though neither seems quite sure whether Ashbery's irony is intentional or not. This uncertainty is an appropriate response to the achieved doubleness of Ashbery's camp, as I will explain shortly. See Perloff 263-65 and Ward 101-2.

2. Huyssen explains that the Great Divide is "the kind of discourse which insists on the categorical distinction between high art and mass culture" (viii). "Ever since the mid-19th century," he notes, "the culture of modernity has been characterized by a volatile relationship between high art and mass culture. . . . Modernism constituted itself through a conscious strategy of exclusion, an anxiety of contamination by its other: an increasingly consuming and engulfing mass culture" (vii).

3. "One and the same civilization produces simultaneously two such different things as a poem by T. S. Eliot and a Tin Pan Alley song, or a painting by Braque and a *Saturday Evening Post* cover. All four are on the order of culture, and ostensibly, parts of the same culture and products of the same society. Here, however, their connection seems to end" (Greenberg 3). Greenberg concludes that kitsch ("popular, commercial art and literature . . . magazine covers, illustrations, ads, slick and pulp fiction, comics . . . tap dancing, Hollywood movies, etc., etc.") is "the epitome of all that is spurious in the life of our times" (9-10).

4. In articles such as Greenberg's "Avant-Garde and Kitsch" and Dwight Macdonald's "Masscult and Midcult," these critics argued that popular culture was not only banal, but that it also posed a serious threat to the canons of educated taste. For more on this topic, see Pells 216-32 and Ross 42-64.

5. The poems were received in many circles as disgraceful. *The Chicago Herald* called them "the songs of half-tipsy wantons" and prayed that Miss Wheeler would "now relapse to Poems of Decency" (qtd. in Lewis 49). In his 1899 *Critical Confessions,* Neal Brown wrote of *Poems of Passion*: "Of what avail is this lawless, wanton, verse? It bears the stigmata of mental debauchery and hysteria and does not teach one valuable lesson. To the psychopathist it may possess a curious scientific interest; but to laymen this demented verse is as abhorrent as the maunderings of a maniac. If it does express the language of a human heart is it not better that that language should remain untranslated, or at least that it should have no such brutal translation?" (191-92).

6. Of Wilcox's boast to have selected her *Poems of Passion* from over twelve hundred poems she wrote on the theme, Brown further notes: "This standard compels us to measure poetical greatness as certain loyal Americans do national greatness—as if it were a matter of barrels of pork and bushels of wheat" (185).

7. "Rather than simply hiding or revealing some homosexual content, [Ashbery's] poems represent and 'behave' differently, no matter what their subject. With their distortions, evasions, omissions, obscurities and discontinuities, Ashbery's poems always have a homotextual dimension" (Shoptaw 4). The term "homotextuality" was coined by Jacob Stockinger in his article "Homotextuality: A Proposal."

8. "Gay people have recognized that they can achieve their rights not by becoming the majority, but by finessing the entire issue of power. Or to put it another way, were gay culture to develop a discourse of power in parity to the dominant society's discourse, it would only end up reproducing the machismo which has oppressed it. The aggressive passivity of camp has been among its most potent tools in giving gay people a voice that we ourselves could hear and then use to speak to others" (Bergman 106-7).

9. In fact it was not only the New Critics and formalist poets who insisted on this kind of control. In the experimentalist camp, the Black Mountain poets were insisting on a slightly different kind of control, according to Ashbery's colleague Frank O'Hara: "[W]ith the influence of Levertov and Creeley you have another element which is making *control* practically the subject matter of the poem. That is your *control* of language, your *control* of the experiences and your *control* of your thought. . . . where they've

pared down the diction so that the experience presumably will come through as strongly as possible, it's the experience of their paring it down that comes through more strongly and not the experience that is the subject" ("Interview" 23).

10. Ella and her husband Robert were both interested in spiritualism and theosophy. In the 1890s, they studied with the Indian mystic Swami Vivekananda as part of an attempt to communicate with their dead infant son. After Robert's death in 1916, Wilcox began a new campaign of séances which she detailed for the readers of her newspaper column. On the advice of her dead husband, she arranged a series of tours of Allied army camps late in 1916. She read poetry, counseled soldiers, and delivered lectures on sexuality, entreating the boys to "Come Back Clean," as she titled one spirited poem (Baird 608).

11. Amusingly enough, Wilcox produced her own doctrinal essay, "A Few Important 'Don'ts'" (1901), addressed in this case to young career women who have just moved to the big city: "Don't think everything you see done by the people you are thrown among is right and fashionable and 'the thing,' because you are in New York. . . . Don't be afraid to express delight and enthusiasm about the things which please you. . . . Although you are to occupy an independent and self-supporting situation, do not think it necessary to dress in a masculine manner or assume mannish dress. Keep yourself as feminine as possible in conduct and attire" (*Everyday Thoughts* 42-43).

Works Cited

Allen, Donald, ed. *The New American Poetry, 1945-1960.* New York: Grove, 1960.

Altieri, Charles. "Ashbery as Love Poet." Schultz 26-37.

———. "Contemporary Poetry as Philosophy: Subjective Agency in John Ashbery and C. K. Williams." *Contemporary Literature* 33 (1992): 214-42.

Ashbery, John. *Girls on the Run.* New York: Farrar, 1999.

———. "The Invisible Avant-Garde." *Reported Sightings: Art Chronicles, 1957-1987.* Ed. David Bergman. New York: Knopf, 1989. 389-95.

———. *The Mooring of Starting Out: The First Five Books of Poetry.* Hopewell, NJ: Ecco, 1997.

———. *Selected Poems.* New York: Viking-Penguin, 1985.

———. *Self-Portrait in a Convex Mirror.* New York: Viking, 1975.

Baird, Julian T., Jr. "Ella Wheeler Wilcox." *Notable American Women, 1607-1950.* Vol. 3. Cambridge, MA: Belknap-Harvard UP, 1971. 607-9.

Ballou, Jenny. *Period Piece: Ella Wheeler Wilcox and Her Times.* Boston: Houghton, 1940.

Bergman, David. "Strategic Camp: The Art of Gay Rhetoric." *Camp Grounds: Style and Homosexuality.* Ed. David Bergman. Amherst: U of Massachusetts P, 1993. 92-109.

Bloom, Harold. "The Charity of Hard Moments." *Figures of Capable Imagination.* New York: Seabury, 1976. 169-208.

Brown, Neal. *Critical Confessions.* Wausau, WI: Philosopher, 1899.

Connor, Steve. "Points of Departure: Deconstruction and John Ashbery's 'Sortes Vergilianae.'" *Contemporary Poetry Meets Modern Theory.* Ed. Antony Easthope and John O. T. Thompson. Toronto: U of Toronto P, 1991. 5-18.

Crase, Douglas. "The Prophetic Ashbery." Lehman, *Beyond* 30-65.

Fink, Thomas A. "The Comic Thrust of Ashbery's Poetry." *Twentieth Century Literature* 30 (1984): 1-14.

Flint, F. S. "Imagisme." *Poetry* 1.6 (1913): 198-200.

Greenberg, Clement. "Avant-Garde and Kitsch." *Art and Culture: Critical Essays.* Boston: Beacon, 1961. 3-21.

Hall, Donald, Robert Pack, and Louis Simpson, eds. *The New Poets of England and America.* New York: Meridian, 1957.

Hoffman, Daniel, ed. *Harvard Guide to Contemporary American Writing.* Cambridge, MA: Harvard UP, 1979.

Huyssen, Andreas. *After the Great Divide: Modernism, Mass Culture, Postmodernism.* Bloomington: Indiana UP, 1986.

Koch, Kenneth. "An Interview with Jordan Davis." *The Art of Poetry: Poems, Parodies, Interviews, Essays, and Other Work.* Ed. David Lehman. Poets on Poetry ser. Ann Arbor: U of Michigan P, 1996. 187-214.

———. *On the Great Atlantic Rainway: Selected Poems, 1950-1988.* New York: Knopf, 1994.

Koethe, John. "The Metaphysical Subject of John Ashbery's Poetry." Lehman, *Beyond* 87-100.

Lehman, David. *The Last Avant-Garde: The Making of the New York School of Poets.* New York: Doubleday, 1998.

———, ed. *Beyond Amazement: New Essays on John Ashbery.* Ithaca, NY: Cornell UP, 1980.

Lepkowski, Frank. "John Ashbery's Revision of the Post-Romantic Quest." *Twentieth Century Literature* 39 (1993): 251-65.

Lewis, Naomi. "The Domestic Bard: Ella Wheeler Wilcox." *Harper's Magazine* March 1962: 47-53.

Macdonald, Dwight. "Masscult and Midcult." *Against the American Grain.* New York: Random, 1952. 3-75.

McCabe, Susan. "Stevens, Bishop, Ashbery: a Surrealist Lineage." *Wallace Stevens Journal* 22 (1998): 148-68.

Moramarco, Fred. "John Ashbery and Frank O'Hara: The Painterly Poets." *Journal of Modern Literature* 5 (1976): 436-62.

O'Hara, Frank. *The Collected Poems of Frank O'Hara.* Ed. Donald Allen. Berkeley: U of California P, 1995.

———. "Interview with Edward Lucie-Smith." *Standing Still and Walking in New York.* Ed. Donald Allen. Bolinas, CA: Grey Fox, 1975. 2-26.

O'Hara, Frank, and Larry Rivers. "How to Proceed in the Arts." *Art Chronicles, 1954-1966.* New York: George Braziller, 1975. 92-98.

Pells, Richard H. *The Liberal Mind in a Conservative Age: American Intellectuals in the 1940s and 1950s.* New York: Harper, 1985.

Perloff, Marjorie. *The Poetics of Indeterminacy: Rimbaud to Cage.* Princeton, NJ: Princeton UP, 1981.

Pound, Ezra. "A Few Don'ts by an Imagiste." *Poetry* 1.6 (1913): 200-206.

Ross, Andrew. *No Respect: Intellectuals and Popular Culture.* New York: Routledge, 1989.

Schultz, Susan M., ed. *The Tribe of John: Ashbery and Contemporary Poetry.* Tuscaloosa: U of Alabama P, 1995.

Shetley, Vernon. *After the Death of Poetry: Poet and Audience in Contemporary America.* Durham, NC: Duke UP, 1993.

Shoptaw, John. *On the Outside Looking Out: John Ashbery's Poetry.* Cambridge, MA: Harvard UP, 1994.

Sontag, Susan. "Notes on 'Camp.'" *Against Interpretation and Other Essays.* 1961. New York: Octagon, 1964. 275-92.

Stockinger, Jacob. "Homotextuality: A Proposal." *The Gay Academic.* Ed. Louie Crew. Palm Springs, CA: ETC, 1978. 135-51.

Towne, Charles Hanson. *Adventures in Editing.* New York: D. Appleton, 1926.

Ward, Geoff. *Statutes of Liberty: The New York School of Poets.* Language, Discourse, Society ser. London: Macmillan, 1993.

Wilcox, Ella Wheeler. *Every-day Thoughts in Prose and Verse.* Chicago: W. B. Conkey, 1901.

———. *Poems of Power.* 1901. London: Gay and Hancock, 1914.

———. *Poetical Works of Ella Wheeler Wilcox.* Toronto: Musson, 1917.

Yingling, Thomas E. *Hart Crane and the Homosexual Text: New Thresholds, New Anatomies.* Chicago: U of Chicago P, 1990.

Vincent N. Lolordo (essay date fall 2002)

SOURCE: Lolordo, Vincent N. "Poets/Readers: Whose Era?" *Wallace Stevens Journal* 26, no. 2 (fall 2002): 211-27.

[*In the following essay, Lolordo focuses on the popular and academic acceptance of Ashbery's work after* Self-Portrait in a Convex Mirror, *arguing that Ashbery's poetry embodies characteristics of both mainstream and avant-garde verse.*]

I

In an early essay, "Examples of Wallace Stevens," R. P. Blackmur attempted to distinguish among modernist poets (Ezra Pound, T. S. Eliot, and Wallace Stevens) on the grounds of the particular variety of obscurity experienced by their reader.[1] In his account, Poundian difficulty takes the form of problems with factual reference, Eliotic the form of problems of reference to beliefs or systems of feelings (on which, for example, the effectiveness of the repeated "Shantih" that closes "The Waste Land" depends). These are both recognizably problems of what George Steiner has called contingent difficulty, the difficulty of "'a word, a phrase or reference which [one] will have to look up'" (27); such a poetry points the reader—via whatever means—outward, toward the world of discourse of which the poem is a interdependent part. Stevens, by contrast, poses difficulties that are specifically those of language: a dictionary, rather than other sources of information, is vital to any reader of his work. To Blackmur, the difficulties of his verse prove not susceptible to "specific sorts of external knowledge and belief" (the dictionary, for Blackmur, is internal to the language) but rather "clarify themselves to the intelligence alone" (89, 91).

Blackmur's particular strand of proto-New Criticism might have taken as its motto Eliot's injunction that the only method is to be very intelligent. Nevertheless, a theory may be elicited from his distinction by reframing it in Bakhtinian terms: Pound's difficulty is that of novelization, Stevens' is that specific to the lyric. Indeed, the very source of each brand of difficulty is its position at the extreme end of the spectrum: Pound's poetry is excessively novelized, Stevens' is excessively lyrical. The high valuation that Blackmur was prepared to give to Stevens at this early date corresponded to his own concern for poetic language: the abstruse quality of Stevensian diction separates his poetry from the hurly-burly of daily language. But it is Pound's poetry that has been aligned with the practice of experimental writing for the past twenty years; and this bears witness to a shift in definition, from the high modernist idea of poetry as a particular language to the more recent account of modernism as a discursive practice that seeks to erase boundaries among different kinds of writing.

Marjorie Perloff's "Pound/Stevens: Whose Era?" was surely a major source of this shift; Perloff argued that the choice between these two poets was defining of modernism—and of its legacy, of "the meaning of poetry itself in current literary history and theory" (2).[2] Twenty years ago, the debate over the meaning and inheritance of modernism looked very different than it does today, as Perloff noted in her talk at the 2000 Modern Studies Association conference. These days, we can have our indeterminacy and our meditative lyricism, too. No new polarity has emerged; indeed, the very idea of an era of literary scholarship defined by poetry—the imaginative legacy left by the New Criticism in the 1950s and 1960s—now seems increasingly distant, separated as we are from that era by the moment of theory.

Perloff restated her old opposition in October 2000, posing Gertrude Stein and Eliot as the two American poets most representative of the radical pre-WWI European modernism to which, she suggests, we are only now returning. Interestingly, she invoked this particular historical moment without overtly reopening the question of the avant-garde—the question that, I will argue, is now most vital to the polarizing debates that still define the contemporary poetry world. To present Stein/Eliot as an either/or is in one important sense deceptive: both writers existed and still exist as "major poets," figures of modernist autonomy rather than avant-garde praxis.[3] Debate in (North) American poetry today is not focused on the question of rival poetics or particular figures who might represent these values. Rather, it concerns itself with publishing venues and their status as value-laden contexts, asking whether poetics can meaningfully be separated from such material concerns.

Here I consciously switch my attention from the school canon—the canon of academic study, within which two writers can coexist comfortably as objects for ideological critique and exegetical subtleties—to the poet's canon (following Alan Golding's distinction). I do so because I take Perloff's project over the past years as an extended, and greatly successful, effort to drive the "poet's canon," as a critical wedge, into the school canon that existed circa 1980. If the Pound/Stevens

polarity pitted synchronic modernism against diachronic literary history, such a gesture, at least in retrospect, seems equally clearly to pose the poet's canon against the continuity-driven canon of the literary academy. But given the growing predominance of practicing poets over a shrinking area of academic poetry studies, it seems of little use to reenact this particular battle. The poet's canon has won even as the academic prestige of poetry has diminished with the recent ascendancy of cultural studies and identity politics, discourses hardly friendly to the "difficulty" of much contemporary poetry. (If Stevens' traditionalism helped him become the favored poet of deconstruction—that is to say, the poet of the moment of "theory"—no one would say that age was the age *of* Stevens.) And the post-theory literary academy's investment in identity politics renders the selection of a single "representative" impossible.

Consequently, to restage Perloff's debate with any two figures—posing, say, the collage scholarship of Susan Howe against the unfurling syntactical displays of Jorie Graham—is finally unsatisfactory. No single binary can encompass the diversity of investments in contemporary poetry. Graham is not the poet of the academy, but the poet long affiliated with a specific institutional site, Iowa; Howe's affiliation with the SUNY-Buffalo poetics program might be read similarly. To pose Graham's "mainstream" against Howe's "margins" considers only a particular institutional reward structure; Howe's poetry is as academically central as Graham's, responding as well to the concerns of poststructuralist historicism as does Graham's to sophisticated formal readings.[4]

Then what if we drop the names? A particularly good example of the kind of contemporary debate that takes this line is the discussion earlier this year on Steve Evans' (privately circulated) "Notes to Poetry."[5] For Evans, the avant-garde is the locus of poetic value, definable both historically and in its present incarnation by "its anti-capitalism and its insistence on autonomous intellectual/poetic production." His admonitory polemic for the new millennium argues that the contemporary avant-garde, directionless since the institutionalization of "language poetry" in the mid-1990s, is vulnerable to the omnivorous appetite of liberal pluralism, the dominant ideology of market society—and of the poetry world. Evans chooses *Fence* as his central target, arguing that the magazine incarnates pluralism by decontextualizing avant-garde strategies and presenting them, apart from the political commitments they should entail, as so many merely formal commodities among others.

My intention here is not to translate "Pound/Stevens" as "avant-garde/mainstream." To do so renders the names "Stevens" and "Pound" almost entirely metaphorical, perhaps designating, say, the National Book Award and St. Elizabeth's, insider and exile, as locations competing for the privilege of telling the truth about American culture—and ignores the fact that *each* writer was both associated with the avant-garde and ultimately canonized as a high modernist. The concept of language-centered writing has come to be understood by criticism as the signified of "the avant-garde" in a way similar to the relation of deconstruction and "theory" within literary-critical debates of the 1980s and later. Yet the relation of Pound to language poetry is as tenuous and mediated as the relation of Stevens to the current practice of "mainstream" literary journals. Charles Bernstein's strongly articulated insistence that Pound's innovative poetics cannot simply be abstracted away from his fascism for liberatory use (see his "Pounding Fascism" in *A Poetics* 120-27) has not, to my knowledge, been countered within experimental poetics. (Such a tacit consensus might be taken as itself indicating a shift in "eras." In her 1982 piece, Perloff used Pound tactically, as an avant-garde precursor: his fascism goes unmentioned in the essay.)

My concerns, ultimately, are not with the specifics of Evans' judgments, but with his focus on the magazine as the central topic of literary-political debate. Such a perspective treats literary history as inherently hostile to avant-garde values, which wither when torn from the ethically rich context from which they spring: the eventual canonization of any once "avant-garde" writer will inevitably obscure the material specifics of his or her original publication context. It does not, however, itself solve the question of the *relation* between formal strategies and their origin in avant-garde sociality.

A skeptical, sociological account might assert that the "mainstream" and the "marginal" in American poetry function as a system of differences without positive values. But movement between these two positions can occur only in a single direction. The work of a poet who emerges in the mainstream may become increasingly experimental, but such shifts are not typically associated with a similar shift in publishing venues and may thus always be dismissed as "merely" formal. By contrast, an experimental writer who chooses to appear in a more mainstream magazine may lose prestige in certain quarters even if his or her work shows no signs of increased conventionality. Nevertheless, the material conditions of publishing are not self-evidently value-laden. Too often critics fall back into a relatively empty notion of oppositionality. The difficulty of maintaining a sociological objectivity is illustrated by Christopher Beach's generally excellent *Poetic Culture,* which contains a chapter pitting Stephen Dobyns against Lyn Hejinian, treating the former as typical of "mainstream" or "workshop" poetry and the latter as representative of "experimental" or "Language" poetry. Beach asserts that Hejinian "wins no prizes and continues to publish in small presses" because her "oppositional" poetry "attacks bourgeois notions of the subject and [its] relation

to discursive formations" (78). Although Hejinian indeed attacks such notions, the opposition Beach locates is merely that of a structural relation between two terms: Hejinian's negative relation to prizes and major presses *defines* her as an "avant-garde" poet as surely as Dobyns' positive relation defines him as a mainstream one.

The question of the avant-garde, then, demands the examination not only of social arguments about the formal, but also of poetry's own internal creation (or figuration) and analysis of the social. To provide evidence of the latter, I will now introduce John Ashbery and his 1991 book-length poem, *Flow Chart.* Ashbery's poem circles obsessively around the notions of centrality and marginality, while constantly converting formal and textual strategies into figures for the social—and vice versa. Ashbery's particular awareness may be ascribed to his peculiar position: my suggestion that no two current poets stood as useful successors to Perloff's Pound and Stevens can now be modified. The current debate most relevant as a successor to Perloff's formulation concerns two versions of this single poet.[6]

II

When Evans (and others) argue that liberal pluralism is "by tendency eclectic and apolitical, allergic to commitment and against principles on principle," their words might equally well describe the lack of "program" Ashbery famously attributed to Frank O'Hara (and by implication to his own work). (Ashbery went on to claim that the "'message'" of O'Hara's poems, "'unlike the message of committed poetry . . . incites one to all the programs of commitment as well as to every other form of self-realisation'" [qtd. in Smith 26 n 4].) While Hank Lazer refers to "the domestication and acceptance of John Ashbery's experimental poetry as a kind of strategic tokenism" (14), other commentators shift the responsibility to the poet himself. Charles Bernstein calls Ashbery's unwillingness to produce an oppositional poetics "a great disappointment for our letters" (157), consciously alluding to William Carlos Williams' famous judgment of "The Waste Land" as "the great catastrophe to our letters. . . . Our work staggered to a halt for a moment under the blast of Eliot's genius which gave the poem back to the academics" (146). The comparison evaluates Ashbery in no uncertain literary-historical terms. Evans' words might then equally describe the "career path" that moves from the title of Yale Younger Poet to the collage work of *The Tennis Court Oath* to the Stevensian meditative verse of *Self-Portrait in a Convex Mirror,* accumulating academic exegesis at a steadily increasing rate.

One aspect of Ashbery's project has been to transcribe the protean moods of the atomic self; and this tendency has been taken to correspond with the socioeconomic fact of Ashbery's post-1976 ascendancy to major or even "greatest American poet" status. Of course, the two Ashberys are not solely their own creation. By the early 1990s, Ashbery could be blurbed (on the back of *Flow Chart*) both as "unfailingly avant-garde" and as the canonical inheritor of the high modern mantle, purifier of "the dialect of the tribe." The two positions coexist easily within what we might think of as the capacious pluralism of Ashbery's work, a poetry as thoroughly novelized as Pound's yet as meditatively lyrical as that of Stevens, one which has eschewed (since *The Tennis Court Oath*) collage strategies and lyric monoglossia alike. Such a pluralism lends itself to appropriation: in "The Story of *Fence*," her first-person account of travels through the wilds of the contemporary poetry world, the editor Rebecca Wolff describes her magazine's title as presenting itself with the inevitability of "the best clichés." Indeed, few clichés remain unembraced by John Ashbery. But his most frequently-cited stance, "a kind of fence-sitting / Raised to the level of an aesthetic ideal" (*Selected* [*Selected Poems*] 88), does not preclude a continuing poetic examination of the relation between the discourse of lyric poetry and the social.[7]

Flow Chart begins by self-consciously charting itself, summoning up an iambic pentameter to locate the speaking subject at some point late in a career: "Still in the published city but not yet / overtaken by a new form of despair, I ask / the diagram" (1). The poem opens on an edge, neither out of the frying pan nor in the fire, acknowledging both the dangers of literary history and an imperative to innovate that might itself be only more poetic history, a temporally paradoxical predicament: the new pursues, seeking to overtake from the past.[8] Throughout, Ashbery addresses the subject of the Major Poet and this figure's relation to the demands of the social world:

> What right have you to consider yourself anything but
>   an enormously eccentric though
> not too egocentric character, whose sins of omission
>   haven't omitted much,
> whose personal-pronoun lapses may indeed have
>   contributed to augmenting the hardship
> silently resented among the working classes? If I
>   thought that for a minute I'd . . .
>
> (150; Ashbery's ellipsis)

By referring to "personal-pronoun lapses," the voice of accusation gestures both at self-critique and at criticism. Noting such an errant use of pronouns, particularly of the lyric "I," a kind of errancy that could not exactly be called "egocentric," has long been a prominent feature of Ashbery criticism. Noting political "sins of omission"—as in Charles Bernstein's stricture—has been another such feature. Thus forcibly pinned into the very person he would rather "lapse" away from—the first—"Ashbery"'s reply sputters out into ellipses. But the

metaphorics of centrality that trail through the accuser's language are a still more serious matter. The two terms (eccentric and egocentric) are potentially opposites, and the opposition is revealing; the eccentric "character" of *Flow Chart* is not centered within the "I" or ego but stands outside it, is etymologically speaking *ek kentros,* outside the center. This is not to argue that Ashbery is claiming (accusing himself of) a marginal identity; his question is different: what would it mean for poetry—and for the act of writing poetry—to have or want a central position?

> So many were hung out to dry, or more accurately,
>   to rot.
> And these marginalia—what other word is there for
>   them?—are the substance of the text,
> by not being allowed to fit in. One can proceed like a
>   ghost
> along corridors and find that doors are closed to one,
>   and then
> what good is being invisible?
>
> (37)

"So many" of us, Ashbery tells us, are marginalized, a group of ghostly outsiders to whom doors remain closed, occupying a corridor (a related, more socially specified space appears earlier on the same page: "the narrow, closetlike conundrum / of their own slender existences"). But this social meaning coexists with the textual reference the same passage enacts. The text gestures at the particular quality of "So many" of its own lines, the consequence of their "not being allowed to fit in." If we take seriously for a moment the possibility that marginalia form "the substance of the text," the formal consequences are radical. Such a work would stand as a response to another, absent form that could never be known through these secondary notations, deriving its own notion of form from the discourse it is parasitic upon.

We might think of this discourse as literary history, a narrative that, for a poet who operates—as he announces in the poem's opening line—inside the "published city" (3) of textuality, has something of the weight that history proper bears for Pound or Stevens:

> *It seems I was reading something*;
> I have forgotten the sense of it or what the small
> role of the central poem made me want to feel. No
>   matter.
> The words, distant now, and mitred, glint. Yet not one
> ever escapes the forest of agony and pleasure that
>   keeps them
> in a solution that has become permanent through
>   inertia. The force
> of meaning never extrudes. And the insects,
> of course, don't mind.
>
> (3-4)

Once established as canonical—positioned as a "central poem"—a text can harden into an alien, senseless literary monument: a fairy-tale location in the timeless "forest of agony and pleasure," where nothing ever changes. The writing that makes up *Flow Chart* seeks to avoid this reification into a "central" poem of stasis. The poem figures reading otherwise, as a process that must be continual, to escape the linguistic inertia that seals up meaning like an insect in amber. Here I equate the "insects" with the glinting "words." The speculative nature, the contingency of this reading is its very point; it suggests a practice in which the writer looks very like a reader of his own text, rereading his own writing as it drifts toward the metaphorical—as it always will—then taking up the implied metaphor (words are insects) to start a new stream of language. It is this ongoing slippage, a quest that slides, placing reader and writer together, on edge, rather than locating or penetrating to some "center," that characterizes the poem's production of meaning.

The forgotten *"something"* being read may be characterized more specifically, given that the "central poem" alludes to a characteristic Stevensian image. In "A Primitive Like an Orb," the complexity and distance of such a hypothesized "central poem," in a logic like that of some medieval proof of God's existence, merely confirms Stevens' faith in its certainty: "The central poem is the poem of the whole, / The poem of the composition of the whole" (*CP* [*Collected Poems*] 442). Ultimately this "central poem" is transformed into a personage, "A giant on the horizon . . . / At the centre on the horizon, concentrum, grave / And prodigious person, patron of origins," and in the lyric's final stanza, Stevens affirms the part/whole relations of traditional representational poetics: "Each one, his fated eccentricity, / As a part, but part, but tenacious particle, / Of . . . the total / Of letters" (*CP* 443). These individual moments of "eccentricity" somehow all add up to a "concentrum": the resort to such a coinage—forging a substantive from an entirely relative adjective, "concentric," which denotes the state of sharing a center—marks the difficulty of such politico-poetic alchemy. By contrast, Ashbery's sense of a shared marginality renders it impossible to find a solid or central position, a fixed ground for judgment. His "I" lacks this perspective; it is part of a "we" who are "other" to the idea of a dominant discourse. Centrality itself, as Charles Bernstein puts it, is "the power of the dominant margin" (188); acknowledging this, the truly marginal poem may *contain* multitudes but declines to *represent* a whole or a central figure that could stand for this whole.

For Ashbery, the marginality of poetry in the order of contemporary discourses is never confused with his own poetic career. The latter periodically emerges with a revealing awkwardness, often undermining those moments in the poem where a certain lyric pathos might otherwise occupy center stage:

> But though reams of work do get done,
> not much listens. I have the feeling my voice is just
>   for me,
> that no one else has ever heard it, yet I keep mumbling
>   the litany
> of all that has ever happened to me. . . .

(81)

"Litany," of course, was first mumbled—published—as the long centerpiece poem of Ashbery's *As We Know.* The section of this work Ashbery chose to excerpt in his *Selected Poems* begins as follows: "Some certified nut / Will try to tell you it's poetry" (253). The "certified" nut—playing on the word—is, of course, no one other than the "major poet."

The poetic career is figured throughout *Flow Chart,* often in terms that both invoke and parody the most traditional of imagery:

> Any day now you must start to dwell in it,
> the poetry, and for this, grave preparations must be
>   made, the walks of sand
> raked, the rubble wall picked clean of dead vine stems,
>   but what
> if poetry were something else entirely, not this purple
>   weather
> with the eye of a god attached, that sees
> inward and outward? What if it were only a small,
>   other way of living,
> like being in the wind?

(145)

The description of poetry as a final dwelling place figures the poetic career in the most somber of terms, as if the practice itself was finally a writing toward death, a process of monumentalization; Ashbery's mordantly comical pun equates "the poetry" with a grave and thus tips the delicate tonal balance, undermining, as it were, the monument. But this is not to suggest that the alternative poetics of the quotidian ("a small, other way of living") is a consistent consolation in the poem. The temptation of the monument constantly returns, as in, for instance, the ambition to "build the palace of reason . . . to be able to construct the small song, our prayer / at the center of whatever void we may be living in: a romantic, nocturnal place / that must sooner or later go away" (76). The image reformulates "the small / role of the central poem" (3); no longer a distant, monumental text, it is now a necessary yet ineffectual prayer, spoken from a position in which centrality seems a tenuous claim indeed.

III

The question of the place of poetry is endemic to *Flow Chart*; at moments it is treated quite literally, with a comic sociological objectivity—as in a remark that "poets are retreating into—or is it out of?—academia, beset by the / usual pit-bulls and well-meaning little old ladies in tennis shoes. And discovering / and assimilating new bastions of indifference and comprehension" (133). The passage hardly needs interpretation; I will simply note that Ashbery's pairs of images unwind with a looseness that serves to emphasize the idea of a system governed by signifying opposition (by difference), rather than the particular values of either side.

Such a reading of textual figurations of the literary is not, of course, itself meant to dismiss the possibility of a more strictly sociological argument (at which I have already gestured). Here I want to briefly introduce the work of Pierre Bourdieu. In Bourdieu's literary sociology, the literary field is the dominated or marginalized part of the field of power. Within the literary, the sector of restricted or autonomous production defines itself through inverting the values of that of large-scale production. The space of literary activity as a whole, then, is marked by struggle between market-driven and market-opposed principles of hierarchy.[9] The latter principle, of course, is that of the avant-garde. Such movements are cemented by opposition; but given the terms of the dominant model of literary history, recognition falls upon the individual and hence acts as a kind of entropy: exhibit, the fate of "language poetry," or the career of John Ashbery. A sociological account of this kind is not concerned with the motivations that might cause an individual poet associated with an avant-garde to send work to a relatively mainstream publication, but with noticing that for such a poet to do so, whatever the motive, is complicit with the existing logic of literary history. Within these terms, such an action is double, counting both as a bet that the game of individual reputation—the game of "eras"—will continue to be the dominant game and an investment in a particular magazine that in its overt denial of group affiliation clearly supports this game. (None of which necessarily prevents a particular author from placing some side bets as well.) But the choice of a particular publication venue is also an attempt to be read in the present: the synchronic game of cultural intervention—the game played most aggressively by the avant-garde—goes on concurrently with the weird diachronic game of reputation (the two games I attempt to show Ashbery's engagement with herein).[10]

It remains possible for literary history to choose its game: to elevate individual authors and forget the avant-garde, collective venues in which they originally appeared. To understand the author-function, as Michel Foucault reminded us, is not to disable it. It is difficult to see what editorial practices might prevent this; certainly, they will need the assistance of a literary history that is able to conceive of a unit of study other than that deadly dichotomy of the "major author" and the amorphous subject of cultural studies. But such a

history cannot ensure the possibility that particular texts or ways of reading might function as a kind of liberatory practice outside the limits of their originary community.

At this point I will step aside: my conclusions are anticipated by Ashbery's *Flow Chart.* I have argued that the poem frees the reader into an active marginality, one maker of meanings among many, while at the same time positioning writing (including its own) as a marginal practice. Its concluding line directs the reader back out into the world by pointing to a space that the poem does not seek to contain: "It's open: the bridge, that way" (216). Such an account accords with the contemporary consensus in experimental poetry, which tells us that an avant-garde or postmodern poem will question and problematize, disrupting certainties and emphasizing differences—will precisely not seek, as did the modern work, to "compel conviction"—all this as part of its project of connecting formal techniques to the social struggles that give them their ultimate purpose and value. I quote Lyn Hejinian from "The Rejection of Closure": "The 'open text,' by definition, is open to the world and particularly to the reader. It invites participation, rejects the authority of the writer over the reader and thus, by analogy, the authority implicit in other . . . hierarchies" (43). One wants to agree—but the question remains: how will such open invitations further a reimagination of social relations?

I want to suggest that for all its revisionary gestures toward modernist ambition, *Flow Chart* finally remains ambivalent about the values of avant-garde poetics. The poem often thematizes claims that are recognizably versions of contemporary ones such as Hejinian's and concludes, I think, that poetic intervention can only affect the ground for discursive exchange—as by allowing the possibility of a relationship that exists outside the discourse of linguistic mastery to continually reemerge:

> What we are to each other is both less urgent and
> more
> perturbing, having no discernible root, no raison
> d'etre, or else flowing
> backward into an origin like the primordial soup it's
> so easy to pin
> anything on, like a carnation to one's lapel. So it
> seems we must
> stay in an uneasy relationship, not quite fitting
> together, not precisely friends or lovers though
> certainly not enemies, if
> the buoyancy of the spongy terrain on which we exist
> is to be experienced
> as an ichor, not a commentary on all that is missing
> from the reflection
> in the mirror. *Did I say that? Can this be me?*
>
> (10)

The slide of language here from metaphorical to literal, and the consequent undermining of the idiom ("to pin /

anything on") mimics the sponginess of the linguistic terrain we inhabit: our shared linguistic conventions. No argument from a concept of origins (reversing the flow) will ease this tension. Instead, we have an "uneasy" present-tense pragmatics; and it is this "not quite fitting" / "together" (our collective marginality, to read the line break strongly) that will preserve us. Rather than a field to be tended by the poet, language is the very ground on which all our relations are conducted, a ground we experience as an "ichor": as a foreign substance that is yet within us, preserving the surprise, the otherness of language and the non-identity of our words and selves: *"Did I say that? Can this be me?"* Another lament on our internal division, another evocation of lyric pathos—"a commentary on all that is missing"—might yet be avoided. Yet this freedom is both solution and problem in Ashbery's poem: the reader of the "open" text is not always properly grateful: "And if I told you / this was your life, not some short story for a contest, how would you react? / Chances are you'd tell me to buzz off and continue writing" (81). If we, the readers, have been writing all along, then belated writerly attempts to free us from the marketplace—presented here in the familiar terms of the literary contest (what Evans calls the "rigged lotteries" of the prize system that establishes and reinforces hierarchies)—may not be entirely welcome. The passage as a whole is still more ambivalent:

> And though one can hear the traffic's
> swish
> as it cuts from one side of the island to the other, one
>   is transfixed,
> facing an army of necessary revisions. "How would it
>   be if I said it this way,
> or would so-and-so's way be better, easy on the adjec-
>   tives?" And if I told you
> this was your life, not some short story for a contest,
>   how would you react?
> Chances are you'd tell me to buzz off and continue
>   writing, except
> it's so difficult; we barely begin and paralysis takes
>   over, forcing us out
> for a breath of fresh air. . . .
>
>   (81)

The earnest self-styled contestant, weighing the do's and don'ts proffered by the minor Hemingways of the workshop or manual ("'easy on the adjectives'"), is easy to mock—except that Ashbery, mixing pronouns with his typical promiscuity, refuses to separate this figure entirely from the writer *qua* writer. Writers here are both spoken for and addressed: "one" is writing, "you" are writing, "we" are writing. The contestant confuses writing—for Ashbery, the project of a life—with the pursuit of literary status; but neither belief will reduce the difficulty of writing and revision itself.[11] As elsewhere in the poem, writing here is figured as a state of would-be fluidity constantly threatened by the force of inertia. The writer is "transfixed" not only by the

process of revision but by the "difficult" process of writing itself, unable to move with the easy flow of the traffic outside: "paralysis takes over" and forces us back into the daily world of banal health.

Ultimately, Ashbery presents the notion of freeing the reader into writing as desirable and impossible, at best as a process that must be repeated over and over again.[12] Readers are or can be writers and vice versa: but the two traditional roles remain, however ridiculous:

>   not that you don't
> already love him enough, more than any writer
>   deserves. He won't thank you for it.
> But you won't mind that either, since his literature
>   will have performed its duty
> by setting you down gently in a new place and then
>   speeding off before
> you have a chance to thank it. We've got to find a
>   new name for him. "Writer" seems
> totally inadequate; yet it is writing, you read it before
>   you knew it. And besides,
> if it weren't, it wouldn't have done the unexpected
>   and by doing so proved that it was quite
> the thing to do, and if it happened all right for you,
>   but wasn't the way you
> thought it was going to be, why still
> that is called fulfilling part of the bargain. And by do-
>   ing so
> he has erased your eternal debt to him. You are free.
>   You can go now.
>
>   (185-86)

The passage is a gleeful send-up, both of those two legendary figures, Author and Reader, and of the by now received revisionary notions about their relationship. The parodic element begins with the clunky false note of Ashbery's sly reference to "his literature." In the midst of these ambitious claims, a secondary meaning sneakily deflates the writer, leaving just another zealot, the type who might aggressively try to interest you in some "literature."[13] The writer "fulfill[s]" the bargain, it should be noted, and so erases our debt to him. In providing this surprising yet pleasurable textual experience, this yet-to-be renamed figure replaces the old notion of the "Writer," that figure on whom we always relied for meaning: the process described and parodied here is that which Roland Barthes so grandly prophesied in "The Death of the Author," the effort toward "suppressing the author in the interests of writing (which is, as will be seen, to restore the place of the reader)" (168). But in Ashbery's scenario, our freedom quickly becomes the tactfully ambiguous freedom to "go."

Have we—returning to Barthes' language—been born as readers, freed from the oppressive mythic regime of the Author to make meaning on our own; or have we simply been dismissed from text? In the end, the perhaps negative freedom with which the passage concludes resonates with the idea of a passive freedom of consumption, the illusory freedom of choice provided by the liberal state, just as strongly as with the conception of positive freedom that stands at the end of the avant-garde project. A stalemate between readerly and writerly poetics—which equally remain circumscribed by the boundary lines of the major poet (and the corresponding mode of publication)—is thus eloquently figured in Ashbery's work. Given my own feelings, already amply stated, I could hardly conclude this piece by any optimistic, and in any case belated, invocation of the Ashbery Era. Nevertheless, to express, whether analytically or as symptom, the dilemmas of the particular historical moment is an achievement that cannot be dismissed. It prompts me to suggest that John Ashbery is surely our most ambivalent living poet.

Notes

1. Blackmur's essay, first published in 1932 in *Hound & Horn,* is an early example of the argument that sought to justify readerly difficulty, a line that would become crucial to the New Critical reception of modernist poetry—and, indeed, to the reception of modernism in the arts. I examine the discourse around modernism and difficulty in my dissertation. See also Diepeveen.

2. Although, as Marjorie Perloff has observed, the New Critics wrote "respectfully—if also quite critically" (1) about both men, here I would choose rather to emphasize that each was somewhat marginal to their canon. In its early stages the New Criticism took Pound to have already declined from the height of "Hugh Selwyn Mauberley" and, without the late achievements before them, considered Stevens a mere aesthete. (The best account of Stevens' reception is John Newcomb's *Wallace Stevens and Literary Canons.*) The two poets only became potentially polar opposites—"major" poets whose work attracted sustained attention—in a postwar environment where Pound was increasingly acknowledged by poets as the crucial precursor of the New American Poetry, Stevens by critics as the foremost living exemplar of the main line of lyric poetry in the English language. This is the background against which Perloff's "Pound/Stevens: Whose Era?" was written.

3. Here I do not mean to deny that the pair otherwise—whether autobiographically or in the literary-historical symbolic—form a perfect opposition. Their well-known encounter is easily allegorized. On November 15, 1924, the patron of the *Criterion,* Lady Rothermere, brought Eliot to pay an unexpected call at 27 Rue de Fleurus. *The Autobiography of Alice B. Toklas* tells the story: "Eliot said that if he printed anything of Gertrude Stein's in the Criterion it would have to be her very latest thing." Stein promptly sat down at her desk. "[S]he . . . began to write a portrait of T. S. Eliot and called it the fifteenth of November, that being this day and so there could be no doubt but that it was her latest thing" (*Selected Writings* 166). The piece was sent to the *Criterion* and appeared in that magazine's January 1926 issue; a year later, writing in the *Nation and Athenaeum,* Eliot associated Stein's writing with jazz and 1920s' mass culture: "'her work is not improving, it is not amusing, it is not interesting, it is not good for one's mind'" (qtd. in Schuchard 137 n 39). The particular terms of this evaluation place Stein outside the literary / artistic domain, the sphere in which value judgments are governed by the faculty of *taste.* Eliot's recognition—or decision—that Stein could not be assimilated to the disciplinary role of the developing modernist literary canon anticipates much of her later reception history.

4. A search of the MLA International Bibliography online turns up 47 articles or book chapters whose "subject" is Howe, 26 whose is Graham. (Much of this scholarship is very recent. More than half of the work on each writer has appeared since 1995: over this span, the count is Howe 26, Graham 17—to contextualize, over the same period the count for Adrienne Rich is 82, for John Ashbery 71. Interestingly, Rich and Ashbery were the two candidates for most significant contemporary poet that Charles Altieri proposed in his 1984 study *Self and Sensibility in Contemporary American Poetry;* some eighteen years later, they remain the living poets most acknowledged by criticism.

5. I focus on this piece as exemplary of definitional debates around the *emerging* avant-garde. The (relative) obscurity of *Fence* is precisely the point: to wait for a magazine to become "established" is to wait for it to have belonged to a previous moment. In any case, I am not the first to mention this debate in other forums; it is alluded to with a certain condescension by Robert Hass in his introduction to *The Best American Poetry, 2001,* as representing the intemperance of youth. For better (if also at times for worse) such intemperance has long defined the avant-garde.

   I will refer only to Evans' piece, "Third Factory: Notes to Poetry IV.1," which was posted at <http://www.umit.maine.edu/~steven.evans/3F-1>; some thirty responses have been archived at <www.umit.maine.edu/~steven.evans/3F-index.htm>.

6. I make this argument in considerably more detail in an article entitled "Charting the Flow: John Ashbery and Literary History," which is the source of much of the second section of this piece.

7. The line is from "Soonest Mended," a poem easily read as addressing the social situation of contemporary poetry. It opens with a weary summary that teeters at the edge of parody: "Barely tolerated, living on the margin / In our technological society" (*Selected Poems* 87).

8. This has long been Ashbery's position. The opening of *Flow Chart* repeatedly echoes his earlier "Self-Portrait in a Convex Mirror"—the poem whose reception quickly elevated Ashbery to critical centrality, making a writing life into a "career"—a poem that could still suggest that since "today is uncharted" (*Selected Poems* 192), "Today has no margins, the event arrives / Flush with its edges, is of the same substance, / Indistinguishable" (200). (Among other images later taken up in *Flow Chart,* "Self-Portrait" ["Self-Portrait in a Convex Mirror"] refers (203) to the inaccessible "diagram still sketched on the wind.") *Flow Chart* maps the space of "today" (left uncharted by the more focused discursive lyric development of the earlier poem). A third related formulation may be noted: near the end of the prose poem "The System," Ashbery speaks of "the razor's edge present which is really a no-time, straying over the border into the positive past and the negative future whose movements alone define it" (*Selected* 158).

9. My account derives primarily from Bourdieu's *The Rules of Art.* Interestingly, *Fence* has proved capable of absorbing this literary sociology and using its aura of value-neutrality to legitimize itself; a recent issue contains a short article by David Kellogg entitled "The Self in the Poetic Field," which takes Bourdieu's cultural sociology as a way of suggesting possibilities for contemporary American poetry. Kellogg argues that the dominant trend among new independent little magazines is a playful eclecticism and that this should be understood not as an attempt to return to a simple, preideological notion of universal literary merit (as a critic like Evans might suggest) but as acknowledging that we exist in an unstable, transitional period. Pluralism, according to this account, has permeated even the avant-garde.

Such an argument works perfectly as part of the journal's position: its pluralism dons the value-neutrality of literary sociology as a disguise and thus eludes the pursuing logic of criticism. In Bourdieu's terms, the willingness of a new player to speak the language of the market reads as a calculated defiance: lacking symbolic capital specific to the field, the new player has less at stake in the field's autonomy and is more likely to appeal to the logic of the dominant. We see a liberal pluralist logic of inclusion under attack by its inverse. To publish a diverse variety of poetry (as does *Fence*) may be a principled stand; but providing such a convenience for the reader is entirely in accordance with hard marketing logic, as if *Fence* were to say: "New all-purpose *Fence*: why buy anything else?"

10. Political or activist concerns necessarily stand in an unpredictable relation to long-term canonicity; perhaps the best example of this phenomenon among American literary careers is that of Harriet Beecher Stowe.

11. Here again the particulars of Ashbery's (perceived) career and more general statements about the activity of writing blur together: while the copiousness of Ashbery's work hardly leads one to think of him as experiencing difficulty writing, the phrase "it's so difficult" more easily adheres to his work, which is resistant both to the local, readerly imposition of coherence and to the literary-historical narratives that seek to position Ashbery, whether as another "major poet" in the tradition or as a marker of some postmodern break. (Nonetheless, "first thought, best thought" is no part of the Ashbery aesthetic. Elsewhere in the poem he cautions, "Something else will break fruitfully / the allotted chain of associations, and it will serve as well—only don't try to pass it off as / an impulse, sincerity" (145). The warning advocates a poetry of association without the (Beat) rhetorical imperative behind it; without the investment in the unified, self-authorizing subject; and without the characteristically Beat refusal of revision.

12. To extend the avant-garde logic of "production for producers" is to see its utopian possibilities to change the social conditions under which some people write and others consume their writing, to make *everybody* a producer: to imagine a polis with a publisher in every neighborhood, people reading each other's work and talking about it, across the space where once stood the backyard fences. And the title of Poet or Writer would disappear. (Here I borrow a fantasy from Marx's *The German Ideology.* John Guillory discusses this particular "thought experiment" in his *Cultural Capital.*) This is not to claim that aesthetic distinctions and the arguments we have over them would vanish; rather, that such judgments would no longer be legitimized in terms of a particular stance vis-à-vis the laws of the market, and consequently the distinction between avant-garde and mainstream literary production would no longer be tenable.

13. "All the rest," one might say, "is literature": the distinction between literature and writing—visible in the figure of the short-story contestant—lies behind this passage. Ashbery, of course, is deeply familiar with the unrelenting attack on *literary* values that distinguished French modernism; in moments such as these his descent from this particular line is most apparent.

Works Cited

Altieri, Charles. *Self and Sensibility in Contemporary American Poetry.* New York: Cambridge University Press, 1984.

Ashbery, John. *Flow Chart.* New York: Alfred A. Knopf, 1991.

———. *Selected Poems.* New York: Viking, 1985.

———. *The Tennis Court Oath.* Middletown, Conn.: Wesleyan University Press, 1962.

Barthes, Roland. "The Death of the Author." *Modern Criticism and Theory.* Ed. David Lodge. New York: Longman, 1988. 167-72.

Beach, Christopher. *Poetic Culture: Contemporary American Poetry Between Community and Institution.* Evanston, Ill.: Northwestern University Press, 1999.

Bernstein, Charles. *A Poetics.* Cambridge, Mass.: Harvard University Press, 1992.

Blackmur, Richard. "Examples of Wallace Stevens." *The Double Agent: Essays in Craft and Elucidation.* Gloucester, Mass.: Peter Smith, 1962. 68-102.

Bourdieu, Pierre. *The Rules of Art.* Stanford: Stanford University Press, 1996.

Diepeveen, Leonard. *The Difficulties of Modernism.* New York: Routledge, 2002.

Evans, Steve. "Third Factory: Notes to Poetry IV.1 (1 January 2001)." <http://www.umit.maine.edu/~steven.evans/3F-1>.

Golding, Alan. *From Outlaw to Classic.* Madison: University of Wisconsin Press, 1995.

Guillory, John. *Cultural Capital.* Chicago: University of Chicago Press, 1993.

Hass, Robert. Introduction. *The Best American Poetry, 2001.* Ed. David Lehman. New York: Scribner, 2001. 17-21.

Hejinian, Lyn. "The Rejection of Closure." *The Language of Inquiry.* Berkeley: University of California Press, 2000. 40-58.

Kellogg, David. "The Self in the Poetic Field." *Fence* 3.2 (Fall/Winter 2000-2001): 97-108.

Lazer, Hank. *Opposing Poetries: Issues and Institutions.* Evanston: Northwestern University Press, 1996.

Lolordo, Vincent N. "A Handful of Specialists": Reading Modernist Difficulty. Ph.D. diss., Harvard University, 2001.

———. "Charting the Flow: John Ashbery and Literary History." 42.4 *Contemporary Literature* (Winter 2001): 750-54.

Newcomb, John. *Wallace Stevens and Literary Canons.* Jackson: University Press of Mississippi, 1992.

Perloff, Marjorie. "Pound/Stevens: Whose Era?" *New Literary History* 13 (1982): 485-510. Rpt. in *The Dance of the Intellect: Studies in the Poetry of the Pound Tradition.* Cambridge and New York: Cambridge University Press, 1985. 1-32.

Schuchard, Ronald, ed. *The Varieties of Metaphysical Poetry,* by T. S. Eliot. New York: Harcourt, Brace, 1993.

Smith, Hazel. *Hyperscapes in the Poetry of Frank O'Hara.* Liverpool: Liverpool University Press, 2000.

Stein, Gertrude. *Selected Writings of Gertrude Stein.* Ed. Carl Van Vechten. New York: Random House, 1962.

Steiner, George. *On Difficulty and Other Essays.* New York: Oxford University Press, 1978.

Stevens, Wallace. *The Collected Poems of Wallace Stevens.* New York: Alfred A. Knopf, 1954.

Williams, William Carlos. *The Autobiography of William Carlos Williams.* New York: Random House, 1951.

Wolff, Rebecca. "The Story of *Fence.*" *Jacket* 12 (2000). <http://jacketmagazine.com/16/index.html>.

Mark Silverberg (essay date spring 2003)

SOURCE: Silverberg, Mark. "Ashbery, O'Hara, and The Neo-Avant-Garde Manifesto." *Arizona Quarterly* 59, no. 1 (spring 2003): 137-65.

[*In the following essay, Silverberg investigates the predominant aesthetic theories of the 1950s and 1960s by comparing Ashbery's essay "The Invisible Avant-Garde" with Frank O'Hara's manifesto, "Personism."*]

> To be what people call anti-art is really to affirm art, in the same way that an atheist affirms God. The only way to be really anti-art is to be indifferent.
>
> Marcel Duchamp

This essay is part of a larger project which considers John Ashbery, Frank O'Hara, and the New York school poets in general, in light of discussions about the neo-avant-garde. Following the work of art critics like Hal Foster, I use the term neo-avant-garde to define those movements of the 1950s and '60s which both revive and revise the achievements of the so-called historical avant-garde (that is, the movements of the early part of the century such as futurism, dada, surrealism). These neo-avant-garde movements—New York school poetry, pop art, conceptual art, etc.—draw on the historical avant-garde's techniques such as collage, montage, assemblage, the readymade, but at the same time are extremely critical of what they came to understand as the avant-garde's ideological orientation, particularly in terms of its antagonistic or oppositional stance. This understanding of the avant-garde is historically specific to the United States in the 1950s and '60s where the avant-garde outsider—whether in the form of abstract expressionist Jackson Pollock, beat poet Allen Ginsberg, or movie star James Dean—was fast becoming an insider and trendsetter, as the mass media reduced cultural radicalism to lifestyle, celebrity, and fashion. At a time when "the break with tradition" had become the tradition and when avant-gardism was reduced to a consumer novelty, a new kind of aesthetic-ideological position needed to be found. In order to look more closely at the aesthetic ideologies of the period, this paper focuses on that genre where ideology is often most bluntly articulated: the manifesto.

* * *

In *Manifestoes: Provocations of the Modern* Janet Lyon argues that the manifesto is the signature genre for avant-garde groups since it is the form which most clearly links the aesthetic and political disruptions of these movements. This linkage can be seen in the way that members of the historical avant-garde adapted what was originally a political form of revolutionary discourse to "signal their own radical departures from bourgeois artistic forms and practices" (5). Lyon and before her Marjorie Perloff in *The Futurist Moment* (1986) outline many of the typical gestures and strategies of these early manifestoes: their heated, passionate, and often militaristic tones; their angry rejections of the past and calls for immediate action; and their ubiquitous use of the pronoun "we," a gesture which supposedly supports the manifesto's claim to speak for the people. Yet paradoxically, as Lyon notes, while many manifestoes claim to be egalitarian they "create audiences through a rhetoric of exclusivity" (2-3). While the putative purpose of many artistic manifestoes is to set out an aesthetic program, this aim often seems ancillary to the purpose of naming an enemy. Through an us-versus-them binary (variously manifested in the oppositional pairings of son/father, life/death, reality/illusion, present/past) the *new* art is contrasted with an *old* form which must be overthrown. Here, for example, is Marinetti's infamous 1909 *Manifesto of Futurism*:

> Up to now literature has exalted a pensive immobility, ecstasy, and sleep. We intend to exalt aggressive action, a feverish insomnia, the racer's stride, the mortal leap, the punch and the slap. . . . We will destroy the museums, libraries, academies of every kind, will fight moralism, feminism, every opportunistic or utilitarian cowardice. . . . We establish *Futurism*, because we want to free this land from its smelly gangrene of professors, archaeologists, *ciceroni* and antiquarians.

> (21, 22)

All these standard militaristic gestures ("the racer's stride, the mortal leap, the punch and the slap"), and many more like them, add up to an image of the avant-garde as an adversary culture, a culture of opposition. Moreover, as Marinetti makes amply clear, the avant-garde is a marginal culture that seeks to become central—to "establish" a new hegemony to replace the old.

This ideology of antagonism was exported from Europe to the United States (generally without its built-in subtleties, ironies, or contradictions) and adapted by the two most vocal and successful American avant-garde movements of the postwar years: abstract expressionism and beat poetry. It is against these movements and this particular image of the avant-garde as necessarily transgressive that John Ashbery, Frank O'Hara, and other New York school poets, formulated their own neo-avant-garde position.

The 1950s and '60s were a time of crisis and reformation for the avant-garde in America according to the most important critics of the day: Leslie Fiedler, Irving Howe, Lionel Trilling, Harold Rosenberg. With the unforeseen success of the avant-garde (figured in the "triumph" of abstract expressionism or the surprising attainments of "Howl," *On the Road,* and the beats in general) adversary culture was becoming popular culture, as corporate and consumer America went about the task of transforming radical art into a useable, saleable form of what Tom Wolfe called "radical chic." Thus Jackson Pollock was conscripted to promote Country Homes real estate and couturier fashion, and the once outcast beat writers were used to sell everything from pulp fiction paperbacks and Hollywood films to "beachnik" swimsuits.[1] Given these conditions, artistic antagonism of the kind expressed repeatedly by someone like Allen Ginsberg became self-parody, its gestures repeatedly reinscribing the dominant culture it sought to defeat. The New York school poets were well aware of the problem of appropriation by the culture industry and like their precursor, long time New York resident Marcel Duchamp, they chose to confront it through a strategy of indifference.

Such a strategy is perfectly illustrated by Duchamp's infamous ready-mades, mass-produced objects such as a urinal, snow shovel, or bottle drier, chosen without concern for aesthetic value but displayed in an institutionally authorized artistic site (a gallery or museum). The quality of these provocative objects that I am interested in here is their unique ability to be at once avant-garde (with its connotations of rebellious and new) and indifferent. In the context of the museum, these stubbornly neutral objects express a nonconfrontational but nonetheless powerful critique of dominant values of artistic personality, gesture, and taste. This critique is issued not through direct challenge but by opening a field of questions: Who should be accredited with making the urinal called *Fountain*? Marcel Duchamp? the J. L. Mott Iron Works from which he purchased it? or the Society for Independent Artists which originally rejected it for their New York show? And what does it mean that this readymade object is signed and dated by "R. Mutt"? and now displayed in several distinguished sites including the Museum of Modern Art in New York? Does this make it art? *Fountain* subtly undermines some of the most cherished ideas about art since Romanticism (individuality, craft, beauty) but does so with indifference, that is, without any of the fanfare or self-aggrandizing gestures of a Marinetti. Similarly, Duchamp's unexpected withdrawal from the art world (he quit painting in 1923, claiming he would spend the rest of his career playing chess) and his indifference to *success,* as it was and is commonly understood, stand as cool but effective critiques of the institution of art.[2]

The idea of a new "aesthetics of indifference" in American art of the 1950s was first described by Moira Roth in an influential 1977 essay in *Artforum.* Her article focuses on Duchamp as paterfamilias for a circle of artists centered around John Cage. This "Indifferent group" (36), which included Robert Rauschenberg, Merce Cunningham and Jasper Johns, along with Duchamp and Cage, produced an art "characterized by tones of neutrality, passivity, irony and, often, negation" (35). Roth understands their indifference as a response to the historical moment, "the political ambience of hysterical anti-Communism and right-wing action" in the McCarthy period. Their neutrality is seen as a hopeless hope, a last ditch option in resisting the "blind and ardent zeal" of the moment. Though unmentioned by Roth, such "right-wing action" was also, of course, expressed in the rampant homophobia of the period, an issue of particular relevance to these artists and a topic which Jonathan Katz takes up in a 1998 response to Roth. Katz's article complicates the earlier critic's position by examining the ways in which *difference* informed this artistic project of indifference. Like Roth, Katz argues that the artists of the Cage circle produced work "calibrated to survive Cold War America," but he reads such productions not as an aesthetic of indifference (which for Katz has politically defeatist overtones), but rather as a "politics of negation": "a strategy of queer resistance to a social context of control and constraint within a culture that offered little room to maneuver, especially for gay men" (51).

In this context, Katz is particularly interested in the telling silences of Cage's and Rauschenberg's work, since silence (an effective form of indifference) became part of a strategy for negotiating the particular dangers of self-expression and self-disclosure for gay artists in the 1950s. For Katz, Cage's notorious *4'33"* (1952), in which a performer sits silently at a piano for 4 minutes and 33 seconds, can be understood not only as a quiet musical critique of the concert hall (à la Duchamp), but also as a way of thematizing or performing the silence that "ensured survival" for homosexuals in the 1950s (Katz 53). Likewise Cage's "Lecture on Nothing," delivered to an audience of abstract expressionist aficionados in 1949 at the celebrated Artist's Club in New York, is both an "indifferent" response to the swaggering, macho seriousness of abstract expressionist art talk and an honest expression of what it was permissible to say at the time:

> I have nothing to say
> and I am saying it   and that is

> poetry   as I need it
> This space of time   is organized
> We need not fear these silences,—
> ....
> ....
> Nothing more than nothing can be said.
> Hearing   or making this in music   is not different
> —   only simpler—   than living this way.

> (109, 111)

In a similar vein, Cage's friend and collaborator Robert Rauschenberg thematizes and performs silence, while issuing an impassive critique in his neutral *White Paintings* of 1951 which were, as Katz notes, "the absolute negation of abstract expressionism in terms of mood, surface, color; a silencing of abstract expressionism, if you will" (65).[3]

In this essay I will build on the insights of both Roth and Katz, but at the same time keep in mind the context of aesthetic histories—that is, the relationship between the avant-garde and the neo-avant-garde and the implosion of avant-garde and commodity cultures in the 1960s. Ashbery and O'Hara produced their work not only because of restraints imposed on gay artists during "arguably the single most actively homophobic decade in American history" (Katz 53) but also because indifference or what I will call (following Ashbery) "independence" became for them the most forceful way to produce new and engaging art. In this sense, indifference to tradition was a way of carrying on an "avant-garde tradition" under a different name, stripped of those (authoritarian, hegemonic, heterosexist) elements which they found so problematic.

The last thing we would call most of the manifestoes of the historical avant-garde is indifferent. And this, Duchamp would argue, is one of their main problems, since to oppose in such a forceful way is necessarily to invest your adversary with power, to make him or her worthy of opposition. To be indifferent, on the other hand, is to express a self-contained disinterest which deprives opponents of their essential importance or seriousness by ignoring them. Such unconcern is, in fact, far more devastating than opposition could ever be.

I would like to proceed by examining two New York school documents as new kinds of manifestoes. While O'Hara's "Personism: A Manifesto" more explicitly states its ideological purpose in its title, Ashbery's **"The Invisible Avant-Garde"** also sets out a manifesto-like position. I do not want to suggest that these texts be viewed "in opposition" to earlier manifestoes, as further documents in a long chain of avant-garde advances through rejection. Instead, the "advance" of the New York school, if we can call it that, is one of awareness both of the strategies of avant-gardist opposition, and of the pitfalls of such a position in their own historical moment. The neo-avant-garde manifesto relies on and departs from older conventions, and it moves in both directions in an attempt not to defeat, but to escape from the problems and contradictions of the avant-garde position in America in the 1960s.

"THE INVISIBLE AVANT-GARDE"

Much of John Ashbery's most intriguing and revealing work is his writing about visual art. As David Bergman remarks in his introduction to **Reported Sightings,** a collection of thirty years of Ashbery's criticism, "Art writing has been a halfway point between the visual and the linguistic and often a place to explore ideas that make their way into the poems" (xii). Moreover, art writing has helped Ashbery, and colleagues such as O'Hara, Barbara Guest, James Schuyler, and Kenneth Koch who also worked regularly as art critics, to develop an aesthetic ideology which informs their poetry at a basic level. One of the things that separates the New York school from contemporary poetic movements like the beats or the confessional poets is a heightened self-consciousness, not only about their own writing, but about the *institution* of writing and what Peter Bürger in his *Theory of the Avant-Garde* calls "the institution of art" in general (lii). Long years of looking at and writing about visual art made these poets highly aware of the ways in which art is institutionalized. Their careers as critics and curators required them to think frequently and deeply about art's commerce with society in ways that would have been foreign to many of their poetic contemporaries. Thus, for these poets, the position they took on the institution of art in general—both within and outside of their poetry—was an essential ingredient to their identity as artists.

Such a position is formulated with unusual clarity (or at least an uncharacteristic lack of ambiguity for Ashbery) in **"The Invisible Avant-Garde,"** a lecture delivered in 1968 at the Yale Art School, and subsequently published in *ArtNews Annual.* While **"The Invisible Avant-Garde"** may not look like a traditional manifesto, it in fact functions in the same way. Like earlier manifestoes, it addresses a specific audience of artists and engages the primary question of artistic praxis: What to do next, how to make meaningful art in this moment given past and present constraints. It also, to a lesser extent than its predecessors, names an enemy—though here the ambiguity we expect from Ashbery is more in evidence, as we will see.

Ashbery begins by observing that in the present moment the avant-garde, which was supposed to be "the very antithesis of tradition" has in fact become "a tradition of sorts" (*RS* [*Reported Sightings*] 389). To make matters worse, the avant-garde has become the most fashionable and marketable tradition around. Thus, Ashbery ironically complains that "the avant-garde can now

barely exist because of the immense amounts of attention and money that are focused on it" (392). The co-option of the avant-garde by the forces of commercialism and by the "acceptance world" (Ashbery's term for a public which rushes to embrace anything that looks modern or scandalous) puts the young artist who wants to do something new in a particularly difficult quandary. For in doing something new and shocking in avant-garde custom, the young artist is liable to wind up "join-[ing] Andy Warhol and Viva and the rest of the avant-garde on *The Tonight Show*" (392).

Ashbery offers two possible solutions to this problem. The first is the way of the enigmatic Italian artist Giorgio de Chirico who, half way through his career, renounced the brilliant experimental work of his youth and became a traditional painter. Such a radical move (Ashbery claims the artist "passed from being one of the greatest painters of this century to a crotchety fabricator of bad pictures" [*RS* 391]) seems to suggest de Chirico's realization that when everyone begins to expect the unexpected, the only way to do something new is to do something old. At a time when it has become "safest to experiment" (393), the revolutionary artist must turn away from experimentation. This kind of reactionary solution is not a satisfactory option for Ashbery since it is ultimately a gesture of bad faith and an act of artistic self-denial:

> I would class de Chirico's late paintings as good traditional art, though as bad art, because they embrace a tradition which everything in the artist's career seemed to point away from, and which he therefore accepted because, no doubt, he felt as an avant-garde artist that only the unacceptable is acceptable.
>
> (392)

The other option that Ashbery offers is to combat acceptance not by turning against it, not by doing the opposite of what's expected, but simply by ignoring it:

> The Midas-like position into which our present acceptance-world forces the avant-garde is actually a disguised blessing which previous artists have not been able to enjoy, because it points the way out of the predicament it sets up—that is, towards an attitude which neither accepts nor rejects acceptance but is independent of it.
>
> (394)

The advantage artists have today is that they are acutely conscious of the often insidious ways art is institutionalized and commercialized in the culture of late capitalism where aesthetic production, as Fredric Jameson notes, "has become integrated into commodity production generally" (4). And this awareness allows artists to develop a theory and practice that takes this situation of "the increasingly essential structural function and position of aesthetic innovation and experimentation" (5) into account. This is exactly what the New York school poets tried to do in developing an aesthetic of independence or indifference as an antidote to the sudden co-option and consumability of the avant-garde.

Ashbery provides several models for this kind of aesthetic indifference. An article for *ArtNews Annual* in 1966 locates a group of such independent artists in those Americans who have abandoned New York for the "privacy and isolation" of Paris: "The Americans in Paris are permanently out of fashion, first ahead of it and now behind it, without ever having gone through an intervening period of acceptance," Ashbery observes in **"American Sanctuary in Paris"** (**RS** 87-88). And this aloofness may account for a particularly engaging quality in their work:

> It is as though they had given up all efforts at trying to please a public, whether French or American, and had gone back to pleasing themselves. For once, you don't have the feeling that the artist is breathing down your neck, or that you are catching the work in a split-second of its trajectory from easel to gallery to museum.

(88)

Ashbery has made a career of collecting models for this kind of aesthetic independence. His interest in painters like Parmigianino, de Chirico, and Michaux; in musicians like Busoni, Satie, and Cage; and in undiscovered writers such as John Clare, David Schubert, John Wheelwright, and Henry Darger all support a fascination with the outsider, the artist who doesn't buck, but *ignores* all current trends. Ashbery has very much incorporated this model of independence into his own poetic practice, as will be examined shortly through a reading of the title poem of his first major collection, *Some Trees* (1956).

Before turning to this poem, we need to look a little closer at the relationship of **"The Invisible Avant-Garde"** to the traditional manifesto in order to understand the basis for Ashbery's aesthetic. As suggested previously, a key role for the manifestoes of the historical avant-garde was to name an enemy in order to set up a self/other dichotomy for self-justification. Ashbery does essentially the same thing, though his enemy is much subtler than the traditional target of avant-gardist attack. In Ashbery's manifesto the enemy is acceptance, and this is a tricky adversary since it no longer looks like an enemy, but instead like a supporter. Such an opponent provides its attack not through indifference or hostility, but by "the efficacious means of over-encouragement" (**RS** 91). Thus the paradox: "Before they [the avant-garde] were fighting against general neglect, even hostility, but this seemed like a natural thing and therefore the fight could be carried on in good faith. Today one must fight acceptance which is much harder because it seems that one is fighting

oneself" (**RS** 393). If the enemy is acceptance, fashion, noise, and acclaim, one way it might be fought, Ashbery seems to be suggesting, is through neutrality, independence, reticence, and secrecy. Ashbery notes that "the period of neglect for an avant-garde artist has shrunk for each generation," so that now "it is no longer possible, or it *seems* no longer possible, for an important avant-garde artist to go unrecognized. And, sadly enough, his creative life expectancy has dwindled correspondingly, since artists are no fun once they have been discovered" (392). I have italicized the word *seems* to suggest that here we find the program Ashbery will follow. He will attempt, though various strategies, to be unrecognized or, more accurately, to produce poetry that is *unrecognizable*. If the artist cannot remain undiscovered, this program suggests, he can at least write poetry that is *undiscoverable,* that refuses to be easily assimilated or *absorbed* (to use a term of Charles Bernstein's) and thus resists commodification.[4] We turn, then, to the title poem of Ashbery's first collection in search of these strategies of reticence.

Like most of Ashbery's poems, **"Some Trees"** is an elusive, mysterious piece, and it claims that mysteriousness (or impermeability in Bernstein's sense) quite consciously as a poetic strategy. Instead of being shocking in the old avant-garde manner (like Kurt Schwitter's Merz poetry, Hugo Ball's sound poems, Tristan Tzara's cut-ups or, for that matter, Allen Ginsberg's "Howl"), **"Some Trees"** is enigmatic and reticent.[5] It chooses a strategy of secrecy which, rather than provoking the reader, resists his or her understanding. As the final poem of this volume suggests, "All beauty, resonance, integrity, / Exist by deprivation or logic / Of strange position" (**"Le livre est sur la table,"** *Mooring* [*The Mooring of Starting Out*] 56). Here is the "logic of strange position" called **"Some Trees"**:

> These are amazing: each
> Joining a neighbor, as though speech
> Were a still performance.
> Arranging by chance
>
> To meet as far this morning
> From the world as agreeing
> With it, you and I
> Are suddenly what the trees try
>
> To tell us we are:
> That their merely being there
> Means something; that soon
> We may touch, love, explain.
>
> And glad not to have invented
> Such comeliness, we are surrounded:
> A silence already filled with noises,
> A canvas on which emerges
>
> A chorus of smiles, a winter morning.
> Placed in a puzzling light, and moving,

Our days put on such reticence
These accents seem their own defense.

(*Mooring* 37)

"Some Trees" is about communion, but who or what is communing, and what the nature of their communication is, remains concealed. Ashbery begins, in what will become a signature gesture, with the ambiguous pronoun "These."[6] Readers may resolve the ambiguity by assuming "these" are the trees (which would follow the rhythmical logic of the poem), but such a resolution leaves many questions. How, for example, is the trees' speech "a still performance"? And what, moreover, are these trees "trying" (notice the Frost-like reticence here) to say? Certainly, the trees' message seems of ontological importance, since it claims to tell "us" *who we are.* Such information might be useful both for the self-knowledge of the poem's "us," and for the critical appreciation of the poem's readers, who remain unsure of the identity of this ambiguous "us."

These uncertainties in the poem are compounded by a number of willful paradoxes and contradictions. How can one arrange, for example, to meet by chance, when such an intention would defeat the random nature of the meeting? How, also, would one meet "as far . . . from the world as agreeing with it," when these positions imply both distance and closeness? Readers might also wonder if "a silence already filled with noises" can still be recognized as a silence. These are not contradictions to be solved, but savored; they are part of the oddly inviting impermeability that absorbs so many of Ashbery's readers.[7] These discrepancies do not suggest discord, but rather an accord which is strangely unplaceable, one of rhythm rather than reason. Thus the last couplet follows a kind of logic of mystery, a logic which seeks to hide as much as to reveal:

Our days put on such reticence
These accents seem their own defense.

The "accents of reticence," words which conceal their meaning in the very act of giving it expression, are the tones which inform "Some Trees." Such tones may remind readers of another gesture of simultaneous defense and revelation from the title poem of a later volume, *Self-Portrait in a Convex Mirror.* Here, in describing Parmigianino's elusive self portrait, Ashbery is also creating a self portrait of his writerly aesthetic:

As Parmigianino did it, the right hand
Bigger than the head, thrust at the viewer
And swerving easily away, as though to protect
What it advertises. A few leaded panes, old beams,
Fur, pleated muslin, a coral ring run together
In a movement supporting the face, which swims
Toward and away like the hand
Except that it is in repose. It is what is
Sequestered. . . .

. . . .
But there is in that gaze a combination
Of tenderness, amusement and regret, so powerful
In its restraint that one cannot look for long.
The secret is too plain. . . .

(*Self-Portrait* [*Self-Portrait in a Convex Mirror*] 68-69)

What is the "plain" secret (notice again the conjunction of revelation and concealment) facing us in Parmigianino's gaze and in Ashbery's poems? What is being "protected" in the painter's ambiguous gesture and in the "accents of reticence" which compose "Some Trees"?

According to critics such as John Shoptaw and Vernon Shetley, there is something very specific at stake which needs protection. Both read "Some Trees" as a hesitant love poem which "exhibits the caution attendant upon unsanctioned behavior" (Shoptaw 22). On this reading, the poem's reticence marks the desire it dare not speak aloud under the regime of homophobia and surveillance in which it was written. Although neither critic mentions it, the work of Jacob Stockinger, who coined the term "homotextuality," would also support this interpretation. Stockinger's article identifies a number of textual features as commonalties of homosexual literary expression. He notes: "the most frequent type of homotextual space is the closed and withdrawn place that is transformed from stigmatizing into redeeming space" (144). These free spaces can also take the form of "the open country side, which is privileged space for the homosexual because it marks both his ostracism and the chance to recuperate his 'unnatural' love in nature" (144). While I find Shetley's and Shoptaw's observations convincing and pertinent, I also think that ultimately we need to give a wider berth of interpretation to Ashbery's interest in concealment.

We must begin by asking who the "you and I" of "Some Trees" refer to. Like so many of Ashbery's "characters" (or more properly pronouns), "you and I" remain ambiguous. While they might refer to homosexual lovers, "you and I" might also refer to reader and author. On this reading, the arranged chance meeting is the encounter of the poem itself, a space that "surrounds" and includes both reader and author: "A silence already filled with noises, / A canvas on which emerges / A chorus of smiles. . . ." What is being protected is more than a secret human love affair, it is also a love affair with language, a poetic process that is unwilling to reduce poems to paraphrasable meanings and simultaneously to consumable products. Through concealment, reticence, and the logic of mystery, Ashbery protects his own poetry from the closure and co-option of a "final" reading. Through this indeterminacy Ashbery also protects his work against the pitfalls of the contemporary avant-garde, against a public eager for artistic products and personalities to consume, a public only too willing to accept the unacceptable. This approach adds to

Shoptaw's or Shetley's insights by suggesting that Ashbery makes the need for concealment into an aesthetic which reaches beyond the very real imperatives of expressing (and concealing) homosexual desire. The need for reticence, secrecy, and independence at the root of **"Some Trees"** reaches up into desires which are both physical and metaphysical. Such reticence is an embodiment of Ashbery's neo-avant-garde aesthetic which replaces the imperatives of shock and rebellion with the principles of withdrawal and indifference. It will be immediately obvious to readers that such reticence is *not* the style of Frank O'Hara. Next, we will turn to O'Hara's manifesto and examine how this poet uses strategies of comedy and camp to achieve a similar goal of dodging the "acceptance world" and creating a space for artistic independence.

PERSONISM: A MANIFESTO

. . . the fact that you move so beautifully more or less takes care of Futurism.

Frank O'Hara, "Having a Coke With You"

The story of the composition of O'Hara's infamous poetic manifesto is a perfect illustration of the myths of his writing method and of the program he sets out—half jokingly, half in earnest—in the manifesto itself. According to his lover and roommate Joe LeSueur, O'Hara wrote "Personism" in less than an hour, with a bourbon and water in hand and Rachmaninoff's Third blaring on the radio. The piece was requested by Don Allen for the "Statements" section of *The New American Poetry* and, after much procrastination, O'Hara finally sat down to write it with his editor on the way across town to pick it up (Gooch 338-39). The manifesto was eventually rejected by Allen, who felt that its aesthetics did not apply to all of O'Hara's work.[8] This was an unfortunate choice, since there is in fact a widely encompassing program hiding behind O'Hara's typically flippant and whimsical prose.

"Personism" is both comical and serious, and in fact posits "the comic" as a serious poetic position—an important New York school stance in general and a key characteristic of the discourse known as camp. For all of the New York school poets, comedy is a way of deflating pretentiousness and challenging what they saw as the polemical seriousness of so much contemporary writing. Such seriousness, as far as O'Hara and his colleagues were concerned, had become institutionalized not only with the New Critics but also with many groups who challenged the New Critics. As "Personism" declares:

Too many poets act like a middle-aged mother trying to get her kids to eat too much cooked meat, and potatoes with drippings (tears). I don't give a damn whether they eat or not. Forced feeding leads to exces-

sive thinness (effete). Nobody should experience anything they don't need to, if they don't need poetry bully for them. I like movies too.

(CP [*The Collected Poems of Frank O'Hara*] 498)

Humor is a way of withdrawing the force feeding hand, of suggesting that poetry need not be somber nor, for that matter, culturally central (as many poets of O'Hara's day tacitly or openly insisted). Poetry, as "Personism" both states and shows, can also be fun: "And after all," O'Hara continues, "only Whitman and Crane and Williams, of the American poets, are better than the movies" (498). Comparing poetry to the movies (which still had the taint of popular culture or kitsch) as opposed to, say, associating it with the very life breath of humanity, as Charles Olson does in probably the most famous manifesto of that decade, "Projective Verse," is to radically deflate the high style and dogmatism of most poetic manifestoes. It is also a way of bridging the gap that Andreas Huyssen calls the "Great Divide" between high art and mass culture.

This is how Olson begins "Projective Verse": "Verse now, 1950, if it is to go ahead, if it is to be of *essential* use, must, I take it, catch up and put into itself certain laws and possibilities of the breath, of the breathing of the man who writes as well as of his listenings" (147). He goes on to proclaim that "the poem itself must, at all points, be a high energy-construct and, at all points, an energy-discharge" (148). The textual and, for that matter, sexual politics of these lines—with their emphasis on manly energies and discharges—probably both amused and annoyed O'Hara for whom Olson becomes something of a synecdoche for a macho seriousness in verse. As Cage and Rauschenberg staged their own art of indifference—silent music, "unexpressive" white paintings—against the macho seriousness and affected authenticity of abstract expressionism, so O'Hara and colleagues position different types of neutral or ironic practices against various forms of "authentic" speech (the projective) and naturalized sincerity (the confessional). It is against these variously "committed" and naturalized positions that Personism stakes its camp poetics and politics.

In a 1965 interview, O'Hara complains that Olson (and we must remember that Olson's dominant position makes him an easy synecdoche for a more general and widespread stance towards poetry) is too "conscious of the Pound heritage and of saying the important utterance, which . . . is not particularly desirable most of the time" (Lucie-Smith 13). Straining for the "important utterance," an occupation so evident in Olson's polemical essays and in poems like the *Maximus* series, is a way of positing poetry as an unremittingly serious and (here the gender politics come in) manly business. Indeed Michael Davidson argues that the poetics and politics of "Projective Verse" (and of the Black

Mountain school in general) was underwritten by a "compulsory homosociality": "a group ethos of male solidarity and sodality that often betrayed homophobic qualities" (198). A comparison of the rhetoric of "Projective Verse" and "Personism" is quite revealing. Here Olson barks orders about prosody as though he were some kind of Poundian poetic drill sergeant:

> ONE'S PERCEPTIONS MUST IMMEDIATELY AND DIRECTLY LEAD TO A FURTHER PERCEPTION. It means exactly what it says, is a matter of, at *all* points (even, I should say, of our management of daily reality as of the daily work) get on with it, keep moving, keep in, speed, the nerves, their speed, the perceptions, theirs, the acts, the split second acts, the whole business, keep it moving as fast as you can, citizen. And if you also set up as a poet, USE, USE, USE the process at all points, in any given poem always, always one perception must must must MOVE, INSTANTER, ON ANOTHER!
>
> (149)

Here, in contrast, are O'Hara's audacious, campy notes on prosody:

> As for measure and other technical apparatus, that's just common sense: if you're going to buy a pair of pants you want them to be tight enough so everyone will want to go to bed with you. There's nothing metaphysical about it.
>
> (*CP* 498)

For O'Hara the "important utterance" and "other technical apparatus" are not particularly desirable because they are constricting (though not in the *good* way of tight pants). Rather, they constrict because they deprive poetry of humor, pleasure, and breadth by confining it to a limited space (Pound's laundry list of "Don'ts", Olson's rules "for only he, the *man* who writes" [150]). Such guidelines are, in essence, elitist forms of control which claim a monopoly over culture. Ideas are important to O'Hara and his New York school colleagues, but they are not the *only* important thing: "I'm not saying that I don't have practically the most lofty ideas of anyone writing today," O'Hara records, "but what difference does that make? They're just ideas. The only good thing about it is that when I get lofty enough I've stopped thinking and that's when refreshment arrives" (*CP* 498). Restrictive rules and serious commitments, which are usually the essence of the traditional manifesto, become the target of satire, and indeed the "enemy" in O'Hara's new manifesto:

> I don't believe in god, so I don't have to make elaborately sounded structures. . . . I don't even like rhythm, assonance, all that stuff. You just go on your nerve. If someone's chasing you down the street with a knife you just run, you don't turn around and shout, "Give it up! I was a track star for Mineola Prep."
>
> (498)

The idea of an aesthetics (and perhaps a politics) of "nerve," presented half-seriously in the above quotation, is worth pausing over because it provides an important key to O'Hara's particular brand of indifference. I would like to read "go[ing] on your nerve" as a queer, camp-inflected version of the dominant avant-garde idea of "risk." While risk implies seriousness, challenge, and certainty, nerve implies jittery uncertainty, a playful impudence. The abstract expressionists, who talked about "risk" constantly, imagined themselves as frontiersmen in the artistic world of conformity. To risk was to reject the current style (in this case the homespun American Regionalism of artists like Pollock's teacher, Thomas Hart Benton) in favor of one's own vision. It was to create something new, as if from scratch—not from past models but from some unnameable interior source. Thus Barnett Newman's claim: "We [abstract expressionists] are freeing ourselves of the impediments of memory, association, nostalgia, legend, myth, or what have you, that have been the devices of Western European painting. Instead of making *cathedrals* out of Christ, man, or 'life,' we are making it [sic] out of ourselves, out of our own feelings" (127). The artist "at risk" is also, ironically, the artist who *knows* he's right, *knows* that he is ahead of his time—thus the egomaniacal tendencies of artists like Jackson Pollock and Ezra Pound. In other words, with "risk" usually goes a kind of authoritarian elitism—the belief that the artist is right and the "mass of dolts" Pound called the general public is lagging far behind. In O'Hara's canny image, the artist at risk is the one likely to shout "Give it up! I was a track star for Mineola Prep" because of his narcissistic belief that he can convince all opponents of his superiority. The nervy artist, on the other hand, just runs. He "lives on his nerves," not openly challenging but rather disregarding the opponent, simply vacating the scene before the conflict emerges. In place of the macho artist at risk, O'Hara imagines a queer artist of nerves who works spontaneously, intuitively, often flippantly, as all the New York school poets habitually did. In fact, as Duchamp has already suggested, such a practitioner who simply ignores or turns his back on the rules of the game is more likely to "touch a nerve" than the next in a long line of avant-garde heirs apparent. Nervy art makes people nervous, and this is one important way of understanding the early dismissive treatment of almost all New York school work.[9] Part of this nervousness, I suspect, derives from the realization that the nervy artist is not *only* being flip. Like the "serious" art of the avant-garde, there is an important element of challenge to "nervy" art—but this challenge is implicit rather than explicit. Instead of openly opposing the dominant mode, nervy art chooses a position of indifference because, as Ashbery notes, "when you get to a situation where everybody is a subversive, sabotage becomes status quo" (*RS* 250). Instead of the overt sabotage of an Allen Ginsberg, O'Hara opts for a provoking indifference, as Ashbery has suggested:

Frank O'Hara's poetry has no program and therefore cannot be joined. It does not advocate sex and dope as a panacea for the ills of modern society; it does not speak out against the war in Vietnam or in favor of civil rights; it does not paint gothic vignettes of the post-Atomic Age: in a word, it does not attack the establishment. It merely ignores its right to exist, and is thus a source of annoyance for partisans of every stripe.

("Frank O'Hara's Question" 6)

At a time when poetry was distinguished by a variety of resolutions and obligations (while the Black Mountain, beat, confessional, feminist, and black arts movements produced very different kinds of poetry, they are all marked by a serious, often solemn, rhetoric of commitment), O'Hara's nervy art looks particularly impertinent. O'Hara rejected overt, public, then-called "political" resolutions in favor of covert personal commitments and tastes. This is why when it first appeared his work seemed irrelevant to many critics—the "vagrant letters and lunch-napkin scribbles" of "a whimsically charming gadfly," as one reviewer put it (Bell 38). What Bell and others were missing were the "exacting sobrieties" (39) necessary for serious poetry. Of course since that time readers have come to see in O'Hara's writing what Kenneth Koch once called "an inspired irrelevance which turns out to be relevant" (*Art of Poetry* 21). Ashbery comments on the same phenomena when he describes the form of an O'Hara poem as "a bag into which anything is dumped and ends up belonging there" (*CP* ix). What we find in O'Hara, finally, is not a lack of commitment, but commitments of unsuspected kinds: to the local, particular, and eccentric; to movie theaters, bars, and public washrooms; to "aspirin tablets, Good Teeth buttons, and water pistols" (Koch, *Art of Poetry* 21).

In the visual arts, Rauschenberg and other "assemblage" artists were following a similar path: rejecting suitable material for serious painting, and instead making "combine paintings" from daily objects and handy junk. (Old bedding, broken furniture, soda bottles, scrap paper, used tires, and stuffed animals are a few of the most famous of Rauschenberg's materials.) While artists like Rauschenberg, Richard Stankiewicz, and John Chamberlain were interested in rusted and raw materials (which had a "gestural" look similar to the abstract expressionists), O'Hara's nervy aesthetic was closer in some ways to pop art which incorporated all kinds of gaudy, commercial, mass-produced, poetically inappropriate junk as artistic material.[10] In one of his earliest published poems, "Today" (1950), O'Hara asserts the importance of the quotidian and the irreverent:

Oh! kangaroos, sequins, chocolate sodas!
You really are beautiful! Pearls,
harmonicas, jujubes, aspirins! all
the stuff they've always talked about

still makes a poem a surprise!
These things are with us every day
even on beachheads and biers. They
do have meaning. They're strong as rocks.

(*CP* 18)

This poetics of inclusiveness, which finds its literary precursor in William Carlos Williams, takes Williams a step further by carrying his prerogative to use the commonplace and mundane into the area of mass culture and the sensibility of camp. "Today"'s affirmation of "things" is reminiscent of a similar assertion by Williams in the opening poem of his first modern collection, "Pastoral" from *Al Que Quiere!* (1917):

When I was younger
it was plain to me
I must make something of myself.
Older now
I walk back streets
admiring houses
of the very poor:
roof out of line with sides
the yards cluttered
with old chicken wire, ashes,
furniture gone wrong;
the fences and outhouses
built of barrel-staves
and parts of boxes, all,
if I am fortunate,
smeared a bluish green
that properly weathered
pleases me best
of all colors.

No one
will believe this
of vast import to the nation.

(*Selected Poems* 15)

The distance between Williams and O'Hara can be measured in the leap from the working class dignity of "Pastoral"'s chicken wire, ashes, and furniture gone wrong to the impertinent sequins, sodas, and jujubes of "Today." Nonetheless, both are committed to a poetics of inclusion—or perhaps a poetics *against* certain kinds of *discrimination* (whether Eurocentric and Eliotic, or heterosexist and Olsonian)—that allowed for a significant "loosening up" in verse which both Williams and O'Hara initiated in their respective days. O'Hara's particular aesthetic of inclusion opened a space not only for a wider range of post-Williamsian/postmodern "things," but also for a new kind of attention to persons. For along with the cheeseburgers, chocolate malteds, papaya juice and poodles in cabs, O'Hara's poems are also populated by people or, more properly, by *names* of the famous, the near-famous, and those who are about to get their five minutes of fame. O'Hara's New York circle of artistic colleagues, lovers, and friends, and the heightened economy of gossip in which all their names circulate, help form the background for the Personist manner which O'Hara's manifesto inaugurates, and to which we will now return.

* * *

Though many critics have discussed "Personism," noting its combination of sincerity and satire, few have tried to seriously understand the nature of the program it half-seriously advances.[11] This is natural, perhaps, given the fact that O'Hara provides so many contradictory signals—offering an idea with one hand only to withdraw or undercut it with the other:

> Abstraction in poetry, which Allen [Ginsberg] recently commented on in *It Is,* is intriguing. . . . Abstraction (in poetry, not in painting) involves personal removal by the poet. . . . Personism, a movement which I recently founded and which nobody knows about, interests me a great deal, being so totally opposed to this kind of abstract removal that it is verging on a true abstraction for the first time, really, in the history of poetry. . . . Personism has nothing to do with philosophy, it's all art. It does not have to do with personality or intimacy, far from it! But to give you a vague idea, one of its minimal aspects is to address itself to one person (other than the poet himself), thus evoking overtones of love without destroying love's life-giving vulgarity, and sustaining the poet's feelings towards the poem while preventing love from distracting him into feeling about the person. That's part of Personism. It was founded by me after lunch with LeRoi Jones on August 27, 1959, a day in which I was in love with someone (not Roi, by the way, a blond). I went back to work and wrote a poem for this person. While I was writing it I was realizing that if I wanted to I could use the telephone instead of writing the poem, and so Personism was born.

>   (*CP* 498-99)

The program of "Personism," which so much of O'Hara's best poetry bears out, is the requirement to write *as if* one were speaking to one other person. It is a stance of conscious artifice. Personism claims to be both opposed to abstraction and truly abstract. It achieves this contradictory feat by basing itself on that least abstract of occasions—the relationship of one individual to another—but also by *abstracting* this relationship from the real world and recomposing it into a poetic relationship. Thus the Personist poem *sounds* personal and intimate, by "evoking overtones of love," but these are just evocations, just material to be manipulated. This removed or abstract use of love, intimacy, and friendship as material allows for a "sustaining [of] the poet's feelings *towards the poem* while preventing love from distracting him into feeling *about the person*" (499, emphasis added). The thing about a Personist poem is that it could be a telephone call (it sounds like that kind of personal, chatty discourse) but it isn't a phone call. Personism was "born" of the decision to write instead of to call, but to make the writing sound like calling. This kind of self-

consciously "intimate" talk (which puts its own discourse, always, between quotation marks) is one of O'Hara's major bequests to twentieth-century poetry. With O'Hara's voice was born the discourse of being "perfectly frank" as Ted Berrigan once put it, with its duplicitous mix of intimacy, openness, and artifice. For ultimately being perfectly frank means being many different things (convincingly!) to many different people.[12]

Personism can also be seen, in a similar way to Ashbery's tactics of reticence and secrecy, as part of a neo-avant-garde project of independence or indifference. While other movements of the time were keenly interested in building public audiences—in speaking to and for a larger group—Personism plans to neglect the public, and in fact to neglect the whole institution or industry of poetry by concentrating instead on one other individual: "It puts the poem squarely between the poet and the person, Lucky Pierre style, and the poem is correspondingly gratified. The poem is at last between two persons instead of two pages" (*CP* 499). Within O'Hara's camp is a new stance, a new way of understanding to whom a poem should speak. Simply talking to one other individual, instead of assuming a poem should speak to many, may be a way, "Personism" tacitly suggests, to defend against the pitfalls of cooption and consumption which were frequently the fates of the postwar avant-garde.

Given all this talk about the intimate and the personal, O'Hara is careful to delimit here, and elsewhere, that Personism is very different from another kind of personal poetry that will later be labeled "confessional." Thus the exclamation: "It does not have to do with personality or intimacy, far from it!" In an interview O'Hara makes clear his attitude towards Robert Lowell and the confessional poem: "I think Lowell has . . . a confessional manner which [lets him] get away with things that are really just plain bad but you're supposed to be interested because he's supposed to be so upset" (Lucie-Smith 13). Despite some claims to the contrary, confessional poetry is essentially a public mode of discourse. It derives its charge and its meaning from breaking the taboo of disclosing private matter in a public forum (we must remember or imagine a time when the personal revelations of a Lowell or Sexton were truly shocking instead of routine poetic content or the daily fare of confessional talk shows). The confessional poem depends on an audience of onlookers or overhearers to feel reverent horror at the agonies of the poet. It works, in other words, on good old-fashioned shock value. The Personist poem, on the other hand, acts with indifference. It is written as though it truly doesn't matter if anyone other than the recipient is reading or listening. One Personist poem, "A Letter to Bunny" (1950), written to O'Hara's friend and muse Bunny Lang, attests to this focus on the singular recipient:

When anyone reads this but you it begins
to be lost. My voice is sucked into a thousand
ears and I don't know whether I'm weakened.
Bunny, when I ran to you in the summer
night and upset us both it was mostly this,
though you thought I was going away. See?
I'm away now, but I'm here.

(*CP* 23)

Like many of O'Hara's poems, "A Letter to Bunny" creates a world which seems intensely private by representing an imagined interpersonal intimacy, an intimacy whose substance, ultimately, is literary. On one hand readers are made to feel that they are part of O'Hara's life, that they are being given personal, confidential access. At the same time, however, they are constantly reminded of their distance from his life. After all, we really don't *know* Bunny (or, for that matter, Larry or Bill or Joan or Jean-Paul)—and the fact that these are real people makes our fictive knowledge of them that much less stable. Part of O'Hara's genius was for creating provocative collisions between these kinds of real and constructed intimacy. It is this tension, the *frisson* of intimacy and distance ("I'm away now, but I'm here") which gives the poetry its unique charge.

Instead of writing against the grain of approval, as Ginsberg does in "Howl" or "America," poems which are set in opposition to "an America gone mad with materialism, a police-state America, a sexless and soulless America" (333) or as Lowell did in 1959 when he brought out *Life Studies* against the best advice of supporters like Allen Tate, O'Hara in "Personism" takes up a stance which, in Ashbery's words "neither accepts nor rejects acceptance but is independent of it." "Howl" and *Life Studies,* for all their reliance on the personal and intimate, are finally public provocations, as the *Howl* obscenity trial and the uproar over Lowell ruining his career with *Life Studies* indicate. In contrast, a poem like "A Letter to Bunny" (which was quite possibly never even intended for publication) declines to speak to or for a greater public; it declines to engage in any kind of debate.

And yet, as O'Hara feared as early as 1950, his voice (like Ashbery's) has been "sucked into a thousand ears"—which begs the poet's own question: has it been weakened? As I suggested at the beginning of this essay, the New York school poets were keenly aware of the potential fate of the avant-garde artist in the era of promotional capitalism. O'Hara knew well from Pollock and Warhol about the transformation of radical art into radical chic. While O'Hara and Ashbery have indeed been "sucked into a thousand ears" of both academic and non-academic auditors they have not been weakened precisely because of their stance of indifference which allows for unique composure even in the face of success.

O'Hara's indifference evolves partly in balancing the public and the private: "We troupers in private know / all about carnival gestures," notes "A Letter to Bunny" (22). The Personist poem, with its flagrant carnival gestures (collapsing Lana Turners like Warhol's multiple Marilyns) and ostensible intimacy ("When anyone reads this but you it begins, / to be lost") is able to enjoy the best of both the public and private worlds, but not succumb to the pitfalls of either. It is a form that implies incomparable presence (voice, self, personality), but at the same time by foregrounding its own artifice it subverts a readerly/consumerist desire for well-packaged, well-marketed presence (à la Ginsberg). Like Ashbery's "shield of a greeting," O'Hara's Personism gives readers "personality" and "presence" with one hand, only to remove them with the other: "I'm away now, but I'm here." This duplicity in Ashbery and O'Hara helps account for the fact that both poets are able to stand as perfect representatives for the Don Allen New American poetry camp (representing a poetics of presence and expressivism) and as crucial precursors for Language poetry with its fundamental challenge to presence, personality, and expressivism. The artifice of indifference helps keep these positions balanced, when we understand indifference not as rejection, but as a viable way to be present *in* language or *with* language without subscribing to a self-aggrandizing "poetics of presence," the too often heard rhetorics of authenticity or revolt that characterized so much of the New American poetry. Indifference allows Ashbery and O'Hara to stake a queer and unstable position beyond the temptations and dangers of "radical" art.

Thanks to Tenney Nathanson and Nick Lolordo for their careful readings and helpful suggestions with drafts of this paper.

Notes

1. See Guilbaut (185) for an analysis of how Country Homes of Tarrytown, New York, used Pollock to help sell luxury housing development units. Guilbaut argues that Pollock was "domesticated by the system of fashion" which made his paintings and himself into desirable commodities (87). This kind of domestication is vividly illustrated in the 1 March 1951 issue of *Vogue* magazine which included a four page fashion spread of models displayed against a backdrop of Pollock canvases. See Hobbs (156-57) for a discussion of the commodification of the Beats and their adoption by television (*Dobie Gillis*), radio soap opera (*Helen Trent*), pulp fiction (*Beatnik Party*) and movies (*The Beat Generation*).

2. We must keep in mind that this is a stance or artifice of indifference. Duchamp was not actually indifferent to the museum. Rather, he chose indifference (as Cage later chose silence) as the most effective way of expressing his concern.

3. Katz's insights into the *White Paintings* are particularly applicable here: "The fact that these paintings were not discussed at the time as oppositional is evidence of their successful incorporation of a politics negation, for oppositionality here lies less in their legibility as acts of resistance than in their indecidable status . . . In a sense, they are absolutely indifferent, but that indifference in turn could, as was in fact the case, spark a wholesale revaluation of hegemonic art practices" (65-66).

4. See Bernstein, particularly the section "Absorption and Impermeability" (18-89). "Canada does not wish to be absorbed into the U.S. / cultural orbit any more than Quebec wishes to be / absorbed by Canada; but then Quebec feminists may not / want to be absorbed by a male-dominated 'free' Quebec. / Identity seems to involve the refusal to be absorbed / in a larger identity . . ." (20). A potential problem with the argument for Ashbery's resistance to commodification is the fact that he has undeniably been absorbed into the academy. As Nick Lolordo has noted in an article on Ashbery's canonical and historical position: "At the present moment, Ashbery appears to have been to the second half of the twentieth century what Eliot was to the first: the most universally acknowledged poet writing in English" (755). As I will argue at the end of this essay, the artifice of indifference allows Ashbery (as it has Duchamp) to maintain a crucial independence regardless of his acceptance by the academy.

5. For details on the philosophy and tactics of "shocking" poetry see Kuenzli. A perfect illustration of the commodification of the avant-garde is the transformation of Tzara's famous recipe for the production of a dadaist poem into a popular novelty item of the 1990s called Magnetic Poetry™. Tzara's original text is as follows:

> To make a dadaist poem
> Take a newspaper.
> Take a pair of scissors.
> Choose an article as long as you are planning to make your poem.
> Cut out the article.
> Then cut out each of the words that make up this article and put them in
> a bag.
> Shake it gently.
> Then take out the scraps one after the other in the order in which they
> left the bag.
> Copy conscientiously.
> The poem will be like you.
> And here you are a writer, infinitely original and endowed with a sensibility that is charming though beyond the understanding of the vulgar.
>
> (qtd. in Kuenzli 58)

Typically, Magnetic Poetry™ takes Tzara's ironic conceptual piece quite literally, offering for a mere twenty dollars a little box of magnetized pre-cut up words which can be assembled, preferably on a refrigerator, into (the box tells us): "provocative work . . . big fun at parties! A real creativity, imagination, and language building tool as well." All that Magnetic Poetry™ is missing is a picture of Tzara, looking suitably bohemian, on the back of the box.

6. Here are a few other examples (selected from many) of poems which open with vague or ambiguous pronouns: "Yes, they are alive and can have those colors" ("A Blessing in Disguise," *Mooring* 184); "Out here on Cottage Grove it matters" ("Pyrography," *SP* 212); "You can't say it that way any more" ("And *Ut Pictura Poesis* Is Her Name," *SP* 235). Several critics, most notably Perloff, have discussed how Ashbery's ambiguous pronouns function to create a "poetics of indeterminacy" or "undecidability." While Perloff's explications of these texts are notable, she is less successful at explaining *why* Ashbery employs this poetic strategy. Perloff relies on placing this work in a tradition of indeterminacy stemming from Rimbaud. While Ashbery's interest in, and debts to, the poets of this tradition are undeniable, I think it is also important to see Ashbery's indeterminacy as a solution to a particular problem artists faced in the 1960s. This problem is articulated, and its solution suggested, in "The Invisible Avant-Garde."

7. Bernstein notes that impermeability and absorption are not mutually exclusive but that, in fact, certain types of impermeability may lead to a deeper and more satisfying readerly absorption. This is because unlike the standard "bourgeois" texts that we are generally invited to be absorbed by ("TV series . . . fastread magazines . . . etc.") nonabsorptive texts and techniques (such as Ashbery's) "may get the reader / absorbed into a more ideologized / or politicized space . . . one that really *can* engross" (53-54). Such antiabsorptive work, then, "does not so much prevent / absorption as shift its plane / of engagement—forcing a shift in attentional focus" (76) which can ultimately "wake / us from the hypnosis of [bourgeois] absorption" (54).

8. "Personism" was published subsequently, along with "Personal Poem," in the little magazine *Yugen* 7 (1961).

9. There are many negative reviews that one could catalogue, but John Simon's comments on Ashbery, Guest, and Koch in a 1962 article in *The Hudson Review* are particularly notable for the critic's annoyance at poets' nerve. For Simon, New York school writing is the "deliberate cultivation of the meaningless, a willed collocation of the disconnected, unspontaneous and ungrammatical: the arrogant assumption that *disjecta membra* can make you *poeta*" (457). He concludes that "these abstract expressionists in words are every bit as undistinguished and indistinguishable as their confreres of the drip, dribble and squirt" (457).

10. In terms of *materials,* O'Hara's choices were closer to the so-called "hard-edge" pop artists (Andy Warhol, Roy Lichtenstein, James Rosenquist, etc.) who were interested in commercial objects rather than cast-offs. However, in terms of *technique* O'Hara shares more in common with the assemblage artists (particularly Rauschenberg) who use their materials in more mixed and layered ways, rather than following the "flat," commercial techniques of the hard-edge artists. Particularly in long poems like *Second Avenue,* "Ode to Michael Goldberg," or "Biotherm" we can detect an assemblage-like aesthetic in O'Hara's work which evokes urban experience by importing its detritus.

11. An important exception is Herring's 2002 *PMLA* article "Frank O'Hara's Open Closet."

12. The line is from Berrigan's poem "Frank O'Hara": ". . . But, his face is open, his eyes / are clear, and, leaning lightly on an elbow, fist below / his ear, he will never be less than perfectly frank, / listening, completely interested in whatever there may / be to hear. Attentive to me alone here. Between friends, / nothing would seem stranger to me than true intimacy" (11). O'Hara's remarkable ability to be many things to many people is confirmed by Larry Rivers in his funeral oration: "Frank O'Hara was my best friend. There are at least sixty people in New York who thought Frank O'Hara was their best friend. . . . At one time or another, he was everyone's greatest and most loyal audience" (138).

Works Cited

Allen, Donald, ed. *The New American Poetry.* New York: Grove, 1960.

Allen, Donald and Warren Tallman, eds. *Poetics of the New American Poetry.* New York: Grove, 1973.

Ashbery, John. "Frank O'Hara's Question." *Bookweek* 25 (September 1966): 6.

————. *The Mooring of Starting Out: The First Five Books of Poetry.* New Jersey: Ecco Press, 1998.

————. *Reported Sightings: Art Chronicles 1957-1987.* Ed. David Bergman. New York: Knopf, 1989.

————. *Selected Poems.* New York: Penguin, 1985.

————. *Self-Portrait in a Convex Mirror.* New York: Viking Press, 1975.

Bell, Pearl K. "The Poverty of Poetry." Rev. of O'Hara's *Collected Poems. Frank O'Hara: To Be True to a City.* Ed. Jim Elledge. Ann Arbor: University of Michigan Press, 1990. 38-39.

Berkson, Bill and Joe LeSueur, eds. *Homage to Frank O'Hara.* Special Issue. *Big Sky* 11/12, 1978.

Bernstein, Charles. "Artifice of Absorption." *A Poetics.* Cambridge: Harvard University Press, 1992. 9-89.

Berrigan, Ted. "Frank O'Hara." Berkson and LeSueur 11.

Bürger, Peter. *Theory of the Avant-Garde.* Ed. Wlad Godzich and Jochen Schulte-Sasse. Trans. Michael Shaw. Theory and History of Literature, Vol. 4. Minneapolis: University of Minnesota Press, 1984.

Cage, John. "Lecture on Nothing." *Silence.* Middletown, CT: Wesleyan University Press, 1961. 109-27.

Davidson, Michael. "Compulsory Homosociality." *Cruising the Performative: Interventions into the Representation of Ethnicity, Nationality, and Sexuality.* Ed. Sue-Ellen Case, Philip Brett, Susan Leigh Foster. Bloomington: Indiana University Press, 1995. 197-216.

Ginsberg, Allen. "Poetry, Violence, and the Trembling Lambs" (1959). Allen and Tallman 331-33.

Gooch, Brad. *City Poet: The Life and Times of Frank O'Hara.* New York: Knopf, 1993.

Guilbaut, Serge. *How New York Stole the Idea of Modern Art: Abstract Expressionism, Freedom, and the Cold War.* Trans. Arthur Goldhammer. Chicago: University of Chicago Press, 1983.

Herring, Terrell Scott. "Frank O'Hara's Open Closet." *PMLA* 117 (2002): 114-27.

Hobbs, Stuart D. *The End of the American Avant Garde.* The American Social Experience Series, Vol. 37. New York: New York University Press, 1997.

Jameson, Fredric. *Postmodernism, or, The Cultural Logic of Late Capitalism.* Durham: Duke University Press, 1991.

Katz, Jonathan. "Identification." Roth and Katz 49-68.

Koch, Kenneth. *The Art of Poetry: Poems, Parodies, Interviews, Essays, and Other Work.* Poets on Poetry. Ed. David Lehman. Ann Arbor: University of Michigan Press, 1996.

Kuenzli, Rudolf E. "The Semiotics of Dada Poetry" *Dada Spectrum: The Dialectics of Revolt.* Ed. Stephen C. Foster and Rudolf E. Kuenzli. Iowa City: University of Iowa Press, 1979. 52-70.

Lolordo, Nick. "Charting the Flow: Positioning John Ashbery." *Contemporary Literature* 42 (2002): 750-74.

Lucie-Smith, Edward. "An Interview with Frank O'Hara." *Standing Still and Walking in New York.* Ed. Donald Allen. Bolinas: Grey Fox Press, 1975. 3-26.

Lyon, Janet. *Manifestoes: Provocations of the Modern.* Ithaca: Cornell University Press, 1999.

Marinetti, F. T. "The Founding and Manifesto of Futurism" *Futurist Manifestos.* Documents of 20th-Century Art. Ed. Umbro Apollonio. New York: Viking, 1973.

Newman, Barnett. "The Plastic Image, 1943-45." *Abstract Expressionism: Creators and Critics*. Ed. Clifford Ross. New York: Harry Abrams, 1990. 125-27.

O'Hara, Frank. *The Collected Poems of Frank O'Hara*. Ed. Donald Allen. Berkeley: University of California Press, 1995. New York: Knopf, 1971.

Olson, Charles. "Projective Verse." Allen and Tallman 147-58.

Perloff, Marjorie. *The Futurist Moment: Avant-Garde, Avant Guerre, and the Language of Rupture*. Chicago: University of Chicago Press, 1986.

Rivers, Larry. "Speech Read at Frank O'Hara's Funeral, Springs, Long Island, July 27, 1966." Berkson and LeSueur 138.

Roth, Moira. "The Aesthetic of Indifference." Roth and Katz 33-47.

Roth, Moira, and Jonathan D. Katz. *Difference/Indifference: Musings on Postmodernism, Marcel Duchamp and John Cage*. Critical Voices in Art, Theory and Culture. Ed. Saul Ostrow. Amsterdam: G+B Arts, 1998.

Shetley, Vernon. *After the Death of Poetry: Poet and Audience in Contemporary America*. Durham and London: Duke University Press, 1993.

Shoptaw, John. *On the Outside Looking Out: John Ashbery's Poetry*. Cambridge: Harvard University Press, 1994.

Simon, John. "More Brass Than Enduring." *Hudson Review* 15 (1962): 455-68.

Stockinger, Jacob. "Homotextuality: A Proposal." *The Gay Academic*. Ed. Louie Crew. Palm Springs, CA: Etc Publications, 1978. 135-51.

Williams, William Carlos. *Selected Poems*. Ed. Charles Tomlinson. New York: New Directions, 1985.

David LeHardy Sweet (essay date 2003)

SOURCE: Sweet, David LeHardy. "John Ashbery." In *Savage Sight/Constructed Noise: Poetic Adaptations of Painterly Techniques in the French and American Avant-Gardes*, pp. 231-74. Chapel Hill, N.C.: U.N.C. Department of Romance Languages, 2003.

[*In the following essay, Sweet focuses on the relationship between Ashbery's poetry and art criticism, and identifies significant changes in American avant-garde art reflected in Ashbery's verse.*]

Although John Ashbery carefully enumerated French avant-garde influences on Frank O'Hara in his introduction to *The Collected Poems of Frank O'Hara*, he has consistently denied the primacy of any such influence in his own work. Yet certain facts about his career undercut this denial—including a ten-year expatriation in Paris where he worked as an art critic for the *Herald Tribune* until 1965—as do the terms of the denial itself, which exclude the likes of Pierre Reverdy, Raymond Roussel, and Giorgio de Chirico, participants in the Avant-Garde to whom he is clearly indebted. What, then, is the avant-garde tradition—in Ashbery's words, the "other tradition"—Ashbery would sidestep even as he acknowledges certain of its by-ways (an "other" other tradition)? Surprisingly, Ashbery himself provides a map of its influence through his writings on avant-garde painters, particularly the French. In this way his own art criticism, like that of so many others, becomes a form of a proto-poetics, while the theoretical relation between painting and poetry repeatedly inserts itself into Ashbery's poetical ruminations on novelty.

ALTERNATIVE AVANT-GARDES PAST AND PRESENT

Ashbery's evasiveness about his own avant-garde genealogy seems to have been a reaction to W. H. Auden's and Harold Bloom's disparaging associations of his "excesses" with Surrealism.[1] By the 1960s official Surrealism was old hat among serious avant-garde practitioners, from the French Situationists to American Pop Artists. Yet, in his own writings on the subject, Ashbery seems determined to retain its unofficial nature as a source of novelty by resuscitating marginal figures and forgotten precursors of the movement—less out of critical premeditation than simple appreciation. At the same time, he upholds the general framework of an anti-literary, anti-artistic attitude inherited from Surrealism by concurring with the poet/painter Henri Michaux (whom he interviewed in 1961) that it provided *"la grande permission"* and was thus to be valued "less for what [its members] wrote than for the permission they gave everybody to write whatever comes into their heads."[2]

Ashbery, then, seems interested in a broader, "acculturated" Surrealism that crosses the perceived limits of its Bretonian program and assimilates itself to new realities: "What has in fact happened is that Surrealism has become a part of our daily lives: its effects can be seen everywhere, in the work of artists and writers who have no connection with the movement, in movies, interior decoration and popular speech. A degradation? Perhaps. But it is difficult to impose limitations on the unconscious, which has a habit of turning up in unlikely places."[3]

Writing at different times in the 1960s, Ashbery discriminates among Surrealism's procedures and practitioners in a way that subtly illuminates his own poetic debts. Indeed, his critical evaluations help to differentiate his own procedures from those most closely identified with the official Surrealism of the 1920s:

Liberté totale in Paris in the 1920s turned out to be something less than total, and if it was not total, then it was something very much like the everyday liberty that pre-Surrealist generations had to cope with. In literature it meant automatic writing, but what is so free about that? Real freedom would be to use this method where it could be of service and to correct it with the conscious mind where indicated. And in fact the finest writing of the Surrealists is the product of the conscious and the unconscious working hand in hand, as they have been wont to do in all ages. But if automatic writing is the prescribed ideal for literature, what about art? Dalí's meticulous handling of infinitesimal brushes excludes any kind of automatism as far as the execution of his paintings goes, and perhaps even their conception was influenced by a desire to show off his dazzling technique to its best advantage. Breton called Miró the most surreal of the Surrealists, yet the deliberate wit and technical mastery of his work scarcely seem like tools to plumb the unconscious.[4]

According to Ashbery, the automatist inadequacies of surrealist painting were rectified only with the advent of the New American Painting, since "automatism was not a viable possibility in art until much later, in the hands of artists like Jackson Pollock."[5] Yet in seeing Abstract Expressionism as the first complete realization of plastic automatism, Ashbery is actually demoting its personal status for him as a poet. One cannot help wondering if this critical maneuver is not in part a way of distinguishing his own avant-garde poetics from the kind of empirical automatism one finds in O'Hara's poetry, particularly in its early, more derivative manifestations in such poems as "Easter" and "Second Avenue," the latter of which Ashbery once described as "a difficult pleasure."[6] Ashbery elaborates his critical view of automatism—albeit primarily as a form of writing—in an essay on Pierre Reverdy in which he claims that "Reverdy's poetry avoids the extremes of Surrealist poetry, and is the richer for it." In the same essay he implies that automatism remained an unachieved ideal for the Surrealists, who adhered to rules that necessarily conflicted with it:

> Though all rules were seemingly abolished, the poets were careful to observe the rules of grammar and syntax: "Take care," wrote Breton. "I know the meaning of each of my words and I observe syntax *naturally*: syntax is not a discipline, as certain oafs believe." But does one always observe these rules when one is writing automatically? And what, in fact, is automatic writing? Isn't all writing automatic? If one corrects a poem after writing it, doesn't one happen automatically on the correction? The discipline as it was practiced by the Surrealists seems arbitrary and sterile.[7]

By questioning the validity and usefulness of Breton's concept of automatic writing, Ashbery is really arguing for an expanded notion of the Avant-Garde and avant-garde procedures that no longer need conform (if they ever did) to the letter of the law of radical spontaneity in all its heroic pomposity. For many of the Surrealists,

spontaneity of expression seemed to involve a constellation of de-personalizing techniques that, in different hands, had the potential of realizing exquisite forms in both plastic and literary media. Even the most anti-literary, anti-artistic practitioners ended up, according to Ashbery, reaffirming a certain artistry: "Picabia, Arp and Schwitters are the most notable Dada artists after Duchamp, and, as with him, one finds it difficult to imagine how their work could ever have been construed as anything but a high form of art." (*RS* [*Reported Sightings*], p. 7) Short of true automatism (a kind of total expression of individual consciousness), the governing principle Ashbery sees behind many surrealist works is a form of "self-abnegation in the interests of a superior realism, one which will reflect the realities both of the spirit (rather than the individual consciousness) and of the world as perceived by it: the state in which *Je est un autre,* in Rimbaud's phrase." (*RS,* p. 26) In the plastic arts, Ashbery detects these self-abnegating techniques in the work of Max Ernst, André Masson, Wolfgang Paalen, and Yves Tanguy in the form of collage, frottage, fumage ("smudges from a candle flame held close to the canvas"), sand painting, and painting upside down (p. 26). He finds literary analogues to such techniques in the writings of Raymond Roussel, elements of which he compared to the meticulous, interlocking shapes found in Tanguy's mysterious landscapes:

> They remind one of the fantastically complicated *"machines célibataires"* described in the novels of Raymond Roussel, one of the writers the Surrealists most admired (though he was not a member of their group). The title of one of Tanguy's early canvases, *"Les Vues"* (1929), may be an allusion to Roussel's long poem *"La Vue,"* whose laborious cataloguing of minutiae prefigures Tanguy's spirit. Roussel's *"demoiselle"* in his novel *Locus Solus*—a kind of aerial pile driver capable of constructing a finely detailed mosaic of teeth—has the same almost insolent awareness of its own improbable being as the central colossus in Tanguy's "My Life, White and Black [fig. 19]."

> (p. 24)

For Ashbery, understanding the distinction between such techniques and presumably "pure" automatism is a prerequisite for understanding his own relation to the French and American Avant-Gardes, a relation that seems to turn on making a critical reappraisal of automatism. On the one hand, he sees automatism as a convenient myth—both for Surrealism's critics and its proponents: a myth no work can fully embody, yet one that points inexorably to a solipsistic austerity or abstraction in art and literature. On the other hand, he does not want to be irrevocably dissociated from that myth; therefore, he makes only the subtlest choice against Bretonian automatism for Rousselian paranomasia, Reverdian polyptoton, and the kind of attenuated phrasing of De Chirico's novel *Hebdomeros*. In the plastic arts, he does not disparage the achievements of the Abstract Expressionists and related avant-garde movements, but suggests their slight impoverishment in comparison to those of such artists as Yves Tanguy and Joseph Cornell, who, unlike the newcomers, ". . . keep all the stories that art seems to want to cut us off from without giving up the inspiring asceticism of abstraction."[8] In short, Ashbery likes the Surrealists as much for what is regressive about their technique as for what is presumably progressive, as much for what contributes to the technical "self-definition" of art[9] as for what detracts from it and thus abolishes formalistic definitions. To be avant-garde in the wake of the radical Avant-Garde is to have a kind of perverse recourse to tradition, illusionism, and obsolete form inasmuch as the moral or ideological implications of those things are now deemed to have been neutralized. "Self-abnegating" techniques move in this direction; yet Ashbery is prepared to go even further, finding avant-garde potentialities even within the most traditional means—by virtue of a kind of non-discrimination between the tradition and the other tradition, the figurative and the abstract, the narrative and the presentational, the speculative and the spontaneous. His description of the relation between the art of Tanguy and Pollock illustrates this tendency:

> . . . the arbitrary distinction between abstract and figurative painting did not exist for Tanguy, who painted real if nonexistent objects, so that his work is in a sense a fusion of the two, always in the interests of a more integral realism. The automatic gestural painting of Pollock, Kline, and their contemporaries looks very different from the patient, minute, old-master technique of Tanguy, yet he was perhaps the Poussin of the same inner landscape of which Pollock was the Turner.
>
> (RS, p. 27)

In a lecture at the Yale Art School published in *Artnews*, 1968, Ashbery offered his most comprehensive statement regarding his relationship to the Avant-Garde by tracing the outlines of an "invisible avant-garde" that presumably included himself. For Ashbery, the true Avant-Garde only properly exists in a condition of cultural tenuousness: unconsolidated and largely unrecognized, disestablished less out of a social hostility against it than uncertainty about it, its quality of *yet becoming*. It was this uncertainty and the risk involved in experimentation that attracted Ashbery to the Avant-Garde as a young poet. But in the late 1960s it became clear to him that the Avant-Garde had established its own tradition, distinct from a presumably established one, yet also very much like it in its enjoyment of growing popularity. As an increasingly celebrated socio-economic phenomenon (exemplified by the career of Andy Warhol), the Avant-Garde had come to resemble a very different—and much larger—military unit than its nineteenth-century label had originally suggested:

What has happened since Pollock? The usual explanation is that "media" have multiplied to such an extent that it is no longer possible for secrets to remain secret for very long, and that this has had the effect of turning the avant-garde from a small contingent of foolhardy warriors into a vast and well-equipped regiment. In fact the avant-garde has absorbed most of the army, or vice versa—in any case the result is that the avant-garde can now barely exist because of the immense amounts of attention and money that are focused on it, and that the only artists who have any privacy are a handful of decrepit stragglers behind the big booming avant-garde juggernaut.[10]

Between the armed camps of the tradition and the other tradition, only deserters, defectors and spies can maneuver, Ashbery argues, for creative autonomy in a culture of oppositional conformities. Putting a new spin on Eliot's theme in the essay "Tradition and the Individual Talent,"[11] Ashbery identifies "acceptance" as a primary menace to the "individual talent," who risks absorption by one or the other of these "traditions." At the same time, certain historic acts of defiance in the face of acceptance are acknowledged to have completely backfired, resulting in bad art—as the case of De Chirico shows, whose late pastiches of Renaissance painting were the objects of Breton's withering scorn. But this latter example might be viewed as an almost proleptic defense against the overwhelming acceptance Ashbery himself would receive after publishing *Self-Portrait in a Convex Mirror* (1972), which earned him the Pulitzer Prize, the National Book Award, and the National Book Critics Circle Award. Recognizing both the danger and potential of widespread acceptance, Ashbery has cultivated a skeptical insouciance with regard to the competing "traditions"—in his own words, "a kind of fence sitting / Raised to the level of an esthetic ideal" as he puts it in the poem **"Soonest Mended"** in *The Double Dream of Spring*.[12]

Ashbery's apparent commitment to "fence sitting" makes it unclear whether the "other tradition" to which he so often refers actually represents the historic Avant-Garde or simply designates the poet's eccentric middle way, a "new" negative capability that skews the terms of "tradition" and "avant-garde." In the process, the terms become reversible as Ashbery assumes a nomadic tangency in relation to these two discursive poles of poetic production—one, established/decaying, the other, emergent/proliferating. As these poles increasingly come to resemble each other in a postmodern or millennial culture of ubiquitous consumption that subsumes all traces of unassimilated space and its cultural ecosystems, Ashbery's mannered idealism becomes a private holdout against the forces of cultural homogenization.

Several poems from *Houseboat Days* (1975), Ashbery's first collection after *Self-Portrait* [*Self-Portrait in a Convex Mirror*], evoke the human cost exacted by a vanguard poetics that succumbs to its own institutional-ization. **"The Other Tradition"** allegorizes the popular-ization of the Avant-Garde as a kind of public demon-stration that overruns a solitary pine grove: "They all came, some wore sentiments / Emblazoned on T-shirts, proclaiming the lateness / Of the hour[.]"[13] The ad-dressee of the poem, whose appearance is significantly delayed by Ashbery but who seems to have been present all along, remains poignantly oblivious to a public ac-claim that simultaneously renders him curiously obsolete: "Only then did you glance up from your book, / Unable to comprehend what had been taking place, or / Say what you had been reading." This reading can only be at variance with the subject's unexpected celebrity conferred by the crowd of the avant-guard juggernaut calling meetings to order and leaving him "expresident of the event." Yet the new participants could never be

> so deceived as to hanker
> After that cool non-being of just a few minutes before
> Now that the idea of a forest had clamped itself
> Over the minutiae of the scene.

Undisconcerted, the fellow poet-addressee finds all this pseudo-attention merely "Charming, but [turns his] face fully toward the night, / Speaking into it like a megaphone, not hearing or caring." Furthermore, in the last lines it is the celebrated poet's "forgetfulness" (unlike the attentive "remembering" of his fans) that alone keeps the crowded avant-garde vessel afloat. It is not that the poet actually forgets either tradition; rather, he deliberately ignores the ideological motivations imputed to their differences. Nor is it a form of Bloom-ian *misprision* whereby the tradition is reaffirmed through reinterpretation, but what David Lehman has called a kind of larceny: the free-handed utilization of "so much raw material, no strings attached, [with] noth-ing to acknowledge or be faithful to,"[14] nor, above all, the didactic residues of Eliotic allusiveness. The key virtue of a true avant-garde poet, then, is disinterested-ness rather than antagonism.

Noting the poem's allusion to Dante's description of Brunetto Latini as one who "Had run his race and won"—albeit across burning sands in the *Inferno*—John Shoptaw, in his extensive study of Ashbery's poetry, has suggested that **"The Other Tradition"** ultimately refers to the reception of Frank O'Hara's poetry.[15] Yet it could as easily be Ashbery himself, given the parallels between the two poets' literary destinies. If O'Hara did not live to "hear" all this appropriative flattery, Ash-bery, who did, tries his best not to "care" about it, cultivating a sort of impertinent obsolescence that reflects his ambivalence about being avant-garde in the wake of the Avant-Garde.

But there is another form of obsolescence Ashbery unequivocally avoids, as revealed in the poem **"And *Ut***

***Pictura Poesis* Is Her Name"** in the same collection. It is the obsolescence of assuming a strictly nostalgic, as opposed to critically open-minded, relation to the competing traditions that frame a poet's innovations. "You can't say it that way any more," the first line of the poem tells us.[16] Although what "it" is is not speci-fied, the pronoun seems to refer to some timeless mes-sage that requires a certain formal refashioning. What is new, and what makes "it" new, is the manner in which it is said.[17] Insofar as the first line seems to comment on the title of the poem itself, the title's own novelty is called into question, as if to say that the only true avant-garde stance is that in which the last thing said is always already outdated. Or does the first line refer only to a part of the title, which fobs off a famous Horatian dictum as a woman's proper name: *Ut Pictura Poesis* (poetry is like painting). Significantly, this dictum also presents the relation between poetry and painting as one of harmonious parallelism or mutual attraction. It is as if the poem were saying that in order to make "it" (poetry, beauty, whatever) new, the avant-garde poet must constantly rethink, restate, resituate his or her poetry in relation to painting, as if painting were poetry's own lover and thus in need of "courting." Furthermore, this lover is, in the modern spirit, independent, anomalous, alienated, as opposed to ac-commodating, constant, domesticated, in the classical spirit. Because classical symmetries or harmonies can-not be vouchsafed in the modern context, the ways in which poems continue to be like pictures are a measure of poetic vitality.

At the same time, if this relation can no longer be elaborated in terms of traditional comparison, neither can it be satisfactorily demonstrated in the form of yet another modernist "poem-painting" with its stark juxta-positioning or cubist cantilevering of verbal elements to create a "presentational" poetry that tries to *be* a kind of painting without referring to it. Thus, although clas-sical aesthetics are out of the question, a residue of classicism's amorous attraction to mere beauty compels the poet to rethink modernist tactics as well—in favor, it would seem, of a somewhat more accommodating, if conditional, communicative strategy. As the poem says: "Bothered about beauty you have to / Come out into the open, into a clearing, / And rest." Instead of a strict poem-painting—i.e., the surrealistic portraiture of the title—Ashbery's poem offers instructions on how to write a new kind of poem-painting, instructions that double as friendly advice on how to "get a girl" (or guy), thus a kind of *ars poetica* as *ars amatoria*. Yet this advice is jolted at different moments in ways that recall the same modernist juxtapositional strategies the poem's discourse would partially circumvent. In short, the poem is a new chimera of Ovidian didacticism and Bretonian juxtapositionism:

Now,
About what to put in your poem-painting:
Flowers are always nice, particularly delphinium.
Names of boys you once knew and their sleds,
Skyrockets are good—do they still exist?
There are a lot of other things of the same quality
As those I've mentioned, Now one must
Find a few important words, and a lot of low-keyed,
Dull-sounding ones. *She approached me*
About buying her desk. Suddenly the street was
Bananas and the clangor of Japanese instruments.
Humdrum testaments were scattered around. His head
Locked into mine. We were a seesaw. [my italics]

The word "seesaw" concretizes the overall strategy of the poem in an oscillating image that also resolves the instructive aspect of the poem with the promise of copulation. As both temporal movement *and* concrete object, the seesaw suggests both Time—here associated with the discursive, narrative, or lyric movement characteristic of literature—and Space—associated with the frozen or "timeless" appearance of the plastic art object. Moreover, the word also suggests an unexpected "rapport" between these two "sister" arts by juxtaposing the past and present tenses of "to see" in a compound noun that implies the temporality of "seeing" itself. In this way Ashbery contorts the modernist assumption that the plastic arts have an instantaneous appeal to the sense of sight, which experiences the relations among a work's visual elements simultaneously, enabling an immediate or accelerated apperception of its plastic properties, unlike the sense of sound, which experiences a work through time.[18] As a primary characteristic of the modern sensibility, this "simultaneism" was the literary Avant-Garde's rationale for the creation of a more "painterly," "objectivist," or "presentational" poetics in the first place. But for Ashbery, seeing ultimately takes just as long as hearing; thus, a certain temporalizing "discursivity" not only accompanies aesthetic judgments about the visual, but helps produce it. Furthermore, the relation between painting and poetry here is analogous to that between "modern" and "traditional" poetics (as the corresponding tenses "see" and "saw" indicate), and it is a quirky synthesis of the two that Ashbery sustains in the interest of a new realism. Ironically, the chief precedent for bridging these constellated categories of time/space, poetry/painting, discursivity/concreteness is surrealist automatism itself in accelerating the creative process and encouraging accidents (sudden, shocking juxtapositions that correspond to Breton's idea of "savage sight" in the sense of an instantaneous, indiscriminate inclusiveness[19]). Ashbery acknowledges this precedent by concluding the poem with an image that echoes surrealist interests, but with a proviso about fostering "understanding" and "communication" in ways that seem less self-consciously marvelous than those the Surrealists envisioned:

Something
Ought to be written about how this affects

You when you write poetry:
The extreme austerity of an almost empty mind
Colliding with the lush, Rousseau-like foliage of its
    desire to communicate
Something between breaths, if only for the sake
Of others and their desire to understand you and desert
    you
For other centers of communication, so that under-
    standing
May begin, and in doing so be undone.

Austere emptiness (the given? being?) and lush communication (the negative? the ideal?) are both components of the final product that seems to have been occasioned by some startling revelation—as if before a painting or beautiful person. The final image almost heuristically displays the elements of surrealist technique with its "empty mind" and excessive desire (described as a Rousseau—one of Breton's favorite painters). Thus, even at this later stage in Ashbery's career, after already re-evaluating his relation both to the Avant-Garde and to the "tradition," one can see the tenacious persistence of the poet's surrealist memory.

POETIC GENEALOGIES: TWO VIEWS OF ASHBERY

I have described Ashbery's tangential relationship with the other tradition as a post-avant-garde stance that nonetheless asserts its avant-garde credentials. Yet from another perspective, this itinerant, "self-reliant" strategy, has a long, Emersonian genealogy deeply ingrained in American letters. In "The Charity of the Hard Moments" Bloom wrests Ashbery's poetics from anything resembling a deflected avant-gardism (or "French silence" in Harold Rosenberg's phrase) and resituates it as a species of American sublime, grandly associated with Walt Whitman and Wallace Stevens, if in a somewhat reduced form. The reduction, however, causes certain headaches for Bloom, who takes considerable pains to formulate the concept of a "counter-sublime" arising from the unavoidable discrepancies of style and impulse between Ashbery and Stevens. The crux of the matter is Ashbery's critical distance (especially in some of his early works) from the coherent and controlling Stevensian persona, who, in privileged moments of poetic invention discovers intelligible and exhilarating orders in the world.[20] Ashbery's counter-sublime involves the dissipation of the poetic persona through different discursive registers that sneakily (and sometimes randomly) enter the fabric of the poem and corrode its habitual identification with an authorial persona. Oddly enough, Bloom sees this corrosion of the self/poem as a form of purification:

For Ashbery, the privileged moment, like their images, are on the dump, and he wants to purify them by clearly placing them there. Say of what you see in the dark, Stevens urges, that it is this or that it is that, but do not use the rotted names. Use the rotted names, Ashbery urges, but cleanse them by seeing that you cannot be apart from them, and are partly redeemed by consciously suffering with them.[21]

The rottedness of Ashbery's language, however, is more rotted than Bloom thinks, deriving as it does from a French symbolist tradition, an idea he dismisses as nonsense.[22] But it is not nonsense and runs deeper than he admits, pertaining also to his American Orpheus, Stevens. The problem is that the "rottedness" Bloom identifies in Ashbery's poetry is less a matter of high and low speech than of language's own impediments to pure communication, to sheer transparency—a transparency Bloom likes to think of as the hallmark of the American sublime. Rather than seeing the fetidity of words—their way of spoiling even in the process of communicating—as something to be suffered for redemptive purposes, French poets writing in the symbolist tradition saw the virtue of allowing language to "stink" a bit, to call attention to itself as a medium, to distract the reader from the domineering assumption of "meaning." (Ironically, Symbolists such as Mallarmé also considered this aspect of language an indication of its purity.) It is a putrefaction lodged at the core of all subsequent avant-garde elaborations, from the cubist one of treating language as an almost physical medium, to the surrealist one of professing a kind of child-like faith in the accidents of language (another form of rot or "de-composition") and therein positing a new, "marvelous" transparency to the medium when used "automatically." Thus, the "putrefaction" of language seems to imply different things: a language voided of certain denotation (i.e., semiotic de-familiarization), or a language overburdened with hermeneutic potentiality by virtue of an almost crystalline encrustation of previous uses, all reflecting, resonating, reinforcing, but also contradicting or canceling each other.

It is precisely this aspect of avant-gardism that some critics see as a distinguishing feature of Stevens' own poetry. In his essay "The Brushstroke's Integrity," Leslie Wolf not only recalls Ashbery to an avant-garde tradition of painterly poetics, but in so doing, resituates his assumed forebear Stevens in that tradition's precondition of emphasizing the linguistic medium *as medium.* Wolf writes:

> The history of this attitude in poetry, from Baudelaire to Rimbaud through Mallarmé and Valéry and the moderns, has included a growing recognition that in order to create an instrument that works in the imagination, the poet must divert his material—the words of his language—from their habitual usage. And if the Symbolism of Mallarmé and Valéry never produced an art equal to the majesty of its theories, it nevertheless delineated clearly the orientation that Pound, Eliot, Crane and Stevens brought to the task of writing poems during the first half of the century.[23]

Wolf goes on to show that this task was facilitated by the example of modern painting, in which the idea of a medium as a desirable impediment to its otherwise presumed function of transparent communication found a conspicuously physical demonstration, particularly in the work of the Cubists. Such work imparted the sense of a medium's materiality, its quality of physical contingency. In short, emphasizing the medium over the message in any art was conceived as a painterly strategy *tout court* (even in music), while emphasizing referentiality—the illusionism of communication—remained literary, discursive, rhetorical or "linguistic" (in Stevens' usage). For Stevens, this "painterly" emphasis on the medium (and as such, the *énonciation*) over a "linguistic" one on the message (the *énoncé*) constituted "abstraction" in poetry—the transporting of reality (habitual meanings) to the imagination by way of material deviations.[24]

Like Bloom, Wolf sees Ashbery as descending from Stevens, although not as American heir-apparent, but as the poet who took Stevens' "French lessons" to an even higher level, upping the ante in a kind of poker game of poetic experimentation. Furthermore, Wolf sees Ashbery's descendant relation to Stevens in parallel with that of the Abstract Expressionists to the Cubists, a parallel relation grounded on the assumption that the late moderns—both painters and poets—essentially accelerate a process of *mediumification*[25] undertaken by their predecessors: "From this point of view, Stevens—Ashbery's favorite poet—is a kind of poetic 'cubist' out of whom has sprung Ashbery's De Kooning: Stevens contradicts the object but retains it as 'motif' in much the way Picasso did; but Ashbery, like De Kooning, 'dares to remove the object further before reconstructing it.'"[26] Thus it is that Wolf, while acknowledging Stevens' influence on Ashbery, modulates that influence as a function of the avant-garde impulse toward "the painterly," which he defines in Greenbergian terms:

> loose, rapid handling, or the look of it; masses that blot and fuse, instead of shapes that stay distinct; large, conspicuous rhythms, broken color; uneven saturations or densities of paint; exhibited brush, knife, finger or rag marks—in short, a constellation of physical features like those defined by Wölfflin when he extracted his notion of the *Malerische* from Baroque art.[27]

Ironically, the Greenbergian definition Wolf uses reveals that while in painting such *mediumification* contributes to the "self-criticism" or "self-definition" of art, in literature it involves a kind of corrosive re-definition in terms of another art: i.e., to think of language as language (semantically destabilized by virtue of tonal, syntactic, or typographic elements) and not as transparent communication is really to think of language in terms of another art, whether as paint or as music.[28]

If the derivation of painterly poetics from a French tradition seems sound, the association of Ashbery's own painterliness with Abstract Expressionism is more problematic. The ways in which De Kooning's art and Ashbery's poetry "abstract" their respective media from the objects they represent to create an "all-over" surface in specific works seems plausible according to the terms Wolf uses. But this consonance is the effect of formal analogizing and lacks a certain documentary grounding that might otherwise reveal a deeper critical sympathy between Ashbery and the New York School. Where this formal parallel starts to break down is precisely where Wolf attempts to move beyond the formal, Greenbergian notion of the painterly and to associate Ashbery with De Kooning on the basis of a Rosenbergian principle of creative "action"—a personal, if unconscious, creative struggle external to the art object and its integral, mediumic necessity, the value of this object, therefore, deriving symbolically from that struggle or process and not from itself. Rosenberg writes:

> What gives the canvas its meaning is . . . the way the artist organizes his emotional and intellectual energy as if he were in a living situation. . . . Since the painter has become an actor, the spectator has to think in a vocabulary of action: its inception, duration, direction—psychic state, concentration and relaxation of the will, passivity, alert waiting. He must become a connoisseur of the gradations among the automatic, the spontaneous, the evoked.[29]

From this standpoint art is important as a record or sign of a certain heroic content with "the artist in attendance pumping it in."[30] Certainly both men's work offers a record of its own production, an abstracting process in which objects and images dissolve, merge, reform or disappear altogether. Furthermore, these records have the same non-hierarchical, all-over effects in their respective media (particularly in Ashbery's *The Tennis Court Oath* [1962], which Bloom angrily rejected as a work of "calculated incoherence"[31]). To this extent an idea of "process" remains compatible with that of the "painterly." But the spirit of heroic self-absorption is absent in Ashbery. It is an American inflation of an idea of automatism to which Ashbery self-consciously responds with self-abnegating strategies derived from pre- and peri-surrealist experiments. Furthermore, Wolf, who writes persuasively about the formal consonance of Ashbery's and De Kooning's art, seems at a loss to explain why such poems as **"The Tennis Court Oath,"** **"Leaving the Atocha Station," "The New Realism,"** and the monumental **"Europe"** all, in his view, "fail to sustain *energy*" (my italics).[32] The answer is simple: the works are based on poetic principles ultimately incompatible with his critical premises. Indeed, the work seems premised on the exhaustion or exhaustive repetition of avant-garde strategies. Yet Wolf deflects this criticism by denying the significance of the one conspicuous strategy of the poems (collage) that might justify this apparent energy drain. As a belated Dadaist, Ashbery resorts to a kind of ritual, deadpan collagism that highlights the self-abnegating character of his poetry as against the self-assertiveness of Abstract Expressionist art in its insistence on personal immediacy, energy, action. The poet David Shapiro has identified collage as the source of this deviation of sensibility:

> One of the curious effects of this transformation of **"The Tennis Court Oath"** into complete and seamless *collage* is the curtailing of the "I" as having much lyric or dramatic nuance. The "I" may now merely be the "I" *not of a persona* but of a piece of *newspaperese* or newspaper, or part of a story pasted, as it were, upon the poem. There is no more of Ashbery to this "I" than the "I" of an alien bit of prose from another source shockingly "fallen into" the poem. The "I" is, indeed, often necessarily linked to the continuous "ego" or *"je"* of the poem, but a radical deflation of its resonance or dignity has occurred. As a matter of fact, Ashbery in this period employs the various kinds of "I" much in the way more conventional masks are employed by Yeats or Eliot, but in Ashbery's extreme case there is only the bitter sense of the two-dimensionality of the collaged "I." This is schizo-analysis.[33]

In a sense, segments of the "I" as an entire, coherent identity are lost inasmuch as the poet's language not only cedes to the words, utterances, or meanings of others (exuberant citation), but to a random agglomeration, an almost mechanical process that transforms those human utterances into ineffable, alien materials. Thus the reverberations of accommodating human voices one recognizes in any modern intertextual procedure become a numbing crush of verbal shards, semi-dead zones of disconnected neuro-linguistic synapses (the postmodern detritus of modern literary imagination). Oblivious to the *énoncés* of "cited" sources, the radical text of Ashbery's **"Europe"** mostly empties the verbal blocks of any discursive, and sometimes even linguistic, significance. What might, in certain other cases, be an affirmation of authorial identity (his or her mastery of sources) not only cedes here to a radical interdiscursivity that deconstructs the authorial self, but one that refuses even the integrity of its components, their capacity for any logical, linguistic, or symbolic sequencing. The effect is that of a simultaneism of speech that fully encroaches on serialization itself, a serial progress that cannot be construed as discursively purposive, but only as plastic accumulation with its effects of verbal cacography. Cacography represents not just a confusion of texts or authors, but a verbal melée or glossalalia, an *écriture affolante* renouncing any principle of contradiction.[34]

By contrast, modern (and mostly scholarly) principles of discursive organization are at pains to preserve a modicum of meaning within the citation, a modicum of the *énoncé* within its appropriated *énonciation,* to yield up a whole identity. The assembled parts narcissistically mirror the self-aggrandizing author, even if the method itself, ironically, recalls that of Echo, who vainly employs the speech of others to requite a nugatory love that is all her own. The interdiscursivity of modern intertextuality/citation is ultimately, then, directed toward exalting the human subject—or, in this case, the author—and thus sustains the notion of the modern discursive entity as a whole, an individual. He is an Apollonian figure with a story to tell—a beginning, middle and end. He has a history, a destiny, and a moral to convey—all of it reinforced through his stupendous command of a plethora of external discursive entities (modern citations) that might otherwise subversively consume him, pull him apart in a sparagmos of contra-dictions (*sic*). In such conditions, who would not say, along with Montaigne, "que sais-je?" (as if he could re-ally be credited for the originality for *that* statement).

But a cacography represents a first literary instance—no matter how ephemeral—of the theoretical death of the author and of the insight that certain constellations of words are no longer the emblems of any single human subject but a kind of universal, human issue that is consumed and excreted like any physical matter, but that just happens to be symbolic. As Salvador Dalí might put it: the only difference between mind and mat-ter is that mind isn't matter. Such word-matter becomes *detached* from human identity, like Van Gogh's shoes from their Van Gogh-ness. As verbal plastic, detached from the self, language empties itself of meaning but also opens itself to other, if arbitrary, hermeneutic potentialities. The latter case may simply involve the arbitrary intervention of a third party—as in Benjamin-ian allegory—to impose a bit of order on the mess (as Reverdy might say). But the former case must remain indecipherable, a schizoid situation in which linguistic particles just leak away (what Deleuze and Guattari call *la fuite*),[35] utterly de-territorializing themselves and reminding the reader of the quotient of madness in any reading of any text in contemporary capitalist society.

ASHBERY'S "EUROPE": POETRY IS GARBAGE

Ashbery's most notorious collage poem is the rambling, 111-section **"Europe,"** which could almost be said, in keeping with the "bitter impression of absence"[36] engendered by Ashbery's self-abnegating techniques, not to have been *written* by the poet at all. The poem is mostly a "cut-up" of author William Le Queux's *Beryl of the Bi-Planes,* a World War I-era girl's book Ashbery "picked up by accident on one of the quais of Paris."[37] Thus, it is less a work of original writing than an extended, plastic adaptation based on a mass-produced object (hence, an "adaptation" that is more original than the work it utilizes as a "source") and thus should be analyzed less as literature than as an object. The ap-propriateness of the source work clearly has less to do with its literary merit than its lack of it—its low genre and accidental discovery. As literature, Le Queux's novel is about as impertinent a choice as that of a urinal as a work of sculpture; indeed, in a post-Duchamp era, the urinal has acquired a kind of iconic status.

But the poem is, ultimately, much more than a ready-made, and its relationship to Duchamp's sensibility and technique is more complex than that of a simple reitera-tion. In a technical sense, the poem is closer to being an elaborately "assisted" found object with neo-Dadaist additions, subtractions, and verbal riddles (a sort of "cryptography"[38]) in the spirit of Raymond Roussel or even Duchamp's *Large Glass.* On the other hand, underneath these collagist manipulations and insertions, Le Queux's banal text remains, in many ways, the physical substrate of the poem—a cheap story reduced to even baser material, its residues of plot, dialogue, and description all interfering with each other and producing verbal noise, shredded print, semantic junk, on to which a literary meaning can be projected in the spirit of allegory, but never quite extracted except as popular genre material. Beneath this artificial heteroge-neity a former cohesion, the sense of a lost un-original, can be faintly detected. Thus the plot of Le Queux's story acquires a certain structuring function[39] like that of the personal encounters between Bill Berkson and Frank O'Hara that punctuate the latter's long poem "Biotherm." But unlike the encounters there, the vague narrative glimpsed in **"Europe"** is totally unimportant, has no aura of personal expression, memory, or even interest. Any semblance of the personal is mortified in **"Europe"** being completely replaced with the pre-fab personae and sentiments of cheap fiction. If the self ap-pears at all, it is in the interstices and accumulations of the poem, in the material collagist adjustments that themselves may only offer further occasions for self-concealment. It is the replacement of the self's *énoncé,* for the body's *énonciation,* but one that may be indistinguishable from those of all other bodies.

To the extent that **"Europe"** retains an aura of Duch-ampian iconoclasm, it does so in the more contemporary spirit of 1960s neo-Dada or "New Realism," the term for art that pitted itself against Abstract Expressionist values of heroic composition for the pre-fabricated compositions of everyday, manufactured objects. Emerging simultaneously and independently in Europe and the United States, the New Realists informally included such artists as Yves Klein, Jean Tinguely, Robert Rauschenberg, Jasper Johns, and even Andy Warhol.[40] The new realism it expressed—even as it reutilized certain dadaist forms—was that of industrial, consumer reality as an inescapable fact of human identity, depriving it of any unique or transcendent meaning beyond that of parody or ritual mimicry. As Ashbery himself wrote in an exhibition catalogue of the New Realists for the Sidney Janis Gallery in 1962, the work represented the "continuing effort to come to grips with the emptiness of modern life." But he also wrote: "The most successful way of doing this seems to be to accord it its due. That is, to recognize that the phenom-ena evoked by the artists in this show are not [just] phenomena, but part of our experience, our lives—created by us and creating us."[41] Unlike their dadaist predecessors, these artists no longer upheld the products of industrial civilization as a provocation to aesthetic values but as confirmation of what those values were becoming. There was little trace in these works of Dada's giddy hysteria in confronting modernity—rather a casual aplomb, a cool facility with its vocabulary of accumulation and consumption. The *otherness* of modernity had infused these works without provoking the usual sense of outrage at a proportional loss of presumed self-expression in a work of art. Such self-expression was now recognized as just another form among many that modern reality provided, ready-made, for the artist to utilize, either in aggregate (Rauschenberg's junk sculptures and photo-silkscreens), in series (Warhol's Campbell's Soup cans), or in simple isolation (Johns's targets and flags). In his review, Ashbery goes on to clarify the appeal of manufactured objects and signs for these artists:

> But why the object? Why are objects any more or less important than anything else? The answer is that they are not, and that, I think, is the secret of their popularity with these artists. They are a common ground, a neutral language understood by everybody, and therefore the ideal material with which to create experiences which transcend the objects. . . . As the French critic Françoise Choay points out, speaking of Duchamp: "On one side the product of industry is denounced in its anonymity, its banality, its essential poverty which deprives it of human and poetic qualifications. On the other hand it still remains an object which a simple decision on the part of the spectator can tear out from its context to give it mystery and opacity. . . . The ready-made is satire, but at the same time it is also a proposition of asceticism and conversion."[42]

One can be shocked or intrigued: the decision is one's own. The meaning one gives it can no longer rely on any organic determination, but is arbitrarily posited—in conformity with Walter Benjamin's concept of allegory.[43] Such is the new realism.

The notion that art was less a natural entity to be heroically discovered in the interest of originality, progress, and other teleological values than an arbitrary selection based on given information opened a huge gap in the American Avant-Garde between the New Realists (and their late, alternative incarnation as Pop Artists) and the Abstract Expressionists. Yet elements of continuity can be identified in their works, albeit primarily in the neo-Dadaists' satirical use of the "painterly" techniques of their predecessors. The two most enlightening examples, apropos of Ashbery, are Johns and Rauschenberg, a number of whose works parallel or anticipate both the poet's attitude toward the recent past and his techniques of literary production in **"Europe."**[44] As critic Leo Steinberg has written of Johns, his "pictures showed essentially Abstract Expressionist brushwork and surface, differing from those

earlier pictures only in the variable of the subject matter, [and thus] seemed to accuse the strokes and drips of the De Kooning school of being after all only a subject matter of a different kind; which threatened the whole foundation of Abstract Expressionist theory."[45] The painting *Liar* seems to make this accusation explicit inasmuch as the painting consists of an accumulation of grey, painterly "strokes and drips" evenly spread across the surface in an all-over manner, but with the imprint of the word "LIAR" along the top, made (presumably) by the "real" block letters illusionistically attached to the canvas by a hinge. In this case, the natural subject of art (in Steinberg's view, art as "analogue of a visual [or subjective] experience of nature" as in Abstract-Expressionist works[46]) is spoofed by the "artificial subject" of Johns's art (the printed word "LIAR"). The device, however, is not without irony, given that the lie also redounds to the block letters themselves, which in order to print the word "LIAR" have to be designed and arranged as mirror opposites of the letters they print. In other works, the painting confesses to its own illusionism, its recourse to conventional forms. It is the paradox of calling oneself a liar.

Another relevant example by Johns is his map paintings of the United States. As in De Kooning's *Women,* the scale of the paintings is monumental and their brushwork conveys a self-consciously gestural, "personal" quality of execution. Yet the subject matter is conspicuously schematic, with the familiar outlines of the forty-eight states and surrounding territories providing a standard template, as it were, for the composition. Furthermore, the postal abbreviations for the states have been systematically, if beautifully, stenciled into their geographically designated spaces. If this recourse to technique were not enough, Johns's "loose, rapid handling" of paint succumbs to another systematics: that of using only primary colors, a criteria derived—with bitter Dada irony—from Abstract Expressionism's near theoretical opposite, Neoplasticism. In each of these ways, then, one discovers an Abstract Expressionist quality of the "painterly" being perversely combined with competing systems of information by which specific contents impose a form and a mode of composition.

Relevant examples by Rauschenberg include junk constructions and "combine" paintings that make use of both painting and ordinary three-dimensional objects and thus promote Steinberg's postmodern idea of painting as a "flat-bed picture plane"[47] (a horizontal and purely cultural "matrix of information,"[48] as against the idea of painting as a vertical analogue of natural vision and against "the mystical qualities of medium made available [to that vision] . . . as compensation for loss of illusionism").[49] The most famous of these "combines," and perhaps the one that directly inspired Steinberg's formulation, is Rauschenberg's *Monogram* with its goat and tire mounted on a horizontal painted surface. Here Rauschenberg has shifted the whole orientation of the painted surface in order to accommodate an otherwise unassimilable found object, a stuffed Angora goat. Other assemblages utilize less conspicuous objects, but nevertheless use them in novel ways, as in *Winter Pool,* where a ladder, instead of combining upper and lower regions, forms a bridge between two painted side panels.

The relevance of such works to Ashbery's poem is their *disorienting* quality of constructed multiplicity—of combining disparate, junk elements and almost casually coordinating them to establish what Rauschenberg has called a "random order."[50] This quality can also be found in the artist's solvent-transfer drawings (the *Inferno* series) and silk-screen paintings, in which numerous images from popular culture are transferred to paper or canvas and, with modifications, combined to form complex, textured wholes—yet with many of their "transferred" elements retaining a kind of floating, mutually-interfering visual autonomy within those wholes. But perhaps the most immediately pertinent example by Rauschenberg is his notorious *Erased De Kooning* (1953). On the face of it, this work would seem an even greater provocation than Johns's by virtue of its actual defacement, even destruction, of a De Kooning drawing. Yet, as in Johns's *Liar,* latent ironies come to the surface of this radical gesture, since Rauschenberg's erasure acquires aesthetic significance by reference to what it eliminates (an irony not lost on De Kooning, who gave his permission[51]).

How do these works relate to Ashbery's **"Europe"**? As Ashbery has written of Johns's procedure, one should try to "build away from the edge of the canvas"[52] of Ashbery's poem by beginning with certain framing or organizational devices at the boundaries, as it were, of the poem and relating them to the various compositional "givens" of Johns's work. In both men's work, it is precisely such given systems of organization that do the most to undermine the self-monumentalizing aspects of the last wave. The primary casualty of Ashbery's systematic mortification of the recent literary past is Eliot's "Waste Land" (although Williams's more sanguine *Paterson* runs a close second).[53] Eliot's masterpiece is evoked, however, only through the most deflationary or superficial of monumentalizing signs, whereby length replaces grandiosity and simple labels replace suggestive titles. Ashbery, then, has precariously premised the literariness of **"Europe"** on an almost arbitrary, involuntary memory rather than on any method of conscientious evocation. The very notion of influence has been flattened out here by labeling a long series of dubious "verses" with a bogus Eliotic subject. **"Europe,"** like "The Waste Land," may indeed refer to a whole history of European culture, but it is the culture of one-dimensional man that is found in the poem (as the chauvinistic prose of Le Queux's novel and other journalistic sources reveals). Given such contents, the title seems just as likely to refer to a map of Europe or the Paris metro stop of the same name. Ashbery's title, then, is schizophrenically evocative *and* flat: like the state-names in Johns's *Map,* it is suggestively applied yet blandly ready-made; like the word "liar" in Johns's painting, **"Europe"** both emulates and mocks its historical predecessor (if more tonelessly here). Yet, in the final analysis, Ashbery's strategy has a sharp dadaist edge. To the extent that the title brings Eliot's poem to mind, it is less for the purpose of enriching Ashbery's own subject than for deflating "The Waste Land" itself. It is as though Ashbery had made the title of Eliot's poem—as opposed to the poem itself—the justification and technique of his own work by taking it quite literally and remaking Europe as if it were an actual garbage heap, real "trash" (in the sense of "literature," too). References to waste and garbage abound in **"Europe,"** but they have little emotional resonance in a poetic landscape plagiaristically fashioned out of snippets of magazine articles and a patently jingoistic novel for English school girls. They simply label contents.

The next organizational feature of the poem that recalls Johns's work is its quantified scale, perfunctorily inflated by the sheer number of sections. If the 100-plus divisions give the work certain Dantesque proportions, Ashbery manneristically attenuates that number to remind us that these divisions correspond to no perfect, classicizing order—simply a distended, entropic series. One may therefore ask whether the accumulated sections really suggest a cosmic, Dantesque vision (in the spirit of Eliot), or if repetition and number have been over-determined. (As the whole of section 2. reads: "A wave of nausea— / numerals[.]"[54]) Symbolic or not, the series is tediously consistent, predictable—as one also finds in Johns's work, which regularly adheres to complete, ordered systems, whether of state-names, digits (0-9), or letters (A-Z). Ashbery ultimately levels the mannered monumentality of his poem by ending it on a number whose very digits suggest mind-numbing repetition: one . . . one . . . one . . .

Consistent with the numbering of the sections is the way the lines of **"Europe"** mostly adhere to the left margin, a sort of baseline to which the poet repeatedly and automatically resorts with each return, as it were, of the typewriter carriage. Automatism here is no longer passionately instinctual but merely mechanical, convenient, all of which helps contribute to the same "impression of absence" that one finds in Johns's paintings (which Steinberg himself described as being "about human absence"[55]). At the same time, however, there are deviations from this course that become all the more conspicuous as a consequence. Certain sections defy the left margin, assuming a kind of all-overness in miniature. Other lines, from section 57, fall into seven couplets to form an eccentric sonnet. Another section has double columns (section 107), while yet another offers a minimalist calligram (section 104). In their eccentric deviation from the general "rule" of the poem, these parodies of poetic forms indicate other preoccupations of the poem that relate less to Johns's schematicism than to a more Rauschenbergian impulse toward assemblage and erasure, collage and disjuncture and their mutual interference (although this impulse is also evident in Johns's work). Evidence of what may be the literal erasure of a text occurs in these "deviations" mentioned above that assume the appearance of certain cubist poems by Reverdy. But unlike those poems, in which an architectonic organization is revealed, Ashbery's sections present something closer to random gaps in what may once have been a coherent, descriptive line or passage:

28.

wishing you were a
the bottle really   before the washed
   handed over to her:
         hundreds
light over her
  hanging her
you can remember

85.

     ghost of stone—massive
        hangs halfway
polishing
       whose winding
Strong, sad half-city
    gardens
                from the bridge of
  stair
         broom
   recent past symbolized
hair banana
does not evoke a concrete image
the splendid

The difficulties of comprehension here are less the result of instilling new insights (say, of form, per Reverdy) than of simply withholding information. Yet the incompleteness produces an almost accidental sense of poetic mystery (as well as funny juxtapositions) not unlike that in Reverdy's poems. Thus, resupplying the missing information would offer a great deal less than withholding it, since such a disclosure would only reduce the poem to the tawdry truth of its sources (in Section 28, a scene of laundering?; Section 85, a travelogue?). In this way the simple technique of erasure imbues the source text with an aura of the poetic it probably does not deserve. Simple in the extreme, erasure reveals the banality inherent to all poetic techniques, the *raison d'être* of which is to provide a shortcut to a desired effect. Yet Ashbery is prepared to go even further with his strategy, obliterating any such effect of aura by completely obliterating linguistic sense

itself. Sections under almost total erasure represent nothing less than a radical demonstration of the effects of the "plastic" attitude in poetry. Such sections are completely deficient as functional linguistic elements, deconstructing any sense of unity or self-containment otherwise attributable to a poem's parts. Both syntax and semantics are lost to the minimal linguistic fragments suspended in the allotted "spaces" of the sections. As such, they almost fuse with adjacent sections, as if to erase their own numbered headings.

But the compositional strategies are not confined to those of erasure or disjuncture and the poem frequently incorporates narrative passages and popular clichés in all their prosaic integrity.[56] More importantly, the poem establishes subtle, self-reflective connections between these narrative chunks and the brittle detrita of the "erased" passages through poeticizing themes of aviation, espionage, and war as found in *Beryl of the Bi-Planes*. In this way the long poem seems less a random collection of verbal junk than a kind of verbal junk sculpture, an assemblage that makes creative use of randomness (an idea corroborated in section 16: "when canvas the must spread / to new junk"). In keeping with statements Ashbery has made about his poetry in general, the poem represents the attempt to keep "meaningfulness up to the pace of randomness. . . ."[57] Meaningfulness seems most able to do this by disguising itself as meaningless clichés (section 15 reads: "He is probably one of the gang") or impertinent blocks of mundane narrative, the absurd clarity of which mock one's incomprehension of the more disjunctive sections. Yet sometimes these clichés and blocks provide a commentary on the poem's procedures through Ashbery's adroit thematization of elements within them.

Such self-commentary occurs early in the poem in section 8—a conspicuously un-versified paragraph (like those found in *Paterson*) that establishes a narrative reference point for other, shorter collage elements derived from the same or similar sources. The passage from *Beryl* describes a scene of "engine trouble" on England's Great North Road, engine trouble that, like the prose block itself, impedes all progress and corrects itself only with the final phrase: "All was now ready for the continuance of the journey," at which point the more regular technique of accelerated, atomistic collagism resumes. The idea here is that the engine of the poem is precisely the randomness and disjunctiveness that this passage of clear and simple prose disrupts with bland coherence (offering a sort of break for the reader not unlike the lunch break enjoyed by the two characters mentioned in the passage). Meaning, then, is what troubles this poem and it is no accident that the literal meanings it sometimes offers are so insipid, drawn from the jingoistic adventure story, the paranoid spy thriller, and the vapid romance. Even at full throttle, as it were, such "meaningful prose" is literarily stunted, even old-fashioned, inasmuch as the source book was written in the context of a war already superseded in historical memory by several others. Thus, as in many of Rauschenberg's early junk sculptures, Ashbery's choice of materials reflects a deliberate anachronism evidenced in the proliferation of bi-planes, telegraphs, Zeppelins, and balloons in this poem of the 1960s.

A culture and technology of national defense provides the substrate of Ashbery's own collagist technology of assemblage and erasure. His technique, then, pits him against the chauvinistic prerogatives of his sources and *he* becomes what Le Queux's characters identify as the "absolute, unthinking / menace to our way of life" (section 7). This way of life is revealed in sections devoted to the honeyed collaboration of the ace pilots Beryl and Ronnie, whose mission is to prevent something called "the silencer" (phallus? fasces?) from falling into the wrong hands. A base narrative of sorts is provided from certain fictional passages the poet leaves relatively intact (many of them ironically versified), allowing the reader to make speculative connections to other, less integral blocks that have been cropped, asseverated, juxtaposed, or shrewdly distorted to reveal the more sinister aspects of such literature. As if in response to Le Queux's themes of espionage and secret messages, Ashbery yields a poetic alternative whereby the secret of banal prose (its *unconscious,* as it were) could only be deciphered through a process of re-scrambling. Some examples of this poetically adulterated, insinuating prose follow:

13. before the truth can be explained
     Nothing can exist.

15. Absolve me from the hatred I never
     she—all are wounded against
     Zeppelin—wounded carrying dying
     three colors over land

16. before I started
     I was forced to
     flying
     she said

30. forget, encouraging your vital organs.
     Telegraph. The rifle—a page folded over.

         More upset, wholly meaningless, the willing
     sheath
         glide into fall .. mercury to passing
         the war you said won—milling around the
     picket fence, and noise of the engine from the sky
     and flowers—here is a bunch
     the war won out of cameos
     And somehow the perfect warrior fallen.

34. you can't understand their terror
     means more to these people waste
     the runt crying in the pile of colored
     snapshots offal in the wind
     that's the way we do it terror

75. Like the public,
     reaction
     from Crystal Palace

80. multitude headquarters shout there
     Because there are no
     because the majority is toxic

A whole culture of terror emerges from these fragments, poetically and plastically assisted to yield what seem their truer, totalitarian impulses. A sort of absolute, unthinking menace to other ways of life thus emanates from the Crystal Palace, as it were, of technological progress—particularly as it is pursued in the national interest. Backward or counter-technologies indicative of such "other ways" become tell-tale signs of sinister plots against the warriors of progress. Among those implicated among the "toxic majority" are the poet and the artist, classical distorters of truth:

107. The steel bolts
      having been replaced
      by *a painting of*
      one of wood!
      Ronnie, thoughtfully,

              of the silencer

          plot to kill us both, dear.

pet

              oh

      it that she was there

But perhaps their paranoia is justified! Nothing so meager as a plot to kill Le Queux's flying deuces, Ashbery's aim is to kill coherence itself and the vision of progress, unity, security such coherence promotes. Yet his purpose has a coherence all its own, an alternative coherence that springs from the need to create an order not out of chaos, but *of* chaos. As a consequence, its effects range across the whole poem, but are only occasionally referred to directly. These references themselves occur at random intervals, although they are never accidental when they do occur. By no means a consistent justification of the work's development, the references are merely pragmatic, a way of joining parts that may or may not go together. Like glue, they are often transparent (in the sense of invisible or disguised), but they also become cloudy and seep out at the joints they hold. It is this seeping out, this calculated self-exposure (like the earlier redundancy of a *painting* of a wooden replacement of a steel bolt) by which the poem admits to its own terroristic impulse toward an alternative order—albeit an order with a certain tolerance for the disorderly. Section 62 suggests the universality of this collagist predicament: "All of us fear the secret / guarded too carefully / An assortment[.]"

Such moments of self-commentary (moments when collagist cacography ascends to a level of virtual citation, implying Ashbery's partial retention of the modern, authorial "I") are subtlest when they occur in the form of un-assisted quotation as in the opening line of section 38: "The roar of the engine, of course, / rendered speech impossible[.]" The engine of Ashbery's collagism does much the same thing, even as it affirms that the "impossible" speech of the poem that results actually conveys the true nature and meaning (or secret) of speech. Other examples are embedded in erased or jerry-rigged sections such as 107: "I don't understand wreckage"; 90: "powerless creating images"; 85: "does not evoke a concrete image"; or 73—which looks like leftover words at the margin of a damaged page, yet assisted (perhaps) with an inserted portion (italicized below):

> A least
> four days
> A surprise
> mothers
> suppose
> *Is not a "images"*
> *to "arrange"*
> [. . .]

Still other sections seem to comment directly on the "traditional" use of newspapers in collage. Section 57 includes the line: "The newspaper is ruining your eyes[,]" while section 39 seems to allegorize the process in a narrative scene: "The newspaper being read / Beside the great gas turbine / The judge calls his assistant over / And together they try to piece the secret message / contained in today's paper." Of course, the best known example of such self-commentary is probably not collage at all but a direct statement of Ashbery's (section 10): "He had mistaken his book for garbage[.]" Although it may be another tongue-in-cheek reference to "The Waste Land," this sentence suggests that a methodological confusion between books and garbage has helped to keep meaningfulness up to pace with randomness, and modern poetry up to pace with junk art.

As a totality, the poem can only be apprehended as a collection of related verbal collage techniques intersecting and interrupting each other in order to thwart the engines of verbal and ideological coherence. The coherence it does offer—a kind of plastic coherence—derives from an appreciation of these variations on collage technique. While literary elements contribute to the poem's effects, any attempt to determine a consistent narrative progress in the work can only yield frustration, "a wave of nausea," or loss of critical identity. It is a dangerous undertaking; its inevitable failure, however, makes a certain case for the poem as well, insofar as the extreme dislocations and garbled multiplicities within yield an almost monolithic sense of

boredom, a critical anaesthesia in which any idea of organic development cedes to one of ironic inertia. From this standpoint, each section of the poem provides another chamber of noise in a hopeless series. The parts, even the subtlest components, have a kind of primary indistinguishability, a tendency to go nowhere but to the next in the series, to "funnily" repeat what comes before and after in a way that produces a vast figure of entropic stasis.

THREE POEMS: "THE SKATERS," "THE NEW SPIRIT," "SELF-PORTRAIT IN A CONVEX MIRROR"

If **"Europe"** capitalizes on erasure and assemblage as primary poetic procedures, Ashbery's two long poems **"The Skaters"** and **"The New Spirit"** provide incipient commentaries on these procedures as a starting point for a more meditative direction in his subsequent work. In doing this, both poems provide insights into Ashbery's developing attitude toward the relation between poetry and the plastic arts as a function of their avant-gardism, as well as toward the changing nature of avant-gardism itself.

Ashbery's well-known opposition between "putting it all in" and "the leaving-out business" first appears in **"The Skaters"** and—like assemblage and erasure in **"Europe"**—generally characterizes his working approach in a poem that oscillates between collagism and a more ruminative mode.[58] Determining which one of these modes occupies the place of the putting-in and the leaving-out businesses is the impossible task the poem sets before the reader in the following lines—despite any rhetorical pretense at dispelling such ambiguity:

> It is time now for a general understanding of
> The meaning of all this. The meaning of Helga,
>   importance of the setting, etc.
> A description of the blues. Labels on bottles
> And all kinds of discarded objects that ought to be
>   described.
> But can one ever be sure of which ones?
> Isn't this a death-trap, wanting to put too much in
> So the floor sags, as under the weight of a piano, or a
>   piano-legged girl
> And the whole house of cards comes dinning down
>   around one's ears!
>
> But this is an important aspect of the question
> Which I am not ready to discuss, am not at all ready
>   to.
> This leaving-out business. On it hinges the very
>   importance of what's novel
> Or autocratic, or dense, or silly.[59]

The "collectibles"—Rousselesque bottle labels and Helga, the discarded objects and other plastic "phenomena" unceremoniously juxtaposed or catalogued in so many modernist poems—would seem to be the substance of this deadly inclusiveness that swamps the imagination. Or is it just the opposite?—the will to explain these phenomena, "the meaning of all this," yet a meaning that can only be all-inclusive through selective abbreviation. And if explanation is a way of putting it all in, aren't those "unexplained" catalogues a mode of "leaving-out" by virtue of not explaining themselves? Turning the problem around again: if catalogues and collages are plastic forms of putting-in, explanation becomes a form of leaving-out, a sort of convenient, summary, semiotic replacement for all that junkyard clutter. As such, explanation can assume either progressive or autocratic properties depending on the spirit of one's replacements. Ironically, the most devastating effects of the explanatory mode (as it assumes the business of leaving-out) come in the guise of modern revolutions of discourse symbolized in the poem by invisible winds of change that trash everything in order, ostensibly, to celebrate trash. This vast cultural purge is filtered through language evoking modernist and avant-garde experiments—not to mention more sinister, political ones that were being undertaken at the same time. Yet the absolutist tenor of the windy rhetoric goes surprizingly well with a variety of ideological positions, whether from the right or left, whether originating in high modernist techniques or low dadaist ones, whether in the heroic self-expression of a Pollock or in the group ethics of process artists—all of whom risk everything in pursuit of prescribed forms of modernity:

> A great wind lifted these cardboard panels
> Horizontal in the air. At once the perspective with the horse
> Disappeared in a *bigarrure* of squiggly lines. The image with the crocodile in it became no longer apparent.
> Thus a great wind cleanses, as a new ruler
> Edits new laws, sweeping the very breath of the streets
> Into posterior trash. The films have changed—
> The great titles on the scalloped awning have turned dry and blight-colored.
> No wind that does not penetrate a man's house, into the very bowels of the furnace,
> Scratching in dust a name on the mirror—say, and what about letters,
> The dried grasses, fruits of the winter—gosh! Everything is trash!
> The wind points to the advantages of decay
> At the same time as removing them far from the sight of men.
> The regent of the winds, Aeolus, is a symbol for all earthly potentates
> Since holding this sickening, festering process by which we are cleansed
> Of afterthought.

(pp. 36-37)

With this sarcastic invalidation of sweeping cultural decrees (identified with that Joycean windbag, Aeolus), Ashbery distances himself from any energetic program of change. Yet the distance is only by half, a measure of self-abnegation, insofar as his own past experiments

also made vigorous "editorial" use of trash. And although it seems a pity to blow the very breath out of the streets, certain effects of the potentates' decrees have a definite appeal to Ashbery's sense of novelty. But in the end, it is novelty—not revolution—that is recommended here, as much for retaining certain qualities of the exquisite as for its own effects of surprise.

> The answer is that it is novelty
> That guides these swift blades o'er the ice
> Projects into a finer expression (but at the expense
> Of energy) the profile I cannot remember.

(p. 34)

If **"The Skaters"** offers an image of this "finer expression" in the form of lines cut in ice, crisscrossing in ways that suggest overlapping and transparent collagist edges, **"The New Spirit"** blurs those edges even further by dissolving collagism itself in a matrix of abstract prose. Ironically, the medium traditionally associated with "explanation" is virtually ubiquitous in this poem, with only occasional lapses into the graphic modulations of free verse. Yet in no sense is Ashbery resorting to mere explanation or even traditional narrative by way of prose: he is appropriating it for avant-garde purposes, or at least those of an idiosyncratic avant-garde.[60] Thus the medium of explanation is drained of didactic potential while avant-garde poetry itself is deprived of graphic energy, the visible disjunctions that formerly signaled novelty. Ashbery also reduces the imagery of the visible, including those catalogues of concrete phenomena that proliferate in **"The Skaters."** They are expressed only as things outside expression: natural elements to be "reclaimed" through the action of art or to reclaim art in turn.[61]

Interestingly, this movement away from the conspicuous physicality and randomness that were indicative of an aesthetics of medium in the painting of the 1950s parallels a certain movement away from visual media and toward verbal discourse in the art of the 1960s, in particular, conceptual and minimal art. In the context of avant-garde poetry, however, any such resumption of discursivity comes provocatively close to resuming the narrative strategies of an older poetics. The old and the new, then, seem to overlap here in the narrow, conditional interests of something even newer (if less presumptuous than its "contributors"). Within these confines, Ashbery's new spirit is conceived. Finding a kind of freedom in circumstances of diminished options is the ironic premise concerning the expressive "self" in this poem: "One is aware of it as an open field of narrative possibilities. Not in the edifying sense of the tales of the past that we are still (however) chained to, but as stories that tell only of themselves, so that one realizes one's self has dwindled and now at last vanished in the diamond light of pure speculation" (p. 41).

A recurring, escalating dialectics of "self" and "other" provides the structural movement of **"The New Spirit."** The fusion, separation, and mannered variation of these meditative categories are the formal modes of the new spirit in its perpetual task, once again, of either putting it all in or leaving it out in the process of going forward.[62] The poem describes the task in the opening lines, initially calling the leaving-out business the "truer" way, but quickly remembering that "forget as we will, something soon comes to stand in their place. Not the truth, perhaps, but—yourself" (*TP* [*Three Poems*], p. 3). While "they" represent everything omitted, the "you" is the domain of everything that puts itself in against the "I's" intention of leaving it out. Thus **"The New Spirit"** seems to be the subject's coming to terms with a tendency—exemplified by the Avant-Garde on one hand and democracy on the other—toward greater inclusion in expressive media that traditionally operate through a process of elimination. Both resignation and a futile bravado characterize the discursive voice of the poem that can only know itself through another but defines itself against that other. Consequently, it is virtually impossible to know whether the "I" and "you," subject and object of the poem, are distinct entities or internalized divisions representing the construction of the self through identification—in a sort of Lacanian mirror-stage—with the object. A strange, hostile complicity surrounds them, like that between the leaving-out and the putting-in. It is a numbing, confused complicity necessitated by perpetually advancing on the future: "I can only say that the wind of the change as it has happened has numbed me, to the point where the false way and the true way are confounded, where there is no way or rather where everything is a way, none more suitable nor more accurate than the last, oblivion rapidly absorbing their outline like snow filling footprints" (p. 17).

Despite its fresh appearance, the title of Ashbery's poem is self-consciously outdated, duplicating in English the original phrase from an essay by Apollinaire, itself laden with traditional, quasi-religious overtones. The new, then, seems almost weary in this poem for its evocations of both the recent, "playful" past and a more archaic one, fraught with eschatology:

> The visitation, was it more or less over? No, it had not yet begun, except as a preparatory dream which seemed to have the rough texture of life, but which dwindled into starshine like all the unwanted memories. There was no holding on to it. But for that we ought to be glad, no one really needed it, yet it was not utterly worthless, it taught us the forms of this our present waking life, the manners of the unreachable. And its judgments, though harmless and playful, were yet the form of utterance by which judgment shall come to be known.
>
> (pp. 7-8)

The preparatory dream, harmless though it may have been, potentially assumes a more sinister, judgmental aspect in keeping with the long, salvific tradition out of which it grew. As ironic heir of *l'esprit nouveau,* the voice of **"The New Spirit"** seems oppressed by this potential and convinced of the necessity—for the sake of its own future—of sustaining a radical avant-garde vision only in the realm of speculation (where the judgments resulting from that vision of inclusion are less irrevocable). **"The New Spirit"** is avant-garde, then, primarily as a meditation on the meaning of the Avant-Garde and the new; it does not repeat the original action of the Avant-Garde—otherwise its own newness would be at risk, especially given its partial dependency on elements of a tradition that are presumably crushed by the success of the Avant-Garde. Such success is, for Ashbery, the Avant-Garde's self-undermining, whereby it becomes a ubiquitous, Faustian endeavor, signalled through obsessive, sweeping *action* to remake the world, to "change life" (again, in Rimbaud's phrase), but using methods that increasingly resemble those of venture capitalism: ". . . there never was a day like this for getting things done, and action pursues its peaceful advance on the lethargic, malarial badlands of the day, draining swamps, clearing scrub forests, putting the hygienic torch to the villages, planting ground-cover crops such as clover, alfalfa, colza, buckwheat and cowpeas." (p. 36)

In the context of the sort of poetic speculation that characterizes Ashbery's version of the Avant-Garde, this sweeping force remains mysteriously docile, the poem's disquisitions providing a more constrained influence in the interest of a conditional future. Like the convulsive Bretonian image of a stilled locomotive in the jungle, the mythic Avant-Garde goes into dormition here preparatory to a form of reverse engineering by which the poem secures alternative futures, personal avant-gardes:

> The wind is now fresh and full, with leaves and other things flying. And to release it from its condition of hardness you will have to take apart the notion of you so as to reconstruct it from an intimate knowledge of its inner workings. How harmless and even helpful the painted wooden components of the Juggernaut look scattered around the yard, patiently waiting to be reassembled! So ends the first lesson: that the concave being, enfolding like air or spirit, does not dissolve when breathed upon but comes apart neatly, like a watch, and the parts may be stocked or stored, their potential does not leak away through inactivity but remains bright and firm, so that in a sense it is just as much *there* as if it were put back together again and even more so: with everything sorted and labeled you can keep an eye on it a lot better than if it were again free to assume protean shapes and senses, the genie once more let out of the bottle, and who can say where all these vacant premises should end? No, it is far better to keep this potential dry, even at the risk of having its immobility come to seem a reproach, the mute appeal of the saber

hung up on the wall. [. . .] Why, its imperfections are just a token of how life moves along, haltingly but somehow always getting there in time, in our time.

(pp. 19-20)

The Juggernaut of the Avant-Garde must be analyzed and, in a sense, tamed. Yet there is also a sense of its fragility, a fear of it evaporating under the breath of discursive expression. Hence, so many precautions about it: as well as "taming" it, the tactful analytics of the poem provide a way of preserving its power. The task, of course, seems merely custodial and suggests a narrowing of ambition for the author of this change, who exists in a state of "erect passivity . . . free to come and go within a limited area, a sort of house-arrest of the free agent intentionally cut off from the forces of renewal" (pp. 20-21). There can be little doubt, however, that the agent has imposed these limits for the sake of the new tradition he has inherited and thus may find genuine "happiness within the limitations" (p. 27). For all its apparent narrowness and inertia, the situation still offers compensations that make it preferable to what went before (i.e., insofar as the latter is construed as simply moving without variation along its projected path toward successful ubiquity). Its space is aerated, protective, more "elevated" than before. Funnily, it has all the earmarks of a new Manhattan apartment where the poet can comfortably take in the life of the streets that sustains his project—only: at a remove, the poet perversely marginalized even as circumstances require that his efforts be somehow broadly encompassing. Only by way of a certain "outward-hanging, ledge over the pitfalls of mankind" (p. 10) is this broadness to be attained. The temptation "to retreat again into the hard dark recesses of yourself" (p. 44) can be difficult to resist when one looks from that ledge into the throng below, described with Eliotic horror as a flood or snake pit (p. 44). The need to think things out, however, is maintained and a workable, compromise solution is found, one that even seems beautiful from the right perspective:

> He thought he had never seen anything quite so beautiful as that crystallization into a mountain of statistics: out of the rapid movement to and fro that abraded individual personalities into a channel of possibilities, remote from each other and even remoter from the eye that tried to contain them: out of that river of humanity comprised of individuals each no better than he should be and doubtless more solicitous of his own personal welfare than of the general good, a tonal quality detached itself that partook of the motley intense hues of the whole gathering but yet remained itself, firm and all-inclusive, scrupulously fixed equidistant between earth and heaven, as far above the tallest point on the earth's surface as it was beneath the lowest outcropping of cumulus in the cornflower-blue empyrean. Thus everything and everybody were included after all, and any thought that might ever be entertained about them; the irritating drawbacks each possessed along with

certain good qualities were dissolved in the enthusiasm of the whole, yet individuality was not lost for all that, but persisted in the definition of the urge to proceed higher and further as well as in the counter-urge to amalgamate into the broadest and widest kind of uniform continuum.

(pp. 48-49)

But true to "time's way of walking sideways out of the event, at the same time proceeding in a straight line toward an actual vanishing point" (p. 23), Ashbery, at the end of the poem, assumes yet another perspective—this time outside the above "liberal" solution. The apartment block the reader has been imaginatively occupying with the poet is now seen from across the parking lot, as it were, and what he discovers is a new tower of Babel, "perfect in its vulgarity" (p. 50) and strangely reminiscent of the Juggernaut of before, only fully reassembled and arrogantly occluding the sky. The compromise one was so pleased to have negotiated now seems an embarrassing surrender to the vast social project of total cultural assimilation. The poet's efforts to establish an idiosyncratic middle way between tradition and anti-tradition have an ironic success or "acceptance" from which he wants to dissociate himself. The only alternative now—again unsatisfactory—is one of absolute negation, of turning one's back on the whole business of assimilation to behold the impassive, uncompromising constellations one had thought were lost to view. New oppositions are posited and the process resumes with the Archer (Ashbery's symbolic self-caricature?) challenging those constellations by "aiming at a still higher and smaller portion of the heavens" (p. 51).

As if in fulfillment of this final image, Ashbery's next long poem is the famous **"Self-Portrait in a Convex Mirror"** in which his poetic sights are representationally focused on a specific historico-aesthetic object: a truly "smaller portion of the heavens" that, nevertheless, possesses "total" reflecting powers (in keeping with the nature of convex mirrors[63]). In this work, Francesco Parmigianino and his own self-portraiture have replaced the slippery, amorphous "you" of **"The New Spirit."** The fact that Ashbery has selected a well-known mannerist painting [fig. 24] in which the highest Renaissance ideals are both confirmed and questioned with singular suavity reveals his assumption that painting continues to offer the adequate correlative of any sustained poetic meditation on problems of artistic production in general. The painting becomes the focus of renewed speculation about the nature of artistic inclusion and exclusion, experimentation and consolidation, democratization and colonization. The boundaries of that speculative activity, however, have shifted to accommodate a broader tradition suggested by the cultural object represented in the poem. It is an object in which "the enchantment of self with self"[64] is unapologetically proclaimed in keeping with a certain Renaissance self-conception that is at odds with the modern aspiration toward the lowest common denominator and the self-abnegating character of such accommodation. What "spars" of otherness are retained in the painting ("eyebeams, muslin, coral") exist only to reinforce that enchantment, a kind of rigorous narcissism bolstered by the most sophisticated illusionistic techniques. Gone are the piano-legged girls, the bottle-labels and other discarded objects that betoken dada and surrealist influences and assume the rough texture of assembled fragments, the marvelous sheen of chimerical juxtapositions, or the cacophonous jangle of simultaneous interdiscursivities. In its most uncompromising formulation, Parmigianino's art is one of intention, reproduction, and discrimination: "The record of what you accomplished by sitting down / 'With great art to copy all that you saw in the glass' / So as to perfect and rule out the extraneous / Forever" (p. 72).

Round like the globe and drawing everything onto its surface, the convex mirror provides the model for this reduction of experience to a "magma of interiors," a deathly, homogenous substance, as the self organizes otherness into self-affirming uniformity. Ashbery, for whom the "strewn evidence . . . the small accidents and pleasures of the day as it moved gracelessly on" (p. 71) still mean something, is nevertheless mesmerized by this exquisite, though "warped" putting-in business by which inclusion becomes ruthless self-expansion. But later in the poem, the idea of the city as the backing or support of this artistic enterprise predominates and, far from being sucked up into that enterprise, city life—at least on the scale of metropolitan New York—works to "siphon off the life of the studio . . ." (p. 75). The city and its dynamism become an almost dogmatic force of cultural change in themselves, pushing relentlessly, yet thoughtlessly toward something new: ". . . a new preciosity / In the wind. Can you stand it, / Francesco? Are you strong enough for it? / This wind brings what it knows not, is / Self-propelled, blind, has no notion / Of itself. It is inertia that once / Acknowledged saps all activity, secret or public" (p. 75). As a negative force, it sweeps all initiative to the suburbs of the mind where imagination languishes in a state of private entropy. But, once again, Ashbery offers an alternative response to these sweeping changes that tend to stifle creative energy: they also divulge new, unexpected values from the more "reticent" aspects of the past (such as mannerist painting) which acquire an unlikely and provocative vitality and which become a part of the change itself.

With the creation and critical success of ***Self-Portrait in a Convex Mirror*** a particular parameter of the continuum between "tradition" and "other tradition" (as Ashbery broadly and provisionally defined them) had been set. And although this more traditionally discursive poem, written in iambic pentameter, may have ulti-

mately satisfied Bloom's definition of a counter-sublime as a way of explaining Ashbery's precarious assimilation to the American romantic tradition, it more accurately reflects the poet's cautious assimilation of the latter to his own avant-garde inclinations. The poem **"Self-Portrait in a Convex Mirror"** is the furthest Ashbery goes—poetically and ideologically—toward realigning his experimentalist propensities with a refulgent, "Stevensian" tradition, but only on the assumption that both categories are in need of revision. The consequence is that avant-gardism becomes less of a practice than an object of sustained meditation, while traditional forms and themes are perversely experimented with. **"Self-Portrait"** [**"Self-Portrait in a Convex Mirror"**] does not set the standard for Ashbery's subsequent poetry, which often vigorously reincorporates the experimental plasticities of collagist, juxtapositional, and other disjunctive strategies (the long, double-columned poem **"Litany"** from *As We Know* represents the most visually conspicuous instance). But it does reveal the limits of his renunciation of the tradition and a certain "nostalgia for nostalgia" (O'Hara's phrase) that emerges in the work of a number of late avant-garde poets. Such a tendency, however, is sanctioned by Ashbery's own, somewhat idiosyncratic investigations of the French and American Avant-Gardes—both literary and artistic—which are shown to be always less monolithic and less radically anti-artistic than their respective manifestos suggest.

Notes

1. See W. H. Auden's foreword to Ashbery's first collection of poems, *Some Trees* (New Haven: Yale University, 1956) and Harold Bloom's "The Charity of the Hard Moments" in *John Ashbery,* ed. Harold Bloom (New York: Chelsea House, 1985), pp. 49-79. Ashbery's own reassessments of his artistic genealogy appear in various sections of his *Reported Sightings: Art Chronicles 1957-1989* (New York: Alfred A. Knopf, 1989). Subsequent citations of this edition will appear in the text and notes as *RS*.

2. John Ashbery, "An Interview with Henri Michaux" (1961) in *RS,* p. 398.

3. Ashbery, "In the Surrealist Tradition" (1964) in *RS,* p. 4.

4. Ashbery, "The Heritage of Dada and Surrealism" (1968) in *RS,* p. 6.

5. Ashbery, "Yves Tanguy" (1974) in *RS,* p. 26.

6. Quoted in Alan Feldman, *Frank O'Hara* (Boston: G. K. Hall, 1979), p. 69.

7. Ashbery, "A Note on Pierre Reverdy," an unpublished essay (c. 1957-1958) quoted in John Shoptaw, *On the Outside Looking Out: John Ashbery's Poetry* (Cambridge: Harvard University Press, 1994), pp. 49-50.

8. Ashbery, "Joseph Cornell" (1967) in *RS*, p. 17.

9. I am referring to the work of Clement Greenberg who saw "flatness" as a definitive or primary quality of modern painting. See his essay "The Crisis of the Easel Picture" in *Art & Culture* (Boston: Beacon Press, 1965), pp. 154-157.

10. Ashbery, "The Invisible Avant-Garde" (1968) in *RS*, p. 392.

11. T. S. Eliot, "Tradition and the Individual Talent" in *Selected Prose of T. S. Eliot,* ed. Frank Kermode (New York: Harcourt, Brace, Jovanovich, 1975), pp. 37-44.

12. Ashbery, "Soonest Mended" in *The Double Dream of Spring* (New York: Ecco Press, 1976), p. 18.

13. Ashbery, "The Other Tradition" in *Houseboat Days* (New York: Viking, 1977), pp. 2-3.

14. David Lehman, "The Shield of a Greeting" in *Beyond Amazement* (Ithaca: Cornell University, 1980), p. 113.

15. Shoptaw, p. 149.

16. Ashbery, "And *Ut Pictura Poesis* Is Her Name" in *Houseboat Days,* pp. 45-46.

17. Shoptaw, p. 193.

18. This assumption can be traced to Lessing's Laocoön, the modernist implications of which are discussed in W. J. T. Mitchell's *Iconology: Image, Text, Ideology* (Chicago: University of Chicago Press, 1986).

19. André Breton, *Surrealism and Painting,* trans. Simon Watson Taylor (New York: Harper & Row, 1972), p. 1.

20. Bloom, "The Charity of the Hard Moments," p. 51.

21. *Ibid.,* p. 65.

22. *Ibid.,* p. 60.

23. Leslie Wolf, "The Brushstroke's Integrity: The Poetry of John Ashbery and the Art of Painting" in *Beyond Amazement,* pp. 232-233.

24. Wolf likens the process of "material deviation" in Hart Crane and Wallace Stevens to Gombrich's notion of contradictory evidence in painting: ". . . the aim is to fight the 'transforming influence' of 'illusion'; for illusion is what allows us to be unconscious of the medium through which we are apprehending reality. Poets like Crane and Stevens—and Ashbery—will not allow us this unconsciousness. One need only consider Crane's arresting adjective-noun combinations—'improved infancy,' 'immaculate venom,' 'petalled word'—or his use of negating prefixes and suffixes—'and your head unrocking to a pulse'—to see one form the poem's 'resistance' may assume. Stevens' strategy is outwardly quieter, if no less insistent. One thinks of the subtle sliding weights moving beneath his strategic repetition of words, transforming them into semantic merry-go-rounds, or the bold contradiction of some of his gestures ('If all the green of spring is blue, and it is'—'Connoisseur of Chaos'). Entangled in a medium whose primary burden in ordinary usage is to refer to external reality, the poet must arrange the 'brushstrokes' of his tableau in such a way that they yield contradictory clues. To do this the poet must, as Stevens directed, approach language abstractly—that is, transport reality into his imagination. That way he can 'use' reality without committing himself to any particular reality. The language must inevitably employ some species of 'deviation'—syntactic dislocation, dissonant diction, variations within repetition—if the poet is to wrest his words from an easy, habitual assimilation." (Wolf, pp. 234-235) I would only add that, in a general way, the Latinate glamour of Stevens' poetic vocabulary oscillates between these abstractly "deviating" and realistically "communicating" alternatives by flaunting its qualities as an elevated style while simultaneously conjuring a sense of its denotative specificity.

25. In using this rather cumbersome term, I nevertheless want to point out its analogous function with art historian Norman Bryson's notion of "style" in painting as an impediment—fostered by historical circumstance—to the copying function painting conventionally assumes in order to capture the supposed "universal visual experience" of the viewer or artist. See Norman Bryson, *Vision and Painting: The Logic of the Gaze* (New Haven: Yale University, 1997 [1983]).

26. Wolf, p. 241 (quoting Wylie Sypher's *Rococo to Cubism in Art and Literature*).

27. *Ibid.,* pp. 224-225 (quoting Greenberg's "After Abstract Expressionism" in *New York Painting and Sculpture*).

28. Ashbery reveals certain symbolist ambitions for his poetry apropos of its relation to music in a statement quoted by Bloom: "I feel I could express myself best in music. What I like about music is its feeling of being convincing, of carrying an argument through to the finish, though the terms of this argument remain unknown quantities. What remains is the structure, the architecture of the argument, scene, or story. I would like to do this in poetry." (Quoted in Bloom's introduction to *John Ashbery,* p. 28).

29. Harold Rosenberg, "The American Action Painters," quoted by Wolf in *Beyond Amazement,* p. 239. Wolf's ellipses.

30. Leo Steinberg's phrase, "Jasper Johns: The First Seven Years of His Art" in *Other Criteria* (New York: Oxford University Press, 1972), p. 54.

31. Bloom, "Charity" in *John Ashbery,* p. 53.

32. Wolf, p. 243.

33. David Shapiro, *John Ashbery: An Introduction to the Poetry* (New York: Columbia University, 1979), pp. 55-56.

34. Antoine Compagnon, *La Seconde Main, ou le travail de la citation* (Paris: Éditions du Seuil, 1979), pp. 381-382.

35. Gilles Deleuze and Félix Guattari, "Capitalism: A Very Special Delirium" (trans. David L. Sweet) in *Chaosophy,* ed. Sylvère Lotringer (New York: Semiotext[e], 1995), pp. 72-73.

36. Ashbery, "The Skaters" in *Rivers and Mountains* (New York: Ecco Press, 1977), p. 39.

37. Shapiro, p. 19. Although this fact is now well known, Shapiro seems to be the first critical expositor of Ashbery's work to have mentioned it.

38. Shoptaw, p. 6. This is Shoptaw's word for the process in which "crypt words" or "crypt phrases" are displaced by misrepresentative marker words or phrases, but are thereby still recoverable in the final poetic text.

39. It should be noted, however, that only about a third of the entire poem can be directly traced to the book, and its plot elements are sparsely deployed. Imre Salusinsky, "The Genesis of Ashbery's 'Europe'" in *NMAL: Notes on Modern American Literature,* Vol. 7, no. 2 (Fall 1983), item #12.

40. Pierre Restany, *Art in America,* Vol. 51 (February 1963), pp. 102-104.

41. Ashbery, "The New Realists" (1962) in *Reported Sightings: Art Chronicles 1957-1987* (New York: Alfred A. Knopf, 1989), pp. 81-82.

42. *Ibid.,* p. 82.

43. Peter Burger, *Theory of the Avant-Garde,* trans. Michael Shaw (Minneapolis: University of Minnesota, 1984), p. 69.

44. In an interview with Fred Moramarco, Ashbery says: "When I came back to New York for two years (1964-65), I first began writing about art and one of the first things I wrote about was a show of Rauschenberg's, and Jasper Johns also had his first exhibition. At that time it seemed as though this was the next logical way in which daring in art could express itself. Somehow the kind of epic grandeur of someone like Pollock already needed to be looked at more closely. I can see now how those junk collages by Rauschenberg influenced me at that point." In Moramarco's essay, "John Ashbery and Frank O'Hara: The Painterly Poets" in *Journal of Modern Literature,* Vol. 5, no. 3 (September 1976), pp. 436-462.

45. Leo Steinberg, "Jasper Johns . . ." in *Other Criteria,* p. 22.

46. Steinberg, "Other Criteria" in *Other Criteria,* p. 84.

47. *Ibid.,* p. 90.

48. *Ibid.,* p. 84.

49. Charles Altieri, "John Ashbery and the Challenge of Postmodernism in the Visual Arts" in *Critical Inquiry,* Vol. 14, no. 4 (Summer 1988), p. 815.

50. Robert Rauschenberg quoted by Lawrence Alloway, "Rauschenberg's Development" in *Robert Rauschenberg* (Washington, D.C.: National Collection of Fine Arts, Smithsonian Institution, 1976), p. 7.

51. Calvin Thompkins, *The Bride and the Bachelors: Five Masters of the Avant-Garde* (New York: Penguin, 1976), pp. 210-211.

52. Ashbery, "Four American Exhibits of 1968" in *RS,* p. 253.

53. Shapiro, pp. 60-61.

54. Ashbery, "Europe" in *The Tennis Court Oath* (Middletown, Connecticut: Wesleyan University Press, 1962), pp. 64-85. Subsequent citations in the text will refer to this edition.

55. Steinberg, *Other Criteria,* p. 52.

56. Shapiro, p. 75.

57. Helen Vendler, "Understanding Ashbery" in *John Ashbery,* p. 185.

58. This assessment is directly confirmed by Ashbery in an interview with Fred Moramarco: "Also, when you mention what I refer to in 'The Skaters' as 'this leaving-out business,' which seems to be a preoccupation of mine—it's also in *Three Poems* and a lot of other work—I see now that it is really a major theme in my poetry, though I wasn't aware of it as it was emerging. It's probably something that came from painting too. A lot of De Kooning's drawings are partly erased. Larry Rivers used to do drawings in which there are more erasures than there are lines. Rauschenberg once asked De Kooning to give him a drawing so that he could erase it. I got to wondering: suppose he did erase it? Wouldn't there be enough left so that it would be something? If so, how much? Or if not, how much could be erased and still have the 'sense' of the original left? I always tend to think that none of the developments in painting rubbed off on me very much, but then, when it comes down to it, I see that, as in this case, a lot of it did." Moramarco, p. 454.

59. Ashbery, "The Skaters" in *Rivers and Mountains* (New York: Ecco Press, 1977), p. 39.

60. Of course the prose poem itself, as David Lehman says, is "a form invested with modernity" by way of Baudelaire's *Spleen de Paris,* Rimbaud's *Illuminations,* and Max Jacob's *Le Cornet à dés.* See Lehman, *The Last Avant-Garde: The Making of the New York School of Poets* (New York: Doubleday, 1998).

61. See pages 36 and 29, respectively, in Ashbery's "The New Spirit" in *Three Poems* (New York: Viking Penguin, 1986).

62. While David Lehman discusses *Three Poems* in *The Last Avant-Garde* as a Kierkegaardian quest for spiritual salvation, I see it more as a quest to determine the spirit of the age, a perpetual search for the new in the spirit of Baudelaire's "Le Voyage." See *The Last Avant-Garde,* pp. 354-357.

63. See Stephen Paul Miller, "'Self-Portrait in a Convex Mirror,' the Watergate Affair, and Johns's Crosshatch Paintings: Surveillance and Reality-Testing in the Mid-Seventies" in *Boundary* 2, 20:2 (Summer 1993), pp. 84-115.

64. Ashbery, "Self-Portrait in a Convex Mirror" in *Self-Portrait in a Convex Mirror* (New York: Viking Press, 1975), p. 72.

Bibliography

Alloway, Lawrence. "Rauschenberg's Development" in *Robert Rauschenberg.* Washington, D.C.: National Collection of Fine Arts, Smithsonian Institution, 1976.

Altieri, Charles. "John Ashbery and the Challenge of Postmodernism in the Visual Arts" in *Critical Inquiry.* Vol. 14, no. 4 (Summer 1988), pp. 805-830.

Ashbery, John. *Houseboat Days.* New York: Viking, 1977.

———. *Reported Sightings: Art Chronicles 1957-1987.* New York: Alfred A. Knopf, 1989.

———. "Reverdy en Amérique" in *Pierre Reverdy: 1889-1960.* Paris: *Mercure de France,* 1962, pp. 109-112.

———. *Rivers and Mountains.* New York: Ecco Press, 1977.

———. *Selected Poems.* New York: Viking/Penguin, 1986.

———. *Self-Portrait in a Convex Mirror.* New York: Viking Press, 1975.

———. *Three Poems.* New York: Viking/Penguin, 1986.

Bloom, Harold. "John Ashbery: The Charity of the Hard Moments" and introduction in *John Ashbery.* Ed. Harold Bloom. New York: Chelsea House, 1985, pp. 49-79.

Breton, André; Taylor, Simon Watson, trans. *Surrealism and Painting.* New York: Harper & Row, 1972.

Bryson, Norman. *Vision and Painting: The Logic of the Gaze.* New Haven: Yale University, 1997 [1983].

Bürger, Peter; Shaw, Michael, trans. *Theory of the Avant-Garde. Theory and History of Literature, Vol. 4.* Minneapolis: University of Minnesota, 1984.

Compagnon, Antoine. *La Seconde Main, ou le travail de la citation.* Paris: Éditions du Seuil, 1979.

Deleuze, Gilles and Guattari, Félix; Sweet, David L., trans. "Capitalism: A Very Special Delirium" in *Chaosophy.* Ed. Sylvère Lotringer. New York: Semiotext(e), 1995.

Eliot, T. S. "The Metaphysical Poets" in *Selected Prose of T. S. Eliot.* Ed. Frank Kermode. New York: Harcourt, Brace, Jovanovich, 1975.

Feldman, Alan. *Frank O'Hara.* Boston: G. K. Hall, 1979.

Greenberg, Clement. "The Crisis of the Easel Picture," in *Art and Culture.* Boston: Beacon Press, 1965, pp. 154-157.

Lehman, David. *The Last Avant-Garde: The Making of the New York School of Poets.* New York: Doubleday, 1998.

———. "The Shield of a Greeting" in *Beyond Amazement: New Essays on John Ashbery.* Ed. David Lehman. Ithaca: Cornell University, 1980, pp. 101-127.

Miller, Stephen Paul. "'Self-Portrait in a Convex Mirror,' the Watergate Affair, and Johns's Crosshatch Paintings: Surveillance and Reality-Testing in the Mid-Seventies" in *Boundary* 2. Vol. 20, no. 2 (Summer 1993), pp. 84-115.

Mitchell, W. J. T. *Iconology: Image, Text, Ideology.* Chicago: University of Chicago, 1986.

Moramarco, Fred. "John Ashbery and Frank O'Hara: The Painterly Poets" in *Journal of Modern Literature.* Vol. 5, no. 3 (September 1976), pp. 436-462.

O'Hara, Frank. *The Collected Poems of Frank O'Hara.* Ed. Donald Allen. Berkeley: University of California, 1995.

Restany, Pierre. *Art in America.* Vol. 51 (February 1963), pp. 102-104.

Rosenberg, Harold. "The American Action Painters" in *The Tradition of the New.* New York: Horizon Press, 1959, pp. 23-39.

Salusinsky, Imre. "The Genesis of Ashbery's 'Europe'" in *NMAL: Notes on Modern American Literature.* Vol. 7, no. 2 (Fall 1983), item #12.

Shapiro, David. *John Ashbery: An Introduction to the Poetry.* New York: Columbia University Press, 1979.

Shoptaw, John. *On the Outside Looking Out: John Ashbery's Poetry.* Cambridge: Harvard University Press, 1994.

Steinberg, Leo. *Other Criteria: Confrontations with Twentieth-Century Art.* Oxford: Oxford University, 1972.

Thompkins, Calvin. *The Bride and the Bachelors: Five Masters of the Avant-Garde.* New York: Penguin, 1976.

Wolf, Leslie. "The Brushstroke's Integrity: The Poetry of John Ashbery and the Art of Painting" in *Beyond Amazement: New Essays on John Ashbery.* Ed. David Lehman. Ithaca: Cornell, 1980, pp. 224-254.

Fred Moramarco (review date March/April 2004)

SOURCE: Moramarco, Fred. "Across the Millennium: The Persistence of John Ashbery." *American Poetry Review* 33, no. 2 (March/April 2004): 39-41.

[*In the following review, Moramarco praises Ashbery's poetic insight in* Other Traditions *and lauds his inventive use of cliché and humor in* Wakefulness, Your Name Here, *and* Chinese Whispers, *but finds* Girls on the Run *monotonous.*]

It's not easy keeping up with John Ashbery's work. *Chinese Whispers* is his twenty-first book of poetry and throughout the nineties and the century's turn they have been coming at us at the rate of nearly one every year. Here are five [*Wakefulness, Girls on the Run, Your Name Here, As Umbrellas Follow Rain, Chinese Whispers*] in four years, plus a book of essays [*Other Traditions*] that deepens our understanding of the underpinnings of his work. (One other title from a smaller press that I've not yet gotten to appeared in 2001.)

For me, Ashbery has always been a poet of lines rather than of poems. Lines like

> the clock ticked on and on, happy about
> being apprenticed to eternity.
>
> (*Wakefulness*)

and

> Please don't tell me it all adds up in the end.
> I'm sick of that one.
>
> (*Your Name Here*)

and

> On wings of windows, parties, songs,
> Comedy and mystery, the world drenches us.
>
> (*Chinese Whispers*)

and

> I remember the world of cherry blossoms looking up
> at the sun and wondering what have I done to
> deserve this or anything else?
>
> (*Your Name Here*)

and, entering the bizarre world of Henry Darger's illustrated novel, *The Story of the Vivian Girls, in What Is Known as the Realms of the Unreal, of the Glandeco-Angelinnian War Storm, Caused by the Child Slave Rebellion,* in his book length poem, which has mercifully shortened Darger's title to *Girls on the Run*:

> Write it now, Tidbit said
> before I get back. And, quivering, I took the pen.

It's as if Darger's figures are talking directly to Ashbery, insisting that he re-transcribe their "story." But you have to use the word "story" loosely here, because in *Girls on the Run,* lines like these often lead us to other lines they seem totally unrelated to; pronouns shift, images undergo metamorphosis: "slush" is paired with "feathers," "graffiti" is found under "frozen mounds of yak butter," and "arroz con pollo" turns into a sailing vessel; elegance exists side by side with the most impossible banalities, and we are in the self-contained world of a disturbed and disturbing mind, one that seems profoundly innocent as well as obsessively driven. As readers of *Girls on the Run* will learn from the dust jacket, this is the mind of Henry Darger (1892-1972) a reclusive "outsider" artist who spent much of his life compulsively drawing figures of little girls with short skirts and penises and writing stories about them. Ashbery attempts to replicate that world—or at least create a parallel sort of a world in his book-length poem—but apart from introducing his loyal audience to the absolutely singular world of a lifelong recluse, this book exercises little hold on the reader. One page reads pretty much like the next, and there is little narrative glue to hold the poem together. On the other hand, narrative glue is never spread on very thick in Ashbery's work, and the shifting ground of *Girls on the Run* is familiar territory for his fans.

Commenting on John Wheelwright's evaluation of Laura Riding's poetry in *Other Traditions,* Ashbery points out that poets "in writing about other poets tend to write about themselves." Then he says this about Wheelwright's own work:

> Even where I cannot finally grasp his meaning, which is much of the time, I remain convinced by the extraordinary power of his language as it flashes by on its way from somewhere to somewhere. At times it seems like higher mathematics; I can sense the 'elegance' of his solutions without being able to follow the steps by which he arrives at them. In short, he is a poet from whom one takes a great deal on faith, but one does it voluntarily. His conviction is contagious.

Surely this observation describes a good many readers' response to Ashbery's work as well. It certainly describes mine. "The language flashes by on its way from somewhere to somewhere." This is quintessential Ashbery, turning language into life, which also, by the way, flashes by on its way from somewhere to somewhere. These books are filled with illuminating flashes.

"No matter how you twist it," he writes in the title poem of *Wakefulness,* "life stays frozen in the headlights." Another quotable and luminous line that ushers us into the world of the awakened that is assembled in this book. The word "wakefulness" has the usually Ashbery resonance: awake, a wake, wakeful, fullness—it's a whole world full of wakes. Dreams and sleeplessness are evoked throughout as are various other transformative states. One thing always leads to another, and becomes another. Change, of course, is life's only constant, though we nearly always resist it. Ashbery has some fun with his own resistance, wanting to pummel it altogether: "Take this, metamorphosis. And this. And this. And this." (**"Baltimore"**). Words themselves seem to change into things, but of course those things are merely other words: "We thought we had seen a few new / adjectives, but nobody was too sure. They might have been gerunds, or bunches of breakfast . . ." (**"Last Night I Dreamed I was in Bucharest"**). Change accelerates, permeates everything: "We, meanwhile, have witnessed changes, and now change / floods in from every angle." But Ashbery goes on to make it clear that he is a jester of change: "Stop me if you've heard this one, but if you haven't, just go about your business." (**"Added Poignancy"**). The clichés that resonate through his poetry in the hands of virtually any other poet would bring the work down, but his purposeful use of them calls our attention to their literalness, and the way, in some senses, they help us to resist change by freezing our repetitive gestures in language. In *Wakefulness* you will find a "pack of liars," "no release in sight" (a shrewd transformation of "no relief in sight") "for what seemed an eternity," "There are no two ways about it," "I put two and two together," "I'm within my rights," "Anyway, what can I tell you?" "if it's the last thing we do," "The rest, as they say, as they say, is history" (the repeated "as they say" makes this a kind of meta-cliché), "it was one for the books," "burns the midnight oil," "all is shot to hell," "it gives me goose bumps," "there is something to be said for everything," and "It is definitely time to move on" (many politicians' favorite).

Sometimes Ashbery deconstructs a cliché as he uses it: "You know I adore ceremony, / even while refusing to stand on it," (**"Homecoming"**) and sometimes he even avoids a cliché and then calls our attention to the avoidance by putting it back in: "We were kept waiting / right up until the announced departure, / and so became part of humanity. Part and parcel, I was going to say." (**"The Earth-Tone Madonna"**). There is a great deal of comedy in this book, but the overall mood of it is not comic. It is more the mood reflected in the photograph on the dust jacket in Vilhelm Hammershoi's painting, *Open Doors, Strandgade 30.* The painting exists on the axis of painting and photography, a turn of the century (19th to 20th) photo realism that anticipates, in a darker, more somber way, the interior spaces in many of Joel Meyerwitz's "Cape Light" photographs. Hammershoi's empty interior spaces, doors open leading to other rooms with doors open, and just a sliver of light peeking through a distant window is something of a metaphor for the poems inside. We're drawn from the emptiness to the light, but the carefully rendered doors with their perfectly recreated brass fittings, the sharp-edged detailed archways, the dark wooden floors, all evoke our admiration as well. In the same way, Ashbery's poems elicit our admiration for his attunement to the language of our time in its extraordinary variety and flexibility. He seems to get it as exactly as Hammershoi "gets" his doorways.

Years ago Ashbery visited one of my classes in contemporary poetry and we were reading his much-anthologized poem, **"Leaving the Atocha Station."** The first line of that poem is "The arctic honey blabbed over the report causing darkness." A student in the class asked him what arctic honey was, and he answered, "It's probably something cold and sweet." I thought of that while I was reading the short poem, **"Laughing Gravy"** in *Wakefulness.* I can hear that same student's voice asking "What is laughing gravy?" and hear Ashbery's answer: "It's probably something funny that you pour over meat." Left over from the early New York School of Poetry days in Ashbery's work is the notion that two words rubbed together create a new entity, whatever those words are.

So in addition to "laughing gravy" we get "wolf factory" (not a place where they make wolves, but a place where wolves work: "All the wolves in the wolf factory paused / at noon, for a moment of silence." (**"Laughing Gravy"**), a "goateed scorpion" (well, maybe if you look close enough) "scarecrow bones" "And a lovely Monkey with lollipop paws," among many other creatures, artifacts, and things that are constructed solely from language. Ashbery's penchant for this kind of linguistically generated reality can be ultimately traced to his early fascination with Raymond Roussel, the French surrealist and subject of his master's thesis. In "How I Wrote Certain of My Books," Roussel outlines a "formula" for creating a distinctive reality from language alone. Each line, each word, impinges on the next, alters its meaning, shapes the future direction of the work. One reads the poetry with an alertness for these interactions. A puzzling poem like **"Many Colors,"** for example, begins this way:

> There is a chastening to it,
> a hymnlike hemline.
> Hyperbole in another disguise.

There is no way to read this stanza literally. "Chastening" to what? *A hymnlike hemline* is one of those Roussel like creations; "Hyperbole in another disguise" seems an interpretation of "a hymnlike hemline." The only way to read it is to try to find the connective tissue: chastening=punish, make better=religion=hymnlike (via sound)=hemline=Hyperbole=via sound and meaning=in another disguise. Now take what you have and find an image for it. Next line:

> Dainty foresters walk through it.

> Holding their hymnlike hemlines?

The title of *Your Name Here* evokes those tourist posters and newspapers where a personalized name can be written in headlines. The dust jacket says specifically that the title was suggested by Spanish bullfight posters which have a blank space where you can put your name in along with other famous bullfighters. Seeing it on the cover of a book of poems, especially a book featuring the photograph of a handsome and exotic Egyptian movie star, in a white dinner jacket and bow tie, gives the viewer a similar sense of vicarious participation. We are invited into this world. John Ashbery is writing about us. So I can paste in my own name: *Fred Moramarco, {poems}* by John Ashbery. How thrilling!

The book's opening poem ushers us into **"This Room,"** (its title) with the Magritte/de Chirico-like opening line:

> The room I entered was a dream of this room

As are all the rooms we enter in poetry. And maybe in "real life" as well. The poem proceeds as one side of a dialogue between poet and reader, the poet posing as jester and clown:

> Surely all those feet on the sofa were mine.
> The oval portrait
> of a dog was me at an early age.

After a few more absurdist details about light, sound, and the food we eat, the poet-narrator asks

> Why do I tell you these things?
> You are not even here.

These clear, simple lines epitomize the paradox of the poet, writing in the solitude of his room, "making up" lines for readers he will never know. "You are not even here," except if you put "your name here" as the book's title invites us to do. Then we can enter this room that is a dream of this room.

But not so fast. The title poem, which concludes the volume, poses a series of questions about perspectives. How can we live in a dream and live in reality at the same time? How can a writer devote his entire life to writing, "the spooky art," as Norman Mailer now calls it, and also live fully in the experiential world? Is human life of central importance in the universe, or are we a cosmic army of ants marching towards nowhere? Put your name here, and answer these questions:

> But how can I be in this bar and also be a recluse?
> The colony of ants was marching toward me, stretching
> Far into the distance, where they were as small as ants.
> Their leader held up a twig as big as a poplar.
> It was obviously supposed to be for me.
> But he couldn't say it with a poplar in his mandibles.

The comedy here takes the usual Ashbery turns. The bar is the social world, the public world, and the reclusive world is the world of the writer. Lines 2 and 3 introduce perspective—a colony of ants, perhaps humanity viewed from a distance, heads toward the writer to give him his subject. The funny self-referential simile—ants as small as ants—only appear that way from afar. Look at them up close and they seem to be able to carry tall trees in their mandibles. The leader of the ants wants to pass this on to the poet, but he is obviously unable to talk, being preoccupied with larger matters. But don't take any of this allegory too seriously. I'm just playing around, Ashbery tells us in the next comic lines:

> Well, let's forget that scene and turn to one in Paris.
> Ants are walking down the Champs-Elysées
> in the snow, in twos and threes, conversing,
> revealing a sociability one never supposed them as having.

Ashbery's playfulness always has a serious edge. Here the ants are even more clearly allegorical, inhabiting the main boulevard of one of the world's most "civilized" cities. Humanity is not an "either/or" phenomenon: it is a "both/and." We are ants who socialize in Paris; angels, as someone said, strapped to the back of mules.

"Poetry," Ashbery is quoted as saying, in a recent issue of *Poetry Flash,* "is mostly hunches." One of those hunches, which permeates nearly all of his work, is that the life we experience individually is remarkably similar under the covering of each of our skins. And these similarities give us a collective life that often remains unexpressed because we live together on the surface. So when we hear an expression of that interior landscape, we recognize ourselves in it, even when it is presented "impersonally," as it is in most of Ashbery's work. In a sense, his work remains the embodiment of T. S. Eliot's "impersonal theory of poetry," as recorded in that seminal essay of Modernism, "Tradition and the Individual Talent." For Eliot, the process of creating art meant for the artist "a continual surrender of himself as he is at the moment to something which is more valuable. The progress of an artist is a continual self-sacrifice, a continual extinction of personality." You will find few direct references in Ashbery's *oeuvre* to specific, identifiable events in his life. Well, yes, we know when he first saw Francesco Parmegianino's *Self Portrait in a Convex Mirror,* and we get several hints from various poems about some aspects of his early family life, but compared to many of his peers, Ashbery's personal life is virtually invisible in his work. So when we come upon a short poem in *Your Name Here* entitled **"The History of My Life"** we sit up and take notice. Especially because the first two lines refer very specifically to a traumatic childhood event:

> Once upon a time there were two brothers.
> Then there was only one: myself.

The sheer clarity and poignancy of these lines—their fairy tale quality, their understated sense of loss, and the childlike simplicity of the diction add up to a deeply felt personal statement, rare in Ashbery's work. The language here is less important, for a change, than the sentiment. As if sensing he is picking at a very deep wound—Ashbery's younger brother died at the age of nine—he quickly lightens up the poem, while at the same time telling us that experiencing the death of a sibling can cause one to grow up a lot before he's ready to:

> I grew up fast, before learning to drive,
> even. There was I: a stinking adult.

"A stinking adult" puts a smile on our face—Ashbery is always vacillating between the unbearable heaviness and unbearable lightness of being, as if moving between the two make both extremes bearable. The inverted syntax ("There was I") followed by a colon and the passé phrase, "a stinking adult" almost makes us see the young wounded John, having to be a "man" before he is ready for it. The poet's formative years—his early rejections, his acceptance of his own value system, and his moving beyond self-deprecation and toward self-acceptance is the subject of the middle stanzas of the poem, a capsule, almost generic, life history:

> I thought of developing interests
> someone might take an interest in. No soap.
>
> I became very weepy for what had seemed
> like the pleasant early years. As I aged
>
> increasingly, I also grew more charitable
> with regard to my thoughts and ideas,
>
> thinking them at least as good as the next man's.

But the poem closes with a fundamental human irony: all the skills, knowledge, self-awareness and self-acceptance that we develop over a lifetime is shadowed by our awareness of our own mortality and its relentless impinging on our consciousness that with each day, we move toward our last.

> Then a great devouring cloud
>
> came and loitered on the horizon, drinking
> it up, for what seemed like months or years.

These last three lines of the poem are a dark *memento mori,* taking us back to the existential loneliness of the first couplet. For all the narrator's talents, achievements and mid-life successes, his life is bracketed by loss—as are all of our lives, in one way or another. "Common sense tells us," Vladimir Nabokov wrote in a haunting sentence from his autobiography, *Speak, Memory,* "that our lives are a parenthesis between two eternities."

The contents of *As Umbrellas Follow Rain,* a book published by a small Massachusetts press, is largely repeated in *Chinese Whispers,* Ashbery's newest book. The title refers to a British version of the game Americans call "Telephone" or "Gossip," where people sit in a circle and someone whispers a story to the person next to him or her and so on around the circle until the last person recites aloud the final version, which usually differs significantly from the original story. Ashbery first refers to this game in a telling passage from **"Self-Portrait in a Convex Mirror,"** where he relates it to the artists' persistent desire to find words or images to convey the present, which necessarily distorts it. The present is constantly in flux and any attempt to "fix" it in a work of art is doomed to a certain kind of failure. Here's the logic of **"Self-Portrait"** [**"Self-Portrait in a Convex Mirror"**]:

> It seems like a very hostile universe
> But as the principle of each individual thing is
> Hostile to, exists at the expense of all the others
> As philosophers have often pointed out, at least
> *This* thing, the mute, undivided present,
> Has the justification of logic, which
> In this instance isn't a bad thing
> Or wouldn't be, if the way of telling
> Didn't somehow intrude, twisting the end result
> Into a caricature of itself. This always
> Happens, as in the game where
> A whispered phrase passed around the room
> Ends up as something completely different.
> *It is the principle that makes works of art so unlike*
> *What the artist intended.*
>
> (emphasis mine)

This passage provides us with a substantial insight into the title *Chinese Whispers,* which refers, I think, to the way a work of art "circulates" in the world, from one reader or viewer to the next, from one critical interpretation to another. It is, to use another of Ashbery's titles, the "flow chart" of the work—how it gets from the mind of the artist into the common cultural currency of the society. So the next time you read an Ashbery poem, whisper a few lines of it to the person next to you, send it around the room, and you'll find yourself at the end with a microcosm of a new Ashbery poem, the language as surprising as a sun shower on a cold winter night when all you expected was a pinker kind of green tea.

Ernesto Suárez-Toste (essay date spring 2004)

SOURCE: Suárez-Toste, Ernesto. "'The Tension Is in the Concept': John Ashbery's Surrealism." *Style* 38, no. 1 (spring 2004): 1-15.

[*In the following essay, Suárez-Toste attributes the surrealistic aspects of Ashbery's poetry to the author's time spent living in France, underscoring the influence of the Oulipo group and the Italian painter and poet Giorgio de Chirico.*]

> [A]fter all it all came from Chirico and he was not a surrealist he is very fanciful and his eye is caught by it and he has no distinction between the real and the unreal because everything is alike to him, he says so, but the rest of them nothing is alike to them and so they do not say so, and that is the trouble with them. [. . .]
>
> —(Gertrude Stein, *Everybody's Autobiography*)

Much has been written about the relationship between John Ashbery's poetry and avant-garde art, particularly the painting of the Abstract Expressionists. Two of the earliest articles dealing with this subject—by Fred Moramarco (1976) and Leslie Wolf (1980)—have considered not only Ashbery's use of *objets d'art* as starting motifs for his poems but also the painterly quality present in much of his poetry itself.[1] That the early-century collage aesthetic has been a major influence on him is beyond doubt, and the most controversial issue nowadays is probably the negative view still taken of his surrealist experiments. A number of annoyed critics have trivialized Ashbery with the label "surrealist" whenever the poems in a volume are unusually dark, displaying a curious fondness for fitting them into the vague category of post-surrealist surrealism.[2] For very similar reasons—and a sense of automatism that Ashbery rejects—this work has been praised by Language poets.

Ashbery himself has shaken off the surrealist label with remarkable energy at times, most likely out of boredom, and has certainly tired of the reductionist connotations which—sadly enough—the term has acquired. Ashbery, who lived in France for ten years, had a first-hand experience of the country where surrealism was born, and it seems clear that his privileged access to "the real thing" has allowed him to appreciate in surrealism aspects that are neglected by the general public. We know from his art criticism that Ashbery distinguishes two kinds of surrealism, and only rejects the label in equal fear of excessively academicist or populist interpretations. Although "the term surrealism has fallen into disfavor," he praised Yves Tanguy as its embodiment on the ground that for him "the arbitrary distinction between abstract and figurative art did not exist" (*Reported Sightings* 27). It is clear from the context that he is referring to surrealism "not in the parochial

1920s sense of the term but in the second, open sense in which it can still be said to animate much of the most advanced art being done today" (see also McCabe 151). Although the most convincing analysis of surrealism as a twofold movement is made in the formally related terms of automatist-abstract and illusionistic-oneiric (see Krauss 91-94), Ashbery's distinction shows a greater personal involvement, not necessarily based on formal criteria. His categorization opposes the outdated and dogmatic received idea of surrealism with an empowering and liberating alternative conception. It is clear enough, though, that the former is related to Bretonian automatism, which he rejects: "The coupling of this acknowledged interest [in surrealism] with the alleged difficulty of his writing has led readers to view Ashbery mistakenly as an American Surrealist, practicing an automatic writing that [. . .] directly expresses his unconscious. Ashbery flatly denies the assertion that he composes by automatic writing" (Fredman 130). I would like to argue here that Ashbery's decade in France influenced him not only through his acquaintance with surrealist art and poetics, but also through his increasing knowledge of the possibilities of the French language and the linguistic experiments conducted by the Oulipo group. This will explain many obscure features of Ashbery's idiom, including the automatic aspect of his poetry and many apparently whimsical collocations. His French experience made him not an American Surrealist but a surrealist American, that is, not a writer whose main perception of the movement came from the 1940s interaction of the New York period of surrealism, but a poet and art critic who lived in Paris for a long part of his life and acquired insider's knowledge of the original movement as it was conceived.[3]

The matter of Ashbery's reception becomes increasingly complicated when dealing with his later work, whose acceptance is widespread. While certain individual examples are acclaimed as masterpieces by consensus (**"Self-Portrait in a Convex Mirror"**), other poems published in these books continue to baffle public and critics alike. I want to focus here on several poems, some of which have so far received little critical attention and, indeed, show how these are touched by surrealism, but in a way that has little or nothing to do with the mainstream movement ("hard-core surrealism" as Ashbery puts it). Alan Williamson has successfully argued that Ashbery uses disjointed narrative and descriptive fragments as deliberate interruptions in his poems, like elements in a collage (120-22). Among these we can spot a clearly defined group whose inspiration seems to have been the characteristic iconographic catalogue of the Italian painter and poet Giorgio de Chirico, co-founder of the school of *Pittura Metafisica* and precursor of surrealism. His literary work has already been related to Ashbery's, regarding the likeness of the prose in *Three Poems* and de Chirico's novel *Hebdomeros* (Fredman 131-32). In the endnotes to *The Double Dream of Spring* Ashbery himself explained that the title was borrowed from one of de Chirico's paintings, and this is something most critics mention but hardly ever elaborate.[4]

However, it would not be exaggerated to suggest that Ashbery at some stage developed a passion for de Chirico's work, and a close look at the poems of the period around 1975 shows how *Self-Portrait in a Convex Mirror* and *Houseboat Days* are sprinkled all over with elements from the Italian's metaphysical landscapes. In 1988 a volume was published in English containing *Hebdomeros* and several other pieces by de Chirico. Ashbery was among the translators, and his 1966 review for *Book Week* of the French edition of *Hebdomeros* (1964) was reprinted as the preface. (His translations date from 1967 to 1975, with the exception of those commissioned for this edition). This shows to how well and how long he knew de Chirico's writing.[5] Not long after Ashbery published *Hotel Lautréamont,* a book that represents his late "surrealistic reassertion" (Moramarco, "Coming" 43).

In fact, it is little wonder that Ashbery has felt attracted to de Chirico, since they share a wide range of obsessions. Traveling and the passing of time have become major preoccupations for both, and they have associated these in a very similar way. Spatial and temporal movement are thus intrinsically connected, the traveling impulse having a cathartic function against the burden of passing time. But at the same time our wandering stands for the permanent sense of loss, the typically metaphysical anxiety. Moreover, they are equally fond of chance associations, but within certain restrictions, scarcely following the Bretonian rule of the unconscious that led to automatic writing. The effect sought by Ashbery's "logic / Of strange position" (*Some Trees* 74) found a consecrated poetics in de Chirico's "metaphysical aesthetic," a vague term coined by the Italian to refer to his special sensibility toward those privileged moments of random intersection between the uncanny and the mundane:

> One must picture everything in the world as an enigma, not only the great questions one has always asked oneself. [. . .] But rather to understand the enigma of things generally considered insignificant. To perceive the mystery of certain phenomena of feeling. [. . .] To live in the world as if in an immense museum of strangeness, full of curious many-colored toys which change their appearance, which, like little children we sometimes break to see how they are made on the inside, and, disappointed, realize they are empty.
>
> ("Eluard Ms." 185-86)

Equally, both feel an unusual interest in the role of memory and the world of dreams, which accounts for their characteristically uneasy atmospheres. They subvert the logic of natural events, and provide an alternative of their own. De Chirico managed to "turn the realities of the seen world and the logic of traditional perspective systems into a theater where dreams could unfold" (Rosenblum 47). But despite his distortions of perspective—another technique he shares with Ashbery—de Chirico is considered a narrative painter, somewhat foreign to the spirit of formal experimentation that swept over the Paris of Cubism and Dada. Ashbery has written of Parmigianino's self-portrait that "The surprise, the tension are in the concept / Rather than its realization" (*Self-Portrait* [*Self-Portrait in a Convex Mirror*] 74). Similarly, Max Morise wrote of de Chirico that "his images are surrealist, but their expression is not" (26). A link between the two painters can be found in Ashbery's own art criticism, where he has proposed Parmigianino as a precursor of de Chirico on account of "his craftsmanship at the service of a sense of the mystery behind physical appearances" (*Reported Sightings* 31).

Affinities of approach and treatment are reinforced by Ashbery's adoption of metaphysical imagery for *Self-Portrait* and especially *Houseboat Days.* In the latter volume a good number of poems feature passages where the voice seems to inhabit a metaphysical landscape/ dreamscape, as if it belonged to one of the passengers inside de Chirico's trains, embedded in his own thoughts but also looking sporadically through the window and thus interrupting the flow by letting the landscape intrude (Ashbery wrote *The Vermont Notebook* during a bus tour, of Massachusetts). Naturally, and given the connotations of metaphysical landscapes, this happens in those moments when the poem's mood is already (or wants to become) nostalgic or melancholy. A long list of items could be extracted from *Houseboat Days* to match de Chirico's favorite iconographic choices: towers, trains, stations, clocks, statues and pedestals, plazas, shadows, arches, maps, spires, machicolations, flagpoles, battlements, etc. But they also share techniques. Richard Howard applied André Gide's extrapolation from heraldry to show how Ashbery slips lines *en abyme* by writing unmediated comments into the poem, often about the poem's own process of becoming (26-27).[6] De Chirico's *The Double Dream of Spring* is an apt example of the same technique. It portrays the artist's studio, showing an unfinished painting within the painting: a painting *en abyme* that echoes the title's suggestion of dreaming within a dream, and thus gives away the circumstances of artistic creation.

Ashbery's poem **"All and Some"** (*Self-Portrait* 64-65) is a case of poem *en abyme* in the way it advances the mood and aesthetics of the following volume by introducing metaphysical imagery and touching upon those concerns that will become crucial in *Houseboat Days.* It is representative of a wide variety of recurrent elements in Ashbery's poetry and therefore a sort of emblem in itself.[7] The scenario is that of a valediction, putting an end to a love story. The opening lines emphasize change and departure from previous habits, which adds to the departure of the lover and also Ashbery's departure from the tradition of valedictions in English poetry: here the poet is the one who stays, and the one with a greater sense of loss. The nostalgic mood later adopted in the poem will suit the inclusion of de Chirico's imagery.

The poem is also representative of the shell games Ashbery plays with language and the readers' expectations. The opening line ("And for those who understand:") seeks to establish a complicity with the reader, based not only on the *in medias res* beginning but also on the apparently selective implications of the statement, and of the title, too. One may feel entitled to wonder, in difficult poetry like Ashbery's, whether we are in for a higher level of difficulty from now on. No one would accept that this is a discouraging opening, for we would hardly deserve the name of readers then. In fact, it works in the opposite way, more like aggressive advertising strategies. Charles Molesworth, in a less celebratory attitude, has denounced the way in which "the author-reader contract is a conspiratorial one for Ashbery, as he writes not simply for those 'in the know,' but for those who can dally at will" (170). Well, it is. We want to be "those" who deserve the confidence of the poet.

Another deceptive phrase in the poem comes in line 22: "But what I mean is. [. . .]" This is another trick played on the reader, for what follows is hardly an explanation of anything. Structurally it recalls those false "tips" by magicians who announce they will teach the audience how to do a trick at home to impress our friends, and end up by complicating it even more. De Chirico is hardly ever so openly self-conscious, although he can introduce unmediated remarks in his canvases. In *The Fatal Temple* he painted a still-life and then mapped it by writing names next to the objects. The names were not those of the objects, but more abstract and symbolic, like *joie* or *souffrance*. In radical contrast to these, by the side of a distorted fish he bluntly wrote *chose étrange*. This is not just an example of unmediated address, it is a fitting technique to introduce an ambiguous irony and rescue the painting from the risk of falling into the sublime. Ashbery, to mention only one example, fearing the same elevation of tone in one of his poems, wrote the deflating two-word sentence "Time farted" immediately after one such passage (**Double Dream** [**The Double Dream of Spring**] 29).

Ashbery and de Chirico also share a strong drive toward originality, emphasizing the importance of a fresh approach to reality and art. In the case of twentieth-century poetry the new has an intrinsic value, and de Chirico relates this to the principle of revelation in art:

one is surprised by one's own inspiration. Ashbery seems to appreciate revelations when he writes about "waking up / In the middle of a dream with one's mouth full / Of unknown words [. . .]" (*Self-Portrait* 55). These lines, moreover, establish a sort of dissociation between the conscious self and the unconscious, suggesting the powerful transformations undergone during dreams. For both de Chirico and Ashbery the role of memory and the world of dreams acquire particular relevance. They do not attempt to describe, but to reproduce, explore, sometimes even subvert them. De Chirico followed Schopenhauer in developing his own theory about madness and art, and held that memory is responsible for the irreversible prosification of the world, for it causes us to become bored with repeated experience:

> Schopenhauer defines the madman as a person who has lost his memory. It is an apt definition because, in fact, that which constitutes the logic of our normal acts and our normal life is a continuous rosary of recollections of relationships between things and ourselves and vice versa. [. . .] By deduction we might conclude that everything has two aspects: a normal one [. . . and] the other, the spectral or metaphysical which can be seen only by rare individuals in moments of clairvoyance or metaphysical abstraction. [. . .]
>
> ("On Metaphysical Art" 450)

Ashbery has his own statement on this subject, which does not altogether lack the mystic tone of de Chirico's, and evidently shares with it the interest in the functions of mental machinery. Moreover, Ashbery's idea of the poem as found object, something which has an existence of its own and which the poet has to discover, fits in with the Italian's welcome to revelation:

> Memory, forgetfulness, and being are certainly things that are happening in our minds all the time which I'm attempting to reproduce in poetry, the actions of a mind at work or at rest. [. . .] My poetry is really trying to explore consciousness to give it perspective. [. . .] I begin with unrelated phrases and notations that later on I hope get resolved in the course of the poem as *it begins to define itself more clearly for me.*
>
> (**"Craft Interview"** [**"Craft Interview with John Ashbery"**] 118-19, emphasis added)

Therefore it is not strange that Ashbery has adopted such experimental modes during his career, with a particularly innovative attitude toward language. De Chirico on his part wrote his novel *Hebdomeros* in French, which was not his mother tongue but allowed him the kind of prose Ashbery has repeatedly praised. Even outside **The Tennis Court Oath** Ashbery has sporadically afforded such defying gestures as resorting to the techniques of the Oulipo writers group; or simply making use of cultural differences in direct translations from the French. In the poem **"Variations, Calypso and Fugue on a Theme of Ella Wheeler Wilcox"** he used the Oulipian strategy of replacing words by their definitions: "On the one hand, a vast open basin—or sea; on the other a narrow spit of land, terminating in a copse, with a few broken-down outbuildings lying here and there. It made no difference that the bey—b-e-y this time, oriental potentate—had ordained their release [. . .]" (*Double Dream* 28). In the opening of this passage Ashbery has described a *bay* ("vast open basin" limited by the "narrow spit of land"), so he pretends that the mention of the *bey* in the third line demands spelling to avoid confusion, and then provides a crossword definition in two words. This is a challenge to the reader's patience, for many would rather miss the point than find out how perversely playful the poet can be. But there is certainly pleasure in the finding, if one happens to be "in the mood for Ashbery."

Ashbery's adoption of Oulipian techniques seems to work on the basis of personal affinity rather than systematic adherence to the movement. In fact, many of these strategies are very similar to those employed in Ashbery's collaborations with Kenneth Koch, like logorally (in the random selection of teleutons in sestinas, for example). Ashbery's self-imposed use of highly demanding forms such as the sestina, the cento, or the pantoum, where form can be said to condition meaning by restricting the paradigm available, pursues a very deliberate aesthetic effect, which in fact constitutes an established genre of Oulipian practice (though it is a genre in permanent flux). In this sense Ashbery is always moving between the automatic-looking experimentalism of *The Tennis Court Oath* and these restrictions, which are defined by Raymond Queneau as the very opposite strategy:

> Another false idea that is current nowadays is the equivalence established between inspiration, the exploration of the subconscious, and liberation; between chance, automatism, and freedom. The kind of freedom that consists of blindly obeying every impulse is in reality a form of slavery. The classical author, who when writing his tragedy follows a certain number of rules that he knows, is freer than the poet who writes whatever comes into his head and is the slave of other rules he is unaware of.
>
> (*Oulipo* 123)

Among other Oulipian techniques there is one more associated with Ashbery's poetry. "Pumectation" can be defined as "the ostensible procedure that a writer uses to mask the procedure he is actually using" (211). This is also called "Imparmigianization" and very aptly so in this context, because Ashbery saw through Parmigianino's use of this technique from the very third line of **"Self-Portrait"** [**"Self-Portrait in a Convex Mirror"**] in the way the hand is advanced "as though to protect / What it advertises" (68). Equally, within **"All and**

Some" we can find this imparmigianization in the already mentioned "But what I mean is. [. . .]" a device that actually helps to conceal the meaning it promises to reveal.

Another technique that seems expressly devised by a would-be saboteur of the Rosetta stone is the exploitation (by means of direct translation) of cultural or idiomatic differences with French. Sarah Lundquist has studied Ashbery's **"French Poems"**—originally written in French so that his own translation into English would avoid "customary word-patterns and associations" (*Double Dream* 95)—and reached the conclusion that he used cognates wherever possible, emphasizing the inherent similarities between the two languages. While this applies to the **"French Poems,"** the opposite is also true outside this small corpus. Perhaps this second technique is limited to very specific expressive possibilities that Ashbery misses in English, but these are hardly "expressive" if the readers overlook them. Of the following two examples one is easily justified, the other less so.

The first one is recurrent in Ashbery's poetry, but he has explained it only once, as if he took his readers' faithfulness for granted. At least this is a meaningful case, where he might have reasonably missed the resources available in French. Two of Ashbery's most recurrent themes, time and the weather or climate, happen to share the same French word (*temps*), and this establishes an "extra" happy connection which somebody with his sensibility toward language cannot help celebrating. Thus in **"The Ice-Cream Wars"** he writes "Time and the weather / Don't always go hand in hand, as here [. . .]" (*Houseboat Days* 60). But other times he stretches the coupling along several lines, or else one of the two terms is merely implicit, as in **"Pyrography"**: "The page of dusk turns like a creaking revolving stage [. . .]" (8). Here the connotations of rusty machinery and heavy, slow movement recall the internal mechanism of a clock, hence time, contrasting with the transition from day into night, which is the most natural in the world, but it is a meaningful mixture if the poet has the polysemic French *temps* in mind. These quotations belong to *Houseboat Days,* and their explanation is found in the title poem of his previous volume, **"Self-Portrait"**: "the weather, which in French is / *Le temps,* the word for time [. . .]" (*Self-Portrait* 70). In any case it becomes clear that he can play with concepts and names at will.

The second example is the allusion to rain in **"Daffy Duck in Hollywood"**:

> The allegory comes unsnarled
> Too soon; a shower of pecky acajou harpoons is
> About all there is to be noted between tornadoes. I
>   have

Only my intermittent life in your thoughts to live
Which is like thinking in another language.

(Houseboat Days 32)

In French, in descriptions of heavy rain, there exists the idiomatic expression *pleuvoir des hallebardes* [to rain halberds], which is closer to the English "cats and dogs" than to other, more logically appropriate terms of measure (*à seaux* [bucketfuls]). These *hallebardes* have an exact equivalent in Spanish (*a chuzos* [spears]), but not in English. Therefore Ashbery's "shower of pecky acajou harpoons" between tornadoes works as a reference to prickling raindrops. The proximity of the phrase "thinking in another language" may provide a clue here.

Naming was a very important task for de Chirico, who learned from his readings of Schopenhauer and Nietzsche that the best way to achieve his metaphysical, defamiliarizing presentation of ordinary events and objects is to see things again with the freshness of the first time. This—of course—applies equally to their names, since these are inevitably charged with banality. In a sense, he needed to begin from a *tabula rasa,* to avoid these connotations: "What is needed above all, is to rid art of all that has been its familiar content until now; all subject, all idea, all thought, all symbol must be put out" ("Eluard Ms." 187). Similarly, Ashbery wrote in 1962 that his purpose in poetry was "à restituer aux choses leur vrai nom, à abolir l'éternel poids mort de symbolisme et d'allegorie" ([to return things their true names, to lift the immemorial burden of symbolism and allegory] qtd. in Longenbach 123n.11). "To return things their true names" is traditionally an orphic function, and to rid names of the accumulated "burden of symbolism" is exactly what de Chirico aspired to do in his paintings.

It is in the second half of **"All and Some"** where we can find a profusion of elements from de Chirico's landscapes. Returning to the nostalgic tone of the valediction, the setting acquires an intensely evocative power, and the poet complains that now no one "Cares or uses the little station any more. / They are too young to remember / How it was when the late trains came in. / Violet sky grazing the gray hill-crests" (*Self-Portrait* 65). A similar melancholy can be attributed to the innumerable train stations in de Chirico's paintings. These perfect settings of anxiety and nostalgia, of departure and arrival, of greetings and farewells, would eventually become emblematic of surrealism, and so, in his description of the 1938 surrealist exhibition in Paris, Georges Hugnet referred to it both as a "railroad station for the imagination and the dream," and "a steam engine that broke a breach in the ramparts of our senses large enough for the heroic charge of our dreams, desires, and needs" (qtd. in Sawin 10-11).

Many of Ashbery's poems feature passages that recreate the wait in stations (**"Melodic Trains"** in *Houseboat Days* [24-26]), or describe a metaphysical landscape seen from a train. **"Pyrography"** (*Houseboat Days* 8-10) is a remarkable example of the image of Ashbery as passenger in one of de Chirico's trains. The "slow boxcar journey" takes us through a country built "partly over with fake ruins, in the image of ourselves: / An arch that terminates in mid-keystone, a crumbling stone pier / For laundresses, an open-air theater, never completed / And only partially designed." The vision of those ruins is very apt to share the feeling evoked in metaphysical paintings. Not ruins as criticism of the decay of modern civilization, but "fake ruins" as a gratuitous demonstration of disdain for functionality, and a further concession to aestheticism. But the introduction of such a landscape is not for aesthetic purposes only, and the metaphysical potential of the ruins triggers Ashbery's imagination into one of his typical reflections on time and what attitude we should adopt to face its passing:

How are we

    to inhabit
This space from which the fourth wall is invariably missing,
As in a stage-set or dollhouse, except by staying as we are,
In lost profile, facing the stars, with dozens of as yet
Unrealized projects, and a strict sense
Of time running out, of evening presenting
The tactfully folded-over bill?

Existential doubts of all sorts, including the fear that we may be little more than a puppet show for some good-humored deity, are softened by the witty image of time as a maître d', with an implicit *carpe diem* message—make the best possible meal, for the bill will invariably be too expensive. Ashbery's description of the setting is extremely apt here. De Chirico's "drama of objects" needs a stage, and Ashbery's typically untypical scenario is very much like a stage-set, an "open field of narrative possibilities" (*Three Poems* 41).

Other poems use the iconography of de Chirico's train stations to describe imaginary settings, as is the case in **"On the Towpath,"** where, as Marjorie Perloff has noted, "unspecified persons perform unspecified and unrelated acts against the backdrop of a constantly shifting landscape whose contours dissolve before our eyes" (72). De Chirico's painting participates in this general indeterminacy by creating the feeling that indeed "something" is happening, that there is a logic ruling these events, but one we are not invited to understand. In that sense he could be said to paint *in medias res.* One of de Chirico's paintings, *Mystery and Melancholy of a Street,* features a typical metaphysical setting where a girl runs up a street (not a rampart but a ramp) and the building behind her shows spires and machicolations. A variation on the same motif, *Mélancolie d'une rue,* pictures a background with a station clock and the shadow of a tower, projected from outside the frame. Compare with the setting of **"On the Towpath"**:

On the earth a many-colored tower of longing rises.
[. . .]
A white figure runs to the edge of some rampart
In a hurry only to observe the distance,
And having done so, drops back into the mass
Of clock-faces, spires, stalactite machicolations.

(*Houseboat Days* 22-23)

The girls in both canvases indeed seem to be running for its own sake, either with a hoop or with a skipping-rope.[8] They run "to observe the distance," that is, not to *see,* but to *keep* the distance with a world in permanent motion: "One must move very fast in order to stay in the same place, as the Red Queen said, the reason being that [. . .] you must still learn to cope with the onrushing tide of time and all the confusing phenomena it bears in its wake" (*Three Poems* 90). This is also applicable to de Chirico's frozen trains, whose arrested motion is strangely foregrounded in the paintings. Regarding the "many-colored tower of longing," de Chirico has several paintings devoted exclusively to a multicolored tower built with narrowing layers of square or circular colonnades, in the fashion traditionally attributed to the tower of Babel. The evocation of Babel, with its verbal confusion, is equally appropriate in both cases, and a motif that keeps reappearing in Ashbery's poetry (acquiring particular relevance in the "New Spirit" section of *Three Poems*).

Finally, the frequent apparition of trains in Ashbery's poems—as in de Chirico's canvases—suggests the way in which he seems to relate them to his obsessions. We find speeding trains and trains in stations; scenes observed from trains and inside other trains, even words read on the windows of passing trains. For both Ashbery and de Chirico railway timetables seem to be simultaneously reliable and somewhat flexible. Trains constitute an alternative timing system and at the same time they are subject to human delay. It is a very fitting treatment of the motif: both need to feel that there is a chance for human control of time, but they know this feeling of control is only illusory: "The train comes bearing joy; / [. . .] / For long we hadn't heard so much news, such noise. / [. . .] / As laughing cadets say, 'In the evening / Everything has a schedule, if you can find out what it is'" (*Some Trees* 9). The train brings joy, and the possibility of a universal logic and harmony. Its own schedule seems to endow life with a meaning yet unrevealed to us. On the other hand, it is laughing cadets, representing inexperienced and playful youth, who voice the statement. Whether the message is reassuring or merely intriguing depends upon readers, and that is probably Ashbery's intention. The message does nothing but mirror the predetermined attitude of the reader, at its best opening new possibilities but not aimed at converting anyone. In "Melodic Trains" (*Houseboat Days* 24-26) the poet comments on all these questions with a similar attitude:

A little girl with scarlet enameled fingernails
Asks me what time it is—evidently that's a toy
   wristwatch
She's wearing, for fun. [. . .]
[. . .]
[. . . A]s though our train were a pencil

Guided by a ruler held against a photomural of the
   Alps
We both come to see distance as something unofficial
And impersonal yet not without its curious justifica-
tion
Like the time of a stopped watch—right twice a day.

Only a child would wear a watch "for fun," says Ashbery in his late forties. The girl is playing at being an adult, but Time will take care of making her one of them. On the other hand, she does not really want to know the time, but rather the time remaining before their arrival. The image of the train as pencil on a photomural (or a map, as in films) makes this clear: when traveling, time and distance become indissociably united, assuming, as he seems to do, that speed is a reliable constant for modern trains. A stopped watch is right twice a day, far more often than a slow or fast one, and yet it is good for nothing, since you cannot check when it is right (unless you have another watch). This implies that human time works on approximations rather than exactness. Then the train schedule becomes a reliable, alternative time-measuring system, like "the philosopher's daily walk that the neighbors set their watches by" (*Three Poems* 32). Ashbery seems to envy the logic behind train timetables, like those "wafer-thin pedestrians / Who know where they are going" (*Self-Portrait* 5). Of course he knows that their security is just a false impression we get from outside, but—just like boys watching ants in the garden—the feeling that they know their mission necessarily filters through the cracks in our confidence.

De Chirico has his own way of feeling he can control time, through the systematic immobilization of trains in his paintings. Often even the smoke cloud rising from the chimney remains vertically static, despite the wind that keeps the station flags in permanent flapping and betrays the incoherence: "Le don étrange de Chirico est d'immobiliser le temps dans le silence de sa mémoire, sur une place où deux personnages se rencontrent ou se séparent à la fin d'une chaude après-midi d'été" ([De Chirico's strange gift is to immobilize time in the silence of his memory, in a square where two characters meet or part at the end of a hot summer afternoon] De Bonnafos).

John Ashbery's poetry, sharing a variety of common concerns with de Chirico—such as the passing of time, the impulse to travel, and the enigma of ordinary objects and situations—has repeatedly demonstrated the influence of the latter's plastic and literary work. This shows through Ashbery's adoption of metaphysical aesthetics whenever he seeks the melancholy, nostalgic tone evoked by the Italian's paintings. The frequency with which this happens coincides fully with Ashbery's periodic translations of de Chirico's literary work from 1967 to 1992, and this surprises no one, given his characteristic permeability to external inspiration. Even less surprising is the choice, considering his interest in art and his recurrent nostalgia for the French language. This choice may be surrealist in origin—insofar as we can call de Chirico a surrealist—but most likely what attracted Ashbery to de Chirico is his selective distance from surrealism, not his membership in the movement. Beyond the interpretation of specific passages which otherwise would be thrown into the surrealist bin, I hope to have contributed to the clarification of Ashbery's surrealist affinities and techniques, emphasizing visuality but also his playful approach to language and poetry. Of particular interest is the way he manages to cultivate—simultaneously or sequentially—different pairs of opposites, a typically surrealist aspiration. He does not really balance or reconcile these opposites, but rather oscillates between them, between automatic-looking experimentation and restrictive Oulipian practices, between the use of cognates and the exploitation of untranslatable idiomatic expressions, between self-revelatory texts *en abyme* and deceiving pumectation, and finally between the most irreconcilable set of contraries: just as Gertrude Stein praised de Chirico for making "no distinction between the real and the unreal" (30), Ashbery wrote of Tanguy that for him "the arbitrary distinction between abstract and figurative painting did not exist [and so he] painted real if nonexistent objects [. . .] in the interest of a more integral realism" (**Reported Sightings** 27). There can be little doubt that Ashbery has succeeded in the same terms.

Notes

1. Wolf aligned Ashbery with Abstract Expressionism, but his poetry has been too diverse to allow any integral identification with a particular movement. David Sweet and David Bergman have successfully corrected his view. Sweet is the author of the most satisfactory analysis of Ashbery's relationship with the painterly avant-garde at large, pointing at his kinship with marginal figures and precursors of surrealism. He argues that Ashbery's "ritual collagism" is characteristic of surrealism and does not fit in with Abstract Expressionism (324). Bergman goes deeper in his rejection of "lack of finish" in Ashbery's surfaces, which he sees instead as overworked in the Mannerist style of Parmigianino, partly revived in this century by de Chirico (xxi-xxii). Bergman refutes Wolf's dismissive treatment of specific works and authors mentioned in the poems, claiming de Chirico as a "touchstone" in Ashbery's career, without further elaborating this point (xiv). I will argue here that the

relevance of de Chirico cannot be overstressed. Indeed, this essay aims primarily to explore his influence on Ashbery and traces the recurrence of metaphysical aesthetics during almost twenty years of Ashbery's poetic production under—I borrow Robert Rosenblum's phrase—de Chirico's "long American shadow."

2. Apparently—perhaps not surprisingly—most critics who are hostile to the early Ashbery are also fierce enemies of surrealism. Hence my use of "trivialized," which in fact means that these critics renounce further exploration once the fearful diagnostic has been reached. There is a whole tradition of Ashbery detractors demanding meaning in his poetry, including Robert Boyers (1978), Charles Molesworth (1979), and James Fenton (1985), among others. Fenton's review is titled "Getting Rid of the Burden of Sense," quoting a line from Ashbery that I also use here, with decidedly different intentions.

3. For a convincing refutation of Ashbery's rejection of other French influences, see Ford.

4. Richard Howard would be an exception here, for he pointed as early as 1970 that de Chirico's "oneiric dissociations are the kind of thing Ashbery himself aspires to" (45).

5. Ashbery's thirty years of art criticism, collected in *Reported Sightings,* would simply not make any sense without his constant references to the Italian, who is praised as a major figure in the development of twentieth-century painting.

6. Howard delights in the way "many writers have provided a clue in the form of an imaginative schema or construct which heightens the work's inner resonance at the same time that it defines the *poetics* by which the contraption operates" (26-27). He explains that for Gide the epitome of this technique was the heraldic suspension of a second, identical blazon in the center of the first. Gide's literary examples are classics like *Hamlet's* "Mousetrap" and *Las Meninas.* For a compelling study of this device see Dällenbach.

7. For David Sweet, "Self-Portrait" marks a climax in Ashbery's participation in a "Stevensian" tradition: "Gone are the piano-legged girls, the bottle-labels and other discarded objects that betoken dada and surrealist influences and assume the rough texture of assembled fragments or the marvelous sheen of chimerical juxtapositions. In contrast, Parmigianino's art involves intention, reproduction, and discrimination" (331). As a poem included in the same volume, "All and Some" advances Ashbery's imminent return to de Chirico's metaphysical sensibility in *Houseboat Days.* Indeed, Sweet admits that "Self-Portrait" actually "does not set the standard for Ashbery's subsequent poetry, which often vigorously reincorporates the experimental plasticities of collagist, juxtapositional, and other disjunctive strategies."

8. There is in Ashbery's poetry at least an instance of a "girl / With the hoop" (*April Galleons* 67).

Works Cited

Ashbery, John. *April Galleons.* New York: Farrar, 1987.

———. "Craft Interview with John Ashbery." *The Craft of Poetry: Interviews from* The New York Quarterly. Ed. William Packard. Garden City: Doubleday, 1974. 111-32.

———. *The Double Dream of Spring.* New York: Ecco, 1970.

———. *Hotel Lautréamont.* New York: Knopf, 1992.

———. *Houseboat Days: Poems.* New York: Viking, 1977.

———. *Reported Sightings: Art Chronicles 1957-1989.* New York: Knopf, 1989.

———. *Self-Portrait in a Convex Mirror: Poems.* New York: Viking, 1975.

———. *Some Trees.* New Haven: Yale UP, 1956.

———. *The Tennis Court Oath: A Book of Poems.* Middletown: Wesleyan UP, 1962.

———. *Three Poems.* New York: Viking, 1972.

———. *The Vermont Notebook.* Los Angeles: Black Sparrow, 1975.

Bergman, David. Introduction. Ashbery, *Reported Sightings* xi-xxiii.

Boyers, Robert. "A Quest without an Object." *Times Literary Supplement* 1 Sept. 1978: 962-63.

De Bonnafos, Edith. "Au-delà de l'image par le mystère." *Grands peintres Hachette: Chirico* 96 (April 1968). N. pag.

Dällenbach, Lucien. *The Mirror in the Text.* Trans. Jeremy Whiteley with Emma Hughes. Chicago: U of Chicago P, 1989. Of *Le récit spéculaire: essai sur la mise en abyme.* Paris: Seuil, 1977.

De Chirico, Giorgio. *The Double Dream of Spring.* 1915. Private collection.

———. "Eluard Manuscript." Trans. various. *Hebdomeros* 175-204.

———. *The Fatal Temple.* 1914. Philadelphia Museum of Art.

———. *Hebdomeros, with Monsieur Dudron's Adventure and Other Metaphysical Writings.* Preface by Ashbery. New York: PAJ Publications; rpt. Cambridge: Exact Change, 1992. *Hebdomeros* 1929 (1-117).

———. *Mélancholie d'une rue.* Private collection.

———. *Mystery and Melancholy of a Street.* 1914. Private collection.

———. "On Metaphysical Art." 1919. Trans. Joshua C. Taylor. *Theories of Modern Art: A Source Book by Artists and Critics.* Ed. Herschel B. Chipp. Berkeley: U of California P, 1968. 448-52.

Fenton, James. "Getting Rid of the Burden of Sense." *New York Times Book Review* 29 Dec. 1985: 10.

Ford, Mark. "*Mount d'Espoir or Mount Despair*: Early Bishop, Early Ashbery, and the French." *Poetry and the Sense of Panic.* Ed. Lionel Kelly. Amsterdam: Rodopi, 2000. 9-27.

Fredman, Stephen. *Poet's Prose: The Crisis of Modern American Verse.* New York: Cambridge UP, 1983.

Howard, Richard. *Alone with America: Essays on the Art of Poetry in the United States since 1950.* Enl. ed. New York: Athenaeum, 1980.

Krauss, Rosalind. *The Originality of the Avant-Garde and Other Modernist Myths.* Cambridge: MIT P, 1986.

Lehman, David, ed. *Beyond Amazement: New Essays on John Ashbery.* Ithaca: Cornell UP, 1980.

Longenbach, James. "Ashbery and the Individual Talent." *American Literary History* 9 (1997): 103-27.

Lundquist, Sara. "'Légèreté et Richesse': John Ashbery's English 'French Poems.'" *Contemporary Literature* 32 (1991): 403-21.

McCabe, Susan. "Stevens, Bishop, and Ashbery: A Surrealist Lineage." *The Wallace Stevens Journal* 22 (Fall 1998): 149-68.

Molesworth, Charles. *The Fierce Embrace: A Study of Contemporary American Poetry.* Columbia: U of Missouri P, 1979.

Moramarco, Fred. "The Painterly Poets: John Ashbery and Frank O'Hara." *Journal of Modern Literature* 5 (1976): 436-62.

———. "Coming Full Circle: John Ashbery's Later Poetry." *The Tribe of John: Ashbery and Contemporary Poetry.* Ed. Susan M. Schultz. Tuscaloosa: U of Alabama P, 1995. 38-59.

Morise, Max. "Les yeux enchantés." *La révolution surréaliste.* 1 Dec. 1924.

Oulipo Compendium. Ed. Harry Matthews and Alastair Brotchie. London: Atlas Press, 1998.

Perloff, Marjorie. "'Fragments of a Buried Life': John Ashbery's Dream Songs." Lehman 66-86.

Rosenblum, Robert. "De Chirico's Long American Shadow." *Art in America* July 1996: 46-55.

Sawin, Martica. *Surrealism in Exile and the Beginning of the New York School.* Cambridge: MIT P, 1995.

Stein, Gertrude. *Everybody's Autobiography*. 1937. New York: Random, 1973.

Sweet, David. "'And *Ut Pictura Poesis* Is Her Name': John Ashbery, the Plastic Arts, and the Avant-Garde." *Comparative Literature* 50 (1998): 316-32.

Williamson, Alan. *Introspection and Contemporary Poetry*. Cambridge: Harvard UP, 1984.

Wolf, Leslie. "The Brushstroke's Integrity: The Poetry of John Ashbery and the Art of Painting." Lehman 224-54.

Helen Vendler (essay date 2004)

SOURCE: Vendler, Helen. "'The Circulation of Small Largenesses': Mark Ford and John Ashbery." In *Something We Have That They Don't: British and American Poetic Relations Since 1925*, edited by Steve Clark and Mark Ford, pp. 182-95. Iowa City: University of Iowa Press, 2004.

[*In the following essay, Vendler observes a similar emphasis on change and random associations in the poetry of Ashbery and Mark Ford, but contends that Ashbery's verse lacks the sense of physicality found in Ford's work.*]

Writers influenced by John Ashbery more often imitate his manner than grasp his import. They can scramble a metaphor, write a melting close, insert pop icons, make a comic allusion. But the essence of Ashbery does not lie in these tricks. When in 1992, I read, with instant joy, Mark Ford's *Landlocked,* I found a poet who had internalized the inner, more than the outer Ashbery. But, as I hope to show, Ford's poetry, even while benefiting from Ashbery's example, retains its own different quirkiness, both in that first volume and in the recent second collection, *Soft Sift* (2001).[1]

Ashbery's importance, to my mind, lies in his being the first notable American poet to free himself, stylistically and thematically, from nostalgia for religious, philosophical, and ideological systems. His modernist predecessors thought such systems necessary to human dignity, and they either remained Christian, like Marianne Moore; returned to Christianity, like T. S. Eliot and John Berryman; adopted an alternate political ideology (fascism in Ezra Pound, political conservatism in Robert Frost, a quasi-socialism in William Carlos Williams, feminism in Adrienne Rich); turned to Buddhism like Allen Ginsberg and Gary Snyder; or to science as a substitutive omni-system, as in the case of A. R. Ammons. Many poets who have tried to do without such systems—Wallace Stevens, Robert Lowell, Elizabeth Bishop, Sylvia Plath, and Charles Wright—nonetheless have expressed explicit imaginative regret for the loss of religious sublimity. One feels the pull, in all these poets, toward a system of belief or an organized form of collectivity, a wish for a way to give honor, dignity, and greater-than-personal significance to human life. Only within and by means of such systems, it seems to many writers, can the human subject be situated and understood.

Ashbery, by contrast, is wholly without a religious creed or a political ideology. And—more crucially—he gets along without the nostalgia for credences, or, to be more precise, he includes systems and creeds in his general mild nostalgia for everything transient, from sunsets to Popeye. But in Ashbery's work a comedy of plenitude and inception, both in theme and language, is constantly—and effortlessly—canceling out the general wash of nostalgia. His little two-line poem says it all: **"The Cathedral Is,"** says the title; "Slated for demolition," says the poem.[2] Sturdy architectural existence in the title; then a white space; then the one-line glee of the wrecking ball. The diction of cathedral-destruction is neither tragic nor sublime, but pragmatic and demotic. What such a poem honors is the human capacity for change (a Stevensian value) and the equally human delight in demolition (which is *not* a Stevensian value: Stevens prefers, as we can see from the beautiful late poem, "St. Armorer's Church from the Outside," the coexistence of the emergent new with the declining old).

Even when "demolition" is in view, Ashbery usually avoids ringing closure (though lingering closure pervades his volumes). He is more likely to start up a new poem in the last several lines of the old than to let the old come to a complete halt. As he writes in **"Grand Galop,"**

But we say, it cannot come to any such end
As long as we are left around with no place to go.
And yet it has ended, and the thing we have fulfilled
  we have become.

Now it is the impulse of morning that makes
My watch tick. As one who pokes his head
Out from a under a pile of blankets, the good and bad
  together,
So this tangle of impossible resolutions and irresolu-
  tions:
The desire to have fun, to make noise, and so to
Add to the already all-but-illegible scrub forest of
  graffiti on the shithouse wall.[3]

Genial though this ending may sound, it is also savage in implication: the *monumentum aere perennius* is unmasked as a "shithouse wall," and the "formèd trace," to use Ezra Pound's phrase,[4] has become a scribble of "graffiti" growing as lawlessly and stuntedly as a scrub forest. Yet, the impulse to write, however denigrated, is affirmed:

And one is left sitting in the yard
To try to write poetry
Using what Wyatt and Surrey left around,
Took up and put down again
Like so much gorgeous raw material.

           (SP [*Selected Poems*] 176)

If the "raw material" is "gorgeous" enough, it will remain so when embodied in our forms as it was in those of the sonneteers. The quest, for instance, is one piece of that perennial "gorgeous raw material," one of the inescapable modes in which life presents itself. In Ashbery then, Childe Roland will approach the dark tower yet once more, but this is how it happens in **"Grand Galop"**:

So it is that by limping carefully
From one day to the next, one approaches a worn,
   round stone tower
Crouching low in the hollow of a gully
With no door or window but a lot of old license plates
Tacked up over a slit too narrow for a wrist to pass
   through
And a sign: "Van Camp's Pork and Beans."

           (SP 178)

The characteristic postmodern pratfall of anticlimax is here, as Ashbery represents the lyric tradition by the "license plates" of former poets, and he parodies the way we say "Spenser's *Faerie Queene*" by signing the location "Van Camp's Pork and Beans." But also visible is the ever-present, if often comically occluded, Ashbery pain: one "limps carefully" from one day of the quest to the next. And the sickening anti-aesthetic of a new order is always rising to view:

Morning saw a new garnet-and-pea-green order
   propose
Itself out of the endless bathos.

           (SP 178)

Yet the implied task of the poet, bafflingly enough, has not changed: it is to find a way of raising human beings to a larger exponential power:

Impossible not to be moved by the tiny number
Those people wore, indicating they should be raised
   to this or that power.
But now we are at Cape Fear . . .

           (SP 179)

We can say, then, that in existence as we find it in Ashbery, nothing is to be taken seriously for long; everything is to be taken seriously in essence as "raw material"; and pain and bathos are forever setting the poet new aesthetic conundrums in "garnet" blood and "pea-green" bile.

What is it that Wyatt and Surrey left lying around? Love and pain, scenery, and an order of archetypes (such as the quest). Ashbery is a poet of all of these. As

he holds the Petrarchan inheritance up to the light, Laura and Stella morph into vulgarly named contemporary girls, just as inherited philosophical questions metamorphose into journalistic banalities:

How to explain to these girls, if indeed that's what
   they are,
These Ruths, Lindas, Pats and Sheilas
About the vast change that's taken place
In the fabric of our society, altering the texture
Of all things in it?

           (SP 182)

There is nothing for the poet to do but drag the clichés into plain view and, like Wyatt and Surrey before him, "babble about the sky and the weather and the forests of change," seeking a contemporary texture of words to match the altered texture of society. "Aloof, smiling and courteous" like life in **"Haunted Landscape"** (**SP** 263), this poet who admires everything and wonders at nothing babbles on, naïveté and sophistication his changes of garments. There is in his poetry a persistent sense of plot aborted, of journeys on circular tracks, of aspiration engaged in and mocked, of synapses of allusion constantly making electrical sparks and then fizzling out. Human meaning is made and exploded, and no larger backdrop of sustained systematic thought or belief guarantees either its fittingness or its permanence. Yet the intelligence that understands itself and its own evolving forms raises human biological organisms to a higher power, even as they helplessly undergo the vicissitudes of their physical being in love, fear, and pain.

Is this what life feels like in Mark Ford's rendering? As I read Ford, I answer "yes" and "no" and "sometimes." Yes, there are, as in Ashbery, many parodic and inconsequential moments, and yes, there are, as in Ashbery, forms of suffering, usually understated, subtending the comic anticlimax. But let me take an example of "No." While Ashbery tends to write within explicitly human terms, Ford is more allegorical in his protean changes. He can be a "misguided angel" (the phrase is the title of a recent poem [SS [*Soft Sift* 17]) or a "huge green amphibian," who in the cartoon-poem "Outing" follows his girlfriend as she shops:

If only it were truly impossible, and less like being a
   huge green amphibian
made to inch my home-sick coils between the different counters
of your favourite store, taking all these fancy cautions
to keep my head down, and out of other shoppers'
   way.
Your ankles I can just make out . . .
The dusty floor is cool, like a fountain,
worn smooth and comfortable by so many feet. . . .
Now as I glide towards the whirr of sliding doors, I
   half-hope
its electric eye won't respond to my irregular approach. Another

spanking clean threshold! "Open Sesame," it cries, "Hold tight!"

(L [*Landlocked*] 51)

Ford's interjection of the clichéd cries, "Open Sesame" from *The Arabian Nights,* and "Hold tight" from *The Waste Land* exhibits the tag-ridden overload of the Ashberian literary synapse, but the comic film of the self as a homesick dragon about to confound the high-placed electronic sensor of the automatic doors has more fairy-tale jollity and more consistency of plot than is natural to Ashbery. Ford's lyrics frequently rest, then, as Ashbery's do not, on a story line—but of course an absurd and allegorical one. The inventiveness in a characteristic early Mark Ford poem—"A Swimming-Pool Full of Peanuts" will be my example—lies in its comic-strip sketches of the protagonist's successive Chaplinesque efforts to deal with a single unexpected situation—coming across a swimming-pool full of peanuts. First the scene is set, in a paratactic style partly borrowed from another influence on early Ford, Frank O'Hara:

> I come across right in the open
> a whole swimming-pool full of peanuts I think
> I've gone mad so I shut my eyes and I count
> to five and look again and they're still resting there
> very quietly an inch or so I suppose below
> the high-water mark they're a light tan colour
> and the tiles around are a lovely cool aqua-blue
> only there's no water just these peanuts.

There follow the speaker's attempts to deal with the anomalous contents of the pool:

> Well this is a hoax . . . / unless they're painted . . . /
>   so I kneel down / and
> with a loud snigger I dip in my finger / just to see it
>   sinks into small grainy
> nuggets.

Queasiness sets in at the thought of what the peanuts might be hiding (piranhas, perhaps?), but he continues his exploration: when "fistful after fistful" of peanuts uncovers nothing underneath, he takes a nine-iron from his golf bag and after fruitlessly swinging away "reckless in that peanut bunker" he jumps in,

> but there's more and more always / so I say let sleep-
>   ing dogs lie / and I crawl
> to the side and haul myself out and . . . / angrily I
>   throw my nine-iron into
> the middle of the pool where it sinks / without trace
>   and I storm back to
> my car and . . .

Ashbery often makes use of a comparable paratactic style but would not have pursued the anecdote so consistently. The deadpan detail includes the saltiness and greasiness of the peanuts, the masculine bravado in the brandishing of the golf club, the intimation of a dark conspiracy between the constructor and the filler

of the pool, and so on. The poem is a perfect mimicry of the absurd medieval trial, the protagonist rising to a furious zeal; but the knight of the swimming pool, in lieu of finding victory, succumbs ingloriously to collapse.

Such a parabolic poem—applicable to any persistent, heroic, deranged, and deranging effort to make sense of the confounding world—aims to make us believe entirely in its frustration while disbelieving its farcical story. It asks us to remember the enormous and angry strivings of youth while judging them, from our later perspective, as absurd and demeaning. The means of Ford's poem are its dogged Disney animation, its lively successive verbs, and its despair of finding—even for a single incident—coherent similes, whether for self ("like a madman . . . like one possessed . . . like a good soldier") or for peanuts ("like sand-flies . . . like golf- / balls . . . like buff-coloured hail"). The Ashberian comic perplexity at the resistance of life to articulated description, and the equally Ashberian drive to describe it nonetheless, compete in Ford. And though the initial premise is absurd, nothing that follows is: Ford makes us believe in the quixotic heroism of our efforts to cope, even though our plight may extort ridiculous self-exposure. "A Swimming-Pool Full of Peanuts" could not have been written without the example of Ashbery and Frank O'Hara, but the young Ford had his own comic élan, more orderly than that of Ashbery, more aggressive and metaphysical than that of O'Hara.

One of Ashbery's most constant attitudes—underlying his display of intelligence and self-mockery that raises us to a higher power—is that of being of (at least) two minds. Dividedness drives almost every Ashbery poem, and is visibly manifest in the vertically split pages of his **"Litany."** A comparable doubleness—but in interestingly altered and much-condensed form—can be seen in Ford; my example is a three-stanza poem from *Landlocked* called "Then She Said She Had to Go," in which the two halves of each stanza of the poem, left and right, are separated by a columnar mid-gutter of white space. Here, to show the gutter, is the first of the three stanzas:

The drawing room was full	The commuters half-turned
At last the angry hostess	to wave good-bye to
approached and	their friend. About their
whispered	feet fell the
black	words
into my	of their
unsuspecting ear	evening newspapers. (L 43)

On the left side of the gutter there appears a scene and there is a matching scene on the right, of precisely equal shape. The first left-hand scene, given above, is located in a "drawing room" where a party is taking place; in the second stanza, the left shows a pastoral field enclosing a wandering cow; in the third, the left gives us a seaside village being drenched by a large sea-swell. In the first right-hand scene, given above, "commuters" wave good-bye to their friends; in the second, the protagonist eats lunch in a hall full of birds; in the third, his girlfriend angrily stalks out of the relationship. We are instructed to read these scenes across as well as down, because the scene on the left always holds its fifth line in common with its partner on the right. In each case, however, the shared line changes meaning, depending on whether we insert it into the left scene or the right.

In the first stanza, for instance, "black words" is the phrase shared by the two matched scenes: although in the left-hand narrative snippet the phrase "black words" has sinister psychological import, the identical phrase, read into the more routine right scenario, has only innocent visual significance. This is an Ashberian demonstration of the comic slipperiness inherent in language. Read separately in either scene, the phrase held in common is in no way ambiguous; but just as "black words" shifts its meaning like a chameleon as it moves from left to right, so does the shared phrase in each of the subsequent two matched sets of stanzas. In the second set, a cow swishes "away flies" on the left, while on the right "away flies" a carrot in the beak of a bird. In the third set, after the ocean floods on the left, "salt water" is found far inland, while on the right, the lover tries to imagine the "salt water" of tears in his girlfriend's eyes.

Whereas the pieces of Ashbery's bicameral mind in the two columns of **"Litany"** never become pervious in this way to each other, Ford wants to insist on the way language leaks across from one mental compartment to another. The first of Ford's puns here is lexical (as "black" is first moral then visual); the second is grammatical (as "flies" is first noun and then verb); and the third zooms from the macro- to the microcosmic (as "salt water" is first oceanic then lachrymal). Such puns suggest how language shimmers in a poet's consciousness, where a word, as it enters into different combinations, behaves with quantum variability—a wave one minute, a particle the next. And it is characteristic of Ford's practice that this lyric is so firmly condensed: he has shown no disposition toward Ashbery's characteristic constantly digressive expansiveness. In fact, Ford has located his writing in the line of the sonnet, saying,

> Every form I try is a variation on a sonnet, or rather an attempt to disguise the fact the poem secretly wants to be a sonnet. . . . In the end they simply end up squashed or stretched sonnets, elastic sonnets, sonnets that have stayed on the train a couple of stops past their destination.[5]

Ford's more recent poetry is less indebted to the Ashberian comic, but continues to practice the silent Ashberian undermining of the ground one stands on. "I plunge" says Ford in a poem entitled "Penumbra," "Towards remote vanishing points, where one man's / Loss unravels and becomes another man's / Devastation" (SS 34). We had expected that one man's loss would become another man's gain, but we were second-guessed—both men lose out. The passage from "loss" to "devastation," by the undertow of circumstance, unsettling our clichés in the process, is pure Ashbery. Here as in Ashbery's verse, the **"Discordant Data"**—to quote the title of a recent Ashbery poem dedicated to Ford[6]—will not add up. Even so, the frustrating wish to create order persists. As Ford puts it in "Living with Equations," "as I emerged from my hip-bath it suddenly dawned / The facts might be remarshalled and shown to rhyme," but the poem nevertheless comes to grief in a very Ashberian way: after a time of more reassuring equations,

> The remainder can only imperceptibly dwindle, retreating
> Backwards until their long lost premises turn inside out.
>
> (SS 13)

The Möbius strip of the human, like a Yeatsian gyre, can only undo itself; but we are at least enabled, by our ability to take the long view, to track the dimensions of our own undoing. Ford's ending here, in its equal avoidance of the comic, the tragic, the sublime, and the just, places his poem in the human-scale aesthetic defined by Ashbery.

Yet one aspect of Ford's work especially differentiates him from Ashbery. Ford includes in his writing a physically sensuous documentation that is not present in the ever-theatrical, ever-virtual John Ashbery. One could say that Wordsworth and Gerard Manley Hopkins, with their sense of skin against wind, breath against earth, lie behind the moments of natural presence we come across in Ford. In the very poem, "Penumbra," where we found the Ashberian satiric bon mot that one man's loss is another man's devastation, we see that Ford brackets that piece of Ashberian dark comedy with bleak scenic passages:

> I lean into the wind that blows
> Off the lake, and scours the sodden fields; the sky's
> Reflections ripple between ruts and bumps . . .
>   Crops,
> Sludge, restless drifts of leaves absorb
> The haggard light.
>
> (SS 34)

The depressive moods of the body, one could say, frame in Ford the comic aphoristic verdict of the mind. And the poet's micro-noticing of "ravaged spores" and "downy nettles" manages to hover, in its adjectives, on the border between the real and surreal without losing a grasp on the actual scene. In this way Ford belongs to the line of British poets, from Shakespeare to Hardy and Hopkins, who are willing to describe unlovely moments in nature; but he differs from them in giving the introspective reflections arising from such depressed physical moments an Ashberian inconsequence and ironic comedy.

In a recent essay, Mark Ford praised in James Tate qualities that can be found in his own work: the "refusal to elide the illogic of experience," the "treacherous instability" of meditation, and the ways in which poems work by "collaging disparate materials into a seamless fluency."[7] And the kind of lyricism that Ford finds in Tate—one both "intimate and impersonal"—is the sort he delights in in Ashbery and desires, I think, for himself. Poetry must be "intimate," or it would scarcely be true to itself; yet it must be "impersonal," so that it can be true for others. Writing in the *New Republic* on Mina Loy, Ford praised a poem that, he said, "embodies a devastating critique of outdated rhetorical conventions and ossified belief-systems," one that "anticipates the decentering fluidities of post-modern poetics."[8] There is perhaps something a little too pat about the approval extended here to something called "post-modern poetics" as though the Shakespeare of *Hamlet* and the Shelley of "The Cloud" were not aware—as they surely were—of "decentering fluidities." Ford is on surer ground when he speaks of every major poet's war on "outdated conventions and ossified belief-systems." Ashbery's war on them has proved, especially in its comic attachment to those very "conventions" and "belief-systems," buoyantly liberating for many younger poets, in England for Ford especially.

I have said one of the aspects distinguishing Ford from Ashbery is the felt presence of the body in an actual landscape. Ford is also likely to set himself in a recognizable location or to narrate a stable incident. Where Ashbery is protean, an absent center through which all discourses move, Ford lets us see himself in a given posture and location, irritated (in a poem called "Plan Nine") by the "dreadful telephone again," facing every morning a supervisor whose "reign of terror / And mind like glue" are relentlessly present (SS 8). Horrible twentieth-century prescriptions for good living are, in the same poem, imposed on a "case" resembling, we are sure, the poet's own, as a "caustic voice" says to "a clutch of bright-eyed interns," "No mohair, no alcohol, / Lots of plain yoghurt certainly, no foreign languages, no tête-à-têtes." One can see, from that parodic mockery of medical discourse, why Ashbery appeals to Ford; and yet such a passage is more firmly located in an actual event—here a medical consultation—than Ashbery's work tends to be.

Ford, though impersonal, is also confessional in a way closer to Hart Crane than to Ashbery. There are recognizable lyrics of disquieting self-exposure, such as "Misguided Angel," which begins with a mock-Miltonic self-challenge:

> Where will you ride in this minute that stretches
> Its wings, and soars aloft, and turns into
> An unplanned, devilish interval?
>
> (SS 17)

Upon this taunt, the "ossified belief-systems" and confusing bewilderment of the flesh immediately put in their appearance:

> Serial
> Misadventures have shattered the grip
> Of barbed rubric and corporate logo; enigmas
> Swarm at the brink of the five senses.

Finally, the poet's initial hyperbolic self-challenge—"Where will you ride in this minute?"—becomes a more actual one, almost a vow, in which the poet admits the three inescapable unfreedoms of the creative mind: one cannot censor one's thoughts, one cannot deny one's wounds, and one cannot escape the "inflexible etiquette" of art. That "inflexible etiquette"—the phrase, in its combination of the necessary and the decorative, could have come from Hart Crane—demands that gesture be brought to coincide with memory:

> There is no controlling
> One's renegade thoughts, nor striking
> The fetters from blistered limbs. Inflexible etiquette
> Demands every gesture be also a memory: you stare
> Into space where fractions and figures still pursue
> Their revenge.
>
> (SS 17)

An unknown frontier lies ahead in which the misguided angel is to stake a claim, but

> Whoever claims
> A stake out there must rise and speak in guttural tones
> Of all they mean—or meant—to do, and why, and
> where.
>
> (SS 17)

We have moved entirely out of the pose of ultimate inconsequence and charming dissolution that is Ashbery's own, and into a Stevensian and Crane-like seriousness in which the poet's muttering will be judged by an exacting ethical standard, at once internal and social.

Hart Crane's verse, as Ford commented in a review of his *Selected Letters,*[9] was motivated by the poet's "need to embody the physical, the mundane, the fleeting." The "mundane" and the "fleeting" are amply present in Ashbery, but the "physical" less so. And it is the "physical," with its irruptions of sensuous transcendence, that appeals to Ford in Crane—what he, quoting Crane, calls the poet's "blanket-like absorption in experience." The quintessential Ford can be found in the grafting of a felt physical ambience on the Ashberian metaphysical one, as well as the grafting of a Fordian allegorical story line on the Ashberian aslant angle of incidence. A recent Ford poem, "Twenty Twenty Vision," remarking centrally that "my doom is never to forget / My lost bearings," opens in a mode of cartoon metaphysics learned from Ashbery:

> Unwinding in a cavernous bodega he suddenly
> Burst out: Barman, these tumblers empty themselves
> And yet I persist.

(SS 29)

Very shortly "Twenty Twenty Vision" turns into a wonderfully exact lyric autobiography, reminiscent by turns of Wordsworth, Eliot, and Crane, but dominated by no one influence.

The fact that we can read such an oblique poem with understanding is due to our training by Ford's precursors in modernism, including Ashbery. But the memorable lyric itself—its story line, its alternately understated and overstated emotional vicissitudes, its surreal scenic vividness—is all Ford's own. I want to quote its closing lines, prefacing them by saying that the Ford narrative departs from the usual Wordsworthian plot by ending, as well as beginning, in medias res by framing both beginning and ending in a setting sun; by symbolizing birth as a death-wound; and by representing the awakening to life as coterminous with the terrible thirst with which "Twenty Twenty Vision" will end:

> *In medias res* we begin
> And end: I was born, and then my body unfurled
> As if to illustrate a few tiny but effective words—
> *But—oh my oh my—avaunt.* I peered
> Forth, stupefied, from the bushes as the sun set
> Behind distant hills. A pair of hungry owls
> Saluted the arrival of webby darkness; the dew
> Descended upon the creeping ferns. At first
> My sticky blood refused to flow, gathering instead
> In wax-like drops and pools: mixed with water and a
>   dram
> Of colourless alcohol it thinned and reluctantly
> Ebbed away. I lay emptied as a fallen
> Leaf until startled awake by a blinding flash
> Of dry lightning, and the onset of this terrible thirst.

(SS 29)

Although the posture here is not heroic, one feels the poet's sheer joy at the discovery of language, even in its most primitive forms of childish response: "but" (the objecting mind); "oh my oh my" (dismay one day, wonder the next); "avaunt" (the first thrill of the literary). For the "terrible thirst" parching the poet's throat from the onset of his vocation, no words, of course, will ever be entirely adequate—but the mind has nevertheless begun to amass its lexicon.

Michael Hofmann once called Mark Ford's work "unmistakably mid-Atlantic," and yet Ford's verse is also "unmistakably"—to this transatlantic reader—English in its attachment to the line of English romantic and modern lyric.[10] In an interview with Graham Bradshaw, Ford repudiated the contemporary genre of the literally autobiographical poem:

> I can't bear poems about grandfathers, or fishing expeditions, or what it's like to move into a new house, unless they're very *very* good poems. . . . I start off prejudiced against them because I find the subject-matter so boring. . . . I guess basically I'm always looking for gaps, little fissures where "a thought might grow," to use Derek Mahon's phrase.[11]

I associate the literal lyric with the United States, where it has lately been thought that specification of gender, ethnicity, class, and family relations adds authenticity to a poem. The classic lyric, from which Ford derives, has in the past engaged in various sorts of despecification so as to make its voice assumable by many readers, and Ford assents to that despecification as he reinvents himself as alligator, angel, or body unfurling into language. In the lyric of the past, the generalized speaker was, however, expected—by an invisible convention—to pursue his thoughts along normal logical lines. Pound, Eliot, Moore, and Crane, by allowing more wayward associations, created a modernism that curved the rails of thought in lyric, while Ashbery, disciple of Rimbaud and Mallarmé, dared to create actual gaps along the length of the rails. Ford, too, makes such leaps in logic native to his poems.

But the enthralling thing about Ford's lyrics is that although he has adopted the newer techniques of curves and gaps in "looping the loop" of consciousness—his phrase (SS 5)—he has allowed these techniques to remain wonderfully hospitable to the old—to Wordsworth, Hopkins, Hardy—not always in the parodic Ashberian way of knowing allusion, but often in the way of natural capacious memory. As Ford said in his Bradshaw interview—using a metaphor for tradition that might have surprised Eliot but not Wordsworth or Hopkins or Ashbery—"You scoop up a bucketful and enjoy as much as you can the various life-forms that happen to be in it."[12] We have the privilege of watching Ford scoop up, from the tide pools of both America and England, the life-forms and language-forms of our era. They are not tabulated by creed or system or ideology into any already known taxonomies of culture, but they group themselves happily in fleeting new convergences of the imagination.

In bringing Ashbery into the precincts of English verse, Ford has loosened the aspects of the English imagination that had remained within the stricter borders of Au-

123

denesque intellectuality, Movement dourness, and Larki-nesque gloomy comedy. For a long time it seemed inconceivable to represent Englishness except within certain contained formal postures; the wilder postures belonged to the provinces, and were tacitly regarded as savage. With his irreproachable literary sophistication, Ashbery has out-Englished the English; but with his Whitmanian expansiveness he has introduced a loose-limbed provincial slouch into the drawing room of Wildean wit. Ford, with comparable parodic savoir-faire, delights in the slippery and the farcical—those mischievous disruptions of the intellectual, the taciturn, the morose, and the well behaved. His cinéma vérité of contemporary English life accompanies his renditions of a postmodern and eclectic sensibility. Ford is at once a veteran of pop culture and a connoisseur of the desperation of high culture, an indoor reader of the past but also an outdoor breather of physically felt atmospheres. His generation of English poets is still in formation but I believe Ford is to be one of its eventual definers, as Ashbery was crucial to postwar writing in the United States.

And in that defining of the contemporary human being, Ford agrees with Ashbery that everything amenable to experience is in perpetual circulation, that culture cannot come to any definitive stability. Yet what circulates, being human, is never merely small: what Ashbery calls the circulation of small largenesses is given its largeness by speculation, reflection, mockery, and irony; by a *dédoublement* in which one is at the same time an angel but misguided; a body, but a penumbra; a bleak connoisseur of facts but at the same time one who "re-marshalls" them into a rhyme that raises all the figures in the equation to a higher (that is, larger) power. Most of all, the contemporary awareness we find in Mark Ford is made large by the vigilant sense (mocked in the two-column scenes of "Then She Said She Had to Go") that any word can come usefully to hand as a particle or a wave, and that the consequent combinatorial potential of language guarantees its ability to represent everything from the sublime to the ridiculous. This is a largeness amply put into circulation by Ashbery, and one that survives translation into Mark Ford's England.

Notes

1. Mark Ford, *Landlocked* (London: Chatto and Windus, 1992), p. 51. Hereafter L. *Soft Sift* (London: Faber and Faber, 2001). Hereafter SS.

2. John Ashbery, *As We Know* (New York: Viking, 1979), p. 93.

3. John Ashbery, *Selected Poems* (New York: Viking Penguin, 1985), p. 175. Hereafter SP.

4. Ezra Pound, *The Cantos* (London: Faber and Faber, 1987), p. 178.

5. Transcript of a letter from Ford, January 31, 1998.

6. John Ashbery, *Wakefulness* (New York: Farrar, Straus and Giroux, 1998), pp. 40-41.

7. Mark Ford, *Times Literary Supplement,* August 29, 1997, p. 26.

8. Mark Ford, *New Republic,* May 26, 1997, p. 39.

9. Mark Ford, *Times Literary Supplement,* September 19, 1997, p. 27.

10. Michael Hofmann, *Times Literary Supplement,* March 6, 1992, p. 23.

11. Mark Ford talking to Graham Bradshaw, in *Talking Verse,* ed. Robert Crawford, Henry Hart, David Kinloch, and Richard Price (St. Andrews and Williamsburg: Verse, 1995), pp. 54-58, especially 57.

12. Ford, *Talking Verse,* p. 58.

Bibliography

Ashbery, John. 1979. *As We Know.* New York: Viking.

———. 1985. *Selected Poems.* New York: Viking Penguin.

———. 1998. *Wakefulness.* New York: Farrar, Straus & Giroux.

Ford, Mark. 1992. *Landlocked.* London: Chatto and Windus.

———. 1992. *Times Literary Supplement,* March 6, p. 23.

———. 1995. "Mark Ford Talking to Graham Bradshaw." *Talking Verse.* Ed. Robert Crawford, Henry Hart, David Kinloch, and Richard Price. St. Andrews and Williamsburg: Verse, pp. 54-58.

———. 1997. *New Republic.* May 26, p. 39.

———. 1997. *Times Literary Supplement,* August 29, p. 26.

———. 1997. *Times Literary Supplement,* September 19, p. 27.

———. 1998. Transcript letter from Ford, January 31, 1998.

———. 2001. *Soft Sift.* London: Faber and Faber.

Pound, Ezra. 1987. *The Cantos of Ezra Pound.* London: Faber and Faber.

Frank B. Farrell (essay date 2004)

SOURCE: Farrell, Frank B. "John Ashbery and Samuel Beckett." In *Why Does Literature Matter?*, pp. 100-28. Ithaca, N.Y.: Cornell University Press, 2004.

[*In the following excerpt, Farrell evaluates motifs of cultural disorder and the passage of time in Ashbery's poetry, noting his incorporation of Martin Heidegger's metaphysical concept of language.*]

For Marjorie Perloff the writers John Ashbery and Samuel Beckett represent what I have called the stronger turn to the linguistic and the grammatical. One finds in their work, she says, the predominance of a more purely linguistic space whose compositional, pattern-generating powers, apart from any links to truth or reference or to the subjective life of experiencing selves, begin to produce connections and possibilities on their own. Perloff's favored writers, she says, take language in a manner that is "compositional rather than referential," where the focus "shifts from signification to the play of signifiers."[1] Since Ashbery and Beckett are powerful writers, if Perloff's account of them is correct then perhaps my overall defense of a weaker linguistic turn, in both philosophy and literature, is problematic. But neither writer offers a good case for her narrative; neither one, therefore, will be useful in demoting the psycho-metaphysical model of literary space I am defending, and in replacing it with a more radically linguistic one.

One feature of the poetry she praises is its resistance to our habit of seeing the linguistic items of a poem as tending toward a (possibly never arrived at) coherence and unity. She quotes James McFarlane as arguing that modernism generally, for all its focus on a threatening disintegration and dissolution, was actually in the service of more centripetal energies, so that objects and topics normally kept separate would collapse in on one another, would overlap and blur.[2] Perloff's more radical modernism, in contrast, would resist just those centripetal energies. In Ashbery, on her reading, readers are defeated when they look for any larger symbolic network because the linguistic fragments are not meant to cohere in that fashion; they are more arbitrarily juxtaposed and are not a teasing out of unifying energies already articulating themselves in the poem. These fragments cannot quite be attached to definite referents in the world; nor can they be attached to each other through the mediation of such a common referential world or through the ties of a more abstract symbolic world.

But is Perloff correct in her reading? It is useful, first of all, to describe a certain kind of poetry that might be called "postmodern." Such poetry would see the items of language as ready to follow, as if along the tracks of a roller coaster, the linguistic grooves by which our utterances typically arrive at meaning, and it would use the disseminating energies of language to frustrate those tendencies, would make the arrival less likely or forever delayed. Its energies would be more lateral and metonymic, with meaning deferred along a chain of words that present themselves as admittedly cultural fragments already part of the discursive field of signs, so that they have the status almost of clichés or near-quotations. Novelty would be generated not by the metaphorical compression of different semantic fields but by an unexpected, unnatural juxtaposition of already articulate cultural units. Instead of feeling that the poet is losing himself in a pre-Oedipal regression we would have a stronger sense of him as expressing attitudes, often ironic or coolly noncommittal, toward his use of words. As with conceptual art, poetry would be there to trigger reflection about concepts of meaning-making. We would be forced to acknowledge, at a certain level of abstraction, the usually hidden machineries by which we invest ourselves in objects and in what we say about them, and we would take a skeptical attitude toward those very machineries. The poet's work would admit that his consciousness is not a generator of meaning but a place where the random discursive elements of culture, including its detritus, happen to be gathering.

There is surely something right in taking this as a description of Ashbery's work. We easily find there a sense that one's poetic phrases are self-consciously bits of cultural discourse, that the move of using certain "beautiful" poetic words has already been played out: "About what to put in your poem-painting: / Flowers are always nice, particularly delphinium. / Names of boys you once knew and their sleds, / Sky rockets are good."[3] There is the disenchanted attitude toward experiences that seem to arrive secondhand: "The light sinks today with an enthusiasm / I have known elsewhere, and known why / It seemed meaningful, that others felt this way / Years ago."[4] There is the cooler, ironic postmodern attitude: "The buildings, piled so casually / Behind each other, are 'suggestions / Which, while only suggestions, / We hope you will take seriously.' . . . / . . . And, is this a silver age? / Yeah, I suppose so" (**"Spring Light,"** in *Houseboat Days,* 68). There are, as Perloff says, often juxtaposings of linguistic items that seem to sit on the page as bits of language and do not contribute to an overall coherent meaning.

Yet what makes Ashbery an important poet goes well beyond this, goes well beyond the role he is assigned in Perloff's story. Actually most of the poems in *Houseboat Days* and *Self-Portrait in a Convex Mirror* do not serve well as models of a linguistic turn, as compositional works arranging linguistic tokens at a considerable remove from their meaning and reference. I will argue that both Ashbery and Beckett are exemplars of, rather than counterexamples to, the account of literary space presented in chapter 1. (This is not an account of Ashbery's work as a whole. Two especially good collections will be examined because they present well a vision of Ashbery that is opposed to Perloff's.)

Here are samples of Ashbery's work.

> How are we to inhabit
> This space from which the fourth wall is invariably
>   missing,
> As in a stage-set or dollhouse, except by staying as
>   we are,

In lost profile, facing the stars, with dozens of as yet
Unrealized projects, and a strict sense
Of time running out, of evening presenting
The tactfully folded-over bill? And we fit
Rather too easily into it, become transparent,
Almost ghosts. One day
The birds and animals in the pasture have absorbed
The color, the density of the surroundings
. . . .
    if we were going to
To be able to write the history of our time, starting
    with today,
It would be necessary to model all these unimportant
    details
So as to be able to include them; otherwise the narra-
    tive
Would have that flat, sandpapered look the sky gets
Out in the middle west toward the end of summer,
The look of wanting to back out before the argument
Has been resolved.

("**Pyrography,**" in *Houseboat Days,* 9-10)

Don't be shocked that the old walls
Hang in rags now, that the rainbow has hardened
Into a permanent late afternoon that elicits too-long
Shadows and indiscretions from the bottom
Of the soul.

("**Business Personals,**" in *Houseboat Days,* 19-20)

One finds in these lines a treatment that might properly be called phenomenological, a study not just of objects but of the background space of appearing that gives them a subtle and hard-to-grasp character as real. There is a suggestion of the advent of a new way that objects are coming to be present for us, of complex moods that characterize our engagement with things, our forms of investment in them. Ashbery makes us focus on that object-determining space by frustrating the process through which we quickly bring the world toward ourselves in ways we already understand it. Or there are places that previously were saturated with meaning but now are emptied out, so that we are aware of that emptying process, of the shape of possible meaningfulness still remaining but unlikely to be filled in. He notes how things, and how we ourselves, become less substantial as individuals and seem to be more transparent to the surrounding space, to absorb its coloring. What makes his work valuable is that the background spaces of appearing that he investigates determine not a familiar form of objectivity, and not the linguistic feel of bits of cultural discourse, but the penumbral, barely evident textures of how things are real for us now. He also gives us a cool-elegiac rather than sentimental-elegiac awareness of endings and loss, when the panning movement of an invisible camera seems to show one from a distance, as the space of one's life seems to be missing a fourth wall, to be exposed to an unexpected

distance and emptiness, and the appearance of evening suggests a settling of accounts, the presentation of a "tactfully folded-over bill," as the life comes into view as what it is.

Even if Ashbery is extremely sophisticated regarding the various linguistic moves that compose his poetry, the stance of the experiencing consciousness, with its forms of openness to the world's ways of appearing, never dissolves here into being a site for the playing through of cultural grammars. It is true that the perceptual spaces he brings into view may not be fully grounded in a detailed geography, may dissolve quickly into other spaces, and often are used metaphorically to talk about conceptual moves or to refer self-reflexively to the writing of poetry. But even with these uses the perceptual spaces usually retain their integrity, a thickness of their own irreducible to the conceptual or poetic functions to which they are put. Note a difference here with what Charles Altieri has said regarding Stein. He claims that it is the *syntactic* resources within the linguistic space of her poetry, such as reversals and repetitions, that embody metaphorically what the poem is trying to say.[5] But in Ashbery it is often the *perceptual* space that serves as a scaffolding or template for ordering and suggesting a more abstract space, one that suggests a conceptualizing about seeing as such, or about poetry. When in the poem just quoted he says that one's narrative, if it does not pay attention to the details that determine the background feel of a scene, will have "that flat, sandpapered look the sky gets out in the middle west toward the end of summer," that phrase is not just a piece of language that is being maneuvered in discursive space. It is bringing into view a scene that has a lasting visual effect. If he goes on to say that such a sky has a "look of wanting to back out before the argument has been resolved," we are forced to examine both the perceptual image we have in mind and the less visible matter that the poem is about. Perhaps a sky can appear in its end-of-summer state to be dissolving into a universal flatness that ignores details and oppositions we ought to have paid attention to. Perhaps a narrative can have a smoothed over, sandpapered feel when we miss the sort of details that affect our subject matter not centrally but in the way that painting the furniture makes a room feel different (as Ashbery mentions in "**Pyrography,**" 9-10). But the perceptual scene does not dissolve into the conceptual one, as it often does in recent art. When the passage talks of a sense of time running out, of evening presenting "the tactfully folded-over bill," we can imagine an evening scene as one having just that quality of an ending that demands a more reflective accounting.

That is why I want to support the somewhat odd pairing of Ashbery with the philosopher John McDowell. The latter, as treated in chapter 3, criticized accounts of belief (he saw such accounts in Rorty and to some extent in Davidson) that portrayed the believer as maneuvering within a conceptual space where bits of language could be measured only against other bits of language, and not against the world. He claimed that a proper account of our mental operations must include both concepts and intuitions; that is, there must be moments in which we have the world itself in evidence, in which we bring it into view as that toward which our processes of belief-formation are directed. Otherwise the conceptual space becomes empty and meaningless or, at least, whatever goes on in there does not have to do with belief and justification. Ashbery remains likewise someone for whom the moment of bringing the world into view is important; the perceptual level does not fold itself neatly back into the conceptual, as it does for those making the turn to language more radically. Ashbery is not simply asking readers to step back and look at his phrases as fragments of cultural discourse, items that should be experienced as having invisible quotation marks around them. He is putting together words in unexpected ways in order to make us see, to experience a subtle perceptual and emotional pattern we have not, ourselves, been able to stabilize linguistically. Yes, there are metapoetic suggestions here about what relation to the world poetry can have now that we are so self-conscious about poetic moves as such. But this awareness is not for Ashbery (as for de Man) a reason to reduce our field to a linguistic (and metalinguistic) one but rather makes more important our attempts at seeing and describing what experience now offers us. What is thus brought into view has a depth to it, a metaphysical character, and is not a mere projection of our linguistic schemes.

Ashbery, then, remains a poet for whom the death of the experiencing subject, as one speaks of in literary theory, is greatly exaggerated. But the consciousness he uncovers is considerably more complex than that of Descartes or Husserl. In Ashbery there is a multiple, mobile, shifting consciousness whose investments in what it is doing poetically, and in its ways of having a meaningful world of objects, express various ironies and refusals and commitments, especially in its attitudes toward the language it uses.[6] He shows an awareness of how language arrives in juxtaposed segments that do not quite cohere; how our moves of investing ourselves in what we say may fail when they try for too much, so that they have to settle for being flatter, less capacious, and yet precise and attentive, even generous; and of how ordinary clichés can suddenly open out into a fresh vision of how matters stand, in the way "the rainbow has hardened into a permanent late afternoon that elicits too-long shadows."

I am arguing, then, that at least in *Houseboat Days* and *Self-Portrait in a Convex Mirror,* the literary space of Ashbery's work is close to what I described in chapter 1. It is phenomenological and metaphysical in the senses articulated there. The space of his work is also translational in that he is concerned with the passing of vague perceptions and moods, of the subtle patterns of our engagement with the world as such, into language, with the gains and losses entailed by that process, the sense of what slips away even as we grasp it. A play with cultural signs that already inhabit a discursive realm would come too late in this process. Ashbery's poetry also reoccupies a transitional space: one repeats aspects of the profound metaphysical work of the child, in the way that the child must come to an overall sense of its relation to an objective world, must satisfy its hunger to grasp what is not the self, and must come through that process to a less grandiose sense of self-identity. (The pity, Ashbery says in another poem, is that the soul is small and "fits its hollow perfectly.") Reoccupying that space as an adult makes one more aware of the initiating moves by which things first emerge into meaningfulness but that we usually miss in our habits of cultural engagement. The poetic space here is also aesthetic in that however much the linguistic baggage of culture circulates through the poems, one still has a sense of crossing over a threshold into a privileged space where a special kind of linguistic arrangement is occurring. (Many forget this fact and suppose that Ashbery's style will be easy to imitate successfully, but it is not so at all.) The poems are often profoundly beautiful. Ashbery gives us a disenchanted, sophisticated attitude toward both language and world, but if one reads his poems aloud there is often a subtle music, a kind of ritual enactment of a stance toward the world that we might come to participate in. So the space of these poems compresses several aspects of literary space as described in chapter I.

More generally, I wish to set Ashbery in the context of the schema presented in that chapter, which described four levels (world, subjectivity, language, practices of social power) that allowed for three radical reductions of certain levels to other ones, as in the radical linguistic or sociological turns. I claimed that these supposedly radical reductions were not radical enough, in that they did not allow modern disenchantment to extend all the way. Instead they assigned a theological status to one of the levels, so that it would project its patterns on the now-thinned-out space occupied by the other levels. When one performs the more thorough disenchantment then no theological stance is possible. But then the radical thinning out of these other levels does not occur and they can retain a richness of content, a metaphysical integrity and depth, even if not a full autonomy, of their own. Ashbery fits better into that schema as one who has made the more thorough disenchantment, rather than as one making the radical linguistic turn that Perloff credits him with. With all his sophistication as someone maneuvering within language, he sees how language is disenchanted just as much as the world and subjectivity are. So he will not assign it a theological role but is free to let the world's ways of appearing and the phenomenological stance of subjectivity retain a depth and richness of their own, as Perloff does not allow for.

Ashbery can be compared on this issue with Davidson. Davidson recognizes that the disenchantment of language, so that it has no magical powers to determine reference and meaning on its own, is not bad news for our hopes of finding ourselves in touch with the world as it is. Ashbery too recognizes that language cannot, and does not have to, carry the weight of a heroic romantic projecting of the self on the world. The poet can be as easily at home in banal, hackneyed language or in slang. But such a use of language is not a celebration of postmodern juxtaposition or collage, or a Rortyan satisfaction in a world well lost. To understand the disenchantment of language is, instead, to understand how one resides within a quiet openness to the world, so long as one patiently attends to the ways in which it brings itself forward. With the radical turn to language one sees only how language destabilizes and deconstructs whatever it touches. But a more thorough disenchantment makes us ironic and skeptical about those linguistic moves as well, so that they lose some of their erosive powers, and world and subjectivity can appear again with a certain depth (even if not the depth that a strong realist would attribute to the former or the Cartesian would attribute to the latter). To understand language as Ashbery does is to see how the synthesizing activity of the individual consciousness in relation to the world is not simply deconstructed, even if we are more aware of energies of fragmentation. The space of poetry remains a space where the experiencing consciousness is bringing materials into a pattern that matters. With the more radical linguistic turn we would emphasize only the centrifugal, dispersive energies of language. With the less radical turn that is demanded by a full disenchantment all the way up, we remain in a richer space (a space the poet takes advantage of) where the synthesizing forces of conscious experiencing are still in play; literary power can often be found in the interplay of those two sorts of opposing forces.

Ashbery asks what kinds of openness to a larger world are still possible if we refuse to settle for what our language gives us now, if we do not try to cover up loss, if we do not try to reduce the space that lets distance and emptiness appear in the first place. It is not that he is nostalgic for what we can no longer have; he acknowledges that the romantic poet's kinds of investment in the world, and especially in the activities of the poetic self, are illusory. But he looks then for more sophisticated kinds of investments in things and in our patterns of engagement with them; and he trains us in coming to embody that more complex subjectivity. In letting go of the world as we once believed it to be, he wonders what we may still retain of it from within our

disenchanted framework, what kinds of openness to the real it would be wrong to give up. That stance is not a regressive one but merely a statement of confidence that the postmodern realm does not exhaust either the world or our worthwhile forms of attention to it.

* * *

I will look at Ashbery's poetry now to see if this description of his work is supported by the poems.

> More chairs
> Were brought, and lamps were lit, but it tells
> Nothing of how all this proceeded to materialize
> Before you and the people waiting outside and in the
> next
> Street, repeating its name over and over, until silence
> Moved halfway up the darkened trunks.

("The Other Tradition," in *Houseboat Days,* 2)

In asking what it is about the time and weather that causes people to note it painstakingly in their diaries, Ashbery says: "Surely it is because the ray of light / Or gloom striking you this moment is hope / In all its mature, matronly form, taking all things into account / So that if one can't say that this is the natural way / It should have happened, at least one can have no cause for complaint" (**"Grand Galop,"** in *Self-Portrait in a Convex Mirror,* 17).

These poetic landscapes have a strangeness about them, and yet there is a mood that holds them together. Ashbery captures as well as anyone our sense of those late-afternoon or evening moments when our focus suddenly widens and we are more aware of the background frame of our present experiences, so that we are conscious of how they "materialize before" us as silence spreads gradually "up the darkened trunks." In the first of the two passages the scene is perhaps a summer cottage where chairs have been brought and lamps lit for guests, but the awareness is of the surrounding space, with its silence or emptiness that is nevertheless insistent and pervasive ("repeating its name"), so that the scene is held there in the light against penumbral forces that both heighten it and would one day dissolve it, that we may sense with a certain late-afternoon dread and yet also find satisfaction in identifying with. Ashbery's flatness of tone is important; there is no call here for existentialist trauma but a cool description of the overall texture of things.

These are moments when we are less taken up into a strategic way of seeing but instead step back and let the shapes of things, including the shapes of our own lives, declare themselves: a "mature, matronly" point of view that is "taking all things into account," that accepts without complaint the way things are, even if they could have been otherwise. We tend to note the light and weather in diaries, Ashbery says, because in certain moods we identify with these phenomena in the way we let objects and events come into view as, if not quite inevitable, still aspects of a natural unfolding, not to be regretted.

> All of our lives is a rebus
> Of little wooden animals painted shy,
> Terrific colors, magnificent and horrible,
> Close together. The message is learned
> the way light at the edge of a beach in autumn is
>   learned.

("**The Wrong Kind of Insurance,**" in *Houseboat Days,*
49)

> Yes, friends, these clouds pulled along on invisible
>   ropes
> Are, as you have guessed, merely stage machinery,
> and the funny thing is it knows we know
> About it and still wants us to go on believing
> In what it so unskillfully imitates, and wants
> To be loved not for that but for itself:
> The murky atmosphere of a park, tattered
> Foliage, wise old treetrunks, rainbow tissue-paper
>   wadded
> Clouds down near where the perspective
> Intersects the sunset, so we may know
> We too are somehow impossible, formed of so many
>   different things,
> Too many to make sense to anybody.
> We straggle on as quotients, hard-to-combine
> Ingredients, and what continues
> Does so with our participation and consent.

("**The Wrong Kind of Insurance,**" 50)

Here again Ashbery is excellent at giving the phenomenology of a certain kind of mood with several components to it: our need to have nature respond to us but our awareness that it now has a flatness, an artificiality to it, as a construct of our seeing, as something already described too often so that it seems a poor imitation of those descriptions; our sense of ourselves as fragmented and unable to give an overall meaningfulness to what is around us; the pressure of a certain aloneness as we recognize these things; a sense of a calm, resolved letting-go as we stare at "light at the edge of a beach in autumn." These passages are not primarily generated by their intralinguistic connections, as Perloff would suggest, but rather by the great difficulty of a perception that Ashbery is trying to put into words. It is true that light at the edge of a beach in autumn is something learned differently from the way other things are learned; the phrase picking that out is making us *look,* instead of being just an already processed item in the culture's economy of representations. We cannot inhabit the perceptual world in the same way as earlier. A cloudy sky at sunset is by now such a cliché that we have to see it as something already meant too often, so that it seems to appear as a stage setting that stagehands, familiar with the task, can wheel

into place quite easily. Nature is repeating scenes that we have already made artificial through our repeated acts of knowing, so that it seems a poor, tattered theatrical.

But then the tone of the poem changes and somehow the scene in the park still matters; that sense of a space already colonized by language weakens, and the park is still a place where the form of our engagement with the world is becoming visible, where the nebulous but insistent character of our selfhood is felt. Our tendency to resist the scene, because its features seem pulled along on invisible ropes in an evidently unskilled fashion, becomes instead a more complex form of identification with the scene that deepens us, as we see that "we too are somehow impossible, formed of so many different things." Nature even when it is processed in what at first is too obvious a manner, even when we can no longer be Wordsworth, can still teach us something that is profound and worth knowing. The elements in the park do not leap to life so as to give the scene a unified, organic, and satisfying way of presenting itself, but neither do we, and that is not a bad thing. Perhaps the psychological movements within us are also like an unskillful stage machinery dragged along on invisible ropes, rather than deeply original. But the tone of the passage shows that these still have an important integrity about them. The self in these passages is a poorly understood scattering of moments like those of the afternoon in the park as portrayed in the poem, moments that have a vague feel or mood that seems to join them but that are flat and without any logic that would link them more reliably. Yet the world before one is still being held together by the viewing consciousness (and not just by the lateral frictions of language), so that what continues "does so with our participation and consent." The reason the "murky atmosphere of a park" and the "tattered foliage" seem meaningful is that they are experienced by a self for whom having an ethically and metaphysically substantial world is still important. For Perloff, on the other hand, it is a severe criticism of Wallace Stevens that he still works within the structure of subject and object, self and world.[7] Presumably her favored poets are beyond that.

There is also the notion here of one's life as "a rebus of little wooden animals," so that we think of a kind of picture puzzle whose solution, requiring a turning of images into words, eludes us but is comprehended, if at all, only in the way we seem to grasp the background mood of a scene. Such a notion places the difficulty not as one emerging within language but as having to do with the border between image and language, with what we grasp in a preunderstanding that is in various respects nonlinguistic, as are the images of a rebus. (And the nature of those images is suggested in the description of the wooden animals as "painted shy, terrific colors, magnificent and horrible.") The perceptual information is already on the way to becoming linguistic, sentential, but it seems mysterious how that process is to complete itself; we have not yet entered a discursive space that breaks off and becomes autonomous. Admittedly the perceptual information of a rebus is used to stand for syllables of a language. An image of someone pouring a pitcher of water joined to an image of a tent may stand for the word *portent,* thus leaving the visual information as such behind. But an Ashbery poem does not become a rebus in that sense. The "light at the edge of a beach in autumn" retains a perceptual thickness that does not translate fully into being a metaphor for language.

Perloff's claim that poetry is more advanced when it is beyond a subject-object structure, as in her criticism of Stevens, fits the narrative being shaped here, for that subject-object structure seems to belong on the less developed side of the distinction I have been examining between different stages of psychological investment. There is on the one hand a stage where one is dealing with individuation, boundaries of self and other, and the overall metaphysical feel of the world over against the self. On the other hand is a stage where the self maneuvers positionally and strategically within cultural grammars, within a circulating movement of linguistic representations, where truth is a matter of (lateral) social agreement or of successful moves in the conceptual game, rather than of reaching forward to grasp reality as it is. Ashbery remains interested in the metaphysical and phenomenological stance of the first stage even as he inhabits the second one, rather than moving more completely into the latter in a way that leaves the former issues behind. Death and the threat of dissolution still matter to the individual's experience of itself in its way of taking in the world. Riding the roller coaster of linguistic and cultural circulation is never enough.

Ashbery as a phenomenologist wants to make us aware of the space of possible meaningfulness, rather than of what appears within it, by presenting it as it has emptied out: "In school / All the thought got combed out: / What was left was like a field. / Shut your eyes, and you can feel it for miles around. / Now open them on a thin vertical path. It might give us—what?—some flowers soon?" (**"What Is Poetry,"** in *Houseboat Days,* 47). There can be an exhilaration in that sudden opening out, in the horizons that can be visible when the mind's normal furniture is no longer in the way, when the mind's general openness to the world, prior to any particular engagement with it, is briefly in view. The danger for the postmodernist stance is that this kind of seeing will be lost. There is in that stance the strong temptation that all available spaces will be filled in by the endlessly productive and disseminating machinery of cultural signs, as in films that cannot allow the quieter opening up of a background space that has its own kind

of insistence. Perhaps it will be said that in this postmodern world of rapidly moving signs, where everything becomes information that is easily transmitted and quickly changes its configurations, where things seem less substantial and more readily consumable as they respond to changing styles, the task of the poet is simply to give the feel of being within that world. But a different task is more important. As the character of experience changes in the ways described, there is the danger that we will lose our capacity for a wide range of experiences: those that emerge in accord with slower, deeper rhythms, in the background perhaps, that require silence and a patient attentiveness before the significant pattern in question is able to appear. Poets are one resource for holding out against the loss of those possible modes of experiencing; they should not be expected to feed us back the styles of processing that the information revolution is training us for. The mark of the importance of Ashbery's poetry is the way it refuses to be simply postmodern, the way it lets the space of possible experience open out in depth without filling it in, the way it chooses scenes that allow that background to come into view.

In another poem (**"Houseboat Days,"** in *Houseboat Days,* 38) Ashbery refers to the "trouvailles" of the senses. The use of that word suggests that our sensory perceptions have a "found" quality that is in some ways artificial, a matter more of our willingness to count things as significant than of what they are in themselves, as when some count ordinary objects as antiques. Unlike with the romantics we are ready to see those sensory findings as giving us rather little, as objects with little staying power. But the empty terrain against which they appear remains something worth attending to, as a matter of understanding ourselves and our forms of knowing.

> Here is nothing, not even
> Lazy slipping away, feeling of being abandoned, a
> Distant curl of smoke above a car
> Graveyard. Instead the shadows stand
> Straight out. Uninvited, light grabs its due;
> What is eaten away becomes etched impression
> Of mutability, but nothing backs it up.

("Fantasia on 'The Nut-Brown Maid,'" in *Houseboat Days,* 74)

That "etched impression of mutability" is what remains as the things appearing within that lighting disappear. Light "grabs its due" so that things must present themselves as they are; we thus see with clarity their metaphysical fragility. As things disappear they leave behind that sense of fragility as a quality of the landscape. The metaphysical lighting does not even allow us the satisfaction of a human sense of loss, a "feeling of being abandoned," a mark of human absence such as the curl of smoke above a junkyard. As Ashbery says in **"Valentine"** (in *Houseboat Days,* 62), things in withdrawing leave an emptiness that is perhaps "bathed in freshness" but may be instead "just a new kind of emptiness."

Ashbery is also a phenomenologist of time-consciousness:

> The insipid chiming of the seconds
> Has given way to an arc of silence
> So old it had never ceased to exist
> On the roofs of buildings, in the sky.
>
> ("**On the Towpath,**" in *Houseboat Days,* 22)

> Yet in the end each of us
> Is seen to have traveled the same distance—it's time
> That counts, and how deeply you have invested in it,
> Crossing the street of an event, as though coming out
>   of it were
> The same as making it happen.
>
> ("**Saying It To Keep It from Happening,**" in *Houseboat Days,* 29)

> Better the months—
> They are almost persons—than these abstractions
> That sift like marble dust across the unfinished works
>   of the studio
> Aging everything into a characterization of itself.
>
> ("**Grand Galop,**" in *Self-Portrait in a Convex Mirror,* 15)

Again, however fine the language is in these passages, what gives them their power is their sense of the self in time, so that the viewpoint of the experiencing subject remains crucial. We are made to notice the difference between attending to measurable calendar time and attending to what seems to sift quietly over things, like dust, in a hardly noticeable, yet perhaps anxiety-producing process that everything around us comes to exemplify. We note the ways we invest ourselves in events or else come through them to the other side, as if crossing a street inattentively, and the way time can seem almost spatial, a silence out of which things are crystallizing. Ashbery talks of his working in an "other tradition," one that would let us attend to the small moments, the indistinct textures of consciousness, the penumbral moods that invest the world, the hard-to-grasp overall feel of the most ordinary scenes, everything that is ordinarily lost in the way we develop the standard narratives of our experience and the standard accounts of what has happened in history. How is moving through an event in one's life like crossing a street? One gets to the other side without being crushed by its streaming forces, but getting to the other side safely is not the same thing as being truly in the event. Crossing a street is at most times a thoughtless undertaking as one's mind is engaged with other things. The point is

that the kind of thought occasioned by the image is not at all well captured by the knowingness of someone who sees words as already in quotation marks, as bits of discourse. (And there is something fine in the notion of phenomenal time, rather than clock time, as like a fine dust that ages everything "into a characterization of itself," with the two opposed meanings of bringing out something's character and replacing the thing with an idea of it.)

Ashbery's phenomenology is in some respects Heideggerian, but instead of Heidegger's feeling that he has found an Ur-vocabulary in the wordplay that the German language offers, such that a new language sensitive to the Being of beings can emerge, Ashbery's attitude is that of coolness, flatness, and detachment. If there is often a sense of elegy and loss, of an emptying out of the terrain, of the passage of time, there is rarely a sense that despair is the proper response or that this emptiness might be filled up by anything the poet might do. Rather the poet accepts the flatness of language, the sense of skepticism about whether his experience, filtered through the cultural languages, is special. Instead of Heidegger's mystical talk of Language as the House of Being, there is a postmodern awareness that our self-consciousness about language is distancing ("The way / Is fraught with danger, you say, and I / Notice the word 'fraught' as you are telling / Me about huge secret valleys some distance from / The mired fighting" ["**Variant,**" in *Houseboat Days,* 4]). Meaning occurs not through a Black Forest regression to the modes of experience of premodern Germany (or to those of pre-Socratic Greece) but through what happens to everyday language almost inadvertently. (To put the matter much too simply, Ashbery is a mix of Heidegger and Derrida: both an openness to the faintly appearing metaphysical character of what is real and a postmodern awareness of how invasive the effects of language are. Critics err in seeing only the Derridean side, but it is important that this side undercuts certain aspects of the Heideggerian one.) For Ashbery it is a matter of integrity to resist and frustrate what may appear to be moments of originality and inspiration, in favor of working with the admitted secondhandedness of the linguistic strings that we maneuver, a secondhandedness that is not a failure of poetic inspiration but belongs to the very character of language. Ashbery's stance is one of belatedly inhabiting a space in which certain experiences are no longer possible (though it is questionable whether they ever were).

> Its scene drifts away
> Like vapor scattered on the wind. The fertile
> Thought-associations that until now came
> So easily, appear no more, or rarely. Their
> Colorings are less intense, washed out
> By autumn rains and winds, spoiled, muddied,
> Given back to you because they are worthless.
>
> ("**Self-Portrait in a Convex Mirror,**" 81)

The pity of it smarts, Makes hot tears spurt: that the
   soul is not a soul,
Has no secret, is small, and it fits
Its hollow perfectly: its room, our moment of attention.

                    ("Self-Portrait in a Convex Mirror," 69)

Instead of a space saturated with proliferating, disseminating signs (as in the description given of Rushdie
as postmodern in chapter 2 and that will be given in
chapter 8 regarding a memoir by Derrida), the space in
which literature happens has an absence about it, a loss
of what once entered it more readily. Thought associations that were easy now come rarely, are less intense,
and are washed out, as the colors of a landscape might
be by autumn rains and winds. They stabilize in the
available field only because what once made them valuable has somehow detached itself from them, has allowed them to appear now as empty and worthless. The
mind appears as gray and less vivid, with a muddying
of boundaries and with shapes that seem to scatter easily like mist. Instead of the often grandiose investments
of the romantic self, with its ability to transcend
boundaries, we have a self that is small and "fits its
hollow perfectly," the room made for it by forces that
have produced this present moment of attention. The
poetic self is not capable of the heroic gestures of
meaning-making that once seemed available not only to
the romantics but also to many of the modernist poets.
But it can honestly and accurately describe the residues
that remain when neither the world nor consciousness
offers space for such gestures. It can capture the fading
character of a world once believed in more intensely,
and it can refuse to imitate, even through parody, the
now-impossible gestures. (This is not an admission of
cultural failure but merely a willingness to acknowledge
both losses and gains in the forms of consciousness we
have come now to inhabit.)

What is thus worth saying is not, as in Perloff's story, a
kind of combustion obtained by rubbing fragments of
language together. Ashbery is still dealing with patterns
that are so fine as to disappear when we try to bring
them forward, that we do not even know we have
captured when we have done so.

   . . . Behind the mask
   Is still a continental appreciation
   Of what is fine, rarely appears and when it does is
      already
   Dying on the breeze that brought it to the threshold
   Of speech.

("A Man of Words," in *Self-Portrait in a Convex Mirror,*
                                                        8)

I have given these extensive quotations from Ashbery
to show that he fits only in a strained manner into Perloff's narrative. It is true, as she claims, that he is not a
symbolic poet in the way that Eliot is. The idea of many

poets in the 1950s and 1960s in America, especially of
the New York School, was to present their experiences
of the world straightforwardly without asking that they
take on significance in a more abstract network of meanings. (The French poet Pierre Reverdy supposedly did
this well and is praised by Ashbery precisely for this
quality.) But if it is clear that Ashbery is not a symbolist poet and does not want to write poetry with all the
religious, cultural, and historical references of *The
Waste Land,* still he is not letting the scenes he describes
simply stand for themselves. The physical landscapes
that he moves through often play a double role; the
space coming into view in them is not just their own
but also the more abstract spaces of language, time,
poetry, semantics, phenomenology, and epistemology.
"Fertile thought-associations" are said to have colorings
that are "washed out by autumn rains and winds,
spoiled, muddied." Certain "abstractions" sift "like
marble dust across the unfinished works of the studio."
A message about human lives is learned "the way light
at the edge of a beach in autumn is learned." A narrative is said to have "that flat, sandpapered look the sky
gets out in the middle west toward the end of summer."
It is difficult to talk about the ways in which language
does its work, about how we take experience in, or
about the workings of poetry. Just as Heidegger uses
lighting and *clearing* to talk of what goes beyond the
characteristics of physical space, so Ashbery's descriptions of the light and the landscape stand both for
themselves and for more abstract spaces. That is why it
is important, for someone who wishes to reflect on how
language does its work in poetry, to remain connected
with prelinguistic spatial and visual patterns of
experiencing; these may still serve as a metaphorical
scaffolding for attempts to comprehend more abstract
realms. Without that scaffolding a crucial resource for
our project of understanding language will have been
lost. If we make the linguistic turn too thoroughly we
defeat our purposes in making it. The energies in Ashbery's poems are clearly centripetal as well as centrifugal. There is not the convergence of meaning on
particular symbolic items, as in Eliot. But there is a
convergence of different spaces, different geographies,
so that they come to occupy the same terrain simultaneously. "And then somehow the loneliness is more real
and more human / You know not just the scarecrow but
the whole landscape / And the crows peacefully peck-
ing where the harrow has passed" (**"Lithuanian Dance
Band,"** in *Self-Portrait in a Convex Mirror,* 53).
Perhaps the "harrow" here is the movement of the poetic
lines. But then it is interesting that what the poem brings
to our attention is the space that opens out once the harrow has passed; what the poem seems to be about is not
the poetic lines but the experiential landscape that they
move across and that appears briefly as an afterimage
as one has followed the poem to its end. Great film-

makers have been able to capture that silent framing against which our gestures appear. Granted that often in recent films the sequences are moves within the language of filmmaking, quotations from earlier films, and so forth, and thus are intertextual. Yet one may wish, in viewing these, that there were moments that opened out toward aspects of the world that, in coming into view, made us equally as aware of the space the harrow has moved across as of the harrow's marks.

Ashbery may bring into his poems bits of cultural discourse, even what looks like a menu copied straight from a nursing home (as in **"Grand Galop," in *Self-Portrait in a Convex Mirror,*** 14). But he also gives us the moments of opening out to a larger vision, where an expansive unfilled space is present behind the words, even if we do not have the mental powers or the linguistic equipment to hold that vision steady or to articulate it.

> . . . To extend one's life
> All day on the dirty stone of some plaza,
> Unaware among the pretty lunging of the wind,
> Light and shade, is like coming out of
> A coma that is a white, interesting country,
> Prepared to lose the main memory in a meeting
> By torchlight under the twisted end of the stairs.

("And Others, Vaguer Presences," in *Houseboat Days,*
48)

> A few black smudges
> On the outer boulevards, like squashed midges
> And the truth becomes a hole, something one has
>   always known,
> A heaviness in the trees, and no one can say
> Where it comes from, or how long it will stay—
> A randomness, a darkness of one's own.

("The Ice-Cream Wars," in *Houseboat Days,* 60-61)

These passages are vintage Ashbery. First our stance is drawn back inward to the linguistic field by the use of language that calls attention to itself: "pretty lunging" or the pairing of "black smudges" with "squashed midges." But then the passages open out to a much wider field, to a feeling of distance, like coming out of a coma or becoming aware of a pervading randomness, a darkness of one's own.

Notes

1. Perloff, *Poetics of Indeterminacy,* 23.

2. Ibid., 29-30. The essay quoted from is James McFarlane, "The Mind of Modernism," in *Modernism* 1840-1930, ed. Malcolm Bradbury and McFarlane (New York: Penguin, 1976), 92.

3. John Ashbery, "And *Ut Pictura Poesis* Is Her Name," in his *Houseboat Days* (New York: Penguin, 1977), 45; copyright © 1972, 1973, 1974, 1975, 1976, 1977

by John Ashbery. The poems in *Houseboat Days* are reprinted by permission of Georges Borchardt, Inc., and Carcanet Press Limited.

4. John Ashbery, "Self-Portrait in a Convex Mirror," in his *Self-Portrait in a Convex Mirror* (New York: Penguin, 1976); copyright © 1972, 1973, 1974, 1975, 1976, 1977 by John Ashbery. The poems in *Self-Portrait in a Convex Mirror* are reprinted by permission of Viking Putnam, a division of Penguin Putnam Inc., and Carcanet Press Limited.

5. Altieri, *Painterly Abstraction,* 240-47.

6. Regarding poetry generally, Altieri is good at seeing how it remains phenomenological and not merely linguistic; how it allows for complex, shifting investments of the self. See his *Painterly Abstraction.*

7. Perloff, *Poetics of Indeterminacy,* 20.

Bibliography

Altieri, Charles. *Painterly Abstraction in Modernist American Poetry.* University Park: Pennsylvania State University Press, 1995.

Ashbery, John. *Houseboat Days.* New York: Penguin, 1977.

———. *Self-Portrait in a Convex Mirror.* New York: Penguin, 1976.

Davidson, Donald. "Belief and the Basis of Meaning." In his *Inquiries into Truth and Interpretation,* 141-54. Oxford: Clarendon Press, 1984.

Derrida, Jacques. *Circumfession.* Translated by Geoffrey Bennington. In Bennington and Derrida, *Jacques Derrida.* Chicago: University of Chicago Press, 1993.

Heidegger, Martin. "The Origin of the Work of Art." In his *Poetry, Language, Thought,* translated by Albert Hofstadter. New York: Harper and Row, 1971.

McDowell, John. *Mind and World.* Cambridge: Harvard University Press, 1994.

McFarlane, James. "The Mind of Modernism." In *Modernism 1840-1930,* edited by Malcolm Bradbury and McFarlane, 71-93. New York: Penguin, 1976.

Perloff, Marjorie. *The Poetics of Indeterminacy.* Evanston, Ill.: Northwestern University Press, 1999.

Rorty, Richard. *Consequences of Pragmatism.* Minneapolis: University of Minnesota Press, 1982.

John Yau (essay date May/June 2005)

SOURCE: Yau, John. "The Poet as Art Critic." *American Poetry Review* 34, no. 3 (May/June 2005): 45-50.

[*In the following essay, Yau explores Ashbery's artistic ideal by examining his art criticism and contrasting it with that of Frank O'Hara.*]

The coordinates of this position might be ill defined, its fragility or strength unassessed, its motivations unconscious; still the position stands, and stands for and against.[1]

—Yves-Alain Bois

The publication of John Ashbery's *Selected Prose,* edited by Eugene Richie (Ann Arbor: The University of Michigan Press, 2004), offers us the opportunity to begin considering what he has, in his position as an art critic, stood for and against. And, once we do so, it may enable us to begin teasing out the relationship between his art criticism and his poetry, how they might have influenced each other. It also allows consideration of the position taken by Frank O'Hara (1926-66), Ashbery's contemporary and close friend, in his art writing. Ashbery and O'Hara are the only two poets of the original five poets associated with the New York School to have made a living from working in the art world. Both James Schuyler and Barbara Guest wrote reviews and essays, but neither of them ever supported themselves as art critics. The fifth poet, Kenneth Koch, taught at Columbia and was never an art critic.

Selected Prose brings together what the author calls "miscellaneous prose pieces written over the last half century." It augments *Reported Sightings: Art Chronicles, 1957-1987,* edited by David Bergman (New York: Alfred A. Knopf, 1989), which includes over one hundred articles and reviews, most of which Ashbery wrote during the years he worked for *ARTnews, Art in America, Newsweek,* and *New York.* The sixty-nine pieces in *Selected Prose* include reviews of poetry and fiction; art criticism; essays on artists who wrote (and vice versa); five essays of varying length on Raymond Roussel (the most on one figure); prefaces and introductions to books; introductions to poetry readings; public lectures; reminiscences; essays on film, music, photography, and architecture; an obituary. They appeared in *Poetry, Portfolio and ARTnews Annual, Book Week, New York Times Book Review, ARTnews, PN Review, Edge, Poetry Project Newsletter,* and *Modern Painters.*

While *Selected Prose* and *Reported Sightings* add up to more than seven hundred pages, the two books represent just a fraction of Ashbery's total activities as an art critic and literary essayist. Based on the six Charles Eliot Norton Lectures that he gave at Harvard University in 1989-90, *Other Traditions* (Cambridge, MA: Harvard University Press, 2000) is around one hundred and fifty pages long, and includes essays on John Clare, Thomas Lovell Beddoes, Raymond Roussel, John Wheelwright, Laura Riding, and David Schubert, writers who, at best, barely have a toe-hold in the canon. According to his bibliographer, David Kermani, Ashbery published over four hundred and fifty articles, reviews, and essays about art between 1957 and 1975. This does not include his contributions to art catalogues,

book reviews and other kinds of writing and writing work he did during this period, his stints as the critic for *New York* (1978-80) and *Newsweek* (1980-85), or catalogue essays and introductions he has written since 1975. As Ashbery readily admits: "Some were written for money to help subsidize my poetry habit." But it is also true that many were written because he was commissioned to write about a subject he "was interested in." It should go without saying that this position is the one every art critic tries to occupy and maintain. Otherwise, writing becomes sheer drudgery.

O'Hara's criticism and related writing is collected in three books totaling around three hundred and seventy-five pages: *Art Chronicles 1954-1966* (New York: George Braziller, 1975), *Standing Still & Walking in New York,* edited by Donald Allen (Bolinas, CA: Gray Fox Press, 1975), and *What's With Modern Art,* with an afterword by Bill Berkson (Austin, TX: Skanky Possum Press, 1999). After graduating from Harvard, where he, Ashbery and Kenneth Koch met, and receiving an M.A. from the University of Michigan, O'Hara moved to New York and worked in the art world from 1952 to 1966. A charismatic figure, he soon became a highly visible, active force in the burgeoning art scene, a dervish toward which different groups, factions, and individuals gravitated. As Philip Guston said, after O'Hara died, "he was our Apollinaire."

Ashbery, who has stated that he "backed into a career as an art critic," began writing art reviews in 1957, though not on a regular basis. In 1960, while living in Paris, he became the art critic for the *New York Herald Tribune* (international edition) and continued in this position until 1965, when he returned to New York and became an executive editor at *ARTnews,* a position he held until 1972. In 1974, after being unemployed for more than a year, he began teaching creative writing at Brooklyn College (1974-1990). While teaching at Brooklyn College, he was the art critic for *New York* (1978-80) and *Newsweek* (1980-85), which means that after he received three major literary awards—National Book Award, Pulitzer Prize, and National Book Critics Circle Award—for *Self-Portrait in a Convex Mirror* (Viking, 1975), he still found it necessary to work at two full-time jobs.

While Ashbery and O'Hara operated in the art world, they functioned as mirror opposites. Ashbery lived and worked in Paris, far from New York, which had overtaken Paris and become the center of the international art world. He was the art critic for a newspaper and a magazine, which is one step removed from the action. O'Hara lived in New York and, at the time of his death, was Associate Curator of Painting and Sculpture at the Museum of Modern Art, New York. Amidst the rise of Pop art and Minimalism, as well as the pronouncements of the death of painting, the failure of the so-called "second generation," and the increasing number of art historians writing criticism, he was a magnet at the center of a storm.

Being an art critic is for the most part a low-paying job. It is particularly insecure if you do not have a position at a university. In the 1950s and '60s, it was far worse than it is now. In an informative interview with the English poet and literary critic Mark Ford, Ashbery talked about the financial side of being an art critic living in Paris:

> I got the job of art critic for the *Herald Tribune,* but that wasn't until May 1960. That didn't pay anything but it did open the way to other things that did pay. Even after five years in the job I was only making about $30 an article, but they could pay slave wages because there were so many Americans in Paris who were dying for that kind of work. So I really just lived from hand to mouth.[2]

In 1961, in addition to his regular job at the *Herald Tribune,* Ashbery became the art critic for *Art International,* a magazine. He also wrote articles for *ARTnews.*

Ashbery may have felt that he backed into his career as an art critic, but his first reviews are not tentative. In his first published review (on Bradley Walker Tomlin[3]), he is poetic and precise, and gets the viewer to want to look again:

> In *Number 8, 1949,* the nervous energy of a pattern which seems to be made up of scythes and swear-words in Chinese is tempered by the sweet blue background. This contrast between form and color was to be the central idea in all the pictures Tomlin painted until his death in 1953.[4]

Often, after summing up the subject he is reviewing, he steps back and argues eloquently for both the difficult and the impossible. He ends his review of Gertrude Stein's *Stanzas in Meditation* (1956) for *Poetry*[5] with the following observation:

> *Stanzas in Meditation* is no doubt the most successful of her attempts to do what can't be done, to create a counterfeit reality more real than reality. And if, on laying the book aside, we feel that it is still impossible to accomplish the impossible, we are also left with the conviction that it is the only thing worth trying to do.

Is it all that surprising that this was the first and last time Ashbery reviewed a book for *Poetry*? Thus, shortly after publishing **Turandot and Other Poems** (1953) and **Some Trees** (1956), he started his career as a critic by defining a worthy aesthetic goal as doing "what can't be done," which is "to create a counterfeit reality more real than reality."

Three years later, in an essay on Pierre Reverdy, Ashbery wrote:

The lines drift across the page as overheard human speech drifts across our hearing: fragments of conversation, dismembered advertising slogans or warning signs in the Metro appear and remain the rock crystal of the poem. And far from banishing poetry to the unconscious, he lets it move freely in and out of the conscious and unconscious. Since we do not inhabit either world exclusively, the result is moving and lifelike.[6]

Elsewhere in this review, while comparing Reverdy to the film director Robert Bresson, who "created an ascetically transparent world,"[7] Ashbery wrote:

> Like Reverdy he has a keen ear for *le langage de la tribu* and a deep feeling for nature. Trees, clouds, lakes, automobiles, the texture of a woman's skin and of her dress are shown for what they are and are also undetachable from the story being told; they are like electrodes in the limpid bath of a precise context.[8]

Already masterful in his ability to shift tones and focus, Ashbery has consciously rejected transparency, received notions of realism in poetry, and confession, all of which were (and still are) believed to be allegorical narratives that naturally culminate in revelation, universal truth, or epiphany. All too often, these states of illuminated insight are familiar and border on cliché. The revelation is not something the poet discovers in the process of writing, but is something he or she already possesses, and must figure out how to package. Such poems are full of detachable symbols and images, triggers that set off the reader's sympathetic Pavlovian response. Ashbery is against both the predictable and the detachable, which allows a poem to be reduced to a theme or be summed up.

Ashbery's interest in both "counterfeit reality" and the "lifelike" helps explain why, nearly twenty years after writing about Stein and Reverdy, he would write his widely acclaimed poem, **"Self-Portrait in a Convex Mirror."** The poem is ostensibly about Parmigianino's *trompe l'oeil* painting, a counterfeit reality that depicts the artist as if he is looking into a convex mirror. By being a "mirror" of the absent painter, the self-portrait displaces the viewer who is standing where the artist once stood. We see his imprisoned reflection looking back at us. On both the visceral level and in a larger sense, the artist's absence reminds us of our immediate and impending departure. At the same time, the painter stares at us, locked inside the wooden sphere, his hand in the foreground, as if protecting him from us and from time. This is one of the ways Ashbery describes the portrait:

> The soul has to stay where it is,
> Even though restless, hearing raindrops at the pane,
> The sighing of autumn leaves thrashed by the wind,
> Longing to be free, outside, but it must stay
> Posing in this place.

Don't poetry and art share the paradox of embodying a frozen time, while outside its domain time ("autumn leaves") keeps surging ahead?

Ashbery's description of Elizabeth Bishop's poetry is particularly apt about both his own writing and Parmigianino's arresting and disturbing painting:

> We live in a quandary, but it is not a dualistic conflict between inner and outer reality; it is rather a question of deciding how much the outer reality is our reality, how far we can advance into it and still keep a toehold on the inner, private one.[9]

Ashbery's observation also applies to his choices as an art critic. For one thing, he has never been known as a critic who either celebrated hyperbolically or grumbled mightily about the work of artists that were or weren't in the spotlight. I suspect this is because early on in his career he recognized that the outer reality (or what the art world is intently focusing on at a particular moment) would subsume him if he advanced too far into it. After all, he chose to live in Paris, not New York. And he never tried to stay young and become the Paul McCartney of art criticism.

* * *

Under the constant pressure of assignments, deadlines, and, for many years, low wages, Ashbery had to repeatedly negotiate, and, out of necessity, define a position. For even in the journalistic world of weekly articles and monthly essays, one cannot remain a passive observer. As Bois makes clear in his brilliant introduction to *Painting as Model,* "Any critical discourse is programmatic in part. . . ." However, when it comes to the criticism of Ashbery and O'Hara, neither the art world nor the literary establishment, mainstream or otherwise, has made any serious attempts to assess their accomplishments, and the positions they have taken. And when they have, both realms have tended to be dismissive. One of the few exceptions is Helen Vendler, whose essay on Ashbery's art criticism[10] is full of astute observations. The other is Marjorie Perloff.[11]

In the fifties, when Ashbery and O'Hara first began publishing in *ARTnews,* it was assumed that, in working for this magazine, one was writing for a general readership. At the same time, they entered into the art world just as it was beginning to morph wildly until, like the incredible Hulk, it became a lurching, contentious, muscle-bound version of its earlier self, with each muscle-bound version spawning yet another more extreme version of itself. The art world was becoming a place for specialists armed with degrees, and writing for a general reader, even if this figure is a fiction, was regarded as frivolous. Among the many developments that had a considerable influence in the art world during the sixties, one must mention the magazine *Artforum,* which was started in San Francisco in 1962 and moved to New York in 1967. There are four figures that had much to do with its rise to prominence as an influential review based in New York: Philip Leider, the founding

editor, the art historians Michael Fried[12] and Rosalind Krauss, and the film theorist Annette Michelson, the influential theorist of cinema. In 1974, for reasons too complicated to go into here, Krauss and Michelson left *Artforum* and shortly afterwards started *October.* Throughout the sixties, the writing that appeared in *ARTnews* and *Art in America* was very different than the kind that appeared in the pages of *Artforum.*

This is how the art historian and theorist Hal Foster describes the opposition between the poet-critics associated with *ARTnews* and the art historians associated with *Artforum:*

> Yet for the critics who most marked *Artforum*—first Fried and [Barbara] Rose, then Michelson and Krauss—[Harold] Rosenberg was all "fustian writing," an aspersion that they also cast at poet-critics like Frank O'Hara and John Ashbery (and later Peter Schjeldahl and Carter Ratcliff) associated with *ARTnews* under its editor Tom Hess. This was not art criticism as "serious discipline."[13]

By "serious discipline," Foster means that none of the poets were either trained in art history or aligned with the formalist critic Clement Greenberg. Essentially, this means that none of them had developed a paradigm that they could apply to different works of art. The assumption is that the poet-critics don't take positions or, if they do, they aren't worth serious consideration because they aren't rooted in a discourse accepted by academia. Foster believes poets are ruled by their mushy sensibilities. Clearly, the art world in which Ashbery and O'Hara were working during the 60s was a bubbling cauldron with everything constantly being pushed to the boiling point.

Foster goes on to elaborate upon his understanding of the opposition:

> Of course such oppositions as formalist versus social-historical methods, and objective versus belle-lettristic styles, long preceded *Artforum,* but for this generation they were compounded most volatilely in its milieu. It was not an even match. Whereas the poet-critics had only an attenuated connection to the belle-lettristic reviews of the French Salons to stand on, the formalist followers of [Clement] Greenberg could draw on the immediate prestige not only of New Criticism in literary studies but also of German art history as established in the American university by such prewar émigrés as Erwin Panofsky. The formalist camp felt that it had a near-scientific view of art history to support its semi-subjective judgments of aesthetic quality (here Fried aligns Greenberg with T. S. Eliot, and Leider relates his *Artforum* to *Scrutiny* under F. R. Leavis). No wonder such criticism appeared so powerful and, to its opponents, so presumptuous. "They were successfully putting over the impression," Ratcliff complains, "that they were writing the final draft of history as it happened."[14]

Three points in Foster's retelling merit further discussion. One is that by aligning themselves with T. S. Eliot and New Criticism, the art historians could claim that they were mainstream intellectuals and thus central. It was they, not the poet-critics, who carried the torch of the "objective correlative" from the literary world to the art world. This view ignores the possibility that the poet-critics associated with *ARTnews* rejected New Criticism, which, after all, was being used to promote poets and poetry with which they had little affinity. Unlike many of their contemporaries, Ashbery and O'Hara did not become followers of Eliot. Clearly, the poetry world was already fractured, with Fried on one side and Ashbery and O'Hara on the other. The second point is that Foster doesn't recognize that American poet-critics didn't need to connect themselves to the belle-lettrist reviews of the French salons, because there was already an American belle-lettrist tradition. It included Parker Tyler, Manny Farber,[15] and James Agee writing movie reviews, Weldon Kees and Fairfield Porter writing art reviews, and Edwin Denby writing dance reviews for various publications. The third point is the more serious charge that the poet-critics were not capable of "serious discipline," and that their writing was "fustian." The implication is that poet-critics are some kind of sensitive plant, and their heads are easily turned.

Given the few examples that I have already cited of Ashbery's lifelong preoccupation with "counterfeit reality," the "lifelike," and about living in a "quandary," and I can assure the reader that there are many more such examples, I would argue that there is a consistency to his approach to art and literature. Ashbery's writing is crystalline, while O'Hara's is simultaneously hyperbolic and self-mocking. Neither is "fustian." I would further add that neither Ashbery nor O'Hara feels compelled to proclaim their seriousness. Their criticism isn't theory driven, but object driven. They are not prone to making generalizations, and both pay close attention to what is in front of them, which is not all that easy or simple to do.

Although not necessarily broadcast from the rooftops, a negative view of poet-critics still predominates in many quarters of the art world. There are many reasons why the work of poet-critics is also largely ignored in the literary world. First of all, poet-critics like Ashbery and O'Hara wrote about art, rather than about poetry or themselves. Both the literary and art worlds have become increasingly fractured and specialized, a contested and in many ways discontinuous field in which there is little consensus among the various factions, and very little overlap between them. The poet-critic exists in two worlds that for the most part don't even bother to recognize each other. At the same time, in each domain there are multiple manifestations of the opposition between those whose practice is defined as "serious discipline" and those who are said to rely on sensibility and something as vague and poetic as the muse. And let's not forget that there are those who believe that if you are a poet engaged in any kind of

writing for a general audience, particularly if you make money from it, you must have compromised your higher self, and tainted forever both your soul and your capacity for serious poetry. Not only is integrity impossible in such a situation, but also no wisdom is to be gained from constantly being in, and negotiating with, the world. According to this view, the only way a poet should exist is as a sequestered being that protects and cultivates his or her sensitivity.[16] Thus, Ashbery and O'Hara did exactly the opposite of what many other poets of their generation did. Instead of retreating from the world and living in the cloistered environment of universities and little magazines, they entered into a situation that was gaining increasing attention from the public. And in terms of the public, the gap between the art world and poetry has only widened since the sixties. Warhol is a household name; O'Hara is not.

Foster's dismissive tone towards poet-critics, and his assertion elsewhere that they lack a paradigm,[17] reveals a lot about the hostilities they have to face. This may be one of the reasons why the poet-critic Raphael Rubinstein felt it was necessary to establish a distance between his writing and that of other poet-critics:

> Like so many other art critics, I am also a poet. I don't believe, however, that writing poetry is any particular qualification for writing about art. In fact, I generally don't like the art criticism of poets, even poets whose work I greatly admire. Frank O'Hara, for instance, is not to me an interesting art critic, though his poetry has taught me as much about art and artists as the work of any single critic.[18]

Whether this constitutes critique or narcissism, Rubinstein's conflicted evaluation of O'Hara's complex position is not an isolated example. In his article, "Frank Appraisal" (*Artforum,* October 1999), which was about the traveling exhibition "In Memory of My Feelings: Frank O'Hara and American Art" (organized by Russell Ferguson for the Museum of Contemporary Art, Los Angeles), Hilton Als is also conflicted about O'Hara. There is the positive view:

> O'Hara believed that his role as a curator was not only to present the artist's view, but to enhance it with a view of his own (and recipients of such curatorial largesse included Jackson Pollock, Arshile Gorky, Franz Kline, and David Smith). He wasn't a trained art historian, which is why his work at MoMA was so refreshing and has never been duplicated: Innocence and joy cannot be duplicated.

And here are just two of Als' negative views:

> The voice of this particular poet: It is overestimated by mediocre graduate students and memoirists, who champion it and, like O'Hara, lack the discipline to write about things other than themselves.

And:

He was the paradigm of the art-world fag that may make you avoid the art world now, and forever.

While Frank O'Hara, who was not an artist, has been the subject of a traveling museum exhibition (How often does this happen?), his name has largely been effaced at the Museum of Modern Art, where he worked for over a decade. At the time of his death, O'Hara had begun working on a retrospective of Jackson Pollock for the Museum. The directorship of the exhibition was taken over by William S. Lieberman. Among the people who contributed research to the exhibition[19] and accompanying exhibition catalogue was the poet-critic William Berkson.[20] A little more than twenty years later, in 1998, the Museum of Modern Art hosted "Jackson Pollock." Kirk Varnedoe, Chief Curator of Painting and Sculpture at the Museum, organized the exhibition, with assistance from Pepe Karmel, Adjunct Assistant Curator in the Museum's Department of Painting and Sculpture. A catalog of nearly three hundred and fifty pages accompanied the exhibition.

In Varnedoe's heavily researched essay on Pollock, O'Hara isn't cited once in the more than two hundred footnotes. It's as if he was never at the museum and didn't write anything about Pollock, even something that Varnedoe disagreed with, or found distasteful. Given that O'Hara was working on Pollock's first retrospective for the museum at the time of his death, that he wrote the first monograph on the artist, *Jackson Pollock* (New York: George Braziller, 1959), and that he championed the black and white paintings of 1951, which many critics saw as a retreat and failure on the artist's part, it is worth noting that three individuals (the poet-critic Raphael Rubinstein, the art historian Hal Foster, and the museum curator Kirk Varnedoe) from very different quarters in the art world seem to agree on one thing; O'Hara's criticism does not warrant attention.

The primary, if largely unstated criticism of O'Hara's art writing is that it is too hyperbolic, too excited and uncritical. It was the opposite of serious and disciplined. Both more judicious and a more careful reader, Berkson describes O'Hara's weaker pieces as being "self-consciously oracular," and that under the pressure of deadlines his "prose stiffened" or became "constricted." The other problem is that O'Hara wore his heart on his sleeve when he wrote about art. In this puritan culture, readers (and other critics) are embarrassed by his excitement. How can you be an art critic if what you are looking at excites you? Being prone to excitement means that you lack restraint and are incapable of being scientific. The one writer who seems to have made the best use of this way of writing about art is Peter Schjeldahl, who has claimed that he no longer writes

poetry and is currently the art critic for the *New Yorker,* a job once held by the fustian Harold Rosenberg. This is how Ashbery, who is not uncritical of O'Hara, saw his friend's relation to art:

> This art absorbed Frank to such a degree, both as critic for *ARTnews* and a curator at the Museum of Modern Art, and as a friend of the protagonists, that it could be said to have taken over his life.[21]

Here, Ashbery seems to be suggesting that O'Hara may have lost hold of the thread connecting him to his inner private life, that he became too externalized. While I won't dispute that O'Hara's writing was often excited and hyperbolic, I believe that he made many observations that are not only significant, but that he also took positions that continue to be instructive:

> The present show also, precisely because it is mainly made up of recent works, reflects another very human situation; the relation between artists of a given tendency is frequently very close. Why this should be a matter of concern to anyone but the artists themselves is beyond me, since the alternatives to this fortuitous happening are blindness or hypocrisy. Nevertheless, the viewer should make more distinctions than the artist, he has the time and room for it, he is merely looking and experiencing, where the artist is creating something, whether in his or another's image, no small feat in any case.[22]

O'Hara believes it is the viewer's responsibility to "make more distinctions," and to see each work for what it is, rather than how it might resemble someone else's work. And yet how many countless times, in reviews of both books and art, has the writer made either a generalization ("painting is dead") or unfavorably compared one person's work to another's? Of course, the point behind the comparison is to elevate one person's work at the expense of another. O'Hara found this behavior unseemly. His non-hierarchical approach to art, to what he called "the living situation" is what distinguishes him from other critics. It is the opposite of what most people think a critic is supposed to do, which is to criticize and judge, make hierarchies. One may believe these hierarchies are based on something more "scientific," but they are hierarchies nevertheless. O'Hara takes a different tack and challenges the public to both look more closely and read more carefully. He wants viewers (and this includes art critics) to locate their understanding of art in their actual experience, rather than in a pre-digested idea about what they are looking at. He is challenging us to suspend judgment and start fresh with each work of art we encounter.[23]

As Ashbery pointed out in his "Introduction" to the *Collected Poems,* O'Hara's poetry was "anti-literary and anti-artistic," which suggests why he liked the art that he did. Being anti-artistic means you are anti-formalist (unlike the art historians writing for *Artforum*), but it doesn't mean that you are against formal mastery. This is what O'Hara has to say about Pollock's *Blue Poles: Number 11* (1952), a late painting which, because structural elements ("blue poles") are used to organize the unruly, clotted field, many art historians see as evidence of the artist's precipitous decline. For them, Pollock has introduced figural elements into his painting, and backed away from all-over abstraction. In contrast to the formalists who believed abstraction was the highest development and representation of any sort was a step down, O'Hara offered this appraisal of Pollock's controversial painting:

> *Blue Poles* is our *Raft of Medusa* and our *Embarkation for Cythera* in one. I say *our*, because it is the drama of an American conscience, lavish, bountiful, and rigid. It contains everything within itself, begging no quarter; a world of sentiment implied, but denied; a map of sensual freedom, fenced; a careening licentiousness, guarded by eight totems native to its origins (*There Were Seven in Eight*). What is expressed here is not only basic to his work as a whole, but it is final.[24]

This is exactly the kind of writing that drives Foster and other art historians up the wall and over the other side. They see it as a prime example of fustian babble, whereas I see it as both metaphorical and analytical, poetic and precise, which I want to make clear is very different than poetic prose. I am not talking about the dreamy fictions of Anaïs Nin here, but about O'Hara's compressed summation of a painting by Pollock. If I have a problem with O'Hara's description, and I do, it is that it is too compressed. It requires the reader to unpack it, and recognize the connections that the writer is making. I think the reason O'Hara wrote this way is because he believed, either naïvely or willfully, that the reader knew as much, and felt as passionately about, culture ("living situation") as he did. For O'Hara, the art history was as much a part of the present as Chinese poetry was for Ezra Pound and the archaic was for Guy Davenport.

O'Hara connects *Blue Poles* to Théodore Géricault's *Raft of Medusa* and Antoine Watteau's *Embarkation for Cythera* because he recognizes the many affinities that these three artists and their cited works share. In terms of biography, Watteau (1684-1721), who was frequently ill, died of tuberculosis at the age of thirty-seven; Géricault (1791-1824), who was injured while riding a horse, died at the age of thirty-two; and Pollock (1912-1956), who was killed while driving a car, died at forty-four. They were young men in the prime of their artistic career. In terms of the reception their art received, it should be remembered that Watteau's training was unconventional, and that his paintings did not fit into any of the established categories. In fact, in order to acknowledge Watteau's accomplishment, the French Academy invented a new term, *Fêtes Galantes,* to describe his wistful, non-narrative paintings. When Géricault's *Raft of Medusa* was first exhibited, it caused a controversy not only because it disregarded classical conventions, but also because it was considered too morbid in its subject matter. Like Watteau and Géricault, Pollock challenged the established conventions that society relied on to define a painting. Willem de Kooning described Pollock as the one who "broke the ice," which could also be said of Géricault and Watteau. All of them were ground-breakers whose work was not immediately accepted. Thus, the three paintings O'Hara connects together are thought of as flawed masterpieces. By not elaborating upon these connections, the poet hurts his own case. There is, however, a precision to his art writing. It isn't simply a matter of him free-associating, and writing down whatever pops into his head. O'Hara may not be the greatest prose stylist in his essays on Pollock, but we don't read Meyer Shapiro for style, do we?

By connecting *Blue Poles* to the American psyche ("a map of sensual freedom, fenced"). O'Hara takes the painting out of the museum and situates it in something as messy as culture. He looks at the painting as if he were Alexis de Tocqueville looking at America. Doesn't his "lavish, bountiful, and rigid" fit right in with de Tocqueville's understanding of democracy? Both men possess innocence and insight. They see what is right in front of everyone's eyes, but which others haven't noticed.

One reason William Carlos Williams hated T. S. Eliot was because he felt that he had returned poetry to the classroom. O'Hara believed that a painting's ultimate destination was the world, not the museum as a sarcophagus or pristine resting place. He didn't think of art as a precious object meant to be sequestered from everyday life. Strong art doesn't need the protection of a sterile environment; it can live in the world. That's what makes it crucial. O'Hara even wrote glowingly about the Guggenheim Museum, New York, a museum whose interior design many dislike:

> Anyhow, I like the whole experience, the "bins" where you come around a semi-wall and find a masterpiece has had its back to you, the relation between seeing a painting or a sequence of them from across the ramp and then having a decent interval of time and distraction intervene before the close scrutiny: in general my idea is that this may not be (as what is) the ideal museum, but in this instance Frank Lloyd Wright was right in the lovable way that Sophie Tucker was to get her gold tea set, which she described as, "It's way out on the nut for service, but it was my dream."[25]

Who else but O'Hara could connect Wright and Tucker, the high and the low? He had a wonderful sense of humor about the situation in which he was active. As much of an aesthete as he was, and he was down to the soles of his feet, he was also a poet who chose to live in the world. He didn't want the security of academia because, I suspect, he knew it would stifle both him and his poetry. This is how he described the elevator at the Guggenheim:

> The elevator is a good idea, too; I wonder if anyone has ever taken it down? And apart from the one-way thing, it takes off the curse of most elevators, which is that when you go up in an elevator you are usually going to some unpleasant experience like work or a job interview, but here you are going up for pleasure.[26]

This is the challenge O'Hara presents to other poet-critics: can writing about art be both demanding work and real pleasure? And if it can be that, then doesn't the act of surviving in New York City become inextricable from the pleasure of what it offers in museums and galleries?

* * *

It is safe to say that John Ashbery has published more articles and reviews in self-supporting magazines and periodicals than any other poet of his or subsequent generations. In contrast to O'Hara, whose reviews appeared in *ARTnews* and in little magazines such as the *Evergreen Review, Horizon, It Is,* and *Kulchur,* Ashbery largely worked for publications that were read by a middlebrow public. Week after week, and over a period of many years, he produced highly informative articles and reviews for the *Herald Tribune, New York,* and *Newsweek.* Thus, in its heterogeneity, the readership for Ashbery's criticism is very different than the one that would have read O'Hara's chronicles in little magazines. One might assume that the reason O'Hara's writing could be so hyperbolic was because he knew an informed, largely sympathetic audience was reading it, while Ashbery knew from the outset that he was writing for strangers. Despite this difference, what Ashbery and O'Hara share is a non-hierarchical approach to the art world, which, I want to emphasize, doesn't mean that they didn't repeatedly stand for and against something.

As a critic working within the art world, Ashbery had to become a commentator whose range of interests, enthusiasms, and preoccupations were recognized, in all senses of the word, by both the reader and those in the position to commission articles and reviews. The Scylla and Charybdis such a critic faces, and I suspect one must make this early on in one's career, is how to resist the temptation to become a social Darwinist who writes approvingly about those whose work has already achieved success in the marketplace. It is not about going against the tide so much as ignoring it, about not letting the outer reality become yours. In what ways can you contribute and perhaps even inflect a world that is not necessarily open to being challenged or criticized? How do you proselytize without becoming proscriptive, dogmatic, or polemical? Certainly it is tempting to become publicly programmatic when you see few if any apparent results from your writing, to become both a knight and martyr. For if you have avoided Scylla (the role of social Darwinist), you (who is always a proselytizer even when writing about successful artists) also have to bypass Charybdis, which is the exciting prospect of becoming judgmental, opinionated, argumentative, and self-righteous, particularly if you are championing those who are not at, or perhaps not even near, the center of the art world's fickle attention.

The art world is full of curmudgeons, each more sanctimonious than the next. It is an efficient way of getting attention, and being remembered. For the rest of us, it is a guilty pleasure because we feel both sympathetic and superior to the bile-spewing critic, and get a vicarious thrill from all that chest-thumping self-righteousness. We secretly like watching people making fools out of themselves in public. It is why clowns entertain some of us.

If these obstacles aren't enough, the successful poet-critic, which is to say one who regularly gets published, will most likely be dismissed or ignored by art historians, theorists, academics, and, in some cases, other poet-critics. In addition, being a successful art critic and published poet means that you have to accept that more people will read your criticism than your poetry. And if this isn't enough, it also means that you realize that the American literary establishment is apt to take your essays seriously only if you write about literature or culture or are from another country and write in English, but will regard your writing about art as akin to being a reviewer of romance novels for a supermarket tabloid. It takes a certain kind of resiliency to be a poet-critic who not only doesn't become a curmudgeon, polemical, stop writing poetry, or start complaining about the inequality of it all, but also still manages to maintain a high level of sophistication, insight, and wit in your essays and reviews.

About the art criticism of Ashbery, the question boils down to this: what does he stand for and against? I would like to approach this question by beginning with a distinction he made in an essay about Artaud:

> His famous pamphlet on Van Gogh (*Van Gogh or The Man Suicided by Society*) is great not because Artaud

was a great critic (which he wasn't because fortunately he could only create, not criticize) but because of what it says about all artists . . .[27]

This is what Ashbery says about artists and the critic's relationship to them: "To create a work of art that the critic cannot even begin to talk about ought to be the artist's chief concern . . ."[28] He is championing art that exists outside of language, particularly when it is academic discourse. It might make his job tougher, but he is against any kind of art that can be explained by a pre-existing discourse. Thus, in this same review of Brice Marden's monochromatic paintings, he writes: "it is not an abstraction but an object made by and for the senses."[29] This observation is in line with his statements about art and poetry that is "life-like," and that moves between the conscious and unconscious.

Ashbery is an heir to Walter Pater, who proposed that all art "aspires to the condition of music." The difference is that Pater is seen as paving the way for abstraction, while Ashbery began publishing poetry and criticism after abstraction's triumph. Thus, he wants an abstract art that is an object made by and for the senses. In other words, he isn't interested in abstraction as an idealized state, but in something messier and closer to life. He believes in art and writing that are autonomous but not removed from reality. This is why many find it nearly impossible to write about his poetry; it keeps slipping through one's fingers and reconstituting itself just beyond one's grasp.

While Ashbery isn't particularly interested in criticizing an artist's work, one should not deduce that he wasn't critical of artists, because he was, but in a way that can only be described as creative.

> Leland Bell is a painter and a polemicist. Seeing him in his studio, vigorously at work on a number of canvases and meanwhile sounding off on his various pet peeves and enthusiasms, one has the feeling of coming upon an almost extinct variety of whooping crane, alive and well in its environment, happily honking around the pond and causing quite a commotion. For polemics, and by extension commitment—to art, that is—is all but extinct in the art world. Where polemics seems to flourish, it often turns out to be the wishful thinking of artists dedicated to the hopeless task of doing away with the art of the past, and must therefore be construed as a romantic metaphor rather than a practical exercise in persuasion.[30]

What is striking about Ashbery's irreducible view of Bell is that it is simultaneously comical, critical, cold, entertaining, and even sympathetic. After all, none of us wants to see any animal, particularly a whooping crane, become extinct. Clearly, the tonal shifts and multiple voices that are an integral part of Ashbery's poetry are

also found in his essays. Even though many of his essays are assignments and commissions that appear in art magazines and weekly journals, he has an original prose voice. He isn't afraid of using a rich complex metaphor or citing a popular term. He isn't a miser who feels compelled to hoard his metaphors for his poems.

One wonders why in his review of *Selected Prose,* Charles McGrath made this observation:

> On the evidence of *Selected Prose,* in fact, it's tempting to conclude that prose is something Ashbery isn't especially good at, which makes him unusual among poets of his stature. Seamus Heaney and Derek Walcott, to take the two most obvious examples, are brilliant critics and essayists, with prose voices as original and as pleasing as their poetic ones. Ashbery's prose writing is clear and competent (he worked as a journalist and art critic for many years) but also dutiful and uninspired. Most of the pieces in this volume are the equivalent of literary chores—and from them you get no sense of how much fun Ashbery can be or what a master of tone and voices he is, able to shift gears in a single line. Most of *Selected Prose* is written in an all-purpose monotone.[31]

On the evidence of McGrath's review, one is tempted to conclude that he never read *Reported Sightings,* and that being, as his byline describes him, "the former editor of the Book Review and a writer at large for The Times" means you don't have to know a whole lot more about your subject than the average reader of your publication.

Written more than decade before the emergence of appropriationists, a number of whom were championed by Hal Foster, Ashbery's observations regarding polemics have a particular relevance in both the art world and literary culture. One doesn't think of what appropriation artists such as Mike Bidlo and Sherrie Levine do as being a "romantic metaphor," and certainly that is not how their work has been framed and written about by art historians involved with postmodern pronouncements such as the death of originality and the death of author. And while it certainly wasn't on his mind when he wrote this in 1970, nearly a decade before the emergence of Language poets and others who (influenced by European theorists) proclaimed the death of the author, as well as mounted heated arguments against the use of the word "I," it should be noted that Ashbery's use of "I" is unlike that of any other poet. Ashbery's "I" is porous and changing, and the reader doesn't sense that it is connected to a fixed personality, as it is in the writing of James Tate, Charles Simic, or Jorie Graham, just to name three obvious examples. I would further suggest that something of the personality of such poets as Bruce Andrews, Charles Bernstein, and

Leslie Scalapino comes through in their work. Thus, whether one uses or doesn't use the "I," and publicly believes in or doesn't comment on the death of the author, isn't really the point, is it? Making statements about these issues is really a way of announcing to others what club you belong to or are trying to be admitted to.

Influenced by contemporary art—and here I am thinking of Jean Hélion and Jasper Johns (two artists he has written about)—Ashbery has submerged his personality in favor of something that is seemingly objective and distanced. His description of Johns's work seems particularly applicable to his own poetry:

> Johns is one of the few young painters of today whose work seems to defy critical analysis, and this is precisely a sign of its power—it can't be explained in any other terms than its own, and is therefore necessary.[32]

For more than four decades Ashbery has defined, defended and championed the difficult and unexplainable, not because he is "a harebrained, homegrown surrealist,"[33] but because he recognizes that the beginning of modernism, which is manifested by the poetry of Baudelaire and the painting of Manet, is marked by the collapse of a collective language. How can you be edifying when there is no collective language or set of symbols to rely on? Within this situation of absence, particularly of moral authority, the writer has two choices: write poems as if there still exists a collective language or try to write poems that achieve complete autonomy. Ashbery chose the latter.

Both T. S. Eliot and Ezra Pound tried to erect a collective language, however gloomy or willed, but Ashbery never tried to achieve a didactic totality. Thus, in his poem, **"Into the Dusk-Charged Air,"** one named river replaces another, and there is no sense of landscape (context) or use of the word "I." Reality is indifferent to us, and its constant, relentless change carries us along, whether we like it or not. Each of us begins in the middle of it:

> Far from the Rappahannock, the silent
> Danube moves along toward the sea.

Without fanfare, Ashbery often challenges some of our most cherished views of art. In his essay on Edwin Dickinson, which appeared in *New York* (October 13, 1980), he made the following observation:

> Coming on this show fresh from the Whitney's [Edward] Hopper retrospective made me wonder once again if we really know who our greatest artists are. I would be the last to deny Hopper's importance, but even in the smallest and most slapdash of these oil sketches, Dickinson seems to me a greater and more elevated painter, and all notions of "cerebralism" and "decadence"—two words critics throw around when they can't find anything bad to say about an artist—are swept away by the freshness of these pictures, in which eeriness and vivacity seem to go hand in hand, as they do in our social life.[34]

Hopper, of course, is the artist everyone points to when they want to prove that a collective language of representation still exists. It is Hopper who many fervently claim most powerfully evokes our urban isolation and alienation, which is all well and good. At the same time, meaning has been detached from Hopper's paintings, making them into a background against which a very programmatic conversation can unfold. Hopper is easy to sum up, while it is impossible to do so with Dickinson. However, without ever denying Hopper's importance, Ashbery brings up "eeriness and vivacity" as aspects of our "social life" we might want to pay more attention to. Hopper hints at his figures' inner life, but everything we see takes place on the painting's surface. It is why so many mainstream poets have used Hopper's paintings as a starting point. With Dickinson, however, it is all but moot to discuss what constitutes inner and outer reality.

One of the painters that Ashbery became friends with while living in Paris was Jean Hélion, whom he championed many times. A provocative, commanding painter who challenges one's assumptions about art, Hélion worked both abstractly and figuratively, and did not "attach much importance to the two categories." He is impossible to categorize, and, in that way, is comparable to Philip Guston. The difference is that Hélion worked in four different modes of abstraction before shifting to figuration; he was both more stylistically restless and less seductive than Guston. Like Guston, Hélion tried to deal with dailiness after he moved away from abstraction.

A friend of Raymond Queneau and Francis Ponge, Hélion published *They Shall Not Have Me* (New York: E. P. Dutton, 1943), a memoir about his experiences as a POW in World War II. His letters to Queneau are full of bright gems about art. He wrote poetry before switching to painting. In the late 1920s, he became known for his abstract paintings that excluded "lyricism, drama, and symbolism."[35] In the early 1950s, Hélion, who, by the way, was a big influence on Leland Bell and his polemical stance, began working on "fanatically realistic still-lifes. . . ." Writing about these works and a portrait he was working on, Ashbery concludes his essay on Hélion with this:

As he once said: "I realize today that it is the abstract which is reasonable and possible. And that it is the pursuit of reality which is madness, the ideal, the impossible."[36]

It so happens that there is a retrospective of Jean Hélion currently on tour. It opened at the Centre George Pompidou, Paris, and will have stops at the Museu Picasso, Barcelona, and the National Academy Museum, New York. The accompanying catalog contains essays by French, English, and American art historians. However, Ashbery's early championing of Hélion—and he was pretty much one of the only American critics to do so—seems to have made no impression on any of the historians, and none of his writings are included in the English version of the catalog. It is just another example of a lost opportunity.[37]

Being a poet and art critic means that much of your writing will appear in fugitive publications, in small magazines, middlebrow magazines with a short shelf life, and catalogs that only a few people will ever see or read. Most of the people who read the poetry probably won't read the essays about art and vice versa. The mainstream literary establishment won't pay much attention and that part of the literary establishment that thinks it is avant-garde or radical also won't pay much attention because art, after all, makes money and therefore it must be corrupt. The art world still largely ignores poet-critics. And yet, despite the absence of attention in this area, and even though nobody might have bothered to notice, it must be apparent by now that Ashbery does take positions in his art criticism and literary essays, and that throughout his publishing life he has done so with remarkable clarity and precision. It seems not to have mattered to Ashbery whether or not someone read what he wrote about art. He would take a stand even if no one were listening. That, I believe, is the definition of integrity.

Notes

1. Yves-Alain Bois, "Introduction: Resisting Blackmail," *Painting as Model* (Cambridge: MIT Press, 1990), p. xi.

2. *John Ashbery in conversation with Mark Ford* (London: Between the Lines, 2003), p. 43.

3. In contrast to many of the other Abstract-Expressionists, Bradley Walker Tomlin (1899-1953) moved in both the commercial world and downtown bohemia. He was both a successful illustrator and a painter. He designed covers for *Vogue* and *House and Garden*. In the last five years of his life, Tomlin used a vocabulary of ribbon-like calligraphic strokes, which are the temperamental opposite of Franz Kline's crashing slathers of paint. Both Philip Guston and Robert Ryman have admired Tomlin's tonalities and matter-of-fact, structural brushstrokes.

4. First published in *ARTnews* (October 1957). Reprinted in *Reported Sightings: Art Chronicles 1957-1987,* edited by David Bergman (New York: Alfred A. Knopf. 1989), p. 193.

5. First published in *Poetry* 90, no. 4 (July 1957). Reprinted in John Ashbery, *Selected Prose,* edited by Eugene Ritchie (Ann Arbor: University of Michigan Press, 2004), p. 15.

6. First published in *Evergreen Review* 4, No. 11 (January-February 1960), Reprinted in *Selected Prose,* p. 21.

7. Ibid. p. 22.

8. Ibid. p. 22.

9. John Ashbery, "Throughout Is This Quality of Thingness: Elizabeth Bishop," *Selected Prose*. First published in *New York Times Book Review* (June 1, 1969). For those who are interested in the degree to which Ashbery has dissolved the distinction between inner and outer realities, I would recommend they compare the early poem, "The Instruction Manual," which makes a clear distinction between these two realms, to his recent poem, "Interesting People of New Foundland," where one is unable to apply such distinctions.

10. Helen Vendler, "Ashbery's Aesthetic: Reporting on Fairfield Porter and Saul Steinberg," *Harvard Review,* No. 22 (Spring 2002).

11. Marjorie Perloff, *Frank O'Hara: Poet Among Painters* (New York: George Braziller, 1977).

12. In addition to being an art historian, Michael Fried is a poet whose books include *To The Center of the Earth.* His forthcoming book is *The Next Bend in the River.* For those who wish to know more about Fried as both a poet and art historian, see the poet and critic Barry Schwabsky's astute review, "Makeshiftedness," in the *London Review of Books,* April 17, 2003.

13. Hal Foster, "Art Critics in Extremis," *Design and Crime* (London: Verso, 2002), p. 108.

14. Ibid., p. 108.

15. Manny Farber's essay "White Elephant Art vs. Termite Art" (1962) is one of the best critiques of the art world's loyalty to the "gemlike inertia of an old, densely wrought European masterpiece." It also continues to be ignored by many art historians.

16. While I myself am not personally acquainted with such poets, I have been assured by many trustworthy individuals that there are numerous poets like this, and that many teach creative writing in prestigious universities all across America, and have received national recognition. I have also been told that these

poets encourage their students to choose a similar path, and cultivate their sensitivities while sequestering themselves from the harsh vagaries of the world.

17. When I mentioned Foster's caveat about poet-critics lacking a paradigm, the poet Robert Kelly responded: "Oh I have a paradigm, I just can't fit it through the door."

18. Raphael Rubinstein, "Preface," *Polychrome Profusion: Selected Art Criticism 1990-2002* (Lenox, MA: Hard Press Editions, 2003), p. 11.

19. *Jackson Pollock* (New York: Museum of Modern Art, 1967). Catalogue, with essay, by Francis V. B. O'Connor. The exhibition showed in New York and traveled to Los Angeles.

20. In his Afterword to *What's With Modern Art* by Frank O'Hara, Bill Berkson's clear-eyed assessment of O'Hara's art criticism is at odds with Raphael Rubinstein's blanket judgment. His generosity, sympathy, criticality, and insightfulness, all of it articulated in beautiful prose, is also evident in his book, *Sweet Singer of Modernism* (Providence: Qua Books, 2004), which collects a number of essays, including exemplary ones on Wayne Thiebaud, Alex Katz, and Piero della Francesca.

21. John Ashbery, "Introduction," *The Collected Poems of Frank O'Hara,* edited by Donald Allen (New York: Knopf, 1971), reprinted in *Selected Prose.*

22. Frank O'Hara, "Art Chronicle," *Art Chronicles 1954-1966* (New York: George Braziller, 1975), p. 5.

23. In this regard, O'Hara and Ashbery have aligned themselves with the positions taken by the art historians Meyer Schapiro and Leo Steinberg. They base their conclusions on looking, rather than theory.

24. Ibid., pp. 37-38.

25. Ibid., "Art Chronicle," p. 2.

26. Ibid., "Art Chronicle," p. 2.

27. First published in *Portfolio and ARTnews Annual 2* (1960). Reprinted in *Selected Prose,* p. 32.

28. "Brice Marden," first published in *ARTnews,* March 1972. Reprinted in *Reported Sightings,* p. 214.

29. Ibid., p. 213.

30. First published in *ARTnews* (February 1970). Reprinted in *Reported Sightings: Art Chronicles 1957-1987,* edited by David Bergman (New York: Alfred A. Knopf, 1989), p. 195.

31. Charles McGrath, "Mapping the Unconscious" in *New York Times Book Review* (March 6, 2005), p. 10. McGrath reviews both *Where Shall I Wander* (New York: Harper-Collins, 2005) and *Selected Prose.*

32. First published in *ARTnews* 65, no. 3 (March, 1966). Reprinted in *Selected Prose,* p. 69.

33. *Selected Prose,* "Second Presentation of Elizabeth Bishop," p. 164.

34. See *Reported Sightings.*

35. From the Manifesto authored by Theo Van Doesburg that appeared in *Art Concret,* No. 1 (April, 1930), p. 1.

36. *Reported Sightings,* "Jean Hélion Paints a Picture," p. 65.

37. Although I haven't been able to verify this, I have been told that an essay by Ashbery is reprinted in the French and Catalan versions of the catalog.

FURTHER READING

Criticism

Altieri, Charles. "Contemporary Poetry as Philosophy: Subjective Agency in John Ashbery and C. K. Williams." *Contemporary Literature* 33, no. 2 (summer 1992): 214-42.

    Assesses the poetry of Ashbery and C. K. Williams according to the theories of Ludwig Wittgenstein and Friedrich Nietzsche.

Ashbery, John, and Mark Ford. *John Ashbery in Conversation with Mark Ford.* London: Between the Lines, 2003, 168 p.

    Book-length interview.

Berger, Charles. "The Sum." *Raritan* 11, no. 4 (spring 1992): 123-36.

    In-depth review of *Flow Chart.*

Blakely, Diann. "It's Got a Good Beat and You Can Write to It." *Antioch Review* 58, no. 3 (summer 2000): 360-66.

    Comments on music as a source of inspiration for Ashbery and other authors.

Chiasson, Dan. "Him Again: John Ashbery." *Raritan* 21, no. 2 (fall 2001): 139-45.

    Considers *Your Name Here* among Ashbery's best work.

Hammer, Langdon. "Frank Bidart and the Tone of Contemporary Poetry." *Southwest Review* 87, no. 1 (2002): 75-89.

Discusses the problem of tone in American poetry since the 1970s, employing Ashbery's work as one example.

Imbriglio, Catherine. "'Our Days Put on Such Reticence': The Rhetoric of the Closet in John Ashbery's *Some Trees.*" *Contemporary Literature* 36, no. 2 (summer 1995): 249-88.

Regards the restraint of Ashbery's early poetry as a repression of his sexuality.

Newman, R. Andrew. "A Poet in Winter: A Fine-Tuned Hand Sketches the Contours of Memory." *Weekly Standard* 10, no. 31 (2 May 2005): 38-9.

Extols Ashbery's contemplation of mortality and memory in *Where Shall I Wander.*

Rubinstein, Raphael. "Ashbery in Dargerland." *Art in America* 88, no. 2 (February 2000): 37, 39.

Offers a positive review of *Girls on the Run.*

Additional coverage of Ashbery's life and career is contained in the following sources published by Thomson Gale: *American Writers Supplement,* Vol. 3; *Contemporary Authors,* Vols. 5-8R; *Contemporary Authors New Revision Series,* Vols. 9, 37, 66, 102, 132; *Contemporary Literary Criticism,* Vols. 2, 3, 4, 6, 9, 13, 15, 25, 41, 77, 125; *Contemporary Poets,* Eds. 1, 2, 3, 4, 5, 6, 7; *Dictionary of Literary Biography,* Vols. 5, 165; *Dictionary of Literary Biography Yearbook,* 1981; *DISCovering Authors Modules: Poets; DISCovering Authors 3.0; Encyclopedia of World Literature in the 20th Century,* Ed. 3; *Literature Resource Center; Major 20th-Century Writers,* Eds. 1, 2; *Major 21st-Century Writers,* (eBook) 2005; *Modern American Literature,* Ed. 5; *Poetry Criticism,* Vol. 26; *Poetry for Students,* Vol. 11; *Poets: American and British; Reference Guide to American Literature,* Ed. 4; *Twayne Companion to Contemporary Literature in English,* Ed. 1:1; and *World Poets.*

Harold Bloom
1930-

American critic, novelist, and editor.

The following entry provides an overview of Bloom's career through 2005. For further information on his life and works, see *CLC*, Volumes 24 and 103.

INTRODUCTION

Bloom is one of the world's most widely recognized and controversial literary critics. Despite his initial association with fellow Yale critics Paul de Man, Geoffrey H. Hartman, and Jacques Derrida, his iconoclastic attitude toward academic tradition has placed him at odds with many of his colleagues. Combining the psychoanalytic principles of Sigmund Freud, the philosophy of Friedrich Nietzsche, and the arcane tenets of Gnosticism, Bloom's eclectic theories stem from his personal passion for reading. His vehement opposition to current trends in the humanities has only served to increase his reputation as an original thinker. Whether Bloom's views elicit debate or assent, his work has helped transform conventional critical and theoretical discourse.

BIOGRAPHICAL INFORMATION

Bloom was born and raised in New York City. The son of William, a garment factory worker, and Paula Lev Bloom, he began reading at an unusually early age. In 1951 Bloom earned a B.A. from Cornell University and received a Ph.D. from Yale University in 1955. He married Jeanne Gould in 1958. The following year his first book, *Shelley's Mythmaking* (1959), was published. This work—which began as his Ph.D. dissertation—won Yale's John Addison Porter Prize in 1956 and introduced Bloom's longstanding defense of Romantic poetry. He accepted a Guggenheim Fellowship from 1962 to 1963 and was honored with a Newton Arvin Award in 1967. *The Anxiety of Influence* (1973) brought him widespread recognition in the academic world and became the first of many of Bloom's commercial successes. Bloom garnered the prestigious Morton Dauwen Zabel Award from the National Institute and American Academy of Arts and Letters in 1981 and in 1985 received a MacArthur Foundation Fellowship. In 2002 Bloom was awarded the Catalonia International Prize

for his lasting contribution to the humanities; he won the Hans Christian Andersen Award in 2005. Bloom has served as the Berg Professor of English at New York University and as Charles Eliot Norton Professor at Harvard. An instructor at Yale University since 1955, he holds the distinguished Sterling Professorship of the Humanities and English.

MAJOR WORKS

In his initial critical analyses, most notably *Shelley's Mythmaking, The Visionary Company* (1961), and *The Ringers in the Tower* (1971), Bloom defended the merit of the Romantic tradition and argued against the New Critical mode of literary exposition that dominated scholastic thought at the time. Generally linked to Matthew Arnold and T. S. Eliot, New Critical theory defined literary tradition as a historical sequence of progression. Adherents of this school of thought perceived Romantic poetry as an emotional response to the natural world, and therefore antithetical to the objective, analytical verse which they championed. In contrast, Bloom's early works extol the visionary and imaginative elements of Romanticism embodied by such poets as William Blake, William Wordsworth, Percy Bysshe Shelley, and William Butler Yeats. Moreover, Bloom's study of Romantic poetry calls for a reassessment of the notion of literary tradition itself. According to Bloom, true literary progression is the result of the overbearing influence exerted upon new authors by their precursors. This concept is the central focus of *The Anxiety of Influence*, which applies Freud's theory of Oedipal conflict to illustrate Bloom's idea that every major poet subconsciously strives to both integrate and surpass the accomplishments of a personally revered, previously established author.

Further refining this idea, *A Map of Misreading* (1975), *Figures of Capable Imagination* (1976), and *Poetry and Repression* (1976) accentuate the esoteric spirituality at the foundation of Bloom's writing. Gnosticism, the mystical school of knowledge practiced by early Jews, Christians, and Sufi Muslims, informs many of his works. Similarly, references to the Kabbalah, an ancient system of Judaic spiritual wisdom, are evident in many of the key tenets of his theoretical model of poetic influence, which he further elucidated in *Kabbalah and Criticism* (1975). *Agon* (1982) elevates religious experience and Gnostic principles to the forefront of Bloom's theoretical approach in concordance with his perspective on literary tradition and the theories of Freud and Nietzsche. Bloom's chief religious concerns are examined more explicitly in *The Book of J* (1990), an interpretation of the Hebrew Bible, and *The American Religion* (1992), a testimony to the subtly pervasive Gnosticism underlying American history.

Bloom's subsequent works focus primarily on the individual authors whose writings support his critical theories. *The Western Canon* (1994) discusses twenty-six authors selected by Bloom as the most significant figures in Western literature. The book has incited considerable controversy due to its emphasis on such traditionally studied writers as William Shakespeare and Jane Austen at the expense of lesser-known and culturally diverse authors. *Shakespeare* (1998) credits the famous playwright with originating modern-day notions of personality, focusing on the character of Falstaff as one of literature's most compelling creations. Divided into sections on poems, novels, short stories, and plays, *How to Read and Why* (2000) is Bloom's personal checklist of seminal literary works and *Genius* (2002) compiles the author's choices for the one hundred most influential authors in world history. Bloom has also edited hundreds of collections of criticism and poetry throughout his career. *The Best Poems of the English Language* (2004), for example, consists of a selection of representative British and American verse by poets born before 1900.

CRITICAL RECEPTION

A visionary and prolific author, Bloom has initiated seminal but polarizing debates among contemporary scholars concerning literary tradition and the Western canon. His theoretical concepts and critical opinions have provoked intense reactions from both his defenders and his detractors. Many reviewers have praised Bloom's audacity and the passion with which he has infused his criticism, crediting him with reinvigorating the discussion and teaching of literatures. Others have deemed his books obnoxious, narcissistic, and reactionary. Bloom's outrage over politically driven curricula in particular has been attacked as closed-minded and elitist. His preoccupation with Gnosticism has been blamed for rendering his theories inaccessible, yet his utilization of complex psychological symbolism has been acknowledged as a major influence on modern literary criticism. Moreover, his enthusiastic endorsement of prominent classical authors, including Shelley and Shakespeare, as well as such contemporary poets as John Ashbery, has persuaded some critics to reevaluate the works of Bloom's subjects in a new light.

PRINCIPAL WORKS

Shelley's Mythmaking (criticism) 1959

The Visionary Company: A Reading of English Romantic Poetry (criticism) 1961

The Ringers in the Tower: Studies in Romantic Tradition (criticism) 1971

The Anxiety of Influence: A Theory of Poetry (criticism) 1973

Kabbalah and Criticism (criticism) 1975

A Map of Misreading (criticism) 1975

Figures of Capable Imagination (criticism) 1976

Poetry and Repression: Revisionism from Blake to Stevens (criticism) 1976

Wallace Stevens: The Poems of Our Climate (criticism) 1977

The Flight to Lucifer: A Gnostic Fantasy (novel) 1979

Agon: Towards a Theory of Revisionism (criticism) 1982

The Breaking of the Vessels (criticism) 1982

Poetics of Influence: New and Selected Criticism of Harold Bloom (criticism) 1988

Ruin the Sacred Truths: Poetry and Belief from the Bible to the Present (criticism) 1989

The Book of J (criticism) 1990

The American Religion: The Emergence of the Post-Christian Nation (criticism) 1992

The Western Canon: The Books and School of the Ages (criticism) 1994

Omens of Millennium: The Gnosis of Angels, Dreams, and Resurrection (criticism) 1996

The Best of the Best American Poetry, 1988-1997 [editor] (anthology) 1998

Shakespeare: The Invention of the Human (criticism) 1998

How to Read and Why (criticism) 2000

Genius: A Mosaic of One Hundred Exemplary Creative Minds (criticism) 2002

The Best Poems of the English Language: From Chaucer through Frost [editor] (anthology) 2004

Where Shall Wisdom Be Found? (criticism) 2004

Jesus and Yahweh: The Names Divine (criticism) 2005

CRITICISM

Lloyd Whitesell (essay date fall 1994)

SOURCE: Whitesell, Lloyd. "Men with a Past: Music and the 'Anxiety of Influence.'" *19th-Century Music* 18, no. 2 (fall 1994): 152-67.

[*In the following essay, Whitesell emphasizes the Oedipal undercurrent and gender-based bias of Bloom's theory of influence, applying it to the classical music genre.*]

For God's sake, let us sit upon the ground, / And tell
sad stories of the death of kings: / How some have
been deposed, some slain in war, / Some haunted by
the ghosts they have deposed.

—William Shakespeare, *King Richard II*

WRESTLING WITH THE DEAD

Harold Bloom's theory of poetic influence as a mythic
struggle between generations has gained an avid audience among music scholars. This well-known theory
locates the modern poet in a context of historical
"belatedness," always in the shadow of the past.[1]
Inescapably haunted by his predecessors, the poet is
driven to define himself through an anxious Oedipal
relation to those looming figures. Recent musical studies have taken up a Bloomian model of influence,
exploring Brahms, the early modernists, and even
Beethoven in such terms.[2]

The insight at the heart of Bloom's theory can be
condensed into the image, resonant and seductive in its
own way, of the solitary artist caught in an insecure,
conflictual, yet intimate relation with the powerful dead.
Bloom maps out the strategies or defense mechanisms
at work as the living poet seeks to rewrite—to "misread"—the works of his forebears and thus to gain
symbolic priority over them.[3] The resulting categorical
apparatus, at once elegant, grandiose, and outlandish,
has not evoked unanimous interest among literary critics and has suffered an uneven fate in the various
importations of Bloom's theory into the musical realm.[4]
It is the central scene of the haunted, anxious artist that
has commanded the widest space of musical reverbera-
tion. This scene will define my focus as well. My point
of contention proceeds from a deep unease with the
unspoken distributions of power, visibility, and subjectivity presented by the central Bloomian scene when
viewed across the axis of gender.[5] Although much of
my attention will be given to literary issues, the
relevance of what I have to say about musical criticism
is not thereby lessened; it is important to know what we
are getting into when we borrow these concepts for
musical use.

The issue of gender is broached near the beginning of
Joseph Straus's *Remaking the Past,* one of the most
ambitious applications of Bloomian theory to music.

> Despite the universalist pretensions of Bloom's theory,
> his discussions are largely confined to works of the
> central canon, that is, to works by white, male poets
> living in England or the United States between 1550 to
> 1950. The centrality in Bloom's theory of the Oedipal
> struggle between sons and fathers suggests the extent
> to which it is a theory designed not for poetry in general
> but for a narrow slice of poetry, a single tradition within
> a much richer and larger poetic world than Bloom
> generally acknowledges.[6]

Unfortunately, the acknowledgement of an unspoken
gender-specificity in the theoretical model, its neglect
of female traditions and its universalization of a
patriarchal canon, does not prevent Straus from allowing virtually identical canonic values to delimit his own
historical project.[7] Furthermore, Straus's brief disclaimer
forecloses even more pressing questions: If gender is a
determining factor in Bloom's theory, what exactly does
it determine? Focused on male creativity, in the service
of male canonization, couched in narratives of masculine
development—does not Bloom's picture of poetic
identity depend quite crucially on a particular idea of
masculinity? How does that gender profile look when
brought to the surface; is it one that critics, male or
female, would care to espouse?

An idea of masculinity begins to take shape from the
very opening pages of *The Anxiety of Influence,* where
Bloom states:

> Strong poets make [poetic] history by misreading one
> another, so as to clear imaginative space for themselves.
> My concern is only with strong poets, major figures
> with the persistence to wrestle with their strong precur-
> sors, even to the death. Weaker talents idealize; figures
> of capable imagination appropriate for themselves. But
> . . . self-appropriation involves the immense anxieties
> of indebtedness.[8]

For Bloom, the poet's worth is conceived first and
foremost in terms of strength; weakness is cause for
dismissal to the lower ranks. Strength is expressed
through a ruthless aggression, with the aim of subduing
those who are thought to threaten the assertion of one's
own identity. Meanwhile, one's "own" identity, even
when established, remains a locus of insecurity and
defensiveness.

What is this portrait, if not the mythical embodiment of
a familiar masculine archetype—one based on dominance, rivalry, and territorial skirmishes? At every level
of representation, from the relentlessly male pronouns
of the surface discourse, to the models of behavior
deeply embedded in the theory, Bloom merges the terms
of artistic self-definition with those of masculine self-
definition.[9] In the process, he mythicizes a particular
profile of manhood/poethood that is highly restrictive
and reversionary, simultaneously brutal and precarious.

"Strength" and "anxiety": the Bloomian regime of
artistic prominence is created by force and laced with
fear. It is the element of fear that has held such strange
and tantalizing appeal for music scholars.[10] As Bloom
would have it, anxiety arises from historical conditions
of "belatedness" and "indebtedness" that threaten poetic
originality. From a more skeptical position, it is possible to see the element of threat in a different light—as
a predicament of beset manhood. For Bloom's artist,
brutality and insecurity go hand in hand; the resulting

attitude is in some defining sense an expression of virility. It is difficult, for me, at least, to see the appeal of such a portrait; to live under the mandates of a fear-driven, force-driven form of masculinity seems confining if not incapacitating, ugly if not nightmarish.

And yet, by romanticizing its central masculine dilemma as the plight of an ironic hero, the theory has gained its perverse appeal. It may be argued that Bloom's idea of "strength" necessitates a studied self-blindness regarding the culpabilities and vulnerabilities of gender. It seems the more urgent and timely task, therefore, to resist such blindness, already so toxically in place in our culture. Before glamorizing the heroic potential of anxiety, I want to be wary of its hidden costs. Before subscribing to a theory of creative behavior in which fear plays such an important role, I want to be extremely clear about the implicative force of that fear. Whom does it terrorize? What kind of power does it confer?

FAMILY ROMANCE

In *The Anxiety of Influence,* Bloom declares: "Poetry (Romance) is Family Romance. Poetry is the enchantment of incest, disciplined by resistance to that enchantment" (p. 95). And in another passage: "Just as we can never embrace (sexually or otherwise) a single person, but embrace the whole of her or his family romance, so we can never read a poet without reading the whole of his or her family romance as poet" (p. 94). In this representation, the interdependencies of poetic meaning are structured by two intertwined metaphors: the bonds of family, and the bonds of sexual desire. Leaving the sexual metaphor—the enchantment and the embrace—for later discussion, I shall turn first to the pervading imagery of the family.

Bloom's reference to incest is programmatically Oedipal. "Battle between strong equals, father and son as mighty opposites, Laius and Oedipus at the crossroads; only this is my subject here" (*Anxiety* [*The Anxiety of Influence*], p. 11). Following Freud, Bloom imagines the path of masculine/creative development in terms of a family drama modeled on the Oedipus myth, with its dual taboos of incest and patricide. Tellingly, however, in Bloom's version it is a family drama *without the mother.* The family configuration is pared down to "father and son"; the essential, productive dynamic within the family is the arc of warring energies set up between its two male poles. Similarly, the full Oedipal narrative is collapsed into the single scene at the crossroads: two men, the young and the old, alone and in combat.

Bloom's familial metaphor entails both a pathway for the transmission of culture and an awareness of obligation to one's forebears. Bloom's archetypal son, however, does not wish to acknowledge such obliga-

tion. One's reputation is to be self-made: "For what strong maker desires the realization that he has failed to create himself?" (*Anxiety,* p. 5). Family indebtedness is seen as a threat, to be resisted through a forceful assertion of individual identity. "To live, the poet must *misinterpret* the father, by the crucial act of misprision, which is the rewriting of the father."[11] This "re-writing" is symbolized in Oedipal terms by patricide: the father is killed to clear space for the son.

Familial bonds of devotion and gratitude have no place in this picture; nor does the domestic sphere in its sheltering, nurturing aspects. Instead, what is foregrounded is the drama of male entitlement. The son appears as an inheritor, but also as a rival for the position of dominance; Laius must be removed in order for Oedipus to ascend the throne. This accounts for the premium placed on "strength," as opposed to other traditional poetic attributes, such as sensibility, fertility, insight. In the Bloomian scenario, the creative potential of the artist is wielded as a form of phallic power.[12]

The feminist critics Sandra Gilbert and Susan Gubar have noted the gender-exclusivity of Bloom's theory, its dedication to a "fierce" masculinity and to a patriarchal distribution of power. Even so, they argue for the usefulness of the theory's terms in relation to a tradition that is itself "overwhelmingly . . . patriarchal": "Bloom's model of literary history . . . is not a recommendation for but an analysis of the patriarchal poetics (and attendant anxieties) which underlie our culture's chief literary movements."[13] I agree that it is possible to use Bloomian insights in the service of a project that seeks to expose the stratagems of the patriarchal unconscious. Bloom's theory, however, does not offer sufficient distance from its own underlying gender motivations to inspire such projects on its own. Bloom glamorizes the male appropriation of creativity; he heroizes a fiercely, fearfully masculine stance. In so doing, he does indeed present a recommendation for cultural patriarchy, albeit in a noticeably threatened, agonized form.

Furthermore, the "attendant anxiety" so crucial to Bloom's theory is not universal even within the various male-dominated canons of Western tradition. Not all of those who have worked within arguably patriarchal traditions have given evidence of such a competitive stance. Nor have all those in favor of a solidly patriarchal poetics been so insecure about their own cultural authority, the adequacy of their own prowess in relation to a "dead but still embarrassingly potent and present ancestor" (*Anxiety,* p. 20). As one counterexample, consider Theodore Roethke's account of how one of his poems came to be written:

> Suddenly, in the early evening, the poem "The Dance" started, and finished itself in a very short time—say thirty minutes, maybe in the greater part of an hour, it

was all done. I felt, I *knew,* I had hit it. I walked around, and I wept; and I knelt down—I always do after I've written what I know is a good piece. But at the same time I had, as God is my witness, the actual sense of a Presence—as if Yeats himself were *in* that room. The experience was in a way terrifying, for it lasted at least half an hour. That house, I repeat, was charged with a psychic presence: the very walls seemed to shimmer. I wept for joy. . . . He, they—the poets dead—were with me.[14]

While Roethke's tale has to do with the moment of inspiration, rather than a more generalized process of influence, one cannot miss the strikingly un-Bloomian attitude he displays toward his poetic forefathers. Their incursion into his creative life is not felt as an overweening, stifling presence, but as a special dispensation, wondrous and electrifying. Roethke's reaction on being thus visited is a mixture of humility, gratitude, and great joy; the fear he feels is not anxiety, but awe. One would not characterize Roethke's attitude as "strong" in the Bloomian sense. Although the point of the narrative is clearly the transmission of authority from one male poet to another, the bond thus established is not conceived in terms of competition or antagonism but of hospitality: the poets dead enter the living poet's house and make it shimmer.

Many other examples could be cited in which a Bloomian reading would be misplaced, no matter how "belated" the artist's relation to his or her cultural lineage. Bloom's mythology should not be taken as an analysis of a general patriarchal dynamic, but as a tendentious position in relation to that dynamic—in fact, as a strong misreading of exactly the type he prescribes. Thus misread, the disposition of male cultural mastery is permanently in crisis, unsteady at the seams, anxious for its own authority. The response open to the presumptive heir is to cultivate a hyperaggressive stance while shoring up defenses: fiercer weapons, stronger armor.

Without doubt, patriarchy has been registering crisis for some time now, not least in nineteenth-century opera. In Wagner's *Ring* cycle, Wotan's dominion—law-bound, patrilineal, with weaponry as its totem—is plagued by internal contradictions and dishonesties and undergoes successive tremors. Eventually bankrupt and moribund, Valhalla merely awaits the final conflagration. It is a woman, outcast from the system, who by her gratuitous act is able to relinquish the token of ill-gotten power and clear the way for a new order. In Bizet's *Carmen* (1875), it is a lower-class woman of gypsy blood, criminally inclined, whose charisma and robust sexual energy work to corrupt the law-abiding, military, and familial allegiances of Don José. José is ultimately frustrated by Carmen's autonomy; his last-ditch act of vengeance serves to remove the threat she poses, even as he himself is ruined.

One hundred years later, Bloom's edifice of male authority is still subject to tremors. His response, like Don José's, is to swerve toward aggression. Meanwhile, the tendentiousness of his theory consists in seeming to admit to vulnerability on one front, while keeping the critical gaze averted from another stretch of patched and teetering defenses. The postulation of a gender-neutral historical distress (belatedness) as primary serves to protect Bloom from acknowledging the intense dynamic of gender anxiety and repression, which never ceases to infuse the discourse of his argument.

To get a clearer picture of this, it will help to look at some common myths of creativity that Bloom has swept aside in order to clear space for his own theory of influence. I turn first to an interview with Benjamin Britten conducted in 1969, nearly contemporaneous with Bloom's first manifesto. The interviewer asks: "To a composer standing at the point of his life where you do today, you have a great inheritance, not only in your own music but also with regard to the past. I would like to ask you how it feels standing in that situation? And are you conscious of this wonderfully exciting but also great *burden* of tradition behind you?" After a long pause, Britten answers: "I'm *supported* by it, Donald. I couldn't be alone. I couldn't work alone. I can only work really because of the tradition that I am conscious of behind me. . . . This may be giving myself away—if so, I can't help it. I feel as close to Dowland . . . as I do to my youngest contemporary. . . . I'm given *strength* by that tradition." He goes on to discuss the importance of the tradition as a source of creative models, of "maps" for the solution of dramatic problems:

> Why, if [a composer] used maps to get to Newmarket, didn't he use maps which show how to write an opera? . . . I think that I would be a fool if I didn't take notice of how Mozart, Verdi, Dvořák . . . had written their Masses. I mean, many people have pointed out the similarities between the Verdi *Requiem* and bits of my own *War Requiem,* and they may be there. If I have not absorbed that, that's too bad.[15]

In complete contrast to Bloom's stringent desire for self-creation, Britten avowedly looks to his precursors for support, company, sustenance, and instruction. His ancestral figures do not press on him as a burden; rather, he is borne up by them, nourished by them. His strength derives from theirs. In effect, Britten's historical rhetoric refers, as does Bloom's, to a symbolic of the family. Britten's family romance, however, is based on nurture, something our culture tends to relegate, materially and symbolically, to the sphere of the "maternal." As mentioned, the mother and the maternal are markedly absent from Bloom's family drama.

One may also consider the attitude exemplified in Robert Schumann's writings: "A true master does not cultivate pupils, but new masters. With reverence I return continually to the works of *this* master [Mozart], whose influence has been so great, so far-reaching." "The study of the history of music, together with lively hearings of masterworks of different eras, is the quickest cure for vanity and self-conceit."[16] Without taking time to characterize Schumann's attitude toward tradition in detail, I wish to emphasize the element of receptivity he finds essential. Poetic stature is achieved not by protecting oneself, but by yielding oneself over to influence; not by seeking the position of dominance, but by embracing the position of submission. Schumann's emphasis on submission and humility in the artist's relation to the past finds important resonances in Theodore Roethke's less abstract, more emotional narrative of kneeling down and weeping for joy in the ancestral presence. It resonates as well with the canonic literary statement of this attitude by T. S. Eliot: "What is to be insisted upon is that the poet must develop or procure the consciousness of the past and that he should continue to develop this consciousness throughout his career. What happens is a continual surrender of himself as he is at the moment to something which is more valuable."[17]

Of course, there may be some who decline to take such humility at face value; there are usually gaps between one's avowals and one's practice. Yet, although these self-descriptions seem naive in a post-Freudian world, their attitudes are certainly not anomalous. As I hope to show in a moment, they participate in a familiar conceptual model of creativity that stands as an alternative to Bloom's model. Besides, what would we hope to uncover in this case by a dig into the unconscious? Anxiety, perhaps? Why should we place more faith in motives of guardedness and dominance than in motives of admiration and affinity? We should remember that our chosen modes of analysis are also reflexive metaphors that tend to turn back on us, influencing the kinds of truth we look for.

The professed attitudes of Schumann, Roethke, and Britten, with their representative emphases on nurture, receptivity, fertility, and gratitude, may be brought together under a broad theory of artistic practice as gift. This theory has been most cogently and comprehensively elaborated by Lewis Hyde, in his book *The Gift: Imagination and the Erotic Life of Property*. Hyde reminds us how the metaphor of beneficence, of free giving and receiving, shapes our common conceptualizations of art. We speak of artistic talent as a "gift," of creative inception as inspiration, evoking a gratuitous element, an invigorating force to which one can only be receptive. Hyde goes on to detail how the audience's experience of art is itself shaped by a dynamic of gift exchange. "Even if we have paid a fee at the door of the museum or concert hall, when we are touched by a work of art something comes to us which has nothing to do with the price."[18]

The experience of art as gift entails a concept of identity fundamentally at odds with the strong, well-defended model under discussion. Hyde quotes Joseph Conrad's description of the artist:

> His appeal is made to our less obvious capacities: to that part of our nature which, because of the warlike conditions of existence, is necessarily kept out of sight within the more resisting and hard qualities—like the vulnerable body within a steel armor. . . . The artist appeals . . . to that in us which is a gift and not an acquisition—and, therefore, more permanently enduring. He speaks to our capacity for delight and wonder, to the sense of mystery surrounding our lives; to our sense of pity, and beauty, and pain; to the latent feeling of fellowship with all creation—to the subtle but invincible conviction of solidarity that knits together the loneliness of innumerable hearts, to the solidarity . . . which binds together all humanity—the dead to the living and the living to the unborn.[19]

The gift circulates along a path of interdependence, awareness of which forms a basis for fellowship rather than competition. Accordingly, the virtue of the artist depends on a stripping away rather than a shoring up of defenses.

A similar emphasis on openness and circulation can be found in the writings of Walt Whitman:

> To be in any form, what is that?
> (Round and round we go, all of us, and ever come back thither,)
> If nothing lay more develop'd the quahaug in its callous shell were enough.
> Mine is no callous shell,
> I have instant conductors all over me whether I pass or stop,
> They seize every object and lead it harmlessly through me.[20]

Whitman's permeable persona presents itself as "a sort of lung, inhaling and exhaling the world." "The initial event of the poem ['Song of Myself'], and of Whitman's aesthetic, is the gratuitous, commanding, strange and satisfying entry into the self of something that was previously separate and distinct. The corresponding gesture on Whitman's part is to give himself away. 'Adorning myself to bestow myself on the first that will take me.'"[21] For Whitman, this attitude of generous, passionate give and take structures not only the poet's relation to the world but also his relation to his "listeners," present and future:

> I bequeath myself to the dirt to grow from the grass I love,
> If you want me again look for me under your boot-soles.
> You will hardly know who I am or what I mean,
> But I shall be good health to you nevertheless,
> And filter and fibre your blood.[22]

He bequeaths his body of writings as a sort of fertile compost, as nutriment for those who will come after him. This is the final sense of art as gift, and the sense that mainly concerns us here: that is, as a gift between generations, influence freely absorbed and freely bestowed.[23] Musical examples of the past-as-nutrient are not hard to find. Ravel concludes his assessment of Satie in such terms: "Influences such as his are as fertile soil, propitious to the growth of rare flowers, wherein the individual consciousness, the indispensable seed, nourished in better surroundings thus provided, may still unfold according to its own essential nature, national, racial, or individual."[24] Likewise, Poulenc "could not do without [Debussy's] music. It is my oxygen."[25]

I admit that my model of gift exchange is bathed in a utopian light. A more balanced picture would acknowledge "the negative side of gift exchange—gifts that leave an oppressive sense of obligation, gifts that manipulate or humiliate, gifts that establish and maintain hierarchies, and so forth."[26] Some may wish to make something of Britten's hesitations at "giving himself away" in the interview quoted above and to project more ambivalence into Schumann's avowals ("A chance reminiscence is preferable to a desperate independence").[27] Bloom's theory, on the other hand, completely inhabits this dark side, while denying the dynamic of gift exchange from which the sense of obligation arises.

Bloom's theory dismisses generosity as a sign of weakness:

> It does happen that one poet influences another, or more precisely, that one poet's poems influence the poems of the other, through a generosity of the spirit, even a shared generosity. But our easy idealism is out of place here. Where generosity is involved, the poets influenced are minor or weaker; the more generosity, and the more mutual it is, the poorer the poets involved.
>
> (*Anxiety,* p. 30)

The gift occasions gratitude; Bloom's poet resists such sentiment and strains instead against a sense of indebtedness. Where Conrad appeals to the vulnerable body, Bloom fortifies the armor; in place of Whitman's open, permeable persona, Bloom chooses the "callous shell." All this shoving aside, this conceptual displacement, is done under the aegis of an anxious masculinity. It comes as no surprise, then, that the conceptual roles being displaced are subject to that dichotomous gravitational pull by which our culture has defined the sphere of the feminine. The "vulnerable body," for instance, defines a highly feminine role that women are allowed but also pressured to perform, and that men are allowed but also pressured to refuse. The gendered character of this role does not inhibit the formulations of Conrad and Whitman; both men use their marginal positions as artists to resist conventional ideological

demands—in effect, to dissolve and expand the traditional roles of masculinity. From a perspective of pronounced gender fear, however, the "vulnerable body" becomes suspect as less than manly. Suspicion likewise falls on the submissive role exemplified in Schumann's and Eliot's aesthetics, and on avowed dependence like Britten's on a supportive, nurturing tradition.

The "weakness" Bloom abhors can thus be read as a stigma of feminization. The "strength" he praises apparently involves being successfully armored against the effeminate traits of nurture, vulnerability, and generosity—all qualities that, under this strict regime, maleness must forgo. I have already remarked how Bloom's family romance manages to elide the mother. A female figure does make a brief appearance, however, in the monstrous person of the Sphinx: "The Sphinx (whose works are mighty) must be a female (or at least a female male). . . . The Sphinx riddles and strangles and is self-shattered at last. . . . But the Sphinx *is* in the way, and must be dislodged" (*Anxiety,* p. 36). Bloom eventually identifies the offending Sphinx as "sexual anxiety"; in the effort to dislodge this anxiety, women too are pushed aside. Bloom's discourse serves to keep women out of the position of creative power; at the same time, it locks men into a pitiable role of brutality, fear, and self-deprivation. The hero in Bloom's script may overthrow the Sphinx (or think he does), but he is never free of the struggle at the crossroads.

DARK PASSION

> Poetry may or may not work out its own salvation in a man, but it comes only to those in dire imaginative need of it, though it may come then as terror. And this need is learned first through the young poet's or ephebe's experience of another poet, of the Other whose baleful greatness is enhanced by the ephebe's seeing him as a burning brightness against a framing darkness, rather as Blake's Bard of Experience sees the Tyger, or Job the Leviathan and Behemoth, or Ahab the White Whale or Ezekiel the Covering Cherub, for all these are visions of the Creation gone malevolent and entrapping, of a splendor menacing the Promethean Quester every ephebe is about to become.
>
> (*Anxiety,* p. 35)

As we can see, there are even stranger beasts in Bloom's imaginary. The Sphinx is not the only terrible opponent standing in the way of true mastery; in fact, Bloom's greater concern is with a more properly male figure—that is,

> the Covering Cherub blocking a new voice from entering the Poet's Paradise. . . . In this discussion he is a poor demon of many names . . . but I summon him first namelessly, as a final name is not yet devised by men for the anxiety that blocks their creativeness. He is that something that makes men victims and not poets, a demon of discursiveness and shady continuities, a pseudo-exegete who makes writings into Scriptures. He

cannot strangle the imagination, for nothing can do that, and he in any case is too weak to strangle anything. The Covering Cherub may masquerade as the Sphinx . . . but the Sphinx . . . must be a female (or at least a female male). The Cherub is male (or at least a male female). The Sphinx riddles and strangles and is self-shattered at last, but the Cherub only covers, he only appears to block the way, he cannot do more than conceal.

(*Anxiety,* pp. 35-36)

Two mythic threats: the sphinxian and the cherubic, the enigmatic and the occult, "sexual anxiety" as distinct from "creative anxiety" (p. 36). But by personifying these threats as gendered monstrosities, or monstrosities of gender, Bloom subsumes both under the commanding influence of sexual difference. In other words, the two threats are hardly distinguishable. On the contrary, it would seem that creative anxiety can be understood only against the backdrop of an equally anxious sorting of sexual possibilities. In fact, the myth of creativity is shaped throughout Bloom's writing by a particular conception of sexuality, however shadowy and concealed. Note, for example, in the quotation that stands as a sort of Dantean warning at the beginning of this section, how one comes to poetry only through strong desire ("dire imaginative need"), awakened by one's youthful experience of a burning, splendid Other—a desire that, strong as it is, is hard to distinguish from terror.

Why should desire be such a terrifying thing? Does its volatility threaten to shatter the artist's strict masculine regime? Or is it that, having peopled the domain of art with an exclusively male citizenry, the admission of strong desire would place one in an awkward position? As I turn to the sexual metaphor in Bloom's theory, it is worth taking a moment to ponder his portrait of the Cherub, this elusive but emblematic figure whose typically obscure outlines may suggest, although in a preliminary, negative way, the fearful object of our discussion. Sexual anxiety is supposed to have been overcome on the way to poetic mastery, yet the anxiety that persists—that of the Cherub—seems to derive much of its character from the residual, sedimented connotations of a specific sexual identity. Consider these elements: the imputation of a contemptible lack of fiber ("too weak to strangle anything"); the blurring or transgression of proper, gender-based roles (to "masquerade" as the Sphinx); the invocation of an unnameable, unrepresentable menace to a victimized masculinity; and an inclination toward concealment, indirection ("discursiveness"), and dubious connections ("shady continuities"). This portrait coaxes the general tenor of gender fear into the unnamed but lurking shape of *homosexual* menace—from which, via an enactment of that very shadiness and indirection, all sexual pungency has been drained.[28]

More needs to be said to bring this object of suspicion into recognizable focus. First, however, I must mention the final element in Bloom's strange portrait:

It is the high irony of poetic vocation that the strong poets can . . . push aside the Sphinx . . . , but they cannot uncover the Cherub. . . . Uncovering the Cherub does not require power so much as it does persistence, remorselessness, constant wakefulness; for the blocking agent who obstructs creativity does not lapse into "stony sleep" as readily as the Sphinx does.

(*Anxiety,* p. 36)

The threat represented by the Cherub is unrelenting and insidious, against which even the mounting of a ceaseless vigilance is no guarantee. This paranoid structure should be kept in mind during the discussion that follows; its significance to the shape and insistence of Bloom's argument will become increasingly clear.

As demonstrated, Bloom's theory takes its momentum from a primal scene of Oedipalized relations between men. The classical Freudian Oedipal narrative elaborates a triangular relation of rivalry and desire, with a woman cast in the mediating role. The men in this narrative establish a bond of rivalry by vying for the same feminine object of desire. With Bloom, however, the loss of the woman's role collapses the triangle into a *pas de deux*. This means that the channels of masculine competition and desire are no longer separately routed; the manly clinch now stands for both struggle and embrace. Not that Bloom welcomes the ensuing implications with anything like open arms. On the contrary, the structural requirement of intense attraction between men is an aspect of his theory that he pushes out of his awareness. Such sidestepping is evident in his more explicit uses of the sexual metaphor: "Just as we can never embrace (sexually or otherwise) a single person, but embrace the whole of her or his family romance, so we can never read a poet without reading the whole of his or her family romance as poet" (*Anxiety,* p. 94). Reading is like embracing; never mind that in every other representation of poetic involvement both parties are male. The gender-inclusivity of this passage, in such high contrast to the surrounding discourse, is rigged to allow for a properly heterosexual disposition of desire.[29] In other instances, desire is not recognized for long; it is shunted along various axes of evasion, to be transmuted into presumably less damaging states of intensity (such as "terror"). "Romantic Love is the closest analogue of Poetic Influence, another splendid perversity of the spirit, *though it moves precisely in the opposite direction*" (*Anxiety,* p. 31; my emphasis). Thus the typical Bloomian poetic bond, whatever its roots in admiration or rapport, finds ultimate expression in disavowal, antagonism, and deflationary violence.

This predicament—whereby intense male bonds are simultaneously mandated and repressed—is in no way peculiar to Harold Bloom. Eve Kosofsky Sedgwick has theorized its significance as an Anglo-American cultural phenomenon. On the one hand, the pathways to cultural authority are constituted by relations between men, in which "the woman figures only as one of the objects in [an] exchange, not as one of the partners."[30] On the other hand,

> At least since the eighteenth century in England and America, the continuum of male homosocial bonds has been brutally structured by a secularized and psychologized homophobia, which has excluded certain shiftingly and more or less arbitrarily defined segments of the continuum from participating in the overarching male entitlement—in the complex web of male power over the production, reproduction, and exchange of goods, persons, and meanings.[31]

The shifting, arbitrary nature of the demarcation of "proper" and "improper" male bonds has meant that the entire continuum has become subject to a subtle disciplinary scrutiny. Not only do those who defy the prevailing norms face the threat of persecution, but even those who try to adhere to the norms are never guaranteed immunity from that threat:

> If such compulsory relationships as male friendship, mentorship, admiring identification, bureaucratic subordination, and heterosexual rivalry all involve forms of investment that force men into the arbitrarily mapped, self-contradictory, and anathema-riddled quicksands of the middle distance of male homosocial desire, then it appears that men enter into adult masculine entitlement only through acceding to the permanent threat that the small space they have cleared for themselves on this terrain may always, just as arbitrarily and with just as much justification, be foreclosed.

This double movement of social coercion, simultaneously toward and away from one's fellow men, results in a regime of definitional anxiety—a dread of making the wrong move, of being seen in the wrong light: "An endemic and ineradicable state of . . . male homosexual panic became the normal condition of male heterosexual entitlement."[32]

The homophobia on which this precarious situation depends can be understood broadly as a reaction, not simply against "deviants" themselves, but against what they stand for. Homophobia represents the fear of dissidence from cultural myths of gender and the systems of power they uphold. Failing to toe the gender line, or doing so with undue attention to one's pedicure, can strike a note of challenge discordant not merely with prevailing fashion but with the prerequisite modes of dominance.

Toward the end of the nineteenth century, the challenge posed by gender failure/dissent crystallized into the figure of the homosexual.[33] Previous conceptions of "deviance" were based on sexual behavior; these were overtaken by conceptions of innate character—that is, of sexual identity. The relatively new category of deviant sexual identity received a notorious imprimatur, along with a human face (at least for English and American audiences), from the theatrical and highly publicized scandal of the Oscar Wilde trials (1895). Until his trials, Wilde had been successful in broadcasting a voice of ironic defiance; the flagrant, virtuosic posing adopted both in his writing and his public persona represented a challenge to dominant pretensions of "decent" gender and class definition.[34] The intense media coverage of the trials, however, presented Wilde's stance as a failure and a debasement. While completely skirting any reference to sexual acts, the newspapers were nevertheless able to portray Wilde as a figure of scandalous departure from wholesome masculine norms, a character of "grossly indecent" tendencies involving shameful (but always unspecified) relations with other men.[35] Wilde thus became the visible representative of a newly imagined type of sexual actor: the male homosexual. At the same time, the spectacle of his ruined reputation, his conviction and incarceration, meant that that very visibility was coupled with punishment. Wilde came to stand for the offender whose ostentation gets what it deserves.

Given this gaudily emblematic status, it comes as something of a surprise to find that the first authority invoked in *The Anxiety of Influence* should be Oscar Wilde. "Oscar Wilde, who knew he had failed as a poet because he lacked strength to overcome his anxiety of influence, knew also the darker truths concerning influence" (pp. 5-6). And this dark knowledge, of which Wilde is to stand as the embittered prophet? Bloom directs us to a passage from *The Picture of Dorian Gray*: "To influence a person is to give him one's own soul. He does not think his natural thoughts, or burn with his natural passions. His virtues are not real to him. His sins, if there are such things as sins, are borrowed. He becomes an echo of someone else's music, an actor of a part that has not been written for him" (quoted in *Anxiety,* p. 6).[36] Through this talk of sin, immorality, and unnatural passion, within a context of the influence of an older man over a younger, wafts the perfume of a transgressive sexuality. Bloom's characterization makes it clear, however, that he is not interested in any challenge Wilde's stance might represent. Wilde is invoked only as a tragic figure of poetic failure. As always, this is understood in terms of failed manhood: connotations of an underlying gender "decadence" are folded into the ostensible dilemma of effete creativity.

Thus, already in his opening pages, Bloom activates sexual undertones. Wilde's image stands as a kind of lightning rod, rechanneling the homoerotic energy that crackles through Bloom's own text. By stigmatizing Wilde as a figure of poetic and masculine abjection,

Bloom seeks to place his own endeavor beyond reproach, separating it from the perverse routes of identification and desire represented by Wilde's career. That is, no matter how dependent Bloom's own argument might be on suspiciously intense relations between men, his phobic targeting of Wilde helps to forestall the imputation of a lapse in masculinity. This discursive strategy occurs, to be sure, on shadowy levels of connotation; the connotative aura around Wilde obviates the need to name his perversion.[37] Yet such "shady continuities" of discourse, if they are meant to ward off the appearance of homosexual longing without speaking its name, prove less than reliable. For what is one to make of the "darker truths concerning influence" provocatively advanced under the mantle of intergenerational, Wildean desire?

Bloom's ephebe comes to poetic authority through a wrestling embrace, through the experience of a dire need close to romantic love in its perversity. His model of influence depends on taut filaments of passion between men, while maintaining a fearful distance from any overt icons or gestures of male same-sex desire. Constrained by the phobic blindness of gender orthodoxy to deny the full spectrum of this (or any) desire, Bloom forces desire into a dark corner, to become the dirty little secret at the heart of his myth of empowerment. The effort to rid the male province of "perversity," the unwanted erotic, results only in its perverse refunneling down channels of rivalry and violence.

In order once again to give an idea of the possibilities being displaced, I turn to the scene of an actual embrace, recalled by Hector Berlioz in his memoirs. The setting is the Paris Opéra, during a performance of *Oedipus* by Sacchini:

> Absorbed though I was . . . I could not help overhearing the dialogue that had begun behind me, between my young friend, who was peeling an orange, and the stranger beside him, who was visibly shaken:
>
> "Good Heavens, sir, calm down."
>
> "No! It is too much! It's overwhelming! Crushing!"
>
> "But, sir, you really mustn't let it *affect* you so. You will make yourself sick."
>
> "No, let me be.—Oh!" . . .
>
> During this dissonant conversation the opera had progressed . . . to the lovely trio "*O joyful moment!*"; the penetrating sweetness of that simple melody had now seized me too; and I began to weep, covering my face with my hands, like a man overcome with grief. No sooner had the trio ended than two muscular arms lifted me off my chair, clasping my chest so tightly that I thought my bones would break; it was the stranger: unable to contain his emotion, and noticing that, of all those around him, I was the only one who shared it, he embraced me fervently and cried out in a fitful voice: "By *God,* sir, how beautiful it is!!!" . . .

> Whereupon, perfectly undisturbed by the mirth of the spectators who had gathered around us . . . we exchanged some words in an undertone; I told him my name, he told me his (it was Le Tessier—I never saw him again) and his profession. He was an engineer! . . . Sensitivity lurks in the oddest nooks![38]

Not only does Berlioz lay himself open to the musical experience as a form of ravishment—by whose sweetness one is seized, shaken, pierced, overwhelmed—but the recognition of the same sensitivity in other men also provides the basis, however fleeting, for the most intimate meeting of souls. Maleness, in this practice, is not predicated on stubborn composure and is not dismayed by the shared, ardent, physical expression of pleasure and its bonds. Moreover, musicality acts as the solvent in which such erotic connections are revealed and amplified.

Tchaikovsky, in trying to convert Nadezhda von Meck to a taste for Mozart, relates the scene of another embrace:

> Once, years [after studying with Mozart], Hummel was giving a concert in Prague. If I remember rightly, he was about twelve years old at that time. On the day of the concert Mozart happened to be in Prague. . . . As he entered the hall, Hummel, who was already sitting at the piano, caught sight of him and recognized him. In a trice he had jumped down from the platform and rushed past the audience to his teacher, started embracing and kissing him, the tears coursing down his cheeks, scandalizing everybody present.[39]

This account directly concerns the ties between generations. Tchaikovsky's myth of Mozart conflates pedagogical influence with a personal attachment stronger than any rules of decorum.

In contrast, the anxious, easily dismayed stance I have been discussing represents a duplicitous negotiation of the dictates of masculinity. The simultaneous pressures toward the cultivation and the disavowal of desiring homosocial relations lead to an untenable position: "The result of men's accession to this double bind is, first, the acute *manipulability,* through the fear of one's own 'homosexuality,' of acculturated men; and second, a reservoir of potential for *violence* caused by the self-ignorance that this regime constitutively enforces."[40] According to Sedgwick, this immanent threat of stigmatization operates as a force of social control—a form of systemwide blackmail. If cultural authority is the carrot, then gender paranoia is the stick by which men are pressed into service. Perversely, however, punishment stalks even the obedient.

The tender question of one's manhood thus works its way insidiously into every level of discourse. The internalization of a chastening, watchful fear exerts its pressure even on one's symbolic self-positionings. In

Bloom's mythic staging, the poet may have trodden the sphinx underfoot, but he still worries about the man at his back. This paranoid structure has so infiltrated the formation of masculine identity that it governs even one's relations with men long dead. Any thought of "mutual generosity" in regard to the ancestral presence lies squeamishly close to the taboo against the free unregulated circulation of male desire. An Eliot-style aesthetic of surrender is doubly suspect, pulling with the forbidden allure of both feminine and homosexual positions of identification. Such uneasy mixtures of allure and suspicion, avowal and disavowal, desire and violence, resonate throughout the strange pronouncements of Bloom's prose:

> Poetry is the anxiety of influence, is misprision, is a disciplined perverseness. . . . Poetry is the enchantment of incest, disciplined by resistance to that enchantment.
>
> *(Anxiety,* p. 95)

> Into this Passion, the Dark Intention that Valentinus called "strengthless and female fruit," the ephebe must fall. If he emerges from it, however crippled and blinded, he will be among the strong poets.
>
> *(Anxiety,* p. 14)

Poetic strength is won through perversely refunneled paths of desire—through a passion which is shadowy and gender-blurring, effete yet a menace. This characterization recalls Bloom's picture of the Cherub who blocks the poet's way into paradise, who goads the poet into "constant wakefulness" (p. 36). I have suggested that this "poor demon" (p. 35) borrows its form from the outlines of the maligned, abominated homosexual. But it would be truer to say that the obstructive, disciplinary figure of the Cherub adumbrates the crippling double bind of masculine identity formation—the irreconcilable demands of modern gender orthodoxy and the damage it exacts.

CROSSROADS

The Bloomian primal scene of generational antagonism, with its mystique of anxious manhood, has become a presence in music criticism. Though audaciously articulated, Bloom's theory feeds into some well-established prejudices. Consider the following remarks by Charles Rosen, which appeared only two years after *The Anxiety of Influence*:

> Originality requires the exploration of a self-created universe coherent and rich enough to offer possibilities beyond the development of an individual manner. An individual style built upon the placid acquiescence in a disintegrating language is stamped . . . with a peculiar character; it is reduced to the exploiting of a limited set of mannerisms (*ostinato,* or repeating basses, in the case of Britten).[41]

Here the familiar emphasis on self-creation and heroic progressivism results in the denigration of a modern "tonal" composer as weak, etiolated, mannered, peculiar. Surely these, too, are subtle insinuations of gender failure.[42]

The musical figure whose reputation has suffered most consistently from such coded imputations is Tchaikovsky. Standing at the same historical nexus as Wilde, as the first "homosexual" composer, he has been subject in his own way to rituals of public denunciation. One form this has taken has been scathing attacks on his expressive aesthetic, which are still heard today:

> In the last movement of the Sixth Symphony . . . the perpetually repeated descending phrase . . . is raised to a hysterical pitch of emotion. . . . There is something quite unbalanced and, in the last resort, ugly, in this dropping of all restraint. This man is ill, we feel: must we be shown all his sores without exception? Will he insist on our not merely witnessing, but sharing, one of his nervous attacks?[43]

The devaluation of an aesthetic of openness and vulnerability becomes an attack on Tchaikovsky the man. Of course, men have been dropping their restraint all through the nineteenth century; but Tchaikovsky acts as a lightning rod for the tension accumulating around masculinity.[44]

The importation of a dynamic of "strength" and "anxiety" into musical poetics bespeaks the same undercurrents of gender fear that trouble Bloom's literary model and incurs the same blindness to them. By glamorizing the Oedipal dilemma, the Bloomian model precludes any perspective from which to analyze the intersections of gender and power that are at issue. In fact, I would argue that three separate factors are being elided in the equation of anxiety toward one's forebears. The first is national. The line of overweening musical tradition is most often figured as German. With most composers, however, other national traditions are also at work, in varying stages of formation and with varying claims to authority. The second factor is gender-based. It is willful to assume that female and male composers experience the same relation to the "masters" of the past. As the composer Ethel Smyth claimed: "There can never be a question of competing with men but an everlasting one of creating something different."[45] Furthermore, not all men share the same implication in reigning myths of gender. The relation of sexual identity to artistic attitudes is only beginning to be explored. The third factor concerns personal psychology, which still must account for differences between contemporaries. Why shouldn't we see the arguably defensive stances of Brahms, Ives, and Boulez as special cases rather than general symptoms? All these factors should be opened up as tools for analysis rather than subsumed under a blanket theoretical category.

Bloom's theory eloquently attests to a sense of endemic paranoia; but instead of being placed in the context of a social fabric, this fearful state is left hanging in mythi-

Violence (Ithaca, N.Y., 1993), pp. 15-52; and Jacques Derrida, "Given Time: The Time of the King," trans. Peggy Kamuf, *Critical Inquiry* 18 (1992), 161-87.

27. Schumann, *Gesammelte Schriften,* I, 152.

28. For discussions of the taboo against naming homosexuality (the "unspeakable" vice), and the consequences for its cultural representation, see Eve Kosofsky Sedgwick, *Epistemology of the Closet* (Berkeley and Los Angeles, 1990), pp. 201-03; Ed Cohen, *Talk on the Wilde Side: Toward a Genealogy of a Discourse on Male Sexualities* (New York, 1993), pp. 97-102, 143-46; D. A. Miller, "Anal Rope," in *Inside/Out: Lesbian Theories, Gay Theories,* ed. Diana Fuss (New York, 1991), pp. 123-27.

29. Another explicit use of the sexual metaphor occasions the only appearance of a female muse: "But what is the Primal Scene, for a poet *as poet*? It is his Poetic Father's coitus with the Muse. . . . There they failed to beget him. He must be self-begotten, he must engender himself upon the Muse his mother" (*Anxiety*, pp. 36-37). The triangle is momentarily reinstated.

30. Claude Lévi-Strauss, *The Elementary Structures of Kinship,* trans. James Harle Bell, John Richard von Sturmer, and Rodney Needham, ed. Rodney Needham (rev. edn. Boston, 1969) (quoted in Sedgwick, *Epistemology of the Closet,* p. 184).

31. Sedgwick, *Epistemology,* p. 185, summarizing her argument in *Between Men: English Literature and Male Homosocial Desire* (New York, 1985).

32. Sedgwick, *Epistemology,* pp. 186; 185.

33. See Michel Foucault, *The History of Sexuality, Volume I: An Introduction,* trans. Robert Hurley (New York, 1980), p. 43. The invention of the classification "homosexual," which can be historically pinpointed, is a response to the gradual formation over time of a concept of subcultural identity based on sexuality. For a look at the research on the growing subculture in the eighteenth century as it relates to music, see Gary C. Thomas, "'Was George Frideric Handel Gay?': On Closet Questions and Cultural Politics," in *Queering the Pitch: The New Gay and Lesbian Musicology,* ed. Philip Brett, Elizabeth Wood, and Gary C. Thomas (New York, 1994), esp. pp. 171-80.

34. See Jonathan Dollimore, *Sexual Dissidence: Augustine to Wilde, Freud to Foucault* (Oxford, 1991), esp. chaps. 1 and 4, on Wilde's "transgressive aesthetic."

35. Cohen, *Talk on the Wilde Side*; see chap. 5, "Typing Wilde: Construing the 'Desire to Appear to Be a Person Inclined to the Commission of the Gravest of All Offenses.'"

36. Bloom neglects to point out that Lord Henry, in delivering these words in his "low, musical voice," is deliberately seeking to exercise his "bad influence" on the young Dorian, and that the speech, spoken with "wilful paradox," is thus a critique of the codes of morality, authenticity, and autonomy to which it refers (Wilde, *The Picture of Dorian Gray* [New York, 1985], pp. 40-42).

37. The name of Oscar Wilde has served through the century as a stand-in for the troublesome name of male homosexual desire. In E. M. Forster's novel *Maurice,* when the eponymous character appeals in desperation to the family doctor, he is only able to blurt out: "I'm an unspeakable of the Oscar Wilde sort" (quoted in Cohen, *Talk on the Wilde Side,* p. 100; see also Sedgwick, *Between Men,* p. 95).

38. Quoted in Piero Weiss and Richard Taruskin, *Music in the Western World: A History in Documents* (New York, 1984), pp. 351-52.

39. Letter from Tchaikovsky to von Meck, 16/28 March 1878, *"To My Best Friend": Correspondence Between Tchaikovsky and Nadezhda von Meck, 1876-1878,* ed. Edward Garden and Nigel Gotteri, trans. Galina von Meck (Oxford, 1993), p. 221.

40. Sedgwick, *Epistemology of the Closet,* p. 186.

41. Rosen, *Arnold Schoenberg* (New York, 1975), pp. 37-38.

42. Let me make it clear that my purpose throughout this article is not to accuse any individual of masculinist or homophobic thinking, but to uncover the sedimented metaphors from which we must learn to extricate ourselves.

43. Martin Cooper, "The Symphonies," in *The Music of Tchaikovsky,* ed. Gerald Abraham (New York, 1946), p. 34; cited in Malcom H. Brown, "The Language of Critical Discourse about Tchaikovsky's Music" (paper given at the annual meeting of the American Musicological Society, Oakland, 11 November 1990).

44. See the amazing passage in Alfred Einstein's book on Romantic music where the scapegoating mechanism is painfully transparent. Tchaikovsky is pathologized and scorned for an "exhibitionism of feeling"—which, by the way, is common to "almost every Romantic." "He was a neurotic, yielding unreservedly to his lyric, melancholy, and emotional ebullitions. . . . A revulsion against such exaggeration had to ensue" (*Music in the Romantic Era* [New York, 1947], pp. 316-17).

45. Ethel M. Smyth, *Female Pipings in Eden* (London, 1934), p. 53.

46. Straus, "The 'Anxiety of Influence' in Twentieth-Century Music," *Journal of Musicology* 9 (1991), 430-31.

47. Gilbert and Gubar, *No Man's Land: The Place of the Woman Writer in the Twentieth Century,* vol. I, *The War of the Words* (New Haven, 1988), p. xii. For a less stark, more nuanced version of this line of think-

ing, see Marianne DeKoven, *Rich and Strange: Gender, History, Modernism* (Princeton, N.J., 1991): "Modernist formal practice has seemed to define itself as a repudiation of, and an alternative to, the cultural implications of late nineteenth- and early twentieth-century feminism and socialism. I will argue here that, on the contrary, modernist form evolved precisely as an adequate means of representing their terrifying appeal. . . . I argue that this ambivalence was differently inflected for male and female modernists" (p. 4).

48. Judith Tick discusses related issues in "Charles Ives and Gender Ideology," in *Musicology and Difference: Gender and Sexuality in Music Scholarship,* ed. Ruth Solie (Berkeley and Los Angeles, 1993), pp. 83-106.

49. Showalter, *Sexual Anarchy: Gender and Culture at the Fin de Siècle* (New York, 1990), p. 3.

50. Sedgwick, *Epistemology of the Closet,* pp. 2, 1.

51. Compare Peter Middleton, *The Inward Gaze: Masculinity and Subjectivity in Modern Culture* (London, 1992). On the turn-of-the-century "crisis of the male," see Showalter, *Sexual Anarchy,* pp. 9-15: "One response . . . was the intensified valorization of male power, and expressions of anxiety about waning virility" (p. 10).

William R. Schultz (essay date 1994)

SOURCE: Schultz, William R. "The Start of a Poetry." In *Genetic Codes of Culture?: The Deconstruction of Tradition by Kuhn, Bloom, and Derrida,* pp. 137-61. New York: Garland Publishing, Inc., 1994.

[*In the following essay, Schultz provides an overview of Bloom's concepts of poetic anxiety, misreading, and artistic creation.*]

INTRODUCTION TO BLOOM'S IDEA OF THE START

Bloom defines the start of a poetry in much more detail than Kuhn does for the more general "science." After having studied Bloom's theory, one can look back at Kuhn's to see some salient ideas more developed by Bloom. Instead of "revolution," Bloom has an idea of a struggle between a precursor and his/her successor. To describe this conflict he develops the ideas of "misreading" or "misprision," "clinamen," and "tessera."

PRELIMINARY IDEA OF THE TRADITION FORM IN BLOOM'S THEORY

It has some features of the genetic code. Before DNA becomes complete, it goes through a process of replication. In Bloom's theory some "revisionary ratios" of poetry develop from previous ones having similar structures. The ratios of one poet relate to the poetry of the predecessor. In non-Bloomian terms, one might refer to the revisionary ratios as recurring structural points in the pattern of poetry making it belong to the canon, the tradition.

Bloom has an idea of "a map of misreading," which can be thought of as a genetic code in two main ways. First of all, each poetry has in it a similar pattern or genetic code; namely, the pattern of revisionary ratios. Secondly, before DNA is complete it duplicates portions of its own structure. Poetry does something like this as well, for Bloom's ratios each have a structure generally like that of the one it develops from; all are dialectical.

The map of misreading is different from the genetic code in an important way. Bloom's notion is actually somewhat more synchronic, because the genetic code is seen as changing in each successive manifestation. Bloom does define six ratios in each successive canonical poetry, yet he almost ignores any discussion of the differences in these ratios from one poetry to the next. Each successive manifestation should be a revision of the recurring figure. Had Bloom described these differences, his view would be more diachronic, even more like a genetic code.

A question to keep in mind, Would Bloom's theory of the anxiety of influence be better if it were more like the genetic code? If so, in what ways?

THE INITIAL RELATIONSHIP BETWEEN PREDECESSOR AND SUCCESSOR

The predecessor does not make way, but paradoxically no creation is possible if the poetic power and difficulty is avoided (154 *AI* [*The Anxiety of Influence*]).

Bloom agrees with Derrida on the way any cultural text acquires its meaning. Concerning Derrida's "Freud and the Scene of Writing," Bloom asserts,

> Psychical life thus is no longer to be represented as a transparency of meaning nor as an opacity of force but as an intra-textual difference in the conflict of meanings and the exertion of forces. For Derrida, writing is pathbreaking . . . Derrida's keenest insight, in my judgment, is that 'writing is unthinkable without repression', . . . Derrida has made of writing an intra-psychical trope, which is a making that necessarily pleases any reader who himself has made of influence an intra-psychical trope or rather a trope for intra-poetic relationships.

(48-49 *MM* [*A Map of Misreading*])

Any text has its meaning through intra-textual differences; these differences begin by differences between texts, author to author.

Bloom's idea that a great poet refuses to make way for a successor requires explanation (154 *AI*). It does not matter if the previous great poet is dead or not, still the poetry has in it as a structural element (part of its end) to speak of poetry as entering a decline or not having any more different rebirths. If one looks in the works of Derrida, one can find the same "resistance to passing," the predecessor's attempt to limit or foretell the limits of future developments (See "Qual quelle," the 1971 essay on Valéry).

The new poet-to-be cannot create great poetry if he/she simply rejects the work of the previous poet, for a new poet to be great must do what the former did, only better. In positive language Bloom does not use, the previous poetry implicitly contains or contains in an encoded way the direction that a new one should take. While the precursor cannot see this direction, the successor can by modifying the code of poetry known to the precursor.

The overpowering by the previous poet forces the successor to "misread" the previous one (51 *AI*). This change in interpretation involves making new aesthetic principles changing the sense of the precursor in relation to his/her precursor. This idea of "misreading" or "misprision" will shortly be discussed in its own right.

Initially, as a person moves toward the act of creation, defences begin to operate, forces against change and growth (92 *MM*). In Freud's psychology the change is blocked because it might disturb the ego as a stable psychic component. For a defence to take place, there must be repression—in a poetic sense. In the simplest terms, repression means that the upcoming poet tries to avoid representing the correctness of the previous poet (287 *PR* [*Poetry and Repression*]; there has been a change from complete admiration to reinterpretation.

Instead of being an instinctual drive or desire, repression serves to prevent the representation of the drive or desire in an image (143 *PR*). In other words what the precursor failed to do is not countered with a direct alternative, at least at the start of a poetry. The opposition to the precursor also requires an acceptance, or else the new person could never hope to join the established ranks of great poets. The "double-bind relationship" necessitates a middle path between identity and opposition: the precursor poem is absorbed as impulse, as intuitive sense of the requirements of form, not entirely explicit, but based on a thorough understanding of the making of the previous form (144 *PR*). In this way Bloom's theory follows Freud's of the id, which is the absorption of the comforts of the mother as impulses. Bloom sees repression as a power, not as something bad, to be corrected; the pattern of the predecessor can only be transferred if the newcomer avoids simple identification or rejection. The middle path is a dialectical one of raising the level of the previous activity.

Sometimes admirers of great poetry do not begin to see it in a new way, resulting in the overdetermination of the poetry (71 *AI*). More detail is known about the poetry than is necessary for subsequent creation, and not enough is known about the poetry as a whole in the series of tradition. Creation cannot occur if the interpreter always has a literal interpretation (108 *AI*).

Bloom gives a Freudian definition of tradition: it is "equivalent to repressed material in the mental life of the individual" (109 *AI*). Literally, this means a poet delays the representation of tradition obstructed by the precursor. A great poet coming into being searches for a wholeness lost by the precursor, although this "larger representation" is "kept in abeyance" through to the end of the poetry (109 *MM*). Cultural repression requires some blindness, some lack of explicitness, or else creation cannot occur: "if any poet knows too well what causes his poem, then he cannot write it, or at least will write it badly. He must repress the causes, including the precursor-poems, but such forgetting . . ." (5 *PR*).

In the preliminary stages of creation there is an internalization of the precursor. The internalization occurs while the upcoming poet believes a new interpretation of the predecessor is the right one and the predecessor is deficient aesthetically. The new interpretation is thought to be "exclusive" and "accurate" (70 *MM*).

Anxiety accompanies the redefinition of the precursor's poetry as deficient. Bloom calls this "the moral problematic of the idea of poetic tradition": how can the predecessor be criticized when he/she is a legitimate great poet standing at the top of accumulated tradition, as if atop a pyramid (141 *MM*)? Could any poetry after this height be the best ever? Could something different be poetry? In general the upcoming poet has "anxiety toward any danger that might 'end' him as a poet" (58 *AI*). In the separation from the previous great poet, there is a danger that the new poetry will be too different and thus not belong to the same kind of cultural product; and there is a danger that the new poetry will be too similar, and thus not be original creation. In entirely Freudian terms, Bloom defines the anxiety of influence: "both a kind of separation anxiety and the beginning of a compulsion neurosis, or fear of a death that is a personified superego" (58 *AI*). The great poet-to-be is set on a quest very much like that spoken of by Campbell (and James Liszka); first separation from the precursor, then initiation into the mysteries of poetic tradition—a rite of passage, and finally the coming into maturity when the new great poet has created a total form that could serve as an alternative to the predecessor's challenge.

In terms almost like Kuhn's, Bloom views the start of a new poetry as questioning the possibility of previous poetry-making (91 *SM* [*Shelley's Mythmaking*]). It was founded on a polarity, a contrast of the product versus the means of its production.

In summary, the upcoming poet experiences much anxiety, much discomfort at not being able to create new great poetry because of the predecessor's perfection. The struggle resembles an Oedipal conflict of generations; killing the father means not wanting to be a mere follower of the poetic father, and marrying the mother means wanting to be one's own source of poetry and of the precursor's poetry. Bloom explicitly rejects the interpretation of his theory as Oedipal because, I believe, he wants to emphasize its poetic meaning. He intends to transplant psychological terms into the context of poetry so that they may be adapted to yield a new critical awareness of poetry.

THE MOMENT OF CONCEPTION, CREATION

Defining the point of change from one poetry to another more than Kuhn did, Bloom sees it as the attempt to rescue or renew poetry. A poem answers a previous poem, and the second is in its turn answered by a future one (1 *PR*).

To create, a poet must form a "Scene of Instruction" (207 *PR*). It is a Freudian term for the conditions in which creation occurs; Bloom translates the psychological idea into poetic terms: "the state of heightened demand that carries a new poet from his origins into his first strong representations" (207).

The riddle of this Primal Scene is a riddle of imaginative priority: how can the successor come to claim he/she forms the riddle? (72 *AI*) "If he [the upcoming poet] is not to be victimized, then the strong poet must 'rescue' the beloved Muse from his precursors" (63 *AI*); this means a new poet offers a changed idea of poetry produced by a new standpoint in tradition.

The moment of creation requires (1) isonomization (equalizing) of one's immediate precursor with the one before, and (2) internalization of the precursor's pattern of poetry. Bloom quotes from J. H. Van den Berg's *Metabletica*: ". . . the impoverishment of things to a uniform substantiality—and the disposal of everything that is not identical with this substantiality into the 'inner self' are both parts of one occurrence" (63 *PR*). That occurrence for Bloom is the moment of creation.

It is an issue of the self-preservation of poetry, for the precursor limited all future poetry and the upcoming poet wants to extend poetry past a limit set by the precursor. The imagination in poetry speaks of itself. Bloom would agree with Victor Shklovsky, who believes "the awareness of form constitutes the subject matter of the novel" (35 Lemon and Reis).

According to Bloom, in the start of a new poetry "the very idea of poetic tradition" is at issue. This idea can be meaningfully elaborated by the following passage from Frederick Griffiths and Stanley Rabinowitz:

> Just as the meaning of a part of the work is not exhausted in itself, but is revealed in its relations with the other parts, a work in its entirety can never be read in a satisfactory and enlightening fashion if we do not put it in relation with other works, previous and contemporary. In a certain sense, all texts can be considered as parts of a single text which has been in the writing since the beginning of time. Without being unaware of the difference between relations established *in presentia* (intratextual relations), and those established *in absentia* (intertextual relations), we must also not underestimate the presence of other texts within the text.
>
> (244 *Novel Epics*)

Applied to Bloom's ideas, the passage suggests that the reinterpretation of a previous poetry depends upon seeing it in a different relation within the growing tradition. The change of this idea of the previous poetry at the same time places the upcoming poet at the new frontier of poetic tradition.

The passage also contains the idea that a canonical text (the last one in the series of tradition) is like a single text "which has been in the writing since the beginning of time." In the Prologue was mentioned the idea that tradition gives the power to the individual mind to be like the single human being who has been developing throughout all of civilization. This interplay of individual and the whole of humanity resembles the capacity of one DNA molecule to carry the instructions evolved through millions of years while yet having the power to alter them.

In passing comments Bloom suggests how a later poet understands the totality of the precursor, or the precursor's aesthetic in principle. "The new poet 'himself' determines the precursor's 'particular' law" (42-43 *AI*). The way the precursor created poetry is known to the successor completely. Yeats described the comprehension in the idea of the Condition of Fire: "in that flame he [the poet] views the last of them [the precursor-questers], and unlike them he both sees and knows what he sees" (115 *MM*). The successor understands the precursor in a way the precursor cannot: the cultural processes as a whole can become a new object of knowledge. To be absolutely self-comprehending seems to be a misnomer. One's own perspective can only truly be seen as a whole by another person; this limitation on the individual is a principle of the role of the psychoanalyst, who can see the psyche of a patient more comprehensively than the patient can, and for which reason the analyst-to-be must himself/herself undergo analysis to see any possible interfering factors hidden from self-conscious view—even that of one trained in psychoanalysis. Similarly, Cassirer uses the phrase physics "cannot jump over its own shadow," meaning all individual minds and all their products must be limited according to a source of knowledge (assumptions), which can give way to another (478 *The Philosophy of Symbolic Forms*, III, Trans. Ralph Manheim, Yale University Press, 1957).

A new poetry starts when the previous poetry is seen as having an origin and end different from what the precursor thought. This origin and this end are understood in relation to the new positive sense of poetic origin and poetic end, given by the upcoming poet to himself. In Bloom's words, "a strong poet invents himself" (7 *PR*). Campbell wrote about the dual focus of myth at both its origin and end, and as a result a myth is not wrong solely at its end but at its start as well. This idea does not mean no progress was made; rather, a change in a step of tradition requires modification of the entire world view, no matter how slightly some of the previous ideas in it may be changed in meaning. Certainly, this change is a revolution in Kuhn's sense. However, he always spoke of the beginning of a science as a victory while also arguing for the complete change of a paradigm to bring about a new world view. It is not completely true to speak of the end of a cultural form as faulty while thinking of the beginning as correct. Perhaps even the notion of faulty does not apply to a tradition form and should be replaced by language emphasizing the raising of the level or understanding of the previous processes, which do correctly lay the ground for successors. Bloom resisted any description of the positive role one form had in preparing the way for a successor.

So the question of the end of a poetic form is ultimately bound to the question of its origin. Changing the end of the former poetry is only done properly when a new origin is conceived. From the first moment of creation, there is a sense of a new end of poetic form, a sense of new destination to replace the old "faulty" one. Kuhn's mentioning of solution modelling indicates that the goals of the previous form are not rejected but re-envisioned. Gablik addresses this issue important for Bloom, although not entirely satisfactorily:

> Even though the kind of experimental thinking we find in art is set (like other forms of thinking) to solve problems in a step sequence, it is never satisfied with this; it must continually achieve new openings and new possibilities. A distinction must be made between a development which is fixed in advance by the end state that it must reach—as with Loewy's and Gombrich's model of progress—and a sequence of events that is open-ended to the future because its specific outcome is not foreseen. Cognitive psychologists have stressed the anticipatory nature of cognitive activity and the constant tendency of the mind to go beyond the information given. Microphysicists, for instance, continually seek new modes of conceptual organization from which the finding of new entities will follow.
>
> (160)

Two types of development are contrasted: "a development which is fixed in advance by the end state that it must reach" and "a sequence of events that is open-ended . . . because its specific outcome is not seen." Although for Gablik the two types of development are in contrast, for Bloom they are not. Both are true if the final cause of the new poetry is sensed by analogy from the previous poetry, yet not actually explicit until the end of that poetry. During the process the understanding of this final cause or end of form becomes progressively clearer, more complete. Quite astute is Gablik's claim about microphysics continually forming new modes of conceptual organization, from which new entities are found. Similarly, in poetry new aesthetic principles allow the poet to find new images, new feelings, a new sense of what poetry does.

To find a direct relation between a successor and a predecessor, Bloom does not read bibliographies of journal articles and also textbooks as Kuhn does. Bloom finds the words of the successor that are the "antithetical use of the precursor's primal words, that must serve as the basis for an antithetical criticism" (66 *AI*). "Antithetical" criticism means "the juxtaposition of contrasting ideas in balanced or parallel structures, phrases, words" (65 *AI*).

MISPRISION OR MISREADING

Kuhn's undeveloped idea of the redefinition of former concepts is for Bloom a more developed doctrine of a transformation in one's total outlook.

Misprision or misreading is not a step before creation: it is creation. The process "clears imaginative space" for the new poet and for poetry (5 *AI*). The previous poetry can no longer be seen as a self-subsistent whole denying real progress after it. In the words of Campbell, "A god [predecessor] outgrown becomes immediately a life-destroying demon. The form [the whole of the poetry] has to be broken and the energies released" (338 *Hero*). Bloom, too, speaks of the "breaking of the vessels," which begins a new poetry (***The Breaking of the Vessels*** 1982). The previous poetry is seen as fundamentally disunified, and then relatively unifiable according to a different start of poetry.

Sometimes Bloom uses ideas from Kabbalah to explain the change in interpretation of previous poetry. According to the Kabbalistic notion of Tzim-Tzum, God, who fills the whole universe, was obliged to make room for the creation by contracting himself. If Bloom had placed more emphasis on the developing needs of the unity of poetic tradition, misreading would be less of an individual's personal choice. The negative prefix, to be discussed further later, means not bad reading but intentional alteration of the meaning actually found; a still better approach would make the change in poetries a matter of an increase in value. For now, it seems as if Bloom's critical practice has two faces; on the one hand, "misreading" allows the critic to stand above any poets, who intentionally alter the interpretation of poetry for their ends, and on the other hand, the idea shows a lack of confidence in the comprehending of one poetry—indeed the whole tradition—by a subsequent poetry.

Misreading for Bloom consists of six revisionary ratios, since a poetry *is* a misreading of a previous poetry. [Of course, by poetry I mean great poetry, in the sense of a tradition form.] Their name suggests a revision of previous poetry, and they also revise one's own previous ratios. At six stages in the making of great poetry, the upcoming poet measures himself/herself against the preceding poet, changing the understanding of that former poet while progressively building an alternative sense of the final goal of poetry. The ratios are spoken of in pairs belonging to the same movement. In the first, the two ratios (clinamen and tessera) strive to correct or complete the dead poetry (122 *AI*). In the second (kenosis and daemonization), the pair works to repress the memory of the dead poetry or to further individuate the new poet (122). In the third (askesis and apophrades), the two poets experience the contest proper, the match to the death and the reconciliation with the dead (122). It is a reconciliation with one's poetic father, one in which the father is seen on a lower or earlier level. The new poet finally has cleared an imaginative space in answer to the limitation (and challenge) of the previous poet.

Bloom forms his idea of misreading into a "map" which can be found on page one of *Poetry and Repression* or page 84 of *A Map of Misreading*. The map represents a definite advance in Bloom's understanding of his own concepts, because the map integrates previous ideas and so defines them further. The map has three overall movements, each movement having three phases of the same names as the overall movements. This holomorphism, the part sharing the structure of the whole form, corresponds to the trait of myths to develop in contexts of three generations and to mirror the threefold context within the myth as a three-stage process. The definition of the whole myth through relations among three generations of myths is mirrored within the myth. Bloom's three movements of a poetry were taken from Kabbalah.

The map can be seen as having four lines of development each synonymous with the others: images in the poem, rhetorical tropes, psychic defenses, and revisionary ratios. Bloom finds characteristic types of images

defining the developing phases of poems. These images come into being by serving as rhetorical tropes of earlier images; these tropes come from the history of literature and rhetoric. The psychic defences come from Freud's psychoanalysis; their ambivalence makes them good analogies for a dialectical development. The revisionary ratios are the most original of Bloom's ideas.

CLINAMEN OR THE SWERVE FROM THE PREDECESSOR

Defining the start of a poetry more than Kuhn did for a science, Bloom defines the first step in a new poetry as "clinamen," a swerve from one's predecessor.

The term "clinamen" comes from Lucretius, meaning a swerve of the atom to make change possible in the universe (14 *AI*). To ground a new poetic step in tradition, a successor must swerve from the predecessor, must make change again possible.

"Clinamen" means "swerve"—the new poet swerves from the previous one, meaning the development does not occur without a change of perspective on former poetry.

Clinamen arises as an attempt to rescue the poetic enterprise from the predicament it was left in by the precursor. In de Man's words, "the polar structure" [at the end of poetries] should itself be questioned if there is to be a "reversal of valorization" (269 Review of Bloom).

Clinamen in one stroke revises the entire accumulated poetic tradition of the human race. The revision, however, is not in detail, nor in fact. In other words, Shelley, for example, does not revise every detail of Wordsworth's poetry. Also, Shelley does not in fact revise all previous poets. Since the subject of poetry is its own tradition, the meaning of this whole can be increased in principle, not in quantity. The increase is an increase in poetic power; Bloom infrequently mentions "greater inwardness" to explain improvement. Derrida claimed to change the entire tradition, and certainly he did not revise every detail, not every figure throughout the history of Western philosophy. There is some way that the whole past tradition can achieve a specific representation and thus be revised, worked on as if clay.

In a somewhat uncharacteristic passage Bloom defines the guiding thread of clinamen more in terms of the continuum [of poetry] than in terms of an individual's will to alter it:

> The clinamen or swerve, which is the Urizenic equivalent of the hapless errors of re-creation made by the Platonic demiurge, is necessarily the central working concept of the theory of Poetic Influence, for what

divides each poet from his Poetic Father (and so saves, by division) is an instance of creative revisionism . . . the clinamen stems from a 'Pataphysical' sense of the arbitrary. The poet so stations his precursor, so swerves his context, that the visionary objects, with their higher intensity, fade into the continuum. The poet has, in regard to the precursor's heterocosm, a shuddering sense of the arbitrary—of the equality, or equal haphazardness, of all objects. This sense is not reductive, for it is the continuum, the stationing context, that is reseen, and shaped into visionary; it is brought up to the intensity of the crucial objects, which then 'fade' into it. . . .

(42 *AI*)

Here Bloom calls clinamen the central concept in his whole theory; elsewhere he calls another one at the ends of poetries (metalepsis in Askesis) the central concept of interpretation. Anyway, both are crucial—both the start and the end. Here, in more detail than almost all other passages, Bloom states the swerve to be a swerve of the *context* of the predecessor. This move shows a totalizing, unifying, comprehending, accumulating operation. Poetry begins as the gathering of its own tradition, and its form is made by reconceiving the past of poetry and redesigning its future. The subject of poetry is its own continuum, its stationing context. As we shall see, the ends of poetries bring about a completed new continuum, imaginative space, to replace the former one.

While a new great poet is re-making the continuum, the sense of it changes and matures. Clinamen is not a mistake because the continuum at the end of the precursor's poetry was facing an unsolvable crisis. The successor sees the precursor's poetry as *having already wandered* from the continuum; the only way to see the former poetry is from a higher level, for it cannot be unified beyond a certain point if its own perspective is used. The wandering of meaning is a point in the ever-developing continuum seen from a more developed point. Even within a poetry does a poet come to see the wandering of meaning until the structural threefold unity of the poetry is complete. The individual poet cannot stop its development but can earn the right to develop it and be developed by it. To come into existence a new poetry must reconceive its stationing context, thus revising tradition as a whole.

It has been my experience that scholars have a hard time understanding, or more politely agreeing, with Bloom's idea of the wandering of meaning *within* a poetry. Bloom claims:

> The great lesson that Kabbalah can teach contemporary interpretation is that meaning in belated texts is always wandering meaning, even as the belated Jews were a wandering people. Meaning wanders, like human tribulation, or like error, from text to text, and within a text, from figure to figure. What governs this wander-

ing, this errancy, is defense, the beautiful necessity of defense. For not just interpretation is defense, but meaning itself is defense, and so meaning wanders to protect itself.

(82 *Kabbalah* . . . [*Kabbalah and Criticism*])

The idea of a revisionary ratio is that a poet revises the precursor's sense of the continuum as well as his/her own while the new one is being formed. In this constantly changing quest, meaning wanders; the continuum guides the poet, as the thread of Ariadne was a guide for the way out of a labyrinth after having been laid down on the way in; this process is rather deconstructive, for a successor lays down the thread while criticizing the predecessor and can return or form a new poetry by following the steps in reverse, as it were. Bloom speaks of this wandering in terms of clinamen; a poem has "an opening awareness that it [the previous poetry] must be mis-read because its [the previous poem's] signification has wandered already" (71 *MM*). This passage in effect places the blame for the change on the precursor, whereas most passages about misreading seem to treat the act of the successor as negative in some way or at least arbitrary and intentional.

In one passage Bloom claims "the precursor went wrong by 'failing to swerve', at just . . . one angle of vision" (130 *AI*). Here, by implication, the swerve is a positive action by the successor. I do not think this statement, however, is very consistent with others. For, if a poet restations the context of the predecessor, not only the end of the previous poetry undergoes misreading but also its start. Hence, it is not accurate to say a swerve should have occurred at a specific point. A whole new basis of poetry is brought about, not just a partial correction of the last phase of a poetry. Perhaps Bloom wanted to speak of the swerve as a function of the virtually self-changing continuum—as it is manifest in the different orientations of two great poets in succession. Poetry becomes different from itself at points, called tropes by Bloom, not in the manner of logical inconsistency but more in the manner of a metamorphosis.

The dead great poets live in their successors. At the end of a successor's own poetry, (s)he finally gets a sense of the whole process of creating a poetry beyond that of the precursor: "A poet dare not regard himself as being late, yet cannot accept a substitute for the first vision he reflectively judges to have been his precursor's also" (19 *MM*). Any poet is bound to the predecessor; more important, any poet must explain the change in poetic vision; once this is explained fully, there is an answer to the precursor: a new poetry. In these senses the predecessor lives on as a directing force up to the end of the successor's poetry.

The dead poets live in their successors in the following way. A new great poet cannot reject everything of the predecessor but must "compound with" his/her reality to be able to create (38 *MM*). In personal psychology the ambivalence appears as identity and opposition to a parent; in poetry, images, characters, situations, and tone may be repeated from a previous author. The total literary use of these elements, however, differs. The Russian Formalist literary critics studied parody as the form in which stylistic change takes place. The idea of parody comes close in meaning to Bloom's rhetorical trope of irony for the revisionary ratio "clinamen." Parody shows that one poet makes of the previous one an object to develop for one's own new purposes.

An example of parody transferring the holy light of literary life is given by Griffiths and Rabinowitz:

> Dostoevsky, as we know, began his career by "re-reading" seminal works of Gogol, by refashioning Gogol's Akakii Akakievich ("The Overcoat") and Major Kovalev ("The Nose") into the more emotionally complex characters of Makar Devushkin ("Poor Folk") and Yakov Petrovich Golyadkin ("The Double"). Nor are we surprised to find other standard Gogolian techniques throughout all of Dostoevsky's work, especially name symbolism. The very name of Dostoevsky's fictitious town "Skotoprigonevsk" ("Cattle Corral") has an absurdly Gogolian ring to it.
>
> (165 *Novel Epics*)

Characters are repeated and become "more emotionally complex." Other techniques from the predecessor are used throughout a writer's works. To further associate parody with irony, I should point out that Bloom, Griffiths and Rabinowitz understand irony to be the form of the relation of one author to the previous one as this relation is known to the second succeeding author: "Gogol discusses irony purely as a matter of communication, not introspection. His accounts of his relations with Pushkin and the Russian audience center on questions of irony" (114). Creating poetry has the significance of revising tradition, the canon of poetry. "They [the Russian Formalists] were very adept," writes the historian Victor Ehrlich, "at assessing the role of an author in the literary process, at determining how boldly he moved beyond the canon inherited from his immediate predecessors" (280).

One of the best studies of parody was carried out by Yury Tynyanov who believes parody is "an act of literary 'warfare'" showing how one author evolves out of another author.[1] An author is both "a product of, and a challenge to" an immediate predecessor. This idea corresponds very much to Bloom's "clinamen" and in general to "revisionary ratio."

Parody or irony can represent the greater literary consciousness of a successor, which is still nonetheless intermingled with the predecessor's. Tzvetan Todorov describes the increase in literary mind:

> For some time James [Henry] followed in Flaubert's wake; when we mentioned his "exercises" it was to evoke precisely those texts in which he perfects the use

of synecdoche (we find such pages to the end of his life.) But in the tales which concern us here, James has gone a step further: he has become conscious of Flaubert's sensationalism (or anti-essentialism), and instead of simply employing it as a means, he has made it the constructive principle of his *oeuvre*. We can see only appearances [when Flaubert's ideas are represented in James' fiction], and their interpretation remains suspect; only the pursuit of the truth can. . . .

> (151 *Poetics of Prose*)

Irony or parody shows the attainment of an aesthetic vantage point above the predecessor.

Fundamentally, Bloom's criticism concentrates on the conflict of poets, whereas other critics discuss the missing positive side of literary evolution. Bloom discusses admirably how one author seems to hinder any followers, this obstruction being built into the end of poetic form as part of its means of closure (the end will be discussed in detail later). It is a way of projecting a vision of the poetic enterprise into the infinite, ideal future, thus safeguarding the integrity, the universality of the vision provided by the form. Cultural forms do this. Bloom does not discuss, however, how one author *helps* another to become a successor. Even though the predecessor may be dead, his/her poetry has within it what the successor needs. The satire, parody, or irony is not merely negative; it does not merely reject what came before; it continues the previous literary art (4 *Novel Epics*). Any great poetry suggests an aesthetic problem, which is at the same time a challenge and opportunity. Faulty presuppositions or aesthetic dead ends point the way to finding new alternative rejuvenating ones. According to Alois Riegl,

> However, in place of those earlier presuppositions for artistic creation it [late Roman art] has substituted new ones which constitute the basis for the gradual development of the practice of linear perspective in the following periods. In order to avoid an easily engendered misunderstanding, it has to be emphasized most emphatically that beside its negative role of demolition in order to make room for the new, late Roman art always had positive aims, which have to date remained unrecognized, because they appear so different from our accustomed ideas of the aims of modern art which to some degree are the aims of classical and Augustan-Trajanic art.

> (11-12)

Parody and irony mean the demolition that is at the same time a construction and extension of the tradition. The fact that Riegl speaks of "presuppositions" should not be overlooked. They permit Riegl to explain how the end of artistic forms can point the way to a new form without actually providing the new principles, and the idea of presuppositions shows the dependence of thought on something outside itself, just beyond. If artistic and other forms are guided by presuppositions, then a successor can accumulate the previous cultural development by becoming aware of the former presuppositions—no one being aware of his/her own. In a non-quantitative sense the accumulation of an entire tradition can occur, because presuppositions supply the means for a successor to totalize, to comprehend what has been done.

Although Bloom's theory allows for a cyclic sense of poetries, Bloom does not develop this sense strongly enough. If he had, he would have explained how one poet does not merely obstruct the successor who then rejects the former; but the poet has his work continued and even prepares the way for this further development.[2]

Unfortunately, despite all the help Bloom can offer to take his readers closer to the well-springs of poetry, he does not describe the positive improvement in poetic tradition enough. Other critics (Mikhail Bakhtin) do describe progress:

> Every *true* reader of Dostoevsky, who perceives his novels not in the monologic mode and who is capable of rising to Dostoevsky's new authorial position, can sense this peculiar *active broadening* of his consciousness, not solely in the sense of an assimilation of new objects (human types, character, natural and social phenomena), but primarily in the sense of a special dialogic mode of communication with the autonomous consciousness of others, something never before experienced, an active dialogic penetration into the unfinalizable depths of man.
>
> (68 *Problems of Dostoevsky's Poetics*)

There is an analogy between poets not being able to create and critics not being able to see the positive help a precursor gives a successor. Creation requires less criticism of the precursor than the constant attention to a new whole of poetry, based on analogy with the predecessor:

> . . . the continuation of *Dead Souls* [novel by Gogol] required more the talents of a poet than of an artist: "But in general one should focus not on *censuring* others but on *contemplating* one's own self. If the creation of the poet does not contain within it this quality, then it is merely . . . the fruit of the temporary state of the artist."
>
> (163 *Novel Epics*)

TRANSFERENCE OF THE PATTERN FROM THE PRECURSOR

The twofold attitude of the anxiety of influence, acceptance and denial, begins the transfer of the pattern of great poetry—perhaps a genetic code—from precursor to successor.

In "Tradition and the Individual Talent" Eliot notices a process of recognition during the creation of great poetry; the poet knows that the pattern of poetry has been pursued and found again.

The pattern of poetry can be transferred because poetry has for its subject its own tradition. Literary critic Leo Bersani finds a transference of the pattern of fiction by Joyce into works of a superior nature: "The Joycean intertext rescues Western literature from the deconstructive effects of the intertext itself. The parodistic replays of Homer, Shakespeare, and Flaubert—not to speak of all the authors 'quoted' in 'Oxen of the Sun'—are neither subversive of nor indifferent to the fact of cultural inheritance; rather, Joyce relocates the items of that inheritance with *Ulysses* as both their center and belated origin."[3] Griffiths and Rabinowitz have noticed "an absorption and reconstitution of canon in *Ulysses*" and "the restaging of the tradition" by Dante. They attribute to Bloom the finding of a similar absorption and reconstitution of tradition by Milton: "Milton's inversion of time may derive from the scene in the *Aeneid* (8.626-728) where the baffled Aeneas looks on a divine shield summarizing the history of a Rome that has not yet been founded."[4] The divine shield is an example of the whole of poetic tradition being represented and then capable of being revised through the representation. A creator cannot give a circumscribing representation of his/her own work, for an infinite regress of such circles would be required. Each new successor circumscribes the poetic process of the predecessor and thereby of the whole tradition. "By arranging his precursors in series," explains Bloom, "Milton figuratively reverses his obligation to them . . ." (138 *MM*); Milton's predecessors are seen as depending on Milton, who has a vantage point. This reversal of perspective on tradition, from seeing oneself as too late to create to seeing oneself as earlier or prior to one's predecessors, is a regular feature of poetry in Bloom's theory.

The pattern cannot be transferred identically, nor can transference be absent if a poet is to become great, to create canonical poetry. Bloom elaborates,

> The compulsion to repeat the precursor's patterns is not a movement beyond the pleasure principle to an inertia of poetic pre-incarnation, to a Blakean Beulah where no dispute can come, but rather is an attempt to recover the prestige of origins, the oral authority of a prior Instruction. Poetic repetition quests, despite itself, for the mediated vision of the fathers, since such mediation holds open the perpetual possibility of one's own sublimity, one's election to the realm of true Instructors.
>
> (59 *MM*)

In the most simple terms a new poet must do what the previous did, only better. More specifically, Bloom is saying that an upcoming great poet attempts to subordinate the predecessor or to see the former as having a lower level of poetic vision; the lower level is spoken of in temporal terms as being "belated"; the superior position is "early" or "prior," which has both temporal and normative or logical meanings. The "mediated vision of the fathers" means the revised interpretation of the previous poetry—this revision being itself a new poetry. The goal of poetry is to form a revised stance of the predecessor's poetry, so that an upcoming poet constantly compares his/her own poetry to that of the predecessor. Whatever goal the new poet has in mind at any time in the unfolding of the poetry, and this goal is constantly maturing, is known by reference to a whole of poetry lost by the precursor [because (s)he could not allow a successor to remake the entirety of poetry, thus violating what had been done]. In this sense the precursor cannot prescribe what the successor must do. In contrast the precursor's aesthetic acts as if it were part of the poetic id, not a poetic superego. The successor understands the precursor as saying, "Be like me but unlike me" (70 **AI**).

Ironically, in an Oedipal fashion, the resistance to the father brings about a closer association with him. The proper rejection of the previous canonical poet causes that pattern to be reproduced in a new way.[5] Oedipus in the classic play was sent away because of his parents' desire to reverse the decreed fate of the boy's killing his father and marrying his mother. In the end the fate was realized ironically; the boy left his foster home for a new land in order to avoid the decreed fate only to go to the land where his real parents were and to make possible the fulfillment of the prophecy. The irony dramatizes the opposition of the father and son's opposition. With reference to Bloom's ideas, the poet is set on the quest of restoring the lost wholeness of the poetic continuum but is unable to do this until a whole poetry is developed as alternative. The irony is that the opposition cannot stop until the newcomer does what the former did, and Bloom sometimes expresses this, as we shall see, as an acceptance of the precursor but on new aesthetic terms.

Victor Shklovsky wrote about Sterne's "conscious manipulation and violation of traditional plot schemata" (169 *Theory of Prose*). The words "traditional plot schemata" suggest the subject of literature consists in the schemata of its tradition. All canonical poetry is constantly revising the whole tradition.

The transference of the pattern or code of poetry in the indefinitely extending series of human history reoccurs in cycles. The upcoming poet tries to understand the poetic production of the predecessor, and in so doing the poet finds a guiding thread to developing an alternative poetry. This complete poetry will in its turn challenge another upcoming poet to understand its processes of production, and again the attempt leads to the creation of still another poetry.

THE GOAL CONSTANT THROUGHOUT THE TRANSFERENCE OF THE PATTERN, CODE

The poet who is becoming great strives to stop being influenced and to become an influence by demanding "a

mental space," a poetry, of his/her own. Though Bloom states the idea anthropomorphically, it can be seen as a necessary function of a tradition form. At the beginning of one's cultural work one must be influenced by the past, but at the end the work must be able to influence a successor to do the same type of work if the activity is to form an indefinitely extending tradition.

Common sense understands poetry as a pretty, perhaps revealing description of ordinary life, real events; Bloom disagrees (182 **SM**). Poetry attempts to understand the production of previous poetry and to restore its lost vision of the poetic continuum, its forbidding of a new total revision. In less abstract terms, the attempt resembles the attempt all people must face to develop their own personalities from their parents. The very first tendencies at identifying with one's parents do not complete the personality until the child can differentiate, perhaps oppose, the new personality and values to those of his/her parents. So a poet-to-be desires to "come into his/her own" as a poet, these words of Bloom's also being commonly used for the maturing of the personality.

According to Bloom the deepest desire of a poet is to be an influence rather than to be influenced (12 **MM**). Analogous to this desire is the desire of animals—all life forms—to reproduce. A comparison can also be made to the desire of people to have their children live beyond them and in turn reproduce, in order to grant the parents a kind of immortality. However, at the beginning of a poetry, as during the years of growing up, influence has a negative connotation for Bloom. Since the influence from the predecessor seems to stop any real creation by a successor, influence means an end to one's chances of having one's own imaginative space or poetry. In Fletcher's words, the poet demands 'a mental space, a referential vacuum, to fill with his own visions' (66 **AI**). Doing what the precursor said could not be done, making the new space, would complete the quest of a poetry.

Thomas Mann has a sense of the goal constant throughout the making of a new canonical literary work[6]:

> . . . The bond with the father, the imitation of the father, the game of being the father, and the transference to father-substitute pictures of a higher and more developed type—how these infantile traits work upon the life of the individual to mark and shape it! I use the word 'shape', for to me in all seriousness the happiest, most pleasurable element of what we call education (Bildung), the shaping of the human being, is just this powerful influence of admiration and love, this childish identification with a father-image elected out of profound affinity. The artist . . . can tell us of . . . a career which after all is often nothing but a reanimation of the hero under very different temporal and personal conditions. . . .

Bloom feels this passage is concerned with the overcoming of the anxiety of influence discussed by Nietzsche and commented on by Mann. For this book, the passage gives a sense of what is constant throughout a poetry: "the transference to father-substitute pictures of a higher and more developed type." In other words, the poet must do what the precursor did, only better—on a higher poetic level. The dead end of the previous poetry sets the task of restoring the lost whole of poetic vision by making possible a newly defined whole or space. This task eventually requires a complete new vision of a similar type (in the passage, "a reanimation of the hero").

From Clinamen to the Next Ratio, Tessera

The swerving from the predecessor leads to the need to use one's new principle to complete the poetic vision of the world, the needs of poetic form, left in doubt by the predecessor; Bloom calls this "tessera," antithetical completion.

The term "tessera" comes from mosaic making: "the fragment say of a small pot which with the other fragments would re-constitute the vessel" (14 *AI*). The vessel means the poetic continuum, described as being broken when seen by the fresh eyes of a newcomer as it excludes the latter. The vessel is the poetic perspective. The repaired pot resembles the new poet's first stage in the recreation of the continuum: "the later poet provides what his imagination tells him would complete the otherwise 'truncated' precursor poem and poet, a 'completion' that is as much misprision as a revisionary swerve is" (66 *AI*). The first step of a poetry reconceives the sense of the tradition to make room for the newcomer, but this solution turns out to be incomplete, as we shall see.

Summary

The start of a poetry can be defined to be a movement of clinamen and tessera, two revisionary ratios. A reinterpretation of the precursor must take place, called "misreading" or "misprision." This act differs from the more partial reinterpretation in daily life, because the new poet revises the entire previous tradition by changing the principles on which the aesthetic was produced. Clinamen uses irony and parody to show its change of style. During this first movement away from the precursor, the upcoming poet realizes he/she must develop a whole vision from the new poetic building block discovered through clinamen. The result is a universalization of clinamen into tessera; at this point in poems the previous types of images are extended to all of nature or life. "Tessera" means the attempt to make an antithetical completion of the precursor. While it does do this, this move is insufficient to gain what the predecessor had lost, as explained by the next pair of revisionary ratios, and so the poet must develop the sense of poetry further.

Notes

1. From 258 Erlich. The passage should be helpful for anyone wishing to understand the evolution or the genealogy of fiction: "The Formalist observations on the role of parody cast an interesting light on the mechanics of literary change. In his masterful study, *Dostoevskij and Gogol*, Tynyanov demonstrated that the relationship between these two writers was a much more complex phenomenon than was generally understood. Dostoevskij's indebtedness to Gogol', he observed, is undeniable, attested as it is by a wealth of Gogolian echoes in Dostoevskij's early novels, e.g. *Poor Folk, The Double, Netochka Nezvanova*. But, according to Tynyanov, there is also another aspect, unnoticed by most literary historians: in his novel *The Friend of the Family* (Selo Stepancikovo) Dostoevskij was parodying the ponderous rhetoric of Gogol's *Correspondence with Friends*. Now parody, continued Tynyanov, is a sign of emancipation, indeed an act of literary 'warfare'. If *Poor Folk* and *The Double* are a proof that Dostoevskij evolved out of Gogol', *The Friend of the Family* clearly indicates that its author was moving beyond Gogol'. Dostoevskij's literary art, concluded Tynyanov, was both a product of, and a challenge to, Gogol's 'romantic naturalism.'"

2. Griffiths and Rabinowitz explain how Dostoevsky extends Gogol's vision: "In presenting epic more as cycle than as genre, as a mode of other genres rather than a form unto itself, we propose a new meaning to the familiar designation of an "epic tradition" in the Russian novel. For it is not just scale and calling that define the category but the quality of memory that attaches the novels to the prophets of other nations—Homer, Virgil, Dante—and novelist to novelist, as in Dostoevsky's implicit sense that he is not just replicating or rivaling Gogol's vision but materially continuing his project, as we shall see" (39 *Novel Epics*).

3. Quoted from 155 *Novel Epics*. The original passage occurs in Leo Bersani's "Against *Ulysses*," *Raritan* 8, no. 2 (Fall 1988): 21.

4. The idea of Griffiths and Rabinowitz is on 155 of *Novel Epics*. Bloom's ideas can be found in *MM*, 138.

5. Bloom's idea is contained in the following passage: "But what is the Primal Scene [discovery of the project of a new poetry], for a poet as poet? It is his Poetic Father's coitus with the Muse. There he was begotten? No—there they failed to beget himself—he must wait for his Son, who will define him even as he has defined his own Poetic Father" (36 *AI*).

6. Quoted from 52 *AI*. The original passage can be found in Mann's *Freud and the Future*. Bloom unfortunately gives no page number nor other publishing information.

List of Abbreviations

BLOOM'S WORKS

AI: *The Anxiety of Influence*

BV: *The Breaking of the Vessels*

KC: *Kabbalah and Criticism*

MM: *A Map of Misreading*

PR: *Poetry and Repression*

SM: *Shelley's Mythmaking*

List of Secondary Works Cited

Bakhtin, Mikhail. *Problems of Dostoevsky's Poetics.* Ed. and trans. Caryl Emerson. Introd. Wayne C. Booth. Minneapolis: University of Minnesota Press, 1984.

Campbell, Joseph. *The Hero with a Thousand Faces.* Bollingen Series XVII. Princeton: Princeton University Press, 1949.

De Man, Paul. "Appendix A: Review of Harold Bloom's *Anxiety of Influence.*" In *Blindness and Insight: Essays in the Rhetoric of Contemporary Criticism.* Introd. by Wlad Godzich. Minneapolis: University of Minneapolis Press, 1971. Also in De Man's "Review of Harold Bloom, *The Anxiety of Influence: A Theory of Poetry.*" *Comparative Literature.* 26: 3 (Summer 1974), 269-75.

Eliot, T. S. "Tradition and the Individual Talent." *The Norton Anthology of English Literature.* Ed. M. H. Abrams. Fifth edition. Vol. 2. N.Y.: W. W. Norton & Company, 1962.

Erlich, Victor. *Russian Formalism: History-Doctrine.* London: Yale University Press, 1955.

Gablik, Suzi. *Progress in Art.* N.Y.: Rizzoli, 1977.

Griffiths, Frederick T. and Stanley J. Rabinowitz. *Novel Epics: Gogol, Dostoevsky, and National Narrative.* Evanston: Northwestern University Press, 1990.

Lemon, Lee T. and Marion J. Reis. *Russian Formalist Criticism: Four Essays.* Trans. and Intro. by Lemon and Reis. London: University of Nebraska Press, 1965.

Liszka, James Jakób. *The Semiotic of Myth: A Critical Study of the Symbol.* Bloomington: Indiana University Press, 1989.

Riegl, Alois. *Late Roman Art Industry.* Trans. from the original Viennese edition with foreword and annotation by Rolf Winkes. 1985. Published by Giorgio Bretschneider Editore. Also, Riegl wrote *Stilfragen* [Questions or Problems of Style]. Also, see Meyer Schapiro, "Style" in *Aesthetics Today.* Ed. Morris Philysson, N.Y.: Meridian, 1961, for a summary of Riegl's views.

Shklovsky, Viktor. *Theory of Prose.* Trans. by Benjamin Sher and Intro. by Gerald L. Bruns. Naperville, Ill.: Dalkey Archive Press, 1992.

Todorov, Tzvetan. *The Poetics of Prose.* Trans. from the French by Richard Howard. Foreword by Jonathan Culler. Ithaca, N.Y.: Cornell University Press, 1977.

Tynyanov, Yury. "Preface." *Russian Prose.* Ed. B. M. Eikhenbaum & Yury Tynyanov. Trans. and Ed. by Ray Parrott. Ann Arbor, Mich.: Ardis, 1985.

Graham Allen (essay date 1994)

SOURCE: Allen, Graham. "Lies against Time: Transumptive Allusion, Diachronic Rhetoric and the Question of History." In *Harold Bloom: A Poetics of Conflict,* pp. 105-33. New York: Harvester Wheatsheaf, 1994.

[*In the following essay, Allen examines the use of psychological symbols in Bloom's vision of literary tradition, noting the absence of historical reference in his criticism.*]

POETIC ECHO: SUBSTANCE AND EFFECT

I

Bloom's revision of traditional conceptions of rhetoric means that when we interpret a poetic (or even a critical) text we are involved in two opposing directions of reading. One direction is the attempt to establish the precise meaning within ('inside') a text; that is to say, we attend to the play between literal and figural uses of language in the text in an attempt to get the poem right, to reproduce the exact structure of the text. This is the level which corresponds to rhetoric conceived as a system of tropes. Bloom points out, however, that every attempt to represent the synchronic significance of a text, every attempt to represent the 'inside', so to speak, of a text, involves us also in a movement 'outside' its specific linguistic structure. We recognise that every pattern of significance we can detect within ('inside') a text depends on a measurement between that text and previous texts. Tropes become echoes of earlier texts.

The movement from synchronic to diachronic dimensions is thus representable as a movement from 'inside' to 'outside'. Bloom shows, however, that such terms as 'inside' and 'outside' are fundamentally insupportable. Every text, due to its dependence for meaning on other texts, has no 'inside' but is rather the product of the relationships (more specifically our measurement) between chains of rhetorical tropes and chains of poetic and critical texts. What is truly 'inside' a text is its relationship to other texts: what traditionally is conceived as a text's 'outside', its ground or context. As Bloom writes: 'To study what poems are about is to interpret their outside relationships. A "subject" is indeed under something else, and a poem's subject thus subjects the poem' (**MM** [*A Map of Misreading*], p. 75).

A deconstructive reading of a poetic text tends to limit us to the synchronic play of that text's finite units of signification. It denies the possibility of fixing those units in a stable and meaningful structure. Bloom argues that texts exist in a vertical as well as a horizontal dimension of meaning. A text 'means' something because of its relationship with other texts (and because of the critical reader's measurement of this relationship). A text is, for Bloom, a concept of Thirdness, and the reading of a text is an event in which meaning hovers somewhere between the three nodes involved in that triadic relationship: the text itself, the tradition against which it tropes itself into being, the interpretation of this relationship by the 'strong' (mis)reader.

Bloom's point is that every poetic trope stands in a diachronic relationship with past tropes, a relationship which need not in any way be signalled on the surface level of the text. The question becomes then, confronting for instance the 'trope of the leaves' in Wallace Stevens's poem 'The course of a particular', to what past instance of this particular trope is the Stevensian example directing itself? In his essay **'Transumption'** (**BV** [*The Breaking of the Vessels*], pp. 73-107) Bloom renews his discussion of the poetic trope of the leaves, studied formerly in chapter 7 of *A Map of Misreading*.[1] According to Bloom, Stevens's poem represents a modern reiteration and revision of a tradition of troping the leaves which stretches back to Homer and the Old Testament.

To speak of the 'trope of the leaves' when reading 'The Course of a Particular' is clearly a rather strange use of the word trope, which traditionally has been associated with certain forms of language use, such as metaphor and metonymy. Yet, as Peter de Bolla explains in discussing the 'Aeolian trope' as located by Bloom in Coleridge's 'France: An ode', the word trope undergoes a form of substitutive transformation or tropism when employed by Bloom; a transformation which explains why Bloom asserts that 'Any critic necessarily tropes or turns the concept of trope in giving a reading of a specific poem' (**BF** [**"The Breaking of Form"**], p. 10). As de Bolla writes, the 'Aeolian trope' is 'a principle of organisation of poetic discourse, a trope in the sense of a principle of substitution which determines the specific language of this poem ["France: An ode"]'. He goes on to explain that Bloom 'wants us to understand that what "figures" this text is a trope in the same way that metaphor might be understood as determining the specificity of an utterance'.[2]

De Bolla's allusion to 'figure' is crucial here. The 'trope of the leaves' in the Stevens poem involves various traditional forms of trope as it progresses through the poem, passing from irony through metaphor and hyperbole to metalepsis, or so Bloom would have us understand the figurative process involved. Yet the only

way in which we can associate the various occurrences of the cry of the leaves to the more traditional forms of trope (irony, metaphor, metalepsis) is to relate each instance to a prior use of the same trope of the leaves 'outside' of the poem. We have to proceed, in a movement now familiar, from a reading of the patterns of misprision 'within' the poem to the scene of instruction staged by the poem's act of misprision.

De Bolla explains that Bloom's use of trope, when discussing such issues as the 'fiction of the leaves' (to employ the phrase Bloom appropriates from Stevens's 'The rock'), pertains to what were traditionally styled 'figures of thought' as opposed to the various forms of 'figures of words'. This is a distinction which leads us to the difference between tropes as swerves from literal language (synchronic) and tropes as the products of willed acts of revision (tropes of tropes—diachronic). As a figure of thought, Bloom's notion of trope becomes an aspect of poetic desire.

De Bolla produces a scheme whereby the synchronic form of the trope is conceived as a 'first-order trope', while the diachronic form is understood as a 'second-order trope'. The difference between these two categories of trope is that while the first-order trope is a swerve from literal usage, the second-order trope is a swerve away from a previous trope.

When reading 'The course of a particular', particularly when reading the 'trope of the leaves' which constitutes its specific rhetorical mode of organisation, we are involved in a tracing of that trope in its various mutations back to a former instance of the 'trope of the leaves' on which it is performing its diachronic, second-order tropism or turning. A certain measurement between the trope in Stevens's poem and its appearance in the prior context is, according to Bloom's theory, *the meaning* of Stevens's employment of the 'fiction of the leaves' and thus, ultimately, of the poem as a whole.

Yet how do we discover the 'outside' (context) towards which Stevens' tropism is directed? This problem takes us back to the theme of the critic's vacillation between empirical reification and dialectical ironisation. Bloom's framing of the diachronic tradition within which the poem exists and has meaning, the list of poetic instances of the 'trope of the leaves' supplied by Bloom (Milton, Shelley, Whitman, *et al.*), is, no matter how persuasive it may appear to his readers, his own invention. As Hollander writes: 'like all phenomena of this sort, we must always wonder what our own contribution was—how much we are always being writers as well as readers of what we are seeing'.[3]

Another question emerges at this point. If the notion of a diachronic rhetoric, and the accompanying notion of transumptive allusion, necessarily involves the interpreter in an arbitrary (in the sense of belated) act of imposition, closure and/or critical persuasion, how is it possible to retain the element of intentionality in our assessment of such apparent acts of poetic rhetoric and allusion?

Hollander spends some considerable time in explaining why and how the notion of transumptive allusion relies on an interpretative assumption concerning intentional acts of poetic will.[4] In his discussion of 'Echo Metaphorical', Hollander distinguishes between quotation, allusion and echo, establishing a cline in which a steady decrease in what we normally would style authorial intention accompanies any progression from the former to the latter. The idea of 'echo' leads out towards the post-structuralist account of intertextuality, a concept which, in some of its guises, possesses a key role in the deconstruction of such traditional metaphysical ideas as the authorial 'subject' and authorial will or intent.

While 'allusion', in Hollander's cline, does not have the direct sense of intention which is traditionally associated with the concept of quotation, it appears to find its location *between* the traditional ideas of intentionality ascribed to quotation, the forms of uncertainty with regard to intention which inhere within the concept of 'echo', and the post-structuralist version of that term: intertextuality. Hollander states: 'one cannot . . . allude unintentionally . . . an inadvertent allusion is a kind of solecism'.[5] Clearly, the concept of intentionality in allusion and echo is inextricably tied to the ability to be able to fix the potential source of an allusion, the ability to interpret a potential intertext as *the* (intended) source. If we can so fix the source of a transumptive echo or allusion, we can equally reincorporate the language of intentionality, whether this has for its focus an author's conscious or various unconscious symbolic actions. Bloom's desire is directed towards such a fixing of origins and sources, and thus such a reassertion of the concept of authorial will and/or intentionality. Yet, as we are observing here, Bloom remains aware of the problems involved in such an interpretative procedure. Bloom states that a trope is 'either the will translating itself into a verbal act or figure of *ethos,* or else the will failing to translate itself and so abiding as a verbal desire or figure of *pathos*'. He adds: 'But, either way, the trope *is* a figure of will rather than a figure of knowledge. The trope is a cut or gap made into the anteriority of language, itself an anteriority in which "language" acts as a figurative substitution for time' (**WS** [*Wallace Stevens*], p. 393).

To cut the poetic trope loose from its relation to a specific past trope or determinate series of tropes denies the performative nature of poetic rhetoric, leaving the nature of that rhetoric open to the deconstructive assertion of the priority of language over the psychological and poetic will. Clearly a diachronic conception of the trope relies on a determinate chain of relationships between signifying units. As Hollander puts it: 'When we speak metaphorically of echoes between texts, we imply a correspondence between a precursor and, in the acoustical actuality, a vocal source'.[6] Yet, as Bloom recognises, the chain of tropes against which a poet such as Stevens can be said to be transumptively troping in 'The course of a particular' remains resistant to definitive determination, complete representation. This is why Bloom's examination of transumptive allusion in poets such as Stevens has led him to talk about transumptive criticism, to highlight the critical act of transumption which necessarily occurs in any interpretation of a poetic act of transumption. As Bloom writes: 'Reading a transumptive chain becomes necessarily a critical exercise in transumptive thought' (**BV,** p. 75).

As Bloom suggests, the meaning produced in any act of diachronic rhetoric occurs in the work that such a troping performs: the *lie against time* which is diachronic rhetoric is produced by the *effect* rather than the *substance* of such transumptive chains. I want to illustrate how Bloom's theory of diachronic rhetoric relies on an understanding or interpretation of the performative *effect* produced by the determinate (and yet often, paradoxically, concealed) chain of tropes established in every poetic instance of what Bloom has called transumptive allusion. In order to do this, it is necessary to look more closely at Bloom's key concept, transumption.

TRANSUMPTION, GNOSTICISM, HISTORY

I

In his essay **'Milton and his precursors'** (**MM,** pp. 125-43), Bloom associates transumption with the psychological defence mechanisms of projection and introjection. As Bloom explains, these processes are performed through the deployment of late words for early words or early words for late words. Bloom's clearest illustration of this process in Milton comes in his reading of *Paradise Lost,* Book 1, lines 283-313 (see **MM,** pp. 130-8); a reading which provides a clear instance of the substitution of a 'late' word for an 'early' word in Milton's reference to the 'Optic Glass' of the 'Tuscan poet' (Galileo) famously discussed, before Bloom, by Dr Johnson. This form of rhetoric is, for Bloom, the most powerful weapon in the battle between the ancients and the moderns.

The manner in which transumptive tropes offer a final defence against the poetic tradition and thus against time, anteriority and otherness is encapsulated in the quotation from George Puttenham Bloom employs.[7] Puttenham defines metalepsis as the 'farrefetcher' and his notion of the fetching of further words expresses exceptionally well the rhetorical strategy Bloom discovers in *Paradise Lost* and in the poetic tradition that poem fostered. In such a strategy the poem's words are pitted against time, against all that comes between the *now* of the poet's own present moment and the origin or source of time and tradition projected by that poet. As Bloom puts it in one review: 'Such a poem swallows up an ever-early freshness as its own, and spits out all sense of belatedness, as belonging only to others.'[8] In other words, metaleptic reversal is a scheme designed to defend the poet against history.

Every poet after Milton, who is the poet in whose poetry 'temporality fully becomes identified with anxiety' (*Agon,* p. 112), wishes to murder time. Bloom explains that 'Metalepsis or transumption can be described as an extended trope with a missing or weakened middle, and for Milton literary tradition is such a trope' (**MM**, p. 139). The preternatural strength of Miltonic metalepsis resides precisely here, in the fact that the entirety of poetic tradition including the Bible itself is conceived of as a weakened middle between the divine origin and the divine, though exponentially darkened, moment in which Milton composes *Paradise Lost* (see **MM**, p. 138).

The technique by which Milton 'murders time' depends on his transumption of particular past texts, particular past tropes; yet the effect of such a poetic practice is to defend Milton against all past text, against all tradition or fallen time. Transumption turns the orthodox and classical notion of *figura*, the form of interpretation which has its origins in the medieval development of a typological reading of the Bible, on its head. Figural interpretation, as exemplified in the work of Erich Auerbach and a number of more recent critics, works on the premiss that later writers can fulfil and complete their earlier precursors. It depends, in other words, on a fundamentally Christian notion of immanence, on the completion of the old by the new. The notion of transumption works on the basis of the inevitable priority and authority which attach to origins and the earlier manifestation of a word or thing.[9] Both *figura* and transumption are lies against time (**PR** [*Poetry and Repression*], p. 88); yet Bloom argues that transumption, because it foregrounds its own status as an interpretative lie against time, is a deidealised approach to the relationship between poetic texts. As Bloom puts it: 'In merest fact, and so in history, no text can fulfil another, except through some self-serving caricature of the earlier text by a later. To argue otherwise is to indulge in a dangerous idealisation . . . [to] refuse the temporal anguish of literary history' (**RST** [*Ruin the Sacred Truths*], p. 43). While transumption acknowledges and yet battles against what Derrida has called supplementarity, the necessary belatedness of all writing, figural interpretation remains trapped in an idealised vision,

which continues to assert that texts can perform that impossible non-supplementary supplementation denied by the full recognition of the belatedness of all text.

What links Bloom's early work on transumptive allusion and his more recent development of a transumptive form of criticism is his engagement with the theory and practice of the ancient Judaeo-Christian heresy, Gnosticism. The reason why Gnosticism has proved such a suitable tradition for Bloom to plunder is perhaps clarified by Hans Jonas, Bloom's main guide in this area of ancient theology. Jonas, in his *The Gnostic Religion,* describes the unique form of interpretation engineered by Gnosticism in its reading of the sacred canon.[10] The Gnostic religion, built on the antagonism between an alien God and an evil demiurge, and paralleled by an agon between the Gnostic adept and the usurping, secondary deity of the natural universe, produces, according to Jonas, an interpretative practice, which can be designated as a form of 'shock tactics'. This interpretative practice, Jonas demonstrates, is pitted directly against the more traditional form of allegorical interpretation. The severity and audacity of this particular manifestation of the revisionary impulse is captured in the Gnostic association of Holy Scripture with the fallen and thoroughly corrupted demiurge.[11] For the Gnostics, to read the Bible is to read the work of the demiurge: to reverse the meaning of the Bible is to pass beyond the word of the demiurge back to the Alien, transmundane Godhead. It is this pattern of alien divinity, demiurge, Gnostic believer and its relation to a form of revisionary reading which so attracts Bloom. The demiurge and his texts can be said to be a 'weakened middle'; a fact which should illustrate the consonance Bloom discovers between the Gnostic worldview, Gnostic forms of misreading and his theory of transumptive criticism.

It must be said here that Bloom's analogy between Gnostic models of misreading and his theory of transumption is not a little tendentious (one must eventually say ideologically determined). Attending to the Gnostic parallels and paradigms employed by Bloom in his development of the theory of transumption highlights the manner in which he constantly seeks to pull his various critical insights into a theory of the essential, unchanging motivations for poetic utterance. A theory of motives orients. Bloom's account of transumption: an account which, as the Gnostic analogies demonstrate, remains highly idiosyncratic, highly patriarchal and highly challengeable. To read Bloom's Gnostic account of transumption is, then, in a sense to read his interpretation of his own critical insight.

As we have seen, Milton's transumptive stance involves a skilful arrangement of precursor poets in a conceptual series. An arrangement of tropes which produces a kind of diachronic spatialisation of time forms the basis, in other words, for Milton's metaleptic reversals. As John Hollander remarks: transumption is that manifestation of 'interpretative or revisionary power which raises the echo even louder than the original'.[12] It is a process of interpreting past tropes which reverses the reliance (the scheme of causality) of the interpretative trope on previous texts and/or tropes. Transumption, at its most successful, produces what Hollander calls an 'ellipsis rather than a relentless pursuit, of further figuration'.[13] When made the exclusive means by which 'strong' poems achieve meaning, however, it necessarily creates a situation in which such an unnaming of the past begins to turn in on itself. The past (and nature) always seems to have the last laugh.

Certainly, if we read transumption as the process by which poems trope on past poetry, and if we read that process as the exclusive technique for the generation of poetic meaning, it becomes clear that there will eventually be far more trope than meaning. This, according to Bloom, is precisely the case and is the inevitable consequence of the kind of transumptive technique instituted by Milton. Bloom writes: 'what he [Milton] could do for himself was the cause of their [the Romantic poets] becoming unable to do the same for themselves. His achievement became at once their starting point, their inspiration, yet also their goad, their torment' (**MM,** pp. 126-7). Transumption, as presented by Bloom, constitutes an internalised history of poetry: the history of poetry becomes equivalent to an intensification of poetic figuration and a decline in poetic meaning. This history, in other words, is centred on a dismal fact. Transumption in Bloom's hands is a phenomenon which could only be employed effectively once, at the moment of its inception. After this moment poetic history necessarily becomes a story of entropic repetition. We need to question Bloom's reading of his own critical trope of transumption. The best way in which we can do this is to look more closely at the internalised history it appears to generate and/or disclose.

II

I have referred to de Bolla's description of the Bloomian 'going beyond' of classical rhetoric as an attempt to bypass the deconstructive focus on the epistemology of the trope. As de Bolla demonstrates, this swerve from deconstructive approaches depends on making rhetoric work on both its axes. De Bolla, as I have stated, develops out of such an approach a description of the transumptive trope as a 'second-order' trope. Such a trope works within the context of a text itself (thus presenting itself as an example of one of the systematised tropes, such as metaphor, metonymy, synecdoche): it also works on a diachronic plane, being the transformation of a particular past trope, a 'first-order' trope.

A transumptive allusion or trope is a poetic lie against time, in that it transforms the tropes on which it is dependent for its meaning. As transumptive readers we, to employ de Bolla's useful terms, have to disfigure or decompose such tropes, measuring the transformations enacted between 'second-order' and 'first-order' tropes, between the transumptive trope and its tropological 'object' (the 'first-order' trope).[14]

Whenever we perform such a transumptive or disfiguring reading we are involved in the only form of literary history Bloom's own severely anti-historical criticism will sanction. Bloom's idea of what constitutes an authentic form of historicism, it should be remembered, depends upon a belief in the possibility of reading from *within* the poetic tradition. Such a mode of 'historicism' depends on a process of disfiguration or, translating the terms back into Bloomian ones, a misreading which is equally a defence and a rhetorical act of persuasion.

De Bolla does not merely help to unpack Bloom's approach to poetic rhetoric, he also helps clarify the implied transformation between Miltonic and Romantic or modern forms of transumption. It is in his distinction between metalepsis and catachresis that de Bolla offers the best opportunity for understanding the difference Bloom would have us observe between Miltonic and Romantic forms of transumption. De Bolla translates these two rhetorical terms into the opposition between *translatio* and *transgressio*.[15] He writes that the latter mode is a 'going beyond', 'a crossing in which the movement between the two domains, the proper and the improper, is only effected with some attendant disturbance'. This kind of 'crossing' or 'translation', he continues, 'cannot be carried out without supplying something that has been elided or erased in the initial crossing'. In such a situation a loss of the 'literal or primary figural base' inevitably occurs. As he writes: 'This in part explains why it is very difficult to isolate second-order tropes formed by catachresis'.[16]

Translating this distinction into the Bloomian account of Miltonic and post-Miltonic forms of transumption, we begin to understand why the trope of transumption undergoes a steady transformation in the post-Enlightenment tradition: a translation which moves such a trope from metalepsis to catachresis. From Milton's explicit arrangement of his precursors in transumptive chains, we move to the ellipsis of all precursors in modern texts. Such a movement can be seen as a translation of Bloom's earlier narrative concerning the history of poetry from pre-Enlightenment meaning to post-Enlightenment belatedness (Milton, and the steady decline after him) into a history of poetic language.

The characteristic feature of modern poetry, then, is its severity of repression, or negation; its generation of meaning through its unnaming of the tropes on which it is increasingly more dependent. No modern poem, according to Bloom, 'merely alludes to another, and what look like overt allusions and even echoes in strong poems are disguises for darker relationships. A strong authentic allusion to another strong poem can be only by and in what the later poem *does not say,* by what it represses' (**BF**, p. 15).

What de Bolla's description of catachretic forms of figuration highlights is that in the interpretation of such forms of rhetoric the reader must 'supply' something to such poems if their transumptive tropes are to be 'disfigured' and so interpreted. This 'something' to be supplied is not merely a reconstituted first-order trope, for such a recuperation of previous tropes merely places the text within a potential or a latent, internalised history. The act of interpretation only properly begins when a measurement is made between the trope and the presumed precursor (first-order) trope. Interpretation only begins, that is, when the interpreter judges the effect of such a relationship between differently context-specific tropes.

The characteristic Bloomian interpretation of such transumptive *histories*—an interpretation which restores them to the psychology of intrapoetic relations—is in no way an inevitable interpretation of such tropological relationships. We cannot escape from the fact (the liberating fact, I would suggest) that the recuperation of such transumptive histories are the product of what Bloom, after Emerson, calls 'the reader's freedom to read'. De Bolla, for example, in analysing the relationship between the trope of desire and the trope of the body in Donne's 'A nocturnal upon St. Lucy's day' and Wordsworth's 'A slumber did my spirit steal', does not, rightly, feel the need to resort to a theory of primary precursorship and intrapoetic agonism in order to explain the relationship between these two poets and their utilisations of these two interrelated tropes.[17] Indeed, pushing the Bloomian theory of diachronic rhetoric towards a theory of properly historical rhetorics, de Bolla emphasises the historical, social and ideological contexts within which specific tropes are troped again. Such contexts, he argues, remain the fundamental criteria for a judgement of the histories internal to any specific second-order trope.[18]

De Bolla brings out the fact that, to judge the meaning of second-order tropes, we must understand the synchronic contexts within which they exist and *mean* before proceeding to compare the differences between them on the basis of such an understanding. The intratextual axis is inextricably linked to the intertextual dimension. Indeed, in making such judgements, the reader enters into the frame of such an interpretative process. The manner in which we perceive these diachronic and synchronic relationships is dependent on the relationship between our discourse, the historical (synchronic) context within which we are positioned, and the influence on that context and thus on our discourse of prior contexts, prior texts.

Bloom's refusal to historicise the *history* of transumptive allusion leads him into an interpretative impasse. Not only do his various theories appear to predetermine the entropic history of language and meaning which takes us from transumption proper to catachresis; without an ability to historicise such a process of intensifying repression and negation, Bloom is forced back on a certain literalisation of his terms. A literalisation, specifically of catachresis, which has led Bloom, in his more recent work, back towards the idealising category of originality.

Before moving on to this area, however, I shall test the points I have made concerning Bloom's account of poetic rhetoric, and particularly transumption, by examining the manner in which Bloom employs the concept in his interpretation of the poetry of Shelley.

COUNTER-READING: TRANSUMPTION AND/IN HISTORY: THE FIGURE OF THE POET AND THE FIGURE OF THE FUTURE IN SHELLEY

In this section I shall demonstrate the manner in which Bloom's ahistorical understanding of his own concept transforms it from a potentially useful and incisive interpretative tool into a principle which blinds Bloom to important elements in Shelley's approach to the issue of poetic influence. I wish through this reading to argue not only that we need to use the concept of transumption to recover the historical dimensions of poetic meaning, but also that if such a concept is to be of use we must understand it as a representation of something— poets' positioning of themselves in relation to tradition—which changes radically through time. Transumption is not merely a technique for understanding the historical dimensions of literary texts, it is a literary technique which is itself subject to historical change.

Bloom's most sustained examination of transumption in Shelley's poetry comes in his **'Shelley and his precursors'**.[19] Here Bloom concentrates on what he describes as 'the transumptive image proper' (**PR**, p. 85), the Judaic trope of God as or in a chariot. This trope, the Merkabah, has its greatest representation in Ezekiel, is taken up in Revelations and then enters into a long series of revisions in the poetic tradition, from Dante through Milton to Shelley. Bloom's implicit argument is that the tradition of 'strong' poetry manifests the primacy of transumption over *figura*. This approach also allows him to produce a reduced account of the overall pattern of Shelley's poetry. What Shelley does with the trope of the chariot comes to symbolise the complete pattern of his poetic career.

Bloom argues that Shelley's failure to revise Milton's priority with regard to this trope in *Prometheus Unbound* finally taught him the true use of such a trope—the transumptive reversal of temporal priority, the effective lying about his position (belated) within tradition. This lesson allowed him, in 'The triumph of life', to attain a limited, highly qualified, agonistic victory over his true precursor, Wordsworth. Accounting for Shelley's engagement with the transumptive trope of the chariot in this way, Bloom is able to produce a developmental narrative of Shelley's career, which hinges on his reading of Wordsworth during the winter of 1814-15 (see **PR,** p. 105).

Bloom's reading functions as a revision of his own earlier readings of Shelley's poetry. Shelley's breakthrough into authentic poethood may come with his acceptance of Wordsworth as precursor, but Bloom argues that Shelley ultimately refused to employ the transumptive trope of the chariot against that precursor (see **PR,** p. 109).

Bloom justifies his reading of Shelley's relation to Wordsworth by moving on to the grand conclusion of *A Defence of Poetry,* a passage I shall turn to at the conclusion of this reading. What needs to be considered here is the basic implication of Bloom's revision of his earlier estimations of Shelley's poetry. Bloom's reading asserts that poetic 'strength' must be judged in terms of the way in which poets succeed in developing a transumptive style, the manner in which they manage to transume their precursors. Bloom's reading suggests that although Shelley attained a degree of control over the trope of transumption, he never managed to exercise it successfully over the poetry of Wordsworth. However, the reader of Shelley's poetry should question this judgement. Reading **'Shelley and his precursors'**, we are forced to entertain the possibility that Bloom may actually be demanding something of Shelley's poetry that it cannot, indeed that it expressly will not, provide.

Such a possibility is bound up with the issue of Shelley's development of what Judith Chernaik calls 'the figure of the poet'.[20] Chernaik writes that 'The emotional power of his [Shelley's] poetry lies in his recognition of the imperatives binding upon the human being powerless to fulfil them, and dependent for what power he has on others of similar frailty'.[21] Shelley's poetry, as Bloom's own reading emphasises, centres on the question of what we might call the positionality of the figure of the poet: an ongoing analysis of the relation between the 'power' that figure is represented as having over itself, the 'power' that outward forces are represented as having over it, and the possible 'power' such a figure might exert over the world. The question which Bloom's account of Shelley and transumption raises is what kind of 'power' does Shelley come to claim for the poet and his work. G. Kim Blank, following Bloom's approach, has reasserted the benefit of analysing Shelley's 'problematic identification with the figurative authority of Wordsworth' in attempting to answer such a question.[22] Blank relies on a narrative of Shelley's career

similar to the one provided by Bloom. He writes of Shelley's career as moving from 'ceremonies of baptism (the rights of admission to Wordsworth's sublime)' to 'exorcism' '(possessed by the "spirit" of Wordsworth, Shelley must free himself from Wordsworth)'. Blank continues: 'The former can be found in Shelley's earliest poetry . . . the latter . . . is evident in some of the poems written in his *annus mirabilis,* from autumn 1818 to early 1820'.[23]

Despite Blank's adoption of Bloomian stances, his comments reaffirm that an analysis of Shelley's direct engagements with Wordsworth's poetry provides the best answers to the question of Shelley's imagining of poetic power and poetic positionality. They also suggest that a useful strategy is to compare and contrast such textual engagements from the period of Shelley's initial reading of Wordsworth's poetry with his later return to the authority of Wordsworth.[24]

If the period around 1814-17 was a transitional one for Shelley then, as Blank demonstrates, a central text in this period becomes Shelley's 'To Wordsworth':

> Poet of Nature, thou hast wept to know
> That things depart which never may return:
> Childhood and youth, friendship and love's first glow,
> Have fled like sweet dreams, leaving thee to mourn.
> These common woes I feel. One loss is mine
> Which thou too feel'st, yet I alone deplore.
> Thou wert as a lone star, whose light did shine
> On some frail bark in winter's midnight roar:
> Thou hast like to a rock-built refuge stood
> Above the blind and battling multitude:
> In honoured poverty thy voice did weave
> Songs consecrate to truth and liberty,—
> Deserting these, thou leavest me to grieve,
> Thus having been, that thou shouldst cease to be.[25]

Although Bloom has not mapped this poem, it is possible to guess what a Bloomian reading of it would be. Such a reading would begin with a mapping of the text's play of image, defence and trope; indeed, the poem does appear to fit within the map of misprision.

The poem starts with images of presence and absence which, in their direct imitation of Wordsworth's characteristic opening move—the recognition of a missing gleam or glory—and yet their implied or latent irony, can be said to be a swerve away from the source, a *clinamen.* Focusing on the images and the rhetorical tropes, a Bloomian reading would remark on the move to synecdochic images of parts for wholes ('Childhood and youth, friendship and love's first glow'), followed by the metonymy of 'One loss'—a metonymy which forms a fine instance of what Bloom calls *kenosis:* an act of self-humbling which humbles the precursor more than the ephebe. The poem then moves on to the striking use of images of 'height' and 'depth' in lines 7-10, a hyperbole of tradition (in terms of the canonical status of the precursor) which begins to create problems in terms of the poem's management of the full movement to poetic 'strength'. Shelley's hyperbolic figuration of Wordsworth ('lone star' shining down on Shelley as ephebe within or actually as the 'frail bark in winter's midnight roar', and then again as a 'rock-built refuge' above 'the blind and battling multitude') leaves Shelley in a rather uncertain position. Shelley positions himself ambiguously between the 'multitude' and the sublime heights of the Wordsworthian precursor. His position between these two extremes ('multitude' = depths, precursor = heights) rules out, from a Bloomian perspective, a description of these lines as Shelley's attainment of a counter-sublime, since Wordsworth's pre-eminent position as guide/teacher remains unquestioned.

The reading at this point becomes rather similar to Bloom's reading of Wallace Stevens's 'The comedian as the letter c'. Failure to manage the *daemonisation* stage of the process of misprision successfully leads to an inconclusive completion of the final two stages in Bloom's map. Passing through the metaphorical (inside/outside) image of the 'weave' of 'Songs consecrate to truth and liberty', Shelley concludes his sonnet not with a final transumption of the precursor—introjecting Wordsworth's power as a property Shelley himself will now take into the future—but with a resistance to such a projection. Blank, who does present a detailed reading of this sonnet, stresses the fact that the conclusion exemplifies that element in 'Shelley's poetry about Wordsworth' in which he 'portrays the older poet as if he were dead',[26] and even more importantly stresses this as only the first stage in Shelley's ultimate resolution of the problem of Wordsworth's poetic authority. Blank describes 'To Wordsworth' as a 'clearing [of] the ground for individual expression'.[27] As a clearing of the ground the poem may be seen as a preparation for Shelley's ultimate achievement of transumptive 'strength', but in terms of the map of misprision it does not offer us an example of that 'strength' in itself. Shelley, at the end of the poem, is left grieving for the 'dead' Wordsworth in a present moment in which his own positionality is uncertain.

This is, of course, only the first phase of a Bloomian reading of 'To Wordsworth'. Having mapped the poem we should move on to a reading in terms of Shelley's scene of instruction with Wordsworth: a reading which would involve a recuperation of the Wordsworthian tropes Shelley is retroping. Such a reading would depend on an 'antithetical' comparison of 'To Wordsworth' with various texts by Wordsworth: these would include *The Excursion*, including the 'Prospectus', and perhaps most significantly Wordsworth's own sonnet to *his* principal precursor, 'London, 1802':

> Milton! thou shoulds't be living at this hour!
> England hath need of thee: she is a fen

> Of stagnant waters; altar, sword, and pen,
> Fireside, the heroic wealth of hall and bower,
> Have forfeited their ancient English dower
> Of inward happiness. We are a selfish men;
> Oh! raise us up, return to us again;
> And give us manners, virtue, freedom, power.
> Thy soul was like a Star, and dwelt apart;
> Thou hadst a voice whose sound was like the sea;
> Pure as the naked heavens, majestic, free,
> So didst thou travel on life's common way,
> In cheerful godliness; and yet thy heart
> The lowliest duties on herself did lay.[28]

Attending to the manner in which Shelley tropes the major tropes in this sonnet helps in understanding the precise criticism Shelley is bringing to bear in his own sonnet. His transumption of Wordsworth's figuration of the positionality of Milton (the redeployment of the figures of the 'star', its separation from and yet influence on the world) establishes Shelley's play on the idea of the tradition of instruction. As Milton was Wordsworth's precursor, so Wordsworth is Shelley's. However, the other major feature of 'London, 1802' taken up by Shelley raises an issue with which the hypothetical Bloomian reading developed so far cannot adequately deal.

Wordsworth's sonnet praises Milton for his occupation of two distinct positions. Milton fulfils the role of the poet as a solitary 'star' and yet he also is praised for his active involvement in common life. Milton, for Wordsworth, is the exemplary poet because he is at one and the same time 'high' and 'low', separate from the common world and yet an active participant within it. Shelley praises the earlier Wordsworth for occupying just such a dual ('high' and 'low') position. Wordsworth was once a teacher and influence (a 'lone star') and yet equally a common man ('honoured poverty'). Examining the Wordsworthian intertexts behind 'To Wordsworth' helps us recognise that Shelley is criticising the later Wordsworth for losing this exemplary dual positionality. Wordsworth has become isolated from the social world and has thus lost his influence upon it.

Hazlitt's similar critique of the 'Lake School' poets some years later actually reverses the figurative structure of Shelley's sonnet. In his chapter on Coleridge in *The Spirit of the Age*, Hazlitt argues that Wordsworth has locked himself up in a watery refuge away from the desert wilderness of contemporary politics and society: 'They [the 'Lakers'] are safely inclosed there. But Mr. Coleridge did not enter with them; pitching his tent upon the barren waste without, and having no abiding place nor city of refuge.'[29] Shelley's earlier account of this retreat reverses the images, placing Wordsworth in a refuge away from the watery realm of contemporary history. What emerges from a comparison between Shelley's and Hazlitt's descriptions of this process is that when we ask where Shelley himself is positioned we find that he occupies a rather similar position to Hazlitt's Coleridge. Shelley is neither in the refuge nor part of the historical ocean/desert. He is neither an influence (star) nor part of the common world of humanity ('blind and battling multitude'). Indeed, like the Poet in *Alastor,* who also is figured being driven along within a 'frail bark', he appears to be the passive victim of influences from both figured realms: he is influenced by the 'star' (precursor) and equally by the sociohistorical realm (rocked within 'winter's midnight roar'). Why the latter source of influence needs to be read as a figuration of the sociohistorical realm becomes clear when we break from Bloom's mode of intratextual reading to an analysis of its intertextual relation to similar figurations in Shelley's work.

P. M. S. Dawson has done much recently to develop our understanding of just how ambiguous Shelley's position was as an intellectual radically committed to social and political revolution. He writes: 'The equivocal class situation of the intellectual stems from the fact that the very logic of the intellectual project will lead him (or her) to prefer the ideals of his class to its practice, but will then leave him to pursue these ideals in a social vacuum.'[30] In the transitional period represented by the *Alastor* volume and the poems immediately succeeding it, Shelley can be said to be working through the implications of and the possibilities available within such an 'equivocal' position. What is most significant for us here is that this developing recognition of and intellectual engagement with his poetic and social position in the poetry of this period appears to depend on or at least construct itself on the same figurative pattern we have located in his sonnet to and about Wordsworth.

In the three translations Shelley composed in 1815, two of which were published in the *Alastor* volume, Shelley extends the themes of 'To Wordsworth',[31] investigating the theme of the community of poets and its relation to the 'multitude / Of blind and maddening men' ('Cavalcante to Dante', ll.5-6) through the same figurations of poetic solitary and watery/stormy social world. In his translation from Moschus, Shelley writes:

> Whose house is some lone bark, whose toil the sea,
> Whose prey the wandering fish, an evil lot
> Has chosen . . .
>
> (ll.10-12)

The vision of earthly tyranny and oppression gained by the 'pure Spirit' at the conclusion of the first part of 'The daemon of the world', also published in the *Alastor* volume, is achieved from a position ('Serene and inaccessibly secure') somewhere in-between the heights and the depths:

> Stood on an isolated pinnacle;
> The flood of ages combating below,

> The depth of the unbounded universe
> Above, and all around
> Necessity's unchanging harmony.
>
> (ll.285-91)

Moving out from the *Alastor* volume itself we can see at least three major examples of the figurative pattern in the following texts written soon after the poems in that volume. The famous description of Prince Athanese returns to the theme of the ideal, dual positionality of the poet, and does so through a redeployment of the figurative pattern I am extracting from 'To Wordsworth':

> Although a child of fortune and of power,
> Of an ancestral name the orphan chief,
>
> His soul had wedded Wisdom, and her dower
> Is love and justice, clothed in which he sate
> Apart from men, as in a lonely tower,
>
> Pitying the tumult of their dark estate.—
> Yet even in youth did he not e'er abuse
> The strength of wealth or thought, to consecrate
>
> Those false opinions which the harsh rich use
> To bind the world they famish for their pride;
> Nor did he hold from any man his dues,
>
> But like a steward in honest dealings tried,
> With those who toiled and wept, the poor and wise,
> His riches and his cares he did divide.
>
> (Poems. ll.29-42)

These lines encapsulate the main features of Shelley's ideal of the figure of the poet. Prince Athanese, replacing the privileges of 'fortune and power' with 'Wisdom', has a sensibility which distinguishes him from common men. Yet his relations to these men is one of pity, instruction and, importantly, involves material as well as spiritual assistance. The image of the Prince 'in a lonely tower' above and yet pitying 'the tumult of their [common men] dark estate' echoes the figures I have examined in 'To Wordsworth', making more explicit the sociohistorical connotations of that poem's version of the 'dark estate', 'winter's midnight roar'. In the two narrative poems of 1817, both of which contain fictional treatments of the French Revolution, *Laon and Cythna* and *Rosalind and Helen* (finished in 1818), the respective poet-figures, Laon and Lionel, are also represented in terms of the twofold position between secluded tower and storm-blown ocean. And yet in these two figures we begin to observe a change in this figurative pattern, the two poet/revolutionary-figures coming to possess a tower-like strength amid the storm environment.

Dawson refers to the passage in which Laon is portrayed 'amid the rocking earthquake steadfast still' standing 'on high Freedom's desert land' like 'A tower whose marble walls the leagued storms withstand'.[32] The truly striking case for our purposes, however, is the following portrayal of Lionel:

He passed amid the strife of men,
And stood at the throne of armed power
Pleading for a world of woe:
Secure as one on a rock-built tower
O'er the wrecks which the surge trails to and fro,
'Mid the passions wild of human kind
He stood, like a spirit calming them;
For, it was said, his words could bind
Like music the lulled crowd, and stem
That torrent of unquiet dream,
Which mortals truth and reason deem,
But is revenge and fear and pride.
Joyous he was; and hope and peace
On all who heard him did abide,
Raining like dew from his sweet talk,
As where the evening star may walk
Along the brink of the gloomy seas,
Liquid mists of splendour quiver.

(Poems. ll.629-46)

Lionel here occupies that desired dual position of separation from the 'passions wild of human kind' and yet direct engagement with the social world. His embodiment of these two interrelated roles make him a 'star' (influence-teacher-guide) to all those around him.

At this point we are perhaps faced with an interpretative decision which takes us to the heart of our response to Bloom's reading of Shelley. Are we to follow a Bloomian reading and interpret these other instances of the figurative pattern we first observed in 'To Wordsworth' as being determined by and having their meaning in Shelley's poetic agon with his precursor, Wordsworth? It is clear that one of the principal sources for this frequently reproduced image-complex in Shelley is Wordsworth's poetry.[33] Indeed, we should go further than this: Wordsworth is crucial for Shelley in this period, both as a major example of poetic authority and as an example or warning of the way not to go as a poet. Wordsworth, in other words, is an ambivalent factor in Shelley's attempt to work through to a proper positioning of himself as a poet.

My brief survey of this image-complex should have demonstrated that the meaning of such a pattern in Shelley's poetry of the period 1814-17 cannot be contained within such an agonistic, intratextual account. The pattern manifests Shelley's personal attempt to confront and find a method of resolving the problematic position of poetry and of the poet him- or herself within contemporary society. What attention to the pattern actually demonstrates, in fact, is that in this early transitional period of his work Shelley was slowly coming to the recognition that, for the poet committed to social revolution, the historical period in which he lived represented a particularly unpropitious time. If the figurations of the desired dual position (the role of influence combined with social rootedness) leave Shelley strangely unpositioned in 'To Wordsworth', this problem is only partially resolved in _Rosalind and Helen_, a poem

in which a poet/hero is imagined within the context of a revolution which, with hindsight, had not fulfilled its promise.

The meaning of this figurative pattern might well be interpreted as the impossibility of proper _presence_ or _position_ (in the sense of radical _influence_) in the present. The present moment does appear to be, to employ Bloom's own phrase 'experientially darkened' in Shelley's poetry of this period. Yet if this is so it is not so much because of Shelley's attempt to transume his precursor; rather, it appears to emerge from that characteristic Shelleyan recognition of the gulf between his ideals and the means to their attainment—the irreconcilability between 'good and the means of good'.

Jerome J. McGann, in his account of the 'second generation' phase of British Romanticism, attempts to revise Bloom's account of the belatedness of these poets by switching the meaning of that term from what we might call a post-formalistic to a properly historical definition.[34] In his 'Shelley's poetry: The judgment of the future', McGann writes: 'From "Alastor" (1816) to the uncompleted "The Triumph of Life" (1822) Shelley's work is marked by a poetic commitment to social melioration and by a reciprocal sense that circumstances seemed forever conspiring against such commitments'.[35] What McGann calls 'Shelley's futurism', which he describes as Shelley's poetic response to such an equivocal position, can usefully be described as his version of transumption, since it is a mode of poetry which does indeed appear to introject the past and project the future at the expense of the present moment. I have not space enough here to analyse the already well-trodden ground of Shelley's utilisation of the Godwinian idea of perfectibility and the education of opinion so fundamental to such an approach. What does need to be stressed is that although such an approach is intricately bound up with an examination of the nature of influence, as a reading of the prefaces to _Laon and Cythna, Prometheus Unbound,_ along with the _Defence_ will amply show, what is being introjected and projected is not a 'power' which can be originated or possessed by any single individual, any particular 'personality'.

Poetry, for Shelley, came to be defined as a medium by and through which the never-to-be-completed drive towards social perfection is channelled. Poets channel this 'power', as Shelley states in the preface to _Prometheus Unbound,_ by clothing it in the 'forms' made available by 'the peculiarity of the moral and intellectual condition of the minds among which they have been produced'. The manner in which poets can introject the past and project the future is, in other words, determined by the influence on them of past and contemporary authors; but what is introjected and projected is neither the property of these past writers nor of the poet being influenced.

All this becomes particularly significant when we move on to Bloom's account of the conclusion of Shelley's *Defence*:

> An unacknowledged legislator is simply an unacknowledged influence, and since Shelley equates Wordsworth with the *Zeitgeist*, it is hardly an overestimate to say that Wordsworth's influence creates a series of laws for a world of feeling and thinking that went beyond the domain of poetry. Very strong poet that he was, Shelley nevertheless had the wisdom and the sadness of knowing overtly what other poets since have evaded knowing, except in the involuntary patterns of their work. Wordsworth will legislate and go on legislating for your poem, no matter how you resist or evade or even unconsciously ignore him.
>
> **(PR,** p. 111)

Bloom, in his final estimate of the shape and significance of Shelley's work, reduces it to the determining influence of Wordsworth. The final paragraph of Shelley's greatest essay on poetry becomes the greatest example of Shelley's inability to turn his transumptive powers on the Father. Wordsworth remains preeminent and is reaffirmed as the influence which 'legislates' the meaning of his poetry. Wordsworth remains beyond transumption, which means that he remains beyond reversal: he is the 'unmoved mover' who controls whatever power Shelley's poetry manages to convince its readers it possesses.

In order to achieve this final assessment Bloom needs to produce a massive revision of what is perhaps Shelley's most famous line: 'Poets are the unacknowledged legislators of the world.' Rejecting the usual interpretation in which the line is read as an assertion that poets are the communicators of a 'power' they may not themselves recognise, Bloom redistributes the lack of acknowledgement (we might say 'blindness') to Shelley himself, thus returning the 'insight' and the 'power' to Wordsworth. Bloom's misreading of the line works to reidentify power with the poet. It also works to impose his theory of the intratextual nature of poetic meaning on a text which, as I have been attempting to assert, rather more conventionally perhaps, attempts to keep separate imitation and influence; attempts, that is, to distinguish between the power poets may exert on one another and the power which 'they may deny and abjure' but which 'they are yet compelled to serve'.

If transumption is an appropriate concept by which to understand Shelley's achieved poetic stance or position, and I would argue that it is, then this is so not because it is the inevitable means by which all post-Miltonic poets gain power or 'strength' but, rather, because it represents effectively the particular response Shelley brought to what he, among others, styled *the spirit of the age*. This spirit of the age included Wordsworth's influence, yet it cannot be reduced to that influence.

Wordsworth himself, for Shelley, was at once the creator and, in another sense, the creation of his age. Poets like Wordsworth, in Shelley's transumptive terms, are products of history as well as being potential producers of future history, and the history of this process is not the history of the 'inter-play of personalities' so much as the inter-play between personality, time and that timeless force Shelley called power. To get closer to Shelley's particular brand of transumption it seems necessary to consider the notion of a form of influence which, because it is directed towards the communication of a mode of social power which each new age must reimagine in its own terms, depends ultimately on the dissolution rather than the imposition of personality on the future. Such an idea, which I believe is Shelley's final position on the issue of influence, allows me to conclude where many accounts of Shelley's work have previously concluded, with the final lines of the 'Ode to the West Wind'. In these lines, Shelley does not project his own 'personality' (in Bloom's sense) into the future, but rather his 'personality', his *voice*, becomes a time-bound medium through which a specifically social 'power', although figured as elemental, is passed on to the future. The 'power' may be constant, akin to the unchanging force behind natural processes, but the medium, the 'words', by which it is communicated and re-embodied is ever changing. Shelley's 'prophecy' is not that his own 'words' will dominate and retain authority over the future, rather it 'trumpet[s]' (heralds—foresees) a future which, unlike the present time, might be capable of embodying the ideal. It seems appropriate to call this poetic stance transumptive; what does not seem appropriate is to call it agonistic:

> Drive my dead thoughts over the universe
> Like withered leaves to quicken a new birth!
> And, by the incantation of this verse,
>
> Scatter, as from an unextinguished hearth
> Ashes and sparks, my words among mankind!
> Be through my lips to unawakened earth
>
> The trumpet of a prophecy! O, Wind,
> If Winter comes, can Spring be far behind?
>
> (Poems. ll.63-70)

TRANSUMPTION, EMERSON AND THE AMERICAN DIFFERENCE

In his article 'Bloom, Freud and America', David Wyatt suggests that the most crucial 'turn' in Bloom's critical career has been his 're-turn' to an analysis of the American tradition in poetry and criticism.[36] Wyatt refers to various comments by Bloom himself which date this crucial redirection of focus to the period around 1965, a dating which makes it coincident with the first appearance in his work of the idea of the anxiety of influence.[37] On the most immediate level, it is possible to state that this attention to the American tradition afforded Bloom the final piece in the historical narrative which underpins his theoretical account of the anxiety of influence. It provides a terminal point in that narrative of the gradual westering of the muse which, in many respects, *is* the theory of the anxiety of influence.

We should remember, as Wyatt does, that a turn is also a trope. If Bloom's work on American tradition is a turn away from his earlier concern with British Romanticism, then it is also a trope. Indeed, it is a 'turn of a previous trope' or the 'trope of a trope': the earlier trope being previously established representations of American tradition. What such a remembering of tropology highlights is that Bloom's invocation of a still nascent American form of 're-centering' interpretation (**MM,** pp. 174-6) has found its fullest expression in the theory of transumption and the idea of a diachronic form of rhetoric: in 'the Emersonian difference, which is to say, the American difference: a diachronic rhetoric, set not only against past tropes, as in Nietzsche, but against the pastness of trope itself, and so against the limitations of traditional rhetoric' (*Agon,* p. 32).

It should already be quite apparent that Bloom's sense of the specificity of the American tradition stems from his reading of Emerson as the 'father' of all American writers, his sense of Emerson as the great American beginning. One could fill many pages with examples of Bloom's representations of Emerson as the 'father' of the American tradition: from statements concerning the literary tradition of America—'an American writer can be Emersonian or anti-Emersonian, but even a negative stance towards Emerson always leads back again to his formulation of the post-Christian American religion of *Self*-Reliance'[38]—to statements concerning the wider cultural identity of America, such as the following: 'The mind of Emerson is the mind of America, for worse and for glory, and the central concern of that mind was the American religion, which most memorably was named "self-reliance"' (*Agon,* p. 145).

This estimate of the place of Emerson in the American tradition allows Bloom to discover within that author's work a variety of transumptive allusion and a form of defensive (and thus diachronic) rhetoric, which he can then style as authentically American. To capture the essence of the transumptive style of reading Bloom extracts from Emerson we should attend to the quotation from 'The oversoul' Bloom employs in his essay **'Ratios'** (**BV,** pp. 7-40), in which he presents one of his most sustained meditations on the power and influence of 'Wrestling Waldo'. The section from the quotation which concerns me at present reads as follows:

> The soul is superior to its knowledge, wiser than any of its works. The great poet makes us feel our own wealth, and then we think less of his compositions. His greatest communication to our mind is to teach us to despise all he has done.

(Quoted **BV,** p. 32)

What Emerson teaches his pupils, then, is that criticism is always prior to literature: the *reader's sublime,* not the *literary sublime,* is the true mode of American tradition. Emerson teaches that the truly seeing soul is, as he states in the famous 'bare-common' passage from 'Nature', 'part or parcel of God'. In the Emersonian scheme, all contexts give way to the priority of the truly seeing soul.

Emerson's strength and rather malforming influence lies in his refusal to choose from among any of the available modes of expression or belief, or at least to set himself against all prior manifestations of the human will. Emerson chose not to choose but rather to rely on his own innate spark, his own 'self'. For Bloom, such a decision makes Emerson the rightful heir of the most extreme forms of revisionism Western traditions have known: Gnosticism and the Lurianic Kabbalah. This decision also tears him loose from the British tradition, Protestant and Romantic, to which he obviously felt most debt and thus most anxiety (see **FCI** [*Figures of Capable Imagination*], p. 75). Emerson's stance, according to Bloom, has generated a subsequent anxiety of influence in the American tradition comparable to the influence-anxieties produced by Milton and Wordsworth in the British tradition.

Bloom finds in the American tradition a fundamental support for his version of literary history. American poetry, we might say, is the last twist in the transumptive chain which stretches from Homer and the Bible through European, post-Enlightenment poetry to the poetry of A. R. Ammons, Elizabeth Bishop and John Ashbery. American poetry, Bloom declares, presents us with 'the last Western Sublime, the great sunset of self-hood in the Evening Land' (**PR,** p. 244). In his preface to **Agon,** Bloom announces that 'The first theologians of agon were the Gnostics of Alexandria, and the final pragmatists of agon were and will be the Americans of Emerson's tradition' (*Agon,* p. viii). In his 1975 review of poetry, Bloom writes that 'America is the evening land, or the last phase of Mediterranean culture, and this late in tradition all reading (and writing) is heavily shadowed by the past.'[39]

Readers of this study should recognise the problem in such representations of the American literary tradition. Bloom wishes to claim a specificity for the American tradition; he wishes, in fact, to retain the possibility of representing discretely different traditions, not merely literary but cultural and/or national. However, such a representation of the American cultural tradition depends on the kind of historical contextualisation which Bloom's version of poetic rhetoric, his Emersonian adherence to the transumptive *reader's sublime,* denies. What is the *cause,* we might ask, for America's place as *the* last great phase of Western culture? What makes the American tradition the culmination of and even the end-game in the history not only of Western revisionism but of Western culture? These questions hover around and within Bloom's whole engagement with American poetry and are continually met by the Bloomian invocation of the great American *beginning*: Wrestling Waldo. The 'peculiar relevance' of Emerson, according to Bloom, 'is that we seem to read him merely by living here, in this place still somehow his, and not our own' (**MM,** p. 171). Emerson, particularly the Emerson of the Optative Mood, the celebrator of an Apollonian 'individualism', is 'the metaphor of "the father", the pragmatic image of the ego ideal, the inescapable precursor, the literary hero, the mind of the United States of America', and if Emerson faded out of view for a while between 1945 and 1965, then he has returned 'as he always must and will, because he is the pragmatic origin of our literary culture'. As Bloom puts it: 'Walt Whitman and Emily Dickinson, Robert Frost and Wallace Stevens, Hart Crane, Elizabeth Bishop and John Ashbery have written the poems of our climate, but Emerson was and is that climate.'[40]

Bloom can represent and analyse American culture because such an activity becomes for him synonymous with reading the work of Emerson, both directly and as it manifests itself in any 'strong' American author. Bloom, it would appear, wishes to remain faithful to what he views as the Emersonian legacy of transumptive criticism and rhetorical acts of *pathos* or persuasion; in other words, the defiant, rhetorical revisionism of all contexts, all prior texts. Emerson is beyond deconstruction (*Agon,* p. 178) because his texts do not present us with *significance* but work to break through into *meaning,* where meaning is defined as 'survival' and 'defence' (**PR** p. 240). Emerson demands that his readers develop a properly American, transumptive mode of criticism, and Bloom would achieve this fideistic critical manoeuvre by developing his attack on all forms of epistemologically or historically oriented modes of reading. Yet, as we have observed, Bloom cannot perform such a critical and theoretical affiliation and, we must say, *repetition,* without presenting the Emersonian tradition as an historically specific tradition. Bloom's account necessarily relies on the language of historical process and contextualisation (the language of periodicity, cultural change and cultural value). Historical projections and presuppositions may be negated by the Bloomian theory of diachronic rhetoric, yet they are indispensable in the employment of such terms as tradition and the form of belatedness Bloom would ascribe to Emerson and his progeny.

Joseph N. Riddel highlights what he calls a 'caesura' in Bloom's presentation of the American tradition. Referring to both Bloom's and Gertrude Stein's projections of the paradoxical combination, in the American tradition, of continuity (last outpost of Western culture, etc.) and discontinuity (new land, virgin soil, etc.) he writes

of a 'catachresis intervening at the crossing or chiasmus' between the 'old' and the 'new'.[41]

Bloom has done much to explain how the figure of catachresis works in the perpetual crossings American poets make in their discontinuous leaps away from and yet paradoxical swervings towards the tradition which engenders them. Riddel's allusion to catachresis, of the dis-membering of the Father, or the discontinuity between present and past states, begins to subvert that explanation, however. What his account can be made to highlight is that, in Bloom's employment of the language of historical specificity, a forgetting of the intertextual links between Emerson and the pre-Emersonian traditions, both American and European, a re-membering of Emersonian 'Giantism', in other words, necessarily threatens the very pitch and tenor of Bloom's whole approach to poetic language and meaning.

The unresolvable claims of discontinuity and continuity threaten either to ruin the specificity of the American tradition by denying it the authentic Father it requires, or to transform Emerson, as representation of that beginning, into a literalised, monumental beginning. In this latter movement, Bloom's work threatens to become a repetition of the Emersonian rhetoric of self-reliance and total discontinuity: de-idealising the American poetic rhetoric of self-reliance in Whitman, Stevens and Ashbery at the expense of a re-idealisation of the Emersonian rhetoric in its representation of Emerson himself (see **MM,** p. 165).

Bloom's attempts to establish Emerson's place within and influence on both American culture and, within that, a still nascent American form of criticism, constitute one of the principal motivations for his recent redefinition of poetic influence. More precisely, we might say that Bloom, confronting an apparent aporia within his own approach, has found it necessary to develop a new theoretical principle in his terminological armoury. This new principle is the theory of historical facticity.

Bloom's interpretative reconstruction of transumptive links between 'strong' American poets reaches a necessary end-point in Emerson and cannot proceed beyond that point without wrecking its entire description of the specificity of that tradition. Bloom, of course, resists the temptation to literalise Emerson's originality and status as Father. For Bloom, Emerson was no literal 'father', no self-begotten original; and yet his 'strength' of repressiveness was so severe that he has become a father to all those Americans living in his wake. Bloom writes: 'But so subtle is Emerson, so much is he our mother as well as our father, that he becomes our child also, for only we can bring forth Wrestling Waldo . . . Emerson's contribution was to invite the gift' (**BV,** p. 36).

What Bloom is attempting to represent in this passage is the uncanniness of Emerson, where the uncanny is that which lies somehow beyond interpretation yet already within every potential reader. The extent of the uncanniness (*originality*) Bloom is ascribing to Emerson can be gauged when we place by the side of this passage the following comment from **Ruin the Sacred Truths**: 'the sublime takes place *between* origin and aim or end, and . . . the only Western trope that avoids both origin and end is the trope of the Father, which is only to say that we do not speak of "Father Nature"' (**RST,** p. 120).

If Emerson is both Father and Mother, then he can be said to be both an antithetical and revisable trope for origins and yet also an unrevisable, unsurpassable trope for origins. Emerson, in this sense, is the Demiurge of American tradition. Emerson is a facticity, which may be equivalent to saying that he is a successful catachresis, a wholly successful unnaming of the past, and so a figure resistant to all contextualisation.

It is interesting to note that in his recent interpretation of the J-writer, Bloom again relies on the 'trope of the Mother' in order to represent the facticity of that, for Bloom, most uncanny and original of all writers. We are brought back to Bloom's 'catastrophe theory' of meaning here, his assertion that meaning can only get started by 'catastrophes at our origins' (**Agon,** p. 43-4).

It would appear that Bloom, wishing to explain cultural history in terms of an agonistic process of (Oedipal) conflict and revision, is forced to rely on the trope (myth) of the primal Mother (literal meaning, origins, death) in order to set the whole process going and to redirect it at specific points along the way. Apart from highlighting the fundamentally patriarchal nature of Bloom's vision of poetry and culture, such a reversion to the 'trope of the Mother' also highlights the impasse built into his critical system, its inability to account properly for transformations in the literary and cultural tradition. Such an impasse is generated by Bloom's refusal to recognise the determining effects of historical contexts on textual traditions. The theory of facticity, as I have suggested, represents Bloom's most recent and most severe attempt to evade such a recognition.

Notes

1. For John Hollander on the metaleptic troping upon the leaves, see *The Figure of Echo: A mode of allusion in Milton and after* (Berkeley, Los Angeles and London: California University Press, 1981), p. 120-2; for Bloom's earlier work on this trope, see MM, pp. 135-9.

2. Peter de Bolla, *Harold Bloom: Towards historical rhetorics* (New York and London: Routledge, 1988), p. 121. I am indebted to de Bolla for my discussion of diachronic rhetoric and transumption in this chapter.

3. John Hollander, op. cit., p. 99.

4. Ibid., pp. 64-72.

5. Ibid., p. 64.

6. Ibid., p. 62.

7. Puttenham is quoted in Hollander, op. cit., p. 142 and by Bloom in MM, p. 103.

8. Harold Bloom, 'James Dickey: From "The other" through *The Early Motion*', in *The Southern Review* 21, 1 (1985), p. 73.

9. For a useful analysis of Bloom's Judaic critique of the concept of *figura,* see Susan Handelman's *The Slayers of Moses: The emergence of rabbinic interpretation in modern literary theory* (Albany: State University of New York Press, 1982), pp. 186-8. For an analysis of Bloom's distinction between transumption and *figura* in the context of modern theories of revisionism, see Jean-Pierre Mileur, *Literary Revisionism and the Burden of Modernity,* pp. 100-19. For Erich Auerbach's work on *figura,* see his 'Figura', in *Scenes in the Drama of European Literature* (1959), 2nd edn (Manchester: Manchester University Press, 1984), pp. 11-76: see also *Mimesis: The representation of reality in western literature* (1946), 3rd edn, trans. William R. Trask (Princeton: Princeton University Press, 1968), pp. 73-6, 156-62, 194-202. For Bloom's criticisms of Auerbach, see PR, pp. 87-92 and RST, pp. 38-50.

10. Hans Jonas, *The Gnostic Religion: The message of the alien god and the beginnings of Christianity* (1958), 2nd edn, revised (London: Routledge, 1992). See the section on 'Gnostic allegory', pp. 91-9.

11. Bloom has pursued his association between American poetics and the Gnostic tradition in various Chelsea House introductions: see, for example, *Nathanael West's 'Miss Lonelyhearts'*, Modern Critical Interpretations (New York: Chelsea House, 1987), pp. 1-9; *Herman Melville's 'Moby-Dick'*, Modern Critical Interpretations (New York: Chelsea House, 1986), pp. 1-11; *Thomas Pynchon's 'Gravity's Rainbow'*, Modern Critical Interpretations (New York: Chelsea House, 1986), pp. 1-9.

12. John Hollander, op. cit., p. 114.

13. Ibid., p. 115.

14. See Peter de Bolla, 'Disfiguring history', in *Diacritics* 16, 4 (1986), pp. 49-58.

15. Peter de Bolla, *Harold Bloom: Towards historical rhetorics,* pp. 134-43.

16. Ibid., p. 133.

17. Ibid., pp. 135-43.

18. Ibid., p. 136.

19. See PR, pp. 83-111. The conclusion of this essay is republished in an extended form in Bloom's Preface to *Shelley's Prose or The Trumpet of a Prophecy* (1954), 3rd edn, ed. David Lee Clark (London: Fourth Estate, 1988).

20. Judith Chernaik, *The Lyrics of Shelley* (Cleveland and London: Case Western Reserve University Press, 1972), pp. 8-31.

21. Ibid., p. 30.

22. G. Kim Blank, *Wordsworth's Influence on Shelley: A study of poetic authority* (London: Macmillan, 1988), p. 4.

23. Ibid., pp. 5-6.

24. Timothy Clark's re-evaluation of the concept of 'sensibility' in Shelley also highlights the period between 1815-1817 as a crucial phase. It was in 1815 that Shelley first began to formulate his 'science of mind' which, as Clark demonstrates, represents a rigorous analysis of the positionality of the poet conceived as a particularly receptive/sensitive being: see Timothy Clark, *Embodying Revolution: The figure of the poet in Shelley* (Oxford: Clarendon Press, 1989).

25. 'To Wordsworth' in *The Poems of Shelley,* vol. 1, 1804-17, Geoffrey Matthews and Kelvin Everest (eds) (London and New York: Longman, 1989). All further references to poems in the *Alastor* volume will be from this edition. All other references will be taken from *Shelley: Poetical works* (1905), ed. Thomas Hutchinson, new edn corrected by G. M. Matthews (Oxford: Oxford University Press, 1970) and will be cited as Poems with line numbers following.

26. G. Kim Blank, op. cit., p. 6.

27. Ibid., p. 69.

28. See 'London, 1802' in *William Wordsworth: The poems,* 2 vols, ed. John O. Hayden, vol. 1 (Harmondsworth: Penguin, 1977), pp. 579-80.

29. William Hazlitt, *Complete Works,* Centenary Edition, 21 vols, *The Spirit of the Age* and *Conversation of James Northcliffe, Esq., R.A.,* vol. 11, ed. P. P. Howe (London and Toronto: J. M. Dent, 1932), pp. 37-8.

30. P. M. S. Dawson, 'Shelley and class', in *The New Shelley: Later twentieth-century views,* ed. G. Kim Blank (London: Macmillan, 1990), pp. 34-41. See also Dawson's *The Unacknowledged Legislator: Shelley and politics* (Oxford: Clarendon Press, 1980).

31. See 'Translated from the Greek of Moschus', 'Sonnet from the Italian of Dante Alighieri' and 'Guido Cavalcanti to Dante Alighieri' in Matthews and Everest. Blank, in *Wordsworth's Influence on Shelley,* argues for the close thematic relationship between the Cavalcanti translation and 'To Wordsworth' (p. 48). Richard Holmes makes a similar point in *Shelley: The pursuit* (1974), 2nd edn (Harmondsworth: Penguin, 1987), p. 308.

32. P. M. S. Dawson, *The Unacknowledged Legislator,* p. 70.

33. A full analysis of the influence of Wordsworth on Shelley's use of this image-complex would, as I have already suggested, need to examine his revisionary reading of *The Excursion.* See *The Excursion* (1814) (Oxford and New York: Woodstock Books, 1991). The manner in which the various roles and positions I have been examining in Shelley's figure of the poet can be said to be separated out among the different characters in Wordsworth's poem is clearly an important issue, one with poetic and ideological implications.

34. Jerome J. McGann, *Romantic Ideology: A critical investigation* (Chicago and London: University of Chicago Press, 1983), p. 111.

35. Ibid., p. 118.

36. David Wyatt, 'Bloom, Freud and America', in *The Kenyon Review* 6, 3 (1984), pp. 59-66.

37. It was in 1965 that Bloom published his first major essay on Emerson and the American tradition 'The central man: Emerson, Whitman, Wallace Stevens' (RT [*The Ringers in the Tower*], pp. 217-33) and there is a degree of reflexivity in Bloom's subsequent dating of the revival of Emerson's reputation in the American canon: see Bloom *Henry David Thoreau's 'Walden',* Modern Critical Interpretations (New York: Chelsea House, 1987), pp. 1-2. See also Bloom's 'Mr. America' in *New York Review of Books,* 22 November 1984, p. 19; this essay is reprinted in revised form as 'Emerson: power at the crossing' in PI [*Poetics of Influence*], pp. 309-23 (see p. 309).

38. *Henry James's 'The Portrait of a Lady',* Modern Critical Interpretations (New York: Chelsea House, 1987), p. 2.

39. 'Harold Bloom on poetry', in *The New Republic,* 29 November 1975, p. 24.

40. *Henry David Thoreau's 'Walden',* op. cit., pp. 1-2.

41. Joseph N. Riddel, 'Juda becomes New Haven', in *Diacritics* 10, 2 (1980), pp. 17-18.

Bibliography

WORKS BY BLOOM

The Ringers in the Tower: Studies in Romantic tradition (Chicago and London: University of Chicago Press, 1971).

A Map of Misreading (New York: Oxford University Press, 1975).

Kabbalah and Criticism (New York: Seabury Press, 1975).

'Harold Bloom on poetry', in *The New Republic,* 29 November 1975, pp. 24-6.

Poetry and Repression: Revisionism from Blake to Stevens (New Haven and London: Yale University Press, 1976).

Figures of Capable Imagination (New York: Seabury Press, 1976).

Wallace Stevens: The poems of our climate (Ithaca and London: Cornell University Press, 1977).

Deconstruction and Criticism, ed. Harold Bloom (New York: Seabury Press, 1979).

Agon: Towards a theory of revisionism (New York: Oxford University Press, 1982).

The Breaking of the Vessels (Chicago and London: University of Chicago Press, 1982).

'Mr. America', in *New York Review of Books,* 22 November 1984, pp. 19-24.

'James Dickey: From "The other" through *The Early Motion*', in *The Southern Review* 21, 1 (1985), pp. 63-78.

Modern Critical Interpretations, 132 vols (New York: Chelsea House, 1985-).

Modern Critical Views, Series 1, 115 vols (New York: Chelsea House, 1985-).

Preface, in *Shelley's Prose or The Trumpet of a Prophecy* (1954), 3rd. edn, corrected, ed. David Lee Clark (London: Fourth Estate, 1988).

Ruin the Sacred Truths: Poetry and belief from the Bible to the present (Cambridge, Mass. and London: Harvard University Press, 1989).

The Book of J, trans. David Rosenberg, interpreted Harold Bloom (London: Faber and Faber, 1991).

Secondary Works

Auerbach, Erich, *Mimesis: The representation of reality in western literature* (1946), 3rd edn, trans. William R. Trask (Princeton: Princeton University Press, 1968).

Auerbach, Eric, *Scenes in the Drama of European Literature* (1959), 2nd edn (Manchester: Manchester University Press, 1984).

Blank, G. Kim, *Wordsworth's Influence on Shelley: A study of poetic authority* (London: Macmillan, 1988).

Bolla, Peter de, 'Disfiguring history', in *Diacritics* 16, 4 (1986), pp. 49-58.

Bolla, Peter de, *Harold Bloom: Towards historical rhetorics* (New York and London: Routledge, 1988).

Chernaik, Judith, *The Lyrics of Shelley* (Cleveland and London: Case Western Reserve University Press, 1972).

Clark, Timothy, *Embodying Revolution: The figure of the poet in Shelley* (Oxford: Clarendon Press, 1989).

Dawson, P. M. S., *The Unacknowledged Legislator: Shelley and politics* (Oxford: Clarendon Press, 1980).

Dawson, P. M. S., 'Shelley and class', in *The New Shelley: Later twentieth-century views,* ed. G. Kim Blank (London: Macmillan, 1990), pp. 34-41.

Handelman, Susan A., *The Slayers of Moses: The emergence of rabbinic interpretation in modern literary theory* (Albany: State University of New York Press, 1982).

Hazlitt, William, *Complete Works,* Centenary Edition, 21 vols, ed. P. P. Howe (London and Toronto: J. M. Dent, 1930-4).

Hollander, John, *The Figure of Echo: A mode of allusion in Milton and after* (Berkeley, Los Angeles and London: California University Press, 1981).

Holmes, Richard, *Shelley: The pursuit* (1974), 2nd edn (Harmondsworth: Penguin, 1987).

Jonas, Hans, *The Gnostic Religion: The message of the alien god and the beginnings of Christianity* (1958), 2nd edn, revised (London: Routledge, 1992).

McGann, Jerome J., *Romantic Ideology: A critical investigation* (Chicago and London: University of Chicago Press, 1983).

Mileur, Jean Pierre, *Literary Revisionism and the Burden of Modernity* (Berkeley and Los Angeles: California University Press, 1985).

Milton, John, *Paradise Lost,* ed. Alastair Fowler (London: Longman, 1971).

Riddel, Joseph N., 'Juda becomes New Haven', in *Diacritics* 10, 2 (1980), pp. 17-34.

Shelley, P. B., *Shelley: Poetical Works* (1905), ed. Thomas Hutchinson, new edn corrected by G. M. Matthews (Oxford: Oxford University Press, 1970).

Shelley, P. B., *The Poems of Shelley,* vol. 1, 1804-17, Geoffrey Matthews and Kelvin Everest (eds) (London and New York: Longman, 1989).

Stevens, Wallace, *Wallace Stevens: The palm at the end of the mind,* ed. Holly Stevens (New York: Vintage Books, 1972).

Wordsworth, William, *William Wordsworth: The Poems,* 2 vols, ed. John O. Hayden (Harmondsworth: Penguin, 1977).

Wordsworth, William, *The Excursion* (1814) (Oxford and New York: Woodstock Books, 1991).

Wyatt, David, 'Bloom, Freud, and America', in *The Kenyon Review* 6, 3 (1984), pp. 59-66.

Susan M. Schultz (essay date spring 1996)

SOURCE: Schultz, Susan M. "'Returning to Bloom': John Ashbery's Critique of Harold Bloom." *Contemporary Literature* 37, no. 1 (spring 1996): 24-48.

[In the following essay, Schultz outlines Bloom's commentary on poet John Ashbery's work and focuses on Ashbery's mixed response to such critical scrutiny.]

In the struggle of the reader both with and against a strong poem, more than an interpretation of a poem becomes the prize. What instruction is more valuable than that which shows us how to distinguish real or illusory dangers to the self's survival, and how to ward off the real menaces?

Harold Bloom, *Agon: Towards a Theory of Revisionism*

I shall keep to myself.
I shall not repeat others' comments about me.

John Ashbery, "Wet Casements"

That critics write about poets is no surprise; what is surprising are those moments when a poet directly confronts and addresses his critics and the content of their work. One of these moments—attenuated, most certainly—occurs in John Ashbery's *Flow Chart* (1991), the book that comes closest to being an autobiography of the poet's career. In this book-length poem, Ashbery takes on the critic most responsible for elevating him into the canon, at some times comically and at others caustically; his critique of his foremost critic is, to steal one of Harold Bloom's favorite words, "strong." This criticism is so strong, and comes so late in the professional relationship between the two men, because—even as Ashbery possesses evident staying power in the twentieth-century canon of American poets—the bloom on Bloom's reputation has, over the past decade, faded. As Marjorie Perloff puts it, rather more dramatically, "Then suddenly the bubble seems to have burst. By the mid-1980s, younger poets were no longer lining up to receive the Bloomian accolade, and graduate students seemed barely to know who Bloom was" (161).

Yet however much critics cultural, feminist, New Historicist, and otherwise (those he refers to in his recent book *The Western Canon* as "the School of Resentment" and a "rabblement of lemmings" [4]) have come to displace Bloom, he cannot so easily be dismissed from the very history he often elides. His rather straightforward Freudian theory of the "anxiety of poetic influence," bolstered by arcane vocabularies borrowed from mystical religious texts, may sound to the ear of today's critics tinny and out of touch with social and historical concerns. But the reputations of Wallace Stevens and John Ashbery, while they would likely have ascended of their own luminosity without Bloom, would not have done so as quickly without his agency.

Among contemporaries, John Ashbery has been the foremost beneficiary of Bloom's marketing strategy. Ashbery, who represents the end of literary history (at least thus far) for Bloom, became one of the unwitting agents of Bloom's own rise in his profession. Bloom's career within the academy has been virtually unparalleled: he has his own department at Yale University and

also teaches at New York University; he won the coveted, if mysteriously proferred, MacArthur Award in 1985; he was, in 1987-88, the Charles Eliot Norton Professor of Poetry at Harvard University (Allen xvii). His books, if you include the Chelsea House collections of essays on writers, which he edits and introduces, number over one hundred, with hundreds more planned. He has been featured in national news magazines and in *The New York Times Magazine* (Begley). This is not to say that Bloom could not have achieved such prominence without Ashbery. But Bloom, like the prophet he sometimes proclaims himself to be, needed a contemporary hero, and Ashbery, often in conjunction with A. R. Ammons, just happened to fill those shoes.

This dual career history becomes more interesting if we consider that Bloom and Ashbery are nearly exact contemporaries (Ashbery was born in 1927, Bloom in 1930) and that Ashbery's career has occasionally dovetailed with that of his critic. Ashbery, for example, also won a MacArthur Award in 1985 and was the Norton Lecturer at Harvard in 1989-90, right after Bloom's stint there ended.[1] The dovetailing of their career paths illustrates the way in which critics and poets have come to play on the same field with one another. This does not mean that the poets are the players and critics the referees; Bloom makes it clear that he, too, is a player. Asked why he had embarked on the outrageously ambitious Chelsea House project of editing and introducing over eight hundred critical anthologies about writers, he told David Lehman, abiding by the strictures of his own theory of influence: "It makes me feel like Milton's Satan. You know, the authors are God, and what keeps me going is this feeling that it's a kind of hopeless struggle with them" (56). Bloom has claimed repeatedly that criticism is creative rather than parasitical, a notion that puts Bloom directly into competition with his poet-hero and renders their relationship more problematic than that of a father-critic and son-poet, as Bloom seems often to portray them, despite their similar ages.

If you believe Bloom's theory, which owes its force to Freudian notions of the oedipal complex, there can be no relationship more problematic than that between fathers and sons; that "complex" is in fact the governing trope for the relationship between poets and their precursors, as Bloom tells it. In Bloom's theory, every "strong" or "great" poet is forced to confront his strong precursors (as Ashbery confronts Stevens, or Stevens, Emerson) and find a way to avoid falling into imitation. How this happens is that the younger poet "misreads" his precursor, in a process that Bloom labels "misprision." The task grows increasingly difficult over time, since poets are more and more the "belated" members of an old tradition: less and less material is original; more and more of it depends on prior poems. Since the publication of *The Anxiety of Influence* in 1973, Bloom has used his theory to map out American literary history, always emphasizing the romantic strain of that literature. His canon moves from Emerson to Whitman to Stevens, not from Eliot and Pound to Charles Olson and Charles Bernstein, as many critics—notably Marjorie Perloff and Jerome J. McGann—would have it. Like Oswald Spengler, Bloom sees history as the repetition of pattern rather than the elaboration of accidents or differences. In that sense, it can be—and has been—argued that his theory is ahistorical.[2]

Bloom's theory allows him to build a very personal canon and to give it the credence of a system, even as he admits to its idiosyncrasies. In a November 1975 review in *The New Republic,* entitled "Harold Bloom on Poetry," Bloom suggests that all canons directly reflect the critic's tastes; he denies the possibility of objectivity in criticism. And so he writes that, were Hugh Kenner writing the review, Kenner would choose to include books by George Oppen, Louis Zukofsky, and Charles Olson, since his "central American poets of the century" were Pound, Eliot, and Williams (24). "I myself prefer E. A. Robinson, Frost, Stevens, and Hart Crane, who seem to me the rightful inheritors of Emerson, Whitman, and Dickinson," Bloom continues. Then this intense admirer of poets curiously distinguishes between himself and "[i]dealizers of poetry, of teaching and of criticism" who say that "*they* read accurately and selflessly," for "such an assertion is always a self-deception" (24). Within the space of a few sentences, he turns this confession of subjectivity into a global rule, placing America in the context of his own theory of belatedness: "America is the Evening Land, or the last phase of Mediterranean culture, and this late in tradition all reading (and writing) is heavily shadowed by the past" (24). By this point, he has mustered a sweeping generalization about world culture as a defense for his own admitted defensiveness: "Where the shadow is so long and so dark, reading and writing inevitably manifest defensive patterns, whatever the overt intentions and ideals of readers or writers" (24). More recently, Bloom has positioned himself as a guardian of aestheticism, besieged by what, in conversation, he calls a "rabblement of lemmings" (Begley 34) whose work is governed more by ideology than by a pure love of literature, which Bloom would claim, contra his critics, has no ideology at all.

Bloom himself writes in *A Map of Misreading* (1975), "As literary history lengthens, all poetry necessarily becomes verse-criticism, just as all criticism becomes prose-poetry" (3). In *Agon: Towards a Theory of Revisionism* (1982), Bloom suggests that strong poems are ones that engender strong critics: "A strong poem, which alone can become canonical for more than a single generation, can be defined as a text that must engender strong misreadings, both as other poems and as literary criticism" (285). Bloom himself acknowl-

edges that his narrative of Ashbery's importance likely differs from Ashbery's own sense of himself; at the same time, he suggests that poets cannot do without their critics, just as they cannot do without their precursors. Ashbery's crucial precursor, for Bloom, is Wallace Stevens, whose poetic fathers (hence one-sided sparring partners) were Emerson and Whitman. In *Figures of Capable Imagination* (1976), Bloom notes Ashbery's likely disapproval of his reading of his work and then goes on nonetheless to assert the truth of that reading, a truth that is also a genealogy: "Ashbery (who is not likely to be pleased by this observation) is at his best when he is neither revitalizing proverbial wisdom nor barely evading an ellipsis, but when he dares to write most directly in the idiom of Stevens" (172). The poet, then, is at his best not when he is most himself (and his use of proverbial clichés does distinguish Ashbery from other poets, including Stevens), but when he fits neatly into Bloom's scheme of influence—when he is most like Stevens. Bloom's argument has had ramifications in the popular press and in literary journals, as well as in academe. Paul Gray's brief 1976 review of *Self-Portrait in a Convex Mirror* in *Time* magazine includes the following comment, which mirrors Bloom's: "This is the gaudy tightrope mode of Wallace Stevens, and few poets since Stevens have been able to escape the pit of arrant gibberish that yawns below" (96). In his review of the book for *Poetry,* Richard Howard invokes Stevens and Bloom, albeit dismissively, noting that "Harold Bloom was so quick to seize upon it ["As You Came from the Holy Land"], exhibit A in the endless catalogue of belatedness which for him constitutes poetry's knowledge of itself" (350). Gray's connection between Stevens and Bloom, as well as Howard's very anxiety about Bloom's interpretation of Ashbery's poem, speaks to the influence of Bloom's theory on discussions of the poet's work in 1976.

Again and again, Bloom aims to *correct* Ashbery's attempts to position himself in ways different from Bloom's. For the poet, according to Bloom's definition of him, necessarily misunderstands his own motivations: "To live as a poet," he writes in *Figures of Capable Imagination,* "a poet needs the illusive mist about him that shields him from the light that first kindled him" (174). To be a critic is, by extension, to penetrate that mist, clarify the situation, or misread the misreading. Bloom's strategy is notable for its being so personal, as if literary history were Bloom's reading of it. Aside from his characteristic opening anecdote about the first time he encountered a poet's work (most notable in this genre is his story about reading Hart Crane at the age of ten),[3] Bloom goes to great pains to separate his own interpretations from Ashbery's, and then to proclaim the truth of his own reading, in contrast to the relative mistiness of the poet's. A poet's value is located in the fact that he compels Bloom to read and reread his work: "But this I think is part of Ashbery's true value; only he and Ammons among poets since Stevens compel me to re-read so often, and then reward such labor" (*Figures* [*Figures of Capable Imagination*] 200). Then, in commenting on thirteen pages in *Three Poems* (1972), Bloom writes, and the emphasis is his, not mine: "I suspect that these [pp. 73-86] are, *for Ashbery,* the most important pages in his book, but except for the lovely pathos of a dreamer's defense, they are too much the work of a poet who wishes to be more of an anomaly than he is, rather than the 'central' kind of a poet he is fated to become, in the line of Emerson, Whitman, Stevens" (206).[4] Ashbery, according to this narrative, is a weak reader of his own work, whereas Bloom's reading represents nothing less than "fate." Bloom's theory depends on a poet's being both an anomaly (a solitary figure caught in a life-and-death tussle with his "fathers") and a predictable part of a chain of being. He would, I suspect, be the last to deny that this chain includes Bloom. The critic poses a further resistance to the poet by making his work more difficult, thus acting like another precursor figure, someone prior to—not contemporary with—the poet:

> One of the functions of criticism, as I understand it, is to make a good poet's work even more difficult for him to perform, since only the overcoming of genuine difficulties can result in poems wholly adequate to an age consciously as late as our own. All that a critic, as critic, can give poets is the deadly encouragement that never ceases to remind them of how heavy their inheritance is.

(Map [*A Map of Misreading*] 10)

There is evidence within Ashbery's poems, as I will show, that he has read or listened to Bloom, that he knows the role he is meant to play in Bloom's theory, and that his attitude toward the theory, and the visionary tradition from which it springs, is one of extreme ambivalence. Ashbery's feelings are mixed, I presume, because (at least in the middle of his career, as it now stands) he may have relied on Bloom, consciously or unconsciously, to make his reputation, at the same time that he wanted to avoid seeming to write his poetry so that it would fit into the critic's preordained scheme of things. A strong poet would never submit to a strong theory; even Bloom would concede that point and, in so doing, emphasize the inherent competition between poets and critics. (Unlike A. R. Ammons, for example, Ashbery has dedicated no poems to Bloom.[5] Nor—and this is doubtless deliberate—does he speak very cogently in interviews about his and Bloom's work. But, as Bloom will tell you, poets are the first to lie about such things.) In a 1977 interview, which he edited in 1980, Ashbery claimed that having an audience had not changed his work, because "After I gained a certain amount of recognition, I realized that this recognition had arrived precisely because of this work which I felt was never going to achieve any, and therefore if I were to continue to get recognition, I would have to continue

in the same way" (Interview 13). In other words, if your success depends on writing as if you were in a vacuum, you must keep doing so even if spectators appear; your success depends upon your lack of an expectation of success. In *Flow Chart,* Ashbery rephrases this sentiment as follows: "Surely, in my younger / days people acted differently about it. There was no barnstorming, just quiet / people going about their business and not worrying too much about / being rewarded at the end when it came down to that" (14). Furthermore, he reports in the 1977 interview: "I rarely discuss my poetry. I find it distasteful. I'd rather not know much about it myself" (14).

Ashbery's strategy during the 1970s when, not coincidentally, both his and Bloom's reputations were made was one of entertaining Bloomian ideas (often wittily) even as his notion of literary history—any history—obviously diverged from Bloom's. Most notably, Ashbery argues against theory as an ahistorical reading of historical (specifically art historical) events. This split emerges most clearly in "Self-Portrait in a Convex Mirror" (1975), where Ashbery writes less about the portrait itself than about the ongoingness of the daily activities surrounding it. Such a notion of time, which has obvious effects on one's conception of "works" of art, links him with certain of his contemporaries, including Elizabeth Bishop who, in her valedictory "Poem," from *Geography III,* argues against momentary "visions," or those which are lifted out of time. Instead, she is most interested in "looks," which are best represented for her in what might otherwise be termed "bad art." Her earlier poem "Large Bad Painting" also bears out this revision of the romantic/modernist notion of art as something that organizes, and hence redeems, history.[6] Like Bishop's, however, Ashbery's "looks" are often redemptive, if not, strictly speaking, visionary.

In "Litany," published in the 1979 collection *As We Know,* Ashbery's own literary criticism appears in the form of a "verse epistle," after Alexander Pope. Better yet, it is an "essay on criticism," or an essay *of* criticism. It may in some ways be as old-fashioned as Pope, for Ashbery suggests that the critic ought not to consider himself more than a handmaiden to the poet:

> Therefore a new school of criticism must be developed.
> First of all, the new
> Criticism should take into account that it is we
> Who made it, and therefore
> Not be too eager to criticize us: we
> Could do that for ourselves, and have done so.

(34)

Ashbery emphasizes the importance of the critic's work to bringing forth poetry's "*enchant[ment]*" (33), and the (tongue-in-cheek) need for critics to address themselves to "*your average baker or cheerleader.*"

What follows Ashbery's emphasis on the relative importance of poetry and criticism is an attempt completely to de-authorize the very genre of criticism:

> Nor
> Should it take itself as a fitting subject
> For critical analysis, since it knows
> Itself only through us, and us
> Only through being part of ourselves, the bark
> Of the tree of our intellect.
>
> (34-35)

The critic ought to confine himself to barking rather than to biting, Ashbery more than implies. But he does not go so far as to name his critics; in these passages he attacks the genre more than any specific perpetrator of it.

In his poems of the 1960s and 1970s, Ashbery distinguishes between ways of organizing time. Bloom knows that the critic's function is to stop time—chart it—in order to tell it better: "Criticism may not always be an act of judging; but it is always an act of deciding, and what it tries to decide is meaning" (*Map* 3). One of his books is, of course, a "map" of misreading. Ashbery, on the other hand, often emphasizes the waywardness of the compass, preferring the journey to its end, the murkiness of daily experience to its apotheosis in masterpieces. In "Soonest Mended," published in the late 1960s in *The Double Dream of Spring,* he writes:

> Night after night this message returns, repeated
> In the flickering bulbs of the sky, raised past us, taken
>   away from us,
> Yet ours over and over until the end that is past truth,
> The being of our sentences, in the climate that fostered
>   them,
> Not ours to own, like a book, but to be with, and
>   sometimes
> To be without, alone and desperate.
> But the fantasy makes it ours, a kind of fence-sitting
> Raised to the level of an esthetic ideal.
>
> (18)

Fence-sitting is not an option that Robert Frost considered; his wall required mending, even if that mending was a convenient fiction for an awkward and ambivalent sense of community. Ashbery here decides not to decide, and his refusal "to grow up," in this poem and others, is equally a refusal to buy fully into a "visionary company," even as the lines also echo that company: "Yet ours over and over until the end that is past truth" retains the visionary sweep of Keats and Crane. Perhaps, he seems to suggest, such vision requires that the poet never (as happened literally in the case of Crane) graduate:

> Better, you said, to stay cowering
> Like this in the early lessons, since the promise of
>   learning

> Is a delusion, and I agreed, adding that
> Tomorrow would alter the sense of what had already
>   been learned,
> That the learning process is extended in this way, so
>   that from this standpoint
> None of us ever graduates from college[.]
>
> (18-19)

Yet Ashbery's debunking of that tradition is constant. In "Self-Portrait in a Convex Mirror," Ashbery is more interested in what gets lost than in what gets captured; he is less taken by theory than by what escapes it:

> Each person
> Has one big theory to explain the universe
> But it doesn't tell the whole story
> And in the end it is what is outside him
> That matters, to him and especially to us
> Who have been given no help whatever
> In decoding our own man-size quotient and must rely
> On second-hand knowledge. Yet I know
> That no one else's taste is going to be
> Any help, and might as well be ignored.
>
> (*Self-Portrait* [*Self-Portrait in a Convex Mirror*] 81-82)

This is as antitheoretical a statement of theory as one might want to locate, and it finds its most apt response in Bloom, for whom such statements are anathema, as when he writes about "Ashbery's zeal in tacitly rejecting a poetry of privileged moments or privileged phrases." This zeal, it is clear to Bloom, is a waste of energy: "But this zeal is misplaced, and almost impossible to sustain, as will be seen in his later development" (*Figures* 177). Ashbery, in other words, came to his senses, which meant that he came to Bloom's senses.

Ashbery's "later development" can be read as a continuation of this antitheoretical line of argument—not so much development as repetition. Temporal reality in Ashbery is always an "emulsion" rather than a "negative" or a "print" or "portrait" in the conventional sense of the term (another way of saying this is that his portraits are more like Gertrude Stein's than like Parmigianino's). Early in *Flow Chart,* Ashbery describes the painting as something potentially moving, not fixed: "the point is one was going to do to it / what mattered to us, and all would be correct as in a painting / that would never ache for a frame but dream on as nonchalantly as we did" (8).

Yet memoirs generally rely on frames rather than nonchalance as their organizing principles, and the notion of a career (great or otherwise) depends on there being development and progress in a person's work. So Ashbery's task in *Three Poems* and *Flow Chart,* his most "autobiographical" books, is a difficult one; he needs to chart his career without fixing it, and he needs to counter Bloom's theoretical description of that career without offering up a countersystem. As can be expected of him, Ashbery performs this act of distancing in large measure through parody, both of his "precursors" and of his critic, who has set himself up as a kind of contemporary precursor.[7]

What we have, then, are competing portraits of a poet's career.[8] The stakes behind these portraits are high. Bloom needs to delineate the form of the strong poet's career as a constant and predictable struggle between sons and fathers, a struggle that threatens to annihilate the son if he does not adequately misread his precursors. Ashbery's self-described career plan is less fraught with oedipal overtones, less easily fixed or mapped. He wants to see it implicated in his ordinary life, not just in the struggle to ascend Parnassus. Ashbery discusses the concept of career in *Three Poems,* a book that he wrote at about the time Bloom was thinking through his notion of anxiety, which he would publish in *The Anxiety of Influence.* Ashbery inaugurates a section of "The System" with the following question: "The great careers are like that: a slow burst that narrows to a final release, pointed but not acute, a life of suffering redeemed and annihilated at the end, and for what? For a casual moment of knowing that is here one minute and gone the next, almost before you were aware of it?" (69). An odd passage, this one; the poet destroys himself for a "casual" and not an apocalyptic moment. It is also a profoundly un-Bloomian moment, denuded of "crisis" and sublimity.

What follows in this prose poem is an argument against reading poetry theoretically, nay, even critically, an argument that shows Ashbery's keen awareness of the power held by the reader of texts: "Besides the obvious question of who knows whether it will still be there, there is the even more urgent one of whose life are we taking into our hands? Is there no way in which these things may be done for themselves, so that others may enjoy them?" (69). The very notion of "career" strikes the speaker as a dangerous one for the way in which it separates the individual from his own activities. The "career" idea is dangerous insofar as it milks "lessons" out of ordinary human experience; to understand a poet's career is very different from understanding his life, or his poems' recounting of that life. To have a career is to have a theory, just as in literary studies having a theory often means having a career:

> But still the "career" notion intervenes. It is impossible for us at the present time not to think of these people as separate entities, each with his development and aim to be achieved, careers which will "peak" after a while and then go back to being ordinary lives that fade quite naturally into air as they are used up, and are as though they never were, except for the "lesson" which has added an iota to the sum of all human understanding. And this way of speaking has trapped each one of us.
>
> (70)

In his development of this idea, Ashbery goes on to suggest that the "career" idea is a fetish, which "hardens

it [the object of contemplation] into a husk around its own being" (70). To talk about life as a ritual strikes Ashbery as a better idea, but one also fraught with dangers, including the destructiveness welcomed by Bloom in his tracing of the poet's career. "[T]he ritual is by definition something impersonal, and can only move further in that direction. It was born without a knowledge of the past. And any attempt to hybridize it can only result in destruction and even death" (70). Theories, like rituals, are impersonal; Bloom's theory, more than many, is ahistorical, lacking in the "knowledge of the past" that might personalize it.

But *Three Poems* is ultimately not the narrative of a secular career but one that traces the possibilities for spiritual development.[9] The speaker of these poems places himself inside and outside of the game, participating in a spectacle in which he also plays a central role. It becomes impossible to fetishize a self that cannot be extricated from its situation either as participant/ poet or as spectator/critic, or so Ashbery seems to hope. Twenty years later, *Flow Chart* tells Ashbery's career narrative in language that tries at all moments not to be fetishistic. And since "tradition" in criticism from T. S. Eliot to Harold Bloom has become fetishized (and so merchandised), Ashbery necessarily avoids expressing reverence for that tradition, even as his poem obsessively engages with it.

By the late 1980s and early 1990s, Ashbery began to stress his independence from Bloom, and it is here that I can begin to unpack the narrative in the nonnarrative of *Flow Chart.* To play with Bloom's notion that great poets misread their precursors, the book might as well be called "Flaw Chart." The title, which offers us both the possibility of organizing history—charting it—and that of refusing to do so—allowing it to flow—can be unpacked as a miniature description of the relationship of poet to critic, as Ashbery sees it. Early on, the speaker wonders when he can meet a friend who is "uncertain where to locate" him (27) and then abruptly enters into a meditation haunted by Stevens and by Bloom (who is included here as a verb). He suggests a movement away from them both:

> I see.
> I'll try another ticket. Meanwhile thanks for the harmonium: its
> inoffensive chords swept me right off my feet near the railroad
> and—nice—are returning to bloom tomorrow and each day after that.
>
> (28)

Any reader of Stevens can tell you that "harmonium" was a crucial word for him; his first book bore it as a title, and he wanted to title his collected poems "The Whole of Harmonium."[10] That the chords from the harmonium might be "returning to bloom" suggests that Ashbery is sending the theory of his having been influenced back to its sender. This leads to a meditation on the relationship between a poet and his "confessor": "I thought nobody needed a confessor any more, but I was wrong I guess, / so, old stump, I'm off until tomorrow or some day early next week, I mean / how much more can I say," which returns him to an "elementary precept" of (again using the natural metaphor) "how we flowered, and lost, and rose up thin again with our thoughts" (28).

In the next section, Ashbery turns more explicitly to a concern with his reputation, particularly with his place in the canon, wondering if he is "the ghost this time" and "wringing his hands" over the question:

> And if I am
> to be cast off, then
> *where?* There has to be a space, even a negative one,
>   a slot
> for me, or does there? But if all space is contained
>   within me, then
> there is no place for me to go, I am not even here, and
>   now, and can join
> no choir or club, indeed I am the sawdust of what's
>   around but nobody can
> even authorize that either.
>
> (29)

Here Ashbery worries over what seems clearly to be an Emersonian principle, that "all space is contained within me," one that he must associate with Bloom, whose use of Emerson is legendary. But the problem with this metaphysical principle is an intensely practical and personal one for Ashbery; if he's merely "the sawdust of what's around," or if he's one of the background singers and not the lead, then no one can "authorize" his place in the canon. Thus Ashbery at once perceives a problem with Bloom's theorizing, which attempts to make history out of metaphysical pronouncements, and expresses a desire for there to be an "authority" like Bloom's for his authorship. Recognizing the illusory nature of present fame, he worries further about "some day several centuries from now / when they open a time capsule" (29). He imagines that no one will want to hear the old stories, yet imagining them reminds him of his own future as part of that history: "Its job is done. We all live in the past now. And so the children / must still hang on somewhere, though no one is quite sure where or how many / or what paths there are to be taken in darkness. Only the fools, the severed heads, know" (30). Severed Orphic heads are one of Bloom's favorite images for the poet; Bloom frames his criticism of Hart Crane (a poet dearer to him even than Stevens) with a discussion of Orphism.[11]

The romantic vision of the poet as a beheaded singer can hardly rest easily with Ashbery, who has spent so much of his career in print finding ways in which to survive the assault of images that his mind generates. Ashbery's famous (or infamous) passivity, it could be argued, defends him against the aggressive mutilation, self and otherwise, that his primary critic glorifies. He wishes, rather, "To pass through pain and not know it," as he writes at the beginning of his long poem "A Wave" (*Wave* 68).

The smallest common denominator of Ashbery's deflation of the importance of tradition and the individual talent is his frequent punning on that tradition; *Flow Chart* is replete with echoes of the Norton anthology poets from Whitman to Eliot to Stevens. The poem opens in "the published city," which quickly harks back to Baudelaire's "fourmillante cité" and to Eliot's wasteland:

> Sad grows the river god as he oars past us downstream
> without our knowing him: for if, he reasons, he can be
> overlooked, then to know him would be to eat him,
> ingest the name he carries through time to set down
> finally, on a strand of rotted hulks.[12]

This is an Eliotic world, most certainly, but the speaker knows that he is reading a text rather than a sanctified tradition; furthermore, he forgets what the big deal is: "*It seems I was reading something*; / I have forgotten the sense of it or what the small / role of the central poem made me want to feel" (3). The "central poem," we scavengers of tradition's echoes will quickly note, belongs to the vocabulary of Stevens, one bandied about liberally by Bloom. So in a book that, from its very girth and weight, appears to be an epic, we are advised from the get-go to look not for the poem's centrality but for its eccentricities. The subtle syntax of this quotation shows Ashbery at once debunking the central poem and wishing that the poem (or poetry) were more central. He is dealing, for better and for worse, with a vision of language that has diminished considerably even since Stevens tried to make a heaven out of it: "the Logos alone will have to suffice. / A pity, since no one has seen it recently" (33-34). Among the book's other pointed puns: "I hear America snowing" (141), rather than "singing," as Walt Whitman would have it; "Another day we read the thunder its own prepared statement," which plays on the final section of *The Waste Land,* namely "What the Thunder Said"; and "I will show you fear in a handful of specialists," a play on Eliot's "dust." In the final item on this doubtless incomplete list, Ashbery writes, "No use trying to cover your tracks using archaic words like 'leman'; the sense / kills and you have the refrain to remind you" (148). Here he recalls the moment when the speaker of *The Waste Land* sits by the shores of Lake Leman and weeps; to adopt Eliot's vocabulary, he suggests, would be a way of "covering" his tracks, perhaps in order that others, like Bloom, might "uncover" them.[13] But there is no "sense" to this reference, and so Ashbery moves on: "Sure but I was just drifting / anyway, faintly out of tune, nothing scared could have happened to me" (148). The phrase "nothing scared could have happened to me" sounds odd, and is probably meant to. Surely Ashbery means to play on the similar sounding word "sacred" and, by revising it to "scared," to belittle the tradition (Bloom's tradition) that he knows he could easily enter by aping. That Ashbery pokes fun at tradition by misreading it bespeaks his ambivalent relationship to Bloom, who is one of the strongest defenders of (a) tradition since T. S. Eliot.

Ashbery attacks the messenger as well as the message, and it is here that he most directly addresses his critic. I would argue, somewhat speculatively, that "the old guy" of the following passage is none other than Harold Bloom:

> an old guy comes up to you and tells you, reading
>   your mind, what a magnificent
> job you've done, chipping away at the noble experi-
>   ment, and then, abruptly,
> you change your plans, backtrack, cancel the rest of
>   the trip
> that was going to promise so much good health and
>   diversion for you; you suddenly
> see yourself as others see you, and it's not such a
>   pretty sight either. . . .
>
>   (124)

Thus Ashbery suggests that the fact of being "seen" as a poet presents such an obstacle to him that he is forced to change direction, to go away from the vantage point at which he has been mapped or "charted." A page earlier, he remarks on his awareness of the way in which he could build his reputation (especially since "[r]epetition makes reputation" [133]), and how that awareness causes him to change direction. His repeated use of the image of a "train" is something I want to comment on.

> All along I had known what buttons to press, but don't
> you see, I had to experiment, not that my life depended
>   on it,
> but as a corrective to taking the train to find out where
>   it wanted to go.
> Then when I did that anyway, I was not so much
>   charmed as horrified
> by the construction put upon it by even some quite
>   close friends,
> some of whom accused me of being the "leopard man"
>   who had been terrorizing
> the community by making howl-like sounds at night,
>   out of earshot
> of the dance floor.
>
>   (123)

That Ashbery is not the contemporary poet who makes "howl-like sounds at night" is quite evident. But his refusal to push the buttons he knew were there to be pushed is especially interesting in light of Bloom's frequent, if not usually noted, attacks on Ashbery.

Bloom is at least as strong a detractor of Ashbery's *The Tennis Court Oath* (1962) as he is a happy advocate for the rest of Ashbery's oeuvre. One of the poems that Bloom excoriates Ashbery for writing is the train-related "Leaving the Atocha Station" (1962), a poem that Ashbery notably leaves out of his *Selected Poems* (1985). This collection of selected poems is, in fact, very thin on the kind of poetry that Bloom disdains. The poem, which is included in Paul Hoover's new Norton anthology, *Postmodern American Poetry* (1994), sounds a lot like recent work by Charles Bernstein; in other words, its value as "experimental," "avant-garde" writing sets it dramatically apart from Bloom's romantic tradition. In *Figures of Capable Imagination,* Bloom quotes from the poem and then attacks it and its readers. The real burden of his criticism is that neither Ashbery nor his readers have properly read Bloom's theory of influence, nor do they recognize the enormous responsibility involved in participating in his tradition. Those who don't are part of the "rabblement," one of Bloom's favorite words:

> This is from the piece called "Leaving the Atocha Sta-
> tion," which (I am told) has a certain reputation among
> the rabblement of poetasters who proclaim themselves
> anti-academic while preaching in the academies, and
> who lack consciousness sufficient to feel the genuine
> (because necessary) heaviness of the poetic past's
> burden of richness. *The Tennis Court Oath* has only
> one good poem, "A Last World."
>
>   (173)

In case the poet dares to contest this tossing of his book on the dump, Bloom quickly adds, "Poets, who congenitally lie about so many matters, *never* tell the truth about poetic influence" (173). Leaving the Atocha station, it seems, was a dangerous thing for Ashbery to do; in Bloom's accounting, it nearly derailed his progress (a concept that Ashbery uses in describing his career as a "development / but not necessarily a resolution at the end" [*Flow Chart* 85]).

Having dismissed Bloom (if I'm correct) as "an old guy" who admires the experiment, Ashbery entertains, but does not quite buy into, the notion that fame is less important than merely being understood:

> the hee-hawing ages in the time it takes to put an idea
>   together
> from its unlikely components, package it, and go on
>   being the genius one was anyway
> but not for too long, or without general consent. It's
>   enough if—
> my friend's mother is the one who believes in me and
>   understands me better
> than anybody, but I'm not going to let it delude me.
>   There's a world out there.
>
>   (126)

The usual option for poets, that of "retreating into—or is it out of?—academia," simply means that they will be "beset by the / usual pitbulls [critics?] and well-meaning little old ladies in tennis shoes [readers outside the academy?]" (133). That gives the poet very little room in which to work, especially one whose poetry doesn't necessarily appeal to a high percentage of the "world out there."

The narrowness, and perhaps nastiness, of these two alternatives, neither of which allows the poet much control over his own destiny, leads Ashbery, in one of the most unexpected passages in *Flow Chart,* to meditate on the Iran-Contra hearings and on Reagan administration underlings whose careers were so obviously at stake.[14] The hearings were noteworthy not simply for their concern with the Reagan administration's radical disrespect for the law, but also for the way in which they revolved around the control and dissemination of information, both within the administration and in the hearings. Politics depends on reputations, and reputations on politics, as Ashbery well knows. And reputations are built, or lost, either on the uncovering of information or on its suppression.

Ashbery briefly imagines himself testifying about his own affairs:

> Those of us who did manage to keep control over our
>   personal affairs
> before it was all over are obviously not going to testify
>   anyway. What would we have said?
> That we confronted the monster eyeball to eyeball and
>   blinked first but only
> after a decent interval had elapsed and were then
>   excused from completing the examination
> before defenestration became an issue?
>
> (176)

This passage could be deciphered several ways; one reading might see it as a defense of Oliver North, who according to his own estimation did not blink first. Ashbery's politics are not clear; he told one critic that he thought Nixon a great president, another that he was not sure he was opposed to the Vietnam War.[15] But in the passage prior to the one quoted above, Ashbery writes critically about Reagan: "but the Reagan / administration insists we cannot go to heaven without drinking caustic soda on the floor / of Death Valley as long as others pay their rent and have somewhere to go without thinking, / behind the curtain of closing down all operations" (175-76). It seems more interesting in the context of a discussion of careers, however, to consider that Ashbery (like his speaker) includes himself among the party of those who kept control over their personal affairs. He is, after all, someone who turned himself "from a / slightly unruly child into a sophisticated and cultivated adult with a number of books / to his credit and many more projects in the works" (177). While these passages say nothing directly about Ashbery's own role in managing his career, they do suggest that he *has* tried to manage it, and that he possesses a keen awareness of the effect of his work on others, even those who make "the old 'elaborate charade' accusation" (128). Oliver North then becomes an example of someone who controlled the narrative about the arms-for-hostages deal; no critic could touch that narrative because it was stronger than the truth (which was that the deal was illegal). Ashbery can only, albeit perhaps grudgingly, admire such control. Where reputations are concerned, control over narrative may ultimately be more important than the content of that narrative.

Ashbery has told one critic that he wrote *Flow Chart* after a friend suggested he write a poem about his mother, who had recently died.[16] His magnificent elegy, a double sestina very close to the end of the book, comes after almost two hundred pages filled with brooding about his career; this is less surprising than appropriate in a book that helps to separate Ashbery from the theory of influence used both for and against him. That it is an elegy for his mother and not his father makes sense to a reading of the poem that takes into account its paradoxical reliance on Bloomian theories. While avoiding Bloom's oedipal model—writing not about his father but about his mother—Ashbery somehow still slips into it. That the poem has as one of its central images a sunflower, one of Blake's most famous images, also permits me to read it as a final song of separation to Harold Bloom, who has written extensively on Blake. It is "she" who inspires the poem, not the tradition. The final sestina ends with the speaker's assertion that his mother has been his central influence, and that that influence is fertile:

> The story that she told me simmers in me still, though
>   she is dead
> these several months, lying as on a bed. The things
>   we used to do, I to thee,
> thou to me, matter still, but the sun points the way
>   inexorably to death,
> though it be but his, not our way. Funny the way the
>   sun can bring you around to her. And as you pause
>   for breath, remember it, now that it is done, and
>   seeds flare in the sunflower.
>
> (193)

The poem's conclusion is profoundly ambivalent; Ashbery seems to concede that poets are the agents in a tradition, even as he wants it to be known that when he gets up to leave, he is that same person he was when he wrote (216). He also avers that poets are known by their reputations and not by themselves: "We are merely agents, so / that if something wants to improve on us, that's fine, but we are always the last / to find out about it, and live up to that image of ourselves as it gets / projected on trees and vine-coated walls and vapors in the night sky: a distant / noise of celebration, forever off-limits" (216). This ambivalence is appropriate in a poem that closes by opening: "By evening the traffic has begun / again in earnest, color-coded. It's open: the bridge, that way" (216).

As I've already suggested, one could easily read this conclusion as evidence for a Bloomian interpretation of the poem; Ashbery here reopens the bridge from which Hart Crane's bedlamite, "shrill shirt ballooning," threw himself. The bow to Crane might be read to reveal Ashbery's anxiety as he ends his career epic thinking about the earlier poet's American epic. The book is, after all, haunted by precursors of all manner and kind. Furthermore, because I have read the poem as (in part) a work of literary criticism, rather than merely as an epic, I can allow myself to submit to Bloom's notion that there is no real difference between poetry and criticism, a position also held by a creature as different from Bloom as the poet-critic Charles Bernstein.[17]

This essay has not attempted to refute Bloom's theory, however, just as it hasn't defended Bloom's notions. The theory, despite Bloom's insistent self-parodying of the last decade, is "strong" in the sense that it tells at least a partial truth about the history of literary influence; how partial that truth is depends on one's sense of allegiance to competing theories of reception, intertextuality, and historicism. The theory works well, however, when applied to the career of the man who marketed it and whose career grew out of it; Bloom stands in the line of succession of critics interested in the romantic backgrounds of modern and contemporary poetry. The "anxiety of influence" theory, then, operates in somewhat the same way that *A Vision* did for Yeats. As a system, it's highly flawed and incomplete; as autobiography, it may work (something that Bloom would not altogether deny).

Career is not history, according to Bloom, but a theoretical construct. Ashbery is brilliant in his realization that this theoretical construct can predetermine the moves that are open to the poet; and so he remarks that "all along" he knew "what buttons to press" but did not push them (123). In that sense, career is not just a theory but also a poem intent on "flowing." Ashbery, more than almost any poet I can think of, has survived his critics. But Ashbery himself, while he's always been attacked from the literary right (by critics like Mark Jarman and Mary Kinzie), has not seen his reputation diminish—and the very vociferousness of the continuing critiques speaks to his importance as a poet.[18] Many of the younger critics who dismiss Bloom find Ashbery every bit as interesting as Bloom does. The answer to this apparent conundrum can be found in lines from Ashbery's verse-criticism, from "Litany," for example, where he claims that criticism that speaks to "*bakers and cheerleaders.*" Or from "Self-Portrait in a Convex Mirror," where he shows himself less interested in the immortality of the work than in the hooting of horns that went on as the work was (and is) made. But even in what I take to be Ashbery's most explicit debunking of Bloom, the *Flow Chart* passage about "the old guy," Ashbery acknowledges that he's indebted to the deal, however rigged it is; the passage bears quoting at length for its appropriately intricate evasions. Watch for the reappearing blossoms, or blooms:

>   you suddenly
> see yourself as others see you, and it's not such a
>   pretty sight either, but at
> least you know now, and can do something to repair
>   the damage, perhaps by
> looking deeper into the mirror, more thoroughly
> to evaluate the pros and cons of your success and
>   smilingly refuse all
> offers of assistance, which would be the wrong kind
>   anyway, no doubt, and set out
> on your own at the eleventh hour, into the vast yawn
>   or cusp that sits
> always next door. And when we have succeeded, not
>   know what to do with it
> except break it into shards that get more ravishing as
>   you keep pounding them. See,
> I am now responsible though I didn't make it. And
>   you
> can come back, I'm harmless now. Anyway, that's
>   how it pleases me to
> detect myself. When the blossoms reappear, as they
>   can, and the consumers,
> someone must pay to keep it poignant. Otherwise one
>   of you will remain an outrider.
> Go finance the rigged deal then, and it can't hurt.
>
>   (124-25)

Notes

I would like to thank the readers for *Contemporary Literature,* whose comments helped to make this a better essay.

1. For information on the specifics of Ashbery's career and awards, see Lesniak 20-22.

2. See John Ernest's marvelous critique of "influence" as a theoretical term in "Fossilized Fish and the World of Unknowing: John Ashbery and William Bronk." Ernest discusses two poets who are in some ways similar, but who have had no influence on each other. Ernest argues, "Fundamentally, narratives of influence are acts of appropriation in the name of historical coherence, acts geared toward identifying the contours of a possible community of understanding" (169).

3. Bloom begins an essay from *Agon,* which became the introduction to the Chelsea House collection of essays, by remembering the first time he read Crane: "I remember reading these lines [from *The Bridge*] when I was ten years old, crouched over Crane's book in a Bronx library. . . . I still have the volume of Crane that I persuaded my older sister to give me on my twelfth birthday, the first book I ever owned" (1). Such is the critic's version of Abe Lincoln's log-cabin-to-the-White-House narrative.

4. Andrew Ross also argues for Ashbery's position as part of a larger tradition, though the tradition to which he assigns the poet is very different from

Bloom's. Ross writes that "at least one of [Ashbery's] volumes [*The Tennis Court Oath*] directly aligns itself with the formal spirit and repertoire of techniques espoused by the historical avant-garde of Europe between the wars" (201).

5. Ammons dedicated "The Arc Inside and Out" to Harold Bloom and also wrote a poem entitled "For Harold Bloom" (*Selected Poems* 101, 105).

6. See especially the last lines of Bishop's "Poem": "Our visions coincided—'visions' is / too serious a word—our looks, two looks: / art 'copying from life' and life itself" (38).

7. Fredric Jameson has famously argued that postmodernism can be characterized by the appearance of pastiche rather than parody: "Pastiche is, like parody, the imitation of a peculiar or unique, idiosyncratic style, the wearing of a linguistic mask, speech in a dead language. But it is a neutral practice of such mimicry, without any of parody's ulterior motives, amputated of the satiric impulse, devoid of laughter and of any conviction that alongside the abnormal tongue you have momentarily borrowed, some healthy linguistic normality still exists" (17). Ashbery, as I hope to show later in this essay, complicates this formulation; while he doesn't always seem to subscribe to the notion of a "healthy linguistic normality" (whatever that may be), his use of other poets' language is often parodic, and quite funny. His is a mimicry with motives, in other words.

8. Speculative studies on the growth of writers' careers and reputations include Lawrence Lipking's *The Life of the Poet,* John Rodden's *The Politics of Literary Reputation,* and Michael Bérubé's *Marginal Forces/ Cultural Centers.*

9. For further discussion of *Three Poems,* see Mills-Courts, Murphy, and Schultz.

10. See Lentricchia on Stevens's change of titles (163).

11. For Bloom's use of Orphism to read Crane, see his introduction to the Chelsea House collection on that poet.

12. Ashbery is playing with the mythical backgrounds to *The Waste Land.* He might extend Eliot's advisory that "Anyone who is acquainted with these works [Jessie Weston's *From Ritual to Romance* and *The Golden Bough*] will immediately recognize in the poem certain references to vegetation ceremonies" (47) to say that "anyone familiar with Eliot's use of mythology will recognize the ceremonies in Ashbery's book."

13. In "The Fire Sermon" section of *The Waste Land,* the speaker relates, "By the waters of Leman I sat down and wept" (36).

14. See Stephen Paul Miller's analogous reading of "Self-Portrait in a Convex Mirror" as a poem about Watergate.

15. Miller reports that Ashbery said to him, "Oh, Nixon was a great president. I wish he was still president" (148).

16. John Shoptaw relates that in the fall of 1987, some few months after the death of Ashbery's mother, "Trevor Winkfield, whose own mother had died recently, suggested that Ashbery write a 'one-hundred page poem about his mother.' Ashbery recalled thinking to himself, 'Say, that's something I haven't done before!' yet hastened to add, 'of course, it's not about my mother'" (141).

17. See Bernstein's *A Poetics,* where he introduces his essays as follows: "if there's a temptation to read the long essay-in-verse ["Artifice of Absorption"] . . . as prose, I hope there will be an equally strong temptation to read the succeeding prose as if it were poetry" (3).

18. Mary Kinzie writes that "Ashbery is the passive bard of a period in which the insipid has turned into the heavily toxic" (17). Mark Jarman considers Ashbery's poetry to be "a kind of musical noise, something like the easy listening jazz of the Windham Hill productions" (159).

Works Cited

Allen, Graham. *Harold Bloom: A Poetics of Conflict.* New York: Harvester, 1994.

Ammons, A. R. *The Selected Poems.* Exp. ed. New York: Norton, 1986.

Ashbery, John. *As We Know.* New York: Viking, 1979.

——. *The Double Dream of Spring.* New York: Ecco, 1970.

——. *Flow Chart.* New York: Knopf, 1991.

——. Interview. With Sue Gangel. *American Poetry Observed: Poets on Their Work.* Ed. Joe David Bellamy. Urbana: U of Illinois P, 1984. 9-20.

——. *Selected Poems.* New York: Viking, 1985.

——. *Self-Portrait in a Convex Mirror.* New York: Viking, 1975.

——. *The Tennis Court Oath.* Middletown, CT: Wesleyan UP, 1962.

——. *Three Poems.* New York: Viking, 1972.

——. *A Wave.* New York: Viking, 1984.

Begley, Adam. "Colossus among Critics: Harold Bloom." *New York Times Magazine* 25 Sept. 1994: 32-35.

Bernstein, Charles. *A Poetics.* Cambridge, MA: Harvard UP, 1992.

Bérubé, Michael. *Marginal Forces/Cultural Centers: Tolson, Pynchon, and the Politics of the Canon.* Ithaca: Cornell UP, 1992.

Bishop, Elizabeth. *Geography III*. New York: Farrar, 1976.

Bloom, Harold. *Agon: Towards a Theory of Revisionism*. New York: Oxford UP, 1982.

——. *The Anxiety of Influence: A Theory of Poetry*. New York: Oxford UP, 1973.

——. *Figures of Capable Imagination*. New York: Seabury, 1976.

——. "Harold Bloom on Poetry." *New Republic* 29 Nov. 1975: 24-26.

——. Introduction. *Modern Critical Views: Hart Crane*. Ed. Harold Bloom. New York: Chelsea House, 1986. 1-15.

——. *A Map of Misreading*. New York: Oxford UP, 1975.

——. *The Western Canon: The Books and School of the Ages*. New York: Harcourt, 1994.

Eliot, T. S. *The Waste Land and Other Poems*. New York: Harcourt, 1962.

Ernest, John. "Fossilized Fish and the World of Unknowing: John Ashbery and William Bronk." Schultz 168-89.

Gray, Paul. "American Poetry: School's Out." *Time* 26 Apr. 1976: 95-98.

Hoover, Paul, ed. *Postmodern American Poetry: A Norton Anthology*. New York: Norton, 1994.

Howard, Richard. "A Formal Affair." *Poetry* 127 (1976): 349-51.

Jameson, Fredric. *Postmodernism, or, The Cultural Logic of Late Capitalism*. Durham, NC: Duke UP, 1991.

Jarman, Mark. "The Curse of Discursiveness." *Hudson Review* 45 (1992): 158-66.

Kinzie, Mary. *The Cure of Poetry in an Age of Prose: Moral Essays on the Poet's Calling*. Chicago: U of Chicago P, 1993.

Lehman, David. "Yale's Insomniac Genius." *Newsweek* 18 Aug. 1986: 56-57.

Lentricchia, Frank. *Modernist Quartet*. New York: Cambridge UP, 1994.

Lesniak, James G., ed. *Contemporary Authors: A Bio-Bibliographical Guide to Current Writers*. New Revision Ser. Vol. 37. Detroit: Gale, 1992.

Lipking, Lawrence. *The Life of the Poet: Beginning and Ending Poetic Careers*. Chicago: U of Chicago P, 1981.

Miller, Stephen Paul. "Periodizing Ashbery and His Influence." Schultz 146-67.

Mills-Courts, Karen. *Poetry as Epitaph: Representation and Poetic Language*. Baton Rouge: Louisiana State UP, 1990.

Murphy, Margueritte S. "John Ashbery's *Three Poems*: Heteroglossia in the American Prose Poem." *American Poetry* 7.2 (1990): 50-63.

Perloff, Marjorie. "Modernist Studies." *Redrawing the Boundaries: The Transformation of English and American Literary Studies*. Ed. Stephen Greenblatt and Giles Gunn. New York: MLA, 1992. 154-78.

Rodden, John. *The Politics of Literary Reputation: The Making and Claiming of 'St. George' Orwell*. New York: Oxford UP, 1989.

Ross, Andrew. "Taking the Tennis Court Oath." Schultz 193-210.

Schultz, Susan M. "'The Lyric Crash': The Theater of Subjectivity in John Ashbery's *Three Poems*." *Sagetrieb* 12.2 (1993): 137-48.

——, ed. *The Tribe of John: Ashbery and Contemporary Poetry*. Tuscaloosa: U of Alabama P, 1995.

Shoptaw, John. "*Flow Chart*: The Unauthorized Autobiography." *New American Writing* 10 (1992): 136-50.

von Hallberg, Robert. *American Poetry and Culture, 1945-1980*. Cambridge, MA: Harvard UP, 1985.

Carol Iannone (essay date spring 1997)

SOURCE: Iannone, Carol. "Harold Bloom and *King Lear*: Tragic Misreading." *Hudson Review* 50, no. 1 (spring 1997): 83-94.

[*In the following essay, Iannone explores Bloom's thoughts on Shakespeare and the reactions of Samuel Johnson and Leo Tolstoy to the Bard, specifically discussing* King Lear *and "the question of the moral dimension in literature."*]

More and more professors of literature seem to be troubled by the state of their profession. A group of eminent professors, including Paul Cantor, John Hollander, and Roger Shattuck, recently founded the Association of Literary Scholars and Critics out of "a deep and widespread concern about the present state of literary studies," according to the organization's statement of purpose. The ALSC's emphasis on "broad conceptions of literature rather than the narrow, highly politicized ones often encountered today" stands in implicit opposition to the Modern Language Association and its enthusiastic sponsorship of these very politicized approaches. In addition, no less a critic than Harold Bloom has weighed in with a hefty tome rather combatively (in the present critical context) titled *The*

Western Canon. This book is at once a repudiation of the social and political theorists of recent decades, a championing of the idea of literary greatness that these theorists have attacked, and an attempt at construction and defense of the author's own "canon" of great writers.

Coming late to his recognition of the decline in his profession, Bloom asserts that the present is by now "the worst of all times for literary criticism." True aesthetic and literary appreciation has been uprooted by what he calls the School of Resentment—"Feminists, Afrocentrists, Marxists, Foucault-inspired New Historicists, or Deconstructors." In their desire to subjugate literature to their idea of social justice, many of the newer critics, says Bloom, "are destroying all intellectual and aesthetic standards." Departments of literature are losing potential students of high quality, and if literary studies are to survive at all, he argues, it will only be in marginal enclaves while "cultural studies" take center stage.

Contrary to some defenders of the tradition who repudiate the idea of a "canon," Bloom does not shy away from the word or its religious connotations, although he defines it idiosyncratically. "The Canon" (his capitalization), Bloom claims, in keeping with his own theoretical preoccupation with literary influence, is the product of a "struggle" carried on "by late-coming authors who feel themselves chosen by particular ancestral figures." Ultimately, the "quest to be canonical" is to defy mortality and "to join communal or societal memory."

Nor does Bloom shrink from setting forth the standards of judgment by which he feels we recognize an author as canonical: "mastery of figurative language, originality, cognitive power, knowledge, exuberance of diction," as well as qualities he names as strangeness, uncanniness, sublimity, incommensurability. He moreover upholds the idea of individual creativity and genius in the face of the newer critics who see the canon as the outgrowth of political power and the product of social forces beyond the individual author.

Bloom has done a service in reviving a sense of aesthetic appreciation, and his effort has been understandably applauded by more traditionally minded critics. While his criticism can be rambling and repetitious, it can also yield nuggets of insight. But in trying to defend the great works from today's moralistic political elites, Bloom succumbs to the opposite fallacy of insisting that literature has no moral significance at all. He argues that literature "will not make one a better or worse person, a more useful or harmful citizen," and asserts that the "silliest way to defend the Western Canon is to insist that it incarnates all of the seven deadly moral virtues that make up our supposed range of normative values and democratic principles."

While few would not sympathize with Bloom's aversion for the simplistic reductionism he has thus described, there is a more expansive moral dimension to literature that must also be restored along with the aesthetic if we are to preserve the significance of great art for our culture and ourselves. Literature may not "save any individual, any more than it will improve our society," but it can make us aware of the moral dimension of our lives, even if only negatively, of the seriousness of our existence, and of the consequences of how we conduct ourselves. Literature works not by precept upon precept, line upon line, but by allowing us to absorb a more expansive articulation of human experience into our own lives, thus deepening the emotional reservoir and enhancing the moral imagination to which we have access.

Bloom's central canonical figure is Shakespeare, and a significant part of Shakespeare's greatness for Bloom is that he is possessed of "a spirit that permeates everywhere, that cannot be defined." It is this very spirit that troubles two other of Bloom's canonical figures: Shakespeare's "freedom from doctrine and simplistic morality," says Bloom, "made Dr. Johnson nervous and Tolstoy indignant." By analyzing Bloom's understanding of Shakespeare, as well as his understanding of Johnson's and Tolstoy's reactions to him, especially in regard to *King Lear,* we can delve more deeply into the question of the moral dimension in literature.

Although he does not say so explicitly, Bloom's understanding of Shakespeare is basically an elaboration of Keats's idea of "negative capability": "when a, man is capable of being in uncertainties, mysteries, doubts, without irritable reaching after fact and reason." Keats felt that Shakespeare possessed this quality to a supreme degree. Says Bloom: "Part of the secret of Shakespeare's canonical centrality is in his disinterestedness; despite all the flailings of the New Historicists and other Resenters," whom Bloom sees as trying to "reduce and scatter" the great bard, Shakespeare "has no theology, no metaphysics, no ethics, and rather less political theory than is brought to him by his current critics."

More specifically, Bloom argues that a "sensitive apprehension of *The Tragedy of King Lear* gives us a sense of having been thrown outward and downward until we are left beyond values, altogether bereft." Bloom insists that there "is no transcendence at the end of *King Lear.* . . . The death of Lear is a release for him, but not for the survivors. . . . And it is no release for us either."

Thus Bloom is ironically able to agree with a certain part of Tolstoy's famous, crabby denunciation of Shakespeare, and of *King Lear* in particular, in *What Is Art?* This unintentionally hilarious screed has got to be a textbook example of the wrong kind of criticism to bring to a work of art:

> Lear walks about the heath and says words which are meant to express his despair: he desires that the winds should blow so hard that they (the winds) should crack their cheeks and that the rain should flood everything, that lightning should singe his white head, and the thunder flatten the world and destroy all germs "that make ungrateful man"! The fool keeps uttering still more senseless words. Enter Kent: Lear says that for some reason during this storm all criminals shall be found out and convicted. Kent, still unrecognized by Lear, endeavors to persuade him to take refuge in a hovel. At this point the fool utters a prophecy in no wise related to the situation and they all depart.

A great admirer of Tolstoy's fiction, Bloom not surprisingly thinks that such criticism, which utterly refuses to enter the imaginative life of the play, "is a disaster," but he finds agreeable Tolstoy's judgment that "Shakespeare, as a dramatist, is neither a Christian nor a moralist." For Tolstoy this is a negative of course while for Bloom it is a positive, and he applauds Tolstoy for inadvertently leading us to "the true grounds of Shakespearean power and offense: freedom from moral and religious overdeterminations." Bloom prefers Tolstoy's "revulsion [from *King Lear*] to any attempts to Christianize Shakespeare's deliberately pre-Christian drama."

Negative capability is a superb two-word description of Shakespeare's power, but Bloom surely overstates the case when he asserts that Shakespeare "has no theology, no metaphysics, no ethics." Granted, the sense of desolation is vivid at the end of *Lear,* yet we are far from being "beyond values." To the contrary, "values" have been restored, albeit at the cost of great suffering. After the awful inversions of the first scene, in which we see the evil daughters triumph and the good daughter banished, in which we see lies, deceit, venality, and hypocrisy trumping honesty, goodness, loyalty, and straightforwardness, by the play's end we see truth emerge and order reinstated. We may feel that the debacle could have been prevented, we may believe that the suffering endured by the characters is disproportionate to their deeds, but we cannot claim to be ignorant of how the disaster occurred. We're made to see the destructiveness of unthinking pride and self-regard, and how what may appear to be the comparatively lesser lapses of selfishness, foolishness, and vanity can give rise to murderousness and cruelty, taking the innocent along with the guilty.

Moreover, if one is so disposed, a Christian element can be discerned in *Lear,* in how, for example, the all-forgiving goodness of Cordelia operates as a redemptive force in the play. The feudal loyalty of Kent, Gloucester, and the Fool sustain Lear in his extremity, but Cordelia's unconditional love seems to bring forth a kind of spiritual restoration of the tormented king. Too, Lear in a fashion loses his life to save it, and grows in his grief until he is truly "every inch a king," larger than before in sympathy and understanding, in what Bloom might call "cognitive power."[1]

Alfred Harbage's 1958 introduction to the Pelican edition, also included in the 1970 edition, offers some plausible support for a Christian understanding. Among other things he points out that the play

> shows obvious signs of its genesis in a Christian culture. . . . On the human level, the implications of the play are more comforting than the data it abstracts. In our actual world, suffering is not always ennobling, evil is not always self-consuming. In every scene where there is pain, there is someone who strives to relieve that pain. At the close, the merciless have all perished; the last sound we hear is the choral voices of the merciful.

Furthermore, whether *Lear* be specifically Christian in temper or not, the play is imbued with the moral weight of tragedy itself. Harbage marvels in his study of Shakespeare, *As They Liked It: An Essay on Shakespeare and Morality* (1947), that even a "cool and judicious aesthetician" like Benedetto Croce can say, "An infinite hatred for deceitful wickedness has inspired this work"; and Harbage ventures in his Pelican introduction that Lear "is religious as all great tragedies are religious." In tragedy, the cosmos is a continuum, sensitive to the doings and disturbances of men, and there are limits at which men learn the truth of their existence. In this regard we think of the words of the Chorus in *Agamemnon*: "God, whose law it is that he who learns must suffer. And even in our sleep pain that cannot forget, falls drop by drop upon the heart, and in our own despite, against our will, comes wisdom to us by the awful grace of God."[2]

By contrast, Bloom derives his reading from what he calls "nature": "The bewildered old king takes his stand on behalf of nature," Bloom says, adding by way of explanation, "In Lear's sense of nature, Goneril and Regan are unnatural hags, monsters of the deep, and so indeed they are." Bloom's reading rather boxes him in, however, and his view of nature seems restrictive, since it leads him to insist that "If we want a human nature that does not prey upon itself, we turn to the authority of Lear, however flawed, however compromised in its hurtful power." But the phrases "monsters of the deep" and "prey upon itself" are echoes of Albany who as the evil about him intensifies cries out: "If that the heavens do not their visible spirits / Send quickly down to tame these vile offenses, / It will come, / Humanity must perforce prey on itself, / Like monsters of the deep." Since Bloom will not look to Cordelia, or for that matter, to Edgar, if not as "visible spirits" able to "tame" the vileness, at least as figures who bring a transfiguring kind of humanity to the suffering before them, he can see only the shattering desolation of the last scene.

And what of the brutal education Lear has been forced, and has heroically forced himself, to undergo? Bloom elsewhere in his discussion of Shakespeare elevates as crucial the idea of the "introspective consciousness" of the Western Canon, but the growth and expansion in Lear's understanding do not seem to register with Bloom. Since in the apparently limited sense of "nature" that Bloom employs, the old king is a "ruined piece of nature" by the play's end, Bloom must of necessity, it would seem, see the whole work as lacking transcendence: "Lear cannot heal us or himself, and he cannot survive Cordelia. . . . Nature as well as the state is wounded almost unto death, and the three surviving characters exit with a dead march."

Ultimately Bloom's view of the play borders on nihilism, or at least solipsism: "What matters most is the mutilation of nature, and our sense of what is or is not natural in our own lives. So overwhelming is the effect at the play's close that everything seems against itself," or as Bloom says elsewhere in his discussion, "beyond poetic justice, beyond good and evil, beyond madness and vanity."

Bloom's attitude amounts to a refusal of tragedy and its implied settlements of the realities with which it deals. He calls himself a student of *gnosis*, which is defined as "a repudiation of known truth," and we might extrapolate to define it in this context as a repudiation of the finally and usually painfully acknowledged limitations and minimal consolations that are the truth of tragedy. Bloom remarks that "Tolstoy demands 'the truth,' and the trouble with Shakespeare, in Tolstoy's perspective, is that he was not interested in the truth." Interestingly, Bloom omits the scare quotes around the second mention of the word in that sentence. Perhaps Shakespeare was not interested in "the truth," in Tolstoy's sense, but the truth in itself is something else again.

Perhaps it is Bloom who is not interested in either "the truth" or the truth. Elsewhere in **The Western Canon,** Bloom tells us that "imaginative literature situates itself somewhere between truth and meaning, somewhere I once compared to what the ancient Gnostics called the *kenoma,* the cosmological emptiness in which we wander and weep, as William Blake wrote." Bloom appreciates literature insofar as he can see it resist meaning in favor of the "uncanny," the "incommensurable" (his frequently used terms for literary greatness), of the non-Socratic Nietzschean experience of ongoing agonistic ecstasy (if that's not an oxymoron). But in order to have this experience he must often rewrite, or "misread" the works before him.

Bloom's reading of Shakespeare seems far more blinkered than Dr. Johnson's, the second of Bloom's canonical figures who balked at Shakespeare's relative amoralism. Bloom generally adores Johnson, and quotes approvingly Johnson's assessment of *Lear*:

> The tragedy of Lear is deservedly celebrated among the dramas of Shakespeare. There is perhaps no play which keeps the attention so strongly fixed; which so much agitates our passions and interests our curiosity. The artful involutions of distinct interests, the striking opposition of contrary characters, the sudden changes of fortune, and the quick succession of events, fill the mind with a perpetual tumult of indignation, pity, and hope. . . . So powerful is the current of the poet's imagination, that the mind, which once ventures within it, is hurried irresistibly along.

But of course Bloom rejects as a criticism Johnson's view that Shakespeare "seems to write without moral purpose." Johnson famously approved the altered eighteenth-century version of the play in which Cordelia is allowed to live and prosper; he defends his choice, lamenting that in the original version "Shakespeare has suffered the virtue of Cordelia to perish in a just cause, contrary to the natural ideas of justice, to the hope of the reader, and, what is yet more strange, to the faith of the chronicles." He asserts further that "since all reasonable beings naturally love justice, I cannot easily be persuaded that the observation of justice makes a play worse."

Nevertheless, Johnson is a more expansive critic than such judgments might make him appear to be. What Johnson says about "moral purpose" is that Shakespeare "sacrifices virtue to convenience, and is so much more careful to please than to instruct, that he seems to write without any moral purpose." The "seems" turns out to be important in light of the next sentence in which Johnson goes on to observe of Shakespeare: "From his writings indeed a system of social duty may be selected for he that thinks reasonably must think morally." In other words, for Johnson, morality is a function of truth and by rendering truth, Shakespeare must needs imply a moral dimension. "Nothing can please many, and please long, but just representations of general nature," Johnson declares with his customary confidence, and his view of "nature" seems quite different from Bloom's, encompassing the totality of human experience:

> Shakespeare is above all writers, at least above all modern writers, the poet of nature; the poet that holds up to his readers a faithful mirrour of manners and of life. His characters are . . . the genuine progeny of common humanity, such as the world will always supply, and observation will always find.

Thus even in the case of the death of Cordelia, although Johnson would prefer to see her virtuousness rewarded, he can brook what Shakespeare has done, for "a play in which the wicked prosper, and the virtuous miscarry, may doubtless be good, because it is a just representation of the common events of human life."

More important than an individual call, however, is the larger point that Johnson at least makes clear his perimeters of judgment; he spells out his difficulties with Shakespeare but is able to appreciate his genius despite them. The difference between Johnson and Bloom is that between a critic who has maintained objectivity with reference to reality and a sense of his own preferences, and one whose subjectivity has grown so large that he takes his own failures of perception to be Shakespeare's. More than the neoclassical Johnson, Bloom seems straitjacketed by his time and his Nietzschean outlook, and unaware of how he confuses his own thought with that of the writers he discusses. To illustrate, take this passage of Johnson on Shakespeare that Bloom quotes:

> Though he had so many difficulties to encounter, and so little assistance to surmount them, he has been able to obtain an exact knowledge of many modes of life, and many casts of native dispositions; to vary them with great multiplicity; to mark them by nice distinctions; and to shew them in full view by proper combinations. In this part of his performance he had none to imitate, but has himself been imitated by all succeeding writers; and it may be doubted, whether from all his successors more maxims of theoretical knowledge, or more rules of practical prudence, can be collected, than he alone has given to his country.

In a gloss on this passage, Bloom transforms it into something more peculiar to his own kind of criticism. He begins acceptably:

> "Theoretical knowledge" is what we might call "cognitive awareness"; "practical prudence" is wisdom. If Shakespeare obtained "exact knowledge" and showed it in full view, he is beyond what philosophers could achieve.

This stretches Johnson a little, but not unacceptably. But then Bloom continues:

> With no inherited contingencies, Shakespeare as originator establishes a contingency that all writers after him must sustain. Johnson realizes, and tells us, that Shakespeare has established the standard for measuring representation ever after. Knowing many modes of life and many casts of native dispositions is not knowing apart from representing.

Now Shakespeare is nudged from being the poet of wisdom and knowledge of life toward the more intraliterary "standard for measuring representation." Bloom continues:

> To vary, mark, and show *is* the knowing, and what is known is what we have learned to call our psychology, of which Shakespeare, as Johnson intimates, is the inventor. If this is holding a mirror up to nature, it is a very active mirror indeed.

Finally then, Shakespeare goes from being Johnson's faithful "mirror" to being the "inventor" of "our psychology" and by implication selfhood, more in keeping with Bloom's idea of absolute "originality" as a criterion for literary genius.

Bloom's subjectivity is not an irrelevant point. As Peter Shaw writes, "Bloom became notorious some twenty-five years ago by maintaining that all interpretations of written works are misreadings of those works. This claim anticipated deconstruction's contention that we cannot ever truly comprehend any piece of writing." As recently as 1990, for example, Bloom asserted in *The Book of J* that all literary interpretations are "fictions," thus clearing the way for his own irresponsible reading of the J document of the Torah as a quasi-Nietzschean declamation of unfettered existence free of moral impositions. If there is no literary truth, then anything can be said about a work, and indeed anything has. As Shaw concludes, "Bloom . . . helped bring about the canon assault that he now finds distasteful."

For in fact, even before the School of Resentment arose, criticism of Shakespeare was already in trouble. As Richard Levin shows in *New Readings vs. Old Plays: Recent Trends in the Reinterpretation of English Renaissance Drama* (1979), the predecessors of the School of Resentment were earlier critics who, starting about 1950 and accelerating through the 1960s, overrode the older, simpler interpretations of Shakespeare with more and more tortured "thematic," "ironic," and "occasionalist" readings. These readings all tended to debunk common sense, traditional values, and the understanding of generations of readers and audiences. It was in this general critical atmosphere that Bloom emerged with his creative misreadings and postmodern resistance to any concept of truth. The battle Bloom is fighting with the School of Resentment is thus a later phase of an earlier battle, one in which he was on the other side.

These later critical developments have to be distinguished from earlier debates in Shakespeare criticism. As Alfred Harbage relates, there have been many disagreements in the history of Shakespeare criticism, including over the nature of the bard's moral sense and over an aesthetically inspired critical "tendency to wrest the plays away from the ordinary reader." After all, Harbage asserts, "It is of the nature of art that it be variously received, and of great art that it mean many things to many men." Harbage insists, however, "There are limits within which sane criticism must reside," and he judges that "All criticism [of Shakespeare] that has had a respectful hearing resides safely within the limits of Shakespeare's meaning." Thus he is able to declare in conclusion,

> The great body of Shakespearean criticism as a whole is a valuable and illuminating product of our culture. It should not in any part be dismissed in a tone of annoyance or contempt. Pre-romantic, romantic, post-romantic—nearly all of it is good in its kind. The critics speak a common language and testify collectively if not individually to the nature of the plays and the nature of human responses.

This was written by a distinguished Harvard professor in 1947. Who could say anything like it today, while critics are busy deconstructing Shakespeare, indicting him for perceived shortcomings in progressive outlook, and manufacturing deliberate misreadings?

Bloom writes in **The Western Canon** that Shakespeare can teach us how to accept death and that the Western Canon can bring one into "confrontation with one's own mortality." But he finds the death of Lear is "no release. . . . Too much has been incarnated in Lear for the manner of his dying to be acceptable to his subjects, and our own investment in Lear's sufferings has become too large for a Freudian 'making friends with death.'"

Bloom wouldn't be the first critic to balk at the intensified losses of the last scene, but it's usually the death of Cordelia, rather than the death of Lear, that forms the sticking point, the death of the tragic hero himself being almost a convention of the genre. Since we have seen how Bloom deliberately resists the redemptive or compensatory elements of the play (Cordelia, Edgar, Lear's own growth toward wisdom), we might conclude that his resistance to tragic closure arises out of his resistance to death itself.

The tragic trajectory constitutes a movement out from self-involvement toward self-transcendence, and involves a surrender of one's life or of one's previous sense of life. If some people want tragedy without suffering, Bloom seems to want suffering without tragedy, that is, without the catharsis, without the release, without the surrender, because that would end the ongoing agonistic struggle, the incommensurable *gnosis* that is for him the essential literary experience and the seal of existence. Bloom prefers the suffering self, rather than the surrender of self which signifies the tragic acceptance of limits. Thus while Bloom's adversaries in the School of Resentment rail against patriarchy, elitism, sexism, heterosexism, racism, and other kinds of hierarchies they see as artificially imposed limits in literature, Bloom's resentment rises to the ultimate limitation, death. While such resistance is certainly understandable, the resistance to the specific address the tragic form makes to such resentment seems less so.

The fact is that while Bloom tries to uphold the Western Canon, his own idiosyncratic modes of reading can only add to its general diminishment because he cuts off the works from the implications they carry for common life and locks them into his own tortured subjectivity. Bloom argues that in order to read great works we must be willing to surrender simple pleasures for complex ones, but once we have done that, we may need to return again to the simple: the simple connections, the simple truths, the simple pleasures of literature. Or as Dr. Johnson says, and Bloom quotes: "'The irregular combinations of fanciful invention may delight a-while, by that novelty of which the common satiety of life sends us all in quest; but the pleasures of sudden wonder are soon exhausted, and the mind can only repose on the stability of truth.'"

Notes

1. The exquisite scene in which Lear recognizes Cordelia shines with this luminous love, as well as with Lear's poignant newfound humility. Pounded and beaten by his ordeal, Lear is aware of how unjustly he has treated his good daughter and he declares his readiness to be punished:

   > Be your tears wet? Yes faith. I pray weep not.
   > If you have poison for me, I will drink it.
   > I know you do not love me; for your sisters
   > Have (as I do remember) done me wrong.
   > You have some cause, they have not.

   Lear is presuming that if the daughters whom he did not wrong have treated him so badly, what can he expect from the one he did wrong? But Cordelia instantaneously transcends any idea of retribution and says simply and movingly:
   > No cause, no cause.

   The way her line completes the pentameter of his last line reflects the renewed linkage of their recently ruptured worlds. Thus Lear's next query seems logical: "Am I in France?", France being Cordelia's kingdom. When he is answered by the loyal Earl of Kent, "No, in your own kingdom, sir," it can be seen as a kind of restoration—Lear's return to sanity, to dignity, to fatherhood, and to acknowledgement of his kingship, despite his unwise abdication.

2. George Orwell agreed with Tolstoy that Shakespeare is not a Christian writer but disagreed that he is an immoral or amoral one. "His moral code might be different from Tolstoy's," says Orwell, "but he very definitely *has* a moral code, which is apparent all through his work. . . . He was like most Englishmen in having a code of conduct but no world-view, no philosophical faculty." This might be another way of talking about negative capability.

   For his part, Croce did feel that Shakespeare's work bore "a strong imprint of Christian ethics."

Milton Birnbaum (review date spring 2000)

SOURCE: Birnbaum, Milton. "A 'Hopeless Romantic?'" *Modern Age* 42, no. 2 (spring 2000): 217-21.

[*In the following review, Birnbaum delineates Bloom's complex relationship with Romanticism, and deems* Shakespeare: The Invention of the Human *overwritten and inconsistent, but ultimately worthwhile for the intensity and enthusiasm of its approach.*]

One would think, or at least hope, that by the time a person has reached the Psalmist's three score and ten, he will have fairly well crystallized his identity. Harold Bloom, born in 1930, apparently is still fairly fluid in determining who he is.

Born in the East Bronx of New York City, into a Jewish Orthodox immigrant family where neither parent could read English, he early developed a passion for reading, a passion fueled by his prodigiously retentive memory.[1] His academic acuity outdistanced that of his fellow students (and probably of his professors) at Cornell University, and, in his graduate studies, later at Yale.

He subsequently joined the English Department at Yale, and began his long and as yet incomplete search for a permanent self-identification and a resting place for his restless mind. His specialty was Romantic literature. At Yale, in a department anchored in New Criticism and Protestantism, he felt somewhat alienated because, as Bloom himself has stated, he was "very Jewish and lower-class Jewish at that."[2] He briefly and somewhat half-heartedly joined the Yale School of Deconstructionists—although he later claimed, "I have always thought of myself as a sect or party of one."[3] Fascinated by Freud's theories, he underwent psychoanalysis. In his affiliation with Yale and later New York University, he became perhaps the best known "celebrity" on the academic scene in the humanities. And yet, though his fame is secure, his literary and philosophic-religious identity remains elusive. He has classified himself as "a gnostic sect of one,"[4] "a wicked old aesthete," a "Late Romantic," "a heretical transcendentalist, gnostic in orientation," and, above all, a "hopeless Romantic." I shall briefly refer to Bloom's references to the "Gnostic" ("gnostic") features, but it is his "Romantic" dimension that I wish to highlight in my discussion and to indicate whether his assessment as a "hopeless Romantic" is accurate.[5]

Shakespeare: The Invention of the Human is a massive book. Its 745 pages attempt to discuss not only the conventional number of thirty-seven plays attributed to the Bard, but also two plays of debatable authorship, *Henry VIII* and *The Two Noble Kinsmen*. May the Muses be thanked for Bloom's omission of Shakespeare's sonnets and narrative poems, but the omission of a bibliography, footnotes, and an index is entirely unfortunate.

At the beginning of the book, Bloom states his chief goal: "Shakespeare will go on explaining us, in part because he invented us, which is the central argumentation in this book." He repeats the central goal of the book at the end in expanded form: "As much a creator of selves as of language, he can be said to have melted down and then remolded the representation of the self in and by language. That assertion is the center of this book. . . ."

If one thinks that Bloom's subtitle to his book is somewhat mystifying, what can one say about Bloom's references to "Gnostic" and "Gnosticism"? He does indicate that "gnosis" is "knowledge" whereas "Gnostic" refers to the religious belief(s) of the early Christians and Jews, not to mention his own brand of Gnosticism—but these particular distinctions are not of much help. Bloom takes it for granted that the reader has read his books on the subject—***Kabbalah and Criticism*** (1975); ***The Flight to Lucifer: A Gnostic Fantasy*** (1979); ***The Breaking of the Vessels*** (1981); ***Omens of Millennium: The Gnosis of Angels*** (1996)—but suppose one has not read them. In effect one remains ignorant of what Bloom means by these terms. His friend and colleague John Hollander is quite right when he says, "His [Bloom's] mode is vatic. . . . He'll get hold of a word and allow this to generate a concept for him, but he's not in a position to say very clearly what he means and what he's doing."[6] After reading Bloom's references to "gnostic," "Gnostic," "Gnosticism," I was reminded of what one critic said after reading Henry James, Sr.'s *The Secret of Swedenborg* (1869); "He [James Sr.] kept his secret very well."

It is to Bloom's evaluation of himself as "a hopeless Romantic" that I wish to devote the main portion of my review. It should be recalled that academic classifications (Romanticism, Classicism, Neohumanism, etc.) are seldom, if ever, pure in their distinctive qualities. A Romantic like John Keats, for example, has some fairly distinguishable classical features—a sense of order and propriety, and the objectivity he stressed as a desideratum for great poets in his famous letter to his brothers in December 1817. At the same time, Keats could write (in his poem "Ode on a Grecian Urn") such a highly subjective and rhapsodically ambiguous statement as "'Beauty is truth, truth beauty.' That is all / Ye know on earth, and all ye need to know." In other words, it is only in their extreme manifestations that the features of a literary nomenclature become clearly distinguished.

The first characteristic of Bloom's Romanticism is his fierce independence and rebelliousness. Like Milton's Satan, he would declare, *"Non serviam."* Unlike Milton's Satan, however, he has a Puckish sense of humor. In an earlier book, he wrote, "I am your true Marxist critic, following Groucho, rather than Karl, and take as my motto, Groucho's grand admonition, 'Whatever it is, I am against it.'"[7] He is against academic Feminism, Marxism, Lacanism, Derrideanism, New Historicism, Popular Culture (and Multi-Culture), the Baconians, Oxfordians, the radically innovative cinematic and stage versions of the Bard's plays, as well as many Freudian allegorical interpretations. He even extends his animadversions to some politicians like Newt Gingrich.

Bloom's chief and most profound rebellion is against Yahweh (Jehovah). Seemingly indifferent that he is being sacrilegious to his faith, Bloom compares Yahweh to secular literary characters: "God in the Hebrew Bible, particularly in Job [*sic*] composes best in rhetorical questions. Hamlet is much given to rhetorical questions, but unlike God's, Hamlet's do not always seek to answer themselves." Bloom even finds similarities between "the jealous God of the Jews, Christians, and Muslims" and Othello; and Othello's rejection of Iago in favor of Cassio as his lieutenant and Yahweh's rejection of Cain. Thus, in his treatment of "the jealous God of the Jews, Christians, and Muslims," Bloom casts his lot with the chief rejector of all, Satan—but I am sure that Bloom would reject being classified as a member of Satan's School of Resentment, and he would probably designate himself as an independent rebel of no particular sect.

This seemingly endless number of resentments is still another manifestation of Bloom's Romanticism, his extreme subjectivity and tendency to enhance the validity of his subjective judgments by both hyperbole and derogation. He exaggerates the "sublimity"[8] of so many states of being that the word loses its force by overapplication. Subjectivity, of course, is common to any critic making critical judgments. When, however, subjectivity is undermined by very tenuous and frequently unsubstantiated claims, then the judgments deteriorate into trivial speculation.

Bloom spends an inordinate amount of time, for example, trying to prove that, up to the writing of *Henry IV,* Part One, Shakespeare was almost obsessed with attempting to outgrow the influence of Christopher Marlowe. With the creation of his "immortal" Falstaff, the Bard finally had declared his dramatic independence and henceforth went on to write his masterpieces: *Hamlet, Othello, King Lear, Macbeth,* and, in addition, *As You Like It, Antony and Cleopatra,* and other masterful plays. Shakespeare's agon, to use one of Bloom's favorite words and the title of one of his books, was over, and the "anxiety of influence" had metamorphosed into the glory of filial independence. But what proof does Bloom really offer for this somewhat Freudian-induced hypothesis of the child figuratively slaying his father? As much proof as the recently successful film *Shakespeare in Love*? Fascinating as a theory, yes. Foolproof? No.

Similarly, Bloom, in his chapter on *Hamlet,* goes off into a fairly long and somewhat pedantic digression that the so-called *UR-Hamlet* was written not by Thomas Kyd or anyone else, but by Shakespeare himself. He digresses in another direction when he speculates (following James Joyce's interpretation) that the standard edition of *Hamlet* was significantly influenced by the death of Shakespeare's father and the death of Shakespeare's only son, Hamnet. Again, the evidence here is highly speculative, rather than determinative.

With no clear-cut set of criteria by which to judge a work of art, moreover, there are bound to be some inconsistencies, depending on one's subjective mood at the moment. On the first page of his book, Bloom writes, "Thomas Carlyle, dyspeptic Victorian prophet, must now be the least favored of all Shakespeare critics who once were respected. And yet the most useful single sentence about Shakespeare is his: 'If called to define Shakespeare's faculty, I should say superiority of intellect.'" On the very next page, however, Bloom says, "In learning, intellect, and personality, Samuel Johnson still is to me first among all Western literary critics." Later on, he calls A. C. Bradley "now absurdly deprecated but still the best English critic on Shakespeare since William Hazlitt,"[9] And much later in the book, he endorses Emerson's words: "Shakespeare is the only biographer of Shakespeare, and even he can tell nothing except to the Shakespeare in us."

His occasional inconsistency reaches more serious proportions when he discusses Hamlet the character. Throughout, one of Bloom's major premises is that character is more important than plot and that what is most important about a character is one's "inwardness." Now it seems to me that with a character like Hamlet, the "real" Hamlet is not revealed with the changing personalities (or perhaps "personae" would be a better word) that Hamlet assumes with the other characters in the play, whether they be his mother, his uncle, Polonius, Ophelia, Horatio, Rosencrantz and Guildenstern, Osric, or the Players. The "real" Hamlet is best revealed by his "inwardness," an inwardness which is best seen in his seven soliloquies. (He is fairly much at ease with Horatio, who he claims, is not, like him, "passion's slave," but perhaps even with Horatio, Hamlet hides his innermost soul.) Curiously, with the exception of the "To be or not to be" soliloquy, Bloom is inexplicably silent about the other six soliloquies. Perhaps Bloom was following the advice he implies in this judgment: "Shakespeare's literary art, the highest we will ever know, is as much an art of omission as it is of surpassing richness. The plays are greatest where they are most elliptical." His first epigraph to his book, taken from Nietzsche, is also uncannily significant: "That for which we find words is something already dead in our hearts. There is always a kind of contempt in the act of speaking."

Perhaps the major vulnerability of purely subjective criticism is that for each of one's endorsing or negating judgments there may be the reader's rejecting response. I myself do not share Bloom's persistent apotheosis of Falstaff. Bloom worships Falstaff because he claims that the fat knight worships life. But Bloom forgets to add that it is his own life that Falstaff worships. I agree with Samuel Johnson that Falstaff's chief value is that he tends to banish melancholy, although with many he tends to induce not only melancholy, but disgust. I do not endorse Bloom's deification of Sir John. To put him in the same company with Sancho Panza (along with Chaucer's Wife of Bath and Rabelais' Pantagruel) is to do an injustice to Don Quixote's companion and, to a lesser extent, the very pragmatic Wife of Bath. Sancho Panza seems to imbibe his master's quixotic idealism as he journeys with the Knight of the Mournful Countenance. At the end of the journey, when his master is dying, chiefly because he has come to recognize the futility of his mission, Sancho urges him to live for further chivalrous forays and says that "he who is vanished today will be the victor tomorrow."[10]

Nor do I share Bloom's judgment that we all share in Macbeth's murderous imagination. Also it seems to me that Bloom's belief that it is Macbeth's proleptic imagination that leads to his doom is highly arguable. Fairly early in the play, it will be recalled, Macbeth, plagued by a guilty conscience that, in killing Duncan, he would be killing not only his king but also his guest and relative, says to his wife that he will go no further in their plan to murder Duncan. It is his wife's appeal to his machismo that reconvinces him to slay his sleeping victim. As for Bloom's claim that the marriage of Macbeth is the happiest in all of Shakespeare's plays, all I can say is that, if this is indeed true, then that statement is the best argument for maintaining one's bachelorhood that I have ever heard.

What Bloom's book really could have used is a balanced recognition of the differences between romanticism and classicism. He would have benefited, for example, from applying the wisdom implicit in Professor George A. Panichas's lucid explanation of the difference he found in his study of Irving Babbitt's "Critical Legacy":

> The need to distinguish between classicism and romanticism constituted, for Babbitt, a judgmental process that centers, and insists, on fundamentals: on fundamentals that must posit critical standards and discipline in an age that has witnessed the weakening of the traditional beliefs. In emphasizing the need for clear-cut definitions, for precise critical analysis, and "hard consecutive thinking," Babbitt hoped to bring attention to the allied need for affirming an enduring scale of values, in the permanent framework of which the job of definition and analysis must be done.[11]

I return to the original question I posed at the beginning of this review: Is Bloom a "hopeless Romantic"? Romantic he definitely is, but "hopeless" he is not. To be a Romantic is not automatically a liability. Despite some of the inherent flaws found in Romanticism—the traits of occasional lack of self-discipline, delving into nostalgia, solipsism and lack of objective standards—any movement that can produce a Wordsworth, a Shelley, a Keats, a Hazlitt, a Lamb is a blessing and not a curse. What must be especially noted about Bloom is

his balancing of his occasional pessimism[12] with his exuberant confirmation of the life-enhancing jollity he finds in Falstaff, Bottom, Feste, Touchstone, *et al.* Bloom is also sufficiently honest to discern that, in the final analysis, "There is no 'real' Hamlet as there is no 'real' Shakespeare; the character, like the writer, is a reflecting pool, a spacious mirror in which we must see ourselves." Consequently one is somewhat prepared for the shocking admission by Bloom when, at the end of the book, he concludes: "It is no longer possible for anyone to read everything of some interest and value that has been published on Shakespeare." One is tempted to agree with this funereally honest statement and perhaps declare that, beyond Melville's poetic tribute to the Bard in "The Coming of Storm" there is nothing else to say:

> No other surprise can come to him
>   Who reaches Shakespeare's core
> That which we seek and shun is there—
>   Man's final lore.

Bardolatry, however, like any other "-latry" (be it "idolatry," "chronolatry," "theolatry"), needs constant reaffirmation to maintain its vitality. In the necessary effort to retain the glory of Shakespeare, and indeed the glories of the Western canon, Harold Bloom has kept the flame blazing—with sublime passion.

Notes

1. "I am probably the largest monster of reading I have ever known. I can read at a shocking rate and I can remember nearly everything." This rather immodest revelation to Adam Begley appeared in Begley's article "Colossus Among Critics: Harold Bloom," *The New York Times Magazine* (September 25, 1994), 34.

2. Begley, 35.

3. Begley, 35.

4. Harold Bloom, *Shakespeare: The Invention of the Human.*

5. Bloom has also edited and written introductions to about four hundred books; his book reviews are found in such publications as *The New York Times Book Review, Bostonia,* etc.; he has appeared on the Charlie Rose Show, the Commonwealth Club of California: he has been featured in *The Chronicle of Higher Education* and has received the prestigious and financially lucrative MacArthur Fellowship.

6. Interestingly enough, although Bloom is fierce in declaring his independence from others—and in the importance of struggling against one's literary predecessors so as to realize one's own creative strength (See his *Agon: Towards a Theory of Revisionism* and *A Mask of Misreading*), he derived the subtitle for his book on Shakespeare from Hazlitt,

and throughout one clearly sees the influence of critics as varied as Samuel Johnson, A. C. Bradley, Harold C. Goddard, and others.

7. *The Western Canon: The Books and School of the Ages* (New York, 1994), 520. Incidentally, it is here in his chapter on Freud that he calls Freud "possibly the best mind of our century." That does not stop him from flaying Freud for insisting that Shakespeare could not possibly have written the plays. It must have been someone of a more aristocratic and superior background. He also berated Freud for misleading allegorical interpretations of the plays.

8. The word "sublime," or variants thereof, occurs frequently: "a vision of the sublime"; "the canonical sublime"; "the negative sublime"; "sublimely demonic"; "sublimely sadistic"; "the tragic sublime"; "enigmatic sublime."

9. As noted above, his favorite critics are Samuel Johnson, William Hazlitt, Samuel T. Coleridge, Harold C. Goddard, A. C. Bradley. It should be noted he particularly favors the Romantic critics.

10. In his chapter on Shakespeare in his earlier *Ruin the Sacred Truths: Poetry and Belief from the Bible to the Present,* a somewhat revised printing (1987, 1989) of The Charles Eliot Norton Lectures given at Harvard in 1987-1988, Bloom gave what seems to me a more balanced judgment of Falstaff. He calls him "a person without the super-ego. . . . Perhaps, even better, Falstaff is not the Sancho Panza of Cervantes but the exemplary figure of Kafka's parable 'The Truth about Sancho Panza.'"

11. *The Critical Legacy of Irving Babbitt* (Wilmington, Del., 1999), 52-53.

12. Note for example the following; ". . . the authentic Shakespearean litany chants variations upon the word 'nothing,' and the uncanniness of nihilism haunts almost every play, even the great, relatively unmixed comedies."

James S. Baumlin (essay date fall 2000)

SOURCE: Baumlin, James S. "Reading Bloom (Or: Lessons Concerning the 'Reformation' of the Western Literary Canon)." *College Literature* 27, no. 3 (fall 2000): 22-46.

[*In the following essay, Baumlin analyzes the Gnostic theology informing Bloom's* The Western Canon, *and applies Bloom's aesthetic to the canonical debate within academic literature.*]

> He will observe this rule concerning the canonical Scriptures, that he will prefer those accepted by all catholic Churches to those which some do not accept; among those which are not accepted by all, he should

prefer those which are accepted by the largest number of important Churches to those held by a few minor Churches of less authority. . . . The whole canon of the Scriptures . . . is contained in the following books. . . .

> (St. Augustine 1958, 41-42)

> All canonizing of literary texts is a self-contradictory process, for by canonizing a text you are troping upon it, which means you are misreading it. Canonization is the most extreme form of what Nietzsche called Interpretation, or the exercise of the Will-to-Power over texts.

> (Bloom 1975, 100)

> My own religious experience and conviction is a form of Gnosis, and in some sense all of this book . . . is a kind of Gnostic sermon. My spiritual concerns, while personal, Jewish, and American, have a universal element in them that stems from a lifetime's study of Gnosis, both ancient and modern. Yet this book, though informed by scholarship, is not a scholarly work but a personal religious testimony that reaches out to our common concerns as the Millennium approaches.

> (Bloom 1996, 2)

A best-selling, award-winning book (albeit heavily criticized by students of the field), Harold Bloom's *The Western Canon: The Books and School of the Ages* (1994) has carried the current curricular debate in English to a nationwide readership of professionals and non-professionals alike.[1] A best-seller, and yet aspects of the book's argument remain, I suspect, a puzzlement to some readers even within the profession, given its many distinctively Bloomian idiosyncrasies—idiosyncrasies that render the book misinterpretable and perhaps even unreadable (that is, apart from the author's related writings and the larger professional dialogue). This is but Bloom's latest on "canonical" literature, and his arguments, though expressed through a critical vocabulary largely of his own making—virtually an idiolect fashioned from Freudian depth psychology, Kabbalah, and Gnosticism—have remained remarkably consistent over the last three decades. An author of many titles, yet Bloom continues to write the same book over and over again. As Martin Heidegger notes, a great thinker is wont to think just one great thought, Bloom's being his Freud-inspired, Gnosis-informed "anxiety of influence." But the Gnostic basis of Bloom's thinking, while influential throughout previous writings and explicitly asserted, reappears in *The Western Canon* without adequate explanation or defense. Readers familiar with his previous writings will find in *The Western Canon* an expansion of Bloom's "one great thought," though novitiates are likely to need glosses. The book's major reviewers (Dean 1994, Ferguson 1995, Kerrigan 1995, Schneidau 1995, and Stewart 1996) offer useful criticisms, but leave crucial aspects insufficiently explained or unexplored; these include the book's complex tone, the nature and extent of Bloom's "literary Gnosticism," and the theology implicit in Bloom's theory of the "isolate selfhood"—a theology which, in turn, grounds his radically individualist, post-Romantic aesthetics.

This essay has a double movement. Through the first half, I shall gloss the argument of *The Western Canon* by reference to Bloom's more explicitly Gnostic writings—particularly *Kabbalah and Criticism* (1975), *Agon* (1982), *Ruin the Sacred Truths* (1989), *The American Religion* (1992), and *Omens of Millennium* (1996)—in order to illuminate aspects of the book's underlying theology. Ultimately, I hope to show that Bloom's "defense" of the "Western Canon" rests upon a deliberate confusion of religious and aesthetic categories. Through the second half, I shall situate Bloom's argument within the broader canon-debate currently occupying our profession. Though Bloom's critical vocabulary, explicitly Gnostic in origin, remains anathema to Western, Judeo-Christian religious orthodoxies, nonetheless it reflects a habit of discourse all too common within English studies—that is, a habit, often unconscious, of sacralizing its discourse and confusing the distinctions between secular and religious texts, traditions, and canons. It is hardly surprising that opponents of the traditional English syllabus resort to a language of sacred parody and exorcism; more curious is the fact that proponents of the traditional syllabus, Bloom among them, cheerfully embrace the role of "secular priesthood" when defending the canon. But let us turn first to an analysis of Bloom's rhetoric.

* * *

For Bloom, poetry and criticism are "a single entity" (1982, 41), joined cognitively and stylistically in the making of meaning. But more than simply assert this unity, Bloom puts it to the test, consciously turning criticism into a literary-stylistic performance. While such literariness may increase a reader's pleasure (especially if one enjoys satire directed at contemporary theorists, Bloom's so-called "School of Resentment"), it also complicates the reader's task. Certainly Bloom's stylistic bravado warps the argument in subtle ways, serving to ironize his more extreme claims and, ultimately, rendering the text unreliable as "philosophical" (as opposed to "literary" or "poetic") discourse.[2] In order to read *The Western Canon* strongly or "knowingly," then, one must first come to terms with its complex, Menippean style. Though heralded as a piece of serious academic criticism, the book modulates into a modern Jeremiad, presenting an unstable mixture of analysis, lamentation, exhortation, satire, confession, personal invective, and prophecy, seeking its unity (and appealing to its readership) less through argument than through the voice and personality of its author.[3] Filled with personal narrative and anecdote, *The Western Canon* takes the author himself as its final subject. (It is

only a slight caricature to subtitle the work, *Bloom Reading*.) But this auto-writing, too, is in keeping with Bloom's aesthetic (for which read "theology," as I shall explain below) of radical individualism. As he writes, "I myself insist that the individual self is the only method and the whole standard for apprehending aesthetic value" (1994, 22).

Doubtless, this refusal to allow ultimate distinctions between literary and critical discourse offers a certain protection. "Must critics take me so seriously?" are words one imagines in response—however ironic these might seem, given Bloom's own theory of "misprision" (1975, 95-126), which prescribes "misreading" as a necessary psychological defense against literary precursors. And occasionally throughout *The Western Canon* Bloom ridicules his previous readers' failures, though this sort of defense eventually wears thin. But once s/he acknowledges the book's complex rhetoric, a reader is less likely to be taken in (or, conversely, offended) by its excesses. I would suggest, further, that Bloom *expects* this book to exceed most readers' capacities, that Bloom *knows* (a good Gnostic, he) that only a few readers possess the heterodox esoteric traditions underlying his otherwise seemingly conservative arguments, and that a majority of his readers would be unsettled, even shocked, were they to grasp the full import of Bloom's "religion of art," as Paul Dean (1994, 59) terms it. My point is that *The Western Canon* is high heterodoxy disguised as tradition, and that it might be to the author's advantage that so few readers would know, or even guess.[4] But whatever the difficulty in pinning Bloom down, of stripping away the ironies and overstatements to expose his most earnest claims, Bloom's recent popularity makes the attempt worth hazarding.

As part of his own private war against contemporary critical theory, Bloom offers to defend the secular literary canon as a system of aesthetics rather than an instrument of politics, ideology, or progressive education. As Bloom avers,

> Ideology plays a considerable role in literary canon-formation, if you want to insist that an aesthetic stance is itself an ideology, an insistence that is common to all six branches of the School of Resentment: Feminists, Marxists, Lacanians, New Historicists, Deconstructionists, Semioticians. There are, of course, aesthetics and aesthetics, and apostles who believe that literary study should be an overt crusade for social change obviously manifest a different aesthetic from my own post-Emersonian version of Pater and Wilde.
>
> (Bloom 1994, 492)

Yet reviewers have questioned the extent to which Bloom's aestheticism remains true to his late Victorian forebears, Walter Pater and Oscar Wilde. Bloom "wants to be an advocate of pure aestheticism," Stanley Stewart notes, and Bloom acknowledges Pater as his "literary 'father'" (1996, 29); nonetheless Bloom violates "his own nonideological ideology" (29), as Stewart suggests, by arguing on behalf of "unbelief" or atheism:

> Unlike Pater, who was deliciously comfortable with Agnosticism as a final perspective on the human situation, [Bloom] is uneasy with his unbelief. He has the good sense to hate the mob of political cheerleaders in the academy, who contaminate literary criteria with social aims. But at the same time, having placed his faith in unbelief, he has become a cheerleader for unbelief. . . . This is why he completely forgets that the heroines of Austen's novels were Christians, in some cases . . . more Christian than their parish rector.
>
> (Stewart 1996, 29-30)

Stewart makes two claims, both of which Bloom would roundly reject. First, he reduces Bloom's Gnostic beliefs to mere atheism, a brand of "perverse and stubborn solipsism" (28), as Stewart writes elsewhere.[5] Second, he states the belief that a "pure aestheticism" must remain uncommitted in all respects and is, therefore, singularly and correctly "agnostic," which Bloom's system is not. The first claim, common enough among Bloom's reviewers, can be treated as a kind of defensive "misreading," whose effect is to free readers from taking the author's Gnostic commitments too seriously (a "stubborn solipsism," after all, poses no threat to readers' personal psychologies). Stewart's second claim—that aesthetic and theological commitments are mutually exclusive—is also common enough among literary critics. Yet Bloom believes otherwise. Arguing elsewhere that "the truest aesthetic is the Valentinian Gnosis" (1982, 56), Bloom offers readers not Pater or Wilde, but rather a "*Post-Emersonian* version" (1994, 492) of aestheticism—Ralph Waldo Emerson being, in Bloom's mind, the great American Gnostic who "champions the literary culture of the isolate individual" (1982, 21). Reviewing **The Western Canon,** Frances Ferguson seems to marvel at the fact that "the self in Bloom's account does not merely recognize aesthetic value; it also . . . *has* aesthetic value, the aesthetic value of the 'isolate selfhood'" (1995, 1152). I would add that the "aesthetic value of the 'isolate selfhood'" should be found to be theological in origin and implication.

Readers have ridiculed Bloom's assertion that "all that the Western Canon can bring one is the proper use of one's own solitude, the solitude whose final form is one's confrontation with one's own mortality" (1994, 30); Herbert N. Schneidau, for one, terms this "a particularly shameless form of romanticizing oneself" (1995, 136-37). Yet by now it should be clear that Bloom's discourse on "the proper use of one's solitude" can be read more strongly as an allegory upon Gnosis. In **Omens of Millennium,** Bloom expresses the "conviction that . . . a great many of us are Gnostics without knowing what it is that we know" (1996, 234). This is a crucial distinction, if true, for it allows him to articulate a theory of "literary Gnosticism" operating independently of the texts and traditions of ancient Gnosticism. For, while "there is no Gnosticism without Gnosis," as he writes in **Agon,** "yet there is a Gnosis without Gnosticism, as Emerson, Blake and others have shown in their lives and writings" (1982, 4). Indeed, seeking to "illustrate how poetic knowledge is a Gnosis; or rather, how much closer poetic knowledge is to Gnosis than to philosophical knowledge of any kind" (11), Bloom begins **Agon** "by attempting an exposition of Gnosis apart from Gnosticism" (4)—a strategy worth emulating here. Recalling his claim that "the truest aesthetic is the Valentinian Gnosis" (56), we are now ready to ask, what sort of "knowing," or Gnosis, lies at the center of a reader's aesthetic experience?

Equating "poetic knowledge" with "self-knowledge" should hardly offend orthodox opinion; humanist educators since the Renaissance have paid lip service to the Socratic *gnothi seauton,* "know thyself," so it would seem unsurprising that Bloom defends canonical literature as a means to nurture "the growing inner self" (1992, 36). But Bloom's is a different sort of "self-knowledge" and, to this extent at least, a different sort of humanism—even, indeed, a different human psychology—than traditionally conceived.[6] In the following passage from **Agon,** Bloom contrasts his theory of "deep reading" with psychoanalysis:

> How much can you know of your own history, when your knowing is itself a crucial movement in that history? The illuminating analogues to this dilemma seem to me to reside in reading poetry, rather than in undergoing psychoanalysis. The peculiar rigors of transference and counter-transference and the waywardness of the unconscious combine to prevent psychoanalysis from becoming a Gnosis, that is, from getting beyond an uneasy knowledge of the multi-layered text of the psyche. But in the deep reading of a poem what you come to know is a concept of happening, a realization of events in the history of your own spark or pneuma, and your knowing is the most important movement in that history. A reader who has known Browning's *Childe Roland,* or Stevens's *The Idea of Order at Key West,* or some comparable poem, will discover that the knowledge is a Gnosis, or can become one.
>
> (Bloom 1982, 8)

"Literary Gnosis" thus begins by recognizing and exploring an author's "knowing," but turns ultimately to recognize a similarly interior event in readers. Invoking ancient Gnosticism's tripartite division of the human being into *hyle* (the material body), *psyche* (the individual mind or soul) and *pneuma* (the uncreated "spark" or, in Gnostic myth, the Primordial Adam, who pre-exists material creation and remains—though alienated from its divine origins—an aspect of the transcendent deity), Bloom turns "the deep reading of a poem" (an alternative "depth psychology"?) into a means of knowing this "Real Me or self or spark" (1992, 15).[7] Undreamed of in Freudian depth psychology, this "*pneuma* or spark, the 'awful Life' that lurks beneath the 'adhesive self' or *psyche*" becomes the ultimate subject of reading, and, Bloom adds, "if this is what the poet speaks to, then this is what must answer that call by a knowing" (1982, 9).

Surely such a concept blurs all practical distinctions between poetry (at least, of a particular kind) and private religious experience (here, too, of a particular kind). As Bloom writes, "literary criticism, as I have learned to practice it, relies finally upon an irreducibly *aesthetic* dimension. . . . Analogously, religious criticism must seek for the irreducibly *spiritual* dimension. . . . Aesthetic values, in my vision, transcend societal and political concerns. . . . Spiritual values similarly transcend the claims of society and politics" (1992, 21). Though Bloom goes on to claim that "literature and religion are not allied enterprises" (21), his own rhetoric gives him the lie. For indeed, "religious criticism," as Bloom argues in the same work,

> has to take literary criticism as its analogue and model, substituting an irreducibly spiritual element for the irreducible effect of the aesthetic. History, sociology, anthropology, and psychology, working together, almost invariably reduce religion in much the same way that they reduce imaginative literature. . . . Religious doctrines and experiences alike share with poems a stance against dying, or to put this most simply, the category of the "religious" is set against death even as the "poetic" seeks a triumph over time.
>
> (Bloom 1992, 36)

The more one reads such a passage, the less stable and clear its distinctions remain; increasingly, they become differences that make no difference. Less hedging is *Kabbalah and Criticism* (1975), where Bloom writes that poetry is a "warding off, defending against death. From our perspective, religion is spilled poetry" (1975, 52).[8] Having turned literary criticism into a form of mysticism, he leaves unwary readers (of *The Western Canon* particularly) to puzzle over such statements as, "the Western worship of God—by Jews, Christians, and Moslems—is the worship of a literary character, J's Yahweh" (1994, 6), and "the Jesus loved by Christians is a literary character largely invented by the author of the gospel of Mark" (30). Are such statements intended to demystify Western religion, or are they refusals, finally, to distinguish poetry from religion, religion from poetry? Once again, Bloom is too much a student of Blake (not to mention of Valentinian gnosis) to make his own "Great Code" easy of access. Still, decades earlier, Bloom had already declared Kabbalah to be "unique among religious systems in that it is, simply, already poetry, scarcely needing translation into the realms of the aesthetic" (1975, 52) and that a "Kabbalistic model . . . means ultimately a Gnostic model" of reading (87).[9]

Reviewing *The Western Canon,* William Kerrigan complains that "none of the canonical poets are Christians. The ones with any religion in them at all turn out to be Gnostics, which makes a certain sense with Whitman and Borges. But Dante?" (1995, 201). Indeed, Bloom's reading of Dante well illustrates his underlying aesthetic/theological system. Observing first that *The Divine Comedy,* "like all of the greatest canonical works, destroys the distinction between sacred and secular writing" (1994, 77), Bloom finds in Dante's Beatrice "a private gnosis, a poet's alteration of the scheme of salvation" (78) and a myth "closer to Gnosticism than to Christian orthodoxy" (85). While more orthodox critics (such as John Freccero, cited by Bloom) read Dante as a "faithful Augustinian," content to emulate the *Confessions* in his "novel of the self" (26), Bloom himself denies any such subservience on the Tuscan poet's part. "It is Beatrice," rather,

> whose presence and function transform Augustine . . . into something figuratively much richer, adding strangeness to truth (if you think it is the truth) or to fiction (if you regard it as that). I myself, as a student of gnosis, whether poetic or religious, judge [*The Divine Comedy*] to be neither truth nor fiction but rather Dante's *knowing,* which he chose to name Beatrice. When you know most intensely, you do not necessarily decide whether it is truth or fiction; what you know primarily is that the knowing is your own.
>
> (Bloom 1994, 93)

With such a claim, we seem to have reached the limits of "literary Gnosticism" and are left to recount the major features of ancient, esoteric Gnosticism itself, aspects of which have been lurking throughout our discussion thus far. The subject is too vast and confusing for an individual, inexpert as I am, to outline, so I turn to Hans Jonas, one of the field's most celebrated scholars.

Outlining the Gnostic cosmology, Jonas writes that "the cardinal feature of gnostic thought is the radical dualism that governs the relation of God and the world, and correspondingly that of man and the world" (1963, 42). He continues:

> The deity is absolutely transmundane, its nature alien to that of the universe, which it neither created nor governs and to which it is the complete antithesis: to the divine realm of light, self-contained and remote, the cosmos is opposed as a realm of darkness. . . . The transcendent God Himself is hidden from all creatures and is unknowable by natural concepts. Knowledge of Him requires supernatural revelation and illumination. . . . The universe, the domain of the Archons, is like a vast prison whose innermost dungeon is the earth, the scene of man's life. . . . The spheres are the seats of the Archons. . . . As guardian of his sphere, each Archon bars passage to the souls that seek to ascend after death, in order to prevent their escape from the world and their return to God. The Archons are also the

creators of the world, except where this role is reserved for their leader, who then has the name of *demiurge* . . . and is often painted with the distorted features of the Old Testament God.

(Jonas 1963, 42-44)

Jonas's last point explains why some readers find Bloom's self-professed Jewish Gnosticism to be a contradiction in terms; indeed, Bloom notes "its rebellion against normative Judaism" (1996, 185), especially in identifying Yahweh with the dark, inferior *demiurge*. Implicitly anti-Jewish in cosmology, its human psychology is equally heretical. Quoting an ancient Gnostic formula that "earthly Man is a mortal god, and that the celestial God is an immortal man" (238), Bloom asks, "yet what can it mean to be a 'mortal god?'" (238). Describing Gnostic or "pneumatic" man, Jonas explains:

> Man . . . is composed of flesh, soul, and spirit. But reduced to ultimate principles, his origin is twofold: mundane and extramundane. Not only the body but also the "soul" is a product of the cosmic powers, which shaped the body in the image of the divine primal (or Archetypal) Man and animated it with their own psychical forces: these are the appetites and passions of natural man. . . . Enclosed in the soul is the spirit, or "pneuma" (called also the "spark"), a portion of the divine substance from beyond which has fallen into the world; and the Archons created man for the express purpose of keeping it captive there. . . . In its unredeemed state the pneuma thus immersed in soul and flesh is unconscious of itself, benumbed, asleep. . . . In brief, it is "ignorant." Its awakening and liberation is effected through "knowledge." . . . The goal of gnostic striving is the release of the "inner man" from the bonds of the world and his return to his native realm of light. The necessary condition for this is that he *knows* about the transmundane God and about himself, that is, about his divine origin as well as his present situation. . . .

(Jonas 1963, 44)[10]

More than Jonas and other scholars, Bloom remains truer to the spirit of esoteric Gnosticism by hesitating to summarize its beliefs or otherwise reduce it to a set of abstract precepts. The pursuit of mysticism, after all, differs from systematic theology in its being experienced rather than studied (or, simply, "believed"). Hence the major texts of ancient Gnosticism—such as the following "Valentinian formula" (Jonas 1963, 44 [*Excerpta* 78.2]), oft-quoted by Bloom—are in essence poems-in-prose, radically metaphoric texts whose truth and meaning lie always elsewhere, beyond language (and, most certainly, beyond discursive reason): "what liberates is the knowledge of who we were, what we became; where we were, whereinto we have been thrown; whereto we speed, wherefrom we are redeemed; what birth is, and what rebirth" (44-45).[11]

What practical consequences might all this have to Bloom's defense of his so-called "Western Canon"? Can Valentinian gnosis offer the basis of a postmodern

literary aesthetics? Can it "save" Bloom's canon? Most obviously, Bloom's aesthetic flies in the teeth of Marxist theory and its critique of liberal humanism (which, traditionally, emphasizes an education in canonical literature).[12] Need I repeat the liberal view? Surely its most common argument—that the secular canon teaches "humane" and "universal" values, offering standards of excellence for all time—is the least persuasive: if aesthetic judgments are arbitrary (as Marxists claim) rather than universal, then a literary canon preserves little more than the tastes and interests of the dominant class (or race, or gender). And the argument that a literary canon preserves cultural memory proves nearly as objectionable: by equating cultural value with the dominant ideology, such a canon serves little more than to silence marginalized cultural voices (so the refutation goes). If not to preserve cultural memory or enforce a standard of taste, might canonical literature offer training in morals and manners? Here we may recall the Victorian Matthew Arnold's hope that literature (of course, the culture's "best" literature) could come to the rescue of modern, post-Christian society, where an established church no longer serves authoritatively as a culture's moral teacher. Why read literature? And why read some literature rather than some other? The liberal "nutshell" answer, as Eagleton puts it, is that "it made you a better person" (1983, 35). Doubtless the atrocities of modern history give the lie to this naive claim: "when the Allied troops moved into the concentration camps . . . to arrest commandants who had whiled away their leisure hours with a volume of Goethe, it appeared that someone had some explaining to do" (35). Yet Bloom seeks to disarm the Marxist critique by denying altogether that literature serves morality, society, or political ideology. Perhaps hyperbolically, Bloom writes, "If we read the Western Canon in order to form our social, political, or personal moral values, I firmly believe we will become monsters of selfishness and exploitation. To read in the service of any ideology is not, in my judgment, to read at all. . . . The true use of Shakespeare . . . is to augment one's own growing inner self" (1994, 28). This sentiment is repeated throughout *The Western Canon*: "Reading the very best writers—let us say Homer, Dante, Shakespeare, Tolstoy—is not going to make us better citizens . . . the aesthetic is, in my view, an individual rather than a societal concern" (15-16).

In short, Bloom offers the most radically private criterion ever adduced for a secular canon: an invitation to experience, through selective reading, a solitude in which "God knows the deep self even as it knows God" (1996, 182). Whereas previous defenses have offered formal/aesthetic or ethical criteria as expressions of shared cultural values (which Marxists effectively reduce to expressions of class tastes and judgments), Bloom's repudiates all cultural, communal, ethical, and interpersonal criteria. And this repudiation, though the logical consequence of his individualist "religion of art" (1994, 59), has caused readers considerable consternation. "This defense is pointless," Schneidau declares: "its propositions are as untestable as Freud's, and too personal and rhetorical to generate real exchanges" (1995, 131). Frances Ferguson argues similarly: Bloom, "on the one hand, describes the canon as if it were a merely personal and individual matter and, on the other, publishes the contents of his canon as if it were useful for other people to know it" (1995, 1149); more succinctly she writes, Bloom "emphasizes individuality and individual consciousness and continually presents them as simultaneously individual and societal" (1151).

Though incontrovertible in themselves, such criticisms proceed from assumptions that Bloom himself explicitly rejects; put simply, both critics replace Bloom's theology with a sociology of art. Whereas Bloom himself "rejects . . . anthropological reductions of religion" (1992, 175), Ferguson invokes the French anthropologist Claude Lévi-Strauss's claim that "everything takes place as if in our civilization every individual's personality were his totem" (1995, 1157)—thereby reducing Bloom's "isolate selfhood" to a fetish or private totem (and rejecting his aesthetic/theological system out of hand). In his defense, Bloom's Gnostic aesthetic, like any private experience, can be neither proved nor disproved discursively, but only tested experientially. (*Placet experiri*, Thomas Mann repeats throughout *Magic Mountain*. "O taste and see," Scripture itself exhorts: clearly, the subjectivities of experience lie at the problematic center of religion, as of aesthetics.) I do not disagree with Bloom's critics, who complain that his Gnostic aesthetic is at once radically private and yet made "available to others" (Bloom 1982, 4); nonetheless **The Western Canon** remains consistent with Bloom's generally post-Romantic, post-Emersonian spirit, which seeks to preserve the individual (and not culture) as the sole theologically-sanctioned origin of meaning and value. While previous defenses of the secular canon assume a communal, cultural ownership of literature, Bloom's defense turns its back on culture, class, race, and gender to reassert the primacy of the solitary reader. And here Bloom would claim to remember what many in our profession seem to neglect: reading's silent interiority.[13]

* * *

Given that "canon" is, as Bloom notes, "a word religious in its origins" (1994, 19), how can we continue to ignore the mystifications that have crept into the profession's curricular debate? Why, indeed, have we embraced such a term when other, more obviously secular terms are available—such as "classic" and "tradition," terms that Samuel Johnson, Matthew Arnold, and T. S. Eliot used in previous discussions of literature and literariness?[14] Used unconsciously or

naively, the term must surely tell against the traditional English syllabus and its defenders since—and here I quote an old *Catholic Encyclopedia*—the word denotes the "authoritative list or closed number of the writings composed under Divine inspiration" (1908, 3.267), the number and contents of which, "Since the Council of Trent, it is not permitted for the Catholic to question" (3.274). (Who among teachers of English would *not* raise the leveling standard when so strict a rule is applied to secular literature?) So when, exactly, did our curricular discussions assume the rhetoric of "canon warfare"? Might that be worth knowing? One might suspect that the "canonization" of traditional course syllabi was a strategy of polemic made popular at the beginning of the 1980s by Leslie A. Fiedler and Houston A. Baker, Jr., editors of *English Literature: Opening Up the Canon*. Their collection heralded a series of articles appearing in *Critical Inquiry* ("Canon and Power in the Hebrew Scriptures," "The Ideology of Canon-Formation," "The Shaping of a Canon," and "Re-Creating the Canon," among numerous others published between 1983-1984) that were themselves followed by waves of articles, essay collections, and monographs. (Indeed, over the past fifteen years, well over 1,000 works have applied the term "canon" to secular literature and literary instruction, a specific usage that, so far as I have observed, is unusual in dictionaries published prior to the 1960s.)[15] Fiedler himself criticized the English curriculum (and liberal humanism) in terms of sacred parody:

> Though some of us continue to speak of "great books," as if humanism were still a living movement instead of one more classroom subject, we all know in our hearts that literature is effectively what we teach in departments of English; or conversely, what we teach in departments of English is literature. Within that closed definitional circle, we perform the rituals by which we cast out unworthy pretenders from our ranks and induct true initiates, guardians of the standards by which all song and story ought to be judged.
>
> (Fiedler 1981, 73-74)

Through such parody, Fielder seeks to demystify the traditional syllabus, casting its proponents in the role of a secular priesthood performing empty rituals of induction and exorcism. Yet the problem, as Bloom's **The Western Canon** reveals, is that proponents of the traditional syllabus often sacralize the literary canon and their roles as readers (and teachers), lending some truth to Fielder's parody. In **Ruin the Sacred Truths** Bloom writes,

> The times are long gone by in which students of Milton's poetry followed the advice of C. S. Lewis, which was to start the day with a Good Morning's Hatred of Satan. Those were the days of my youth, when professors of literature were a secular clergy. I used to scoff

at such a clerisy, but now the mocker is mocked, the biter bitten, and I would as soon be surrounded by a secular clergy as by a pride of displaced social workers.

(Bloom 1989, 93)

I assume that Bloom wishes to be taken seriously here, as in his later **The Western Canon,** where he writes that "if the governing class, in the days of my youth, freed one to be a priest of the aesthetic, it doubtless had its own interest in such a priesthood" (1994, 23). Here, too, I do not think that Bloom's language is entirely satirical, though he refers elsewhere (and obviously ironically) to various "high priests of the anticanonizers" (22) and "apostles . . . for social change" (492).

If professors of English wish to attack (or, in Bloom's case, defend) textual traditions and teaching in a language of priestly ritual and exorcism, so be it. Yet the implications may well be glimpsed by comparing the current debate to the sectarian conflicts of the European Protestant Reformation—during which time Christianity split into two, three, four, and more churches, each with its distinctive "rule of faith" and set of claims regarding Scriptural Canon. Parallels might also be found in the Old Testament canon—controversies between Palestinian and Alexandrian (or Hellenized) Jews of the First and Second Centuries A.D. (Bruns 1984, 462; see also Childs 1979)—as well as in the New Testament controversies of the Third and Fourth Centuries A.D., when a restricted, orthodox canon triumphed over the texts and teachings of "heretics," Montanist, Manichaean, and Gnostic alike. Not trained as an historian of the early Christian church, I am hardly qualified to make such parallels myself, but I can say that our own age is at least the fourth to confront a culture-wide crisis of "canon," though apparently in the secular realm of English studies. (Let me also apologize here and now for the oversimplifications that I shall perform on Reformation theology: alas, the need to highlight distinctions sometimes brings one too quickly to the brink of caricature.) Throughout the remainder of this essay, I shall speculate on the consequences of having anointed our *Norton Anthologies* with holy oil.

As distinguished from the shorter, more restrictive Protestant Bible, the Catholic Canon is hierarchized into "protocanonical" works (that is, works of the "first" or highest inspiration, the synoptic Gospels for instance) and "deuterocanonical" (that is, works previously contested but finally accepted as inspired, such as the Apocalypse). Within the historical process of canon-formation, some works initially deemed *antilegomena* (that is, disputed though not entirely rejected as authoritative) were ultimately canonized, some others declared apocryphal, and the rest excluded, though exclusion from the Catholic Canon never in itself meant

that such works could not profitably be read by the faithful; it has, however, meant that such works should be read only in certain ways—for education in charity, say, and not for authoritative and "safe" (that is, "saving") doctrine.[16] Paradoxically this older, Catholic model of canonicity once offered the possibility of slow expansion, of a sifting-through and partial assimilation of the "non-canonical" (as, indeed, *antilegomenon* can become deuterocanonical). But note again that the Scriptural Canon—for Catholic and Protestant alike—has remained closed for centuries.

How, then, might such a Scriptural model compare to contemporary curricular trends in English literature? Assuming slow expansion within a hierarchized literary system, one might think that works of African-American, Native-American, and other non-traditional literatures can still become "canonized," though only within a hierarchical arrangement that, as Bloom would have it, necessarily keeps Shakespeare "first" (or "protocanonical"), Dante "second," Dickinson "twelfth," and so on.[17] While the African novelist Chinua Achebe is admitted into Bloom's "Western Canon" (1994, 560), I would suspect that he stands only as a "deutero" or a sort of 2 Maccabees. And while the position of *antilegomenon* suffices to maintain emerging, even controversial works and authors within the traditional literary syllabus, still we must ask, at what price? Early Christian culture, for example, slowly assimilated the pagan literatures of Greece and Rome, but only after banishing (or allegorizing, thereby disarming) their gods.[18] Judged by today's multicultural debate, the Mosaic First Commandment too often exacts too high a price for such assimilation: marginalized or multicultural literatures may be read, but the African gods themselves, the Great Mother, the Native American Earth Spirit, and even History (served by the high priests of Marxism) must fall in sacrifice. I exaggerate only slightly: when Achebe is declared to speak from *within* the "Western canon," his Eurocentrist critique is at least partially domesticated and tamed. I would think that some texts speak loudest when "standing outside" the dominant discourse—for example, the early Gnostic texts informing Bloom's own mysticism, which have been declared heretical and excluded from all orthodox canons, whether Jewish, Catholic, or Protestant. Part of their allure, surely, lies in their dangerous marginality, such texts supplementing as well as undermining the wisdom of Scripture by their "alien" voice and message. Indeed, Kabbalah and Gnosticism both offer powerful historical instances of *counter-canons*—that is, of texts and traditions that cannot be assimilated into orthodoxy, and that gain whatever power they wield precisely by remaining unassimilated. Heresy (from the Greek αιρεσι "to choose" or "take," implying an independent course of action or thought) is *an assertion of freedom,* though a dangerous freedom when pitted against religious (or literary) orthodoxy; one would think that Bloom, in fine Blakean fashion, might rather embrace the heretic's freedom over the canonist's law.

Hence a weakness of Bloom's *The Western Canon* may well be its failure to acknowledge the anti-canonical as a significant and powerful cultural/textual status. Using slightly different terms, John Guillory has made arguments much to this same effect:

> It has seemed necessary to many progressive critics to present certain texts by minority authors as intrinsically noncanonical, as unassimilable to the traditional canon. The separatist strategy follows from the same basic assumption of pluralist canonical critique as the integrationist, that the process of the inclusion or exclusion of texts is identical to the representation or nonrepresentation of social groups. . . . The noncanonical is a newly constituted category of text production and reception, permitting certain authors and texts to be taught as noncanonical, to have the status of noncanonical works in the classroom. . . . It is only as canonical works that certain texts can be said to represent hegemonic social groups. Conversely, it is only as noncanonical works that certain other texts can truly represent socially subordinated groups.
>
> (Guillory 1993, 9)[19]

And thus heresy—a freedom of thought and expression independent of orthodox canons—may be more potent than Bloom intimates. Perhaps the opposition most worth our attention arises not in the distinction between "canonical" and "non-canonical," but rather between "canonical" and "anti-canonical," since the "non-canonical" is too easily dismissed as defective (and therefore largely powerless); in contrast, the "anti-canonical" remains dangerously independent of orthodoxy and, for this reason, can make claims to express an authority of its own.

Of course the real problem, to which Reformation history alerts us, is that even the Christian Church could not settle on a singular, definitive canon. Instead, there arose three major systematic theologies during the Sixteenth Century: the old Catholicism, which located truth in "tradition" and church institution, granting the church (that is, a professional priesthood) sole authority in interpreting Scripture; Lutheranism (a belated second), which located truth in the text itself (rather than in "tradition": *sola fide, sola Scriptura*), thus treating Scripture as if it were a self-contained, even self-interpreting, meaning system; and Calvinism (a more radical third), which supplemented the revealed truth of Scripture with the "inner word" or light of the private, individual conscience. I do not wish to turn the various Reformation theologies into so many allegories of contemporary critical method: metaphors of a Catholic "old philology," a Lutheran "formalism," and a Calvinist "reader-response" do not hold. (Yet there are currently about as many literary, critical, interpretive methods as there are contemporary religious sects, each with its own canon and creed.)

By speaking of a Catholic, a Lutheran, and a Calvinist Canon I am no longer referring simply to a catalog of Scripture but, rather, to a prior criterion or "rule of faith," a *regula fidei* that offers to justify and preserve one's religious canon and doctrine by asserting—indeed, by guaranteeing—its divinely-inspired, divinely-sanctioned authority. As Richard H. Popkin observes (and his observation holds for both the history of the Reformation and our current canon debate), "the problem of justifying a standard of true knowledge does not arise as long as there is an unchallenged criterion" (1964, 3).[20] Yet Protestant arguments against Catholic tradition proceeded (perhaps necessarily) by means of a radical skepticism that ultimately served to deny *any* theology—reflexively, its own included—a means to claim, and to demonstrate, the absolute authority of its own "rule of faith." In other words, the instruments of skepticism and critique became inevitably self-reflexive, as the course of the Reformation so poignantly demonstrated. For "the intellectual core of this battle of the Reformation," Popkin writes, "lay in the search for justification of infallible truth in religion by some sort of self-validating or self-evident criterion. Each side was able to show that the other had no 'rule of faith' that could guarantee its religious principles with absolute certainty" (14).

If this summary of the Reformation's crisis (and ultimate failure) in establishing a single, sure "rule of faith" seems remote from our current canon debate, let me point out that the ecclesiastical word "canon" denotes precisely this, a "rule of faith." The Greek κανων means literally a "rule" or "measuring-rod" which, applied to Scripture, determines the place of any text or passage within a restricted catalog of authoritative books (the existence and preservation of which establishes both the belief-system and the corporate identity of its followers). So a Scriptural Canon is not simply a list of books: it is, rather, *a criterion by means of which any book is to be tested* for its authority (theologically, its "divine inspiration") and, thus, for its *guaranteed place* in such a list. And during the Reformation, it was the difference among competing criteria that led to schism and, ultimately, to centuries of religious warfare. The Reformation should teach us that arguments used to undermine "traditional" conceptions of hierarchy and canonicity cannot logically establish new canons in turn.[21] By various means, one can argue that Shakespeare is *not* superior to other, "non-canonical" authors; but it does not therefore follow that other authors merit reading in his place. The very relativism adduced to undermine Shakespeare's curricular dominance necessarily, logically, extends to all. Arguments used to destroy, doubt, or undermine the "Western Canon" must surely dash any future or alternative attempts to build anew, whether that new canon be post-colonial, gay-feminist, popular-cultural, or what-have-you. Bloom suggests as much when he writes, "pragmatically, the 'expansion of the Canon' has meant the destruction of the Canon" (1994, 6-7)—its destruction, that is, not as a catalog of books but as a strict "rule" or "measuring rod," guaranteeing aesthetic value or excellence. So our profession seems caught in a dilemma: either we must refuse the concept of canonicity altogether (thereby disabling the value-claims of any marginal, non-traditional, non-canonical text), or else we must continue our battles over literary hierarchy and canonicity *within* the current hierarchy itself. No other alternative seems available, so long as we remain unwilling to affirm the culturally dangerous status of heresy—the status, that is, of the anti-canonical. Only an affirmation of the anti-canonical (or of counter-canons, as opposed simply to the non-canonical) can transform the current canon-debate into a genuine dialectic.

If I may be allowed a local example, my own department of English recently replaced its B.A. requirement for an upper-division single-author course (in effect, a course in Chaucer, Shakespeare, or Twain) with a course in non-European, non-American, "non-canonical" literature. In other words, "Shakespeare" (read this name as a synecdoche) has been replaced by "Chinua Achebe" (read this name, too, as a synecdoche). Previously, our department declared "Shakespeare" (synecdoche) "protocanonical"; now, "Shakespeare" (synecdoche) would become a curricular "elective," "Achebe" (synecdoche) a "requirement." Why might this happen? To the suggestion that perhaps *neither* "Shakespeare" *nor* "Achebe" should be declared a "requirement," leaving the student to choose, at least one member of an *ad hoc* curriculum review committee responded, "But aren't we more qualified than our students to determine what they need to become literate individuals?" *Shouldn't we tell them* what courses, periods, or authors are vital? *Aren't we* the authorities? The problem is that we, as a committee (or department, or field, or even profession) have lost the ability (and perhaps the will) to articulate a singular criterion—a "canon" or "rule of faith"—by which such a choice could even be made. Once literary-aesthetic criteria are relativized (which the current debate has achieved), no single author, text, tradition, class, cultural status, or ideology can be argued into a secure position of value or dominance. To topple one is necessarily to topple them all: this is not political or conservative reactionism, but a fact of logic. Only by forgetting their own skeptical bases can arguments *against* one canon be turned to arguments for another. Popkin describes this "active forgetting" among Protestant Reformers who insisted, nonetheless,

> on the complete certainty of their cause. In order to ac-
> complish their ecclesiastical revolution, they had to
> insist that they, and they alone, had the only assured
> means of discovering religious knowledge. The break

> with authority was not in favor of a tolerant individual-
> ism in religion, . . . but in favor of a complete
> dogmatism in religious knowledge.
>
> (Popkin 1964, 13)

With but minor changes in vocabulary, such a passage mirrors our current curricular impasse.

I can conclude only that the theological origins and connotations of the term "canon" are precisely the cause of its attractiveness, among both reformers and defenders of the traditional curriculum. In the Burkean sense, "canon" has become one of our profession's "god terms" (though some might say "devil term") and, as such, has become larger than the lives of those participating in the debate. Terms such as these no longer serve us; we serve them. Half the history of the human creature (including, certainly, the European warfare of the Reformation) offers a catalog of atrocities performed in the service of an idea. Few of us would fight for anything less—or more—than a word or concept. One might think that I exaggerate: I am only talking about a syllabus, after all, an English reading list or curriculum. A colleague of mine was fond of saying that academicians argue so vociferously in committees and professional journals "because the stakes are so low." Perhaps. But we do not see it this way. Our curricular arguments are filled with the emotions of missionary zeal. Is there any wonder, then, that arguments concerning the English curriculum have assumed the language and tenor of theological debate?

Thus far, our profession has remained largely (and salutarily) "latitudinarian" in its response to multiculturalism and the plurality of interpretive methods. If we continue to follow the *via media*—that historically Anglican theological compromise, taking the "middle road" between high traditionalism and radical reform—we may yet pull through. Proponents of either extreme will be dissatisfied; no one side will get entirely what it wants. Yet "the center cannot hold," if Bloom prophesies aright; and, if so, the profession of English stands on the verge of yet further schism that may well create two or more academic departments (call them "sects," if you will) out of what is currently a single, though hardly unified, field.[22] So Bloom himself prognosticates:

> The study of Western literature will . . . continue, but
> on the much more modest scale of our current Classics
> departments. What are now called "Departments of
> English" will be renamed departments of "Cultural
> Studies" where *Batman* comics, Mormon theme parks,
> television, movies, and rock will replace Chaucer,
> Shakespeare, Milton, Wordsworth, and Wallace Stevens.
>
> (Bloom 1994, 519)[23]

So long as we do not share a singular "rule of faith," we shall either have to maintain a tolerant, latitudinarian attitude, agreeing to disagree, or else part company in order to elect our own separate presbyters and write our own "canon laws." Of course, the history of our profession is one of competing subjects and methods that have become, ultimately, separate disciplines. At the school where I currently teach, a single department at one time (say, thirty years ago) included professors of classics, communication, foreign languages, philosophy, and journalism as well as English; reflecting national trends and a steady growth in enrollment, first philosophy, then foreign and classical languages, then communication, and then—just a few years ago—journalism "split off." Schism and sectarianism seem bred into our bones.

Notes

1. Having sold 86,000 hardcover copies within four years of publication (its paperback distributor, Riverhead Press, has refused to provide figures, though one imagines soft-cover sales well in excess of 100,000), no other scholarly book—certainly not in English studies—is likely to have sold so well over the past decade. Though other works on the subject are equally deserving of an audience—see for example, Guillory (1993), which typifies current professional attitudes—Bloom's has outsold them all, by as much as 200-to-1. A work so popular, yet so controversial within its own field, should not be read in isolation from its critical contexts.

   Through the following, I wish to highlight these many contexts. But while I take issue with Bloom's conclusions, still I seek to be fair, observing where critics overstate or err. Bloom, too, must be given his due.

2. As Bloom asserted two decades earlier, "I knowingly urge critical theory to stop treating itself as a branch of philosophical discourse, and to adopt instead the pragmatic dualism of the poets themselves. . . . A theory *of* poetry must belong *to* poetry, must *be* poetry, before it can be of any use in interpreting poems" (1975, 109).

3. Bloom's reviewers have observed his penchant for irony. "If pressed," Herbert N. Schneidau notes, "Bloom would no doubt assert that the book is really another strong poem, brought into being by the motive for metaphor rather than by thoughtful concern for genuine issues" (1995, 136). Schneidau probably overstates Bloom's lack of conviction or "thoughtful concern," just as William Kerrigan seems to overrate Bloom's success as a satirist. "With this book," as Kerrigan claims, Bloom "earns the title of supreme academic humorist of our day and towards the end so canonizes himself: 'I am your true Marxist critic, following Groucho rather than Karl . . .'" (1995, 198-99; see also Stewart 1996, 28). Still, treating Bloom as an "academic humorist" somewhat softens the book's several excesses—its "extraordinary inflationary valuations" and "patently empty rhetorical gestures," as Paul Dean (1994, 60) puts it—as

well as its *ad hominem* attacks against the "Resenters," attacks which, to most students of literature, read more like caricature than serious academic criticism.

4. As St. Augustine writes, "many and varied obscurities and ambiguities deceive those who read casually, . . . so obscurely are certain sayings covered with a most dense mist. I do not doubt that this situation was provided by God to conquer pride by work and to combat disdain in our minds" (1958, 37). Dare I invoke an Augustinian model of reading? Like a secular scripture, Bloom's writing is encoded in subtle ways, its esoteric vocabulary offering to welcome initiates only. At the very least, I would argue that Bloom's rhetoric enables him at once to assert, *and to protect,* the heterodox message lying at the book's core. (Then again, how can anyone accuse an ironist of anything *except irony?* Only serious claims can be seriously accused.)

5. "Bloom embraces Gnosticism," Roger Poole declares, "because it is the most extreme form of cultural pessimism he can find in the whole gamut of theological thinking" (1983, 25). In fact Poole, like Stewart, deprecates Bloom's Gnostic commitments (or "obsessions" [19], as Poole terms them): the theories "inaugurated by *Kabbalah and Criticism* one might be tempted to see as explicitly theological, if it were not that Bloom's theological thinking moves by way of various forms of anti-theology" (19). "Violently attacked and quickly uprooted from the early Christian communities" (22), Gnosticism is, Poole claims, "wrongly described as a Christian heresy," since it offers an atheism in the place of theology: "if theology, by definition, is the study of God, then the teachings of Gnosticism must in some way be antithetical to theology, if only because they start from the premise that the world they are discussing is separate from God's creation" (21-22). Poole's logic here appears somewhat Jesuitical. Heterodox, heretical, but hardly offered as an atheism, Bloom's professions deserve more careful consideration, if only because the fate of his aesthetic arguments rests upon very specific theological assumptions, however weird or unsettling these may seem to more orthodox readers. In *Agon* he professes, "I write this book as a Jewish Gnostic, trying to explore and develop a personal Gnosis and a possible Gnosticism, perhaps even one available to others" (1982, 4). And indeed, in *Omens of Millennium*—one of his latest—Bloom offers to expound "Gnosticism as the spiritual alternative available right now to Christians, Jews, Muslims, and secular humanists" (1996, 234). Surely this sounds more evangelical than atheistic.

6. As Jeffrey Nealon writes, "the reemergence of subjective agency as a crucial category in recent literary and cultural studies can be seen as a direct response to the decentering of the subject enacted by the first wave of poststructuralism" (1997, 129). While *The Western Canon* is certainly part of this "direct

response," Bloom's own "ideology of the 'human,'" to steal a phrase from Terry Eagleton (1983, 200), diverges from humanist tradition by redrawing the map of human psychology. Granted, Bloom's humanism remains strongly committed to individual subjective agency and to a "conviction," as Kurt Spellmeyer puts it, "that the self is enduring and real" (1996, 907). But while most recent humanist critiques of poststructuralism assert that "the body, and not language, is the source of the self and the doorway into the living world" (Spellmeyer 1996, 908), for Bloom it is not the body *per se,* but rather the indwelling pneuma or Gnostic "spark," that constitutes one's "deep" self and one's source of value; so we shall see.

7. Note that *The American Religion* preceded *The Western Canon* by two years, making them virtually two consecutive chapters of the same larger book. There Bloom writes that

> freedom, in the context of the American Religion, means being alone with God or with Jesus, the American God or the American Christ. In social reality, this translates as solitude, at least in the inmost sense. The soul stands apart, and something deeper than the soul, the Real Me or self or spark, thus is made free to be utterly alone with a God who is also quite separate and solitary, that is, a free God or God of freedom. What makes it possible for the self and God to commune so freely is that the self is no part of the Creation, or of evolution through the ages. The American self is not the Adam of Genesis but is a more primordial Adam, a Man before there were men or women. Higher and earlier than the angels, this true Adam is as old as God, older than the Bible, and is free of time, unstained by mortality. . . . No American pragmatically feels free if she is not alone, and no American ultimately concedes that she is part of nature.

> (Bloom 1992, 15)

8. Even when most adamant in making distinctions, Bloom cannot abandon the analogies between religious and aesthetic experience. "Poetry and belief," as he writes in *Ruin the Sacred Truths,* "are antithetical modes of knowledge, but they share the peculiarity of taking place *between* truth and meaning, while being somewhat alienated both from truth and from meaning" (1989, 12). Such a passage is worth pausing over. What does it mean that poetry and belief are "modes of knowing" "alienated" from truth? Perhaps both are "alienated" in that their words *awaken something else* in the individual; that is, the words are not themselves constitutive of gnosis. St. Augustine offers a rather orthodox explanation in *The Teacher*: "whenever words are spoken, we either know what they mean or we do not. If we know, they recall rather than teach something to us; if we do not know, they cannot even recall something, though they may lead us to inquire" (1968, 49). Surprisingly, this seems to accord with Bloom's aesthetic: as a pneumatic awakening within the individual, the gnosis of reading recounts an interior

"happening" or experience rather than a passive reception of "information" *per se.* Bloom himself quotes the Gnostic *Gospel of Thomas* (composed during the first century A.D., possibly in Syria), "which promises resurrection through an act of understanding: 'whoever discovers the interpretation of these sayings will not taste death'" (1996, 166). It is not the "sayings" themselves, but their right reading, that saves.

9. As R. Wilson notes, Valentinus (fl. C. 150) was "founder and first head of one of the leading schools of heretical Christian Gnosticism" (1967, 226), identified by Irenaeus (*Adversus Haereses* 3.2.9) as the author of the *Evangelium Veritatis* or "Gospel of Truth," among other Gnostic treatises. Though their origins and mythologies differ (in some ways radically), Bloom's own practice encourages me to downplay the distinctions between Valentinian and Lurianic or Kabbalistic versions of Gnosis.

10. To his own question, "yet what can it mean to be a 'mortal god?'" Bloom provides an answer similar to Jonas: "Since gnosis is the redemption of the 'interior man' or 'interior woman,' inwardness is the heart or center of the mortal godhead" (1996, 238).

11. Taken as the text of Bloom's "Gnostic sermon" in *Omens of Millennium* (1996, 233-53), this passage is also explored in *Kabbalah and Criticism* (1975, 58-64) and serves as epilogue to his "Gnostic fantasy" novel, *The Flight to Lucifer.* As I have mentioned, Bloom consistently treats Gnosticism mythically or poetically, rather than as a set of precepts. Appropriately, then, Bloom's most expansive presentation of the Gnostic mythos is fictionalized: I refer to his *Flight to Lucifer* (for a useful summary see Poole 1983, 19-23).

12. Terming liberal humanism "at once largely ineffectual, and the best ideology of the 'human' that present bourgeois society can muster," Eagleton treats contemporary English departments as extensions of "the ideological apparatus of the modern capitalist state" (1983, 200)—in place of which Marxists have proposed departments of "'cultural criticism,' for which there are no selves." as Bloom complains, "whether in writers or readers, but only politics: gender, racial, class, ethnic" (1986, 19-20).

13. "Now, as he read, his eyes glanced over the pages and his heart searched out the sense, but his voice and tongue were silent" (1955, 6.3): thus Augustine expresses wonder at St. Ambrose's habit, apparently novel for the time, of silent reading. By such example, Augustine himself learned to seek out the living "spirit" within the otherwise "dead letter" of Scripture.

14. As Guillory notes, "canon" was "not until recently a common term in critical discourse," displacing

> the expressly honorific term "classic" precisely in order to isolate the "classics" as the object of critique. The concept of the canon names the traditional curriculum

of literary texts by analogy to that body of writing historically characterized by an inherent logic of *closure*—the scriptural canon. The scriptural analogy is continuously present, if usually tacit, whenever canonical revision is expressed as "opening the canon."

(Guillory 1993, 6)

Indeed, as late as Frank Kermode's *The Classic* (1975) "it was still possible," Guillory notes, "to discuss canon formation exclusively by reference to the word 'classic'" (1993, 344). For Bloom, though, the term "tradition" (translating the Hebrew *Kabbalah*) is already "deeply contaminated by the daemonic" (1975, 97) and serves readers no better.

15. Listing publications from 1981 to 1998, the recent *MLA Bibliography* on CD-ROM finds over 1,500 works through its subject/title search of the term "canon." Admittedly, I have not read them all—nor have I checked all dictionaries for usage, though works at hand point to the term's relative novelty. *Webster's New International Dictionary,* 2nd edition (1957) does not refer "canon" to a list or catalog of *secular* literature, though the 3rd edition (1966) does; even the magisterial *Oxford English Dictionary* (1928) neglects this secularized usage. *The Encyclopedia Britannica* (1968) does not include "catalog of books" among its meanings, though more recent "specialist" encyclopedias and dictionaries tend to reflect this now-fashionable usage. The *Oxford Companion to the English Language,* for example, defines "classics" as "an established canon of literary works" (1992, 216), while the *Encyclopedia of Contemporary Literary Theory* devotes several pages (1993, 514-16) to discussions of "canon," "canon-formation," and "canonical interpretation" (though citing no scholarship prior to 1979). Even so brief a survey should remind us of the modishness of our critical vocabularies.

16. According to Article VI of the Anglican *Book of Common Prayer* ("Of the Sufficiency of the Holy Scriptures for Salvation"), "in the name of the Holy Scripture we do understand those canonical Books of the Old and New Testament, of whose authority was never any doubt in the Church" (1953, 603). Following its list of received works, Article VI states,

> and the other Bookes (as Hierome saith) the Church doth read for example of life and instruction of manners; but yet it doth not apply them to establish any doctrine; such are these following: The Third Book of Esdras, The Fourth Book of Esdras, The Book of Tobias, The Book of Judith, The rest of the Book of Esther, The Book of Wisdom, Jesus the Son of Sirach, Baruch the Prophet, The Song of the Three Children, The Story of Susanna, Of Bel and the Dragon, The Prayer of Manasses, The First Book of Macabees, The Second Book of Macabees.

(The Book of Common Prayer 1953, 604)

17. Unabashed, Bloom writes, "Shakespeare *is* the secular canon, or even the secular scripture; forerunners and legatees alike are defined by him alone for

canonical purposes" (1994, 23-24). Even the Bard's most ardent admirers are likely to find such a claim embarrassing.

18. As St. Augustine declares, "we should not think that we ought not to learn [pagan] literature because Mercury is said to be its inventor, nor that because the pagans dedicated temples to Justice and Virtue . . . we should therefore avoid justice and virtue. Rather, every good and true Christian should understand that wherever he may find truth, it is his Lord's" (1958, 54). Such assimilation or "baptizing" of pagan literary culture represents, as Bloom would say, "misprision" at its boldest.

19. With obvious relevance to Bloom's expanded lists, Guillory adds,

> the inclusion of noncanonical works in the canon misrepresents the social significance of the canon by failing to recognize it as the inevitable embodiment of hegemonic cultural values. On this account canonical and noncanonical works are by definition mutually exclusive; they confront each other in an internally divided curriculum in the same way that hegemonic culture confronts nonhegemonic subcultures in the larger social order.

(Guillory 1993, 20)

I find it ironic, then, that Bloom includes the Apocrypha in his infamous catalog of books, thus finally "canonizing"—albeit in the secular realm— one of the more enduring strands of Western heterodoxy.

20. Similarly, the myth of a "Western Canon" would seem to imply an original and once unchallengeable "Catholic" standard. I use the term "myth," by the way, because no singular, authoritative catalog of secular literature has ever existed; and Bloom's own attempt at such a list cannot, so far as I can tell, serve any useful pedagogic purpose. Paul Dean calls the list "silly" (1994, 58). Indeed it is.

21. In "An Idea and an Ideal of a Literary Canon," Charles Altieri restates, albeit coincidentally, these many Reformation arguments. Skepticism or "systematic suspicion," as he suggests, reduces all value- or truth-claims to "subjectivity," at the same time rendering all future arguments for canon impossible. "Canons," he writes,

> are an institutional form for exposing people to a range of idealized attitudes. . . . If a critic refuses to take such idealizations at face value or to locate grounds on which they can be discussed as idealizations before systematic suspicion is applied, he in effect binds himself within his own narrow circle. . . . He has, then, no terms by which to explain his evaluation. . . . Thousands of years of culture have come to this—a stimulus to subjectivity.

(Altieri 1983, 42)

Earlier Altieri had asserted, "once we emphasize disbelief, we cannot maintain traditional notions of the canon" (1983, 38). Poignantly, then, he concludes with reference to a "faithful" readership: "by seeing how canons can be normative, by understanding the judgments that form them, we are likely to make demands on ourselves to be strong readers who are also faithful readers" (58). I cannot help but refer his phrase, "faithful readers," to an implicit theology of discourse. Whether or not Altieri intends his argument to be driven (as Bloom's is) by theology, clearly his language is shaped by such.

22. It would be difficult (and dangerous) "to understate our disciplinary disunity," as Marshall Gregory puts it (1997, 41). Howard Felperin—himself a deconstructive critic—notes that Marxism and the varieties of poststructuralist criticism pose "a fundamental threat to the institutional and pedagogical practices" (1989, 183) of liberal humanism and, thus far, have successfully resisted assimilation within the humanist traditions that they seek, ultimately, to supplant (for an influential call for such supplanting, see Easthope 1991).

23. Commenting on this passage, Schneidau writes, "This is meant to appall, but as pedagogy it has a certain appeal. Much better to see the cultural implications of *Batman* than to compartmentalize criticism with the canonical works; better even this caricature of Cultural Studies than moribund English departments where aging vestals tend votive flames" (1995, 133). Note once again the fall into sacred parody (though here at Bloom's expense).

Works Cited

Altieri, Charles. 1983. "An Idea and an Ideal of a Literary Canon." *Critical Inquiry* 10: 37-60.

Augustine. 1955. *Augustine: Confessions and Enchiridion.* Trans. Albert C. Outler. Philadelphia: Westminster.

———. 1958. *On Christian Doctrine.* Trans. W. D. Robertson, Jr. Indianapolis: Bobbs-Merrill.

———. 1968. *The Teacher.* Vol 59 of *The Fathers of the Church: A New Translation,* trans. Robert P. Russell. Washington, D.C.: The Catholic University of America Press.

Bloom, Harold. 1975. *Kabbalah and Criticism.* New York: Seabury.

———. 1980. *The Flight to Lucifer: A Gnostic Fantasy.* New York: Vintage.

———. 1982. *Agon: Towards a Theory of Revisionism.* New York: Oxford University Press.

———. 1989. *Ruin the Sacred Truths: Poetry and Belief from the Bible to the Present.* Cambridge: Harvard University Press.

———. 1992. *The American Religion: The Emergence of the Post-Christian Nation.* New York: Simon and Schuster.

———. 1994. *The Western Canon: The Books and School of the Ages.* New York: Harcourt.

———. 1996. *Omens of Millennium: The Gnosis of Angels, Dreams, and Resurrection.* New York: Riverhead.

Book of Common Prayer, The. 1953. New York: Seabury.

Bruns, Gerald L. 1984. "Canon and Power in the Hebrew Scriptures." *Critical Inquiry* 10: 462-80.

Catholic Encyclopedia, The. 1908. 15 vols. New York: Robert Appleton.

Childs, Brevard S. 1979. *Introduction to the Old Testament as Scripture.* Philadelphia: Fortress.

Dean, Paul. 1994. "Shakespeare and Company." *The New Criterion* 13: 58-63.

Eagleton, Terry. 1983. *Literary Theory: An Introduction.* Minneapolis: University of Minnesota Press.

Easthope, Anthony. 1991. *Literary into Cultural Studies.* London: Routledge.

Felperin, Howard. 1989. "The Anxiety of American Deconstruction." In *Deconstruction: A Critique,* ed. Rajnath. Hong Kong: MacMillan.

Ferguson, Frances. 1995. "Canons, Poetics, and Social Value: Jeremy Bentham and How to Do Things with People." *MLN* 110: 1148-164.

Fiedler, Leslie A. 1981. "Literature as an Institution: The View from 1980." In *English Literature: Opening Up the Canon,* ed. Leslie A. Fiedler and Houston A. Baker. Selected Papers from the English Institute, New Series, No. 4. Johns Hopkins University Press.

Fiedler, Leslie A., and Houston A. Baker, Jr., eds. 1981. *English Literature: Opening Up the Canon.* Selected Papers from the English Institute, New Series, No. 4. Baltimore: Johns Hopkins University Press.

Gregory, Marshall. 1997. "The Many-Headed Hydra of Theory vs. The Unifying Mission of Teaching." *College English* 59: 41-58.

Guillory, John. 1983 "The Ideology of Canon-Formation: T. S. Eliot and Cleanth Brooks." *Critical Inquiry* 10: 173-98.

———. 1993. *Cultural Capital: The Problem of Literary Canon Formation.* Chicago: University of Chicago Press.

Jonas, Hans. 1963. *The Gnostic Religion: The Message of the Alien God and the Beginnings of Christianity.* 2nd ed. Boston: Beacon.

Kermode, Frank. 1975. *The Classic: Literary Images of Permanence and Change.* London: Viking.

Kerrigan, William. 1995. "Bloom and the Great Ones." *Clio* 25: 195-206.

Lévi-Strauss, Claude. 1966. *The Savage Mind.* Chicago: University of Chicago Press.

MacArthur, Tom. 1992. *The Oxford Companion to the English Language.* Oxford: Oxford University Press.

Makaryk, Irena R., ed. 1993. *Encyclopedia of Contemporary Literary Theory: Approaches, Scholars, Terms.* Toronto: University of Toronto Press.

Nealon, Jeffrey. 1997. "The Ethics of Dialogue: Bakhtin and Levinas." *College English* 59: 129-48.

Ohmann, Richard. 1983. "The Shaping of a Canon: U. S. Fiction, 1960-1975." *Critical Inquiry* 10: 199-222.

Poole, Roger. 1983. "The Yale School as a Theological Enterprise." *Renaissance and Modern Studies* 27: 1-29.

Popkin, Richard H. 1964. *The History of Scepticism from Erasmus to Descartes.* New York: Harper.

Schneidau, Herbert N. 1995. "Harold Bloom and the School of Resentment; or, Canon to the Right of Them." *Arizona Quarterly* 52: 127-41.

Searle, John. 1994. "The Storm Over the University." In *Falling into Theory: Conflicting Views on Reading and Literature,* ed. David H. Richter. New York: St. Martin's Press.

Spellmeyer, Kurt. 1996. "After Theory: From Textuality to Attunement with the World." *College English* 58: 893-913.

Stewart, Stanley. 1996. "Canonizing Bloom: A Review Essay." *Cithara* 35: 27-33.

Wilson, R. McL. 1967. "Valentinus and Valentinianism." In *The Encyclopedia of Philosophy,* ed. Paul Edwards. New York: Macmillan.

Leslie Schenk (review date summer/autumn 2001)

SOURCE: Schenk, Leslie. Review of *How to Read and Why,* by Harold Bloom. *World Literature Today* 75, nos. 3/4 (summer/autumn 2001): 236-37.

[*In the following review, Schenk characterizes* How to Read and Why *as poorly written, culturally biased, and unworthy of Bloom's earlier achievements.*]

It is sad and indeed embarrassing to witness a respected literary critic's faculties begin to wobble. Already in Harold Bloom's celebrated **Western Canon,** there were at least two monumental assumptions that were dubious: that in this global day and age one could write about a Western Canon without any reference whatever to an Eastern Canon, and that by far the greater bulk of Western literature was written in English. No mention of Sweden's Selma Lagerlöf or Hungary's Jókai Mór. Similarly biased, Bloom's prophecies about which new works might live included more Americans than any other nationality—by the nature of things, highly unlikely.

In his next book, **Shakespeare,** Bloom claimed our Bard had invented "the human." But surely the Greeks got there first, as did Chaucer, Rabelais, Dante, not to mention Mencius, Murasaki Shikibu, and the Sanskrit poet Valmiki, who first put the Ramayana Saga together? Worse, Bloom attacked that other poet who wrote "Hath not a Jew eyes? Hath not a Jew hands, organs, dimensions, senses, affections, passions?" as being an anti-Semite! Oblivious to Shakespeare's gift for being able to put himself into everyone else's shoes, Bloom justified this fatuous blunder by quoting the anti-Semitisms the other characters in *The Merchant of Venice* had to say. By what sleight of hand can Shakespeare be identified with one rather than the other of two contradictory extremes? What it does prove, it seems to me, is the poet's cool objectivity in being able to create his art outside as well as inside his characters. To clinch his argument, Bloom reminds us that Shylock insisted to the end that contracts should be honored, as though that were a particularly Jewish trait and not the universal rule still today. He did not seem to notice that the other characters in *The Merchant* were in their various ways considerably more despicable, more immoral than was Shylock, for all their feelings of superiority, nor that "if you prick us, do we not bleed?" may well be a reference to another Jew, the one who died on a cross. At least Bloom did not by analogy condemn Shakespeare as being anti-Italian because of Iago.

All this being said, Bloom's performance in **How to Read and Why** is so totally and inadmissibly below par that one can only wonder why it was published in the first place. To cash in on his mostly well-deserved past reputation? Mortimer Adler once wrote *How to Read a Book,* destined for university students and a sophisticated audience, and what a difference! Bloom's title alone might be appropriate for beginners in elementary school, but not for educated adults, the readership he has always written for and does again now. First, none of us would be able to read this book if we did not already know "how to read," as well as how and why to chew over and assimilate the contents of what we read. Second, those of us who already know hows and whys learn nothing new from it; we can only balk at wispy suggestions totally lacking in usefulness or viable connection with Bloom's purpose, however denoted by his title; we don't need to be reminded to ponder what we read. Third, are there really any grown-ups left anywhere in the civilized world still unaware that Shakespeare heads all lists of great writers?

Worse, Bloom often puts authors' intentions into his own brief words, which many authors themselves might not be able to do. But is the main reason to read Nathanael West's *Miss Lonelyhearts* really to "understand better our obsession with guns and violence"? Nor is it by doing little indigestible digests, often giving plots away, that Bloom is going to persuade potential readers to open Proust or Turgenev, Mann or Melville, Bellow or Malouf. His direct quotations from authors might by themselves serve to do this, but not in the grim context of his explanatory notes, which are simply not as good as those in individual Readers' Guides available left and right. Besides, anybody who bandies about snippets from the world's most renowned authors is bound to come up with gems.

Bloom claims that reading is "the most healing of pleasures," which sounds wonderfully soothing at first; but the more you look at that phrase, the less you can make of it. Healing? Healing *what*? What *other* pleasures heal? Reading returns us "to otherness." What does *that* mean? It makes us "wholly ourselves." What does *that* mean? I still rub my eyes at having found in *The Western Canon* that "Shakespeare is the inventor of psychoanalysis; Freud, its codifier." This is fairly flattering to both, but it is also utter nonsense. I think the preceding are fair examples of how Bloom can write initially impressive words whose meanings ultimately dissolve into mere black ink on white paper, duds, not really setting off any of the magical recognition of truths that that combination of ingredients can set off in readers' minds. Sparking imagination through ink and paper is what literature is all about, and Bloom gives no sign of being aware of that aspect of artistic endeavor. Odd that anyone who claims to value good writing should write so many words that thud.

To boot, a distressing aspect of this book is carried over from his previous literary surveys, as mentioned above. Western literature is the only literature there is, literature in English is better than all other literatures combined, American writers deserve more attention than British writers—let alone the Indians who turn out some of the best novels in English these days—and, worst blooper of all, male writers deserve much more space than female writers, no matter what. Are Jane Austen, Virginia Woolf, Molly Keane, Nancy Mitford, Djuna Barnes, Edna St. Vincent Millay, and company given their due credit? No, they aren't, which I (a male) find unforgivable. I could go on, but won't.

In case my relentless panning of this book hasn't convinced you, consider: Geoff Dyer of *The Independent* has said Bloom shoots himself in the foot with his own canon. I wish I had thought of that. *The Guardian Weekly* has bluntly stated that "Harold Bloom dismisses the trilogy [*Henry VI*] as an exercise in Marlovian rhetoric that no longer lives. Untrue." And Michael

Gorra in the *New York Times* found Bloom's judgments "questionable at best." So I am not alone. If you have come this far with me, it is surely in good part because you already have your own ideas of how and why you read, and you will fully understand my conclusion: thumbs down.

Joseph Epstein (essay date summer 2002)

SOURCE: Epstein, Joseph. "Bloomin' Genius." *Hudson Review* 55, no. 2 (summer 2002): 213-21.

[*In the following essay, Epstein contends that Bloom's pompous attitude and ineffective theories have not detracted from his fame and notoriety as a literary critic.*]

Harold Bloom, the Yale professor and literary critic, has been on a helluva roll. His last two major books, **The Western Canon: The Books and School of the Ages** and **Shakespeare: The Invention of the Human,** have both been bestsellers—unusual in itself for works of such high intellectual pretension—and when the latter came out, in a thickish paperback edition, its publisher saw fit to send out a vast number of copies in its own special floor display, *à la* John Grisham or Danielle Steel. Bloom has won a MacArthur Fellowship, better known as a genius grant or a Big Mac; been chosen to deliver the Charles Eliot Norton Lectures at Harvard; been awarded the gold medal for criticism of the American Academy of Arts & Letters, of which he is himself a member. Michael Dirda, in the *Washington Post,* called Harold Bloom one of the three most important literary critics writing in English in the twentieth century: the other two being the Cambridge don F. R. Leavis and the American man-of-letters Edmund Wilson.

Harold Bloom's success is of a peculiarly American kind and yet not easily fathomed. As a critic, he is not all that accessible and is capable of producing sentences, paragraphs, lengthy stretches that are quite incomprehensible. ("Like Thoreau, Whitman has a touch of the *Bhagavad-Gita,* but the Hindu vision is mediated by Western hermeticism, with its Neoplatonic and Gnostic elements." Yeah, sure, as the kids say, right!) He claims to be of the school of aesthetic critics, remarking that, in an ideological age, "I feel quite alone these days in defending the autonomy of the aesthetic." Yet he himself doesn't seem to have a clue about how to produce anything approaching the aesthetically pleasing in his own writing. In an interview in the *Paris Review,* he declared that he never revises his prose, and nothing in his work refutes this impressive claim. Any critic ready to avail himself of such gargoylesque words as "psychokabbalistic" and "pneumognostic," who can refer to a passage in Montaigne as an "apotropaic talisman," and can write about the cosmos having been "reperspectivized by Tolstoy," may be many things, but he ain't no aesthete.

Nor does Bloom, in his writing, project an attractive, let alone a seductive, character. He is the type not of the charmingly nutty but of the exhaustingly garrulous professor. His writing displays all the symptoms of an advanced case of Professor's Disease—dreaded PD—and to the highest power. Such is Bloom's loquacity that he discovered himself, in the midst of his own psychoanalysis, "paying him [his own analyst] to give him lectures several times a week on the proper way to read Freud."

Bloom writes like a man accustomed to speaking to his inferiors—to students, that is, a captive audience beholden to him for grades and promotion. To them he may lay down the law, brook no argument, take great pleasure in his own performance, be utterly unworried about someone coughing politely and saying, "Excuse me, pal, but what you just said seems to me a bunch of bullshit!" One has the sense that everything Bloom writes he has probably said before, scores, perhaps hundreds of times, to students; it all comes out of that great booming Bloombox, the academic equivalent of a great Boombox, but this one with no Off switch and no control whatsoever over the volume.

Harold Bloom resembles no one so much as Zero Mostel, with something of the same physique and verbal mania but none of the amusing punchlines. Such laughs as are to be found in Bloom are all unconsciously created on his part. In *The Western Canon,* he reports that whenever he re-reads *Bleak House* he cries whenever Esther Summerson does, "and I don't think I'm being sentimental." In the same book he also reports that he uses the poems of Walt Whitman to assuage grief. "I remember one summer, in crisis, being at Nantucket with a friend who was absorbed in fishing, while I read aloud to both of us from Whitman and recovered myself again." Poor friend, one feels, poor fish.

Critics come in vastly varying styles: from subtle, self-effacing, and sardonic, to oracular, vatic, apocalyptic, to plain damned intelligent. The one quality indispensable to the critic, however, is authoritativeness. He must show no hesitation, making commandingly clear that he knows whereof he speaks. Edmund Wilson put the case for authority in criticism best: "The implied position of the people [that's critics] who know about literature (as in every other fine art) is simply that they know what they know, and that they are determined to impose their opinions by main force of eloquence or assertion on the people who do not know [that's the rest of us]."

Bloom has had no problem mastering the tone of authoritativeness. If he came off any more *ex cathedra* in his judgments, he'd be Pope. In his literary judgments, he is all assertion and no proof whatsoever. Samuel Johnson is, for Bloom, "unmatched by any critic in any nation before or after him." Then there is Oscar Wilde, "who was right about everything." Tolstoy's story "Hadji Murad" is his "personal touchstone for the sublime of prose fiction, to me the best story in the world, or at least the best I have ever read." And then there is Emily Dickinson, who, "at the height of her powers," is "the best mind to appear among western poets in nearly four centuries." What's that qualificatory *nearly* doing there, one wonders. And why not round it off, and make it an even half millennium?

Harold Bloom presents himself as a genius—a genius battling his way through the dark forces of the ignorant. His claim is to universal knowledge. He is the man who ranges across literatures, absorbs religious ideas, swallows whole cultures, happily making pronunciamentos upon them as he passes. His pretension rate is quite outside the solar system. In *The Book of J,* for example, he argued that the real author of the Hebrew Bible was a woman who belonged to the Solomonic elite and wrote during the reign of Rehoboam. Although every serious scholar on the subject shot holes in this notion, Bloom remains unshaken in his sense of his own rightness on the matter, and placidly refers, to this day, to the "J writer" as if his own speculation is the unshakeable truth.

Born in 1930, Harold Bloom began his professional life as a critic of Romantic poetry, and quite a good one, as his book *The Visionary Company* still shows. But his ambition grew out of all bounds, and he soon became the intellectual equivalent of that character in P. G. Wodehouse of whom Wodehouse writes that he looked like someone who was poured into his clothes but forgot to say when. The sensible Bloom occasionally peeks through, even in his recent books. "You cannot teach someone to love great poetry if they come to you without that love," he writes in *The Western Canon.* "How can you teach solitude?" But for many years now bombast, rant, and confident obscurity have been his reigning notes.

"The personality of the critic is much deprecated in our time," Bloom wrote in *The Western Canon.* Sad, because the great critic—that would be Dr. Bloom—is engaged in a dramatic struggle at a depth and with an accompanying danger beyond our imagining. For you and me reading is not the hell that it is for Harold Bloom, who, in *Kabbalah and Criticism,* writes that "reading is defensive warfare, however generously or joyously we read, and with whatever degree of love, for in such love or such pleasure there is more-than-usual acute ambivalence." If you are what Bloom calls a "strong reader," it gets even worse, as he notes in his *A Map of Misreading*: "Such a reader, at once blind and transparent with light, self-deconstructed yet fully knowing the pain of his separation both from text and from nature, doubtless will be more than equal to the revisionary labors of contraction and destruction, but hardly to the antithetical restoration that increasingly becomes part of the burden and function of whatever valid poetry we have left or may yet receive." It's almost enough to make a person turn in his library card.

Writing, it turns out, isn't much easier. Although Bloom allowed, in a *Paris Review* interview, that he doesn't often revise and accepts no editing, he also holds that writing carries its own *Sturm und Drang.* "One writes to keep going, to keep oneself from going mad," Bloom told that same *Paris Review* interviewer. "One writes to be able to write the next piece of criticism or to live through the next day or two. Maybe it's an apotropaic gesture, maybe one writes to ward off death." As with writing criticism, so with teaching literature: "The various times I have taught her [Emily Dickinson's] poems have left me with fierce headaches, since the difficulties force me past my limits." Imagine, if you will, the headaches of his students.

Harold Bloom is that most comic of unconscious comic figures: the academic Dionysian, calling for higher fires, more dancing girls, music, and wine, all from an endowed chair. His literary taste runs to the hot-blooded and long-winded, his natural appetite is for the apocalyptic. Blake, Whitman, Nietzsche, D. H. Lawrence, Norman Mailer, these are among the writers who light our aging professor's fire. "Strangeness, as I keep discovering," he writes in *The Western Canon,* "is one of the prime requirements for entrance into the Canon." Apart from Shakespeare, Bloom's great culture heroes are Emerson and Freud, who, in combination, yield a gasbag with a dirty mind. "Why criticism has not addressed itself to the image of masturbation in Whitman," Bloom writes, "I scarcely know." A critic's work, as you can see, is never done.

"Criticism," Bloom has said, "is either a genre of literature or it is nothing." But criticism becomes literature only when it satisfies one of two standards. The first is that it be so well written that it gives some of the same pleasure that literature itself does. William Hazlitt, Edmund Wilson, V. S. Pritchett, and a few other critics qualify here. Harold Bloom, whose writing is charitably described as "difficult" by John Hollander, his colleague at Yale, does not. The second way criticism can qualify as literature is through the elucidating power of its ideas. Samuel Johnson, Matthew Arnold, T. S. Eliot, F. R. Leavis and perhaps Northrop Frye qualify. It is here that Bloom would no doubt wish to stake his claim.

Bloom has been known as a man with a Big Idea. His Big Idea has not had the luck of instant luminosity that other Big Ideas—the class struggle, the Oedipus complex—have had. The idea itself is named in the first of three books he devoted to it, *The Anxiety of Influence* (the other two books are *A Map of Misreading* and *Kabbalah and Criticism*). Written in prose with the translucency of isinglass, these three books, as the Germans say, *zie lassen sich nicht lesen*—do not permit themselves to be read. Still, one can make out their broader lineaments. The Big Idea, which was more modestly and lucidly first put forth by W. Jackson Bate, the biographer of Dr. Johnson and Coleridge, is that writers feel greatly haunted if not daunted by their predecessors, causing them to feel sorely belated, as if everything they wish to do has already been done before them. Weaker writers are crushed by this, the idea holds, but strong writers go on to challenge and in many instances surpass their precursors.

As a theory of literary influence, based on the psychology of authorship, Bloom's Big Idea has not been taken up either by his fellow academics or by practicing critics. So far as one can determine, *The Anxiety of Influence* has had very little influence and appears to have caused anxiety chiefly in Harold Bloom, who claims that few people really understand it. A characteristic passage from the book may indicate why this is:

> But what is the Primal Scene, for a poet *as poet*? It is his Poetic Father's coitus with the Muse. There he was begotten? No—there they failed to beget him. He must be self-begotten, he must engender himself upon the Muse his mother. But the Muse is as pernicious as the Sphinx or Coevering Cherub, and may identify herself with either, though more usually with the Sphinx. The strong poet fails to beget himself—he must wait for his Son, who will define him even when he has defined his own Poetic Father. To beget here means to usurp, and is the dialectical labor of the Cherub. Entering here into the center of our sorrow, we must look closely at him.

Bloom sees literary influence everywhere, and his claims have the crisp clarity that only freedom from evidence or consecutive argument give. In *The Western Canon,* Bloom writes that he is "inclined to believe that Shakespeare induced a considerable anxiety in Freud." He next tells us that "Shakespeare is everywhere in Freud, far more present when unmentioned than when he is cited." The plot quickens, thickens, and sickens: "Freud, as prose-poet of the post-Shakespearean, sails in Shakespeare's wake; and the anxiety of influence has no more distinguished sufferer in our time than the founder of psychoanalysis, who always discovered that Shakespeare had been there long before him, and all too frequently could not bear to confront this humiliating truth." But how do we know? We know, as the song from the old Walt Disney movie has it, because Uncle Harold (for Remus) tells us so.

Finding the anxiety of influence in your favorite writer—or friends and relatives, for that matter—may work better as an after-dinner game, or way to break up dull parties, than it does in actual criticism, though Bloom thought, when he first published the book, that it would change poetic history and provide "a wholly different practical criticism." As with almost all Bloom's criticism, the theory of the anxiety of influence has a nice arbitrariness about it. Tennyson, Arnold, Hopkins, and Rossetti, Bloom tells us, felt anxiety over the influence of Keats, though among them, according to him, only Tennyson triumphed. Dostoyevsky, like Freud, had to struggle free of the influence of Shakespeare, though through five volumes of his biography this notion seems to have eluded Dostoyevsky's highly intelligent biographer Joseph Frank, who makes no mention of it whatsoever. T. S. Eliot and Wallace Stevens both felt anxious about the influence of Walt Whitman. Ezra Pound had to square off against Robert Browning.

No one denies that literary influence exists, which of course it does, but it almost always does in ways too subtle for genuinely precise tracing. "I am not fond of the word *influence,*" Valéry wrote, "which indicates ignorance or a hypothesis and plays a great and convenient role in criticism." The real question is does influence always necessitate anxiety, a struggle, an *agon* (a favorite Bloom word), a misreading of a writer's precursors? Nobody but Harold Bloom seems to think so. Near as one can make out, as an idea, the anxiety of influence chiefly gets in the way, so that, for example, in his biography of Balzac, Graham Robb feels compelled to note: "The 'anxiety of influence' is not much in evidence in Balzac's jottings [his early writings]. . . . Rather, he seems to be cheered on by his predecessors, most of whom he came across in primers and anthologies. . . . If anything, Balzac was *under-*whelmed by the intellectual achievements of humanity."

Bloom seems happiest viewing the world locked in endless struggle. He sees himself, for example, in bayonet battle with the younger generation of English professors, among them feminists, new historicists, deconstructionists, Marxists, the rather pathetic motley that Bloom calls the School of Resentment. He also sees fundamentalist religion, the wider and wider spread use of the computer, television and "the University of Resentment (already well along in consolidation)" combined "into one rough beast," presaging a future that would cancel out not only a literary canon but literature itself. True enough, something like a School of Resentment does exist and it is destroying literature as an academic subject, but in attacking these academics, Bloom portrays himself as the lonely heroic outsider, single-handedly taking on the charging horde of barbarians. Not quite so.

Harold Bloom is an establishment man. He is the consummate literary politician, riding to hounds—now there is a subject for a David Levine cartoon—with those literary personages who have themselves already

been declared winners. In contemporary literature, eschewing heterodoxy, he takes few chances, and none that are likely to cost him future emoluments or useful friends. Thus he attacks Alice Walker but lays off Toni Morrison. He everywhere pretends to contemn the stridently political in literature, yet in an appendix to **The Western Canon** called **"A Canonical Prophecy"** he lists Tony Kushner's *Angels in America*—a play that is all politics and little else—as a likely canonical work of the future. If one runs down the names of contemporary poets he admires in this same appendix, these turn out for the most part to be the usual suspects, the old gang, that happy mutual admiration society that each year awards one another Pulitzer, Lannan, and other jolly prizes.

The mystery is that Harold Bloom, for all his nearly perfect unreadability, today finds himself in that small but lucky elite of writers whose books sell without being actually read. I have been plowing my way through **Shakespeare: The Invention of the Human** for weeks now, and I can only report that it is difficult to imagine anyone reading through it who has not been paid to write about it. The Shakespeare book, too, has a large, useless idea at its center—namely, that Shakespeare invented our feelings and way of feeling and so, through his plays, invented (or, as Bloom sometimes says, "reinvented") human personality. Reading Bloom on this point is, as John Carey, writing in the *Times* of London, puts it, "like chatting with an acquaintance and gradually realizing he believes death rays are issuing from his television screen."

Much the greater part of Bloom's book on Shakespeare is a great ramble, play by play, in which Bloom piles opinionation upon opinionation, agreeing with this critic, arguing with that, inserting bits of quite uninteresting academic autobiography, establishing his own superiority, providing as heavy-breathing a solipsistic performance as one is likely to find off a Beverly Hills psychoanalytic couch. "It is very difficult, even painful to have done with Falstaff," Bloom writes toward the conclusion of his chapter on *Henry IV,* "for no other literary character . . . seems to me so infinite in provoking thought and arousing emotion." Choice selections of the characteristically impenetrable Bloomian prose are the raisins in this indigestible pudding of a book: "Shakespeare's uniqueness, his greatest originality, can be described either as a charismatic cognition, which comes from an individual before it enters group thinking, or as a cognitive charisma, which cannot be routinized." As a work of Bardolatry, **Shakespeare: The Invention of the Human** succeeds in giving even Shakespeare a bad name. "If Bloom himself is anything to go by," John Carey writes, "an ability to laugh at yourself is far from being an inevitable result of reading Shakespeare."

Bloom has a book in the works on genius. That he would next turn to this subject makes a certain amount of sense: a great critic is, after all, a reader of genius. Which is the claim that Harold Bloom has for many years made for himself, in books both arcane and ambitious. A critic for whom Bloom hasn't much regard, T. S. Eliot, once said that the best method for being a critic is to be very intelligent. Harold Bloom isn't very intelligent—he is merely learned, though in a wildly idiosyncratic way. He has staked out his claim for being a great critic through portentousness, pomposity, and extravagant pretension, and, from all appearances, seems to have achieved it.

This comes about, in part, through a lack of competition. What Randall Jarrell, half in rue, once called The Age of Criticism—the cavalcade of whose names include T. S. Eliot, Edmund Wilson, F. R. Leavis, Lionel Trilling, Cleanth Brooks, E. R. Curtius, Erich Auerbach, and René Wellek—seems to have been over for more than two decades, to be replaced by . . . well, by not much. In Europe there is George Steiner, who has all Bloom's pomposity and pretension and even more of his portentousness but none of what a wag—me, actually—once referred to as the latter's modesty and lighthearted humor. Christopher Ricks and Denis Donoghue write careful and serious literary criticism, but neither seems to want to set up shop as omniscient in the way Bloom does. Helen Vendler has restricted herself to the realm of poetry in English, both past and present, and her own book on Shakespeare's sonnets makes no claims outside attempting to understand how they work. Frank Kermode, though very learned, writes with a modesty that is almost the reverse of Bloom's assertiveness.

Proust says that in art, medicine, and fashion, there have to be new names, by which he meant that new names will arise whether they are worthy or not of being known. The same principle operates in literary criticism, where the name that has now popped up is that of Harold Bloom. But his is a reputation much in need of puncturing, if only to release the bloat and if literary criticism is once again to be taken—and is to take itself—seriously.

Lawrence Danson (review date spring 2003)

SOURCE: Danson, Lawrence. Review of *Harold Bloom's Shakespeare,* edited by Christy Desmet and Robert Sawyer. *Shakespeare Quarterly* 54, no. 1 (spring 2003): 114-17.

[*In the following review, Danson surveys the largely negative critical responses to Bloom's* Shakespeare: The Invention of the Human *in an assessment of the collection* Harold Bloom's Shakespeare, *which is composed of essays in response to Bloom's book.*]

Harold Bloom needs enemies, and where they don't exist he invents them with, yes, Falstaffian amplitude. How else, except against all comers, in buckram or Kendall green, could he pronounce, heroically and begging no man's pardon, the greatness of Falstaff or Hamlet? There's something comical (but "rancid," too, to use one of Bloom's talismanic words) about this brilliant critic's impassioned defense of things that scarcely need defending. Sure, there are dissenters from the view that Richard III lacks inwardness while Hamlet is transcendent. But *Shakespeare: The Invention of the Human* is less interested in arguing with particular critics than in opposing a whole spectral school of resentment, undifferentiated masses of historicists "Old and New," a legion of "academic puritans and professorial power freaks" who hate us youth.[1] Bloom is a writer of astounding power, but his book could have been better, and shorter, without his pose as *vox clamantis in deserto.* My favorite review of it—reprinted in the collection called *Harold Bloom's Shakespeare*—is Hugh Kenner's, which advises taking it in small doses.

Most of the eighteen essays in this collection [*Harold Bloom's Shakespeare*] began life as contributions to a seminar at the annual meeting of the Shakespeare Association of America in 2000. They have been meticulously edited, judiciously arranged, and introduced by Christy Desmet and Robert Sawyer. Many of the book's contributors find something, or everything, to dislike about Bloom's *Shakespeare.* Some are surprisingly temperate, given that Bloom leaves hardly a wither unwrung. The opening section reprints reviews by Jay L. Halio, Terence Hawkes, William W. Kerrigan, and the aforementioned Kenner, along with a purpose-built contribution from Gary Taylor. Halio is the only unconflicted admirer in the volume (he praises "Bloom's largeness of vision—truly immense, as no other critic's of our time is" [20]). Kerrigan is Bloomian with very interesting reservations. Only at the end of his essay does Kerrigan say anything about Bloom's commentaries on specific plays: he likes the *Lear* chapter and thinks Bloom has good things to say about four acts of *A Midsummer Night's Dream,* but he "butchers *Measure for Measure,*" takes a "preposterous tack [on] . . . Othello and Desdemona," finds "nothing relevant to talk about" in *Macbeth*; and the *Hamlet* chapter is "a whole lot of hot air" (41). In fact, Bloom is secondary to Kerrigan's real purpose, which is indicated by his subtitle: "Harold Bloom Rescues Shakespeare from the Critics." Like Bloom, Kerrigan is a great lumper-together: for him, new historicists are members of a "sect" (35), a "movement" (37), "a critical school programmatically excluding literary greatness" (38). He cites some really bad stuff by way of example, but his killer tactics are unfair to a lot of scholars who think you can love Shakespeare's work and also be interested in his historical situation. Kerrigan claims that Bloom has a "heroic disregard for academic fashion" (33). Hardly: without a fashionable cabal to oppose, much of Bloom's book, as well as Kerrigan's essay, would seem a tempest without even a teapot.

Still, people who invent enemies can also make enemies. Bloom insults Gary Taylor in the third sentence of his acknowledgments: Taylor's Oxford Shakespeare "perversely seeks, more often than not, to print the worst possible text";[2] and Kerrigan gets in his licks, too: "There is no more pathetic book in modern criticism than Gary Taylor's *Reinventing Shakespeare* (1989)" (38). Taylor's reply is the anger peak of this collection. Writing annoyingly in the third person, Taylor claims that "Bloom is effectively quoting and endorsing Taylor's work" (50)—an interesting accusation considering "Taylor's" belief that "Shakespeare's reputation is on life support and would die if it were removed from the machine that is artificially prolonging its life" (51). Taylor, for his part, would gladly, righteously, pull the plug on the moribund Bard. He's more sanguine about Thomas Middleton's health. Middleton supposedly tops Shakespeare because Middleton has better attitudes: in *Measure for Measure,* for instance, Shakespeare endorses King James's retrograde attitude toward freedom of speech, but Middleton's plays promote open criticism of folks in authority. Taylor's credo—"I have to admit that, as Bloom and Kerrigan charge, I do resemble Shakespeare's villains. Yes, I am like Edmund: I do not believe in the importance of 'legitimate' birth, I do not believe in primogeniture, and I do not believe in the sanctity of patriarchal wedlock. If that makes me evil, I am evil" (61)—makes the school of resentment sound like clown college.

Terence Hawkes (the only representative of British cultural materialism in this volume) also thinks Shakespeare—at least as taught in British schools—is a bad influence. Hawkes is witty and sharp, as always, but his fast-talking, media-savvy style ("Hamlet 'n' Falstaff 'R' Us!") isn't adequate to its task of dismantling the monumental Bloom. Hawkes focuses on the issue of character criticism: "Bloom's book is Bradley and water, with quite a bit of wind as well" (28). In fact it's the other way round: Bradley was a Bloom spritzer. He scarcely approached Bloom's vision of Shakespeare's Giant Forms, which, liberated from the constraint of mere plays, disdain in their self-sufficient humanity all historical contingency.

The next section focuses specifically on this subject of character criticism. It opens with Richard Levin's sensible essay "Bloom, Bardolatry, and Characterolatry." Levin, who has been a mighty scourge of the critics Bloom scourges, doesn't play favorites: many of Bloom's comments on Shakespeare's characters "ascend (or descend) to pure hype" (75). He traces a genealogy of bardolatry, and he says important things about

Bloom's popular success and about why it matters. On Bloom's appeal to the parents of the people who become our students: "[The] striking difference between the book's reception inside and outside the academy should concern us, since it marks the extent to which our vanguard critics have separated themselves from, and alienated, a significant part of the public that used to be included in our audience and our constituency" (77).

In this section, Sharon O'Dair urges that we supplement the idea of interiorized characters with a view more like that held by social psychologists, who see us all as types or, to use the word O'Dair picks up from Bloom, "cartoons." Mustapha Fahmi, drawing on the work of Mikhail Bakhtin and Charles Taylor, discusses a dialogic idea of character (and character criticism), which he opposes to Bloom's idea of monological characters. Herbert Weil's essay about Shakespeare's characters in the theater complements Fahmi's: he claims that Bloom's devotion to the charismatic individual "rarely attends to the interplay among characters or to the quicksilver variations in dynamics that can occur on stage" (126). William Morse begins his essay about Nietzsche and Bloom by applauding Bloom's insistence on "the aesthetic power of art" (109), but I'd have thought that Bloom's antitheatrical prejudice (exempting his primal vision of Ralph Richardson as Falstaff) conflicts with Morse's starry-eyed claim that "in the theater . . . we are more complexly alive, more fully human, than when we are normally 'ourselves'" (110).

Edward Pechter's "Romanticism Lost: Bloom and the Twilight of Literary Shakespeare" is the most substantial essay in the next section, called "Anxieties of Influence," and one of the most substantial in the volume. Pechter challenges Bloom's "consensus" view that Romanticism installed character and author at the center of the Shakespearean enterprise. According to Pechter, the major emphasis of Romantic criticism of Shakespeare is "a 'perceiving subject' who engages the text within the collective history of a long and complex interpretive tradition. . . . The Romantics were not 'looking behind' the text for authors, but in front of it for audiences capable of engaging—speculatively, inventively—with desires for a future in front of *them*" (153). Bloom, then, is not the Last Romantic but a lost Romantic, who has weakly misread his ostensible precursors.

Other essays in this section are less successful in dealing with Bloom's influences. Why not? An army of John Livingston Loweses couldn't track Bloom through his snows. Certainly it won't do to claim (with Robert Sawyer) that Bloom steals his ideas from Swinburne or Wilde—or from Valerie Traub or Jonathan Goldberg—and that by failing to push those ideas where Sawyer thinks they ought to go, Bloom exposes his "homophobia" (174). And it's certainly bad news—to use a Bloomianism—when James R. Andreas Sr. accuses Bloom of a "Judaeocentric" vision that keeps him from evenhandedly decrying insults to characters of every race, gender, and nationality (184).

In the final section, "Shakespeare as Cultural Capital," Christy Desmet discusses Bloom's ubiquitous Chelsea House series. In this section I especially liked Lawrence F. Rhu's essay on Bloom in relation to Stanley Cavell. Rhu is one of several contributors who make an issue—as Bloom does—of Bloom's Judaism. David M. Schiller's essay discusses Bloom's *Merchant of Venice*—the "limit," he claims, of Bloom's bardolatry (247). It's not the clearest of the essays under review, but it's less darkly mysterious than the shiver-provoking final sentence of Bloom's chapter on *Merchant*: "Shakespeare was up to mischief, but you have to be an anti-Semitic scholar, Old Historicist or New, to appreciate fully the ambition of such mischief"—my vote for the most bizarre moment in Bloom's book.³

Linda Charnes has pride of last place in *Harold Bloom's Shakespeare*. I like her admission—boldly set out with lots of *italics* and SMALL CAPS—that the Bloom fuss is partly about academics' jealousy of a fellow academic who's had the nerve to make himself richer and more famous than the rest of us could be in our wildest imagining. But as the essays in this collection suggest, it's about a lot more than that, too. ***Shakespeare: The Invention of the Human*** is all the things it's been accused of being: bloated, repetitious, windmill-tilting, closed-minded, unoriginal, and politically retrograde. It's also grandly inventive. What it invents is not the abstract "human" and not even a new Shakespeare but the Shakespearean critic as righteous prophet, a post-millennial sage sneering and thundering, humorlessly claiming the mantle of Falstaff while playing the part of Timon: in all, a figure who forces other teachers of literature to reconsider not their ideas about a particular play but the bases of their own claims to cultural authority.

Notes

1. Harold Bloom, *Shakespeare: The Invention of the Human* (New York: Riverhead Books, 1998), 191, 271, and 282.

2. Bloom, xi.

3. Bloom, 191.

Martin Bidney (essay date summer 2003)

SOURCE: Bidney, Martin. "War of the Winds: Shelley, Hardy, and Harold Bloom." *Victorian Poetry* 41, no. 2 (summer 2003): 229-44.

[*In the following essay, Bidney investigates the defensive nature of Bloom's claim in* A Map of Misreading *that the poetry of Thomas Hardy was strongly influenced by Percy Bysshe Shelley's work.*]

Central to the efforts of some major Hardy critics to promote their varied theoretical agendas in recent decades has been a shared emphasis on the affinities and influence linking the poetry of Percy Shelley to that of Thomas Hardy. Poet-critic Joseph Brodsky thinks that if T. S. Eliot had read Hardy instead of Laforgue, English poetical history in this century "might be somewhat more absorbing": "For one thing, where Eliot needs a handful of dust to perceive terror, for Hardy, as he shows in 'Shelley's Skylark,' a pinch is enough."¹ Since Brodsky has written his Hardy essay largely to defend the sort of traditional verse craft he personally excels in, the Shelley-Hardy "pinch" may symbolize what Brodsky considers the more-than-Eliotic emotional power of these two kindred poets' technical mastery and Brodsky-like formal control. For J. Hillis Miller, by contrast, Shelley is Hardy's worthy precursor as Millerian deconstructor. Hardy's work "might almost be defined as from beginning to end a large-scale interpretation of Shelley, one of the best and strongest we have," offering "a double reading of Shelley," seeing him "as both idealist" and "skeptic," much the same kind of open-ended deconstructor as Hardy, or as Miller himself.²

For Harold Bloom, finally, Hardy (grouped with Wallace Stevens as the only two "strong poets" writing in English during the twentieth century) has Shelley as his "prime precursor."³ Hardy's "'During Wind and Rain,' as good a poem as our century has given us," is "grandchild of the 'Ode to the West Wind'" (*Misreading* [*A Map of Misreading*], p. 20). As Bloom sees it, the influence between these two strong poets "works in the depths, as all love antithetically works" (*Misreading,* p. 21). The Shelley-Hardy dynamic of attachment and rebellion is presented as a revealingly pervasive instance of the Bloomian father-son effect of anxiety-arousing influence. For the neo-Freudian Bloom, as for the formal traditionalist Brodsky and the deconstructive Miller, Shelley and Hardy are poets of a very high order, and the depth of their kinship will add conviction to whatever literary theory it is taken to illustrate.

I choose to focus here on some features of Bloom's presentation, and I do so for two reasons, one relating to Bloom and the other to Shelley and Hardy. The first reason is that Bloom's rhetoric regarding the Shelley-Hardy filiation is a fascinating psychoanalytical crux in the essay where it appears, **"Poetic Origins and Final Phases,"** Chapter I of *A Map of Misreading*. We will see that when the topic of Hardy's reaction to Shelley is introduced, Bloom's rhetoric grows suddenly so heated in its pre-emptive attack on possibly unsympathetic or unconvinced readers, that it raises questions: Why the Bloomian defensiveness? What vulnerability might it shield? An attempt to answer these queries will disclose the second reason why Bloom's arguments are so striking: they can lead us, in ways of which Bloom is not consciously aware, to detailed evidence for a new kind of precursor-disciple tension in the Shelley-Hardy relationship, one involving more playful parody than Bloom has found there. In the process of learning about Bloom, we discover a new dimension of Hardy's response to Shelley.

Bloom introduces his Shelley-Hardy section (about five pages in **"Poetic Origins"** [**"Poetic Origins and Final Phases"**] by emphasizing that the two poets' kinship must not be sought in shared features of style such as rhymes and meters but in the likeness-and-difference of their underlying thinking, what Emerson would call their "meter-making arguments." Stylistic parallels are an ineffective key to real affinity, an inadequate indicator of true indebtedness-and-rebellion:

> Poets need not *look* like their fathers, and the anxiety of influence more frequently than not is quite distinct from the anxiety of style. Since poetic influence is necessarily misprision, a taking or doing amiss of one's burden, it is to be expected that such a process of malformation and misinterpretation will, at the very least, produce deviations in style between strong poets.
>
> (*Misreading,* p. 20)

Not such stylistic trappings as meters but "meter-making" or form-determining "arguments" show influence working "in the depths"; that these arguments are profoundly subject to "tyrannies of inheritance," to pressures of father-son or mentor-disciple conflict, is, Bloom says, "the saddest truth I know about poets and poetry" (*Misreading,* pp. 20-21).

What does Hardy see as Shelley's meter-making argument or unifying thesis? Here is Bloom's answer:

> Hardy's Shelley is very close to the most central of Shelleys, the visionary skeptic, whose head and whose heart could never be reconciled, for they both told truths, but contrary truths. In *Prometheus Unbound,* we are told that in our life the shadow cast by love is always ruin, which is the head's report, but the heart in Shelley goes on saying that if there is to be coherence at all, it must come through Eros.
>
> (*Misreading,* p. 22)

Hardy's characteristic swerve, as Bloom sees it, is to grant the Shelleyan conflict between heart and head, between what we love and what we know, but to insist, contra Shelley, that the split is irremediable, that there is not "to be coherence at all":

> In Hardy's best poems, the central meter-making argument is what might be called a skeptical lament for the hopeless incongruity of ends and means in all human

acts. Love and the means of love cannot be brought together, and the truest name for the human condition is simply that it is loss:
>
> And brightest things that are theirs. . . .
> Ah, no; the years, the years;
> Down their carved names the raindrop plows.
>
> These are the closing lines of "During Wind and Rain," as good a poem as our century has given us. The poem, like so many others, is a grandchild of "Ode to the West Wind." . . . A carrion-eater, Old Style, would challenge my observations, and to such a challenge I could offer, in its own terms, only the first appearance of the refrain
>
> Ah, no; the years O!
> How the sick leaves reel down in throngs!
>
> (*Misreading,* pp. 20-21)

For Bloom, these two lines of verse encapsulate Hardy's deviation from Shelley's "argument." Shelley, too, had seen sick autumn leaves reel down in throngs, "Pestilence-stricken multitudes," but he had hoped, or prayed, that through his "Ode" he might serve as "trumpet of a prophecy" bearing vernal hope to humanity just as the buried leaves would be resurrected in spring by the breath of the brusque fall wind's gentler "azure sister" (ll. 5, 69, 9).[4] To this prospect of deliverance, Hardy's dirge four times replies, "Ah, no . . .":

DURING WIND AND RAIN

They sing their dearest songs—
He, she, all of them—yea,
Treble and tenor and bass,
  And one to play;
With the candles mooning each face. . . .
  Ah, no; the years O!
How the sick leaves reel down in throngs!

They clear the creeping moss—
Elders and juniors—aye,
Making the pathways neat
  And the gardens gay;
And they build a shady seat. . . .
  Ah, no; the years, the years;
See, the webbed white storm-birds wing across.

They are blithely breakfasting all—
Men and maidens—yea,
Under the summer tree,
  With a glimpse of the bay,
While pet fowl come to the knee. . . .
  Ah, no; the years O!
And the rotten rose is ript from the wall.

They change to a high new house,
He, she, all of them—aye.
Clocks and carpets and chairs
  On the lawn all day,
And brightest things that are theirs. . . .
  Ah, no; the years, the years;
Down their chiselled names the rain-drop ploughs.[5]

The reader of this lyric may find that at least three of Bloom's points so far have made good sense. Hardy may be deviating from Shelley's major "argument" in the way Bloom claims. Hardy's throngs of hectic autumnal leaves, evoked in a context of troubled musings and in a mood of existential crisis, may also recall the leaves in Shelley's "Ode."[6] And the deviation of Hardy's "argument" from Shelley's, coupled with his apparent carryover of some Shelley-like imagery in a new context, may suggest the mentor-disciple or father-son tension Bloom finds.

But three problems with Bloom's presentation are perhaps even more evident. First, "During Wind and Rain" is far from being "as good a poem" as the twentieth century "has given us"; in my view it is not even one of Hardy's finest. "During Wind and Rain" does not genuinely earn the emotional response it wants to arouse; the recurrent "Ahs" should be those of the listener, not the speaker, and one may feel that to plant multiple audience responses in the poem is a far too easy and transparent tactic.[7] Further, "During Wind and Rain" does not illustrate Hardy's characteristic "argument" as well as, say, the much better known and more successful "Neutral Tones." If the central Hardy "argument" is the conflict between heart and head, ends and means, love and loss, such a thesis is not well manifested in "During Wind and Rain"—a poem about the aging and death that the "years" bring, not about the loss of love or the shattering of illusions. We always knew we would age and die. "Neutral Tones," in contrast, powerfully deals with the inadequacies and illusoriness of love as we experience it: here, the mootness of the question "which lost the more by our love" (l. 8) is even depressingly emblematized by a "pond edged with grayish leaves" (l. 16), some more post-Shelleyan dead fall foliage.[8]

A second problem is that despite Bloom's assurance that style does not count much as an indicator of deep indebtedness to one's mentor and therefore should not be invoked in dealing with the Hardy-Shelley sonship struggle, "During Wind and Rain" does seem to owe a good deal to Shelley's style, both for better and for worse. Though strong in its Shelleyan inventive musicality, the Hardy poem weakly, uncritically, incorporates repetitive features that typically mar Shelley's less effective exclamatory lyrics, such as "A Lament" which I quote in full:

I

O world! O life! O time!
On whose last steps I climb,
    Trembling at that where I had stood before;
When will return the glory of your prime?
    No more—Oh, never more!

II

Out of the day and night
A joy has taken flight;
    Fresh spring, and summer, and winter hoar,
Move my faint heart with grief, but with delight
    No more—Oh, never more!

Shelley offers an impressively Hardy-like rhythmic virtuosity of stanza invention, but the O's and Oh's or Ah's can become equally tiresome in both writers.

The third oddity in Bloom's treatment of the Shelley-Hardy connection appears the most puzzling, but it may prove to shed light on the other two. "A carrion-eater, Old Style, would challenge my observations [about the Shelley-Hardy link]," Bloom says, "and to such a challenge I could offer, in its own terms, only the first appearance of the refrain: 'Ah, no; the years O! / How the sick leaves fall down in throngs!'" (***Misreading***, p. 21). A few pages earlier the disgusting "carrion-eaters" are defined for us: "Critics may be wary of origins, or consign them disdainfully to those carrion-eaters of scholarship, the source hunters, but the poet-in-a-poet is as desperately obsessed with poetic origins, generally despite himself, as the person-in-a-person at last becomes obsessed with personal origins" (***Misreading***, pp. 17-18). Carrion-eaters, then, are scholarly source hunters considered as deadheads; and source hunters of the (particularly unimaginative or literalist) "Old Style," are—Bloom explains—the sort that would "challenge my observations" regarding poetic origins.

This is helpful, but it is not sufficient. For a really clear concept of carrion-eating, we need to see Bloom's use of the image as his own inventive deviation from his mentor, Shelley. In *Adonais* Shelley describes as "carrion kites" the sort of hostile reviewers, inimical interpreters, whom he holds responsible for the death of Adonis/Keats, with whose martyrdom—and presumed posthumous triumph—Shelley closely identifies:

Nor let us weep that our delight is fled
Far from these *carrion kites* that scream below;
He wakes or sleeps with the enduring dead;
Thou canst not soar where he is sitting now.—
Dust to the dust! but the pure spirit shall flow
Back to the burning fountain whence it came,
A portion of the Eternal, which must glow
Through time and change, unquenchably the same,
Whilst thy cold embers choke the sordid hearth of
    shame.

(*Adonais*, xxxviii, ll. 334-342 [emphasis added])

In context, then, a carrion-eater, for Bloom, is no mere narrowly pedantic or lifeless interpreter but rather a cannibalistically menacing one. It is as if the unappreciative reader of Bloom's account of Hardy's debt to Shelley stands accused of vicariously re-cannibalizing Keats/Adonis/Shelley and perhaps the latter's spokesman Bloom, and Hardy too. Carrion kites and hostile readers are omnivorously greedy for dead meat.

While the carrion-eater image lets Bloom identify with a whole group of martyred, misunderstood poetic/mythic luminaries, it may, at the same time, defensively project his own unease with the two chief weaknesses of his argument. First, there is the disquieting possibility that if Hardy's leaf-throng poem is not as good as Bloom thinks, the power of the Shelley-Hardy tradition it illustrates is not as well shown as he hopes. Second, there appears to be evidence that the Shelley-Hardy influence works not only "in the depths" of their lyrics but equally on the less impressive surface level of a sometimes flawed exclamatory style.

But Bloom's discussion is useful not only for its psychological and rhetorical interest. Indirectly, it can help us to open up greater depth in the Shelley-Hardy relationship, depth of a pre-eminently Bloomian kind, that of indebtedness, anxiety, and a consequent agonistic distortion or shrinking, on the son/ephebe's part, of the poetic father's grand achievement.[9] The creative-destructive distortion to which I refer will add to Bloomian theory the recognizably Bakhtinian pleasures of parody and dialogic mockery.[10] Hardy's Bloomian reaction to Shelley may be less melancholy than Bloom thought. After Bloom has gotten us started by inciting our curiosity to read "as good a poem as [the twentieth] century has given us," and then after we have read "During Wind and Rain," pages 465-466 in the *Complete Poems,* we find immediately before it on pages 464-465 "The Wind's Prophecy,"[11] whose title proclaims its Shelleyan provenance by appropriating a Shelleyan rhetorical triumph: "Be through my lips to unawakened earth / The trumpet of a *prophecy*! O, *Wind*! / If Winter comes, can Spring be far behind?" ("Ode to the West Wind," ll. 68-70 [emphases added]). A reading of the two poets' wind-lyrics together reveals a pair of intimately related poetic-psychological exhibits. The two crucial words of Shelley's final clarion call, "prophecy" and "Wind," become the title of Hardy's defiant, bold response.[12] In Shelley's end is Hardy's beginning.

The clash of Shelley's and Hardy's meter-making arguments, their underlying themes or theses, may be clearer here than anywhere, though the Shelley represented in the "Ode" is more affirmative than the skeptical Shelley Bloom found in *Prometheus Unbound*: in that work, as Bloom says, coherence, if it comes at all, can come only through Eros, while in "Ode to the West Wind" the coherence is shown to be achieved—according to Bloom himself—through the related but deeper concept of "dialogue." Summing up his "West Wind" discussion as well as some other chapters in *Shelley's Mythmaking,* Bloom expresses this in the Buberian language he favors in that book:

> That "principle within the human being, and perhaps within all sentient beings," is what I have taken in these chapters to be the mythopoeic principle. In turn I

judge that to be the will of a human or any sentient being to stand in relation to all that is sentient and to what is the ground of all that is sentient, as I am confronting a Thou rather than an I experiencing an It. And conversely, since relation is mutual, that being will himself be confronted as a Thou and not as an It.[13]

"What rises in the final stanza" of "West Wind" is, for Bloom, a Shelleyan "faith" that "holds to the humanizing possibility of mythmaking and affirms again the value of the relationship which can create poems" (*Shelley's Mythmaking,* p. 86). However hedged about, it is a faith in some kind or degree of dialogue.

Since "dialogue" means that a speaker and an interlocutor experience a worthwhile personlike interchange, the word usefully describes a poem where the persona and the wind are united through what is felt (in the "myth") as a mutual receptivity. It is a commonplace of Shelley criticism[14] that mutual receptivity enables the poet to relate to the wind's unifying powers as they interanimate the four elements: the "dreaming earth," "aery surge," "blue Mediterranean," and symbolic "sparks" of the first, second, third, and fifth stanzas (ll. 10, 19, 30, 67), with the fourth stanza serving as transition from the three physical elements to the fourth metaphoric one (Shelley's words as fires).

The unifying, reconciling, interanimating power of mutual receptivity is quickly shown in other oft-cited harmonizing schemas: interracial, interreligious, psychological. The leaves, like varied races of Humanity, are "Yellow, and black, and pale, and . . . red" (l. 4). The religiously syncretic wind drives an Apollonian chariot and inspires a Dionysian "Maenad"; it biblically resurrects leaves and blows a trumpet of judgment; it is "Destroyer and preserver" like Shiva and Vishnu, yet also a lifegiving "Spirit" like Brahma or Jehovah or the Holy Ghost (ll. 6, 21, 14). I would add that the poem achieves the ultimate in dialogue by resolving the persona's oedipal tensions. Recalling the early time when in fancied childhood omnipotence he felt himself to be the wind's "comrade" and its equal in speed, then the alienation and punishment that left the "tameless" and "swift" boy bloody and struggling, striving with the fatherlike wind-spirit in "sore need," the reconciled poet finally asks no greater bliss than to be the forest-lyre and trumpet of the Spirit's melody and prophecy, the spokesman of that greater vision with which he now identifies in vigor and prospective joy (ll. 49, 56, 52, 57, 69). Dialogic openness has found its reward, the Wind its prophet.

If, following M. H. Abrams' classic essay "The Correspondent Breeze: A Romantic Metaphor,"[15] we emphasize the lyre over the trumpet, we can even say that, by the poem's conclusion, dialogue has turned to a quasi-spiritual romantic love or courtship in the Song of

Solomon tradition, as the poet implores, "Be thou, Spirit fierce, / My spirit! Be thou me, impetuous one!" (ll. 61-62). As Aeolian lyre, the persona fills the traditional feminine role for the masculine World-Wind. Much in the manner of Coleridge's "To an Eolian Harp," masculine- and feminine-like roles for the Spirit and speaker in Shelley's "Ode" turn the dialogic interlocutors into loving soul mates. The poet's incantation has called up the Spirit that then responds by animating the poet's own spirit—Abramsian "correspondent breezes." The wind's prophecy is the revelation that its nature is kindred to our own and is in harmony with our deepest dreams.

Hardy has no patience with any of the three closely interrelated metaphoric implications of Shelley's "Ode": human-natural dialogue; romantic masculine-feminine loving interchange of natural wind and human harp; correspondent breezes in world and mind. "The Wind's Prophecy" parodies these ideas with gusto as Hardy's derisive wind laughs and grins. By writing his poem, like Shelley's, in five stanzas, Hardy can satirize Shelley, in rhetorical putdowns, five times in a row. An additional reason for the five sallies is equally Shelleyan: the first four stanzas focus on the four elements, as do four of the stanzas in the "Ode," and the fifth may be taken to summarize the elements' combined purpose. That purpose, in Hardy's Cervantes-like parodic treatment, is skeptically to ridicule Shelley's faith in the usefulness of trying to conduct dialogues or love affairs either with individual elements or with a spirit-wind that might humanizingly reconcile elemental powers with the speaker's fantasized wishes through its responsive animating activity as a "correspondent breeze." Mocking Shelley's metaphysical dialogue, cosmicized romance, and personification of natural forces as responsive to our passionate desires, Hardy mischievously introduces what may well be the most polemically relentless non-correspondent breeze ever contributed to the rivalrous romanticist tradition.[16]

The first stanza of "The Wind's Prophecy" seems elementally allotted to air, as the poet on a depressing country walk fastens his interpretive hope on the brightly glimmering gulls:

> I travel on by barren farms,
> And gulls glint out like silver flecks
> Against a cloud that speaks of wrecks,
> And bellies down with black alarms.
> I say: 'Thus from my lady's arms
> I go; those arms I love the best!'
> The wind replies from dip and rise,
> 'Nay; toward her arms thou journeyest.'
>
> (ll. 1-8)

The wind tells the poet he does not know what he is talking about; he thinks he has just visited the love of his life, but actually he is walking toward her.[17] The

bright glint of traveling silver gulls is deceptive if taken to confirm the poet's idealizing reveries of what he has experienced. The wind knows best, and what it knows is always the opposite of what you thought you knew. The wind will make this point five times in five stanzas, effectively dismissing any likelihood of a satisfying dialogue with the perplexed lover, but showing a fine appetite for parodic humor that the reader, too, will relish.

A gloomy gray shore or "verge" introducing stanza two gives a dark portrayal of the second element, earth, which the speaker tries to brighten a bit with idealizing fantasy as a distant light comes into focus:

> A distant verge morosely gray
> Appears, while clots of flying foam
> Break from its muddy monochrome,
> And a light blinks up far away.
> I sigh: 'My eyes now as all day
> Behold her ebon loops of hair!'[18]
> Like bursting bonds the wind responds,
> 'Nay, wait for tresses flashing fair!'
>
> (ll. 9-16)

Again, the wind claims to know best: the speaker's true lady love will be no brunette but a blonde. Fantasized hopes, always misleading, will never be confirmed by nature's voice.

Stanza three, the sea stanza, offers no glinting gulls or blinking lights to dazzle hope, nothing but the noise of breakers heard as insistent marine violence:

> From tides the lofty coastlands screen
> Come smitings like the slam of doors,
> Or hammerings on hollow floors,
> As the swell cleaves through caves unseen.
> Say I: 'Though broad this wild terrene,
> Her city home is matched of none!'
> From the hoarse skies the wind replies:
> 'Thou shouldst have said her sea-bord one.'
>
> (ll. 17-24)

For a moment the twice-cowed speaker has stopped trying to educe encouragement directly from the land- or seascape; instead, as if seeking now to avoid refutations from the wind, he links his wishful thinking to the faraway city home of his desired beloved. But the wind, never outsmarted, always wins: the destined lady will live, in the most contrarious way, by the sullen shore.

In the fourth, fire stanza, can the morning star possibly offer some correspondence to the poet's dream where the other three elements have so obviously failed?

> The all-pervading clouds exclude
> The one quick timorous transient star;
> The waves outside where breakers are
> Huzza like a mad multitude.

'When the sun ups it, mist-imbued,'
I cry, 'there reigns the star for me!'
The wind outshrieks from points and peaks:
'Here, westward, where it downs, mean ye!'

(ll. 25-32)

It is another ludicrous putdown. If a man wishes on an eastern star, nature rudely tells him to turn around to the west instead. The "mad multitude" of waves seem to utter their wild huzzas at the lyric dreamer's expense. Well might the star be "timorous"; its fire is the last of the four elements to be ridiculed as prophets, interlocutors, or guides to romance.

Elements come together, or perhaps gang up, in the summary conclusion: the birdlike vulturine headland, the rocky chasms and steeps, the fiery shine of the pharos or lighthouse by the sea, combine to provide a picture that might suggest—what? Unity in variety? Unity underlying, or despite, variety? Reliability amid change? To these questions the comprehensive dismissive reply, as always, will be "Of course not."

Yonder the headland, vulturine,
Snores like old Skrymer in his sleep,
And every chasm and every steep
Blackens as wakes each pharos-shine.
'I roam, but one is safely mine,'
I say. 'God grant she stay my own!'
Low laughs the wind as if it grinned:
'Thy love is one thou'st not yet known.'

(ll. 33-40)

For the fifth time the voice of nature has laughed the poet's interpretive pretensions to scorn, and now we can even enjoy hearing the wind gleefully chortling and imagine it grinning. Five times the would-be cosmicizing, nature-interpreting lover has been targeted, hit, and comically knocked off his ducking-stool. The wind continues, presumably, to prophesy, and what it can be counted on to predict is that there will never be a shortage of naively confident, hopeful but misguided fantasizers.

Though "During Wind and Rain" may well recall Shelleyan autumnal pestilence-stricken multitudes in its brief mention of sick throngs of fall leaves, one could easily suppose the poem to have been written without any conscious thought of Shelley. But it is hard to imagine how Hardy could have conceived and crafted the resolutely anti-Aeolian "Wind's Prophecy," so mockingly (anti-)Shelleyan in its borrowed and allusive title, fourfold elemental imagery, and five-stanza structure, if he had not intended it as a lively parodic reply to Shelley's dialogic dreams, cosmic romance-rapture, and harmonious correspondent breezes. Apart from the parody-tempting context provided by the idealized wind's wish-fulfilling "prophecy" in Shelley's five-stanza "Ode," what could possibly have been the literary or psychological motive for Hardy's poetic format, a sequence of five laughing-and-grinning putdowns?

Note that Hardy's poem does not express the central argument of nature's mere indifference that is elsewhere so pervasive in his work. Nature here is not indifferent at all but actively, derisively, wittily anti-Shelleyan, determined to shrink the pretensions, the pretenses, of Shelley's "Spirit" in an oedipal rivalry of ephebe against mentor, disciple against precursor.[19] There is a dialogue in the poem between man and nature, as between Shelley and Hardy; it is not a correspondent-breeze dialogue but a competitive, contestatory, rivalrous one, far less Buberian than Bloomian. The two poems I have compared are among the most vividly agonistic Bloomian exhibits one could wish to find. But their ludic, parodic prankishness lightens the mood of the mentor-disciple confrontation, thus in part Bakhtinizing Bloom.[20]

In suggesting that a Bloomian understanding of the Shelley-Hardy filiation could benefit from Bakhtinian awareness, I should clarify just what I mean by Bakhtinian. To make a rough but useful distinction, it is what I would call the "Cervantean" rather than the better-known "Rabelaisian" Bakhtin that I consider applicable here. Although the Russian critic is best known to Americans for *Rabelais and His World,* the outlook maintained in that work—which contains "an element of 'utopian' radicalism"—is not typical of Bakhtin's larger corpus of writing: as Gary Saul Morson and Caryl Emerson observe, the "grotesque body" celebrated in the Rabelais book "eats, drinks, laughs, and curses—but does not necessarily contemplate the world or hold dialogues with it"; the "carnival word" in this book "does not really communicate" but only "*mediates,* much as excrement is said to mediate (between body and earth); and it is far from the case that words are the more potent fructifier."[21] By contrast, in the treatment of *Don Quixote* that exemplifies the delights and tensions of dialogic exchange as Bakhtin more characteristically explores them in "Discourse in the Novel," the "respectable language of the chivalric romance" is "only one of the participants in a dialogue of languages."[22] To the truly dialogic "Cervantean" Bakhtin, as opposed to the more one-sidedly defiant and utopian (thus oddly monologic) "Rabelaisian" one, Hardy's "The Wind's Prophecy" would appear an exuberantly heteroglossic work, with the parodically Shelleyan voice of the amiable, naively hopeful, charming but quixotic lover countered in every stanza by the brusquely, entertainingly dismissive replies of the wind, his Sancho Panza.

A final question arises. Since "The Wind's Prophecy" appears right next to "During Wind and Rain" in Hardy's *Collected Poems* (this is true whatever edition one chooses, and it is something nearly impossible not to notice), and since the former poem, starting with the bold allusion in its title to the concluding clarion call of Shelley's prophetic wind, is far more comprehensively (anti-)Shelleyan than the latter, why didn't Bloom include "The Wind's Prophecy" among his comparative data for **"Poetic Origins and Final Phases"**? To choose pages 465-466 over the more obviously relevant adjacent pages 464-465 might seem a Freudian slip or parapraxis, a possibly revealing repression. But if Bloom has possibly repressed an awareness of "The Wind's Prophecy" as Hardy's reply to Shelley, why would the repression occur?

I would hazard the guess that in order to give a High Romantic pedigree to Hardy, whom he considers one of the only two "strong" poets of the twentieth century, Bloom—consciously or not—was seeking a Hardyan rewriting of Shelley that would be more moving, more elevated in tone, more serious in mood, more imbued with pathos, than Hardy's gleeful parody of Shelley consisting of ironic poetical putdowns. But, happily for the reader, the larger picture of Hardy's indebtedness to Shelley reveals a literary son-father relationship that could withstand a high intensity of exuberant, uninhibited lyrical teasing. To be so artfully teased by such a talent as Thomas Hardy is a masterly tribute to his Romantic master.

Notes

1. Joseph Brodsky, "Wooing the Inanimate: Four Poems by Thomas Hardy," *On Grief and Reason: Essays* (New York: Farrar Straus Giroux, 1995), p. 314.

2. J. Hillis Miller, *The Linguistic Moment: From Wordsworth to Stevens* (Princeton: Princeton Univ. Press, 1985), pp. 115, 267. Peter Widdowson, *On Thomas Hardy: Late Essays and Earlier* (New York: St. Martin's Press, 1998), applauds Miller's deconstructive resistance of the pervasive critical "temptation to link poem with poem in some grand scheme" (p. 147). Insistence on correlating the sequence of Hardy's lyrics with the events in his own life in a grand scheme of psychological development has led critics to read "The Wind's Prophecy" exclusively as a gloomy assessment of Hardy's own love life and so to miss the dimension of refreshing parody that I will focus on here; see examples in Harold Orel, *The Final Years of Thomas Hardy, 1912-1928* (Lawrence: Univ. Press of Kansas, 1976), pp. 36-37, and Paul Zietlow, *Moments of Vision: The Poetry of Thomas Hardy* (Cambridge: Harvard Univ. Press, 1974), pp. 194-196.

3. Harold Bloom, *A Map of Misreading* (New York: Oxford Univ. Press, 1975), pp. 9, 19. Hereafter cited as *Misreading*.

4. All Shelley citations are from *The Poems of Shelley*, ed. Thomas Hutchinson (1965; Oxford: Oxford Univ. Press, 1965).

5. All Hardy citations are from *Collected Poems* (New York: Macmillan, 1919; repr. 1925, 1946), which seems the likeliest edition for Bloom to have used. But see also note 11 below.

6. But Armstrong's annotations to the poem in Thomas Hardy, *Selected Poems,* ed. Tim Armstrong (London: Longman, 1993) suggest that the Shelley borrowing may be no more central or crucial than are possible allusions to the song that ends Shakespeare's *Twelfth Night,* to Henry Vaughan's "The Burial," to Elizabeth Barrett Browning's "Isobel's Child," and to a Horace ode (pp. 228-230).

7. My view, though a minority position, is vigorously supported by Widdowson: "Quite how one gets to the position of being able to judge 'During Wind and Rain' as one of the 'best poems of the century', as some critics have done, is quite beyond me" (*On Thomas Hardy,* p. 151). Dennis Taylor, *Hardy's Poetry, 1860-1928* (New York: Columbia Univ. Press, 1981) says, "'During Wind and Rain' achieves an immediacy and vividness not felt in the other poems" (p. 36). But against this, consider the very real difficulty of reciting the lyric without producing emotionally false and discordant notes: See if you can say, "Ah, no; the years O!" and "Ah, no; the years, the years" without some degree of constraint and embarrassment. (An additional problem when reading the poem aloud is that if the word "aye" in lines 9 and 23 is pronounced to rhyme with "gay" and "day" as the rhymes require, it takes on the meaning of "ever" or "always"—as in the phrase "for aye," meaning "forever"—while the sense of the stanzas appears to require the meaning of "yes" and the corresponding pronunciation of "aye" to rhyme with "eye.") In addition to the Taylor reference, Armstrong (Hardy, *Selected Poems,* p. 228) cites Tom Paulin, *Thomas Hardy: The Poetry of Perception* (London: Macmillan, 1975), p. 205 ("one of the best poems of this century") and Thom Gunn, "Hardy and the Ballads," *Agenda* 19 (1972): 2-3, on the poem's superiority, and cites Hardy's own description of the poem, in a letter, as one of his best; see *The Collected Letters of Thomas Hardy,* ed. Richard Little Purdy and Michael Millgate, 7 vols. (Oxford: Oxford Univ. Press, 1975-88), 6:96. Possibly the poet's self-appraisal has helped found a long tradition of over-laudatory assessments of "During Wind and Rain," so that by the year 2000 we hear: "Never mind that it is one of Hardy's greatest poems, it is one of the great poems of the world"; see Douglas Dunn, "Thomas Hardy's Narrative Art: The Poems and Short Stories," in Phillip Mallett ed., *The Achievement of Thomas Hardy* (London: Macmillan, 2000), p. 153. I would grant, however, that the reading in Paulin, *Thomas Hardy,* pp. 205-210, does beautifully elucidate the implications of the five stanzas' respective scenarios, which Paulin calls "illuminated transparencies" (p. 210).

8. Patricia O'Neill, "Pedigree of Self-Making: Shelley's Influence on Browning and Hardy," dissertation, Northwestern University, 1986, working in a Bloom-

ian context, finds "Neutral Tones" an antithetical refashioning of, and response to, Shelley's "Lines: 'When the Lamp is Shattered'" (pp. 153-157).

9. Paulin, *Thomas Hardy: The Poetry of Perception,* pp. 51-61, offers, though not in the Bloomian context I employ here, a fine array of evidence for Hardy's continual quarrel with Shelley's idealizing concept of love.

10. See M. M. Bakhtin, *The Dialogic Imagination: Four Essays,* ed. Michael Holquist, trans. Caryl Emerson and Michael Holquist (Austin: Univ. of Texas Press, 1981).

11. *Complete Poems* seems to me the likeliest edition of Hardy's collected poetry for Bloom to have used, but my observation that the two poems are printed sequentially holds good for all editions of the complete poetry. In another edition which Bloom could have consulted, *The Writings of Thomas Hardy in Prose and Verse with Prefaces and Notes* (Anniversary Edition) 21 vols. (New York and London: Harper, 1921), "The Wind's Prophecy" is on pages 135-136 and "During Wind and Rain" on pages 137-138 of *Moments of Vision* in volume 21. In *The Complete Poems of Thomas Hardy* (London: Macmillan, 1976—just one year after *A Map of Misreading*) the two poems are numbers 440 and 441 (pp. 494-496).

12. Armstrong's annotations (Hardy, *Selected Poems,* pp. 226-228) include no reference to Shelley, nor does any other critic note parallels or quarrels with Shelley in "The Wind's Prophecy." Suggesting that the poem "looks forward to Hardy's marriage" and "describes Hardy's premonitions on his 1870 journey to Cornwall," Armstrong adds, "Hardy's cousin Tryphena Sparks has been suggested (without real proof) as the city lover in the east contrasted with the as yet unseen one in the west" (Hardy, *Selected Poems,* p. 226), a suggestion originally made by Lois Deacon and Terry Coleman, *Providence and Mr. Hardy* (New York: Oxford Univ. Press, 1972), pp. 84-85. Problems with the Deacon-Coleman thesis are revealed by F. B. Pinion, *A Commentary on the Poems of Thomas Hardy* (New York: Barnes and Noble, 1976): Tryphena Sparks "did not have a 'city home' which was 'matched of none' (she was a student at Stockwell Training College); nor was her hair 'ebon'" (p. 144). But Donald Davie, *Thomas Hardy and British Poetry* (New York: Oxford Univ. Press, 1972), pp. 19-22 thinks these two writers show "conclusively" that Tryphena is the "dark-haired girl behind the traveler eastward, whom he thinks of as his chosen; Emma is the blonde who, unknown to him, awaits him at his destination, St. Juliot in Cornwall." Davie believes he has also detected an undercurrent of industrial imagery in the poem which suggests "revenge" of "natural elements" against an "advanced technological culture." Yet, admitting that "the poem itself does not ask to be put together in this way," he concludes

that it "fails to satisfy; and our interest in it is clinical." But I find the poem highly satisfying when read for what it is, an exuberant parody of Shelley, to which certain extensively transformed biographical elements may have contributed.

13. Harold Bloom, *Shelley's Mythmaking* (1959; Ithaca: Cornell Univ. Press, 1969), p. 89.

14. My main points about elements, races, and religions are found in notes 1, 3, and 6 to "Ode to the West Wind" in *Shelley's Poetry and Prose,* ed. Donald Reiman and Sharon Powers (New York: Norton, 1977), p. 221. My aim in this paragraph is not to be original but to suggest a number of immediately available meanings of the sort Hardy might have noted and "antithetically" confronted.

15. M. H. Abrams, "The Correspondent Breeze: A Romantic Metaphor," *KR* 19 (1957): 113-130; rev. and repr. in *English Romantic Poets: Modern Essays in Criticism,* ed. M. H. Abrams (New York: Oxford Univ. Press, 1960), pp. 37-54.

16. For an intercultural sample of additional non-correspondent breezes see my "The Aeolian Harp Reconsidered: Music of Unfulfilled Longing in Tjutchev, Mörike, Thoreau, and Others," *Comparative Literature Studies* 22 (1985): 329-343.

17. J. Hillis Miller, in *Tropes, Parables, Performatives: Essays on Twentieth-Century Literature* (Durham: Duke Univ. Press, 1991), interestingly relates the wind's perspective to that of the "ghosts" in Hardy's poetry, whose retrospective insights regarding the "ineluctable consequences of events," however disillusioning these insights may be, are for Hardy "the only way to make the present tolerable," so that he tries to "look at the present as if one were a ghost" (p. 114).

18. "In all five stanzas, amazingly, the vigour and accuracy of the first half is opposed by the 'literary' slackness of the second; 'clots of flying foam' against 'ebon loops,'" according to Kenneth Marsden, *The Poems of Thomas Hardy: A Critical Introduction* (New York: Oxford Univ. Press, 1969), p. 53. Similarly, commenting on the two halves of the fourth stanza, Trevor Johnson, *A Critical Introduction to the Poems of Thomas Hardy* (New York: St. Martin's Press, 1991), deplores the transition from a "superb picture of sky and seascape, which Tennyson might have envied," to the disappointing final "exchange" which tries to take words "by the scruff and yank them about" (pp. 106-107). Johnson thinks the "unrivalled evocation[s] of the wild North Atlantic coast of Cornwall" in the first halves of the five stanzas could be "detached" to "great advantage" from the "turgid prophesyings of the wind" in the second halves (p. 107): he wants to tear every stanza in two and throw out the second half. These critics rightly note the dramatic difference between the diction in the first and second halves of each stanza, but

because they fail to hear the humor of the parodic putdowns, they do not perceive that the "lower" style of the second part (which they call slack or turgid) is perfect for comic contrast. Hardy proves, as Samuel Beckett confirms, that one can be a philosophical pessimist and at the same time a master of humor.

19. Unawareness of the Shelley context may help explain why Taylor says simply, "'The Wind's Prophecy' is a flawed poem. Its ominous import is obscure and its descriptions seem out of proportion to its subject" (*Hardy's Poetry, 1860-1928,* p. 36). Yet the poem's import is not only ominous but grotesquely parodic. As for the disproportion between the romantically, lyrically interpreted landscape and its "real" satirical meaning, this is not a flaw but the whole point of the parody. Taylor has a valuable discussion, though, of ways in which he feels "'The Wind's Prophecy' may have contributed to the peculiarly dramatic effect" of the conclusion to "During Wind and Rain" (p. 37).

20. The relation of Bakhtinian to Bloomian theory is a rich topic that critics have barely begun to explore. Elizabeth Sauer, "The Partial Song of Satanic Anti-Creation: Milton's Discourses of the Divided Self," in Janet Lungstrum and Elizabeth Sauer, eds., *Agonistics: Arenas of Creative Contest* (Albany: SUNY Press, 1997), pp. 226-239, combines the two in her discussion of Milton's *Paradise Lost,* as the Bloomian agon of Satan versus God is contrasted to the Bakhtinian ludic-dialogic multiplicity of viewpoints provided by the poem's multiple narrators, dispersing power among "a plurality of centers of consciousness" (p. 228). Michel André Bernstein, "The Poetics of Ressentiment," in Gary Saul Morson and Caryl Emerson, eds., *Rethinking Bakhtin: Extensions and Challenges* (Evanston: Northwestern Univ. Press, 1989), pp. 197-223, combines Bakhtin and Bloom in a different but equally fascinating way by showing how characters like Dostoevsky's Underground Man feel enraged that their Bloomian belatedness is precisely their "*post festum* existence," their arrival on the literary-historical scene at a time when Bakhtinian ludic dialogue is stale or dead. Thus the Underground Man feels frustrated at "deriving his very desires from, and then only being able to articulate them through, images and situations borrowed from works like 'Pushkin's *Silvio* and Lermontov's *Masquerade'*" (p. 212). My own path toward a synthesis of Bloom and Bakhtin would begin with the ludic element in *Agon: Towards a Theory of Revisionism* (Oxford: Oxford Univ. Press, 1982) where Bloom himself seems working toward a Bakhtinian plurality of competitive games for every agonist when he approvingly says that, in Nietzsche's view, "the spirit portrays itself as agonistic, as contesting for supremacy, with other spirits, with anteriority, and finally with every earlier version of itself." Bloom adds, "The first theologians of agon were the Gnostics of Alexandria, and the final pragmatists of agon have been and will be the

Americans of Emerson's tradition." I see Bloom's "American religion of competitiveness" as combining a Bakhtinian ludic joy with agonistic rivalry (see *Agon,* p. viii).

21. Gary Saul Morson and Caryl Emerson, *Mikhail Bakhtin: Creation of a Prosaics* (Stanford: Stanford Univ. Press, 1990), pp. 444, 447; see M. M. Bakhtin, *Rabelais and His World,* trans. Hélène Iswolsky (Cambridge: MIT Press, 1968).

22. Morson and Emerson, p. 367, citing "Discourse in the Novel" in M. M. Bakhtin, *The Dialogic Imagination,* see p. 386.

Cary Nelson (review date spring 2004)

SOURCE: Nelson, Cary. "Boomlay, Boomlay, Boomlay, BLOOM." *Virginia Quarterly Review* 80, no. 2 (spring 2004): 243-52.

[*In the following review, Nelson highlights what he judges as Bloom's omissions and idiosyncratic selections in* The Best Poems of the English Language.]

The poems I have chosen to memorize over the years answer to an odd mixture of social occasions and opportunities. When asked to perform a poem at non-academic parties, I have found Lewis Carroll's "Jabberwocky," not among the poems Harold Bloom includes in *The Best Poems of the English Language* (2004), to serve me best. My audience is not literary, but it can still readily grasp the capacity of sound and syntax alone to generate narrative meaning. Meanwhile the poem can be embodied in gesture and expression, so the mysterious power to incarnate words may also be on display. As a longtime poetry teacher, moreover, I have not found it possible to get through a semester without quoting Gerard Manley Hopkins's "The Windhover." The plosive excesses of his sprung rhythm haunt a wide range of poems whose effects become audible in the wake of this most extreme example of English's capacity for alliteration. On the other hand, though I am equally committed to, coembedded with, Hopkins's "Spring and Fall," I prefer to recite it to myself. I am not entirely sure why—perhaps because it is one of very few poems that offer me consolation I can accept. "Márgarét, áre you grieving / Over Golden-grove unleaving?" And, finally, like many steeped in high literary traditions, I have some favorite pieces of doggerel whose capacity to burlesque literary ambition and bring it down to earth is a necessary cultural and personal antidote. My all-time favorite remains H. H. Lewis's "Thinking of Russia":

> I'm always thinking of Russia
> I can't keep her out of my head.
> I don't give a damn for Uncle Sham.

I'm a left wing radical Red.

Lewis's rude little quatrain, needless to say, finds no place in Bloom's recent hyperbolically titled ***The Best Poems of the English Language,*** though Bloom's anthology is no less of a challenge to its readers' sensibilities than Lewis's poem is. The pressures to number the company of the elect presumably prohibit Bloom's or anyone else's version of Lewis—perhaps a favorite limerick—from getting into the book. But it is worth remembering that the pleasures of the poetic always exceed prevailing standards for excellence. Bloom tells us he has compiled the book he has always wanted to have by his side. Will anyone feel the same? Surely it is as much a compilation of our favorite poems we would want by our side on that proverbial desert island as it is whatever the best of the best poems might be. The personal favorites collection each of us might assemble would not be transferable to other readers. Neither, for that matter, would anyone's large collection of "best" poems match anyone else's. Bloom certainly knows that. Indeed he sees his enterprise as a corrective to rampant bad judgment and nonaesthetic criteria. The difference in part is that Bloom believes he has got it right. I might take on a "some of the best" anthology, but nothing could convince me my taste was divine. If Bloom harbors any such doubt, he has successfully suppressed all public evidence of it for many years.

It is not just that different readers—and different historical periods—evidence different tastes, interests, and standards. It is also that history has bequeathed us so many different poetic styles, voices, forms, rhythms, and subjects that contests between them are undecidable. You could of course decide in advance that the best poems have to be sonnets. Or you could rule out satire. Or you could choose bests in many different categories of form and content—the best love poems, the best villanelles, and so forth. If no one consistent aesthetic standard is likely to encompass even a single reader's reasons for experiencing poetic pleasure, the aesthetic variation out there in the field is still greater.

What Bloom has done in this curious collection is to combine idiosyncratic preferences in tone and subject matter with large exclusionary categories. The glaring omissions that will immediately strike most contemporary readers derive from Bloom's scorched-earth policy toward women and minority writers. The 1996 edition of *The Norton Anthology of Poetry* includes over twenty women poets from the beginning of English poetry to the year 1819, the year Bloom's first female poet was born. Here are the names of the women poets included in the *Norton* and the year each was born: Anne Askew (1521), Queen Elizabeth (1533), Isabella Whitney (ca. 1540s), Mary Sidney (1568), Aemilia Lanyer (1569), Mary Wroth (ca. 1587), Anne Bradstreet (ca. 1612), Margaret Cavendish (1623), Katherine Philips (1632),

Aphra Behn (ca. 1640), Anne Killigrew (1660), Anne Finch (1661), Lady Mary Wortly Montagu (1689), Mary Leapor (1722), Anna Laetitia Barbauld (1743), Hannah More (1745), Phillis Wheatley (1753), Helen Maria Williams (1761), Joanna Baille (1762), Mary Tighe (1722), Felicia Dorothy Hemans (1793), Elizabeth Barrett Browning (1806), and Emily Brontë (1818). Their names are not to be found in Bloom's table of contents. In their place he repeats his notorious complaint, first broadcast in a *Boston Review* essay, that "extrapoetic considerations of race, ethnicity, gender, sexual orientation, and assorted ideologies increasingly constitute the grounds for judgment in the educational institutions and the media of the English-speaking world" (13). He offers instead what he calls a search for "the Sublime." for instances of "Loftiness."

How might a woman embody the sublime? To what form of loftiness might she aspire? Perversely, the first poem by a woman, five hundred pages into Bloom's anthology, gives us one version of his answer:

> Mine eyes have seen the glory of the coming of the Lord:
> He is trampling out the vintage where the grapes of wrath are stored:
> He hath loosed the fateful lightning of his terrible swift sword . . .

It is Julia Ward Howe's 1862 "Battle-Hymn of the Republic," which did indeed become the unofficial anthem of the Northern Army in the American Civil War. Summoning symbols of transcendent patriarchal power to the army's side, the poem bids men to die "While God is marching on." Women, it seems, can aspire to bless the state. It is a text, incidentally, that cannot be read aloud; it can only be sung, lest lines like "They have builded Him an altar in the evening dews and damps" or "As ye deal with my contemners, so with you my grace shall deal" lead one to falter. The poem belongs in any historical anthology of American poetry, for it is lodged in the heart of the country and exists in scores of versions rewritten for new occasions. But is it one of "the best poems of the English language"? When editing the *Anthology of Modern American Poetry* (Oxford 2000), I found I could not bring myself to include it because it has, to my ears, too many bad lines. For me, then, aesthetics trumped history in this case, which is Bloom's self-declared principle as well. You may judge on which side the truth falls.

"Battle-Hymn of the Republic" initiates a whole series of problematic Bloomian decisions about women's poetry. Our memory of both 19th- and 20th-century poetry in English has been thoroughly overhauled over the last thirty years, and a whole series of women poets have been reevaluated and recovered. The results include both poems of significant historical and cultural interest and poems that rank as major achievements. Bloom ignores most of these writers, but on the few occasions when he does include their work, he often refuses what we have learned about it and renews their incorporation within male condescension.

Thus Edna St. Vincent Millay gets doubly undermined. First Bloom tells us, "I confess to finding her more interesting as a life story than as a poet" (929), the traditional way of dismissing her. Then he prints only "If I should learn, in some quite casual way," a sonnet that is not only antiromantic—Millay's most notable mode—but also self-undermining for its female speaker, who reports that if she learned of her man's death, she would not "cry / Aloud" but rather attend to "Where to store furs and how to treat the hair." Bloom might well have paired it with a Millay poem debunking male subjectivity or, still better, used one of Millay's powerful poems in which an articulate female speaker opts for cold and sophisticated romantic deflation. Those, moreover, are the sonnets more intricately in dialogue with their Renaissance predecessors. But Bloom is willing to set aside his thirty-year preoccupation with issues of influence and literary allusion to choose a Millay poem that is not as good as a number of her others. He simply cannot help himself.

Bloom set a remarkably counterproductive limit to his collection, drawing a line in the sand at the year 1899. No poet born later would gain admittance. The calendar has a certain cultural logic, to be sure, one that exceeds the merely arbitrary, but it does not map onto literary history except by way of a willful misreading. There are dates that set meaningful—if always debatable—limits to literary periods, but a birth date of 1899 has instead an irrational impact. It does not stop before modernism, but it does not carry through until modernism's conclusion either. The British have often felt Yeats's death in 1939 on the eve of World War II combined literary and political history in a way that decisively signaled the end of an era. In the United States we have both the arrival of the Beats and the emergence of confessional poetry in the 1950s, both of which overturn Eliot's mask of impersonality and place literary modernism decisively in the past. One may choose earlier events, like the use of the atomic bomb or the revelation of the Holocaust, to close the modern period, but a birth year tells us little about literary history.

There are two unstated but no doubt significant motives underlying Bloom's decision. First, it prevents him from confronting the need to pay reprint fees. Poems published in 1922 or earlier are now in the public domain, as are poems by writers dead for seventy years or more. T. S. Eliot, born in 1888, published *The Waste Land* in 1922. Hart Crane, born in 1899, died in 1932. *The Waste Land* and *The Bridge* are now in the public

domain, as are Robert Frost's and Wallace Stevens's early work. The absence of anything from Eliot's *Four Quartets* may have more to do with the fact that it is expensive to reprint than with any claim that it just isn't as good as "Battle-Hymn of the Republic." As I argue at length in *Office Hours* (2004), reprint fees can kill off an anthology substantially devoted to the 20th century. Bloom might well have acknowledged this problem rather than disguising it.

The other reason for setting the 1899 cutoff date is more sinister. It helps Bloom to eliminate much of the Harlem Renaissance. In Bloom's mind, those of our African American poets who did not much like the United States have apparently returned to where they or their ancestors came from: "If poets born in the twentieth century were included here, many would be from Canada, the West Indies, Australia, New Zealand, and Africa" (xxv). No mention of Native American poets, no mention of the black poets who radically transformed the sonnet into a form for political protest or incorporated blues and jazz rhythms into poetry for the first time, all innovations requiring us to broaden our aesthetic horizons.

When Henry Louis Gates introduced the *Norton Anthology of African American Literature,* he remarked that simply winning attention for Melvin Tolson's *Libretto for the Republic of Liberia* (1953) would justify the entire book. The poem is partly a black rejoinder to *The Waste Land,* offering an alternative set of literary and historical allusions from worlds that do not impinge on Eliot's imagination. When I reprinted it in *Anthology of Modern American Poetry,* I commissioned a remarkable set of annotations from Edward Brunner, making it fully accessible to readers for the first time. There is some doubt about when Tolson was born. It may have been 1899, but 1900 is more likely. So Bloom can hide behind the inanity of the calendar and consider Tolson barred by law. Sterling Brown, born in 1901, and Langston Hughes, born in 1902, are luckily ruled out of contention as well. And so Bloom's "best" poems are by white poets. It was the implacable authority of the calendar, folks; Harold had no choice.

But as the list of women poets from earlier periods demonstrates, Bloom had no small measure of choice even within the limits he set for himself. Lola Ridge, born in 1873, could also rewrite the Renaissance sonnet for the modern age:

> What if the heat of this enormous hive
> Plotted and combed with fire, shall not suffice,
> To stay the bleak offensive of the ice . . .

Amy Lowell, born in 1874, wrote some of the most powerful and metaphorically inventive love poems of the century: "I parted you from your leaves, / Until you stood up like a white flower." Mina Loy, born in 1882, wrote "Songs to Joannes," which is now widely regarded as one of the major achievements of experimental modernism. Angelina Weld Grimké, born in 1880, wrote love poems and protest poems, often haunting and intricate. In Anne Spencer's "White Things" we have one of the towering poetic indictments of whiteness; she was born in 1882.

Grimké and Spencer were also black, but Bloom had James Weldon Johnson (1871) and Paul Laurence Dunbar (1872) as options as well. But perhaps the most outrageous omission of an African American poet—within Bloom's own announced standards—is Claude McKay, born in Jamaica in 1889. McKay broke with the sonnet tradition in 1919 and continued to do so for another two decades. If Millay rearticulated centuries of rhetorical eloquence to a feminized irony, McKay did the same for anger. His full poetic output is only available now, in his *Collected Poems,* edited for the first time by William Maxwell and published in 2004. His ground-breaking sonnets, however, have been reprinted in anthologies for more than fifty years. Here is "Mulatto" (1925):

> Because I am the white man's son—his own,
> Bearing his bastard birth-mark on my face,
> I will dispute his title to his throne,
> Forever fight him for my rightful place,
> There is a searing hate within my soul,
> A hate that only kin can feel for kin,
> A hate that makes me vigorous and whole,
> And spurs me on increasingly to win.
> Because I am my cruel father's child,
> My love of justice stirs me up to hate,
> A warring Ishmaelite, unreconciled.
> When falls the hour I shall not hesitate
> Into my father's heart to plunge the knife
> To gain the utmost freedom that is life.

If Bloom's wholesale elimination of poems by women and minorities is disgusting and deplorable, however, it is not especially interesting. It is simply part of the conservative backlash against muticulturalism. In Bloom's much-attacked *Boston Review* piece, he turned a military metaphor from Thucydides—"They have the numbers; we, the heights"—into a cultural claim, one intended to evoke a horde of multiculturalists about to overwhelm those few white cultural stalwarts in possession of the truth. It was reprinted as the introduction to Bloom's ***The Best of the Best American Poetry: 1988-1997,*** where he castigates Adrienne Rich for her inclusion of "enemies of the aesthetic who are in the act of overwhelming us" (16) in her own anthology, *The Best American Poetry 1996.* Bloom has in mind, among others, such Native American poets as Sherman Alexie and Adrian Louis. Always convinced he has one hand securely grasping the eternal verities, Bloom regrettably

has the other hand embedded in racist cultural temptations he might better have resisted. His fellow backlasher, Marjorie Perloff, lampoons most African American poets, all too political for her taste, but tries to cover herself by praising those few who write in her preferred abstract, experimental tradition. Bloom cannot do the same, since black poets do not exist in the aesthetic of his book, but, like all canny contemporary misogynists, he finds one woman to praise. In his case it is Léonie Adams, about whom he remarks, "I am unable to understand why Léonie Adams is not more read and discussed than she is now. Four of her best poems are given here, but I wish I had space for more" (936). Neither Hopkins nor Yeats, among others, gets a similar wistful "were there but world enough and time" plea for more space.

Yet the price he pays in ***The Best Poems of the English Language*** is deeper than laying himself open to charges of assembling a collection grounded in unconscious racism and misogyny. His 1899 cutoff propels him into modernism but then severely curtails its representation. The deaf ear he turns to African American and feminist music incapacitates him further. The unquestioned masterpieces in the book—and there are scores of them—are mostly altogether familiar and entirely canonical. Any of us would include them in such a book, from the General Prologue to *The Canterbury Tales* through Shakespeare's sonnets and Keats's Odes to *The Bridge.* What matters in the end are the surprises he provides, and those are mostly surprises of omission. When they are not surprises of omission, they are, alas, too often surprises of commission, hilarious choices that leave one astonished. In the place of Amy Lowell's enraptured love poems and Claude McKay's towering protest poems we are offered Trumbull Stickney's "Mnemosyne," which Bloom aptly describes as "a perfect example of American nostalgia" (814):

> It's lonely in the country I remember
>
> The babble of our children fills my ears,
> And on our hearth I stare the perished ember
> To flames that show all starry thro my tears.

This bathos Bloom promotes to empyrean heights. One may only express relief that, if the "Battle-Hymn of the Republic" sounds in our ears as we march toward the next Baghdad, we at least have Stickney to remind us there are reasons to be embarrassed at being an American.

So why are a number of Bloom's additions to the company of the blest such clunkers? What drives him to look elsewhere when he encounters strong poems that might well belong in his book? What unifies the poems he admires and what unifies the poems he rejects? The first clue might be recognized in the poems he chooses for the poets who are in his anthology. Herman Melville is there with his gnomic "The Portent," which forecasts the deluge of the Civil War, and with his riveting and visceral nature poem "The Maldive Shark," but not with "Shiloh," "Ball's Bluff," "Malvern Hill," "Memorial on the Slain at Chickamauga," "The March into Virginia," or "An Uninscribed Monument on One of the Battlefields of the Wilderness." Neither in the selection of poems nor in the headnote is there anything to suggest Melville is fundamentally a poet of the Civil War. Whitman gets "When Lilacs Last in the Dooryard Bloom'd" but not "The Wound-Dresser," "Vigil Strange I Kept on the Field One Night," or any of his other Civil War poems. Tennyson does not get "The Charge of the Light Brigade." which might well have pride of place with Howe's "Battle-Hymn."

The pattern persists into the 20th century. Kipling gets "The Vampire," a poem I like because it received a feminist rejoinder, but not "Tommy," "Recessional," or the later "Epitaphs of the War." Allen Tate gets "Aeneas at Washington" and "The Mediterranean," both refreshing reminders of Tate's rhetorical dexterity, but at the price of eliminating the canonical "Ode to the Confederate Dead." For some writers, especially those whose work peaked as they died at war, there would seem little choice. But there Bloom's choices become not simply strange but actually perverse. Isaac Rosenberg is represented with two rather indirect poems, "Returning, We Hear the Larks" and "A Worm Fed on the Heart of Corinth," while his wartime masterpieces "Break of Day in the Trenches" and "Dead Man's Dump" are nowhere to be found. Siegfried Sassoon is not represented at all. With Wilfred Owen, again, he is either to be given war poems or cast out of the book, and Bloom permits him "Strange Meeting" and "Anthem for Doomed Youth," but the one poem central to every discussion of the literature of the war, Owen's "Dulce et Decorum Est," is rejected. Far from being a typical poem of the First World War, for the average poem was patriotic and prowar, Owen's is also one of very few poems to manage graphic descriptions of death. Yet it clings to literariness despite the barbarity of what it witnesses. Its omission from the anthology is inexcusable. But Bloom is not fond of poems so visceral, so recklessly material. His ideal voice is *Hamlet*'s Polonius, as if rewritten by Hart Crane. In other words, Bloom likes philosophical platitudes refracted through layers of frenzied imagery and high rhetoric. At the end he admits "a lifelong addiction to high poetry" (942). Poetry for Bloom is about transcendent truths, the twists and turns of consciousness thoroughly abstracted from time and place. It is not just war poems he dislikes—though the absence of Richard Lovelace's "To Lucasta, Going to

the Wars" is astonishing, for it haunts every subsequent wartime departure from a lover—but all poems tied to historical events and social struggles.

Yeats is thus here with "The Second Coming" but not with "Easter 1916" or "An Irish Airman Foresees His Death." Perhaps even "Leda and the Swan" seemed too physical for this editor. One would not know from Bloom's collection that race has been a central theme in English and American poetry for a century and a half. Not that every major poem about race in America is readily available, either in anthologies or elsewhere. Aaron Kramer's "Denmark Vesey," the most ambitious poem about African American history ever written by a white American, has languished in a chapbook for half a century; it will finally be reprinted in *Wicked Times*, Kramer's selected poems, in 2004. If there are any doubts, one may confirm that Bloom seems to have forgotten abolitionist poetry. In much the same vein, one would not know from Bloom's anthology that labor struggles have been played out in poems even longer. Poems on governmental themes stretch back further still. Bloom asks the standard—and often dishonestly answered—question of each poem he considers: "Has it transcended the history of its own time and the events of the poet's life, or is it now only a period piece?" (21). But of course the ravages of war and the inequities of social life are not short-term subjects. They permeate human history almost without relief. Poems on such subjects often enough have difficulty holding onto the specifics of time and place, they seem so relevant to future generations.

"Ultimately," Bloom writes, "we seek out the best poems because something in many, if not most, of us quests for the transcendental and extraordinary, however secular, however well within the realm of the natural" (xxvi). Why, in the light of this, he refuses to include either Hopkins's "The Windhover" or his "Spring and Fall," among the poems I cited at the outset, I can hardly guess, though perhaps the former is too harsh in the way it deploys its consonants; perhaps it is not sufficiently abstract and lyrical. Presumably it is the anti-lyrical character of her verse that leads Bloom to omit Gertrude Stein. And one assumes it is the willfully intermittent lyricism and factually irradiated character of Pound's *Cantos* that explains their absence, though in Pound's case he offers a further explanation: "*The Cantos* contain material that is not humanly acceptable to me, and if that material is acceptable to others, then they themselves are thereby less acceptable, at least to me" (859). But the inclusion in Pound's *Cantos* of humanly unacceptable allegiances is precisely why one might want to anthologize them. They teach us what poetry can be and has been and prevent us from deluding ourselves about the nature of poetic idealization. Other omissions—among them the rejection of William

Carlos Williams's "The Red Wheelbarrow" and Pound's "In a Station of the Metro"—also make it impossible to represent poets' careers fairly or to track the very patterns of influence Bloom finds so central to poetic tradition.

Part of what recent theories that Bloom hates have taught us is that the transcendental is not transcendent. It is produced in time, by people facing difficulty and aspiration. It occurs as often as not in poems confronting specific historic occasions, just as so many abstract notions—justice, decency, faith—are formulated out of need, in the face of their historical betrayal. Part of what the poems Bloom casts into the abyss regularly do is offer the most telling and concise historical testimony possible. They do so, as Bloom recognizes for the poems he admires, by radical exploitation of the figurative power of the language. In poetry an era can sometimes be compressed into a stanza. Miraculously, it will sometimes seem that none of that era's complications have been slighted. Extraordinary? Certainly, but the extraordinariness is of insight, compression, and representation—and of a complementary power of implication—not the extraordinary illusion of leaving lived time behind.

Linda Munk (review date summer 2004)

SOURCE: Munk, Linda. "'Resentment-Pipers': The Case of Harold Bloom." *University of Toronto Quarterly* 73, no. 3 (summer 2004): 934-40.

[*In the following review, Munk declares* Genius *an angry, self-obsessed reaction to recent changes in literary criticism.*]

> I have spent my life teaching literature, and increasingly I have become surrounded by academic imposters who call themselves 'cultural critics.' They are nothing of the sort: they are resentment-pipers.
>
> Harold Bloom, *Genius* (2002)

> From street to street he piped advancing,
> And step for step they followed dancing,
> Until they came to the river Weser
> Wherein all plunged and perished!
> —Save one who, stout as Julius Caesar,
> Swam across and lived to carry
> (As he, the manuscript he cherished)
> To Rat-land home his commentary.
>
> Robert Browning, 'The Pied Piper of Hamelin'

> Everyone has, or should have, a desert island list against that day when, fleeing one's enemies one is cast ashore . . .
>
> Harold Bloom, *The Western Canon* (1994)

We begin in 1992, the year Bloom published *The American Religion*:

> Moral criticism, political criticism, social criticism have now usurped the place of the aesthetic in what passes for literary criticism in our academies. The function of religious criticism at the present time is to keep the spiritual in religion from following the aesthetic in literature into the discard trays of the politically correct School of Resentment. Anti-intellectualism pervades American political, social, and moral life, and its answering chorus is the political correctness of the academic pseudo-Left.

Bloom's phrasing ('have now usurped the place of') invokes Emerson's 'Divinity School Address': 'The idioms of his [Jesus Christ's] language, and the figures of his rhetoric, have usurped the place of his truth; and churches are not built on his principles, but on his tropes.' In Bloom's case, the 'dogmas' of the 'School of Resentment' and its followers, 'the rabblement of lemmings who now dominate American campuses,' have usurped 'the place of the aesthetic'; and departments of literature are built on 'the overdeterminations of race, class, and gender.' Lemmings, Arctic rodents about six inches long, are remarkable for their 'prolific character' and their annual migration to the sea (*OED*).

The School of Resentment is composed of six 'branches,' we read in *The Western Canon* (1994): 'Feminists, Marxists, Lacanians, New Historicists, Deconstructionists, Semioticians.'

> I am not concerned . . . with the current debate between the right-wing defenders of the Canon, who wish to preserve it for its supposed (and nonexistent) moral values, and the academic-journalistic network I have dubbed the School of Resentment, who wish to overthrow the Canon in order to advance their supposed (and nonexistent) programs for social change.

We meet up with 'the rabblement of lemmings,' who one day 'will cease to hurl themselves off the cliffs' and into the sea. In the mean time, 'Shakespeare criticism is in full flight from his aesthetic supremacy and works at reducing him to the "social energies" of the English Renaissance.'

> The School of Resentment is compelled by its dogmas to regard aesthetic supremacy, particularly in Shakespeare's instance, as a prolonged cultural conspiracy undertaken to protect the political and economic interests of mercantile Great Britain from the eighteenth century until today. . . . One sees why Foucault has won such favor with apostles of Resentment; he replaces the canon with the metaphor he calls the library, which dissolves hierarchies.

Reading Alice Walker's novel *Meridian* for the second time, Bloom had an 'epiphany.' There is a 'correct test for the new canonicity' (for the counter-canon, 'resentment's alternative to the Canon'): 'it must not and cannot be reread, because its contribution to societal progress is its generosity in offering itself up for rapid ingestion and discarding.' The deepest cut is the word *societal*.) And yet and yet, a counted number of pulses only is given to us . . .

> As there is only so much time, do we reread Elizabeth Bishop or Adrienne Rich? Do I again go in search of lost time with Marcel Proust, or am I to attempt yet another rereading of Alice Walker's stirring denunciation of all males, black and white? My former students, many of them now stars of the School of Resentment, proclaim that they teach social selflessness, which begins in learning how to read selflessly.

> Pragmatically, the 'expansion of the Canon' has meant the destruction of the Canon, since what is being taught includes by no means the best writers who happen to be women, African, Hispanic, or Asian, but rather the writers who offer the resentment they have developed as part of their sense of identity. There is no strangeness and no originality in such resentment . . .

Bloom's most recent book is ***Genius: A Mosaic of One Hundred Exemplary Creative Minds*** (2002). It weighs in at 814 pages; and yet we're given no index, no notes, no bibliography. *Genius* must therefore be reread, whether a reviewer with only so much time likes it or not. 'This is a book about genius,' Bloom writes, 'in which I juxtapose many figures, in the hope of isolating in each the specific originality that renders us reluctant to yield him or her up to the ongoing vanishing of our high culture.' This is a book about resentment: resentment against 'the neo-Christian New Criticism of T. S. Eliot and his academic followers'; resentment against 'Frenchified critics' like 'Foucault and his resentful followers,' whose 'pernicious historicism . . . has destroyed humanistic study in the English-speaking world'; and resentment against the 'academic-journalistic network' Bloom names the 'School of Resentment.'

Ignoring the book's pasteboard scaffolding (and Bloom's cheapening of Kabbalah), I turn first to 'our self-ruined academies of instruction':

> Groupthink is the blight of our Age of Information, and is most pernicious in our obsolete academic institutions, whose long suicide since 1967 continues.

> If genius is the God within, I need to seek it there, in the abyss of the aboriginal self, an entity unknown to nearly all our current Explainers, in the intellectually forlorn universities and in the media's dark Satanic mills.

> You would not then appoint Falstaff to the faculty at West Point or at Sandhurst. Would you appoint him at Yale? Even if by gift and guile, he were to be tenured there, he would have to become a department of one, a teacher without colleagues, though with students enough.

(As a 'department of one' at Yale, Falstaff would be related to Milton, Blake, Dante, and Dickinson; each is 'a sect of one' and 'a party of one.') In Bloom's reading of Shakespeare, Falstaff 'dies for love: a teacher's love':

Well, what is a teacher's love? In the English-speaking academic world, closely ruled by campus Puritans, we now have knitting-circles of Madame Defarges, sadistically awaiting the spectacle of the guillotine, fit punishment for 'sexual harassment,' that poor parody of the Socratic Eros. Though seventy-one, and so someone for whom virtue and exhaustion have become synonymous, I continue to believe that an eros more dualistic even than that of Socrates is appropriate, indeed essential, for effective teaching.

> The *Alice* books are not secret manuals of sexual harassment, and the Madame Defarges who staff the Sexual Harassment Committee in each and every one of our English-speaking universities would never be able to knit Lewis Carroll into their indictments.

Bloom is now 'seventy-one,' we've learned on page 24. On page 98 the senex repeats himself: 'At seventy-one, I am perhaps not yet ready for the *Paradiso* (where being of the Jewish persuasion I am not going to end anyway).' Now page 178, in case the January topos has slipped our minds: 'I am aware that I testify as a person of seventy-one, nine years old at the time of Freud's death.' He's reached his anecdotage: 'When I was young, critics saw Stevens as a kind of poetic dandy, addicted to finicky language. This yielded, during my middle years, to Snow Man Stevens, endlessly negative. . . . Now, in old age, I am offered a newly historicized Stevens, socially overdetermined.'

On page 194 of *Genius* we confront Bloom's twin obsessions—'old age' and 'Frenchified' critics: 'At seventy-one, a literary critic has learned that he can speak only for himself, and not for what is fashionable, so let me begin by dismissing "French Nietzsche," and send that off to the dustbin with "French Freud."' Moreover 'our still-current French intellectual disease' (!) has produced 'French Emily Brontë':

> Though the ongoing rabblement of mock-feminists, pretend Marxists, and sub-historians swarm around *Wuthering Heights,* in order to give us what could be called French Emily Brontë, they scarcely can get near a work that renders void all moral, social, and political contexts.

Migratory instincts have carried Bloom's 'rabblement' from the Heights to the sea: 'Christian moralist critics are as irrelevant as our Frenchified cultural studies rabblement; Ahab is Melville's longest reach toward Shakespeare, and toward the aesthetic dignity we must still designate as genius.' Compare an excerpt from ***The Western Canon***:

> As for redefining them [Shakespeare and Dante], good fortune to you. That enterprise is now considerably advanced by 'the New Historicism,' which is French Shakespeare, with Hamlet under the shadow of Michel Foucault. We have enjoyed French Freud or Lacan, and French Joyce or Derrida. Jewish Freud and Irish Joyce

are more to my taste, as is English Shakespeare or universal Shakespeare. French Shakespeare is so delicious an absurdity that one feels an ingrate for not appreciating so comic an invention.

As there is only so much space allotted to *Genius* in *UTQ,* I move to Bloom's chapter on 'Shakespeare's daughter,' Jane Austen:

> I begin by declaring my pragmatic disinterest in the supposed relationship between her novels and her country's imperial policies and procedures. I have met a remarkable number of persons who teach—I will not say literature, but cultural studies—and who tell me that they have never read *Mansfield Park,* and yet tell me also that what matters most about Austen's novel is its financial 'dark side,' Sir Thomas Bertram's ownership of a sugar plantation in Antigua.

(It is a truth universally acknowledged that what matters most about *Mansfield Park* is its 'dark side'—'Sir Thomas Bertram's ownership of a sugar plantation in Antigua'—just as everyone knows that 'only the Dickinson fortune and social position made her possible.')

> The academic world, which rewards cheerleading and loathes genius, is the worst possible audience for, or authority upon, Emily Dickinson, as the vast mass of current contemporaries pathetically demonstrate. 'Hurrah for Emily!' the pom-pom wavers cheer: 'She slept with sister-in-law Sue!'

(Here's one more, this time from *The Western Canon*: 'Miss Dickinson of Amherst does not set out to help Mrs. Elizabeth Barrett Browning complete a quilt. Rather, Dickinson leaves Mrs. Browning far behind in the dust.')

'Genius is not always lovable,' Bloom writes in *Genius.* 'Wharton, like T. S. Eliot and the shattering Dostoevsky, belongs to that small band of writers I am compelled to admire, but do not like. Celine, whom I find unreadable, is a different phenomenon: he is my garbage bin, with Wyndham Lewis and all but a few fragments of Ezra Pound.' In his short chapter on Eliot, Bloom cites two of the poems written before 1925— 'Preludes,' and 'La Figlia Che Piange,' a poem in which 'Eliot catches the precise nuances of personal betrayal, of bad faith, of our weariness of our own hypocrisies.'

> As for what now would be called his cultural criticism, I grimace and pass by. There remains his anti-Semitism, which is very winning if you happen to be an anti-Semite; if not, not.
>
> Joyce, unlike Eliot, was not an anti-Semite, and the actual Poldy is vital, gentle, affectionate, endlessly kind, and even heroic when he stands up for his Jewishness in a pub confrontation.
>
> I am delighted by Freud's *The Future of an Illusion,* though it may be his weakest book, if only because I relish the image of T. S. Eliot, respectable anti-Semite, reading it in a fury. Freud too would have been delighted.

Freud's pragmatic motto, in relation both to Catholics and to normative Jews, might well have been: 'Outrage, outrage, always given them outrage.' T. S. Eliot indeed was outraged, but then even a far less gifted Jew than Freud would have been enough for Eliot to deplore. The only Jewish genius who pleased Eliot was Christopher Marlowe's Barabas, *The Jew of Malta,* who dies in boiling oil, though to be just to the abominable Eliot, one should mention his fondness for Groucho Marx.

Whence could spring so deep a malice? There is no originality in such resentment.

For the past three decades Bloom has been circling around Freud's crucial essay of 1925-26, 'Inhibitions, Symptoms and Anxiety.' 'Freud famously defined anxiety as being *Angst vor etwas,* or anxious expectations,' we read in *The Western Canon.* 'There is always something in advance of which we are anxious, if only of expectations that we will be called upon to fulfill.' Freud writes: 'Anxiety [*Angst*] has an unmistakable relation to expectation; it is anxiety about [*vor*] something' (*Pelican Freud Library,* vol 10). When Bloom sets out to give outrage to this one and to that one, what does he expect? 'A literary work also arouses expectations that it needs to fulfill or it will cease to be read,' he writes in *The Western Canon.*

The wry trope Bloom identifies with is 'high irony,' which he links to anxiety and 'daemonic energy.' 'In high irony,' he notes in *Genius,* 'anxiety becomes vitalizing for the ego: it provides daemonic energy, and fuels the genius of Macbeth—and of Sigmund Freud.' What arouses the anxious expectations (and vitalizes the ego) of Harold Bloom?

> Nor does the subtly ironic Shelley literally believe that the fiery particle of Keats's mind was snuffed out by a resentful article or two in wintry Scotland. Keats was a pugnacious personality, and while I am nothing of the sort, even I am energized by the endless idiocy of my bad reviewers. 'I hate to be praised in a newspaper,' remarked the sagacious Emerson, and nothing is more soul-destroying than any praise from the *New York Times Book Review.*

Nothing is more soul-satisfying than 'a resentful article or two' in the *New York Times Book Review*: 'even I am energized by the endless idiocy of my bad reviewers.'

It's a closed circuit, the anxiety of anxiety. Expectation—of betrayal, injury, insult, resentment, contempt, rejection, helplessness, belatedness, loss, failure, abandonment—constitutes anxiety, *Angst vor etwas.* Freud writes in 'Inhibitions, Symptoms and Anxiety': 'Anxiety is . . . on the one hand an expectation of a trauma, and on the other a repetition of it in a mitigated form.' It's a *Teufelskreis,* an engine recoiling on itself, an ironic situation.

R. V. Young (essay date winter 2005)

SOURCE: Young, R. V. "Harold Bloom: The Critic as Gnostic." *Modern Age* 47, no. 1 (winter 2005): 19-29.

[In the following essay, Young suggests that Bloom's reliance upon Gnostic beliefs as the foundation of his criticism denies the influence of Christianity upon classical literature.]

A Christian critic confronting the work of Professor Harold Bloom may well find himself in a frame of mind analogous to the apostle, St. John: "Master, we saw one casting out devils in thy name, who followeth not us; and we forbade him" (Mk. 9. 37). This critic may well fear the same rebuke that St. John received: "But Jesus said: Do not forbid him. For there is no man that doth a miracle in my name and can soon speak ill of me. For he that is not against you is for you" (Mk. 9. 38-39; Lk. 9. 49-50). Bloom is, after all, the defender of the Western canon and scourge of "the Party of Resentment"—the Marxists, the feminists, and the new historicists who all strive to reduce literature to the ideological effluent of the material substructure or to patriarchal repression or to hegemonic power relations. This same Bloom is also, however, the author of *The American Religion* (1992), which identifies the faith of our country as Emersonian Gnosticism, and of *The Book of J* (1990), which speculates that "the original author of what we now call Genesis, Exodus, and Numbers" was a skeptical Hittite woman, whom he has subsequently decided to identify with Bathsheba.[1] At this point our Christian critic may reflect upon another Dominical utterance from the gospels: "He that is not with me is against me; and he that gathereth not with me scattereth" (Mt. 12.30; Lk. 11.23).

Such is the dilemma posed by an era in which Harold Bloom, who proclaims himself a Gnostic and whose principal contribution to literary theory is a Freudian interpretation of the history of literary influence, is regarded as "a staunch defender of the Western literary tradition," "a powerful warrior on the literary field, always ready to raise his lance in the name of the Western tradition."[2] Bloom has not changed; he is in the situation of an aging revolutionary whose revolution has been overtaken and subverted by the next generation. Robespierre, one will recall, came to his end under the blade of the guillotine. It is a grimly ironic truth that Bloom's own Gnostic Freudian treatment of literature and, above all, of authors, opened the gates to the postmodern assassins of the Party of Resentment, who now conduct their scornful ritual over the "death of the author." Finally, it is precisely his hostility to Christianity and his effort to displace it, spiritually and intellectually, which has resulted in the most grievous damage to the literary tradition that Bloom claims to love. While he gazes unblinkingly at the devastation wrought upon the tradition by the postmodern assault, he is blind to the intimate and indispensable bond between the secular "canon" and the Faith informing its necessary model, the scriptural canon. Western civilization is the cultural embodiment of Christendom; when its cultural heart stops beating, all that is left is a corpse.

Bloom deserves commendation for identifying so explicitly and accurately the Gnostic roots of his spiritual orientation. Deriving from γνωσις (gnôsis), a Greek word for "seeking to know," "inquiry," "investigation," or simply "knowledge," Gnosticism essentially offers salvation on the basis of occult knowledge. As Elaine Pagels points out, one of the central texts of ancient Gnosticism, the apocryphal Gospel of Thomas, identifies itself as a "secret gospel."[3] The secrets that Gnosticism imparts involve a denial of the Judæo-Christian doctrine of God and creation and a catastrophic vision of humanity's relation to the spiritual powers that dominate the material world.

Gnosticism is a religious conspiracy theory. In what remains the definitive scholarly work on the subject, Hans Jonas points out that a "radical dualism" is the key to every facet of reality:

> The deity is absolutely transmundane, its nature alien to that of the universe, which it neither created nor governs and to which it is the complete antithesis: to the divine realm of light, self-contained and remote, the cosmos is opposed as the realm of darkness. The world is the work of lowly powers which though they may mediately be descended from Him do not know the true God and obstruct the knowledge of Him in the cosmos over which they rule.[4]

As a result, human beings are prisoners in a world of frustration and deception: "The universe . . . is like a vast prison whose innermost dungeon is the earth, the scene of man's life."[5] Salvation requires the recognition that we are better than the situation into which we have been cast, and "The goal of gnostic striving is the release of the 'inner man' from the bonds of [the] world and his return to his native realm of light"—often entailing "intentional violation of the demiurgical norms"; that is, the natural laws of a wicked creation.[6]

Perhaps the version of Gnosticism most familiar to Christian readers is the Manichæanism with which St. Augustine was involved in his young manhood and which he eventually rejected and refuted.[7] His experience is emblematic of the experience of the early Church; like the Church as a whole. St. Augustine had to recognize that the evil that mattered most was personal sin separating him from God; that is, salvation entails repentance, through the help of divine grace. The Gnostics' teaching, on the contrary, places the origin of evil, of pain and suffering, in the conditions of the material creation; salvation involves overcoming ignorance and escaping these external conditions by finding divinity within. Marxism is a good example of the similarity between Gnosticism and many modern ideologies: misery results from unfavorable economic conditions; "salvation" comes by seizing the means of production and remaking the material world that men inhabit in order to change their nature.[8] A sympathetic historian of Gnosticism, Elaine Pagels, calls attention to another version of modernity that shares the Gnostic outlook: "Many gnostics . . . insisted that ignorance, not sin, is what involves a person in suffering. The gnostic movement shared certain affinities with contemporary methods of exploring the self through psychotherapeutic techniques."[9]

Early Christian fathers like Irenæus tended to treat Gnosticism as if it were a Christian heresy, but Bloom is acutely aware that, despite its use of Christian language, figures, and stories, Gnosticism is the utter antithesis of Christianity. If the creation and the author of creation are evil, then human beings are only evil through contamination by the world, not because of the inherent sinfulness of their fallen nature. The Christian begins the path toward salvation in the humble realization of his own culpable estrangement from his loving Creator to whom he must submit absolutely and on whose gracious mercy he depends utterly. The Gnostic finds the beginning of the path to salvation in the realization that the world is a great imposture, a prison of pain and frustration. His escape lies in recovering the intrinsic goodness within himself, the principle of illumination that he shares with other enlightened spirits. "If you are not to be hedged in by God's incomprehensible power," Bloom writes, "then you must dissent from the doctrine of Creation. You must learn to speculate about origins, and the aim of your speculation will have to be a vision of catastrophe, for only a divine catastrophe will allow for your own, your human freedom."[10] *Your own, your human freedom*—not "the liberty of the glory of the children of God" (Romans 8.21).

Now the worship of a distant aloof spirit with no relation to all that disappoints and appalls in the material creation would be a rather abstract business, except that we come to know this ultimate luminous being by its likeness in ourselves—in the selves we recover through the growing awareness that we, too, are alienated from the wicked world of injustice and suffering. "Many gnostics," writes Elaine Pagels, "would have agreed in principle with Ludwig Feuerbach, the nineteenth-century psychologist, that 'theology is really anthropology.'"[11] Worship of the "good" Gnostic God, of the God who does not create and is thus relieved of responsibility for the problem of evil, is essentially worship of the self. This point is not lost on Bloom:

> Freedom, in the context of the American Religion, means being alone with God or with Jesus, the American God or the American Christ. In social reality, this translates as solitude, at least in the inmost sense. The soul stands apart, and something deeper than the soul, the Real Me or self or spark, thus is made free to be utterly alone with a God who is also quite separate and solitary, that is a free God or God of freedom. What makes it possible for the self and God to commune so freely is that the self already is of God: unlike body and even soul, the American self is no part of the Creation, or of evolution through the ages. . . . No American pragmatically feels free if she is not alone, and no American ultimately concedes that she is part of nature.[12]

Christianity teaches that the only freedom that counts is freedom from sin, the spiritual cancer that consumes us from within unless we are irradiated by divine grace. Our only freedom is the freedom God grants us. Bloom maintains that this doctrine must be rejected on behalf of our own, human freedom—a freedom that is simply ours and that separates "the Real Me" from all the mishaps of our bodies and disgraces of our souls, a freedom that will not serve even God. *Especially not God*. St. Augustine has another name for this "freedom"; "Two loves have, then, made these two cities. Love of self, namely, even to the contempt of God made the earthly [city], while love of God, even to contempt of self, made the heavenly."[13]

From here to Freud is only a short step. Psychoanalysis, especially according to Freud's later "structural" model of psychic processes comprising the ego, the id, and the superego, basically substitutes itself for examination of conscience and the work of grace. Analysis, instead of enabling the soul to conform to the divine wisdom of repentance, relieves the neurotic conscious mind of the pressure of inhibitions; that is, from the repression of instinctual drives or libidinous urges in the id or unconsciousness. As in Gnosticism, "salvation" is a matter of liberation of a true self that has been thwarted and occluded by a negative environment. Christian salvation from the bondage of sin is displaced, in the argot of vulgar Freudianism, by the satisfaction or self-fulfillment of "getting rid of your hang-ups." Bloom frames the issue with considerably more elegance, but without a really substantial difference:

> The pragmatic mode akin to art and ideology for most of us is no longer religion but Eros, or even the religion of Eros, or for many of us, psychoanalysis. This means that most of my own readers will have confronted revisionism primarily in their erotic lives, which are quite simply now our spiritual lives.[14]

The ancient Gnostics, Sigmund Freud, and Harold Bloom all share a loathing of the Christian vision of reality, which sees mankind's willful disobedience and fallen nature as the principal source of his misery and of the evil in a world created good. We are twice beholden to God as our creator and as our redeemer, and our only hope of restoration to his favor is submission to Him with self-effacing love. The alternative is the Gnostic and Freudian view, endorsed by Bloom, which urges us to satisfy our desires so far as we can amidst a hostile, threatening, and above all frustrating natural environment. Our hope lies not in acknowledging and submitting to the moral reality of our situation, but in overcoming or even transforming it.

Such a vision of human nature and the human condition has grave implications for a theory of literature, for a man's understanding of life and literature cannot possibly be hermetically sealed off from each other. In this respect the study of literature—as well as the rest of the humanistic disciplines—differs decisively from the scientific investigation of natural phenomena. Two equally competent microbiologists, one an atheist and one a Christian, will arrive at identical results in an experiment involving DNA if their equipment and laboratory conditions are equal. A Christian and an atheist will not, however, arrive at the same interpretation of Shakespeare's *King Lear.*

While we may debate endlessly over the precise modes and effects of mimesis or dramatic representation, it is undeniable that literature is in some important sense *about* life. Our conception of the one is inextricably linked to our understanding of the other. Now while an error about the nature and the purpose of human life has severe consequences for enterprises of far graver import than literature, one of the chief benefits of literary study is to provide a forum in which we may consider life's crucial questions and choices in a comparatively disinterested manner. *King Lear* is always there for my contemplation, and if I am wrong in my initial assessment, I can always reconsider it. The errors I make about the treatment of my parents, or my children, or my brothers and sisters—these I may find the grace to repent, but rarely to undo.

A central concern of this traditional mimetic theory of literature is necessarily validity in representation. Works of literature arise out of an attempt to grasp the truth of human experience in a verbal form that engages not only abstract rational apprehension, but also the senses and emotions. Literature thus enhances knowledge and understanding by representing what is concrete and specific in our lives in a mode available for imaginative contemplation, which is as important for the understanding of our lived experience as rational knowledge. The author must strive to be true to—to give an honest assessment of—not necessarily the "facts," whether historical or scientific—but the moral and the spiritual realities of human nature. Various poets give us varied accounts of the world because they are looking at different kinds of events in the lives of men and women, or they are looking at the same events from distinctive points of view. No poet, not even Shakespeare, "who,"

Dryden rightly says, "of all modern, and perhaps ancient poets, had the largest and most comprehensive soul"[15]—none can capture every facet of human life, because poets are finite, limited creatures like all of us. When a poet such as, say, Wordsworth writes under the influence of an earlier poet, such as Milton, the later poet reminds us of his predecessor because he is adopting elements of style, structure, and theme: but he is different because he has a distinctive, concrete perspective on a specific facet of human life. Wordsworth has not made Milton obsolete, but, while not as great a poet as Milton, Wordsworth is certainly worth reading because we encounter aspects of our own experience in *The Prelude* that are not available in *Paradise Lost.* Digital recording may have made analogue recording obsolete, but Bartok has not made Bach obsolete. To be sure, different works of literature are more or less satisfying, profound, moving, or convincing, and some are wholly inadequate or even despicable. We should apportion the time and the effort we devote to various authors with these factors in mind. Our criteria of judgment ought to be, however, the degree to which each has devised a faithful and compelling vision of the particularly human realities of our experience.

It ought to give us pause, then, that the first principle of Bloom's theory of literature is willful error, or, as he calls it, "misprision." Authors who count, in his view, are not true, but "strong," with the result that the relationships among them are all fundamentally antagonistic. What is more, both the writing and the reading of poetry are less concerned with coming to terms with a reality external to the self than with asserting the self's inner compulsions upon reality:

> Influence, as I conceive it, means that there are *no* texts, but only relationships *between* texts. These relationships depend upon a critical act, a misreading or misprision, that one poet performs upon another, and that does not differ in kind from the necessary critical acts performed by every strong reader upon every text he encounters.[16]

From a Gnostic perspective literature as expropriation is the only logical response to the condition of humanity. Trapped in a dark, dangerous, delusory realm—the state of a creature in the creation—why would anyone wish to achieve an imaginative harmony with reality by means of a faithful representation? Rather, an author must impose his *authority* and wrestle a recalcitrant external world into a shape agreeable to his own desires, and other men and women and their devices are a very prominent part of that rival reality:

> Let me reduce my argument to the hopelessly simplistic; poems I am saying, are neither about "subjects" nor about "themselves." They are necessarily about *other poems*; a poem is a response to a poem, as a poet is a response to a poet, or a person to his parent. Trying to write a poem takes the poet back to the origins of what

a poem *first was for him,* and so takes the poet back beyond the pleasure principle to the decisive encounter and response that began him.[17]

Bloom is at his best as a critic of the Romantic poets, but he teases all of its Gnostic implications out of the Romantic notion that literature is self-expression rather than imitation of nature—the lamp rather than the mirror. The poet in the classical mimetic tradition is content to imitate the handiwork of God and pay homage to his poetic forebears: the Romantic, expressive poet—at least in Bloom's radical revision (to use his own term)—is discontented with a disappointing creation, which must be transformed, and threatened by his poetic predecessors, who must be displaced.[18]

Bloom envisions this conflict in Oedipal terms: "To live, the poet must *misinterpret* the father, by the crucial act of misprision, which is the re-writing of the father."[19] Moreover, the Freudian resonance is increased by what finally emerges as a preoccupation with death, or rather with the evasion of death. The discarding of literary representation is necessary to Bloom's theory of poetry because, he says, "a poem is written to escape dying. Literally, poems are refusals of mortality."[20] Bloom maintains overtly that poetry is an attempt to deny the reality of death: he opposes to "the darkest of Freudian formulae, that 'the aim of all life is death'" what he insists is "the inherent belief of all strong poets, . . . that death is only a failure in imagination."[21] Ironically, this blatant delusion is not incompatible with Freud, whose notion of the death instinct may be regarded as the embodiment of the ultimate destination of Gnostic pride: despair. Freud, like Bloom, is an antagonist of the Christian virtue of hope. In *The Future of an Illusion*—the "illusion" is revealed religion, specifically Christianity—Freud calls on man to escape "the retardation of sexual development and the early application of religious influence," which he attributes to repressive Christian civilization, and settle for a purely earthly existence:

> And as for the great necessities of late, against which there is no remedy, these he will simply learn to endure with resignation. Of what use to him is the illusion of a kingdom on the moon, whose revenues have never yet been seen by anyone? As an honest crofter on this earth he will know how to cultivate his plot in a way that will support him. Thus by withdrawing his expectations from the other world and concentrating all his liberated energies on this earthly life he will probably attain to a state of things in which life will be tolerable for all and no one will be oppressed by culture any more.[22]

If Bloom is an example of anything, however, it is that man cannot "learn to endure with resignation" what Freud euphemistically calls those "great necessities of fate," and find it "tolerable." Bloom is certainly correct, therefore, in finding the mechanisms of Freudian analysis of the mind a grand scheme for denying mortal-

ity, in the struggle between Eros and death; "strong poets" are simply the most gifted illusionists.

To treat literature as a means of warping reality rather than figuring it forth affects adversely both the interpretation of individual poems and understanding of the place of literature in education and culture. One may surmise that Bloom's insistence on a competitive, agonistic paradigm for all reading and writing represents less an observation of the historical development of literature than a response to his own inner "agon"—the struggle between his often sensible, sometimes inspired intuitions about particular literary works and his preoccupation with making all these works lie down in the same Procrustean bed of Freudian angst. Indeed, psychoanalytic theory compels Bloom to conform his healthy insights about specific poems to the assumption that all "strong poets" suffer from a psychic malaise, an ego obsession that reduces them all to the level of Woody Allen.

The theory is a clanking bit of Rube Goldberg machinery. In 1973, in *The Anxiety of Influence,* Bloom introduced his "Six Revisionary Ratios," an odd assortment of terms and concepts wrenched out of their contexts in classical antiquity and turned into intimidating jargon: *Clinamen, Tessera, Kenosis, Dæmonization, Askesis, Apophrades.*[23] Bloom's synopsis of one of these "ratios" should provide a sufficient sample to indicate the flavor of the recipe:

> *Clinamen,* which is poetic misreading or misprision proper; I take the word from Lucretius, where it means a "swerve" of the atoms so as to make change possible in the universe. A poet swerves away from his precursor, by so reading his precursor's poem as to execute a *clinamen* in relation to it. This appears as a corrective movement in his own poem, which implies that the precursor poem went accurately up to a certain point, but then should have swerved, precisely in the direction that the new poem moves.[24]

There is a rather amusing irony in the fact that Bloom has chosen for his primary "ratio" one of the most ridiculed terms in the Epicurean lexicon. Cicero calls the hypothesis of a "lateral swerve" among the atoms falling forever through space "wishing rather than arguing." If lateral movement among these atoms explains how the earth and its living inhabitants emerged from the collisions of atoms, what explains the "swerve" in the first place?[25] Or as the commentary in one edition of *De rerum natura* puts it: "Epicurus adopted a mechanistic system because he hoped by that means to eliminate fears and superstitions; and then introduced into that system an unmechanistic element, chance, in order to get rid of the blighting effects on the soul of philosophical determinism."[26]

Bloom's psychoanalytic use of the term is similarly equivocal; it suggests that the "strong poet" is governed by psychic-chance precisely at the point at which he most assertively "revises" his paternal predecessor. Despite his repeated denials that his theory of influence is in any strict sense Freudian, Bloom's flourish of psychoanalytic terms nevertheless implicates even the strongest of poets in the toils of irreconcilable chance and necessity. Moreover, we may well ask *why* "the precursor poem . . . should have swerved" at the same point as its successor. Why is it necessary that the "poetic father" be "misread," misprized, and displaced? Following Emerson and the extreme wing of the Romantic movement, Bloom assumes that each poet— each "strong poet" at least—stakes a claim to divinity. Since the divine is the absolute, no "divine" poet can brook the competition of another "god"; his creation must be unique and total. Such is the result of the Gnostic denigration—or, if you will, *misprision*—of the material creation: since the world is imperfect and evil, the poet is not imitating God's creation, but substituting his own; and the work of prior poets is from the perspective of each of their successors part of that botched realm of distress, dissatisfaction, and death.

To be sure, there are some fairly daring statements of the poet's creative powers in the Western literary tradition. Sir Philip Sidney favorably compares the poet's handiwork to Nature's: "Her world is brasen, the Poets only deliuer a golden"; but Sidney is careful to qualify his assertion:

> Neyther let it be deemed too sawcie a comparison to ballance the highest poynt of mans wit with the efficacie of Nature: but rather give right honor to the heavenly Maker of that maker, who, having made man to his owne likenes, set him beyond and over all the workes of that second nature, which in nothing hee sheweth so as in Poetrie, when with the force of a diuine breath he bringeth things forth far surpassing her dooings, with no small argument to the incredulous of that first accursed fall of *Adam*: sith our erected wit maketh vs know what perfection is, and yet our infected will keepeth vs from reaching vnto it.[27]

For all the Gnostic overtones of Sidney's neo-Platonism, the Creation remains God's perfect conception, which fallen man in a fallen world can only imitate.

By contrast, Bloom proffers us what he calls "Whitman's accurate insight that all the gods, Jehovah included, were once men, rising to superb blasphemy." Bloom quotes from Section 41 of *Song of Myself,* which culminates thus: "The supernatural of no account, myself waiting my time to be one of the supremes."[28] Once the ultimate goodness has been detached from creation, and nature is deemed not merely fallen, but innately evil, no standard of judgment remains either for morals or literature. If nature is the devising of the wicked "god" of darkness and material corruption, then there is no natural law, no essential distinction between right and wrong, good and evil. In literature, the fidelity of a representation to nature or the human experience of reality no longer counts as a measure of the poet's success. All that remains is sheer force of will, and Bloom, for all his protests against "Gallic modes of recent interpretation," is not so different from Michel Foucault in claiming "that the love of poetry is another variation of the love of power."[29]

The tendency of this Gnostic theoretical posture is to cripple Bloom's interpretive skills even when his literary intuitions are at their most acute. His discussion of Jane Austen is quite sensible and sensitive: he astutely dismisses efforts to bind her novels in the chains of socio-economic determinism, and even his comparison between Anne Elliot in *Persuasion* and Rosalind in *As You Like It* sheds light on both works. For Bloom, however, the central preoccupation of Austen's fiction is not the development and the manifestation of character in her heroines, but rather something he calls "Protestant will." Defending her from the strictures of Emerson, Bloom says that she "understood that the function of the convention was to liberate the will, even if convention's tendency was to stifle individualism, without which the will was inconsequential." He continues by maintaining that "Austen's major heroines—Elizabeth [Bennett], Emma [Woodhouse], Fanny [Price], and Anne—possess such inward freedom that their individualities cannot be repressed."[30] But in fact, Elizabeth and Emma have will to excess at the beginning of their respective tales; they must both acquire the virtue of humility, an element of good character, in order to find happiness. "Individuality"—Austen would probably say "willfulness"—is especially what Emma Woodhouse must forsake in submitting to the institution of marriage and the tutelage as well as the love of George Knightly. Fanny Price, on the other hand, is a character of such self-effacing patience that only extraordinary strength of moral character can steel her will to resist both the blandishments of Henry Crawford and the injunctions of her formidable uncle, Sir Thomas Bertram.

Bloom's insistence on seeing all literature in terms of Gnostic agon blinds him to the obvious in these novels, and this comment on *Persuasion* is simply bizarre:

> Since Austen is anything but an accidental novelist, we might ask why she chose to found *Persuasion* upon a mutual nostalgia. After all, the rejected Wentworth is even less inclined to a renewed affection than Anne is, and yet the fusion of memory and imagination triumphs over his will also. Was this a relaxation of the will in Jane Austen herself?[31]

Although Bloom makes some persuasive comparisons between Jane Austen and Wordsworth, he is certainly wrong to imply that Austen's fiction constitutes a prose *Prelude,* a "growth of the novelist's mind." *Persuasion* is by no means an account of "a schism in the self" of the novelist "with memory taking the side of imagination in an alliance against the will."[32] The novel is about how Anne Elliot reawakened Frederick Wentworth's love by demonstrating fortitude, patience, and maturity—in other words, character—that set her apart from all the other young women in the book. Of course memory is important in recalling to his imagination his abiding affection for her, but his choice comes of the realization that, even after eight years, with the freshness of her youthful beauty perhaps somewhat faded, her goodness and constancy make her more worthy the love of a prudent, sincere man than do the girlish charms of the frivolous Louisa Musgrove. The function of the trip to Lyme and Louisa's serious accident resulting from her recklessness is to fix the contrast between the two women in Wentworth's mind. Determined to see all literature as the expression of Gnostic discontent with creation, Bloom simply cannot see that *Persuasion,* like all of Jane Austen's novels, is fundamentally about character, not will, "Protestant" or otherwise.

Bloom's interpretation of Shakespeare, whom he rightly extols, is vitiated by the contamination of the same peculiar Gnostic ideology. The thesis of **Shakespeare: The Invention of the Human** is contained in the subtitle. Taken as routinely metaphoric shorthand for Shakespeare's innovative and unique gift for dramatic characterization, it is both unexceptionable and unoriginal. The Bard's unparalleled achievement in the depiction of vivid plausible individuals has been a given of literary scholarship since at least the days of Dr. Johnson. Wayne Booth, for example, in a discussion of "Types of Narration," first published in 1961, casually makes what he clearly takes to be a commonplace, self-evident remark: "Ever since Shakespeare taught the modern world what the Greeks had overlooked in neglecting character change (compare *Macbeth* and *Lear* with *Oedipus*), stories of character development and degeneration have become more popular."[33] What Bloom adds to this formulation, in addition to a certain portentousness, is the Gnostic disdain for creation in favor of personal re-creation on the part of the divine self:

> Literary character before Shakespeare is relatively unchanging; women and men are represented as aging and dying, but not as changing because their relationship to themselves, rather than to the gods or God, has changed. In Shakespeare, characters develop rather than unfold, and they develop because they reconceive themselves.[34]

Bloom is not saying that all Shakespeare's characters are like failed politicians or business executives who "reinvent themselves," in the current vulgar argot. He explicitly insists on treating what looks like a metaphor literally and makes it clear that he is considering our greatest writer in terms beyond mere literary criticism:

> I join Johnsonian tradition in arguing . . . that [Shakespeare] went beyond all precedents (even Chaucer) and

invented the human as we continue to know it. A more conservative way of stating this would seem to me a weak misreading of Shakespeare: it might contend that Shakespeare's originality was in the *representation* of cognition, personality, character. But there is an overflowing element in the plays, an excess beyond representation, that is closer to the metaphor we call "creation." The dominant Shakespearean characters—Falstaff, Hamlet, Rosalind, Iago, Lear, Macbeth, Cleopatra among them—are extraordinary instances not only of how meaning gets started, rather than repeated, but also of how new modes of consciousness come into being.[35]

It is improbable that Dr. Johnson or many of his successors in "Johnsonian tradition" would find acceptable the notion that Shakespeare, rather than God, created our humanity; but Bloom's rejection of the divine creation of the world and its living denizens leads him to regard all worship as a form of idolatry, of obeisance to an idealized self: "A substantial number of Americans who believe they worship God actually worship three major literary characters; the Yahweh of the J Writer . . . , the Jesus of the Gospel of Mark, and Allah of the Koran."[36] Bloom recommends that "Bardolatry, the worship of Shakespeare, ought to be even more a secular religion than it already is."[37]

Bloom's Gnosticism, his twisted view of reality, undermines the soundness of his literary judgment, and he is in peril of answering seriously L. C. Knights's jocular question, "How Many Children Had Lady Macbeth?"[38] Nothing displays the folly of denying the divinely ordained limits of reality more forcibly than Bloom's obsession with Falstaff, whom he treats as somehow more real or authentic than actual human beings. Like Hamlet, Falstaff has a life outside the plays in which he is a character: "these two charismatics are *in* their plays, but not *of* them; Hamlet is a person, and Claudius and Ophelia are fictions—or Falstaff is a person, while Hal and Hotspur are fictions."[39] Reject God's natural creation, and you will find yourself setting up an alternative "nature" to rival it, not unlike Mammon in Book II of *Paradise Lost.* Not only does Bloom "exalt Falstaff above his plays" (as if he were the matinee idol who steps off the screen in the movie-within-the-movie in *Purple Rose of Cairo*), but also he calls this "salvation" and brooks no heresy: "Those who do not care for Falstaff are in love with time, death, the state, and the censor. They have their reward."[40]

Bloom has fallen into the same error in making Falstaff the hero of the Falstaffiad as he does in making Satan the hero of *Paradise Lost,* and it was an error that C. S. Lewis clarified years before Harold Bloom had published a line:

> Before considering the character of Milton's Satan it may be desirable to remove an ambiguity by noticing that Jane Austen's Miss Bates [in *Emma*] could be

described either as a very entertaining or a very tedious person. If we said the first, we should mean that the author's portrait of her entertains us while we read; if we said the second, we should mean that it does so by being a portrait of a person whom the other people in *Emma* find tedious and whose like we also should find tedious in real life. For it is a very old critical discovery that the imitation in art of unpleasing objects may be a pleasing imitation.[41]

Unlike Miss Bates, Falstaff is not "tedious"; he remains, however, like Miss Bates, a fiction. He is in fact a brilliantly conceived and executed representation of the kind of man who is jovial, engaging, and likable, but also irresponsible, greedy, and exploitative. Prince Hal, on the other hand, embodies the melancholy truth that popular, effective rulers are often inscrutable and ruthless. Most readers and theatre-goers are going to *like* Falstaff more than Hal, but even Bloom would be reluctant to trust the fat knight with his car keys or his credit card. Why should King Henry V—no longer "Hal"—entrust to him a position of power and influence at court? We can appreciate the irony in applying the phrase "the mirror of all Christian Kings" to Henry V and still acknowledge that dismissing Falstaff is the King's only alternative to becoming another Richard II.

What makes Shakespeare such a great poet and dramatist is not that he "invented" the human or human personality, but that his plays embody so concretely and convincingly the tensions between personality and character, moral integrity and personal inclination that are among the most vexing aspects of the human condition. We know almost everything about the deficiencies of Bloom's criticism when he defends Falstaff's unreliable, self-centered dishonesty, dissolution, and corruption by remarking that *personality* is more important to him than *character*.[42]

In conclusion, the Christian surveying the numerous books by Harold Bloom will find much to admire and much to raise his spirits in Bloom's shrewd mockery of the institutional nihilism that pervades the postmodern literary establishment. What is more he amply displays the quality he most admires in poets; he is a very "strong" reader of literary texts and often sweeps his own readers along with the passion and the eloquence of his rhetoric. His theory of literature, however, his view that literary influence may be reduced to an intergenerational struggle between "strong poets" turns literature into a psychic manifestation of the poet, above all of his anguished flight from the inevitably of death, rather than a representation of reality. Bloom's theory, with all its secular Freudian trappings, is fundamentally a Gnostic theology rejecting the divine creation, regarded as the source of human death and despair. Poetry is the protest against this unsatisfactory creation, which reminds human beings of their creaturely status. This warped vision of the human situation distorts

Harold Bloom's view of literary works, especially of the moral standing of literary characters, making him an unreliable guide to the Western Canon he so prizes, whose greatest classics are Christian in their spiritual sources and traditional in their moral orientation. In fine, a man's view of literature is inevitably controlled by his vision of life.

Notes

1. *The Western Canon: The Books and School of the Ages* (New York/San Diego/London, 1994), 5.

2. These phrases come from Jennie Rothenberg, "Ranting Against Cant," an interview with Harold Bloom in *Atlantic Unbound,* http://www.theatlantic.com/unbound/interviews/int2003-07-16.htm.

3. *The Gnostic Gospels* (New York, 1981 [1979]), xiii.

4. *The Gnostic Religion* (2nd ed. Boston, 1963), 42.

5. *Ibid.,* 43.

6. *Ibid.,* 44, 46.

7. See *Confessions* IV-VII.

8. See Eric Voegelin, *The New Science of Politics: An Introduction* (Chicago & London, 1987 [1952]) for an account of modern ideologies as versions of Gnosticism.

9. *The Gnostic Gospels,* 149. Cf. R. V. Young, *At War with the Word: Literary Theory and Liberal Education* (Wilmington, Del., 1999), esp. 14-18 for further reflections on Gnosticism in contemporary intellectual life.

10. *Agon: Towards a Theory of Revisionism* (New York/Oxford, 1982), 78.

11. *The Gnostic Gospels,* 148.

12. *The American Religion: The Emergence of the Post-Christian Nation* (New York, 1992), 15.

13. *De Civilate Dei* 14. 28, *Patrologia Latina* 41. 436: "Fecerunt itaque civitates duas amores duo; terrenam scilicet amor sui usque ad contemptum Dei, cœlestem vero amor Del usque ad contemptum sui."

14. *Agon,* 49.

15. *Of Dramatic Poesy and Other Critical Essays,* ed. George Watson (London, 1962), 1, 67.

16. *A Map of Misreading* (Oxford/New York/Toronto, 1975), 3.

17. *Ibid.,* 18.

18. For standard accounts of the transition from classic to romantic, see M. H. Abrams, *The Mirror and the Lamp: Romantic Theory and the Critical Tradition* (New York, 1953); and Walter Jackson Bate, *From Classic to Romantic: Premises of Taste in Eighteenth-Century England* (New York, 1961 [1946]). For a

more sober account of what Bloom calls the "anxiety of influence," see Walter Jackson Bate, *The Burden of the Past and the English Poet* (New York, 1970).

19. *A Map of Misreading,* 19.

20. *Ibid.*

21. *Ibid.,* 13.

22. *The Future of an Illusion* (1927), trans. W. D. Robson-Scott (Garden City, N.Y., n.d.), 85, 89.

23. *The Anxiety of Influence: A Theory of Poetry* (2nd ed., New York/Oxford, 1997), 14-16.

24. *Ibid.,* 14.

25. *De Fato* 20.46: "'Declinat', inquit, 'atomus'. Primum cur? . . . Quae ergo nova causa in natura est quae declinet atomum (aut num sortiuntur inter se quae declinet, quae non?) aut cur minimo declinent intervallo, maiore non, aut cur declinent uno minimo, non declinent duobus aut tribus? Optare hoc quidem est, non disputare."

26. William Ellery Leonard and Stanley Barney Smith, ed., *T. Lucreti Cari De Rerum Natura Libri Sex* (Madison, Wis., 1942), 333.

27. *An Apology for Poetry,* in *Elizabethan Critical Essays,* ed. G. Gregory Smith (London, 1904), 1, 156, 157.

28. *The Western Canon,* 270.

29. The first phrase comes from *The Breaking of the Vessels* (Chicago and London, 1982), 29; the second from *Agon,* 17.

30. *The Western Canon,* 258.

31. *Ibid.,* 259.

32. *Ibid.*

33. *The Rhetoric of Fiction* (2nd ed., Chicago & London, 1983), 157.

34. *Shakespeare: The Invention of the Human* (New York, 1998), xvii.

35. *Ibid.,* xviii.

36. *Ibid.,* xviii-xix.

37. *Ibid.,* xvii.

38. *Explorations* (London, 1946), 1-39. See Bloom, *Shakespeare,* 522, where he does speculate on Lady Macbeth's marital history.

39. *Shakespeare,* 279.

40. *Ibid.,* 314, 288.

41. *A Preface to Paradise Lost* (New York, 1961 [1942]), 94.

42. *Shakespeare,* 313. This paragraph and its predecessor are in part adapted from R. V. Young. "Shakespeare with Tears," an essay-review of Harold Bloom. *Shakespeare: The Invention of the Human, Ben Jonson Journal* 6 (1999): 319-25.

Adam Kirsch (review date 2005)

SOURCE: Kirsch, Adam. "Power Games." *Parnassus* 28, nos. 1 & 2 (2005): 224-33.

[*In the following review, Kirsch addresses the disparity between the introductory discussion in* The Best Poems of the English Language *and the poems collected in the book, and comments on Bloom's tendency to read every poem as a statement about poetry.*]

Thirty years ago, Harold Bloom surely seemed the American critic least likely to become the public face of Serious Literature. He had nothing in common with the professorial populists who have always found eager pupils in the American reading public—Mortimer Adler and Mark Van Doren, Clifton Fadiman and Jacques Barzun. On the contrary, Bloom's major work was passionately, theatrically difficult. Today, *The Anxiety of Influence* seems like one of those hulking computers of the same vintage, a technology so eccentrically jury-rigged that no one but its inventor knows how to use it. Though the book's title has become a catchphrase, the terminology of Bloom's system—kenosis and apophrades, metalepsis and transumption—remains as hermetic as ever.

Most of Bloom's readers, however, know nothing of his taxing early work. For in the last ten years, Bloom has been reborn as the author of huge, culturally nutritious books like *How to Read and Why, Genius,* and *The Western Canon.* Judging by their titles, and their commercial success, it would be easy to call these books "middlebrow." But the really surprising thing about the Bloom phenomenon is how unmiddlebrow, how idiosyncratic and unaccommodating, his bestsellers are. Not only does he not dumb down his ideas for the reader, he usually seems to write without the reader in mind at all.

This sounds like integrity, and partly is. Ever since *The Western Canon,* Bloom's trademark has been his refusal to compromise his literary judgment for any commercial or political consideration. Ironically, that is just what accounts for his popular success: Reading Bloom is a way of declaring one's allegiance to pure aesthetic standards. Indeed, the very first sentence of the introduction to his new anthology, *The Best Poems of the English Language: From Chaucer through Frost,* defies "all considerations of political correctness and incorrectness."

But Bloom's indifference is not restricted to the political. What is most striking about his books is their failure to address themselves to the needs of their likely readers. Certainly anyone who comes to Bloom in search of the introduction to literature he seems to promise is bound to be baffled and disappointed. No matter what the subject, exposition, information, and consecutive argument are virtually absent; what Bloom offers, instead, is disconnected, often esoteric speculation. In *The Western Canon,* for instance, the chapter on Emily Dickinson focuses on the trope of the "blank" in Dickinson, Emerson, Coleridge, and Stevens; the chapter on Chaucer is restricted to a comparison of the Wife of Bath and the Pardoner with Falstaff and Iago. In each case, Bloom's analysis—leaving its merits to one side—assumes a nearly professional level of engagement with the subject and the critical debate. This careless disregard of the common reader for whom he ostensibly writes is one of many glaring contrasts between Bloom and the critic he claims as his role model, Samuel Johnson.

Bloom's negligence has never been more obvious than in *Best Poems* [*The Best Poems of the English Language*]. His introduction promises "the anthology I've always wanted to possess," and such a book—with all its surprises of inclusion and omission—would be a useful critical provocation. Unfortunately, that is not at all what he has produced. In fact, Bloom's introductory notes regularly award their highest praise to poems that he has not bothered to include. As always, Bloom is not shy of superlatives: "Probably [Drayton's] most memorable achievement is the highly Spenserian *The Muses Elizium*"; "Herrick's masterpiece is the wonderful 'Corinna's Going A-Maying'"; "Lovelace's most remarkable poem . . . is 'Love Made in the First Age'"; "Crashaw's best secular poem is 'Music's Duel'"; "[Dryden's] masterpieces [are] the political satire *Absalom and Achitophel* and the mock-heroic satire *Mac Flecknoe*"; "Rochester's great poem is 'A Satire Against Mankind'"; "the matching of 'The Divine Image' and 'The Human Abstract' [in *Songs of Innocence and Experience*] seems to be the crucial one." Yet not a single one of the poems named appears in *Best Poems,* in whole or in part. So much for "the anthology I've always wanted to possess." And this is not to mention the outright editorial mistakes: In at least two cases (Bryant's "Thanatopsis" and Pound's "Seafarer"), Bloom promises poems that are simply missing.

Bloom's introductory notes are the volume's selling point, but they are haphazard and disproportionate to the point of randomness. Ezra Pound, for instance, receives eight pages of commentary to one page of poetry; H. D., five pages to two; and W. C. Williams, eight to five and a half. Bloom's note on Spenser is fifteen pages long, and discusses many episodes in *The Faerie Queene* in considerable detail, even though he has included only one episode from one canto. Time and again, the reader is left with the feeling that he is reading a recycled lecture or essay. This kind of discourtesy seriously limits the utility and the appeal of *Best Poems.*

In subordinating the poems to his own commentary, however, Bloom is just repeating on the editorial plane what has long been the principle of his criticism. For he has never been the kind of critic who aims to be, in Randall Jarrell's phrase, "the telescope through which the children see the stars." That is one reason why the mantle of public educator sits so uncomfortably on him. The teacher draws attention to the subject; Bloom demands attention for himself.

If Bloom is not a great critic, it is not simply because he is too obtrusive. It is primarily because of the faulty metaphor that lies at the heart of his criticism: power. Poetry, for Bloom, has always been about accruing and exerting power. His highest accolade is not "great," still less "true" or "beautiful," but "strong"; as he declares in *The Anxiety of Influence,* "my concern is only with strong poets." And whenever he attempts to sell the reader on reading, a frequent gesture in his recent work, Bloom imagines literature as a vitality-transfusion: "We read in search of more life"; "To be augmented by the genius of others is to enhance the possibilities of survival"; "We read Shakespeare, Dante, Chaucer, Cervantes, Dickens, Proust, and all their peers because they . . . enlarge life." In his aesthetics of power, Bloom shows the influence of his idol Emerson, as in "Self-Reliance": "Power ceases in the instant of repose; it resides in the moment of transition from a past to a new state, in the shooting of the gulf, in the darting to an aim."

Power, in this Emersonian sense, is not an ability or sensibility, as it was for Matthew Arnold when he spoke (in a phrase quoted in *Best Poems*) of the "extraordinary power with which Wordsworth feels the joy offered to us in nature . . . and renders it so as to make us share it." Instead, power is autotelic, something willed for its own sake and productive only of itself: Power is the sensation of power. In this conception, and in identifying power above all with art, Bloom is equally a follower of Emerson's disciple, Nietzsche, whose name is not much mentioned in Bloom's recent work, but who, along with Freud, looms large in his early criticism.

Indeed, the theory of the anxiety of influence is Bloom's elaboration of an aphorism from *The Will to Power*. "The phenomenon 'artist' is still the most transparent—to see through it to the basic instincts of power. . . ." Taking up this hint, Bloom sketched his theory of poetry as a series of power struggles, in which the self-assertion of the young poet or "ephebe" takes the form of misreading his predecessors. The anxiety of influence is not something that leaves its mark on a poem; rather, the poem is nothing but that anxiety. The sole reason a poet writes is to assert his power against his precursors, and the critic is the umpire who decides whether his assertion has been successful. The Freudian-Nietzschean sternness of this view was much insisted upon by the young Bloom, as, for instance, in **A Map of Misreading**: "Poems, I am saying, are neither about 'subjects' nor about 'themselves.' They are necessarily about *other poems*."

Bloom's recent, more popular work does not take such grim pleasure in forcing the reader to confront this poetic reality principle. But the principle remains, and continues to guide Bloom's readings of individual poems. **Best Poems** offers some unusually interesting examples, since it leads Bloom to write about poets not on his oft-repeated list of favorites (Blake, Shelley, Whitman, Stevens). Take, for instance, Bloom's introduction to Thomas Gray, which is mainly a close reading of the "Elegy Written in a Country Churchyard." "What moves me most about the superb *Elegy*," he writes, is "the pathos of a poetic death-in-life, the fear that one either has lost one's gift before life has ebbed or that one may lose life before the poetic gift has expressed itself fully." In this reading, the "Elegy" becomes "Gray's version of *Lycidas*," which is one of Bloom's touchstones because of its overt anxiety about such "poetic death-in-life": "But the fair guerdon when we hope to find, / And think to burst out into sudden blaze, / Comes the blind Fury with th'abhorred shears / And slits the thin-spun life." But while this is an element in Gray's poem, it is surely not the essence:

> For who, to dumb forgetfulness a prey,
> This pleasing anxious being e'er resigned,
> Left the warm precincts of the cheerful day,
> Nor cast one longing lingering look behind?
>
> On some fond breast the parting soul relies,
> Some pious drops the closing eye requires;
> Even from the tomb the voice of Nature cries,
> Even in our ashes live their wonted fires.

The longing that Gray imagines is not for poetic immortality, but for affectionate remembrance. And the pathos lies not in a fear of losing one's gift, but in the realization that, once affection can no longer be reciprocal, it becomes an unenforceable charity. That is why "Lycidas" left Johnson cold, while he found in the "Elegy" "sentiments to which every bosom returns an echo": Milton indeed writes as a poet, but Gray writes as a man.

Bloom, however, either cannot see or refuses to acknowledge this distinction, because his central metaphor does not allow for the possibility that a poet can write as something other than a poet, or about anything other than poetry. Even when a poet clearly means to address what Bloom denigrates as "a subject"—that is, a subject other than his or her own power—Bloom is compelled to translate that subject back into the terms of his own metaphor. In **Genius**, for instance, Bloom discusses Elizabeth Bishop's "The Unbeliever," built around the image of a man asleep on

the top of a mast. In this precarious position, the unbeliever envies the clouds and gulls, comfortable at an altitude that is potentially lethal to him: "I must not fall," he says to himself, "The spangled sea below wants me to fall." This is one of Bishop's best metaphors for the desperation so pervasive in her work; what the unbeliever disbelieves is not just God, but the very possibility of safety. Yet for Bloom, this too is a poem about poetry: The "cloud, seagull, unbeliever," he writes, "I interpret as three kinds of poets."

Bloom's belief that all poems are about other poems naturally makes him exceptionally alert to allusion. He is aided in this by his voracious erudition and prodigious memory. But because he imagines poetry as an entirely closed system, related to nothing outside itself, Bloom inflates the concept of allusion until it virtually replaces representation. In his introduction to the Whitman section of **Best Poems,** he dwells on some lines from "Crossing Brooklyn Ferry":

> Was wayward, vain, greedy, shallow, sly, cowardly, malignant,
> The wolf, the snake, the hog, not wanting in me,
> The cheating look, the frivolous word, the adulterous wish, not wanting. . . .

Bloom may be right to hear in this list an echo of Edgar's self-condemnation in *King Lear*: "hog in sloth, fox in stealth, wolf in greediness, dog in madness, lion in prey." But when he goes on to suggest that Whitman thus casts himself as Edgar and "his readers as a composite Lear . . . redeemed by Whitman's prophetic thoughts of them," the reader resists. For Bloom does not allow for the possibility that, in using animals as types of human vice, Whitman no less than Shakespeare might be drawing on actual observation of those animals. In other words, if Whitman calls himself a wolf, a snake, and a hog, it may be because he was thinking of wolves, snakes, and hogs, and not because he was thinking about Shakespeare. Animals are not belated.

A similar distortion arises in Bloom's discussion of Hart Crane's "Voyages II." In Crane's famous line "The seal's wide spindrift gaze toward paradise," Bloom detects "a yearning for the mother"—because, in *Moby-Dick,* Melville writes about young seals separated from their mothers. In the previous line, where Crane imagines "the vortex of our grave," Bloom finds an invocation of Blake's "conceptual image of 'the vortex,' which closes the perceptual gap between subject and object." As a result, Crane's explicit meaning—the vortex is the whirlpool created by the sinking of the lovers' ship—simply vanishes. Indeed, Bloom writes that Crane "refers to" Blake, as though allusion and reference were the same thing.

Bloom's readings, in other words, are misreadings. According to Bloom's own theory, of course, misreadings are essential to the life of poetry. "To live," he writes in *A Map of Misreading,* "the poet must *misinterpret* the father, by the crucial act of misprision, which is there-writing of the father." This is the "swerve" away from the precursor that Bloom, borrowing from Lucretius, named "clinamen." The poet's misprision is justified by his poem. And the critic's misprision is justified by—what?

This question leads directly to the dubious core of Bloo-mian criticism. Almost from the beginning, Bloom has elided the distinction between the poet's reading and the critic's. He is quite open about this: "The influence-relation governs reading as it governs writing, and reading is therefore a miswriting just as writing is a misreading. As literary history lengthens, all poetry necessarily becomes verse-criticism, just as all criticism becomes prose-poetry." The anxiety of influence is not, after all, exclusive to artists: "We all suffer" from it, "whether we are poets or not."

And, in fact, the anxiety of influence—so obviously reductive as an account of the poet's relation to his predecessors—is quite suggestive as an account of the critic's relation to his text. It is the critic, not the poet, whose writing must be subservient to another writing, and who yearns to break free from this humiliating dependence. The only kind of poem that is really doomed to be "about other poems" is what Bloom called, in *The Anxiety of Influence,* "the poem we write as our reading." And the hermeneutic waywardness that Bloom demonstrates in *Best Poems* is understandable only as his own clinamen, his aggressive swerve into originality.

If the critic is also subject to the anxiety of influence—is, indeed, much more its victim than the poet—it seems fair to ask which predecessor most haunts the ephebe Bloom. Samuel Johnson would be the obvious answer: Time and again Bloom stakes his claim to Johnson, as when he writes with blithe narcissism in *Best Poems* that Johnson "loved Pope's poetry with the personal passion I myself bring to the reading of Wallace Stevens and Hart Crane." But when Bloom himself asks this question about a poet, he proceeds with Freudian suspicion, rejecting the analysand's facile affirmations and attending to his violent negations.

In writing about T. S. Eliot, for example, Bloom repeats the conclusion he has advanced many times before: "Eliot asserted poetic descent from Dante and Baude-laire, and from Jacobean dramatists and metaphysical poets. The actual deep influences upon his poetry are Whitman and Tennyson." In particular, Bloom believes that the "paradigm" for *The Waste Land* was "When Lilacs Last in the Dooryard Bloom'd." And he acutely points out several images that Eliot seems to have taken from Whitman: "Where the hermit-thrush sings in the pine-trees" is indubitably an echo of Whitman's hermit-thrush, who warbles the song of death "From the fragrant cedars and the ghostly pines so still." And Eli-ot's "Who is the third who walks always beside you?" is at least reminiscent of Whitman's "with the knowl-edge of death as walking one side of me, / And the thought of death close-walking the other side of me, / And I in the middle as with companions. . . ." These parallels notwithstanding, however, there could be few poems more different in style, technique, atmosphere, and spirit than these two. So implausible is Bloom's comparison—repeated in book after book, and never supported with anything like an argument—that one looks for an ulterior motive; and it is not far to seek. For if there is a villain in *Best Poems,* and in Bloom's criticism as a whole, it is surely Eliot. Beginning his career in what he calls "the Eliotic Fifties," Bloom was dismayed to find that all of his favorite poets—Milton, Blake, Shelley—were "out of favor because the Vicar of Christ for the universities, T. S. Eliot, disliked [them]." In his early books, *Shelley's Mythmaking* and *The Visionary Company,* Bloom helped to overturn this ban. But the resentment remains. Bloom's note on Eliot in *Best Poets* begins, "I confess a lifelong hostility to T. S. Eliot, whose literary criticism did real harm, and whose cultural criticism showed, at times, a vicious proto-Fascism."

There are surely valid reasons, moral and literary, to dislike Eliot, some of which are widely shared. But Bloom's comparison of *The Waste Land* with "Lilacs," always made in a tone of triumphant accusation or debunking, suggests a personal animus. In some way, the purpose of the comparison is to take away author-ship of Eliot's great poem and assign it to a poet with whom Bloom closely identifies himself. That Bloom intends such a symbolic theft seems more likely when one considers his habit of attributing Eliot's famous sayings to other people. In *The Western Canon,* Bloom credits William Empson with "poetry in our time has become a mug's game," which Eliot said in *The Use of Poetry and the Use of Criticism* ("As things are, and as fundamentally they must always be, poetry is not a career, but a mug's game"). In *How to Read and Why,* he credits John Hollander with the notion that "no authentic verse is free," which is an aphorism of Eliot's quoted by Ezra Pound ("no *vers* is *libre* for the man who wants to do a good job"). These textbook Freudian slips are obviously aggressive. Add to them Bloom's habit of insulting Eliot in passing whenever possible—"Eliot's celebrated essay [on Marvell] is in fact quite bad"; "*Atalanta in Calydon* . . . remains considerably more readable than Eliot's *Murder in the Cathedral*"—and the identity of Bloom's own dreaded precursor becomes clear as day.

I suspect that what troubles Bloom about Eliot is not simply his authority, or the literary values he used it to establish. Neither is it the immense superiority of Eliot's prose to his own, or even the obvious fact that Eliot was a great poet as well as a critic, so that his criticism enjoys an immortality that Bloom's cannot hope to achieve. The real reason Eliot stands as Bloom's antithetical precursor is that he foretold what must become of a critic like Bloom—a critic who is not a poet, but passionately wants to assert his own personality. "The moment you try to put the impressions [created by a poem] into words." Eliot wrote in "The Perfect Critic," "you either begin to analyze and construct . . . or you begin to create something else." That something else is exactly what Bloom calls "the poem we write as our reading." And Eliot knew that such a "poem" must be obsessed with power, because its author "suffer[s] from a defect of vitality or an obscure obstruction which prevents nature from taking its course." What Bloom writes, indeed, is "not criticism, but is not the expulsion, the ejection, the birth of creativeness." It seems that all along, when he thought he was defining the poet, Bloom was actually defining himself: "not so much a man speaking to men as a man rebelling against being spoken to by a dead man."

FURTHER READING

Criticism

Bloom, Harold, and Eli Lehrer. "Literary Critic Bloom Finds Life in the Bard." *Insight on the News* 14, no. 44 (30 November 1998): 21-3.

Interview detailing Bloom's passion for William Shakespeare's work.

Desmet, Christy. "Harold Bloom as Shakespearean Pedagogue." In *Harold Bloom's Shakespeare,* edited by Christy Desmet and Robert Sawyer, pp. 213-25. New York: Palgrave, 2001.

Analyzes Bloom's study of William Shakespeare.

Kearns, Cleo McNelly. Review of *The American Religion,* by Harold Bloom. *Theology Today* 49, no. 4 (January 1993): 542-44.

Lauds the treatment of spirituality in *The American Religion.*

Shankar, Lavina Dhingra. Review of *Asian-American Women Writers,* edited by Harold Bloom. *MELUS* 24, no. 4 (winter 1999): 183-84.

Terms Bloom's introduction to *Asian-American Women Writers* problematic, but cites the book as valuable.

Weisman, Karen A. "Birthing an Ecstatic Anxiety: Harold Bloom's *Western Canon* and its Readers." *Salmagundi,* no. 112 (fall 1996): 216-25.

Deems *The Western Canon* an overreaction to the prevalence of culturally diverse literature.

Wittenberg, David H. "Misreading as Canon Formation: Remembering Harold Bloom's Theory of Revision." *Qui Parle* 10, no. 1 (fall/winter 1996): 21-42.

Demonstrates Bloom's role in forging the ostensibly objective literary connections upon which his theories are based.

Wittreich, Joseph. Review of *Ruin the Sacred Truths,* by Harold Bloom. *Comparative Literature Studies* 30, no. 2 (1993): 206-11.

Pronounces *Ruin the Sacred Truths* "another jewel in Bloom's already weighty crown."

Additional coverage of Bloom's life and career is contained in the following sources published by Thomson Gale: *Contemporary Authors,* Vols. 13-16R; *Contemporary Authors New Revision Series,* Vols. 39, 75, 92, 133; *Contemporary Literary Criticism,* Vols. 24, 103; *Dictionary of Literary Biography,* Vol. 67; *Encyclopedia of World Literature in the 20th Century,* Ed. 3; *Literature Resource Center; Major 20th-Century Writers,* Ed. 2; *Major 21st-Century Writers,* (eBook) 2005; and *Reference Guide to American Literature,* Ed. 4.

George Steiner
1929-

(Full name Francis George Steiner) French-born American critic, essayist, novelist, short fiction writer, editor, and memoirist.

The following entry presents criticism of Steiner's works from 1990 to 2004. For discussion of Steiner's career prior to 1990, see *CLC*, Volume 24.

INTRODUCTION

Recognized as one of the major literary critics of the twentieth century, Steiner has investigated the interconnections between language and culture in light of contemporary history. His writings reflect the breadth and depth of his thought on topics ranging from the Holocaust and communism to translation of literary works and the virtues of high culture. Written in a style that appeals to a wide, nonacademic audience, Steiner's work stands in contrast to the nihilism and narrow politics that characterizes much contemporary literary criticism. Despite Steiner's impressive erudition and his powerful insights, scholars are sharply divided about his contributions to comparative literature.

BIOGRAPHICAL INFORMATION

The son of Jewish émigrés from Austria, Steiner was born in Paris, France. In 1940 his family fled to the United States to escape the advancing Nazis during World War II. They settled in New York City, where Steiner became an American citizen in 1944. After graduating from the French Lycée in Manhattan, Steiner completed his bachelor's degree at the University of Chicago in 1948 and his master's degree at Harvard University in 1950. During the early 1950s, Steiner lived in England, where he was a member of the editorial staff of the *Economist* between 1952 and 1956. Meanwhile, he received a Rhodes scholarship and earned his doctorate in philosophy at Oxford University in 1955. That year he also married historian Zara Alice Shakow, with whom he has two children. In 1956 he accepted a two-year fellowship at the Institute for Advanced Study at Princeton University and published his first short story, "The Deeps of the Sea," which won the O. Henry Award. After the publication of his first book, *Tolstoy or Dostoevsky* in 1959, Steiner returned to England to accept a founding fellowship at Churchill

College, Cambridge University, where he has taught since 1961. Steiner has also served as Professor of English and Comparative Literature at the University of Geneva, Switzerland, from 1974 to 1994, and he has held numerous visiting professorships at several American and European universities, most recently at Oxford and Harvard. Throughout his academic career, Steiner has been a prolific writer. He not only has regularly contributed articles and reviews to journals and newspapers such as the *New Yorker* and the *Times Literary Supplement,* but also has produced a considerable body of literary and cultural criticism, most notably *The Death of Tragedy* (1961), *Language and Silence* (1967), *In Bluebeard's Castle* (1971), *After Babel* (1975), *Heidegger* (1978), *Antigones* (1979), and *Real Presences* (1989). In addition, Steiner has periodically written award-winning fiction including the novel *The Portage to San Cristóbal of A. H.* (1981), which was produced as a stage play in 1982, and the short stories collected in *Anno Domini* (1964) and *Proofs, and Three Parables* (1992). Since the mid-1990s, Steiner has published the essay collections *No Passion Spent* (1996) and *Grammars of Creation* (2001), an autobiography, *Errata* (1997), and the nonfiction *Lessons of the Masters* (2003). Steiner has received many academic and international honorifics for his scholarly accomplishments, including appointment to France's Légion d'Honneur, membership in the American Academy of Arts and Sciences, and election to the British Academy.

MAJOR WORKS

The bulk of Steiner's writing is broadly drawn, thematic literary criticism characterized by his insights into such twentieth-century cultural and philosophical concerns as the Holocaust, the problems of translation, and the limitations of language. Widely regarded as a classic study by scholars of Russian literature, *Tolstoy or Dostoevsky* contrasts the biographies and philosophies of both writers within the larger contexts of the epic tradition and the irreconcilable tension between theology and history. *The Death of Tragedy* surveys tragic literature from ancient times through the mid-twentieth century, tracing the decline of the genre. *Language and Silence* ponders the inadequacy of language and literature to effectively deal with the dehumanizing effects of World War II and the Holocaust, contemplating the significance of silence as an alternate response. The focus of the essays collected in *Extra-Territorial* (1971) shifts to the cultural and linguistic implications of multilingualism and translation, which also inform the thesis of *After Babel*. Widely regarded as a groundbreaking work in translation studies and perhaps Steiner's most important book, *After Babel* articulates the mysterious nature of language and the linguistic and circumstantial problems of translation, drawing upon a wealth of examples that span the globe and history. Similar in scope to Steiner's first book, *Heidegger* outlines the philosopher's ontological thought, explicating its nuances in straightforward prose. Among Steiner's most provocative works, *Real Presences* deliberately invokes the terminology of Eucharistic theology and attempts to refute the literary theory of deconstruction on its own terms and using its own methods. Positing that every literary text "incarnates . . . a real presence of significant being," this book probes the consequences and implications of such a thesis, demonstrating the ephemeral nature of literary criticism and cataloging the inherent nihilism of deconstruction. Spanning a seventeen-year period, the previously published essays collected in *No Passion Spent* cover diverse subjects ranging from the changing status of dreams ("The Historicity of Dreams") and the history of classical literature translated into English ("Homer in English") to Jewish history ("Totem or Taboo"), ethnic identity ("Our Homeland, the Text"), and a meditation on the importance of critical reading ("The Uncommon Reader").

Steiner's later critical writings include *Grammars of Creation,* which surveys literary and artistic development in Western culture to show the evolution and subsequent devolution of a "theological, canonic world order," and *Lessons of the Masters,* which investigates the progression of cultural pedagogy from the perspectives of past and present teachers and students. Like much of his criticism, Steiner's fiction reflects upon the significance of key events in the twentieth century, namely the end of World War II and the fall of communism. In *The Portage to San Cristóbal of A. H.,* Steiner's only novel, a group of Nazi-hunters scours the globe for a ninety-year-old Adolf Hitler, who survived the bunker in Berlin in 1945 and lives in the jungle of South America. Developing ideas rather than characters, the novel uses the dictator to explore the various meanings historically attributed to Hitler as expressed through the attitudes of Israeli secret agents, French diplomats, Russian spies, and German lawyers. In the novel's final section, designed to represent the allure and duplicity of evil, Hitler eloquently defends his anti-Semitic philosophy and ultimately implies that the Nazi belief in Aryan supremacy mirrors the Jewish belief of being God's chosen people. *Proofs, and Three Parables* comprises a novella and three short stories. Its title a play on words on several levels, *Proofs* illuminates the psychological effects of the fall of communism in Eastern Europe. Mainly set in Italy, the novella recounts

a debate regarding the merits of Marxism and the Church between a communist who is losing his eyesight and a priest, underscoring the importance of a search for understanding rather than justification. Both "Desert Island Discs" and "Noël, Noël" center on the implications of listening, and the brief final story, "A Conversation Piece," presents different interpretations of the biblical story of Abraham and Isaac by several Jews on their way to a gas chamber. Steiner's *Errata* resists the conventions of traditional autobiography, tracing instead the evolution of his thought and interests in a thematic fashion. Although the first four chapters recall incidents in Steiner's life as a boy in Paris, an adolescent in Manhattan, and an undergraduate in Chicago, the subsequent chapters are ruminations on various subjects including his Jewish identity, music, the horrors of modern history, religion, and his teachers and intellectual companions.

CRITICAL RECEPTION

Critics have offered divergent reactions to Steiner's philosophical speculation, textual commentary, and accessible style. On one hand, most commentators have marveled at the breadth and depth of Steiner's thought, particularly his fresh insights on various intersections among the disciplines of philosophy, linguistics, sociology, literature, and the fine arts. On the other hand, many reviewers have dismissed Steiner's literary criticism as elitist, regressive, or overtly religious. Indeed, the theological implications of Steiner's hermeneutics have perplexed most poststructuralist literary scholars, who have questioned its value in the age of deconstruction, although some have also pointed out the central role Steiner has assigned to "the text" in his understanding of religion and its influence on his philosophy. In addition, critics have debated the merits of Steiner's cultural criticism, generally finding his critiques of American cultural phenomena limited and discounting his perception that contemporary Western culture is in crisis or decay. Much scholarship has centered on how Steiner's Jewish identity and his understanding of the Holocaust has influenced not only his literary criticism but also his fiction, causing Steiner to bring charges of moral irresponsibility and blatant anti-Semitism against his detractors. Despite occasional controversies, Steiner's critical reading of cultural texts of all kinds has generally received broad acclaim.

PRINCIPAL WORKS

Tolstoy or Dostoevsky: An Essay in the Old Criticism (criticism) 1959
The Death of Tragedy (criticism) 1961

Anno Domini: Three Stories (short stories) 1964

The Penguin Book of Modern Verse Translation [editor] (anthology) 1966

Language and Silence: Essays on Language, Literature, and the Inhuman (criticism) 1967

Extra-Territorial: Papers on Literature and the Language Revolution (criticism) 1971

In Bluebeard's Castle: Some Notes towards the Re-Definition of Culture (criticism) 1971

After Babel: Aspects of Language and Translation (criticism) 1975

Heidegger (criticism) 1978

On Difficulty, and Other Essays (criticism) 1978

Antigones (criticism) 1979

*The Portage to San Cristóbal of A. H. (novel) 1981

George Steiner: A Reader (criticism) 1984

†*Real Presences* (criticism) 1989

Proofs, and Three Parables (novella and short stories) 1992

The Deeps of the Sea, and Other Fiction (novel and short stories) 1996

No Passion Spent: Essays 1978-1996 (essays) 1996

Errata: An Examined Life (memoirs) 1997

Grammars of Creation: Originating in the Gifford Lectures for 1990 (criticism) 2001

Lessons of the Masters (criticism) 2003

*This work was adapted by Christopher Hampton and staged as a play titled *George Steiner's The Portage to San Cristóbal of A. H.* in 1982.

†This work was originally delivered as a lecture titled *Real Presences: The Leslie Stephen Memorial Lecture* at Cambridge University on November 1, 1985.

CRITICISM

George Steiner and Nicolas Tredell (interview date 20 July 1990)

SOURCE: Steiner, George, and Nicolas Tredell. "George Steiner in Conversation." *PN Review* 17, no. 4 (March/April 1991): 24-31.

[*In the following interview, which was originally conducted in 1990, Steiner discusses his early cultural development, the relationship between art and religion, and the value of literary deconstruction methods.*]

CHURCHILL COLLEGE, CAMBRIDGE 20 JULY 1990

[*Tredell*]: *In your books, you've given some glimpses of your early life—of the 'polyglot matrix', as you call it in* **After Babel** *(1975, p. 116), in which you were raised, of the influence of your father, of your schooling at ly-* cées *in Paris and New York, of the growing threat of Fascism. Could you give us an outline of your early cultural development?*

[Steiner]: Yes. The first and central point is that it was physically very safe and privileged in Paris. Psychologically, my father had no doubt at all, from the late twenties on, that the catastrophe was coming, and among my earliest memories are those of Hitler's voice on the radio being picked up by my parents with a sense of absolute and terrible certainty. So I was educated under the pressure of trying to get ready to move. My father saying, on a Monday you start packing your steamer trunk and on a Tuesday your hand baggage, stuck with me even before I quite understood it. And the polyglot matrix gave a kind of wonderful sense of not being afraid of being caught in any one place. Very systematically, my father suggested to me that the more languages you knew, the more you learned of other cultures and other ways, the more you might have a chance of acting, of making a contribution, without necessarily being where you were as a child. I'd like to stress that this, far from introducing any particular sense of instability and schizophrenia, helped enormously—it took away a lot of fear. Another key moment was when I had been rushed home from school one day because of a fascist demonstration during one of the many anti-Blum uprisings and scandals in Paris. My mother very rightly began closing the windows and bringing down the blinds. I desperately wanted to see the mob in the street, as any little child would. My father came home and with extreme calm ordered my mother to open the windows and the blinds, stood next to me and said: 'Never be afraid, this is called history.' That was one of the real turning-points in my life. It placed what was happening in a fascinating and positive context. So these were very important elements, together with being taught by my father to begin reading the classics at a very, very early age. He would take a Homer, look at some lines with me in English or in French, or in the great German Voss translation which he loved best, and we'd come to one of those unbearably exciting passages, the arrow, the spear, flying through the air, and I couldn't bear it any more, I was out of my mind with excitement. And he'd say, with tremendous regret, I don't know how to explain this, there is no translation of this passage, it's missing. And I'd almost shout for help, and he'd say, let's find out, and do the Greek words with me. And that simple device was, of course, tremendous. It gave me the idea that you had better learn to translate for yourself if you wanted to find out how the story went on. There was also the unashamed proud élitism of the French system, where the teacher says to the six-year old children who only partially understood him: You have walked this morning through the Rue de la Fontaine, Place Descartes, Place Victor Hugo and Square Pascal, and one in a million of you might one day contribute something worth preserving. I owe everything to that. And I have no grimmer sadness about what has happened to Western education than the fact that children are no longer allowed the great vision of eventual possibility, harsh as it is in one way, but in another way fantastically bracing and encouraging.

You then went to New York and to the lycée *there?*

In 1940, we were unable to get to England, where I was supposed to go. I had as a kind of unofficial godfather, because in Judaism you don't have official godfathers, Lewis Namier, who was a very close friend of my father. Namier, because he had some students there, put me down for Harrow. It is my humble conviction that, had I gone there, I don't think I would have found my way. Owing to Herr Hitler, I was unable to benefit from Lewis Namier's generous foresight and had to go to New York and to the *lycée* there in which some of those who were important figures in modern culture were earning their precarious living in exile, before they found university posts, by teaching little boys and girls. So I heard lectures by Maritain, by Gilson, by Lévi-Strauss, by Perrin the physicist. It was an extremely heady, complicated, stimulating atmosphere. The *lycée* was official pro-Vichy, the students of course extremely Gaullist, and there is nothing healthier than to fear being beaten up by political opponents. It related again to what my father had said: Never be afraid, this is called history. I found history a very exciting business.

When you went to the University of Chicago, you switched for a time to the study of science. Why was that?

That had very special and bizarre reasons. Robert Hutchins, who was a great reformer in American education, a very, very Thomist, very fascinating figure, said that American undergraduate education was a complete waste of time for the literate. It was essentially designed for the semi-literate. So you had a system where you came and volunteered to sit any final exam in any of the fourteen basic subjects you had to take. If you got an alpha, you didn't need to take the course, a delightful idea. So I sat all fourteen and got alphas in all but three, mathematics, physics and chemistry, which, coming out of a Greek-Latin French system, I failed with below gamma. So that's what I felt I had to study. I switched completely to science, and it was beautifully taught. Hutchin's rule was that the greater and more eminent you were as a man, the more you had to allow a little time for beginners. I learned physics from Enrico Fermi, who loved lecturing to idiots because physics itself was beginning again, so he wanted to know how you teach it. I had eminent teachers in chemistry and biology and worked day and night because I was so embarrassed, so ashamed. That led to a quite extraordinary ending of the whole matter. I did well on the Finals and rushed to see the science advisor of the university,

a very distinguished man, saying I'd like to do science. He called in my papers, and he said: You got good marks, and you're an idiot. You learnt the maths by heart, and there isn't a spark of real insight in this. I was still in a period, 1948-9, when it was atoms or nothing. If you weren't good enough to do physics, particularly nuclear physics, in Chicago, you were called a bottlewasher. And of course I couldn't have coped even with the beginning of graduate work, because indeed my mathematics was learned by rote. I still remember the sense of shock, of numbing sadness, as I resigned myself to philosophy and literature. And let me say that the embarrassment about being so helpless in real mathematics has always stayed with me, and it may be that my passions for music and chess are, to do tuppenny psychoanalysis, vestiges of the sadness over the mathematics. We're meeting in a science college full of mathematicians, and I am unashamedly sad and in some ways envious as they pass by.

You went on to Harvard and to Oxford to do graduate work in literature, spent four years on The Economist *in London, and then, in 1956, went to the Institute of Advanced Study in Princeton, where you finished your first published book,* **Tolstoy or Dostoevsky** *(1959). That book was written against what was then still the dominant ideology in literary studies, the New Criticism. What were your objections to the New Criticism?*

The lack of a historical body and context, the autistic play with the text, the lack above all of the possibility of intentionality. By then, I'd come into close contact with Lukács in Budapest, I was beginning to study Hegel and Marx intensely, I was reading Husserl a lot. The New Criticism seemed to me a wonderful therapeutic, pedagogic device, but finally false to the possibilities of the text. And its incapacity to handle works like *The Brothers Karamazov* or *War and Peace* or *The Death of Ivan Ilych* seemed to me palpable. I was trying to see why the New Critical tools snap, like very thin metal files which are not up to the job, when you have the real stone in front of you. And *Real Presences,* '**The Grammars of Creation**' which are the Gifford Lectures I've just given, my fiction, everything I've written, they're all in *Tolstoy or Dostoevsky,* in the statement which begins all my formal work, that true criticism is a debt of love, and my sense that where the God-question is not fully admitted as a question, there are dimensions which are simply not accessible to style, to discourse.

Developing that point, one particular anticipation of your future work, and of your current quarrel with deconstruction in **Real Presences,** *occurs in this passage from* **Tolstoy or Dostoevsky***: 'The most stringent test of the aliveness of an imagined character—of its mysterious acquisition of a life of its own outside the book or play in which it has been created and far exceeding the* *mortality of its creator—is whether or not it can grow with time and preserve its coherent individuality in an altered setting. Place Odysseus in Dante's* Inferno *or in Joyce's Dublin and he is Odysseus still . . .' (p. 104). Now the objection that would be made today is that this continuity and coherence, even within a text, let alone between texts, is a retrospective simplification, a construction, a synthetic act of the imagination which really leaves out all the differences between, say, Homer's Odysseus and Joyce's Bloom.*

I don't accept that. Because we start at different points of questioning. Flaubert dies screaming—he was in pain—I'm dying like a dog and *cette putaine* Emma Bovary will live. Deconstruction has nothing to tell me about that scream, nothing whatever. The notion that Odysseus or Falstaff or Hamlet or Emma Bovary or Anna Karenina are only semantic markers is entirely coherent. It cannot be disproved. But I know it's rubbish. If that were so, more of us could have a crack at creating those semantic markers. The survival of a fictional persona, the way it absorbs one's own life so that it is much more alive than you and I—these figures have life infinitely beyond yours and mine, and a physical life strangely enough—all this entails a possible analogy, and I'm using analogy in a strict, almost theological sense, with the act of creation. Now that is another vocabulary, another language game: let's be Wittgensteinian for a moment. Derrida has his game. Nothing in Derrida's game is better than in my game. I think mine accounts much more for one's actual experience of the figure in the text. Indeed, if I ask myself why we lack, in our time, epigones of this order of real presence, maybe the language game I'm within at least offers hypotheses of a post-Nietzchean, post-Freudian linguistic moment. The other can offer no hypotheses, it can merely say hoorah. *And it may be right.* I do not say, as my teachers like Maritain and Gilson, the great Thomists, could say: I am right. No, I am saying that what I ask and what I suggest addresses itself more to actual experiences than do the dances over the emptiness of Monsieur de Man and Monsieur Derrida. This is not to say either that they aren't right or that there isn't only an emptiness to dance over. I do not know. But I am accountable to the naive immediacy of my experiences, when I read a major text, when a major melody enters into me. Proust, dying, wants to see the yellow spot on the wall in Vermeer's *View of Delft* because he says: to have seen that is to know the essence of life. Now you can deconstruct that, and, by the way, in so many more interesting ways than the deconstructionists. You could make of it a symptom of asthmatic decay. Very interesting. A doctor might want to tell us something about that. You could deconstruct it in the name of dandyish aestheticism, of the religion of art *contra* humanism, Maurice de Guérin and Baudelaire against Matthew Arnold. And I wonder if what you have done is not to wholly, wholly diminish it. In *A*

La Recherche, on the night of the death of the great writer Bergotte—and this is one of the last pages Proust writes—his books are open in the *vitrines* of the Paris bookstores in the silent city, and the narrator says the open books are the wings of the death angels honouring the writer who will never die. If that is the rhetoric of a language game, then I would like to know why there are many human beings who can, and indeed do, live and die by Proust. I wonder what book you have in your pocket when things go very, very wrong, or—an even harsher test in some ways—are ecstatically wonderful.

But aren't you moving towards using literature and art as a substitute for religion?

Certainly not as a substitute. At a certain range and reach, I see a continuum between art and religion. Plato teaches me in the *Phaedo* that the thirst for beauty is insatiable. It can never be slaked. That makes such obvious sense to me. When Baudelaire says that in and through the music, you will know what is on the other side of death, I'm sure I cannot paraphrase it, but it seems to me an imperative of common sense. When Lawrence says, you have to be so terribly religious to be an artist, the fire of God has gone through me this morning—as Blake would, of course—I don't think these men are mixing up art and religion, I don't think they're bluffing. I don't think they're deceiving themselves. They are reporting. All I can do is report on my thirst. My whole fifteen books have been a report on being very, very thirsty. And perhaps it would have been better if I could have had the Coca-Cola of complete relativism and playfulness. Please mark my prediction. Monsieur Sollers attacked me years ago when he was running a journal called *Tel Quel*: Monsieur Sollers is now a friend who, with Levinas, is editing an orthodox Jewish magazine called *L'Infini*. We've gone from *Tel Quel* to *L'Infini*. Monsieur Derrida will perhaps end in Jewish rabbinism, as Geoffrey Hartman has done. What a detour! A fine, exciting detour! But that's been clear from the start. Deconstruction is a thirst. Why is it so Jewish? Why has this country contributed almost nothing? Because it doesn't have a Jewish intellectual tradition? It's a complicated question. Why have all these people come out of the Talmudic tradition in order to mock it? They are thirsty. And it's almost embarrassing, the simplicity of the logic. If you begin with such craving, where else are you going to end but with *L'Infini*? I almost wish they'd stuck to their guns: if you are an anarchic, nihilistic dancer, don't for God's sake sit down! No, for me, there are very deep relations between art and religion, but art is not a substitute for religion. I fear the Arnoldian argument on substitution. Not a substitute, but an approach. Threshold. Door-handle.

Your next book, **The Death of Tragedy** *(1961), is very rich and wide-ranging, but perhaps also limiting—when* *you say, for instance: 'Tragedy speaks not of secular dilemmas which may be resolved by rational innovation, but of the unalterable bias towards inhumanity and destruction in the drift of the world' (p. 291). Isn't that too narrow a definition of tragedy?*

The book does not sufficiently distinguish between what I now call 'absolute tragedy' and the natural tragi-comic pulse which is there in most of the great plays that we call tragedies—namely, the act of trust in the world, in its continuation: that Cyprus will be better governed by Cassio after Othello's death, that Fortinbras will, though with less intellectual distinction, possibly be a decent king of Denmark: the great Shakespearean pulse of life. But there are a handful of absolute tragedies in which there is no upbeat—among them, the *Bacchae* of Euripides, the *Antigone* of Sophocles. *Timon of Athens,* which I now work on more and more, seems to me the only absolute tragedy in Shakespeare because it says, let language end. It is the only time in the whole Shakespearean canon that we do not even have the hope that language might persist. Timon's epitaph speaks of the end of language, which is the end of the Shakespearean universe. Absolute tragedies would also include *Woyzeck,* and certain plays of Racine where there is the vision that man is an unwelcome guest in the universe, hunted, harried, tortured and eliminated. We now assign to Theognis—but competent scholars tell me it may be much older—the famous saying which Sophocles and then endless others will quote: It is best not to have been born, and, saving that, to die young. The worst is to live. That famous triple statement, for me, defines the enactment of absolute tragedy. To look at a human situation in the light of that. I should have been much more rigorous in **The Death of Tragedy** and I should have made it clear that this tiny handful of tragedies are almost in the nature of experiments out of the night. They are testings of ultimate blackness. They can only be sustained for a very short period—though you might argue that the fact that you can write the play is a subversion of this absolute. I could add further recent examples of absolute tragedy—by Edward Bond, whom I admire enormously, and the last Beckett parables, the black mouth screaming, the extinction of the world and of speech within final sorrow. And let me say something more. You quoted this bias towards the inhuman. If you had told me that the world would not move a finger when Pol Pot was burying alive 100,000 men, women and children, and it was being reported to us, which was not true at the time of Auschwitz—sorry, I stick by that statement.

This leads on to a crucial, harrowing concern of your work, which you eloquently address in **Language and Silence** *(1967) and elsewhere—the co-existence, and indeed the possible complicity, of culture and barbarism. Isn't that concern in tension with your desire to conserve high culture?*

In constant, unresolved tension. Had I only observed that one could torture in the morning and play Schubert at night, this would have been more or less valid. I ventured to go further and ask: what is it inside the playing of Schubert which may relate to the capacity to torture? That, to me, is the much more urgent question. Is it that people trained to imagine abstractly—and to abstract means to get out of, draw away from, separate, cut from—are made less human? That is what I keep asking, and I've never had anyone answering it. Does the cry in *Lear,* as it enters into me, silence the cry in the street? Or muffle it? Or make it messily boring? This creates a constant tension, and I have no answer to your question, I have a sense of bewilderment. My consequent position should have been an ultimately anti-cultural one. Mother Teresa does not need to read Shakespeare or Dostoevsky. One person—this is the later Wittgenstein torment—in a hospital taking care of the incontinent during the night is presumably, by my own convictions, nearer to God than the greatest teacher or writer. And I cannot resolve that tension. I'm a mandarin. I was trained into this clerisy whose role is to pass on the excellence of the really creative, the really great; trained to be what Pushkin called the mailman, the courier bringing the mail from the great to others who may live by it and love it. I would give anything to be able to say that I now see a way through the antinomian contradiction. I do not see a way through. I see little clearings at the edge. For example, I think one can teach at risk and live one's loves at a certain risk. One can try to make imagining extremely concrete, and hope—it's a pious hope, perhaps something like what Trilling meant by the liberal imagination, what Leavis meant by his whole life-teaching, by life-enhancement—that the more scrupulous reader will not take for granted the barbarism around him.

A concern related to the co-existence of culture and barbarism, which you've taken up in, for instance, the essays **'Night Words'** *in* **Language and Silence,** *and* **'Eros and Idiom'** *in* **On Difficulty** *(1978), is with, in Pound's phrase, 'frankness as never before', the new explicitness in literature in the 20th century, and especially since the 1960s.*

I loathe that new explicitness, and let me quickly define the grounds. First of all, it makes it much more difficult to write well. That's a really mundane ground, but one which I could demonstrate without any difficulty. It has become much harder to say anything fresh or to educate the reader's imagination to work with, to collaborate with, the writer. There is more sexual charge in Casaubon and Dorothea's failed honeymoon in *Middlemarch* than in all of modern pornography and frank fiction. Secondly, the emptying-out of the ballast of self, in psychoanalysis, in total confessional revelation, the making public of that which is your own strength, your own darkness, your own infirmity. Like many people who are slightly or otherwise handicapped, I have a cardinal, central sense of the privilege of wrestling alone. And that's how you make it or don't make it. I think we are defined by the weight of secrecy that we can carry, by that which is inviolably discreet within us. I have a deep distaste for psychoanalysis, for the pouring into another person's monied lap of one's aching, final secrets. The psychoanalytic, the revelatory, the confessional, harness the cheapest of human instincts which is that of voyeurism. I'll take a step further. The question of censorship seems to me an urgent and open one. If you were to ask me to balance between, on the one hand, the dissemination of child pornography, sado-masochistic literature in every window as it is now by the completely new instruments of video, and, on the other hand, the errors, the injustices, the corruptions which attach to any body that censors, ineluctably because it is a human interest body with its own power relations, I still opt for those errors which seem to me reparable, challengeable, reversible in a perfectly Miltonic and Millian sense. Nobody has tried to meet the argument of my work, which is a very simple one. If we are in deprivation, socially, physically, economically, explicit material is hot oil being dropped into dynamite. We do not have other escapes, we do not have ironic distances from this material. I want the argument to be looked at in terms of the power of images, of sounds of words. Where does that power fall? The revolutions in Eastern Europe would not have happened without *Dallas,* without the soap operas that were beamed across the walls. People wanted to eat that way, to dress that way, they were ready to do almost anything so that they too could one day step into a car and drive off. This is being hailed as a triumph for free communication. If that is so, I have a right to ask what happens when images of the flogging and burning of the child can be bought in every video shop and shown on every screen. You can't have it both ways. If, as we know, the media of communication are the most powerful means of political suggestion open to man, then the whole question of what you're communicating and to whom is a fair question.

Aren't there, however, some novels which have benefited from, perhaps couldn't even have been written without, the new explicitness? I'm thinking, for instance, of a novel for which you've expressed your admiration, Doris Lessing's The Golden Notebook.

Very good point. First of all, would that we didn't have *Lady Chatterley,* which is a weak book. Or *Nana.* In most cases, the great moments of emancipation have been paid for by the quality of the work—which doesn't detract from the courage or martyrdom of the authors. I don't think of *The Golden Notebook* as necessarily a novel, but we do have the one important passage on the solitary practices of women, one of the first times when this is explored. And there are other books which indeed

have benefited from the abolition of certain rather absurd taboos. By the way, those taboos are exaggerated. We now know that the Victorians were much tougher and franker than our textbooks would suggest to us. But nevertheless, there were absurd taboos, and there have been important emancipations. There have been some magnificent, I think oblique, realizations. I would not want Updike's best fiction to be impossible, Philip Roth's certainly not—one of the great comic artists of our time—nor Bellow, so restless, so classical. I suppose I would want Mailer's *Deer Park* to be available. There are not many. Great artists were able to say what they wanted before then. You're not going to tell me we know more about sex than Dante or Shakespeare or Rabelais did. However, perhaps we can relax more with our readers in a shared pact of adultness. But compared to that, the servitudes, the number of writers under pressure who feel that they have to have orgasm when it isn't even within the reach or need of that particular book or of their way of feeling or of being. It is the blackmail of visceral totality which really worries me now and which is producing massive cruelty and trash.

Could we move on to that fecund and copious work, **After Babel,** *which is to come out in a new edition. A key aspect of the original book was your scepticism about Chomsky's postulate of universal deep structures of language. How do you feel about that today?*

More strongly than ever. I live among more and more languages, and, since 1974, in a totally polyglot society, Geneva, and I teach in it and dream in it and have my human relations in it. Are there any universal deep structures? We haven't come up with any concrete ones. I'm still waiting. But suppose there are: I still maintain that they are of the order of the fact that we need oxygen to breathe and cannot breathe carbon dioxide. Whether they can go much beyond that in concreteness, I do not know. Transformational generative grammars have nothing to say about the poem, and that, to me, is the tuning-fork test of linguistic theory.

There's a strong sense in **After Babel,** *which again this anticipates your quarrel with deconstruction, that translation—and in that book, translation is, for you, the paradigm of all interpretation—involves the attempt to recover some kind of original meaning. Now it's the existence of any such meaning that deconstruction denies.*

Of course. Absolutely denies. I would like to say an original presence. Almost a mute one. Let me move laterally a little here because you ask very difficult and central questions. Why am I a Racinian, perhaps more than a Shakespearean? Because there are moments where speech in Racine is the only thing left in the universe. Human beings are using very simple words that bring them to the edge and then to silence. If you had to put to me the famous *Desert Island Discs* situation, where you can take only one play with you, I would choose *Bérénice*. It captures the moment of utter desolation when you're standing in front of another human being whom you love more than anything in the universe and know it's the last time. No bears chasing you, no castles being stormed by moving woods, no hurricanes spouting, no pother, no anything: language has ended quietly, calmly, with a word like *adieu,* and then a man and a woman are looking at each other. This is the kind of act of presence which may be more primary even than the most nakedly truthful speech. This act of presence involves a sense of the sacramental, and hence a sense of the theology of the Incarnation for which Shakespeare finds the words—bodying forth—an untranslatable two words. We could spend a lifetime pondering that phrase. The bodying forth of what? I think, of a real presence, which if you're that way inclined can be theological, but doesn't need to be. It can be immanent, the bodying forth of the other human being, of the other visage, of the other hand which you can no longer touch, which you will never touch again. Why don't we give an example from, yes, from the realm of inspired kitsch which forms all of us. I was formed as a boy by a film called *Brief Encounter.* Did I see it four times, six times, I kept going in New York, drenched in tears of course. I can't put on the Rachmaninov to this day without having those tears come back. When they both know it's the last time, and there's the whistle of the train, and the smoke of the teakettle comes between them, and they will never touch hands again, it's nearer to Racine than almost anything English culture has produced. A Racinian film. So it can be the most humble of experiences: what it must be like when you see, for the last time, a child who is dying and who doesn't know it. It's not speech then, it is real presence, but speech is rooted in it, and the speech of supreme poetry more than any other.

There seems to be a certain equivocation in **After Babel,** *which very much relates to current debates between deconstructionists and liberal humanists, as to how far language shapes human beings and how far human beings shape language. What are your views on that?*

Heidegger's *die Sprache spricht,* language speaks us, and his sense that the poet is the one most open to this passage of language through him, was a flash of illumination that came to me very young—without full understanding, of course, but it seemed to me a revelation of what was happening when a great poem, a great piece of meaning, which can also be music, passed through me. The idea that we are bespoken, we are uttered by, this. I know the full power of counter-

arguments, which don't convince me. Nothing that men seem able to say about it makes any sense. The Rabbinic idea that language much precedes man, since God has been speaking to the universe before we appear on the sixth day, and that we are largely there so that, at a much lower level of form, the breath of speech which is *Ruah* can continue going on through man when God keeps quiet, which he does forever after the sixth day—this seems to me a marvellously reasonable hypothesis, compared to the notion that it's birdsong we imitate or that the larynx develops certain synaptic, cellular networks which, for reasons unbeknown to anybody, come out as syntax. Let the others do better and I shall most respectfully be taught and change my mind. They haven't done better so far and they don't help me with a poem at all, which is always the test.

With that test in mind, could we focus on your desire— which you mention for instance, in your contribution to a TLS *symposium on 'Modern literary theory: its place in teaching' (6 February 1981, p. 135) to question Leavis's dictum that 'linguistics has nothing to contribute to our understanding of literature'. What do you think linguistics can contribute?*

The first books I like to give my students are Empson's. *Seven Types of Ambiguity* and more, to me, *The Structure of Complex Words* and some of the essays, show someone who smelt grammar like a palpable agency moving within the poem. When I heard Roman Jakobson, in a seminar, repeat to his students, do not come to tell me about the grammar of the poem if you do not know about the poetry of the grammar, it helped me enormously. And Jakobson could do it, he could take a Shakespeare sonnet and show that the grammar of poetry and the poetry of grammar are deeply congruent. Then there is Kenneth Burke on the grammar of rhetoric and of argument, and people who are less well-known in this country, like Contini and Timpanaro, who are highly alert to the interactions of linguistics and literature. Linguistics can tell us a lot about structure, about constraint. Take Chomsky's fascinating axiom that there can't be an endless sentence. It's very important, to the reader of *Finnegans Wake,* of Hölderlin, of late Proust, to understand what Chomsky is saying and what deep structural rule he's suggesting. I learnt much from Christine Brooke-Rose's *The Grammar of Metaphor*: it has behind it the lineaments of a trained linguistic awareness. And Donald Davie's early books *Purity of Diction in English Verse* and *Articulate Energy* mean a great deal to me, I teach them all the time. I do want my students, when they do, say *Lycidas* with me, to show me they've learnt what a gerund is, what an ablative absolute is, what an anaphoric structure is, because they would not, I think, be allowed in a basic music class if they did not know there was a scale, a key, a dominant and a subdominant. And the idea that you can read literature from Milton to Geoffrey Hill, from Ovid to Robert Lowell, without knowing the lineaments of prosody and of grammar seems to me silly. In those respects, I'm sure Leavis is wrong. On the other hand, if we're told nonsense, such as, there will be a new generation of computers that will be able to give us a Shakespeare play or a Balzac novel, if we are told by Derrida that all texts are a pre-text of semiotic textuality, then I know Leavis is right. He didn't even need to see this kind of barbaric yawping. But a great deal can be learnt at the interface of linguistics and literary criticism.

You've brought up the topic of teaching, and I'd like to take issue with a comment you made in the 1976 essay 'Text and Context', which is collected in **On Difficulty.** *You say in that essay: 'The attempt to impose "textual" habits or a transcendental convention of the "classical" on a mass public, as it is now being made in many of our universities, is a self-defeating hypocrisy' (p. 15). I'd like to set against that another of your statements, made in 1974, but to take the liberty, if I may, of altering one word. The statement then runs: 'Is there even a shred of evidence to show that the capacity for literary insight and enjoyment, up to a certain modest standard of competence, is mysteriously or genetically specific? Or are we, actually, dealing with a long tradition of bad teaching, patronising sloth and socially conditioned recalcitrance?' Now I'm quoting, as you'll recognize, from your address to the AGM of the Headmasters' Conference in October 1974 (published in* Conference, *vol. 12, no. 1, February 1975, p. 9), and I've substituted 'literary' for 'mathematical'.*

Fine. You have every right to substitute one for the other. I was speaking to headmasters and trying to prevent mass depression, which I've sometimes been known to induce in generous audiences. I don't know the answer. Could we, given ideal conditions, do much better in bringing to far more young men and women and children access to the best? Yes, we must, at some level, believe this. Yes, if we had teachers almost capable of themselves creating something. It's not infinitely elastic. I still think that, even under ideal conditions, Shakespeare's *Sonnets,* Dante's *Paradiso,* Spinoza's *Ethics,* Bach's *Well-Tempered Clavier,* are not infinitely 'bringable'. There were, at the best scholarly estimates, nine people at the Crucifixion, *ca.* 610 at the premiere of *Hamlet,* 1200 at the first performance of the *Missa Solemnis* and a billion-and-a-half watching the World Cup Final. Yours and my brain cannot take in a billion-and-a-half. This is not a statistical fact, it is a sociological fact of the most enormous importance. Eliot said human beings can stand very little reality. I'm not sure that they can stand very much irreality— the mind-demanding abstraction, demanding purity and intensity of meditation. The idea which was inculcated

in me, by my father, by the great French educational system, was that you sit alone on a chair in a quiet room—Pascal's formula—being neither afraid nor empty. Nothing in our culture now wants that. It even regards it as highly asocial and potentially dangerous. Those East European societies based on that Messianic heresy of Judaic élitism that was Marxism have now collapsed. In those societies, the article on Hegel or the poem by Pasternak or the next production of *Othello* or the next Shostakovitch quartet were among the most important political issues, for which human beings risked their lives. That was an enviable condition. And if that is gone, if there is no longer the provocation, *provocare,* the summons, the calling—a beautiful word we don't use any more—the calling of that challenge to us in the West, then God help us. Then indeed there is a possibility that the best of liberal hopes and instincts will become the emporium of the McDonald hamburger and the fast food chain. And fast food is a formidable image, because, as we know, the idea of nurture has food in it, and the dialectic between humane nurture and fast food is the one we are now going to have to live.

Those Eastern European Communist orders emerged from a continent devastated by Fascism, and your most powerful exploration of the genesis of Fascism is your novel **The Portage to San Cristóbal of A. H.** *(1981). Relating that to your earlier point about the desirability of teachers being almost capable of creation, how do you see your own fiction?*

In a great creative artist, there is an innocence which I simply do not have. Such an artist has something which we don't have a terribly good word for, a supreme intelligence, an innocent necessity, of shaping. My fiction, which has had a very good run for it, and is now alive in many languages, comes out of an argument, out of an idea, out of what might have been an essay. I hope this is a little less true of some of the most controversial parts of *The Portage* [*The Portage to San Cristóbal of A. H.*] These are not things I could have said in any other form. The novel wrote itself in three days and three nights, at a moment of very deep personal crisis. So I've known a little whiff of the real thing. And of course if one could do the real thing all the time, one would. I hope I have never deflected from the statement near the beginning of *Tolstoy or Dostoevsky,* that no-one would write a book of criticism if he could write one sentence of *War and Peace* or *The Brothers Karamazov.* But the other job is infinitely worth doing. It's to be the pilot-fish in front of the master shark, or one of those wonderful birds that sit on the rhinoceros and go *pit-pit,* so that everybody knows the real one is coming. Ask a critic, a teacher, for whom he has helped to open the way. There are half-a-dozen major figures whose rhinoceros horns I've at least been lucky enough to chirp on. And that's exciting, that's what I look back on with pride. Figures like Benjamin, Adorno, Lévi-Strauss, Hermann Broch, are now available, and everyone uses them as if they'd always known about them. I hate those who close books. To be told you're mistaken, fine, but far better that error than the English-English 'Come off it', the love of cutting-down which has crippled this insular culture. This is my deep difference with Leavis—the number of books he closed for others. That's unforgivable. You don't need to say you like them, you don't need to touch on them, but don't close them by fiat.

As well as introducing those modern masters, you've also sought to show—especially in **Antigones** *(1984)—the rich afterlife of ancient classics in Western culture. A new Classics building opened here in Cambridge last month, Tony Harrison's translations of Greek drama circulate widely, Oliver Taplin's recent book* Greek Fire *and the related TV series, of which you were one of the presenters, have been successful. Do you see a general revival of interest in Classics?*

There is something of a revival. I don't know that we can be at all confident about it, however. What stands in its way is not only its élitist and formal character, but the fact that we're not in a pagan period at all. In order to have a strong Nietzchean paganism, you have to go around shouting that Christ was a crook and an impostor. If that's no longer an issue, then it's very difficult to return to the counter-statement of the immanent proliferation which is paganism. And as psychoanalysis ebbs, which it certainly is doing, something of the grip of classical mythology may ebb with it. Will this mean a greater catholicity of awareness of, say, African, Far Eastern, Amerindian myth, as Lévi-Strauss believes? It doesn't look that way. Few read the four volumes of Latin American and Amerindian myths which Lévi-Strauss hoped would be the new *mythologiques,* as Freud's Oedipus had been. But as the new Europe comes into difficult, confused existence, it looks as if certain classical authors and their afterlives, particularly Virgil and Homer, speak to the European condition as others have not. The *civilitas* of continuity may give us certain shared points of reference. There is a politics of the classical which has a new, though still marginal and preliminary, actuality. And the Victorian sense of being part of a Roman-Greek Hellenistic world would have made easier the entrance into Europe than what has happened since in this country. In that respect, the Victorians were more modern than we.

You suggested earlier in our conversation that you might be more of a Racinian than a Shakespearean, and you've expressed doubts elsewhere about this most exalted *of English cultural icons, for instance in your 1986 W. P. Ker lecture,* '**A Reading Against Shakespeare**'. *Could you sum up your doubts about him?*

There's a French fairy tale about Patapouf, who's big and furry and rolls, and Fil de Fer, the iron thread who cuts. Shakespeare is Patapouf beyond Patapoufs: all the universe is in there. Racine is Fil de Fer: he cuts and cuts and cuts, to essentialize, and that's a dangerous Heideggerian term, to achieve a final, ultimate identity. I have problems, which are my problems, with an art that has so much waste and contingency in it. This is the mark of a French and very classical Greek-Aeschylean-Sophoclean education. I couldn't live a day without Shakespeare, of course. The *Sonnets* never leave me. They have an intensity which is ultimate for me. I read Dante, the *Sonnets,* and Proust, whenever I have the slightest doubt about human intelligence and transcendence. But the doubts about Shakespeare of a Wittgenstein, of a Tolstoy, of a Lukács, of an Eliot, who is anti-Shakespeare, who prefers Dante, do not seem to me trivial or not worth attending to. And if they were more attended to, it would be even more exciting to see the infinite gift to our language that is Shakespeare.

One could relate your uneasiness about the waste and contingency in Shakespeare to the uneasiness about deconstructive dissemination which has vividly emerged several times as we've talked, and which is of course powerfully focused in **Real Presences** *(1989), a book that has perhaps been implicitly present throughout our discussion. But one might ask, given your stress in* **After Babel** *on linguistic plurality and proliferation: why not welcome deconstruction? Doesn't deconstruction, after all, celebrate that plurality and proliferation?*

Could we first of all say of **Real Presences** that there is no recent book which does not honour deconstruction more? I give the deconstructionists a glorious run for it and say how much we owe to them. But finally they are guilty of an ethical, almost religious, breach of values. They put the text below the commentary, they take away from us the task of living a text by the abolition of the responding responsibility of the reader. If that is all there is to reading—if, as de Man says, every good reading is a misreading—then indeed I am in a world which I am perhaps no longer brave enough or playful enough to live with. Perhaps **Real Presences** is a certain cry of muddled despair at my own incapacity to handle the possibility of nothingness. Paul Celan I put above almost any other poet of this century. I've looked at what Lacoue-Labarthe and Derrida do with Celan, and they can't really get anywhere because his work resists by saying: I come out of an order of experience which no playfulness has any purchase on. A Celan, a Walter Benjamin, should have written **Real Presences**. I certainly delight in plurality, in the richness of possible interpretations, but in this I am both with Blake's holiness of the minute particular and Leavis's 'Yes, but . . .'. After all, Leavis never denied that there could be plurality, but he thought that if we spoke to each other nakedly and patiently enough in front of the work, we would limit the disagreements to a fruitful area where they would have the dignity of promise. The deconstructionists and pragmatists would take that away from us. When a Rorty says anything goes, a Chesterton answers—and Chesterton is an out-of-fashion, anti-Semitic, hectoring writer, but he said one thing which haunts me a lot, which helps me as a teacher: when you stop believing, the trouble isn't that you believe nothing—that would be fine—it's that you'll believe anything. And that, I think, is a very strong point. With this kind of playful irresponsibility, the inhuman is near. I have refrained from publishing a single word about Paul de Man, because I think we're too near the shock of the event and because I'm so involved in the Heidegger paradox. But I now have to review for the *TLS* these massive journals of Eliade, and it seems that Eliade was a Romanian Iron Guard sympathizer who made racist and anti-Jewish pronouncements. (See *TLS,* 4 October 1990, pp. 1015-16). If deconstruction is right, this is of no interest whatsoever. It's a moment of one game contrasted with other games. I can't live by that. And by the way, Derrida doesn't either any more. Why should he bother to write so much in defence of de Man? It's a complete contradiction of his own doctrine. He's not deconstructing Paul: it's a long lovesong of aching sophistic agony. So we're all in a bit of trouble. I hope that the Gifford Lectures which I've just completed, and which I hope to write up and publish as *The Grammars of Creation,* will mean that, in future, I'll be able to fail a little better in answering you and that my incomplete replies to your questions will be a little more worth disagreeing with. That is the Leavisian hope, that is the Arnoldian hope, that is the Platonic hope of the maieutic dialogue. What I try to do in the Gifford Lectures is to concentrate on a single question: why does the language invite, allow and solicit the sentence 'God created the universe' and refuse the sentence 'God invented the universe'? I have tried to think about creation and invention in art, philosophy and music, but also in society, in political institutions. This seems to lead back to things right at the beginning of my work. And as I look around for help, I notice that there isn't much, that this question has scarcely been touched. The reason I mention it is the sense of boundless gratitude one has for the difficulty of what we have to think about. Never or rarely, I believe, has there been a period in which the fundamentals have become so daily again, so that it's not whether you get it right— you don't—but whether you get it wrong fruitfully. And of course the sentence 'to get it wrong fruitfully' does

postulate logically the possibility of getting it right. And that's where the cut, the diacritical cut, in everything you've asked comes.

Nathan A. Scott Jr. (essay date summer-autumn 1990)

SOURCE: Scott Jr., Nathan A. "Steiner on Interpretation." *Religion & Literature* 22, nos. 2-3 (summer-autumn 1990): 9-20.

[*In the following essay, Scott discusses the theological implications of Steiner's literary criticism, contrasting them with poststructuralist hermeneutics.*]

Of the major literary critics of our period there is, apart from Northrop Frye, but one other whose work requires us to reach toward such a term as "greatness," and this is George Steiner. The shocking massiveness of his learning that extends across the entire gamut of humanistic studies, the prodigiousness of his competence in the major Western languages, the speculative power of his hermeneutical reflections, the brilliance of his textual commentary, the piercing eloquence of his prose—all this helps to make *The Death of Tragedy, Language and Silence, In Bluebeard's Castle, Extra-Territorial, After Babel, Antigones,* and his various other books form a kind of *oeuvre* that, in its puissant majesty, is virtually without parallel. And yet there is an enormous amount of ill-will toward him that is harbored within the university community on both sides of the Atlantic. As one of his friendlier critics remarked not long ago, "he can seem too vehement, hortatory, overbearing; he raises his voice in public." Moreover, beyond the special kind of intensity and earnestness that belong to his public persona, conventional academicians cannot forgive his polymathic virtuosity, and thus—of this chap who writes on chess and mountain-walking and philosophy and imaginative literature and poetics and various other adjacent subjects—they ask dismissively, "But what is his field?"

So, expectably, captiousness and animadversion and rancor have frequently shaped the reception of his work. But the integrity that belongs to his vision of the hermeneutical enterprise is undauntable, and it has been a privilege over the past thirty years to watch that vision consolidate itself in the many remarkable books he has produced. Yet, though he is commonly thought to be committed to linguistics and cultural criticism and theoretical poetics and intellectual history and philosophical anthropology, it is curious that his reflections on the religious tendency of the literary imagination have rarely been seen to have a kind of exemplarity deserving of careful advertence. In his book of 1971,

Extra-Territorial, he lays it down that "most of serious literature from the jubilant close of Pindar's Third Pythian Ode to Eluard's *dur désir de durer,* and underlying a coherent response to that literature, is a gamble on transcendence" (161). Or, again, in his Introduction to *George Steiner: A Reader* he wants to declare that most of the great literature of the West expresses "a more or less articulate consciousness of the presence or absence of God in and from human affairs" (8). And from his very first book (*Tolstoy or Dostoevsky,* 1959) on, so constantly has such an insistence been a part of his fundamental testimony that he makes us feel that he is very doubtful indeed about the possibility in any strict sense of a secular poetics. For, as he would say, whether one turns to the *Oresteia* or to Dante's *Commedia,* to the poetry of Hölderlin or Montale or Paul Celan, to *The Brothers Karamazov* or *Light in August,* what we are finally by way of encountering is a *mysterium tremendum* which, like that archaic torso of Apollo in Rilke's famous poem, bids us to "change your life."

Steiner, in other words, is not inclined in any degree at all to treat with that "Byzantine acrobatics" whereby the "deconstructive" mode of poststructuralist hermeneutics radically dissociates literary art from its circumambient world and exhibits it as without any specifiable stability of meaning or any capacity for reference and predication. As he says in his recent book, *Real Presences,* "Where it is consequent, deconstruction rules that the very concept of *meaning-fulness,* of a congruence, even problematic, between the signifier and the signified, is theological or onto-theological . . ." (119). And in this one particular he wants resoundingly to register his assent to contemporary scepticism, for what has come to be with him a matter of primary principle is that "any coherent account of the capacity of human speech to communicate meaning and feeling is, in the final analysis, underwritten by the assumption of God's presence" (3). In short, a logocentric universe is not for him the odious specter that it is for Jacques Derrida, since he conceives it to be precisely the immanence of the *Logos* within the world-order (requiring, as it does, a "transcendent metaphysics") that has guaranteed the possibility of that covenant between word and world which forms the basis of the entire cultural project of the Western tradition, the whole sense so deeply endemic to our mode of civility that reality is "sayable."

This "deed of semantic trust" (91) has, of course, been radically impugned by many of the foremost strategists of modernity. Already in the late years of the nineteenth century Mallarmé was insisting that the essential genius of language lies in its self-reflexiveness, in its non-referentiality, in its absolute separation from any kind of phenomenality. And in due course his poetic presentiment was in various ways to be given systematic form by that line of *Sprachphilosophie* reaching from Fritz Mauthner to Saussure and on to Wittgenstein and Frege and Quine and Kripke. The latest chapter in this developing history of *Sprachkritik* is that being currently written by deconstructionist ideology of the present time which asserts that literary texts can tell us nothing at all about anything outside the world of textuality itself. Indeed, as the new savants would have it, the signifiers of which all discourse is comprised only bear upon themselves the traces of still other signifiers, so that the very distinction between the signifier and the signified proves in the end to be an utter delusion. To seek the meaning of any given signifier is only to be confronted with an alternative signifier, and thus any kind of terminal meaning is forever scattered and "not yet," so much so that even the reality of one's own selfhood must be found to be something thoroughly insubstantial and vaporous. Which is to say that our condemnation is to "the prison-house of language." "*It is,*" says Steiner (and the italics are his), "*this break of the covenant between word and world which constitutes one of the very few genuine revolutions of spirit in Western history and which defines modernity itself*" (93).

In this late time of "the 'after-Word,'" when *logos* and cosmos are no longer considered to meet and when "the very concept and realizability of reference, nomination, predication . . . are put in question" (102), Steiner refuses any simple optimism about the possibility of subverting deconstructionist ideology. As he says, "*On its own terms and planes of argument . . . the challenge of deconstruction does seem to me irrefutable*" (132). Which is by no means for him to concede that there are no grounds, substantial grounds indeed, for rebuttal. But he chooses not to waste time on polemic: since what Paul Ricoeur calls "the dismantled fortress of consciousness" is not to be "restored or made stormproof by replacing this or that fallen brick" (133), he wants instead to register a passionate plea that we risk "a wager on transcendence." He sees with absolute clarity that the most essential repudiation lying at the heart of the whole deconstructive enterprise is a theological repudiation, and thus, as he feels, the one kind of faith (in unfaith) may be countered only by another kind of faith. Indeed, that he for the title of his book of 1989 should have borrowed from the lexicon of eucharistic theology the term ("real presence") that speaks of the habitancy of the body and blood of Christ within the two species of the Christian sacrament was on his part a carefully considered tactic (though one wonders why "presence" is pluralized), for what he wants most principally to suggest is that, ultimately, the predicative power that hermeneutics has traditionally attributed to human discourse is underwritten by a theological guarantee, by a radical faith in the immanence of God, this immanence itself in turn making possible significant junctures between word and world.

Contemporary nihilism, after Nietzsche and Foucault and Derrida, declares that our metaphysical situation is that of living amidst absolute nullity, at what the late Roland Barthes liked to call *le degré zéro.* So it says that language lies, in so far as it persuades the innocent that it offers access to anything other than itself: it says that "the games of meaning cannot be won. No prize of transcendence, no surety, awaits even the most skilful, inspired player" (127), since "language inevitably undoes the figures of possible, momentary sense which emerge, like ephemeral and mendacious bubbles, from the process of articulation" (123). But Steiner's rejoinder says, no, our metaphysical situation is defined by the habitancy, the immanence, within our world of a transcendent otherness which, as in myriad ways it touches human existence, makes us know that the foundations of the house of being are in no way at all of our making. And it is this otherness that calls forth those rites of recognition that are enacted by the kind of language we call "literature." "For poets," says Steiner, "these matters are straightforward: over and over, a Dante, a Hölderlin, a Montale tell us of what poetry is saying when, exactly when, words fail it. So does the light at the Vermeer casement. And all great music" (216). By which he does indeed mean to say, shockingly indecorous as it may seem in our phase of civility, that all truly serious *poiesis,* that everything in literature and the arts that we find to be of compelling stature, is of a religious inspiration and intends one or another kind of religious reference. He puts it in this way: he says:

> Referral and self-referral to a transcendent dimension, to that which is felt to reside either explicitly—this is to say ritually, theologically, by force of revelation—or implicitly—outside immanent and purely secular reach, does underwrite created forms from Homer and the *Oresteia* to *The Brothers Karamazov* and Kafka. It informs art from the caves at Lascaux to Rembrandt and to Kandinsky. Music and the metaphysical . . . have been virtually inseparable. It is in and through music that we are most immediately in the presence . . . of the verbally inexpressible but wholly palpable energy in being that communicates to our senses and to our reflection what little we can grasp of the naked wonder of life.
>
> . . . Western painting, sculpture and much of what is incarnate in architecture, have, until the Enlightenment, been religious and, more specifically, Scriptural, both in motivation and representational content. Epic poetry and tragic drama . . . are altogether inseparable from the postulate of "more things in heaven and earth." Tragedy, in particular—and it may be, until now, the most eloquent, concentratedly questioning of all aesthetic genres—is God-haunted from Aeschylus to Claudel. . . . There is, as Socrates hints, a corollary in the *tristia* of high comedy. The gods are most present in their hiddenness when they smile.
>
> (216-19)

So Steiner's conclusion is that "it is the enterprise and privilege of the aesthetic to quicken into lit presence the continuum between temporality and eternity, between matter and spirit, between man and 'the other'" (227). It belongs, in other words, to the essential gravity of major art to remind us that the metaphysical situation to which we are ultimately committed is one established by ours being a world indwelt by a Presence that calls us into something like what Martin Buber spoke of as the relation between I and Thou. True, the literature of our vexed modernity is sometimes to be found insisting (as in the manner of a Kafka or a Beckett) on the *absence* of God, but, even amid the density of that absence, Steiner, by no mere dialectical pirouette, suggests that we will be struck by an "edge of presence" (229).

Now one cannot but be struck by the tack he takes in the interesting argument he put forward in a great essay he issued in 1979 in *New Literary History,* "**'Critic'/ 'Reader,'**" available now in ***George Steiner: A Reader,*** where he in effect treats the hermeneutical situation itself as bearing an analogical relationship to the metaphysical situation, since it, too, as one enters the world of a text, involves an encounter between presence and presence, between the presence of the reader and that *présence transcendante* which is the "jinnee" in "the well-wrought urn" of the poem or the novel.

In the 1940s and 50s, when the pieties and shibboleths of the New Criticism held sway in the critical forum, one used to hear young disciples of Cleanth Brooks and Allen Tate pridefully declaring their aim to be that of "taking the text apart and putting it back together again," whereas today those who have received their tutelage from Paul De Man and Derrida and Stanley Fish are likely to congratulate themselves simply on their deftness in taking texts apart. But, in either case, from the perspective of Steiner this view of the literary text as merely a neutral object awaiting dissection and mastery, far from representing any sort of bracing rigor, appears to bespeak only a kind of brash philistinism. For, as he urges, "the letter is the vessel . . . of the spirit" ("**'Critic'**" ["**'Critic'/'Reader'**"] 95), and thus I am certain that he would want to subscribe to the line that was being taken a generation ago in a brilliant essay of Fr. Walter Ong's, "The Jinnee in the Well Wrought Urn," that appeared in *Essays in Criticism* and was reissued in Ong's *The Barbarian Within.* Here, Fr. Ong calls into question that modern theory of the poem-as-object, with its emphasis on the work of art *as such,* the whole notion that "it is neither the potter who made it nor the people, real or fictional, to whose lives it is tangent, but the well-wrought urn itself which counts" (*Barbarian,* 15). And he wants to declare his own sense of how imperfect is the justice done the actuality of aesthetic experience by this modern idolatry of the art-object. Fr. Ong is careful to acknowledge that the artistic situation does itself claim for the work of art a certain measure of autonomy: he knows it to be the case that the poem bids for an intransitive kind of attention. But he contends that, precisely in the degree to which the object is taken with ultimate seriousness, our contemplation of it inevitably involves us in a very profound disappointment. For, given the essentially personal orientation of our humanity, we cannot finally perform a genuinely intransitive act of attention before anything less than a person. Contemplation of this sort requires that someone else be *there,* for it involves love—which cannot be "projected into an unpeopled void." Yet, curiously, the end of the aesthetic transaction is not psychological disaster, since, as he maintains, "in proportion as the object of art pretends to be serious," it drives us to the point of considering it, indeed, as "a surrogate for a person"—as a surrogate not (as I take him to mean) for the actual scribe who wrote the sonnet or the story but for him whom Wayne Booth in *The Rhetoric of Fiction* calls "the implied author" (71-76) and whose real profile is to be found not in the biography of the historical person but in the texts which he created. "In proportion as the work of art is capable of being taken in full seriousness," says Fr. Ong, "it moves further and further along an asymptote to the curve of personality" (24)—or at least of a person behaving "enough like one to betray the bias of the human heart" (25). Which is to say that the world of literary experience is a personalist universe, a world of dialogue—where the poem is a word spoken and a word heard, this speaking and hearing enabling us to reach the interior not of an "object" but of a personal vision of reality.

So, this being the case, Steiner wants to remind us that, when we are face to face with the *donné* presented by the poem, we do not (or ought not) *attack* it as if it were merely an object to be dismembered for inspection, since the real question is how it is to be granted entrance into the narrows of the heart. "We light the lamp at the window" (*Presences* [*Real Presences*] 149), when a guest approaches our threshold. "We lay a clean cloth on the table. . . ." And he argues that we must indeed summon the chivalric spirit of a most scrupulous *cortesia,* if "the living significations of the aesthetic [are to] seek [us] out [and find us]" (147): we must give true welcome to the poem when it calls at our door. The "critic" will, of course, take a step backward from that which is before him: he will "externalize" it as he tries to decide how to "grasp" it. And, if he is honest, he will in no way at all attempt to conceal the particular angle—whether it be historicist or psychoanalytic or formalist or some other—from which he views the text. Moreover, not only will he undertake to achieve an "ordering sight" ("'Critic'" 69) of, or "objectivity" of perspective on, what he faces: he will also be trying to decide how to rank his text, since, "however eminent, however theoretic in bias, [he] assigns and ascribes

valuations every time he views and designates. . . . He marks down . . . Milton, and marks up Donne. He 'rates' Hölderlin above, say, Mörike; he underwrites new issues, such as the modernist movement, as . . . offering a higher yield to attention and sensibility than the late Romantics or Georgians" ("'Critic'" 73-74)—and so on and so on. Which is to say that, as he "selects and 'prices,'" the "critic" tends to establish a "syllabus" which instructs us regarding those texts which will be found to be most richly rewarding.

The "reader," on the other hand, situates himself in relation to the text quite differently: he does not objectivize it into any sort of *datum,* since for him its otherness is that not of an object but of a "real presence": so his relationship to it cannot be that "of reification, of competition, and, by logical extension, of supersedure" ("'Critic'" 86). Because his aim is deeply to internalize the text, he strives to obliterate the distance from it that the critic would actualize, sometimes undertaking indeed to commit it to memory, to learn it *by heart,* thus permitting it to become an agency in his own consciousness and to "generate a shaping reciprocity" between itself and his own deepest selfhood. In this way he seeks to be a shepherd and servant to the texts he treasures.

Amongst the actual clerisy in the field of *litterae humaniores* some will incline more to the one than to the other type of study, but Steiner makes us feel that he regards a "criticism" unpenetrated by "reading" as destined ultimately for a sad kind of dryness and infertility, since it is only by way of "reading" that we are led to subscribe to that "contract of implicit presence" ("'Critic'" 95) which comports with the sort of loving trusteeship of the canon that constitutes the profoundest obligation of a truly humane criticism. Always the interpreter needs to solicit that tact of mind and heart which *cortesia* would accord to the presence incarnate within the text. As Steiner says,

> There are questions we do not ask of our "caller," of the summoner's presence in the poem or the music, lest they diminish both the object of our questioning and ourselves. There are cardinal discretions in any fruitful encounter with the offering of form and of sense. . . . Maturity of mind and of sensibility in the face of the aesthetic demands "negative capability" (Keats). It allows us to inhabit the tentative. . . . The philological space . . . is that of the expectant, of the risks of trust taken in the decision to open a door.
>
> (*Presences* 176-77)

Indeed, we might say that for Steiner the hermeneutical moment occurs when that presence which is incarnate within the text comes knocking at our door to bid for reception and to seek tenancy within the house of our being. And just what is it that would take up residence within us? Steiner's answer to this question can be come

by only as close attention is paid to his way of reckoning with the prior question as to why it is that there
should be poetry or painting or music at all. To which
his answer is that the motive animating artistic creation

> is radically agonistic. It is rival. In all substantive art-
> acts there beats an angry gaiety. . . . The human maker
> rages at his coming *after,* at being, forever, second to
> the original and originating mystery of the forming of
> form. The more intense, the more maturely considered
> the fiction, the painting, the architectural project, the
> more palpable inside it will be the tranquil fury of sec-
> ondarity. The more sensible will be the master maker's
> thrust towards a rivalling totality. The mortal artist
> would beget, . . . he would encompass, he would
> make an articulate *summa* of the world, as the unname-
> able rival, the "other craftsman" (Picasso's expression)
> did in those six days. The most concise of *haikus,* the
> briefest of Webern's studies, an early Kandinsky of a
> rider in a nightwood, so concentrated in scale that we
> must bend close, can do just that. They create a counter-
> world so entire, so imprinted with the mark of their
> craftsman's hand . . . that we in turn give it echo,
> sanctuary of remembrance, by discovering in it a
> habitation for our most intimate needs and recogni-
> tions.
>
> (***Presences*** 204)

The poet's *mundus contra mundum* is not, of course,
wrought *ex nihilo.* "Fictions and formal imaginings do
select, recombine from among the world's warehouse."
But the novelist or poet or dramatist does produce a
second creation which, as it re-enacts the *fiat* of the
original creation, becomes a means of epiphany, since it
brings us into the neighborhood of that "out of which,
inexplicably, have come the self and the world into
which we are cast" (215). In short, when we enter into
transaction with the work of art, what seeks tenancy
within us is the "radiant opacity" of that transcendent
Otherness of which Rilke's "angels" bring him news in
the *Duino Elegies.* Which is why, as Steiner would
argue, the logic of poetics can never be, wholly and
without remainder, a logic of immanence, for *poiesis*
does in the nature of the case bring us into contact with
"possibilities of meaning and of truth that lie outside
empirical seizure or proof" (225). "Can there be an
understanding of that which engenders 'texts' and which
makes their reception possible which is not underwritten by a postulate of transcendence?" (223). To this
question he wants resoundingly to propose a negative
answer.

So, given his view of the unique kind of nourishment
offered the soul by the arts of the word (as well as by
the plastic and musical arts), it is not surprising that
Steiner gives such short shrift to that new *mystique*
invented by the deconstructionists which declares the
work of the commentator and exegete to have a status
equal to and perhaps even superior to that of the primary
text. In a symposium on "Literary Theory in the

University" published in *New Literary History* in the
winter of 1983 he said, "I regard as pretentious
absurdity current claims for the equivalence in importance or specific gravity of text and commentary" (445).
Ours is, of course, a time in which there seems to be no
end to commentary. "Books of literary interpretation
and criticism . . . are about previous books on the same
or closely cognate themes. Essay speaks to essay, article
chatters to article in an endless gallery of querulous
echo" (***Presences*** 39). The secondary and tertiary are so
much the great narcotic of the age that they are often
by way of seducing us into forgetfulness of the primary
fact that the poem, the novel, the drama is "the literal
'ground and rationale of being' of the interpretations
and judgments which it elicits." And when the new
theorists undertake indeed to argue in effect that the
work of art is merely the accidental and subordinate
"'pre-text' of all subsequent . . . 'textualities,' 'inter-
textualities' . . . and 'counter-textualities'" (***Presences***
151), they are not only trivializing the source-texts, but
they are in fact also seeking to "domesticate . . . [and]
secularize the mystery and summons of creation"
(***Presences*** 39). So Steiner absolutely refuses to assist
in any way at all in the burial of the original source-text
by exegesis. "The poem comes before the commentary.
The construct precedes the deconstruction" (***Presences***
150). And it, therefore, has right of way.

Now Steiner's whole structure of thought—which it has
been possible only partially to review in this brief essay—is profoundly antithetical to those styles of
doctrine and expression that are currently modish in the
forums of hermeneutical theory. He continues to believe,
for example, what he said in his first book, ***Tolstoy or
Dostoevsky,*** that "No man is more wholly wrought in
God's image or more inevitably His challenger than the
poet" (7). And, in a period when the human subject is
considered to be but a cypher at the behest of the norms
and protocols governing his linguistic culture, Steiner's
unabashed romanticism will to many seem to be vatic
and obscurantist in the extreme. Nor will the intransigent
scepticism with which he faces "the carnival and satur-
nalia of post-structuralism" be readily forgiven, nor his
equally intransigent loyalty to the great humanistic
tradition, the tradition of Augustine and Dante, of Hegel
and Hölderlin and Coleridge, of Humboldt and Benjamin and Heidegger. Moreover, despite his immense
distaste for anything resembling "vulgar" Marxism, his
sympathy for the effort of the Frankfurt School (Lukács,
Adorno, *et al*) to situate literature and the arts within
the matrix of history and his belief that this effort holds
forth significant lessons for the liberal imagination—
this has often aroused misgiving and suspicion. And
there are not a few for whom it is nettling that, by dint
of the circumstances of his upbringing, he can find his
own polyglot background to be "circumscribed by Leningrad, Odessa, Prague and Vienna on the one side, and
by Frankfurt, Milan and Paris on the other"

("Introduction" 13). So his hectoring eloquence, with its occasional Latinate prolixity, is resisted and has sometimes provoked ugly charges of "pomposity" and "theatricality" and "egotism": in this late, bad time it is sometimes thought to be a breach of the decorums for a man (in the manner of a Lionel Trilling or an Erich Heller) to address himself to the generality of cultivated people and to abjure the brutal, barbarous jargon that is today deemed to be the requisite parlance for criticism.

But that which seems often to make Steiner's critics most nervous is his habit of driving hermeneutical questions into a theological dimension. Surely, *surely,* says Ihab Hassan, for example, "Steiner is too much part of our secular, agnostic, vaguely rationalist, uneasily humanist, community of letters to evince an unseemly preoccupation with transcendence" (331). But it is clear that Steiner's sense of what is seemly and unseemly does not comport with Hassan's, for his is a hermeneutic that never ceases to insist upon the ultimately religious import of literary art. Yet his argument dances round the whole question of transcendence in ever so gingerly a way: so chary an argument is it indeed that it never quite becomes a true argument, never quite manages to be more than a matter of sheer assertion. Though he conceives it to be the primary principle of hermeneutics that the possibility of junction between word and world is guaranteed by the immanence of the Transcendent, he never undertakes to set forth what it really means to speak of the world as indwelt by God. The affidavit that he offers in this connection is sometimes deeply moving, but it never rises above the level of personal testimony, whereas the role it plays in his discourse does in fact require a systematic elaboration of the grounds on which his testimony is based.

Coleridge spent the period between the early spring and late summer of 1815 setting down those reflections that form the *Biographia Literaria,* and they record, of course, in part the sense by this point he had won as a literary theorist of how blighting for his age had been the whole legacy of neo-classical rationalism. The empiricist tradition of Locke and Hume had been so scornful of those versions of experience offered by literary art that it had bullied the literary community into supposing (as evidenced, say, by the Addison of the *Spectator* papers) that, far from recasting his inherited language and in the process reconstituting the world, the poet could legitimately elect only the role of copyist who reproduces the natural order as faithfully as possible. And thus the vision of the literary enterprise as involving an act of *poiesis* had been displaced by a primitive kind of mimeticism. But it is precisely the doctrine of *poiesis* that Coleridge in the *Biographia* is declaring it to be his intention to reinstate by way of a theory of imagination. Since the creativity of the artist, however, was in his view but an instance of the creativity displayed in all man's basic transactions with the

world, by 1815 he knew that what he had to do was not merely to produce a reinterpretation of the poetic act but also to call into question the whole system of British empiricist philosophy which took the mind to be nothing more than the passive recipient of sense data. So the kind of metaphysical enterprise to which he thereafter committed himself in *The Friend* (1818) and the *Philosophical Lectures* (1819) and *Aids to Reflection* (1825) and the three volumes of papers now known as the *Opus Maximum* was by him felt to be a matter of obligation.

Now it is a part of George Steiner's distinction to be, after Walter Benjamin, perhaps the only other major literary theorist since Coleridge whose literary reflections do in effect ask for completion by a metaphysical and theological project. And it is our inability to discern in his publications to date what the contours of this project might be expected to entail that accounts for the special kind of discontent with which his hermeneutical theory leaves us. Indeed, it is this discontent that prompts a great eagerness for his Gifford Lectures which he began to deliver in April of 1990, for one remembers, of course, that Lord Gifford, who died in 1887, in that section of his will that endowed the lectures (to be delivered in the four Scottish universities—Edinburgh, Glasgow, Aberdeen, and St. Andrews) laid it down that the lecturers shall take "Natural Theology" as their subject. When Karl Barth took this platform at Aberdeen in 1937 and 1938, since he conceived natural theology to be the work of the Devil, he elected as his subject *The Knowledge of God and the Service of God According to the Teaching of the Reformation,* and a few of his successors have at times found one or another way of dodging Lord Gifford's challenge. But, since Steiner's scrupulousness in this matter is to be taken for granted and since if he keeps faith with the founder's intention he will be by way of doing precisely what his work to date invites him to do, the publication of his own Gifford Lectures is to be awaited with very considerable interest.

Note

A small portion of my brief review of Steiner's *Real Presences* that appeared in *First Things* 1:3 (1990) has been incorporated here with the permission of the Editor.

Works Cited

Barth, Karl. *The Knowledge of God and the Service of God According to the Teaching of the Reformation.* Trans. J. L. M. Haire and Ian Henderson. New York: Scribner's, 1939.

Barthes, Roland. *Writing Degree Zero.* Trans. Annette Lavers and Colin Smith. New York: Hill and Wang, 1968.

Booth, Wayne C. *The Rhetoric of Fiction*. Chicago: U of Chicago P, 1961.

Cohen, Ralph, ed. "Literary Theory in the University: A Survey." *New Literary History* 14 (1983):411-51.

Hassan, Ihab. "The Whole Mystery of Babel: On George Steiner." *Salmagundi* 70-71 (1986), 316-33.

Ong, Walter, S. J. *The Barbarian Within*. New York: Macmillan, 1962.

Steiner, George. *Tolstoy or Dostoevsky*. New York: Knopf, 1959.

————. *The Death of Tragedy*. New York: Knopf, 1961.

————. *Language and Silence: Essays on Language, Literature, and the Inhuman*. New York: Knopf, 1967.

————. *In Bluebeard's Castle: Some Notes towards the Redefinition of Culture*. New Haven: Yale UP, 1971.

————. *Extra-Territorial: Papers on Literature and the Language Revolution*. New York: Atheneum, 1971.

————. *After Babel: Aspects of Language and Translation*. New York: Oxford UP, 1975.

————. *Antigones*. New York: Oxford UP, 1984.

————. "Introduction" and "'Critic'/'Reader.'" *George Steiner: A Reader*. New York: Oxford UP, 1984.

————. *Real Presences*. Chicago: U of Chicago P, 1989.

Ronald A. Sharp (review date winter 1991)

SOURCE: Sharp, Ronald A. "Creation and the Courtesy of Reading." *Kenyon Review* 13, no. 1 (winter 1991): 187-92.

[*In the following review, Sharp outlines the main points of Steiner's hermeneutical model in* Real Presences, *anticipating likely responses to the book by intellectuals.*]

Debates about deconstruction have been raging in the academy for nearly two decades. Though academic literary criticism has now taken a decisive turn towards historicism and cultural studies, which work from vastly different assumptions than those of a Derrida or a De Man, the legacy of deconstruction remains potent. Nor, according to George Steiner, has its "summons to nihilism" ever been adequately answered. Those who were not persuaded by its claims defended their positions with ever shriller appeals to common sense, fantasizing that this fashion, like all other theoretical fashions, would also pass.

Real Presences takes deadly aim at deconstruction, but it also takes it in deadly earnest, refusing to pass it off as a fashion or to refute it on pragmatic or even on logical grounds. For "*on its own terms and planes of argument,*" Steiner says, "the challenge of deconstruction does seem to me irrefutable" (132). What is required, he suggests, is a recourse no less radical than that of deconstruction: a leap of faith, a "wager on transcendence" (214). "We must ask of ourselves and of our culture whether a secular, in essence positivist, model of understanding and of the experience of . . . the aesthetic is tenable in the light, or if you will, in the dark of the nihilistic alternative" (134). Five years ago, in his Leslie Stephen Memorial Lecture at Cambridge, Steiner argued that every text, every work of art "*incarnates . . . a real presence of significant being*" (Cambridge: Cambridge UP, 1986, 19). In this book, he considers the consequences and implications of that argument, and concludes that the only grounds on which deconstruction can be refuted are moral and theological. In both the creation of art and in its reception there must be "a presumption of presence" (214).

Steiner has been so controversial for so long, on so many issues, and for so many reasons, that one wonders whether his less sympathetic readers will even notice the boldness of his claims in this dazzling new book. But surely Steiner is courting double trouble in arguing for a moral and theological foundation of literary criticism—indeed of all aesthetic experience and interpretation, since he insists that he is talking not just about literature but about all the arts. One has only to glance at a review like Roger Kimball's in *The New York Times Book Review* (30 July 1989: 11) to see something of the enormous naïveté and viciousness of the knee-jerk response. Steiner understands all too well that most modern intellectuals see red at the prospect of ethical criticism, that they are "more or less at ease with the manifold discourse of uncertainties" because they perceive "in this multiplicity . . . a guarantor of tolerance" and they suspect "in any thirst for absolutes not only an infantile simplicity but the old, cruel demons of dogma" (199-200).

Nor is Steiner unaware of the risks in arguing for a conception of presence in the age of Derridean absence. Such an attempt to reclaim the high ground that deconstruction both deserted and undermined makes him vulnerable to "the whole gamut of muddle and embarrassment" (178). But the stakes are momentous. Wayne Booth, in his blurb for *Real Presences,* does not exaggerate when he says that this "challenging, ambitious, highly original, learned and moving work . . . reappraises the whole of modern thought, with the aim of restoring our belief that art reveals a transcendent reality."

The very ambition of such an argument is, sadly, enough to make most intellectuals suspicious if not embarrassed—a response that would strike Steiner as deeply characteristic of our contemporary quagmire of uncertainty, of our minimalist hesitation and timidity. In the "secondary city" that constitutes our current intellectual habitation, we have grown accustomed to the endless flood of critical commentary on the arts and to the proliferation of commentaries on commentaries. We are scarcely shocked by the fact that "in the field of modern literature alone, Russian and Western universities are thought to register some thirty thousand doctoral theses *per annum,*" or that "an average college or university library will need to stock some three to four thousand periodicals in the humanities" (25). This "Byzantine dominion of secondary and parasitic discourse over immediacy, of the critical over the creative" (38), has its apotheosis in the ostensible triumph of theory. For Steiner these are all symptoms of our craving for "remission from direct encounter with the 'real presence' . . . which an answerable experience of the aesthetic must enforce on us. . . . In the agency of the critic, reviewer or mandarin commentator, we welcome those who can domesticate, who can secularize the mystery and summons of creation" (39). The secondary has become our "narcotic. Like sleepwalkers, we are guarded by the numbing drone of the journalistic, of the theoretical, from the harsh, imperious radiance of sheer presence" (49). Will we not flinch, then, when a Steiner comes along urging us to lower our guard?

If we are to regain our full humanity, we must, according to Steiner, relearn what is involved in the authentic experience of aesthetic creation. It is to the illumination of that task that he turns in the third and final chapter of **Real Presences.** The first chapter outlines the horrors of the secondary city and develops a wry and purely heuristic fantasy of banning all commentary on art; in the second chapter Steiner provides a kind of intellectual history of how we came to our present pass.

Historians of various stripes will undoubtedly quarrel with Steiner's choice of seminal moments and events, but his outline strikes me as wonderfully suggestive. We are now, he says, at one of those rare periods in which there is a true break in the history of human perception. From the 1870s to the 1930s one begins to observe the first massive cracks in the ancient trust that there is a relation between word and world, between language and reality. Until the 1870s even the most extreme versions of skepticism maintained their trust in language, in the relation between *logos* and *cosmos*. The earliest watersheds in the disintegration of that consensus are "Mallarmé's disjunction of language from external reference and . . . Rimbaud's deconstruction of the first person singular" (94). Perhaps most decisively in Rimbaud's "je est un autre" ("I is an/other") we encounter the breakdown of the very notion of an identifiable self. This move not only undermines any conception of authorship (*auctoritas*); it also severs the aesthetic from the ethical. For if a self is finally a fiction, where could one possibly locate responsibility,

for either an author or a reader? It is this break, Steiner claims, that "defines modernity itself" (93). We now live *after* the word, in an age of "*epilogue*" (94).

It should not be surprising, then, to discover that Derrida associates meaningful semantic signs with divinity. "The age of the sign," Steiner quotes him as claiming, "is essentially theological" (120). Steiner agrees; indeed, he rests his argument on the necessity of establishing just such a theologically based view of language, which Derrida, of course, would consider hopelessly naïve and nostalgic. But for Steiner there is no middle ground: "The break with the postulate of the sacred is the break with any stable, potentially ascertainable meaning of meaning" (132).

Four years ago, in a retrospective piece in which he justly suggests that no other contemporary critic has more "speculative power, verbal texture, [or] cultural insight" than Steiner, Ihab Hassan contends that "Steiner is too much part of our secular, agnostic, vaguely rationalist, uneasily humanist, community of letters to evince an unseemly preoccupation with transcendence" ("The Whole Mystery of Babel: On George Steiner," *Salmagundi,* 70-71, [Spring-Summer 1986]: 333, 331). Though Hassan certainly underestimates the importance of the transcendent in Steiner, one can understand why. Steiner is, after all, as sophisticated and cosmopolitan as anyone on the current intellectual/literary scene. P. F. Strawson may be right when he claims that Steiner "has perhaps read more widely in cognate fields than anyone else alive" ("Take the B Train," rev. of *Heidegger* and *On Difficulty and Other Essays,* by George Steiner, *New York Review of Books,* 19 April 1979: 36). For much of his career Steiner has been ridiculed by Lilliputians envious of his staggering learning and irked by the fact that he has managed to stay in touch not only with the latest developments in virtually all of the arts but also with the frontiers of a dozen academic fields. Small wonder, then, that it should cause a certain cognitive dissonance to hear this most contemporary of our contemporaries proclaiming on the first page of his new book, published late in the twentieth century, that "any coherent understanding of what language is and how language performs" must finally be "underwritten by the assumption of God's presence" (3).

Steiner is, of course, aware that a notion of "real presence"—a conception borrowed, after all, from eucharistic theology—may appear to be mystical; but he insists on appealing to common sense, particularly to the actual experience of anyone who has ever been inhabited by a melody, a painting, or a poem. What is it that "happens inside oneself," he wants to know, "as one affords vital welcome and habitation to the presences in art, music and literature" (178)? "The encounter with the aesthetic is, together with certain modes of religious and metaphysical experience, the most 'ingressive', transformative summons available to human experiencing. . . . If we have heard rightly the wing-beat and provocation of that visit, the house is no longer habitable in quite the same way as it was before" (143). We may feel embarrassment in "bearing witness to the poetic, to the entrance into our lives of the mystery of otherness in art," but that embarrassment, Steiner insists, "is of a metaphysical-religious kind" (178).

The focus of Steiner's last and most important chapter is on the mysterious but sacred process by which we actually encounter a work of art when we are honoring the ethics of reception. It is in these pages that Steiner's ability to describe exactly what it is like to be seriously engaged with a poem, a statue, or a concerto is in full flower. Though in many ways this chapter develops a phenomenology of serious reading, the central form for Steiner, here and throughout the book, is music, which is not only the most irreducible of the arts but also, as Levi-Strauss has said, the closest kin to "the supreme mystery of man."

Since understanding for Steiner is a profoundly moral act, the experience of art must always be one of "answerability," of "responding responsibility" (8). Steiner does not put it in precisely this way, but it seems to me that his model here is a kind of gift exchange, according to which the experiencing of a work of art is analogous to the proper reception of a gift. The reader, that is to say, opens himself or herself to the "real presence," the spirit of the text, providing the sort of welcome that is associated with the full ritualistic significance of hospitality. "The informing agency is that of *tact,* of the ways in which we allow ourselves to touch or not to touch, to be touched or not to be touched by the presence of the other" (148). Steiner is at his best here as he weaves elaborate and resonant parallels with the arts of hospitality in human relations generally:

> We lay a clean cloth on the table when we hear the guest at our threshold. . . . What we must focus . . . on the text, on the work of art, on the music before us, is . . . a courtesy of the most robust and refined sort. . . . The numinous intimations which relate hospitality to religious feeling in countless cultures and societies, the intuition that the true reception of a guest, of a known stranger in our place of being touches on transcendent obligations and opportunities, helps us to understand the experiencing of created form.
>
> (148-49, 155)

Steiner realizes that he has not refuted deconstruction, and he is fully aware that he has had to revert to "constant enlistment of images, similes, metaphors" which deconstructionists could readily deconstruct. But on the secular level, given their premises, deconstructionist claims simply cannot be answered. Steiner concedes that his own position cannot be proved either logically or evidentially, but that, he says, is true of

"every essential aspect of human existence" (214)—of explanations of birth as well as death, of eros as well as identity. Without presence, "certain dimensions of thought and creativity are no longer attainable. . . . We must read *as if*" (229).

If we do so, if we take this interpretive leap of faith, we will not find the meaning of this poem or that painting to be unitary and absolute. Interpretation for Steiner is always provisional and tentative, never complete. He does not seek to replace deconstruction's infinite open-endedness with a reactionary assertion of stable, singular, and exhaustive meaning. Instead he presents a third alternative, whereby the assumption of presence in art both makes meaning possible and prevents dogmatic reductionism. "There is, there can be no end to interpretive disagreement and revision," he says. "But where it is seriously engaged in, the process of differing is one which cumulatively circumscribes and clarifies the disputed ground. It is . . . the irreducible autonomy of presence, of 'otherness', in art and text which denies either adequate paraphrase or unanimity of finding" (214).

The hermeneutic model here is human relations more generally, and here again Steiner strikes me as both acute and compelling. "Our encounter with the freedom of presence in another human being . . . will always entail approximation. . . . The congruence is never complete. It is never uniform with its object. If it was, the act of reception would be wholly equivalent to that of original enunciation. Our guest would have nothing to bring us. . . . The falling-short is a guarantor of the experienced 'otherness'. . . ." (175) Steiner refers in this connection to Keats's conception of "negative capability," which is an imperative to be open simultaneously to meaning and to mystery, or in Steiner's terms, a summons to "inhabit the tentative" (176). The proper posture "is that of the expectant, of the risks of trust taken in the decision to open a door" (177).[1]

That Steiner himself decided to open a door and take a risk in this book is perfectly clear. Though no one else could have written it, though his signature is everywhere in it, and its connection with his earlier work is profound, ***Real Presences*** is Steiner's most daring book because its entire argument rests on a claim that, as he well knows, most intellectuals will not take seriously. To call this book reactionary would be a bit like calling *King Lear* reactionary on the issue of suffering. Unlike most other critics of deconstruction, Steiner faces up to its darkest implications without flinching. If he comes out on the other side, it is because he has passed through its corroding fires rather than circumventing them.

One wishes that Steiner had been more precise in his use of the terms *transcendent, metaphysical,* and *theological,* which he tends to use interchangeably; and one also wishes that he were not quite so reticent about whether his "as if" is indeed an equivalent to faith. But *Real Presences* is that rarest of contemporary works: a book that is unembarrassed about its wide learning, but humble about its own status in relation to great art; that is unafraid to take on the largest issues, but willing to argue its ambitious claims patiently and illustrate them with richly textured references to personal experience; that is undaunted by critical theory, but insistent that it not overshadow the truly creative. Both in its luxuriant details and its extraordinary reach, *Real Presences* is, with the possible exception of *After Babel,* Steiner's most ambitious and important book. That it is also likely to be controversial is as much as to say that it was written by George Steiner.

Note

1. Steiner's effort to reunite ethics and criticism, and to do so partly by analogy with human relationships, shares something with Wayne Booth's massive *The Company We Keep: An Ethics of Fiction* (Berkeley: U of California P, 1988).

Frank Burch Brown (review date January 1991)

SOURCE: Brown, Frank Burch. "The Startling Testimony of George Steiner." *Theology Today* 47, no. 4 (January 1991): 419-23.

[*In the following review, Brown assesses the content, logic, and rhetoric of* Real Presences.]

Those who are watching the signs of the times will have noticed that, as this century enters its last decade, a number of scientists, philosophers, politicians, and artists have once again become openly interested in God and in various modes of religiosity. Nevertheless, the testimony offered in the latest book by one of our leading interpreters of literature and culture is, in this regard, both unexpected and audacious.

George Steiner's *Real Presences* [. . .] is a signal work whose importance is disproportionate to its modest length of 236 pages. Its author, writing in a manner that is unmistakably personal, impassioned, and religiously engaged, sets himself apart from the literary theorists currently in ascendancy—theorists for whom the terms "religious" and "theological" invariably connote something rigid and dead. Although Steiner's specific claims and lines of reasoning are by no means unproblematical, they deserve the considerable attention they are likely to receive from theologians and humanists alike.

What Steiner proposes and explores is the idea that any coherent account of meaning in language and experience must be "underwritten by the assumption of God's presence." Focusing on the arts in particular, he argues that both the making of meaningful art and the experience of significant artworks implicitly assume the "necessary possibility" of transcendence. Artistic creation emulates and distantly rivals the activity of God, the primordial and perhaps perpetual creator. In turn, our encounter with creative artworks puts us in touch with meanings that are most meaningful. These meanings (to put the matter baldly) have to do with the mysteries of life, death, and God. Transcending the sheerly pragmatic and empirical, they are vital to all serious engagement with the arts. Accordingly, Steiner suggests that any reasonably adequate hermeneutics or aesthetics is bound to be at least incipiently theological. To reckon responsibly with great literature, music, and art is to invoke a theology concerned with the real presence in the symbolic object and with the genuine mystery in the form.

While Steiner's overt theologizing comes as a surprise, it must be said that he gave advance notice—particularly in the introduction to his volume of 1984 entitled *George Steiner: A Reader.* There, Steiner observes that, from the time of his first book, *Tolstoy or Dostoevsky* (1959), he has always seen a connection between the possibility of meaningful art and the possibility of transcendence. In the same context, he announces his intention to flesh out this thesis more fully, in the conviction that we probably cannot get much further in our "poetics of understanding" without "an acknowledged transcendence." Our leading thinkers and readers, such as Walter Benjamin and Martin Heidegger, draw heavily on the fund of an undeclared theology. It is time, he says, to make a deposit on this hidden spiritual, metaphysical, and linguistic loan, to offer at least the collateral of an avowed faith.

After 1984, but still prior to *Real Presences,* several of Steiner's occasional pieces seem to have been deposits intended to reduce this theological indebtedness. There is, for instance, his remarkable review of *The Literary Guide to the Bible,* edited by Robert Alter and Frank Kermode, which appeared January 11, 1988 in *The New Yorker.* Steiner takes this opportunity to argue forthrightly that, for all the obvious merits of the urbane, academic literary criticism that is now brought to bear on Holy Scripture, such criticism remains relatively trivial because it fails to acknowledge the terror and *mysterium tremendum* of theophany, prophecy, and passion narrative. It is not possible, Steiner declares, to distinguish neatly between a literary and a theological-religious experiencing of biblical texts. Therefore, literary biblical criticism, even when secular, needs somehow to face the religious claims of the text, including the "plain question of divine inspiration."

All this comes from the pen (or processor) of someone whose institutional connections are thoroughly academic and secular. Extraordinary Fellow of Churchill College,

Cambridge, and professor of English and Comparative Literature at the University of Geneva, Steiner also has affiliations with Harvard, Oxford, Princeton, and Chicago. Surrounded by predominantly secular colleagues, Steiner must repeatedly remind himself—and others—not to flinch from the task of what amounts to a kind of religious testimony. Confessing his lingering metaphysical-religious embarrassment at bearing witness "to the poetic, to the entrance into our lives of the mystery of otherness in art and in music," Steiner nevertheless asserts: "the attempt at testimony must be made and the ridicule incurred."

Far easier to be detached and ironic. To be otherwise is to come under the suspicion of craving "not only an infantile simplicity but the old, cruel demons of dogma." Anticipating this suspicion, Steiner lets it be known that there is nothing he fears more than religious fundamentalism and kitsch ideologies. As a non-Orthodox Jewish intellectual nurtured on Central European humanism of a sort that was virtually extinguished in the Second World War, Steiner abhors an authoritarian mind-set. His particular allegiance to "truth-fictions" precludes treating them as dogmas.

Even so, Steiner rejects any mentality that would retreat from all fidelities into skeptical irresponsibility and obscurantism. He disdains our present preoccupation with intellectual games, as evidenced in our countless books about books about books. He declines to take part in the sophisticated but cynical playfulness of what he describes as the newest dance around the Ark, in which the dancers suppose they know that the Ark is empty.

If we are to play, Steiner challenges us to make our play serious in the end. He asks for us to join him in making a wager that meaning, as in myth and music, exceeds the bounds of clear-cut ideas and empirical verification. This would be a wager that God (or what "God" names) underwrites the trust we inevitably place in words and in what lies beyond words, whether tragic or redemptive.

Steiner realizes that the basic premises underlying such claims are no more susceptible of proof than they are of falsification. Perhaps this is why his discourse in ***Real Presences*** makes little use of rigorous argumentation and why his exposition is so flagrantly unsystematic. Be that as it may, he clearly hopes that if he can provoke us into being more *responsible* in our response to artistic and cultural legacies—if he can tempt us to approach works of art with a sort of love and welcoming courtesy (*cortesia*)—we may undergo a "nativity of consciousness."

Aware that such notions can easily sound romantic and vaporous, Steiner defends himself partly by attacking as illusory the notion that so-called theories of language and art can somehow aspire to the clarity and rigor of theories in the natural sciences. At the same time, Steiner makes a considerable effort to describe and confront honestly the major developments in modern thought that would call into question basic assumptions underlying any kind of theology of meaning or metaphysics of presence.

Obviously Steiner, unlike the deconstructionists, wants to find a way to own these metaphysical assumptions rather than to disown them. Yet he acknowledges that this has become more and more difficult. By the late nineteenth century, a truly fundamental break in human perception appears. The break comes with an increasing loss of trust in the possibility of significant relations between word and world. Adopting a skepticism more radical than any before, we begin to think of language as closed in on itself. Thus, we enter a time of after-Word, of epilogue and absence (which Steiner's talk of presences never tries to obscure). At least among many of the intelligentsia, there is consciousness not of a real presence of Logos/God, but only of "the play of sounds and markers amid the mutations of time." Such skepticism lies at the heart of the theological and metaphysical repudiations central to deconstruction and anticipated by Nietzsche, Mallarmé, Rimbaud, and numerous others.

Steiner cannot pretend to be able to refute such extreme skepticism on its own terms. Nor has he any wish to replace it with credulity that sees itself as basking in pure presence beyond all absence. Such an option is not open to one who, having once described himself as (metaphorically speaking) a "survivor" of the holocaust, has devoted a significant portion of his fiction and prose to themes of loss and tragedy. No, the most Steiner can do is attempt to awaken a dormant sense of the "edge of presence" in God's absence, and a concomitant sense that "where God's presence is no longer a tenable supposition and where His absence is no longer a felt, indeed overwhelming weight, certain dimensions of thought and creativity are no longer attainable."

It is striking that the rhetoric Steiner employs to stir us from metaphysical slumber incorporates at least as many Christian images as Jewish, weaving them together in a nontraditional or cross-traditional pattern. Just as Steiner refers to Moses, the Ark of the Covenant, the Talmud, rabbinical commentary, and modern messianic hopes, he also refers to sacrament, annunciation, nativity, epiphany, real presence, passion, resurrection. While his Jewish heritage may influence Steiner's judgment that the day which best symbolizes our human existence can be called Saturday (a day he then alludes to in terms of "Sabbatarian" pain and hope), Steiner carefully locates this day in relation to two Christian days and the realities they symbolize: Friday (the day of injustice and radical suffering) and Sunday (the day of resurrection, love, and justice). The Christian theologian and scholar could well envy this ability to think and imagine in terms of multiple traditions.

As has already been observed—and as might be expected in a work of this kind—the testimony of *Real Presences* is at times peculiar and imbalanced. There is an admitted masculine bias in Steiner's agonistic picture of artistic and divine creativity, which is frustratingly sketchy. And Steiner gives little consideration to the possible limitations of his exclusively Western range of reference. With respect to Western art and thought, he settles too quickly for sweeping generalizations that hide the heterogeneity of traditions. He is too ready to dismiss popular arts as uniformly vacuous. And though he regards classics as open to critique, Steiner is very much inclined (like Paul Tillich before him) to give them all a halo of religious significance. Finally, he does little to explain why the very possibility of meaning *per se* should depend on the real presence of God. The momentum that Steiner needs in order to break free of the pull of secularism can carry him too far, albeit on a trajectory hard to trace.

In some circles, Steiner's ideas will doubtless be dismissed as plainly supernaturalist, elitist, and sexist; as theocentric, logocentric, and phallocentric. Yet *Real Presences* is much more exploratory than any easy criticism—or easy adulation—would suggest, subtly unsettling conventional notions of God, word, and human capacities and desires. It is also more artfully written than commentary can possibly convey. Perhaps the most important thing about the book, however, is not what is finally said, or exactly how it is said, but the fact that it is said at all, and by someone of widely recognized intellectual stature. Whatever Steiner's faults as a witness, his new work helps to legitimize and motivate nondogmatic theological reflection within the academic study of history and culture. By calling attention to persistent religious implications in language and art, Steiner testifies memorably for those who refuse to accept epilogue as the last word.

Harold Fromm (review date summer 1991)

SOURCE: Fromm, Harold. Review of *Real Presences*, by George Steiner. *Georgia Review* 45, no. 2 (summer 1991): 398-403.

[*In the following review, Fromm questions the necessity and efficacy of* Real Presences, *finding the book "troubling."*]

George Steiner's *Real Presences* is an heroic, somewhat desperate attempt to part the Red Sea of postmodernism and conduct the faithful to a new Promised Land of postdeconstructive meaningfulness. Can it be done without seeming reactionary? Can it be done at all? Should it even be attempted?

The last question is the easiest to address: Western society, particularly the Anglo-American variety, appears to have lost all the traditional generators of cultural value—apart from moneymaking—that give meaning to daily life. The older, established religions cling to obsolete metaphysics that are seldom reflected in practice; the more vital denominations are neoevangelical crudities that worship money, varieties of fascism, or both. High culture is widely regarded as obsolescent; opera and concert music as anachronistic, elitist, and Eurocentric; and "the ideology of the aesthetic" (to use Terry Eagleton's sinister phrase) as little more than a smokescreen for upper-class patriarchal hegemony over the lower orders.

The arts in general, which had served as surrogates for declining religious beliefs since the Enlightenment, have been taken over by a rootless academia that has largely sold itself as a commodity agent of the Information Society in return for professional success. As Steiner himself puts it, "In their scale of bureaucratic formalization, of funding, in their eager pretence to theoretical rigour and cumulative discovery, the humanities in our universities and institutes of advanced studies strive obsessively to rival the high good fortunes of the exact and the applied sciences. This striving, and the mendacious notion of research which it entails, are themselves founded in the positivism and 'scientism' of the nineteenth century." The result for Steiner is that the living arts have become grist for unending secondary and tertiary commentary, in the form of criticism and scholarship: in place of the "real presence" of the work of art itself, "essay speaks to essay, article chatters to article in an endless gallery of querulous echo. . . . How can personal sensibility go upstream, to the living springs of 'first being?' Does such an image of the primal have any legitimacy?"

Indeed, except for performances by actors or musicians—whom Steiner regards as the primary interpreters of the arts, interpreters whose hermeneutics are "real presences," *lived* rather than talked about—the criticism industry has supplanted original works with open-ended and parasitic secondariness. Reading, writing, and conferences *about* art now take the place of the artworks themselves, while providing incomes for the commentators whose commentary squelches the primary sources. But the literary (and other) theory that has dominated the humanities in recent years is not really theory at all, Steiner tells us, because it is not subject to verifiability or potential falsification. Most of what passes for theory in the humanities, he believes, is actually a form of pseudoscientific *description*, often mixed with polemics.

Although Steiner does not see the arts as falling into the rationalist paradigms established by Descartes, Newton, or Kant, he does find that until recently a belief in the connection between word and world—a belief that words pointed to a reality apart from the acts of verbal reference—had been able to coexist with the long philosophic tradition of skepticism as well as with rationalism's narrowing of the areas in which certainty could be obtained. Moreover, the assumed referentiality of words gave cosmic weight to poetry and philosophy as well as to the hard sciences. But according to Steiner, "It is this break of the covenant between word and world which constitutes one of the very few genuine revolutions of spirit in Western history and which defines modernity itself."

After discussing such stepping stones toward this modernity as Wittgenstein, psychoanalysis, Saussurean linguistics, and Heidegger, Steiner moves on to deconstruction—which he uses as a generic term for the replacement of "real presences" with the absence that results from the attack on logocentrism. The argument of this attack is that words refer only to other words and never to independent "things" in an outside world (which is unknowable apart from these words); thus, it has become customary to say that the guarantee of a reality always assumed to stand behind our words is no longer in operation. Of course, there never really was such a guarantee, which at best was purely phantasmal and hypothetical, but now that it has been explicitly repudiated, talk has come to be considered as not much more than talk, with literally nothing behind it except more talk. "God the Father of meaning, in His authorial guise, is gone from the game: there is no longer any privileged judge, interpreter or explicator who can determine and communicate the truth, the true intent of the matter."

Steiner is by no means prepared to quarrel with this widespread point of view, which more than half of his book is at pains to delineate, even though he sees deconstruction as self-invalidating because of its *own* logocentrism. After his deft but dispirited exposition of current academic paradigms of reality, however, his main interest is to find some basis for value with which to circumvent the infinite reverberations of nothingness that many intellectuals are willing to grant as the nature of the case. This is one rough job, not to be pulled off by some fly-by-night academic clone—and thus we come back to my original questions: should it and can it be done?

For starters, George Steiner is nobody's clone, academic or otherwise. On the contrary, he is a prime contender for the role of Western culture's number one polymath, wise in both the arts and sciences. As one of the most sensitive registers of the arts we have, he is hardly in a position to feel that the cause of his aesthetic experi-

ences is simply Nothing. Nor is it negligible that for him it is music that lies at the heart of everything most potent and real; how can a person who feels its presence in the involuntary pulsations of his blood believe that so powerful a sense of Being is simply so much baloney?

As affect-driven as art may seem, however, for Steiner it is "a phenomenon *of freedom*"—that is, it chooses to come into being out of virtual nothingness because of a pressing ethical mission in the artist. This freedom is matched by the comparable freedom of aesthetic response in the reader or listener, and the resulting experience takes place somewhere between the absolute meaning that deconstruction denies and the endless free-play that it claims is all there is. After rightly complaining that contemporary academic criticism is unconcerned with the personal nature of this experience—with its cultural, bodily, and erotic roots—Steiner expresses a willingness to face ridicule as he attempts to explain "that the embarrassment we feel in bearing witness to the poetic, to the entrance into our lives of the mystery of otherness in art and in music, is of a metaphysical-religious kind" because of our intuition that artists look freshly at Being itself, while the population at large experiences life in the terms these artists have already set forth.

In the course of his exposition, Steiner leads us to a dilemma: on one hand, the deconstructive dismantling of logocentrism is, he freely admits, irrefutable. On the other hand, the deconstructive explanation is "false to human experience," an experience involving an irreducible "autonomy of presence, of 'otherness'" in works of art (most powerfully in music) which is felt as pure meaningfulness, transcendent and god-ridden: the energy of Being itself, "a logic of sense other than that of reason," and "finally religious."

Steiner's increasing importation of religious language should come as no great surprise to careful readers, since he informs them on the very first page of this book that "the capacity of human speech to communicate meaning and feeling is, in the final analysis, underwritten by the assumption of God's presence." Yet they may well feel both astonished and betrayed when they reach the final numinous pages, coming as these do after so judicious and forthright an exposition of the self-contradictions of contemporary intellectual life. Indeed, Steiner himself is fully aware that he is in for trouble: "I know," he observes, "that this formulation will be unacceptable not only to most of those who will read a book such as this, but also to the prevailing climate of thought and of feeling in our culture." Why does this powerful book end up by resolving itself into an elaborate failure despite its author's prescience and genius?

To begin with, as eloquent, rich, deeply felt, and informed as Steiner's argument may be, there is little in it that is new. In 1976, for instance, Murray Krieger's *Theory of Criticism* came to similar conclusions. And since then, there have been many other books and essays written about not only the nihilism of deconstruction but its increasing self-invalidation as well. Steiner, however, goes much farther than Krieger and the others through what amounts to an unlooked-for introduction of a variety of "Credo quia impossibile est," intimating (like Tertullian) that one must believe even though the opposing stance is irrefutable. That is, the matter of art is in the last analysis a question of faith in one's own experience, which reports that the power of music is no illusion but the most real thing in the world.

What *is* novel here is Steiner's regressive importation of "transcendent," "God," "religion," and "theology," words he uses only in the vaguest, most metaphorical and mystified ways. Never literally meaning any of them, he wants the aroma—the aura—they exude. No consequences (beyond an Arnoldian high seriousness now in disfavor) follow from his use of these words because they are completely empty except as affective figures of speech: his God is not really God, his transcendence has no literal characteristics he can clearly name apart from his own feelings, his religion has no tenets or contents. In place of any discursive support he merely provides heated assertions and instant fiats. This is the old game of highbrow intellectuals taking over certain anachronistic doctrines—from Catholicism, say, or Marxism—and transforming them into unrecognizable and rarefied cults that the Pope or Marx would radically repudiate. There is thus a certain element of disingenuousness in maneuvers of this sort, whereby you can have your cake (by not subscribing to the vulgar version) and eat it too (by reappropriating its afflatus for an elitist ritual and claiming that yours is the *authentic* version). But the adoption of a defiantly resurrected antique vocabulary changes nothing, except that instead of saying "absence" at point *b* in your sentence, you say "presence"; instead of "nonrepresentational," you say "transcendent." Does such wordplay really matter?

Still, however regressive Steiner may seem, he is hardly to be dismissed as a reactionary, since he acknowledges the internal logic of the mentality for which "deconstruction" is a generic name. But he doesn't think it accounts for enough, because it excludes too much of what we experience as reality: people in fact communicate very decently every day, understand what they read quite adequately, and get along in the quotidian world remarkably well—even, I might add, without the "presence" that Steiner is trying to rescue. Deconstruction's flaw, one could well argue, has always been that it speaks about a *perfect* communication that never existed, whereas imperfect communication is all we

ever needed. Deconstruction had interesting things to say, but by the time it became apparent that the movement had set itself up as a new transcendental signifier, it was already on the wane. The answer to deconstruction is not to slap it in the face with God and presence and similar shopworn mystifications, but either to show its faulty thinking (or irrelevance), or to let it quietly die. Although Steiner's approach may provide uplift, it serves no one well. People who think they know all about God and transcendence will also think that in Steiner they have acquired a new ally (which they haven't, since he would regard them as infra dig), and people who don't care very much about those things will yawn and turn elsewhere for enlightenment.

Real Presences is thus a troubling book: a preeminent intelligence feelingly reviews old problems, intimates new solutions, yet finally produces an intellectual's counterpart of "Just say no to drugs!" But it takes more than recycled mythologies to kick destructive habits, to inaugurate new cultural epochs, or to make the center regain its hold. Meanwhile, we can likely live a good enough life without delusive foundations, or if not we can keep on waiting for Godot.

Paul Hollander (review date winter 1994)

SOURCE: Hollander, Paul. "Coping with the Loss of Political Faith." *Modern Age* 36, no. 2 (winter 1994): 183-90.

[*In the following review, Hollander critiques the novella* Proofs, and Three Parables, *focusing on its representation of the psychological dimension of communism's decline in Eastern Europe.*]

It is a curious aspect of Western intellectual and literary life that, while the disillusionment with the Soviet Union between the 1930s and 1950s had stimulated a substantial outpouring of writings, the subsequent discrediting of other communist systems has not produced similar public soul-searching. In vain would one look for volumes addressing retrospectively the grotesque infatuation with Mao's China, Castro's Cuba, communist Vietnam, and Sandinista Nicaragua, each of which had earlier inspired an abundance of devotional literature. Similarly forgotten are the accolades stimulated by "African socialism" and its putative embodiments in countries such as Tanzania, communist Angola, and Mozambique.

It is not easy to explain why many Western intellectuals found it easier to confront their misguided affection for the Soviet Union (and the communist movements it supported abroad) than to acknowledge similar lapses of judgment and common sense as regards the other communist states which, at least initially, modeled themselves after the Soviet Union. Not even the recent collapse of Soviet communism has sufficed to inspire public discussion and candid examination of why and how such regimes could have attracted and enchanted segments of the educated public in the West and especially many intellectuals.

In the United States, at any rate, the cultural-institutional after-effects of the 1960s best explain why such discussions failed to take place. During the 1960s the attitude of anti-anti-communism among large portions of the American intelligentsia became institutionalized, a disposition that became part of an entrenched and expanded adversary culture. Since the public display or avowal of anti-communist sentiment came to be discouraged and virtually proscribed among self-respecting liberal academic intellectuals (and their audiences), the atmosphere has been far from congenial for public self-scrutiny aimed at understanding why communist systems and ideologies—despite their massive and proven flaws—exercised such abiding attraction for so many American intellectuals. In turn the impressive growth in the numbers of those who came to constitute the adversary culture, clustered around universities and other cultural institutions, made it easier for erstwhile admirers of these systems to live with their old beliefs and avoid feeling compunction over political misjudgments which were so widely shared. There have been millions of people with similar beliefs, biases, hopes, and disappointments not in the least inclined to reevaluate these beliefs since they constituted a critical mass large enough to sustain them. Even if the communist systems collapsed and became totally discredited among their own people anti-communism was not to be rehabilitated in these circles.

Although a fair amount has been written of late about the political and economic costs and consequences of the collapse of communism (as distinct from its attractions for Western intellectuals and their followers), little is known about the emotional impact this collapse had on those who used to believe in the communist ideals and their existing incarnations. George Steiner's *Proofs* [*Proofs, and Three Parables*] may well be the first successful literary attempt in the West to chronicle and probe the psychological dimensions of and responses to the decay of communism.

The other "three parables" in this volume deal with different topics and are on the whole far less memorable; they are exercises in erudition and literary, or literary-philosophical, virtuosity. They have little in common with one another or with *Proofs*.

Proofs may be read as a meditation on the interaction between spiritual needs, political commitment, and disillusionment in contemporary Western societies. It is a "parable" of the political beliefs and attachments of Western intellectuals and their pursuit of meaning in an increasingly secular and consumption-oriented world. Although none of the characters (former supporters of the Italian Communist Party) are portrayed—sociologically speaking,—as typical intellectuals, they act and talk as if they were.

Proofs is the story of the changing *and* unchanging political attitudes of an Italian master printer, also known as "*Professore*" on account of his erudition and articulateness. He is an appealing and interesting figure who combines modesty, meticulousness, devotion to work, and a rigidly but satisfactorily routinized life with intense political convictions and an abstracted idealism. His political ideals and attitudes are more characteristic of the mind set of a privileged academic intellectual than an Italian working class printer. Like many memorable literary heroes he, too, is a somewhat tragic character, compassionate yet fallible, unprotected by his theoretical knowledge from a basic wrongheadedness, irresistibly drawn to bonds and beliefs which sooner or later will fail him. On top of it all, his eyesight—the key to his work and pursuit of meaning in life (the printed matter)—is beginning to fail him and gets worse as the story unfolds. It is not clear what precisely this metaphoric device intends to convey: it could mean that he achieves greater insight with poorer eyesight, or his worsening vision could symbolize his resistance to confronting the new, unwelcome political realities.

This is also a novella about a group of people politically associated with the printer who are also trying to cope with the loss of faith and the erosion of political community set into motion by the developments in the Soviet Bloc and its final collapse. They include Anna B. (the statistician), a priest (Father Carlo Tessone), a school teacher, and an engineer. They do not seem to include authentic representatives of the proletariat. Evidently the group is constituted by what might be called quasi-intellectuals or aspiring intellectuals and one authentic, if exceptional, member of the working classes, the learned printer. Grappling with the political events of the late 1980s in what used to be the Soviet Bloc, the actors debate the major political-philosophical conflicts and dilemmas of our times.

The events in Eastern Europe deliver the final blow to their faith; the group disbands. Concurrently, the hero, the erudite proof reader, undergoes a process of physical decline and especially a deterioration of his eyesight. The story somewhat unexpectedly ends with his pursuit of admission (or re-admission) into the new and unauthentic incarnation of what used to be the Italian communist party, now called the "Party of the Democratic Left."

Contemporary political infatuation and disaffection with communism is a vast topic particularly when it includes both those who lived under such systems and those who admired them from afar. Paradoxically, the outlook of those who had lived under the now defunct communist regimes is more accessible, less intriguing, and easier to grasp than the convoluted sentiments of former true believers in the West. Steiner wisely chose to concentrate on a sample of the latter, whose beliefs are presented in the process of erosion or collapse.

Such groups of true believers would have been difficult to locate, or plausibly conjure up, in the former communist states. True believers have long been extinct in the countries where the attempt was made to realize their beliefs. It defies the imagination and even memory, at this historical juncture, to visualize any group of people in what used to be the Soviet Bloc, who would gather regularly to discuss reverentially the ideas of Marx, as do the characters in this book in their Circle for Revolutionary Theory and Praxis.

Similar groups are far from extinct in the West. They are most readily found (under various designations) on or about college campuses rather than in big cities and least of all in working-class neighborhoods. They are descendants of what used to be the "New Left" and the counterculture; their most striking attribute is a combination of the (by now) traditional hatred of capitalism with a loss of faith in reason and rationality that represents a radical departure from the perspectives of the Marxism of the old left.

Western responses to the fall of communism are morbidly fascinating, untainted as they are by the actual experience of living under these systems. Such beliefs have been more "pure" and driven primarily by unfulfilled spiritual longings, a misdirected idealism, and more or less obscure psychological needs. In the East it was harder to separate disinterested or "pure" belief from opportunism, since survival, let alone success, required a show of belief and support for the system. Western communists, including party members—unlike their counterparts in countries run by these parties—could not, as a rule, expect better jobs, housing, or other tangible benefits on account of their political beliefs and positions. On the other hand, it has become of late useful in the United States for one's career in academia to adhere to some form of watered down leftism, to signal that one is a member in good standing of the adversary culture. These attitudes do not require taking Marxist ideas seriously. It has been sufficient to convey that one dislikes American society and capitalism in order to be accepted by a subculture which has gradually become dominant in academic institutions and has come to play a part in distributing the rewards academics seek and receive.

Steiner chose the Italian master printer with a life of long commitment to the theory and practice of communism (insofar as Party work was a form of practice) and the group around him to present a literary case study of what happens to true believers when the objects of belief disintegrate. In doing so he leads the reader into a long forgotten political culture: the world of Party loyalists and activists diligently and dutifully attending meetings, reverently poring over the "classics," analyzing current events through the lens of their political correctness. They are people for whom joining the Party was a pivotal event of their lives, an admission "into that freemasonry of hope," providing access to community and brotherhood. Following the death of Stalin the characters in this story "had become orphans huddled in somber bewilderment." Subsequently, despite his fine mind and germinating doubts, the *Professore* defends Soviet intervention in Hungary in 1956 since its purpose was to crush the "CIA financed coup" which has "the evident potential for a Fascist resurgence."

Despite a long record of disciplined loyalty the point comes when *Professore* can no longer stomach the dictates of the Party and the deeds of its great role model and ally; he is incapable of approving of the Soviet intervention in Czechoslovakia in 1968. (We do not learn from the narrative why that was less acceptable than the Soviet crackdown in Hungary, why it became the final disillusioning experience he could not rationalize in the time-honored ways). Awaiting his expulsion from the Party, "he had sat in his room, motionless, made stone. He had sat like a paralytic, his temples pounding as in cold fever. Knowing that he was being read out of the scroll of the saved, of the elect to hope and meaning. The loneliness of that hour branded him irreparably. It was more solitary than death."

It was the disillusionment with Soviet policies that led to the formation of the Circle for Marxist Revolutionary Theory and Praxis, numbering less than twenty active members. In it the faithful gathered to salvage and renew their commitment and continue their earnest discussions of matters largely theoretical. Thus, Comrade Anna B., by occupation a statistician at the psychiatric social service of the General Clinic, treats her comrades to an analysis of "the radical differences in social infrastructure and peer-group communication as between coffee drawn from, and consumed near, a mechanical dispenser and that brewed in one's own kitchen and poured into one's own cups for a neighbor . . . :" She also raises a troubling question, "What had Marxist and Gramscian sociology to contribute to a better understanding of these gender-bounded and gender-oriented socializations? Had Kautsky or C. Wright Mills said anything to the point?"

The tone and the topics of these meetings conjure up the ambience of campus-based feminist (and other radical-left) groups in the United States rather than the plausible gatherings of former Party activists in a quasi-working class setting in a large Northern Italian city. We are reminded of communications in faculty lounges or English department meetings rather than of the deliberations and debates of former communist activists in an Italian center of industry and commerce. Still, given the content and the quality of these discussions, one inclines to overlook the questionable authenticity of their setting.

Five pages are devoted to the Western television coverage of the events in Eastern Europe. We are left in no doubt what Steiner thinks of Western television and its reflections of the less than admirable aspects of Western culture and society, including the undignified scramble for publicity among intellectuals. For example:

> The titles, credit and presenter's overture had been breathless. Picture, action sequences, interviews, exclusive documentary footage would be shown over the next two hours to mark 'the greatest blossoming of freedom history had ever known.' There would be expert commentaries from Minister X, Professor Y, and novelist Z. They would, in turn, join a panel assembling further luminaries. . . . As the celebrated compère spoke, his mouth an almost perfect o of bounteous excitement, bursts of Beethoven deployed their great wings on the soundtrack and the chorale of the Ninth rose towards the fiercely spotlit Brandenburg gate. . . . Shots of teenagers from the east tumbling into West Berlin supermarkets, rocking in wonder before the shelves, emptying them in a sleep-walker's sweep. Bright-tinted toothpaste, lacquer for toenails, soft toilet paper in the hues of rainbow . . . jeans bleached or mended. . . .

> The first of the pundits in a professorial study. Yes. He agreed entirely. An earthquake. Promethean. The liberation of the man's spirit from the shackles of Marxist-Leninist folly and despotism . . . the camera glided tastefully behind the sage's brow to show a panorama of the Milan skyline. . . . A second break for ads. . . . The round-table which was to crown the programme had harvested politicians, more professors, the winner of this season's stellar prize for fiction. . . .

The unmistakable tone of irony is not to suggest that Steiner wants to trivialize the significance of the failure of communism. Rather, he uses the opportunity to convey his aversion to Western mass culture and media, a theme which his protagonists subsequently pick up.

The sparkling dialogues and disputes in the Circle go to the heart of the contemporary conflicts between communism and capitalism, the discontents of modernity, the various conceptions of human nature, and the quest for meaning in our times. There is, for instance, a lively debate in the Circle over the East Germans and other East Europeans abandoning their polluting Trabant vehicles at Western borders as they seek to escape their socialist societies in 1989. One member of the group asks, ". . . [W]hy do they have all those foul machines in the first place? Polluting, wasting raw materials, consuming fossil fuels. It's pure lunacy. As bad as capitalism. . . . Even the worst of these automobiles is totally beyond the reach of the Third World. . . ." He goes on to argue—as do the politically correct social critics in this country—that "superfluity enslaves," but at least he perceives wastefulness in both socialist and capitalist systems.

For the *Professore* the issue is different and more subversive: "Why can a Marxist economy, in a country with a history of industrial strength and a skilled labor force, [i.e. East Germany] not produce a satisfactory internal combustion engine and chassis? Isn't that the real question?"

More fundamental disagreements arise between *Professore* and Father Carlo, the politically incorrect or regressive priest. They clash over ends and means, the nature of American society, the subordination of the present to the future, and on the question as to who was the greater victimizer, the Church or the Party. For the Father, the fate of a single human being is decisive:

> A figure like one million means nothing. . . . Twenty-five million . . . we are told was the number of men, women, and children Stalin starved, froze, tortured to death. . . . So I focus on single human being . . . a nun they arrested for counterrevolutionary attitudes and sabotage . . . in 1937. They transported her to Kolyma, to the Arctic Circle. . . . Her feet froze to the ground . . . other women in the labour squad had to chop down her body with an axe. Her eyes were still open.

> So I do my best to make Sister Evgenia stand for 24,999,999 human beings done to hopeless death. . . . There is not, just now . . . a day when they are not digging up mass graves in the forests of the Ukraine, skulls by the ten thousands, each with a neat little bullet hole in its back. . . . That's what came of your Messiah for man. A savagery beyond understanding. . . . Arise ye prisoners of starvation. . . . So we can push you into the limepits. Break your chains. So we can flog you to death with them.

The crimes of the churches were committed

> . . . in the name of a revealed, transcendent verity. The fires were no less hot or the censorship less suffocating. I know that. . . . But those who did these hideous things were laboring to save souls. . . . They held themselves, poor imbeciles, to be God's agents. The stakes were so high, so pure and free of earthly benefit . . . but at the heart of Communism, there is a demeaning of man and woman worse than the tyrannies and depravities of Christendom, foul as these are. . . . At the heart of Communism is the lie. The central, axiomatic lie: a kingdom of justice, a classless brotherhood, a release from servitude here and now. That's the great lie. The systematic bribing and betraying of human hope.

But the learned printer will not lightly let go of what had given meaning to his life:

> Consider the source of our error. Of that great lie. And mark you, I don't accept that it was. Or that there were only venal butchers at the top. . . .
>
> Marxism did man supreme honour. The Moses and Jesus and Marx vision of the just earth, of a neighbor's love, of human universality, the abolition of barriers between lands, classes, races . . . that vision was . . . an overestimate of man. . . . A possibly fatal, possibly deranged, but none the less magnificent, jubilant over-estimate of man. The highest compliment ever paid to him. The Church held man in doleful contempt. He is a fallen creature. . . . Marxism has taken him to be almost boundless in his capacities. . . . A reacher to the stars. Not mired in original sin . . . the big error, the overestimate of man from which the mistake came, is the single most noble notion of the human spirit in our awful history.

Steiner brilliantly captures the animating spirit of Marx-ist idealism that enthralled generations of Western intel-lectuals still reluctant to give it up. Capitalism cannot be forgiven for using a far less inspiring conception of human nature that continues to offend intellectuals:

> The free market takes man at his mean average. And *mean* is the word. It invests in his animal greed. . . . It caresses his appetites for goods and comforts and mechanical toys and holidays in the sun. . . . Capital-ism has not left man where it found him, it has lessened him. We are become a pack snarling for luxuries, grunt-ing at the trough. That second car. A larger refrigerator. We are indeed possessed. . . . By unnecessary, idiotic wants. . . . That is the very genius of capitalism: to package, to put a price tag on men's dreams. . . .
>
> How accurately America has priced man, reducing him to well-being, making peace between human desires and fulfillment. Stalin starved millions. . . . But America made the hungry, the drugged, the ugly invis-ible. Which is worse? It buttered the souls of man . . . they have thirty different sorts of bread over there. . . .

These are familiar enough critiques of capitalism and American society pouring forth since the 1960s. There is an unexpectedly spirited rebuttal from Father Carlo:

> The old Party-line blood-libel on human nature and America. . . . To me it sounds like the society which says to every man and woman: Be what you want to be. Be yourself. This world was not made only for geniuses or neurotics, for the obsessed or the in-spired. . . . If you choose to try and be an artist or a thinker or a pure scholar, that's fine. . . . If you prefer to be a couch-potato, an auto-mechanic, a break dancer . . . a broker . . . a truck driver or even a drifter, that's fine too. Perhaps even better. Because it so hap-pens that ideological passion and ascetic illumination . . . have not brought only light and aid to this ap-proximate world of ours. They have sown interminable hatred and self-destruction. And when America said, 'just be yourself' . . . it is saying 'Go after the Nobel

prize if that's what fires your soul. Or that heated swim-ming pool.' Not because America believes that heated swimming pools are the Parthenon or even a necessity. But because they seem to bring pleasure, and not very much harm. . . . America is just about the first nation and society in human history to encourage common fallible, frightened humanity to feel at home in its skin.

The dialogue clarifies both the mainsprings of anti-Americanism *and* the attraction the United States continues to exercise around the world despite the bitter denunciation of intellectuals, American or foreign:

> . . . There are in American affairs black pages, stupidi-ties in plenty. But on balance America does stand as the one and only great power and community, which, unlike any other I know of, is aiming to leave the globe a little better off, a little more hopeful than it finds it. Hope has, in fact been America's gross national product and export. . . . Ask if you dare the millions who have survived under Marxism-Leninism, whether they would rather endure such a regime a day longer or be penniless immigrants to America, or even tenants to an American slum. You know the answer.

American society has often been rebuked for not taking ideas and intellectuals seriously enough. *Professore* is one among such critics. He once observed that "to exile a man because he differs from you on Hegel and on points in Party orthodoxy is proudly to honor the hu-man spirit." Communist movements and systems have taken ideas very seriously which earned them the admiration of intellectuals not living under them. Those who did were acquainted with the sometimes fatal results of this seriousness.

Father Carlo also addresses the horrors of mass culture, another venerable theme in the critiques of America:

> Like you, *Professore,* I cannot abide Rock music. My stomach turns at most television, at the plastic and porn; fast food and illiteracy that pours out. . . . But I wonder whether even these things are inflicting on man a fraction of the pain, of the despair which all our Athens, all our high culture have inflicted. . . . They lectured on Kant and played Schubert and went off the same day to stuff millions into gas ovens.
>
> America may not be for you or me. Not for a Com-munist dreamer and glutton for the printed word. Not for a mendicant friar. . . . But I cannot see by what authority, by what right, you or I can cram *our* values . . . down other men's throats. You claim to be argu-ing from love of the common man. . . . But that love is filled with contempt and oppression. The pursuit of quality, your blueprint for excellence come with a lash. The price is too high. We have seen that.

But the master printer persists:

> I am a socialist. I am and remain a Marxist. Because otherwise I could not be a proof reader. . . . If California triumphs there will be no need of proof read-ers. Machines will do it better. . . . Carlo, you must

see what I'm driving at. Utopia simply means *getting it right*! Communism means taking the errata out of history. Out of man. . . . I believe in my beliefs. What else is there for me now?

As the Circle reluctantly dissolves in the wake of the events in Eastern Europe in 1989-1990 the members grasp at various straws. As Anna B. speaks of 'the movement' ". . . the phrase made it plain that it was not the nine members of the Circle actually present . . . but a vast throng progressing out of time, out of perennial enslavements . . . and millenarian uprisings, the Communards and the innocent and the kneeling shot down on that grand square in St. Petersburg in 1905, a column without end of the mutinous and the vanquished giving their lives to the cause. . . ."

As to the *Professore,* he was to convey at this last meeting that

> No tearing down the wall, no overthrow of a regime, not even the collapse of the USSR, could refute the verities shared by those whom he now addressed. On the contrary. A new phase of imperialist exploitation, racism and wage slavery, in short, an Americanization of the planet would attest to the unshakable foresight of Marxist theory. . . . Marxist revolutionary theory had (not) been disproved or made obsolete. The exact opposite was the case. . . . Never had there been more need of theoretical clarity. . . .

> The day would come when its membership (of the Circle) would no longer total twenty or a dozen but hundreds and thousands thereafter!

At the end of the story, as the printer applies for reinstatement in the Party, the irony and the absurdity of this quest for faith and community are brought home. No longer tormented by the "deranged conviction that a deserted universe, like a house unlocked after the removal vans had gone, would sink into oblivion . . ." he walks out of the dingy building (where his pursuit of membership took him) more sure-footed, his eyesight improved.

It is not clear whether or not the author intends for the printer to represent either a struggling and fallible individual in search of meaning in a world that offers little assurance about the ends of life, or Western intellectuals unable or unwilling to come to grips with a world which discredited their dearest beliefs. In any event, *Proofs* offers the reader a penetrating summary of the major political-ideological dilemmas and divides of our times. More than that, it lays bare the discontents and conflicts which will not go away with the collapse of communist systems and which also help us to understand why Western sympathizers hold on to their moral indignation and discredited ideals.

Henry L. Shapiro (review date fall 1994)

SOURCE: Shapiro, Henry L. Review of *Proofs, and Three Parables,* by George Steiner. *Studies in Short Fiction* 31, no. 4 (fall 1994): 693-94.

[*In the following review, Shapiro draws thematic connections among the stories comprising* Proofs, and Three Parables.]

George Steiner is a great celebrator, and this elegantly written, slim volume [*Proofs, and Three Parables*] is a paean to the art of interpretation. The title of the 73-page **"Proofs"** is a play on words (not so much about alcohol, though it is certainly about ideological intoxication), a straddling of "proof" as demonstration and as perfectible page of print. The protagonist is an unrivaled reader of proof who is a communist, in great danger of losing both his eyesight and his political faith in the days of the fall of the Soviet Union. A large part of the story, which takes place in Italy, consists of a debate between him and a friend on the merits of Marxism versus the Church, the laws of history and the laws of God. It is all familiar, yet put with lapidary brilliance. It is not clear which man is right, which wrong. It is not clear whether either man is right. There may be a *tertium quid.* What shines through as incontrovertible is that the quest for understanding is of supreme importance, that insight must not be dismissed a priori as subjectivity writ large. The goal of proofreading, as of political thought, is *"getting it right."*

Obliged to take time off by his fading eyesight, the protagonist cannot help going in to his office and correcting his replacement's proofreading. He is told that these are mere handbills, not fine books, and that his passion is misplaced. His response is inspiring:

> On the contrary. It is just here that it matters more than ever before. To act otherwise is utter contempt. Contempt for those who cannot afford to look at a fine book, at quality paper or crafted type. Contempt for those who have a right under God, yes, under God, to have a flawless hand-bill, also for a sale of manure! It is just for those who live in rural holes, in slums, that we should do the best work. So that some spark of perfection will enter their wretched days. Can't you understand how much contempt there is in a false accent or a misplaced serif? As if you spat at another human being.

It is possible to read this as mere fanaticism. Let us rather connect it with the much briefer last story in the volume, **"A Conversation Piece,"** in which the great tale of God's commanding Abraham to slay Isaac is viewed from different perspectives. The exercise cannot but remind the reader of the political/theological debate in **"Proofs."** It is equally well done. And when, at the end, a woman condemns it as a pointless masculine game, the reply is also inspiring:

Thought is the dance of the mind. The spirit dances when it seeks out meaning, and the meaning of that meaning. Perhaps there is in the forty-ninth letter of the forty-ninth verse of the forty-ninth chapter of the Book of Books, which lies hidden in the Torah as the Torah rolls lie cloaked inside their shrine, a truth so mighty that God Himself must pause when He remembers it. The dance-steps of the soul are words, woman. The lords of the dance are we. Are we not dancing now?

It is rather difficult to understand the sense in which the other two very short stories are parables—conveyors of a moral or spiritual message. Both seem mere *tours de force*. **"Desert Island Discs"** and **"Noël, Noël"** are structured around a heightened sense of hearing, as **"Proofs"** deals with the perfection of vision. In the latter, an unearthly sound deranges the narrator, who turns out to be four-footed and murderous. In the former, the sounds selected to take to the desert island include Fortinbras's belch, "the one at the end of the interminable coronation carouse," and the neighing of a horse at the place where three roads meet and Oedipus encounters his father. It is ever so clever, but is that all it is? A bit later, three of the Marx brothers appear, not including the Karl who was central to **"Proofs."** Is the point that "the dance-steps of the soul" may be simultaneously playful and meaningfully structured, that the ludic and the fateful may be one?

Robert Boyers (essay date 1994)

SOURCE: Boyers, Robert. "Steiner as Cultural Critic: Confronting America." In *Reading George Steiner*, edited by Nathan A. Scott Jr., and Ronald A. Sharp, pp. 14-42. Baltimore: The Johns Hopkins University Press, 1994.

[*In the following essay, Boyers surveys Steiner's critiques of American culture, probing their insights in light of their limitations.*]

George Steiner's views of the United States are not easy to sort out. Although often accused of a Eurocentric bias, he obviously knows a great deal about American culture and has spent considerable time teaching and lecturing at American universities. Educated at the University of Chicago and at Harvard—where he won the Bell Prize in American Literature—he won a Rhodes Scholarship from Illinois and is a member of the American Academy of Arts and Sciences. He often writes on American themes for leading magazines, and though he devotes considerably more attention to European writing and ideas than to American topics, he is clearly comfortable with the work of Updike and Penn Warren, Plath and Doctorow. Sharply critical of American education, he is also deeply respectful of American scholarship and has gone out of his way to

support, explain, or contend seriously with the work of leading American intellectuals. Sometimes dismissive of American ideals, he is clearly troubled by the implications of his inveterate resistance to things American and thoughtful about issues that many of his contemporaries refuse to acknowledge. Rightly convinced that his own obsessive regard for genius and for the best that has been thought and said "will strike the vast majority of *educated* Americans as effete or even (politically, socially) dangerous nonsense," he persists in carrying the argument into the literate American heartland, absorbing one rebuke after another.

Of course the American theme in Steiner is ordinarily subordinated to broader themes. He has never devoted an entire book to American culture, and the overwhelming majority of the nearly two hundred articles and reviews he has written for the *New Yorker*—to cite just one important venue—are on European topics. If Steiner had more fully developed his views of the United States, we would no doubt find it easier to sort them out. What to some readers seems gratuitously provocative in Steiner's formulations might then seem not only more plausible but also necessary. When Steiner asserts that American philosophy is "of a distinctly secondary order," his readers would probably be rather more tolerant if he had devoted more than a few paragraphs to the subject. When he dismisses out of hand the American "creative writing centers" and "poetry workshops," he would no doubt receive a different response if he grappled with what actually goes on under such auspices and demonstrated that compelling art and ideas are not generated in those precincts. No one doubts Steiner's courage, his willingness to provoke and to open debate. But his work on American themes especially has failed to elicit from most American intellectuals the respectful attention accorded to his far more substantial writings on literary, linguistic, and philosophic issues.

Some would no doubt contend that, for all his large Arnoldian ambition, Steiner is not at his best when he operates as a cultural critic. The thinness of his writing on the American theme would then be accounted part of a broader failure. This is a tempting notion, but clearly it will persuade only those for whom Steiner's provocations are mostly fruitless. Others, for whom a briskly essayistic book such as **In Bluebeard's Castle** continues to speak with telling cogency, will simply prefer to wish for fuller substantiation. Such readers will regard Steiner's scattered observations on America as refreshingly free of cant and will note the degree to which his arguments have informed subsequent critiques of American culture that are at once more detailed and less consistently suggestive.

Noting that Steiner's characteristic mode as a cultural critic is not brash assertion but nimble speculation, many say of his criticism—quite as Raymond Williams once noted of Edmund Burke's—that it is "an articulated experience, and as such it has a validity that can survive even the demolition of its general conclusions." What proportion of those "general conclusions" one would deny is of course open to question, but just as it is clear that Steiner often avoids full substantiation of important insights, it is also clear that his speculations are the product of extraordinarily wide reading and a grasp of diverse particulars. Unlike many of those who casually dismiss his cultural criticism, Steiner names names, pronounces firm judgments, constructs intricately ramifying arguments. The "articulated experience" of which Williams wrote is in Steiner a reflection of total commitment to the life of culture. That commitment, in turn, rests upon deep investment in particular loved objects, traditions, artists, thinkers, and agencies of renewal. That there are important limitations in Steiner's cultural criticism no one will doubt; that these limitations are largely disabling, or have principally to do with the relative proportion of assertion to evidence, will hardly seem credible to careful students of the work.

* * *

The resistance to Steiner's work on the United States has some relationship to a political and theoretical attack on cultural criticism which has lately held sway in parts of the American academy. Theodor Adorno, himself one of the century's most brilliant cultural critics, raised objections to "the notion of culture as such," and particularly to the fetishization of culture and other "isolated categories such as mind, life, and the individual." Making the case for an alternative "dialectical criticism," Adorno saw in what he took to be the more venerable mode features sometimes cited in attacks on Steiner. "The cultural critic," Adorno writes, "can hardly avoid the imputation that he has the culture which culture lacks." Thus the "arrogance" of a criticism that presumes to pass judgment from a perspective that "exempts itself from evaluation" and speaks as from "a higher historical stage." Fatally tempting to practitioners of this criticism, Adorno argues, is to take up a "position" within the established "culture industry" and, while ostentatiously refusing to make a "commodity" of themselves, to "reproduce the socially prevalent categories." The consequence of such practice is the debasement of culture to "cultural goods" and the promotion of that "hideous philosophical rationalization" which is "cultural values," with all that implies of a willingness to "place culture at the will of the market" or to pretend an escape from the market by a turn "towards the past."

Adorno's probing of cultural criticism nonetheless issues in an appreciation of its indispensable significance, even as he presses for its subsumption by a "dialectical" criticism less susceptible to the dangers he

catalogues. Rejecting a fashionable "theory" that "knows the place of every phenomenon and the essence of none," he avows the need for a cultural criticism—like Steiner's—that can maintain "a spontaneous relation to the object." Here, in Adorno's treacherously elusive presentation, one finds the negation of the polemical negation to which his critique had seemingly been bound. That sort of dialectical turn is of course largely absent from the work of Steiner's critics, who see in him only what is "reactionary" or "arrogant." Whereas Adorno grasps the relationship between strengths and limitations in the most bracing criticism, refusing to be dominated by categories such as "reactionary" or "elitist" yet reflecting upon them, American academics are often misled by such terms. To say of Steiner that his views are elitist is to say what is untrue, namely, that he writes from a fixed ideological position, which he promotes with single-minded determination. To say of his work on American culture that it is arrogant because its tone is occasionally aggressive is not to see that the fatal arrogance is only present where the mind of the critic truly "exempts itself from evaluation" and accepts more or less unconsciously that the important questions have been answered. Cultural criticism as anatomized by Adorno is infinitely more various and unpredictable than the caricature of Arnoldianism pilloried by most "advanced" critics today. But the climate in which that caricature has taken hold is generally inimical to thinking clearly about the actual merits and deficiencies of someone such as Steiner.

In one of its primary aspects, Steiner's work on American themes, like his cultural criticism generally, is frankly a part of the classic Arnoldian project. As a reviewer and practical critic, he has tried to see the objects of his attention as they really are and, in so doing, to identify the major work produced in his own time. More ambitiously, in books and essays, he has sought—in Arnold's words—"to make an intellectual situation of which the creative power can profitably avail itself," and in this he has seen criticism as a useful though entirely secondary enterprise. More willfully provocative than Arnold, and decidedly less sanguine about the effectuality of sweetness and reasonableness, he has been no less obsessed than Arnold by the prospect of "living by ideas" and exercising "the free play of the mind upon all subjects." More open to the anomalous and eccentric, he has also been less inclined than Arnold to disparage the polemical and the immoderate. Reluctant to accept Arnold's "central standard" and "the application of principles" as essential to the business of judgment, Steiner is more frankly committed to intuition and vehement speculation, at once more abrasively contentious and more willing to be corrected. His observations on American culture are "Arnoldian" in the sense that they proceed from a concern for the health of culture and a belief in the continuing validity of distinctions between high and low, serious and frivolous, enduring and transitory. But Steiner is very much his own man, and few Western writers have offered so thoughtful a welcome to different kinds of twentieth-century art and thought, from Heidegger to Gershom Scholem, from Nabokov to Montale. The notion that, in rejecting American rock music and other expressions of "popular" culture, Steiner shows that he is hopelessly stuck in an outworn Arnoldian posture is no more credible than the same notion when applied—as it has been—to Adorno.

When Steiner returns, again and again, to such themes as the decay of literacy, and speaks with revulsion of the new "leveling," he invites the charge that he presumes to have "the culture which culture lacks." To some, this presumption seems not only offensive but also a mark of Steiner's distance from the egalitarian civilization he wishes to study and address. *In Bluebeard's Castle,* far more than other books by Steiner, is marked by his assertion that high accomplishment is the province of "the gifted few," that there cannot be "value without hierarchy," that in the United States especially primary and secondary education are committed to an "organized amnesia," which has made it ever more difficult for the sophisticated mandarinate to perform its higher functions. Those without a proper grasp of "physics, astronomy and algebraic analysis," Steiner asserts, can hope to read seventeenth- and eighteenth-century literature "only at the surface." The literary tradition, in which one work echoes, mirrors, alludes to another, "is now passing quickly out of reach" as "glossaries lengthen, . . . footnotes become more elementary and didactic, . . . marvelous spontaneities of enacted feeling become 'literary' and twice-removed." In calling attention to these conditions, Steiner hopes to sound an alarm. His critics are turned off by the hyperbole.

Adorno cautioned against the idea that the cultural critic could transcend by sheer force of will the conditions he deplored. To this caution Steiner offers a compelling if not wholly persuasive response. First, while it is true that a total "transcendence" is neither possible nor desirable for the cultural critic, he can surely propose an alternative model and embody it so fiercely in the very tone and sinew of his prose as to compel acknowledgment of difference. Steiner knows as well as Adorno did how hard it is to resist the encroachment of mass culture into every area of life. Adorno's pained attention to Tin Pan Alley and to American jazz is matched by Steiner's more circumspect treatment of rock music and the technologies of the mass media. But far more important is Steiner's insistent evocation of the alternative self that alone can in any sense resist the culture that is studied. Although in Steiner there is argument, even brash polemic, one is struck more forcefully by the sheer *presence* of an unfamiliar personal vehemence, passion, obsessiveness. Steiner's language enacts resistance in its very disregard of the decorums that

mandate caution, impeccable generosity of sentiment, at all costs moderation. Steiner speaks with the driving fullness of one possessed by feelings increasingly unfamiliar to contemporary intellectuals. His capacity to evoke his otherness, his willingness to see himself as "hunter," his unembarrassed identification with those "for whom a great poem, a philosophic design, a theorem, are, in the final reckoning, the supreme value"—these features of Steiner's work embody difference and make Adorno's caution about transcendence irrelevant here. Steiner need not pretend to transcend the culture he describes. While participating in it, he obviously does not belong to it in any way that would make his limitations typical or symptomatic.

Steiner also responds—again implicitly—to Adorno's caution by evoking the power of contemporary culture, its ability to effect massive transformations in every domain of experience. Nothing is more alien to Steiner than the posture of the drawing-room critic holding himself aloof from the changes taking place just outside his window. Steiner's engagement with his culture is aggressive. The very speed of his sentences as they follow hard on one another, the voracity with which he grabs now at one vivid item, then another: these represent to us not only Steiner's singularity but also his indomitable curiosity, the visceral satisfaction he takes in immersion without submission. With sometimes hammering insistence, Steiner dwells upon changes inevitably taking place in our "central habits of consciousness." He argues that it is the vision of the contemporary sciences, *their* energy and "forward dreams," that increasingly "define us." This is not the observation of one who hopes to transcend his own cultural moment. When Steiner speaks of "our reduced condition," when he worries over the degree to which "we are in metamorphosis," he does not exempt himself or anyone else from these conditions. Like very few other critics, Steiner registers the fact of change, tests it on his pulses, responds with sometimes ferocious, never detached fascination. Nor is there anything merely conventional in Steiner's speaking of "our" condition as a common fate. For all of his resistance to much that he describes, he acknowledges that there is no viable way to transcend modernity. One can opt out only by willfully blinding oneself to what is central in our experience. For one who wishes above all to see, neither mystic withdrawal nor aristocratic disdain will serve.

What of the charge that Steiner "presumes to have the culture which culture lacks"? Is it not the case that Steiner declares himself privileged in ways remote from most others? Does he not associate himself all too readily with "a small number, a conscious élite"? The charge is in one sense impossible to answer. To accuse a culture of deliberately denying or tearing down hierarchies of value is obviously to assume that one is in touch with cultural imperatives in the name of which the accusation is leveled. To furnish vivid examples of declining literacy is of course to imply that the critic himself suffers no such debility. But if this seems offensive, then those offended must ask themselves why a forthright assault on recent developments in the culture should seem so unsavory. If the critic only pretended to have the culture that culture lacks, then indeed he would seem presumptuous. But if the very terms in which he indicts the culture seem cogent, the facts more or less unassailable, why then so grave a discomfort with his speaking truthfully?

We have learned to be suspicious of anyone's claim to be simply telling the truth. Steiner makes no such claim. He offers instead a strenuous discourse on various themes in which sometimes tendentious, sometimes unimpeachable observations inform an attempt "to get certain perplexities into focus." That is the heart of Steiner's cultural criticism. Is it grandiose for him to declare his willingness to "press home the debate with the unknown"? The objection has little validity if it reflects only a collision of different intellectual styles, what Irving Howe has called "the Anglo-Saxon" rejecting "the Continental." Beyond that, a serious objection would need to demonstrate that Steiner is not genuinely engaged with the unknown, that he does not ask hard questions for which there are as yet no reliable answers. When he reflects on the relationship between political tyranny and the specific density of certain works of imagination, can any reader feel certain that the relationship is not worth pondering? When he asks whether particular taboos, discernible in American academic life especially, do not portend proscriptions on political, genetic, or theological research, is it clear that he is simply making interesting noises? Intelligent readers in many countries believe that it is necessary to ask such questions, and many wonder why so few writers are willing to ask them. In part it is the burden of Steiner's criticism to ask that question as well and to offer various plausible reasons, which have stimulated debate throughout Western Europe and even in the United States.

The fact that numerous seminars at major universities have been devoted to—or built around—discussion of Steiner's cultural criticism is hardly proof that it is of enduring value or even of serious ephemeral interest. Adorno might well see in the fact nothing more than Steiner's success in making himself a spokesman for the culture industry and brilliantly reproducing the cultural values of a dominant elite. But the very existence of a coherent elite is today more than ever open to question, and one can only wonder who might be said to belong to it. Academics? Poets? Museum directors? Editors of quarterly magazines? However one draws the ranks, it is clear that an elite is today more than ever a dubious fiction and that even the once useful concept of a culture industry invites such confusion and impreci-

sion as to be quite dangerous. If Steiner's cultural criticism has had some resonance—it has surely attracted loud and violent detraction—that cannot be because he has articulated values held by a powerful establishment. Few of the best known cultural figures in the country share Steiner's views on most matters. Leading literary intellectuals in the United States surely do not regard Steiner as a representative voice, and, however much he is admired by many writers, only rarely is he mentioned in their periodicals of choice. Although in England Steiner has certainly remained "visible" in leading magazines such as the *Times Literary Supplement* and *Granta,* he has never achieved among intellectuals the venerable status of an Isaiah Berlin or a Frank Kermode. Even in France, where his works have been warmly received, no one would claim for him a "representative" status. More important, the cultural establishment in these countries is so much a matter of competing factions as to resist any sort of representative voice.

Of course the values informing Steiner's cultural criticism were once central to intellectual elites in Europe, and even to some extent in the United States. So much Steiner himself contends. But those values were then upheld with a confidence no longer conceivable. Steiner, after all, must now take those values to be under assault not from "philistines," but from the very intellectual class whose convictions they were once thought to express. That fact rightly suggests that the values themselves have undergone important changes. What were once elite establishment values are now truly minority values and are in process of being repudiated by many who know quite as much as Steiner does about the formation of cultural elites. Whereas for Arnold a "classic" spoke with an accent sure to be recognized by decently educated readers, for Steiner there can be no "classic" without the accompanying apparatus of argument designed to challenge a general resistance to "perfection" and "tradition." Whereas for Arnold the "value" of great works had something to do with their enabling sweetness and light, Steiner denies that "value" is likely to have any relation to humane virtues. Whereas Arnold could believe that, in speaking for himself, he was speaking for others, Steiner must know that he fights a rear-guard action in a culture for which the rear has been pushed to the margins.

If Steiner's cultural criticism is proof against Adorno's sharpest strictures, it is nonetheless built upon a suspect concept of "culture." For Steiner, "a culture 'lived' is one that draws for continuous, indispensable sustenance on the great works of the past, on the truths and beauties achieved in the tradition." In such a culture, some constituents at least will be willing to "gamble on transcendence" (though not the "transcendence" indicted by Adorno). The gamble can only be sustained by a conviction that certain things are immeasurably more important to our civilization than other things, that the fulfillment of identity is tied to participation in a still living tradition: only the tradition, with all it entails of past glories and forward dreams, can free and make vital what Pindar called "the divinity that is busy within my mind." Adorno feared that such investment in culture, such concern with "divinity" and "transcendence," would inevitably distract attention from "the true horrors," the exclusions and injustices everywhere present in the domain of culture. For Steiner to argue on behalf of "the gamble" must, in Adorno's terms, only ensure that "culture" remain the domain of the few, as it has been. To pursue the "concrete judgments" that can as yet only be reached by the few must further embed one's criticism in the very society from which one would stand apart. For Adorno, the danger to which cultural critics such as Steiner must succumb is that of supposing culture to be an autonomous realm. Adorno argues that culture, as an autonomous realm, is deprived of "the ferment which is its very truth—negation." Insofar as Steiner purports to encompass culture, to assume that it is a realm of sufficiency constituted by the vitally sufficient judgments and creations of a traditionally informed elite, he cannot see culture as he should: as a necessarily indeterminate object "not yet illuminated by reason."

In defense of Steiner, it might here be objected that no Continental or American cultural critic would be exempt from Adorno's condemnation. In calling for a dialectical criticism, Adorno demands that cultural criticism refine itself out of existence. Then culture would no longer be an idea offering comfort by reminding adherents of the unbridgeable divorce between high and low. The necessary critic, it follows, must not be content with the "superficial" satisfaction of exposing the philistinism or shallowness of those passing before him. What the critic would then do to promote the desired "negation" is nowhere clearly articulated by Adorno, but his primary demands do surely call into question certain assumptions to which Steiner subscribes. Although Steiner's writing on American themes is but an aspect of his cultural criticism, it is surely useful here to look at that work with Adorno's demands in view. For perhaps Steiner's cultural criticism is, in ways Adorno himself would have appreciated, a good deal closer to the ideal than his opponents would allow.

* * *

Consider Steiner's most sustained, and notorious, essay on American culture, the long piece **"The Archives of Eden,"** which appeared in the quarterly *Salmagundi* in 1980. The centerpiece of the magazine's special issue "Art and Intellect in America," the piece was there subjected to mostly hostile criticism by such writers as Cynthia Ozick, Susan Sontag, Leslie Fiedler, Dwight Macdonald, and Christopher Lasch. Subsequent re-

sponses, printed in the "Letters" pages of the magazine, showed considerable support for Steiner's arguments among European readers, but something less than approval among most Americans. As in other controversies focused on Steiner's cultural criticism, his harshest critics complain that his speculations are largely without foundation. Others complain that the implications of his "position" are unsavory and that he should know better than to let them stand. Still others complain about the tone of the essay, its arrogance and stridency. Defenders of the piece, and of others like it, generally have little to say of the tone or manner of presentation, preferring to argue the broad merits of Steiner's case, citing the impressive thoroughness with which he assembles the materials of a very complex argument. Accepting that Steiner could not have provided substantiating detail for all of the contentions he makes in such an essay, many respondents are grateful to have the lineaments of the argument and the various "leads" Steiner provides. Those familiar with his earlier work note his continuing emphasis on themes developed in previous books and essays.

Steiner's essay opens with a quotation from a Puritan text on the Great Migration to America, and it cites other contemporaneous speculations on "whether the establishment of the New England polity was not a signal of the end of secular time, for this was the *ne plus ultra* of mundane innovation." He goes on in the opening paragraph to refer to "the reign of everlastingness as foretold in Revelation," of exceeding "terrestrial possibilities," of "ambiguities in the trope of final renovation." Steiner's language is charged with the intensity and hope of those whose vision he records. Elsewhere, things are rather less strenuously energetic, but the overall coloration of the writing is vivid; the temper, vehement. Steiner often selects for quotation the most dramatic formulations he can find, and his own prose shows his fondness for words such as "antinomian," "prodigality," and "infection." His rhetorical questions typically pose very large issues and genuinely challenge the reader in a way not often associated with the milder uses to which that accessible device is often turned. When Steiner asks "can it be an accident that" or "is American culture not precisely what" or "How much" does this or that "matter," he means us to feel that our serious response is urgently required. Even if we have not the information to proceed confidently—so the tone and persistence of the questioning would suggest—we cannot but feel that our thinking on these matters may not be put off and should follow in the general courses Steiner has set down.

Whereas in other writers tentativeness often bespeaks a retreat to calm reflection and stock-taking, in Steiner the statement that "one is bound to get magnitudes and relations wrong" simply concedes that, though one may make mistakes, there is much to be said for aggressively following one's hunches and inviting correction or debate. If a part of the landscape one is covering "is strewn with critical hyperbole and modishness," one ought still to move vigorously forward: to be forewarned is not to be forestalled or intimidated. In his cultural criticism, the rhetoric of Steiner is often one of thrust and thrust. There is little parry and counterthrust, however often Steiner notes potential objections to his line of inquiry. For all of his obviously genuine desire to get things right by consulting every conceivably relevant source and alternative opinion, he moves with a relentless determination toward the fullness of his argument. He has a marked fondness for conclusive insights that permit him to use such terms as "indisputable," "preeminent," and "decisive." Although Steiner routinely questions his own formulations and wonders aloud whether "there is anything but ignorance or shortsightedness" to them, the driving insistence of his writing makes it difficult to think of him as a modest fellow. Tentativeness in Steiner is part of an aggressive rhetorical posture.

There is no law that requires of the cultural critic a becoming modesty. Of course a number of Steiner's best-known predecessors would hardly have seemed modest to their respective audiences. For all of the occasional sweetness and light of Arnold, he purported to know what was what, and he used his touchstones to arrive at literary judgments that were remarkably inflexible by any standard. When Arnold presumes in *Culture and Anarchy* to speak for "Culture" and asks his reader to "consider these people [philistines], then, their way of life, their habits, their manners, the very tones of their voice . . . the things which give them pleasure . . . the thoughts which make the furniture of their minds," and goes on to ask "would any amount of wealth be worth having with the condition that one was to be just like these people by having it?," he is here speaking immodestly, with the untroubled conviction of being right. When Clement Greenberg in "Avant Garde and Kitsch" argues that "the urban masses set up a pressure on society to provide them with a kind of culture fit for their own consumption," he does not apologize for suggesting what may seem offensive or mistaken. He knows that the culture of "the urban masses" feeds an appetite for kitsch and other kinds of junk. Even Adorno is not at all beyond arrogant and inflexible reflections on matters that might have seemed open to legitimate dispute. Jazz fans, for example, seem to Adorno to contribute to "the disintegration of culture" by helping to erase "the distinction between autonomous 'high' and commercial 'light' art." Adorno claims that glorifying "a highly rationalized section of mass production" is "philistine": "Anyone who allows the growing respectability of mass culture to seduce him into equating a popular song with modern art because of a few false notes squeaked by a clarinet; anyone who mistakes a triad studded with 'dirty notes' for atonality, has

already capitulated to barbarism." Clearly, Steiner's brashness and his attraction to decisive formulations and ringing judgments are very much in the grain of the cultural criticism practiced by many distinguished forebears. Although one would be loath to designate these as constitutive features of cultural criticism, it is clear that a liberal distaste for such elements ought itself to be subjected to further scrutiny.

Steiner's **"Archives of Eden"** is also marked by another characteristic feature of his cultural criticism, namely, an attempt to "think the contradictions" of an argument. Throughout the essay Steiner not only concedes that he may be in error but also forcefully undercuts some of his most "decisive" charges. This has nothing to do with self-contradiction. When Steiner indicts the American counterculture he does so with a consistency that is nowhere diminished by confusion. When he associates an authentic culture with "the transmission forward of the best that reason and imagination have brought forth in the past and are producing now," he does not muddy the argument by allowing for exceptions that would invalidate his own emphatic preferences. Steiner's position on most matters is about as coherent as an intelligent position can be. To think the contradictions is for him to acknowledge perspectives radically different from his own. This he does in a spirit of considerable generosity and tolerance. "Liberalism" is not for him the enemy; it is another perspective, different from his own. It entails decencies that he admires, that he would embrace insofar as they are compatible with other imperatives to which he feels at least comparable allegiance. It is reasonable, he feels, for a liberal to oppose elites, though he himself can oppose them only to the extent that he need not thereby renounce his convictions about the way that culture is transmitted. Thinking the contradictions here involves trying to establish what are and are not compatible ideas. At its most severe it involves an attack on those who not only "want it both ways" but are unwilling to concede that the most appealing values often conflict with one another and entail painful choices. Thinking the contradictions can be for Steiner the practice of exposing "puerile hypocrisy" or an ever more contagious confusion. It is also a part of the ongoing quest to establish hierarchies of value by questioning the nature of first- and second-order priorities.

That thinking the contradictions is not in Steiner quite what Adorno meant by dialectical thinking is clear. Steiner is not intent upon doing away with the large contradictions and incompatibilities to which he pays attention. His sense is that such antinomies necessarily persist and that culture expresses them without ever really knowing how to eradicate them. Efforts to think beyond the contradictions, though sometimes exhilarating, are too often undertaken by overtly coercive regimes. The very different prospect envisioned by

Adorno, of a dialectical thinking that would install negation at the heart of a culture's sense of itself, does not for Steiner offer a sufficiently coherent view of culture. Neither does negation as a presiding principle offer an adequate underpinning for a common experience in which human beings drink deeply from, and are regularly nourished by, the things they love. Steiner is too much the obsessed servant of particular loved texts, musical scores, metaphysical proofs, theorems, to be as comfortable as Adorno with a dialectical thinking that is largely theoretical and consistently geared to avoiding any kind of domination. To be "dominated" by a great painting is not for Steiner an experience one should wish to renounce or overcome—much though he believes that possession at best entails an aggressive component, a *taking* possession in which the work is itself transformed, no longer the object that at first confidently imposed itself. Although Adorno warned against the infatuation of theory, his fear of "enthrallment in the cultural object" makes his criticism quite different from Steiner's, for which self-possession is fully enabled by the loved objects that take permanent root in the mind.

The "contradiction" central to **"Archives of Eden"** turns on the professed desire of Americans to extend culture to everyone and what Steiner takes to be the consequent "disaster" of American "pseudo-literacy," "the awful state of intellectual affairs" in the United States. The essay is not in the main an attack on institutions but on self-deceptions and lies that affect American education and in turn perpetuate myths about the great American experiment. The self-deceptions are discernible in many kinds of American "promotional" discourse. Often they are most vivid in the practice and rationalization of the American professoriate, which can routinely "trivialize" and "water down" what it teaches while pretending to have sacrificed nothing of consequence. Or they are vivid in the claim that one can "educate" a person without asking him to read much or to master a range of intellectual disciplines. In exposing these self-deceptions, Steiner is not at great pains to provide documentation, believing that the evidence is fully available and widely accepted. Although many will disagree with what he makes of these matters, the *fact* that trivialization and watering down take place seems to him unanswerable. So, too, with the fact that many in the American educational establishment express contempt or indifference to "content-oriented" courses and profess instead simply to teach students how to think—as if thinking could be taught at a university level to people who typically have almost nothing to think *about.* Although Steiner offers here and there an anecdote or a reference, the force of the argument is largely dependent upon his willingness to speak truthfully about what others also see, however accustomed they may be to denying it. If some American readers utterly reject the argument, that may reflect their continu-

ing refusal to acknowledge the facts or their feeling that Steiner makes more of those facts than is warranted.

Another significant contradiction has to do with the gap between American "custodial" achievement and the relative indifference of most Americans to high culture. The United States has been for some time preeminent for "the scope, generosity, technical brilliance and public prestige" of its cultural enterprise. So Steiner contends. The "didactic energies" and curatorial achievements of the American museum world are remarkable. So are the "scale" and "pitch of quality" of American musical performance, the organization and activity of American libraries, the resourcefulness and thoroughness of the country's archives. Although it is possible, Steiner says, that in some domains the United States "will not produce first-rate contributions," it is clear that in some areas at least the culture has already produced works of "classic occasion."

If all this is so, Steiner goes on, why do works of the first magnitude matter so little in the United States? Why the "contradiction" between a culture brilliantly organized to preserve and present the best that has been thought and said and a society utterly unable to view a rich cultural tradition as the principal source of its strength? Steiner knows that this question, like others growing out of it, may well rest upon "oversimplification." But such questions are central to his thinking on the vicissitudes of liberal culture, and the American instance seems to him particularly troubling, given the manifest strengths of the culture and the diversity of its intellectual and artistic elite.

Two elements come together in the argument about the United States as "the archives of Eden," and it is not always as clear as Steiner assumes that they belong together. On the one hand, there is the contention that the American genius tends to organization, coherence, preservation: it is committed to culture as a "thing out there," something to be packaged—willfully, professionally, efficiently prepared and disseminated. On the other hand, Steiner contends that Americans tend not to take to heart the works of spirit and beauty that are routinely made accessible to them. Inclined, conditioned, to regard great works of thought and imagination as "adjunct" to real life, as "artifact" or "monument," Americans typically are reluctant to let themselves go in the presence of the real thing or to regard an obsession with a powerful work as anything but remediable affliction. The American citizen at his best is inclined to "have" culture as a "something" potentially valuable, perhaps even in some way indispensable, but in no way intrinsic to his intimate sense of self or his valuation of the society in which he lives.

Steiner clearly believes that the one issue is, in important respects, essential to a grasp of the other, but it may also be that neither can be tested without treating it independently. Take the argument about the intrinsic character of the American genius. In suggesting that the national genius is more inclined to organization than to "organic" creativity, Steiner places primary emphasis on the country's institutional achievements. This is inevitable. As long as Steiner can point to the extraordinary investment Americans have made in their cultural institutions, he can speak persuasively about a major dimension of their ambition. The number and quality of their symphony orchestras, the acquisitive reach and largesse of their museums, and other manifestations do surely help to make Steiner's point. Americans are not only good at preservation and presentation but also throw themselves into these enterprises with perhaps unrivalled conviction and efficiency.

What of the other side of Steiner's assertion, that Americans are more inclined or suited to organization than to organic creativity? The one aspect of the assertion is of meager polemical interest without the other, and the other is, to say the least, not only provocative but highly questionable. Not many will deny that culture is packaged and sometimes watered down and conspicuously consumed in the United States. But many will deny that Steiner can mean what he says when he suggests that, "in some cardinal domains at least, America will not produce first-rate contributions." Steiner is quite right to admit that in undertaking a broad assault on all of American culture he is necessarily reduced to an "intuitively vague, partial account," that there is nothing for him but to "generalize and drop names in an impressionistic register of guesswork and prejudice." And yes, such an inquiry may surely elicit fruitful debate and rebuttal. But what makes Steiner's vagueness or partiality acceptable whereas another's would be irresponsible? What makes Steiner's "prejudice" worth contending with, his name-dropping more than a facile ploy?

First, and most obviously, there are the important concessions and exceptions built into Steiner's argument. We note his attempt to make a case for the "authority" of the American novel and observe him grappling with the dominance of American painting in the mid-1950s. However briefly he handles these matters, he does clearly see the weaknesses in his thesis. Just so does he acknowledge "innovative" genius in American dance and architecture and wonder whether it is his "incompetence" in mathematics that leads him to doubt the validity of American claims there. These doubts, acknowledgments, and concessions are telling signs of good faith in an argument so willfully provocative as to need as many signs of this order as it can muster.

Yet the persistence in vagueness and partiality remains troubling. For Steiner to conclude the generalizing and merely suggestive name-dropping with a statement such as "this is not an overwhelming harvest" is peremptory almost to the point of arbitrariness. One cannot say, after all, that a culture with considerable claims to contemporary preeminence in literature, the visual arts, dance, mathematics, and the sciences is nonetheless deficient in creativity. Nor is it tenable to assert that the creativity that does exist is not organically related to nurturant factors in American life and institutions. Perhaps it is true, as Steiner contends, that no American painter will "emerge as possessing a stature, an innovative or recreative strength," to match that of a Duchamp or Picasso (the example of Duchamp is itself highly dubious). But perhaps—and here one confronts the limits of this kind of speculation—it is *not* true. Perhaps, moreover, the "overwhelming harvest" Steiner wishes to see has already been realized in a degree his own "prejudice" cannot allow. Suppose that he is right when, in citing the "authority" of the American novel, he asserts that "the summits are *not* American." Is there any reason to go on from that to deny that there has anyway been an "overwhelming harvest" in twentieth-century American literature, from Dos Passos, Hemingway, Faulkner, O'Connor, Ellison, and Bellow in fiction to Eliot, Pound, Stevens, Bishop, Frost, and Lowell in poetry, or Mailer, Baldwin, Trilling, Gass, and Wilson in the essay? The vagueness in Steiner's argument is troubling largely because it leaves important parts of the relevant questions not only unanswered but also unformulated.

Steiner hopes that, in asking "unappetizing" and sometimes even "indefensible" questions, he will elicit the "fertile instigation to understanding" which is "No, but." The hope is often repeated in the body of his cultural criticisms, and he does surely believe that some of what he proposes will be shown to require revision. But, we ask again, What makes the largely unsupported generalizations and hunches worth attending to? First, the assertions are not wholly unsupported. To drop names is a kind of support. To set up comparisons is another: Steiner does not merely state that Faulkner and Hemingway are not the summits of modern prose fiction; he offers in "evidence" the names of Mann, Kafka, Joyce, and Proust. We are free to disagree, but not to deny that a comparative framework may be useful. Part of the American provinciality that Steiner indicts is the reluctance to accept the validity of such contexts, with all they imply of hierarchy and ranking. But Steiner is as good as his word in insisting again and again that there can be no judgment and no understanding without frameworks for comparison. Although he rarely pursues the comparisons in his cultural criticism—where he has other purposes to fulfill—he does so with enormous care and shrewdness in his literary and philosophical criticism. In works such as **"Archives of Eden,"** the generalizations and hunches stir us in the degree that we can sense the pressure of a careful and shaping reflection just behind them. If indeed audacity is required to make in passing the kinds of sweeping judgment Steiner makes, that is not to deny that the judgments are cogent and that the logic of the argument is usually unassailable.

The best reason for attending to Steiner's sometimes unsupported generalizations is that they furnish and enable an argument that is really more important than its parts. One can reject his statement that in the United States there has not been "a major philosophic presence with the possible exception . . . of C. S. Peirce" and still take very seriously indeed his broader charge that in the United States even educated people have never been deeply persuaded "that abstract thought is the true motor of felt life." Ought Steiner, then, to have seen how unnecessary was the statement about "a major philosophic presence" and omitted it? Some of his critics would surely say so. But the statement, if not essential to the broader argument, does have a good deal to do with it, and it does in itself not only provoke but also raise a legitimate issue rarely accredited today. The larger argument does not depend on the collateral issue because the linkage is suggestive, not a matter for conclusive determination.

So Steiner asks us to accept that certain propositions are usefully arguable. "The climate of American feeling," he says, is resistant to ontological thinking. This *may* be a consequence of the failure of the country to have produced "a major philosophic presence." The major philosopher "is one whose discourse, as it were, successive generations carry on their person." In Europe—think of the public stature of a Sartre, a Gramsci—philosophic debate is an "emphatic" element "of political and generational identity," as it cannot be in the United States. And so on. Some say this business of making things usefully arguable cannot be a sufficient goal for so palpably extensive an enterprise. After all, it is argued, we do not need Steiner to propose what we are able to consider without him, such as the possible connection between the intrinsic merit of a work and the long-term effects it may have. But the intervention of Steiner may well seem critical in a way his critics do not acknowledge—in reminding us, for example, that these are not merely academic issues, that observations on the state of philosophic thinking may bear heavily on much else, that the willingness of educated people to take seriously matters vital to the life of their culture is very much in doubt. A number of the American writers who expressed disdain for Steiner's attacks on cultural disorder and blithe academicism in the 1970s showed themselves quite ready twenty years later to sound their own alarms. Among these are two of the most accomplished American cultural critics, Irving Howe and David Bromwich, both men of the liberal Left, both once sharply critical of Steiner's work. To see how far such writers have come, one need only note that in his 1991 essay "The Value of the Canon," Howe finds himself having to cite for support Georg Lukács, Leon Trotsky, and Antonio Gramsci in order to make the point that "students should read great books." Obvious? No doubt, says Howe, but necessary, given "where we are." Looking back, it may well seem to many of his critics that Steiner saw first where American education and intellectual life were headed and that the tone of feverish urgency one finds in his cultural criticism is not at all excessive.

So let us consider again Steiner's contention that the very character of "a community of rational men and women" is involved in their willingness to "think being" and to feel its experience "pervaded by explicit philosophic argument." In citing what he takes to be vulnerabilities in the philosophic record of the United States, Steiner vividly calls our attention to a problematic dimension of the national character. In saying that there is no American "enquirer into the meaning of meaning to set beside Heidegger or Wittgenstein or Sartre," he presses us to accept as valid—as full of implication—the relationship between one thing and another ordinarily seen as distinct. For Steiner—and this is what he truly hopes to make "usefully arguable"—educated people for whom there is no point in making comparisons, for whom it is not important whether American philosophy may rightly be said to have merely an academic interest, do in fact tell us a great deal about "America." The many educated Americans for whom these are not usefully arguable issues help us to see that Steiner has long been on to questions few other critics have been willing to address.

Steiner's work as cultural critic has often borne on the character of the intellectual and artistic elites that help determine the direction of a culture. His writing on things American is in this sense characteristic. What Steiner takes to be central to American culture has much to do with the attitudes of its cultural elites. If in his view American music "has been of an essentially provincial character," this has much to do with continuing ideas of "newness" and innovation which move American composers to operate outside "formal and substantive" continuities more usually embraced elsewhere, even by bold spirits. In his cultural criticism Steiner often follows the implications of ideas—newness, frankness—that routinely exercise artists and intellectuals. What benefits, he wonders, follow from a culture's insistence that "fairness" predominate in its organization of educational priorities? What indispensable strengths are there in works of imagination which hope to "make it new" by denying their relationship to previous works? How clear are the distortions and spiritual deficits, the intellectual weaknesses and delusions, consequent upon those predominating ideas and commitments? Even those uncomfortable with Steiner's sense that the health of a culture can be gauged in its attitude toward an elite minority will agree that an elite does influence the temper of a culture. If members of that elite deny that it is their business to exert cultural influence, or that their interests are in any way different from those of other citizens, that denial is surely of significance to the cultural critic. So Steiner would have us understand.

No doubt, Steiner's constant circling back to the idea of an elite minority is hard for most American readers to stomach. Accustomed to thinking well of people who speak frankly, many of these readers are nonetheless unable to forgive Steiner for believing that most of us do not amount to much and that "it is a Socrates, a Mozart, a Gauss or a Galileo who, in some degree, compensate for man." Those—"the vast majority of educated Americans"—who regard this kind of thinking as "dangerous nonsense" are likewise convinced that there is nothing so special in the numerous lesser members of Steiner's elite who attempt to transmit insight and beauty, in the classroom or in works of secondary "paraphrase." To his critics, the elite of Steiner is typically self-important and out of touch with much that lifts the spirit of most thoughtful people. For Steiner, the elite figure is to be understood as "infected with the leprosy of abstract thought," an "obsessed servant" of texts, "a loving, a clairvoyant parasite" living on, passing on a feeling for ultimate things. Such a figure "abides," as others cannot, "the hideous fact that hundreds of thousands could be fed on the price a museum pays for one Raphael or Picasso." On the other hand, the critics of Steiner, feeling a decent revulsion at the "hideous fact," as at his confident enunciation of priorities, often dismiss his concerns as "effete," his instincts as so willfully mandarin as to separate him from all but a handful of his contemporaries.

What does Steiner see as the proper relation between his elite and the culture? On the American scene the proper relation is at present only a remote ideal, and it must remain so for as long as the intelligentsia refuses to behave like a responsible elite. So Steiner contends. Citing Julien Benda and "The Treason of the Clerics," Steiner refers to those who have "sought pardon" for their gifts and advantages "by seeking to strip themselves of their own calling," going in for a "masochist exhibitionism" and "seeking to howl with the wolves of the so-called counter culture." In practice, this stripping and howling have amounted to protestations of solidarity with the oppressed, the young, the disaffected, even with groups in the Third World who openly express contempt for the intellectual traditions and institutions of the West. The posturing of many academic intellectuals especially has had the effect of generating an "apologetic" and "defensive" attitude in the intelligentsia, which knows that people without feeling for the intrinsic benefits of higher education are often deeply resentful of intellectual elites. To reach those who are skeptical or downright contemptuous toward

the very disciplines and traditions they represent, many believe it is necessary and good to stress their primary commitment to equality, gregariousness, pluralism, and openness.

Steiner regards the preference expressed in such commitments as "thoroughly justifiable." The person who genuinely believes in the merits of an open society and in his own primary responsibility to work to enhance the pride of formerly oppressed peoples, to spread ideas of distributive and social justice, and to deny the validity of hierarchy, and who "makes this choice and lives accordingly deserves nothing but attentive respect." Steiner instead condemns those—"and they have been legion in American academe or the media—who want it both ways." He condemns, that is to say, "the puerile hypocrisy and opportunism" of those "who profess to experience, to value, to transmit authentically the contagious mystery of great intellect and art while they are in fact dismembering it." The academic who professes to teach "literature" while offering students an easily digestible and patently mediocre work on the grounds that it contains acceptably humane sentiments and liberally accredited identity images is such a hypocrite. The hip, ever so sophisticated literary journalist who professes to find in a rock lyric as telling an expression of the modern condition as any to be found in Joseph Skvorecky or Thomas Bernhard is another. So, too, the intellectual who wants to know who gave anyone "the right" to "invalidate" the tastes of others by presuming to set in place evaluative contexts to which even "popular" art may be submitted. In these instances Steiner sees treason or betrayal: principally, on the part of those who "espouse—a justly sacramental verb—" a commitment to great art and thought, "while seeking to deny the conditions of person and of society from which they have come to us, from which they continue to come."

The most obvious rejoinder to Steiner would ask why we should not wish to have it "both ways." Americans often believe, quite as Steiner has shown, that the pursuit of happiness is compatible with just about any other worthwhile goal and that the ordinary is not a "despotism" but a perspective useful for undercutting disproportionate attention to the rare and pretentious. Why should American academics desist from teaching in the name of democratic and liberal values if only those values, worn prominently on every sleeve, will win for them the hearing they crave? Why should a robust feeling for the contemporaneous and immediate interfere with a sober interest in the past, or disable the effort to make it seem relevant? Why should a distaste for the consecration of culture to the discovery of "genius" be absolutely inimical to the study or appreciation of important art? To put these and other such questions in this way is clearly to move toward an answer. Those who want things both ways ought at least to see what they can do, and Steiner would be foolish to deny that some have already enjoyed considerable success in their efforts. Steiner has no fully persuasive evidence that "the correlations between extreme creativity . . . and political justice are, to a significant degree at least, negative." His sense of the past is such that he is necessarily inclined to read the correlations as negative, but—as any American would surely remind him—*that* was *then,* and *this* is *now.* If, as he says, "the flowering of the humanities is not worth the circumstances of the inhuman"—or the unjust?—then it not only makes sense to regard that flowering as a secondary priority but also to try to make the humanities flower under very different auspices. Many artists and intellectuals have sought to have it both ways, and not simply by trying to promote in their works a respect for social justice. Many, after all, have harnessed their creative obsessions to the achievement of personal advantage or comfort. Steiner's language of infection does not always do justice to the creative experience even of artists and thinkers he admires. That language of extremity may also distort our understanding of the appetites underlying the devoted transmission of culture. So Steiner's critics contend.

Just as there is no fully persuasive reason why people should not try to have things "both ways," there is also no denying that Steiner is right to speak of hypocrisy and shallowness in American culture. Given the enormous numbers enrolled in American colleges and universities, it is astonishing how slight in the United States are the sales of serious fiction and poetry, how little first-rate theater can be sustained in American cities, how small a proportion of Americans can speak or read even a single foreign language, how few are the daily newspapers that carry "hard" news and adult commentary, how entirely even the leading professional schools in the arts and sciences are content to be vocational training grounds whose students are in the broad sense uneducated, how even reputable institutions routinely graduate students who have read little and are not able to compose coherent papers. To be sure, there is a wide public response to blockbuster museum shows, the success of American musical training, the international prestige of American medicine, and so on. No one denies that the United States has accomplished a great deal. But Steiner rightly points to so many fundamental deficiencies in American culture that his attack cannot be easily dismissed. Neither should anyone too readily dismiss what he says of the "sheer dishonesty" involved in the promotion of American open-admission universities or programs. The absence of academic standards in many of these institutions is no secret. We are learning, moreover, that most of these colleges and universities not only fail to teach very much college-level material but also do not succeed in creating the kind of pride and commitment to growth that might otherwise be said to "compensate" for

academic deficiencies. If the "populist ideal of general education" for all is not "totally superficial and mendacious," it has yet failed to achieve generally satisfactory results. The hypocrisy of those who claim success and refuse to address the deteriorating state of the culture is obvious. Here Steiner has for many years touched upon a sensitive and critical issue.

The shallowness of American culture is an elusive matter. Many have taken it on, none with greater cogency than Tocqueville. Philip Rieff's observations on "The Triumph of the Therapeutic" were similarly instructive. So, too, the testimony of leading poets and novelists. Consider Randall Jarrell, who wrote in "A Girl in a Library" of a nineteen-year-old college student who—"very human"—dozes over her books or, awake, "studies" to get ahead. Jarrell's girl passively insinuates herself into the poet's mind, which "shrinks from its object" and concludes that "this is a waist the spirit breaks its arm on." Steiner's reflections on American culture are very much in this vein, not quite so ironically playful, but comparably fierce and, even in their generous moments, unforgiving. Like Steiner and others confronted with the numbing common sense, "the sovereign candour of American philistinism," Jarrell in his poem calls as witness not an American friend but a European—specifically, in Jarrell's poem, Pushkin's Tatyana Larina—so that together they may agree that when "the Angel comes," it is "better to squawk like a chicken / Than to say with Truth, 'But I'm a *good* girl.'" In his own calls to Pushkin, Kierkegaard, Wittgenstein, and Heidegger, Steiner has seemed routinely to invoke the European spirit as witness against the pervasive shallowness of American cultural life. So he reminds us that in the standard American version, "a psychiatric social worker waits on Oedipus, . . . a family counselling service attends on Lear," and Dostoevsky is reassured that there are "cures for epilepsy." Caricature, to be sure, but telling caricature, and by now familiar among critics of the United States, though Steiner was among the first of his generation to frame the case in these terms.

Steiner's critique of American culture does not lead on to programmatic recommendations. For one thing, Steiner insists that the culture is too diverse to be neatly contained within any single formula. For another, the choices and circumstances that have made the United States what it is have much to be said for them: Steiner is perfectly serious when he repeats that the so-called American way is "thoroughly justifiable." His admiration for particular American achievements is considerable. When his critics complain about the absence of persuasive judgments or recommendations in Steiner's work on the United States, they usually say that it is finally hopeless to judge by looking back or consulting European models. Also hopeless is Steiner's idea that one can judge by drawing comparisons between the

American experience and the experience of oppressive societies. Few of Steiner's assertions have met with as much resistance as his contention that great art and thought are more likely to come from politically repressive circumstances than from relatively open societies. Although Steiner cites Borges—"Censorship is the mother of metaphor"—and Joyce—"we artists are olives; squeeze us"—he is routinely accused of building a theory on what is in others merely a vagrant suggestion. Steiner, it is said, cannot expect to do justice to the American condition armed with notions taken over from cultural settings that will not transfer to distant shores. His refusal of programmatic overtures is therefore often regarded as evasion, even by academic intellectuals who would never dream of demanding from other cultural critics a practical program.

What must be stressed, of course, is that Steiner does not expect Americans to quit their ways and take up his urgencies. His task is to point out the cultural consequences of particular assumptions and to see the United States as a peculiar, in some ways exemplary, phenomenon in the history of the West. In citing Borges and Joyce, he does not recommend that American writers find ways to labor under censorship or tyranny. His view of exigency does not lead him to deny the first-rate work that is produced in pleasant circumstances. Although he persistently applies to American culture standards taken over from other precincts, he most strenuously judges the United States by its own high claims. It is not only the candor but also the aggressive contemporaneity of American intellectuals that Steiner anatomizes and seeks to understand. His oppositional critique is everywhere a response to inflated or misleading claims, as well as to the betrayal of promises Americans themselves have often made.

* * *

There is no use in trying to defend Steiner against recent proponents of so-called cultural studies. People who believe that a university curriculum should be principally built on the interests and demands of the population at large may have a valid case to make, but there is no way that they can seriously confront Steiner without finding a way to take seriously once again the idea of culture that informs his stance. Academics who automatically sneer at "humanists" who "imagine that the general progress of civilization has something to do with appreciating great art"—here I quote a prominent postmodern thinker—are themselves an important part of the problem Steiner confronts. So also are those for whom the idea of an elite minority is said to be reprehensible and disgusting, though they are themselves frequently contemptuous of generalist intellectuals such as Steiner, Irving Howe, and John Bayley, who write not solely for a professional literary class but for a common reader. Although Steiner has aggressively

locked horns with many of those who casually consign "humanists" to the dustbin of history, it is unlikely that at present he will carry the day in the American academy.

Of course there are many kinds of readers, and even in the American academy substantial numbers continue to regard Steiner as a model of intellectual range and brilliance, whose cultural criticism on the whole is deeply stirring. Those who would make a case for the cultural criticism obviously follow some of his own procedures so as to place him where he belongs. This seems fair, and helpful. When one says that he belongs with Adorno, or Arnold, one is aware that the points of legitimate comparison are partial at best. Place him alongside other cultural critics and the impression of disparity remains. Yet at his best—and he is often at his best—Steiner does often call to mind other prominent cultural critics. Is there a single model against which to measure his achievement? Probably not; no two writers could be as different from each other as Adorno and Arnold, and other such figures are no less singular. At the same time, one does often have the sense that cultural criticism is an enterprise characterized by a particular sentiment. That sentiment, one feels, would underwrite and enable the work of a writer in such a way as to make it useful or inspiriting to his contemporaries at least. Steiner's posture might not be—in this sense—so eccentric as to prevent his doing the essential work of the cultural critic.

What posture? What work, exactly? Elias Canetti, speaking in 1936 of Hermann Broch, describes the true writer as "the thrall of his time," one who "sticks his damp nose into everything," who is "insatiable," "unintimidated by any single task," attentive always to the "diversity of the world." Canetti also demands that the writer "stand against his time, . . . not merely against this or that," but against the very "law" of his time. This opposition, Canetti goes on, "should be loud," and the writer will thus have to "kick and scream like an infant," though "no milk of the world, not even from the kindest breast, may quench his opposition and lull him to sleep. If he forgets his opposition, he has become an apostate."

Canetti's profile was not intended to describe the cultural critic, but a certain kind of exemplary writer. That much is clear. So, too, is it obvious that, as in any typology, individual particulars may not apply in every relevant instance. Yet, taken together, the qualities cited by Canetti say a great deal about our experience of the best cultural critics, and of Steiner's work most especially. Which critics in our day have so consistently and lucidly opposed the "law" of their time? Which have been so "insatiable" and "loud" while managing to hold a very broad and serious readership? If Canetti's profile helps us to identify the sentiment underlying cultural criticism, it surely helps us to see what Steiner is about.

So, too, do elements in the profile trouble us. Can a writer who invokes the tradition as Steiner does be said to be "the thrall of his time"? Can one who rejects so much be genuinely and openly attentive to "diversity"? Is the demand for a radically "oppositional" stance not an encouragement to iconoclasm and posturing? These are useful cautionary questions, to be sure. But Steiner would seem proof against the objections they convey.

For one thing, Steiner is compulsively engaged with the thought and main currents of his time. He writes about not only new books and theories but also basic changes in the culture, from the impact of rock music to recent developments in sexual practice. The easy notion of the traditionalist as one who buries himself in the past to avoid having to confront the terrors of the present is totally inapplicable to Steiner. His hostility to aspects of contemporary culture is matched by his exhilaration in taking on fresh ideas. Just so, though his work is everywhere informed by a furious moral earnestness, he is deeply curious about everything and willing to look closely at things from which others fastidiously recoil.

In the 1960s Steiner took seriously the long-term implications of pornography, sexual candor, and sexual license in a way that ostensibly liberated critics were then unwilling to follow. Later he carefully considered the relation between racism and art and made a case for writers such as Céline, whose noxious views are everywhere implicated in their writings. In the 1980s he launched an outspoken assault against the Israeli betrayal of the Zionist dream, against Israel's adoption of a "Bismarckian nationalism" in which other human beings are made "disinherited," "wretched," and "homeless"—with the consequence that "Judaism has become homeless to itself." More recently he has considered the curious rebirth of religious perspectives in advanced Western precincts from which it was thought that religion had been permanently eviscerated. In all, an abundant harvest, a record of extraordinary candor and sustained engagement. The polemical uses to which the concept of diversity has lately been put should not obscure the genuine diversity of the passions of Steiner and his openness to issues others are reluctant to tackle.

The oppositional dimension in Steiner's work is hardly a manifestation of unbridled compulsiveness or negativism. Steiner has found much to praise. He has also found ways to be generous to opponents, and he typically has selected for strenuous criticism the most brilliant, audacious, and well-armed adversaries. Consider that Steiner has taken on, at the height of their influence, such figures as Leavis, Chomsky, and Derrida. If

his attack on selected aspects of the culture has sometimes seemed intransigent, his insatiable appetite for positive models and his instinct for precise discriminations are no less apparent. Those who find him overbearing, relentless, and unembarrassed by the aura of learning and avidity he conveys might again think to place Steiner within the tradition of largely European cultural criticism to which he belongs—a tradition to which numerous Americans have themselves made notable contributions. Having done that, they will perhaps reflect more scrupulously on Steiner's connections with the Elias Canetti to whom Susan Sontag, in an essay exemplary for its sympathy, attributes such qualities as self-confidence, insolence, impatience, ambition, and passion. "I try to imagine someone saying to Shakespeare, 'Relax!'" says Canetti. Of Steiner's cultural criticism, we may well say what Sontag writes of Canetti's: "His work eloquently defends tension, exertion, moral and amoral seriousness."

Edith Wyschogrod (essay date 1994)

SOURCE: Wyschogrod, Edith. "The Mind of a Critical Moralist: Steiner as Jew." In *Reading George Steiner*, edited by Nathan A. Scott Jr., and Ronald A. Sharp, pp. 151-79. Baltimore: The Johns Hopkins University Press, 1994.

[*In the following essay, Wyschogrod explains how Steiner's Jewish identity and understanding of the Holocaust affect his approach to literary texts, centering on the role of silence and biblical narratives in shaping the author's theories.*]

Jewish thinkers think about the Holocaust. They think about it all the time. When thought shifts its venue so thinking centers on other issues, it still remains a thinking of the Holocaust in the manner of not thinking it. Those who refuse to privilege the Holocaust because it might threaten the positive value of traditional learning still ponder how they might have transmitted Torah in secret in the camps and ghettos of Eastern Europe. Epistemological reference point and moral obsession. Holocaust thinking is concerned neither with matters of fact nor with the relations of ideas, but is instead a kind of perpetual moral wakefulness, a cogitating of new scales for calibrating quanta of evil. George Steiner's work is in this vein: a Holocaust hermeneutics of language and culture.

Does the ubiquity of the Holocaust in Jewish thinking not vitiate all hermeneutical projects? Is a hermeneutics of culture possible after the Holocaust? If culture has been emptied of all meaning and value, the Eleatic principle, whatever is not can neither be thought nor spoken about, would seem to hold. An event of ultimate negation leaves nothing worth remembering or interpreting, not even the event of negation itself. But, if a hermeneutics of culture is possible, then thought is the master of the Holocaust, and its existence as sheer nihilation is sublated.

For those who choose the first alternative and interpret the Holocaust as sheer nullity, as ontological abyss, reason must be demolished, and either total silence or antisystem must replace systematic philosophy. Thus Theodor Adorno argues that if thinking "is to be true today . . . it must also be a thinking against itself. If thought is not measured by the extremity that eludes the concept, it is from the outset in the nature of the musical accompaniment with which the SS liked to drown out the screams of its victims."[1] Steiner's analyses of language and culture are efforts to avoid the extreme of nihilism on the one hand and the subjection of the Holocaust to the norms of categorical thinking which the Holocaust has itself made suspect on the other.

Two questions inform Steiner's hermeneutics: What must thinking be if it is to remain heedful of itself as inseparable from the Holocaust? What is the result of such heedful thinking when it is attentive to the artifacts of culture? For Steiner, to think is to interpret, and to interpret is to translate, not only from one language to another but from one temporal framework to another. "The French word *interprète* concentrates all the relevant values. . . . *Interprète/interpreter* are commonly used to mean *translator.*"[2] One who explicates the meaning of a poem, a musical composition, a painting, is no less embarked on translation than one who renders a text from Finnish to French, for both are engaged in semiotic transposition. "*Inside or between languages, human communication equals translation*" (*AB* [*After Babel*], 47).

As for the event of the Holocaust—Steiner prefers *Whirlwind* because *Holocaust* means ceremonial sacrifice (*R* [*George Steiner: A Reader*], 14)—what linguistic matrix could provide *le mot juste* that would express sheer annihilation? Steiner argues that Christian imagery, with its graphic depiction of hell, is the language of reference, the source language that, with the loss of transcendence, is translated in wildly parodic form, into the receptor language of actual existence: "Needing hell we have learned how to build and run it on earth" (*BC* [*In Bluebeard's Castle*], 55). I believe Steiner's formulation can itself be translated into the older literary-critical language of T. S. Eliot: the Holocaust is the "objective correlative" of a lost transcendence.

Steiner is interested not only in the theological antecedents of the Holocaust but also in how it regiments the reading of the Western cultural past. If, as Steiner believes, the psychological stage for the Holocaust is set by "the brain-hammering strangeness . . . of the monotheistic idea" (37), then this idea must be brought to light in all its protean manifestations, including the amorphous literary genres of modernity and postmodernity. Steiner is not proposing a naïve didacticism, a moral decoding of literature, nor is he attributing biblical theological constructs to the Hellenic literature that developed independently of them. Instead, a discursive space is opened in which the relation of literature to ethics in what he calls a postculture may be considered. Thus, far from envisioning a simplistic renewal of ancient values, Steiner is attentive to thinkers who exhibit the epistemic conditions for the breakdown of earlier idealities, as well as to the literary and philosophical texts in which these idealities are first articulated. Steiner scans the history of culture by remaining attentive to the tracks of transcendence and the efforts to eradicate them which, often enough, erupt in violent acts of semiotic transposition. His style is one of cascading metaphor and rhapsodic intensity, and the lineage of texts is as meticulously enumerated in his work as the chains of begettings in the book of Genesis.

In *Real Presences* there is a marked radicalization of his affirmation of transcendence. Meaning as articulated in cognitive language or artistic expression is validated by the assumption of the presence of God or by the felt presence of his absence even when translated into the *cri de coeur* of a contemporary postculture. Steiner reads texts through the nearly illegible spoors of transcendence that are their accompanying or countertexts and does so because the Holocaust, like no previous historical event, attests the pressure of a divine selfwithholding. I shall argue that this semantic transposition, this reading of text with and through its countertext in both his early and later work, constitutes a Jewish hermeneutics of Western culture.

Although Steiner does not discuss the matter, the contrast between a conceptual language that is quintessentially Jewish, "the Jewish word," and the languages of the world is a recurrent theme in nineteenth-century Jewish literature from the pale of settlement. The Judaization of the outsider's language entails its ethical and religious transformation through an *ascesis* that involves acquaintance with Torah and Jewish suffering. For example, a Yiddish language poem, "The Alien Word," describes the pilgrimage of the personified figure of a strange language who "come[s] from the broad / field that sits on the world," and "from the crooked stone / [whose] water is like the clean heaven,"[3] to enlist the transformative powers of the founder of Hasidism, the Baal Shem Tov, Master of the Holy Name:

> Before the thought of the Baal Shem Tov
> Transfixed, oft stood

A word, alien,
And humbly small. . . .

"Hush, won't you? What do you want?"
He was asked by the Besht. . . .

"I want to become
An Israelite word"[4]

The alien word must learn the "alphabet" and "cantillation." It must also acquire the power of Torah interpretation and reexperience the woes of Israel until at last

. . . . the Besht sees
an Israelite crease

On the narrow brow
of the alien word.
Well-pleased
he stroked his beard

And he did bless him.[5]

Steiner's thought often Judaizes in something like the sense ascribed to the term in the verses cited, not because it exhibits great familiarity and commerce with traditional rabbinic sources, but because for him the Judaizition of culture is culture's passing through the prism of moral self-questioning. It can be so construed by virtue of two criteria proposed by the late Steven S. Schwarzschild: first, "the primacy of Practical Reason," the idea that human beings are moral agents before they are cognitive subjects and that logic, epistemology, and metaphysics are therefore the instruments of ethics; and second, the transcendence of the rational, the hypothesis that the ideal cannot be realized in the world of phenomena and "that everything in the world is fallible and subject to critique."[6] Thus for Steiner tragedy is concerned with the blind working of fate alien to the Judaic sense of the world. By contrast, "the Judaic spirit [exemplified in Job] is vehement in its conviction that the order of the universe and of man's estate is accessible to reason" (**DT** [**The Death of Tragedy**], 4).

In what follows, I first describe Steiner's perception of Judaism by examining the autobiographical statements in his writings, as well as his critical stance toward several modes of contemporary Jewish existence, religious orthodoxy, and Zionism. Next, I focus on the way in which the Holocaust affects his approach to literary texts. In so doing, I consider the problem of translation as a dialogical relation between what is to be interpreted (literary text, music, and the like) and the language of present-day reception of the text. Crucial to my argument is the contention that there is an accompanying countertext that shapes the discourse of the critic, the presence/absence of transcendence in the age of the Holocaust. In this connection, I discuss the role of silence in contemporary hermeneutics, "the failure of the word in the face of the inhuman" (**LS** [**Language**

and Silence], 51). Finally, I develop the idea of what I call a biblical hermeneutical mytheme that I define as a biblical story—building the tower of Babel, Jacob wrestling with the angel, stories of Moses and Aaron, and the like—that is not the *subject* of interpretation, but its instrument. I give to the term *mytheme* something of the meaning it has in Claude Lévi-Strauss, a malleable "element halfway between a percept and a concept."[7] In my usage, however, mythemes are not atomic simples, but complex narratives, which Steiner uses to bring to the fore the workings of cultural processes and the meanings of texts. I argue, too, that this use of biblical stories is an expression of Steiner's Jewishness, which enters the fabric of his work.

THE JEW OF CENTRAL EUROPE

If the Holocaust is to inscribe itself into interpretation, the interpreter must become a passageway for its annihilating power in the sense intended by Eckhardt when he speaks of self-emptying to create a space for the Holy Spirit, or in the sense of Heidegger when he thinks of the poet as the passageway for language. Yet, for Heidegger, not everyone can become the instrument of language. The poet is especially receptive to the meaningfulness and musicality of language and, in the present age, to the absence of the gods. Just as the poet is steeped in language, the critic who is to translate/interpret Western culture must be immersed in it; speak its principal tongues, French, English, and German; understand the interrelationships of its multiple literatures—their roots in Hellenism and Hebraism, the Roman world, and Latin Christendom—and, when possible, grasp the symbolism and local lore of Europe's regional subcultures. Through the accident of birth and rigorous self-shaping, Steiner has acquired these requisites.

This understanding is not the result of an inborn gift, but of the formative influences, the polishing effect of *Bildung,* an untranslatable term for the process of civilizing natural man through educating him in matters of manners and morals, as well as shaping his cultural literacy as it was defined in late nineteenth- and early twentieth-century Germany. Although Steiner is not of German Jewish descent—his father was born in Prague, and his mother's ancestry was probably Galician—central European Jewry was bound through language and culture to this ideal. The *Bildungsroman* of a somewhat earlier period combines the goals of Greek *paideia* and of the *Wanderjahre* as appropriated by German Romanticism into a single narrative of youth and was standard fare in the homes of German-speaking Jews. (Women were *erzogen,* "bred"; they may have been *gebildet,* "learned," but, if so, they were likely to have been thought bluestockings.) Wilhelm von Humboldt thought of *Bildung* as harmonizing intellect and morality. Greek thought and language were seen to refine sensibilities so that practical reason, in harmony with classical norms, could transcend national differences and overcome man's sensual nature.[8] Wary of *Bildung* because of its failure in shaping the morality of German national consciousness, Steiner is nevertheless its beneficiary.

Steiner himself was born in Paris and raised in both Paris and New York and thus is a generation removed from the *Bildung* ideal, which is still likely to have informed the ethos of his parental home. He recalls, somewhat nostalgically, a polyglot childhood in which he spoke English, French, and German concurrently and with equal facility. All, he writes, are "perfectly equivalent centres of myself" (*AB,* 115). If the idea of *Bildung* permeates German and central European Jewish life, the line of access to literary culture is skewed differently for central European Jews: "Strong particles of Czech and Austrian-Yiddish continued active in my father's idiom. And beyond these," Steiner avers, "like a familiar echo of a voice just out of hearing, lay Hebrew" (116). This "polyglot matrix" stamped his personal identity, "the formidably complex, resourceful cast of feeling of Central European and Judaic humanism" (116). It is Judaic humanism in a post-Holocaust version that guides Steiner's critical vision.

Steiner is thoroughly familiar with Heidegger's critique of humanism in the latter's *Letter on Humanism.* There Heidegger claims that, with its stress upon rationality as the essence of the human, humanism is parasitic upon a metaphysical conception of man and, as such, precludes a receptiveness to Being. In his book on Heidegger, Steiner shows that for Heidegger "the issue is . . . the *Seinsfrage,* . . . the gradual coming nearer to man of 'Being' and questioning" (*MH* [*Martin Heidegger*], 54). Unlike Heidegger, for Steiner humanism is bound up with the study of the canonical literary texts of the West insofar as they deal with the image of humanity and with human conduct. But humanistic learning has not become humane culture, has not served as a buffer against the reality of the concentration camps. "Before we can go on teaching we must surely ask ourselves: are the humanities humane and, if so, why did they fail before the night?" (*LS,* 66).

One reason Steiner offers for the failure of the tradition is the gap between university culture and historical actuality, the abstractness of the written text and the concreteness of real events. With the focus of consciousness upon texts, a psychological investment in the imaginary may diminish rather than enhance moral acuity in the real world of affairs. To the extent that we are absorbed by the fictive creations of imagination, "the death in the novel may move us more potently than the death in the next room" (61).

A second reason is the all too ready acceptance of what Steiner calls the myth of "the garden of imagined literary culture," an idealized depiction of Western civilization that developed between the 1820s and 1915 (*BC,* 5). Steiner's description of it reads like a bill of lading enumerating English and German Enlightenment values: a high level of literacy, a society ruled by law, a reaping of the benefits of science. But this myth of present comfort and future promise concealed a substructure of poverty, class distinction, and the exploitation of underdeveloped countries (7). Steiner does not apply this analysis to the internal structure of the Jewish communities of Europe. Gershom Scholem, however, writes bitterly of German Jewry's acceptance of a comparable image of progress. Jews bought the myth of advancement and integration into middle-class society, Scholem contends, without recognizing its exclusionary character. Because of their intellectual heritage, post-Enlightenment German Jews saw themselves as fitting snugly into German intellectual life, but the short-lived "love affair of the Jews and the Germans remained one-sided and unreciprocated." For Scholem (although, as I shall show, not for Steiner) only a Jewish homeland could put an end to these false hopes.[9]

RECONQUERING THE FUTURE

If humanism fails as Steiner's perspicuous criticisms would seem to indicate, should the dead past not bury its dead? Is it not pointless to collect the ashes of a defunct civilization? Or are there within that civilization embers that may still be fanned? Steiner responds that the sciences, and the languages of mathematics and logic, constitute "the 'forward dreams' which define us" (128). This may appear to be something of a tour de force in light of the woes that have come to be associated with the principal outcomes of scientific research: the development of ever more lethal weaponry and the destruction of the environment, points that Steiner concedes are by now commonplaces (135). But there are reasons for this hope quite apart from Steiner's admiration for what intelligence can produce.

To be sure, Steiner as polymath and *enfant terrible* embraces the sciences, as well as mathematics, out of sheer love for the "deep elegance, . . . quickness and merriment of the spirit" (*BC,* 129) that they exhibit. But, I would urge, there is something deeper in Steiner's enthusiasm for science and mathematics than an eros for the feats of intellect. A clue is to be found in several dilatory remarks in his writings on chess linking it to mathematics and music. It could be argued that Steiner's love for the game is a kind of fetishism reflecting a central European's passion for the game. But, for Steiner, even if mathematics, music, and chess are value-free in the sense of offering no moral prescriptions, they are freighted with moral meaning. To be sure, they do not in natural language or visual imagery body forth a view of the human, yet each in its unique fashion opens up a vision of infinitude. Thus, Steiner exults, there are more possible moves in a game of chess than, it is calculated, "the generally assumed sum of atoms in the universe" (*FF* [*Fields of Force*], 54). This is compounded when the grand master plays numerous boards simultaneously (*E* [*Extra-Territorial*], 56).[10] Mathematics, music, and chess at the highest reaches may be practically useless and morally neutral, but each, by virtue of its endless possible combinations of sounds or symbolic relations, marks off a potentially unending stream of time. Although Steiner does not carry the argument in this direction, Emmanuel Levinas asserts (with Descartes) that the infinite always exceeds any idea we can have of it and that, by going beyond the bounds of consciousness, the infinite's sheer excessiveness and uncontainability opens up the dimension of transcendence.[11] In the case of science the infinite is expressed as what lies ahead: for scientists, "their evenings point self-evidently to tomorrow" (*BC*, 135). The importance of this shred of hope is obvious when one reflects that these activities restore a sense of the future and that "genocide is the ultimate crime because it pre-empts on the future" (*LS,* 164).

Is science then to replace the humanist tradition? If so, why does Steiner continue to write unceasingly of Homer and the tragic spirit, of Virgil and Dante, Shakespeare and Ben Jonson, Racine and Corneille, Ibsen and Beckett? Does he support a version of Derrida's argument that the old metaphors of philosophy and literary culture are like worn-out coins, but that these metaphors are the only currency we have?[12] Steiner's continuing attachment to Western culture is restrained by the crucial caveat that our mode of reading be altered so as to ethicize, to morally impassion, the process of interpretation. Kafka's injunction is definitive for him. Steiner cites Kafka thus: "If the book we are reading does not wake us, as with a fist hammering on our skull, why then do we read it . . . what we must have are those books which come upon us like ill-fortune, and distress us deeply, like the death of one we love better than ourselves, like suicide. A book must be an ice-axe to break the sea frozen inside us" (67). "A neutral humanism," Steiner contends, "is either a pedantic artifice or a prologue to the inhuman" (66).

Thus far, I have argued that the Holocaust functions as a perpetual placing in question of Western culture as a source of meaning and value, but, despite this moral obbligato that accompanies the artifacts of literary and visual culture, Steiner does not reject the aesthetic productions that the West has created. Instead, developing a double response, he turns to what C. P. Snow calls the "other" culture, that of science and mathematics (as well as to music and chess) as a reserve of value because of their purchase upon the future. At the same time, he calls for a new hermeneutics of culture that would break open our moral sensibilities, for Nietzsche's hammer and Kafka's ice-axe as interpretive

tools. I shall soon turn to what I think such a hermeneutic entails for Steiner. At present it suffices to notice that—and in this he sees himself in league with Israelite prophecy—Steiner exposes the growing gap between the text and the existential claims it places upon the reader.

ZIONISM, ORTHODOXY, AND THE "JEW OF CULTURE"

To understand Steiner as Jew, it is important to examine his reasons for rejecting two by now standard Jewish responses to the events of the twentieth century, responses for which he is not without sympathy despite his harsh criticism of them: Zionism and Jewish orthodox practice in their post-Holocaust forms. In what is perhaps the most autobiographically revealing text concerned with these matters, **"A Kind of Survivor,"** he argues that, crucial to his view of himself as Jew, is the "burden of ancient loathing" and "savagery" that he bequeaths to his children. Steiner argues that the orthodox believer looks at his children "not as hostages that bear the doom of his love, but in pride and rejoicing. . . . They are alive not because of a clerical oversight in a Gestapo office, but because they no less than the dead are part of God's truth" (141). What is more, Steiner sees himself as excluded from a communion based upon observance of the Law.

His summary account of orthodox piety ignores a fissuring of consciousness even in the most rigorously fundamentalist communities that both affirm transcendence and, no less than he, quake for their children. At the same time, Steiner misses the diversity and inflectedness of many of the theological responses of modern orthodoxy to the Holocaust. Although their abundance precludes anything more than summary mention of some principal positions, these allusions may suggest their range.[13] Emil Fackenheim, in what is by now a staple of inner Jewish dialectic, argues that traditional Judaism must be maintained in order not to grant Hitler a posthumous victory through a post-Holocaust surrender of Jewish faith. Michael Wyschogrod responds that, in the absence of living faith, the Holocaust constitutes no reason to continue Jewish life and practice. If Judaism is to remain alive, it must affirm its positive content despite the Holocaust. Irving Greenberg sees the covenant as having been traduced by the Holocaust, so the loss of religious observance is understandable, but he finds solace in the numerous defiant expressions of faith. Eugene Borowitz (a traditionally minded Reform theologian) argues that, if there is no transcendent criterion of holiness, then there is no standard by virtue of which Auschwitz can be judged evil. A central figure in shaping religious Zionism, Rabbi Abraham ha-Cohen Kook, sees in the eclectic spirit of both secular and religious Jewish thought a kernel of sanctity, an outgrowth of Kook's mystical doctrine that the souls of all Jews, despite their diversity, are holy. While Kook's Jewish ecumenicity is an exception in Jewish right-wing circles, his position allows for a positive attitude toward Steiner. Although Steiner's view of Jewish orthodoxy is sympathetic, if wistful and nostalgic, it nevertheless slides into dismissiveness without addressing orthodoxy's recent theological literature.

Steiner's rejection of Zionism as an option for himself is bound up with his general suspicion of nationalisms. Acknowledging the necessity of nationhood and self-defense, Steiner nevertheless maintains that "the nation-state bristling with arms is a bitter relic, an absurdity in the century of crowded men. And it is alien to some of the most radical, most humane elements in the Jewish spirit" (154). The essay in which this comment appears was written in 1965 and so antedates the crystallization of the issues that sparked the Peace Now movement in Israel, but his familiarity with Buber's work makes it more than likely that he was then aware of the Yihud group that supported a binational Jewish-Arab state founded by Judah Magnes and endorsed by Martin Buber and Ernst Simon. Unlike either of these groups, Steiner argues from the standpoint of a Diaspora Jew opposed to all nationalisms while endorsing the survival of a Jewish national state. There is no thought on his part of dissolving the state on the one hand, nor is it clear to him how a state is to survive without the accouterments of power and sovereignty on the other.

The mood of uneasiness with Zionism in the early work gives way to denunciation in the essay **"Our Homeland, the Text,"** written twenty years later (1985). There Steiner does not criticize specific Israeli policies or actions, but thinks in terms of historical laws from which he derives, in quasi-deductive fashion, imagined historical outcomes of Jewish nationhood. First, for him all nationalisms—Zionism no less than others—must degenerate into violence, which can end in genocide. Thus he writes that "there is no singular vice in the practices of the State of Israel. These follow ineluctably on the simple institution of the modern nation-state, on the political-military necessities by which it exists with and against its nationalist competitors" (**HT** [**"Our Homeland, the Text"**], 22). Second, along with violence, the displacement of peoples is simply a byproduct of nationalism from which Zionism is not exempt. Third, paradoxically Steiner shares with Zionism its ideal of post-Holocaust Jewish self-preservation. Employing what could be called an endangered-species argument, he contends that after the Holocaust the lives of Jews must not be concentrated in any one place because such close ingathering makes them vulnerable to extermination. What is more, in the long run it is a law of history that "nation[s] are laid waste" (21) and the best way to avoid this is to scatter. His final and for him most existentially compelling point is that, even if

nations disappear, texts and their transmitters endure. The relation to texts is not a mere concession to survival, but the expression of Jewish greatness. The text is home; "each text rightly established and expounded . . . a homecoming of Judaism to itself and to its keeping of the books" (19).

It can be argued that Steiner's position is itself a species of Romanticism bound up with nineteenth-century notions of national greatness. To be sure, instead of economic and military strength, intellectual excellence and the willingness to produce and care for the treasures of culture now qualify a people for its place in the sun. Yet the ideal of national greatness persists. What is more, it is hard to see how the mission of rescuing culture squares with Steiner's critique of its previous failure to prevent the Holocaust. Nor is it easy to understand how there can be safety in dispersion when the Holocaust occurred in the widely scattered Jewish communities of Europe. Steiner's ultimate agendum is, I suspect, bound up with his understanding of what he believes to be the moral task of Jews: to remind humankind that the treasures of its collective memory must be judged in light of its excesses of bestiality and that so dangerous a job can only fall to its victim-priests, men and women who have been shaped by culture and who have also suffered its depredations.

In short, Steiner chooses to become what Phillip Rieff has called "a Jew of Culture," one who is the reverent caretaker of culture in a period of far-reaching social change.[14] His or her function is to fend off the barbarians at the gate by sustaining at least the memory of the authoritative interdicts that once governed Western societies. On this reading, the university, like the Talmudic academies at Sura and Pumbeditha, transmits the lessons of antiquity in a setting of relative isolation. In Steiner's terms, the Jew "is a cleric. . . . No other tradition or culture has ascribed a comparable aura to the conservation and transcription of texts" (17).[15] Like Luther's Christian, the lover of texts both rules and serves: as critic, such a one is master and judge of the text; as reader, she or he is placed at the text's disposal (**R,** 95).

Steiner, like Rieff, believes that Jews have a special talent for what has been called a hermeneutics of suspicion. "The long confinement of the Ghetto, the sharpening of wit and nervous insight against the whetstone of persecution, had accumulated large reserves of consciousness" (**LS,** 145) that enabled Jews to transfigure the content of Western thought. Steiner goes on to say: "That which has been destroyed . . . embodied a particular genius, a quality of intelligence and feeling which none of the major Jewish communities now surviving has preserved or recaptured. Because I feel that specific inheritance urgent in my own reflexes, in the work I try to do, I am a kind of survivor" (145).

This position is argued with varying nuances and different degrees of intensity by other Jewish critics of art and literature, including Lionel Trilling, Clement Greenberg, and, more recently, Harold Bloom, who writes that "many of us shape an inchoate and still heretical new Torah out of the writings of Freud, Kafka and Gershom Scholem."[16] The persistence of the Jew of culture in eastern Europe—Adam Michnik in Poland and George Conrad in Hungary—is astonishing in light of the minuscule numbers of Jews in those countries. Although he does not touch on Steiner's 1965 essay specifically, Gershom Scholem criticizes alienation as an existentially viable Jewish stance. The idea that Jews as alienated exemplify the human condition does not assure an appreciation of the Jewish contribution to culture on the part of a hostile world, Scholem asserts. Far from reflecting on the human lot generally, the state of homelessness remains for those who are truly rooted a term of opprobrium and serves only to sever the outsider's connection with his or her own traditions.[17] Scholem's argument successfully disposes of the view that, because estrangement contributes to the creation of culture and Jews are estranged, gratitude for their contributions will ameliorate their life circumstances. But Scholem slides over the issue of whether the culture to which the Jew contributes is worth saving. What is more, as I argued earlier, the *Bildung* that shapes Jewish scholarship (including Scholem's own) results in an indissoluble amalgam with non-Jewish elements that is often disingenuously described as purely Jewish thinking.

AMBIGUITY AND A HOLOCAUST HERMENEUTIC

Steiner's stationing himself alternately within each extreme of a pair of oppositions—central European and Jewish, for example—moving from horn to horn of some existential dilemma, and his refusal to resolve it by fixing upon an Aristotelean mean or midpoint, suggests that something like a hermeneutical tactic is at work. I hope to show that this tactic is one of carefully thought out, deliberate ambiguity. I shall argue that Heidegger's phenomenological description of ambiguity is the backdrop against which Steiner's appropriation of ambiguity must be grasped, and I shall discuss key instances of its use in the context of Steiner's Jewish concerns. Finally, I hope to suggest some lines of comparison between Steiner's view of culture and that of Jacques Derrida, an Algerian Jew, in which ambiguity plays a key role. Despite Steiner's fierce criticism of deconstruction in ***Real Presences*** on the grounds that deconstruction dissolves meaning into sheer textuality, his invoking of the Holocaust to call into question the artifacts of culture suggests closer affinities with Derrida than this later appraisal allows.

In *Being and Time,* Heidegger analyzes ambiguity—the German original, *Zweideutigkeit,* connotes not only undecidability but also doubleness and duplicity—in the context of the phenomenon of fallenness or the way in which *Dasein,* human Being, loses itself through absorption in social existence and the world of things. Fallenness is a state of bewitchment, a fascination that plunges *Dasein* into inauthentic existence, into anonymity, into the sphere of faceless others, into the they-self. The term is not to be understood as indicating a capitulation to sin or a descent from primordial purity, but as descriptive of *Dasein*'s situation as a being thrown into the world. Ambiguity is a manifestation of fallenness, which for Heidegger is "the impossibility to decide what is disclosed in genuine understanding and what is not."[18] In ambiguity nothing is concealed from the understanding. Ambiguity is simply the "uprooted" condition of *Dasein* in its everydayness, a *Dasein* that is "everywhere and nowhere."

Although Steiner does not discuss ambiguity specifically in his book about Heidegger, he takes up the issue of fallenness. Taking his cue from Heidegger's assertion that fallenness is something positive and not merely privative of some prior ontological fullness, Steiner asserts that "the 'positivity of fallenness' in Heidegger's analysis is an exact counterpart to the celebrated *felix culpa* paradox, to the doctrine which sees in Adam's 'happy fall' the necessary precondition for Christ's ministry and man's ultimate resurrection. Through the inauthenticity of its being-in-the world, *Dasein* is compelled to search out the authentic" (***MH,*** 99). Like the fallenness of which it is an expression, ambiguity or *Zweideutigkeit* exposes the doubleness of human existence, a loss and return to self, which Steiner will transform into a tactic of textual interpretation.

Steiner interprets fallenness less as loss than as an opportunity for self-transcendence. The fallenness that belongs to everydayness (what Virginia Woolf called the dailyness of life) can be grasped authentically through care and solicitude, so that *Dasein* is brought face to face with itself. But, for Steiner, the doubleness of ambiguity, the back-and-forth movement of binary oppositions, occurs because interpretation cannot avoid dwelling upon the question that accompanies these oppositions. A Holocaust hermeneutics requires that texts justify themselves in the light of their actual or potential failure to create a conscience that would preclude, or at least protest, the extermination of peoples. Interpretation for Steiner is a kind of inquisition that bears down on texts with the force of Kafka's ice-axe. Thus Steiner writes that "a theory of culture, an analysis of our present circumstances, which do not have at their pivot a consideration of the modes of terror that brought on the death, through war, starvation, and deliberate massacre, of some seventy million human beings in Europe and Russia, between the start of the first World War and the end of the second, seem to me irresponsible" (***BC,*** 30).

A hermeneutics of ambiguity, when maintained in its purity, can produce a result that runs directly counter to its intent. By stationing oneself within a moral extreme so repugnant as to appear to lack a point of opposition, the moral import of the analysis may be lost. Thus, one could ask, what would count as the lexical opposite of Nazi anti-Semitism? Philo-Semitism? Liberal democracy? I shall consider this problem in greater detail in connection with Hitler's speech in Steiner's novel *The Portage to San Cristóbal of A. H.* At present it suffices to notice that texts not only present philological, historical, and aesthetic problems but also disclose themselves to interpretation in their moral ambiguity.

The binary oppositions, the either/or that cultural artifacts present, are a major focus of Steiner's critical writings. Consider the tension of the terms *particularity* and *universality* as they are used in the context of the social and political philosophy of Steiner. For him they are not logical or epistemological categories, but freighted with moral meaning. For example, Marx, Trotsky, and Jewish Marxist intellectuals such as Georg Lukács and Ernst Bloch are thinkers who appeal to universal categories and utopian ideals that offset the destructive character of eastern European regional loyalties, whose divisiveness Steiner perceived long before the emergence of ethnic conflict in post-*perestroika* Europe. By contrast, as I suggested in connection with his remarks on Jewish nationhood, Steiner sees "nationalism [as] the venom of our age. . . . It drives the new states of Asia and Africa like crazed lemmings" (*LS,* 152). On the other hand, Steiner concedes, genocides are often directed against particular peoples when utopian ideals founder. Thus Stalin's terror was aimed against not only ideological enemies but also kulaks, Jews, and other ethnic groups.

There is little doubt that Steiner leans strongly toward a definition of humankind that would blur national distinctions. Yet his penchant for universalism does not preclude his conceding that particularism functions as a moral counterpoise to the excesses of universalist utopias. The tension of these opposites—what propels Steiner in one direction or another in a rebounding dialectic—is the potential of each for sparking the destruction of peoples. No hermeneutical perspective is exempt from the Holocaust question that makes ambiguous every interpretive stance and implicates the interpreter, at least potentially, in its conceptual opposite.

Steiner identifies Judaism as the intellectual root of the West's most profound moral expressions of universalism. Jews, he argues, invented monotheism, individual conscience, and messianism. With Freud, he posits a causal relationship between all three and the rise of modern anti-Semitism. "By killing the Jews, Western culture would eradicate those who had 'invented' God"

and suppressed instinctual life (*BC,* 41). The demands of the Hebrew prophets for justice are incised into individual consciousness, where they suppress instinctual expression, as well as self-love. What is more, the message of atheistic socialism is an outgrowth of prophetic eschatological promise. Nothing is more akin to the prophetic quest for justice than the Socialist vision of the destruction of the bourgeoisie, he argues. In an impassioned passage, Steiner declares that "monotheism at Sinai, primitive Christianity, messianic socialism: these are the three supreme moments in which Western culture is presented with . . . 'the claims of the ideal.' These are the three stages, profoundly interrelated, through which Western consciousness is forced to experience the blackmail of transcendence" (44).

Yet it is Israel, a particular people, that is the recipient of punishment for having inflicted bad conscience upon the West. It is here that ambiguity is born: Steiner's Jew is Israel in its *Leibhaftigkeit,* its flesh and blood particularity, and at the same time an archetype of humankind as such. As Steiner describes him, the Jew is a taxonomical anomaly (in Mary Douglas's language):[19] particular and universal, and as such bearer of a negative sacrality that has resulted in near extinction.

Similar considerations govern Steiner's relation to literary texts. He extols the multilingual, transnational character of the writings of Borges, Beckett, and Nabokov, as well as modernist abstraction in literature and painting, as expressing a desirable universalism. Thus Nabokov is seen as "a great writer driven from language to language by social upheaval and war, . . . an apt symbol for the age of the refugee" (*E,* II).[20] Yet Steiner acknowledges the impoverishment that results when myths that are time-bound and site-specific are lost or supplanted. To be sure, for him such specificity is generally tied to Greek or Latin sources that are shaped by the traditions of epic and pastoral poetry, but they are, for all that, the mythical "antecedents" that enable members of a society to achieve identity (*BC,* 3). Even Kafka—who is, for Steiner, the premier polyglot writer of our time—is enriched by the particularities of place, including "the Zlatá ulička, the Golden Lane of the Emperor's alchemists, and . . . the castle on Hradčany Hill," which Steiner associates with that of Kafka's *The Castle* (*LS,* 120). Steiner's preference for polyglot writers and his cavalier dismissal of what he calls "neoprimitive" non-Western cultural, literary, and artistic creations, should not obscure the role mythic sources play in his interpretive framework.[21] Without them, the classical world of Homer, Hesiod, Pindar, and Greek tragedy would disappear.

It can be argued against Steiner that in the realm of action the hermeneutics of ambiguity paralyzes choice. "The reader is one who (day and night) is absent from action" (*HT,* 5), he writes. It is astonishing that Steiner, who is so acutely aware of the failure of European intellectuals to take decisive steps against Nazism and of the American intellectual's failure to speak out when the facts about the existence of concentration camps began to trickle in, does not address the problem raised by Sartre in *Les Mains Sales,* withdrawal from action because speculation by its very nature opens numerous seemingly equivalent moral options. Unable to select from among them, the intellectual seeks by fatuous argument to evade the world's work, just the outcome that Steiner seeks to avoid.

Another difficulty inherent in a hermeneutics of ambiguity is the possibility that one of the poles in a pair of oppositions is so repugnant that stationing oneself within it risks a certain rubbing off of its taint on the interpreter. Steiner incurs this danger when he analyzes Nazi racial theory and focuses on one of its assumptions, that the idea of a master race is parasitic on the biblical doctrine of election. Thus he writes that "the concept of a chosen people, of a nation exalted above others by particular destiny, was born in Israel. In the vocabulary of Nazism there were elements of a vengeful parody on the Judaic claim" (*LS,* 153). Steiner recycles this assertion in fictional form in *The Portage to San Cristóbal of A. H.,* but, as one reviewer suggests, in the mouth of Adolph Hitler, a central figure in the novel and rather favorably depicted, the contention, controversial even in the analytic writings, begins to acquire an eerie plausibility.[22] When Hitler pronounces oracularly, "To slaughter a city because of an idea, because of a vexation over words. Oh that was . . . a device to alter the human soul. Your invention. One Israel, one *Volk,* one leader" (*P* [*The Portage to San Cristóbal of A. H.*], 163), the parodic character of the words is obscured by their rhetorical force.

The risk Steiner takes in showcasing the Hitler speech is especially puzzling in the light of his own fierce criticism, in his essay on Louis Ferdinand Céline, of racist fiction that echoes the racist prose writings of an author (*E,* 39). Those who because of failed insight or deliberate bad faith want to rehabilitate the literary reputation of Céline overlook the moral spillover of his extreme bigotry, which, as Steiner contends, damages the aesthetic surface of his work. In this context Steiner reiterates one of his most compelling insights: the creation of beauty can be conjoined in a single sensibility with a sadistic politics. It is the task of the critic to bring this out and to return literature to its vocation. The innovative literary techniques of Céline do not exonerate the anti-Semitism of his fiction.[23]

If these arguments hold, why does Steiner highlight the perverse politics of Hitler? When Steiner is asked about the provocative character of the Hitler speech in an interview with D. J. R. Bruckner,[24] he responds that

equal time has been granted to the "litany of suffering" spoken by the Nazi hunter Lieber. It is of course possible to interpret Lieber's words as a rebuttal of Hitler's arguments, but to do so is to grant these arguments a certain legitimacy, to presuppose conditions of debate in which all participants fall within the framework of recognizably moral discourse. Perhaps Steiner saw this when he added that Milton's Satan and Dostoevsky's Grand Inquisitor proffer no "real answers" because evil is imponderable. *Teku,* the name of one of the novel's characters and the Hebrew word for a query whose answer lies beyond human wisdom, suggests the imponderability of evil that haunts moral inquiry.

Like Richard Rorty, Steiner recognizes that there is no profit to be had in juxtaposing incommensurable discourses, in this case those of Hitler and the Nazi hunter Lieber. But, unlike Rorty, once it is conceded that the discourses have no common measure, Steiner would find it bizarre to conclude as Rorty does that Nazis are "folks just like us" who simply base their actions on a social consensus different from that of liberal democracies and that "lightening up" might help us to demystify the difference.[25] For Rorty, "human beings are centerless networks of beliefs and desires and their vocabularies and opinions are determined by historical circumstance,"[26] whereas Steiner holds that radical evil is incomprehensible. Still, Steiner appears to believe that we can, however obliquely, experience something of its imponderability when we give the position, however odious, its discursive space.

I proposed earlier that Steiner's work be examined in the context of other Jewish critics of culture. On the face of it, Steiner's predilection for the classical tradition suggests affinities with conservative Jewish figures such as Leo Strauss and Allan Bloom or the non-Jewish Eric Voegelin. Yet for none of these is a Holocaust-driven hermeneutics of ambiguity, in the sense in which I have described it, a feature of his work. Despite Steiner's harsh criticisms of deconstruction in *Real Presences,* the bulk of his critical writings, those informed by the problem of the Holocaust, exhibit affinities with Derrida's effort to expose the false consciousness of language and text. In fact, Steiner concedes, given its premises, "deconstruction does seem to me irrefutable" (*RP* [*Real Presences*], 132).

For Derrida ambiguity is inescapable and follows at least in part from his contention that texts conceal the law of their composition. Texts are duplicitous in the etymological sense, exhibiting a doubleness that goes all the way down. Thus they have no "true" meaning that can be brought into full presence. What cannot be made present (their mode of temporalization, the fact and manner of their dissimulation, in short the way in which they are fissured or differ from their supposed essences) is covered over by concepts such as unity, identity, and presence. Derrida does not wish simply to reverse the order of opposed philosophical concepts. For example, in considering the opposed terms *speech* and *writing,* philosophers since Plato have interpreted writing as ancillary to speech. But Derrida does not simply want to rehabilitate writing, but rather to show that language is always already writing-like (graphematic) even when spoken.[27]

Although Derrida is generally interested in the esoteric properties of language, in tracking the spoors of its metaphysical presuppositions, in his "Otobiographies" he considers a word's potential for debasement, an ambiguity that is bound up with the future unfolding of the word's semiotic potential.[28] In a passage that could have been written by Steiner, Derrida comments on a text of Nietzsche that discusses the necessity for a guide or *Führer* to supplant democratic education: "Doubtless it would be naive and crude simply to extract the word 'Führer' . . . and let it resonate all by itself in its Hitlerian consonance, with the echo it received from the Nazi orchestration of the Nietzschean reference, as if the word had no other context. But it would be just as peremptory to deny that something . . . passes from the Nietzschean Führer, who is not merely a schoolmaster and master of doctrine, to the Hitlerian Führer."[29] Derrida goes on to say that philosophical language is unstable, so interpretation is inherently undecidable. For example, there are left and right Hegelians, Heideggerians, and Nietzscheans such that "the one can always be the other, the double of the other."[30]

In *Real Presences,* Steiner asserts that the understanding of language and the experience of meaning are "underwritten by the assumption of God's presence" (*RP,* 3). Thus, the perpetual question posed by the Holocaust is resolved by positing a divine center with which meaning and value are in accord. Nothing, it would seem, could be further removed from Derridean usage. Yet, even in his most manifestly theological work, Steiner is driven to posit a counterlogos to explain language's clouded doubleness, the speech that articulates the death camps, actualizes and "deconstructs the humane," and is not merely privative but a demonic positivity. Does not the counterlogos play the role of the Egyptian god Thoth in his guise as poisoner of language in Derrida's essay "Plato's Pharmacy"? Steiner's remark that deconstruction "ironizes into eloquence, the underlying nihilistic findings of literacy . . . as these *must* be stated and faced in the time of epilogue" (132) could well be applied to aspects of his own work.

JEWISH HERMENEUTICAL MYTHEMES

If Derrida's view of language focuses on writing, on the physical topos of the page, then the white spaces of writing must constitute a key feature of language. For Steiner, language is primarily utterance, and the *Urna-*

tur of language is silence: first, the silence that antedates speech, what there was before there was utterance; second, the circumambient silence of transcendence that surrounds and limits all language; and, finally, the silence of night, the Holocaustal silence of an absent Presence. Of the first silence, Steiner writes, "the human person has broken free from the great silence of matter" (*LS,* 36).

The second and third modes of silence are perceived and made sensuously present through the works of three central European Jewish figures: Franz Kafka, Hermann Broch, and Arnold Schoenberg. Not only do references to them abound, but the analyses of their works are conducted with unusual intensity, as if physically to ingest the core of their aesthetic and moral visions. Steiner writes:

> Kafka used every word, in a language which he experienced as alien, as if he had purloined it from a secret, dwindling store and had to return it before morning intact. Hermann Broch . . . recognizes in the act of poetry, in a commitment to language, a blasphemy against life and the needs of man. One would also want to include the new uses of silence in the music of Schoenberg . . . and in particular the "failure of the word" which is the dramatic substance and climax of Schoenberg's *Moses and Aaron.*
>
> (*E,* 72)

Steiner sees the three as virtuosi of silence, and his effort to give an account of their work (and that of others who wrestle with silence) is mediated by biblical "hermeneutical mythemes" as I defined this term earlier: complex stories that are not the subject of interpretation, but interpretive instruments. Because they recur frequently in Steiner's work, I shall focus particularly on the tales of Babel, Jacob's wrestling with the angel, and the struggle between Moses and Aaron.

For Steiner the story of Babel is the controlling figure for hermeneutical activity itself. The salient features of the story from the standpoint of its interpretive function are the existence of a single language spoken by the whole earth, the effort of the people to build a city and a tower that would reach to the heavens in order to make a name for themselves, God's anger at their overweening ambition, their dispersion, and the multiplication of the earth's languages. The move from the Edenic transparency of a single language to manifold languages constitutes a primal act of humanization.[31] To be human is to translate, to reach for a semiotic equivalence across the phonic and lexical differences of numerous languages. The true genius of our age, on Steiner's account, is the genius of Babel, the polyglot writer who needs no visa to pass across the frontiers of several languages. Steiner is often quoted as saying that trees have roots and men have legs (*LS,* 152), implying that mobility in space and language, rather than static rootedness, is quintessentially human.

I noted earlier that there is, for Steiner, a prelapsarian silence and the deathly quiet of a postapocalyptic world, the world after Babel. This double silence is found in opposing predictions of the Kabbalah: that there would come a time when the pellucid language of divine speech would return, but also when words would cease to have any meaning, would "'become only themselves, and as dead stones in our mouths'" (*AB,* 474). Steiner reads Broch's *The Death of Virgil* as an envisagement of this final silence. The work centers on Virgil's decision to destroy the manuscript of the *Aeneid* because language can never be adequate to "human suffering and the advance of barbarism" (*LS,* 103). Thus the work is itself a chronicle about the failure of language in the face of humankind's anguish and pain. For Steiner, Kafka also lives at the edge of this silence, for even if "Kafka names all things anew," these acts of nomination take place "in a second Garden full of ash and doubt" (50). The stillness that succeeds the tumult of Babel is a fall deeper than the fall into multiple tongues from a single divine language.

Jacob's wrestling with the angel is the hermeneutical mytheme through which Steiner explicates the emergence of psychic individuation and artistic creation. To understand Steiner's view, it is important to notice that, in order to account for artistic creation, he does not introduce the myth of Prometheus, who breaches the chasm between heaven and earth with his theft of fire from the gods. Instead, Steiner turns to Jacob, who wrestles with an angel ("man" in the newer translations) throughout the course of a night, forces the angel to bless him, and receives the name Israel. Prometheus is hideously punished for his theft, but Jacob's striving with God and mortals goes unpunished. Steiner uses the Jacob story almost allegorically: to force the divine blessing from God is the equivalent of commandeering the poetic word. Thus Steiner can say of Kafka: "Overarching the whole Kafka enigma is the conflict between Judaic iconoclasm—the injunction that there can be only one true revealed body of writing—and the impulse to fiction, to rivalry with the Torah."[32] Grappling with the creator, seizing the transcendent word and exploiting it, is literary creation.

Steiner's focus on the Moses story is bound up with Schoenberg's opera *Moses and Aaron,* so much so that Steiner's use of it is incomprehensible without attending to Schoenberg's reconfiguring of the biblical narrative. For Schoenberg, the same story is explicans and explicandum, both the opera's subject and the hermeneutical mytheme through which Steiner explicates his theory of fiction. I want to suggest, following Robert Alter, that the significance of the original biblical version of the story may be discovered in a *Leitwort,* a theme or motif revealed by a key word (or a synonym for it) that expresses and develops the meaning of the story.[33] It could be argued plausibly that the key word of

the original biblical story is "obedience." But in Schoenberg's free rendering of the Moses tales, the key lexical items are the terms *image* and *idea,* which, for Steiner, will undergo a significant shift to become *speech* and *silence.*

Schoenberg's work, composed in the period 1930-32 and never completed, is a complex of interwoven musical, verbal, and theatrical elements that transcends the genre of opera. Act one distinguishes the role of Moses, the prophet in direct contact with God, from that of Aaron, the channel to the people of the divine word delivered by Moses. (Moses often speaks his lines, whereas Aaron sings his.) In the absence of empirical proof, the people reject the new God until Aaron performs concrete miracles and promises a land of milk and honey. Act two explicates the crisis of meaning instigated by Aaron's fashioning of the golden calf. An orgiastic display of sex and human sacrifice is the result of sacralizing a material thing. Horrified, Moses castigates Aaron for making an image out of an idea, but Aaron disdains the tablets of the Law as themselves images. This act ends with Moses' outcry: "O Wort, du Wort, das mir fehlt."[34]

One need not posit explicit borrowing in order to see that Schoenberg's interpretation exhibits the neo-Kantian mind set condensed in Hermann Cohen's oft-cited remark about the impossibility of loving anything but an idea. What Cohen meant is that the concept of monotheism is the highest expression of ideality and therefore the most worthy object of human love. For Cohen, if God were to become actual, he would acquire the properties of phenomenal existence, and thus, in the nature of the case, he can have no actuality.[35] This is the position that Schoenberg's Moses pits against the idolatry of the concrete.

Steiner can no longer adopt a straightforwardly neo-Kantian reading of the Moses cycle in light of the linguistic turn taken by contemporary philosophy. It is now increasingly difficult to speak of words as mirroring an antecedent reality. If words cannot refer straightforwardly to things, if a theory of truth that posits a positive relation of meaning and reference is suspect, then the crisis of meaning appears to be unsurpassable. For Steiner, the Moses cycle reveals the possibility that language is incapable of capturing signification and that therefore all language lies, or, more precisely, fabulates. "Golden-tongued" Aaron tolerates the lie of the golden calf, but for Moses, the stutterer, "no words are available with which to articulate the essential, the election to suffering that is history, and the real presence of God as it was signified to him in the tautology out of the Burning Bush. . . . Human saying lies" (*RP,* 112).

Far from lamenting the lie of language, Steiner finds in it the human opportunity to wrest, from the aporia between transcendence and words, the possibility of literary fiction. In everyday usage, to lie is to say that which is not. But, if we had only the capacity to express what is, all human existence would be an endless and mindless chain of positive iteration. Only by imagining what is not can we register dissent, protest against the world, and imagine counterworlds. Thus both ethics and literature depend upon our ability to express counterfactuality (*AB,* 217-18).³⁶ The lie that the Moses and Aaron story reveals differs from the "noble lie" told by the rulers of Plato's *Republic* in the interest of a higher truth in that the former is intrinsic to language itself. Nor is the lie that is subject to dialectical sublation the lie that Steiner discovers. Steiner's lie is the event that comes to pass when human artistry exercises a godlike prerogative by imagining worlds that are not. The field for counterfactual speculation is infinite, so writing and interpretation are infinite tasks in the Kantian sense.

Steiner's rejection of some standard expressions of Judaism (Zionism and religious orthodoxy) does not preclude his developing a Jewish hermeneutics of culture and texts. Jewish "rootless cosmopolitanism" is construed positively as the condition for a post-Holocaust Jewish central European humanism. Yet even positions that are endorsed may in the end be made ambiguous by the power of the Holocaust. What is more, Steiner invents a biblical hermeneutic in which narratives are hermeneutical instruments: Babel, a vehicle for grasping interpretation as translation; Jacob and the angel, a means for understanding individuation and artistic creation; Moses and Aaron, a way of seeing the relation of fiction to lying, counterfactuality, and negation.

Notes

1. Theodor Adorno, *Negative Dialectics,* trans. E. B. Ashton (New York: Continuum Publishing, 1973), 365.

2. George Steiner, *After Babel: Aspects of Language and Translation* (London: Oxford University Press, 1975), 27-28. Hereafter cited in the text as *AB*. Works by Steiner are abbreviated and cited in the text as follows: *The Death of Tragedy* (New York: Knopf, 1961). Cited as *DT. Language and Silence: Essays on Language, Literature, and the Inhuman* (New York: Atheneum, 1967). Cited as *LS. Extraterritorial: Papers on Literature and the Language Revolution* (New York: Atheneum, 1971). Cited as *E. In Bluebeard's Castle: Some Notes towards the Redefinition of Culture* (New Haven: Yale University Press, 1971). Cited as *BC. Fields of Force: Fischer and Spassky in Reykjavik* (New York: Viking Press, 1973). Cited as *FF. On Difficulty and Other Essays* (New York: Oxford University Press, 1978). *Martin Heidegger* (New York: Viking Press, 1978). Cited as *MH. The Portage to San Cristóbal of A. H.* (New York: Simon and Schuster, 1981). Cited as *P. George*

Steiner: A Reader (New York: Oxford University Press, 1984). Cited as *R.* "Our Homeland, the Text," *Salmagundi* 66 (Winter-Spring 1985): 4-25. Cited as *HT. Real Presences* (Chicago: University of Chicago Press, 1989). Cited as *RP.*

3. This poem is found in Yiddish in J. I. Siegel, *Letzte Lieder* (Montreal: J. I. Siegel Foundation, 1955), 327. I am indebted to my student Mr. Harold Berman for calling my attention to it. The translation is mine.

4. Ibid.

5. Ibid.

6. Schwarzschild's position is explicated in Kenneth Seeskin, *Jewish Philosophy in a Secular Age* (New York: State University of New York Press, 1990), 4-5.

7. Claude Lévi-Strauss, *The Savage Mind* (Chicago: University of Chicago Press, 1966), 18.

8. See George Mosse, "Scholem as a German Jew," *Modern Judaism* 10, no. 2 (May 1990): 123. Mosse shows that the thought of Gerschom Scholem, whose works on Kabbalah and Hasidism are frequently cited by Steiner, was permeated by the concept despite Scholem's late repudiation of German national culture on the ground that Jews, contrary to their self-delusions, were excluded from it.

9. Gershom Scholem, "Jews and Germans," in *On Jews and Judaism in Crisis: Selected Essays* (New York: Schocken Books, 1976), 86. The essay was first written as a lecture, "Juden and Deutsche," and delivered at the World Jewish Congress, Brussels, 2 August 1966. It was translated by Werner J. Dannhauser.

10. During the 1950s and 60s, Paul Wyschogrod, my father-in-law, a chess grand master and a student of the late nineteenth- and early twentieth-century Hungarian grand master Geza Maroczy, played as many as thirty boards blind-folded, often at the Rossolimo Chess Club frequented by Steiner (*E,* 56). But he frequently spoke of multiple board playing as mere flummery that impressed the crowd, insisting that the real challenge in chess was the encounter of two master players.

11. See Emmanuel Levinas, "Philosophy and the Idea of Infinity," in his *Collected Philosophical Papers,* trans. Alphonso Lingis (The Hague: Martinus Nijhoff, 1987), 47-60.

12. Jacques Derrida, "White Mythology: Metaphor in the Text of Philosophy," in *Margins of Philosophy,* trans. Alan Bass (Chicago: University of Chicago Press, 1982), 207-72.

13. Accounts of the theological positions I summarize can be found in Eugene Borowitz, *Choices in Modern Jewish Thought* (New York: Behrman House, 1983), 187-217; and Kenneth Seeskin, *Jewish Philosophy in a Secular Age* (Albany: State University of New York

Press, 1990), 169-225. For a variety of positions on the Holocaust in Jewish theology in the 1970s, including those of Emil Fackenheim and Irving Greenberg, see *Auschwitz: Beginning of a New Era? Reflections on the Holocaust,* ed. Eva Fleischner (New York: K'tav Publishing, 1977). An assessment of Jewish theology in the last decade, including the role of the Holocaust, is in Kenneth Seeskin's "Jewish Philosophy in the 1980's," *Modern Judaism* 11, no. 1 (February 1991): 157-72.

14. See Philip Rieff, "'Fellow Teachers,'" *Salmagundi* 20 (Summer-Fall 1972): 5-85. There were numerous German Jewish "Jews of Culture" in New York City from the 1940s to the early 70s. Some, like Hannah Arendt, Ernst Cassirer, and Hans Jonas, entered mainstream American intellectual life. Others, who produced works of considerable sophistication, remain virtually unknown. Sigmund Krakauer, a Frankfurt School film critic, has only recently received serious attention in film circles. Hermann Broch, a novelist neglected in the English-speaking world, has begun to come into prominence, largely through Steiner's own efforts. Erich Gutkind, author of an important theological work, *The Body of God: First Steps towards an Anti-Theology* (New York: Horizon Press, 1969), tends to be remembered as a footnote in Scholem's *On Jews and Judaism in Crisis.* Interactions between this circle and American Jewish intellectuals were sporadic. When Rieff speaks of "Jews of Culture" he appears to have in mind American Jews such as Lionel Trilling, Irving Howe, and himself, whereas Steiner thinks of the cultivated refugee novelists, poets, and scholars who lived and died in obscurity.

15. In "A Challenge to Jewish Secularism," *Jewish Spectator* 55 (Summer 1990), Jonathan Sacks, Chief Rabbi of Britain, reproaches Steiner for extending the notion of Torah to include texts in general. Against Steiner, Sacks writes that if Jews found a homeland in the text, "it was not *a* but *the* text, the Torah, the written record of the Divine covenant. . . . The texts of the Greeks were to be studied. At worst they led to heresy. At best they were *bittul Torah,* a distraction from Torah-learning" (28). Sacks's criticism is suggested *in nuce* in his *Traditional Alternatives: Orthodoxy and the Future of the Jewish People* (London: Jews' College Publications, 1989), 238, 242, passim. One could infer from this that, in creating a reverence for texts, Judaism has succeeded too well. But Sacks overstates his case when he argues that Steiner's pantextuality divinizes all great texts. Although art is a wrestling with transcendence, this does not entail for Steiner a literal canonization of literary texts. To the contrary, Steiner questions their failure to prevent historical catastrophes. Eugene Borowitz's remarks in "A Soft Word to Writers," in his *How Can a Jew Speak of Faith Today?* (Philadelphia: Westminster Press, 1969), predate Sacks' criticism but remain sugges-

tive: "If Jews want the intellectual in the community they must cherish him for what he is and let him be that. He must always be allowed his distance, judging, criticising, using his intelligence in a never-ending search for greater honesty and understanding" (155). I am most grateful to Nathan Scott, an editor of the present volume, for calling my attention to Sacks' article.

16. Harold Bloom, "The Pragmatics of Contemporary Jewish Culture," in *Post-Analytic Philosophy,* ed. John Rajchman and Cornel West (New York: Columbia University Press, 1985), 126. Something of this sacralization occurs in Thomas J. J. Altizer's interpretation of Western literary history as a sequence of episodes in a progressively expanding Christian and post-Christian canon. Thus in *Genesis and Apocalypse: A Theological Voyage towards Authentic Christianity* (Louisville, Ky.: Westminster/ John Knox Press, 1990), he writes: "Apocalyptic faith . . . has been renewed . . . in each of the great revolutionary transformations of Christian or Western history, as reflected not only in the epic poetry of Dante and Milton, but also . . . in the vision of Blake" (9).

17. Scholem, "Jews and Germans," 82.

18. Martin Heidegger, *Being and Time,* trans. John Macquarrie and Edward Robinson (New York: Harper and Row, 1962), 217.

19. Mary Douglas, in *Purity and Danger: An Analysis of Concepts of Pollution and Taboo* (Harmondsworth: Penguin Books, 1970), discusses the fear of liminal or borderline forms of life in nonliterate societies.

20. In a review of Brian Boyd's biography of Nabokov in the *New Yorker,* 10 December 1990, Steiner surfaces some reservations: "There is compassion in Nabokov, but it is far outweighed by lofty or morose disdain" (157).

21. Despite the range of his erudition with regard to Western texts, it is possible that Steiner's knowledge of non-Western cultures, especially South Asian, pre-Colombian, and African ones, is limited. It is otherwise difficult to account for such remarks as "it is a truism or ought to be that the world of Plato is not that of the shamans . . . that the inventions of Mozart reach beyond drumtaps and Javanese bells" (*LS,* 120).

22. See Morris Dickstein's account of *The Portage to San Cristóbal of A. H.* in the *New York Times Book Review,* 2 May 1982, 13, 21. Robert M. Adams, in his review of the same work in the *New York Review of Books* 29 (12 August 1982): 11, argues that romanticizing such arguments is wrong and, in this case, an attention-getting device. Bernard Bergonzi, writing in the *Times Literary Supplement,* 12 June 1981, states that, although it risks antagonizing certain Jewish readers, he finds it "a fiction of . . .

power and thoughtfulness" (680). Robert Boyers, "Steiner's Holocaust: Politics and Theology," *Salmagundi* 66 (Winter-Spring 1985): 26-49, defends Steiner's Hitler portrait, arguing that negative criticism results from forgetting its fictional character, whereas Hyam Macoby, "George Steiner's 'Hitler,'" *Encounter* 58, no. 5 (May 1982): 27-34, sees it as unjustifiable propaganda.

23. In my *Saints and Postmodernism* (Chicago: University of Chicago Press, 1990), 249-51, I argue that Julia Kristeva's writings on Céline exhibit a doubleness, an expression of abhorrence, but also a willingness to speak the transgressive words through the mouth of another, which Steiner excoriates in other recent efforts to rehabilitate Céline.

24. D. J. R. Bruckner, "Talk with George Steiner," *New York Times Book Review,* 2 May 1982, 13, 20.

25. The gist of Rorty's remarks and the phrases cited were contained in his talk at Queens College of the City University of New York, April 1991, and my recollection of them is confirmed by several colleagues who were present.

26. Richard Rorty, *Objectivity, Relativism, and Truth,* Philosophical Papers, vol. I (Cambridge: Cambridge University Press, 1991), 191.

27. For an analysis of the secondary status of writing, see Jacques Derrida, "Plato's Pharmacy," in *Dissemination,* trans. Barbara Johnson (Chicago: University of Chicago Press, 1981), 63-171.

28. See Jacques Derrida, *The Ear of the Other: Octobiography, Transference, Translation,* trans. Peggy Kamuf (Lincoln: University of Nebraska Press, 1988), 1-40. "Otobiographies" is translated by Avital Ronell.

29. Ibid., 28.

30. Ibid., 32.

31. See Walter Benjamin, "The Task of the Translator," in *Illuminations,* trans. Harry Zohn (New York: Schocken Books, 1969). Benjamin, whose view of translation strongly influences Steiner, argues that "where a text is identical with truth or dogma," it is "unconditionally translatable." In that sense "the interlinear version of the Scriptures is the prototype or ideal of all translation" (82).

32. George Steiner, in his review of a biography of Kafka by Pietro Citati: "Man of Letter," *New Yorker,* 28 May 1990, 109.

33. Robert Alter, *The Art of Biblical Narrative* (New York: Basic Books, 1981), 180. Geoffrey H. Hartman, in considering the story of Jacob and the angel, makes a similar point about a leitmotif that for him extends through the story's chain of interpretations. In his "The Struggle for the Text," in *Midrash and Literature,* ed. Geoffrey H. Hartman and Sanford Bu-

dick (New Haven: Yale University Press, 1986), he argues that although "we cannot define Scripture . . . we have redefined fiction in the light of Scripture" (12).

34. Steiner notes how rarely the opera has been produced (*LS,* 130). The extraordinary Hans Neugebauer production at the New York City Opera on 6 October 1990 was its long-awaited New York stage debut.

35. See my "The Moral Self: Emmanuel Levinas and Hermann Cohen," in *Daat: A Journal of Jewish Philosophy and Kabbalah* (Winter 1990): 41.

36. For an account of possibility and counterfactuality as the space of fiction and ethics, see my *Saints and Postmodernism,* 52-58.

Ronald A. Sharp (essay date 1994)

SOURCE: Sharp, Ronald A. "Steiner's Fiction and the Hermeneutics of Transcendence." In *Reading George Steiner,* edited by Nathan A. Scott Jr., and Ronald A. Sharp, pp. 205-29. Baltimore: The Johns Hopkins University Press, 1994.

[*In the following essay, Sharp illuminates the relationship between Steiner's fiction and criticism by considering his representation of the Holocaust in* The Portage to San Cristóbal of A. H. *and his methodologies of interpretation and translation articulated in* After Babel *and* Real Presences.]

Among the many extraordinary moments in George Steiner's novel, ***The Portage to San Cristóbal of A. H.,*** surely it is Hitler's final speech that has generated the most controversy. As though the subject were not risky enough in itself, Steiner concludes the novel by including in Hitler's self-defense many of the ideas—and not a few of the phrases—that Steiner had himself used in his own essays. ***In Bluebeard's Castle: Some Notes towards the Redefinition of Culture,*** for example, had described three stages of "the blackmail of transcendence" by which Jews had pressed on Western civilization "a summons to perfection": the invention of "monotheism at Sinai, primitive Christianity, [and] messianic socialism."[1] The demands of this idealism proved so great that the civilization built up "murderous resentments" against the Jews, branding them "the 'bad conscience' of Western history" (**BC** [***In Bluebeard's Castle***], 45), and later trying to exterminate them and the threatening idealism they had come to represent. In his speech at the end of ***The Portage*** [***The Portage to San Cristóbal of A. H.***], Hitler uses Steiner's very phrase ("Three times the Jew has pressed on us the blackmail of transcendence"), then goes on to an explanation of the three stages, which in many respects resembles Steiner's.[2] Although some critics have drawn the astonishing and surely mistaken conclusion that Steiner must therefore have been sanctioning Hitler's position,[3] clearly Steiner's gesture of self-quotation is significant, and it bears directly on any consideration of the relationship between his fiction and essays.

Nobody is more aware than Steiner of this past decade's reconsideration of the relationships among genres, of its withering critique of essentialistic conceptions of generic purity, and of its insistence that a precise distinction between "creative" and "critical" writing cannot be sustained. Steiner does, finally, want to preserve the latter distinction, but not without a deep sense of both the difficulty of drawing boundaries and the rich potential for serious play across those boundaries.

There are many ways in which the defining features of Steiner's work are tied up with precisely this violation of boundaries. His critics say that his criticism is preposterously overwritten and that his fiction is too concerned with ideas. A more charitable way to put the point might be to say that in his critical and theoretical work he often writes like a novelist and that in his fiction his concern with ideas makes him seem theoretical. For Steiner to foreground ideas in his fiction and his own style in his criticism is to invite a certain misunderstanding. But clearly he does so with full awareness, and one wonders if his critics on this point are not relying on unexamined formalistic assumptions that all too simplistically distinguish the aesthetic from the intellectual, or the imaginative from the theoretical, ignoring the crucial crossovers.

Nor is this the only regard in which critics have been mystified by Steiner. To ask—as apparently his colleagues at Cambridge did rather uncharitably a decade ago—"What exactly is his field?" was not simply to ask whether he was a Renaissance specialist or a Modernist, but rather whether he was in "English" at all. Who is this man writing about Tolstoy and Lévi-Strauss and Benjamin, to say nothing of chess, music, mountain climbing, topology, the Holocaust, and linguistics? Even in our current academic/literary configurations, where the old model of historical "fields" has been increasingly eroded, Steiner continues to stand betwixt and between. In some ways he writes for that mythical figure, the "general reader"; in some ways he writes for the most esoteric specialist. He is often accused of being arrogant in his writing, but, as we shall see, he is as nakedly modest as any critic alive. Although there may be a grain of truth in caricatures of him as pompously delivering papal declarations, there is no critic whose work is so deeply grounded in the serious posing of original but unanswered questions.

"Consciously or not," says Steiner in the "Introduction" to *George Steiner: A Reader,* "I thought of myself as some kind of courier carrying urgent letters and signals to those few who might respond with interest and, in their turn, pass on the challenging news."[4] The image of Hermes shuttling across borders, crossing frontiers, ranging from field to field seems perfectly apt not only to Steiner's passionate antagonism to nationalism and his commitment to the values of the cosmopolitan Diaspora but also to his central work as a literary and cultural critic and a writer of fiction. For it is the ideal of translation, in this radical, fundamental sense that Steiner develops in *After Babel: Aspects of Language and Translation*—as a carrying across from one field or locus or realm into another—that is Steiner's model for all hermeneutic acts, as well as his most pervasive trope for comprehending experience, in both his fiction and his essays. To see him whole we need to understand just how deeply this notion of translation informs his vision and his sense of his work as an agent of movement or exchange across borders—from one language to another, from field to field, across cultures and historical periods and genres, across the permeable but important boundary between the creative and the critical, and, most significantly in his recent work, from the secular world of immanence to what he often calls the *"mysterium tremendum"* of transcendence.

To illuminate the connections between Steiner's fiction and criticism, I want to focus on his most ambitious work of fiction, *The Portage*; on its connection with his most ambitious theoretical work, *After Babel*; and on his recent critical book, *Real Presences.* Although the debates about Paul de Man remind us of the dangers of glibly speculating about relations between hermeneutics and actual historical horrors, with Steiner there is no escaping the intimate connection between his understanding of the Holocaust and his theory of interpretation and thus translation.

According to Steiner, the Holocaust—or, as he now prefers to call it, the "Shoah"—enacted "the travesty of all meaningfulness."[5] "A thousand years you men have argued, ravelled, spun words," says a woman on her way into the Nazis' gas chambers in Steiner's fable **"A Conversation Piece"**: "You have read yourselves blind, crooked your backs, poring over the single letter or the missing vowel . . . as if truth could be caught in your fingers. You have burrowed for meaning like starved mice and pounded the words so fine they have fallen to dust. . . . To what end? Have you found those syllables which make up the secret name of God? . . . Was it all for *this*?"[6] To have posed this skeptical declaration, this chilling interrogation on the way to the gas chambers is to suggest that the question of meaning and interpretation—the whole hermeneutic dilemma—must be taken up in the urgent historical context of the Holocaust, an event that for Steiner forever transformed not only our sense of the possibilities of human conduct but also our very sense of language—of its import, its power to deceive and corrupt and destroy.

In ***The Portage,*** molding and transforming the conventions of the thriller, the historical novel, and the *roman philosophique,* Steiner explores the disquieting implications for interpretation of the whole phenomenon of Hitler. To put the matter in this way is to suggest a crass readiness to move too quickly from brutal historical fact to speculation and theory—a tendency that this novel does not, emphatically, demonstrate. But for Steiner, Hitler inevitably poses the most fundamental problems of meaning: How can we make sense of him and what he did, particularly because he was, in Steiner's view, a master manipulator of language and meaning himself?

The fundamental structural premise of ***The Portage*** is that Hitler is a text to be interpreted. Discovered alive in a remote South American jungle by an Israeli search party at the beginning of the novel, Hitler is carried through the heart of darkness on a wildly symbolic mission of retrieval, which becomes a brilliant parable and enactment of translation as a carrying over from one place to another: a transportation, a "portage." The task of making sense of Hitler and his capture, of comprehending this infinitely reverberating bundle of signification, is both monumental and terrifying. The very structure of the novel can be seen as a network of variously congruent or discordant translations of Hitler into meaningful constructs that the various interpreters unknowingly revert to in order to comprehend what finally remains elusive.

For the younger generation, for example, Hitler is "a figure out of the dim past, somewhere between the neolithic and the almost equally remote day-before-yesterday . . . all part of a school syllabus and television past. Totally unreal. Categorized for examination purposes or entertainment" (*P* [***The Portage to San Cristóbal of A. H.***], 142-43). For the Americans he becomes not a historical text, but a psychological one, a mere pattern of pathology. "The psychologists will have their day" if the Americans get hold of him, says the French under-secretary of state: "'The Rehabilitation of Adolf Hitler; the elucidation of his childhood traumas.' The triumph of the therapeutic" (142). In the Röthling chapter, Hitler becomes a legal text, somebody who has generated a file of "convolutions, proliferating codices, minority reports and thousand-page addendum . . . the prodigality of conjectured happening, the ramifications of invoked precedent and counterexample docketed in his file were such as no other legal body could hope to equal" (121-22).

The rush to make sense of Hitler breeds a chaos of interpretations, of desperate attempts to move in on the prey and capture him. "So many signals were poring in, so many indices of feverish advance somewhere just beyond the horizon" (147). The battered radio transmitter that the search party uses to keep in touch with the outside world becomes an emblem of the frailty of our instruments of communication and comprehension. Barely functional because eaten through by jungle rot, at one point it is "picking up a signal though it could no longer amplify or sort it out" (55).

Beyond the jungle the Soviets are scrambling to translate the discovery of Hitler into their own official version of reality, a version that one Nikolai Gruzdev had his fingernails ripped out for earlier contradicting. When he is asked now whether he thinks Hitler could possibly be alive, he responds in a way that points again to the shaken foundations of meaning in every sense: "I will say whatever you wish me to say. Possible, gentlemen? Everything is possible. *Everything*" (38). It is a point Steiner himself had made in his 1966 essay **"Postscript"**: that after the Holocaust we are "now instructed as never quite before—and it is here that history *is* different—of the fact that 'everything is possible.'"[7]

The French, in their turn, see only the prospect of an embarrassing reopening of the question of their wartime complicity with the Nazis. In the United States the secretary of state reverts to bureaucratic jargon about "the current eventuality," and "the accused's mental condition and degree of responsibility" (154), while a journalist seeks his assurance "that due process will be followed and, most especially, that the accused will be given every legal aid for his defense" (155).

That otherwise important matters such as due process and the right to legal defense seem utterly beside the point here is simply to say that, like the other "translations" of Hitler, this one trivializes the appallingly complex reality of its text. Steiner drives home this point in the ultimate vulgarizations of the American Marvin Crownbacker, who appears one day in the squalid hut of an intelligence operative, Rodriguez Kulken, very close to the scene of the search party. "This was the biggest story of the century," he tells Kulken:

> Bigger than Lindberg. . . . Bigger than Jonestown . . . this was the hottest news break since Jesus got off his slab. This was like being at tombside . . . they'll have to come to us, Mr. Kulken, 'cause we'll have the contracts, the sole and exclusive right to deal with and negotiate for the sale of subsidiary and other rights within all territories covered by said agreement, i.e. newspaper and magazine serialization, anthology digest quotation and abridgement, dramatic, film, radio and television, microphotographic reproduction and picturization, reproduction by phonograph records and other mechanical means whether by sight, sound or a combination thereof.
>
> (107)

Last on the outrageous list, as though all the other items had not already been instances of translation: "translation into any foreign language and that, sir, includes Bantu, Toltec, Easter Island and/or Yiddish" (107).

"To *trans/late*," says Steiner in the "Introduction" to his *Penguin Book of Modern Verse Translation,* is "to carry over from what has been silent to what is vocal, from the distant to the near. But also to carry back."[8] "When he can't walk," says Benasseraf about Hitler, "we'll *carry* him. . . . We'll take turns *carrying* him. Like the ark" (23; emphasis mine).

After Babel, which grew directly out of Steiner's speculations in his early anthology of verse translation, is an extended meditation on both the "burden" and the "splendour" of Babel,[9] a meditation that takes its bearings from the claim that translation between and within languages is the model of all understanding and interpretation. Understanding, that is to say, is correct or effective translation. Culture is understood by Steiner to be a tissue of translations, an enormously complex web constituted by the continual reordering and reshaping of previous meanings and configurations of meanings. "It is no overstatement," he claims, "to say that we possess civilization because we have learnt to translate out of time" (*AB* [*After Babel*], 30-31).[10]

The stakes of translation could not, then, be higher, a point on which Steiner cites the authority of Goethe writing to Carlyle: "Say what you will of its inadequacy, translation remains one of the most important, worthwhile concerns in the totality of world affairs" (*MVT* [*The Penguin Book of Modern Verse Translation*], 25). Goethe's emphasis matches Steiner's precisely, giving equal weight to both the inadequacy of translation and its necessity. In this respect *The Portage* is at one level a fable about the perplexities and possibilities, the limitations and urgencies, of translation. However inadequate, "the attempt to translate must be made," says Steiner, "the risks taken, if that tower in Babel is to be more than ruin" (29).

Once the search party in *The Portage* captures its man, it confronts the soul-rending task of what to make of him. Interpretation and evaluation, comprehension and judgment can no more tidily be separated with regard to Hitler than with a work of literature, so here the issue of accurate judgment shades quickly into the question of justice.[11] "For Thou art judge," Elie Barach prays early in the book. "Thine is the vengeance and Thine the pardon. . . . Guard us from certitude. . . . Do not ask of us, O Lord, that we do vengeance or show mercy. The task is greater than we are. It passes understanding" (*P,* 22). We shall see, when we turn later to *Real Presences,* that this sense of humility when confronted with judging another human being has its analogue in acts of literary interpretation and evaluation, which, Steiner will argue, must finally be underwritten by the transcendent. But however perilous the act of translation may be, however fraught with difficulty and uncertainty and the possibility of radical misunderstanding, it must be undertaken. One does what one can, as

the search party does at the end of the novel when it does indeed put Hitler on trial. "Where there is a temple," Elie tells Asher just before the trial,

> let the rabbi speak. Where there is only a rabbi let the unlearned hold their peace. Where there are ten simple men left, let them join in counsel. Where there is but one man left, let him be steadfast as the temple was, let him seek out the meaning of the Law as the rabbi did, let him take counsel with himself as if a score of just men inhabited his heart. We have only ash in hand to kindle a great fire.
>
> (157)

One begins a translation, then, in trust, which constitutes the first of the four stages or motions that Steiner outlines for the act of translation in *After Babel.* The parallels with *The Portage* are striking. Translation begins with the assumption, not so obvious as it might at first appear, that "there is 'something there' to be understood . . . an investment of belief . . . epistemologically exposed and psychologically hazardous" (*AB,* 296). The very premise of the search party, that Hitler is alive in the jungle, seems the maddest gamble, exposing them to every conceivable form of doubt about the meaning of their venture. In one sense, then, their situation represents a dramatic enactment of precisely that radical exposure and hazard of which Steiner speaks in *After Babel,* though in the novel it is both intensified and symbolized by the enormity of physical danger that they confront throughout their mission. "No man," a local priest had explained to them, "could live in the unmapped quicksand and green bogs beyond the falls," nobody could survive the black rains that "lashed the clothing off their back," or the infernal swarms of insects as the members of the search party literally crawled the last thirty miles "inchwise. On their knees and with loosening bowels" (*P,* 17-18). But these men are in the obsessive grip of a vision, directed by their leader via radio from Tel Aviv: Emmanuel Lieber, a survivor who had "crawled out from under the burnt flesh in the death pits of Bialka" with "a perception so outside the focus of man's customary vision" that he could pursue his "one incessant dream" with a will utterly "inviolate to any other claim of life" (16-17).

"The second move," says Steiner, "is incursive and extractive. . . . Comprehension, as its etymology shows, 'comprehends' not only cognitively but by encirclement and ingestion. . . . We 'break' a code; decipherment is dissective, leaving the shell smashed and the vital layers stripped" (*AB,* 297-98). Desperately, those on the periphery try to break the search party's code. Kulken, for example, lies awake listening "through the static and the oily wash of music" from the regional radio stations to "a code out of Revelation, an alphabet reversed and permuted out of Chronicles and Malachi" (*P,* 79). In Steiner's dramatization, the effort of decipherment is not only aggressive and dissective but also bone-shatteringly arduous work. "There were nights when his fingers had swollen to pale grubs just transcribing the stuff, trying to separate the syllables as they crackled or whispered out of the jungle. There had been thorns in his ears; he had felt them bleed" (80). That Steiner can sustain this symbolic rendering of the spiritual dynamics of translation/interpretation without compromising either the sheer literary suspense or the urgent historicity of the central plot is not least among the triumphs of this inspired fable; what is even more remarkable is that the subtext about translation achieves a power and resonance of its own that is virtually mythic in its portrayal of interpretation as a primal hunt for meaning.

Nor do the obstacles to be overcome cease with the seizure of the object. If the first step outlined in *After Babel* is trust and the second is aggression, the third is incorporation. "The import, of meaning and of form, the embodiment, is not made in or into a vacuum. The native semantic field is crowded" (*AB,* 98), as witness the array of semantic fields waiting hungrily on the jungle's periphery: Kulken and Crownbacker with their P.R., Röthling with his legal precedents, the French, Soviet, and American officials ready with their own structures of understanding to absorb and domesticate even this wild new piece of reality. But they are all anxious because "the act of importation can potentially dislocate or relocate the whole of the native structure. . . . No language, no traditional symbolic set or cultural ensemble imports without risk of being transformed" (299). It is here, I think, that we can begin to understand *The Portage* itself as a radical act of translation: a meditation on Hitler and the crisis of meaning, which aims to reshape our understanding of both the Holocaust and the nature of meaning itself.

The fourth and final stage of translation is "the enactment of reciprocity in order to restore balance" (300). The initial movement of trust and the fact that "we come home laden" cause "disequilibrium throughout the system by taking away from 'the other' and by adding . . . to our own. . . . The hermeneutic act must compensate . . . it must mediate into exchange. . . . The over-determination of the interpretive act is inherently inflationary . . . [and] enlarges the stature of the original . . . the latter is left more prestigious" (300-301). It is in this context that we can best understand those attacks on *The Portage* that claim the novel lends Hitler something of Steiner's own authority. For Steiner certainly does, at one level, enlarge the stature of Hitler, though it is important to emphasize that to do so is not to sanction or endorse Hitler—which has been a preposterous charge against Steiner and a complete misreading of *The Portage*—but rather to give Hitler his full due as an object of understanding. It is not that Steiner is impishly flirting with controversy or yielding

to sensationalism, but rather that his view of language and understanding itself compels him to examine what might seem to be outrageous ambiguities, ironies, and resonances.

In a telling phrase in *After Babel* Steiner describes the third, the penultimate, stage of translation as "the *portage* home of the foreign 'sense' and its domestication in the new linguistic-cultural matrix. . . . It instances . . . the issue of 'alternity'" (333; emphasis mine), an issue central not only to this novel and his theory of translation but to all of his work. *After Babel* begins with an apparently innocent question: Why are there so many languages? It is a question that Steiner, in a fashion characteristic of his best work, wants to dissociate from the deadening context of the obvious. As with so many of his searching questions, this one is meant to awaken our astonishment at what might before have seemed familiar. For Steiner it is a source of constant amazement to reflect that there are literally thousands of natural languages. "Why," he asks, "should human beings speak thousands of different, mutually incomprehensible tongues?" (49). His answer is that the main function of language is not to communicate information. "The outwardly communicative, extrovert thrust of language is secondary," he says. "The primary drive is inward and domestic" (231-32). The main function of language, then, is to create alternities, by which he means "the 'other than the case,' the counter-factual propositions, images, shapes of will and evasion with which we charge our mental being and by means of which we build the changing, largely fictive milieu of our somatic and social existence" (222). Language, he says, "is the main instrument of man's refusal to accept the world as it is" (217-18), which means that concealment, protection of one's identity and interior life are perhaps even more central functions of language than the outward movement of communication. "Distinct groups intent on keeping from one another the inherited, singular springs of their identity, and engaged in creating their own semantic worlds" speak different languages precisely in order to shape and preserve those identities and semantic worlds (232).

If the essential genius of language is thus "creative [and] 'counter-factual'" (235), then the relation between lies and creativity becomes crucial. Steiner draws our attention to that relation in his numerous references to Hitler as a monstrous master of language. Gideon, for example, says of Hitler that "there is nothing he could not do with words. They danced for him" (*P,* 97). Steiner further emphasizes the relation in his controversial partial identification with Hitler through two types of allusion: having Hitler use some of the ideas and language from Steiner's own essays, and, even more shockingly, giving Hitler a withered arm, which Steiner himself has. In a manner that in curious ways recalls the coy self-allusions of Byron, both gestures violate the boundaries of historical and fictional actuality with the same kind of devilish abandon with which they leap across genres. The messiness of language is not, for Steiner, its defect but its vital energy; ambiguity, polysemy, the capacity to lie are "not pathologies of language but the roots of its genius" (**AB,** 235).

Falsity, then, becomes "an active, creative agent. The human capacity to utter falsehood, to lie, to negate what is the case, stands at the heart of speech" (214), which is one reason that Steiner's fascination with Hitler and the problem of meaning should not be passed off as indulgence or as insensitivity to historical suffering in the name of theory. "Central to everything I am and believe and have written," Steiner tells an interviewer for the *New York Times Book Review,* "is my astonishment, naive as it seems to people, that you can use human speech both to bless, to love, to build, to forgive and also to torture, to hate, to destroy and to annihilate."[12] "You must not let him speak," Lieber tells his men after they have caught Hitler:

> Gag him if necessary. . . . If he is allowed speech he will trick you and escape. . . . His tongue is like no other. . . . All that is God's, hallowed be His name, must have its counterpart, its backside of evil and negation. So it is with the Word. . . . When He made the Word, God made possible also its contrary. . . . He created on the night side of language a speech for hell. . . . Let him speak to you and you will think of him as a man. . . . Words are warmer than fresh bread; share them with him and your hate will grow to a burden.
>
> (*P,* 44-46)

Robert Boyers, in his rebuttal to critics who have read Hitler's monologue as a vindication by Steiner, points out that one cannot interpret that speech outside the context established earlier by Lieber's monologue, from which I just quoted. "Hitler's speech," Boyers says, "is not a formal presentation of ideas; it is an elaborate self-defense mounted by a *character*. . . . The final speech demonstrates that a Hitler can appropriate a Steiner for his purposes by willfully ignoring, and thus violating, the *spirit and intent of Steiner's original utterances* and turning them to totally alien purposes."[13] Although Boyers does not make this point, his phrasing provides an almost perfect indication of what I take to be central here: that by violating the spirit and intent of Steiner's original, Hitler has, as it were, rendered a bad *translation* of Steiner. To put the matter in this way is obviously to suggest that Steiner is scrambling conventional divisions of chronology, to say nothing of the relations between fictional and historical realms. But it seems clear to me that, in a novel everywhere concerned with the problem of translation, we ought to read Hitler's self-defense as still another attempt—not unlike

Röthling's and Crownbacker's and all the others'—to make sense out of the whole phenomenon of Hitler. In light of Lieber's earlier warning that Hitler will twist the truth, it seems much more plausible to take Hitler's use of the ideas and language of Steiner not as Steiner's attempt to vindicate Hitler, but rather as a wildly inaccurate translation of Steiner himself. There may be grains of truth in what Hitler says—and Steiner does clearly intend his speech to be provocative in this sense of challenging complaisant views—but the final result is an appallingly self-serving distortion on Hitler's part, a distortion that any careful reader of Steiner will recognize. Nonetheless, this extraordinary, Borgesian gesture of literary self-consciousness is consistent with Steiner's characteristic crossing of boundaries, with his continual translation.

This movement from one world to another is a familiar theme in **The Portage** in other ways as well. In the throes of a raging malarial fever in the darkest depths of the jungle, Gideon, who had suffered terribly in the Holocaust, begins imagining another world. "Listen *zadik,*" he tells Elie, "we'll go to the seaside you and I. Sit on a bench all day till the wind blows us clean. And say marvelous words like 'What time is it' or 'Stop picking your nose' or 'Do you want chocolate ice or vanilla?' Words human beings use" (*P,* 99). The world beyond the jungle feels like the merest dream, as though reality as it had been understood before the Holocaust were itself a kind of marvelous alternity or, as Steiner might put it, a kind of dreaming backward. "A man whose child has been burnt alive, whose wife has led another of his children into the gas, should use the future tense sparingly" (69).

Earlier in the novel Gideon confronts this sharp sense of disjunction when he looks at a post card containing scenes from his Parisian life before the war. The world that floods back into his memory is one of sidewalk cafés, of "Boursin with its shade of garlic and a pear . . ., bread . . . new as morning . . . her hair smoke-brown as September grass" (67). How, Steiner, wants to know, can that world be reconciled with the one Gideon now inhabits, or with the world of the Holocaust? The post card "arrested in a waking dream the otherness of the world, the illusion of total possibility without which the soul falls to a dusty heap" (68). This is the same language that Steiner uses to describe alternity, that urge to the extraterritorial that is both the glory and the bane of human imagining. Steiner sees it as a principle of radical freedom, dangerous because unpredictable, leading—painful as it may be to contemplate—to the creations of both a Sophocles and a Hitler. "If the Word can create, can it not," Steiner asks, "unmake and annihilate?" (*R [George Steiner: A Reader]*, 17). From the vantage point of the Holocaust, the familiar world seems a dream, but the world Hitler created must also be understood as a dream—a cruel and perverse imagining, but an alternity nonetheless. "It was he," says Lieber of Hitler, "who turned the dream into day" (*P,* 51)—a point that could as easily be made of a great artist.

Steiner underlines the association between alternity and the mad creations of Hitler by surrounding the fictional Hitler with a brooding radiance, which arises as much out of silence as anything else, an intensity of being that is shockingly Heideggerian, with something of the awful immensity of Blake's tiger or Yeats's "rough beast." The jungle itself embodies the fierce contraries of life and death, creation and destruction, which leap to life when a bat is killed: "The ground sprang alive. In a moment the white maggots were at its belly and a dung beetle had its scissors in the dead wing" (90). Even the lair where Hitler is snared has the aura of the extraterritorial: "Pure hell I'd imagine. . . . No one really knows. . . . So far as we can tell there's never been a party beyond the falls. . . . And they're a thousand miles from nowhere" (12). Hitler resides in a moral or imaginative territory that is literally off the charts, a place where "the maps went mute" (17). It is because of that fact, because the terrible enormity of his being and his creations cannot be readily comprehended in the usual languages of human understanding, that to understand him requires an act of translation, which, like any great translation, alters the contours and structure of the language into which it is translated.

"One of the things I cannot grasp," says Steiner in his early essay **"Postscript,"** "is the time relation." He is "trying to get . . . into some kind of bearable perspective" the horrors visited upon two men during the Holocaust:

> At a previous point in rational time, Professor Mehring was sitting in his study, speaking to his children. . . . And flayed alive . . . Langner was, in some sense, the same human being who had, a year earlier, . . . walked the daylight street, done business, looked forward to a good meal, read an intellectual monthly. But in what sense? Precisely at the same hour in which Mehring or Langner was being done to death, the overwhelming plurality of human beings . . . were sleeping or eating or going to a film or making love or worrying about the dentist. This is where my imagination balks. The two orders of simultaneous experience are so different, so irreconcilable to any common norm of human values, their co-existence is so hideous a paradox . . . that I puzzle over time.

> (*PS* ["**Postscript**"], 156)

Time and again in **The Portage** we confront these contrasts between two worlds that seem utterly irreconcilable. It is precisely that sense of hysterically outrageous juxtaposition, welding Nazi brutalities hideously together with images of domestic tranquility

and noble aspiration, that makes Lieber's epic catalogue of horrors so powerful. It is this same principle of contrast that makes the opening movement of the novel so jarringly effective, moving seamlessly as it does from the discovery of Hitler in the hellish jungle to the polished sheen of oiled book bindings and fine-grained furniture in the inner sanctum of an élite British university.

Perhaps the most recurrent theme in Steiner's writing about the Holocaust is the inadequacy of what he calls "pragmatist-positivist levels of argument" (*LLM* ["**The Long Life of Metaphor: An Approach to 'the Shoah'**"], 61). "Understandably," he says in *In Bluebeard's Castle,* "in an effort to make the insane material susceptible and bearable to reason, sociologists, economists, political scientists have striven to locate the topic in a rational, secular grid." But none of these approaches can explain the "active indifference . . . of the vast majority of the European population," or the Nazi decision to liquidate the Jews instead of exploiting them "towards obvious financial and practical ends," or the "persistence of violent anti-Semitism where no Jews or only a handful survive. . . . The mystery, *in the proper theological sense,* is one of hatred without present object" (*BC,* 34-36; emphasis mine). Steiner is not denying the need for "pragmatical systematic studies" of the Holocaust; he is simply underlining their limitations and their failure to illuminate "the deeper-lying roots of the inhuman" (*LLM,* 57-58).

This is not the place to examine the details of Steiner's complex and controversial attempts to provide more illuminating explanations. For our purposes the important point is that for Steiner the origins of the Holocaust are as complex as its meaning, and any hypothesis about them that is worth pursuing "cannot be 'proved'; the evidence for it is not of an empirical or quantifiable kind. . . . Only a theological-metaphysical scale of values . . . can hope to throw some light—I do not lay claim to more—on the aetiology, on the causal dynamics of Jew-hatred and of the Auschwitz experience" (59). The only language, that is to say, into which the Holocaust can be intelligibly translated, is the theological.[14]

Anyone who has followed Steiner's recent forays into hermeneutics should be struck by this claim that the only way to understand the Holocaust is to approach it from the perspective of the theological. For Steiner has been making roughly the same argument with regard to interpretation itself, which in recent years has had its own crisis confronting the question of meaning. "Today," Steiner says in the 1984 "Introduction" to *George Steiner: A Reader,* "more and more of my work is an attempt . . . to discover whether and in what rational framework it is possible to have a theory and practise of understanding (hermeneutics) and a theory and practise of value-judgements (aesthetics) without a theological reinsurance or underwriting" (*R,* 8). Any serious theory of interpretation, Steiner insists, requires the underwriting of "a theology or, at the least, of a transcendent metaphysics. . . . I cannot arrive at any rigorous conception of a possible determination of either sense or stature," he says in his 1985 Leslie Stephen Memorial Lecture at Cambridge, "which does not wager on a transcendence, on a real presence, in the act and product of serious art."[15]

After all the concessions to ambiguity in *After Babel,* after all the disclaimers that communication is the central function of language, after all the encyclopedic cataloguing of the difficulties and limits of translation, Steiner still concludes that "translation is desirable and possible" (*AB,* 253). However multifaceted and elusive the great work of art may be, however difficult it may be to comprehend the Holocaust, the attempt must be made, as Steiner's nearly obsessive rethinking and reworking of the Shoah over the years and in a variety of forms suggest. Despite, or perhaps because of, the crisis of meaning created by the Holocaust and deconstruction, a leap of faith is required in any act of interpretation, something like that first stage of trust in the four steps of translation that Steiner outlines. "Without some axiomatic leap towards a postulate of *meaning-fulness,*" he says in the Leslie Stephen Memorial Lecture, "there can be no striving toward intelligibility or value-judgement however provisional." Consequently, "we must read *as if.* We must read as if the text before us had meaning" (*LSML* ["**Real Presences: The Leslie Stephen Memorial Lecture**"], 17-18). If the text is a serious one, this meaning will be neither single nor ahistorical, and it will never be exhausted by commentary or interpretation. But without this "as if," without this "axiomatic conditionality," "literacy becomes transient Narcissism" (18-19).

Steiner's recent critical book *Real Presences* works explicitly from this premise, developing a fascinating and, as always, controversial argument about the necessary relationship of art and the transcendent. Although space prevents me from examining that argument more fully in this essay, I want to emphasize that the question of how one bridges those two realms is closely connected with the question of translation.[16] What we are confronting here is the central paradox, for Steiner, of translation: its difficulties are virtually limitless, but it remains a vital and essential task and must be undertaken with all the skill and knowledge and sensitivity and wisdom that one can muster.

But "the ideal [of translation], never accomplished," Steiner has said, "is one of total counterpart or repetition—an *asking again*—which is not, however, a tautology" (*AB,* 302; emphasis mine). Precisely because of translation's insistent paradox—its ideal can never be

accomplished but must always be pursued—it is the question, the "asking," that becomes the signature of Steiner's distinctive style of translation. Without exploring the central influence of Heidegger in this regard, it is worth noting the connection, for Steiner's explication of the role of questions in Heidegger has more than a little relevance for his own work. "Questions . . . are only worth asking," Steiner says, "of that which is worth questioning, of that 'which is questionable in a sense implying not the guarantee of an answer, but at least that of an informing response.'"[17]

That an answer may not be forthcoming is not a problem for Steiner. Time and again in his work it is his brilliant and provocative formulation of questions that matters most and cuts most deeply. I referred earlier to his attempt to recover from the deadening context of the obvious the question of why there are so many languages in the world. Steiner is constantly urging us to see issues freshly, to recognize, as he says of Heidegger, that "the font of genuine thought is astonishment" and that "questioning" is "the translation of astonishment into action" (*H* [*Heidegger*], 57). "Again," Steiner says about a question he has just posed in *Antigones,* "I ask: Why should this be so? . . . I am not certain that we have registered an appropriate sense of astonishment" (*A* [*Antigones*], 122-23).

In the last section of *In Bluebeard's Castle,* as he turns to the final set of issues that he wants to examine, Steiner poses a question, then says something quite remarkable: "This is the last question I want to touch on. And by far the most difficult. I can state it and feel its extreme pressure. But I have not been able to think it through in any clear or consequent manner" (*BC,* 135). We need to pause over this frank admission of the limits of one's understanding and notice how rare it is—rare at any time, but particularly so in our present critical climate. Given the extent to which skeptical presuppositions now inform critical thinking and practice, it is rather ironic that one does not encounter more humility. One reason, of course, is that it has become conventional to assume an equality of author and critic, text and commentary, a situation that obviously elevates the status of the critic. It is thus doubly ironic that in such a universe of critical discourse someone such as Steiner, who has vigorously opposed the erosion of this distinction and the consequent elevation of the critic, should be considered arrogant.

From his earliest essays and books to his most recent, Steiner has, more than any other critic I know, continually emphasized both the provisionality of his claims and the limits of his understanding. What has misled his more uncharitable readers is that this consistent skepticism and stringent sense of limits have not led Steiner to renounce the quest for understanding, much less to deny its possibility. On the contrary, it has led him to seek it with such relentless passion and single-ness of purpose that he sometimes adopts a prophetic voice, which is often misinterpreted as an indication of self-righteousness. What that voice does indicate is an extraordinary intensity and earnestness, both of which can threaten people, to say nothing of the vastness of Steiner's learning. What business does this man have working constantly outside his "field"? Time and again Steiner is taken to task by specialists in this or that academic field for some alleged inaccuracy, and indeed there are instances when the charges are warranted. But it seems to me that in the vast majority of cases the real grievance is unstated: Where does Steiner derive the authority to make pronouncements about my territory? Where does this man get off violating every conceivable established boundary?

It would be difficult to exaggerate the frequency with which Steiner thematizes questioning, both in his fiction and his essays, and it would be equally difficult to exaggerate the centrality that questions—carefully formulated but often unanswered ones—occupy in his work as a whole. He does, of course, often try to answer the questions that he poses, but the sense of provisionality is so insistent, the assertions are so obviously being kept at risk, that Steiner's humility is easily mistaken for disingenuousness, particularly in light of his vast learning, his impatience with cant, and his occasional—and they *are* only occasional—lapses into papal pronouncement.

This unfamiliar combination of ambition and modesty, of lofty purpose and humility, is not only a function of the paradox of translation; it is also related to the issue of transcendence. "At most," Steiner says in the final paragraph of ***In Bluebeard's Castle,*** "one can try to get certain perplexities into focus. Hope may lie in that small exercise" (141). The posture puts one readily in mind of a kind of theological humility, a stance toward understanding transcendent meaning and mystery, which has its clear analogue in Steiner's hermeneutics. Repeatedly, reading Steiner, one is grateful for the questions he poses, for the way he brings complex issues into focus, teases out strands of an argument, tries out hypotheses, speculates boldly but always provisionally. In one sense there is an important parallel, in terms of humility, with Socrates, who knew enough, he said, to know how much he did not know. But in another sense Steiner's humility is un-Socratic in much the same way that he says Heidegger's is:

> To question truly is to enter into harmonic concordance with that which is being questioned. Far from being initiator and sole master of the encounter, as Socrates, Descartes and the modern scientist-technologist so invariably are, the Heideggerian asker lays himself open to that which is being questioned and becomes the vulnerable locus, the permeable space of its disclosure. (Again, the parallel with religious mod-

els, . . . with the risk of nakedness implicit in the dialectic of prayer, is unmistakable.)

(*H*, 56)

The questioner lays himself open, that is to say, to the "real presence" of that which is being questioned, which discloses itself in the act of translation. The questioner's humility arises both from the inherent difficulty of his task and from his respect for the "real presence" that he now approaches. Interpretation thus becomes for Steiner a kind of secular petition, a "re-petition," as he calls it, an "asking again," in which one trains one's most concentrated, virtually prayerful attention not on God but on the text, which becomes the divine analogue. Of course "text" encompasses here not only literary texts but also cultural and historical ones, in the full modern sense derived from semiotics. Steiner's assiduous concern with the Holocaust, for example, should be understood in this context as just such a "re-petition," and it arises from that same radical sense of astonishment. Anxious lest the Holocaust come to be perceived as "a rational fact of life, a platitude," not unlike our jaded sense that of course there are many languages, Steiner argues that "we must keep in sharp focus its hideous novelty. . . . We must keep vital in ourselves a sense of scandal so overwhelming that it affects every significant aspect of our position in history and society. . . . I cannot stress this enough" (***BC***, 48).

The danger of hectoring is clear, not only because the Holocaust is so inherently painful to contemplate but also because a certain repetition is required if that sense of scandal is to be kept vital. The line between vitalizing re-petition and dulling repetition is a fine one. Moreover, Steiner presses his quest for understanding into precisely those aspects of the subject that have been forbidden because they are so controversial. There is indeed a certain feistiness about Steiner, a love of "mental fight," which occasionally slips over into an indulgent flirtation with controversy for its own sake. Frequently, Steiner speaks in a prophetic voice that, like all prophetic voices, is easily parodied. Edward Said refers to Steiner's "absurdly theatrical generalizations"; Ihab Hassan suggests that "he can seem too vehement, hortatory, overbearing" and that "he raises his voice in public"; Terrence Des Pres says that Steiner "wears his learning on his breastplate"; and Morris Dickstein claims that his "most ambiguous trait" is "the moral anguish he wears on his sleeve."[18]

Together with his occasional impishness and what Steiner himself might call his dark, Dostoevskyan (as opposed to Tolstoyan) streak, his feistiness has touched more than a few raw nerves among his critics. But one has to wonder if the more extreme reactions to Steiner's incessant probing of the Holocaust might not be related to a phenomenon that he has so often explored in his fiction and essays: the fear of the Jew as the "bad conscience" of the human race.[19] For the questions he raises are not only unpleasant; they are repeated, recast, reasked with the kind of urgency that we would do well to see not as hectoring and sensationalism, but rather as re-petition in the theological sense to which I referred.

One is reminded in this connection of a memorable character in Elie Wiesel's *Night*: Moché the Beadle, who was the young Elie's religious teacher before he was taken away with all the other "foreign Jews" by the Hungarian police. When Moché miraculously escaped and returned to Elie's town with horrifying stories of babies being used as machine-gun targets, nobody believed him. But what sticks with Elie about Moché is his teacher's notion "that every question possessed a power that did not lie in the answer. 'Man raises himself toward God by the questions he asks Him,' he was fond of repeating."[20]

"We have the obligation," says Steiner in a symposium on the responsibility of intellectuals,

> of pressing the unpleasant questions, the questions which are in bad taste, the embarrassing questions, the taboo questions. Being so privileged as we are it is almost our imperative job not to ask the nice questions, not to ask the comfortable questions. At the moment, of course, looking about us even in the most liberal of societies, there is an astonishing list of taboo questions, the raising of which ruins one's professional hopes, or one's friendships, or whatever. Well, if that is what matters most then the intellectual is in the wrong business.[21]

The fury unleashed upon the publication of *The Portage* and the production of its theatrical version on the London stage testifies to Steiner's point.[22] Hitler's monologue does indeed constitute an upping of the ante, but the gamble is in the service of pressing precisely these kinds of unpleasant, embarrassing, even taboo questions. It is not exactly true that Steiner translated his essayistic concern with both translation and the Holocaust to fiction fairly late in his career, for there are important respects in which the three stories that constitute *Anno Domini,* originally published in 1964, also deal with these issues. But in *The Portage* Steiner seems to have found a way of making questioning, in this theological sense of re-petitioning, a fundamental structural principle that is tied up with the central tropes of translation and alternity. Teku's one-word response to Hitler's speech, "proved" (*P,* 170), comports both an appropriate ambiguity and a final interrogative posture that is consistent with the Talmudic meaning, as Steiner explains it in an interview, of Teku's name: "that there are issues here beyond our wisdom to answer or decide" (*NYTBR*, 20).

Steiner has been cautious about moving more fully into the writing of fiction, but I think we see with *The Portage* an increasing attraction, as he puts it, to "the kind of patience of apprehension and open-endedness of asking which fiction can enact."[23] Fiction becomes a more appropriate genre to create and explore alternities, to explore those theological dimensions of the Holocaust and of the drama of meaning that Steiner now considers impervious to empirical study and rational analysis. The disjunction between those realms, which is the deepest source of the astonishment that issues in questioning, is explored in his recent story, **"A Conversation Piece."**

In the tradition of midrash, Steiner reexamines the story of Abraham and Isaac from a multiplicity of viewpoints, including Sarah's, and in the process he weaves a dense and suggestive fable about the status of meaning in a world that, he is again astonished to acknowledge, could actually have included the Holocaust. The story begins *in medias res,* with a character citing an early seventeenth-century commentary on the biblical narrative, so we have the sense of entering the middle of an endless conversation whose object is interpreting the sacrifice of Isaac. The characters try to untangle the perplexities of freedom, faith, and obedience; they meditate and quote commentaries on the nature of silence, nationhood, and temptation; they cite authorities on the similarity of God and Satan; they speculate about Christ and sacrifice and the exclusion of women, trying all the while to understand, to comprehend, to wrestle some sense out of things. What we find ourselves in the midst of, then, is an apparently seamless web of glosses, interpretations, translations, revisions, re-petitions. We enter immediately into this dense thicket of textuality, so we quickly find ourselves moving in the same environment of interpretation, the same insistent context of translation, that Steiner images in the jungles of *The Portage.*

When, at the end of the story, it becomes devastatingly clear that the setting for this narrative is Hitler's gas chambers, which are at precisely that moment being turned on, the question is raised whether all this burrowing for meaning is not utterly in vain, and an outrageous luxury to boot. Steiner is pressing here the full weight of the argument for viewing interpretation and the problem of meaning in an exclusively historical, secular context. But the final speech of the story, which directly follows and responds to this powerfully persuasive and moving cry of skeptical anguish, gives voice to an equally compelling counterpoint: "Thought is the dance of the mind. The spirit dances when it seeks out meaning, and the meaning of that meaning. . . . The dance-steps of the soul are words. . . . The lords of the dance are we. Are we not dancing now?" (*CP* ["**A Conversation Piece**"], 177). Are we not, this character asks, performing a kind of spiritual dance even now as we debate the nature of meaning? Interpretation from this perspective is an emphatically and inevitably spiritual activity, one that unavoidably involves the transcendent, and thus stands in a relation of dynamic tension with the secular and exclusively historical view. This tension also parallels something of the paradox of translation, which is for Steiner both fraught with difficulty and absolutely crucial, both an impossibility and, when it truly happens, a kind of miracle.

In another of his recent fictions, the brief piece **"Desert Island Discs,"** Steiner seems to be coming even more fully into his own by examining what happens when he brings into juxtaposition an extraordinary range of events, images, ideas, tones, and planes of reality. From a surrealistic sound archive, the main character makes six selections, listening to recordings of such disparate sounds as Fortinbras's belch after a banquet following Hamlet's death, the scratching of Clausius's pen nib as he writes the fundamental equation of entropy, and the laugh of a woman in a dark London alley as her lover "drank of her."[24] The metaphor of music is critical here, for—and this is a recurrent theme both in the fiction and in the essays—Steiner considers music "the most 'iconic,' the most 'really present' essent known to man," and thus "that which most absolutely resists paraphrase or translation" (*C/R* ["'Critic'/'Reader'"], 443).[25]

"The evident reason for the irreducibility of the iconic," says Steiner, "is that that which declares and conceals itself in the text . . . is of the order of being rather than of meaning, or, more accurately, that it has force incarnate in but also in excess of sense" (442-43). Although the iconic is found in its purest form in music, "infolding and resistance of this kind characterize all living texts," says Steiner (443). The best interpretation will attempt to translate meaning, but it will also, when it fully succeeds, translate the original text's "being," and, though this is translation's greatest challenge, it its also its greatest triumph: to translate what is, paradoxically, untranslatable. By working with richly suggestive imagistic and conceptual juxtapositions and trying to render something very much like their unique and multifarious "melodies," Steiner in this story seems to be exploring, more daringly than ever before, the notion of "real presences" and their habitation within the odd and assorted nooks and crannies of both everyday and high intellectual/artistic life. As his concern with the transcendent moves into the foreground of his work, Steiner more turns to music as the *mysterium tremendum* of our relations to meaning, and thus increasingly he seems drawn to that "patience of apprehension and open-endedness of asking" that fiction, more than the essay, provides.

Notes

1. George Steiner, *In Bluebeard's Castle: Some Notes towards the Redefinition of Culture* (New Haven: Yale University Press, 1971), 44-45. Hereafter cited in the text as *BC*.

2. George Steiner, *The Portage to San Cristóbal of A. H.* (New York: Simon and Schuster, 1981), 166. Hereafter cited in the text as *P*. The novel originally appeared as a separate issue of *Kenyon Review*, n.s., vol. 1, no. 2 (Spring 1979). It won a PEN-Faulkner Stipend in 1983 and has been translated or pirated into nearly a dozen languages, though there is a prohibition on either a German or a Hebrew version of the novel and the play based upon it. In addition to *The Portage*, "A Conversation Piece," and "Desert Island Discs," all of which I discuss in this essay, Steiner's fiction includes *Anno Domini: Three Stories* (New York: Atheneum, 1964), reissued by Overlook (New York, 1986) and Faber and Faber (London, 1985); "The Deeps of the Sea," *Botteghe Oscure* 18 (1956): 303-21, which in 1958 was awarded an O. Henry Prize; and two more recent fables, "Noël" and "Proofs," which, together with "A Conversation Piece" and "Desert Island Discs," have just appeared in a new collection, *Proofs and Three Parables* (New York: Granta Books/Penguin, 1993).

3. See, e.g., Morris Dickstein, "Alive and Ninety in the Jungles of Brazil," a review of *The Portage to San Cristóbal of A. H.*, by George Steiner, *New York Times Book Review*, 2 May 1982, 13, 21; and Alvin H. Rosenfeld, *Imagining Hitler* (Bloomington: Indiana University Press, 1985), 83-102.

4. George Steiner, "Introduction," in *George Steiner: A Reader* (New York: Oxford University Press, 1984), 21. Hereafter cited in the text as *R*.

5. George Steiner, "The Long Life of Metaphor: An Approach to 'the Shoah,'" *Encounter* 68, no. 2 (February 1987): 56; hereafter cited in the text as *LLM*.

6. George Steiner, "A Conversation Piece," *Granta*, no. 15 (1985): 177; hereafter cited in the text as *CP*.

7. George Steiner, "Postscript," in *Language and Silence: Essays on Language, Literature, and the Inhuman* (1967; reprint, New York: Atheneum, 1974), 157. Hereafter cited in the text as *PS*.

8. George Steiner, "Introduction," in *The Penguin Book of Modern Verse Translation* (Harmondsworth: Penguin Books, 1966), 35. Hereafter cited in the text as *MVT*.

9. George Steiner, *After Babel: Aspects of Language and Translation* (1975; reprint, New York: Oxford University Press, 1976), 474. Hereafter cited in the text as *AB*. The second edition of this book was published after this essay was completed.

10. Steiner's most exhaustive application of *After Babel*'s claim that interpretation is translation is in *Antigones: How the Antigone Legend Has Endured in Western Literature, Art, and Thought* (1984; reprint, New York: Oxford University Press, 1986), esp. 214-25. Hereafter cited in the text as *A*.

11. Steiner explores the mutual dependence of the interpretation and evaluation of literary works in "'Critic'/'Reader,'" *New Literary History* 10 (Spring 1979): 423-52. Hereafter cited in the text as *C/R.*

12. D. J. R. Bruckner, "Talk with George Steiner," *New York Times Book Review,* 2 May 1982, 20. Hereafter cited in the text as *NYTBR.*

13. Robert Boyers, *Atrocity and Amnesia: The Political Novel since 1945* (New York: Oxford University Press, 1985), 169-70; emphasis mine.

14. It is in this context that we ought to consider Steiner's controversial claims that the Nazi extermination camp "embodies, often down to minutiae, the images and chronicles of Hell in European art and thought"; that all the death camps of the twentieth century are *"Hell made immanent,"* transferred from "below the earth to its surface"; and that, with the waning of religious belief, "needing Hell, we have learned to build it and run it on earth" (*BC,* 53-56).

15. George Steiner, *Real Presences: The Leslie Stephen Memorial Lecture* (Cambridge: Cambridge University Press, 1986), 23. Hereafter cited in the text as *LSML.* The much-expanded, book-length version of this lecture/pamphlet is *Real Presences* (Chicago: University of Chicago Press, 1989). Hereafter cited in the text as *RP.*

16. I take up these issues in greater detail in "Creation and the Courtesy of Reading," my review of *Real Presences* in *Kenyon Review,* n.s. 13 (Winter 1991): 187-92; and in my essay "Interrogation at the Borders: George Steiner and the Trope of Translation," *New Literary History* 21 (Autumn 1989): 133-62.

17. George Steiner, *Heidegger* (London: Fontana, 1978), 29. Hereafter cited in the text as *H.*

18. Edward Said, "Himself Observed," review of *George Steiner: A Reader, Nation* 240 (2 March 1985): 244; Ihab Hassan, "The Whole Mystery of Babel: On George Steiner," *Salmagundi,* nos. 70-71 (Spring-Summer 1986): 332; Terrence Des Pres, "Kulturkritiker," review of *Antigones* by George Steiner, *Nation* 240 (2 March 1985): 241; and Dickstein, "Alive and Ninety in the Jungles of Brazil," 21. Although Dickstein is negative throughout his review, Hassan is extremely enthusiastic, as is Des Pres in his assessment of *Antigones:* "There is no doubt about his brilliance" (241). Said's view is more mixed. Steiner, he says, "is without peer in rendering and reflecting on patterns and motifs in modern, mainly German, culture" (244). "There is much to be learned from what he says" (246). According to Said, *After Babel* "demonstrates a learning and insight that are remarkably exhilarating" (245). But Said's condescension is often flagrant, as in his claim that "Steiner is . . . a kind of humanistic relic" (246).

19. See esp. Steiner, "The Long Life of Metaphor"; *The Portage to San Cristóbal of A. H.*; and "A Season in Hell," in *In Bluebeard's Castle,* 29-56.

20. Elie Wiesel, *Night,* trans. Stella Rodway (1960; reprint, New York: Bantam, 1982), 2-3. For important parallels, see George Steiner, "A Kind of Survivor," in *Language and Silence,* 140-54.

21. George Steiner, "The Responsibility of Intellectuals: A Discussion," *Salmagundi,* nos. 70-71 (Spring-Summer 1986): 194.

22. Christopher Hampton's production of *The Portage,* with Alec McCowen playing Hitler, was first produced in London during the winter of 1982. It has subsequently been produced throughout the United States as well.

23. Letter from George Steiner, 18 January 1988. Compare Steiner's answer to an interviewer's question about why he would want to "use a novel to raise the moral issues canvassed in *The Portage to San Cristóbal of A. H.*": "I believe that a work of art, like metaphors in language, can ask the most serious, difficult questions in a way which really makes the readers answer for themselves; that the work of art far more than an essay or a tract involves the reader, challenges him directly and brings him into the argument" (Bruckner, "Talk with George Steiner," 13).

24. George Steiner, "Desert Island Discs," *Granta,* no. 18 (1985): 26.

25. In *The Portage* Gervinus Röthling says that music is "irreducible to language" (113), an observation that is played off against the vulgar lyrics of a pop song that both Kulken and the search party hear on the radio. Hitler is almost desperate to hear music. "Let me hear the music," he says. "I haven't heard music" (72). Compare *In Bluebeard's Castle*: "In the absence or recession of religious belief, close-linked as it was to the classic primacy of language, music seems to gather, to harvest us to ourselves" (122); "A Reading against Shakespeare": "Outside language lie the imperative spheres of the transcendental, of aesthetic, ethical and, perhaps, metaphysical awareness. Outside language, also, lies music, whose expressive, inferential access to these spheres is, precisely, that denied to verbal discourse" (14); *Real Presences: The Leslie Stephen Memorial Lecture*: "It is more than likely that the performance and personal reception of music are now moving to that cultural pivot once occupied by the cultivation of discourse and letters. . . . At decisive points, ours is today a civilization 'after the word'" (6); and the "Introduction," in *George Steiner: A Reader*: "Music . . . grows indispensable [to me], as if it had become the elect companion of identity, the homecoming to that inside oneself which time has in its keeping" (18).

Dow Marmur (essay date February 1995)

SOURCE: Marmur, Dow. "The Struggle between Text and Land in Contemporary Jewry: Reflections on George Steiner's 'Our Homeland, the Text.'" *History of European Ideas* 20, nos. 4-6 (February 1995): 807-13.

[*In the following essay, Marmur explicates the tension between the Talmud and modern-day Israel informing contemporary Jewish thought, demonstrating how Steiner privileges the former over the latter.*]

The Jews came late to Modernity, but once they got to it, they embraced it with alacrity and enthusiasm. German-speaking Europe was the centre of it.[1] Three exponents of this Modernity, often mentioned together—Marx, Freud and Einstein—are in the forefront of those who testify to the rapid progress of Jews, once their integration into European society seemed possible.

But despite the many outstanding personalities and their enormous impact, it proved to be a very superficial integration. Two of the three—Freud and Einstein—did not die in the countries of their birth, but ended up as refugees from Nazism. Had Marx been their contemporary, he would have suffered the same fate, notwithstanding the baptism to which his father subjected him. For as much as Jews may have embraced Modernity, and as much as they may have even helped to shape it, ultimately it not only let them down, but it also became a significant, perhaps decisive, tool in persecuting them.[2]

In retrospect, may Jews seemed surprisingly unconcerned with the ambiguity of their situation. Most recognised only when it was too late that, as hard as they may have tried, they were not accepted by the majority culture. However, some did acknowledge the precariousness of their status as Jews. Their mixed feelings often expressed themselves in simultaneous affirmation of European culture and Zionist ideology; Einstein was most decidedly a Zionist, and even Freud might have flirted with it. But very few were sufficiently committed to choose the land of their ancestors, Palestine, instead of remaining within the milieu of German-speaking Central Europe into which they were born and in which they were educated.[3]

Those who did go to Palestine early on—Gershom Scholem, for example—came to help shape the new State of Israel intellectually and morally while continuing to contribute richly to Western scholarship and its culture.[4] But even late-comers to Palestine, such as Martin Buber—another refugee from Nazi Germany—found in the land of their ancestors a home without having to pay the price of isolation from their international networks. Their critique of the Jewish past, arising out of their return to Jewish soil, was in many ways ahead of its time. Because they saw Judaism from the old/new perspective of rootedness in The Land, they could judge it—and its relationship to the rest of the world—in a new light; they became Jewish pioneers of a peculiarly Jewish version of post-Modernism.

Thus it was only while in exile from Europe and at home in Palestine, that Buber wrote of the religion of Israel as a 'Covenant of God, people and land'.[5] In this way he acknowledged that the authentic Jew must also be rooted in the soil that, tradition claims, God gave to Israel. Buber's understanding of Judaism, corroborated and elaborated upon by many others,[6] constitutes the starting point of this paper, the aim of which is to suggest that The Text gains new meaning when studied in The Land and from the perspective of The Land.

With the recognition that Jews are not only the people of The Book that is the Torah but also the people of The Land which God gave to their ancestors in covenant—and which every Jew underwrites by "standing at Sinai again" through the study of Torah—the reading of the Bible and the other primary sources of Judaism undergoes a radical change. The purely universal is replaced, if not by a strictly particularist understanding, then decidedly by an exegesis that brings out the tensions and the ambiguities.

* * *

The term 'post-Modern', at least in the context of contemporary Judaism, points to a critique of Modernity that is neither pre-Modern nor anti-Modern. It does not deny Modernity, yet is critical of it, and it does not lead to an affirmation of pre-Modern fundamentalism. It is from this perspective that I hope to reflect on the tension between Text and Land in contemporary Jewish thought.

In order to provide a focus, I shall make special reference to George Steiner. For his biography[7] reflects the burden of Jewish homelessness, and his understanding of the Holocaust is, in many ways, an indictment against Modernity in general and language in particular.[8] Nevertheless, he seems to be drawing different conclusions from what I perceive to be the thrust of contemporary Jewish thought.[9] It is as if he so yearned for the resolution of the tension between Text and Land that, despite his critique, he decided to opt for the former. And he is by no means the only Jewish literary critic who has chosen that path.

Steiner's view of the relationship between Land and Text, as expressed in his essay, **"Our Homeland, The Text,"**[10] begins with Hegel's understanding of the biblical Abraham as 'a wanderer on the earth, a passer-by severed from the familial, communal and organic context of love and of trust . . . a shepherd of the winds, traversing each land with indifferent lightness of foot'.[11]

Steiner does not seem to challenge Hegel's analysis. He ignores the fact that 'of all the promises made to the patriarchs, it was that of The Land that was most prominent and decisive'.[12] But he does draw different conclusions from Hegel. Steiner does not question the philosopher's anti-Jewish bias by pointing out, for example, that Abraham, the first Jew, is not to be confused with Ahasuerus, the wandering Jew. The former, rooted in history, leaves his country of birth in order to *come home* to the Land that God promised him; the latter, on the other hand, a creature of myth, is the aimless wanderer among hostile strangers. Instead, Steiner tries to make a virtue out of the patriarch's— and, perhaps, also his own—homelessness. In this way he comes to strengthen Hegel's distortion:

> What is to Hegel an awesome pathology, a tragic, arrested stage in the advance of human consciousness towards a liberated homecoming from alienation, is, to others, the open secret of the Jewish genius and of its survival. The text is home; a commentary a return.[13]

In his search for scriptural support, Steiner, more like a preacher than a literary critic, selects this sentence in the Book of Joshua (1:8) as 'the supreme commandment to Judaism':[14]

> Let not this Book of the Teaching cease from your lips, but recite it day and night, so that you may observe faithfully all that is written in it. Only then will you prosper in your undertakings and only then will you be successful.[15]

Steiner does not seem to be bothered by the fact that normative Judaism repeatedly struggles with the question as to which is 'the supreme commandment to Judaism'. Not being able to resolve the issue, it deliberately puts all the commandments side by side—if not for everybody to obey all of them, then, at least, for each Jew to make her or his own selection, always recognising that what has not been chosen may be equally authentic and equally binding. Tension and ambiguity are endemic to Judaism, including the tension between Text and Land; to seek to resolve the tension may mean to distort Judaism.

Selective use enables Steiner to ignore the overwhelming evidence in Jewish literary sources which points to an unequivocal affirmation of The Land. Telling his readers that 'no other tradition or culture has ascribed a comparable aura to the conservation and transcription of texts', and citing specifically the attachment to Hebrew words and letters so characteristic of the Jewish mystical tradition, he is explicit as to where he wants to take us:

> The point is that sometimes hallucinatory techniques and disciplines of attention to the text, the mystique of fidelity to the written word, the reverence bestowed on its expositors and transmitters, concentrated within

Judaic sensibility unique strengths and purities of disinterested purpose. It is these which have made so many Jewish men and, more recently, women most native to modern intelligence. It is these that have generated the provocative pre-eminence of the Jew in modernity, be it humanistic or scientific. The 'bookish' genius of Marx and of Freud, of Wittgenstein and of Levi-Strauss, is a secular deployment of the long schooling in abstract, speculative commentary and clerkship in the exegetic legacy. . . . Under Roman persecutive, Akiba[16] made his refuge a 'place' or 'house of the book'. A secularised but closely derived system of values was to make of Central European Jewry and its American after-glow the intellectual-spiritual heartland of modernity.[17]

This, I believe deliberate, misunderstanding of the nature of Judaism enables Steiner to juxtapose Jerusalem, if not to Athens then to—his own choice of cities—Prague, Budapest, Vienna, Leningrad, Frankfurt and New York. He can now opt for these in preference to Jerusalem that is Zion, because they represent to him, 'An "Israel" of truth-seeking. Each seeking out of a moral, philosophic, positive verity, each text rightly established and expounded, is an *aliyah*,[18] a homecoming of Judaism to itself and its keeping of the books'.[19] Those Jews who, contrary to Steiner, have chosen a commitment to Jewish statehood and, unlike many of us, settled in Zion have rendered 'Judaism homeless to itself'.[20] In this way Steiner comes to articulate his anti-Zionist politics in the garb of literary criticism: 'Ironically, the threat of that "final solution" might prove to be the greatest yet if the Jews were now to be compacted in Israel'.[21]

In the last paragraph of his essay, George Steiner offers yet another reason why the Jews' return to The Land is a threat to Jewish literacy and, by inference, to Western culture: 'Locked materially in a material homeland, the text may, in fact, lose its life-force'.[22] The custodians of The Word may squander their patrimony in the process of seeking to reclaim it. Not only does this imply that the other nations of the world who have had the normality that Jews now strive for are incapable of literary creativity, but it also misses the most obvious point about contemporary Jewish life, namely that returning to the Land of Israel has led to an unprecedented revival of Jewish learning and Jewish creativity.

The beginnings of normality that came with the establishment of the State of Israel have enabled Jews to speak out of their own tradition and in their own language, rather than seeking to emulate others. In the same way as the growing empowerment of women has given rise to new literary and critical creativity, so has the 'emergence from powerlessness'[23] through statehood manifested itself in a new outpouring of Jewish creativity. This is not only true of Judaic scholarship but also of the contribution of Israelis to the study of contemporary culture, as well as to fiction and poetry.

By ignoring the paradigm shift that has taken place in contemporary Jewish creativity as a result of the Jews' return to The Land that God promised Abraham and Moses, George Steiner has himself become part of the old paradigm, which effectively has ceased with the Holocaust, and which sees the Jew as the clever—and, therefore, often dangerous—alien in Western society and culture. Steiner—the exponent of Modernity, which he, like its critics, has identified with the Jewish condition of exile—has failed to recognise that Judaism, no longer seeking merely *space* in exile but insisting on a *place* of its own,[24] like all the other nations, has entered the post-Modern era and has come to view the world from a radically different perspective than hitherto.

Hans Küng, the Catholic theologian, understands this better than George Steiner, the Jewish literary critic, when Kung writes:

> The resurgence of the state of the Jews is the unmistakable signal for an epoch-making paradigm shift in Judaism, in which once again everything is changing. For Judaism, too—after Modern assimilation and Modern anti-Semitism with the absolute nadir of the Holocaust—*the post-Modern era has begun*. Of course, even now certain constants will remain for believing Jews: it is still a matter of the same *people* with the remembrance of the same *covenant* in connection with the same *land*.[25]

Küng, being rooted in biblical religion, is able to appreciate the spiritual dimension of The Land. By contrast, Steiner can only quote with approval Heinrich Heine's description of Judaism as *das aufgeschriebene Vaterland,* implying that Jewish territoriality has been replaced by Jewish literacy.[26] In so doing, he, firstly, ignores the fact that the purpose of study in Judaism is never merely theoretical, but must always manifest itself in observance, and that much of that observance is, in the eyes of Jewish tradition, only possible in The Land. Criticism is only a means by which the message of The Text can be translated into action; it is not an end in itself.

Secondly, Steiner chooses not to recognise that the notion of the portable Torah as a substitute for The Land must always be viewed in the context of 'an interim ethic'.[27] 'Extraterritorial' is not only the title of one of Steiner's books,[28] but it seems to be a kind of credo which he associates with his Jewishness and which he ascribes both to like-minded Jews and to Jewish tradition as a whole. The evidence to the contrary, however, is overwhelming.[29]

* * *

Nevertheless, Steiner's position cannot be dismissed. Diaspora and Modernity have not only brought pain to the Jewish people; they have also come to shape Judaism and, perhaps, much of Western culture. Even W. D. Davies, writing about the centrality of The Land in Judaism, recognises the tension: 'Much of the theology and history of Judaism in its main expressions points to The Land as of its essence: the history of Judaism, however, seems also to offer serious qualifications of this'.[30] Zionism has tended to ignore the qualifications in favour of the essence; George Steiner affirms the qualifications and denies the essence. Both are partially right, but both are also radically wrong, for they seek to resolve the tension and, therefore, distort Judaism.

Davies' understanding is much more helpful:

> We have appealed to history in support of the claim that exile as much as, if not more than, life in The Land has significantly marked Jewish history. The force of that appeal must in no way be belittled. Taken in isolation, however, it is misleading, because in the Jewish experience, both religious and secular, exile has always coexisted with the hope of a return to The Land. It might well be argued that the Jewish people would probably have gradually disintegrated and ceased to be without that hope.[31]

At no time was the threat of disintegration greater than after the Holocaust. Hope alone would no longer sustain the Jewish people. It is at that point in history that return to The Land becomes a political possibility; the State of Israel is proclaimed barely three years after the end of World War II. And with that event, Jews are able to move from the Modernity that has so savagely decimated them to a new, post-Modern, era reminiscent, perhaps, of biblical times.

The new situation is fraught with many dangers, but it has also the promise of opportunities. If the emergence from powerlessness can teach us to exercise power 'with the memory of powerlessness',[32] the tension between Text and Land can gain new significance in Modern thought. It may also enable the testimony of Jewish exponents of Sacred Writ to offer fresh insights to all who wish to hear them.

Notes

1. See, for example, H. I. Bach, *The German Jew: A Synthesis of Judaism and Western Civilization 1730-1930* (New York: Oxford University Press for The Littman Library, 1984).

2. See Zygmunt Bauman, *Modernity and the Holocaust* (Ithaca, New York: Cornell University Press, 1989). Though in his comprehensive, *Judaism* (New York: Crossroads, 1992), Hans Kung, the Christian theologian, does not refer to Bauman, the Jewish sociologist, he comes to a similar conclusion when he writes:

> So the Holocaust is a warning to *all* modern nations. Why? Because rationality, technology and industrialisation, the whole complicated organisation of industrial

mass-murder invested here by the 'engineers' Himmler and Heydrich—although without doubt a German invention and a perversion of German thoroughness—was completely in line with a secularist *European Modernity* which had become godless.

(p. 591)

3. Few intellectuals, if any, went to America in order to achieve that which Europe might deny them. The mass emigration of Jewish intellectuals and artists across the Atlantic only took place after the Nazis' ascendance to power.

4. See in particular Gershom Scholem, *On Jews and Judaism in Crisis* (New York: Schocken Books, 1978).

5. Martin Buber, *On Zion: The History of an Idea* (London: East and West Library, 1973), p. 29.

6. Thus Andre Neher in David Burrell and Yehezkel Landau (eds), *Voices from Jerusalem: Jews and Christians Reflect on the Holy Land* (New York, Mahwah: Paulist Press, 1992), p. 19. Also W. D. Davies, *The Territorial Dimension of Judaism* (Minneapolis: Fortress Press, 1991), p. 37.

7. Born in 1929 in Paris to German-Jewish parents: educated in France, the United States and Britain; Fellow of Churchill College, Cambridge and Professor of Comparative Literature in Geneva.

8. See his *Language and Silence* (London: Faber & Faber, 1967).

9. The most recent, and perhaps the most interesting, formulation of contemporary Jewish theology is Eugene B. Borowitz, *Renewing the Covenant: A Theology for the Postmodern Jew* (Philadelphia, New York, Jerusalem: The Jewish Publication Society, 1991).

10. In *Salmagundi,* No. 66 (Winter-Spring 1985), pp. 4ff.

11. *Op. cit.,* p. 6.

12. W. D. Davies, *op. cit.,* p. 9.

13. *Ibid.,* p. 7.

14. *Ibid.,* p. 4.

15. I have used the new translation of the Jewish Publication Society of America. Steiner uses a different English version.

16. Rabbi Akiba (c.50-135 CE) was one of the most outstanding scholars of his age and a decisive influence on the development of Jewish law and lore. He died a martyr's death after the failure of the Bar Kochba rebellion against the Roman occupation of Judea.

17. *Op. cit.,* pp. 17ff.

18. Hebrew for 'ascent'. The current term for emigration to Israel. The same word is also used when a person ascends the lectern in the synagogue to recite the benedictions before the reading of a portion of the Torah (Pentateuch) at every Sabbath and Festival service.

19. *Op. cit.,* p. 19.

20. *Ibid.,* p. 22.

21. *Ibid.,* p. 23.

22. *Ibid.,* p. 24.

23. A phrase coined by the Holocaust historian Yehuda Bauer and favoured by the Holocaust theologian Emil Fackenheim.

24. For the distinction between *space* and *place,* see Walter Brueggemann, *The Land* (Philadelphia: Fortress Press, 1977), pp. 3ff. Also Dow Marmur, *The Star of Return* (New York, Westport, Connecticut, London: Greenwood Press, 1991), pp. 41ff.

25. *Op. cit.,* p. 519. For Kung's definition of paradigm shift in the context of Jewish history, see p. 55f, and Index.

26. *Our Homeland, the Text,* p. 5.

27. W. D. Davies, *op. cit.,* p. 82.

28. George Steiner, *Extraterritorial: Papers on Literature and the Language Revolution* (London: Faber & Faber, 1972).

29. In addition to books already mentioned in these Notes, I would like to draw the reader's attention to Eliezer Schweid, *The Land of Israel: National Home or Land of Destiny* (London, Toronto: Associated University Presses, 1985) and to Christopher J. H. Wright, *God's People in God's Land: Family, Land and Property in the Old Testament* (Grand Rapids, Michigan: William B. Eerdmans Publishing Company, 1990).

30. *Op. cit.,* p. 79.

31. *Ibid.*

32. Irving Greenberg, *The Third Great Cycle in Jewish History* (New York: National Jewish Resource Center, 1981), p. 25.

Christopher J. Knight (essay date spring 1996)

SOURCE: Knight, Christopher J. "George Steiner's Religion of Abstraction." *Religion & Literature* 28, no. 1 (spring 1996): 49-84.

[*In the following essay, Knight delineates Steiner's understanding of religion and its influence on his thought, illustrating the primacy of textuality in Steiner's theology.*]

If Steiner's religious thinking were to be reduced to a sentence, it might well be Jesus' command, "Be perfect as your heavenly Father is perfect" (Matt. 5.48). This commandment is, as Geza Vermes argues, solidly based in "Jewish teaching on the imitability of God's loving-kindness and the duty to follow him" (204), and, as such, is one more testimony to the merit of seeing Jesus as part of the Jewish tradition. In 1935, Thomas Walter Manson wrote, "We are so accustomed . . . to make Jesus the object of religion that we become apt to forget that in our earliest records he is portrayed not as the object of religion, but as a religious man" (Vermes 184). Steiner himself sees Jesus this way, as a religious man, specifically a Jew, compelled by an extraordinary idealism that should be intolerable to most. In his novel *The Portage to San Cristóbal of A. H.,* Steiner has Hitler say of Jesus,

> Demand of human beings more than they can give, demand that they give up their stained, selfish humanity in the name of a higher ideal, and you will make of them cripples, hypocrites, mendicants for salvation. The Nazarene said that his kingdom, his purities were not of this world. . . . Ask of man more than he is, hold before his tired eyes an image of altruism, of compassion, of self-denial which only the saint or the madman can touch, and you stretch him on the rack. Till his soul bursts. What can be crueler than the Jew's addiction to the ideal?
>
> (165-66)

Here, Hitler says nothing that Steiner himself has not said elsewhere, albeit in a more modulated tone. Steiner identifies Jesus with the summons to perfection, a way of life that sets itself in aggressive contradistinction to the lives of ordinary men and women. The desire is to escape reality's dross and to move toward the Ideal. In *Bluebeard's Castle,* Steiner writes:

> The Books of the Prophets and the Sermon on the Mount and parables of Jesus which are so closely related to the prophetic idiom, constitute an unequaled act of moral demand. Because the words are so familiar, yet too great for ready use, we tend to forget or merely conventionalize the extremity of their call. Only he who loses his life, in the fullest sense of sacrificial self-denial, shall find life. The kingdom is for the naked, for those who have willingly stripped themselves of every belonging, of every sheltering egoism. There is no salvation in the middle places. For the true disciple of the prophets and of Jesus, the utmost ethical commitment is like common breath. To become a man, man must make himself new, and in so doing stifle the elemental desires, weaknesses, and claims of the ego. Only he who can say with Pascal, *"le moi est haissable,"* has ever begun to obey the Gospels' altruistic imperative.
>
> (42)

Steiner views the summons to perfection not only as articulative of "the religious element" in its essence (**TD** [*Tolstoy or Dostoevsky*] 329), but also as particularly identifiable with Judaism. In the first instance, it might be noted that as a non-practicing Jew, Steiner's references to religion have generally been non-parochial. In his first book, *Tolstoy or Dostoevsky,* he urges his reader to understand his references to religion "in its most spacious connotations" (329). This conception of religion as an expression of larger, abstract purposes has held good throughout his career. Still, as his work has increasingly discussed the Shoah, it has also increasingly made reference to his own Jewishness. This has not really altered his sense of the religious impulse as broad-based, though it has resulted in an increasing identification of Judaism not only with the murdered victims of German hatred and the world's indifference but also with the challenge of Abstraction. Moses was the first, Jesus was the second and Marx was the third of three Jews, each of whom demanded that the world reform itself, that it put aside its suspect practices and gods and attend to the call of the Ideal: "Three times, Judaism has confronted Western man with the merciless claims and exactions of the ideal. Three times—in its invention of monotheism, in the message of the radical Jesus, in Marxism and messianic-socialism—Israel has asked of ordinary men and women more than human nature wishes to give; more, it may be, than it is organically and psychically able to give. Nothing is more cruel than the blackmail of perfection" (**LLM** [**"The Long Life of Metaphor: Shoah"**] 59).

Steiner finds several reasons for identifying Judaism with the realm of Abstraction. First, there is the reason of its God, this Presence who, after Mount Sinai, has been most notable for His Absence, an absence which has been the central fact of Judaic history, though perhaps never so noticed and painful as in the period of the Shoah. "In post-Shoah Judaism," Steiner states, "the question of the language of prayer—how can it be anything but cynical, accusatory or despairing?—is radically posed" (**LLM** 143). How can one pray to a God who has abandoned one? This is the question that every post-Shoah Jew must struggle with, though the question is not, in Jewish history, without antecedent, for it was heard earlier on Golgotha: "*Eli, la'ma sabach-tha'ni?*" (Matt. 27.46). Belief here makes extraordinary demands, as it always has, for how does one orient one's life toward that which appears seldom more palpable than the most ancient testimony and the most suspect intuition? "The demands made of the mind are, like God's name, unspeakable. Brain and conscience are commanded to vest belief, obedience, love in an abstraction purer, more inaccessible to ordinary sense than is the highest of mathematics" (**BC** [*In Bluebeard's Castle*] 37). By contrast, the Christian's core of beliefs seems absolutely physical. Steiner remarks on this, noting how difficult it must have been for the ancient Israelites to hold to what, at the time, would have seemed a fantastic notion (i.e., one God). He says that Christianity, in effect, found a way to make the demands on the imagination less arduous by offering a blend of monotheism and polytheism, a blend of abstraction and household saints: "it allowed scope for the pluralistic, pictorial needs of the psyche. Be it in their Trinitarian aspects, in their proliferation of saintly and angelic persons, or in their vividly material realization of God the Father, of Christ, of Mary, the Christian churches have, with very rare exception, been a hybrid of monotheistic ideals and polytheistic practices" (**BC** 39). The more stringent monotheistic ideal predates Christianity, and it still seems unmindful of human needs, originating as it does from this "jealous God," who visits "the iniquity of the fathers upon the children to the third and fourth generation" (Exodus 20.5). This may be one more reason why the God of Moses must have received from the early Israelites only a lukewarm welcome. Or as Steiner writes: "What we must recapture to mind, as nakedly as we can, is the singularity, the brainhammering strangeness, of the monotheistic idea. Historians of religion tell us that the emergence of the concept of the Mosaic God is a unique fact in human experience, that a genuinely comparable notion sprang up at no other place. The abruptness of the Mosaic revelation, the finality of the creed at Sinai, tore up the human psyche by its most ancient roots. The break has never really knit" (**BC** 37).

Another reason for identifying Judaism with the realm of Abstraction connects with the Mosaic God's commandment against "graven image[s]." In *The Critique of Judgement,* Kant wrote that there was perhaps "no more sublime passage in the Jewish Law" than this (I 127), his reason being that it forced the Jewish people away from the commonplace idols of more primitive communities, and instead forced them to stretch their imaginations and to reach out to the realm of the sublime:

> The fear that, if we divest this representation of everything that can commend it to the senses, it will thereupon be attended only with a cold and lifeless approbation and not with any moving force or emotion, is wholly unwarranted. The very reverse is the truth. For when nothing any longer meets the eye of sense, and the unmistakable and ineffaceable idea of morality is left in possession of the field, there would be need rather of tempering the ardour of an unbounded imagination to prevent it rising to enthusiasm, than of seeking to lend these ideas the aid of images and childish devices for fear of their being wanting in potency.
>
> (I 127-28)

Steiner agrees. "To all but a very few," he writes, "the Mosaic God has been from the outset, even when passionately invoked, an immeasurable Absence, or a metaphor modulating downward to the natural sphere of poetic, imagistic approximation. But the exaction stays in force—immense, relentless. It hammers at human consciousness, demanding that it transcend itself, that it reach out into a light of understanding so pure that it is itself blinding" (**BC** 38). Images may be inescapable, but we can resist, thinks Steiner, the temptation to caress and worship them, and to think

that they are all there is and that there is no copula between the realm of images and the meanings of meaning. It is why he is so hostile to poststructuralism and its celebration of a linguistic indeterminacy, for he fears that it leaves us mired in the detritus of language, with our backs turned away from the source of our being. In a discussion comparing Derrida and Levinas, Steiner writes: "When Derrida postulates that semantic markers can be ascribed decidable and eventually stabilized sense only if 'the sign is taken to look to God,' he is in total accord with Levinas. But for deconstruction, of course, such an assumption is an absurd atavism and a ludicrous quest for beginnings, for an *auctoritas* that never was. For Levinas, no less self-evidently, a theory and practice of sense is underwritten by that very turn towards the 'face of God'" (**"Levinas"** 244-45).

For Steiner, theology entails a grammar, a closed system: "Grammatical postulates and demonstrations of God's existence . . . can have validity only inside closed speech systems" (**RP** [*Real Presences*] 57). The system either finds its validation in the Deity, or it does not find it at all. But the sense is that all things, when understood in the light, or invisible center, which is God, acquire meaning, a meaning more measurable than that locatable in an indeterminate system driven by forces that are as rapacious as they are blind. And this, says Steiner, helps to explain the necessity of taboos, not only the Judaic taboo against graven images but also more general religious restrictions against blasphemy, or any other action which would invert the hierarchy of the divine and the mundane through making God's name one name among others. The "depth of the Judaic prohibition on the enunciation of the name or, more strictly speaking, of the Name of the Name, of God," says Steiner, relates to the fact that once this name is spoken, it "passes into the contingent limitlessness of linguistic play, be it rhetorical, metaphoric or deconstructive," where it finds "no demonstrable lodging" (**RP** 57). But this restriction exacts a price, for it makes the Jewish God appear all that much more abstract and inaccessible, a God almost more wisely addressed, or acknowledged, through silence. Certainly, Steiner encourages the view that silence is the most fitting response to Divinity. He even imagines prayer as passing through into silence, as the supplicant is forced to adopt the language of his Interlocutor, "the silence of live meaning" (**BC** 106). Language, thinks Steiner, severs us "from the silences that inhabit the greater part of being" (**LS** [*Language and Silence*] x). Silence, on the other hand, gives us "access" to "the categories of felt being" (**RP** 103). It need not be a dead-end, and may be an avenue toward the Light (**LS** 21); and for those who are most attentive to the world's unspoken articulacies, silence can be a form of active answering (**RP** 7). Still, to make silence the primary avenue by which God may be known furthers, again, the sense of His abstractness. Nor does it escape the charge of being rhetorical, for a polemics on behalf of silence remains a gesture lodged in language. Even when silence's gestures appear most pure, they still constitute a kind of language. This does not mean that we cannot imagine a realm outside the bounds of human linguistics. We can, and we do well to if we wish to avoid a spiritual impoverishment. For Steiner, the prohibition against graven images was a reminder of the need to seek out meaning even in the midst of a sea of images. In his essay **"Graven Images,"** he celebrates a host of Jewish art historians—Adolph Goldschmidt, Fritz Saxl, Erwin Panofsky, Meyer Schapiro, Max Friedländer, E. H. Gombrich, and Aby Warburg—precisely for their ability to search out the meanings of meaning, which even if it did not offer itself plainly, did evidence itself in shadow, in the symbolic iconography of a Flemish canvas that if one, such as a Panofsky, knew how to read it, could make the world seem luminescent with meaning. That these men were able to read as well as they did Steiner partly attributes to the Hebraic prohibition against graven images, a prohibition which helped teach them, as Kant would have it, the power of the imagination:

> The question leaps to mind: Why this dominance of a veritable galaxy of Jewish talent in art history and art interpretation? A possible answer . . . lies to hand. Prohibited throughout its earlier religious and ritual history from the making and contemplation of graven images, emancipated Judaism turned to the study of Western art with a peculiar thirst but also with a vehement, if perhaps subconscious, bias. The art to which it turned had to be "meaningful"—it had to be subject to intelligible readings and, ultimately, to rational analysis, as were the canonic texts in the Judaic tradition. There was in Warburg's obsession and in the great library that he gathered and handed on more than a touch of the Talmudic. But so there is, he would point out, in the assemblage of occult symbols, in the unwavering posture of intellectual and moral inquiry that Dürer delineated in his representation of human sorrow.
>
> (98)

Steiner's allusion to the Talmud also calls forth another reason for identifying Judaism with Abstraction, and this has to do with its being such a remarkably text-based religion. Of course, the Talmud calls up an image of a text that has taken on a life of its own, and Steiner admits the fact: "Dialogue with the ultimately, but only ultimately, unfathomable text is the breath of Jewish history and being. It has proved to be the instrument of improbable survival. At the same time, the Talmudic genius and method have, very possibly, generated within Judaic sensibility certain philological-legalistic sterilities and circularities. The dance turns never-endingly on itself" (**RP** 41). This image of the Talmud as emblematically textual has not gone unnoticed by commentators sympathetic to the poststructuralist point of view. Susan Handelman, in *The Slayers of Moses: The Emergence of Rabbinic Interpretation in Modern Literary Theory* (1982), is most identified with the theory that finds a strong rabbinical element in poststructuralism's celebration of textuality, for her thinking here is both the most developed and presumptive. But other critics, including Frank Kermode and Hartman, have also promoted the thesis that Talmudic commentary's strength lies in its offering a way of reading that accents "revision, rather than more violent ways of denial, or trying to start *de novo*" (Hartman in Salusinszky 87). Steiner would not dispute the point, but at the same time, it has been his contention that this method is different from deconstructive readings in that it assumes a theological order. In **"'The Critic'/'Reader,'"** he writes: "the rabbinical exegete or Calvin on the Gospels can proceed without apology or rationalizing metaphor, 'as if' the real presence were unambiguously operative in his text. He can, in short, make explicit the assumption, implicit in all true reading, that the warranty of meaning, that which finally underwrites the capacity of language to have sense and force beyond sense, is of a theological order" (**GSR** [*George Steiner Reader*] 90). Here, Steiner does not distinguish between Jewish and Christian commentary, conceiving more similarity than difference in the methodologies. Ten years later, in *Real Presences* (1989), however, his shading acquires a different hue.

In *Real Presences* and other recent work, Steiner demonstrates greater readiness to make strong distinctions between Jewish and Christian practices, including the difference in commentary styles. He still views Talmudic practice as predicating a theological order, but he also seems to be borrowing something from poststructuralism in general and Handelman in particular, most notably the latter's view that "Paul and the Church Fathers after him replaced the prolonged Rabbinic meditation on and meditation of the Text with the pure unmediated presence of Jesus, who resolves all oppositions, stabilizes meaning, provides ultimate identity, and collapses differentiation" (Cunningham 399). For instance, compare this statement to the following in *Real Presences*:

> Note the radical difference between Catholic and Judaic textuality. There is no temporal singularity, no enigma of historicity ("why in this one place, why at that one time?") in the Judaic sense of the Creation and of the Mosaic reception and transmission of the Law. There is a strict, utterly mysterious temporality in the coming and ministry of Christ. Being so naturally, if inexplicably, immersed in actual time, the meanings of that coming, the normative consequences of the sayings of Christ and of the writings of the Apostles, must, as it were, be stabilized in eternity. The Torah is indeterminately synchronic with all individual and communal life. The Gospels, Epistles and Acts are not.
>
> (44)

The antithesis, while not unhelpful, seems a little too pat. We know of Christ, like we know of Moses, through narratives handed down, sometimes lost and then later found, redacted, translated, and filtered through commentary, conflict and ritual. We make a mistake if we think that all the Christian needs to do is go back to the source, the Gospel narratives, themselves a form of commentary, or textuality, written decades after Jesus' death and often at odds with one another as to even the basic facts. As Valentine Cunningham says in response to Handelman, "What, I wonder, would Lancelot Andrewes have made of being dismissed as one not meditating on the text in prolonged ways or of accepting the a-textually 'unmediated presence of Jesus'!" (399). Textuality is textuality, whether it be Jewish or Christian, though we perhaps force the matter when we compare Jewish texts of law to Christian texts of revelation. As Vermes writes: "If Judaism is described exclusively on the basis of such legal or near-legal documents as the Mishnah, the Talmud or the *Shulhan Arukh,* it will appear more legalistic and casuistic than spiritual; but so would Christianity if seen one-sidedly mirrored in the codes of canon law, penitential books or manuals of moral theology of the various churches" (195). These texts announce their secondariness, their textuality, in a way, for instance, that neither Genesis nor Mark does. And yet we would be naive to think the latter narratives transparencies. They are not. Steiner knows this, of course; but it does not stop him from wishing to make a distinction that places Christianity on the side of time-stopping revelation and Judaism on the side of textuality (and, by extension, on the side of Abstraction). As he writes in **"Our Homeland, the Text,"** "whether they are seen as positive or negative, the 'textual' fabric, the interpretative practices in Judaism are ontologically and historically at the heart of Jewish identity" (7), of an identity that "scorn[s] the natural sphere" in favor of "its extreme commitment to abstraction, to word and text" (6).

Crucial to Steiner's identification of Judaism with textuality is the downplaying, even rejection, of a Messiah. That is, while Steiner is keenly aware of the messianic elements in such historical movements as Christianity, Marxism, Zionism and even Judaism proper, he thinks the concept of a Messiah a bogus one, whether understood in the frame of Jewish longing or Christian remembrance and promise. In the instance of Judaism, he believes that its messianic tenets have always been ambivalent, and that, in the period of the post-Shoah, they must be simply set aside, as something now widely recognized as unrealizable: "The Old Testament and the Talmud, rabbinic teachings and Jewish historicism are unquestionably brimful of the messianic promise and of the awaiting of the Messiah in moods both anguished and exultant. But does the Jew, in psychological and historical fact truly believe in the coming? More searchingly: does he truly thirst for it? Or is it, was it perhaps from the very first, what logicians or grammatologists might designate as a 'counter-factual optative,' a category of meaning never to be realized?" (**TGD**

["**Through That Glass Darkly**"] 37). It is not that radical an opinion, actually, even among more committed Jewish thinkers. Gershom Scholem, for instance, thinks that while the personal Messiah "is undoubtedly connected with the historical origins of the messianic hope," "[i]t has become immaterial for wide circles of Jews, even for some who harbor strong religious feelings" (*On Jews and Judaism* 287-88). Here, even as Scholem thinks of himself as a messianist, he sees the Messiah surviving mainly as a symbol, "as a summation of everything implied by the messianic ideal" (288). This is the way things should be thinks Steiner, believing the ideal too anti-historical, too much a threat to the delivery of tomorrow's "morning paper":

> Given the choice, the Jew prefers tomorrow's news, however grim, to the arrival of the Messiah. We are a people unquenchably avid of history, of knowledge in motion. We are the children of Eve whose primal curiosity has modulated into that of the philosophic and natural sciences. In denying the messianic status of Jesus, in subverting early Christian beliefs in the proximity of the eschatological, the Jew gave expression to the genius of restlessness central to his psyche. We were, we remain nomads across time.

> (**TGD** 37-38)

Scholem once wrote that "[a]ny discussion of the problems relating to Messianism is a delicate matter, for it is here that the essential conflict between Judaism and Christianity has developed and continues to exist" (*The Messianic Idea* 1). The statement reflects both his temperance and wisdom. On the matter of messianism, however, Steiner steers a different course. In **"Through That Glass Darkly,"** the oppositions he celebrates mostly entail a far from delicate dismissal of Christian messianism. Again, his point is that Christianity would have stopped time—though it is not clear how—had it not been for the refusal of the Jews to recognize Jesus as the Messiah: "The Jewish rebuke to Christ prevents the coming of the messianic realm. It pries and forces open the ravenous jaws of history" (41). This forgets that Christians imagine their existences as situated between a First and Second Coming (or Parousia), and thereby see themselves historically. History and Logos co-exist, even as the former is imagined as living in and moving toward the latter. It is true, as Scholem writes, that what for Judaism "stood unconditionally at the end of history as its most distant aim was for" Christianity "the true center of the historical process" (*The Messianic Idea* 1); and that this has had consequences in the way the two theologies conceive this Ideal. Notably, says Scholem, Jews have long "maintained a concept of redemption as an event that takes place publicly, on the stage of history and within the community," whereas Christians have tended to imagine "redemption as an event in the spiritual and unseen realm, an event which is reflected in the soul, in the private world of each individual, and which effects an inner transformation which need not correspond to anything outside" (*The Messianic Idea* 1). Also, says Scholem, the experience of the messianic has, for Jews, long been associated with the state of exile; and that whereas Christians know Christ as a historical person, the Jewish image of the Messiah is necessarily abstract and entails no longing backward but only a looking forward: "Thus in Judaism the Messianic idea has compelled a *life lived in deferment,* in which nothing can be done definitively, nothing can be irrevocably accomplished. One may say, perhaps, the Messianic idea is the real anti-existentialist idea" (*The Messianic Idea* 35). Clearly, then, there are differences, but to push these differences, as Steiner does, to the point where Christianity's embrace of Logos is seen as all-in-all, and Judaism's embrace of History is also seen as all-in-all, is to distort matters too much. Here, Judaism seems less anti-existential than quintessentially existential. "In what measure, at what level of consciousness," Steiner asks, "was the Jewish refusal of Jesus, at the time and thereafter, a symptom of radical psychic commitment to historical freedom, to the creative *daimon* of existential destiny on a changing earth?" (**TGD** 38). We are expected to answer that the refusal of Jesus' messianic claim was a conscious, profound and sound affirmation of history over telos, even over Judaism's own form of messianism. Or as Steiner himself says: "We Jews have said 'No' to the claims made for and, in certain opaque moments by, the man Jesus. He remains for us a spurious messiah. The true one has not come in his stead. Today, who but a fundamentalist handful awaits his coming in any but a formulaic, allegoric sense, a sense bitterly irrelevant to the continuing desolation of the human situation?" (**TGD** 49).

For Steiner, this rejection of Jesus the Messiah is not a rejection of Jesus the man, or his teachings. About the latter, Steiner's views parallel Vermes's, that the Sermon on the Mount and other such teachings are continuous with Judaic practices of the time, particularly "the charismatic Judaism of wonder-working holy men such as the first-century BC Honi and Jesus' younger contemporary, Hanina ben Dosa, modelled on the biblical prophets such as Elijah and Elisha" (Vermes 4). These teachings can, says Steiner, be found to "correspond very nearly point for point with cardinal tenets of the Torah and with the ethics, unsurpassed, of the Prophets, most especially Isaiah. Where there are departures from the canonic norm, in respect, for example, of the need to keep company with the publicans and the sinful, or in regard to the primacy of healing and salvational acts over the sanctity of the Sabbath, such dissents do not go signally beyond queries and challenges to Pharisiac observance as we find them among other Jewish 'liberals' or apocalyptic at the time" (**TGD** 34). Steiner views Jesus as a paragon of virtue, the mouthpiece of "a purified, humanly resourceful and compassionate Judaism" (**TGD** 34), who summoned

men and women to live not by their appetites but by an ideal of self-sacrifice and love for one another. That the message got distorted, suggests Steiner, is less the fault of Jesus than of Paul, John and those who came after. He should probably agree with Vermes, when the latter writes: "Today as in past centuries, the believing Christian's main New Testament source of faith lies, not so much in Mark, Matthew and Luke and their still sufficiently earthly Jesus, as in the centuries of speculation by the church on the theological Gospel of John with its eternal Word become flesh, and perhaps, even more on the letters of Paul with their drama of death, atonement, and resurrection. The Christ of Paul and John, on the way toward deification, overshadows and obscures the man of Galilee" (210). Certainly, Paul comes across as the villain in Steiner's accounts, the one most responsible for the early Christian sect's separation from the larger Jewish community. In Paul, Steiner detects element of Jewish self-hatred, a flaw that found its tragic denouement in the Shoah, as hatred originally directed inward found itself, after the divorce of communities, directed outward: "The beginning of the macabre history of Jewish self-hatred is inextricably inwoven with those of Christianity. . . . [T]he thought presses on one that Christianity is at fundamental points a product and externalization of just this Jewish self-hatred" (**TGD** 40). Whether this be true or not, Steiner believes the Shoah has its roots in those passages (he names Romans 9-11, Ephesians 2, and 1 Thessalonians) wherein Paul appears to blame the Jews for Christ's crucifixion. In **"Through That Glass Darkly,"** he writes: "1 Thessalonians, 2, 15, proclaims the Jew to be a deicide, a slayer of his own Prophets and, therefore, one 'contrary' or 'enemy to all men.' Vatican II sought to attenuate or even cancel this sentence of death in the troubled light of modern squeamishness and the Holocaust. In view of the 'final solution' which this Pauline verdict determines. But the text is not accident: it lay, it continues to lie, at the historical and symbolic roots of Christendom" (49-50). Here, Steiner's vehement rejection of Paul contrasts with Vermes's more equitably managed view:

> To be fair, it has to be said that Paul, despite the many harsh polemical comments against Judaism, shies off in the end from damning his people for ever. His inventive poetic mind imagines that the rejection of Christ is a dreadful but only temporary lapse. The apostle of the Gentiles by attempting to graft the whole converted non-Jewish world on to the Jewish stock, thus making them the heirs of all the divine promises granted to Abraham and his posterity, secretly hoped that the elevation of the Gentiles would excite the jealousy of the Jews, and bring them to *teshuvah* and submission to Christ so that "all Israel" might be saved.
>
> (212-13)

In short, Steiner blames the split between the Christian and Jewish communities on 1) self-hatred among the early Christians for their own antecedents; 2) Paul's placement of blame upon the Jews for Jesus' crucifixion; 3) the Jews' refusal to acknowledge Jesus as the Messiah; and 4) Christianity's later inclination toward political power. About this last point, I have as yet said nothing. But it is an important point for Steiner, and explains not only his dislike for the Church, but also his discomfort with the state of Israel, particularly as it presents itself as both a religious and political entity. In the first instance, Steiner says that "[i]t is altogether possible that Judaism would have lost its identity, would have diffused itself in Christianity, if the latter had been true to its Judaic catholicity. Instead, Christendom became, itself, a political-territorial structure, prepared, on all practical counts, to serve, to hallow, the genesis and militancy of secular states" (**OHT** [**"Our Homeland, the Text"**] 21). The suggestion that Judaism would have been absorbed into Christianity had the latter remained outside the political matrix is plausible, I suspect, given the interrelation between Christianity's understanding of Jesus' messianic dimension and the coercive force of the First Council of Nicaea and the First Council of Constantinople, respectively convened by the emperors Constantine I and Theodosius I. But whether or not this might have happened, Steiner's main point is that no corporate entity like a Church can do justice to the anarchic energy of a Jesus, to the intolerable demands that his teachings make upon us. "Can," he quotes Dostoevsky, "any established church house the Galilean trouble-maker?" (**SR** [**"The Scandal of Revelation"**] 59). He thinks not, not this prophet who, in the spirit of Amos (7.14), demanded of his disciples that they go out into the world taking "nothing for their journey except a staff; no bread, no bag, no money in their belts; but to wear sandals and not put on two tunics" (Mark 6. 8-9). To seek the homeland which is God requires that we not put down roots, that we remain restless searchers. To do otherwise is to convert the unearthly imperative into something much more tame—forms and rituals, empty of meaning and force:

> For the majority of "practicing" Christians—and what does "practicing" entail in this concept?—the Crucifixion remains an unexamined inheritance, a symbolic marker of familiar but vestigial recognitions. This marker is reversed and invoked in conventional idiom and gestures. Its concrete status, the enormity of suffering and injustice it incarnates, would appear to have faded from felt immediacy. How many educated men or women now hear Pascal's cry that humanity must not sleep because Christ hangs on his Cross till the end of the world? A "rationalized" Christianity hovers between an untenable literalism and symbolic insubstantiality, in the indistinct spaces of fitful imagining which we call myth.

(**SR** 62-63)

There is, then, something implacable about Steiner's project, for which he makes no apologies. Instead, when pressed to adopt a more liberal posture, he becomes

more goading, telling us, for instance, that "[t]he death of Socrates outweighs the survival of Athens" (**GSR** 196). Or that the nation of Israel has become "a death trap": "The messianic vision was, precisely, that which strove to overcome the homicidal tribalism that inhabits man. Having to be peregrine on this earth, the Jew developed that inward restlessness, those antennae for danger to which he owes his survival. For the Jew, the nation-state is not a fulfillment but a death trap" (**"A Jew's Grief,"** 20). This last analysis has not won Steiner very many friends, certainly not among Jewish intellectuals. Morris Dickstein speaks of *The Portage to San Cristóbal of A. H.,* and its theories about Israel in its relation to nationalism and the Shoah, "as a sideshow distraction from the serious business of thinking through the unspeakable horrors of the Nazi era" ("Alive and 90," 21); and Lionel Abel writes that "no Jew, religious or secular, can follow George Steiner, nor can Steiner follow himself. He still has to decide how it is possible to secularize the Torah and yet regard it as true, or how to make sacred the untrue text. Without bringing off one or the other of these impossible feats, there cannot be Homeland for him" (371). Steiner is, of course, obsessed with the question of homeland, but he thinks, unlike Abel and even unlike Scholem and Levinas, whose thinking he clearly respects, that the Jew's true homeland is not to be found in a piece of property alongside the Mediterranean, no matter how imbued with Jewish history, but rather in the text: "In post-exilic Judaism, but perhaps earlier, active reading, answerability to the text on both the meditative-interpretative and the behavioural levels, is the central motion of personal and national homecoming. The Torah is met at the place of summons and in the time of calling (which is night and day). The dwelling assigned, ascribed to Israel is the House of the Book. Heine's phrase is exactly right: *das aufgeschriebene Vaterland.* The 'land of the fathers,' the patrimonie, is the script" (**OHT** 5).

Abel has reason to worry that Steiner's allegiance to the text extends beyond Jewish sacred texts, and that these latter texts do not receive an attention distinctive enough to make clear their specialness. Steiner has long postulated a connection between literary texts and the spiritual, and his interest has been more with secular than sacred texts. Still, in **"Our Homeland, the Text,"** Steiner makes a concerted attempt to deal with the issues of text and textuality as they pertain to Jewish experience and longings—specifically the longing connected to the *aliyah.* He begins by drawing a connection between Judaism and the text as they both bespeak the condition of exile. It is easy, given the long history of the Diaspora, to understand the first connection; the second, however, needs spelling out. Steiner starts off by proposing the possibility that the Torah itself "is a place of privileged banishment from the tautological immediacy of Adamic speech, of God's direct, unwritten address to man" (**OHT** 5). Here, the condition of something being written already confers on it the status of exile, of that which has traveled a distance from its first home. God's Word has an immediacy or originality about it which escapes transcription and confers a secondariness even upon sacred writings. Among the Hebrews, no less than the Greeks, says Steiner, there is "a distrust of the written word, a critical regret at the passing of orality" (**OHT** 8). For them, "the written is always a shadow after the fact, a post-script" (**OHT** 8). Nor does Steiner stop at writing. He also attributes a quality of belatedness and exile to reading, particularly in relation to praxis: "Reading, textual exegesis, are an exile from action, from the existential innocence of *praxis*, even when the text is aiming at practical and political consequence. The reader is one who (day and night) is absent from action" (**OHT** 5). Writing and reading, then, are noticeably textual, locatable in their own diaspora. This diaspora, argues Steiner, is not so unlike the Jewish people's own Diaspora, for their situation has historically also been one of textuality. Or as Steiner writes: "The 'textuality' of the Jewish condition, from the destruction of the Temple to the foundation of the modern state of Israel, can be seen, has been seen by Zionism, as one of tragic impotence. The text was the instrument of exilic survival; that survival came within a breath of annihilation. To endure at all, the 'people of the Book' had, once again, to be a nation" (**OHT** 5).

Steiner, however, rejects the Zionist conclusion. He acknowledges that Jews are divided by their "unhoused at-homeness in the text" (specifically the Hebraic text) and "the territorial mystery of the native ground" (**OHT** 5), but he sees no reason for thinking that Israel as homeland is preferable to the Book. This conviction has only been strengthened by the events of the previous decades, events which, thinks Steiner, have demonstrated that an Israel conceived along the lines of nineteenth-century nationalism will invariably fall into all the traps—the inequities, the militarism, the bureaucratic subterfuge and liming of brutalities—included in the territory. Looking back to Theodor Herzel's *Fudenstaat,* a founding document in the Zionist movement, Steiner is struck by how much "the language and the vision are proudly mimetic of Bismarckian nationalism" (**OHT** 22), and what an ominous foreshadowing this was of present-day Israel:

> Israel is a nation-state to the utmost degree. It lives armed to the teeth. It has been compelled to make other men homeless, servile, disinherited, in order to survive from day to day (it was, during the millennia, the dignity of the Jew that he was too weak to make any other human being unhoused, as wretched as himself). The virtues of Israel are those of beleaguered Sparta. Its propaganda, its rhetoric of self-deception, are as

> desperate as any contrived in the history of nationalism. Under external and internal stress, loyalty has been atrophied to patriotism, and patriotism made chauvinism.
>
> (**OHT** 22)

The homecoming has been a disappointment, at least to the extent that Zionism provoked a messianic promise which it has, so far, failed to keep. The future may change this, and it may be perverse to suggest that Israelites, any more than other people, should prefer the abandon of the nomadic life to the comforts and pleasures of material at-homeness. Steiner does, in fact, think Jews remarkably different from other people, even to the point of promoting a racialism that, among late twentieth-century intellectuals, is almost unheard of: "if one is a Jew, one has quite extraordinary experience, perhaps illusory, perhaps not, of going down a street in a distant land, even where one does not know the language, and the other Jew in the street is one one recognizes by the way he walks. I know this to be true of my own experience" (**TT** ["**Totem or Taboo**"] 393). Still, whether or not this is the case, Steiner thinks that the Jew's religion and proud heritage must make him or her a partisan of transcendence, in a way foreign to the majority of non-Jews. He cites here Hegel's description of Abraham as seeking an "almost autistic intimacy with God," and as one "radically uninterested in or even hostile to other men, to those outside the covenant of his search" (**OHT** 6). The search is the most important thing, and others are not expected to take a like interest in it. From the Jew's perspective, thinks Steiner, they do not: "More than any other people, Jews claim, indeed they seem to achieve, nearness to the concept of God. They do so at the suicidal cost of mundane renunciation, of self-ostracism from the earth and its family of nations" (**OHT** 6). Steiner still seems to be speaking in the voice of Hegel here, though it is not clear. He does concur with Hegel's description, but not his conclusion. The reason is that while Hegel found the Jews an exceptional people, he also thought them the victims of "an awesome pathology, a tragic, arrested stage in the advance of human consciousness towards a liberated homecoming" (**OHT** 7). Steiner thinks otherwise, believing this same movement away from the world and toward transcendence a sign "of the Jewish genius and of its survival" (**OHT** 7). He may be right, but the cost has been great.

Still, there remains the question that if the Jew is not to think of Israel as his or her homeland because its model is conventional nationhood, why should this person think better of the text, which, as we have seen, is also equated with exile? Steiner has an answer, though it seems to entail an evasion. I say this because Steiner, as we have seen, has long railed against the essential parasitism of commentary, imagining such activity as occluding that which should be held primary. And yet, when it comes to Jewish commentary upon the Torah, he takes a somewhat different stance, approving what before he previously scorned (and sometimes still does). The point is, in **"Our Homeland, the Text,"** he demonstrates a readiness, perhaps influenced by Handelman and other poststructuralists, to see commentary not as a killing of the thing one loves, but as a way to keep it alive in people's hearts. Or as he writes: "The text is home; each commentary a return. When he reads, when, by virtue of commentary, he makes of his reading a dialogue and life-giving echo, the Jew is, to purloin Heidegger's image, 'the shepherd of being.' The seeming nomad in truth carries the world within him, as does language itself" (**OHT** 7). Without commentary, texts—original and incarnated—would be forgotten and, in effect, die. The sacred would wither away into anthropology. Yet so long as the holy books "are read and surrounded by a constancy of secondary, satellite texts," their authority cannot be abrogated, and we can say of the secondary texts that they "rescue the canon from the ebbing motion of the past tense, from that which would draw live meaning into inert and merely liturgical monumentality" (**OHT** 7).

Everything that Steiner says in **"Our Homeland, the Text"**, suggests a privileging of sacred writ over all else, though with Steiner one never quite knows whether it is he or the rhetoric that is speaking. This is not to accuse him of dishonesty. It is, rather, to acknowledge the brilliance of his writing and to wonder whether this brilliance does not, at times, reverse the order of horse and cart. Dickstein puts this matter more harshly than I would, but because I think he is on to something, I will quote him: "Mr. Steiner's writings often have this hollow feeling to them, as if his language were running away from him, and as though this gifted rhetorician were treating the blood and bone of history as a literary text, a conceptual challenge, an occasion for ingenious exercises in interpretation" (13, 21). This comes from the review of Steiner's controversial novel, and the statement's harshness is undoubtedly connected to that fact. But there is a strong element of truth in it, and in an essay like **"Our Homeland, the Text,"** the rhetorical performance is of such an extraordinary caliber that even Steiner, near its conclusion, must pull back and confess that "this, of course, is only a part of the truth" (**OHT** 22), that while it makes wonderful poetic sense to identify Jews as the people of the Book, thirsting for transcendence, it must be acknowledged that "[t]he overwhelming majority of Jews . . . seek neither to be prophets nor clerics deranged by some autistic, otherworldly addiction to speculative abstractions and the elixir of truth" (**OHT** 22-23). Then, in a statement that seemingly has forgotten from whence the matter originated, he writes: "What mandarin fantasy, what ivory-tower nonsense, is it to suppose that alone among men, and after the unspeakable horrors of destruction

lavished among him, the Jew should not have a land of his own, a shelter in the night?" (**OHT** 23). This, of course, is to grant the opposing view its legitimacy, not to acquiesce to it. And in the remainder of the essay, Steiner returns to his theme, albeit in a more modulated, even chastened—"*Personally,* I have no right to this answer" (**OHT** 23)—tone.

I raise this matter of rhetoric now because, as suggested above, Steiner's preference of the homeland of the text over that of the state employs rhetorical strategies—i.e., the drawing of a line of inheritance that connects Jewish sacred texts back to the Word of God—that could be used just as well to justify the excellence of the state; and that have, in fact, been so used, as for instance by Levinas, when he argues that the state of Israel achieves its "true sovereignty" through its institutionalizing the justice of God, the justice that makes it possible "for a man to see the face of an other" (Hand 260-61):

> Like an empire on which the sun never sets, a religious history extends the size of its modest territory, even to the point where it absorbs a breath-taking past. But, contrary to national histories, this past, like an ancient civilization, places itself above nations, like a fixed star. And yet we are the living ladder that reaches up to the sky. Doesn't Israel's particular past consist in something both eternal and ours? This peculiar right, revealed by an undeniable Jewish experience, to call our own a doctrine that is none the less offered to everyone, marks the true sovereignty of Israel. It is not its political genius nor its artistic genius nor even its scientific genius (despite all they promise) that forms the basis of its majority, but its religious genius! The Jewish people therefore achieves a State whose prestige none the less stems from the religion which modern political life supplants.
>
> (260)

For Levinas, there is the homeland of Israel, for Steiner, that of the text, sacred and secular (political, artistic, scientific). Both scholars employ an argument that begs the question, and begs it in a similar way, so it is perhaps wrong for Steiner to promote the text over the state by claiming that the text is articulative of something—i.e., divinity—that a state can never be. Which text? Which state? Not Israel, thinks Steiner, but maybe its texts. That is, while he argues that all texts have a quality of the secondary, of the exilic, about them, some texts—most notably, sacred texts—exhibit a greater sense of recognition, of a recall of a mystery which, in our postlapsarian condition, escapes too rapidly into the crevices of our quotidianness. Before the Fall, things were otherwise. Then, "[t]hings were as Adam named them and said them to be. Word and world were one" (**OHT** 8). But "[a]fter the Fall," says Steiner, "memories and dreams, which are so often messianic recollections of futurity, become the storehouse of experience and of hope. Hence the need to re-read, to re-call (revocation) those texts in which the mystery of a beginning, in which the vestiges of a lost self-evidence—God's 'I am that I am'—are current" (**OHT** 8). For someone whose Jewishness has been described as "secular" (RGS [*Reading George Steiner*] 267), this predicates a lot of argument on what almost amounts to a literal reading of the Bible. Steiner knows this, and undoubtedly does not wish to proceed too far this way, but he is almost obliged to, given the emphasis placed on the textuality of Jewish experience. By claiming that Judaism "holds Christianity, and, indeed, mankind . . . hostage," that its rejection of Christ "has condemned man to the treadmill of history" (**TGD** 41), Steiner is in danger of making too much of Jewish textuality, to the point that his blueprint threatens a permanent exile to the people of the Book. He is proud of this textuality, proud that "[i]n Judaism, the letter is the life of the spirit" (**OHT** 17), and proud that "the God to whom the Jew would stand so near is, by virtue of implacable abstraction, of the unfathomable elevation attributed to Him, furtherest from man" (**OHT** 6). But unless there be some reversal of direction, away from an argument that has so much poststructuralist coloring about it, there can be no real talk of homecoming. Textuality will have won out.

In his later work, Steiner moves in seemingly contradictory directions. He likes opposing Jewish textuality to Christian a-textuality, and suggesting that this shows the greater fortitude and wisdom of the Jewish people. But by composing a binary grounded in an antithesis, something is also lost, not only as far as Christianity (now opposed to History) is concerned, but also as far as Judaism is concerned. That is, by placing Christianity on the side of Logos, and Judaism on the side of History, Steiner threatens to cut off Jewish experience from what first makes it meaningful: the claim to be God's chosen people. Steiner is ambivalent about this claim, and has angered many Jews by the linkage made, in ***The Portage to San Cristóbal of A. H.,*** between it and the claim of Nazism. (Hitler: "My racism was a parody of yours, a hungry imitation. What is a thousand-year *Reich* compared with the eternity of Zion? Perhaps I was the false Messiah sent before. Judge me and you must judge yourselves. *Übermenschen,* chosen ones!" [164]) Still, without this claim, and without some credence in it, the propensity to see both Jewish *and* Christian Scripture as sacred would quickly lose its valency. Steiner is not yet ready to give up this much. Still, his general ambivalence makes his appeal to *Genesis* and the Fall seem forced, and makes his argument that between God and the Jews "the concepts of contract and of covenant are not metaphoric" (**OHT** 8) seem rhetorical. Nevertheless, Steiner chooses not to abandon the Jew to a textuality that is all post-script, and he or she is said to act out a "prescript," "to inhabit the literal text of his [or her] foreseen being" (**OHT** 12). More fully, Steiner writes:

No other community in the evolution and social history of man has, from its outset, read, re-read without cease, learnt by heart or by rote, and expounded without end the texts which spell out its whole destiny. These texts, moreover, are felt to be of transcendent authorship and authority, infallible in their *pre*-diction, as oracles in the pagan world, notoriously, are not. The script, therefore, is a contract with the inevitable. God has, in the dual sense of utterance and of binding affirmation, 'given His word.' His *Logos* and His bond to Israel. It cannot be broken or refuted.

(**OHT** 12)

It is because Jews conceive of their relation to God as contractual, says Steiner, that they have cultivated a clerical mode, attentive to the conservation and dissemination of the contract as well as the obligations enjoined by it: "The mystery and the practises of clerisy are fundamental to Judaism. No other tradition or culture has ascribed a comparable aura to the conservation and transcription of texts. In no other has there been an equivalent mystique of the philological" (**OHT** 17). All this has importance to Judaism's doctrinal demands and more general zeitgeist. Steiner is more interested in the latter, in the consequences ensuing from the Jewish people's subservience to the Book. For him, there is, as noted, something exilic about books. They also encourage our own separation from the activity and commotion about us. Reading a book, we step out of the "real" world, and into an extraterritorial space. This departure, or chosen exile, often increases our detachment regarding the world as found. We become more disinterested. It is this relation between bookishness and detachment, or disinterest, that helps to explain, says Steiner, the Jewish character, particularly as it has been shaped by its long, historical relation to the Book: "It is because he lives, enacts privately and historically, a written writ, a promissory note served on him when God sought out Abraham and Moses, it is because the 'Book of Life' is, in Judaism, literally textual, that the Jew dwells apart" (**OHT** 12). Jewish bookishness, however, does not stop with the Bible; it carries over into a more general respect for books, and this respect, in turn, has dialectically molded and distinguished the Jewish character. Thus Steiner speaks of "the sometimes hallucinatory techniques and disciplines of attention to the text, the mystique of fidelity to the written word, the reverence bestowed on its expositors and transmitters, concentrated within Judaic sensibility unique strengths and purities of disinterested purpose" (**OHT** 17).

For Steiner, it is this latter phase—where would-be clerics, raised in the tradition of the Book, begin to take an interest in secular texts—that has always most interested him. It is a phase that only begins to acquire bulk in the late nineteenth and early twentieth centuries, after the processes of assimilation (itself related to the factors of urbanization and the growth of the middle class) made it possible for Jews to participate in the larger intellectual life of Europe and North America. Earlier, I mentioned Steiner's conviction that Jewish intellectual life experienced something like a golden age during this period. If it were so, it is, he says, because Jewish clerical traditions easily adapted themselves to the disciplines of humanistic scholarship, mathematics, and science. The accomplishments were not, at first, as significant in the arts because the Hebraic restrictions regarding mimesis discouraged them (**"Graven Images"**). This, however, has changed in the present century, as witnessed by the extraordinary achievements of Kafka, Proust, Chagall, Celan, Schoenberg, Mandelstam, Gershwin, Rothko, Bellow, Roth, et al. In any event, this history of bookishness, first religious and then less so, must be credited with placing a disproportionate number of Jewish intellectuals at the forefront of modern culture: "The 'bookish' genius of Marx and of Freud, of Wittgenstein and of Lévi-Strauss, is a secular deployment of the long schooling in abstract, speculative commentary and clerkship in the exegetic legacy (while being at the same time a psychological-sociological revolt against it). The Jewish presence, often overwhelming, in modern mathematics, physics, economic and social theory, is direct heir to that abstinence from the approximate, from the mundane, which constitutes the ethos of the cleric" (**OHT** 17). Steiner can be, as his readers know, chauvinistic about this achievement. It is, for instance, a little disconcerting to find that he thinks there is little in United States culture that merits attention once the contributions of the Puritans and the Jews have been accounted for. Or as Steiner says in regard to post-War American culture: "Think away the arrival of the Jewish *intelligentsia,* think away the genius of Leningrad-Prague-Budapest-Vienna and Frankfurt in American culture of the past decades, and what have you left? For the very concept of an *intelligentsia,* of an élite minority infected with the leprosy of abstract thought, is radically alien to the essential American circumstance" (**AE** [**"Archives of Eden"** 73-74]). This kind of thinking, so captive to ethnic and cultural stereotypes and the partisanship that goes with them, has a tragic enough history already, so it is a little dispiriting to see Steiner participating in it.

In any event, this clerical tradition, that first engaged sacred and later secular texts, carried with it not only an expertise in hermeneutics, but also the faith—or maybe just the hope—that the text *sui generis* remains somehow valuable and sacred. It is faith which initially probably cannot imagine the text as existing other than a conduit of first meanings. Later, when it can imagine this, it must change its relation to texts, either by dramatically narrowing down the range of texts thought worthy of serious investigation or by changing its strategy vis-à-vis texts. This might mean moving away from a hermeneutics that engages texts ontologically and toward one that engages them otherwise, for

instance ethnographically, historically, psychologically, sociologically, etc. The fact is, current criticism has thought it best to pursue the second avenue, to alter its strategy vis-à-vis texts. Steiner, however, still thinks it worthwhile, even important, to pursue the first avenue. He knows that this means ignoring the majority of texts, though it is not clear that he has fully weighed the consequences of this exclusion. Those critics who have chosen otherwise would no doubt find his selectivity this way neglectful and elitist. He, in turn, would fault them for prematurely withdrawing from the most important of investigations: the pursuit of the meanings of meaning. Steiner knows that one cannot here make the claim—as it has been made for sacred texts—that secular texts issue from the very first source of meaning. But if they are not this—i.e., God-spoken—they may still be understood as participating in the sacred, to the extent, or in the sense, that this is identified with Order in its most transcendent, and thereby Divine, manifestation. If God has spoken Himself in the world, either through the prophets or the world itself, then we must assume that the voice is distinctive enough that those who seek it out, who are receptive, and honest with themselves and others, can hear it, if not all the time, at least some of the time, and that what they hear concurs, more or less, with what others of like attentiveness also hear. It is the assumption that underwrites religious life in general; and while artists ostensibly pursue other purposes, they have long been identified with a similar attentiveness or hearing, though this history seems to be coming to a close. It *has* closed for many, if not the majority, of artists working in the West. This latter fact helps to explain Steiner's own disenchantment with contemporary Western art—"God, look at our literature in free Britain. Mountains of trivia and pretentiousness!" (**RI** [**"The Responsibility of Intellectuals"**] 180)—particularly when compared to its Eastern European and Russian counterparts. The point is, Steiner's interest as a critic specifically addresses that ambit of art that makes claims, if seldom explicitly, for what might be imagined as a largely unheard music, of a divine presence underwriting the world's dailiness. Here, "[w]hat is implicit is the notion of and expression of 'real presence'" (**GSR** 85). This leads the critic, or reader, to proceed "*as if* the text was the housing of forces and meanings, of meanings of meaning, whose lodging within the executive verbal form was one of 'incarnation.' He reads *as if*—a conditionality which defines the 'provisional' temper of his pursuit—the singular presence of the life meaning in the text and work of art was 'a real presence' irreducible to analytic summations and resistant to judgement in the sense in which the critic can and must judge" (**GSR** 85).

Steiner's most eloquent statement this way is found in *Real Presences* (1989), a book that must be thought of as near, if not *the,* pinnacle of his work so far, so beautifully does he articulate the argument that inscribes not simply art but all meaning in an Absolute. The book's success partly follows from the fact that, unlike some of the earlier books, Steiner achieves a less acrid, more conciliatory, tone. Of course, there is enough acridity for those who want it—e.g., "[t]he entire notion of research in modern letters is vitiated by the evidently false postulate that tens of thousands of young men and women will have anything new and just to say about Shakespeare or Keats or Flaubert" (35)—and by ordinary standards, there should seem a lot. Still, on the whole, the book is a more measured and thoughtful effort than his previous work in cultural criticism, *In Bluebeard's Castle.* Included among its strengths are not only the lucidity of the analysis but also the willingness to front the embarrassment that holds forth in the academy with regard to questions about ultimate meaning, and particularly about the Deity. He is perfectly cognizant that ours is a time "in which embarrassment terrorizes even the confident" and that the prevailing criticisms prefer to "'play it cool'" (**RP** 178), avoiding those risks that might easily be confused with intellectual naiveté. Steiner is not immune to these embarrassments, yet he thinks the question of meaning—i.e., of what we take, or do not take, to be the foundation of what we say and do—is of such extraordinary importance that it is worthwhile to put fears momentarily aside. Thus in *Real Presences,* Steiner proposes what only a neophyte or a *provocateur* would dare to suggest—that is, "that any coherent understanding of what language is and how language performs, that any coherent account of the capacity of human speech to communicate meaning and feeling is, in the final analysis, underwritten by the assumption of God's presence" (**RP** 3).

It is a daring thesis, and Steiner does not imagine it attracting many sympathetic readers among academicians. Toward the end, he says as much and offers a reason: "I know that this formulation will be unacceptable not only to those who will read a book such as this, but also to the prevailing climate of thought and of feeling in our culture. It is just this unacceptability which characterizes what I have called a time of 'epilogue,' an immanence within the logic of the 'afterword'" (**RP** 228). By this, he means that in the present, after the lessons of Mallarmé, Stein, Joyce and Derrida, our current paradigm of meaning is less transcendent than self-reflexive, of words calling forth other words calling forth other words, in an unending round robin of textuality. And it is not only words which are imagined as operating this way, but so are events, including the events of our lives, mired in a history that moves nowhere except further into the recesses, or black holes, of contingency. There are stoics among us who are not threatened by such a paradigm, and who tend to pooh-pooh the expressed misgivings of those who are. There are others who, while less stoical, view matters as out of their hands, and who resign themselves to whatever

scenario appears most aggressive and powerful. Forcefulness here gets identified with things as they are, or as they are entropically predetermined to be. Steiner himself is cognizant of this, and knows that the scenario he offers may, to the present generation and its heirs, appear passé, or nostalgic, something better sloughed off like an old skin. If this happens, as it already is happening, then, believes Steiner, the whole nature of our thinking about aesthetics will change dramatically: "It may well be that the forgetting of the question of God will be the nub of cultures now nascent. It may be that the verticalities of reference to 'higher things,' to the impalpable and mythical which are still incised in our grammars, which are still the ontological guarantors of the arcs of metaphor, will drain from speech. . . . Should these mutations of consciousness and expression come into force, the forms of aesthetic making as we have known them will no longer be productive" (**RP** 230). It is almost a truism, something that those on both sides of the debate can agree on: our definition of aesthetics is crucially intertwined with the way we understand the meanings of meaning. Things only get contestable when we try to fill in the equation.

In the present climate, Steiner's conviction that all things, aesthetics included, lean either toward or away from an Absolute, the determinant of their worth, is almost quarrelsome. No matter, he thinks, for while it may be possible to imagine the universe as something like an unending, directionless flux, the fact that this scenario offers so little in the way of human consolation, so little to offset the blunt fact of death—not only our own but that of those nearest to us—almost forces us to imagine things otherwise. Steiner's religiosity is never less than tentative, yet he still thinks a Pascalian wager almost required. In *Real Presences* he writes that a "wager on the meaning of meanings, on the potential insight and response when one human voice addresses another, when we come face to face with the text and the work of art or music, which is to say when we encounter the *other* in its condition of freedom, is a wager on transcendence" (4). The wager is that these interactions not only mean something (for contingency theory says nothing less), but that they are reflections of a larger meaning, underwriting and reinforcing them to the degree that they are truthful. The wager, then, predicates not only meaning but meaningfulness. Steiner writes: "This wager—it is that of Descartes, of Kant and of every poet, artist, composer of whom we have explicit record—predicates the presence of a realness, of a 'substantion' (the theological reach of this word is obvious) within language and form. It supposes a passage, beyond the fictive or the purely pragmatic, from meaning to meaningfulness. The conjecture is that 'God' *is,* not because our grammar is outworn; but that grammar lives and generates because there is the wager on God" (**RP** 4).

The reference to grammar has a Wittgensteinian ring to it, particularly the Wittgenstein of the *Tractatus,* wherein the philosopher postulates an invisible form, or grammar, that conjoins representations and their objects: "It is clear that however different from the real one an imagined world may be, it must have something—a form—in common with the real world" (35). Steiner himself believes this, believes that what we say and do—even our skepticisms and stoicisms—postulates a "tenor of *trust*" (**RP** 89) whereby we take for granted all sorts of benevolent facts about the world, including that of its logicality and our ability to imitate this. Also included is our belief, affirmed each time we write or speak a sentence, that words, singular or networked, can refer (even with startling accuracy and beauty) to things beyond themselves, and thereby make sense to others. "There would," Steiner sensibly says, "be no history as we know it, no religion, metaphysics, politics or aesthetics as we have lived them, without an initial act of trust, of confiding, more fundamental, more axiomatic by far than any 'social contract' or covenant with the postulate of the divine. This instauration of trust, this entrance of man into the city of man, is that between word and world" (**RP** 89). To say otherwise only throws us into the paradox of the Cretan calling all Cretans liars, whereby we would have to imagine that while all claims to speak the truth of things are essentially specious, this one claim must be thought otherwise. It makes for a spissatus-like truth. Thus, it seems wiser to grant the "Hebraic-Hellenic copula," so syntactically crucial to the history of our thought and language, a continuing centrality (**RP** 119). Here, Steiner argues that every time we join subject to predicate with the purpose of putting sense in a form recognizable to others, we also do something else: we affirm our belief in an equation which transcends the strict grammars of language and nature; we affirm our belief that the world holds together. Steiner quotes Derrida to the effect that "[t]he age of the sign is essentially theological" (**RP** 119), but whereas Derrida launches a revolt against this knowledge, Steiner wants to build on it. "The archetypal paradigm," he says, "of all affirmations of sense and of significant plenitude—the fullness of meaning—is a *Logos*-model" (**RP** 119). Things originate with the *Logos.* We do not call on it so much as it calls on us; it summons us. Steiner writes: "That which comes *to call on us*—that idiom . . . connotes both spontaneous visitation and summons—will very often do so unbidden. Even where there is a readiness, as in the concert hall, in the museum, in the moment of chosen reading, the true entrance into us will not occur by an act of will" (**RP** 179).

For Steiner, the relation between sacred and secular texts of the highest sort is, as noted, an overlapping one. Distinguishing them both is this quality of summons, though one assumes the summons will be greater in Isaiah than in Henry James. In one sense, Steiner ac-

cepts this, which leads him to recoil from the whole premise of *The Literary Guide to the Bible,* with its implicit embarrassment regarding the claims that sacred texts, including the Hebrew and Christian Bibles, make: "The separation, made in the name of current rationalism and agnosticism, between a theological-religious experiencing of Biblical texts and a literary one is radically factitious. It cannot work" (**"The Good Books,"** 97). In a second sense, however, he finds the distinction hard to make, for it is precisely this imputation of summons that he believes characterizes art work at its most profound. He writes: "The relations between the sacred and the legally or ethically prescriptive ('the worded') on the one hand, and the poetic or fictive on the other, have always been vexed. What matters is that literary invention should be regarded, be it with welcome or with mistrust . . . , as one of the foundational triad. In the poem, in the prayer, in the law, the reach of words is made very nearly equivalent to the humanity of man" (**RP** 189). Steiner seeks here to offer a definition of civilization, not to chart the difference between the sacred and the aesthetic, but even from this, it is clear that he imagines an unusual intimacy between the two. They both summon us to an experience that is thought to originate not only outside of ourselves but also outside of our world. Or as Steiner, making more explicit the relation between the aesthetic and the theological, writes: "The ascription of beauty to truth and to meaning is either a rhetorical flourish, or it is a piece of theology. It is a theology, explicit or suppressed, masked or avowed, substantive or imaged, which underwrites the presumption of creativity, of signification in our encounters with text, music, art. The meaning of meaning is a transcendent postulate. To read the poem responsibly ('respondingly'), to be answerable to form, is to wager on a reinsurance of sense" (**RP** 216). The suggestion is that while not all texts reputed to be sacred are so (i.e., command our full-fledged respect), not all aesthetic texts—which of course make no overt claims of inspiration—need be thought as existing outside the realm of the sacred. In the first instance, Steiner grants that "much in the Old Testament burns with tribal folly" and brutality (**SR** 69), while, in the second instance, he argues that art, when it appears (in Joyce's words) "grave and constant," may well be thought of as sacred, or at least religious:

> I am arguing that the "gravity" and the "constancy" are, finally, religious. As is the category of meaningfulness. They are religious in two main senses. The first is obvious. The *Oresteia, King Lear,* Dostoevsky's *The Devils* no less than the art of Giotto or the Passions of Bach, inquire into, dramatize, the relations of man and woman to the existence of the gods or of God. It is the Hebraic intuition that God is capable of all speech-acts except that of monologue which has generated our arts of reply, of questioning, and counter-creation. After the

Book of Job and Euripides' *Bacchae,* there *had* to be, if man was to bear his being, the means of dialogue with God which are spelt out in our poetics, music, art.

The gravity and constancy at the heart of major forms and of our understanding of them are religious in a second, more diffuse sense. They enact . . . a root-impulse of the human spirit to explore the possibilities of meaning and of truth that lie outside empirical seizure or proof.

(**RP** 225)

Crucial to Steiner's grasp of the religious element in our texts, be they sacred, judicial or aesthetic, is the suggestion of dialogue. They begin in response to a summons, to something larger than ourselves requiring us to bend toward it, to give answer. The summons may, as in Scripture, have the force of God's impress, or it may, as in the art of a Schoenberg, Rothko or Kieslowski, have a lesser force, more akin to intuition than revelation. Still, whether it be one or the other, a response appears called for. This response may take the form of a respectful silence, the sort advocated by Wittgenstein and often spoken of approvingly by Steiner: "For the *Tractatus,* the truly 'human' being, the man or woman most open to the solicitations of the ethical and the spiritual, is he who keeps silent before the essential" (**RP** 103). Or the response may take the form of the poet's or the musician's most expressive articulation of what it means to be human, what it means to be un-housed, to dwell apart from, and largely ignorant of, the source of our being: "Serious painting, music, literature or sculpture make palpable to us, as do no other means of communication, the unassuaged, unhoused instability and estrangement of our condition" (**RP** 139). In the latter instance, the artist's work can also function as a summons to others capable of responding to that which in the art transcends its own boundaries and somehow gives voice to the source of its inspiration. Thus it is, says Steiner, that "[t]he encounter with the aesthetic is, together with certain modes of religious and of metaphysical experience, the most 'ingressive,' transformative summons available to human experiencing. . . . [T]he shorthand image is that of an Annunciation, of 'a terrible beauty' or gravity breaking into the small house of our cautionary being" (**RP** 143). At this level, art is both a response and an enticement to a response, implying a dialogic equation that makes our relation with the Creator more than simply a passive experience. William James, in *The Varieties of Religious Experience,* once wrote:

The religious phenomenon, studied as an inner fact, and apart from ecclesiastical or theological complications, has shown itself to consist everywhere, and at all its stages, in the consciousness which individuals have of an intercourse between themselves and higher powers with which they feel themselves to be related. This intercourse is realized at the time as being both active and mutual. If it be not effective; if it be not a give and take relation; if nothing is really transacted while it lasts; if the world is in no whit different for its having taken place; then prayer, taken in this wide meaning of a sense that something is transacting, is of course a feeling of what is illusory, and religion must on the whole be classed, not simply as containing elements of delusion,—these undoubtedly everywhere exist,—but as being rooted in delusion altogether, just as materialists and atheists have always said it was.

(465)

Steiner, I think, would agree. We pray and we make art because we anticipate a response. We imagine an Other, a Deity, whose investment in us is not unlike our investment in Him. We assume that the world's final shape is not predetermined and that we can make a difference. If this be not the case, then the purposes of religion and art (as conceived here) must appear terribly empty. But we—or many of us—proceed as if this is the case. We see this in the rabbi's unending dialogue with the sacred texts; and we see this in the artist's assumption of authorship, a model taking the Creator as its inspiration. "I take the aesthetic act," says Steiner, "the conceiving and bringing into being of that which, very precisely, could not have been conceived or brought into being, to be an *imitatio,* a replication on its own scale, of the inaccessible first *fiat*" (**RP** 201). The reasons for this imitation can be complicated. The motivation can be one of emulation, or it can be one of rivalry, of an attempt to provoke God, to make Him step out from behind the plane of His invisibility. In either case, the gesture postulates that we are not mere passive adjuncts to reality but that we ourselves can author our own responses: "A *Logos*-aesthetic and hermeneutic is one of reference to authorship, to the potential of 'authority' contained within that word and concept. All *mimesis,* thematic variation, quotation, ascription of intended sense, derives from a postulate of creative presence" (**RP** 101). Inherent in this postulate is the sense that our authored responses to the world, our answering to the Deity, entail the demands of responsibility, of answerability. Question and answer here bespeak the same equation. "There can be," writes Steiner in **Heidegger,** "no life-giving precision, no responsibility when question and answer do not relate, where they do not spring from a common ontological center" (31). The artist engages in a back-and-forth dialogue with the universe, and with the Author of this universe. And yet, whatever confidence the artist places in this dialogue, he or she cannot escape the fact that we dwell apart from the home of being and are unhoused:

It is poetics, in the full sense, which informs us of the visitor's visa in place and time which defines our status as transients in a house of being whose foundations, whose future history, whose rationale—if any—lie wholly outside our will and comprehension. It is the capacity of the arts, in a definition which must, I believe, be allowed to include the living forms of the speculative (what tenable vision of poetics will exclude

Plato, Pascal, Nietzsche?), to make us, if not at home, at least alertly, answerably peregrine in the unhoused-ness of our human circumstance. Without the arts, form would remain unmet and strangeness without speech in the silence of the stone.

(**RP** 140)

For Steiner, men and women are unhoused, but often do not know it. The artist knows it, and this puts him or her in alliance with the rabbi or priest. They each seek to find the way home, be it through sacred texts, moral action or aesthetic form. For the artist, it is mostly via the last of these that he or she works, attempting to seduce us into a recognition of what has been lost but might be recovered. The work will mean nothing for us, however, if we ourselves "do not redefine, if we do not re-experience, the life of meaning in the text, in music, in art" (**RP** 49-50). This life has nothing to do with newness or with originality as generally conceived; rather, it has to do with something like a return to first being. "Originality" in art, says Steiner, "is antithetical to novelty. The etymology of the word alerts us. It tells of 'inception' and of 'instauration,' of a return, in substance and in form, to beginnings. In exact relation to their originality, to their spiritual-formal force of in-novation, aesthetic inventions are 'archaic.' They carry in them the pulse of the distant source" (**RP** 27). This is why art, at its most powerful, must be conceived as a form of anagnorisis, of recognition in its fullest and most transcendent sense: "We must come to recognize, and the stress is on *re*-cognition, a meaningfulness which is that of a freedom of giving and of reception beyond the constraints of immanence" (**RP** 50). This is the way toward homecoming, the way toward what Steiner, in **"Our Homeland, the Text,"** refers to as the "'Israel' of truth-seeking" (**OHT** 19). This is not a physical place, not a state alongside the Mediterranean, but that *trópos* which signifies the place wherein all contradictions vanish, and the universal reigns. Of course, religions can and have pointed the way. Steiner gives credit to Judaism for its invention of monotheism and the primacy its bestows upon the Book; and he probably would agree with Vermes when he credits Christianity, or better yet Jesus, for "the underlying universalism" of his "doctrine of *imitatio Dei*, a God whose providence includes all, and his primary concern for the individual, thus permitting an easier dispensa-tion from the mostly communal and social aspects of the Law of Moses" (213).[1] But Steiner's religiosity feels ultimately uncomfortable when housed in doctrine. He cannot quite accept a Judaism that, in its orthodox manifestation, "continues in its often jejune formalism, in its feverish atrophy in ritualistic minutiae," that, in its Zionist manifestation, encourages the state of Israel's "savagery and corruption," and that, in its liberal manifestation, seems spiritually and metaphysically inert (**TGD** 48). Nor can he accept a Christianity, which since the Shoah, is "sick at heart" and "lamed, possibly

terminally, by the paradox of revelation and of doctrine which generated not only the Shoah but the millennia of anti-Jewish violence, humiliation and quarantine which are its obvious background" (**TGD** 47). In the end, for Steiner, there can be "no synagogue, no *ecclesia,* no *polis,* no nation, no ethnic community which is *not* worth *leaving*" (**TT** 397). It is a melancholy conclu-sion, predicated on his belief that a nation, in time, will always act in an unacceptable manner, and that "[a] synagogue will one day excommunicate Spinoza, it must" (**TT** 397). It is better, he thinks, to place one's trust directly in the Absolute, and to distrust all those instances wherein two or more are gathered in the name of some cause, or lord: "Personally, I believe that anarchy is one of the ideals and hopes and utopias of anyone who wants to do serious thinking and work. It is when you find yourself agreeing with another person you should begin to suspect that you are talking nonsense. I repeat: there is no community of love, no family, no interest, caste, profession, or social class not worth resigning from" (**TT** 397-98).

For me, there is something too hubristic about Steiner's stance, about the suggestion that one's salvation is an individual matter, unrelated to the good works and faithfulness of others. William James once noted that "[o]ur faith is faith in someone else's faith, and in the greatest matters this is most the case." It is difficult to believe in anything, not to mention something invisible, without some form of concurrence. As is his wont, Steiner prefers to go it alone, to conceive of the Deity as an abstraction characterized as much by its absence as by its presence. This sense of absence is heightened by the Shoah, when so many Jews experienced "the dark of God's absence" (**LS** 167). And while this emo-tion is, obviously, not to be discounted, there also seems something personal about Steiner's stress on God's absence. Or maybe I am misreading him here, and his stress on God's absence has more to do with the fact that there is something almost archaic about the Hebrew Bible's God, making it easier to imagine Him in the past tense. Even before the Shoah, this God, says Steiner, seemed notably absent. In *Bluebeard's Castle,* he writes, "To all but a very few the Mosaic God has been from the outset, even when passionately invoked, an immeasurable Absence, or a metaphor modulating downward to the natural sphere of poetic, imagistic ap-proximation" (38). This is the way Steiner imagines Him: an unfathomable First Cause and Principle of Perfection, almost more tellingly revealed in the work of the greatest artists than of those more ostensibly religious. "Above all," he writes in **"Language Under Surveillance,"** "it is in art and literature that the Mes-sianic challenge, the potential of human ripening and deliverance, is enacted and transmitted across time" (36). Free from the matrix of power, and working in isolation, the artist here feels, as few others do, "responsible toward the claims and provocations of the ideal" (36). The demand on the artist is to acknowledge the Ideal, that place which counts as home. In *Antigones,* Steiner speaks of the "co-ordinates of Idealism" as "exile and attempted homecoming" (14). Until one completes the journey of becoming (which, by definition, never ends), a person exists as an exile from being. Mindful of this, the artist, more than others, holds to the path. But as described by Steiner, it is a rather solitary adventure, not suitable for those of a social or non-intellectual temper. Thus, he praises Benjamin for withdrawing from life (**R** [**"The Remembrancer"**] 38) and Lukács for making a homeland of the mind (**MH** [**"Making a Homeland for the Mind"**] 67). And when Steiner considers his own demise, he thinks that "[a] man need not be buried in Israel. Highgate or Golders Green or the wind will do" (**LS** 154).

In the interim, Steiner is increasingly drawn to music, thinking it an embodiment of the Ideal. "Personally," he writes in the "Introduction" to his *Reader* [*George Steiner Reader*], "I find myself *needing* music more and more. The number of books one feels one *must* read diminishes; it is re-reading that matters. Music, on the contrary, grows indispensable, as if it had become the elect companion of identity, the homecoming to that inside oneself which time has in its keeping" (**GSR** 18). It is a thought that he has expressed throughout his writings, though in the fullness of the claim, it also harkens back to his statement, in *Bluebeard's Castle,* that music increasingly served him and those he knew as a substitute for a religion no longer thought tenable:

> one does know of a good many individual and familial existences in which the performance or enjoyment of music has functions as subtly indispensable, as exalting and consoling, as religious practices might have, or might have had formerly. It is this indispensability which strikes one, the feeling (which I share) that there is music one cannot do without for long, that certain pieces of music rather than, say, books, are the talisman of order and of trust inside oneself. In the absence or recession of religious belief, close-linked as it was to the classic primacy of language, music seems to gather, to harvest us to ourselves.
>
> (**BC** 122)

For me, the stance mistakenly conflates two things—religion and music—which, whatever their affinities, need, more importantly, to be understood as separate. If the consolations that music offers do not seem pale in comparison to those offered by this or that religion, then the religion must itself be weakly imagined. To return to James's suggestion, if the practice of religion changes nothing in the world, if everything is as it was found, and if there be no felt experience of real conversation between oneself, or-selves, and the Deity, then yes, music can be compared to religion, for the consolation that each offers, in this instance, is of a largely psychological, or therapeutic, nature; it is a

consolation enwrapped in the individual's own estimation of self, and its "harvest" may well be understood reflexively, as a homecoming "to ourselves." Steiner would, no doubt, resent this representation of his thinking, but his extolling of music to the point that it becomes something akin to an object of worship forces us to ask, if not to Whom, then to What are we answerable, and in exactly what way? In *Real Presences,* he writes that "music puts our being as men and women in touch with that which transcends the sayable, which outstrips the analysable. Music is plainly uncircumscribed by the world as the latter is an object of scientific determination and practical harnessing. The meanings of the meaning of music transcend. It has long been, it continues to be, the unwritten theology of those who lack or reject any formal creed. Or to put it reciprocally: for many human beings, religion has been the music which they believe in" (218). It is an extraordinary rhetorical flight, but once it is over, what are we left with? Are we to worship music? mathematics? or the Abstraction that they imply? Steiner comes close to suggesting that we are to do just this. This view, for instance, is implicit in the praise that he bestows on the "Jewish abstractionists," by whom he means Lukács, Bloch, Benjamin, Adorno, Marcuse, Wittgenstein and others. In an essay on Lukács, he writes:

> Unhoused, peregrine, domestic in ostracism, he is one of that tragic constellation—Ernst Bloch, Walter Benjamin, Adorno, Herbert Marcuse—of Jewish abstractionists, possessed by a messianic rage for logic, for systematic order in the social condition of man. Lukács's Marxism is, in essence, a refusal of the world's incoherence, of the murderous stupidities whereby men and women misconduct their lives. Like the other Jewish self-exiles whose radicalism out of Central Europe has so incisively marked the century, Lukács is an heir in immanence to the transcendent absolute of Spinoza.
>
> (**MH** 67)

And it is implicit in his monkish, but not monkish, fantasy about a temperate clime, distant from the "hellish" world, where one can indulge in the pursuit of abstraction for its own sake:

> It is perfectly conceivable that there is a small strip on the world's map (this was Herodotus's view, also Thucydides', also Plato's) where the climate is more or less bearable, temperate, where there is enough protein to eat, where there are *slaves*—that is, subject peoples who allow you to get on with the business of thinking, which means that you can spend your day doing something fantastic, like examining the geometry of conic sections (which is what Archimedes dies for), that you can do this quite insane and obsessive thing—to give your life to abstraction, to a speculation, to pure mathematics. Perhaps there is one part of the earth that produces complex theorems, algebraic

theorems, of a very involved and difficult and totally useless nature, that produces not religious faith but that immense luxury we call metaphysical speculative systems.

(**TT** 396)

This happy "strip" where abstraction is indulged appears more a temptation than an answer. Throughout his career, Steiner has reminded us of the cost of abstraction, of the cry more soundly heard when it originates in a novel rather than next door. And in the passage just quoted, Steiner ends by saying that "[c]limatically, food-wise, survival-wise, this is not open to everyone" (**TT** 396). Still, the temptation has always been a particularly seductive one for Steiner, and it colors what he has to say about "real presences" underwriting the text. He makes reference to God often enough, but it is a God lacking in warmth and other, decidedly anthropomorphic, characteristics that we like to attribute to "Him": caring, mercy, justice, etc. Instead, Steiner's God easily slips into the dress of abstraction, identified in terms— e.g., Being, *Logos,* Presence—more likely to warm the hearts of a convention of philosophers than a congregation of ordinary men and women seeking something, or rather Someone, to place their trust in. Steiner's critics have noted this. Robert P. Carroll, referring to ***Real Presences*** (where "the question of God [is addressed] more fully than in anything else" Steiner has written), says that its God is likable to "'transcendence,' that is, the undefined, unknown God, rather than the overdetermined, overdefined God of traditional Jewish religion and Christian ecclesiastical creeds" (RGS 266). And Harold Fromm, taking a harsher view, says that "his God is not really God, his transcendence has no literal characteristics he can clearly name apart from his own feelings, his religion has no tenets or contents" (402). Finally, Graham Ward notes that Steiner's "ontology of reading is described in distinctly Catholic (Heidegger's theological background) terms: 'transubstantial,' 'real presence,' 'sacramental,' 'incarnation,' 'icon,' and 'revelation'"; but that much is also unresolved here for the reason that "he is attempting to interlace a sociology and an ontology of literature" (RGS 192). In short, says Ward, Steiner's "wants a synthesis of the ontic and the ontological, and it is all too easy to create the synthesis by being 'eloquent of God'" (RGS 92).

Steiner's theology finds itself drawn away by other interests. It invokes the terms of theology, but in the end it is really about other things. It is about literature, music, philosophy, rhetoric, and the Shoah. But it is also about longing, and this I find its most interesting aspect and greatest strength. That is, what I find so attractive about Steiner's work here is just how emotionally involved he is in wanting the world to make sense, to hold together. It is true that this is not necessarily a religious project, but the asking of such questions is, it seems to me, at the heart of theology, particularly a

theology that thinks the asking of questions one of the most valuable things we can do. Steiner has suggested that Judaism is itself a-theological, that its textuality makes it ill at ease with the construction of answers that are inherently a-historical. In **"The Long Life of Metaphor,"** he writes that "the very notion of 'theology,' in the post-Pauline, post-Johannine, and post-Augustinian sense, has no real counterpart in Jewish religious feeling. The most authentic and lasting strength in Jewish sensibility is not a reflection or metaphysical discourse on the nature and attributes of God, but a 'living in His presence'" (55). Again, for Steiner, Judaism's relation to God is thought more dialogic, and Christianity's more duty-bound. It is, as said earlier, a hard antithesis to maintain, dismissing (among other things) the importance of the Torah in the life of the observant Jew and the importance of prayer in the life of the observant Christian. It is better to admit the importance of questioning to both religions, something that Steiner himself does, in effect, when in **"Anglican Inadequacies,"** he approvingly quotes the Protestant theologian Donald MacKinnon: "If Christianity survives it will be in part at least because the lonely figure, dying in agony upon the cross, crying out in dereliction to the Father, whom he believes to have forsaken him, remains ceaselessly interrogating men and women, outside as much as within the Christian churches, concerning his significance and that of his supreme hour. 'What think you of this man?'" (1238). In truth, George Steiner has, as Robert Carroll points out, always combined a "knowledge of things Jewish with a sensitivity to things Christian" (RGS 269), and it is this, rather than what Ward describes as an inexplicable "Christocentric" imagery, that best explains the beautiful closing passage in ***Real Presences***:

> But ours is the long day's journey of the Saturday. Between suffering, aloneness, unutterable waste on the one hand and the dream of liberation, of rebirth on the other. In the face of the torture of a child, of the death of love which is Friday, even the greatest art and poetry are almost helpless. In the Utopia of the Sunday, the aesthetic will, presumably, no longer have logic or necessity. The apprehensions and figurations in the play of metaphysical imagining, in the poem and the music, which tell of pain and hope, of the flesh which is said to taste of ash and of the spirit which is said to have the savour of fire, are always Sabbatarian. They have risen out of an immensity of waiting which is that of man. Without them, how could we be patient?

(**RP** 232)

True, Steiner employs an Easter allegory, but he also intersects it with the Jewish Sabbath, and it is the Sabbath—the Saturday characterized by waiting for the "Utopia of Sunday" (the release day from history's bondage), as well as the art and music composed in this period—that is the reality in place: "ours is the long day's journey of the Saturday." It is an image that might be critiqued for the way it sets Judaism and Christianity in opposition, but it is also one that quite beautifully yokes them together. In doing so, it also calls forth all Steiner's own longings and doubts, which, as I say, need not be thought of as a-theological, and are certainly not thought of so here.

Note

1. In *Language and Silence,* Steiner points to another side of Judaism, that which advocates a boundless "radical humanism." Jesus is in this camp, and so is Marx:

> But if the poison [i.e., of sectarianism] is, in ancient part, Jewish, so perhaps is the antidote, the radical humanism which sees man on the road to becoming man. This is where Marx is most profoundly a Jew— while at the same time arguing the dissolution of Jewish identity. He believed that class and economic status knew no frontiers, that misery had a common citizenship. He postulated that the revolutionary process would abolish national distinctions and antagonisms as industrial technology had all but eroded regional autonomy. The entire socialist utopia and dialectic of history is based on an international premise.
>
> (LS 153)

Abbreviations

A: *Antigones*

AE: "Archives of Eden"

BC: *In Bluebeard's Castle*

GSR: *George Steiner Reader*

LLM: "The Long Life of Metaphor: Shoah"

LS: *Language & Silence*

MH: "Making a Homeland for the Mind"

OHT: "Our Homeland, the Text"

PSC: *The Portage to San Cristóbal of A. H.*

R: "The Remembrancer"

RGS: *Reading George Steiner,* ed. Nathan A. Scott, Jr. and Ronald A. Sharp

RP: *Real Presences*

RI: "The Responsibility of Intellectuals," a discussion moderated by Robert Boyers

SR: "The Scandal of Revelation"

TD: *Tolstoy or Dostoevsky*

TGD: "Through That Glass Darkly"

TT: "Totem or Taboo"

Works Cited

Abel, Lionel. "So Who is to Have the Last Word? (On Some of the Positions Taken by George Steiner)," *Partisan Review,* v. 53, no. 3 (Spring 1987): 358-71.

Boyers, Robert, moderator. "The Responsibility of Intellectuals: A Discussion." *Salmagundi,* no. 70-71 (Spring/ Summer 1986): 164-95.

Carroll, Robert P. "Toward a Grammar of Creation: On Steiner the Theologian," in Scott and Sharp, 262-274.

Cunningham, Valentine. *In the Reading Gaol: Postmodernity, Texts, and History.* Cambridge, MA: Basil Blackwell, 1994.

Dickstein, Morris. "Alive and 90 in the Jungles of Brazil," *The New York Review of Books* (2 May 1982): 13, 21.

Hand, Séan, ed. *The Levinas Reader.* Cambridge: Basil Blackwell, 1992.

Handelman, Susan A. *The Slayers of Moses: The Emergence of Rabbinic Interpretation in Modern Literary Theory.* Albany: State University of New York Press, 1982.

Kant, Immanuel. *The Critique of Judgement.* Trans. James Creed Meredith. Oxford: Oxford UP, 1986.

James, William. *The Varieties of Religious Experience.* New York: Penguin, 1982.

Scholem, Gershom. *The Messianic Idea in Judaism, And Other Essays on Jewish Spirituality.* New York: Schocken Books, 1974.

————. *On Jews and Judaism in Crisis: Selected Essays.* Ed. Werner J. Dannhauser. New York: Schocken Books, 1976.

Scott, Nathan A. and Ronald A. Sharp, eds. *Reading George Steiner.* Baltimore: Johns Hopkins UP, 1994.

Sharp, Ronald A. "Steiner's Fiction and the Hermeneutics of Transcendence," in Scott and Sharp, 205-29.

Steiner, George. "Anglican Inadequacies," *Times Literary Supplement* (7 November 1986): 1238.

————. *Antigones: How the Antigone Legend Has Endured in Western Literature, Art, and Thought.* Oxford: Oxford UP, 1986.

————. "The Archive of Eden," *Salmagundi,* no. 50-51 (Fall/Winter 1981): 57-89.

————. *George Steiner: A Reader.* New York: Oxford UP, 1984.

————. "The Good Books," *The New Yorker* (11 January 1988): 94-98.

————. "Graven Images," *The New Yorker* (2 February 1987): 95-98.

————. *In Bluebeard's Castle: Some Notes Towards the Redefinition of Culture.* New Haven: Yale UP, 1971.

————. "A Jew's Grief," *Harper's Magazine* (October 1988): 18-20.

———. *Language and Silence: Essays on Language, Literature and the Inhuman.* New York: Atheneum, 1972.

———. "Language Under Surveillance: The Writer and the State," *The New York Times Book Review* (12 January 1986): 12, 36.

———. "Levinas," *Cross Currents* (Summer 1991): 243-48.

———. "The Long Life of Metaphor: An Approach to the Shoah," *Encounter,* vol. 68 (February 1987): 55-61.

———. "Making a Homeland for the Mind," *Times Literary Supplement* (22 January 1982): 67-68.

———. *Martin Heidegger.* Chicago: U of Chicago P, 1991.

———. "Our Homeland, the Text," *Salmagundi,* no. 66 (Winter/Spring 1985): 4-25.

———. *The Portage to San Cristóbal of A. H.,* New York: Simon and Schuster, 1981.

———. *Real Presences: Is There Anything in What We Say?* London: Faber and Faber, 1989.

———. "The Scandal of Revelation," *Salmagundi,* no. 98-99 (Spring/Summer 1993): 42-70.

———. "Through That Glass Darkly," *Salmagundi,* no. 93 (Winter 1992): 32-50.

———. *Tolstoy or Dostoevsky: An Essay in the Old Criticism.* New York: Knopf, 1959.

———. "Totem or Taboo," *Salmagundi,* no. 88-89 (Fall 1990/Winter 1991): 385-98.

Vermes, Geza. *The Religion of Jesus the Jew.* Minneapolis: Fortress P, 1993.

Ward, Graham. "Heidegger in Steiner," in Scott and Sharp, 180-204.

Wittgenstein, Ludwig. *Tractatus Logico-Philosophicus.* Trans. C. K. Ogden. London: Routledge, 1988.

James Wood (review date 30 September 1996)

SOURCE: Wood, James. "Real Absences." *New Republic* 215, no. 14 (30 September 1996): 32-8.

[*In the following review, Wood objects to the cultural analyses of* No Passion Spent, *finding the rhetoric imprecise, thought solipsistic, and logic faulty.*]

George Steiner's prose is a remarkable substance; it is the sweat of a statue that wishes to be a monument. Readers of his essays in *The New Yorker* will be familiar with that prose's laborious imprecisions and melodra-mas; the platoon-like massing of its adjectives, its cathedral hush around the great works. Nabokov once complained that one of Steiner's essays was "built on solid abstractions and opaque generalisations"; but things are worse than that, as his new book of essays [*No Passion Spent*] demonstrates.

George Steiner has a fear of exhibiting even rhetorical ignorance, and this is accompanied by a superstitious worship of "greatness," where greatness has been detached from its referent and has become a portable magic, like feng shui. **"An Uncommon Reader,"** in his new book, provides two amusing examples on successive pages. Steiner is discoursing on the decline of "classic codes of literacy." ("Do not even ask a relatively well-prepared student to respond to the title of 'Lycidas.'") Every true reader, he avers, "carries within him a nagging weight of omission:" the books that he has not read. Apparently there are books that even George Steiner has not read. And yet he knows that they are great: "the eight volumes, unread, of Sorel's great diplomatic history of Europe and the French Revolution haunt me." Or a page earlier: "I have, a dozen times, slunk by Sarpi's leviathan history of the Council of Trent (one of the pivotal works in the development of western religious-political argument). . . . I shall never manage the sixteen thousand pages of Amiel's (profoundly interesting) journal currently being published. There is so little time in 'the library that is the universe' (Borges's Mallarméen phrase)." David's lament for Jonathan, he tells us, is "unsurpassed in any poetry."

All this greatness is memorialized in rippling and indiscriminate lists, whose tic is a consumer's indefinite article. Just as one asks for a coffee, a piece of pie and a Coke, Steiner asks for "a Socrates, a Mozart, a Gauss or a Galileo who, in some degree, compensate for man"; or "a Mantegna, a Turner or a Cézanne . . . a Racine, a Dostoevsky, a Kafka." He charges that "the pressure of presence throughout the world of the mind and of moral feeling exercised on civilization by a Marx, a Freud, even a Lévi-Strauss, is of a calibre which American culture does not produce." This is not a trivial habit of style. There is only "a coffee," but there is no such thing as "a Mozart." There is Mozart, singular and non-transferable, a concretion, not a vapor. Steiner's use of lists, and his use of the indefinite article, suggests that the meal of greatness can be had in any order and in any combination; the important thing is to fill oneself up and be bloatedly grateful.

It may be that Steiner, detecting his own vulgarity in these matters, compensates by wrapping great works in veils. Since greatness is a magic, one must be wary of offending it, in particular by unthinking worldliness. "If we choose, we can put on Opus 131 while eating breakfast," he quivers in his book *In Bluebeard's*

Castle. This is not a good thing. Steiner is here denouncing the coarsening freedoms of modernity, specifically American modernity. One of his persistent sensations, doubtless accurate, is that reading as it was pursued a hundred years ago in bourgeois families has been superseded by listening to music. This technological proximity to great music is all very well, but one should not be too intimate with holiness. Steiner enunciates the dangers, in two languages: "There can be an unprecedented intimacy, but also a devaluation (*désacralisation*)."

* * *

Steiner's melodrama of transcendence accounts for his air of excited gravity. He approaches each work as if leading a coup to restore a monarch to the throne. First he must synchronize his beating heart with the reader's: "We are entering on large, difficult ground"; "Here extreme precision is needed"; "Let me be absolutely clear on this"; "Again, this is a most complex topic." Generally, the coup fails. The less precise his prose is, the more it speaks of the importance of precision. An emblematic moment occurs in his essay **"Absolute Tragedy."** Steiner urges on us the blackness of our times ("this century has witnessed a carnival of bestiality"), and suggests that pure tragedy's lack of mercy may be our most appropriate literary form. "If this perception can, must be dwelt on, if it must be 'thought' (in Heidegger's active sense of that word), do there not attach to it the potential, the likelihood of a renascence of tragic drama?" "Heidegger's active sense of that word": here is the essence of Steiner. The operatic flounce, the sentimental wrestle ("if this perception can, must be dwelt on"); the allusion, quite irrelevant, to Heidegger, followed by the ascription of the importance of thinking to the word itself rather than a demonstration of its activity. What is "active" here, except a pulse?

The prose is a servant of the thought, and the thought is . . . a servant. Great work is to be worshiped and protected, and great work requires great questions. His commonest sentence is a question: "Is it possible that. . . ." "Could it be that. . . ." Could it be that anti-Semitism is the Gentile's guilty revenge on the impossible demands of Mosaic monotheism, Christianity and messianic socialism, all Jewish "inventions"? Could it be that great art thrives best in elitist structures, in totalitarian societies? Is it possible that great art does not merely co-exist with barbarism and evil, but in some way encourages it? These are some of the questions of Steiner's work. He seems to relish their unanswerability, as if that made them better questions, and as if the fact that nobody has ever answered them means that nobody has ever asked them. Steiner is in love with the glamour of the unsayable. He has sensations rather than arguments. In his essay **"Real Presences,"** he notes

that all value-judgments about works of art are unproveable and arbitrary. *"Anything can be said about anything,"* he italicizes. Indeed. *And nothing can be said about nothing.* There are times, as Auden warned, when "to ask the hard question is simple."

Steiner's new book lets us see that his work since *Language and Silence* (1967) has been impressively repetitive. The first essay in his new collection, **"An Uncommon Reader,"** from 1978, expands a sensation central to both *In Bluebeard's Castle* (1971) and *Real Presences* (1988). Steiner has felt, since the 1960s, that our age is "in retreat from the word." The word, for Steiner, signifies a certain authority of meaning and a body of assumed knowledge. This retreat is partly, and trivially, a matter of fashion. Education is no longer rooted in the Greek and Latin classics. We listen to music but we do not read aloud to one another. Culture is now democratically accessible. Most people own paperbacks, and few people have libraries of hardback volumes. In place of *"cortesia"* there is now "informality." Culture was once kept alive by stern schooling and by the cultivation of memory, especially through learning poetry by heart. (This was the education that Steiner received in the *lycée* system in Paris.) "Memory is, of course, the pivot," but in most students there has been an "atrophy of memory." Quite forgivably, Steiner's thought bears the characteristic impress of a university teacher who has not recovered from the shock that he received in the 1960s when the counterculture (a phrase Steiner spits, when he can) ambled into his *cortesia,* and who has refueled his shock at the pump of postmodernism, whose excesses seem to repeat philosophically what the 1960s attempted politically.

The retreat has deeper lineaments. Never mind the counterculture. Writers no longer write for the glory beyond death: "The very notion of *fama,* of literary glory achieved in defiance of and as rebuttal to death, embarrasses." This is, above all, a crisis of meaning. Modernism snapped the idea of a natural link between a word and its meaning, and Freudianism has undermined our sense of control over that meaning. Meanwhile the belief in God, which guarantees a telos, has fallen away. The greatest danger, as Steiner sees it, comes from the philosophical skepticism that travels under the name of deconstruction, post-modernism or post-structuralism. The modernists strove against the decay of meaning, but deconstruction embraces it, embraces the free play of meanings. The text is a bubble of signifiers constantly revealing its own contradictions and wistful ambitions, and the contemporary critic's only job seems to be to prick it. Where modernism was unafraid to make hierarchies, deconstruction erodes them and postmodernism ignores them. Truth is radically unstable. *Auctoritas* is gone.

There are too many professors of literature who see around them only collapsing vertebrae for Steiner's complaint to be other than conventional; and an argument on behalf of distinction—Steiner's argument—is surely cheapened by not itself having much distinction. In fairness, though, it should be noted that Steiner departs from these other complainers in three ways. He is philosophically more literate than most, competently dragging the heavy iron of the Germanic tradition into his corner whenever he can. And he is much more open to new work, in various languages, than is usual among English-language critics. There are people who speak happily of their years at Cambridge University in the '60s, when the young Steiner filled lecture rooms, burrowing into his cellular erudition and prompting students to discover writers who were hardly known to them: Borges, Barthes, Garcia Marquez, Beckett. An essay on translation in this volume shows Steiner passionate and not too imprecise, arguing the merits of the Austrian novelist Thomas Bernhard and pleading for his translation into English. In 1982, when this essay was written, only one of Bernhard's novels had traveled out of German. Now most of them are available in English, and Steiner had something to do with this.

But Steiner differs from other Jeremiahs most spectacularly in his response to the malaise. The solution is Steiner's doctrine of the Real Presence. He proffered this in his Cambridge lecture of 1985, **"Real Presences,"** which he expanded into a book of the same title. He thinks that the solution is frankly theological. It is, alas, vaguely religious. His prose, always smeary, becomes diligently evasive in the course of this particular sensation. Deconstruction, for Steiner, is a nihilism, and "the summons of nihilism demand answer." The answer is faith. In the face of a deconstructionist who claims that *Madame Bovary* is just a set of signifiers, or Mahler's Fourth Symphony just complex notations on staves, Steiner demands that we read and listen "as if"—as if these great works have a transcendent meaning which is irreducible. This, suggests Steiner, is what Flaubert meant when, dying, he complained that "that whore Emma Bovary" would outlive him.

We will have to believe, Steiner teaches, that these and other great works "incarnate" a meaning in the same way that in the Christian communion the bread and wine incarnate the flesh and blood of Christ. (That is what the doctrine of the Real Presence refers to.) Meaning is guaranteed by a belief in the transcendent, in the divine. Speaking strictly, we cannot know that this is so, but just as Pascal made his wager, we must make ours: "Where we read truly, where the experience is to be that of meaning, we do so as if the text (the piece of music, the work of art) *incarnates* (the notion is grounded in the sacramental) *a real presence of significant being*. This real Presence, as in an icon, as in the enacted metaphor of the sacramental bread and wine, is finally irreducible to any other formal articu-

late. . . ." A little earlier, Steiner refers to Descartes's *"sine qua non* that God will not systematically confuse or falsify our perception and understanding of the world" and adds that "without some such fundamental presupposition" in regard to sense and value, we cannot understand great work. He calls this "our Cartesian-Kantian wager, our leap into sense. . . ." It is this theological underpinning that funds not only true reading, but also the art of translation and the blasphemy of nihilistic or "absolute" tragedy.

This is no more than the milk of optimism. Even a philosophical amateur knows that Kant and Descartes did not construct a wager like Pascal's. They constructed proofs for the existence of a God in which they believed and trusted. Those proofs are expressions not of will, but of mind: they are true or false; they may be verified or refuted. The Pascalian wager, by contrast, is an unhappily wary manner in which to win God. As Santayana said (in *Character and Opinion in the United States*), "betting on the improbable because you are offered big odds is an unworthy parody of the real choice between wisdom and folly." And it is a nonsensical manner in which to win meaning. Pascal could, he supposed, lose heaven. How can one lose meaning? Who wins the meaning that the gambler might lose? Moreover, and unlike Pascal's, Steiner's wager is pithless: his language is a religious skin only. He takes the language of hard religious belief, softens it into mere metaphor, then convinces himself that what he has is a hard metaphor that is the equivalent of religious belief.

But it is not an equivalent, nor should it be. Attend to Steiner's evasions: he writes that where we read truly, we do so not *because* the text incarnates meaning but *as if* it incarnates meaning. Again, he writes that we must follow Descartes's "wager"—but we must follow it only vaguely: "some such fundamental presupposition." Any similar fundamental presupposition will do, as long as it is very fundamental. And while on the one hand the text is taken to "incarnate" meaning, a word with a specific (Christian) gravity of embodiment, in the next sentence this incarnation is no more than an "enacted metaphor."

This is intellectually feeble. The doctrine of the Real Presence, in Christian practice, is guaranteed by belief in the greater incarnation of Christ, who is believed to be God made into man. There are, broadly, three kinds of belief in the Real Presence. Catholicism believes that in the communion service, which repeats Jesus's last supper, the bread and wine become the flesh and blood of Christ while remaining outwardly unchanged ("transubstantiation"); Protestantism believes that Jesus's body is present in the bread and wine ("consubstantiation"); and there are Christians, like the Zwinglians of old, who believe that neither happens, but that the communion service memorializes Christ's last supper. Is George Steiner a Zwinglian? It is only this last belief that comes close to the idea of an enacted metaphor. Most orthodox belief takes incarnation to mean what it says, since Christ's incarnation is taken to mean what it says. The Real Presence is founded on God-given truth; and even the Zwinglian doctrine is founded on the possibility of memorializing God-given truth. None of these positions is a wager. And none is an enacted metaphor, unless Christ is an enacted metaphor.

"Incarnation" is not a word that should be used lightly, as Steiner does here. Not because to do so is blasphemous, but because to do so is meaningless. Incarnation promises the presence and guarantee of God. Nowhere does Steiner appear to believe in this final presence. His wager is not a wager on a presence real and final enough to guarantee meaning. Wagering on merely "a significant being" seems a mug's game.

Steiner is like a patient who reinfects himself by putting dirty bandages on his wounds. His own religiose language infects his doctrine of meaning, for it forces the very question that is necessary for this doctrine but entirely unnecessary outside it: Does Steiner believe in God? Or does he not? Either he is wagering meaning on God, or he is merely wagering meaning by gambling with language. But the latter is not far from what we do every day, habitually, without a theological language. A "leap into sense," which Steiner promises, is not the same as a leap into God. A leap into sense is how the secular day begins, and necessity has turned the leap, for most of us, into a daily stroll. A stroll, because we do not need to wager on sense when all our life it has seemed that this is a bet that has already been won for us. To wager thus would actually be senseless: the sun rises every day.

* * *

It is not obvious that great criticism or great art needs Steiner's theological postulate to live in the stability of truth and the transcendence of beauty. Steiner ignores the many great post-Renaissance artists who have gotten along without a theology or a language of theology, and have radiantly made do with a theology of art. This is what Proust hints in his essay on Ruskin, when he separates his own non-theological aestheticism from the Christian aestheticism of Ruskin, whose principal religion "was religion," as Proust puts it, and whose "wholly religious life was spent wholly aesthetically." Proust, who uses language exactly, calls Ruskin's aesthetic a "supernatural aesthetic." Steiner wants to enjoy a supernatural aesthetic without the obligation of supernatural belief. Ruskin worried about drinking tea while looking at Titian because Titian truly incarnated a Real Presence. Steiner fusses about eating breakfast while listening to Opus 131 because Opus 131 is an enacted metaphor . . . of something or other.

One feels that Steiner is asking us to believe not in the presence of the divine but in the easier presence of undefined greatness. The test is easy to apply. Were Steiner proposing a doctrine of meaning, it would have to be a universal doctrine, just as Christianity is a universal doctrine. If great work incarnates a Real Presence, then minor or even bad work must do so also, for meaning, divine or otherwise, cannot be present only in masterpieces. Schubert's C major Quintet, which Steiner mentions ritualistically again and again, must incarnate meaning as, say, must a novel by Danielle Steele. The quality of the meaning is another matter; but vulgar meaning is not without any meaning at all. Ruskin worshiped and wrote about not only the stones of Venice, but also the stones and trees on simple hillsides, since both were incarnations of God's creativity. Nothing in the whole body of Steiner's work suggests that he could bring himself to apply his Real Presence democratically.

Steiner is dismissive of those who would hold him to theological accountability. At the end of his **"Preface to the Hebrew Bible,"** he wonders aloud if the Bible is merely literature or the bearer of divine witness and revelation. Those who believe the latter, he says, are "fundamentalists." Those who believe the former, he thinks, are secularists. Having vandalized each side of this binarism, he decides that we need a third position—that nice and useful Real Presence. In fact, all that Steiner does here is bloat the Bible with mystery, but a mystery arrived at by the most vulgar route. What awes him, and finally convinces him that the Bible is quasi-divine ("*as if* divine"), is that he cannot imagine someone writing the Psalms or the Book of Job and then going to lunch.

That really is his argument, accompanied by swirls and swoons. He can just about imagine "Shakespeare remarking at home or to some intimate on whether or not work on *Hamlet* or *Othello* had, that day, gone well or poorly, as the case might be," and "then enquiring as to the price of cabbages," though this boggles his mind. But what he cannot do—or will not do?—is imagine the same about the writers of the Bible. "The picture of some man or woman, lunching, dining, after he or she had 'invented' and set down these and certain other biblical texts, leaves me, as it were, blinded and off balance." He forgets that the worldliness of these texts—the Psalmist crying to God in one breath and calling to his sheep in the next—is one of their highest beauties.

The scriptures make him feel somewhat religious; therefore they are somewhat religious. That is Steiner's thrust, that is his Real Presence. He leaps into sublimity by deciding that the sublime cannot be vulgar, that you cannot write a Psalm and then eat. But he exaggerates vulgarity in order to exaggerate sublimity's lack of it; and in the end all he offers is a hedged secularism written up religiously. Elsewhere in his book he confesses to similar mystical goose bumps in relation to Kafka. That the parable "Before The Law" was written "by a gentleman in a bowler hat going to and from his daily insurance business, defies my grasp." And indeed it does. Truly this is not thought, but a fear of thought.

II.

The retreat from the word has one other determinant: the Holocaust. In the Holocaust, art blithely coexisted with utmost evil. "We know of personnel in the bureaucracy of the torturers and the ovens who cultivated a knowledge of Goethe, a love of Rilke. . . . Nothing in the next-door world of Dachau impinged on the great winter cycle of Beethoven chamber music played in Munich." Heidegger wrote great philosophy almost within earshot of a concentration camp. In *In Bluebeard's Castle,* and in several essays in the new book, Steiner lays out the impotences that flow from this terrible knowledge. We can no longer believe in a necessary connection between high art and high behavior. "Voltaire and Arnold regarded as established the crucial lemma that the humanities humanize." But we have lost this certainty. "We have lost a characteristic élan, a metaphysic of 'forward dreaming' (of which Ernst Bloch's *Das Prinzip Hoffnung* is the inspired statement)."

Perhaps, Steiner speculates, art encourages barbarism, for it wraps its audience in falsities that bloom larger for them than the dilemmas of reality. The obsessiveness of great art and great thought promotes a mandarinism careless of the world. A recurrent figure in Steiner's work is Archimedes, who would not relinquish his work on the algebra of conic sections even as the Romans came to kill him in his garden in Syracuse. Anthony Blunt, the British art historian and Soviet spy, inspired one of Steiner's best pieces for *The New Yorker,* and in it he orates on the scandalous disjunction of civilized activity and treason: "I would like to think for a moment about a man who in the morning teaches his students that a false attribution of a Watteau drawing . . . is a sin against the spirit and in the afternoon or evening transmits to the agents of Soviet intelligence classified, perhaps vital information given to him in sworn trust by his countrymen and intimate colleagues. What are the sources of scission?"

As in much of Steiner's work, this is offered to us with first-night flamboyance, as if we were his virgins in knowledge. As in his discussion of religious faith, he erects melodramatic binarisms and does vulgar damage to precise thinking. The binarism is always at an hysterical pitch: philosophy or the death-camps; Watteau or treason; breakfast or Opus 131; a Real Presence or nihilism. Steiner's ruminations are not novel and they cloud thought. More calmly, and with deeper understanding,

writers and philosophers have long considered the irresponsible power of art; it is a commonplace of theories of tragedy and of the sublime. Hazlitt, in his celebrated essay on *Coriolanus* and elsewhere, pointed out that poetry "delights in power, in strong excitement, as well as in truth," and that this "gives a Bias to the imagination often inconsistent with the greatest good," that "in Poetry it [the imagination] triumphs over Principle, and bribes the passions to make a sacrifice of common humanity."

Steiner has at times usefully reminded us of art's complicities with the inhumane. But Steiner is himself in love with the inhumane. This is gravely said. The despotic negligence, the God-like separateness, the vicious mysteries, the sickness or the madness of Kierkegaard or Kafka or Weil—these are the qualities that Steiner cherishes. He wants to be the voice out of the whirlwind; and if this cannot be, he will spend his life chasing the whirlwind. The political system that seems best to protect the life of great art, he thinks, is elitist, anti-democratic, unjust and possibly even totalitarian. This is where he would rather live, the better for whirlwind-chasing. In **"An Uncommon Reader,"** written in 1978, he notes that one country where the old codes of "classic literacy" survive—remembrance, learning by heart, fiercely held private libraries, ideas to live and die for—is the (then) Soviet Union. Were Steiner to have to choose, he would choose, for art's sake, something closer to the Soviet dispensation than to the American, democratic, meliorist dispensation.

The very idea of speculating about choosing between these systems—as if such momentousness were up for grabs, as if this were all a kind of ghastly, mutilated consumerism—is not only null but offensive. Since we are fortunate enough not to have to choose between tyranny and freedom, we should not choose rhetorically between them. But this is just what Steiner does in **"The Archives of Eden,"** his notorious essay of 1978, reprinted here. Steiner is like someone who, seeing a blind man in the street, says, "I would rather be deaf than blind." He begins by charging America with having produced very little of great artistic or intellectual achievement. Its classical music is eccentric; its philosophy is limited, with no great work done in the areas of metaphysics or ethics; its mathematics, where there has been real achievement, has been largely by imported Europeans; its fine art of any quality is simply an epilogue to European modernism and surrealism; its theology lacks anyone of Karl Barth's stature. Only America's literature has what he calls "claims to classic occasion." But in this century, "the summits are *not* American: they are: Thomas Mann, Kafka, Joyce, Proust." There is not, in America, (to be Steiner-ish for a moment) a Stravinsky or a Schoenberg, a Kandinsky or a Picasso, a Heidegger, a Wittgenstein, a Sartre.

* * *

Steiner proceeds characteristically, eating his way through great works as a bat in flight blindly gobbles insects, a thousand a minute. America, he decides, is a culture devoted to the custody of European work. It has the best museums and galleries, the greatest research centers, the finest holdings of manuscripts; but it is not a place where great creation is going on. Also, America in this century has become the richest and freest land on earth, while Europe has twice erupted into warfare and barbarism. This correlation between creativity and catastrophe suggests much about the relative qualities of these two societies, and the place that art is accorded in them. Steiner speculates that since art is always the preserve of the few, a society devoted to the liberation of the many, such as America, will not be the cradle for art's prospering. The American ideal is that of "material progress and recompense. *Fortuna* is fortune."

Liberal democratic meliorism is no home for the greatness that is always made by the few for the few. Such a society, aflame with "libertarian cant," may actually conspire against the production of great work. Meanwhile, it seems to be the case that great art is either produced in conditions of elitism (Pericles's Athens, Racine's France) or, in the modern age, in the nearest equivalent of this, which are the totalitarian regimes of Latin America or the Soviet Union. (Steiner's essay has grown crow's-feet since 1978.) He quotes Borges, who once said "Censorship is the mother of metaphor," and Joyce, who said: "We artists are olives; squeeze us." He points out that the Russian novel in this century has an urgency and a desperation that American fiction cannot rival.

One of the many slynesses of Steiner's sensations is that he affects the motions of argument while actually standing completely still. One is never in any doubt as to which side Steiner is on in this grotesque fight, but he must pretend to see things from the American side. To be sure, he simpers, there will be prices to pay on both sides. You can have torture, injustice and restricted access in Europe; or you can have wealth, health and the mindless pursuit of happiness in America. And to be sure, he pretends, only a monster would choose Europe. "No play by Racine is worth a Bastille, no Mandelstam poem an hour of Stalinism." America has done the decent thing: "If a choice must be made, let humane mediocrity prevail." Steiner is merely being honest in laying out the costs. What he cannot stand are those— "and they have been legion in American academe or the media"—who "want it both ways." For those who espouse the highest standards while preaching the liberal democracy that undermines those very standards, Steiner has only contempt.

There are a number of responses to this vicious incoherence. The swiftest and most majestic was provided by Joseph Brodsky, who knew firsthand the tyrannies that are only pornographic to Steiner. Years ago Brodsky and Steiner appeared on a British television program. Steiner set out his anti-democratic stall. He spoke for fifteen minutes. Small and quivering, cold-eyed, he emanated a punitive hysteria. He spoke in rolling discourses, hardly pausing for breath, vigorous with triumphalist evasions. He resembled one of those petit-bourgeois maniacs or upstarts who crowd the drawing-rooms and sniff the action in Dostoevsky's novels. He presented the argument of **"The Archives of Eden."** Then he stopped. And quietly, with thick dignity, Brodsky responded: "Yes, but liberty is the greatest masterpiece."

That is all that needs to be said. By insisting on his own lovely metaphor, Brodsky was reminding Steiner that although censorship may be "the mother of metaphor," censorship is not itself a metaphor. For when torture is discussed speculatively by someone who has known only freedom, it is being discussed metaphorically. This is the real affront of Steiner's essay. It is a rhetoric of choice indulged in by a man who is fortunate enough to have never had to choose; and his choice is for a system in which people have never been allowed to choose. He makes a choice for not being able to choose. His essay is thus an exhausted liberty.

But it is also a nonsense. One cannot choose tyranny. No one would actually do so; so Steiner's argument is strictly meaningless. But to make it seem meaningful, he must give us the illusion that one can choose between such things. He despises those who "want it both ways." The implication is clear. Steiner is the more honest for wanting it only one way, and this is the way of elitist, even totalitarian regimes. He moves from the speculative to the prescriptive. It is as if Steiner, having decided that he would rather be blind than deaf, asks to be forcibly blinded, the better to develop his hearing.

"If a choice must be made," he writes. But a choice must not be made, and has never been made. This rhetoric of choice pushes Steiner toward facile linkages: we want or choose a dispensation (America has apparently "chosen" humane mediocrity) and this dispensation uncomplicatedly "produces" certain works of art and thought. Ironically, this great anti-American here speaks a language of pure consumerism, of choice and product. Culture is a factory floor, and he is the bullying foreman.

But Steiner conflates elitism and totalitarianism. He begins by comparing Europe and America. By the end of the essay he is speaking of the Soviet Union. Most of his examples of European greatness are not Russian, yet the force of his melodrama is toward squaring off totalitarianism against American freedom. (This is a binarism he indulges with equal melodrama in his recent novella, *Proofs* [*Proofs, and Three Parables*] in which two men discuss the pros and cons of the American and Russian systems.) But much of modern European art, while labored on in the midst of injustice, has been created in conditions that are closer to democracy than to tyranny. And much ordinary art—Britain in the twentieth century: not a single one of Steiner's examples of greatness is British—has been produced in elitist, class-sodden cultures.

* * *

Steiner is not, in fact, making a political contrast at all, though he thinks he is. He is not setting banal freedom against special illiberality. He is comparing several very ancient societies with one relatively new one. This is not a comparison. Borges actually and politically repressed is very different from Joyce yearning for (if he really did yearn for) intellectual repression. One lived in a police state and one lived in democratic Europe. Steiner thinks, for example, that it is a neat jibe to end his essay by pledging his faith in Archimedes's garden in Syracuse. "My hunch is that it [the labor of greatness] lies in Syracuse still—Sicily, that is, rather than New York." But the two Syracuses have much in common. Both are places of liberal democracy, even if the Italian version is corruptly unstable. What divides them is antiquity, not politics. Indeed, if one set out to become a great writer, then Syracuse, New York, might be a more hospitable place than Syracuse, Sicily. A great writer did grow up in Syracuse, New York, and briefly attended university there. His name was Stephen Crane.

Had Steiner, in 1978, fought like with like—posed a newish totalitarian society against a newish liberal one—what would have been America's proper rival? South Africa, perhaps. And to anyone familiar with its literature (doubtless not "great" enough to attract Steiner's attention) South Africa gives the lie to the idea that totalitarianism produces, in some uncomplicated causal way, great work. On the contrary, in South Africa totalitarianism has produced an enfeebled, minor literature with occasional peaks. And it is a literature whose constant subject has been, inevitably and limitingly, power and repression and the corruptions of society. J. M. Coetzee said this about it in his Jerusalem Prize speech of 1987: "It is a less than fully human literature, unnaturally preoccupied with power and the torsions of power. . . . It is exactly the kind of literature you would expect people to write from a prison."

Steiner complains that America is a museum culture. But Steiner is himself a museum of European monuments. In Steiner's museum all the monuments are in conspiracy with each other. One monument leads to another. Without Kafka, says Steiner, "we would not have Beckett's clowns." But those of us who cherish literary greatness see that, contra Steiner, greatness is not always dynastic. The critic's truest wager is made not on an unarguably great God, but on the foundling, the unparented work that no one has yet raised to greatness. America is incomprehensible to George Steiner because it is a country which has produced masterpieces but not dynasties of monuments. It is a country that has often had to cast off European monuments in order to create American masterpieces. It is a country in which passionate languages of art have been spoken without need of theology. George Steiner offers a parody of Europeanness while fighting a parody of Americanness. America eludes him. In America's museums and libraries are the great European works that populate Steiner's family of giants; but its true vitalities fly.

Hans H. Rudnick (review date spring 1997)

SOURCE: Rudnick, Hans H. Review of *No Passion Spent,* by George Steiner. *World Literature Today* 71, no. 2 (spring 1997): 471-72.

[*In the following review, Rudnick praises Steiner's achievement in* No Passion Spent.]

Milton's Samson in *Samson Agonistes,* who had steadfastly fought against the Philistines, who had burdened himself with guilt through the hubris of a freely acting man, and who found the path to God's grace through insight, repentance, and following the divine will, inspired the title of George Steiner's latest collection of lectures, introductions, essays, and reviews [*No Passion Spent*]. The last three words that conclude the sonnet at the end of *Samson Agonistes* are "all passion spent." Steiner *agonistes,* most eloquent and erudite of all defenders of the Judeo-Christian tradition, demonstrates valiantly that his passion is not spent and that his thinking and judgment are based on the *auctoritas* of time-honored Western values *sine ira et studio.*

The hoi polloi without exile experience who have lately added "comparative literature" to their academic title without being able to read or write a word in any other major Western language accuse Steiner (who is fluent in at least four major living languages) of "elitism" without noticing their own cultural blindness. Paradigms and archeologies, economies and supplements have replaced plain learning and the genesis of historically grown knowledge as shortcuts to obtaining admittance into the community of scholars. Where are, Steiner asks with reference to Péguy, "des lecteurs qui sachent lire," who, like Chapman, Golding, Florio, North, and Urquhart, through their masterful translations, prepared the "ingestions" of Homer, Ovid, Montaigne, Plutarch, and Rabelais into English? Where are, one might add, the likes of Wellek, Guillén, Friederich, Remak, and Miner?

In his lecture **"What Is Comparative Literature?"** Steiner emphasizes that "comparative literature listens and reads after Babel" and that "a persistent engagement with natural languages, an inquiry into the reception and influence of texts, an awareness of thematic analogies and variants, are part of all literary studies."

Homme savant, Mensch, praeceptor, supreme stylist and thinker, Steiner is *sans pareil.* Literature and anything that has a cultural relation with it are Steiner's métier. In twenty-one chapters, from the Torah and Homer, Shakespeare, Kierkegaard and Freud, Péguy and Weill, Kafka, Husserl, and Heidegger, to the Last Suppers of Jesus and Socrates, Steiner explains, argues, and makes us think about our shared cultural past, our relationship to language and literature, and our religion and moral behavior. His profound understanding of phenomenology and its history, extremely important for any person of letters because of its unquestionably fruitful relationship to literature in its "zurück zu den Sachen" premise and subsequent significant further development by Husserl's former students (Heidegger, Gadamer, Ingarden, and Fink, to name only a few) and major French philosophers (Sartre, Merleau-Ponty, Levinas, and Derrida, whose revolutionary and central concept of *différance* he properly understands), also leads Steiner consistently to highlight the moral *débâcle* of Heidegger's shameful failure as a human being while nevertheless recognizing his intellectual brilliance as a major twentieth-century philosopher and *lecteur* who returned in his studies *ad fontes.*

Steiner himself, always eager to know "wie es einst gewesen," judges *la condition humaine* without concession to fads and trends. The consistently evolved values of the Western tradition remain his touchstone. He knows "American culture has stood, from its outset, on giant shoulders"—namely, the Judeo-Christian tradition. He then observes, "The tenor of American feeling is closer to the bias for magic, for pragmatic *bricolage,* current in non-western traditions than it is in the world of Plato and of Kant. . . . The twentieth century offers graphic evidence: there is, quite simply, no American metaphysician, no 'thinker on being', no inquirer into the meaning of meaning to set beside Heidegger or Wittgenstein or Sartre. . . . The inheritance of ontological astonishment (*thaumazein*) and systematic response remains unbroken from Heraclitus to Sartre's *Les Mots.* It runs through Aquinas, Descartes, Hume, Kant, Hegel and Nietzsche. There is no American membership in this list."

Steiner courageously asks us to look into the mirror, take inventory, and pose the *quo vadis* question. That does not make him an elitist, but rather a caring critic who wants us to recognize and honor our own heritage.

John C. Hawley (review date summer 1997)

SOURCE: Hawley, John C. "A Metaphorical Transcendence." *Cross Currents* 47, no. 2 (summer 1997): 254-55.

[*In the following review, Hawley evaluates what he perceives to be strengths and weaknesses of* No Passion Spent.]

One of the many criticisms that George Steiner makes of American culture, especially in his infamous 1981 essay **"The Archives of Eden,"** which is included here [*No Passion Spent*], is that "the dominant apparatus of American high culture is that of custody" (281). Our libraries, he writes, are the "Alexandria of western civilization," and we have produced nothing that marks an advance on Europe. Perhaps after reading a few of this book's twenty-one essays, readers will suspect that Steiner has set himself much the same task for which America merits his dismissive scorn. His allusive (and thereby elusive) style shows evidence of a reversal of the editing process: jumping within sentences from Dostoevsky to Racine to Heidegger to Cezanne, he gives the impression that this is a palimpsest of revisions in which nothing is deleted, and much tenuously related cross-referencing is laboriously accreted.

The high cultural smokescreen that this throws up raises the question of Steiner's choice of audience. For whom but elitists is he writing such sentences as the following: "Send me 'the wretched refuse of your teeming shore,' urges the Statue of Liberty. Could it be that Europe did just that?" (284) "It is the sovereign candour of American philistinism which numbs a European sensibility" (290), he intones, extolling European culture as the highpoint of human history—and paradoxically, as the womb of the Holocaust. In the face of the horrifying distancing of art from life implied by Beethoven festivals that continued within earshot of Dachau, Steiner suggests that language of any sort is no longer adequate—or is, perhaps, too perfect in its representation of a fractured, attenuated civilization.

But *he* keeps writing—and seems to find little escape from the conclusion of an aesthete: those who appreciate beauty and who can maintain a salvific gap between themselves and the illiterate masses must accept, and perhaps revel in, their own isolation. Yet he also embodies the aesthete's need to send coded messages into the darkness, hoping to identify and gather those of like sensitivity into a gnostic coven. In *The Death of Tragedy* (1961) Steiner had written that "literary criticism has about it neither rigour nor proof. Where it is honest, it is passionate, private experience seeking to persuade." Such a view at least explains one of his own aims in this new collection, which is to persuade readers that "the genius of Leningrad-Prague-Budapest-Vienna and

Frankfurt" (285) was the needed but insufficient antidote to what many other immigrants brought to the United States—"the gene of tired common sense" (284), by which he generally means commerce and mediocrity. "In the new Eden (of America)," he says, "God's creatures move in herds" (297), and elsewhere, "there is no community of love, no family, no interest, caste, profession or social class not worth resigning from" (237).

The overall effect suggests a William Bennett or Dinesh D'Souza (or even a Matthew Arnold) after thorough training at a French *lycée* (where Steiner received his education) or a German *Gymnasium,* who ends up with an endowed chair at a major European university and then battens down the hatches against the onslaught of the barbarians. "Schooling today," he writes in **"The Uncommon Reader,"** "notably in the United States, is planned amnesia" (15). Any educator will admit that Steiner has a point here, but the solution implied in the following lament is reactionary: "the entire economy, the architecture of privilege, in which the classic act of reading took place, has become remote" (12). Symptoms of, and vectors for, this migration from "the architecture" that housed such culture present themselves to Steiner in such diverse forms as deconstruction (in which the notion of shared and verifiable systems of intelligence breaks down—and is then celebrated) and the replacement of books by the Internet and cyberspace.

This is his diagnosis of contemporary crises of meaning. And what of his prescription? In an essay that was elsewhere developed into a book, **Real Presences,** Steiner offers a surprisingly postmodern attempt at hermeneutics that smacks of deconstructive *jouissance* by disguising itself as a return to eternal verities. Admitting that he cannot see how a secular theory of meaning can withstand close scrutiny over time, he nonetheless posits the desirability of carrying on "as if" this were not the case (34, 38). But the transcendent that he posits is purely metaphorical and imagined—and, therefore, not really transcendent either in the religious sense or as a Kierkegaardian leap into possible absurdity. He casts it principally as a recovery of the ethical in culture.

Steiner focuses insistently upon the cultural heritage of Judaism as central to what he defines as civilization. The examples he offers cannot be denied, but what are his expectations from statements like the following, and to whom are they addressed?—"It will not, I believe, be possible for European culture to regain its inward energies, its self-respect, so long as Christendom is not made answerable to its own seminal role in the preparation of the Shoah. . . . In one perspective, such questions are of another dimension than those which pertain to literacy. In another, they are inseparable" (xi). What possible answerability does he have in mind? And

would it erase the destabilizing words of Darwin, Freud, Nietzsche, Heisenberg, et al, and return "us" (by whom he pointedly means Western civilization—Asia and Africa do not exist in this volume, and South America only as an extension of Spain) to the wonderful Hellenic-Hebraic world of yore? Or does he, in fact, have no vehicle or outcome, in mind other than a sure-fire lock on his place at the side of the angels? "There *is* a sense," he writes, "—I believe it to be decisive—in which the Cross stands beside the gas ovens" (395). True, in a limited and importantly metaphorical sense (though, "decisive"?); but believing Christians might also find in the gas ovens (and in Christian complicity therewith) the very reason for the Cross.

Gilbert Adair (review date 6 September 1997)

SOURCE: Adair, Gilbert. "A Fiery, Frozen Alp." *Spectator* 279, no. 8823 (6 September 1997): 39.

[*In the following review, Adair assesses the themes, style, and structure of* Errata.]

George Steiner reminds me of Switzerland, rather. What I mean by that faintly incongruous analogy is that, just as the British no longer care much for Switzerland—'too clean,' they say disparagingly, 'too boring' (as if the caked grubbiness of their own native land were one of its principal charms)—so too, even while paying lip service to his eminence, do they tend to be suspicious, not to say downright derisive, of Steiner's stupendous erudition. 'Doesn't wear his learning lightly' is only the most commonly heard put-down.

But why should Steiner wear his learning lightly? It's not, after all, as if the journalists and media folk who are most sniffy about him wear their ignorance lightly. In a world obsessed with Diana and Dodi, Liam and Patsy, the Spice Girls and Tara Whatsherface, Steiner's ivory tower is where, for some of us (admittedly, fewer and fewer), it's still all happening.

Steiner himself is aware of, and by no means indifferent to, his increasing marginalisation as a thinker. In this self-styled 'memoir' of his [*Errata*] (and I'll return to those quotation marks in a moment) he confesses somewhat wistfully to his insensitivity to the facile allure of popular culture. 'The cardinal role of the ephemeral, of the populist . . . in our culture has, too often, passed me by.' His plurality of convictions, his intellectual cosmopolitanism, the lack in his work of what he calls 'the authority of the native, monoglot spirit', have gradually alienated him from the ever-decreasing circles of cultural specialism. His fundamental humanism, as well as his essentially unshakeable faith in the inherited idioms of the human tribe—a page of text by Steiner is instantly distinguishable from one by any other contemporary thinker of note by its relative sparsity of inverted commas—has exiled him from the more extreme forms of literary theory. And 'the virus of the absolute' by which he was contaminated once and for all in his adolescence has no place in the catechism of postmodernity.

In fact, *Errata*—a fairly unfathomable title—constantly teeters on the brink of becoming a polemical defence of elitism, a word which 'has been incessantly thrust at me', but it never quite makes it. Steiner's style—that measured professorial tone which has no qualms about committing to print a sentence like this (on one of his classics teachers at the French *lycée* in Manhattan): 'Nor was our halting pursuit of the Greek aorist and optative the sole spur to Boorsch's hebdomadal raid on New York'—is congenitally ill-equipped for controversy.

Equally, the book never succeeds in becoming a memoir in the proper sense. Even in its opening chapters, where certain significant facets of Steiner's life are indeed examined—his Austrian childhood, his father's sceptical Zionism, his initiation into sex by a prostitute (in Cicero, Illinois, of which he typically writes 'a town justly ill-famed but by virtue of its name reassuring to me'—one has to smile sometimes)—the relevant passages tend to function as no more than three- or four-page prefaces to totally unautobiographical discourses on the great themes that have always exercised him. Here again, as in earlier and better books, is Steiner on the survival, against incalculable odds, of the Jewish race; on the importance of Babelic multilingualism and multiculturalism; on the origins of evil; on the misanthropy, if one may phrase it thus, of God. By the time he gets into his stride, he has utterly forgotten that he is supposed to be writing a memoir (many of the essays read like lectures), and the autobiographical strain all but vanishes.

So what, finally, is *Errata*? Put ungenerously, it's just another George Steiner book, not sufficiently different in style and subject-matter (or subject-matters) from those preceding it in the canon to allow one to welcome it as anything but a minor addition to it. Put more generously, as I myself would wish it to be put, it's a restatement, as passionate as ever, of his refusal to, in his own word, *negotiate,* his wholly admirable refusal to budge from the position, however unmodish it has become, that 'study, theological-philosophic argument, classical music, poetry, art, all that is difficult because it is excellent, are the excuse for life'.

What he is offering us, then, and whether we think we need it or not, is a call to order, a work of warning, of vigilance. And I was unjust when, above, I referred to Steiner's 'ivory tower'. It is, rather, an ivory watchtower.

Edward Skidelsky (review date 19 March 2001)

SOURCE: Skidelsky, Edward. "Beware the False Prophet." *New Statesman* 14, no. 648 (19 March 2001): 52-3.

[*In the following review, Skidelsky investigates the lines of reasoning and aesthetic principles informing* Grammars of Creation, *faulting the book's ahistorical context and theological undertones.*]

Remember the genius? In his black Victorian hat and cape, with his flowing white beard, he was the scourge of philistinism and a terror to his wife and children. What has happened to him? Why do we regard this figure, once so venerated, with a combination of amusement and censure?

We have become more modest, more democratic, in our attitude to creation. Poets are no longer the unacknowledged legislators of mankind; they are merely the curators of a dead tradition. Philosophers no longer strive to penetrate the mysteries of existence, but only to resolve certain esoteric conceptual confusions. Artists content themselves with devising witty and provocative visual effects, a job that is increasingly indistinguishable from advertising. In all these spheres, talent is no longer regarded as an excuse for bad behaviour. Biographies regularly appear lambasting the shoddy private conduct of this or that artist or writer.

But behind all these changes lies a single fact: we no longer believe in the possibility of what was once called genius. We no longer believe that it is possible to create something out of nothing; we have lost what Proust called "the faith that creates". This loss is often dignified with the name "postmodernism". The work of art, according to postmodernist theory, is not a creation *ex nihilo*—out of nothing—but through a mere rearrangement of items already in existence. This theory was first developed in relation to architecture, an art form that has always relied heavily on traditional elements, but was subsequently extended to the other arts. The prototype of the postmodern artist is perhaps the DJ, who mixes records made by others. It is the DJ, and not the creative musician, who has become the representative figure of modern youth culture.

These are among the themes of George Steiner's new book, *Grammars of Creation.* Much of it is familiar stuff. The awestruck reverence before the Great Works of Art; the intimations of some peculiarly deep but never quite defined relationship between genius and evil; the nervous flurry of reference—all these are well-known "Steinerisms". Some people find them insufferable. But I view them as part of an elaborate game that Steiner plays with his reader. Steiner knows how to pull off a good act. His pyrotechnics are redeemed by a sense of irony—easy to miss in his prose, but which becomes apparent in his verbal performances. He once began an Oxford lecture on "the siren song in European literature" by telling the audience that he had recently consulted an entry of the same title in an encyclopaedia of world literature. There was an audible murmur of derision (ha, so he really is a fraud after all). Steiner allowed it to die down before delivering his riposte: "The entry was seriously incomplete!" He then proceeded to recite a long list of works—many of them astonishingly obscure—not mentioned in the encyclopaedia. The audience laughed, and the lecture continued in the same vein.

Steiner is the intellectual equivalent of a Rothschild: he has a well-stuffed mind and is not embarrassed to display it. This renders him vulnerable to the very English kind of anti-Semitism that conveys itself in hints about "vulgarity" and "ostentation". These charges are silly, as well as mean. Steiner's showmanship should be enjoyed for what it is—a knowing and self-conscious act—rather than subjected to snooty disapproval.

Grammars of Creation has no argument as such. It is a series of intellectual arabesques around the theme of creation. The creation in question is that of both the artist and God. The work of art is a genuine "second creation", the artist an imitator on in more Luciferian versions, a usurper of God. It was neo-Platonism that first discerned this analogy between the artist and God; the idea was revived in the Renaissance and assumed its modern form in the aesthetics of the German enlightenment. But there is a crucial difference between classical and modern versions of the analogy. Plato's demiurge imposes form on the raw material of chaos, and Plotinus's artist-creator imitates him in this primal act of form-giving. But the God of Christianity and Judaism does not merely form the universe from some pre-existent stuff: He creates it *ex nihilo*. "In the beginning God created the Heaven and the earth."

The great innovation of Romantic aesthetics was to apply this idea of creation *ex nihilo* to the production of artworks. Understood literally, this application is, of course, false; no artist actually creates his work from nothing. But as a metaphor for the kind of originality after which the Romantic artist strives, it has proved hugely potent. The Romantic artist seeks not merely to rearrange elements given by tradition—think of all those tedious nymphs and satyrs that adorn classical poetry and painting—but to create a new heaven and a new earth. His creation strains after the vitality of the real world; his characters are judged successful only if they "come alive". In his struggle to create *ex nihilo*, the Romantic artist is preordained to defeat. The writer's medium is language—and language, as Steiner writes, "transports with it the cargo of the world". However hard he tries, the writer can never replicate the absolute originality of God; the world is too much with him.

The same is true of the artist and musician. The most successful parts of *Grammars of Creation* examine the struggle of individual poets and novelists—Paul Celan, in particular—against the constraints of language. It is in these passages that Steiner's talent for tactful and imaginative close reading comes alive.

Less appealing is the aesthetic theory that underlies the particular interpretations. Is it really true that poetry seeks to transcend the historicity of language, to achieve "liberation from imposed, borrowed, eroded reference"? Were that indeed the case, one might wonder why more poets did not avail themselves of the easy expedient of writing in Esperanto. Esperanto is a language with no history; its words are mere counters, without resonance or depth. Writing in Esperanto, poets would achieve without difficulty that "immaculateness" that historical languages inhibit.

Yet the very notion of "Esperanto poetry" is repellent; it suggests, as Wittgenstein once remarked, a corpse. Why this should be so is an extremely interesting question. At the very least, it suggests that there is something radically wrong with Steiner's conception of poetry. Far from scorning the historicity of language, the poet should, of all people, delight in it. It is only because words have a history, because they teem with ideas not of the poet's choosing, that poetry is at all possible. As English transforms itself into the *lingua franca* of the global market, as it approaches more and more the condition of Esperanto, poetry in English becomes not easier, but progressively more difficult to write.

Steiner's remarks on poetry belong to the venerable and tarnished tradition of German aesthetics. They express Schopenhauer's conviction that art's purpose is to liberate us from the tedium and brutality of life. This view of art implies a hierarchy. On the bottom rung lies architecture, constrained as it is by the brute facts of engineering and economics. Sculpture and painting, still tied to the physical world but freer from constraint, lie higher up. Literature and poetry—above all lyric poetry—lie higher still. Unlike a painting or a sculpture, a poem does not inhere in a particular physical artefact. A poem need not exist anywhere but in the mind of its creator. Yet even the most exultant lyric cannot entirely escape the world, since its medium, language, refers us inexorably back. Only in music is the bond of reference cracked once and for all.

Music, for Steiner as for Schopenhauer, is the highest of the arts. All art aspires to the condition of music. Yet even music cannot evade the constraints of empirical reality; chamber music, as Steiner once wittily remarked, implies the existence of chambers. Higher than all the arts lies mathematics, the paragon of free creation. "Together with music, pure mathematics, in its disinterested irrelevance, is probably the crowning enigma of our so often dubious presence in the world."

The first thing that strikes one about this schema is its complete lack of historical reference. This is no oversight. Art, for Steiner, is fundamentally an escape from history. He is not therefore very interested in the different historical conditions under which art has been produced, or in the varying historical conceptions of the artist and his task. Steiner's view of European literature is panoptic; he sees it laid out, as it were, on a map before his feet. His references criss-cross wildly from one end to the other. Coleridge was a disciple of the medieval Sufi Ibn 'Arabi; Kafka was a kabbalist. This indifference to accidents of time and place is expressive of Steiner's basic belief that all great minds exist in timeless communion with one another. Creative genius is an undifferentiated substance. Its manifestations may vary, but its essence is always and everywhere the same. This attitude leaves Steiner ill-equipped to resolve what Ernst Gombrich has called the "riddle of style". Why is it that different ages have evolved such hugely different ways of representing the world? Why is it that, as the art historian Heinrich Wölfflin put it, "not everything is possible in every period"?

Disturbing, too, is the distinct note of religious exultation in *Grammars of Creation.* Steiner's hierarchy of the arts and sciences resembles one of those mystic ladders of medieval art, up which the neophyte must climb on his way to salvation. The higher up the ladder one ascends, the greater one's liberation from the bondage of the senses. Steiner's aesthetics is theological through and through. "The armature of poiesis," he writes, "has been theological."

Yet theology, in Steiner, is not merely the armature of poiesis; it is poiesis. Theology has been thoroughly aestheticised and art, in turn, has become a kind of ersatz theology. Art is a sop to our spiritual hankerings; it supplies us, at little cost, with all the thrills and perils of transcendence. It was precisely this kind of false religiosity that Nietzsche famously discerned in Wagner, and which led him to reject his former mentor in favour of the modest and unpretentious Bizet. Steiner might take heed from his example.

Hugh Lawson-Tancred (review date 31 March 2001)

SOURCE: Lawson-Tancred, Hugh. "Conceptions of Conception." *Spectator* 286, no. 9008 (31 March 2001): 39-40.

[*In the following review, Lawson-Tancred contrasts the philological approach to the question of creativity in Steiner's* Grammars of Creation *with the psychological methods expressed by* The Origins of Creativity, *edited by Karl H. Pfenninger and Valerie R. Shubik.*]

A spectre is haunting the study of the mind: the spectre of neuroscience. Are we, after the explosive development in the last 20 years of MRI, PET and other non-

invasive technologies for eavesdropping on the cortex, at last in a position to realise the hopes of scientific radicals and the fears of cultural conservatives that we can pinpoint in some convolution of the ideogenetic tissue the precise point of origin of, say, the 'atonal' section of the development in the finale of the G minor symphony or the appearance of the messenger from Corinth at the climax of the *Oedipus Rex*? Is even the definitive human achievement of aesthetic generation about to cross the snow line and become the pabulum of formula-laden articles in technical journals rather than the claret-driven musings of High Table? Two new books offer between them one vantage point for framing an answer. George Steiner, doyen of critical, literary and humanistic culturalism, has put a dust jacket on his Gifford lectures of 1990 [*Grammars of Creation*], and OUP have brought out the latest popular compendium [*The Origins of Creativity*] of interdisciplinary potshots at the elusive target of the mind-brain interface.

There are, of course, certain difficulties that have to be overcome in reading Steiner. He is uncompromising in his use of not only the content (fleeting references to out-of-the-way writers and an alarming acquiescence in the normality of Hegel and even Heidegger) but also the mannerisms of continental cultural discourse (interjection of rhetorical questions in brackets, use of the indefinite article before great names, as in 'in a Keats . . . or a Schubert'). These habits are buttressed by not infrequent recourse to a tone of portentous oracularity which it is notoriously easy to find transparently specious. Indeed such is his predilection for polysyllabic obscurantism that he might almost appropriate the expostulation of the apocryphal jurisprudentialist who protested against allegations of gratuitous philological exhibitionism. In the case of *Grammars of Creation,* these difficulties are compounded by the fact that his argument is structured more in the manner of a novel or a play than of an expository treatise, with a wide range of subsidiary themes making their exits and their entrances more at the whim of dramatic propriety than from the exigencies of exposition.

Nevertheless, it would be a mistake to dispatch this work peremptorily to the exile of Pseud's Corner (even if he does think negative entropy is the same as chaos). Steiner is engaged in an exercise of grammatology, the attempt to use the interconnected nuances of a range of highly charged abstractions, their 'semantic fields', to throw light on deep, or at any rate salient, assumptions about fundamental cultural values.

> 'Creation' is cardinal in theology, in philosophy, in our grasp of art, music and literature. My inquiry is founded on the assumption that the semantic field of this word is most active and questionable where religious-mythological narratives of the origins of the world, in Genesis, for example, or in Plato's *Timaeus,* press upon our attempts to understand the coming into articulate

being of philosophic visions and poetics. How do stories of the inception of the Kosmos relate to those which recount the birth of the poem, of the work of art or melody? In what regards are theological, metaphysical and aesthetic conceptions of conception kindred or divergent?

The inquiry is conducted in a loosely evolutionary way, mingling history with thematic analysis. Beginning with Athens and Jerusalem (on whose similarities and differences Steiner is always stimulating), he uses the *Timaeus,* 'the bible of Neo-platonism', to effect the transition to the Scholastics, where the baton is taken over, strikingly, by the doctrines of the Incarnation and the Eucharist, which Steiner perceives as subliminally present in later Renaissance and Romantic conceptions of creativity. This cues a fascinating discussion of Dante as the apex of the synthesis of the theological, aesthetic and philosophical conceptions of creation. He contrasts, for instance, the central role of Virgil in the *Inferno* and *Purgatorio* with the reluctance of 'a Shakespeare' to engage in the creation of creators.

As we move away from the Dantean synthesis, the salient interaction of semantic fields shifts from that of the theological and the aesthetic senses of 'creation' to the rivalry of the sibling notions of creation and invention, which are fruitfully commingled and confused. As Steiner rightly says, 'definitions blur'. In this climate of definitional obscurity, who else can make his appearance but the dreaded figure of Hegel? But, just as we expect a plunge into the full rigours of the *Phenomenologie,* the centre stage is cheekily stolen by Hölderlin's even more impenetrable essay on the *Verfahrungsweise* of the mind of the poet. Here are all the great themes—the antinomy of Being and Not-Being (the Nothing notheth not), the negation of negation, the sublation of the non-existent by the incipient—but above the heavy orchestration rises the shrill motif of the duel between the mind of the Romantic poet and the *Unendlich,* the infinity, amongst others, of the aesthetic possibilities from which the creator is forced to choose, a conceit prefiguring the insistence, in the later discussion, on the eidetic destructiveness of creativity, bolstered by reflections, with the occasional ukase, on the answerability of the artist for the thing made and the harnessing of temporality itself to the imperium of the creative actuality.

We are now at the start of the home straight, as Steiner carries us at full tilt from the luxuriant verbiage of the Biedermeier philosophers into the *Sprachkritik* of Hofmannsthal and Kraus, pausing only for a vignette on the last night in the life of Evariste Galois (whose death at 21 held up the development of 19th-century mathematics by perhaps five decades) and a discursus on the ontogeny of the lyric poems of a Yeats or a Larkin. The discussion of the criticism of language in early 20th-century Vienna (with Wittgenstein being assigned a fashionably non-central role) gives dialectic precision to Steiner's central, Frankfurtian theme of the murder of meaning in the death camps of the Shoah (as he rightly prefers to call the Holocaust), a subject which, here, is looked at mostly retrospectively through the heart-rending example of Paul Celan and his post-war struggles, as a Jewish poet, to come to terms with the use of the German language. The sustained intensity, the intellectual energy, of this discussion is extraordinary, so much so that one can forgive its obviously excessive Germanocentrism (what, we ask, about Croce, Saussure, Collingwood et al.?).

But, before the end, Steiner has another surprise to pull. Our own age is denied access to the key semantic resonances of the seminal concepts of our hereditary culture by the barbarism of our recent past and the godlessness of our debased present, but, lo, at dusk the owl of Minerva does indeed take flight. We may be in the late afternoon of a culture, no longer at ease with the self-definition of our species by the dignity of speech, but a mutation is subterraneanly taking place. In Paris, London, Berlin, Washington and a myriad other centres the work of archiving and garnering the past is proceeding apace and a kind of ultra-Alexandrian preoccupation with the shoring up of every scrap is leading inevitably, through the medium of the Internet, to a quantum change in the core triadic relationship of author, work and readership. Technology precedes metaphysics.

Steiner's travel sketches of the Web are as brilliantly suggestive and tantalising as everything else in this dazzling tour de force but, ultimately, as unsatisfying. The eventual conclusion, reprised slightly out of key in the brief and inchoate coda, is aporetic. Can atheists create? Can there be origination if, in an authentic sense, there is no death? This all smacks alarmingly of the apotheosis of the sixth-form prize essay, suspicion of which has taken some repressing at earlier junctures in the argument. And, to my taste at least, there is a certain vacuity to the, admittedly provisional, definition of creativity that we finally reach as the exercise of a certain form of freedom which intrinsically entails the renunciation of other, perhaps equally valid, creative options. This negative result tells us what creativity is not, but not much about what it is, nor are we brought much further by the sprinkled references to such marginal figures as Duchamp, Schwitters and Tinguely. It is hard not to smile at the murine output of so mountainous a parturition.

So we turn to *The Origins of Creativity,* a collection of a dozen or so pieces from a fairly wide spectrum of pundits. The contributors come from both the arts and the sciences and discuss both the experience of creation and its theoretical explanation, but the relation between these two dichotomies is very much orthogonal. Thomas Cech, for instance, tells us what it was like to make the discovery that RNA can itself catalyse metabolic processes, a finding for which he won the Nobel Prize, while the glass artist Dale Chihuly, the painter Françoise Gilot and the composer Bruce Adolphe all let us into the secret of how they get their best ideas. This shared creativity of arts and sciences is given a formal framework by the development by Gunther Stent of his familiar thesis that the supposed contrast between the indispensability of the artist to the work of art and the irrelevance of the scientist to the scientific discovery is factitious. Considerable attention is paid to the developmental context of the creative mind, with Janina Galler deploring the consequences of lack of stimulus as being perhaps even more deleterious than simple malnutrition; George Palade writing lucidly on the golden flower of 20th-century art; and, most substantially, the always readable Howard Gardner surveying a range for successful creators from Stravinsky to Gandhi. The hard science is provided by Antonio Damasio on sensory processing and imagination, Karl Pfenninger on brain evolution and Charles Stevens on the separation of image components in visual processing.

The show, however, is stolen and the tone is set by Mandelbrot, who contributes a lively review of his more recent ideas and whose spirit dominates the concluding synthesis provided by the editors. This is unusually schoolmasterly in its castigations of the perceived waywardness of this or that contributor—a bit like criticising the dress of one's dinner guests—but it makes it very plain that the upshot of the whole is that fractal order is the key to creativity.

> So what is creativity? Creativity must be the ability to generate in one's brain (the association cortex) novel contexts and representations that elicit associations with symbols and principles of order. Such symbols or principles of order are innate to the human brain or part of the repertoire of acquired dispositional representations in the brains that form one's culture or society. Creativity further must include the ability to translate the selected representations into a work of art or science. Much of these abilities depends upon the highly developed human association cortex.

This definition would appear to have the required scientific sobriety but it surely leaves more questions open than closed. No doubt, as these scholars are hardly the first to have noticed, perception of certain archetypal patterns does at some level underlie the phenomenon of aesthetic satisfaction. But such forms are hardly a necessary condition for that state and their mere postulation or even enumeration is hardly a sufficient explanation of it. The relevance of the new sciences to the study of creativity is amply documented by this collection, but the genie has not exactly been put back in its bottle.

My conclusion is that the mystery has survived at least these onslaughts. Neither philological musing nor the

psychology lab have yet put a marker on why it is that we do what we most value doing. Pass the claret.

Frank G. Novak Jr. (review date winter 2002)

SOURCE: Novak Jr., Frank G. Review of *Grammars of Creation,* by George Steiner. *Studies in the Novel* 34, no. 4 (winter 2002): 482-86.

[*In the following review, Novak summarizes the principal themes of* Grammars of Creation *but observes that the book raises more questions than it answers.*]

In *Grammars of Creation,* George Steiner delivers an eloquent eulogy on the death of art and meaning as they have been known in the West. Part meditation, part lament, the book suggests a multiplicity of connections and cites numerous examples of art, literature, and thought from pre-history to the present. A glance at the index reveals the formidable range and depth of Steiner's erudition: from Abelard to Zola, Borges to Wittgenstein, Parmenides to Proust. The array of topics and issues Steiner considers is equally impressive: an inquiry into the meaning of "creation" as contrasted with "invention"; reflections on time, death, and the divine; definitions of the "classic"; consideration of the "grammars" of music, painting, architecture, and literature; contrasts between the communal nature of scientific achievement and the autonomous work of the artist and philosopher; speculations concerning the impact of computer technology on knowledge and the book; theories about the mutation of man as a "language-animal"; forebodings on the prospects for art and thought in an atheistic age. The book contains extended discussions of Plato's *Timaeus,* the meaning of the book of Job, Dante's "triplicity," the differences between Dante and Shakespeare, and the varieties of artistic solitude.

Steiner states that one purpose of his book is to provide "an *in memoriam* for lost futures and a stab at understanding their transmutation into something 'rich and strange'" (15). Another primary purpose is to consider the nature of creation: the differences and connections between "creation" and "invention" and the effect of "the eclipse of the messianic" on the concept of creation (16). Insofar as these particular purposes are achieved, however, the book disappoints; more questions are posed than answered, and future prospects for art and thought are uncertain. The work never succeeds in unraveling the differences between invention and creation; after three hundred pages of dense analysis and speculation, their differences remain blurred, ambiguous. How will communal invention replace autonomous creation as the primary mode of producing meaning? What will emerge as the "executive forms" of art in a world radically remade by cybernetic technology? If religious faith, a sense of the "messianic," and longings for immortality are in "eclipse," what can provide a basis for humane values and purposeful living? Rather than providing encouragement, Steiner's "valediction" to Western culture identifies much that is troubling. He does not offer a prescription for renewal, and he is dubious about the future of intellectual life and the arts in an "atheist" age beset by unprecedented technological and human transformations.

In vintage Steiner form, the book possesses brilliance and value in its epigrammatic statements, what the author himself would term its "lapidary" pronouncements, especially those that define and extol the nature of the "classic" work of art. There are pages in which Steiner's famous critical acumen magnificently erupts, such as the comparison of Dante and Shakespeare and the discussion of "typologies of solitude." However, the strands of Steiner's extended argument are difficult to follow. Sections of the book exist as coherent, self-contained essays, yet the overall logic and organization remain murky (perhaps because the book is a "recasting" of Steiner's 1990 Gifford lectures); this difficulty is compounded by the absence of chapter and section titles. For example, there are multiple, synonymous formulations of what constitutes a "classic" interspersed throughout the book; and Steiner continually adverts to the "grammars" of mathematics and music without providing definitions or amplifications as he does with the language "grammar" of literature. The book lacks the intense focus and the magisterial conclusiveness of such landmark Steiner essays as **"The Cleric of Treason"** and **"The Archives of Eden."** Instead, Steiner here presents an allusive, wide-ranging discussion containing myriad connections and subtle resonances that culminates in paradox, ambiguity, and uncertainty.

A summation of Steiner's sinuous, elusive argument may be helpful to the prospective reader. Contemporary art and thought, in Steiner's view, are in crisis—lacking the values and purposes that once impelled them. He laments the loss of "beginnings" in the West, instead, a sense of "a core-tiredness" and "terminality" pervades the modern outlook (3). As a result of "violence, oppression, economic enslavement and social irrationality," Western culture has experienced a "collapse of humaneness" (6, 4). Learning and culture have been ineffectual in combating the barbarity and horrific cataclysms of the twentieth century. Humankind thus confronts "the distinct possibility of a reversal of evolution, of a systematic turn-about towards bestialization." Steiner sets out to evaluate the "impact of this darkened condition on grammar," which he defines as "the articulate organization of perception, reflection, and experience, the nerve structure of consciousness when it communicates with itself and with others" whether in literature, music, or painting (6). One "impact" is the ir-

relevance of the future tense which Steiner relates to the dubious "status of hope" in the modern world (7). Another involves what Steiner terms "the eclipse of the messianic," with "messianic" involving "man's access to perfectibility, to a higher and, presumably, enduring condition of reason and of justice" (10). Much of the ensuing discussion considers the role of authorship and the status of the "classic" at this decisive moment in cultural history, "the time of the long eclipse of humane hopes and the dislocation of the future tense" (27).

Steiner also launches an inquiry into the nature of "creation" as the essential element of "humaneness," culture, and community. After considering issues of meaning and creation in Job and *Timaeus,* Steiner turns to Dante to show how his work is vital to "our understanding and reception of the truth of art" (67), how it embodies the "*iconic*"—art as "a real presence . . . a true fiction" (77). Steiner asserts that Dante provides "privileged access to almost the entirety of our theme" (84). Precisely what this "theme" comprises is unclear, but Dante appears to be important as a presence that is both individual (the artist as godlike creator) and communal (reflecting the multitudinous "reciprocities of influence") and who thereby dissolves "the discriminations between the invented and the created" (99, 112). Steiner extols the "triplicity" of Dante: "he organizes, makes irreducibly vital, the reciprocities of religious, metaphysical, and aesthetic codes in respect of being and of generation" (78). In short, it seems, Dante is a key figure because he represents the vitality of what has been "lost."

Along with the collapse of hope and "humaneness" in the twentieth century, the pervasive influence of scientific development has also undermined the concept of "creation." Steiner views scientific/technological achievement as a "collaborative, pluralistic" process, as a "composite . . . combinatorial enterprise" (216-17). Identifying another characteristic feature, Steiner states that the sciences "are in incessant progress . . . an advance across measurable time" as one discovery builds upon another (250); a particular individual discovery may be important but is not crucial. In contrast to the scientist who must collaborate with associates and build upon previous discoveries, "individual authorship" in art and thought involves the "solitude and singularity of the artist" (219-20). Steiner catalogues various "typologies of solitude," the conditions of creation, represented by such writers as Montaigne, Dickinson, Kafka, Nietzsche, and Proust. Their individual, enduring achievements in literature and philosophy fundamentally differ from scientific discoveries that possess a "sequential inevitability" and an "anonymity" (230-31) and that will eventually be superseded. He writes: "Creativity in the arts and in philosophic proposal is, in respect of the survival of consciousness, of another order than is invention in the sciences" (259).

In this context, Steiner considers the "paradox" of the classic work. He questions: "is it possible to think new?" (147). Have there been "fundamentally new, unprecedented enactments, motions of intelligible meaning . . . added to the repertoire?" These appear to be rhetorical questions, answered in the negative: "What have we added to, what have we 'created new' in respect to Hector's sorrow over Andromache, to the rage of Moses or David's stricken love for Jonathan?" (155). "What . . . is an advance on Homer or Sophocles, on Plato or Dante? What stage-play has progressed beyond *Hamlet,* what novel surpasses *Madame Bovary* or *Moby Dick*?" (252). Steiner argues that "[t]he shock of great literature is that of the *déjà-vu*"; its "themes, motifs, narrative, and dramatic situations" are characterized by "recursiveness," the "eternal return" (156-57). Thus, literature may be "the most inventive but least creative of artifacts" (159). Paradoxically, however, literature is continually made "new": in contrast to the progressive nature of science wherein technological advances and new discoveries render the old obsolete and irrelevant, the products of individual authorship are incessantly renewed by readers in the form of "renovating response" and "new appropriations" (249). Steiner proclaims: "All texts, all works of art and of music empowered by survival and transmission, open to renascence and renewal by virtue of reception, possess values neither superseded nor cancelled out by later works. Neither historical chronology nor technical sophistication renders a classic obsolete (this being the definition of a 'classic')" (256-57). "The Homeric epic, the Platonic dialogue, the Vermeer townscape, the Mozart sonata do not age and grow obsolescent as do the products of invention" (262). The classic, the enduring work of art or thought, therefore, derives from both invention and creation; it is both old and new; it is a monument continually renovated and renewed, endlessly relevant.

Because of "this conceptual eternity and reversibility," the classics "have underwritten Western education and taste. They define our network of reference and recognition" (258). Identifying what he terms "a central postulate," Steiner asserts that there are two experiences that liberate humankind from death: "One way is that of authentic religious beliefs. . . . The other is that of the aesthetic. It is the production and reception of works of art, in the widest sense, which enables us to share in the experiencing of duration, of time unbounded. Without the arts, the human psyche would stand naked in the face of personal extinction" (259). There can be no community without music, art, myth, and poetry. As his discussion of Dante argues, art in its classic form—insofar as it embodies the "iconic"—expresses the transcendent and the immortal.

Steiner queries: "Has poiesis its classic future?" (259). Will the classic be silent, forgotten in the emerging new world, one devoid of hope and a need for the future tense? Will the traditional "grammars of creation" in art and thought continue to be viable? Steiner identifies several ominous signs, bleak prospects in a cultural landscape where "[g]rammars of nihilism flicker . . . on the horizon" (11). He states that "the current changes in the experience of communication, of information, of knowledge, of the generation of meaning and of form, are probably the most comprehensive and consequential since *homo sapiens'* development of language itself" (263). These changes, he suspects, are causing the "mutation" of humankind as a "language-animal" (265). He discerns a "slippage of elemental trust in the word" (267), a condition in which "[t]he long standing, pre-1914 claims to spiritual sense and communicability have been lost" (273). The undermining of the "logo-centric system," Steiner writes, "constitutes a seismic dislocation . . . more severe and consequential than any other in modernity" (278). Consequently, "the concepts of creation and of invention . . . are being fundamentally affected" (283). The status of the classic and the role of authorship have suffered devaluation, ridicule, and attack. Steiner detects in the modern outlook a "bias towards the communal, the participatory, and the collective," and "an accelerating erosion of both solitude and attendant privacy," the conditions necessary for creation (316-17). The concept of creation itself is seen as "ambiguous, mythological, and even taboo" (336). Invention has supplanted creation. A pervasive Dadaism has infected modern art and thought. These forces also threaten the status of the book itself as "the medium of significant life and revelation" (309). Steiner fears that the *magnum opus,* the great novelistic achievement of a Melville or a Proust, has become "archaic, nostalgic": "Incompletion and the fragment, not the monumental, are the pass-words to modernism" (320).

Despite such profound transformations, Steiner insists that "human exultation and sorrow, anguish and jubilation, love and hatred, will continue to demand shaped expression," and "[t]he human intellect will persist in posing questions which science has ruled illicit or unanswerable." He again queries: "Can there, will there be major philosophy, literature, music, and art of an atheist provenance?" (337). Can there be an "atheist counterpart to a Michelangelo fresco or *King Lear*?" (338). These are certainly provocative and disturbing questions, but Steiner adduces little evidence to show that the vitality of the classics is waning or that the "creation" of "monuments of unageing intellect" has ceased. Are the works of Homer, Shakespeare, Flaubert, and Mann read less these days? Are they any less "alive"? Have they somehow lost those qualities that distinguish them as classics? Steiner theorizes that humans are becoming less and less "language-animals," but he apparently assumes that technological advance has not altered basic mind, feeling, and need. What are the implications of both these changes and these constants for canonical classics and contemporary, if not future, expressions of art and thought? Steiner provides no direct, precise answers to such troubling, intractable questions.

However, I believe that he does address them in a broader, general sense; indeed, the book both adumbrates an answer and represents an assertion of hope. For this work exhibits the power of eloquence, learning, and devotion. Steiner discloses what is timeless, relevant, and vital in the monumental classics. Despite the murderous horrors of the past century (not to mention those that have attended the present), Steiner demonstrates, as he writes in **"The Archives of Eden,"** that the creators of classics "compensate for man. It is they who, on fragile occasion, redeem the cruel, imbecile mess which we dignify with the name of history." Steiner himself embodies that rare, great critic whom he describes as "a loving, clairvoyant parasite feeding on the life of art." For through Steiner's words, in his thoughtful and sensitive formulations, by means of his own "grammar" of criticism and interpretation, Plato and Dante speak anew, Shakespeare and Proust repopulate the imagination. His own "music of thought" (17) summons artists and philosophers as well as scholars and critics to redeem the present and to create the future.

Geoffrey Heptonstall (review date January 2002)

SOURCE: Heptonstall, Geoffrey. "George Steiner's Passionate Reason." *Contemporary Review* 280, no. 1632 (January 2002): 54-5.

[*In the following review, Heptonstall commends* Grammars of Creation *for its erudite synthesis of Western aesthetics, metaphysics, and theology.*]

Creation speaks to the future, to the unborn. The primary Creation, according to Genesis, was voiced into being. When God spoke something—everything—created came into being so that the voice could be heard. The essential meaning of inspiration is an intake of breath. Implicitly it is divine breath. 'He breathed in air / He breathed out light', wrote Adrian Mitchell evoking Charlie Parker's music. This snatch of poetry resonates with understanding of the process of artistry. A world entire is described.

It has been Dr. Steiner's life-work to map this world. In this book [*Grammars of Creation*] he offers a lexicon of affirmation. It is a timely reminder of the need in this peopled world for humane creation. The range of reading called in witness is extraordinary. To master such material, allowing for trivial error, is a rare contribu-

tion. This is more than a book. There is a liberal education in the synthesis of voices. Shuffling the cards of aesthetics, metaphysics and theology, Dr. Steiner elucidates a way through the labyrinth of all that we have known as Western culture. Yet the sense of an ending has become an insistent warning. It will not fade with the victories over transient absolutisms. An inconfidence, a self-loathing even, seems to have entered the stream of our consciousness. Here as elsewhere the author, himself a noted creator of original literature, is concerned that the affirmation is being refused where it might expect to be heard.

For obvious and justified reasons, the *Shoah* is fundamental to the Steinerian thesis. The crushing of the Jewish renaissance went to the core of European culture. History will not go away even when barbarism is defeated. The victory in certain lights does seem indeed to be a hollow miracle. Much that previously was held culturally essential has suffered a prolonged retreat. A libertarian materialism consciously rejects the community of wisdom which has been the guarantor of values down the ages. Aquinas, a key figure in Dr. Steiner's pantheon, is ridiculed for asking irrelevant questions about angels. The truth is that Aquinas helped shape our relations to the physical and moral worlds we cannot escape.

This was known to James Joyce, whose creative urges were not the least material. For creation should not be confused with technique or invention. In this regard we in our time are strangely unenlightened. If that were the end of the argument the problem would be terminal. The possibility of cultural extinction is real. It is the uncompromising vitality of creation which remains the hope. 'The grammars of creation are, in the final analysis, those of the erotic'. It is there in the personal exchange between artist and audience, between artist and subject, between subject and audience. We are moved, disturbed even, by images which speak to private, perhaps unconscious, experience. The created is radically related to the uncreated. The artist imagines what might have been, or what might never have been. What we read or see or hear contains the pause, the space, the silence which is integral to the created artifact.

In minimal art, it would seem, are the latent possibilities, the alternatives, which are the essence of creation. Beckett, John Cage, Emily Dickinson, Mondrian: these are the vital witnesses, as authentic artists, to a growing sense of crisis. The exuberance of modernism failed to resolve this. Picasso himself warned of the charlatans who would follow. This may be less problematic than Dr. Steiner will allow. There have been poetasters and quack-theorists from the moment imagination emerged in human consciousness. Their public success is transient, whereas the music of John Cage reaches obliquely towards unknown harmonies. He was right to question their possible existence. Certainty at this time is simply noise. We do face a cacophony of gestures which for the time being have an ascendancy. This is inevitable in a publicity-conscious culture. To see these forms as enclosing all the currency of creativity is, surely, a cardinal error. There remains a multitude of authentic voices which continue to hold the public imagination. The mountebank shows are entertaining, but their character is as reactionary as the amateurs who think there is no architecture beyond Palladio. Is anyone, except a fool, fooled by any of this?

Reading George Steiner is an engagement with intuitions given public voice. What the reader had vaguely supposed emerges from the shadows by the light of passionate reason. The distinction of this book is its capacity to cohere and sustain a complex pattern of argument. It speaks for the revaluation of matters we dare not ignore.

Carver T. Yu (review date July 2002)

SOURCE: Yu, Carver T. Review of *Grammars of Creation*, by George Steiner. *Theology Today* 59, no. 2 (July 2002): 332, 334.

[*In the following review, Yu highlights the central theme of* Grammars of Creation, *noting the work's complex prose style.*]

To many of his critics, George Steiner is fighting a losing battle against the overwhelming tide of nihilism, which comes not so much from epistemological despair as from the close encounter with *Nihil*. The Holocaust alone was enough to explode any attempt to make sense of anything. Everywhere there are signs that, beneath the surface of meaning and values, there is the grammar of negation and nothingness. Hopeless as it may seem, Steiner fights on. He testifies to something fundamental to humanity: an irrepressible demand for meaning, even in the face of what appears to be utterly meaningless and unbearably absurd. ***Grammars of Creation,*** originating from the Gifford Lectures for 1990, is a defense for meaning and the transcendent before its cultured despisers. Tirelessly, Steiner shows us pointers to the transcendent, without which human creativity is impossible.

Why is there something and not nothing? "Human beings are persuaded that the totality of sensory-empirical data is not the whole story." Such conviction is the begetter of culture and history. *Homo sapiens* is also *homo quarens,* who asks and keeps asking. "Thus in philosophy, no less than in theology or poetics, the beginning of the story is also the story of the beginning." Without the story of the beginning, there will be no beginning of a story, and there will be no history. However, according to Steiner, "We have no more beginnings." The eclipse of beginning results in the eclipse of future tenses in the twentieth century: "Shall, will and if are pass-words to hope." The loss of hope is a severe cultural consequence. This book is "an *in memoriam* for lost futures" and the loss of hope in our present age.

The challenge of deconstruction, Steiner admits, does seem irrefutable on its own terms and planes of arguments. But a positivist model of understanding and experience of meaningful form (the aesthetic) is implicitly nihilistic. If human creativity is to survive, such a nihilistic alternative has to be rejected. Any attempt to answer this challenge "requires a readiness to envisage foundations beyond the empirical." Steiner is the Dante of our modern age, who "rounds in glory the investigation of creativity and creation, of divine authorship and human *poesis,* of the concentric spheres of the aesthetic, the philosophical, and the theological." He piles illustrations upon illustrations to show that any coherent understanding of language is underwritten by the assumption of God's presence; the experience of aesthetic meaning—whether of literature, the arts, or musical form—implies the possibility of this "real presence."

On the other hand, when creation is displaced by invention, which denies creativity and allows the technical to take over, "a seismic dislocation" radiates into all aspects of human existence. Technical critique of language puts language on trial, resulting in the "death of language and silence at the end." On another level, the mass media and information technology trivialize language. Steiner reminds us, "A total negation of the semantic, a logos-nihilism . . . occurs towards the final moments of *Timon of Athens.*" The dialectics of the inhuman in Nazism and Stalinism take over precisely when truth is rendered speechless. With a vivid story, Steiner indicates the possible connection between anti-language and death camps: "Dying of thirst, an inmate watched his torturer slowly spill on the floor a glass of fresh water. 'Why are you doing this?' The butcher replied: '*There is no "why" here.*' Signifying . . . the divorce between humanity and language, between reason and syntax, between dialogue and hope." Death camps are symptomatic of a culture that obliterates the asking of "why." The warning is clear: "*The God-hypothesis will not be mocked without cost.*"

Steiner's approach is rather simple, though his presentations convoluted. We are presented with a wager between the empiricist negation of the transcendent, leading to nihilism, and the metaphysical quest for meaning, which affirms creativity. Steiner does not argue; he shows. Those looking for linear arguments will be disappointed.

The book is both difficult and easy. Difficult, because it is massive and compressed, its style intimidating and forbidding. Steiner could have made it more accessible to those less cultured than his peers. Worse still, his presentations appear at times repetitive and almost disorganized. It is easy, however, for there is no involuted logical argument to tease out. There are just cycles of insights around a central theme. In any case, this is a powerful book, full of penetrating comments and compelling illustrations. One feels the passion, the persuasive force, and the richness. It is a rewarding book for those undeterred by heavy readings.

Robert Boyers (essay date summer-fall 2002)

SOURCE: Boyers, Robert. "A Refusal to Mourn the Fate of the Muses." *Salmagundi,* nos. 135-36 (summer-fall 2002): 157-66.

[*In the following essay, Boyers refutes significant points of Steiner's cultural criticism regarding the crisis and decay of contemporary European culture.*]

Early and late in his recent Nexus lecture [**"The Muses' Farewell,"** given May 24, 2000, at the Catholic University in Tilburg, The Netherlands] George Steiner proposes that "every secular generation" inevitably registers, feels in its very bones, a sense of decline and decay. Contemporary artists and critics who debate the crisis in their culture inevitably replay the laments or anxieties of Milton and Nietzsche, Sartre and Matthew Arnold, Leopardi and Valery. Fear for the future of European high culture at the beginning of a twenty-first century may be no more justified, no more "objectively valid," than comparable fears expressed over and over again in the past, but the fear is felt and acknowledged as if it were not a tired sentiment with a long and dubious pedigree.

Of course no one can be certain about what is and is not "objectively valid" in the domain of the arts and humanities. It does no good to suppose that simple or complex inferences drawn from this or that instance will enable us to predict with perfect precision what is to come. No more than Milton could be trusted to be right about Shakespeare's inferiority to Sophocles can any other writer be trusted to know that the novel is finished, exhausted, fresh ideas utterly inconceivable under any likely sun, poetry bound to be thin and uninspired. No doubt it is tempting for writers endowed with every power of retrospection to survey the century just ended and to note everywhere signs of decay and awfulness, portents, presumably, of more to come. But such signs are often misleading. Inhumanity does not proceed according to some grim, inexorable plan or calculus. The creative imagination does not run down

or flourish in perfect accord with social conditions or philosophical programs. The death of god, however widely and deeply felt, may not quite amount to the same thing as the death or silence of the muses.

No doubt temperament determines, to a considerable degree, one's inclination to read the available portents in one way or another. A temperament formed by the tragic or high apocalyptic traditions of European culture will feel more sharply than an optimistic American sensibility the dark authority of portents, the foreshadowings of imminent collapse. This is not to reduce to triviality the differences between actual cultures. Surely no one will doubt that at particular times or places the predominant tastes and literacies are more auspicious to the creation of masterpieces than is the case elsewhere. But the disposition to be awed by the prevailing signs, to read into them large meanings and predictive powers, is an important feature of a certain style of cultural criticism. To say that George Steiner shares, with Nietzsche and Adorno, Thomas Bernhard and Paul Celan, that disposition and style, is not to suggest that the crisis in European culture is at best an invented idea or the stock formula of a standard disposition. But it is to propose that the evidence supporting such a reading of the available facts is largely unreliable.

Take, for example, the proposition that the vitality of European high culture is a function, or a reflection, of the masterpieces produced under its auspices. A century and a half ago, Arnold spoke bleakly of anarchy and decline at a time when European culture was entering a period of extraordinary vitality, when the novels of Stendhal and Flaubert, Dickens and George Eliot, were already in the air he breathed. In 1900 George Santayana condemned what he called "the poetry of barbarism," citing as his two primary exemplars the two greatest poets of mid- and late-nineteenth century Anglo-America, Robert Browning and Walt Whitman, failing utterly to recognize what George Steiner calls the "transcendent pre-suppositions" informing the works of these poets. Spengler wrote of the decline of the west when Mann and Proust, Joyce and Kafka were creating permanent works of unsurpassable vitality nourished by, built around the very idea of decline and fall their supreme fictions anatomized. Pound and Eliot had good reason to lament a "botched" civilization "gone in the teeth" as they contemplated a Europe devastated by war, but they participated in a modernist revolution that was as vital in its energies as any era before or since. And though George Steiner himself once noted the irrevocable disasters brought upon the German language by Nazi propagandists, he later acknowledged that, in the novels of Günter Grass especially, the language had demonstrated a capacity for renewal that the available cultural information would never have predicted.

As we enter a new century, George Steiner notes that we are "unsurprised" by "ideological venom and falsehood," by the "jargon" and "portentous bluff" that are endemic in the Euro-American academy. The past, apparently, will not save us. "The idiom of 'truth, beauty and goodness,'" Steiner argues, is no longer viable, "a dusty cliche." And surely there is reason, we say, to ask with Steiner "what is there left for Europe to create," reason to suppose that this time European culture faces an authentically "unprecedented condition" to which it will not have an adequate response.

And yet it is surely possible, as before, that the very terms and premises invoked to speak of such matters are in their own way misleading. Does "unsurprised" invariably signify "unmoved" or "resolved not to notice"? Who, precisely, is unsurprised by current varieties of brutality and mayhem? Not, surely, the many writers and intellectuals who have, in the last decade, repeatedly argued on behalf of humanitarian intervention in the military campaigns waged by ideologically venomous regimes in Bosnia, Kosovo and other countries. And when were the mandarinates in the European past not themselves inured to injustice and brutality and resolved to behave as if the songs they sang and the systems they created and the lives they led might have a logic or beauty or validity largely independent of the conditions around them? When, precisely, was the idiom of truth, beauty and goodness not susceptible to corruption or cliche? Were there not numerous hacks and time servers in whose hands the Elizabethan sonnet was good for nothing but cheap sentimentality and inanity? When were the graces of language and learning not used to deceive or flatter or boast, even as, in one or two or a dozen remarkable instances, those same graces might yield something true, something inestimably bracing because so utterly not what was typically generated even by high learning and refined expression? Is not the question "What is there left for Europe to create?" a question better asked in somewhat less expansive, more intimate versions, as in "What is there left for me to create?" or "Who will conceivably be interested in this new thing that I am doing or making or thinking?"

In many respects, in many books and essays, George Steiner has himself taught us to think seriously about these issues. Certainly he has alerted us to the perils of creation in the late twentieth century and shown us how to appreciate the master thinkers and writers improbably granted to us at a time when we had little reason to expect them. At the same time, he has alerted us to the merely provisional character of speculations aroused by issues of creativity and decline, insisting that we think through, again and yet again, questions that are apt to seem hollow or fatuous. For the thinking through can alone provide a means of resistance to false optimism or, what amounts to the same thing, an easy despair.

And so, it may well be necessary at this juncture to respond with some further resistance to George Steiner's Nexus lecture, which draws heavily on a body of work that has disturbed and provoked us for nearly half a century, in books like *Language and Silence, In Bluebeard's Castle* and *No Passion Spent.*

Consider, for example, the assertion that the idiom of truth, beauty and goodness has, "to a large extent, become a dusty cliche." The assertion would seem to suggest not only that serious artists and thinkers would be well advised to avoid the use of such terms, but that they must also manage not to assess artworks or, indeed, life choices armed with standards associated with those terms. Serious persons who wish to maintain any vestige of self respect will know, presumably, what is no longer permissible, and will discipline or restrain their impulse to respond to anything with the assistance of outworn terms or categories.

Now it is true, of course, that the idiom to which George Steiner refers has become suspect. The very terms cited do often seem hollow or pretentious in ways that may not have seemed obvious to earlier generations. Where writers in the twentieth century have nonetheless used such terms, they have often bracketed them, signalled to readers by one means or another their awareness of the problematic nature of concepts like beauty and goodness, their subordination to particular, by no means universal or permanent, paradigms. But the terms have survived, as also their meaning and their force. When a writer like Susan Sontag can say in a single breath, as she did in a recent Nexus conference at Tilburg, that of course she understands the central importance of Andy Warhol in the art of the twentieth century while reserving the right to detest his work, she is in effect resorting to, drawing upon, the categories implied in the idiom of truth, beauty and goodness. She is reserving the right to assert, in her way, a judgment upon work that is effective without being good, powerful without being beautiful, truthful about the circumstances of art in the late twentieth century without attempting to get at the important truths to which the best art ought at least to aspire. The idiom of truth, beauty and goodness may seem all too susceptible to cliche, but it remains, for most serious artists and writers, indispensable.

What follows from this observation is at least the suspicion that great art continues to exist as an idea that informs the practices of creative artists. If many writers have been emancipated "from the constricting reveries of the messianic," as George Steiner says, other artists have not been so emancipated, and many who are unable to sustain any semblance of a transcendental reverie know what they do not have and long to recover what has been denied to them. The sense of a vital *something* that has been lost is present in late twentieth century European writers as diverse as Ingeborg Bachmann and

Peter Handke, W. G. Sebald and Danilo Kis. The spectre of a "post-theological indeterminacy" does not, apparently, utterly obstruct the instinct for revelation, does not undermine absolutely the desire to move beyond surfaces. If major art is to be known, as George Steiner suggests, by its drive to engage with god questions, its willingness to wrestle with metaphysical despair, its openness to some possibility of joy or genuine mystery, its resistance to escapism, then it is fair to say that something very like major art is today being produced in Europe. George Steiner is surely well advised to wonder how it can be that conditions so ill-suited to the sentiments of wonder and mystery and conviction may nonetheless nurture, or fail at least to impede, the generation of such sentiments. But we have before us ample evidence that the arts informed by those sentiments are alive and more or less well. The existence of the meretricious, the shabby, the slick, the condescending, the all-too-knowing, the merely ironic, should not distract us from the other facts, facts we name when we refer to major writers like Bachmann and Handke, Sebald and Norman Manea, Milosz and Heaney, Saramago and Kundera.

Or to Adam Zagajewski, the great Polish poet whose most recent volume of poems in English translation is entitled *Mysticism for Beginners*. About Zagajewski's work the poet Edward Hirsch has written that it veers "between the temporal and the eternal," that the poet is "a seeker, a celebrant in search of the divine, the unchanging, the absolute," offering us poems "filled with radiant moments of plenitude," "spiritual emblems, hymns to the unknown, levers for transcendence." And yet, we may well add, they are poems very much of the earth, committed to the world and its ephemera as much as to the prospect of the radiant and the absolute. Struck by the cruelties of the world, by the spectacle of human beings "quickened by envy, / anger, desire," buffeted perpetually by the wind that "kills hope," Zagajewski nonetheless discovers moments "full of boundless, senseless / silly joy," moments that seem to know "something we didn't," and precious for that very reason. Craving, as he often says, "transformation," he is watchful for small signs, gradual cosmic motions, like "the dusk, slow and systematic, / erasing the outlines of medieval houses" on Tuscan hills. Alert to silence and vacancy, skeptical about the existence of a "fulfilled revelation of language," as George Steiner has it, adept at getting by without final foundations, he makes himself a humble learner, enrolls in what he calls "the elementary course," applies himself to a "mysticism for beginners," so that the sudden happiness he sometimes glimpses will seem "less opaque," the faces of others "almost beautiful." Impatient, though also in love, with the merely present and palpable, the cozy and familiar, he watches for some hint of "depths," a "mystery" that is more than "just blue sky," a plenitude beyond mere sufficiency.

Zagajewski is not, strictly speaking, a mystic poet, and he does not work from a fully elaborated visionary poetics. But he surely has considerable access to the idiom of truth, beauty and goodness. The end of beauty may have seemed inevitable to Duchamp when he looked at the landscape bequeathed to his generation at the time of the First World War, but Zagajewski knows that "we must live," that "though we are made of shadow", there is that which is "all light," and he is determined to take it in. This is not atavism, not the "archaism and nostalgia" which George Steiner describes as "sterile." Zagajewski has not quite discovered "a language north of the future," but he quietly opens a path to a way of seeing that may allow us to believe in such a language.

Zagajewski's quiet but sensuously charged forays, like the works of other poets and artists, allow us to wonder at George Steiner's suggestion that creative persons will be inhibited by the fear that "European civilization" cannot conceivably "produce another Shakespeare, another Mozart or Michelangelo." "Even a mediocre scientist," Steiner argues, unlike a poet or painter or composer, "is part of an onward-going, exponentially progressive enterprise." By contrast, the arts and humanities are "retrospective," have no "contract with tomorrow." Or so Steiner contends.

But in what sense precisely is the "executive performance" of writers and artists inevitably "retrospective"? And is it quite clear that a contemporary artist like Zagajewski will be fatally afflicted by the anxiety of influence, in a degree exceeding anything earlier writers will have experienced? Will a painter like Anselm Kiefer feel the utter foreclosure of any possible progressive orientation as he registers the weight of the tradition he inherits?

Surely it seems more reasonable to believe that working artists, by virtue of the work they do, have "a contract with tomorrow" as viscerally compelling as anything a scientific practitioner is likely to experience. For most serious working artists the operant sentiment is not principally a concern about immortality or about an "exponentially progressive enterprise." Often artists are concerned more or less exclusively with the conception and shaping of what they take to be the next episode in a narrative, the discovery of how to close or build momentum in a poem, the orchestration of color in the left foreground of a canvas. This is obvious, but possibly worth saying all the same. Tomorrow, for most working artists, is the moment they can see at last the next inevitable move, the moment when the figure in the carpet is revealed to them, the conceptual grid underwriting the poem or painting made plausibly manifest without becoming unduly obvious or literal. Artists are more apt to worry over idiom, pigment and incident than about whether or not their works are fit to stand with Shakespeare's or Picasso's. Nor is it any sign of mediocre ambition for artists to dwell principally on local matters, on details of execution or inflections of voice. For most serious artists the preoccupation with masterpieces has never been more than an aspect of the creative process, and even those who suspect that their works will endure devote rather little time to polishing their pedestals. The absorption in the creative project at hand is too overmastering to allow most artists to be distracted by what can only seem hopelessly remote and vainglorious.

Just so, if there is a crisis in European culture, it would seem to have rather little to do with the absence of "demonstrable" truth values in the arts and humanities. The standards of veracity that obtain in the hard sciences quite clearly vary from one science to another. Experimental and theoretical explanatory models are so different that efforts at "consilience" are bound most often to fail. Scientists themselves cite the proliferation of hyphenated disciplines and sub-disciplines like evolutionary psychology and physical anthropology, arguing that the unity of science is a myth and that so-called scientific explanations tend to come in many varieties of proprietary dialects. It is more or less hopeless to suppose that the arts and humanities can be improved or made more rigorous by the appropriation of a hypothetically universal set of scientific truth values which are themselves partial and unstable and are, in any case, generally alien to the very spirit of the artworks they might conceivably inspire. The sciences can at most furnish what is already discernible in many of the arts, namely, a range of metaphors and ideas, images and contexts: not system, not ethos, not "demonstrable verity," but material and suggestion are the most that the sciences can usefully contribute to the arts.

And if this seems somehow unduly pessimistic, consider that efforts to bring art and science together have usually failed. Freud had interesting things to say about Dostoyevski, but little insight into the internal dynamics of works of art. The application of relativity theory to modernist fiction and poetry has never been more than suggestive, and figures very little in the way we read and think about Joyce or Eliot or Woolf. The father of contemporary consilience theory, Edward O. Wilson, has written that "works of art that prove enduring are intensely humanistic," thereby revealing a total failure to grasp what George Steiner has often taught us about the strange seductiveness of in-humanist writers like Celine. No, if there is a crisis in European culture, it is not "science" that will answer to the problem.

Which leaves us asking, again, what precisely is the problem? Perhaps it is nothing more or less than the multiplicity of perspectives and discourses—yes, that awful word *discourses* again—that hold partial sway in what was not long ago a more unitary high culture.

Perhaps what seems to be the problem is the very fact of multiplicity. Science had once promised to do away with the fragmentation of knowledge, to provide what Wilson calls "one class of explanations, a seamless web of cause and effect." But now that promise has lost most of its lustre. In the arts and humanities there had been a seeming if always artificial consensus about value and standards, a consensus based on the idea of a reliable canon, a "great tradition" which conferred order upon a situation always threatened by the new and unforeseen. If the consensus that went by the name of "the canon," as George Steiner contends, was never more than "an historical, ideologically contextual and transitory consensus from which dissent [was], very likely, the most valuable by-product," it was nevertheless comforting for most educated persons to believe in the necessary fiction: to believe that some things were higher, better, truer, more beautiful, more enduring than others, and that the world presented something other than a pluralism of more or less equivalently valid or "interesting" or "authentic" expressions.

At the beginning of a new century we find that the educated classes are more or less willing to dispense with the necessary fiction of canon and consensus. They want still to value some things more than others, to believe in degrees of competence and, even, in excellence, but they are uncomfortable with distinctions between high and low, true and untrue, permanent and transitory. What George Steiner calls our "post-theological indeterminacy" is experienced by most educated Europeans, surely by most Americans, as a chaos of competing forms and sensibilities whose authenticity and allure cannot be determined by a recourse to canonic touchstones, many of which have been discredited or seem no longer compelling. It does no good to say that for every empty, trivial, shoddy piece of work on display at the latest Biennale there are others that demonstrate someone's concern for standards of beauty or technical virtuosity or visionary scope. The very fact that the world will sometimes value the shabby more than the sublime, that cultural institutions are generally committed to showing or publishing or discussing or teaching *everything,* that pluralism has become a promiscuous openness to virtually *any* idea or sensation, is enough to make many of us feel that European high culture, the domain of the muses, is about at an end.

Of course George Steiner does his best to rally us with the speculation that "the deserts may have very new horizons." But I find it difficult to accept that Heaney and Kiefer, Zagajewski and Manea, Lucien Freud and Handke, are, all of them, residents of a cultural desert. And precisely there, as we name names and engage with the particular works of our best artists, may lie our best hope of understanding whether there is any substantial reason to lament the fate of the European muses. My own instinct is to say that there is not.

Gene Fendt (review date fall 2002)

SOURCE: Fendt, Gene. Review of *Grammars of Creation,* by George Steiner. *Southern Humanities Review* 36, no. 4 (fall 2002): 385-90.

[*In the following review, Fendt assesses Georges Bernanos's* Under Satan's Sun *in terms of the critical criteria outlined in Steiner's* Grammars of Creation, *implicitly validating the latter's thesis.*]

It was entirely accidental that I should have been sent both of these books [*Grammars of Creation*; *Under Satan's Sun* by Georges Bernanos] at the same time, but supposing that the universe is an accident, this world an accident, its life forms a further accident, such a minor accident might be seen to carry within it exactly "the scandal of its hazard": "no logic to its necessity," the "compelling needlessness" that marks all creation—artistic or divine. But it is precisely these phrasal regimens that George Steiner suggests are among those we lose as the grammars of creation fade from our consciousness under the more constant "anonymous, collective inertial motion" of science's experimentation and discovery. In the repetition and recombination of an infinite (but bounded?) set of variables even the most empiricist, materialist, and logically atomistic of thinkers can tell narratives of *discovery,* but *creation* thereby reduces to illusory play, and then "invention," which has, for ages, been at play between "creation" and "discovery," loses its moorings—and becomes mere accident, happening: "The crux is this: 'invention.'" So just here, too, in beginning what is to be a "review," we might feel such needlessness to be "a threat or a liberation," and perhaps both sides of our feeling are lit by the flickering grammars of nihilism. In the near future, one begins to feel, "review" will be the only term of art—or science, for the future tense is becoming "incredible." What remains is explication.

There is another accident behind this sending of the two books, which I would like to review before beginning—if this word beginning is not too trammeled up already in the question of how we may speak of creation without invention or invention without repetition, a repetition so archaic that now, as Steiner says, we play a glass-bead game with stones we imagine once to have been precisely and exquisitely cut. In looking backward at this last accident, it almost seems possible that a reduction (a leading back) through the trammels of causality will explain every aspect of this threatening novel by Bernanos. Just so, nothing creative, or even inven-

tive, can come out of this review. That further accident is the combination of a remark of Steiner's, that "we have not begun to gauge the damage to man—as a species . . . inflicted by events since 1914," and a fact about Bernanos: that all of his major fiction was written in the period after that war—from 1926, when *Under Satan's Sun* was first published, to 1937, when another war began. Or should we say broke out?

We should say broke out, if I read Bernanos correctly. Things break out in this novel. It is hard to tell who is speaking. The novel begins with a 57-page prologue called "Mouchette's Story," but that prologue begins with a poet, Paul-Jean Toulet, who loves that time of evening "when the horizon has lost its sharp outline, . . . and from the highest point of the heavens right down to earth, there stretches an immense and already icy solitude. . . . It was the time when the poet distilled his inner life, making it yield its fragrant and poisoned secret essence." He seems to be sitting at a café on a boulevard; he is, perhaps, thirty or forty years too early to meet Camus's judge-penitent (from *The Fall*)—unless he is the judge-penitent. But what am I thinking? The novel I suppose to be this poet's distillation. But he disappears, entirely, after that paragraph; unless he is the distillate, or distills himself into the world—the world of the novel, of course; that is all I could mean. "We talk of chance, but the face of chance looks very much like our own."

The heroine (such a perfect accident, that word) of this prologue is a little blonde who thinks she can have anything, but there is much of her kind of distillate around, even in the small country towns of the story. What follows is the usual chemistry leading to a murder that is almost accidental, through a seduction and adultery that are purposed partly as cover, partly as game, partly because she can, and—"once again her gaze broke away from his and seemed to turn inward, with nothing specifically human in it but a barely detectable look of vanity and obstinacy"—to conclude with . . . But I should not give away what the conclusion is; and I do not think the conclusion is about the girl in any case. She finds her village-deputy lover to be quite stupid, for he is not afraid of hell (he swears he does not believe in it) but is afraid of his wife. She quietly wonders at him: "afraid of *her* but not of *me!*"; she goes loudly into a fit of madness; she collapses; the child is stillborn. She disappears for 80 pages.

Part one, "The Temptation of Despair," begins with two older priests discussing one of their younger protegés—one simple and ascetic to the point of an embarrassing raggedness; his underwear is not spotless; we are given to understand he did not do well in Latin or theology. In the middle of this part the young priest, walking at evening to a town six miles away to hear confessions, gets lost and turned around and the narrative breaks in such ways that he seems walking in a nightmare in the increasing night. The story is not told, but breaks forth; "the novelist who tells all communicates knowingness, not knowledge" (Steiner 43). This part seems to be written into the night with letters of darkness. The priest falls—was it three times?—he turns, turns again; falls delirious, the delirium is mimetic. The priest finds he is not alone in the dead of night; a lively short man, a horse trader, comes upon him. You know who he is. A conversation starts, breaks. The priest is thankful to be found: "It's been a long hard night for me, longer and harder than you could imagine." It is not even half over.

"Purgatory is the natural locus of the arts," says George Steiner; Orpheus forever almost leading love out of darkness. Is artistic creation an *imitatio Dei* we must be cured of, itself curing? As if Dante, leaving Vergil behind, could leave art, too, behind and enter, really, the Paradise of light. Dante enacts this in the *Commedia,* Steiner reminds us (with glorious detail in section two of his book)—as if the word, in wording, could world. So, Steiner concludes, the "paradox of true invention is intimately grounded in the transmutation of the nature of truth through divine incarnation in Jesus." But we who live on the other side of faith find this solution, this grounding, as "lost or forgotten as is Adamic speech." What will our speech be, then, if this one was true? How should we think of language now? The Word never worlded, but the world, whirling its permutations, in one beast changed into word; suppose it, can we? That would be the other of the grammars of creation.

> "Anybody else would have been going around in circles on a night like this. But I know all this area."
>
> "Do you live around here?" . . .
>
> "I don't live anywhere, really."
>
> (Bernanos 113)

The figure of the night is friendly, full of an unknown tenderness, subtly humiliating, terrifying, a dizzying doppelgänger. "What is there to say? It was his own pale face, . . . his instinctive way of moving his hand toward his heart; it was his eyes, and in them he could see fear." Perhaps that is what speaks even in review? What should be the fear? "Our works and days are lunatic with *reden* [talk] and *Gerede* [chit-chat], with loquacity and its 'palpable designs upon us'" (Steiner 203). Bernanos palpates this doppelgänger; the priest receives the horse-trader's kiss on his mouth.

On this other side of creation's old grammars, in the new age Steiner would say was born under "the eclipse of the messianic," in which all of the Western redemption narratives are withering away—as in one of them the state was eventually to do—

What do [we] make of the inner life? A dreary battlefield of the instincts. Of morality? A hygiene of the senses. Grace is now merely a reasonable argument appealing to our intelligence, temptation an urge. . . . Man is supposed to seek only what is pleasurable and useful, with his conscience guiding his choice. . . . That childish way of seeing things explains nothing. In such a world of sentient and reasoning animals, either there's nothing left for the saint, or we have to declare him mad. And so we do.

> (Bernanos 163)

The last character to appear in the novel, in part two, "The Saint of Lumbres," is a famous novelist—described variously as "the past master of irony" and "the old hypocrite"—of the Académie Française. If the book had not been written before Bertrand Russell grew aged, I should have said this part of the novel was a roman à clef. The novelist comes to visit the now-aged living saint, and the young priest who meets him, "trying to put things in a way that was within [his] grasp, in [his] kind of language," finds himself stymied at each turn, flustered, shamed. Uncreation has been the ironist's daily bread for as long as the saint has fed, as the novelist describes it, "on the bread of illusion." The old hypocrite knows his life to have been "a kind of morose delight shot through with fits of lucid despair," yet imagines the old priest to be someone he might yet get something of: "Perhaps I should borrow from sanctity whatever is pleasant in it." He finds the saint dead; he thinks it a dirty trick.

Then the novel is a trick, too. I do not speak of the particular, but of the species. And that genus, art? In a grammar without creation, what is invention? Without invention, what is repetition? "How can recombination, unlimited as its play may be, satisfy . . . that 'thirst for the virgin soil of time'" (Steiner 156)? And if now, even later in the night than Professor Steiner's new book [*Grammars of Creation*], we find the air full of ashes and ourselves forced to eat them, is it sensible to hope, or even

> suppose that atheism will come to possess and energize those who are masters of articulate form and builders of thought[?] Will their works rival the dimensions, the life-transforming strengths of persuasion we have known? What would be the atheist counterpart to a Michelangelo fresco or *King Lear*? It would be impertinent to rule out the possibility.

I will be impertinent: if Steiner's study shows anything, it shows how impossible it is to escape from the grammars of creation; Bernanos over half a century earlier exhibited the face of that character's feeling:

> Let others be laid to rest by friendly hands under a fresh white sheet; the priest was still standing in his black darkness, listening to the cries of his children. He still had something to say.

Indeed, both Bernanos and Steiner have something more to say than I have been able, in this merely recombinant review, to make clear. After the accident of reading them together I find it difficult at times to tell which will have been the priest, which the professor:

> Human language cannot be forced into any abstract expression of the certainty of a real presence, since all our certainties are deductions, and our experience of others, at the close of a long life, is mostly just the end of a long journey around our own nothingness.
>
> . . . . .
>
> Love knows of absences more vehement . . . than any presence.

And then there was one more striking accident, in Professor Steiner's closing reflections on the end of art in the new world order; as if, in fact, there is an order, and one can feel it coming like a Greek fate, or the consequence of original sin:

> One step remained to be taken. In 1960, in the forecourt of the Museum of Modern Art in New York, Jean Tinguely set alight his intricate, soaring *Hommage à New York*. The metal construct collapsed in brightness ("a brightness falls from the air"). Other "self-destructs" were to follow.

Edward Skidelsky (review date 8 December 2003)

SOURCE: Skidelsky, Edward. "The Lost Disciples." *New Statesman* 16, no. 786 (8 December 2003): 48-9.

[*In the following review, Skidelsky faults* Lessons of the Masters *for its rhetorical abstraction, "shallow eclecticism," and lack of social or historical contexts.*]

George Steiner has chosen a deliberately unfashionable subject [in *Lessons of the Masters*.] The position of the teacher in the modern world is an awkward, anomalous one. Institutes of education avoid the term, preferring to talk about "facilitators" or "learning partners". "Teacher", they claim, sounds stuffy and authoritarian. (What would they make of "master"?) Yet the desire for discipleship, for intellectual submission, remains as powerful as ever. As undergraduates, I and many of my friends felt like disciples in search of a master. Our tutors remained frustratingly aloof, their advice restrained and professional. Doubtless they were wise to act in this way; they had their careers to manage, their privacy to protect. Acolytes can be a nuisance. But reading about masters and disciples in Steiner's book left me feeling strangely envious, as though I had missed one of the great experiences of youth. It is perhaps only by surrendering to a master and then rebelling that one attains to full intellectual autonomy. Of all religious themes, that of losing one's life in order to save it comes closest to the heart of this peculiar relationship.

Unfortunately, *Lessons of the Masters* far from fulfils the promise of its subject. It displays all of Steiner's well-known intellectual vices and few of his virtues. Mystagogy has all but replaced thought; the profound depths of the master-disciple relationship are endlessly insinuated but never explained. This cultivation of mystery lies at the centre of Steiner's religion of art; one does not, as Bagehot said, let daylight in on magic. Like a temple priest, Steiner officiates before a sanctum that remains for ever closed. All that is visible from the outside is the mummery of learning and wordplay. "Valid teaching is ostensible. It shows. This 'ostentation', so intriguing to Wittgenstein, is embedded in etymology: Latin *dicere* 'to show' and, only later, 'to show by saying'; Middle English *token* and *techen* with its implicit connotations of 'that which shows'. (Is the teacher, finally, a showman?)" And so on. Such passages evade refutation; there is nothing there to refute. Like the Cheshire cat disappearing behind his smile, Steiner has disappeared behind his own manner.

The book is full of intriguing questions. Why is the theme of mastery and discipleship absent from Shakespeare? Why does it suddenly revive in the late 19th and early 20th centuries, in the George circle and in the cults surrounding Gurdjieff and Madame Blavatsky? There are interesting passages on the French educational tradition, on the affinities of Hassidism and Zen and on Henry Adams. But because nothing is pursued for more than a few pages, the overall impression is one of shallow eclecticism. Steiner would have done better to concentrate on three or four central figures. As it is, we are left with nothing but generalities. Steiner's summary of his findings is banal: sometimes masters destroy their disciples; sometimes disciples destroy their masters; sometimes masters and disciples get on. One could have guessed as much.

But this thin, abstract quality stems above all from the almost complete lack of social or historical background. Apart from the occasional allusion to the effects of mass consumption and the internet, there is hardly any sense that the relationship between master and disciple might change significantly from one age to another. This is why Steiner can leap directly from Abelard to Heidegger, from Tycho Brahe to Franz Kafka. There is no intermediary level between the eternal and the personal. Steiner's perspective is similar to that which Augustine ascribes to God; he sees the entirety of human history spread out before him in a line, even and undifferentiated. He ignores the one crucial insight of Marxist aesthetics, that—as he himself once quipped— there is no chamber music without chambers.

Steiner's lack of historical sense is most evident in his outbursts against the "two movements or pathologies" that have "eroded trust between Master and disciple". These turn out, unsurprisingly, to be radical feminism and political correctness. Many of Steiner's charges are accurate; his concern for the disappearance of irony is particularly welcome. But jeremiads are no substitute for understanding. Steiner dismisses the movements in question as mere "witch-hunts" or "treason". He is unwilling to acknowledge that the entire bent of European civilisation since the Enlightenment has been hostile to the master-disciple relationship. The title "master" implies personal, charismatic authority. Its connotations are religious and hierarchical; it tallies uncomfortably with the liberal ideal of symmetrical relations between free and equal citizens. It is also at variance with the modern ideal of *Wissenschaft,* or organised knowledge. "Wisdom" is what a master traditionally imparts; the techniques of modern science and scholarship call for a less personal, more transparent form of instruction. The very word "master" carries a distinctly reactionary charge. It is no accident that Steiner's one example of the 20th-century use of the term is taken from a letter by the philosopher and writer Pierre Boutang to Charles Maurras, then incarcerated for collaboration with Vichy.

* * *

But even if the word has all but disappeared, the phenomenon has not. Behind many a modern university lecturer lurks a master. Much of the furore over "sexual harassment" can be traced to this disjuncture between our official ideals and our historical inheritance. In the past, the sexual charisma of the master was understood as an aspect of his authority, the disciple's desire for him as part of his desire for wisdom. The master's responsibility was to direct this desire away from his own person towards its true object. Hence Socrates, at the climax of the Symposium, refuses to sleep with Alcibiades. But the modern liberal professor has no authority to transmit, no wisdom to impart. His charisma, if he has any, is shorn of its pedagogic alibi. He no longer has any overriding reason not to use it for purposes of seduction, nor have his students any overriding reason not to assist him in so doing. A relationship of reciprocal *eros* has become one of mutual exploitation.

It was along these lines that the late Bernard Williams interpreted David Mamet's play *Oleanna,* in which a student falsely accuses her professor of sexual abuse. The play was commonly understood—and is understood by Steiner—as a straightforward denunciation of the "mendacious hysteria" of campus sexual politics. But its message, Williams argued, is rather more complex.

The student comes to the professor looking for authority, but is told that all authority is a mask for power. She infers, logically, that the professor's own authority over her is also a mask for power, and specifically sexual power. Her accusations, although literally false, express what can plausibly be seen as the essential truth of their relationship. (Besides, the professor has also taught her that truth and falsehood are nothing but social constructs.) The professor, in short, is not merely a victim; he is the unsuspecting agent of his own ruin. He cannot justify or even acknowledge his own charisma; he is undone by his unwitting "mastery".

Mamet biases the issue by making his professor an ultra-trendy postmodernist and relativist, thereby shifting the blame on to these particular fashions. Steiner does much the same. But the problem they confront is far more general. The disappearance of the masters is not the work of an intellectual fad. It has deep causes; it is bound up with many of the things we value most in liberal civilisation. Would Steiner, for all his magisterial affectations, feel entirely comfortable, I wonder, hearing the title "master" applied to himself?

Paul Dean (review date January 2004)

SOURCE: Dean, Paul. "The Steiner School." *New Criterion* 22, no. 5 (January 2004): 73-5.

[*In the following review, Dean sympathizes with some of the concerns addressed by* Lessons of the Masters *despite alleging it contains numerous "flaws and absurdities."*]

A book about great teachers [**Lessons of the Masters**]—by George Steiner? One's eyes narrow suspiciously. But no, he is in chastened mood. "Why have I been remunerated," he asks, "for what is my oxygen and *raison d'étre*?" Tactfully he avoids answering that question, evoking instead his weekly seminars at Geneva, where he and his students (now dispersed "on five continents") would study *Phaedrus* or *The Tempest* and he would "introduce (falteringly) *The Brothers Karamazov.*" The university teacher, heir of Socrates, Jesus, and Buddha, thus enjoys "touches of grace and hope." Why, he later concedes, "even at a humble level—that of the schoolmaster—to teach, to teach well, is to be accomplice to transcendent possibility": for who knows whether that solemn little boy in the back row might not turn out to be a budding George Steiner?

Speaking as someone who has operated "at a humble level" for as long as Steiner was in Geneva, I may tell him that I, too, have taught *Phaedrus* and *The Tempest*—and the passage from Proust on the death of Bergotte which he also mentions. Not *Karamazov,* admittedly, but one can only do so much at a humble level. Even so, I cheer myself with the reflection that my students would not, as he does, believe Plato's Socrates as a character to be "comparable if not superior to" Falstaff, Hamlet, or Anna Karenina, or claim that the Platonic dialogues are "as intricately plotted as Henry James's," or think that Hermann Hesse's *The Glass Bead Game* is a novel to admire. In the customarily wide range of Steiner's survey, one figure eludes him. Shakespeare is silent, he thinks, about the master/disciple relationship. (He forgets, apparently, Falstaff's role as a kind of parodic Socrates to Prince Hal.) Of course, as Steiner says, Shakespeare was suspicious of academic authority; he never attended a university seminar, and had Hamlet gone to Geneva rather than Wittenberg he might have been spared much perplexity.

Amid the pomposity, portentousness, and vacuousness of Steiner's prose—"the sweat of a monument" as James Wood brilliantly describes it in his lethal essay on Steiner in *The Broken Estate*—some important points struggle for survival. Yes, a great teacher does have a quasi-seductive appeal to the intellect. Yes, a great teacher is ultimately lonely, because if he has been successful his pupils can do without him (think of the moving evaporation of Virgil from the *Divine Comedy*). Wittgenstein has a penetrating passage in *Culture and Value:*

> A teacher may get good, even astounding, results from his pupils while he is teaching them and yet not be a good teacher; because it may be that, while his pupils are directly under his influence, he raises them to a height which is not natural to them, without fostering their own capacities for work at this level, so that they immediately decline again as soon as the teacher leaves the classroom. Perhaps this is how it is with me; I have sometimes thought so.

It was also true, I should say, of Leavis, who is often linked with Wittgenstein as a great twentieth-century teacher. And yes, the influence of great teaching is incommunicable; the *dicta* of Nadia Boulanger, one of the few women in a book whose title and incidental usages largely confine pedagogic greatness to males, are colorless, but it was her charisma, her physical presence, that mattered.

* * *

This is why Steiner's remarks about computer technology are as wrong as they could well be:

> The screen can teach, examine, demonstrate, interact with a precision, a clarity, and a patience exceeding that of a human instructor. Its resources can be disseminated and enlisted at will. It knows neither

prejudice nor fatigue. In turn, the apprentice can question, object, answer back in a dialectic whose pedagogic value may come to surpass that of spoken discourse.

No, no, and no again! For it is the presumed infallibility and inexhaustibility of the machine (Steiner must be able to afford much better ones than I can) which make it impossible for it to be a teacher of any kind, let alone a great one. The *mutual* taking of risks, the acceptance of error, the frustrations of nerve and intellect, the renewal of will, the awareness of limited time and the corresponding sense of urgency are fundamental to the learning process. Teaching is a human act grounded in a human relationship. To call a computer a teacher is to pervert the word.

Among the most telling strokes in the book are the remarks on the American education system—much of which apply in Britain, too—with its belief in what Steiner, in a rare moment of epigrammatic crystallization, calls "the rights of all to be gifted." The *ad hoc* instruction of Eliot by Pound, and, less happily, of Hemingway by Gertrude Stein, ossified into "creative writing" classes. "What would 'non-creative writing' be?" Steiner wonders, forgetting that the answer lies all around him in the products of those same classes.

He is on stronger ground in deploring the "travesty of responsible argument and scholarship" represented by "Pseudo-curricula" which "have been institutionalized at the price of indispensable disciplines." A longer quotation shows him writing with unusual force and clarity:

> The point is that for better or worse . . . our heritage in the west is that of Jerusalem, Athens, and Rome. The alphabet of our recognitions is that developed by "dead white males." Our literary, philosophical, aesthetic touchstones are those of a European or North American core, often vividly influenced from outside and now qualified and enriched by ethnic plurality. To regard Sophocles or Dante or Shakespeare as somehow tainted by imperialist, colonialist mentality is idiocy pure and simple. To discard western poetry or the novel from Cervantes to Proust as "male chauvinistic" is blindness.

Amen to that, and he puts the blame precisely where it ought to be, on the university teachers who have abdicated their function at the behest of politically motivated minority pressure groups who have maneuvered themselves into positions of financial and administrative power. He adds, though perhaps more confidently than the circumstances warrant, "The Sciences know no such folly," inhabiting a world where "The correctness is that of the equation, not the politics of cowardice." Yet the sciences too are humane disciplines, and we can all think of cases in which research funds have been deployed to promote some politically expedient but morally dubious cause.

* * *

As suggested above, the British system is in comparable disarray. The Education Secretary, Charles Clarke, has expressed open contempt for universities that wish to retain teachers of philosophy or medieval history (while conceding that a few museum specimens might be allowed to remain for the amusement of the public). Teachers at all levels, from reception class to postgraduate seminar, are hamstrung by a curriculum that demands that the maximum number of students be catered for at the minimum cost, and that hates ambition, excellence, vision, or originality. The possibility, not just of great teaching, but of adequate teaching, is menaced, for the liberties which are its lifeblood are denied. Steiner quotes a Harvard wisecrack on Jesus, "A fine teacher, but didn't publish"; neither he nor Socrates would get tenure today. For all their absurdities and flaws, Steiner and his book reflect a noble and, one fears, a doomed heritage.

FURTHER READING

Criticism

Basney, Lionel. Review of *Errata,* by George Steiner. *Sewanee Review* 107, no. 1 (winter 1999): xxvii-xxix.
> Observes the paucity of biographical information about Steiner in *Errata.*

Eagleton, Terry. "Commentary." *New Literary History* 35, no. 1 (winter 2004): 151-59.
> Challenges Steiner's view that the advent of modernity heralded the death of tragedy.

Hagen, W. M. Review of *Errata,* by George Steiner. *World Literature Today* 73, no. 4 (autumn 1999): 833-34.
> Describes the effects of ignoring the conventions of autobiography in *Errata.*

Hensher, Philip. "Let Us Now Praise Obscure Men." *Spectator* 276, no. 8738 (13 January 1996): 29-30.
> Surveys *No Passion Spent* and the collection *The Deeps of the Sea,* offering faint praise.

Kennedy, John. Review of *Grammars of Creation,* by George Steiner. *Antioch Review* 60, no. 1 (winter 2002): 161-62.
> Praises the breadth of *Grammars of Creation.*

Lojek, Helen. "Brian Friel's Plays and George Steiner's Linguistics: Translating the Irish." *Contemporary Literature* 35, no. 1 (spring 1994): 83.
> Compares the conceptual significance of translation in *After Babel* with that in Brian Friel's play *Translations.*

Mathewes, Charles T. Review of *Lessons of the Masters,* by George Steiner. *Virginia Quarterly Review* 80, no. 2 (spring 2004): 267-68.
> Questions both the organization and the purpose of *Lessons of the Masters.*

McEntyre, Marilyn Chandler. Review of *No Passion Spent,* by George Steiner. *Theology Today* 54, no. 2 (July 1997): 230-31.
> Highlights the themes of several essays in *No Passion Spent* within the context of "what it is to read well."

Neuhaus, Richard John. "The End of Endings." *First Things,* no. 115 (August/September 2001): 47-56.
> Surveys thematic similarities in *Grammars of Creation* and Paul S. Fiddes's *The Promised End.*

Popkin, Michael. "George Steiner's *Portage*: Holocaust Novel or Thriller?" In *Apocalyptic Visions Past and Present: Selected Papers from the Eighth and Ninth Annual Florida State University Conferences on Literature and Film,* edited by JoAnn James and William J. Cloonan, pp. 13-24. Tallahassee: The Florida State University Press, 1988.
> Studies the confluence between conventions of Holocaust literature and spy thrillers in *The Portage to San Cristóbal of A. H.,* demonstrating the inadequacy of language to explain the Holocaust.

Schwartz, Joseph. Review of *Real Presences,* by George Steiner. *Modern Philology* 89, no. 3 (February 1992): 452-56.
> Elucidates several epistemological and ethical inferences drawn from *Real Presences,* summarizing the book's central arguments.

White, Nick. "The Ventriloquial Paradox: George Steiner's *The Portage to San Cristóbal of A. H.*" *New Theatre Quarterly* 18, no. 1 (February 2002): 66-90.
> Describes the circumstances surrounding the 1982 stage adaptation of *The Portage to San Cristóbal of A. H.* and the ensuing controversy about the protagonist's, and ultimately Steiner's, perceptions of the Holocaust.

Young, Michael. "Real Presence and the Conscience of Words: Language and Repetition in George Steiner's *Portage to San Cristóbal of A. H.*" *Style* 26, no. 1 (spring 1992): 114-28.

Investigates the role of linguistic repetition in two key speeches in *The Portage to San Cristóbal of A. H.*

Additional coverage of Steiner's life and career is contained in the following sources published by Thomson Gale: *Contemporary Authors,* Vols. 73-76; *Contemporary Authors New Revision Series,* Vols. 31, 67, 108; *Contemporary Literary Criticism,* Vol. 24; *Dictionary of Literary Biography,* Vols. 67, 299; *DISCovering Authors Modules: Novelists*; *Encyclopedia of World Literature in the 20th Century,* Ed. 3; *Literature Resource Center*; *Major 20th-Century Writers,* Eds. 1, 2; *Major 21st-Century Writers,* (eBook) 2005; *Reference Guide to Holocaust Literature*; and *Something about the Author,* Vol. 62.

How to Use This Index

The main references

Calvino, Italo
 1923-1985 .... CLC 5, 8, 11, 22, 33, 39,
                                              73; SSC 3, 48

list all author entries in the following Thomson Gale Literary Criticism series:

AAL = *Asian American Literature*
BG = *The Beat Generation: A Gale Critical Companion*
BLC = *Black Literature Criticism*
BLCS = *Black Literature Criticism Supplement*
CLC = *Contemporary Literary Criticism*
CLR = *Children's Literature Review*
CMLC = *Classical and Medieval Literature Criticism*
DC = *Drama Criticism*
FL = *Feminism in Literature: A Gale Critical Companion*
GL = *Gothic Literature: A Gale Critical Companion*
HLC = *Hispanic Literature Criticism*
HLCS = *Hispanic Literature Criticism Supplement*
HR = *Harlem Renaissance: A Gale Critical Companion*
LC = *Literature Criticism from 1400 to 1800*
NCLC = *Nineteenth-Century Literature Criticism*
NNAL = *Native North American Literature*
PC = *Poetry Criticism*
SSC = *Short Story Criticism*
TCLC = *Twentieth-Century Literary Criticism*
WLC = *World Literature Criticism, 1500 to the Present*
WLCS = *World Literature Criticism Supplement*

The cross-references

See also CA 85-88, 116; CANR 23, 61;
DAM NOV; DLB 196; EW 13; MTCW 1, 2;
RGSF 2; RGWL 2; SFW 4; SSFS 12

list all author entries in the following Thomson Gale biographical and literary sources:

AAYA = *Authors & Artists for Young Adults*
AFAW = *African American Writers*
AFW = *African Writers*
AITN = *Authors in the News*
AMW = *American Writers*
AMWR = *American Writers Retrospective Supplement*
AMWS = *American Writers Supplement*
ANW = *American Nature Writers*
AW = *Ancient Writers*
BEST = *Bestsellers*
BPFB = *Beacham's Encyclopedia of Popular Fiction: Biography and Resources*
BRW = *British Writers*
BRWS = *British Writers Supplement*
BW = *Black Writers*
BYA = *Beacham's Guide to Literature for Young Adults*
CA = *Contemporary Authors*
CAAS = *Contemporary Authors Autobiography Series*
CABS = *Contemporary Authors Bibliographical Series*
CAD = *Contemporary American Dramatists*
CANR = *Contemporary Authors New Revision Series*
CAP = *Contemporary Authors Permanent Series*
CBD = *Contemporary British Dramatists*
CCA = *Contemporary Canadian Authors*
CD = *Contemporary Dramatists*
CDALB = *Concise Dictionary of American Literary Biography*

CDALBS = *Concise Dictionary of American Literary Biography Supplement*
CDBLB = *Concise Dictionary of British Literary Biography*
CMW = *St. James Guide to Crime & Mystery Writers*
CN = *Contemporary Novelists*
CP = *Contemporary Poets*
CPW = *Contemporary Popular Writers*
CSW = *Contemporary Southern Writers*
CWD = *Contemporary Women Dramatists*
CWP = *Contemporary Women Poets*
CWRI = *St. James Guide to Children's Writers*
CWW = *Contemporary World Writers*
DA = *DISCovering Authors*
DA3 = *DISCovering Authors 3.0*
DAB = *DISCovering Authors: British Edition*
DAC = *DISCovering Authors: Canadian Edition*
DAM = *DISCovering Authors: Modules*
   DRAM: *Dramatists Module;* **MST:** *Most-studied Authors Module;*
   MULT: *Multicultural Authors Module;* **NOV:** *Novelists Module;*
   POET: *Poets Module;* **POP:** *Popular Fiction and Genre Authors Module*
DFS = *Drama for Students*
DLB = *Dictionary of Literary Biography*
DLBD = *Dictionary of Literary Biography Documentary Series*
DLBY = *Dictionary of Literary Biography Yearbook*
DNFS = *Literature of Developing Nations for Students*
EFS = *Epics for Students*
EXPN = *Exploring Novels*
EXPP = *Exploring Poetry*
EXPS = *Exploring Short Stories*
EW = *European Writers*
FANT = *St. James Guide to Fantasy Writers*
FW = *Feminist Writers*
GFL = *Guide to French Literature,* Beginnings to 1789, 1798 to the Present
GLL = *Gay and Lesbian Literature*
HGG = *St. James Guide to Horror, Ghost & Gothic Writers*
HW = *Hispanic Writers*
IDFW = *International Dictionary of Films and Filmmakers: Writers and Production Artists*
IDTP = *International Dictionary of Theatre: Playwrights*
LAIT = *Literature and Its Times*
LAW = *Latin American Writers*
JRDA = *Junior DISCovering Authors*
MAICYA = *Major Authors and Illustrators for Children and Young Adults*
MAICYAS = *Major Authors and Illustrators for Children and Young Adults Supplement*
MAWW = *Modern American Women Writers*
MJW = *Modern Japanese Writers*
MTCW = *Major 20th-Century Writers*
NCFS = *Nonfiction Classics for Students*
NFS = *Novels for Students*
PAB = *Poets: American and British*
PFS = *Poetry for Students*
RGAL = *Reference Guide to American Literature*
RGEL = *Reference Guide to English Literature*
RGSF = *Reference Guide to Short Fiction*
RGWL = *Reference Guide to World Literature*
RHW = *Twentieth-Century Romance and Historical Writers*
SAAS = *Something about the Author Autobiography Series*
SATA = *Something about the Author*
SFW = *St. James Guide to Science Fiction Writers*
SSFS = *Short Stories for Students*
TCWW = *Twentieth-Century Western Writers*
WLIT = *World Literature and Its Times*
WP = *World Poets*
YABC = *Yesterday's Authors of Books for Children*
YAW = *St. James Guide to Young Adult Writers*

Literary Criticism Series
Cumulative Author Index

MULT; DLB 175, 206, 278; LATS 1:2;
MTCW 2; MTFW 2005; NFS 17; SSFS
18

al-Farabi 870(?)-950 .... **CMLC 58**
See also DLB 115

Alfau, Felipe 1902-1999 .... **CLC 66**
See also CA 137

Alfieri, Vittorio 1749-1803 .... **NCLC 101**
See also EW 4; RGWL 2, 3; WLIT 7

Alfonso X 1221-1284 .... **CMLC 78**

Alfred, Jean Gaston
See Ponge, Francis

Alger, Horatio, Jr. 1832-1899 .... **NCLC 8, 83**
See also CLR 87; DLB 42; LAIT 2; RGAL
4; SATA 16; TUS

Al-Ghazali, Muhammad ibn Muhammad
1058-1111 .... **CMLC 50**
See also DLB 115

Algren, Nelson 1909-1981 ..... **CLC 4, 10, 33;**
SSC 33
See also AMWS 9; BPFB 1; CA 13-16R;
103; CANR 20, 61; CDALB 1941-1968;
CN 1, 2; DLB 9; DLBY 1981, 1982,
2000; EWL 3; MAL 5; MTCW 1, 2;
MTFW 2005; RGAL 4; RGSF 2

**al-Hariri, al-Qasim ibn 'Ali Abu
Muhammad al-Basri**
1054-1122 .... **CMLC 63**
See also RGWL 3

Ali, Ahmed 1908-1998 .... **CLC 69**
See also CA 25-28R; CANR 15, 34; CN 1,
2, 3, 4, 5; EWL 3

Ali, Tariq 1943- .... **CLC 173**
See also CA 25-28R; CANR 10, 99

Alighieri, Dante
See Dante
See also WLIT 7

al-Kindi, Abu Yusuf Ya'qub ibn Ishaq c.
801-c. 873 .... **CMLC 80**

Allan, John B.
See Westlake, Donald E(dwin)

Allan, Sidney
See Hartmann, Sadakichi

Allan, Sydney
See Hartmann, Sadakichi

Allard, Janet .... **CLC 59**

Allen, Edward 1948- .... **CLC 59**

Allen, Fred 1894-1956 .... **TCLC 87**

Allen, Paula Gunn 1939- .... **CLC 84, 202;**
NNAL
See also AMWS 4; CA 112; 143; CANR
63, 130; CWP; DA3; DAM MULT; DLB
175; FW; MTCW 2; MTFW 2005; RGAL
4; TCWW 2

Allen, Roland
See Ayckbourn, Alan

Allen, Sarah A.
See Hopkins, Pauline Elizabeth

Allen, Sidney H.
See Hartmann, Sadakichi

Allen, Woody 1935- .... **CLC 16, 52, 195**
See also AAYA 10, 51; AMWS 15; CA 33-
36R; CANR 27, 38, 63, 128; DAM POP;
DLB 44; MTCW 1; SSFS 21

Allende, Isabel 1942- ... **CLC 39, 57, 97, 170;**
HLC 1; SSC 65; WLCS
See also AAYA 18; CA 125; 130; CANR
51, 74, 129; CDWLB 3; CLR 99; CWW
2; DA3; DAM MULT, NOV; DLB 145;
DNFS 1; EWL 3; FL 1:5; FW; HW 1, 2;
INT CA-130; LAIT 5; LAWS 1; LMFS 2;
MTCW 1, 2; MTFW 2005; NCFS 1; NFS
6, 18; RGSF 2; RGWL 3; SATA 163;
SSFS 11, 16; WLIT 1

Alleyn, Ellen
See Rossetti, Christina

Alleyne, Carla D. .... **CLC 65**

Allingham, Margery (Louise)
1904-1966 .... **CLC 19**
See also CA 5-8R; 25-28R; CANR 4, 58;
CMW 4; DLB 77; MSW; MTCW 1, 2

Allingham, William 1824-1889 ...... **NCLC 25**
See also DLB 35; RGEL 2

Allison, Dorothy E. 1949- .... **CLC 78, 153**
See also AAYA 53; CA 140; CANR 66, 107;
CN 7; CSW; DA3; FW; MTCW 2; MTFW
2005; NFS 11; RGAL 4

Alloula, Malek .... **CLC 65**

Allston, Washington 1779-1843 .... **NCLC 2**
See also DLB 1, 235

Almedingen, E. M. .... **CLC 12**
See Almedingen, Martha Edith von
See also SATA 3

Almedingen, Martha Edith von 1898-1971
See Almedingen, E. M.
See also CA 1-4R; CANR 1

Almodovar, Pedro 1949(?)- .... **CLC 114;**
HLCS 1
See also CA 133; CANR 72; HW 2

Almqvist, Carl Jonas Love
1793-1866 .... **NCLC 42**

**al-Mutanabbi, Ahmad ibn al-Husayn Abu
al-Tayyib al-Jufi al-Kindi**
915-965 .... **CMLC 66**
See Mutanabbi, Al-
See also RGWL 3

Alonso, Damaso 1898-1990 .... **CLC 14**
See also CA 110; 131; 130; CANR 72; DLB
108; EWL 3; HW 1, 2

Alov
See Gogol, Nikolai (Vasilyevich)

al'Sadaawi, Nawal
See El Saadawi, Nawal
See also FW

al-Shaykh, Hanan 1945- .... **CLC 218**
See also CA 135; CANR 111; WLIT 6

Al Siddik
See Rolfe, Frederick (William Serafino
Austin Lewis Mary)
See also GLL 1; RGEL 2

Alta 1942- .... **CLC 19**
See also CA 57-60

Alter, Robert B(ernard) 1935- .... **CLC 34**
See also CA 49-52; CANR 1, 47, 100

Alther, Lisa 1944- .... **CLC 7, 41**
See also BPFB 1; CA 65-68; CAAS 30;
CANR 12, 30, 51; CN 4, 5, 6, 7; CSW;
GLL 2; MTCW 1

Althusser, L.
See Althusser, Louis

Althusser, Louis 1918-1990 .... **CLC 106**
See also CA 131; 132; CANR 102; DLB
242

Altman, Robert 1925- .... **CLC 16, 116**
See also CA 73-76; CANR 43

Alurista .... **HLCS 1; PC 34**
See Urista (Heredia), Alberto (Baltazar)
See also CA 45-48R; DLB 82; LLW

Alvarez, A(lfred) 1929- .... **CLC 5, 13**
See also CA 1-4R; CANR 3, 33, 63, 101,
134; CN 3, 4, 5, 6; CP 1, 2, 3, 4, 5, 6, 7;
DLB 14, 40; MTFW 2005

Alvarez, Alejandro Rodriguez 1903-1965
See Casona, Alejandro
See also CA 131; 93-96; HW 1

Alvarez, Julia 1950- .... **CLC 93; HLCS 1**
See also AAYA 25; AMWS 7; CA 147;
CANR 69, 101, 133; DA3; DLB 282;
LATS 1:2; LLW; MTCW 2; MTFW 2005;
NFS 5, 9; SATA 129; WLIT 1

Alvaro, Corrado 1896-1956 .... **TCLC 60**
See also CA 163; DLB 264; EWL 3

Amado, Jorge 1912-2001 ... **CLC 13, 40, 106;**
HLC 1
See also CA 77-80; 201; CANR 35, 74, 135;
CWW 2; DAM MULT, NOV; DLB 113,
307; EWL 3; HW 2; LAW; LAWS 1;
MTCW 1, 2; MTFW 2005; RGWL 2, 3;
TWA; WLIT 1

Ambler, Eric 1909-1998 .... **CLC 4, 6, 9**
See also BRWS 4; CA 9-12R; 171; CANR
7, 38, 74; CMW 4; CN 1, 2, 3, 4, 5, 6;
DLB 77; MSW; MTCW 1, 2; TEA

Ambrose, Stephen E(dward)
1936-2002 .... **CLC 145**
See also AAYA 44; CA 1-4R; 209; CANR
3, 43, 57, 83, 105; MTFW 2005; NCFS 2;
SATA 40, 138

Amichai, Yehuda 1924-2000 .. **CLC 9, 22, 57,**
116; PC 38
See also CA 85-88; 189; CANR 46, 60, 99,
132; CWW 2; EWL 3; MTCW 1, 2;
MTFW 2005; WLIT 6

Amichai, Yehudah
See Amichai, Yehuda

Amiel, Henri Frederic 1821-1881 .... **NCLC 4**
See also DLB 217

Amis, Kingsley (William)
1922-1995 ...... **CLC 1, 2, 3, 5, 8, 13, 40,**
44, 129
See also AITN 2; BPFB 1; BRWS 2; CA
9-12R; 150; CANR 8, 28, 54; CDBLB
1945-1960; CN 1, 2, 3, 4, 5, 6; CP 1, 2,
3, 4; DA; DA3; DAB; DAC; DAM MST,
NOV; DLB 15, 27, 100, 139; DLBY 1996;
EWL 3; HGG; INT CANR-8; MTCW 1,
2; MTFW 2005; RGEL 2; RGSF 2; SFW
4

Amis, Martin (Louis) 1949- .... **CLC 4, 9, 38,**
62, 101, 213
See also BEST 90:3; BRWS 4; CA 65-68;
CANR 8, 27, 54, 73, 95, 132; CN 5, 6, 7;
DA3; DLB 14, 194; EWL 3; INT CANR-
27; MTCW 2; MTFW 2005

Ammianus Marcellinus c. 330-c.
395 .... **CMLC 60**
See also AW 2; DLB 211

Ammons, A(rchie) R(andolph)
1926-2001 ...... **CLC 2, 3, 5, 8, 9, 25, 57,**
108; PC 16
See also AITN 1; AMWS 7; CA 9-12R;
193; CANR 6, 36, 51, 73, 107; CP 1, 2,
3, 4, 5, 6, 7; CSW; DAM POET; DLB 5,
165; EWL 3; MAL 5; MTCW 1, 2; PFS
19; RGAL 4; TCLE 1:1

Amo, Tauraatua i
See Adams, Henry (Brooks)

Amory, Thomas 1691(?)-1788 .... **LC 48**
See also DLB 39

Anand, Mulk Raj 1905-2004 ...... **CLC 23, 93**
See also CA 65-68; 231; CANR 32, 64; CN
1, 2, 3, 4, 5, 6, 7; DAM NOV; EWL 3;
MTCW 1, 2; MTFW 2005; RGSF 2

Anatol
See Schnitzler, Arthur

Anaximander c. 611B.C.-c.
546B.C. .... **CMLC 22**

Anaya, Rudolfo A(lfonso) 1937- ...... **CLC 23,**
148; HLC 1
See also AAYA 20; BYA 13; CA 45-48;
CAAS 4; CANR 1, 32, 51, 124; CN 4, 5,
6, 7; DAM MULT, NOV; DLB 82, 206,
278; HW 1; LAIT 4; LLW; MAL 5;
MTCW 1, 2; MTFW 2005; NFS 12;
RGAL 4; RGSF 2; TCWW 2; WLIT 1

Andersen, Hans Christian
1805-1875 .... **NCLC 7, 79; SSC 6, 56;**
WLC
See also AAYA 57; CLR 6; DA; DA3;
DAB; DAC; DAM MST, POP; EW 6;
MAICYA 1, 2; RGSF 2; RGWL 2, 3;
SATA 100; TWA; WCH; YABC 1

Anderson, C. Farley
See Mencken, H(enry) L(ouis); Nathan, George Jean

Anderson, Jessica (Margaret) Queale
1916- .... **CLC 37**
See also CA 9-12R; CANR 4, 62; CN 4, 5, 6, 7

Anderson, Jon (Victor) 1940- .... **CLC 9**
See also CA 25-28R; CANR 20; CP 1, 3, 4; DAM POET

Anderson, Lindsay (Gordon)
1923-1994 .... **CLC 20**
See also CA 125; 128; 146; CANR 77

Anderson, Maxwell 1888-1959 .... **TCLC 2, 144**
See also CA 105; 152; DAM DRAM; DFS 16, 20; DLB 7, 228; MAL 5; MTCW 2; MTFW 2005; RGAL 4

Anderson, Poul (William)
1926-2001 .... **CLC 15**
See also AAYA 5, 34; BPFB 1; BYA 6, 8, 9; CA 1-4R, 181; 199; CAAE 181; CAAS 2; CANR 2, 15, 34, 64, 110; CLR 58; DLB 8; FANT; INT CANR-15; MTCW 1, 2; MTFW 2005; SATA 90; SATA-Brief 39; SATA-Essay 106; SCFW 1, 2; SFW 4; SUFW 1, 2

Anderson, Robert (Woodruff)
1917- .... **CLC 23**
See also AITN 1; CA 21-24R; CANR 32; CD 6; DAM DRAM; DLB 7; LAIT 5

Anderson, Roberta Joan
See Mitchell, Joni

Anderson, Sherwood 1876-1941 .. **SSC 1, 46; TCLC 1, 10, 24, 123; WLC**
See also AAYA 30; AMW; AMWC 2; BPFB 1; CA 104; 121; CANR 61; CDALB 1917-1929; DA; DA3; DAB; DAC; DAM MST, NOV; DLB 4, 9, 86; DLBD 1; EWL 3; EXPS; GLL 2; MAL 5; MTCW 1, 2; MTFW 2005; NFS 4; RGAL 4; RGSF 2; SSFS 4, 10, 11; TUS

Andier, Pierre
See Desnos, Robert

Andouard
See Giraudoux, Jean(-Hippolyte)

Andrade, Carlos Drummond de ..... **CLC 18**
See Drummond de Andrade, Carlos
See also EWL 3; RGWL 2, 3

Andrade, Mario de .... **TCLC 43**
See de Andrade, Mario
See also DLB 307; EWL 3; LAW; RGWL 2, 3; WLIT 1

Andreae, Johann V(alentin)
1586-1654 .... **LC 32**
See also DLB 164

Andreas Capellanus fl. c. 1185- .... **CMLC 45**
See also DLB 208

Andreas-Salome, Lou 1861-1937 ... **TCLC 56**
See also CA 178; DLB 66

Andreev, Leonid
See Andreyev, Leonid (Nikolaevich)
See also DLB 295; EWL 3

Andress, Lesley
See Sanders, Lawrence

Andrewes, Lancelot 1555-1626 .... **LC 5**
See also DLB 151, 172

Andrews, Cicily Fairfield
See West, Rebecca

Andrews, Elton V.
See Pohl, Frederik

Andreyev, Leonid (Nikolaevich)
1871-1919 .... **TCLC 3**
See Andreev, Leonid
See also CA 104; 185

Andric, Ivo 1892-1975 .... **CLC 8; SSC 36; TCLC 135**
See also CA 81-84; 57-60; CANR 43, 60; CDWLB 4; DLB 147; EW 11; EWL 3; MTCW 1; RGSF 2; RGWL 2, 3

Androvar
See Prado (Calvo), Pedro

Angela of Foligno 1248(?)-1309 .... **CMLC 76**

Angelique, Pierre
See Bataille, Georges

Angell, Roger 1920- .... **CLC 26**
See also CA 57-60; CANR 13, 44, 70, 144; DLB 171, 185

Angelou, Maya 1928- ... **BLC 1; CLC 12, 35, 64, 77, 155; PC 32; WLCS**
See also AAYA 7, 20; AMWS 4; BPFB 1; BW 2, 3; BYA 2; CA 65-68; CANR 19, 42, 65, 111, 133; CDALBS; CLR 53; CP 4, 5, 6, 7; CPW; CSW; CWP; DA; DA3; DAB; DAC; DAM MST, MULT, POET, POP; DLB 38; EWL 3; EXPN; EXPP; FL 1:5; LAIT 4; MAICYA 2; MAICYAS 1; MAL 5; MAWW; MTCW 1, 2; MTFW 2005; NCFS 2; NFS 2; PFS 2, 3; RGAL 4; SATA 49, 136; TCLE 1:1; WYA; YAW

Angouleme, Marguerite d'
See de Navarre, Marguerite

Anna Comnena 1083-1153 .... **CMLC 25**

Annensky, Innokentii Fedorovich
See Annensky, Innokenty (Fyodorovich)
See also DLB 295

Annensky, Innokenty (Fyodorovich)
1856-1909 .... **TCLC 14**
See also CA 110; 155; EWL 3

Annunzio, Gabriele d'
See D'Annunzio, Gabriele

Anodos
See Coleridge, Mary E(lizabeth)

Anon, Charles Robert
See Pessoa, Fernando (Antonio Nogueira)

Anouilh, Jean (Marie Lucien Pierre)
1910-1987 . **CLC 1, 3, 8, 13, 40, 50; DC 8, 21**
See also AAYA 67; CA 17-20R; 123; CANR 32; DAM DRAM; DFS 9, 10, 19; DLB 321; EW 13; EWL 3; GFL 1789 to the Present; MTCW 1, 2; MTFW 2005; RGWL 2, 3; TWA

Anselm of Canterbury
1033(?)-1109 .... **CMLC 67**
See also DLB 115

Anthony, Florence
See Ai

Anthony, John
See Ciardi, John (Anthony)

Anthony, Peter
See Shaffer, Anthony (Joshua); Shaffer, Peter (Levin)

Anthony, Piers 1934- .... **CLC 35**
See also AAYA 11, 48; BYA 7; CA 200; CAAE 200; CANR 28, 56, 73, 102, 133; CPW; DAM POP; DLB 8; FANT; MAICYA 2; MAICYAS 1; MTCW 1, 2; MTFW 2005; SAAS 22; SATA 84, 129; SATA-Essay 129; SFW 4; SUFW 1, 2; YAW

Anthony, Susan B(rownell)
1820-1906 .... **TCLC 84**
See also CA 211; FW

Antiphon c. 480B.C.-c. 411B.C. .... **CMLC 55**

Antoine, Marc
See Proust, (Valentin-Louis-George-Eugene) Marcel

Antoninus, Brother
See Everson, William (Oliver)
See also CP 1

Antonioni, Michelangelo 1912- .... **CLC 20, 144**
See also CA 73-76; CANR 45, 77

Antschel, Paul 1920-1970
See Celan, Paul
See also CA 85-88; CANR 33, 61; MTCW 1; PFS 21

Anwar, Chairil 1922-1949 .... **TCLC 22**
See Chairil Anwar
See also CA 121; 219; RGWL 3

Anzaldua, Gloria (Evanjelina)
1942-2004 .... **CLC 200; HLCS 1**
See also CA 175; 227; CSW; CWP; DLB 122; FW; LLW; RGAL 4; SATA-Obit 154

Apess, William 1798-1839(?) .... **NCLC 73; NNAL**
See also DAM MULT; DLB 175, 243

Apollinaire, Guillaume 1880-1918 .... **PC 7; TCLC 3, 8, 51**
See Kostrowitzki, Wilhelm Apollinaris de
See also CA 152; DAM POET; DLB 258, 321; EW 9; EWL 3; GFL 1789 to the Present; MTCW 2; RGWL 2, 3; TWA; WP

Apollonius of Rhodes
See Apollonius Rhodius
See also AW 1; RGWL 2, 3

Apollonius Rhodius c. 300B.C.-c.
220B.C. .... **CMLC 28**
See Apollonius of Rhodes
See also DLB 176

Appelfeld, Aharon 1932- ... **CLC 23, 47; SSC 42**
See also CA 112; 133; CANR 86; CWW 2; DLB 299; EWL 3; RGSF 2; WLIT 6

Apple, Max (Isaac) 1941- .... **CLC 9, 33; SSC 50**
See also CA 81-84; CANR 19, 54; DLB 130

Appleman, Philip (Dean) 1926- .... **CLC 51**
See also CA 13-16R; CAAS 18; CANR 6, 29, 56

Appleton, Lawrence
See Lovecraft, H(oward) P(hillips)

Apteryx
See Eliot, T(homas) S(tearns)

Apuleius, (Lucius Madaurensis)
125(?)-175(?) .... **CMLC 1**
See also AW 2; CDWLB 1; DLB 211; RGWL 2, 3; SUFW

Aquin, Hubert 1929-1977 .... **CLC 15**
See also CA 105; DLB 53; EWL 3

Aquinas, Thomas 1224(?)-1274 ..... **CMLC 33**
See also DLB 115; EW 1; TWA

Aragon, Louis 1897-1982 .... **CLC 3, 22; TCLC 123**
See also CA 69-72; 108; CANR 28, 71; DAM NOV, POET; DLB 72, 258; EW 11; EWL 3; GFL 1789 to the Present; GLL 2; LMFS 2; MTCW 1, 2; RGWL 2, 3

Arany, Janos 1817-1882 .... **NCLC 34**

Aranyos, Kakay 1847-1910
See Mikszath, Kalman

Aratus of Soli c. 315B.C.-c.
240B.C. .... **CMLC 64**
See also DLB 176

Arbuthnot, John 1667-1735 .... **LC 1**
See also DLB 101

Archer, Herbert Winslow
See Mencken, H(enry) L(ouis)

Archer, Jeffrey (Howard) 1940- .... **CLC 28**
See also AAYA 16; BEST 89:3; BPFB 1; CA 77-80; CANR 22, 52, 95, 136; CPW; DA3; DAM POP; INT CANR-22; MTFW 2005

Archer, Jules 1915- .... **CLC 12**
See also CA 9-12R; CANR 6, 69; SAAS 5; SATA 4, 85

Archer, Lee
See Ellison, Harlan (Jay)

Archilochus c. 7th cent. B.C.- .... **CMLC 44**
See also DLB 176

Arden, John 1930- .... **CLC 6, 13, 15**
    See also BRWS 2; CA 13-16R; CAAS 4;
    CANR 31, 65, 67, 124; CBD; CD 5, 6;
    DAM DRAM; DFS 9; DLB 13, 245;
    EWL 3; MTCW 1

Arenas, Reinaldo 1943-1990 .. **CLC 41; HLC 1**
    See also CA 124; 128; 133; CANR 73, 106;
    DAM MULT; DLB 145; EWL 3; GLL 2;
    HW 1; LAW; LAWS 1; MTCW 2; MTFW
    2005; RGSF 2; RGWL 3; WLIT 1

Arendt, Hannah 1906-1975 .... **CLC 66, 98**
    See also CA 17-20R; 61-64; CANR 26, 60;
    DLB 242; MTCW 1, 2

Aretino, Pietro 1492-1556 .... **LC 12**
    See also RGWL 2, 3

Arghezi, Tudor .... **CLC 80**
    See Theodorescu, Ion N.
    See also CA 167; CDWLB 4; DLB 220;
    EWL 3

Arguedas, Jose Maria 1911-1969 .... **CLC 10, 18; HLCS 1; TCLC 147**
    See also CA 89-92; CANR 73; DLB 113;
    EWL 3; HW 1; LAW; RGWL 2, 3; WLIT 1

Argueta, Manlio 1936- .... **CLC 31**
    See also CA 131; CANR 73; CWW 2; DLB
    145; EWL 3; HW 1; RGWL 3

Arias, Ron(ald Francis) 1941- .... **HLC 1**
    See also CA 131; CANR 81, 136; DAM
    MULT; DLB 82; HW 1, 2; MTCW 2;
    MTFW 2005

Ariosto, Lodovico
    See Ariosto, Ludovico
    See also WLIT 7

Ariosto, Ludovico 1474-1533 ... **LC 6, 87; PC 42**
    See Ariosto, Lodovico
    See also EW 2; RGWL 2, 3

Aristides
    See Epstein, Joseph

Aristophanes 450B.C.-385B.C. .... **CMLC 4, 51; DC 2; WLCS**
    See also AW 1; CDWLB 1; DA; DA3;
    DAB; DAC; DAM DRAM, MST; DFS
    10; DLB 176; LMFS 1; RGWL 2, 3; TWA

Aristotle 384B.C.-322B.C. .... **CMLC 31; WLCS**
    See also AW 1; CDWLB 1; DA; DA3;
    DAB; DAC; DAM MST; DLB 176;
    RGWL 2, 3; TWA

Arlt, Roberto (Godofredo Christophersen)
    1900-1942 .... **HLC 1; TCLC 29**
    See also CA 123; 131; CANR 67; DAM
    MULT; DLB 305; EWL 3; HW 1, 2;
    IDTP; LAW

Armah, Ayi Kwei 1939- . **BLC 1; CLC 5, 33, 136**
    See also AFW; BRWS 10; BW 1; CA 61-
    64; CANR 21, 64; CDWLB 3; CN 1, 2,
    3, 4, 5, 6, 7; DAM MULT, POET; DLB
    117; EWL 3; MTCW 1; WLIT 2

Armatrading, Joan 1950- .... **CLC 17**
    See also CA 114; 186

Armitage, Frank
    See Carpenter, John (Howard)

Armstrong, Jeannette (C.) 1948- .... **NNAL**
    See also CA 149; CCA 1; CN 6, 7; DAC;
    SATA 102

Arnette, Robert
    See Silverberg, Robert

Arnim, Achim von (Ludwig Joachim von Arnim) 1781-1831 .. **NCLC 5, 159; SSC 29**
    See also DLB 90

Arnim, Bettina von 1785-1859 ...... **NCLC 38, 123**
    See also DLB 90; RGWL 2, 3

Arnold, Matthew 1822-1888 ..... **NCLC 6, 29, 89, 126; PC 5; WLC**
    See also BRW 5; CDBLB 1832-1890; DA;
    DAB; DAC; DAM MST, POET; DLB 32,
    57; EXPP; PAB; PFS 2; TEA; WP

Arnold, Thomas 1795-1842 .... **NCLC 18**
    See also DLB 55

Arnow, Harriette (Louisa) Simpson
    1908-1986 .... **CLC 2, 7, 18**
    See also BPFB 1; CA 9-12R; 118; CANR
    14; CN 2, 3, 4; DLB 6; FW; MTCW 1, 2;
    RHW; SATA 42; SATA-Obit 47

Arouet, Francois-Marie
    See Voltaire

Arp, Hans
    See Arp, Jean

Arp, Jean 1887-1966 .... **CLC 5; TCLC 115**
    See also CA 81-84; 25-28R; CANR 42, 77;
    EW 10

Arrabal
    See Arrabal, Fernando

Arrabal (Teran), Fernando
    See Arrabal, Fernando
    See also CWW 2

Arrabal, Fernando 1932- ... **CLC 2, 9, 18, 58**
    See Arrabal (Teran), Fernando
    See also CA 9-12R; CANR 15; DLB 321;
    EWL 3; LMFS 2

Arreola, Juan Jose 1918-2001 .... **CLC 147; HLC 1; SSC 38**
    See also CA 113; 131; 200; CANR 81;
    CWW 2; DAM MULT; DLB 113; DNFS
    2; EWL 3; HW 1, 2; LAW; RGSF 2

Arrian c. 89(?)-c. 155(?) .... **CMLC 43**
    See also DLB 176

Arrick, Fran .... **CLC 30**
    See Gaberman, Judie Angell
    See also BYA 6

Arrley, Richmond
    See Delany, Samuel R(ay), Jr.

Artaud, Antonin (Marie Joseph)
    1896-1948 .... **DC 14; TCLC 3, 36**
    See also CA 104; 149; DA3; DAM DRAM;
    DFS 22; DLB 258, 321; EW 11; EWL 3;
    GFL 1789 to the Present; MTCW 2;
    MTFW 2005; RGWL 2, 3

Arthur, Ruth M(abel) 1905-1979 ..... **CLC 12**
    See also CA 9-12R; 85-88; CANR 4; CWRI
    5; SATA 7, 26

Artsybashev, Mikhail (Petrovich)
    1878-1927 .... **TCLC 31**
    See also CA 170; DLB 295

Arundel, Honor (Morfydd)
    1919-1973 .... **CLC 17**
    See also CA 21-22; 41-44R; CAP 2; CLR
    35; CWRI 5; SATA 4; SATA-Obit 24

Arzner, Dorothy 1900-1979 .... **CLC 98**

Asch, Sholem 1880-1957 .... **TCLC 3**
    See also CA 105; EWL 3; GLL 2

Ascham, Roger 1516(?)-1568 .... **LC 101**
    See also DLB 236

Ash, Shalom
    See Asch, Sholem

Ashbery, John (Lawrence) 1927- .. **CLC 2, 3, 4, 6, 9, 13, 15, 25, 41, 77, 125, 221; PC 26**
    See Berry, Jonas
    See also AMWS 3; CA 5-8R; CANR 9, 37,
    66, 102, 132; CP 1, 2, 3, 4, 5, 6, 7; DA3;
    DAM POET; DLB 5, 165; DLBY 1981;
    EWL 3; INT CANR-9; MAL 5; MTCW
    1, 2; MTFW 2005; PAB; PFS 11; RGAL
    4; TCLE 1:1; WP

Ashdown, Clifford
    See Freeman, R(ichard) Austin

Ashe, Gordon
    See Creasey, John

Ashton-Warner, Sylvia (Constance)
    1908-1984 .... **CLC 19**
    See also CA 69-72; 112; CANR 29; CN 1,
    2, 3; MTCW 1, 2

Asimov, Isaac 1920-1992 ..... **CLC 1, 3, 9, 19, 26, 76, 92**
    See also AAYA 13; BEST 90:2; BPFB 1;
    BYA 4, 6, 7, 9; CA 1-4R; 137; CANR 2,
    19, 36, 60, 125; CLR 12, 79; CMW 4;
    CN 1, 2, 3, 4, 5; CPW; DA3; DAM POP;
    DLB 8; DLBY 1992; INT CANR-19;
    JRDA; LAIT 5; LMFS 2; MAICYA 1, 2;
    MAL 5; MTCW 1, 2; MTFW 2005;
    RGAL 4; SATA 1, 26, 74; SCFW 1, 2;
    SFW 4; SSFS 17; TUS; YAW

Askew, Anne 1521(?)-1546 .... **LC 81**
    See also DLB 136

Assis, Joaquim Maria Machado de
    See Machado de Assis, Joaquim Maria

Astell, Mary 1666-1731 .... **LC 68**
    See also DLB 252; FW

Astley, Thea (Beatrice May)
    1925-2004 .... **CLC 41**
    See also CA 65-68; 229; CANR 11, 43, 78;
    CN 1, 2, 3, 4, 5, 6, 7; DLB 289; EWL 3

Astley, William 1855-1911
    See Warung, Price

Aston, James
    See White, T(erence) H(anbury)

Asturias, Miguel Angel 1899-1974 .... **CLC 3, 8, 13; HLC 1**
    See also CA 25-28; 49-52; CANR 32; CAP
    2; CDWLB 3; DA3; DAM MULT, NOV;
    DLB 113, 290; EWL 3; HW 1; LAW;
    LMFS 2; MTCW 1, 2; RGWL 2, 3; WLIT 1

Atares, Carlos Saura
    See Saura (Atares), Carlos

Athanasius c. 295-c. 373 .... **CMLC 48**

Atheling, William
    See Pound, Ezra (Weston Loomis)

Atheling, William, Jr.
    See Blish, James (Benjamin)

Atherton, Gertrude (Franklin Horn)
    1857-1948 .... **TCLC 2**
    See also CA 104; 155; DLB 9, 78, 186;
    HGG; RGAL 4; SUFW 1; TCWW 1, 2

Atherton, Lucius
    See Masters, Edgar Lee

Atkins, Jack
    See Harris, Mark

Atkinson, Kate 1951- .... **CLC 99**
    See also CA 166; CANR 101; DLB 267

Attaway, William (Alexander)
    1911-1986 .... **BLC 1; CLC 92**
    See also BW 2, 3; CA 143; CANR 82;
    DAM MULT; DLB 76; MAL 5

Atticus
    See Fleming, Ian (Lancaster); Wilson,
    (Thomas) Woodrow

Atwood, Margaret (Eleanor) 1939- ... **CLC 2, 3, 4, 8, 13, 15, 25, 44, 84, 135; PC 8; SSC 2, 46; WLC**
    See also AAYA 12, 47; AMWS 13; BEST
    89:2; BPFB 1; CA 49-52; CANR 3, 24,
    33, 59, 95, 133; CN 2, 3, 4, 5, 6, 7; CP 1,
    2, 3, 4, 5, 6, 7; CPW; CWP; DA; DA3;
    DAB; DAC; DAM MST, NOV, POET;
    DLB 53, 251; EWL 3; EXPN; FL 1:5;
    FW; GL 2; INT CANR-24; LAIT 5;
    MTCW 1, 2; MTFW 2005; NFS 4, 12,
    13, 14, 19; PFS 7; RGSF 2; SATA 50;
    SSFS 3, 13; TCLE 1:1; TWA; WWE 1;
    YAW

Aubigny, Pierre d'
    See Mencken, H(enry) L(ouis)

Aubin, Penelope 1685-1731(?) .... **LC 9**
    See also DLB 39

MTFW 2005; NCFS 4; NFS 4; RGAL 4; RGSF 2; SATA 9; SATA-Obit 54; SSFS 2, 18; TUS

Baldwin, William c. 1515-1563 .... **LC 113**
See also DLB 132

Bale, John 1495-1563 .... **LC 62**
See also DLB 132; RGEL 2; TEA

Ball, Hugo 1886-1927 .... **TCLC 104**

Ballard, J(ames) G(raham) 1930- . **CLC 3, 6, 14, 36, 137; SSC 1, 53**
See also AAYA 3, 52; BRWS 5; CA 5-8R; CANR 15, 39, 65, 107, 133; CN 1, 2, 3, 4, 5, 6, 7; DA3; DAM NOV, POP; DLB 14, 207, 261, 319; EWL 3; HGG; MTCW 1, 2; MTFW 2005; NFS 8; RGEL 2; RGSF 2; SATA 93; SCFW 1, 2; SFW 4

Balmont, Konstantin (Dmitriyevich) 1867-1943 .... **TCLC 11**
See also CA 109; 155; DLB 295; EWL 3

Baltausis, Vincas 1847-1910
See Mikszath, Kalman

Balzac, Honore de 1799-1850 ... **NCLC 5, 35, 53, 153; SSC 5, 59; WLC**
See also DA; DA3; DAB; DAC; DAM MST, NOV; DLB 119; EW 5; GFL 1789 to the Present; LMFS 1; RGSF 2; RGWL 2, 3; SSFS 10; SUFW; TWA

Bambara, Toni Cade 1939-1995 .... **BLC 1; CLC 19, 88; SSC 35; TCLC 116; WLCS**
See also AAYA 5, 49; AFAW 2; AMWS 11; BW 2, 3; BYA 12, 14; CA 29-32R; 150; CANR 24, 49, 81; CDALBS; DA; DA3; DAC; DAM MST, MULT; DLB 38, 218; EXPS; MAL 5; MTCW 1, 2; MTFW 2005; RGAL 4; RGSF 2; SATA 112; SSFS 4, 7, 12, 21

Bamdad, A.
See Shamlu, Ahmad

Bamdad, Alef
See Shamlu, Ahmad

Banat, D. R.
See Bradbury, Ray (Douglas)

Bancroft, Laura
See Baum, L(yman) Frank

Banim, John 1798-1842 .... **NCLC 13**
See also DLB 116, 158, 159; RGEL 2

Banim, Michael 1796-1874 .... **NCLC 13**
See also DLB 158, 159

Banjo, The
See Paterson, A(ndrew) B(arton)

Banks, Iain
See Banks, Iain M(enzies)
See also BRWS 11

Banks, Iain M(enzies) 1954- .... **CLC 34**
See Banks, Iain
See also CA 123; 128; CANR 61, 106; DLB 194, 261; EWL 3; HGG; INT CA-128; MTFW 2005; SFW 4

Banks, Lynne Reid .... **CLC 23**
See Reid Banks, Lynne
See also AAYA 6; BYA 7; CLR 86; CN 4, 5, 6

Banks, Russell (Earl) 1940- .... **CLC 37, 72, 187; SSC 42**
See also AAYA 45; AMWS 5; CA 65-68; CAAS 15; CANR 19, 52, 73, 118; CN 4, 5, 6, 7; DLB 130, 278; EWL 3; MAL 5; MTCW 2; MTFW 2005; NFS 13

Banville, John 1945- .... **CLC 46, 118**
See also CA 117; 128; CANR 104; CN 4, 5, 6, 7; DLB 14, 271; INT CA-128

Banville, Theodore (Faullain) de 1832-1891 .... **NCLC 9**
See also DLB 217; GFL 1789 to the Present

Baraka, Amiri 1934- .... **BLC 1; CLC 1, 2, 3, 5, 10, 14, 33, 115, 213; DC 6; PC 4; WLCS**
See Jones, LeRoi
See also AAYA 63; AFAW 1, 2; AMWS 2; BW 2, 3; CA 21-24R; CABS 3; CAD; CANR 27, 38, 61, 133; CD 3, 5, 6; CDALB 1941-1968; CP 4, 5, 6, 7; CPW; DA; DA3; DAC; DAM MST, MULT, POET, POP; DFS 3, 11, 16; DLB 5, 7, 16, 38; DLBD 8; EWL 3; MAL 5; MTCW 1, 2; MTFW 2005; PFS 9; RGAL 4; TCLE 1:1; TUS; WP

Baratynsky, Evgenii Abramovich 1800-1844 .... **NCLC 103**
See also DLB 205

Barbauld, Anna Laetitia 1743-1825 .... **NCLC 50**
See also DLB 107, 109, 142, 158; RGEL 2

Barbellion, W. N. P. .... **TCLC 24**
See Cummings, Bruce F(rederick)

Barber, Benjamin R. 1939- .... **CLC 141**
See also CA 29-32R; CANR 12, 32, 64, 119

Barbera, Jack (Vincent) 1945- .... **CLC 44**
See also CA 110; CANR 45

Barbey d'Aurevilly, Jules-Amedee 1808-1889 .... **NCLC 1; SSC 17**
See also DLB 119; GFL 1789 to the Present

Barbour, John c. 1316-1395 .... **CMLC 33**
See also DLB 146

Barbusse, Henri 1873-1935 .... **TCLC 5**
See also CA 105; 154; DLB 65; EWL 3; RGWL 2, 3

Barclay, Alexander c. 1475-1552 .... **LC 109**
See also DLB 132

Barclay, Bill
See Moorcock, Michael (John)

Barclay, William Ewert
See Moorcock, Michael (John)

Barea, Arturo 1897-1957 .... **TCLC 14**
See also CA 111; 201

Barfoot, Joan 1946- .... **CLC 18**
See also CA 105; CANR 141

Barham, Richard Harris 1788-1845 .... **NCLC 77**
See also DLB 159

Baring, Maurice 1874-1945 .... **TCLC 8**
See also CA 105; 168; DLB 34; HGG

Baring-Gould, Sabine 1834-1924 ... **TCLC 88**
See also DLB 156, 190

Barker, Clive 1952- .... **CLC 52, 205; SSC 53**
See also AAYA 10, 54; BEST 90:3; BPFB 1; CA 121; 129; CANR 71, 111, 133; CPW; DA3; DAM POP; DLB 261; HGG; INT CA-129; MTCW 1, 2; MTFW 2005; SUFW 2

Barker, George Granville 1913-1991 .... **CLC 8, 48**
See also CA 9-12R; 135; CANR 7, 38; CP 1, 2, 3, 4; DAM POET; DLB 20; EWL 3; MTCW 1

Barker, Harley Granville
See Granville-Barker, Harley
See also DLB 10

Barker, Howard 1946- .... **CLC 37**
See also CA 102; CBD; CD 5, 6; DLB 13, 233

Barker, Jane 1652-1732 .... **LC 42, 82**
See also DLB 39, 131

Barker, Pat(ricia) 1943- ...... **CLC 32, 94, 146**
See also BRWS 4; CA 117; 122; CANR 50, 101; CN 6, 7; DLB 271; INT CA-122

Barlach, Ernst (Heinrich) 1870-1938 .... **TCLC 84**
See also CA 178; DLB 56, 118; EWL 3

Barlow, Joel 1754-1812 .... **NCLC 23**
See also AMWS 2; DLB 37; RGAL 4

Barnard, Mary (Ethel) 1909- .... **CLC 48**
See also CA 21-22; CAP 2; CP 1

Barnes, Djuna 1892-1982 .... **CLC 3, 4, 8, 11, 29, 127; SSC 3**
See Steptoe, Lydia
See also AMWS 3; CA 9-12R; 107; CAD; CANR 16, 55; CN 1, 2, 3; CWD; DLB 4, 9, 45; EWL 3; GLL 1; MAL 5; MTCW 1, 2; MTFW 2005; RGAL 4; TCLE 1:1; TUS

Barnes, Jim 1933- .... **NNAL**
See also CA 108; 175; CAAE 175; CAAS 28; DLB 175

Barnes, Julian (Patrick) 1946- . **CLC 42, 141**
See also BRWS 4; CA 102; CANR 19, 54, 115, 137; CN 4, 5, 6, 7; DAB; DLB 194; DLBY 1993; EWL 3; MTCW 2; MTFW 2005

Barnes, Peter 1931-2004 .... **CLC 5, 56**
See also CA 65-68; 230; CAAS 12; CANR 33, 34, 64, 113; CBD; CD 5, 6; DFS 6; DLB 13, 233; MTCW 1

Barnes, William 1801-1886 .... **NCLC 75**
See also DLB 32

Baroja (y Nessi), Pio 1872-1956 .... **HLC 1; TCLC 8**
See also CA 104; EW 9

Baron, David
See Pinter, Harold

Baron Corvo
See Rolfe, Frederick (William Serafino Austin Lewis Mary)

Barondess, Sue K(aufman) 1926-1977 .... **CLC 8**
See Kaufman, Sue
See also CA 1-4R; 69-72; CANR 1

Baron de Teive
See Pessoa, Fernando (Antonio Nogueira)

Baroness Von S.
See Zangwill, Israel

Barres, (Auguste-)Maurice 1862-1923 .... **TCLC 47**
See also CA 164; DLB 123; GFL 1789 to the Present

Barreto, Afonso Henrique de Lima
See Lima Barreto, Afonso Henrique de

Barrett, Andrea 1954- .... **CLC 150**
See also CA 156; CANR 92; CN 7

Barrett, Michele .... **CLC 65**

Barrett, (Roger) Syd 1946- .... **CLC 35**

Barrett, William (Christopher) 1913-1992 .... **CLC 27**
See also CA 13-16R; 139; CANR 11, 67; INT CANR-11

Barrett Browning, Elizabeth 1806-1861 ... **NCLC 1, 16, 61, 66; PC 6, 62; WLC**
See also AAYA 63; BRW 4; CDBLB 1832-1890; DA; DA3; DAB; DAC; DAM MST, POET; DLB 32, 199; EXPP; FL 1:2; PAB; PFS 2, 16, 23; TEA; WLIT 4; WP

Barrie, J(ames) M(atthew) 1860-1937 .... **TCLC 2, 164**
See also BRWS 3; BYA 4, 5; CA 104; 136; CANR 77; CDBLB 1890-1914; CLR 16; CWRI 5; DA3; DAB; DAM DRAM; DFS 7; DLB 10, 141, 156; EWL 3; FANT; MAICYA 1, 2; MTCW 2; MTFW 2005; SATA 100; SUFW; WCH; WLIT 4; YABC 1

Barrington, Michael
See Moorcock, Michael (John)

Barrol, Grady
See Bograd, Larry

Barry, Mike
See Malzberg, Barry N(athaniel)

Barry, Philip 1896-1949 .... **TCLC 11**
See also CA 109; 199; DFS 9; DLB 7, 228; MAL 5; RGAL 4

Bart, Andre Schwarz
See Schwarz-Bart, Andre

Barth, John (Simmons) 1930- ... CLC 1, 2, 3, 5, 7, 9, 10, 14, 27, 51, 89, 214; SSC 10, 89
  See also AITN 1, 2; AMW; BPFB 1; CA 1-4R; CABS 1; CANR 5, 23, 49, 64, 113; CN 1, 2, 3, 4, 5, 6, 7; DAM NOV; DLB 2, 227; EWL 3; FANT; MAL 5; MTCW 1; RGAL 4; RGSF 2; RHW; SSFS 6; TUS

Barthelme, Donald 1931-1989 ... CLC 1, 2, 3, 5, 6, 8, 13, 23, 46, 59, 115; SSC 2, 55
  See also AMWS 4; BPFB 1; CA 21-24R; 129; CANR 20, 58; CN 1, 2, 3, 4; DA3; DAM NOV; DLB 2, 234; DLBY 1980, 1989; EWL 3; FANT; LMFS 2; MAL 5; MTCW 1, 2; MTFW 2005; RGAL 4; RGSF 2; SATA 7; SATA-Obit 62; SSFS 17

Barthelme, Frederick 1943- ...... CLC 36, 117
  See also AMWS 11; CA 114; 122; CANR 77; CN 4, 5, 6, 7; CSW; DLB 244; DLBY 1985; EWL 3; INT CA-122

Barthes, Roland (Gerard) 1915-1980 .... CLC 24, 83; TCLC 135
  See also CA 130; 97-100; CANR 66; DLB 296; EW 13; EWL 3; GFL 1789 to the Present; MTCW 1, 2; TWA

Bartram, William 1739-1823 .... NCLC 145
  See also ANW; DLB 37

Barzun, Jacques (Martin) 1907- ..... CLC 51, 145
  See also CA 61-64; CANR 22, 95

Bashevis, Isaac
  See Singer, Isaac Bashevis

Bashkirtseff, Marie 1859-1884 .... NCLC 27

Basho, Matsuo
  See Matsuo Basho
  See also RGWL 2, 3; WP

Basil of Caesaria c. 330-379 .... CMLC 35

Basket, Raney
  See Edgerton, Clyde (Carlyle)

Bass, Kingsley B., Jr.
  See Bullins, Ed

Bass, Rick 1958- .... CLC 79, 143; SSC 60
  See also ANW; CA 126; CANR 53, 93, 145; CSW; DLB 212, 275

Bassani, Giorgio 1916-2000 .... CLC 9
  See also CA 65-68; 190; CANR 33; CWW 2; DLB 128, 177, 299; EWL 3; MTCW 1; RGWL 2, 3

Bastian, Ann .... CLC 70

Bastos, Augusto (Antonio) Roa
  See Roa Bastos, Augusto (Jose Antonio)

Bataille, Georges 1897-1962 .... CLC 29; TCLC 155
  See also CA 101; 89-92; EWL 3

Bates, H(erbert) E(rnest) 1905-1974 .... CLC 46; SSC 10
  See also CA 93-96; 45-48; CANR 34; CN 1; DA3; DAB; DAM POP; DLB 162, 191; EWL 3; EXPS; MTCW 1, 2; RGSF 2; SSFS 7

Bauchart
  See Camus, Albert

Baudelaire, Charles 1821-1867 . NCLC 6, 29, 55, 155; PC 1; SSC 18; WLC
  See also DA; DA3; DAB; DAC; DAM MST, POET; DLB 217; EW 7; GFL 1789 to the Present; LMFS 2; PFS 21; RGWL 2, 3; TWA

Baudouin, Marcel
  See Peguy, Charles (Pierre)

Baudouin, Pierre
  See Peguy, Charles (Pierre)

Baudrillard, Jean 1929- .... CLC 60
  See also DLB 296

Baum, L(yman) Frank 1856-1919 .. TCLC 7, 132
  See also AAYA 46; BYA 16; CA 108; 133; CLR 15; CWRI 5; DLB 22; FANT; JRDA;

MAICYA 1, 2; MTCW 1, 2; NFS 13; RGAL 4; SATA 18, 100; WCH

Baum, Louis F.
  See Baum, L(yman) Frank

Baumbach, Jonathan 1933- .... CLC 6, 23
  See also CA 13-16R; CAAS 5; CANR 12, 66, 140; CN 3, 4, 5, 6, 7; DLBY 1980; INT CANR-12; MTCW 1

Bausch, Richard (Carl) 1945- .... CLC 51
  See also AMWS 7; CA 101; CAAS 14; CANR 43, 61, 87; CN 7; CSW; DLB 130; MAL 5

Baxter, Charles (Morley) 1947- . CLC 45, 78
  See also CA 57-60; CANR 40, 64, 104, 133; CPW; DAM POP; DLB 130; MAL 5; MTCW 2; MTFW 2005; TCLE 1:1

Baxter, George Owen
  See Faust, Frederick (Schiller)

Baxter, James K(eir) 1926-1972 .... CLC 14
  See also CA 77-80; CP 1; EWL 3

Baxter, John
  See Hunt, E(verette) Howard, (Jr.)

Bayer, Sylvia
  See Glassco, John

Bayle, Pierre 1647-1706 .... LC 126
  See also DLB 268, 313; GFL Beginnings to 1789

Baynton, Barbara 1857-1929 .... TCLC 57
  See also DLB 230; RGSF 2

Beagle, Peter S(oyer) 1939- .... CLC 7, 104
  See also AAYA 47; BPFB 1; BYA 9, 10, 16; CA 9-12R; CANR 4, 51, 73, 110; DA3; DLBY 1980; FANT; INT CANR-4; MTCW 2; MTFW 2005; SATA 60, 130; SUFW 1, 2; YAW

Bean, Normal
  See Burroughs, Edgar Rice

Beard, Charles A(ustin) 1874-1948 .... TCLC 15
  See also CA 115; 189; DLB 17; SATA 18

Beardsley, Aubrey 1872-1898 .... NCLC 6

Beattie, Ann 1947- ..... CLC 8, 13, 18, 40, 63, 146; SSC 11
  See also AMWS 5; BEST 90:2; BPFB 1; CA 81-84; CANR 53, 73, 128; CN 4, 5, 6, 7; CPW; DA3; DAM NOV, POP; DLB 218, 278; DLBY 1982; EWL 3; MAL 5; MTCW 1, 2; MTFW 2005; RGAL 4; RGSF 2; SSFS 9; TUS

Beattie, James 1735-1803 .... NCLC 25
  See also DLB 109

Beauchamp, Kathleen Mansfield 1888-1923
  See Mansfield, Katherine
  See also CA 104; 134; DA; DA3; DAC; DAM MST; MTCW 2; TEA

Beaumarchais, Pierre-Augustin Caron de 1732-1799 .... DC 4; LC 61
  See also DAM DRAM; DFS 14, 16; DLB 313; EW 4; GFL Beginnings to 1789; RGWL 2, 3

Beaumont, Francis 1584(?)-1616 .. DC 6; LC 33
  See also BRW 2; CDBLB Before 1660; DLB 58; TEA

Beauvoir, Simone (Lucie Ernestine Marie Bertrand) de 1908-1986 .... CLC 1, 2, 4, 8, 14, 31, 44, 50, 71, 124; SSC 35; WLC
  See also BPFB 1; CA 9-12R; 118; CANR 28, 61; DA; DA3; DAB; DAC; DAM MST, NOV; DLB 72; DLBY 1986; EW 12; EWL 3; FL 1:5; FW; GFL 1789 to the Present; LMFS 2; MTCW 1, 2; MTFW 2005; RGSF 2; RGWL 2, 3; TWA

Becker, Carl (Lotus) 1873-1945 ..... TCLC 63
  See also CA 157; DLB 17

Becker, Jurek 1937-1997 .... CLC 7, 19
  See also CA 85-88; 157; CANR 60, 117; CWW 2; DLB 75, 299; EWL 3

Becker, Walter 1950- .... CLC 26

Beckett, Samuel (Barclay) 1906-1989 .. CLC 1, 2, 3, 4, 6, 9, 10, 11, 14, 18, 29, 57, 59, 83; DC 22; SSC 16, 74; TCLC 145; WLC
  See also BRWC 2; BRWR 1; BRWS 1; CA 5-8R; 130; CANR 33, 61; CBD; CDBLB 1945-1960; CN 1, 2, 3, 4; CP 1, 2, 3, 4; DA; DA3; DAB; DAC; DAM DRAM, MST, NOV; DFS 2, 7, 18; DLB 13, 15, 233, 319, 321; DLBY 1990; EWL 3; GFL 1789 to the Present; LATS 1:2; LMFS 2; MTCW 1, 2; MTFW 2005; RGSF 2; RGWL 2, 3; SSFS 15; TEA; WLIT 4

Beckford, William 1760-1844 .... NCLC 16
  See also BRW 3; DLB 39, 213; GL 2; HGG; LMFS 1; SUFW

Beckham, Barry (Earl) 1944- .... BLC 1
  See also BW 1; CA 29-32R; CANR 26, 62; CN 1, 2, 3, 4, 5, 6; DAM MULT; DLB 33

Beckman, Gunnel 1910- .... CLC 26
  See also CA 33-36R; CANR 15, 114; CLR 25; MAICYA 1, 2; SAAS 9; SATA 6

Becque, Henri 1837-1899 .... DC 21; NCLC 3
  See also DLB 192; GFL 1789 to the Present

Becquer, Gustavo Adolfo 1836-1870 .... HLCS 1; NCLC 106
  See also DAM MULT

Beddoes, Thomas Lovell 1803-1849 .. DC 15; NCLC 3, 154
  See also BRWS 11; DLB 96

Bede c. 673-735 .... CMLC 20
  See also DLB 146; TEA

Bedford, Denton R. 1907-(?) .... NNAL

Bedford, Donald F.
  See Fearing, Kenneth (Flexner)

Beecher, Catharine Esther 1800-1878 .... NCLC 30
  See also DLB 1, 243

Beecher, John 1904-1980 .... CLC 6
  See also AITN 1; CA 5-8R; 105; CANR 8; CP 1, 2, 3

Beer, Johann 1655-1700 .... LC 5
  See also DLB 168

Beer, Patricia 1924- .... CLC 58
  See also CA 61-64; 183; CANR 13, 46; CP 1, 2, 3, 4; CWP; DLB 40; FW

Beerbohm, Max
  See Beerbohm, (Henry) Max(imilian)

Beerbohm, (Henry) Max(imilian) 1872-1956 .... TCLC 1, 24
  See also BRWS 2; CA 104; 154; CANR 79; DLB 34, 100; FANT; MTCW 2

Beer-Hofmann, Richard 1866-1945 .... TCLC 60
  See also CA 160; DLB 81

Beg, Shemus
  See Stephens, James

Begiebing, Robert J(ohn) 1946- .... CLC 70
  See also CA 122; CANR 40, 88

Begley, Louis 1933- .... CLC 197
  See also CA 140; CANR 98; DLB 299; TCLE 1:1

Behan, Brendan (Francis) 1923-1964 .... CLC 1, 8, 11, 15, 79
  See also BRWS 2; CA 73-76; CANR 33, 121; CBD; CDBLB 1945-1960; DAM DRAM; DFS 7; DLB 13, 233; EWL 3; MTCW 1, 2

Behn, Aphra 1640(?)-1689 .. DC 4; LC 1, 30, 42; PC 13; WLC
  See also BRWS 3; DA; DA3; DAB; DAC; DAM DRAM, MST, NOV, POET; DFS 16; DLB 39, 80, 131; FW; TEA; WLIT 3

Behrman, S(amuel) N(athaniel) 1893-1973 .... CLC 40
  See also CA 13-16; 45-48; CAD; CAP 1; DLB 7, 44; IDFW 3; MAL 5; RGAL 4

Bekederemo, J. P. Clark
See Clark Bekederemo, J(ohnson) P(epper)
See also CD 6

Belasco, David 1853-1931 .... **TCLC 3**
See also CA 104; 168; DLB 7; MAL 5;
RGAL 4

Belcheva, Elisaveta Lyubomirova
1893-1991 .... **CLC 10**
See Bagryana, Elisaveta

Beldone, Phil "Cheech"
See Ellison, Harlan (Jay)

Beleno
See Azuela, Mariano

Belinski, Vissarion Grigoryevich
1811-1848 .... **NCLC 5**
See also DLB 198

Belitt, Ben 1911- .... **CLC 22**
See also CA 13-16R; CAAS 4; CANR 7,
77; CP 1, 2, 3, 4; DLB 5

Belknap, Jeremy 1744-1798 .... **LC 115**
See also DLB 30, 37

Bell, Gertrude (Margaret Lowthian)
1868-1926 .... **TCLC 67**
See also CA 167; CANR 110; DLB 174

Bell, J. Freeman
See Zangwill, Israel

Bell, James Madison 1826-1902 .... **BLC 1;**
TCLC 43
See also BW 1; CA 122; 124; DAM MULT;
DLB 50

Bell, Madison Smartt 1957- ...... **CLC 41, 102**
See also AMWS 10; BPFB 1; CA 111, 183;
CAAE 183; CANR 28, 54, 73, 134; CN
5, 6, 7; CSW; DLB 218, 278; MTCW 2;
MTFW 2005

Bell, Marvin (Hartley) 1937- .... **CLC 8, 31**
See also CA 21-24R; CAAS 14; CANR 59,
102; CP 1, 2, 3, 4, 5, 6, 7; DAM POET;
DLB 5; MAL 5; MTCW 1

Bell, W. L. D.
See Mencken, H(enry) L(ouis)

Bellamy, Atwood C.
See Mencken, H(enry) L(ouis)

Bellamy, Edward 1850-1898 ..... **NCLC 4, 86,**
147
See also DLB 12; NFS 15; RGAL 4; SFW
4

Belli, Gioconda 1948- .... **HLCS 1**
See also CA 152; CANR 143; CWW 2;
DLB 290; EWL 3; RGWL 3

Bellin, Edward J.
See Kuttner, Henry

Bello, Andres 1781-1865 .... **NCLC 131**
See also LAW

**Belloc, (Joseph) Hilaire (Pierre Sebastien
Rene Swanton)** 1870-1953 .... **PC 24;**
TCLC 7, 18
See also CA 106; 152; CLR 102; CWRI 5;
DAM POET; DLB 19, 100, 141, 174;
EWL 3; MTCW 2; MTFW 2005; SATA
112; WCH; YABC 1

Belloc, Joseph Peter Rene Hilaire
See Belloc, (Joseph) Hilaire (Pierre Sebastien Rene Swanton)

Belloc, Joseph Pierre Hilaire
See Belloc, (Joseph) Hilaire (Pierre Sebastien Rene Swanton)

Belloc, M. A.
See Lowndes, Marie Adelaide (Belloc)

Belloc-Lowndes, Mrs.
See Lowndes, Marie Adelaide (Belloc)

Bellow, Saul 1915-2005 ...... **CLC 1, 2, 3, 6, 8,**
10, 13, 15, 25, 33, 34, 63, 79, 190, 200;
SSC 14; WLC
See also AITN 2; AMW; AMWC 2; AMWR
2; BEST 89:3; BPFB 1; CA 5-8R; 238;
CABS 1; CANR 29, 53, 95, 132; CDALB
1941-1968; CN 1, 2, 3, 4, 5, 6, 7; DA;
DA3; DAB; DAC; DAM MST, NOV,

POP; DLB 2, 28, 299; DLBD 3; DLBY
1982; EWL 3; MAL 5; MTCW 1, 2;
MTFW 2005; NFS 4, 14; RGAL 4; RGSF
2; SSFS 12; TUS

Belser, Reimond Karel Maria de 1929-
See Ruyslinck, Ward
See also CA 152

Bely, Andrey .... **PC 11; TCLC 7**
See Bugayev, Boris Nikolayevich
See also DLB 295; EW 9; EWL 3

Belyi, Andrei
See Bugayev, Boris Nikolayevich
See also RGWL 2, 3

Bembo, Pietro 1470-1547 .... **LC 79**
See also RGWL 2, 3

Benary, Margot
See Benary-Isbert, Margot

Benary-Isbert, Margot 1889-1979 .... **CLC 12**
See also CA 5-8R; 89-92; CANR 4, 72;
CLR 12; MAICYA 1, 2; SATA 2; SATA-
Obit 21

Benavente (y Martinez), Jacinto
1866-1954 .... **DC 26; HLCS 1; TCLC 3**
See also CA 106; 131; CANR 81; DAM
DRAM, MULT; EWL 3; GLL 2; HW 1,
2; MTCW 1, 2

Benchley, Peter 1940- .... **CLC 4, 8**
See also AAYA 14; AITN 2; BPFB 1; CA
17-20R; CANR 12, 35, 66, 115; CPW;
DAM NOV, POP; HGG; MTCW 1, 2;
MTFW 2005; SATA 3, 89, 164

Benchley, Peter Bradford
See Benchley, Peter

Benchley, Robert (Charles)
1889-1945 .... **TCLC 1, 55**
See also CA 105; 153; DLB 11; MAL 5;
RGAL 4

Benda, Julien 1867-1956 .... **TCLC 60**
See also CA 120; 154; GFL 1789 to the
Present

Benedict, Ruth (Fulton)
1887-1948 .... **TCLC 60**
See also CA 158; DLB 246

Benedikt, Michael 1935- .... **CLC 4, 14**
See also CA 13-16R; CANR 7; CP 1, 2, 3,
4, 5, 6, 7; DLB 5

Benet, Juan 1927-1993 .... **CLC 28**
See also CA 143; EWL 3

Benet, Stephen Vincent 1898-1943 ..... **PC 64;**
SSC 10, 86; TCLC 7
See also AMWS 11; CA 104; 152; DA3;
DAM POET; DLB 4, 48, 102, 249, 284;
DLBY 1997; EWL 3; HGG; MAL 5;
MTCW 2; MTFW 2005; RGAL 4; RGSF
2; SUFW; WP; YABC 1

Benet, William Rose 1886-1950 ..... **TCLC 28**
See also CA 118; 152; DAM POET; DLB
45; RGAL 4

Benford, Gregory (Albert) 1941- ..... **CLC 52**
See also BPFB 1; CA 69-72, 175; CAAE
175; CAAS 27; CANR 12, 24, 49, 95,
134; CN 7; CSW; DLBY 1982; MTFW
2005; SCFW 2; SFW 4

Bengtsson, Frans (Gunnar)
1894-1954 .... **TCLC 48**
See also CA 170; EWL 3

Benjamin, David
See Slavitt, David R(ytman)

Benjamin, Lois
See Gould, Lois

Benjamin, Walter 1892-1940 .... **TCLC 39**
See also CA 164; DLB 242; EW 11; EWL
3

Ben Jelloun, Tahar 1944-
See Jelloun, Tahar ben
See also CA 135; CWW 2; EWL 3; RGWL
3; WLIT 2

Benn, Gottfried 1886-1956 .. **PC 35; TCLC 3**
See also CA 106; 153; DLB 56; EWL 3;
RGWL 2, 3

Bennett, Alan 1934- .... **CLC 45, 77**
See also BRWS 8; CA 103; CANR 35, 55,
106; CBD; CD 5, 6; DAB; DAM MST;
DLB 310; MTCW 1, 2; MTFW 2005

Bennett, (Enoch) Arnold
1867-1931 .... **TCLC 5, 20**
See also BRW 6; CA 106; 155; CDBLB
1890-1914; DLB 10, 34, 98, 135; EWL 3;
MTCW 2

Bennett, Elizabeth
See Mitchell, Margaret (Munnerlyn)

Bennett, George Harold 1930-
See Bennett, Hal
See also BW 1; CA 97-100; CANR 87

Bennett, Gwendolyn B. 1902-1981 .... **HR 1:2**
See also BW 1; CA 125; DLB 51; WP

Bennett, Hal .... **CLC 5**
See Bennett, George Harold
See also DLB 33

Bennett, Jay 1912- .... **CLC 35**
See also AAYA 10; CA 69-72; CANR 11,
42, 79; JRDA; SAAS 4; SATA 41, 87;
SATA-Brief 27; WYA; YAW

Bennett, Louise (Simone) 1919- .... **BLC 1;**
CLC 28
See also BW 2, 3; CA 151; CDWLB 3; CP
1, 2, 3, 4, 5, 6, 7; DAM MULT; DLB 117;
EWL 3

Benson, A. C. 1862-1925 .... **TCLC 123**
See also DLB 98

Benson, E(dward) F(rederic)
1867-1940 .... **TCLC 27**
See also CA 114; 157; DLB 135, 153;
HGG; SUFW 1

Benson, Jackson J. 1930- .... **CLC 34**
See also CA 25-28R; DLB 111

Benson, Sally 1900-1972 .... **CLC 17**
See also CA 19-20; 37-40R; CAP 1; SATA
1, 35; SATA-Obit 27

Benson, Stella 1892-1933 .... **TCLC 17**
See also CA 117; 154, 155; DLB 36, 162;
FANT; TEA

Bentham, Jeremy 1748-1832 .... **NCLC 38**
See also DLB 107, 158, 252

Bentley, E(dmund) C(lerihew)
1875-1956 .... **TCLC 12**
See also CA 108; 232; DLB 70; MSW

Bentley, Eric (Russell) 1916- .... **CLC 24**
See also CA 5-8R; CAD; CANR 6, 67;
CBD; CD 5, 6; INT CANR-6

ben Uzair, Salem
See Horne, Richard Henry Hengist

Beranger, Pierre Jean de
1780-1857 .... **NCLC 34**

Berdyaev, Nicolas
See Berdyaev, Nikolai (Aleksandrovich)

Berdyaev, Nikolai (Aleksandrovich)
1874-1948 .... **TCLC 67**
See also CA 120; 157

Berdyayev, Nikolai (Aleksandrovich)
See Berdyaev, Nikolai (Aleksandrovich)

Berendt, John (Lawrence) 1939- ...... **CLC 86**
See also CA 146; CANR 75, 93; DA3;
MTCW 2; MTFW 2005

Beresford, J(ohn) D(avys)
1873-1947 .... **TCLC 81**
See also CA 112; 155; DLB 162, 178, 197;
SFW 4; SUFW 1

Bergelson, David (Rafailovich)
1884-1952 .... **TCLC 81**
See Bergelson, Dovid
See also CA 220

Bergelson, Dovid
See Bergelson, David (Rafailovich)
See also EWL 3

Bitov, Andrei (Georgievich) 1937- ... **CLC 57**
See also CA 142; DLB 302

Biyidi, Alexandre 1932-
See Beti, Mongo
See also BW 1, 3; CA 114; 124; CANR 81;
DA3; MTCW 1, 2

Bjarme, Brynjolf
See Ibsen, Henrik (Johan)

Bjoernson, Bjoernstjerne (Martinius)
1832-1910 .... **TCLC 7, 37**
See also CA 104

Black, Robert
See Holdstock, Robert P.

Blackburn, Paul 1926-1971 .... **CLC 9, 43**
See also BG 1:2; CA 81-84; 33-36R; CANR
34; CP 1; DLB 16; DLBY 1981

Black Elk 1863-1950 .... **NNAL; TCLC 33**
See also CA 144; DAM MULT; MTCW 2;
MTFW 2005; WP

Black Hawk 1767-1838 .... **NNAL**

Black Hobart
See Sanders, (James) Ed(ward)

Blacklin, Malcolm
See Chambers, Aidan

Blackmore, R(ichard) D(oddridge)
1825-1900 .... **TCLC 27**
See also CA 120; DLB 18; RGEL 2

Blackmur, R(ichard) P(almer)
1904-1965 .... **CLC 2, 24**
See also AMWS 2; CA 11-12; 25-28R;
CANR 71; CAP 1; DLB 63; EWL 3;
MAL 5

Black Tarantula
See Acker, Kathy

Blackwood, Algernon (Henry)
1869-1951 .... **TCLC 5**
See also CA 105; 150; DLB 153, 156, 178;
HGG; SUFW 1

Blackwood, Caroline (Maureen)
1931-1996 .... **CLC 6, 9, 100**
See also BRWS 9; CA 85-88; 151; CANR
32, 61, 65; CN 3, 4, 5, 6; DLB 14, 207;
HGG; MTCW 1

Blade, Alexander
See Hamilton, Edmond; Silverberg, Robert

Blaga, Lucian 1895-1961 .... **CLC 75**
See also CA 157; DLB 220; EWL 3

Blair, Eric (Arthur) 1903-1950 .... **TCLC 123**
See Orwell, George
See also CA 104; 132; DA; DA3; DAB;
DAC; DAM MST, NOV; MTCW 1, 2;
MTFW 2005; SATA 29

Blair, Hugh 1718-1800 .... **NCLC 75**

Blais, Marie-Claire 1939- .... **CLC 2, 4, 6, 13, 22**
See also CA 21-24R; CAAS 4; CANR 38,
75, 93; CWW 2; DAC; DAM MST; DLB
53; EWL 3; FW; MTCW 1, 2; MTFW
2005; TWA

Blaise, Clark 1940- .... **CLC 29**
See also AITN 2; CA 53-56, 231; CAAE
231; CAAS 3; CANR 5, 66, 106; CN 4,
5, 6, 7; DLB 53; RGSF 2

Blake, Fairley
See De Voto, Bernard (Augustine)

Blake, Nicholas
See Day Lewis, C(ecil)
See also DLB 77; MSW

Blake, Sterling
See Benford, Gregory (Albert)

Blake, William 1757-1827 . **NCLC 13, 37, 57, 127; PC 12, 63; WLC**
See also AAYA 47; BRW 3; BRWR 1; CD-
BLB 1789-1832; CLR 52; DA; DA3;
DAB; DAC; DAM MST, POET; DLB 93,
163; EXPP; LATS 1:1; LMFS 1; MAI-
CYA 1, 2; PAB; PFS 2, 12; SATA 30;
TEA; WCH; WLIT 3; WP

Blanchot, Maurice 1907-2003 .... **CLC 135**
See also CA 117; 144; 213; CANR 138;
DLB 72, 296; EWL 3

Blasco Ibanez, Vicente 1867-1928 . **TCLC 12**
See Ibanez, Vicente Blasco
See also BPFB 1; CA 110; 131; CANR 81;
DA3; DAM NOV; EW 8; EWL 3; HW 1,
2; MTCW 1

Blatty, William Peter 1928- .... **CLC 2**
See also CA 5-8R; CANR 9, 124; DAM
POP; HGG

Bleeck, Oliver
See Thomas, Ross (Elmore)

Blessing, Lee (Knowlton) 1949- .... **CLC 54**
See also CA 236; CAD; CD 5, 6

Blight, Rose
See Greer, Germaine

Blish, James (Benjamin) 1921-1975 . **CLC 14**
See also BPFB 1; CA 1-4R; 57-60; CANR
3; CN 2; DLB 8; MTCW 1; SATA 66;
SCFW 1, 2; SFW 4

Bliss, Frederick
See Card, Orson Scott

Bliss, Reginald
See Wells, H(erbert) G(eorge)

Blixen, Karen (Christentze Dinesen)
1885-1962
See Dinesen, Isak
See also CA 25-28; CANR 22, 50; CAP 2;
DA3; DLB 214; LMFS 1; MTCW 1, 2;
SATA 44; SSFS 20

Bloch, Robert (Albert) 1917-1994 .... **CLC 33**
See also AAYA 29; CA 5-8R, 179; 146;
CAAE 179; CAAS 20; CANR 5, 78;
DA3; DLB 44; HGG; INT CANR-5;
MTCW 2; SATA 12; SATA-Obit 82; SFW
4; SUFW 1, 2

Blok, Alexander (Alexandrovich)
1880-1921 .... **PC 21; TCLC 5**
See also CA 104; 183; DLB 295; EW 9;
EWL 3; LMFS 2; RGWL 2, 3

Blom, Jan
See Breytenbach, Breyten

Bloom, Harold 1930- .... **CLC 24, 103, 221**
See also CA 13-16R; CANR 39, 75, 92,
133; DLB 67; EWL 3; MTCW 2; MTFW
2005; RGAL 4

Bloomfield, Aurelius
See Bourne, Randolph S(illiman)

Bloomfield, Robert 1766-1823 ..... **NCLC 145**
See also DLB 93

Blount, Roy (Alton), Jr. 1941- .... **CLC 38**
See also CA 53-56; CANR 10, 28, 61, 125;
CSW; INT CANR-28; MTCW 1, 2;
MTFW 2005

Blowsnake, Sam 1875-(?) .... **NNAL**

Bloy, Leon 1846-1917 .... **TCLC 22**
See also CA 121; 183; DLB 123; GFL 1789
to the Present

Blue Cloud, Peter (Aroniawenrate)
1933- .... **NNAL**
See also CA 117; CANR 40; DAM MULT

Bluggage, Oranthy
See Alcott, Louisa May

Blume, Judy (Sussman) 1938- .... **CLC 12, 30**
See also AAYA 3, 26; BYA 1, 8, 12; CA 29-
32R; CANR 13, 37, 66, 124; CLR 2, 15,
69; CPW; DA3; DAM NOV, POP; DLB
52; JRDA; MAICYA 1, 2; MAICYAS 1;
MTCW 1, 2; MTFW 2005; SATA 2, 31,
79, 142; WYA; YAW

Blunden, Edmund (Charles)
1896-1974 .... **CLC 2, 56; PC 66**
See also BRW 6; BRWS 11; CA 17-18; 45-
48; CANR 54; CAP 2; CP 1, 2; DLB 20,
100, 155; MTCW 1; PAB

Bly, Robert (Elwood) 1926- .... **CLC 1, 2, 5, 10, 15, 38, 128; PC 39**
See also AMWS 4; CA 5-8R; CANR 41,
73, 125; CP 1, 2, 3, 4, 5, 6, 7; DA3; DAM
POET; DLB 5; EWL 3; MAL 5; MTCW
1, 2; MTFW 2005; PFS 6, 17; RGAL 4

Boas, Franz 1858-1942 .... **TCLC 56**
See also CA 115; 181

Bobette
See Simenon, Georges (Jacques Christian)

Boccaccio, Giovanni 1313-1375 ... **CMLC 13, 57; SSC 10, 87**
See also EW 2; RGSF 2; RGWL 2, 3; TWA;
WLIT 7

Bochco, Steven 1943- .... **CLC 35**
See also AAYA 11; CA 124; 138

Bode, Sigmund
See O'Doherty, Brian

Bodel, Jean 1167(?)-1210 .... **CMLC 28**

Bodenheim, Maxwell 1892-1954 .... **TCLC 44**
See also CA 110; 187; DLB 9, 45; MAL 5;
RGAL 4

Bodenheimer, Maxwell
See Bodenheim, Maxwell

Bodker, Cecil 1927-
See Bodker, Cecil

Bodker, Cecil 1927- .... **CLC 21**
See also CA 73-76; CANR 13, 44, 111;
CLR 23; MAICYA 1, 2; SATA 14, 133

Boell, Heinrich (Theodor)
1917-1985 ..... **CLC 2, 3, 6, 9, 11, 15, 27, 32, 72; SSC 23; WLC**
See Boll, Heinrich (Theodor)
See also CA 21-24R; 116; CANR 24; DA;
DA3; DAB; DAC; DAM MST, NOV;
DLB 69; DLBY 1985; MTCW 1, 2;
MTFW 2005; SSFS 20; TWA

Boerne, Alfred
See Doeblin, Alfred

Boethius c. 480-c. 524 .... **CMLC 15**
See also DLB 115; RGWL 2, 3

Boff, Leonardo (Genezio Darci)
1938- .... **CLC 70; HLC 1**
See also CA 150; DAM MULT; HW 2

Bogan, Louise 1897-1970 .... **CLC 4, 39, 46, 93; PC 12**
See also AMWS 3; CA 73-76; 25-28R;
CANR 33, 82; CP 1; DAM POET; DLB
45, 169; EWL 3; MAL 5; MAWW;
MTCW 1, 2; PFS 21; RGAL 4

Bogarde, Dirk
See Van Den Bogarde, Derek Jules Gaspard
Ulric Niven
See also DLB 14

Bogosian, Eric 1953- .... **CLC 45, 141**
See also CA 138; CAD; CANR 102; CD 5,
6

Bograd, Larry 1953- .... **CLC 35**
See also CA 93-96; CANR 57; SAAS 21;
SATA 33, 89; WYA

Boiardo, Matteo Maria 1441-1494 .... **LC 6**

Boileau-Despreaux, Nicolas 1636-1711 . **LC 3**
See also DLB 268; EW 3; GFL Beginnings
to 1789; RGWL 2, 3

Boissard, Maurice
See Leautaud, Paul

Bojer, Johan 1872-1959 .... **TCLC 64**
See also CA 189; EWL 3

Bok, Edward W(illiam)
1863-1930 .... **TCLC 101**
See also CA 217; DLB 91; DLBD 16

Boker, George Henry 1823-1890 . **NCLC 125**
See also RGAL 4

Boland, Eavan (Aisling) 1944- .. **CLC 40, 67, 113; PC 58**
See also BRWS 5; CA 143, 207; CAAE
207; CANR 61; CP 1, 7; CWP; DAM
POET; DLB 40; FW; MTCW 2; MTFW
2005; PFS 12, 22

Boll, Heinrich (Theodor)
See Boell, Heinrich (Theodor)
See also BPFB 1; CDWLB 2; EW 13; EWL 3; RGSF 2; RGWL 2, 3

Bolt, Lee
See Faust, Frederick (Schiller)

Bolt, Robert (Oxton) 1924-1995 ...... **CLC 14; TCLC 175**
See also CA 17-20R; 147; CANR 35, 67; CBD; DAM DRAM; DFS 2; DLB 13, 233; EWL 3; LAIT 1; MTCW 1

Bombal, Maria Luisa 1910-1980 .... **HLCS 1; SSC 37**
See also CA 127; CANR 72; EWL 3; HW 1; LAW; RGSF 2

Bombet, Louis-Alexandre-Cesar
See Stendhal

Bomkauf
See Kaufman, Bob (Garnell)

Bonaventura .... **NCLC 35**
See also DLB 90

Bonaventure 1217(?)-1274 .... **CMLC 79**
See also DLB 115; LMFS 1

Bond, Edward 1934- .... **CLC 4, 6, 13, 23**
See also AAYA 50; BRWS 1; CA 25-28R; CANR 38, 67, 106; CBD; CD 5, 6; DAM DRAM; DFS 3, 8; DLB 13, 310; EWL 3; MTCW 1

Bonham, Frank 1914-1989 .... **CLC 12**
See also AAYA 1; BYA 1, 3; CA 9-12R; CANR 4, 36; JRDA; MAICYA 1, 2; SAAS 3; SATA 1, 49; SATA-Obit 62; TCWW 1, 2; YAW

Bonnefoy, Yves 1923- . **CLC 9, 15, 58; PC 58**
See also CA 85-88; CANR 33, 75, 97, 136; CWW 2; DAM MST, POET; DLB 258; EWL 3; GFL 1789 to the Present; MTCW 1, 2; MTFW 2005

Bonner, Marita .... **HR 1:2**
See Occomy, Marita (Odette) Bonner

Bonnin, Gertrude 1876-1938 .... **NNAL**
See Zitkala-Sa
See also CA 150; DAM MULT

Bontemps, Arna(ud Wendell)
1902-1973 .. **BLC 1; CLC 1, 18; HR 1:2**
See also BW 1; CA 1-4R; 41-44R; CANR 4, 35; CLR 6; CP 1; CWRI 5; DA3; DAM MULT, NOV, POET; DLB 48, 51; JRDA; MAICYA 1, 2; MAL 5; MTCW 1, 2; SATA 2, 44; SATA-Obit 24; WCH; WP

Boot, William
See Stoppard, Tom

Booth, Martin 1944-2004 .... **CLC 13**
See also CA 93-96, 188; 223; CAAE 188; CAAS 2; CANR 92; CP 1, 2, 3, 4

Booth, Philip 1925- .... **CLC 23**
See also CA 5-8R; CANR 5, 88; CP 1, 2, 3, 4, 5, 6, 7; DLBY 1982

Booth, Wayne C(layson) 1921-2005 . **CLC 24**
See also CA 1-4R; CAAS 5; CANR 3, 43, 117; DLB 67

Borchert, Wolfgang 1921-1947 .... **TCLC 5**
See also CA 104; 188; DLB 69, 124; EWL 3

Borel, Petrus 1809-1859 .... **NCLC 41**
See also DLB 119; GFL 1789 to the Present

Borges, Jorge Luis 1899-1986 ... **CLC 1, 2, 3, 4, 6, 8, 9, 10, 13, 19, 44, 48, 83; HLC 1; PC 22, 32; SSC 4, 41; TCLC 109; WLC**
See also AAYA 26; BPFB 1; CA 21-24R; CANR 19, 33, 75, 105, 133; CDWLB 3; DA; DA3; DAB; DAC; DAM MST, MULT; DLB 113, 283; DLBY 1986; DNFS 1, 2; EWL 3; HW 1, 2; LAW; LMFS 2; MSW; MTCW 1, 2; MTFW 2005; RGSF 2; RGWL 2, 3; SFW 4; SSFS 17; TWA; WLIT 1

Borowski, Tadeusz 1922-1951 .... **SSC 48; TCLC 9**
See also CA 106; 154; CDWLB 4; DLB 215; EWL 3; RGSF 2; RGWL 3; SSFS 13

Borrow, George (Henry)
1803-1881 .... **NCLC 9**
See also DLB 21, 55, 166

Bosch (Gavino), Juan 1909-2001 ..... **HLCS 1**
See also CA 151; 204; DAM MST, MULT; DLB 145; HW 1, 2

Bosman, Herman Charles
1905-1951 .... **TCLC 49**
See Malan, Herman
See also CA 160; DLB 225; RGSF 2

Bosschere, Jean de 1878(?)-1953 ... **TCLC 19**
See also CA 115; 186

Boswell, James 1740-1795 ... **LC 4, 50; WLC**
See also BRW 3; CDBLB 1660-1789; DA; DAB; DAC; DAM MST; DLB 104, 142; TEA; WLIT 3

Bottomley, Gordon 1874-1948 ..... **TCLC 107**
See also CA 120; 192; DLB 10

Bottoms, David 1949- .... **CLC 53**
See also CA 105; CANR 22; CSW; DLB 120; DLBY 1983

Boucicault, Dion 1820-1890 .... **NCLC 41**

Boucolon, Maryse
See Conde, Maryse

Bourdieu, Pierre 1930-2002 .... **CLC 198**
See also CA 130; 204

Bourget, Paul (Charles Joseph)
1852-1935 .... **TCLC 12**
See also CA 107; 196; DLB 123; GFL 1789 to the Present

Bourjaily, Vance (Nye) 1922- .... **CLC 8, 62**
See also CA 1-4R; CAAS 1; CANR 2, 72; CN 1, 2, 3, 4, 5, 6, 7; DLB 2, 143; MAL 5

Bourne, Randolph S(illiman)
1886-1918 .... **TCLC 16**
See also AMW; CA 117; 155; DLB 63; MAL 5

Bova, Ben(jamin William) 1932- ...... **CLC 45**
See also AAYA 16; CA 5-8R; CAAS 18; CANR 11, 56, 94, 111; CLR 3, 96; DLBY 1981; INT CANR-11; MAICYA 1, 2; MTCW 1; SATA 6, 68, 133; SFW 4

Bowen, Elizabeth (Dorothea Cole)
1899-1973 . **CLC 1, 3, 6, 11, 15, 22, 118; SSC 3, 28, 66; TCLC 148**
See also BRWS 2; CA 17-18; 41-44R; CANR 35, 105; CAP 2; CDBLB 1945-1960; CN 1; DA3; DAM NOV; DLB 15, 162; EWL 3; EXPS; FW; HGG; MTCW 1, 2; MTFW 2005; NFS 13; RGSF 2; SSFS 5; SUFW 1; TEA; WLIT 4

Bowering, George 1935- .... **CLC 15, 47**
See also CA 21-24R; CAAS 16; CANR 10; CN 7; CP 1, 2, 3, 4, 5, 6, 7; DLB 53

Bowering, Marilyn R(uthe) 1949- .... **CLC 32**
See also CA 101; CANR 49; CP 4, 5, 6, 7; CWP

Bowers, Edgar 1924-2000 .... **CLC 9**
See also CA 5-8R; 188; CANR 24; CP 1, 2, 3, 4, 5, 6, 7; CSW; DLB 5

Bowers, Mrs. J. Milton 1842-1914
See Bierce, Ambrose (Gwinett)

Bowie, David .... **CLC 17**
See Jones, David Robert

Bowles, Jane (Sydney) 1917-1973 ..... **CLC 3, 68**
See Bowles, Jane Auer
See also CA 19-20; 41-44R; CAP 2; CN 1; MAL 5

Bowles, Jane Auer
See Bowles, Jane (Sydney)
See also EWL 3

Bowles, Paul (Frederick) 1910-1999 . **CLC 1, 2, 19, 53; SSC 3**
See also AMWS 4; CA 1-4R; 186; CAAS 1; CANR 1, 19, 50, 75; CN 1, 2, 3, 4, 5, 6; DA3; DLB 5, 6, 218; EWL 3; MAL 5; MTCW 1, 2; MTFW 2005; RGAL 4; SSFS 17

Bowles, William Lisle 1762-1850 . **NCLC 103**
See also DLB 93

Box, Edgar
See Vidal, (Eugene Luther) Gore
See also GLL 1

Boyd, James 1888-1944 .... **TCLC 115**
See also CA 186; DLB 9; DLBD 16; RGAL 4; RHW

Boyd, Nancy
See Millay, Edna St. Vincent
See also GLL 1

Boyd, Thomas (Alexander)
1898-1935 .... **TCLC 111**
See also CA 111; 183; DLB 9; DLBD 16, 316

Boyd, William (Andrew Murray)
1952- .... **CLC 28, 53, 70**
See also CA 114; 120; CANR 51, 71, 131; CN 4, 5, 6, 7; DLB 231

Boyesen, Hjalmar Hjorth
1848-1895 .... **NCLC 135**
See also DLB 12, 71; DLBD 13; RGAL 4

Boyle, Kay 1902-1992 .... **CLC 1, 5, 19, 58, 121; SSC 5**
See also CA 13-16R; 140; CAAS 1; CANR 29, 61, 110; CN 1, 2, 3, 4, 5; CP 1, 2, 3, 4; DLB 4, 9, 48, 86; DLBY 1993; EWL 3; MAL 5; MTCW 1, 2; MTFW 2005; RGAL 4; RGSF 2; SSFS 10, 13, 14

Boyle, Mark
See Kienzle, William X(avier)

Boyle, Patrick 1905-1982 .... **CLC 19**
See also CA 127

Boyle, T. C.
See Boyle, T(homas) Coraghessan
See also AMWS 8

Boyle, T(homas) Coraghessan
1948- .... **CLC 36, 55, 90; SSC 16**
See Boyle, T. C.
See also AAYA 47; BEST 90:4; BPFB 1; CA 120; CANR 44, 76, 89, 132; CN 6, 7; CPW; DA3; DAM POP; DLB 218, 278; DLBY 1986; EWL 3; MAL 5; MTCW 2; MTFW 2005; SSFS 13, 19

Boz
See Dickens, Charles (John Huffam)

Brackenridge, Hugh Henry
1748-1816 .... **NCLC 7**
See also DLB 11, 37; RGAL 4

Bradbury, Edward P.
See Moorcock, Michael (John)
See also MTCW 2

Bradbury, Malcolm (Stanley)
1932-2000 .... **CLC 32, 61**
See also CA 1-4R; CANR 1, 33, 91, 98, 137; CN 1, 2, 3, 4, 5, 6, 7; CP 1; DA3; DAM NOV; DLB 14, 207; EWL 3; MTCW 1, 2; MTFW 2005

Bradbury, Ray (Douglas) 1920- .... **CLC 1, 3, 10, 15, 42, 98; SSC 29, 53; WLC**
See also AAYA 15; AITN 1, 2; AMWS 4; BPFB 1; BYA 4, 5, 11; CA 1-4R; CANR 2, 30, 75, 125; CDALB 1968-1988; CN 1, 2, 3, 4, 5, 6, 7; CPW; DA; DA3; DAB; DAC; DAM MST, NOV, POP; DLB 2, 8; EXPN; EXPS; HGG; LAIT 3, 5; LATS 1:2; LMFS 2; MAL 5; MTCW 1, 2; MTFW 2005; NFS 1, 22; RGAL 4; RGSF 2; SATA 11, 64, 123; SCFW 1, 2; SFW 4; SSFS 1, 20; SUFW 1, 2; TUS; YAW

Braddon, Mary Elizabeth
1837-1915 .... **TCLC 111**
See also BRWS 8; CA 108; 179; CMW 4;
DLB 18, 70, 156; HGG

Bradfield, Scott (Michael) 1955- .... **SSC 65**
See also CA 147; CANR 90; HGG; SUFW
2

Bradford, Gamaliel 1863-1932 .... **TCLC 36**
See also CA 160; DLB 17

Bradford, William 1590-1657 .... **LC 64**
See also DLB 24, 30; RGAL 4

Bradley, David (Henry), Jr. 1950- .... **BLC 1;
CLC 23, 118**
See also BW 1, 3; CA 104; CANR 26, 81;
CN 4, 5, 6, 7; DAM MULT; DLB 33

Bradley, John Ed(mund, Jr.) 1958- . **CLC 55**
See also CA 139; CANR 99; CN 6, 7; CSW

Bradley, Marion Zimmer
1930-1999 .... **CLC 30**
See Chapman, Lee; Dexter, John; Gardner,
Miriam; Ives, Morgan; Rivers, Elfrida
See also AAYA 40; BPFB 1; CA 57-60; 185;
CAAS 10; CANR 7, 31, 51, 75, 107;
CPW; DA3; DAM POP; DLB 8; FANT;
FW; MTCW 1, 2; MTFW 2005; SATA 90,
139; SATA-Obit 116; SFW 4; SUFW 2;
YAW

Bradshaw, John 1933- .... **CLC 70**
See also CA 138; CANR 61

Bradstreet, Anne 1612(?)-1672 ...... **LC 4, 30;
PC 10**
See also AMWS 1; CDALB 1640-1865;
DA; DA3; DAC; DAM MST, POET; DLB
24; EXPP; FW; PFS 6; RGAL 4; TUS;
WP

Brady, Joan 1939- .... **CLC 86**
See also CA 141

Bragg, Melvyn 1939- .... **CLC 10**
See also BEST 89:3; CA 57-60; CANR 10,
48, 89; CN 1, 2, 3, 4, 5, 6, 7; DLB 14,
271; RHW

Brahe, Tycho 1546-1601 .... **LC 45**
See also DLB 300

Braine, John (Gerard) 1922-1986 . **CLC 1, 3,
41**
See also CA 1-4R; 120; CANR 1, 33; CD-
BLB 1945-1960; CN 1, 2, 3, 4; DLB 15;
DLBY 1986; EWL 3; MTCW 1

Braithwaite, William Stanley (Beaumont)
1878-1962 .... **BLC 1; HR 1:2; PC 52**
See also BW 1; CA 125; DAM MULT; DLB
50, 54; MAL 5

Bramah, Ernest 1868-1942 .... **TCLC 72**
See also CA 156; CMW 4; DLB 70; FANT

Brammer, Billy Lee
See Brammer, William

Brammer, William 1929-1978 .... **CLC 31**
See also CA 235; 77-80

Brancati, Vitaliano 1907-1954 .... **TCLC 12**
See also CA 109; DLB 264; EWL 3

Brancato, Robin F(idler) 1936- .... **CLC 35**
See also AAYA 9, 68; BYA 6; CA 69-72;
CANR 11, 45; CLR 32; JRDA; MAICYA
2; MAICYAS 1; SAAS 9; SATA 97;
WYA; YAW

Brand, Dionne 1953- .... **CLC 192**
See also BW 2; CA 143; CANR 143; CWP

Brand, Max
See Faust, Frederick (Schiller)
See also BPFB 1; TCWW 1, 2

Brand, Millen 1906-1980 .... **CLC 7**
See also CA 21-24R; 97-100; CANR 72

Branden, Barbara .... **CLC 44**
See also CA 148

Brandes, Georg (Morris Cohen)
1842-1927 .... **TCLC 10**
See also CA 105; 189; DLB 300

Brandys, Kazimierz 1916-2000 .... **CLC 62**
See also CA 239; EWL 3

Branley, Franklyn M(ansfield)
1915-2002 .... **CLC 21**
See also CA 33-36R; 207; CANR 14, 39;
CLR 13; MAICYA 1, 2; SAAS 16; SATA
4, 68, 136

Brant, Beth (E.) 1941- .... **NNAL**
See also CA 144; FW

Brant, Sebastian 1457-1521 .... **LC 112**
See also DLB 179; RGWL 2, 3

Brathwaite, Edward Kamau
1930- .... **BLCS; CLC 11; PC 56**
See also BW 2, 3; CA 25-28R; CANR 11,
26, 47, 107; CDWLB 3; CP 1, 2, 3, 4, 5,
6, 7; DAM POET; DLB 125; EWL 3

Brathwaite, Kamau
See Brathwaite, Edward Kamau

Brautigan, Richard (Gary)
1935-1984 .... **CLC 1, 3, 5, 9, 12, 34, 42;
TCLC 133**
See also BPFB 1; CA 53-56; 113; CANR
34; CN 1, 2, 3; CP 1, 2, 3, 4; DA3; DAM
NOV; DLB 2, 5, 206; DLBY 1980, 1984;
FANT; MAL 5; MTCW 1; RGAL 4;
SATA 56

Brave Bird, Mary .... **NNAL**
See Crow Dog, Mary (Ellen)

Braverman, Kate 1950- .... **CLC 67**
See also CA 89-92; CANR 141

Brecht, (Eugen) Bertolt (Friedrich)
1898-1956 ..... **DC 3; TCLC 1, 6, 13, 35,
169; WLC**
See also CA 104; 133; CANR 62; CDWLB
2; DA; DA3; DAB; DAC; DAM DRAM,
MST; DFS 4, 5, 9; DLB 56, 124; EW 11;
EWL 3; IDTP; MTCW 1, 2; MTFW 2005;
RGWL 2, 3; TWA

Brecht, Eugen Berthold Friedrich
See Brecht, (Eugen) Bertolt (Friedrich)

Bremer, Fredrika 1801-1865 .... **NCLC 11**
See also DLB 254

Brennan, Christopher John
1870-1932 .... **TCLC 17**
See also CA 117; 188; DLB 230; EWL 3

Brennan, Maeve 1917-1993 ... **CLC 5; TCLC
124**
See also CA 81-84; CANR 72, 100

Brenner, Jozef 1887-1919
See Csath, Geza
See also CA 240

Brent, Linda
See Jacobs, Harriet A(nn)

Brentano, Clemens (Maria)
1778-1842 .... **NCLC 1**
See also DLB 90; RGWL 2, 3

Brent of Bin Bin
See Franklin, (Stella Maria Sarah) Miles
(Lampe)

Brenton, Howard 1942- .... **CLC 31**
See also CA 69-72; CANR 33, 67; CBD;
CD 5, 6; DLB 13; MTCW 1

Breslin, James 1930-
See Breslin, Jimmy
See also CA 73-76; CANR 31, 75, 139;
DAM NOV; MTCW 1, 2; MTFW 2005

Breslin, Jimmy .... **CLC 4, 43**
See Breslin, James
See also AITN 1; DLB 185; MTCW 2

Bresson, Robert 1901(?)-1999 .... **CLC 16**
See also CA 110; 187; CANR 49

Breton, Andre 1896-1966 .. **CLC 2, 9, 15, 54;
PC 15**
See also CA 19-20; 25-28R; CANR 40, 60;
CAP 2; DLB 65, 258; EW 11; EWL 3;
GFL 1789 to the Present; LMFS 2;
MTCW 1, 2; MTFW 2005; RGWL 2, 3;
TWA; WP

Breytenbach, Breyten 1939(?)- .. **CLC 23, 37,
126**
See also CA 113; 129; CANR 61, 122;
CWW 2; DAM POET; DLB 225; EWL 3

Bridgers, Sue Ellen 1942- .... **CLC 26**
See also AAYA 8, 49; BYA 7, 8; CA 65-68;
CANR 11, 36; CLR 18; DLB 52; JRDA;
MAICYA 1, 2; SAAS 1; SATA 22, 90;
SATA-Essay 109; WYA; YAW

Bridges, Robert (Seymour)
1844-1930 .... **PC 28; TCLC 1**
See also BRW 6; CA 104; 152; CDBLB
1890-1914; DAM POET; DLB 19, 98

Bridie, James .... **TCLC 3**
See Mavor, Osborne Henry
See also DLB 10; EWL 3

Brin, David 1950- .... **CLC 34**
See also AAYA 21; CA 102; CANR 24, 70,
125, 127; INT CANR-24; SATA 65;
SCFW 2; SFW 4

Brink, Andre (Philippus) 1935- . **CLC 18, 36,
106**
See also AFW; BRWS 6; CA 104; CANR
39, 62, 109, 133; CN 4, 5, 6, 7; DLB 225;
EWL 3; INT CA-103; LATS 1:2; MTCW
1, 2; MTFW 2005; WLIT 2

Brinsmead, H. F(ay)
See Brinsmead, H(esba) F(ay)

Brinsmead, H. F.
See Brinsmead, H(esba) F(ay)

Brinsmead, H(esba) F(ay) 1922- ...... **CLC 21**
See also CA 21-24R; CANR 10; CLR 47;
CWRI 5; MAICYA 1, 2; SAAS 5; SATA
18, 78

Brittain, Vera (Mary) 1893(?)-1970 . **CLC 23**
See also BRWS 10; CA 13-16; 25-28R;
CANR 58; CAP 1; DLB 191; FW; MTCW
1, 2

Broch, Hermann 1886-1951 .... **TCLC 20**
See also CA 117; 211; CDWLB 2; DLB 85,
124; EW 10; EWL 3; RGWL 2, 3

Brock, Rose
See Hansen, Joseph
See also GLL 1

Brod, Max 1884-1968 .... **TCLC 115**
See also CA 5-8R; 25-28R; CANR 7; DLB
81; EWL 3

Brodkey, Harold (Roy) 1930-1996 .. **CLC 56;
TCLC 123**
See also CA 111; 151; CANR 71; CN 4, 5,
6; DLB 130

Brodsky, Iosif Alexandrovich 1940-1996
See Brodsky, Joseph
See also AITN 1; CA 41-44R; 151; CANR
37, 106; DA3; DAM POET; MTCW 1, 2;
MTFW 2005; RGWL 2, 3

Brodsky, Joseph . **CLC 4, 6, 13, 36, 100; PC
9**
See Brodsky, Iosif Alexandrovich
See also AMWS 8; CWW 2; DLB 285;
EWL 3; MTCW 1

Brodsky, Michael (Mark) 1948- .... **CLC 19**
See also CA 102; CANR 18, 41, 58; DLB
244

Brodzki, Bella ed. .... **CLC 65**

Brome, Richard 1590(?)-1652 .... **LC 61**
See also BRWS 10; DLB 58

Bromell, Henry 1947- .... **CLC 5**
See also CA 53-56; CANR 9, 115, 116

Bromfield, Louis (Brucker)
1896-1956 .... **TCLC 11**
See also CA 107; 155; DLB 4, 9, 86; RGAL
4; RHW

Broner, E(sther) M(asserman)
1930- .... **CLC 19**
See also CA 17-20R; CANR 8, 25, 72; CN
4, 5, 6; DLB 28

Buchan, John 1875-1940 .... **TCLC 41**
See also CA 108; 145; CMW 4; DAB;
DAM POP; DLB 34, 70, 156; HGG;
MSW; MTCW 2; RGEL 2; RHW; YABC
2

Buchanan, George 1506-1582 .... **LC 4**
See also DLB 132

Buchanan, Robert 1841-1901 .... **TCLC 107**
See also CA 179; DLB 18, 35

Buchheim, Lothar-Guenther 1918- .... **CLC 6**
See also CA 85-88

Buchner, (Karl) Georg
1813-1837 .... **NCLC 26, 146**
See also CDWLB 2; DLB 133; EW 6;
RGSF 2; RGWL 2, 3; TWA

Buchwald, Art(hur) 1925- .... **CLC 33**
See also AITN 1; CA 5-8R; CANR 21, 67,
107; MTCW 1, 2; SATA 10

Buck, Pearl S(ydenstricker)
1892-1973 .... **CLC 7, 11, 18, 127**
See also AAYA 42; AITN 1; AMWS 2;
BPFB 1; CA 1-4R; 41-44R; CANR 1, 34;
CDALBS; CN 1; DA; DA3; DAB; DAC;
DAM MST, NOV; DLB 9, 102; EWL 3;
LAIT 3; MAL 5; MTCW 1, 2; MTFW
2005; RGAL 4; RHW; SATA 1, 25; TUS

Buckler, Ernest 1908-1984 .... **CLC 13**
See also CA 11-12; 114; CAP 1; CCA 1;
CN 1, 2, 3; DAC; DAM MST; DLB 68;
SATA 47

Buckley, Christopher (Taylor)
1952- .... **CLC 165**
See also CA 139; CANR 119

Buckley, Vincent (Thomas)
1925-1988 .... **CLC 57**
See also CA 101; CP 1, 2, 3, 4; DLB 289

Buckley, William F(rank), Jr. 1925- . **CLC 7,
18, 37**
See also AITN 1; BPFB 1; CA 1-4R; CANR
1, 24, 53, 93, 133; CMW 4; CPW; DA3;
DAM POP; DLB 137; DLBY 1980; INT
CANR-24; MTCW 1, 2; MTFW 2005;
TUS

Buechner, (Carl) Frederick 1926- . **CLC 2, 4,
6, 9**
See also AMWS 12; BPFB 1; CA 13-16R;
CANR 11, 39, 64, 114, 138; CN 1, 2, 3,
4, 5, 6, 7; DAM NOV; DLBY 1980; INT
CANR-11; MAL 5; MTCW 1, 2; MTFW
2005; TCLE 1:1

Buell, John (Edward) 1927- .... **CLC 10**
See also CA 1-4R; CANR 71; DLB 53

Buero Vallejo, Antonio 1916-2000 ... **CLC 15,
46, 139; DC 18**
See also CA 106; 189; CANR 24, 49, 75;
CWW 2; DFS 11; EWL 3; HW 1; MTCW
1, 2

Bufalino, Gesualdo 1920-1996 .... **CLC 74**
See also CA 209; CWW 2; DLB 196

Bugayev, Boris Nikolayevich
1880-1934 .... **PC 11; TCLC 7**
See Bely, Andrey; Belyi, Andrei
See also CA 104; 165; MTCW 2; MTFW
2005

Bukowski, Charles 1920-1994 ... **CLC 2, 5, 9,
41, 82, 108; PC 18; SSC 45**
See also CA 17-20R; 144; CANR 40, 62,
105; CN 4, 5; CP 1, 2, 3, 4; CPW; DA3;
DAM NOV, POET; DLB 5, 130, 169;
EWL 3; MAL 5; MTCW 1, 2; MTFW
2005

Bulgakov, Mikhail (Afanas'evich)
1891-1940 ..... **SSC 18; TCLC 2, 16, 159**
See also BPFB 1; CA 105; 152; DAM
DRAM, NOV; DLB 272; EWL 3; MTCW
2; MTFW 2005; NFS 8; RGSF 2; RGWL
2, 3; SFW 4; TWA

Bulgya, Alexander Alexandrovich
1901-1956 .... **TCLC 53**
See Fadeev, Aleksandr Aleksandrovich;
Fadeev, Alexandr Alexandrovich; Fadeyev,
Alexander
See also CA 117; 181

Bullins, Ed 1935- ... **BLC 1; CLC 1, 5, 7; DC
6**
See also BW 2, 3; CA 49-52; CAAS 16;
CAD; CANR 24, 46, 73, 134; CD 5, 6;
DAM DRAM, MULT; DLB 7, 38, 249;
EWL 3; MAL 5; MTCW 1, 2; MTFW
2005; RGAL 4

Bulosan, Carlos 1911-1956 .... **AAL**
See also CA 216; DLB 312; RGAL 4

**Bulwer-Lytton, Edward (George Earle
Lytton)** 1803-1873 .... **NCLC 1, 45**
See also DLB 21; RGEL 2; SFW 4; SUFW
1; TEA

Bunin, Ivan Alexeyevich 1870-1953 ... **SSC 5;
TCLC 6**
See also CA 104; DLB 317; EWL 3; RGSF
2; RGWL 2, 3; TWA

Bunting, Basil 1900-1985 ...... **CLC 10, 39, 47**
See also BRWS 7; CA 53-56; 115; CANR
7; CP 1, 2, 3, 4; DAM POET; DLB 20;
EWL 3; RGEL 2

Bunuel, Luis 1900-1983 ... **CLC 16, 80; HLC
1**
See also CA 101; 110; CANR 32, 77; DAM
MULT; HW 1

Bunyan, John 1628-1688 ..... **LC 4, 69; WLC**
See also BRW 2; BYA 5; CDBLB 1660-
1789; DA; DAB; DAC; DAM MST; DLB
39; RGEL 2; TEA; WCH; WLIT 3

Buravsky, Alexandr .... **CLC 59**

Burckhardt, Jacob (Christoph)
1818-1897 .... **NCLC 49**
See also EW 6

Burford, Eleanor
See Hibbert, Eleanor Alice Burford

Burgess, Anthony . **CLC 1, 2, 4, 5, 8, 10, 13,
15, 22, 40, 62, 81, 94**
See Wilson, John (Anthony) Burgess
See also AAYA 25; AITN 1; BRWS 1; CD-
BLB 1960 to Present; CN 1, 2, 3, 4, 5;
DAB; DLB 14, 194, 261; DLBY 1998;
EWL 3; RGEL 2; RHW; SFW 4; YAW

Burke, Edmund 1729(?)-1797 .... **LC 7, 36;
WLC**
See also BRW 3; DA; DA3; DAB; DAC;
DAM MST; DLB 104, 252; RGEL 2;
TEA

Burke, Kenneth (Duva) 1897-1993 ... **CLC 2,
24**
See also AMW; CA 5-8R; 143; CANR 39,
74, 136; CN 1, 2; CP 1, 2, 3, 4; DLB 45,
63; EWL 3; MAL 5; MTCW 1, 2; MTFW
2005; RGAL 4

Burke, Leda
See Garnett, David

Burke, Ralph
See Silverberg, Robert

Burke, Thomas 1886-1945 .... **TCLC 63**
See also CA 113; 155; CMW 4; DLB 197

Burney, Fanny 1752-1840 .... **NCLC 12, 54,
107**
See also BRWS 3; DLB 39; FL 1:2; NFS
16; RGEL 2; TEA

Burney, Frances
See Burney, Fanny

Burns, Robert 1759-1796 ... **LC 3, 29, 40; PC
6; WLC**
See also AAYA 51; BRW 3; CDBLB 1789-
1832; DA; DA3; DAB; DAC; DAM MST,
POET; DLB 109; EXPP; PAB; RGEL 2;
TEA; WP

Burns, Tex
See L'Amour, Louis (Dearborn)

Burnshaw, Stanley 1906- .... **CLC 3, 13, 44**
See also CA 9-12R; CP 1, 2, 3, 4, 5, 6, 7;
DLB 48; DLBY 1997

Burr, Anne 1937- .... **CLC 6**
See also CA 25-28R

Burroughs, Edgar Rice 1875-1950 . **TCLC 2,
32**
See also AAYA 11; BPFB 1; BYA 4, 9; CA
104; 132; CANR 131; DA3; DAM NOV;
DLB 8; FANT; MTCW 1, 2; MTFW
2005; RGAL 4; SATA 41; SCFW 1, 2;
SFW 4; TCWW 1, 2; TUS; YAW

Burroughs, William S(eward)
1914-1997 .. **CLC 1, 2, 5, 15, 22, 42, 75,
109; TCLC 121; WLC**
See Lee, William; Lee, Willy
See also AAYA 60; AITN 2; AMWS 3; BG
1:2; BPFB 1; CA 9-12R; 160; CANR 20,
52, 104; CN 1, 2, 3, 4, 5, 6; CPW; DA;
DA3; DAB; DAC; DAM MST, NOV,
POP; DLB 2, 8, 16, 152, 237; DLBY
1981, 1997; EWL 3; HGG; LMFS 2;
MAL 5; MTCW 1, 2; MTFW 2005;
RGAL 4; SFW 4

Burton, Sir Richard F(rancis)
1821-1890 .... **NCLC 42**
See also DLB 55, 166, 184; SSFS 21

Burton, Robert 1577-1640 .... **LC 74**
See also DLB 151; RGEL 2

Buruma, Ian 1951- .... **CLC 163**
See also CA 128; CANR 65, 141

Busch, Frederick 1941- ... **CLC 7, 10, 18, 47,
166**
See also CA 33-36R; CAAS 1; CANR 45,
73, 92; CN 1, 2, 3, 4, 5, 6, 7; DLB 6, 218

Bush, Barney (Furman) 1946- .... **NNAL**
See also CA 145

Bush, Ronald 1946- .... **CLC 34**
See also CA 136

Bustos, F(rancisco)
See Borges, Jorge Luis

Bustos Domecq, H(onorio)
See Bioy Casares, Adolfo; Borges, Jorge
Luis

Butler, Octavia E(stelle) 1947- .. **BLCS; CLC
38, 121**
See also AAYA 18, 48; AFAW 2; AMWS
13; BPFB 1; BW 2, 3; CA 73-76; CANR
12, 24, 38, 73, 145; CLR 65; CN 7; CPW;
DA3; DAM MULT, POP; DLB 33; LATS
1:2; MTCW 1, 2; MTFW 2005; NFS 8,
21; SATA 84; SCFW 2; SFW 4; SSFS 6;
TCLE 1:1; YAW

Butler, Robert Olen, (Jr.) 1945- ...... **CLC 81,
162**
See also AMWS 12; BPFB 1; CA 112;
CANR 66, 138; CN 7; CSW; DAM POP;
DLB 173; INT CA-112; MAL 5; MTCW
2; MTFW 2005; SSFS 11

Butler, Samuel 1612-1680 .... **LC 16, 43**
See also DLB 101, 126; RGEL 2

Butler, Samuel 1835-1902 .... **TCLC 1, 33;
WLC**
See also BRWS 2; CA 143; CDBLB 1890-
1914; DA; DA3; DAB; DAC; DAM MST,
NOV; DLB 18, 57, 174; RGEL 2; SFW 4;
TEA

Butler, Walter C.
See Faust, Frederick (Schiller)

Butor, Michel (Marie Francois)
1926- .... **CLC 1, 3, 8, 11, 15, 161**
See also CA 9-12R; CANR 33, 66; CWW
2; DLB 83; EW 13; EWL 3; GFL 1789 to
the Present; MTCW 1, 2; MTFW 2005

Butts, Mary 1890(?)-1937 .... **TCLC 77**
See also CA 148; DLB 240

Buxton, Ralph
See Silverstein, Alvin; Silverstein, Virginia
B(arbara Opshelor)

Cankar, Ivan 1876-1918 .... **TCLC 105**
See also CDWLB 4; DLB 147; EWL 3

Cannon, Curt
See Hunter, Evan

Cao, Lan 1961- .... **CLC 109**
See also CA 165

Cape, Judith
See Page, P(atricia) K(athleen)
See also CCA 1

Capek, Karel 1890-1938 .... **DC 1; SSC 36; TCLC 6, 37; WLC**
See also CA 104; 140; CDWLB 4; DA; DA3; DAB; DAC; DAM DRAM, MST, NOV; DFS 7, 11; DLB 215; EW 10; EWL 3; MTCW 2; MTFW 2005; RGSF 2; RGWL 2, 3; SCFW 1, 2; SFW 4

Capote, Truman 1924-1984 . **CLC 1, 3, 8, 13, 19, 34, 38, 58; SSC 2, 47; TCLC 164; WLC**
See also AAYA 61; AMWS 3; BPFB 1; CA 5-8R; 113; CANR 18, 62; CDALB 1941-1968; CN 1, 2, 3; CPW; DA; DA3; DAB; DAC; DAM MST, NOV, POP; DLB 2, 185, 227; DLBY 1980, 1984; EWL 3; EXPS; GLL 1; LAIT 3; MAL 5; MTCW 1, 2; MTFW 2005; NCFS 2; RGAL 4; RGSF 2; SATA 91; SSFS 2; TUS

Capra, Frank 1897-1991 .... **CLC 16**
See also AAYA 52; CA 61-64; 135

Caputo, Philip 1941- .... **CLC 32**
See also AAYA 60; CA 73-76; CANR 40, 135; YAW

Caragiale, Ion Luca 1852-1912 ...... **TCLC 76**
See also CA 157

Card, Orson Scott 1951- .... **CLC 44, 47, 50**
See also AAYA 11, 42; BPFB 1; BYA 5, 8; CA 102; CANR 27, 47, 73, 102, 106, 133; CPW; DA3; DAM POP; FANT; INT CANR-27; MTCW 1, 2; MTFW 2005; NFS 5; SATA 83, 127; SCFW 2; SFW 4; SUFW 2; YAW

Cardenal, Ernesto 1925- .... **CLC 31, 161; HLC 1; PC 22**
See also CA 49-52; CANR 2, 32, 66, 138; CWW 2; DAM MULT, POET; DLB 290; EWL 3; HW 1, 2; LAWS 1; MTCW 1, 2; MTFW 2005; RGWL 2, 3

Cardinal, Marie 1929-2001 .... **CLC 189**
See also CA 177; CWW 2; DLB 83; FW

Cardozo, Benjamin N(athan) 1870-1938 .... **TCLC 65**
See also CA 117; 164

Carducci, Giosue (Alessandro Giuseppe) 1835-1907 .... **PC 46; TCLC 32**
See also CA 163; EW 7; RGWL 2, 3

Carew, Thomas 1595(?)-1640 . **LC 13; PC 29**
See also BRW 2; DLB 126; PAB; RGEL 2

Carey, Ernestine Gilbreth 1908- ...... **CLC 17**
See also CA 5-8R; CANR 71; SATA 2

Carey, Peter 1943- .... **CLC 40, 55, 96, 183**
See also CA 123; 127; CANR 53, 76, 117; CN 4, 5, 6, 7; DLB 289; EWL 3; INT CA-127; MTCW 1, 2; MTFW 2005; RGSF 2; SATA 94

Carleton, William 1794-1869 .... **NCLC 3**
See also DLB 159; RGEL 2; RGSF 2

Carlisle, Henry (Coffin) 1926- .... **CLC 33**
See also CA 13-16R; CANR 15, 85

Carlsen, Chris
See Holdstock, Robert P.

Carlson, Ron(ald F.) 1947- .... **CLC 54**
See also CA 105; 189; CAAE 189; CANR 27; DLB 244

Carlyle, Thomas 1795-1881 ..... **NCLC 22, 70**
See also BRW 4; CDBLB 1789-1832; DA; DAB; DAC; DAM MST; DLB 55, 144, 254; RGEL 2; TEA

Carman, (William) Bliss 1861-1929 ... **PC 34; TCLC 7**
See also CA 104; 152; DAC; DLB 92; RGEL 2

Carnegie, Dale 1888-1955 .... **TCLC 53**
See also CA 218

Carossa, Hans 1878-1956 .... **TCLC 48**
See also CA 170; DLB 66; EWL 3

Carpenter, Don(ald Richard) 1931-1995 .... **CLC 41**
See also CA 45-48; 149; CANR 1, 71

Carpenter, Edward 1844-1929 .... **TCLC 88**
See also CA 163; GLL 1

Carpenter, John (Howard) 1948- ... **CLC 161**
See also AAYA 2; CA 134; SATA 58

Carpenter, Johnny
See Carpenter, John (Howard)

Carpentier (y Valmont), Alejo 1904-1980 . **CLC 8, 11, 38, 110; HLC 1; SSC 35**
See also CA 65-68; 97-100; CANR 11, 70; CDWLB 3; DAM MULT; DLB 113; EWL 3; HW 1, 2; LAW; LMFS 2; RGSF 2; RGWL 2, 3; WLIT 1

Carr, Caleb 1955- .... **CLC 86**
See also CA 147; CANR 73, 134; DA3

Carr, Emily 1871-1945 .... **TCLC 32**
See also CA 159; DLB 68; FW; GLL 2

Carr, John Dickson 1906-1977 .... **CLC 3**
See Fairbairn, Roger
See also CA 49-52; 69-72; CANR 3, 33, 60; CMW 4; DLB 306; MSW; MTCW 1, 2

Carr, Philippa
See Hibbert, Eleanor Alice Burford

Carr, Virginia Spencer 1929- .... **CLC 34**
See also CA 61-64; DLB 111

Carrere, Emmanuel 1957- .... **CLC 89**
See also CA 200

Carrier, Roch 1937- .... **CLC 13, 78**
See also CA 130; CANR 61; CCA 1; DAC; DAM MST; DLB 53; SATA 105

Carroll, James Dennis
See Carroll, Jim

Carroll, James P. 1943(?)- .... **CLC 38**
See also CA 81-84; CANR 73, 139; MTCW 2; MTFW 2005

Carroll, Jim 1951- .... **CLC 35, 143**
See also AAYA 17; CA 45-48; CANR 42, 115; NCFS 5

Carroll, Lewis ..... **NCLC 2, 53, 139; PC 18; WLC**
See Dodgson, Charles L(utwidge)
See also AAYA 39; BRW 5; BYA 5, 13; CDBLB 1832-1890; CLR 2, 18; DLB 18, 163, 178; DLBY 1998; EXPN; EXPP; FANT; JRDA; LAIT 1; NFS 7; PFS 11; RGEL 2; SUFW 1; TEA; WCH

Carroll, Paul Vincent 1900-1968 ..... **CLC 10**
See also CA 9-12R; 25-28R; DLB 10; EWL 3; RGEL 2

Carruth, Hayden 1921- ..... **CLC 4, 7, 10, 18, 84; PC 10**
See also CA 9-12R; CANR 4, 38, 59, 110; CP 1, 2, 3, 4, 5, 6, 7; DLB 5, 165; INT CANR-4; MTCW 1, 2; MTFW 2005; SATA 47

Carson, Anne 1950- .... **CLC 185; PC 64**
See also AMWS 12; CA 203; DLB 193; PFS 18; TCLE 1:1

Carson, Ciaran 1948- .... **CLC 201**
See also CA 112; 153; CANR 113; CP 7

Carson, Rachel
See Carson, Rachel Louise
See also AAYA 49; DLB 275

Carson, Rachel Louise 1907-1964 .... **CLC 71**
See Carson, Rachel
See also CA 77-80; CANR 35; DA3; DAM POP; FW; LAIT 4; MAL 5; MTCW 1, 2; MTFW 2005; NCFS 1; SATA 23

Carter, Angela (Olive) 1940-1992 ...... **CLC 5, 41, 76; SSC 13, 85; TCLC 139**
See also BRWS 3; CA 53-56; 136; CANR 12, 36, 61, 106; CN 3, 4, 5; DA3; DLB 14, 207, 261, 319; EXPS; FANT; FW; GL 2; MTCW 1, 2; MTFW 2005; RGSF 2; SATA 66; SATA-Obit 70; SFW 4; SSFS 4, 12; SUFW 2; WLIT 4

Carter, Nick
See Smith, Martin Cruz

Carver, Raymond 1938-1988 ..... **CLC 22, 36, 53, 55, 126; PC 54; SSC 8, 51**
See also AAYA 44; AMWS 3; BPFB 1; CA 33-36R; 126; CANR 17, 34, 61, 103; CN 4; CPW; DA3; DAM NOV; DLB 130; DLBY 1984, 1988; EWL 3; MAL 5; MTCW 1, 2; MTFW 2005; PFS 17; RGAL 4; RGSF 2; SSFS 3, 6, 12, 13; TCLE 1:1; TCWW 2; TUS

Cary, Elizabeth, Lady Falkland 1585-1639 .... **LC 30**

Cary, (Arthur) Joyce (Lunel) 1888-1957 .... **TCLC 1, 29**
See also BRW 7; CA 104; 164; CDBLB 1914-1945; DLB 15, 100; EWL 3; MTCW 2; RGEL 2; TEA

Casal, Julian del 1863-1893 .... **NCLC 131**
See also DLB 283; LAW

Casanova, Giacomo
See Casanova de Seingalt, Giovanni Jacopo
See also WLIT 7

Casanova de Seingalt, Giovanni Jacopo 1725-1798 .... **LC 13**
See Casanova, Giacomo

Casares, Adolfo Bioy
See Bioy Casares, Adolfo
See also RGSF 2

Casas, Bartolome de las 1474-1566
See Las Casas, Bartolome de
See also WLIT 1

Casely-Hayford, J(oseph) E(phraim) 1866-1903 .... **BLC 1; TCLC 24**
See also BW 2; CA 123; 152; DAM MULT

Casey, John (Dudley) 1939- .... **CLC 59**
See also BEST 90:2; CA 69-72; CANR 23, 100

Casey, Michael 1947- .... **CLC 2**
See also CA 65-68; CANR 109; CP 2, 3; DLB 5

Casey, Patrick
See Thurman, Wallace (Henry)

Casey, Warren (Peter) 1935-1988 .... **CLC 12**
See also CA 101; 127; INT CA-101

Casona, Alejandro .... **CLC 49**
See Alvarez, Alejandro Rodriguez
See also EWL 3

Cassavetes, John 1929-1989 .... **CLC 20**
See also CA 85-88; 127; CANR 82

Cassian, Nina 1924- .... **PC 17**
See also CWP; CWW 2

Cassill, R(onald) V(erlin) 1919-2002 .... **CLC 4, 23**
See also CA 9-12R; 208; CAAS 1; CANR 7, 45; CN 1, 2, 3, 4, 5, 6, 7; DLB 6, 218; DLBY 2002

Cassiodorus, Flavius Magnus c. 490(?)-c. 583(?) .... **CMLC 43**

Cassirer, Ernst 1874-1945 .... **TCLC 61**
See also CA 157

Cassity, (Allen) Turner 1929- .... **CLC 6, 42**
See also CA 17-20R; 223; CAAE 223; CAAS 8; CANR 11; CSW; DLB 105

Chapman, John Jay 1862-1933 .... **TCLC 7**
   See also AMWS 14; CA 104; 191

Chapman, Lee
   See Bradley, Marion Zimmer
   See also GLL 1

Chapman, Walker
   See Silverberg, Robert

Chappell, Fred (Davis) 1936- .... **CLC 40, 78, 162**
   See also CA 5-8R, 198; CAAE 198; CAAS 4; CANR 8, 33, 67, 110; CN 6; CP 7; CSW; DLB 6, 105; HGG

Char, Rene(-Emile) 1907-1988 .... **CLC 9, 11, 14, 55; PC 56**
   See also CA 13-16R; 124; CANR 32; DAM POET; DLB 258; EWL 3; GFL 1789 to the Present; MTCW 1, 2; RGWL 2, 3

Charby, Jay
   See Ellison, Harlan (Jay)

Chardin, Pierre Teilhard de
   See Teilhard de Chardin, (Marie Joseph) Pierre

Chariton fl. 1st cent. (?)- .... **CMLC 49**

Charlemagne 742-814 .... **CMLC 37**

Charles I 1600-1649 .... **LC 13**

Charriere, Isabelle de 1740-1805 .. **NCLC 66**
   See also DLB 313

Chartier, Alain c. 1392-1430 .... **LC 94**
   See also DLB 208

Chartier, Emile-Auguste
   See Alain

Charyn, Jerome 1937- .... **CLC 5, 8, 18**
   See also CA 5-8R; CAAS 1; CANR 7, 61, 101; CMW 4; CN 1, 2, 3, 4, 5, 6, 7; DLBY 1983; MTCW 1

Chase, Adam
   See Marlowe, Stephen

Chase, Mary (Coyle) 1907-1981 .... **DC 1**
   See also CA 77-80; 105; CAD; CWD; DFS 11; DLB 228; SATA 17; SATA-Obit 29

Chase, Mary Ellen 1887-1973 .... **CLC 2; TCLC 124**
   See also CA 13-16; 41-44R; CAP 1; SATA 10

Chase, Nicholas
   See Hyde, Anthony
   See also CCA 1

Chateaubriand, Francois Rene de 1768-1848 .... **NCLC 3, 134**
   See also DLB 119; EW 5; GFL 1789 to the Present; RGWL 2, 3; TWA

Chatelet, Gabrielle-Emilie Du
   See du Chatelet, Emilie
   See also DLB 313

Chatterje, Sarat Chandra 1876-1936(?)
   See Chatterji, Saratchandra
   See also CA 109

Chatterji, Bankim Chandra 1838-1894 .... **NCLC 19**

Chatterji, Saratchandra .... **TCLC 13**
   See Chatterje, Sarat Chandra
   See also CA 186; EWL 3

Chatterton, Thomas 1752-1770 .... **LC 3, 54**
   See also DAM POET; DLB 109; RGEL 2

Chatwin, (Charles) Bruce 1940-1989 .... **CLC 28, 57, 59**
   See also AAYA 4; BEST 90:1; BRWS 4; CA 85-88; 127; CPW; DAM POP; DLB 194, 204; EWL 3; MTFW 2005

Chaucer, Daniel
   See Ford, Ford Madox
   See also RHW

Chaucer, Geoffrey 1340(?)-1400 .. **LC 17, 56; PC 19, 58; WLCS**
   See also BRW 1; BRWC 1; BRWR 2; CD-BLB Before 1660; DA; DA3; DAB; DAC; DAM MST, POET; DLB 146; LAIT 1; PAB; PFS 14; RGEL 2; TEA; WLIT 3; WP

Chavez, Denise (Elia) 1948- .... **HLC 1**
   See also CA 131; CANR 56, 81, 137; DAM MULT; DLB 122; FW; HW 1, 2; LLW; MAL 5; MTCW 2; MTFW 2005

Chaviaras, Strates 1935-
   See Haviaras, Stratis
   See also CA 105

Chayefsky, Paddy .... **CLC 23**
   See Chayefsky, Sidney
   See also CAD; DLB 7, 44; DLBY 1981; RGAL 4

Chayefsky, Sidney 1923-1981
   See Chayefsky, Paddy
   See also CA 9-12R; 104; CANR 18; DAM DRAM

Chedid, Andree 1920- .... **CLC 47**
   See also CA 145; CANR 95; EWL 3

Cheever, John 1912-1982 ..... **CLC 3, 7, 8, 11, 15, 25, 64; SSC 1, 38, 57; WLC**
   See also AAYA 65; AMWS 1; BPFB 1; CA 5-8R; 106; CABS 1; CANR 5, 27, 76; CDALB 1941-1968; CN 1, 2, 3; CPW; DA; DA3; DAB; DAC; DAM MST, NOV, POP; DLB 2, 102, 227; DLBY 1980, 1982; EWL 3; EXPS; INT CANR-5; MAL 5; MTCW 1, 2; MTFW 2005; RGAL 4; RGSF 2; SSFS 2, 14; TUS

Cheever, Susan 1943- .... **CLC 18, 48**
   See also CA 103; CANR 27, 51, 92; DLBY 1982; INT CANR-27

Chekhonte, Antosha
   See Chekhov, Anton (Pavlovich)

Chekhov, Anton (Pavlovich) 1860-1904 .... **DC 9; SSC 2, 28, 41, 51, 85; TCLC 3, 10, 31, 55, 96, 163; WLC**
   See also AAYA 68; BYA 14; CA 104; 124; DA; DA3; DAB; DAC; DAM DRAM, MST; DFS 1, 5, 10, 12; DLB 277; EW 7; EWL 3; EXPS; LAIT 3; LATS 1:1; RGSF 2; RGWL 2, 3; SATA 90; SSFS 5, 13, 14; TWA

Cheney, Lynne V. 1941- .... **CLC 70**
   See also CA 89-92; CANR 58, 117; SATA 152

Chernyshevsky, Nikolai Gavrilovich
   See Chernyshevsky, Nikolay Gavrilovich
   See also DLB 238

Chernyshevsky, Nikolay Gavrilovich 1828-1889 .... **NCLC 1**
   See Chernyshevsky, Nikolai Gavrilovich

Cherry, Carolyn Janice 1942-
   See Cherryh, C. J.
   See also CA 65-68; CANR 10

Cherryh, C. J. .... **CLC 35**
   See Cherry, Carolyn Janice
   See also AAYA 24; BPFB 1; DLBY 1980; FANT; SATA 93; SCFW 2; SFW 4; YAW

Chesnutt, Charles W(addell) 1858-1932 .... **BLC 1; SSC 7, 54; TCLC 5, 39**
   See also AFAW 1, 2; AMWS 14; BW 1, 3; CA 106; 125; CANR 76; DAM MULT; DLB 12, 50, 78; EWL 3; MAL 5; MTCW 1, 2; MTFW 2005; RGAL 4; RGSF 2; SSFS 11

Chester, Alfred 1929(?)-1971 .... **CLC 49**
   See also CA 196; 33-36R; DLB 130; MAL 5

Chesterton, G(ilbert) K(eith) 1874-1936 . **PC 28; SSC 1, 46; TCLC 1, 6, 64**
   See also AAYA 57; BRW 6; CA 104; 132; CANR 73, 131; CDBLB 1914-1945; CMW 4; DAM NOV, POET; DLB 10, 19, 34, 70, 98, 149, 178; EWL 3; FANT; MSW; MTCW 1, 2; MTFW 2005; RGEL 2; RGSF 2; SATA 27; SUFW 1

Chettle, Henry 1560-1607(?) .... **LC 112**
   See also DLB 136; RGEL 2

Chiang, Pin-chin 1904-1986
   See Ding Ling
   See also CA 118

Chief Joseph 1840-1904 .... **NNAL**
   See also CA 152; DA3; DAM MULT

Chief Seattle 1786(?)-1866 .... **NNAL**
   See also DA3; DAM MULT

Ch'ien, Chung-shu 1910-1998 .... **CLC 22**
   See also CA 130; CANR 73; MTCW 1, 2

Chikamatsu Monzaemon 1653-1724 ... **LC 66**
   See also RGWL 2, 3

Child, L. Maria
   See Child, Lydia Maria

Child, Lydia Maria 1802-1880 .. **NCLC 6, 73**
   See also DLB 1, 74, 243; RGAL 4; SATA 67

Child, Mrs.
   See Child, Lydia Maria

Child, Philip 1898-1978 .... **CLC 19, 68**
   See also CA 13-14; CAP 1; CP 1; DLB 68; RHW; SATA 47

Childers, (Robert) Erskine 1870-1922 .... **TCLC 65**
   See also CA 113; 153; DLB 70

Childress, Alice 1920-1994 . **BLC 1; CLC 12, 15, 86, 96; DC 4; TCLC 116**
   See also AAYA 8; BW 2, 3; BYA 2; CA 45-48; 146; CAD; CANR 3, 27, 50, 74; CLR 14; CWD; DA3; DAM DRAM, MULT, NOV; DFS 2, 8, 14; DLB 7, 38, 249; JRDA; LAIT 5; MAICYA 1, 2; MAIC-YAS 1; MAL 5; MTCW 1, 2; MTFW 2005; RGAL 4; SATA 7, 48, 81; TUS; WYA; YAW

Chin, Frank (Chew, Jr.) 1940- .... **AAL; CLC 135; DC 7**
   See also CA 33-36R; CAD; CANR 71; CD 5, 6; DAM MULT; DLB 206, 312; LAIT 5; RGAL 4

Chin, Marilyn (Mei Ling) 1955- .... **PC 40**
   See also CA 129; CANR 70, 113; CWP; DLB 312

Chislett, (Margaret) Anne 1943- ...... **CLC 34**
   See also CA 151

Chitty, Thomas Willes 1926- .... **CLC 11**
   See Hinde, Thomas
   See also CA 5-8R; CN 7

Chivers, Thomas Holley 1809-1858 .... **NCLC 49**
   See also DLB 3, 248; RGAL 4

Choi, Susan 1969- .... **CLC 119**
   See also CA 223

Chomette, Rene Lucien 1898-1981
   See Clair, Rene
   See also CA 103

Chomsky, (Avram) Noam 1928- ..... **CLC 132**
   See also CA 17-20R; CANR 28, 62, 110, 132; DA3; DLB 246; MTCW 1, 2; MTFW 2005

Chona, Maria 1845(?)-1936 .... **NNAL**
   See also CA 144

Chopin, Kate .... **SSC 8, 68; TCLC 127; WLCS**
   See Chopin, Katherine
   See also AAYA 33; AMWR 2; AMWS 1; BYA 11, 15; CDALB 1865-1917; DA; DAB; DLB 12, 78; EXPN; EXPS; FL 1:3; FW; LAIT 3; MAL 5; MAWW; NFS 3; RGAL 4; RGSF 2; SSFS 2, 13, 17; TUS

Chopin, Katherine 1851-1904
   See Chopin, Kate
   See also CA 104; 122; DA3; DAC; DAM MST, NOV

Chretien de Troyes c. 12th cent. - . **CMLC 10**
   See also DLB 208; EW 1; RGWL 2, 3; TWA

Christie
   See Ichikawa, Kon

Clough, Arthur Hugh 1819-1861 .. **NCLC 27, 163**
See also BRW 5; DLB 32; RGEL 2

Clutha, Janet Paterson Frame 1924-2004
See Frame, Janet
See also CA 1-4R; 224; CANR 2, 36, 76, 135; MTCW 1, 2; SATA 119

Clyne, Terence
See Blatty, William Peter

Cobalt, Martin
See Mayne, William (James Carter)

Cobb, Irvin S(hrewsbury)
1876-1944 .... **TCLC 77**
See also CA 175; DLB 11, 25, 86

Cobbett, William 1763-1835 .... **NCLC 49**
See also DLB 43, 107, 158; RGEL 2

Coburn, D(onald) L(ee) 1938- .... **CLC 10**
See also CA 89-92

Cocteau, Jean (Maurice Eugene Clement)
1889-1963 ...... **CLC 1, 8, 15, 16, 43; DC 17; TCLC 119; WLC**
See also CA 25-28; CANR 40; CAP 2; DA; DA3; DAB; DAC; DAM DRAM, MST, NOV; DLB 65, 258, 321; EW 10; EWL 3; GFL 1789 to the Present; MTCW 1, 2; RGWL 2, 3; TWA

Codrescu, Andrei 1946- .... **CLC 46, 121**
See also CA 33-36R; CAAS 19; CANR 13, 34, 53, 76, 125; CN 7; DA3; DAM POET; MAL 5; MTCW 2; MTFW 2005

Coe, Max
See Bourne, Randolph S(illiman)

Coe, Tucker
See Westlake, Donald E(dwin)

Coen, Ethan 1958- .... **CLC 108**
See also AAYA 54; CA 126; CANR 85

Coen, Joel 1955- .... **CLC 108**
See also AAYA 54; CA 126; CANR 119

The Coen Brothers
See Coen, Ethan; Coen, Joel

Coetzee, J(ohn) M(axwell) 1940- ..... **CLC 23, 33, 66, 117, 161, 162**
See also AAYA 37; AFW; BRWS 6; CA 77-80; CANR 41, 54, 74, 114, 133; CN 4, 5, 6, 7; DA3; DAM NOV; DLB 225; EWL 3; LMFS 2; MTCW 1, 2; MTFW 2005; NFS 21; WLIT 2; WWE 1

Coffey, Brian
See Koontz, Dean R.

Coffin, Robert P(eter) Tristram
1892-1955 .... **TCLC 95**
See also CA 123; 169; DLB 45

Cohan, George M(ichael)
1878-1942 .... **TCLC 60**
See also CA 157; DLB 249; RGAL 4

Cohen, Arthur A(llen) 1928-1986 ...... **CLC 7, 31**
See also CA 1-4R; 120; CANR 1, 17, 42; DLB 28

Cohen, Leonard (Norman) 1934- ...... **CLC 3, 38**
See also CA 21-24R; CANR 14, 69; CN 1, 2, 3, 4, 5, 6; CP 1, 2, 3, 4, 5, 6, 7; DAC; DAM MST; DLB 53; EWL 3; MTCW 1

Cohen, Matt(hew) 1942-1999 .... **CLC 19**
See also CA 61-64; 187; CAAS 18; CANR 40; CN 1, 2, 3, 4, 5, 6; DAC; DLB 53

Cohen-Solal, Annie 1948- .... **CLC 50**
See also CA 239

Colegate, Isabel 1931- .... **CLC 36**
See also CA 17-20R; CANR 8, 22, 74; CN 4, 5, 6, 7; DLB 14, 231; INT CANR-22; MTCW 1

Coleman, Emmett
See Reed, Ishmael (Scott)

Coleridge, Hartley 1796-1849 .... **NCLC 90**
See also DLB 96

Coleridge, M. E.
See Coleridge, Mary E(lizabeth)

Coleridge, Mary E(lizabeth)
1861-1907 .... **TCLC 73**
See also CA 116; 166; DLB 19, 98

Coleridge, Samuel Taylor
1772-1834 ...... **NCLC 9, 54, 99, 111; PC 11, 39, 67; WLC**
See also AAYA 66; BRW 4; BRWR 2; BYA 4; CDBLB 1789-1832; DA; DA3; DAB; DAC; DAM MST, POET; DLB 93, 107; EXPP; LATS 1:1; LMFS 1; PAB; PFS 4, 5; RGEL 2; TEA; WLIT 3; WP

Coleridge, Sara 1802-1852 .... **NCLC 31**
See also DLB 199

Coles, Don 1928- .... **CLC 46**
See also CA 115; CANR 38; CP 7

Coles, Robert (Martin) 1929- .... **CLC 108**
See also CA 45-48; CANR 3, 32, 66, 70, 135; INT CANR-32; SATA 23

Colette, (Sidonie-Gabrielle)
1873-1954 .... **SSC 10; TCLC 1, 5, 16**
See Willy, Colette
See also CA 104; 131; DA3; DAM NOV; DLB 65; EW 9; EWL 3; GFL 1789 to the Present; MTCW 1, 2; MTFW 2005; RGWL 2, 3; TWA

Collett, (Jacobine) Camilla (Wergeland)
1813-1895 .... **NCLC 22**

Collier, Christopher 1930- .... **CLC 30**
See also AAYA 13; BYA 2; CA 33-36R; CANR 13, 33, 102; JRDA; MAICYA 1, 2; SATA 16, 70; WYA; YAW 1

Collier, James Lincoln 1928- .... **CLC 30**
See also AAYA 13; BYA 2; CA 9-12R; CANR 4, 33, 60, 102; CLR 3; DAM POP; JRDA; MAICYA 1, 2; SAAS 21; SATA 8, 70; WYA; YAW 1

Collier, Jeremy 1650-1726 .... **LC 6**

Collier, John 1901-1980 . **SSC 19; TCLC 127**
See also CA 65-68; 97-100; CANR 10; CN 1, 2; DLB 77, 255; FANT; SUFW 1

Collier, Mary 1690-1762 .... **LC 86**
See also DLB 95

Collingwood, R(obin) G(eorge)
1889(?)-1943 .... **TCLC 67**
See also CA 117; 155; DLB 262

Collins, Billy 1941- .... **PC 68**
See also AAYA 64; CA 151; CANR 92; MTFW 2005; PFS 18

Collins, Hunt
See Hunter, Evan

Collins, Linda 1931- .... **CLC 44**
See also CA 125

Collins, Tom
See Furphy, Joseph
See also RGEL 2

Collins, (William) Wilkie
1824-1889 .... **NCLC 1, 18, 93**
See also BRWS 6; CDBLB 1832-1890; CMW 4; DLB 18, 70, 159; GL 2; MSW; RGEL 2; RGSF 2; SUFW 1; WLIT 4

Collins, William 1721-1759 .... **LC 4, 40**
See also BRW 3; DAM POET; DLB 109; RGEL 2

Collodi, Carlo .... **NCLC 54**
See Lorenzini, Carlo
See also CLR 5; WCH; WLIT 7

Colman, George
See Glassco, John

Colman, George, the Elder
1732-1794 .... **LC 98**
See also RGEL 2

Colonna, Vittoria 1492-1547 .... **LC 71**
See also RGWL 2, 3

Colt, Winchester Remington
See Hubbard, L(afayette) Ron(ald)

Colter, Cyrus J. 1910-2002 .... **CLC 58**
See also BW 1; CA 65-68; 205; CANR 10, 66; CN 2, 3, 4, 5, 6; DLB 33

Colton, James
See Hansen, Joseph
See also GLL 1

Colum, Padraic 1881-1972 .... **CLC 28**
See also BYA 4; CA 73-76; 33-36R; CANR 35; CLR 36; CP 1; CWRI 5; DLB 19; MAICYA 1, 2; MTCW 1; RGEL 2; SATA 15; WCH

Colvin, James
See Moorcock, Michael (John)

Colwin, Laurie (E.) 1944-1992 .... **CLC 5, 13, 23, 84**
See also CA 89-92; 139; CANR 20, 46; DLB 218; DLBY 1980; MTCW 1

Comfort, Alex(ander) 1920-2000 .... **CLC 7**
See also CA 1-4R; 190; CANR 1, 45; CN 1, 2, 3, 4; CP 1, 2, 3, 4, 5, 6, 7; DAM POP; MTCW 2

Comfort, Montgomery
See Campbell, (John) Ramsey

Compton-Burnett, I(vy)
1892(?)-1969 .... **CLC 1, 3, 10, 15, 34**
See also BRW 7; CA 1-4R; 25-28R; CANR 4; DAM NOV; DLB 36; EWL 3; MTCW 1, 2; RGEL 2

Comstock, Anthony 1844-1915 ...... **TCLC 13**
See also CA 110; 169

Comte, Auguste 1798-1857 .... **NCLC 54**

Conan Doyle, Arthur
See Doyle, Sir Arthur Conan
See also BPFB 1; BYA 4, 5, 11

Conde (Abellan), Carmen
1901-1996 .... **HLCS 1**
See also CA 177; CWW 2; DLB 108; EWL 3; HW 2

Conde, Maryse 1937- ..... **BLCS; CLC 52, 92**
See also BW 2, 3; CA 110; 190; CAAE 190; CANR 30, 53, 76; CWW 2; DAM MULT; EWL 3; MTCW 2; MTFW 2005

Condillac, Etienne Bonnot de
1714-1780 .... **LC 26**
See also DLB 313

Condon, Richard (Thomas)
1915-1996 .... **CLC 4, 6, 8, 10, 45, 100**
See also BEST 90:3; BPFB 1; CA 1-4R; 151; CAAS 1; CANR 2, 23; CMW 4; CN 1, 2, 3, 4, 5, 6; DAM NOV; INT CANR-23; MAL 5; MTCW 1, 2

Condorcet .... **LC 104**
See Condorcet, marquis de Marie-Jean-Antoine-Nicolas Caritat
See also GFL Beginnings to 1789

Condorcet, marquis de
Marie-Jean-Antoine-Nicolas Caritat
1743-1794
See Condorcet
See also DLB 313

Confucius 551B.C.-479B.C. .... **CMLC 19, 65; WLCS**
See also DA; DA3; DAB; DAC; DAM MST

Congreve, William 1670-1729 ... **DC 2; LC 5, 21; WLC**
See also BRW 2; CDBLB 1660-1789; DA; DAB; DAC; DAM DRAM, MST, POET; DFS 15; DLB 39, 84; RGEL 2; WLIT 3

Conley, Robert J(ackson) 1940- .... **NNAL**
See also CA 41-44R; CANR 15, 34, 45, 96; DAM MULT; TCWW 2

Connell, Evan S(helby), Jr. 1924- . **CLC 4, 6, 45**
See also AAYA 7; AMWS 14; CA 1-4R; CAAS 2; CANR 2, 39, 76, 97, 140; CN 1, 2, 3, 4, 5, 6; DAM NOV; DLB 2; DLBY 1981; MAL 5; MTCW 1, 2; MTFW 2005

Connelly, Marc(us Cook) 1890-1980 . **CLC 7**
See also CA 85-88; 102; CAD; CANR 30; DFS 12; DLB 7; DLBY 1980; MAL 5; RGAL 4; SATA-Obit 25

Cox, William Trevor 1928-
See Trevor, William
See also CA 9-12R; CANR 4, 37, 55, 76, 102, 139; DAM NOV; INT CANR-37; MTCW 1, 2; MTFW 2005; TEA

Coyne, P. J.
See Masters, Hilary

Cozzens, James Gould 1903-1978 . **CLC 1, 4, 11, 92**
See also AMW; BPFB 1; CA 9-12R; 81-84; CANR 19; CDALB 1941-1968; CN 1, 2; DLB 9, 294; DLBD 2; DLBY 1984, 1997; EWL 3; MAL 5; MTCW 1, 2; MTFW 2005; RGAL 4

Crabbe, George 1754-1832 .... **NCLC 26, 121**
See also BRW 3; DLB 93; RGEL 2

Crace, Jim 1946- .... **CLC 157; SSC 61**
See also CA 128; 135; CANR 55, 70, 123; CN 5, 6, 7; DLB 231; INT CA-135

Craddock, Charles Egbert
See Murfree, Mary Noailles

Craig, A. A.
See Anderson, Poul (William)

Craik, Mrs.
See Craik, Dinah Maria (Mulock)
See also RGEL 2

Craik, Dinah Maria (Mulock)
1826-1887 .... **NCLC 38**
See Craik, Mrs.; Mulock, Dinah Maria
See also DLB 35, 163; MAICYA 1, 2; SATA 34

Cram, Ralph Adams 1863-1942 ..... **TCLC 45**
See also CA 160

Cranch, Christopher Pearse
1813-1892 .... **NCLC 115**
See also DLB 1, 42, 243

Crane, (Harold) Hart 1899-1932 .... **PC 3; TCLC 2, 5, 80; WLC**
See also AMW; AMWR 2; CA 104; 127; CDALB 1917-1929; DA; DA3; DAB; DAC; DAM MST, POET; DLB 4, 48; EWL 3; MAL 5; MTCW 1, 2; MTFW 2005; RGAL 4; TUS

Crane, R(onald) S(almon)
1886-1967 .... **CLC 27**
See also CA 85-88; DLB 63

Crane, Stephen (Townley)
1871-1900 ...... **SSC 7, 56, 70; TCLC 11, 17, 32; WLC**
See also AAYA 21; AMW; AMWC 1; BPFB 1; BYA 3; CA 109; 140; CANR 84; CDALB 1865-1917; DA; DA3; DAB; DAC; DAM MST, NOV, POET; DLB 12, 54, 78; EXPN; EXPS; LAIT 2; LMFS 2; MAL 5; NFS 4, 20; PFS 9; RGAL 4; RGSF 2; SSFS 4; TUS; WYA; YABC 2

Cranmer, Thomas 1489-1556 .... **LC 95**
See also DLB 132, 213

Cranshaw, Stanley
See Fisher, Dorothy (Frances) Canfield

Crase, Douglas 1944- .... **CLC 58**
See also CA 106

Crashaw, Richard 1612(?)-1649 .... **LC 24**
See also BRW 2; DLB 126; PAB; RGEL 2

Cratinus c. 519B.C.-c. 422B.C. ..... **CMLC 54**
See also LMFS 1

Craven, Margaret 1901-1980 .... **CLC 17**
See also BYA 2; CA 103; CCA 1; DAC; LAIT 5

Crawford, F(rancis) Marion
1854-1909 .... **TCLC 10**
See also CA 107; 168; DLB 71; HGG; RGAL 4; SUFW 1

Crawford, Isabella Valancy
1850-1887 .... **NCLC 12, 127**
See also DLB 92; RGEL 2

Crayon, Geoffrey
See Irving, Washington

Creasey, John 1908-1973 .... **CLC 11**
See Marric, J. J.
See also CA 5-8R; 41-44R; CANR 8, 59; CMW 4; DLB 77; MTCW 1

Crebillon, Claude Prosper Jolyot de (fils)
1707-1777 .... **LC 1, 28**
See also DLB 313; GFL Beginnings to 1789

Credo
See Creasey, John

Credo, Alvaro J. de
See Prado (Calvo), Pedro

Creeley, Robert (White) 1926-2005 .. **CLC 1, 2, 4, 8, 11, 15, 36, 78**
See also AMWS 4; CA 1-4R; 237; CAAS 10; CANR 23, 43, 89, 137; CP 1, 2, 3, 4, 5, 6, 7; DA3; DAM POET; DLB 5, 16, 169; DLBD 17; EWL 3; MAL 5; MTCW 1, 2; MTFW 2005; PFS 21; RGAL 4; WP

Crenne, Helisenne de 1510-1560 .... **LC 113**

Crevecoeur, Hector St. John de
See Crevecoeur, Michel Guillaume Jean de
See also ANW

Crevecoeur, Michel Guillaume Jean de
1735-1813 .... **NCLC 105**
See Crevecoeur, Hector St. John de
See also AMWS 1; DLB 37

Crevel, Rene 1900-1935 .... **TCLC 112**
See also GLL 2

Crews, Harry (Eugene) 1935- ..... **CLC 6, 23, 49**
See also AITN 1; AMWS 11; BPFB 1; CA 25-28R; CANR 20, 57; CN 3, 4, 5, 6, 7; CSW; DA3; DLB 6, 143, 185; MTCW 1, 2; MTFW 2005; RGAL 4

Crichton, (John) Michael 1942- .... **CLC 2, 6, 54, 90**
See also AAYA 10, 49; AITN 2; BPFB 1; CA 25-28R; CANR 13, 40, 54, 76, 127; CMW 4; CN 2, 3, 6, 7; CPW; DA3; DAM NOV, POP; DLB 292; DLBY 1981; INT CANR-13; JRDA; MTCW 1, 2; MTFW 2005; SATA 9, 88; SFW 4; YAW

Crispin, Edmund .... **CLC 22**
See Montgomery, (Robert) Bruce
See also DLB 87; MSW

Cristofer, Michael 1945- .... **CLC 28**
See also CA 110; 152; CAD; CD 5, 6; DAM DRAM; DFS 15; DLB 7

Criton
See Alain

Croce, Benedetto 1866-1952 .... **TCLC 37**
See also CA 120; 155; EW 8; EWL 3; WLIT 7

Crockett, David 1786-1836 .... **NCLC 8**
See also DLB 3, 11, 183, 248

Crockett, Davy
See Crockett, David

Crofts, Freeman Wills 1879-1957 .. **TCLC 55**
See also CA 115; 195; CMW 4; DLB 77; MSW

Croker, John Wilson 1780-1857 .... **NCLC 10**
See also DLB 110

Crommelynck, Fernand 1885-1970 .. **CLC 75**
See also CA 189; 89-92; EWL 3

Cromwell, Oliver 1599-1658 .... **LC 43**

Cronenberg, David 1943- .... **CLC 143**
See also CA 138; CCA 1

Cronin, A(rchibald) J(oseph)
1896-1981 .... **CLC 32**
See also BPFB 1; CA 1-4R; 102; CANR 5; CN 2; DLB 191; SATA 47; SATA-Obit 25

Cross, Amanda
See Heilbrun, Carolyn G(old)
See also BPFB 1; CMW; CPW; DLB 306; MSW

Crothers, Rachel 1878-1958 .... **TCLC 19**
See also CA 113; 194; CAD; CWD; DLB 7, 266; RGAL 4

Croves, Hal
See Traven, B.

Crow Dog, Mary (Ellen) (?)- .... **CLC 93**
See Brave Bird, Mary
See also CA 154

Crowfield, Christopher
See Stowe, Harriet (Elizabeth) Beecher

Crowley, Aleister .... **TCLC 7**
See Crowley, Edward Alexander
See also GLL 1

Crowley, Edward Alexander 1875-1947
See Crowley, Aleister
See also CA 104; HGG

Crowley, John 1942- .... **CLC 57**
See also AAYA 57; BPFB 1; CA 61-64; CANR 43, 98, 138; DLBY 1982; FANT; MTFW 2005; SATA 65, 140; SFW 4; SUFW 2

Crowne, John 1641-1712 .... **LC 104**
See also DLB 80; RGEL 2

Crud
See Crumb, R(obert)

Crumarums
See Crumb, R(obert)

Crumb, R(obert) 1943- .... **CLC 17**
See also CA 106; CANR 107

Crumbum
See Crumb, R(obert)

Crumski
See Crumb, R(obert)

Crum the Bum
See Crumb, R(obert)

Crunk
See Crumb, R(obert)

Crustt
See Crumb, R(obert)

Crutchfield, Les
See Trumbo, Dalton

Cruz, Victor Hernandez 1949- ... **HLC 1; PC 37**
See also BW 2; CA 65-68; CAAS 17; CANR 14, 32, 74, 132; CP 1, 2, 3, 4, 5, 6, 7; DAM MULT, POET; DLB 41; DNFS 1; EXPP; HW 1, 2; LLW; MTCW 2; MTFW 2005; PFS 16; WP

Cryer, Gretchen (Kiger) 1935- .... **CLC 21**
See also CA 114; 123

Csath, Geza .... **TCLC 13**
See Brenner, Jozef
See also CA 111

Cudlip, David R(ockwell) 1933- .... **CLC 34**
See also CA 177

Cullen, Countee 1903-1946 . **BLC 1; HR 1:2; PC 20; TCLC 4, 37; WLCS**
See also AFAW 2; AMWS 4; BW 1; CA 108; 124; CDALB 1917-1929; DA; DA3; DAC; DAM MST, MULT, POET; DLB 4, 48, 51; EWL 3; EXPP; LMFS 2; MAL 5; MTCW 1, 2; MTFW 2005; PFS 3; RGAL 4; SATA 18; WP

Culleton, Beatrice 1949- .... **NNAL**
See also CA 120; CANR 83; DAC

Cum, R.
See Crumb, R(obert)

Cumberland, Richard
1732-1811 .... **NCLC 167**
See also DLB 89; RGEL 2

Cummings, Bruce F(rederick) 1889-1919
See Barbellion, W. N. P.
See also CA 123

Cummings, E(dward) E(stlin)
1894-1962 .. **CLC 1, 3, 8, 12, 15, 68; PC 5; TCLC 137; WLC**
See also AAYA 41; AMW; CA 73-76; CANR 31; CDALB 1929-1941; DA; DA3; DAB; DAC; DAM MST, POET; DLB 4, 48; EWL 3; EXPP; MAL 5; MTCW 1, 2; MTFW 2005; PAB; PFS 1, 3, 12, 13, 19; RGAL 4; TUS; WP

Davies, William Henry 1871-1940 ... **TCLC 5**
See also BRWS 11; CA 104; 179; DLB 19, 174; EWL 3; RGEL 2

Da Vinci, Leonardo 1452-1519 ..... **LC 12, 57, 60**
See also AAYA 40

Davis, Angela (Yvonne) 1944- .... **CLC 77**
See also BW 2, 3; CA 57-60; CANR 10, 81; CSW; DA3; DAM MULT; FW

Davis, B. Lynch
See Bioy Casares, Adolfo; Borges, Jorge Luis

Davis, Frank Marshall 1905-1987 ...... **BLC 1**
See also BW 2, 3; CA 125; 123; CANR 42, 80; DAM MULT; DLB 51

Davis, Gordon
See Hunt, E(verette) Howard, (Jr.)

Davis, H(arold) L(enoir) 1896-1960 . **CLC 49**
See also ANW; CA 178; 89-92; DLB 9, 206; SATA 114; TCWW 1, 2

Davis, Natalie Zemon 1928- .... **CLC 204**
See also CA 53-56; CANR 58, 100

Davis, Rebecca (Blaine) Harding
1831-1910 .... **SSC 38; TCLC 6**
See also CA 104; 179; DLB 74, 239; FW; NFS 14; RGAL 4; TUS

Davis, Richard Harding
1864-1916 .... **TCLC 24**
See also CA 114; 179; DLB 12, 23, 78, 79, 189; DLBD 13; RGAL 4

Davison, Frank Dalby 1893-1970 ..... **CLC 15**
See also CA 217; 116; DLB 260

Davison, Lawrence H.
See Lawrence, D(avid) H(erbert Richards)

Davison, Peter (Hubert) 1928-2004 . **CLC 28**
See also CA 9-12R; 234; CAAS 4; CANR 3, 43, 84; CP 1, 2, 3, 4, 5, 6, 7; DLB 5

Davys, Mary 1674-1732 .... **LC 1, 46**
See also DLB 39

Dawson, (Guy) Fielding (Lewis)
1930-2002 .... **CLC 6**
See also CA 85-88; 202; CANR 108; DLB 130; DLBY 2002

Dawson, Peter
See Faust, Frederick (Schiller)
See also TCWW 1, 2

Day, Clarence (Shepard, Jr.)
1874-1935 .... **TCLC 25**
See also CA 108; 199; DLB 11

Day, John 1574(?)-1640(?) .... **LC 70**
See also DLB 62, 170; RGEL 2

Day, Thomas 1748-1789 .... **LC 1**
See also DLB 39; YABC 1

Day Lewis, C(ecil) 1904-1972 . **CLC 1, 6, 10; PC 11**
See Blake, Nicholas; Lewis, C. Day
See also BRWS 3; CA 13-16; 33-36R; CANR 34; CAP 1; CP 1; CWRI 5; DAM POET; DLB 15, 20; EWL 3; MTCW 1, 2; RGEL 2

Dazai Osamu .... **SSC 41; TCLC 11**
See Tsushima, Shuji
See also CA 164; DLB 182; EWL 3; MJW; RGSF 2; RGWL 2, 3; TWA

de Andrade, Carlos Drummond
See Drummond de Andrade, Carlos

de Andrade, Mario 1892(?)-1945
See Andrade, Mario de
See also CA 178; HW 2

Deane, Norman
See Creasey, John

Deane, Seamus (Francis) 1940- ...... **CLC 122**
See also CA 118; CANR 42

de Beauvoir, Simone (Lucie Ernestine Marie Bertrand)
See Beauvoir, Simone (Lucie Ernestine Marie Bertrand) de

de Beer, P.
See Bosman, Herman Charles

De Botton, Alain 1969- .... **CLC 203**
See also CA 159; CANR 96

de Brissac, Malcolm
See Dickinson, Peter (Malcolm de Brissac)

de Campos, Alvaro
See Pessoa, Fernando (Antonio Nogueira)

de Chardin, Pierre Teilhard
See Teilhard de Chardin, (Marie Joseph) Pierre

de Crenne, Helisenne c. 1510-c.
1560 .... **LC 113**

Dee, John 1527-1608 .... **LC 20**
See also DLB 136, 213

Deer, Sandra 1940- .... **CLC 45**
See also CA 186

De Ferrari, Gabriella 1941- .... **CLC 65**
See also CA 146

de Filippo, Eduardo 1900-1984 ... **TCLC 127**
See also CA 132; 114; EWL 3; MTCW 1; RGWL 2, 3

Defoe, Daniel 1660(?)-1731 .... **LC 1, 42, 108; WLC**
See also AAYA 27; BRW 3; BRWR 1; BYA 4; CDBLB 1660-1789; CLR 61; DA; DA3; DAB; DAC; DAM MST, NOV; DLB 39, 95, 101; JRDA; LAIT 1; LMFS 1; MAICYA 1, 2; NFS 9, 13; RGEL 2; SATA 22; TEA; WCH; WLIT 3

de Gourmont, Remy(-Marie-Charles)
See Gourmont, Remy(-Marie-Charles) de

de Gournay, Marie le Jars
1566-1645 .... **LC 98**
See also FW

de Hartog, Jan 1914-2002 .... **CLC 19**
See also CA 1-4R; 210; CANR 1; DFS 12

de Hostos, E. M.
See Hostos (y Bonilla), Eugenio Maria de

de Hostos, Eugenio M.
See Hostos (y Bonilla), Eugenio Maria de

Deighton, Len .... **CLC 4, 7, 22, 46**
See Deighton, Leonard Cyril
See also AAYA 6; BEST 89:2; BPFB 1; CDBLB 1960 to Present; CMW 4; CN 1, 2, 3, 4, 5, 6, 7; CPW; DLB 87

Deighton, Leonard Cyril 1929-
See Deighton, Len
See also AAYA 57; CA 9-12R; CANR 19, 33, 68; DA3; DAM NOV, POP; MTCW 1, 2; MTFW 2005

Dekker, Thomas 1572(?)-1632 ..... **DC 12; LC 22**
See also CDBLB Before 1660; DAM DRAM; DLB 62, 172; LMFS 1; RGEL 2

de Laclos, Pierre Ambroise Franois
See Laclos, Pierre-Ambroise Francois

Delacroix, (Ferdinand-Victor-)Eugene
1798-1863 .... **NCLC 133**
See also EW 5

Delafield, E. M. .... **TCLC 61**
See Dashwood, Edmee Elizabeth Monica de la Pasture
See also DLB 34; RHW

de la Mare, Walter (John)
1873-1956 . **SSC 14; TCLC 4, 53; WLC**
See also CA 163; CDBLB 1914-1945; CLR 23; CWRI 5; DA3; DAB; DAC; DAM MST, POET; DLB 19, 153, 162, 255, 284; EWL 3; EXPP; HGG; MAICYA 1, 2; MTCW 2; MTFW 2005; RGEL 2; RGSF 2; SATA 16; SUFW 1; TEA; WCH

de Lamartine, Alphonse (Marie Louis Prat)
See Lamartine, Alphonse (Marie Louis Prat) de

Delaney, Franey
See O'Hara, John (Henry)

Delaney, Shelagh 1939- .... **CLC 29**
See also CA 17-20R; CANR 30, 67; CBD; CD 5, 6; CDBLB 1960 to Present; CWD; DAM DRAM; DFS 7; DLB 13; MTCW 1

Delany, Martin Robison
1812-1885 .... **NCLC 93**
See also DLB 50; RGAL 4

Delany, Mary (Granville Pendarves)
1700-1788 .... **LC 12**

Delany, Samuel R(ay), Jr. 1942- ...... **BLC 1; CLC 8, 14, 38, 141**
See also AAYA 24; AFAW 2; BPFB 1; BW 2, 3; CA 81-84; CANR 27, 43, 116; CN 2, 3, 4, 5, 6, 7; DAM MULT; DLB 8, 33; FANT; MAL 5; MTCW 1, 2; RGAL 4; SATA 92; SCFW 1, 2; SFW 4; SUFW 2

De la Ramee, Marie Louise (Ouida)
1839-1908
See Ouida
See also CA 204; SATA 20

de la Roche, Mazo 1879-1961 .... **CLC 14**
See also CA 85-88; CANR 30; DLB 68; RGEL 2; RHW; SATA 64

De La Salle, Innocent
See Hartmann, Sadakichi

de Laureamont, Comte
See Lautreamont

Delbanco, Nicholas (Franklin)
1942- .... **CLC 6, 13, 167**
See also CA 17-20R; 189; CAAE 189; CAAS 2; CANR 29, 55, 116; CN 7; DLB 6, 234

del Castillo, Michel 1933- .... **CLC 38**
See also CA 109; CANR 77

Deledda, Grazia (Cosima)
1875(?)-1936 .... **TCLC 23**
See also CA 123; 205; DLB 264; EWL 3; RGWL 2, 3; WLIT 7

Deleuze, Gilles 1925-1995 .... **TCLC 116**
See also DLB 296

Delgado, Abelardo (Lalo) B(arrientos)
1930-2004 .... **HLC 1**
See also CA 131; 230; CAAS 15; CANR 90; DAM MST, MULT; DLB 82; HW 1, 2

Delibes, Miguel .... **CLC 8, 18**
See Delibes Setien, Miguel
See also DLB 322; EWL 3

Delibes Setien, Miguel 1920-
See Delibes, Miguel
See also CA 45-48; CANR 1, 32; CWW 2; HW 1; MTCW 1

DeLillo, Don 1936- ..... **CLC 8, 10, 13, 27, 39, 54, 76, 143, 210, 213**
See also AMWC 2; AMWS 6; BEST 89:1; BPFB 1; CA 81-84; CANR 21, 76, 92, 133; CN 3, 4, 5, 6, 7; CPW; DA3; DAM NOV, POP; DLB 6, 173; EWL 3; MAL 5; MTCW 1, 2; MTFW 2005; RGAL 4; TUS

de Lisser, H. G.
See De Lisser, H(erbert) G(eorge)
See also DLB 117

De Lisser, H(erbert) G(eorge)
1878-1944 .... **TCLC 12**
See de Lisser, H. G.
See also BW 2; CA 109; 152

Deloire, Pierre
See Peguy, Charles (Pierre)

Deloney, Thomas 1543(?)-1600 .... **LC 41**
See also DLB 167; RGEL 2

Deloria, Ella (Cara) 1889-1971(?) ..... **NNAL**
See also CA 152; DAM MULT; DLB 175

Deloria, Vine (Victor), Jr.
1933-2005 .... **CLC 21, 122; NNAL**
See also CA 53-56; CANR 5, 20, 48, 98; DAM MULT; DLB 175; MTCW 1; SATA 21

del Valle-Inclan, Ramon (Maria)
See Valle-Inclan, Ramon (Maria) del
See also DLB 322

Del Vecchio, John M(ichael) 1947- .. **CLC 29**
See also CA 110; DLBD 9

de Man, Paul (Adolph Michel)
  1919-1983 .... **CLC 55**
  See also CA 128; 111; CANR 61; DLB 67;
  MTCW 1, 2

DeMarinis, Rick 1934- .... **CLC 54**
  See also CA 57-60, 184; CAAE 184; CAAS
  24; CANR 9, 25, 50; DLB 218; TCWW 2

de Maupassant, (Henri Rene Albert) Guy
  See Maupassant, (Henri Rene Albert) Guy
  de

Dembry, R. Emmet
  See Murfree, Mary Noailles

Demby, William 1922- .... **BLC 1; CLC 53**
  See also BW 1, 3; CA 81-84; CANR 81;
  DAM MULT; DLB 33

de Menton, Francisco
  See Chin, Frank (Chew, Jr.)

Demetrius of Phalerum c.
  307B.C.- .... **CMLC 34**

Demijohn, Thom
  See Disch, Thomas M(ichael)

De Mille, James 1833-1880 .... **NCLC 123**
  See also DLB 99, 251

Deming, Richard 1915-1983
  See Queen, Ellery
  See also CA 9-12R; CANR 3, 94; SATA 24

Democritus c. 460B.C.-c. 370B.C. . **CMLC 47**

de Montaigne, Michel (Eyquem)
  See Montaigne, Michel (Eyquem) de

de Montherlant, Henry (Milon)
  See Montherlant, Henry (Milon) de

Demosthenes 384B.C.-322B.C. ...... **CMLC 13**
  See also AW 1; DLB 176; RGWL 2, 3

de Musset, (Louis Charles) Alfred
  See Musset, (Louis Charles) Alfred de

de Natale, Francine
  See Malzberg, Barry N(athaniel)

de Navarre, Marguerite 1492-1549 ... **LC 61;
  SSC 85**
  See Marguerite d'Angouleme; Marguerite
  de Navarre

Denby, Edwin (Orr) 1903-1983 .... **CLC 48**
  See also CA 138; 110; CP 1

de Nerval, Gerard
  See Nerval, Gerard de

Denham, John 1615-1669 .... **LC 73**
  See also DLB 58, 126; RGEL 2

Denis, Julio
  See Cortazar, Julio

Denmark, Harrison
  See Zelazny, Roger (Joseph)

Dennis, John 1658-1734 .... **LC 11**
  See also DLB 101; RGEL 2

Dennis, Nigel (Forbes) 1912-1989 ...... **CLC 8**
  See also CA 25-28R; 129; CN 1, 2, 3, 4;
  DLB 13, 15, 233; EWL 3; MTCW 1

Dent, Lester 1904-1959 .... **TCLC 72**
  See also CA 112; 161; CMW 4; DLB 306;
  SFW 4

De Palma, Brian (Russell) 1940- ...... **CLC 20**
  See also CA 109

De Quincey, Thomas 1785-1859 ..... **NCLC 4,
  87**
  See also BRW 4; CDBLB 1789-1832; DLB
  110, 144; RGEL 2

Deren, Eleanora 1908(?)-1961
  See Deren, Maya
  See also CA 192; 111

Deren, Maya .... **CLC 16, 102**
  See Deren, Eleanora

Derleth, August (William)
  1909-1971 .... **CLC 31**
  See also BPFB 1; BYA 9, 10; CA 1-4R; 29-
  32R; CANR 4; CMW 4; CN 1; DLB 9;
  DLBD 17; HGG; SATA 5; SUFW 1

Der Nister 1884-1950 .... **TCLC 56**
  See Nister, Der

de Routisie, Albert
  See Aragon, Louis

Derrida, Jacques 1930-2004 .... **CLC 24, 87**
  See also CA 124; 127; 232; CANR 76, 98,
  133; DLB 242; EWL 3; LMFS 2; MTCW
  2; TWA

Derry Down Derry
  See Lear, Edward

Dersonnes, Jacques
  See Simenon, Georges (Jacques Christian)

Der Stricker c. 1190-c. 1250 .... **CMLC 75**
  See also DLB 138

Desai, Anita 1937- .... **CLC 19, 37, 97, 175**
  See also BRWS 5; CA 81-84; CANR 33,
  53, 95, 133; CN 1, 2, 3, 4, 5, 6, 7; CWRI
  5; DA3; DAB; DAM NOV; DLB 271;
  DNFS 2; EWL 3; FW; MTCW 1, 2;
  MTFW 2005; SATA 63, 126

Desai, Kiran 1971- .... **CLC 119**
  See also BYA 16; CA 171; CANR 127

de Saint-Luc, Jean
  See Glassco, John

de Saint Roman, Arnaud
  See Aragon, Louis

Desbordes-Valmore, Marceline
  1786-1859 .... **NCLC 97**
  See also DLB 217

Descartes, Rene 1596-1650 .... **LC 20, 35**
  See also DLB 268; EW 3; GFL Beginnings
  to 1789

Deschamps, Eustache 1340(?)-1404 .. **LC 103**
  See also DLB 208

De Sica, Vittorio 1901(?)-1974 .... **CLC 20**
  See also CA 117

Desnos, Robert 1900-1945 .... **TCLC 22**
  See also CA 121; 151; CANR 107; DLB
  258; EWL 3; LMFS 2

Destouches, Louis-Ferdinand
  1894-1961 .... **CLC 9, 15**
  See Celine, Louis-Ferdinand
  See also CA 85-88; CANR 28; MTCW 1

de Tolignac, Gaston
  See Griffith, D(avid Lewelyn) W(ark)

Deutsch, Babette 1895-1982 .... **CLC 18**
  See also BYA 3; CA 1-4R; 108; CANR 4,
  79; CP 1, 2, 3; DLB 45; SATA 1; SATA-
  Obit 33

Devenant, William 1606-1649 .... **LC 13**

Devkota, Laxmiprasad 1909-1959 . **TCLC 23**
  See also CA 123

De Voto, Bernard (Augustine)
  1897-1955 .... **TCLC 29**
  See also CA 113; 160; DLB 9, 256; MAL
  5; TCWW 1, 2

De Vries, Peter 1910-1993 ..... **CLC 1, 2, 3, 7,
  10, 28, 46**
  See also CA 17-20R; 142; CANR 41; CN
  1, 2, 3, 4, 5; DAM NOV; DLB 6; DLBY
  1982; MAL 5; MTCW 1, 2; MTFW 2005

Dewey, John 1859-1952 .... **TCLC 95**
  See also CA 114; 170; CANR 144; DLB
  246, 270; RGAL 4

Dexter, John
  See Bradley, Marion Zimmer
  See also GLL 1

Dexter, Martin
  See Faust, Frederick (Schiller)

Dexter, Pete 1943- .... **CLC 34, 55**
  See also BEST 89:2; CA 127; 131; CANR
  129; CPW; DAM POP; INT CA-131;
  MAL 5; MTCW 1; MTFW 2005

Diamano, Silmang
  See Senghor, Leopold Sedar

Diamond, Neil 1941- .... **CLC 30**
  See also CA 108

Diaz del Castillo, Bernal c.
  1496-1584 .... **HLCS 1; LC 31**
  See also DLB 318; LAW

di Bassetto, Corno
  See Shaw, George Bernard

Dick, Philip K(indred) 1928-1982 ... **CLC 10,
  30, 72; SSC 57**
  See also AAYA 24; BPFB 1; BYA 11; CA
  49-52; 106; CANR 2, 16, 132; CN 2, 3;
  CPW; DA3; DAM NOV, POP; DLB 8;
  MTCW 1, 2; MTFW 2005; NFS 5; SCFW
  1, 2; SFW 4

Dickens, Charles (John Huffam)
  1812-1870 .... **NCLC 3, 8, 18, 26, 37, 50,
  86, 105, 113, 161; SSC 17, 49, 88; WLC**
  See also AAYA 23; BRW 5; BRWC 1, 2;
  BYA 1, 2, 3, 13, 14; CDBLB 1832-1890;
  CLR 95; CMW 4; DA; DA3; DAB; DAC;
  DAM MST, NOV; DLB 21, 55, 70, 159,
  166; EXPN; GL 2; HGG; JRDA; LAIT 1,
  2; LATS 1:1; LMFS 1; MAICYA 1, 2;
  NFS 4, 5, 10, 14, 20; RGEL 2; RGSF 2;
  SATA 15; SUFW 1; TEA; WCH; WLIT
  4; WYA

Dickey, James (Lafayette)
  1923-1997 .... **CLC 1, 2, 4, 7, 10, 15, 47,
  109; PC 40; TCLC 151**
  See also AAYA 50; AITN 1, 2; AMWS 4;
  BPFB 1; CA 9-12R; 156; CABS 2; CANR
  10, 48, 61, 105; CDALB 1968-1988; CP
  1, 2, 3, 4; CPW; CSW; DA3; DAM NOV,
  POET, POP; DLB 5, 193; DLBD 7;
  DLBY 1982, 1993, 1996, 1997, 1998;
  EWL 3; INT CANR-10; MAL 5; MTCW
  1, 2; NFS 9; PFS 6, 11; RGAL 4; TUS

Dickey, William 1928-1994 .... **CLC 3, 28**
  See also CA 9-12R; 145; CANR 24, 79; CP
  1, 2, 3, 4; DLB 5

Dickinson, Charles 1951- .... **CLC 49**
  See also CA 128; CANR 141

Dickinson, Emily (Elizabeth)
  1830-1886 ... **NCLC 21, 77; PC 1; WLC**
  See also AAYA 22; AMW; AMWR 1;
  CDALB 1865-1917; DA; DA3; DAB;
  DAC; DAM MST, POET; DLB 1, 243;
  EXPP; FL 1:3; MAWW; PAB; PFS 1, 2,
  3, 4, 5, 6, 8, 10, 11, 13, 16; RGAL 4;
  SATA 29; TUS; WP; WYA

Dickinson, Mrs. Herbert Ward
  See Phelps, Elizabeth Stuart

Dickinson, Peter (Malcolm de Brissac)
  1927- .... **CLC 12, 35**
  See also AAYA 9, 49; BYA 5; CA 41-44R;
  CANR 31, 58, 88, 134; CLR 29; CMW 4;
  DLB 87, 161, 276; JRDA; MAICYA 1, 2;
  SATA 5, 62, 95, 150; SFW 4; WYA; YAW

Dickson, Carr
  See Carr, John Dickson

Dickson, Carter
  See Carr, John Dickson

Diderot, Denis 1713-1784 .... **LC 26, 126**
  See also DLB 313; EW 4; GFL Beginnings
  to 1789; LMFS 1; RGWL 2, 3

Didion, Joan 1934- . **CLC 1, 3, 8, 14, 32, 129**
  See also AITN 1; AMWS 4; CA 5-8R;
  CANR 14, 52, 76, 125; CDALB 1968-
  1988; CN 2, 3, 4, 5, 6, 7; DA3; DAM
  NOV; DLB 2, 173, 185; DLBY 1981,
  1986; EWL 3; MAL 5; MAWW; MTCW
  1, 2; MTFW 2005; NFS 3; RGAL 4;
  TCLE 1:1; TCWW 2; TUS

di Donato, Pietro 1911-1992 .... **TCLC 159**
  See also CA 101; 136; DLB 9

Dietrich, Robert
  See Hunt, E(verette) Howard, (Jr.)

Difusa, Pati
  See Almodovar, Pedro

Dillard, Annie 1945- ...... **CLC 9, 60, 115, 216**
  See also AAYA 6, 43; AMWS 6; ANW; CA
  49-52; CANR 3, 43, 62, 90, 125; DA3;
  DAM NOV; DLB 275, 278; DLBY 1980;

LAIT 4, 5; MAL 5; MTCW 1, 2; MTFW 2005; NCFS 1; RGAL 4; SATA 10, 140; TCLE 1:1; TUS

Dillard, R(ichard) H(enry) W(ilde)
1937- .... **CLC 5**
See also CA 21-24R; CAAS 7; CANR 10; CP 2, 3, 4, 5, 6, 7; CSW; DLB 5, 244

Dillon, Eilis 1920-1994 .... **CLC 17**
See also CA 9-12R, 182; 147; CAAE 182; CAAS 3; CANR 4, 38, 78; CLR 26; MAICYA 1, 2; MAICYAS 1; SATA 2, 74; SATA-Essay 105; SATA-Obit 83; YAW

Dimont, Penelope
See Mortimer, Penelope (Ruth)

Dinesen, Isak ..... **CLC 10, 29, 95; SSC 7, 75**
See Blixen, Karen (Christentze Dinesen)
See also EW 10; EWL 3; EXPS; FW; GL 2; HGG; LAIT 3; MTCW 1; NCFS 2; NFS 9; RGSF 2; RGWL 2, 3; SSFS 3, 6, 13; WLIT 2

Ding Ling .... **CLC 68**
See Chiang, Pin-chin
See also RGWL 3

Diphusa, Patty
See Almodovar, Pedro

Disch, Thomas M(ichael) 1940- ... **CLC 7, 36**
See Disch, Tom
See also AAYA 17; BPFB 1; CA 21-24R; CAAS 4; CANR 17, 36, 54, 89; CLR 18; CP 7; DA3; DLB 8; HGG; MAICYA 1, 2; MTCW 1, 2; MTFW 2005; SAAS 15; SATA 92; SCFW 1, 2; SFW 4; SUFW 2

Disch, Tom
See Disch, Thomas M(ichael)
See also DLB 282

d'Isly, Georges
See Simenon, Georges (Jacques Christian)

Disraeli, Benjamin 1804-1881 ... **NCLC 2, 39, 79**
See also BRW 4; DLB 21, 55; RGEL 2

Ditcum, Steve
See Crumb, R(obert)

Dixon, Paige
See Corcoran, Barbara (Asenath)

Dixon, Stephen 1936- .... **CLC 52; SSC 16**
See also AMWS 12; CA 89-92; CANR 17, 40, 54, 91; CN 4, 5, 6, 7; DLB 130; MAL 5

Dixon, Thomas, Jr. 1864-1946 ..... **TCLC 163**
See also RHW

Djebar, Assia 1936- .... **CLC 182**
See also CA 188; EWL 3; RGWL 3; WLIT 2

Doak, Annie
See Dillard, Annie

Dobell, Sydney Thompson
1824-1874 .... **NCLC 43**
See also DLB 32; RGEL 2

Doblin, Alfred .... **TCLC 13**
See Doeblin, Alfred
See also CDWLB 2; EWL 3; RGWL 2, 3

Dobroliubov, Nikolai Aleksandrovich
See Dobrolyubov, Nikolai Alexandrovich
See also DLB 277

Dobrolyubov, Nikolai Alexandrovich
1836-1861 .... **NCLC 5**
See Dobroliubov, Nikolai Aleksandrovich

Dobson, Austin 1840-1921 .... **TCLC 79**
See also DLB 35, 144

Dobyns, Stephen 1941- .... **CLC 37**
See also AMWS 13; CA 45-48; CANR 2, 18, 99; CMW 4; CP 4, 5, 6, 7; PFS 23

Doctorow, E(dgar) L(aurence)
1931- .... **CLC 6, 11, 15, 18, 37, 44, 65, 113, 214**
See also AAYA 22; AITN 2; AMWS 4; BEST 89:3; BPFB 1; CA 45-48; CANR 2, 33, 51, 76, 97, 133; CDALB 1968-1988; CN 3, 4, 5, 6, 7; CPW; DA3; DAM

NOV, POP; DLB 2, 28, 173; DLBY 1980; EWL 3; LAIT 3; MAL 5; MTCW 1, 2; MTFW 2005; NFS 6; RGAL 4; RHW; TCLE 1:1; TCWW 1, 2; TUS

Dodgson, Charles L(utwidge) 1832-1898
See Carroll, Lewis
See also CLR 2; DA; DA3; DAB; DAC; DAM MST, NOV, POET; MAICYA 1, 2; SATA 100; YABC 2

Dodsley, Robert 1703-1764 .... **LC 97**
See also DLB 95; RGEL 2

Dodson, Owen (Vincent) 1914-1983 .. **BLC 1; CLC 79**
See also BW 1; CA 65-68; 110; CANR 24; DAM MULT; DLB 76

Doeblin, Alfred 1878-1957 .... **TCLC 13**
See Doblin, Alfred
See also CA 110; 141; DLB 66

Doerr, Harriet 1910-2002 .... **CLC 34**
See also CA 117; 122; 213; CANR 47; INT CA-122; LATS 1:2

Domecq, H(onorio Bustos)
See Bioy Casares, Adolfo

Domecq, H(onorio) Bustos
See Bioy Casares, Adolfo; Borges, Jorge Luis

Domini, Rey
See Lorde, Audre (Geraldine)
See also GLL 1

Dominique
See Proust, (Valentin-Louis-George-Eugene) Marcel

Don, A
See Stephen, Sir Leslie

Donaldson, Stephen R(eeder)
1947- .... **CLC 46, 138**
See also AAYA 36; BPFB 1; CA 89-92; CANR 13, 55, 99; CPW; DAM POP; FANT; INT CANR-13; SATA 121; SFW 4; SUFW 1, 2

Donleavy, J(ames) P(atrick) 1926- .... **CLC 1, 4, 6, 10, 45**
See also AITN 2; BPFB 1; CA 9-12R; CANR 24, 49, 62, 80, 124; CBD; CD 5, 6; CN 1, 2, 3, 4, 5, 6, 7; DLB 6, 173; INT CANR-24; MAL 5; MTCW 1, 2; MTFW 2005; RGAL 4

Donnadieu, Marguerite
See Duras, Marguerite

Donne, John 1572-1631 ... **LC 10, 24, 91; PC 1, 43; WLC**
See also AAYA 67; BRW 1; BRWC 1; BRWR 2; CDBLB Before 1660; DA; DAB; DAC; DAM MST, POET; DLB 121, 151; EXPP; PAB; PFS 2, 11; RGEL 3; TEA; WLIT 3; WP

Donnell, David 1939(?)- .... **CLC 34**
See also CA 197

Donoghue, Denis 1928- .... **CLC 209**
See also CA 17-20R; CANR 16, 102

Donoghue, P. S.
See Hunt, E(verette) Howard, (Jr.)

Donoso (Yanez), Jose 1924-1996 ... **CLC 4, 8, 11, 32, 99; HLC 1; SSC 34; TCLC 133**
See also CA 81-84; 155; CANR 32, 73; CDWLB 3; CWW 2; DAM MULT; DLB 113; EWL 3; HW 1, 2; LAW; LAWS 1; MTCW 1, 2; MTFW 2005; RGSF 2; WLIT 1

Donovan, John 1928-1992 .... **CLC 35**
See also AAYA 20; CA 97-100; 137; CLR 3; MAICYA 1, 2; SATA 72; SATA-Brief 29; YAW

Don Roberto
See Cunninghame Graham, Robert (Gallnigad) Bontine

Doolittle, Hilda 1886-1961 . **CLC 3, 8, 14, 31, 34, 73; PC 5; WLC**
See H. D.
See also AAYA 66; AMWS 1; CA 97-100; CANR 35, 131; DA; DAC; DAM MST, POET; DLB 4, 45; EWL 3; FW; GLL 1; LMFS 2; MAL 5; MAWW; MTCW 1, 2; MTFW 2005; PFS 6; RGAL 4

Doppo, Kunikida .... **TCLC 99**
See Kunikida Doppo

Dorfman, Ariel 1942- .... **CLC 48, 77, 189; HLC 1**
See also CA 124; 130; CANR 67, 70, 135; CWW 2; DAM MULT; DFS 4; EWL 3; HW 1, 2; INT CA-130; WLIT 1

Dorn, Edward (Merton)
1929-1999 .... **CLC 10, 18**
See also CA 93-96; 187; CANR 42, 79; CP 1, 2, 3, 4, 5, 6, 7; DLB 5; INT CA-93-96; WP

Dor-Ner, Zvi .... **CLC 70**

Dorris, Michael (Anthony)
1945-1997 .... **CLC 109; NNAL**
See also AAYA 20; BEST 90:1; BYA 12; CA 102; 157; CANR 19, 46, 75; CLR 58; DA3; DAM MULT, NOV; DLB 175; LAIT 5; MTCW 2; MTFW 2005; NFS 3; RGAL 4; SATA 75; SATA-Obit 94; TCWW 2; YAW

Dorris, Michael A.
See Dorris, Michael (Anthony)

Dorsan, Luc
See Simenon, Georges (Jacques Christian)

Dorsange, Jean
See Simenon, Georges (Jacques Christian)

Dorset
See Sackville, Thomas

Dos Passos, John (Roderigo)
1896-1970 ... **CLC 1, 4, 8, 11, 15, 25, 34, 82; WLC**
See also AMW; BPFB 1; CA 1-4R; 29-32R; CANR 3; CDALB 1929-1941; DA; DA3; DAB; DAC; DAM MST, NOV; DLB 4, 9, 274, 316; DLBD 1, 15; DLBY 1996; EWL 3; MAL 5; MTCW 1, 2; MTFW 2005; NFS 14; RGAL 4; TUS

Dossage, Jean
See Simenon, Georges (Jacques Christian)

Dostoevsky, Fedor Mikhailovich
1821-1881 .. **NCLC 2, 7, 21, 33, 43, 119, 167; SSC 2, 33, 44; WLC**
See Dostoevsky, Fyodor
See also AAYA 40; DA; DA3; DAB; DAC; DAM MST, NOV; EW 7; EXPN; NFS 3, 8; RGSF 2; RGWL 2, 3; SSFS 8; TWA

Dostoevsky, Fyodor
See Dostoevsky, Fedor Mikhailovich
See also DLB 238; LATS 1:1; LMFS 1, 2

Doty, M. R.
See Doty, Mark (Alan)

Doty, Mark
See Doty, Mark (Alan)

Doty, Mark (Alan) 1953(?)- .... **CLC 176; PC 53**
See also AMWS 11; CA 161, 183; CAAE 183; CANR 110

Doty, Mark A.
See Doty, Mark (Alan)

Doughty, Charles M(ontagu)
1843-1926 .... **TCLC 27**
See also CA 115; 178; DLB 19, 57, 174

Douglas, Ellen .... **CLC 73**
See Haxton, Josephine Ayres; Williamson, Ellen Douglas
See also CN 5, 6, 7; CSW; DLB 292

Douglas, Gavin 1475(?)-1522 .... **LC 20**
See also DLB 132; RGEL 2

Dunbar, Paul Laurence 1872-1906 ... **BLC 1; PC 5; SSC 8; TCLC 2, 12; WLC**
See also AFAW 1, 2; AMWS 2; BW 1, 3; CA 104; 124; CANR 79; CDALB 1865-1917; DA; DA3; DAC; DAM MST, MULT, POET; DLB 50, 54, 78; EXPP; MAL 5; RGAL 4; SATA 34

Dunbar, William 1460(?)-1520(?) .... **LC 20; PC 67**
See also BRWS 8; DLB 132, 146; RGEL 2

Dunbar-Nelson, Alice .... **HR 1:2**
See Nelson, Alice Ruth Moore Dunbar

Duncan, Dora Angela
See Duncan, Isadora

Duncan, Isadora 1877(?)-1927 .... **TCLC 68**
See also CA 118; 149

Duncan, Lois 1934- .... **CLC 26**
See also AAYA 4, 34; BYA 6, 8; CA 1-4R; CANR 2, 23, 36, 111; CLR 29; JRDA; MAICYA 1, 2; MAICYAS 1; MTFW 2005; SAAS 2; SATA 1, 36, 75, 133, 141; SATA-Essay 141; WYA; YAW

Duncan, Robert (Edward)
1919-1988 .... **CLC 1, 2, 4, 7, 15, 41, 55; PC 2**
See also BG 1:2; CA 9-12R; 124; CANR 28, 62; CP 1, 2, 3, 4; DAM POET; DLB 5, 16, 193; EWL 3; MAL 5; MTCW 1, 2; MTFW 2005; PFS 13; RGAL 4; WP

Duncan, Sara Jeannette
1861-1922 .... **TCLC 60**
See also CA 157; DLB 92

Dunlap, William 1766-1839 .... **NCLC 2**
See also DLB 30, 37, 59; RGAL 4

Dunn, Douglas (Eaglesham) 1942- .... **CLC 6, 40**
See also BRWS 10; CA 45-48; CANR 2, 33, 126; CP 1, 2, 3, 4, 5, 6, 7; DLB 40; MTCW 1

Dunn, Katherine (Karen) 1945- .... **CLC 71**
See also CA 33-36R; CANR 72; HGG; MTCW 2; MTFW 2005

Dunn, Stephen (Elliott) 1939- .. **CLC 36, 206**
See also AMWS 11; CA 33-36R; CANR 12, 48, 53, 105; CP 3, 4, 5, 6, 7; DLB 105; PFS 21

Dunne, Finley Peter 1867-1936 ...... **TCLC 28**
See also CA 108; 178; DLB 11, 23; RGAL 4

Dunne, John Gregory 1932-2003 ..... **CLC 28**
See also CA 25-28R; 222; CANR 14, 50; CN 5, 6, 7; DLBY 1980

Dunsany, Lord .... **TCLC 2, 59**
See Dunsany, Edward John Moreton Drax Plunkett
See also DLB 77, 153, 156, 255; FANT; IDTP; RGEL 2; SFW 4; SUFW 1

Dunsany, Edward John Moreton Drax Plunkett 1878-1957
See Dunsany, Lord
See also CA 104; 148; DLB 10; MTCW 2

Duns Scotus, John 1266(?)-1308 ... **CMLC 59**
See also DLB 115

du Perry, Jean
See Simenon, Georges (Jacques Christian)

Durang, Christopher (Ferdinand)
1949- .... **CLC 27, 38**
See also CA 105; CAD; CANR 50, 76, 130; CD 5, 6; MTCW 2; MTFW 2005

Duras, Claire de 1777-1832 .... **NCLC 154**

Duras, Marguerite 1914-1996 . **CLC 3, 6, 11, 20, 34, 40, 68, 100; SSC 40**
See also BPFB 1; CA 25-28R; 151; CANR 50; CWW 2; DFS 21; DLB 83, 321; EWL 3; FL 1:5; GFL 1789 to the Present; IDFW 4; MTCW 1, 2; RGWL 2, 3; TWA

Durban, (Rosa) Pam 1947- .... **CLC 39**
See also CA 123; CANR 98; CSW

Durcan, Paul 1944- .... **CLC 43, 70**
See also CA 134; CANR 123; CP 1, 7; DAM POET; EWL 3

Durfey, Thomas 1653-1723 .... **LC 94**
See also DLB 80; RGEL 2

Durkheim, Emile 1858-1917 .... **TCLC 55**

Durrell, Lawrence (George)
1912-1990 ..... **CLC 1, 4, 6, 8, 13, 27, 41**
See also BPFB 1; BRWS 1; CA 9-12R; 132; CANR 40, 77; CDBLB 1945-1960; CN 1, 2, 3, 4; CP 1, 2, 3, 4; DAM NOV; DLB 15, 27, 204; DLBY 1990; EWL 3; MTCW 1, 2; RGEL 2; SFW 4; TEA

Durrenmatt, Friedrich
See Duerrenmatt, Friedrich
See also CDWLB 2; EW 13; EWL 3; RGWL 2, 3

Dutt, Michael Madhusudan
1824-1873 .... **NCLC 118**

Dutt, Toru 1856-1877 .... **NCLC 29**
See also DLB 240

Dwight, Timothy 1752-1817 .... **NCLC 13**
See also DLB 37; RGAL 4

Dworkin, Andrea 1946-2005 ..... **CLC 43, 123**
See also CA 77-80; 238; CAAS 21; CANR 16, 39, 76, 96; FL 1:5; FW; GLL 1; INT CANR-16; MTCW 1, 2; MTFW 2005

Dwyer, Deanna
See Koontz, Dean R.

Dwyer, K. R.
See Koontz, Dean R.

Dybek, Stuart 1942- .... **CLC 114; SSC 55**
See also CA 97-100; CANR 39; DLB 130

Dye, Richard
See De Voto, Bernard (Augustine)

Dyer, Geoff 1958- .... **CLC 149**
See also CA 125; CANR 88

Dyer, George 1755-1841 .... **NCLC 129**
See also DLB 93

Dylan, Bob 1941- .... **CLC 3, 4, 6, 12, 77; PC 37**
See also CA 41-44R; CANR 108; CP 1, 2, 3, 4, 5, 6, 7; DLB 16

Dyson, John 1943- .... **CLC 70**
See also CA 144

Dzyubin, Eduard Georgievich 1895-1934
See Bagritsky, Eduard
See also CA 170

E. V. L.
See Lucas, E(dward) V(errall)

Eagleton, Terence (Francis) 1943- .. **CLC 63, 132**
See also CA 57-60; CANR 7, 23, 68, 115; DLB 242; LMFS 2; MTCW 1, 2; MTFW 2005

Eagleton, Terry
See Eagleton, Terence (Francis)

Early, Jack
See Scoppettone, Sandra
See also GLL 1

East, Michael
See West, Morris L(anglo)

Eastaway, Edward
See Thomas, (Philip) Edward

Eastlake, William (Derry)
1917-1997 .... **CLC 8**
See also CA 5-8R; 158; CAAS 1; CANR 5, 63; CN 1, 2, 3, 4, 5, 6; DLB 6, 206; INT CANR-5; MAL 5; TCWW 1, 2

Eastman, Charles A(lexander)
1858-1939 .... **NNAL; TCLC 55**
See also CA 179; CANR 91; DAM MULT; DLB 175; YABC 1

Eaton, Edith Maude 1865-1914 .... **AAL**
See Far, Sui Sin
See also CA 154; DLB 221, 312; FW

Eaton, (Lillie) Winnifred 1875-1954 .... **AAL**
See also CA 217; DLB 221, 312; RGAL 4

Eberhart, Richard 1904-2005 ...... **CLC 3, 11, 19, 56**
See also AMW; CA 1-4R; 240; CANR 2, 125; CDALB 1941-1968; CP 1, 2, 3, 4, 5, 6, 7; DAM POET; DLB 48; MAL 5; MTCW 1; RGAL 4

Eberhart, Richard Ghormley
See Eberhart, Richard

Eberstadt, Fernanda 1960- .... **CLC 39**
See also CA 136; CANR 69, 128

Echegaray (y Eizaguirre), Jose (Maria Waldo) 1832-1916 .... **HLCS 1; TCLC 4**
See also CA 104; CANR 32; EWL 3; HW 1; MTCW 1

Echeverria, (Jose) Esteban (Antonino)
1805-1851 .... **NCLC 18**
See also LAW

Echo
See Proust, (Valentin-Louis-George-Eugene) Marcel

Eckert, Allan W. 1931- .... **CLC 17**
See also AAYA 18; BYA 2; CA 13-16R; CANR 14, 45; INT CANR-14; MAICYA 2; MAICYAS 1; SAAS 21; SATA 29, 91; SATA-Brief 27

Eckhart, Meister 1260(?)-1327(?) .. **CMLC 9, 80**
See also DLB 115; LMFS 1

Eckmar, F. R.
See de Hartog, Jan

Eco, Umberto 1932- .... **CLC 28, 60, 142**
See also BEST 90:1; BPFB 1; CA 77-80; CANR 12, 33, 55, 110, 131; CPW; CWW 2; DA3; DAM NOV, POP; DLB 196, 242; EWL 3; MSW; MTCW 1, 2; MTFW 2005; NFS 22; RGWL 3; WLIT 7

Eddison, E(ric) R(ucker)
1882-1945 .... **TCLC 15**
See also CA 109; 156; DLB 255; FANT; SFW 4; SUFW 1

Eddy, Mary (Ann Morse) Baker
1821-1910 .... **TCLC 71**
See also CA 113; 174

Edel, (Joseph) Leon 1907-1997 .. **CLC 29, 34**
See also CA 1-4R; 161; CANR 1, 22, 112; DLB 103; INT CANR-22

Eden, Emily 1797-1869 .... **NCLC 10**

Edgar, David 1948- .... **CLC 42**
See also CA 57-60; CANR 12, 61, 112; CBD; CD 5, 6; DAM DRAM; DFS 15; DLB 13, 233; MTCW 1

Edgerton, Clyde (Carlyle) 1944- ...... **CLC 39**
See also AAYA 17; CA 118; 134; CANR 64, 125; CN 7; CSW; DLB 278; INT CA-134; TCLE 1:1; YAW

Edgeworth, Maria 1768-1849 ... **NCLC 1, 51, 158; SSC 86**
See also BRWS 3; DLB 116, 159, 163; FL 1:3; FW; RGEL 2; SATA 21; TEA; WLIT 3

Edmonds, Paul
See Kuttner, Henry

Edmonds, Walter D(umaux)
1903-1998 .... **CLC 35**
See also BYA 2; CA 5-8R; CANR 2; CWRI 5; DLB 9; LAIT 1; MAICYA 1, 2; MAL 5; RHW; SAAS 4; SATA 1, 27; SATA-Obit 99

Edmondson, Wallace
See Ellison, Harlan (Jay)

Edson, Margaret 1961- ...... **CLC 199; DC 24**
See also CA 190; DFS 13; DLB 266

Edson, Russell 1935- .... **CLC 13**
See also CA 33-36R; CANR 115; CP 2, 3, 4, 5, 6, 7; DLB 244; WP

Edwards, Bronwen Elizabeth
See Rose, Wendy

Edwards, G(erald) B(asil)
1899-1976 .... **CLC 25**
See also CA 201; 110

Edwards, Gus 1939- .... **CLC 43**
See also CA 108; INT CA-108

Edwards, Jonathan 1703-1758 .... **LC 7, 54**
See also AMW; DA; DAC; DAM MST;
DLB 24, 270; RGAL 4; TUS

Edwards, Sarah Pierpont 1710-1758 .. **LC 87**
See also DLB 200

Efron, Marina Ivanovna Tsvetaeva
See Tsvetaeva (Efron), Marina (Ivanovna)

Egeria fl. 4th cent. - .... **CMLC 70**

Egoyan, Atom 1960- .... **CLC 151**
See also AAYA 63; CA 157

Ehle, John (Marsden, Jr.) 1925- ...... **CLC 27**
See also CA 9-12R; CSW

Ehrenbourg, Ilya (Grigoryevich)
See Ehrenburg, Ilya (Grigoryevich)

Ehrenburg, Ilya (Grigoryevich)
1891-1967 .... **CLC 18, 34, 62**
See Erenburg, Il'ia Grigor'evich
See also CA 102; 25-28R; EWL 3

Ehrenburg, Ilyo (Grigoryevich)
See Ehrenburg, Ilya (Grigoryevich)

Ehrenreich, Barbara 1941- .... **CLC 110**
See also BEST 90:4; CA 73-76; CANR 16,
37, 62, 117; DLB 246; FW; MTCW 1, 2;
MTFW 2005

Eich, Gunter
See Eich, Gunter
See also RGWL 2, 3

Eich, Gunter 1907-1972 .... **CLC 15**
See Eich, Gunter
See also CA 111; 93-96; DLB 69, 124;
EWL 3

Eichendorff, Joseph 1788-1857 .... **NCLC 8**
See also DLB 90; RGWL 2, 3

Eigner, Larry .... **CLC 9**
See Eigner, Laurence (Joel)
See also CAAS 23; CP 1, 2, 3, 4; DLB 5;
WP

Eigner, Laurence (Joel) 1927-1996
See Eigner, Larry
See also CA 9-12R; 151; CANR 6, 84; CP
7; DLB 193

Eilhart von Oberge c. 1140-c.
1195 .... **CMLC 67**
See also DLB 148

Einhard c. 770-840 .... **CMLC 50**
See also DLB 148

Einstein, Albert 1879-1955 .... **TCLC 65**
See also CA 121; 133; MTCW 1, 2

Eiseley, Loren
See Eiseley, Loren Corey
See also DLB 275

Eiseley, Loren Corey 1907-1977 .... **CLC 7**
See Eiseley, Loren
See also AAYA 5; ANW; CA 1-4R; 73-76;
CANR 6; DLBD 17

Eisenstadt, Jill 1963- .... **CLC 50**
See also CA 140

Eisenstein, Sergei (Mikhailovich)
1898-1948 .... **TCLC 57**
See also CA 114; 149

Eisner, Simon
See Kornbluth, C(yril) M.

Ekeloef, (Bengt) Gunnar
1907-1968 .... **CLC 27; PC 23**
See Ekelof, (Bengt) Gunnar
See also CA 123; 25-28R; DAM POET

Ekelof, (Bengt) Gunnar 1907-1968
See Ekeloef, (Bengt) Gunnar
See also DLB 259; EW 12; EWL 3

Ekelund, Vilhelm 1880-1949 .... **TCLC 75**
See also CA 189; EWL 3

Ekwensi, C. O. D.
See Ekwensi, Cyprian (Odiatu Duaka)

Ekwensi, Cyprian (Odiatu Duaka)
1921- .... **BLC 1; CLC 4**
See also AFW; BW 2, 3; CA 29-32R;
CANR 18, 42, 74, 125; CDWLB 3; CN 1,
2, 3, 4, 5, 6; CWRI 5; DAM MULT; DLB
117; EWL 3; MTCW 1, 2; RGEL 2; SATA
66; WLIT 2

Elaine .... **TCLC 18**
See Leverson, Ada Esther

El Crummo
See Crumb, R(obert)

Elder, Lonne III 1931-1996 ..... **BLC 1; DC 8**
See also BW 1, 3; CA 81-84; 152; CAD;
CANR 25; DAM MULT; DLB 7, 38, 44;
MAL 5

Eleanor of Aquitaine 1122-1204 ... **CMLC 39**

Elia
See Lamb, Charles

Eliade, Mircea 1907-1986 .... **CLC 19**
See also CA 65-68; 119; CANR 30, 62; CD-
WLB 4; DLB 220; EWL 3; MTCW 1;
RGWL 3; SFW 4

Eliot, A. D.
See Jewett, (Theodora) Sarah Orne

Eliot, Alice
See Jewett, (Theodora) Sarah Orne

Eliot, Dan
See Silverberg, Robert

Eliot, George 1819-1880 ...... **NCLC 4, 13, 23,**
41, 49, 89, 118; PC 20; SSC 72; WLC
See Evans, Mary Ann
See also BRW 5; BRWC 1, 2; BRWR 2;
CDBLB 1832-1890; CN 7; CPW; DA;
DA3; DAB; DAC; DAM MST, NOV;
DLB 21, 35, 55; FL 1:3; LATS 1:1; LMFS
1; NFS 17, 20; RGEL 2; RGSF 2; SSFS
8; TEA; WLIT 3

Eliot, John 1604-1690 .... **LC 5**
See also DLB 24

Eliot, T(homas) S(tearns)
1888-1965 ...... **CLC 1, 2, 3, 6, 9, 10, 13,**
15, 24, 34, 41, 55, 57, 113; PC 5, 31;
WLC
See also AAYA 28; AMW; AMWC 1;
AMWR 1; BRW 7; BRWR 2; CA 5-8R;
25-28R; CANR 41; CBD; CDALB 1929-
1941; DA; DA3; DAB; DAC; DAM
DRAM, MST, POET; DFS 4, 13; DLB 7,
10, 45, 63, 245; DLBY 1988; EWL 3;
EXPP; LAIT 3; LATS 1:1; LMFS 2; MAL
5; MTCW 1, 2; MTFW 2005; NCFS 5;
PAB; PFS 1, 7, 20; RGAL 4; RGEL 2;
TUS; WLIT 4; WP

Elisabeth of Schönau c.
1129-1165 .... **CMLC 82**

Elizabeth 1866-1941 .... **TCLC 41**

Elizabeth I 1533-1603 .... **LC 118**
See also DLB 136

Elkin, Stanley L(awrence)
1930-1995 .. **CLC 4, 6, 9, 14, 27, 51, 91;**
SSC 12
See also AMWS 6; BPFB 1; CA 9-12R;
148; CANR 8, 46; CN 1, 2, 3, 4, 5, 6;
CPW; DAM NOV, POP; DLB 2, 28, 218,
278; DLBY 1980; EWL 3; INT CANR-8;
MAL 5; MTCW 1, 2; MTFW 2005;
RGAL 4; TCLE 1:1

Elledge, Scott .... **CLC 34**

Eller, Scott
See Shepard, James R.

Elliott, Don
See Silverberg, Robert

Elliott, George P(aul) 1918-1980 .... **CLC 2**
See also CA 1-4R; 97-100; CANR 2; CN 1,
2; CP 3; DLB 244; MAL 5

Elliott, Janice 1931-1995 .... **CLC 47**
See also CA 13-16R; CANR 8, 29, 84; CN
5, 6, 7; DLB 14; SATA 119

Elliott, Sumner Locke 1917-1991 ..... **CLC 38**
See also CA 5-8R; 134; CANR 2, 21; DLB
289

Elliott, William
See Bradbury, Ray (Douglas)

Ellis, A. E. .... **CLC 7**

Ellis, Alice Thomas .... **CLC 40**
See Haycraft, Anna (Margaret)
See also CN 4, 5, 6; DLB 194

Ellis, Bret Easton 1964- ...... **CLC 39, 71, 117**
See also AAYA 2, 43; CA 118; 123; CANR
51, 74, 126; CN 6, 7; CPW; DA3; DAM
POP; DLB 292; HGG; INT CA-123;
MTCW 2; MTFW 2005; NFS 11

Ellis, (Henry) Havelock
1859-1939 .... **TCLC 14**
See also CA 109; 169; DLB 190

Ellis, Landon
See Ellison, Harlan (Jay)

Ellis, Trey 1962- .... **CLC 55**
See also CA 146; CANR 92; CN 7

Ellison, Harlan (Jay) 1934- ... **CLC 1, 13, 42,**
139; SSC 14
See also AAYA 29; BPFB 1; BYA 14; CA
5-8R; CANR 5, 46, 115; CPW; DAM
POP; DLB 8; HGG; INT CANR-5;
MTCW 1, 2; MTFW 2005; SCFW 2;
SFW 4; SSFS 13, 14, 15, 21; SUFW 1, 2

Ellison, Ralph (Waldo) 1914-1994 .... **BLC 1;**
CLC 1, 3, 11, 54, 86, 114; SSC 26, 79;
WLC
See also AAYA 19; AFAW 1, 2; AMWC 2;
AMWR 2; AMWS 2; BPFB 1; BW 1, 3;
BYA 2; CA 9-12R; 145; CANR 24, 53;
CDALB 1941-1968; CN 1, 2, 3, 4, 5;
CSW; DA; DA3; DAB; DAC; DAM MST,
MULT, NOV; DLB 2, 76, 227; DLBY
1994; EWL 3; EXPN; EXPS; LAIT 4;
MAL 5; MTCW 1, 2; MTFW 2005; NCFS
3; NFS 2, 21; RGAL 4; RGSF 2; SSFS 1,
11; YAW

Ellmann, Lucy (Elizabeth) 1956- ..... **CLC 61**
See also CA 128

Ellmann, Richard (David)
1918-1987 .... **CLC 50**
See also BEST 89:2; CA 1-4R; 122; CANR
2, 28, 61; DLB 103; DLBY 1987; MTCW
1, 2; MTFW 2005

Elman, Richard (Martin)
1934-1997 .... **CLC 19**
See also CA 17-20R; 163; CAAS 3; CANR
47; TCLE 1:1

Elron
See Hubbard, L(afayette) Ron(ald)

El Saadawi, Nawal 1931- .... **CLC 196**
See al'Sadaawi, Nawal; Sa'adawi, al-
Nawal; Saadawi, Nawal El; Sa'dawi,
Nawal al-
See also CA 118; CAAS 11; CANR 44, 92

Eluard, Paul .... **PC 38; TCLC 7, 41**
See Grindel, Eugene
See also EWL 3; GFL 1789 to the Present;
RGWL 2, 3

Elyot, Thomas 1490(?)-1546 .... **LC 11**
See also DLB 136; RGEL 2

Elytis, Odysseus 1911-1996 .... **CLC 15, 49,**
100; PC 21
See Alepoudelis, Odysseus
See also CA 102; 151; CANR 94; CWW 2;
DAM POET; EW 13; EWL 3; MTCW 1,
2; RGWL 2, 3

Emecheta, (Florence Onye) Buchi
1944- ...... **BLC 2; CLC 14, 48, 128, 214**
See also AAYA 67; AFW; BW 2, 3; CA 81-
84; CANR 27, 81, 126; CDWLB 3; CN
4, 5, 6, 7; CWRI 5; DA3; DAM MULT;
DLB 117; EWL 3; FL 1:5; FW; MTCW
1, 2; MTFW 2005; NFS 12, 14; SATA 66;
WLIT 2

Emerson, Mary Moody
1774-1863 .... **NCLC 66**

Emerson, Ralph Waldo 1803-1882 . **NCLC 1, 38, 98; PC 18; WLC**
See also AAYA 60; AMW; ANW; CDALB 1640-1865; DA; DA3; DAB; DAC; DAM MST, POET; DLB 1, 59, 73, 183, 223, 270; EXPP; LAIT 2; LMFS 1; NCFS 3; PFS 4, 17; RGAL 4; TUS; WP

Eminescu, Mihail 1850-1889 .. **NCLC 33, 131**

Empedocles 5th cent. B.C.- .... **CMLC 50**
See also DLB 176

Empson, William 1906-1984 ... **CLC 3, 8, 19, 33, 34**
See also BRWS 2; CA 17-20R; 112; CANR 31, 61; CP 1, 2, 3; DLB 20; EWL 3; MTCW 1, 2; RGEL 2

Enchi, Fumiko (Ueda) 1905-1986 ..... **CLC 31**
See Enchi Fumiko
See also CA 129; 121; FW; MJW

Enchi Fumiko
See Enchi, Fumiko (Ueda)
See also DLB 182; EWL 3

Ende, Michael (Andreas Helmuth)
1929-1995 .... **CLC 31**
See also BYA 5; CA 118; 124; 149; CANR 36, 110; CLR 14; DLB 75; MAICYA 1, 2; MAICYAS 1; SATA 61, 130; SATA-Brief 42; SATA-Obit 86

Endo, Shusaku 1923-1996 ..... **CLC 7, 14, 19, 54, 99; SSC 48; TCLC 152**
See Endo Shusaku
See also CA 29-32R; 153; CANR 21, 54, 131; DA3; DAM NOV; MTCW 1, 2; MTFW 2005; RGSF 2; RGWL 2, 3

Endo Shusaku
See Endo, Shusaku
See also CWW 2; DLB 182; EWL 3

Engel, Marian 1933-1985 .... **CLC 36; TCLC 137**
See also CA 25-28R; CANR 12; CN 2, 3; DLB 53; FW; INT CANR-12

Engelhardt, Frederick
See Hubbard, L(afayette) Ron(ald)

Engels, Friedrich 1820-1895 .. **NCLC 85, 114**
See also DLB 129; LATS 1:1

Enright, D(ennis) J(oseph)
1920-2002 .... **CLC 4, 8, 31**
See also CA 1-4R; 211; CANR 1, 42, 83; CN 1, 2; CP 1, 2, 3, 4, 5, 6, 7; DLB 27; EWL 3; SATA 25; SATA-Obit 140

Ensler, Eve 1953- .... **CLC 212**
See also CA 172; CANR 126

Enzensberger, Hans Magnus
1929- .... **CLC 43; PC 28**
See also CA 116; 119; CANR 103; CWW 2; EWL 3

Ephron, Nora 1941- .... **CLC 17, 31**
See also AAYA 35; AITN 2; CA 65-68; CANR 12, 39, 83; DFS 22

Epicurus 341B.C.-270B.C. .... **CMLC 21**
See also DLB 176

Epsilon
See Betjeman, John

Epstein, Daniel Mark 1948- .... **CLC 7**
See also CA 49-52; CANR 2, 53, 90

Epstein, Jacob 1956- .... **CLC 19**
See also CA 114

Epstein, Jean 1897-1953 .... **TCLC 92**

Epstein, Joseph 1937- .... **CLC 39, 204**
See also AMWS 14; CA 112; 119; CANR 50, 65, 117

Epstein, Leslie 1938- .... **CLC 27**
See also AMWS 12; CA 73-76, 215; CAAE 215; CAAS 12; CANR 23, 69; DLB 299

Equiano, Olaudah 1745(?)-1797 . **BLC 2; LC 16**
See also AFAW 1, 2; CDWLB 3; DAM MULT; DLB 37, 50; WLIT 2

Erasmus, Desiderius 1469(?)-1536 ..... **LC 16, 93**
See also DLB 136; EW 2; LMFS 1; RGWL 2, 3; TWA

Erdman, Paul E(mil) 1932- .... **CLC 25**
See also AITN 1; CA 61-64; CANR 13, 43, 84

Erdrich, (Karen) Louise 1954- .. **CLC 39, 54, 120, 176; NNAL; PC 52**
See also AAYA 10, 47; AMWS 4; BEST 89:1; BPFB 1; CA 114; CANR 41, 62, 118, 138; CDALBS; CN 5, 6, 7; CP 7; CPW; CWP; DA3; DAM MULT, NOV, POP; DLB 152, 175, 206; EWL 3; EXPP; FL 1:5; LAIT 5; LATS 1:2; MAL 5; MTCW 1, 2; MTFW 2005; NFS 5; PFS 14; RGAL 4; SATA 94, 141; SSFS 14; TCWW 2

Erenburg, Ilya (Grigoryevich)
See Ehrenburg, Ilya (Grigoryevich)

Erickson, Stephen Michael 1950-
See Erickson, Steve
See also CA 129; SFW 4

Erickson, Steve .... **CLC 64**
See Erickson, Stephen Michael
See also CANR 60, 68, 136; MTFW 2005; SUFW 2

Erickson, Walter
See Fast, Howard (Melvin)

Ericson, Walter
See Fast, Howard (Melvin)

Eriksson, Buntel
See Bergman, (Ernst) Ingmar

Eriugena, John Scottus c.
810-877 .... **CMLC 65**
See also DLB 115

Ernaux, Annie 1940- .... **CLC 88, 184**
See also CA 147; CANR 93; MTFW 2005; NCFS 3, 5

Erskine, John 1879-1951 .... **TCLC 84**
See also CA 112; 159; DLB 9, 102; FANT

Eschenbach, Wolfram von
See Wolfram von Eschenbach
See also RGWL 3

Eseki, Bruno
See Mphahlele, Ezekiel

Esenin, Sergei (Alexandrovich)
1895-1925 .... **TCLC 4**
See Yesenin, Sergey
See also CA 104; RGWL 2, 3

Eshleman, Clayton 1935- .... **CLC 7**
See also CA 33-36R, 212; CAAE 212; CAAS 6; CANR 93; CP 1, 2, 3, 4, 5, 6, 7; DLB 5

Espriella, Don Manuel Alvarez
See Southey, Robert

Espriu, Salvador 1913-1985 .... **CLC 9**
See also CA 154; 115; DLB 134; EWL 3

Espronceda, Jose de 1808-1842 ..... **NCLC 39**

Esquivel, Laura 1951(?)- ... **CLC 141; HLCS 1**
See also AAYA 29; CA 143; CANR 68, 113; DA3; DNFS 2; LAIT 3; LMFS 2; MTCW 2; MTFW 2005; NFS 5; WLIT 1

Esse, James
See Stephens, James

Esterbrook, Tom
See Hubbard, L(afayette) Ron(ald)

Estleman, Loren D. 1952- .... **CLC 48**
See also AAYA 27; CA 85-88; CANR 27, 74, 139; CMW 4; CPW; DA3; DAM NOV, POP; DLB 226; INT CANR-27; MTCW 1, 2; MTFW 2005; TCWW 1, 2

Etherege, Sir George 1636-1692 . **DC 23; LC 78**
See also BRW 2; DAM DRAM; DLB 80; PAB; RGEL 2

Euclid 306B.C.-283B.C. .... **CMLC 25**

Eugenides, Jeffrey 1960(?)- .... **CLC 81, 212**
See also AAYA 51; CA 144; CANR 120; MTFW 2005

Euripides c. 484B.C.-406B.C. .... **CMLC 23, 51; DC 4; WLCS**
See also AW 1; CDWLB 1; DA; DA3; DAB; DAC; DAM DRAM, MST; DFS 1, 4, 6; DLB 176; LAIT 1; LMFS 1; RGWL 2, 3

Evan, Evin
See Faust, Frederick (Schiller)

Evans, Caradoc 1878-1945 ... **SSC 43; TCLC 85**
See also DLB 162

Evans, Evan
See Faust, Frederick (Schiller)

Evans, Marian
See Eliot, George

Evans, Mary Ann
See Eliot, George
See also NFS 20

Evarts, Esther
See Benson, Sally

Everett, Percival
See Everett, Percival L.
See also CSW

Everett, Percival L. 1956- .... **CLC 57**
See Everett, Percival
See also BW 2; CA 129; CANR 94, 134; CN 7; MTFW 2005

Everson, R(onald) G(ilmour)
1903-1992 .... **CLC 27**
See also CA 17-20R; CP 1, 2, 3, 4; DLB 88

Everson, William (Oliver)
1912-1994 .... **CLC 1, 5, 14**
See Antoninus, Brother
See also BG 1:2; CA 9-12R; 145; CANR 20; CP 2, 3, 4; DLB 5, 16, 212; MTCW 1

Evtushenko, Evgenii Aleksandrovich
See Yevtushenko, Yevgeny (Alexandrovich)
See also CWW 2; RGWL 2, 3

Ewart, Gavin (Buchanan)
1916-1995 .... **CLC 13, 46**
See also BRWS 7; CA 89-92; 150; CANR 17, 46; CP 1, 2, 3, 4; DLB 40; MTCW 1

Ewers, Hanns Heinz 1871-1943 ..... **TCLC 12**
See also CA 109; 149

Ewing, Frederick R.
See Sturgeon, Theodore (Hamilton)

Exley, Frederick (Earl) 1929-1992 .... **CLC 6, 11**
See also AITN 2; BPFB 1; CA 81-84; 138; CANR 117; DLB 143; DLBY 1981

Eynhardt, Guillermo
See Quiroga, Horacio (Sylvestre)

Ezekiel, Nissim (Moses) 1924-2004 .. **CLC 61**
See also CA 61-64; 223; CP 1, 2, 3, 4, 5, 6, 7; EWL 3

Ezekiel, Tish O'Dowd 1943- .... **CLC 34**
See also CA 129

Fadeev, Aleksandr Aleksandrovich
See Bulgya, Alexander Alexandrovich
See also DLB 272

Fadeev, Alexandr Alexandrovich
See Bulgya, Alexander Alexandrovich
See also EWL 3

Fadeyev, A.
See Bulgya, Alexander Alexandrovich

Fadeyev, Alexander .... **TCLC 53**
See Bulgya, Alexander Alexandrovich

Fagen, Donald 1948- .... **CLC 26**

Fainzilberg, Ilya Arnoldovich 1897-1937
See Ilf, Ilya
See also CA 120; 165

Fair, Ronald L. 1932- .... **CLC 18**
See also BW 1; CA 69-72; CANR 25; DLB 33

Fairbairn, Roger
See Carr, John Dickson
Fairbairns, Zoe (Ann) 1948- .... **CLC 32**
See also CA 103; CANR 21, 85; CN 4, 5, 6, 7
Fairfield, Flora
See Alcott, Louisa May
Fairman, Paul W. 1916-1977
See Queen, Ellery
See also CA 114; SFW 4
Falco, Gian
See Papini, Giovanni
Falconer, James
See Kirkup, James
Falconer, Kenneth
See Kornbluth, C(yril) M.
Falkland, Samuel
See Heijermans, Herman
Fallaci, Oriana 1930- .... **CLC 11, 110**
See also CA 77-80; CANR 15, 58, 134; FW; MTCW 1
Faludi, Susan 1959- .... **CLC 140**
See also CA 138; CANR 126; FW; MTCW 2; MTFW 2005; NCFS 3
Faludy, George 1913- .... **CLC 42**
See also CA 21-24R
Faludy, Gyoergy
See Faludy, George
Fanon, Frantz 1925-1961 .... **BLC 2; CLC 74**
See also BW 1; CA 116; 89-92; DAM MULT; DLB 296; LMFS 2; WLIT 2
Fanshawe, Ann 1625-1680 .... **LC 11**
Fante, John (Thomas) 1911-1983 .... **CLC 60; SSC 65**
See also AMWS 11; CA 69-72; 109; CANR 23, 104; DLB 130; DLBY 1983
Far, Sui Sin .... **SSC 62**
See Eaton, Edith Maude
See also SSFS 4
Farah, Nuruddin 1945- ...... **BLC 2; CLC 53, 137**
See also AFW; BW 2, 3; CA 106; CANR 81; CDWLB 3; CN 4, 5, 6, 7; DAM MULT; DLB 125; EWL 3; WLIT 2
Fargue, Leon-Paul 1876(?)-1947 .... **TCLC 11**
See also CA 109; CANR 107; DLB 258; EWL 3
Farigoule, Louis
See Romains, Jules
Farina, Richard 1936(?)-1966 .... **CLC 9**
See also CA 81-84; 25-28R
Farley, Walter (Lorimer)
1915-1989 .... **CLC 17**
See also AAYA 58; BYA 14; CA 17-20R; CANR 8, 29, 84; DLB 22; JRDA; MAI-CYA 1, 2; SATA 2, 43, 132; YAW
Farmer, Philip Jose 1918- .... **CLC 1, 19**
See also AAYA 28; BPFB 1; CA 1-4R; CANR 4, 35, 111; DLB 8; MTCW 1; SATA 93; SCFW 1, 2; SFW 4
Farquhar, George 1677-1707 .... **LC 21**
See also BRW 2; DAM DRAM; DLB 84; RGEL 2
Farrell, J(ames) G(ordon)
1935-1979 .... **CLC 6**
See also CA 73-76; 89-92; CANR 36; CN 1, 2; DLB 14, 271; MTCW 1; RGEL 2; RHW; WLIT 4
Farrell, James T(homas) 1904-1979 . **CLC 1, 4, 8, 11, 66; SSC 28**
See also AMW; BPFB 1; CA 5-8R; 89-92; CANR 9, 61; CN 1, 2; DLB 4, 9, 86; DLBD 2; EWL 3; MAL 5; MTCW 1, 2; MTFW 2005; RGAL 4
Farrell, Warren (Thomas) 1943- ...... **CLC 70**
See also CA 146; CANR 120
Farren, Richard J.
See Betjeman, John

Farren, Richard M.
See Betjeman, John
Fassbinder, Rainer Werner
1946-1982 .... **CLC 20**
See also CA 93-96; 106; CANR 31
Fast, Howard (Melvin) 1914-2003 .. **CLC 23, 131**
See also AAYA 16; BPFB 1; CA 1-4R, 181; 214; CAAE 181; CAAS 18; CANR 1, 33, 54, 75, 98, 140; CMW 4; CN 1, 2, 3, 4, 5, 6, 7; CPW; DAM NOV; DLB 9; INT CANR-33; LATS 1:1; MAL 5; MTCW 2; MTFW 2005; RHW; SATA 7; SATA-Essay 107; TCWW 1, 2; YAW
Faulcon, Robert
See Holdstock, Robert P.
Faulkner, William (Cuthbert)
1897-1962 .... **CLC 1, 3, 6, 8, 9, 11, 14, 18, 28, 52, 68; SSC 1, 35, 42; TCLC 141; WLC**
See also AAYA 7; AMW; AMWR 1; BPFB 1; BYA 5, 15; CA 81-84; CANR 33; CDALB 1929-1941; DA; DA3; DAB; DAC; DAM MST, NOV; DLB 9, 11, 44, 102, 316; DLBD 2; DLBY 1986, 1997; EWL 3; EXPN; EXPS; GL 2; LAIT 2; LATS 1:1; LMFS 2; MAL 5; MTCW 1, 2; MTFW 2005; NFS 4, 8, 13; RGAL 4; RGSF 2; SSFS 2, 5, 6, 12; TUS
Fauset, Jessie Redmon
1882(?)-1961 .. **BLC 2; CLC 19, 54; HR 1:2**
See also AFAW 2; BW 1; CA 109; CANR 83; DAM MULT; DLB 51; FW; LMFS 2; MAL 5; MAWW
Faust, Frederick (Schiller)
1892-1944 .... **TCLC 49**
See Brand, Max; Dawson, Peter; Frederick, John
See also CA 108; 152; CANR 143; DAM POP; DLB 256; TUS
Faust, Irvin 1924- .... **CLC 8**
See also CA 33-36R; CANR 28, 67; CN 1, 2, 3, 4, 5, 6, 7; DLB 2, 28, 218, 278; DLBY 1980
Faustino, Domingo 1811-1888 ...... **NCLC 123**
Fawkes, Guy
See Benchley, Robert (Charles)
Fearing, Kenneth (Flexner)
1902-1961 .... **CLC 51**
See also CA 93-96; CANR 59; CMW 4; DLB 9; MAL 5; RGAL 4
Fecamps, Elise
See Creasey, John
Federman, Raymond 1928- .... **CLC 6, 47**
See also CA 17-20R, 208; CAAE 208; CAAS 8; CANR 10, 43, 83, 108; CN 3, 4, 5, 6; DLBY 1980
Federspiel, J(uerg) F. 1931- .... **CLC 42**
See also CA 146
Feiffer, Jules (Ralph) 1929- ...... **CLC 2, 8, 64**
See also AAYA 3, 62; CA 17-20R; CAD; CANR 30, 59, 129; CD 5, 6; DAM DRAM; DLB 7, 44; INT CANR-30; MTCW 1; SATA 8, 61, 111, 157
Feige, Hermann Albert Otto Maximilian
See Traven, B.
Feinberg, David B. 1956-1994 .... **CLC 59**
See also CA 135; 147
Feinstein, Elaine 1930- .... **CLC 36**
See also CA 69-72; CAAS 1; CANR 31, 68, 121; CN 3, 4, 5, 6, 7; CP 2, 3, 4, 5, 6, 7; CWP; DLB 14, 40; MTCW 1
Feke, Gilbert David .... **CLC 65**
Feldman, Irving (Mordecai) 1928- ..... **CLC 7**
See also CA 1-4R; CANR 1; CP 1, 2, 3, 4, 5, 6, 7; DLB 169; TCLE 1:1
Felix-Tchicaya, Gerald
See Tchicaya, Gerald Felix

Fellini, Federico 1920-1993 .... **CLC 16, 85**
See also CA 65-68; 143; CANR 33
Felltham, Owen 1602(?)-1668 .... **LC 92**
See also DLB 126, 151
Felsen, Henry Gregor 1916-1995 ..... **CLC 17**
See also CA 1-4R; 180; CANR 1; SAAS 2; SATA 1
Felski, Rita .... **CLC 65**
Fenno, Jack
See Calisher, Hortense
Fenollosa, Ernest (Francisco)
1853-1908 .... **TCLC 91**
Fenton, James Martin 1949- .... **CLC 32, 209**
See also CA 102; CANR 108; CP 2, 3, 4, 5, 6, 7; DLB 40; PFS 11
Ferber, Edna 1887-1968 .... **CLC 18, 93**
See also AITN 1; CA 5-8R; 25-28R; CANR 68, 105; DLB 9, 28, 86, 266; MAL 5; MTCW 1, 2; MTFW 2005; RGAL 4; RHW; SATA 7; TCWW 1, 2
Ferdowsi, Abu'l Qasem
940-1020(?) .... **CMLC 43**
See Firdawsi, Abu al-Qasim
See also RGWL 2, 3
Ferguson, Helen
See Kavan, Anna
Ferguson, Niall 1964- .... **CLC 134**
See also CA 190
Ferguson, Samuel 1810-1886 .... **NCLC 33**
See also DLB 32; RGEL 2
Fergusson, Robert 1750-1774 .... **LC 29**
See also DLB 109; RGEL 2
Ferling, Lawrence
See Ferlinghetti, Lawrence (Monsanto)
Ferlinghetti, Lawrence (Monsanto)
1919(?)- .... **CLC 2, 6, 10, 27, 111; PC 1**
See also BG 1:2; CA 5-8R; CAD; CANR 3, 41, 73, 125; CDALB 1941-1968; CP 1, 2, 3, 4, 5, 6, 7; DA3; DAM POET; DLB 5, 16; MAL 5; MTCW 1, 2; MTFW 2005; RGAL 4; WP
Fern, Fanny
See Parton, Sara Payson Willis
Fernandez, Vicente Garcia Huidobro
See Huidobro Fernandez, Vicente Garcia
Fernandez-Armesto, Felipe .... **CLC 70**
Fernandez de Lizardi, Jose Joaquin
See Lizardi, Jose Joaquin Fernandez de
Ferre, Rosario 1938- ...... **CLC 139; HLCS 1; SSC 36**
See also CA 131; CANR 55, 81, 134; CWW 2; DLB 145; EWL 3; HW 1, 2; LAWS 1; MTCW 2; MTFW 2005; WLIT 1
Ferrer, Gabriel (Francisco Victor) Miro
See Miro (Ferrer), Gabriel (Francisco Victor)
Ferrier, Susan (Edmonstone)
1782-1854 .... **NCLC 8**
See also DLB 116; RGEL 2
Ferrigno, Robert 1948(?)- .... **CLC 65**
See also CA 140; CANR 125
Ferron, Jacques 1921-1985 .... **CLC 94**
See also CA 117; 129; CCA 1; DAC; DLB 60; EWL 3
Feuchtwanger, Lion 1884-1958 .... **TCLC 3**
See also CA 104; 187; DLB 66; EWL 3
Feuerbach, Ludwig 1804-1872 ..... **NCLC 139**
See also DLB 133
Feuillet, Octave 1821-1890 .... **NCLC 45**
See also DLB 192
Feydeau, Georges (Leon Jules Marie)
1862-1921 .... **TCLC 22**
See also CA 113; 152; CANR 84; DAM DRAM; DLB 192; EWL 3; GFL 1789 to the Present; RGWL 2, 3
Fichte, Johann Gottlieb
1762-1814 .... **NCLC 62**
See also DLB 90

Freeman, Mary E(leanor) Wilkins 1852-1930 .... **SSC 1, 47; TCLC 9**
See also CA 106; 177; DLB 12, 78, 221; EXPS; FW; HGG; MAWW; RGAL 4; RGSF 2; SSFS 4, 8; SUFW 1; TUS

Freeman, R(ichard) Austin 1862-1943 .... **TCLC 21**
See also CA 113; CANR 84; CMW 4; DLB 70

French, Albert 1943- .... **CLC 86**
See also BW 3; CA 167

French, Antonia
See Kureishi, Hanif

French, Marilyn 1929- .. **CLC 10, 18, 60, 177**
See also BPFB 1; CA 69-72; CANR 3, 31, 134; CN 5, 6, 7; CPW; DAM DRAM, NOV, POP; FL 1:5; FW; INT CANR-31; MTCW 1, 2; MTFW 2005

French, Paul
See Asimov, Isaac

Freneau, Philip Morin 1752-1832 .. **NCLC 1, 111**
See also AMWS 2; DLB 37, 43; RGAL 4

Freud, Sigmund 1856-1939 .... **TCLC 52**
See also CA 115; 133; CANR 69; DLB 296; EW 8; EWL 3; LATS 1:1; MTCW 1, 2; MTFW 2005; NCFS 3; TWA

Freytag, Gustav 1816-1895 .... **NCLC 109**
See also DLB 129

Friedan, Betty (Naomi) 1921- .... **CLC 74**
See also CA 65-68; CANR 18, 45, 74; DLB 246; FW; MTCW 1, 2; MTFW 2005; NCFS 5

Friedlander, Saul 1932- .... **CLC 90**
See also CA 117; 130; CANR 72

Friedman, B(ernard) H(arper) 1926- .... **CLC 7**
See also CA 1-4R; CANR 3, 48

Friedman, Bruce Jay 1930- ...... **CLC 3, 5, 56**
See also CA 9-12R; CAD; CANR 25, 52, 101; CD 5, 6; CN 1, 2, 3, 4, 5, 6, 7; DLB 2, 28, 244; INT CANR-25; MAL 5; SSFS 18

Friel, Brian 1929- .... **CLC 5, 42, 59, 115; DC 8; SSC 76**
See also BRWS 5; CA 21-24R; CANR 33, 69, 131; CBD; CD 5, 6; DFS 11; DLB 13, 319; EWL 3; MTCW 1; RGEL 2; TEA

Friis-Baastad, Babbis Ellinor 1921-1970 .... **CLC 12**
See also CA 17-20R; 134; SATA 7

Frisch, Max (Rudolf) 1911-1991 ... **CLC 3, 9, 14, 18, 32, 44; TCLC 121**
See also CA 85-88; 134; CANR 32, 74; CD-WLB 2; DAM DRAM, NOV; DLB 69, 124; EW 13; EWL 3; MTCW 1, 2; MTFW 2005; RGWL 2, 3

Fromentin, Eugene (Samuel Auguste) 1820-1876 .... **NCLC 10, 125**
See also DLB 123; GFL 1789 to the Present

Frost, Frederick
See Faust, Frederick (Schiller)

Frost, Robert (Lee) 1874-1963 .. **CLC 1, 3, 4, 9, 10, 13, 15, 26, 34, 44; PC 1, 39, 71; WLC**
See also AAYA 21; AMW; AMWR 1; CA 89-92; CANR 33; CDALB 1917-1929; CLR 67; DA; DA3; DAB; DAC; DAM MST, POET; DLB 54, 284; DLBD 7; EWL 3; EXPP; MAL 5; MTCW 1, 2; MTFW 2005; PAB; PFS 1, 2, 3, 4, 5, 6, 7, 10, 13; RGAL 4; SATA 14; TUS; WP; WYA

Froude, James Anthony 1818-1894 .... **NCLC 43**
See also DLB 18, 57, 144

Froy, Herald
See Waterhouse, Keith (Spencer)

Fry, Christopher 1907-2005 ... **CLC 2, 10, 14**
See also BRWS 3; CA 17-20R; 240; CAAS 23; CANR 9, 30, 74, 132; CBD; CD 5, 6; CP 1, 2, 3, 4, 5, 6, 7; DAM DRAM; DLB 13; EWL 3; MTCW 1, 2; MTFW 2005; RGEL 2; SATA 66; TEA

Frye, (Herman) Northrop 1912-1991 .... **CLC 24, 70; TCLC 165**
See also CA 5-8R; 133; CANR 8, 37; DLB 67, 68, 246; EWL 3; MTCW 1, 2; MTFW 2005; RGAL 4; TWA

Fuchs, Daniel 1909-1993 .... **CLC 8, 22**
See also CA 81-84; 142; CAAS 5; CANR 40; CN 1, 2, 3, 4, 5; DLB 9, 26, 28; DLBY 1993; MAL 5

Fuchs, Daniel 1934- .... **CLC 34**
See also CA 37-40R; CANR 14, 48

Fuentes, Carlos 1928- .. **CLC 3, 8, 10, 13, 22, 41, 60, 113; HLC 1; SSC 24; WLC**
See also AAYA 4, 45; AITN 2; BPFB 1; CA 69-72; CANR 10, 32, 68, 104, 138; CDWLB 3; CWW 2; DA; DA3; DAB; DAC; DAM MST, MULT, NOV; DLB 113; DNFS 2; EWL 3; HW 1, 2; LAIT 3; LATS 1:2; LAW; LAWS 1; LMFS 2; MTCW 1, 2; MTFW 2005; NFS 8; RGSF 2; RGWL 2, 3; TWA; WLIT 1

Fuentes, Gregorio Lopez y
See Lopez y Fuentes, Gregorio

Fuertes, Gloria 1918-1998 .... **PC 27**
See also CA 178, 180; DLB 108; HW 2; SATA 115

Fugard, (Harold) Athol 1932- . **CLC 5, 9, 14, 25, 40, 80, 211; DC 3**
See also AAYA 17; AFW; CA 85-88; CANR 32, 54, 118; CD 5, 6; DAM DRAM; DFS 3, 6, 10; DLB 225; DNFS 1, 2; EWL 3; LATS 1:2; MTCW 1; MTFW 2005; RGEL 2; WLIT 2

Fugard, Sheila 1932- .... **CLC 48**
See also CA 125

Fujiwara no Teika 1162-1241 .... **CMLC 73**
See also DLB 203

Fukuyama, Francis 1952- .... **CLC 131**
See also CA 140; CANR 72, 125

Fuller, Charles (H.), (Jr.) 1939- .... **BLC 2; CLC 25; DC 1**
See also BW 2; CA 108; 112; CAD; CANR 87; CD 5, 6; DAM DRAM, MULT; DFS 8; DLB 38, 266; EWL 3; INT CA-112; MAL 5; MTCW 1

Fuller, Henry Blake 1857-1929 .... **TCLC 103**
See also CA 108; 177; DLB 12; RGAL 4

Fuller, John (Leopold) 1937- .... **CLC 62**
See also CA 21-24R; CANR 9, 44; CP 1, 2, 3, 4, 5, 6, 7; DLB 40

Fuller, Margaret
See Ossoli, Sarah Margaret (Fuller)
See also AMWS 2; DLB 183, 223, 239; FL 1:3

Fuller, Roy (Broadbent) 1912-1991 ... **CLC 4, 28**
See also BRWS 7; CA 5-8R; 135; CAAS 10; CANR 53, 83; CN 1, 2, 3, 4, 5; CP 1, 2, 3, 4; CWRI 5; DLB 15, 20; EWL 3; RGEL 2; SATA 87

Fuller, Sarah Margaret
See Ossoli, Sarah Margaret (Fuller)

Fuller, Sarah Margaret
See Ossoli, Sarah Margaret (Fuller)
See also DLB 1, 59, 73

Fuller, Thomas 1608-1661 .... **LC 111**
See also DLB 151

Fulton, Alice 1952- .... **CLC 52**
See also CA 116; CANR 57, 88; CP 7; CWP; DLB 193

Furphy, Joseph 1843-1912 .... **TCLC 25**
See Collins, Tom
See also CA 163; DLB 230; EWL 3; RGEL 2

Fuson, Robert H(enderson) 1927- .... **CLC 70**
See also CA 89-92; CANR 103

Fussell, Paul 1924- .... **CLC 74**
See also BEST 90:1; CA 17-20R; CANR 8, 21, 35, 69, 135; INT CANR-21; MTCW 1, 2; MTFW 2005

Futabatei, Shimei 1864-1909 .... **TCLC 44**
See Futabatei Shimei
See also CA 162; MJW

Futabatei Shimei
See Futabatei, Shimei
See also DLB 180; EWL 3

Futrelle, Jacques 1875-1912 .... **TCLC 19**
See also CA 113; 155; CMW 4

Gaboriau, Emile 1835-1873 .... **NCLC 14**
See also CMW 4; MSW

Gadda, Carlo Emilio 1893-1973 ...... **CLC 11; TCLC 144**
See also CA 89-92; DLB 177; EWL 3; WLIT 7

Gaddis, William 1922-1998 ... **CLC 1, 3, 6, 8, 10, 19, 43, 86**
See also AMWS 4; BPFB 1; CA 17-20R; 172; CANR 21, 48; CN 1, 2, 3, 4, 5, 6; DLB 2, 278; EWL 3; MAL 5; MTCW 1, 2; MTFW 2005; RGAL 4

Gaelique, Moruen le
See Jacob, (Cyprien-)Max

Gage, Walter
See Inge, William (Motter)

Gaiman, Neil (Richard) 1960- .... **CLC 195**
See also AAYA 19, 42; CA 133; CANR 81, 129; DLB 261; HGG; MTFW 2005; SATA 85, 146; SFW 4; SUFW 2

Gaines, Ernest J(ames) 1933- .. **BLC 2; CLC 3, 11, 18, 86, 181; SSC 68**
See also AAYA 18; AFAW 1, 2; AITN 1; BPFB 2; BW 2, 3; BYA 6; CA 9-12R; CANR 6, 24, 42, 75, 126; CDALB 1968-1988; CLR 62; CN 1, 2, 3, 4, 5, 6, 7; CSW; DA3; DAM MULT; DLB 2, 33, 152; DLBY 1980; EWL 3; EXPN; LAIT 5; LATS 1:2; MAL 5; MTCW 1, 2; MTFW 2005; NFS 5, 7, 16; RGAL 4; RGSF 2; RHW; SATA 86; SSFS 5; YAW

Gaitskill, Mary (Lawrence) 1954- .... **CLC 69**
See also CA 128; CANR 61; DLB 244; TCLE 1:1

Gaius Suetonius Tranquillus
See Suetonius

Galdos, Benito Perez
See Perez Galdos, Benito
See also EW 7

Gale, Zona 1874-1938 .... **TCLC 7**
See also CA 105; 153; CANR 84; DAM DRAM; DFS 17; DLB 9, 78, 228; RGAL 4

Galeano, Eduardo (Hughes) 1940- . **CLC 72; HLCS 1**
See also CA 29-32R; CANR 13, 32, 100; HW 1

Galiano, Juan Valera y Alcala
See Valera y Alcala-Galiano, Juan

Galilei, Galileo 1564-1642 .... **LC 45**

Gallagher, Tess 1943- .... **CLC 18, 63; PC 9**
See also CA 106; CP 3, 4, 5, 6, 7; CWP; DAM POET; DLB 120, 212, 244; PFS 16

Gallant, Mavis 1922- ..... **CLC 7, 18, 38, 172; SSC 5, 78**
See also CA 69-72; CANR 29, 69, 117; CCA 1; CN 1, 2, 3, 4, 5, 6, 7; DAC; DAM MST; DLB 53; EWL 3; MTCW 1, 2; MTFW 2005; RGEL 2; RGSF 2

Gallant, Roy A(rthur) 1924- .... **CLC 17**
See also CA 5-8R; CANR 4, 29, 54, 117; CLR 30; MAICYA 1, 2; SATA 4, 68, 110

Gellhorn, Martha (Ellis)
1908-1998 .... **CLC 14, 60**
See also CA 77-80; 164; CANR 44; CN 1, 2, 3, 4, 5, 6 7; DLBY 1982, 1998

Genet, Jean 1910-1986 .. **CLC 1, 2, 5, 10, 14, 44, 46; DC 25; TCLC 128**
See also CA 13-16R; CANR 18; DA3; DAM DRAM; DFS 10; DLB 72, 321; DLBY 1986; EW 13; EWL 3; GFL 1789 to the Present; GLL 1; LMFS 2; MTCW 1, 2; MTFW 2005; RGWL 2, 3; TWA

Gent, Peter 1942- .... **CLC 29**
See also AITN 1; CA 89-92; DLBY 1982

Gentile, Giovanni 1875-1944 .... **TCLC 96**
See also CA 119

Gentlewoman in New England, A
See Bradstreet, Anne

Gentlewoman in Those Parts, A
See Bradstreet, Anne

Geoffrey of Monmouth c. 1100-1155 .... **CMLC 44**
See also DLB 146; TEA

George, Jean
See George, Jean Craighead

George, Jean Craighead 1919- .... **CLC 35**
See also AAYA 8; BYA 2, 4; CA 5-8R; CANR 25; CLR 1; 80; DLB 52; JRDA; MAICYA 1, 2; SATA 2, 68, 124; WYA; YAW

George, Stefan (Anton) 1868-1933 . **TCLC 2, 14**
See also CA 104; 193; EW 8; EWL 3

Georges, Georges Martin
See Simenon, Georges (Jacques Christian)

Gerald of Wales c. 1146-c. 1223 ... **CMLC 60**

Gerhardi, William Alexander
See Gerhardie, William Alexander

Gerhardie, William Alexander
1895-1977 .... **CLC 5**
See also CA 25-28R; 73-76; CANR 18; CN 1, 2; DLB 36; RGEL 2

Gerson, Jean 1363-1429 .... **LC 77**
See also DLB 208

Gersonides 1288-1344 .... **CMLC 49**
See also DLB 115

Gerstler, Amy 1956- .... **CLC 70**
See also CA 146; CANR 99

Gertler, T. .... **CLC 34**
See also CA 116; 121

Gertsen, Aleksandr Ivanovich
See Herzen, Aleksandr Ivanovich

Ghalib .... **NCLC 39, 78**
See Ghalib, Asadullah Khan

Ghalib, Asadullah Khan 1797-1869
See Ghalib
See also DAM POET; RGWL 2, 3

Ghelderode, Michel de 1898-1962 ..... **CLC 6, 11; DC 15**
See also CA 85-88; CANR 40, 77; DAM DRAM; DLB 321; EW 11; EWL 3; TWA

Ghiselin, Brewster 1903-2001 .... **CLC 23**
See also CA 13-16R; CAAS 10; CANR 13; CP 1, 2, 3, 4, 5, 6, 7

Ghose, Aurabinda 1872-1950 .... **TCLC 63**
See Ghose, Aurobindo
See also CA 163

Ghose, Aurobindo
See Ghose, Aurabinda
See also EWL 3

Ghose, Zulfikar 1935- .... **CLC 42, 200**
See also CA 65-68; CANR 67; CN 1, 2, 3, 4, 5, 6, 7; CP 1, 2, 3, 4, 5, 6, 7; EWL 3

Ghosh, Amitav 1956- .... **CLC 44, 153**
See also CA 147; CANR 80; CN 6, 7; WWE 1

Giacosa, Giuseppe 1847-1906 .... **TCLC 7**
See also CA 104

Gibb, Lee
See Waterhouse, Keith (Spencer)

Gibbon, Edward 1737-1794 .... **LC 97**
See also BRW 3; DLB 104; RGEL 2

Gibbon, Lewis Grassic .... **TCLC 4**
See Mitchell, James Leslie
See also RGEL 2

Gibbons, Kaye 1960- .... **CLC 50, 88, 145**
See also AAYA 34; AMWS 10; CA 151; CANR 75, 127; CN 7; CSW; DA3; DAM POP; DLB 292; MTCW 2; MTFW 2005; NFS 3; RGAL 4; SATA 117

Gibran, Kahlil 1883-1931 . **PC 9; TCLC 1, 9**
See also CA 104; 150; DA3; DAM POET, POP; EWL 3; MTCW 2; WLIT 6

Gibran, Khalil
See Gibran, Kahlil

Gibson, Mel 1956- .... **CLC 215**

Gibson, William 1914- .... **CLC 23**
See also CA 9-12R; CAD; CANR 9, 42, 75, 125; CD 5, 6; DA; DAB; DAC; DAM DRAM, MST; DFS 2; DLB 7; LAIT 2; MAL 5; MTCW 2; MTFW 2005; SATA 66; YAW

Gibson, William (Ford) 1948- ... **CLC 39, 63, 186, 192; SSC 52**
See also AAYA 12, 59; BPFB 2; CA 126; 133; CANR 52, 90, 106; CN 6, 7; CPW; DA3; DAM POP; DLB 251; MTCW 2; MTFW 2005; SCFW 2; SFW 4

Gide, Andre (Paul Guillaume)
1869-1951 ...... **SSC 13; TCLC 5, 12, 36, 177; WLC**
See also CA 104; 124; DA; DA3; DAB; DAC; DAM MST, NOV; DLB 65, 321; EW 8; EWL 3; GFL 1789 to the Present; MTCW 1, 2; MTFW 2005; NFS 21; RGSF 2; RGWL 2, 3; TWA

Gifford, Barry (Colby) 1946- .... **CLC 34**
See also CA 65-68; CANR 9, 30, 40, 90

Gilbert, Frank
See De Voto, Bernard (Augustine)

Gilbert, W(illiam) S(chwenck)
1836-1911 .... **TCLC 3**
See also CA 104; 173; DAM DRAM, POET; RGEL 2; SATA 36

Gilbreth, Frank B(unker), Jr.
1911-2001 .... **CLC 17**
See also CA 9-12R; SATA 2

Gilchrist, Ellen (Louise) 1935- .. **CLC 34, 48, 143; SSC 14, 63**
See also BPFB 2; CA 113; 116; CANR 41, 61, 104; CN 4, 5, 6, 7; CPW; CSW; DAM POP; DLB 130; EWL 3; EXPS; MTCW 1, 2; MTFW 2005; RGAL 4; RGSF 2; SSFS 9

Giles, Molly 1942- .... **CLC 39**
See also CA 126; CANR 98

Gill, Eric .... **TCLC 85**
See Gill, (Arthur) Eric (Rowton Peter Joseph)

Gill, (Arthur) Eric (Rowton Peter Joseph)
1882-1940
See Gill, Eric
See also CA 120; DLB 98

Gill, Patrick
See Creasey, John

Gillette, Douglas .... **CLC 70**

Gilliam, Terry (Vance) 1940- .... **CLC 21, 141**
See Monty Python
See also AAYA 19, 59; CA 108; 113; CANR 35; INT CA-113

Gillian, Jerry
See Gilliam, Terry (Vance)

Gilliatt, Penelope (Ann Douglass)
1932-1993 .... **CLC 2, 10, 13, 53**
See also AITN 2; CA 13-16R; 141; CANR 49; CN 1, 2, 3, 4, 5; DLB 14

Gilligan, Carol 1936- .... **CLC 208**
See also CA 142; CANR 121; FW

Gilman, Charlotte (Anna) Perkins (Stetson)
1860-1935 ...... **SSC 13, 62; TCLC 9, 37, 117**
See also AMWS 11; BYA 11; CA 106; 150; DLB 221; EXPS; FL 1:5; FW; HGG; LAIT 2; MAWW; MTCW 2; MTFW 2005; RGAL 4; RGSF 2; SFW 4; SSFS 1, 18

Gilmour, David 1946- .... **CLC 35**

Gilpin, William 1724-1804 .... **NCLC 30**

Gilray, J. D.
See Mencken, H(enry) L(ouis)

Gilroy, Frank D(aniel) 1925- .... **CLC 2**
See also CA 81-84; CAD; CANR 32, 64, 86; CD 5, 6; DFS 17; DLB 7

Gilstrap, John 1957(?)- .... **CLC 99**
See also AAYA 67; CA 160; CANR 101

Ginsberg, Allen 1926-1997 .... **CLC 1, 2, 3, 4, 6, 13, 36, 69, 109; PC 4, 47; TCLC 120; WLC**
See also AAYA 33; AITN 1; AMWC 1; AMWS 2; BG 1:2; CA 1-4R; 157; CANR 2, 41, 63, 95; CDALB 1941-1968; CP 1, 2, 3, 4, 5, 6; DA; DA3; DAB; DAC; DAM MST, POET; DLB 5, 16, 169, 237; EWL 3; GLL 1; LMFS 2; MAL 5; MTCW 1, 2; MTFW 2005; PAB; PFS 5; RGAL 4; TUS; WP

Ginzburg, Eugenia .... **CLC 59**
See Ginzburg, Evgeniia

Ginzburg, Evgeniia 1904-1977
See Ginzburg, Eugenia
See also DLB 302

Ginzburg, Natalia 1916-1991 .... **CLC 5, 11, 54, 70; SSC 65; TCLC 156**
See also CA 85-88; 135; CANR 33; DFS 14; DLB 177; EW 13; EWL 3; MTCW 1, 2; MTFW 2005; RGWL 2, 3

Giono, Jean 1895-1970 .... **CLC 4, 11; TCLC 124**
See also CA 45-48; 29-32R; CANR 2, 35; DLB 72, 321; EWL 3; GFL 1789 to the Present; MTCW 1; RGWL 2, 3

Giovanni, Nikki 1943- ...... **BLC 2; CLC 2, 4, 19, 64, 117; PC 19; WLCS**
See also AAYA 22; AITN 1; BW 2, 3; CA 29-32R; CAAS 6; CANR 18, 41, 60, 91, 130; CDALBS; CLR 6, 73; CP 2, 3, 4, 5, 6, 7; CSW; CWP; CWRI 5; DA; DA3; DAB; DAC; DAM MST, MULT, POET; DLB 5, 41; EWL 3; EXPP; INT CANR-18; MAICYA 1, 2; MAL 5; MTCW 1, 2; MTFW 2005; PFS 17; RGAL 4; SATA 24, 107; TUS; YAW

Giovene, Andrea 1904-1998 .... **CLC 7**
See also CA 85-88

Gippius, Zinaida (Nikolaevna) 1869-1945
See Hippius, Zinaida (Nikolaevna)
See also CA 106; 212

Giraudoux, Jean(-Hippolyte)
1882-1944 .... **TCLC 2, 7**
See also CA 104; 196; DAM DRAM; DLB 65, 321; EW 9; EWL 3; GFL 1789 to the Present; RGWL 2, 3; TWA

Gironella, Jose Maria (Pous)
1917-2003 .... **CLC 11**
See also CA 101; 212; EWL 3; RGWL 2, 3

Gissing, George (Robert)
1857-1903 .... **SSC 37; TCLC 3, 24, 47**
See also BRW 5; CA 105; 167; DLB 18, 135, 184; RGEL 2; TEA

Gitlin, Todd 1943- .... **CLC 201**
See also CA 29-32R; CANR 25, 50, 88

Giurlani, Aldo
See Palazzeschi, Aldo

Gladkov, Fedor Vasil'evich
See Gladkov, Fyodor (Vasilyevich)
See also DLB 272

Gladkov, Fyodor (Vasilyevich)
    1883-1958 .... **TCLC 27**
    See Gladkov, Fedor Vasil'evich
    See also CA 170; EWL 3
Glancy, Diane 1941- .... **CLC 210; NNAL**
    See also CA 136, 225; CAAE 225; CAAS
    24; CANR 87; DLB 175
Glanville, Brian (Lester) 1931- .... **CLC 6**
    See also CA 5-8R; CAAS 9; CANR 3, 70;
    CN 1, 2, 3, 4, 5, 6, 7; DLB 15, 139; SATA
    42
Glasgow, Ellen (Anderson Gholson)
    1873-1945 .... **SSC 34; TCLC 2, 7**
    See also AMW; CA 104; 164; DLB 9, 12;
    MAL 5; MAWW; MTCW 2; MTFW 2005;
    RGAL 4; RHW; SSFS 9; TUS
Glaspell, Susan 1882(?)-1948 ..... **DC 10; SSC
    41; TCLC 55, 175**
    See also AMWS 3; CA 110; 154; DFS 8,
    18; DLB 7, 9, 78, 228; MAWW; RGAL
    4; SSFS 3; TCWW 2; TUS; YABC 2
Glassco, John 1909-1981 .... **CLC 9**
    See also CA 13-16R; 102; CANR 15; CN
    1, 2; CP 1, 2, 3; DLB 68
Glasscock, Amnesia
    See Steinbeck, John (Ernst)
Glasser, Ronald J. 1940(?)- .... **CLC 37**
    See also CA 209
Glassman, Joyce
    See Johnson, Joyce
Gleick, James (W.) 1954- .... **CLC 147**
    See also CA 131; 137; CANR 97; INT CA-
    137
Glendinning, Victoria 1937- .... **CLC 50**
    See also CA 120; 127; CANR 59, 89; DLB
    155
Glissant, Edouard (Mathieu)
    1928- .... **CLC 10, 68**
    See also CA 153; CANR 111; CWW 2;
    DAM MULT; EWL 3; RGWL 3
Gloag, Julian 1930- .... **CLC 40**
    See also AITN 1; CA 65-68; CANR 10, 70;
    CN 1, 2, 3, 4, 5, 6
Glowacki, Aleksander
    See Prus, Boleslaw
Gluck, Louise (Elisabeth) 1943- .. **CLC 7, 22,
    44, 81, 160; PC 16**
    See also AMWS 5; CA 33-36R; CANR 40,
    69, 108, 133; CP 1, 2, 3, 4, 5, 6, 7; CWP;
    DA3; DAM POET; DLB 5; MAL 5;
    MTCW 2; MTFW 2005; PFS 5, 15;
    RGAL 4; TCLE 1:1
Glyn, Elinor 1864-1943 .... **TCLC 72**
    See also DLB 153; RHW
Gobineau, Joseph-Arthur
    1816-1882 .... **NCLC 17**
    See also DLB 123; GFL 1789 to the Present
Godard, Jean-Luc 1930- .... **CLC 20**
    See also CA 93-96
Godden, (Margaret) Rumer
    1907-1998 .... **CLC 53**
    See also AAYA 6; BPFB 2; BYA 2, 5; CA
    5-8R; 172; CANR 4, 27, 36, 55, 80; CLR
    20; CN 1, 2, 3, 4, 5, 6; CWRI 5; DLB
    161; MAICYA 1, 2; RHW; SAAS 12;
    SATA 3, 36; SATA-Obit 109; TEA
Godoy Alcayaga, Lucila 1899-1957 .. **HLC 2;
    PC 32; TCLC 2**
    See Mistral, Gabriela
    See also BW 2; CA 104; 131; CANR 81;
    DAM MULT; DNFS; HW 1, 2; MTCW 1,
    2; MTFW 2005
Godwin, Gail 1937- ...... **CLC 5, 8, 22, 31, 69,
    125**
    See also BPFB 2; CA 29-32R; CANR 15,
    43, 69, 132; CN 3, 4, 5, 6, 7; CPW; CSW;
    DA3; DAM POP; DLB 6, 234; INT
    CANR-15; MAL 5; MTCW 1, 2; MTFW
    2005

Godwin, Gail Kathleen
    See Godwin, Gail
Godwin, William 1756-1836 .. **NCLC 14, 130**
    See also CDBLB 1789-1832; CMW 4; DLB
    39, 104, 142, 158, 163, 262; GL 2; HGG;
    RGEL 2
Goebbels, Josef
    See Goebbels, (Paul) Joseph
Goebbels, (Paul) Joseph
    1897-1945 .... **TCLC 68**
    See also CA 115; 148
Goebbels, Joseph Paul
    See Goebbels, (Paul) Joseph
Goethe, Johann Wolfgang von
    1749-1832 . **DC 20; NCLC 4, 22, 34, 90,
    154; PC 5; SSC 38; WLC**
    See also CDWLB 2; DA; DA3; DAB;
    DAC; DAM DRAM, MST, POET; DLB
    94; EW 5; GL 2; LATS 1; LMFS 1:1;
    RGWL 2, 3; TWA
Gogarty, Oliver St. John
    1878-1957 .... **TCLC 15**
    See also CA 109; 150; DLB 15, 19; RGEL
    2
Gogol, Nikolai (Vasilyevich)
    1809-1852 .... **DC 1; NCLC 5, 15, 31,
    162; SSC 4, 29, 52; WLC**
    See also DA; DAB; DAC; DAM DRAM,
    MST; DFS 12; DLB 198; EW 6; EXPS;
    RGSF 2; RGWL 2, 3; SSFS 7; TWA
Goines, Donald 1937(?)-1974 ... **BLC 2; CLC
    80**
    See also AITN 1; BW 1, 3; CA 124; 114;
    CANR 82; CMW 4; DA3; DAM MULT,
    POP; DLB 33
Gold, Herbert 1924- ... **CLC 4, 7, 14, 42, 152**
    See also CA 9-12R; CANR 17, 45, 125; CN
    1, 2, 3, 4, 5, 6, 7; DLB 2; DLBY 1981;
    MAL 5
Goldbarth, Albert 1948- .... **CLC 5, 38**
    See also AMWS 12; CA 53-56; CANR 6,
    40; CP 3, 4, 5, 6, 7; DLB 120
Goldberg, Anatol 1910-1982 .... **CLC 34**
    See also CA 131; 117
Goldemberg, Isaac 1945- .... **CLC 52**
    See also CA 69-72; CAAS 12; CANR 11,
    32; EWL 3; HW 1; WLIT 1
Golding, Arthur 1536-1606 .... **LC 101**
    See also DLB 136
Golding, William (Gerald)
    1911-1993 ..... **CLC 1, 2, 3, 8, 10, 17, 27,
    58, 81; WLC**
    See also AAYA 5, 44; BPFB 2; BRWR 1;
    BRWS 1; BYA 2; CA 5-8R; 141; CANR
    13, 33, 54; CD 5; CDBLB 1945-1960;
    CLR 94; CN 1, 2, 3, 4; DA; DA3; DAB;
    DAC; DAM MST, NOV; DLB 15, 100,
    255; EWL 3; EXPN; HGG; LAIT 4;
    MTCW 1, 2; MTFW 2005; NFS 2; RGEL
    2; RHW; SFW 4; TEA; WLIT 4; YAW
Goldman, Emma 1869-1940 .... **TCLC 13**
    See also CA 110; 150; DLB 221; FW;
    RGAL 4; TUS
Goldman, Francisco 1954- .... **CLC 76**
    See also CA 162
Goldman, William (W.) 1931- ...... **CLC 1, 48**
    See also BPFB 2; CA 9-12R; CANR 29,
    69, 106; CN 1, 2, 3, 4, 5, 6, 7; DLB 44;
    FANT; IDFW 3, 4
Goldmann, Lucien 1913-1970 .... **CLC 24**
    See also CA 25-28; CAP 2
Goldoni, Carlo 1707-1793 .... **LC 4**
    See also DAM DRAM; EW 4; RGWL 2, 3;
    WLIT 7
Goldsberry, Steven 1949- .... **CLC 34**
    See also CA 131

Goldsmith, Oliver 1730-1774 .... **DC 8; LC 2,
    48, 122; WLC**
    See also BRW 3; CDBLB 1660-1789; DA;
    DAB; DAC; DAM DRAM, MST, NOV,
    POET; DFS 1; DLB 39, 89, 104, 109, 142;
    IDTP; RGEL 2; SATA 26; TEA; WLIT 3
Goldsmith, Peter
    See Priestley, J(ohn) B(oynton)
Gombrowicz, Witold 1904-1969 .... **CLC 4, 7,
    11, 49**
    See also CA 19-20; 25-28R; CANR 105;
    CAP 2; CDWLB 4; DAM DRAM; DLB
    215; EW 12; EWL 3; RGWL 2, 3; TWA
Gomez de Avellaneda, Gertrudis
    1814-1873 .... **NCLC 111**
    See also LAW
Gomez de la Serna, Ramon
    1888-1963 .... **CLC 9**
    See also CA 153; 116; CANR 79; EWL 3;
    HW 1, 2
Goncharov, Ivan Alexandrovich
    1812-1891 .... **NCLC 1, 63**
    See also DLB 238; EW 6; RGWL 2, 3
Goncourt, Edmond (Louis Antoine Huot) de
    1822-1896 .... **NCLC 7**
    See also DLB 123; EW 7; GFL 1789 to the
    Present; RGWL 2, 3
Goncourt, Jules (Alfred Huot) de
    1830-1870 .... **NCLC 7**
    See also DLB 123; EW 7; GFL 1789 to the
    Present; RGWL 2, 3
Gongora (y Argote), Luis de
    1561-1627 .... **LC 72**
    See also RGWL 2, 3
Gontier, Fernande 19(?)- .... **CLC 50**
Gonzalez Martinez, Enrique
    See Gonzalez Martinez, Enrique
    See also DLB 290
Gonzalez Martinez, Enrique
    1871-1952 .... **TCLC 72**
    See Gonzalez Martinez, Enrique
    See also CA 166; CANR 81; EWL 3; HW
    1, 2
Goodison, Lorna 1947- .... **PC 36**
    See also CA 142; CANR 88; CP 7; CWP;
    DLB 157; EWL 3
Goodman, Paul 1911-1972 ..... **CLC 1, 2, 4, 7**
    See also CA 19-20; 37-40R; CAD; CANR
    34; CAP 2; CN 1; DLB 130, 246; MAL
    5; MTCW 1; RGAL 4
GoodWeather, Harley
    See King, Thomas
Googe, Barnabe 1540-1594 .... **LC 94**
    See also DLB 132; RGEL 2
Gordimer, Nadine 1923- ...... **CLC 3, 5, 7, 10,
    18, 33, 51, 70, 123, 160, 161; SSC 17,
    80; WLCS**
    See also AAYA 39; AFW; BRWS 2; CA
    5-8R; CANR 3, 28, 56, 88, 131; CN 1, 2,
    3, 4, 5, 6, 7; DA; DA3; DAB; DAC; DAM
    MST, NOV; DLB 225; EWL 3; EXPS;
    INT CANR-28; LATS 1:2; MTCW 1, 2;
    MTFW 2005; NFS 4; RGEL 2; RGSF 2;
    SSFS 2, 14, 19; TWA; WLIT 2; YAW
Gordon, Adam Lindsay
    1833-1870 .... **NCLC 21**
    See also DLB 230
Gordon, Caroline 1895-1981 . **CLC 6, 13, 29,
    83; SSC 15**
    See also AMW; CA 11-12; 103; CANR 36;
    CAP 1; CN 1, 2; DLB 4, 9, 102; DLBD
    17; DLBY 1981; EWL 3; MAL 5; MTCW
    1, 2; MTFW 2005; RGAL 4; RGSF 2
Gordon, Charles William 1860-1937
    See Connor, Ralph
    See also CA 109

Gordon, Mary (Catherine) 1949- .... **CLC 13, 22, 128, 216; SSC 59**
See also AMWS 4; BPFB 2; CA 102; CANR 44, 92; CN 4, 5, 6, 7; DLB 6; DLBY 1981; FW; INT CA-102; MAL 5; MTCW 1

Gordon, N. J.
See Bosman, Herman Charles

Gordon, Sol 1923- .... **CLC 26**
See also CA 53-56; CANR 4; SATA 11

Gordone, Charles 1925-1995 .. **CLC 1, 4; DC 8**
See also BW 1, 3; CA 93-96, 180; 150; CAAE 180; CAD; CANR 55; DAM DRAM; DLB 7; INT CA-93-96; MTCW 1

Gore, Catherine 1800-1861 .... **NCLC 65**
See also DLB 116; RGEL 2

Gorenko, Anna Andreevna
See Akhmatova, Anna

Gorky, Maxim .... **SSC 28; TCLC 8; WLC**
See Peshkov, Alexei Maximovich
See also DAB; DFS 9; DLB 295; EW 8; EWL 3; TWA

Goryan, Sirak
See Saroyan, William

Gosse, Edmund (William)
1849-1928 .... **TCLC 28**
See also CA 117; DLB 57, 144, 184; RGEL 2

Gotlieb, Phyllis (Fay Bloom) 1926- .. **CLC 18**
See also CA 13-16R; CANR 7, 135; CN 7; CP 1, 2, 3, 4; DLB 88, 251; SFW 4

Gottesman, S. D.
See Kornbluth, C(yril) M.; Pohl, Frederik

Gottfried von Strassburg fl. c.
1170-1215 .... **CMLC 10**
See also CDWLB 2; DLB 138; EW 1; RGWL 2, 3

Gotthelf, Jeremias 1797-1854 .... **NCLC 117**
See also DLB 133; RGWL 2, 3

Gottschalk, Laura Riding
See Jackson, Laura (Riding)

Gould, Lois 1932(?)-2002 .... **CLC 4, 10**
See also CA 77-80; 208; CANR 29; MTCW 1

Gould, Stephen Jay 1941-2002 .... **CLC 163**
See also AAYA 26; BEST 90:2; CA 77-80; 205; CANR 10, 27, 56, 75, 125; CPW; INT CANR-27; MTCW 1, 2; MTFW 2005

Gourmont, Remy(-Marie-Charles) de
1858-1915 .... **TCLC 17**
See also CA 109; 150; GFL 1789 to the Present; MTCW 2

Gournay, Marie le Jars de
See de Gournay, Marie le Jars

Govier, Katherine 1948- .... **CLC 51**
See also CA 101; CANR 18, 40, 128; CCA 1

Gower, John c. 1330-1408 .... **LC 76; PC 59**
See also BRW 1; DLB 146; RGEL 2

Goyen, (Charles) William
1915-1983 .... **CLC 5, 8, 14, 40**
See also AITN 2; CA 5-8R; 110; CANR 6, 71; CN 1, 2, 3; DLB 2, 218; DLBY 1983; EWL 3; INT CANR-6; MAL 5

Goytisolo, Juan 1931- .... **CLC 5, 10, 23, 133; HLC 1**
See also CA 85-88; CANR 32, 61, 131; CWW 2; DAM MULT; DLB 322; EWL 3; GLL 2; HW 1, 2; MTCW 1, 2; MTFW 2005

Gozzano, Guido 1883-1916 .... **PC 10**
See also CA 154; DLB 114; EWL 3

Gozzi, (Conte) Carlo 1720-1806 .... **NCLC 23**

Grabbe, Christian Dietrich
1801-1836 .... **NCLC 2**
See also DLB 133; RGWL 2, 3

Grace, Patricia Frances 1937- .... **CLC 56**
See also CA 176; CANR 118; CN 4, 5, 6, 7; EWL 3; RGSF 2

Gracian y Morales, Baltasar
1601-1658 .... **LC 15**

Gracq, Julien .... **CLC 11, 48**
See Poirier, Louis
See also CWW 2; DLB 83; GFL 1789 to the Present

Grade, Chaim 1910-1982 .... **CLC 10**
See also CA 93-96; 107; EWL 3

Graduate of Oxford, A
See Ruskin, John

Grafton, Garth
See Duncan, Sara Jeannette

Grafton, Sue 1940- .... **CLC 163**
See also AAYA 11, 49; BEST 90:3; CA 108; CANR 31, 55, 111, 134; CMW 4; CPW; CSW; DA3; DAM POP; DLB 226; FW; MSW; MTFW 2005

Graham, John
See Phillips, David Graham

Graham, Jorie 1950- .... **CLC 48, 118; PC 59**
See also AAYA 67; CA 111; CANR 63, 118; CP 4, 5, 6, 7; CWP; DLB 120; EWL 3; MTFW 2005; PFS 10, 17; TCLE 1:1

Graham, R(obert) B(ontine) Cunninghame
See Cunninghame Graham, Robert (Gallnigad) Bontine
See also DLB 98, 135, 174; RGEL 2; RGSF 2

Graham, Robert
See Haldeman, Joe (William)

Graham, Tom
See Lewis, (Harry) Sinclair

Graham, W(illiam) S(idney)
1918-1986 .... **CLC 29**
See also BRWS 7; CA 73-76; 118; CP 1, 2, 3, 4; DLB 20; RGEL 2

Graham, Winston (Mawdsley)
1910-2003 .... **CLC 23**
See also CA 49-52; 218; CANR 2, 22, 45, 66; CMW 4; CN 1, 2, 3, 4, 5, 6, 7; DLB 77; RHW

Grahame, Kenneth 1859-1932 ...... **TCLC 64, 136**
See also BYA 5; CA 108; 136; CANR 80; CLR 5; CWRI 5; DA3; DAB; DLB 34, 141, 178; FANT; MAICYA 1, 2; MTCW 2; NFS 20; RGEL 2; SATA 100; TEA; WCH; YABC 1

Granger, Darius John
See Marlowe, Stephen

Granin, Daniil 1918- .... **CLC 59**
See also DLB 302

Granovsky, Timofei Nikolaevich
1813-1855 .... **NCLC 75**
See also DLB 198

Grant, Skeeter
See Spiegelman, Art

Granville-Barker, Harley
1877-1946 .... **TCLC 2**
See Barker, Harley Granville
See also CA 104; 204; DAM DRAM; RGEL 2

Granzotto, Gianni
See Granzotto, Giovanni Battista

Granzotto, Giovanni Battista
1914-1985 .... **CLC 70**
See also CA 166

Grass, Guenter (Wilhelm) 1927- ... **CLC 1, 2, 4, 6, 11, 15, 22, 32, 49, 88, 207; WLC**
See Grass, Gunter (Wilhelm)
See also BPFB 2; CA 13-16R; CANR 20, 75, 93, 133; CDWLB 2; DA; DA3; DAB; DAC; DAM MST, NOV; DLB 75, 124; EW 13; EWL 3; MTCW 1, 2; MTFW 2005; RGWL 2, 3; TWA

Grass, Gunter (Wilhelm)
See Grass, Guenter (Wilhelm)
See also CWW 2

Gratton, Thomas
See Hulme, T(homas) E(rnest)

Grau, Shirley Ann 1929- .... **CLC 4, 9, 146; SSC 15**
See also CA 89-92; CANR 22, 69; CN 1, 2, 3, 4, 5, 6, 7; CSW; DLB 2, 218; INT CA-89-92; CANR-22; MTCW 1

Gravel, Fern
See Hall, James Norman

Graver, Elizabeth 1964- .... **CLC 70**
See also CA 135; CANR 71, 129

Graves, Richard Perceval
1895-1985 .... **CLC 44**
See also CA 65-68; CANR 9, 26, 51

Graves, Robert (von Ranke)
1895-1985 .. **CLC 1, 2, 6, 11, 39, 44, 45; PC 6**
See also BPFB 2; BRW 7; BYA 4; CA 5-8R; 117; CANR 5, 36; CDBLB 1914-1945; CN 1, 2, 3; CP 1, 2, 3, 4; DA3; DAB; DAC; DAM MST, POET; DLB 20, 100, 191; DLBD 18; DLBY 1985; EWL 3; LATS 1:1; MTCW 1, 2; MTFW 2005; NCFS 2; NFS 21; RGEL 2; RHW; SATA 45; TEA

Graves, Valerie
See Bradley, Marion Zimmer

Gray, Alasdair (James) 1934- .... **CLC 41**
See also BRWS 9; CA 126; CANR 47, 69, 106, 140; CN 4, 5, 6, 7; DLB 194, 261, 319; HGG; INT CA-126; MTCW 1, 2; MTFW 2005; RGSF 2; SUFW 2

Gray, Amlin 1946- .... **CLC 29**
See also CA 138

Gray, Francine du Plessix 1930- ..... **CLC 22, 153**
See also BEST 90:3; CA 61-64; CAAS 2; CANR 11, 33, 75, 81; DAM NOV; INT CANR-11; MTCW 1, 2; MTFW 2005

Gray, John (Henry) 1866-1934 ...... **TCLC 19**
See also CA 119; 162; RGEL 2

Gray, John Lee
See Jakes, John (William)

Gray, Simon (James Holliday)
1936- .... **CLC 9, 14, 36**
See also AITN 1; CA 21-24R; CAAS 3; CANR 32, 69; CBD; CD 5, 6; CN 1, 2, 3; DLB 13; EWL 3; MTCW 1; RGEL 2

Gray, Spalding 1941-2004 .... **CLC 49, 112; DC 7**
See also AAYA 62; CA 128; 225; CAD; CANR 74, 138; CD 5, 6; CPW; DAM POP; MTCW 2; MTFW 2005

Gray, Thomas 1716-1771 .... **LC 4, 40; PC 2; WLC**
See also BRW 3; CDBLB 1660-1789; DA; DA3; DAB; DAC; DAM MST; DLB 109; EXPP; PAB; PFS 9; RGEL 2; TEA; WP

Grayson, David
See Baker, Ray Stannard

Grayson, Richard (A.) 1951- .... **CLC 38**
See also CA 85-88; 210; CAAE 210; CANR 14, 31, 57; DLB 234

Greeley, Andrew M(oran) 1928- ...... **CLC 28**
See also BPFB 2; CA 5-8R; CAAS 7; CANR 7, 43, 69, 104, 136; CMW 4; CPW; DA3; DAM POP; MTCW 1, 2; MTFW 2005

Green, Anna Katharine
1846-1935 .... **TCLC 63**
See also CA 112; 159; CMW 4; DLB 202, 221; MSW

Green, Brian
See Card, Orson Scott

Green, Hannah
See Greenberg, Joanne (Goldenberg)

Guicciardini, Francesco 1483-1540 ..... **LC 49**
Guild, Nicholas M. 1944- .... **CLC 33**
See also CA 93-96
Guillemin, Jacques
See Sartre, Jean-Paul
Guillen, Jorge 1893-1984 . **CLC 11; HLCS 1; PC 35**
See also CA 89-92; 112; DAM MULT, POET; DLB 108; EWL 3; HW 1; RGWL 2, 3
Guillen, Nicolas (Cristobal)
1902-1989 .... **BLC 2; CLC 48, 79; HLC 1; PC 23**
See also BW 2; CA 116; 125; 129; CANR 84; DAM MST, MULT, POET; DLB 283; EWL 3; HW 1; LAW; RGWL 2, 3; WP
Guillen y Alvarez, Jorge
See Guillen, Jorge
Guillevic, (Eugene) 1907-1997 .... **CLC 33**
See also CA 93-96; CWW 2
Guillois
See Desnos, Robert
Guillois, Valentin
See Desnos, Robert
Guimaraes Rosa, Joao 1908-1967 .... **HLCS 2**
See Rosa, Joao Guimaraes
See also CA 175; LAW; RGSF 2; RGWL 2, 3
Guiney, Louise Imogen
1861-1920 .... **TCLC 41**
See also CA 160; DLB 54; RGAL 4
Guinizelli, Guido c. 1230-1276 ...... **CMLC 49**
See Guinizzelli, Guido
Guinizzelli, Guido
See Guinizelli, Guido
See also WLIT 7
Guiraldes, Ricardo (Guillermo)
1886-1927 .... **TCLC 39**
See also CA 131; EWL 3; HW 1; LAW; MTCW 1
Gumilev, Nikolai (Stepanovich)
1886-1921 .... **TCLC 60**
See Gumilyov, Nikolay Stepanovich
See also CA 165; DLB 295
Gumilyov, Nikolay Stepanovich
See Gumilev, Nikolai (Stepanovich)
See also EWL 3
Gump, P. Q.
See Card, Orson Scott
Gunesekera, Romesh 1954- .... **CLC 91**
See also BRWS 10; CA 159; CANR 140; CN 6, 7; DLB 267
Gunn, Bill .... **CLC 5**
See Gunn, William Harrison
See also DLB 38
Gunn, Thom(son William)
1929-2004 . **CLC 3, 6, 18, 32, 81; PC 26**
See also BRWS 4; CA 17-20R; 227; CANR 9, 33, 116; CDBLB 1960 to Present; CP 1, 2, 3, 4, 5, 6, 7; DAM POET; DLB 27; INT CANR-33; MTCW 1; PFS 9; RGEL 2
Gunn, William Harrison 1934(?)-1989
See Gunn, Bill
See also AITN 1; BW 1, 3; CA 13-16R; 128; CANR 12, 25, 76
Gunn Allen, Paula
See Allen, Paula Gunn
Gunnars, Kristjana 1948- .... **CLC 69**
See also CA 113; CCA 1; CP 7; CWP; DLB 60
Gunter, Erich
See Eich, Gunter
Gurdjieff, G(eorgei) I(vanovich)
1877(?)-1949 .... **TCLC 71**
See also CA 157
Gurganus, Allan 1947- .... **CLC 70**
See also BEST 90:1; CA 135; CANR 114; CN 6, 7; CPW; CSW; DAM POP; GLL 1

Gurney, A. R.
See Gurney, A(lbert) R(amsdell), Jr.
See also DLB 266
Gurney, A(lbert) R(amsdell), Jr.
1930- .... **CLC 32, 50, 54**
See Gurney, A. R.
See also AMWS 5; CA 77-80; CAD; CANR 32, 64, 121; CD 5, 6; DAM DRAM; EWL 3
Gurney, Ivor (Bertie) 1890-1937 ... **TCLC 33**
See also BRW 6; CA 167; DLBY 2002; PAB; RGEL 2
Gurney, Peter
See Gurney, A(lbert) R(amsdell), Jr.
Guro, Elena (Genrikhovna)
1877-1913 .... **TCLC 56**
See also DLB 295
Gustafson, James M(oody) 1925- ... **CLC 100**
See also CA 25-28R; CANR 37
Gustafson, Ralph (Barker)
1909-1995 .... **CLC 36**
See also CA 21-24R; CANR 8, 45, 84; CP 1, 2, 3, 4; DLB 88; RGEL 2
Gut, Gom
See Simenon, Georges (Jacques Christian)
Guterson, David 1956- .... **CLC 91**
See also CA 132; CANR 73, 126; CN 7; DLB 292; MTCW 2; MTFW 2005; NFS 13
Guthrie, A(lfred) B(ertram), Jr.
1901-1991 .... **CLC 23**
See also CA 57-60; 134; CANR 24; CN 1, 2, 3; DLB 6, 212; MAL 5; SATA 62; SATA-Obit 67; TCWW 1, 2
Guthrie, Isobel
See Grieve, C(hristopher) M(urray)
Guthrie, Woodrow Wilson 1912-1967
See Guthrie, Woody
See also CA 113; 93-96
Guthrie, Woody .... **CLC 35**
See Guthrie, Woodrow Wilson
See also DLB 303; LAIT 3
Gutierrez Najera, Manuel
1859-1895 .... **HLCS 2; NCLC 133**
See also DLB 290; LAW
Guy, Rosa (Cuthbert) 1925- .... **CLC 26**
See also AAYA 4, 37; BW 2; CA 17-20R; CANR 14, 34, 83; CLR 13; DLB 33; DNFS 1; JRDA; MAICYA 1, 2; SATA 14, 62, 122; YAW
Gwendolyn
See Bennett, (Enoch) Arnold
H. D. .... **CLC 3, 8, 14, 31, 34, 73; PC 5**
See Doolittle, Hilda
See also FL 1:5
H. de V.
See Buchan, John
Haavikko, Paavo Juhani 1931- ... **CLC 18, 34**
See also CA 106; CWW 2; EWL 3
Habbema, Koos
See Heijermans, Herman
Habermas, Juergen 1929- .... **CLC 104**
See also CA 109; CANR 85; DLB 242
Habermas, Jurgen
See Habermas, Juergen
Hacker, Marilyn 1942- ...... **CLC 5, 9, 23, 72, 91; PC 47**
See also CA 77-80; CANR 68, 129; CP 3, 4, 5, 6, 7; CWP; DAM POET; DLB 120, 282; FW; GLL 2; MAL 5; PFS 19
Hadewijch of Antwerp fl. 1250- ... **CMLC 61**
See also RGWL 3
Hadrian 76-138 .... **CMLC 52**
Haeckel, Ernst Heinrich (Philipp August)
1834-1919 .... **TCLC 83**
See also CA 157
Hafiz c. 1326-1389(?) .... **CMLC 34**
See also RGWL 2, 3; WLIT 6

Hagedorn, Jessica T(arahata)
1949- .... **CLC 185**
See also CA 139; CANR 69; CWP; DLB 312; RGAL 4
Haggard, H(enry) Rider
1856-1925 .... **TCLC 11**
See also BRWS 3; BYA 4, 5; CA 108; 148; CANR 112; DLB 70, 156, 174, 178; FANT; LMFS 1; MTCW 2; RGEL 2; RHW; SATA 16; SCFW 1, 2; SFW 4; SUFW 1; WLIT 4
Hagiosy, L.
See Larbaud, Valery (Nicolas)
Hagiwara, Sakutaro 1886-1942 .... **PC 18; TCLC 60**
See Hagiwara Sakutaro
See also CA 154; RGWL 3
Hagiwara Sakutaro
See Hagiwara, Sakutaro
See also EWL 3
Haig, Fenil
See Ford, Ford Madox
Haig-Brown, Roderick (Langmere)
1908-1976 .... **CLC 21**
See also CA 5-8R; 69-72; CANR 4, 38, 83; CLR 31; CWRI 5; DLB 88; MAICYA 1, 2; SATA 12; TCWW 2
Haight, Rip
See Carpenter, John (Howard)
Hailey, Arthur 1920-2004 .... **CLC 5**
See also AITN 2; BEST 90:3; BPFB 2; CA 1-4R; 233; CANR 2, 36, 75; CCA 1; CN 1, 2, 3, 4, 5, 6, 7; CPW; DAM NOV, POP; DLB 88; DLBY 1982; MTCW 1, 2; MTFW 2005
Hailey, Elizabeth Forsythe 1938- ..... **CLC 40**
See also CA 93-96, 188; CAAE 188; CAAS 1; CANR 15, 48; INT CANR-15
Haines, John (Meade) 1924- .... **CLC 58**
See also AMWS 12; CA 17-20R; CANR 13, 34; CP 1, 2, 3, 4; CSW; DLB 5, 212; TCLE 1:1
Hakluyt, Richard 1552-1616 .... **LC 31**
See also DLB 136; RGEL 2
Haldeman, Joe (William) 1943- .... **CLC 61**
See Graham, Robert
See also AAYA 38; CA 53-56, 179; CAAE 179; CAAS 25; CANR 6, 70, 72, 130; DLB 8; INT CANR-6; SCFW 2; SFW 4
Hale, Janet Campbell 1947- .... **NNAL**
See also CA 49-52; CANR 45, 75; DAM MULT; DLB 175; MTCW 2; MTFW 2005
Hale, Sarah Josepha (Buell)
1788-1879 .... **NCLC 75**
See also DLB 1, 42, 73, 243
Halevy, Elie 1870-1937 .... **TCLC 104**
Haley, Alex(ander Murray Palmer)
1921-1992 .... **BLC 2; CLC 8, 12, 76; TCLC 147**
See also AAYA 26; BPFB 2; BW 2, 3; CA 77-80; 136; CANR 61; CDALBS; CPW; CSW; DA; DA3; DAB; DAC; DAM MST, MULT, POP; DLB 38; LAIT 5; MTCW 1, 2; NFS 9
Haliburton, Thomas Chandler
1796-1865 .... **NCLC 15, 149**
See also DLB 11, 99; RGEL 2; RGSF 2
Hall, Donald (Andrew, Jr.) 1928- ...... **CLC 1, 13, 37, 59, 151; PC 70**
See also AAYA 63; CA 5-8R; CAAS 7; CANR 2, 44, 64, 106, 133; CP 1, 2, 3, 4, 5, 6, 7; DAM POET; DLB 5; MAL 5; MTCW 2; MTFW 2005; RGAL 4; SATA 23, 97
Hall, Frederic Sauser
See Sauser-Hall, Frederic
Hall, James
See Kuttner, Henry

Hall, James Norman 1887-1951 ..... **TCLC 23**
See also CA 123; 173; LAIT 1; RHW 1;
SATA 21

Hall, Joseph 1574-1656 .... **LC 91**
See also DLB 121, 151; RGEL 2

Hall, (Marguerite) Radclyffe
1880-1943 .... **TCLC 12**
See also BRWS 6; CA 110; 150; CANR 83;
DLB 191; MTCW 2; MTFW 2005; RGEL
2; RHW

Hall, Rodney 1935- .... **CLC 51**
See also CA 109; CANR 69; CN 6, 7; CP
1, 2, 3, 4, 5, 6, 7; DLB 289

Hallam, Arthur Henry
1811-1833 .... **NCLC 110**
See also DLB 32

Halldor Laxness .... **CLC 25**
See Gudjonsson, Halldor Kiljan
See also DLB 293; EW 12; EWL 3; RGWL
2, 3

Halleck, Fitz-Greene 1790-1867 .... **NCLC 47**
See also DLB 3, 250; RGAL 4

Halliday, Michael
See Creasey, John

Halpern, Daniel 1945- .... **CLC 14**
See also CA 33-36R; CANR 93; CP 3, 4, 5,
6, 7

Hamburger, Michael (Peter Leopold)
1924- .... **CLC 5, 14**
See also CA 5-8R, 196; CAAE 196; CAAS
4; CANR 2, 47; CP 1, 2, 3, 4, 5, 6, 7;
DLB 27

Hamill, Pete 1935- .... **CLC 10**
See also CA 25-28R; CANR 18, 71, 127

Hamilton, Alexander
1755(?)-1804 .... **NCLC 49**
See also DLB 37

Hamilton, Clive
See Lewis, C(live) S(taples)

Hamilton, Edmond 1904-1977 .... **CLC 1**
See also CA 1-4R; CANR 3, 84; DLB 8;
SATA 118; SFW 4

Hamilton, Elizabeth 1758-1816 ... **NCLC 153**
See also DLB 116, 158

Hamilton, Eugene (Jacob) Lee
See Lee-Hamilton, Eugene (Jacob)

Hamilton, Franklin
See Silverberg, Robert

Hamilton, Gail
See Corcoran, Barbara (Asenath)

Hamilton, (Robert) Ian 1938-2001 . **CLC 191**
See also CA 106; 203; CANR 41, 67; CP 1,
2, 3, 4, 5, 6, 7; DLB 40, 155

Hamilton, Jane 1957- .... **CLC 179**
See also CA 147; CANR 85, 128; CN 7;
MTFW 2005

Hamilton, Mollie
See Kaye, M(ary) M(argaret)

Hamilton, (Anthony Walter) Patrick
1904-1962 .... **CLC 51**
See also CA 176; 113; DLB 10, 191

Hamilton, Virginia (Esther)
1936-2002 .... **CLC 26**
See also AAYA 2, 21; BW 2, 3; BYA 1, 2,
8; CA 25-28R; 206; CANR 20, 37, 73,
126; CLR 1, 11, 40; DAM MULT; DLB
33, 52; DLBY 2001; INT CANR-20;
JRDA; LAIT 5; MAICYA 1, 2; MAIC-
YAS 1; MTCW 1, 2; MTFW 2005; SATA
4, 56, 79, 123; SATA-Obit 132; WYA;
YAW

Hammett, (Samuel) Dashiell
1894-1961 .... **CLC 3, 5, 10, 19, 47; SSC
17**
See also AAYA 59; AITN 1; AMWS 4;
BPFB 2; CA 81-84; CANR 42; CDALB
1929-1941; CMW 4; DA3; DLB 226, 280;
DLBD 6; DLBY 1996; EWL 3; LAIT 3;

MAL 5; MSW; MTCW 1, 2; MTFW
2005; NFS 21; RGAL 4; RGSF 2; TUS

Hammon, Jupiter 1720(?)-1800(?) .... **BLC 2;
NCLC 5; PC 16**
See also DAM MULT, POET; DLB 31, 50

Hammond, Keith
See Kuttner, Henry

Hamner, Earl (Henry), Jr. 1923- ...... **CLC 12**
See also AITN 2; CA 73-76; DLB 6

Hampton, Christopher (James)
1946- .... **CLC 4**
See also CA 25-28R; CD 5, 6; DLB 13;
MTCW 1

Hamsun, Knut .... **TCLC 2, 14, 49, 151**
See Pedersen, Knut
See also DLB 297; EW 8; EWL 3; RGWL
2, 3

Handke, Peter 1942- .... **CLC 5, 8, 10, 15, 38,
134; DC 17**
See also CA 77-80; CANR 33, 75, 104, 133;
CWW 2; DAM DRAM, NOV; DLB 85,
124; EWL 3; MTCW 1, 2; MTFW 2005;
TWA

Handy, W(illiam) C(hristopher)
1873-1958 .... **TCLC 97**
See also BW 3; CA 121; 167

Hanley, James 1901-1985 ..... **CLC 3, 5, 8, 13**
See also CA 73-76; 117; CANR 36; CBD;
CN 1, 2, 3; DLB 191; EWL 3; MTCW 1;
RGEL 2

Hannah, Barry 1942- .... **CLC 23, 38, 90**
See also BPFB 2; CA 108; 110; CANR 43,
68, 113; CN 4, 5, 6, 7; CSW; DLB 6, 234;
INT CA-110; MTCW 1; RGSF 2

Hannon, Ezra
See Hunter, Evan

Hansberry, Lorraine (Vivian)
1930-1965 ... **BLC 2; CLC 17, 62; DC 2**
See also AAYA 25; AFAW 1, 2; AMWS 4;
BW 1, 3; CA 109; 25-28R; CABS 3;
CAD; CANR 58; CDALB 1941-1968;
CWD; DA; DA3; DAB; DAC; DAM
DRAM, MST, MULT; DFS 2; DLB 7, 38;
EWL 3; FL 1:6; FW; LAIT 4; MAL 5;
MTCW 1, 2; MTFW 2005; RGAL 4; TUS

Hansen, Joseph 1923-2004 .... **CLC 38**
See Brock, Rose; Colton, James
See also BPFB 2; CA 29-32R; 233; CAAS
17; CANR 16, 44, 66, 125; CMW 4; DLB
226; GLL 1; INT CANR-16

Hansen, Martin A(lfred)
1909-1955 .... **TCLC 32**
See also CA 167; DLB 214; EWL 3

Hansen and Philipson eds. .... **CLC 65**

Hanson, Kenneth O(stlin) 1922- .... **CLC 13**
See also CA 53-56; CANR 7; CP 1, 2, 3, 4

Hardwick, Elizabeth (Bruce) 1916- . **CLC 13**
See also AMWS 3; CA 5-8R; CANR 3, 32,
70, 100, 139; CN 4, 5, 6; CSW; DA3;
DAM NOV; DLB 6; MAWW; MTCW 1,
2; MTFW 2005; TCLE 1:1

Hardy, Thomas 1840-1928 .... **PC 8; SSC 2,
60; TCLC 4, 10, 18, 32, 48, 53, 72, 143,
153; WLC**
See also BRW 6; BRWC 1, 2; BRWR 1;
CA 104; 123; CDBLB 1890-1914; DA;
DA3; DAB; DAC; DAM MST, NOV,
POET; DLB 18, 19, 135, 284; EWL 3;
EXPN; EXPP; LAIT 2; MTCW 1, 2;
MTFW 2005; NFS 3, 11, 15, 19; PFS 3,
4, 18; RGEL 2; RGSF 2; TEA; WLIT 4

Hare, David 1947- . **CLC 29, 58, 136; DC 26**
See also BRWS 4; CA 97-100; CANR 39,
91; CBD; CD 5, 6; DFS 4, 7, 16; DLB
13, 310; MTCW 1; TEA

Harewood, John
See Van Druten, John (William)

Harford, Henry
See Hudson, W(illiam) H(enry)

Hargrave, Leonie
See Disch, Thomas M(ichael)

**Hariri, Al- al-Qasim ibn 'Ali Abu
Muhammad al-Basri**
See al-Hariri, al-Qasim ibn 'Ali Abu Mu-
hammad al-Basri

Harjo, Joy 1951- ..... **CLC 83; NNAL; PC 27**
See also AMWS 12; CA 114; CANR 35,
67, 91, 129; CP 7; CWP; DAM MULT;
DLB 120, 175; EWL 3; MTCW 2; MTFW
2005; PFS 15; RGAL 4

Harlan, Louis R(udolph) 1922- .... **CLC 34**
See also CA 21-24R; CANR 25, 55, 80

Harling, Robert 1951(?)- .... **CLC 53**
See also CA 147

Harmon, William (Ruth) 1938- .... **CLC 38**
See also CA 33-36R; CANR 14, 32, 35;
SATA 65

Harper, F. E. W.
See Harper, Frances Ellen Watkins

Harper, Frances E. W.
See Harper, Frances Ellen Watkins

Harper, Frances E. Watkins
See Harper, Frances Ellen Watkins

Harper, Frances Ellen
See Harper, Frances Ellen Watkins

Harper, Frances Ellen Watkins
1825-1911 ..... **BLC 2; PC 21; TCLC 14**
See also AFAW 1, 2; BW 1, 3; CA 111; 125;
CANR 79; DAM MULT, POET; DLB 50,
221; MAWW; RGAL 4

Harper, Michael S(teven) 1938- ... **CLC 7, 22**
See also AFAW 2; BW 1; CA 33-36R; 224;
CAAE 224; CANR 24, 108; CP 2, 3, 4, 5,
6, 7; DLB 41; RGAL 4; TCLE 1:1

Harper, Mrs. F. E. W.
See Harper, Frances Ellen Watkins

Harpur, Charles 1813-1868 .... **NCLC 114**
See also DLB 230; RGEL 2

Harris, Christie
See Harris, Christie (Lucy) Irwin

Harris, Christie (Lucy) Irwin
1907-2002 .... **CLC 12**
See also CA 5-8R; CANR 6, 83; CLR 47;
DLB 88; JRDA; MAICYA 1, 2; SAAS 10;
SATA 6, 74; SATA-Essay 116

Harris, Frank 1856-1931 .... **TCLC 24**
See also CA 109; 150; CANR 80; DLB 156,
197; RGEL 2

Harris, George Washington
1814-1869 .... **NCLC 23, 165**
See also DLB 3, 11, 248; RGAL 4

Harris, Joel Chandler 1848-1908 ..... **SSC 19;
TCLC 2**
See also CA 104; 137; CANR 80; CLR 49;
DLB 11, 23, 42, 78, 91; LAIT 2; MAI-
CYA 1, 2; RGSF 2; SATA 100; WCH;
YABC 1

**Harris, John (Wyndham Parkes Lucas)
Beynon** 1903-1969
See Wyndham, John
See also CA 102; 89-92; CANR 84; SATA
118; SFW 4

Harris, MacDonald .... **CLC 9**
See Heiney, Donald (William)

Harris, Mark 1922- .... **CLC 19**
See also CA 5-8R; CAAS 3; CANR 2, 55,
83; CN 1, 2, 3, 4, 5, 6, 7; DLB 2; DLBY
1980

Harris, Norman .... **CLC 65**

Harris, (Theodore) Wilson 1921- .... **CLC 25,
159**
See also BRWS 5; BW 2, 3; CA 65-68;
CAAS 16; CANR 11, 27, 69, 114; CD-
WLB 3; CN 1, 2, 3, 4, 5, 6, 7; CP 1, 2, 3,
4, 5, 6, 7; DLB 117; EWL 3; MTCW 1;
RGEL 2

Harrison, Barbara Grizzuti
1934-2002 .... **CLC 144**
See also CA 77-80; 205; CANR 15, 48; INT
CANR-15

Harrison, Elizabeth (Allen) Cavanna
1909-2001
See Cavanna, Betty
See also CA 9-12R; 200; CANR 6, 27, 85,
104, 121; MAICYA 2; SATA 142; YAW

Harrison, Harry (Max) 1925- .... **CLC 42**
See also CA 1-4R; CANR 5, 21, 84; DLB
8; SATA 4; SCFW 2; SFW 4

Harrison, James (Thomas) 1937- ...... **CLC 6,
14, 33, 66, 143; SSC 19**
See Harrison, Jim
See also CA 13-16R; CANR 8, 51, 79, 142;
DLBY 1982; INT CANR-8

Harrison, Jim
See Harrison, James (Thomas)
See also AMWS 8; CN 5, 6; CP 1, 2, 3, 4,
5, 6, 7; RGAL 4; TCWW 2; TUS

Harrison, Kathryn 1961- .... **CLC 70, 151**
See also CA 144; CANR 68, 122

Harrison, Tony 1937- .... **CLC 43, 129**
See also BRWS 5; CA 65-68; CANR 44,
98; CBD; CD 5, 6; CP 2, 3, 4, 5, 6, 7;
DLB 40, 245; MTCW 1; RGEL 2

Harriss, Will(ard Irvin) 1922- .... **CLC 34**
See also CA 111

Hart, Ellis
See Ellison, Harlan (Jay)

Hart, Josephine 1942(?)- .... **CLC 70**
See also CA 138; CANR 70; CPW; DAM
POP

Hart, Moss 1904-1961 .... **CLC 66**
See also CA 109; 89-92; CANR 84; DAM
DRAM; DFS 1; DLB 7, 266; RGAL 4

Harte, (Francis) Bret(t)
1836(?)-1902 ... **SSC 8, 59; TCLC 1, 25;
WLC**
See also AMWS 2; CA 104; 140; CANR
80; CDALB 1865-1917; DA; DA3; DAC;
DAM MST; DLB 12, 64, 74, 79, 186;
EXPS; LAIT 2; RGAL 4; RGSF 2; SATA
26; SSFS 3; TUS

Hartley, L(eslie) P(oles) 1895-1972 ... **CLC 2,
22**
See also BRWS 7; CA 45-48; 37-40R;
CANR 33; CN 1; DLB 15, 139; EWL 3;
HGG; MTCW 1, 2; MTFW 2005; RGEL
2; RGSF 2; SUFW 1

Hartman, Geoffrey H. 1929- .... **CLC 27**
See also CA 117; 125; CANR 79; DLB 67

Hartmann, Sadakichi 1869-1944 ... **TCLC 73**
See also CA 157; DLB 54

Hartmann von Aue c. 1170-c.
1210 .... **CMLC 15**
See also CDWLB 2; DLB 138; RGWL 2, 3

Hartog, Jan de
See de Hartog, Jan

Haruf, Kent 1943- .... **CLC 34**
See also AAYA 44; CA 149; CANR 91, 131

Harvey, Caroline
See Trollope, Joanna

Harvey, Gabriel 1550(?)-1631 .... **LC 88**
See also DLB 167, 213, 281

Harwood, Ronald 1934- .... **CLC 32**
See also CA 1-4R; CANR 4, 55; CBD; CD
5, 6; DAM DRAM, MST; DLB 13

Hasegawa Tatsunosuke
See Futabatei, Shimei

Hasek, Jaroslav (Matej Frantisek)
1883-1923 .... **SSC 69; TCLC 4**
See also CA 104; 129; CDWLB 4; DLB
215; EW 9; EWL 3; MTCW 1, 2; RGSF
2; RGWL 2, 3

Hass, Robert 1941- ... **CLC 18, 39, 99; PC 16**
See also AMWS 6; CA 111; CANR 30, 50,
71; CP 3, 4, 5, 6, 7; DLB 105, 206; EWL
3; MAL 5; MTFW 2005; RGAL 4; SATA
94; TCLE 1:1

Hastings, Hudson
See Kuttner, Henry

Hastings, Selina .... **CLC 44**

Hathorne, John 1641-1717 .... **LC 38**

Hatteras, Amelia
See Mencken, H(enry) L(ouis)

Hatteras, Owen .... **TCLC 18**
See Mencken, H(enry) L(ouis); Nathan,
George Jean

Hauptmann, Gerhart (Johann Robert)
1862-1946 .... **SSC 37; TCLC 4**
See also CA 104; 153; CDWLB 2; DAM
DRAM; DLB 66, 118; EW 8; EWL 3;
RGSF 2; RGWL 2, 3; TWA

Havel, Vaclav 1936- ..... **CLC 25, 58, 65, 123;
DC 6**
See also CA 104; CANR 36, 63, 124; CD-
WLB 4; CWW 2; DA3; DAM DRAM;
DFS 10; DLB 232; EWL 3; LMFS 2;
MTCW 1, 2; MTFW 2005; RGWL 3

Haviaras, Stratis .... **CLC 33**
See Chaviaras, Strates

Hawes, Stephen 1475(?)-1529(?) .... **LC 17**
See also DLB 132; RGEL 2

Hawkes, John (Clendennin Burne, Jr.)
1925-1998 .. **CLC 1, 2, 3, 4, 7, 9, 14, 15,
27, 49**
See also BPFB 2; CA 1-4R; 167; CANR 2,
47, 64; CN 1, 2, 3, 4, 5, 6; DLB 2, 7, 227;
DLBY 1980, 1998; EWL 3; MAL 5;
MTCW 1, 2; MTFW 2005; RGAL 4

Hawking, S. W.
See Hawking, Stephen W(illiam)

Hawking, Stephen W(illiam) 1942- . **CLC 63,
105**
See also AAYA 13; BEST 89:1; CA 126;
129; CANR 48, 115; CPW; DA3; MTCW
2; MTFW 2005

Hawkins, Anthony Hope
See Hope, Anthony

Hawthorne, Julian 1846-1934 .... **TCLC 25**
See also CA 165; HGG

Hawthorne, Nathaniel 1804-1864 ... **NCLC 2,
10, 17, 23, 39, 79, 95, 158; SSC 3, 29,
39, 89; WLC**
See also AAYA 18; AMW; AMWC 1;
AMWR 1; BPFB 2; BYA 3; CDALB
1640-1865; CLR 103; DA; DA3; DAB;
DAC; DAM MST, NOV; DLB 1, 74, 183,
223, 269; EXPN; EXPS; GL 2; HGG;
LAIT 1; NFS 1, 20; RGAL 4; RGSF 2;
SSFS 1, 7, 11, 15; SUFW 1; TUS; WCH;
YABC 2

Hawthorne, Sophia Peabody
1809-1871 .... **NCLC 150**
See also DLB 183, 239

Haxton, Josephine Ayres 1921-
See Douglas, Ellen
See also CA 115; CANR 41, 83

Hayaseca y Eizaguirre, Jorge
See Echegaray (y Eizaguirre), Jose (Maria
Waldo)

Hayashi, Fumiko 1904-1951 .... **TCLC 27**
See Hayashi Fumiko
See also CA 161

Hayashi Fumiko
See Hayashi, Fumiko
See also DLB 180; EWL 3

Haycraft, Anna (Margaret) 1932-2005
See Ellis, Alice Thomas
See also CA 122; 237; CANR 90, 141;
MTCW 2; MTFW 2005

Hayden, Robert E(arl) 1913-1980 ..... **BLC 2;
CLC 5, 9, 14, 37; PC 6**
See also AFAW 1, 2; AMWS 2; BW 1, 3;
CA 69-72; 97-100; CABS 2; CANR 24,
75, 82; CDALB 1941-1968; CP 1, 2, 3;
DA; DAC; DAM MST, MULT, POET;
DLB 5, 76; EWL 3; EXPP; MAL 5;
MTCW 1, 2; PFS 1; RGAL 4; SATA 19;
SATA-Obit 26; WP

Haydon, Benjamin Robert
1786-1846 .... **NCLC 146**
See also DLB 110

Hayek, F(riedrich) A(ugust von)
1899-1992 .... **TCLC 109**
See also CA 93-96; 137; CANR 20; MTCW
1, 2

Hayford, J(oseph) E(phraim) Casely
See Casely-Hayford, J(oseph) E(phraim)

Hayman, Ronald 1932- .... **CLC 44**
See also CA 25-28R; CANR 18, 50, 88; CD
5, 6; DLB 155

Hayne, Paul Hamilton 1830-1886 . **NCLC 94**
See also DLB 3, 64, 79, 248; RGAL 4

Hays, Mary 1760-1843 .... **NCLC 114**
See also DLB 142, 158; RGEL 2

Haywood, Eliza (Fowler)
1693(?)-1756 .... **LC 1, 44**
See also DLB 39; RGEL 2

Hazlitt, William 1778-1830 ...... **NCLC 29, 82**
See also BRW 4; DLB 110, 158; RGEL 2;
TEA

Hazzard, Shirley 1931- .... **CLC 18, 218**
See also CA 9-12R; CANR 4, 70, 127; CN
1, 2, 3, 4, 5, 6, 7; DLB 289; DLBY 1982;
MTCW 1

Head, Bessie 1937-1986 ...... **BLC 2; CLC 25,
67; SSC 52**
See also AFW; BW 2, 3; CA 29-32R; 119;
CANR 25, 82; CDWLB 3; CN 1, 2, 3, 4;
DA3; DAM MULT; DLB 117, 225; EWL
3; EXPS; FL 1:6; FW; MTCW 1, 2;
MTFW 2005; RGSF 2; SSFS 5, 13; WLIT
2; WWE 1

Headon, (Nicky) Topper 1956(?)- ..... **CLC 30**

Heaney, Seamus (Justin) 1939- ..... **CLC 5, 7,
14, 25, 37, 74, 91, 171; PC 18; WLCS**
See also AAYA 61; BRWR 1; BRWS 2; CA
85-88; CANR 25, 48, 75, 91, 128; CD-
BLB 1960 to Present; CP 1, 2, 3, 4, 5, 6,
7; DA3; DAB; DAM POET; DLB 40;
DLBY 1995; EWL 3; EXPP; MTCW 1,
2; MTFW 2005; PAB; PFS 2, 5, 8, 17;
RGEL 2; TEA; WLIT 4

Hearn, (Patricio) Lafcadio (Tessima Carlos)
1850-1904 .... **TCLC 9**
See also CA 105; 166; DLB 12, 78, 189;
HGG; MAL 5; RGAL 4

Hearne, Samuel 1745-1792 .... **LC 95**
See also DLB 99

Hearne, Vicki 1946-2001 .... **CLC 56**
See also CA 139; 201

Hearon, Shelby 1931- .... **CLC 63**
See also AITN 2; AMWS 8; CA 25-28R;
CANR 18, 48, 103, 146; CSW

Heat-Moon, William Least .... **CLC 29**
See Trogdon, William (Lewis)
See also AAYA 9

Hebbel, Friedrich 1813-1863 . **DC 21; NCLC
43**
See also CDWLB 2; DAM DRAM; DLB
129; EW 6; RGWL 2, 3

Hebert, Anne 1916-2000 .... **CLC 4, 13, 29**
See also CA 85-88; 187; CANR 69, 126;
CCA 1; CWP; CWW 2; DA3; DAC;
DAM MST, POET; DLB 68; EWL 3; GFL
1789 to the Present; MTCW 1, 2; MTFW
2005; PFS 20

Hecht, Anthony (Evan) 1923-2004 .... **CLC 8, 13, 19; PC 70**
See also AMWS 10; CA 9-12R; 232; CANR 6, 108; CP 1, 2, 3, 4, 5, 6, 7; DAM POET; DLB 5, 169; EWL 3; PFS 6; WP

Hecht, Ben 1894-1964 ..... **CLC 8; TCLC 101**
See also CA 85-88; DFS 9; DLB 7, 9, 25, 26, 28, 86; FANT; IDFW 3, 4; RGAL 4

Hedayat, Sadeq 1903-1951 .... **TCLC 21**
See also CA 120; EWL 3; RGSF 2

Hegel, Georg Wilhelm Friedrich 1770-1831 .... **NCLC 46, 151**
See also DLB 90; TWA

Heidegger, Martin 1889-1976 .... **CLC 24**
See also CA 81-84; 65-68; CANR 34; DLB 296; MTCW 1, 2; MTFW 2005

Heidenstam, (Carl Gustaf) Verner von 1859-1940 .... **TCLC 5**
See also CA 104

Heidi Louise
See Erdrich, (Karen) Louise

Heifner, Jack 1946- .... **CLC 11**
See also CA 105; CANR 47

Heijermans, Herman 1864-1924 .... **TCLC 24**
See also CA 123; EWL 3

Heilbrun, Carolyn G(old) 1926-2003 .... **CLC 25, 173**
See Cross, Amanda
See also CA 45-48; 220; CANR 1, 28, 58, 94; FW

Hein, Christoph 1944- .... **CLC 154**
See also CA 158; CANR 108; CDWLB 2; CWW 2; DLB 124

Heine, Heinrich 1797-1856 .... **NCLC 4, 54, 147; PC 25**
See also CDWLB 2; DLB 90; EW 5; RGWL 2, 3; TWA

Heinemann, Larry (Curtiss) 1944- .. **CLC 50**
See also CA 110; CAAS 21; CANR 31, 81; DLBD 9; INT CANR-31

Heiney, Donald (William) 1921-1993
See Harris, MacDonald
See also CA 1-4R; 142; CANR 3, 58; FANT

Heinlein, Robert A(nson) 1907-1988 . **CLC 1, 3, 8, 14, 26, 55; SSC 55**
See also AAYA 17; BPFB 2; BYA 4, 13; CA 1-4R; 125; CANR 1, 20, 53; CLR 75; CN 1, 2, 3, 4; CPW; DA3; DAM POP; DLB 8; EXPS; JRDA; LAIT 5; LMFS 2; MAICYA 1, 2; MTCW 1, 2; MTFW 2005; RGAL 4; SATA 9, 69; SATA-Obit 56; SCFW 1, 2; SFW 4; SSFS 7; YAW

Helforth, John
See Doolittle, Hilda

Heliodorus fl. 3rd cent. - .... **CMLC 52**

Hellenhofferu, Vojtech Kapristian z
See Hasek, Jaroslav (Matej Frantisek)

Heller, Joseph 1923-1999 . **CLC 1, 3, 5, 8, 11, 36, 63; TCLC 131, 151; WLC**
See also AAYA 24; AITN 1; AMWS 4; BPFB 2; BYA 1; CA 5-8R; 187; CABS 1; CANR 8, 42, 66, 126; CN 1, 2, 3, 4, 5, 6; CPW; DA; DA3; DAB; DAC; DAM MST, NOV, POP; DLB 2, 28, 227; DLBY 1980, 2002; EWL 3; EXPN; INT CANR-8; LAIT 4; MAL 5; MTCW 1, 2; MTFW 2005; NFS 1; RGAL 4; TUS; YAW

Hellman, Lillian (Florence) 1906-1984 .. **CLC 2, 4, 8, 14, 18, 34, 44, 52; DC 1; TCLC 119**
See also AAYA 47; AITN 1, 2; AMWS 1; CA 13-16R; 112; CAD; CANR 33; CWD; DA3; DAM DRAM; DFS 1, 3, 14; DLB 7, 228; DLBY 1984; EWL 3; FL 1:6; FW; LAIT 3; MAL 5; MAWW; MTCW 1, 2; MTFW 2005; RGAL 4; TUS

Helprin, Mark 1947- .... **CLC 7, 10, 22, 32**
See also CA 81-84; CANR 47, 64, 124; CDALBS; CN 7; CPW; DA3; DAM NOV,
POP; DLBY 1985; FANT; MAL 5; MTCW 1, 2; MTFW 2005; SUFW 2

Helvetius, Claude-Adrien 1715-1771 .. **LC 26**
See also DLB 313

Helyar, Jane Penelope Josephine 1933-
See Poole, Josephine
See also CA 21-24R; CANR 10, 26; CWRI 5; SATA 82, 138; SATA-Essay 138

Hemans, Felicia 1793-1835 ..... **NCLC 29, 71**
See also DLB 96; RGEL 2

Hemingway, Ernest (Miller) 1899-1961 .... **CLC 1, 3, 6, 8, 10, 13, 19, 30, 34, 39, 41, 44, 50, 61, 80; SSC 1, 25, 36, 40, 63; TCLC 115; WLC**
See also AAYA 19; AMW; AMWC 1; AMWR 1; BPFB 2; BYA 2, 3, 13, 15; CA 77-80; CANR 34; CDALB 1917-1929; DA; DA3; DAB; DAC; DAM MST, NOV; DLB 4, 9, 102, 210, 308, 316; DLBD 1, 15, 16; DLBY 1981, 1987, 1996, 1998; EWL 3; EXPN; EXPS; LAIT 3, 4; LATS 1:1; MAL 5; MTCW 1, 2; MTFW 2005; NFS 1, 5, 6, 14; RGAL 4; RGSF 2; SSFS 17; TUS; WYA

Hempel, Amy 1951- .... **CLC 39**
See also CA 118; 137; CANR 70; DA3; DLB 218; EXPS; MTCW 2; MTFW 2005; SSFS 2

Henderson, F. C.
See Mencken, H(enry) L(ouis)

Henderson, Sylvia
See Ashton-Warner, Sylvia (Constance)

Henderson, Zenna (Chlarson) 1917-1983 .... **SSC 29**
See also CA 1-4R; 133; CANR 1, 84; DLB 8; SATA 5; SFW 4

Henkin, Joshua .... **CLC 119**
See also CA 161

Henley, Beth .... **CLC 23; DC 6, 14**
See Henley, Elizabeth Becker
See also CABS 3; CAD; CD 5, 6; CSW; CWD; DFS 2; DLBY 1986; FW

Henley, Elizabeth Becker 1952-
See Henley, Beth
See also CA 107; CANR 32, 73, 140; DA3; DAM DRAM, MST; DFS 21; MTCW 1, 2; MTFW 2005

Henley, William Ernest 1849-1903 .. **TCLC 8**
See also CA 105; 234; DLB 19; RGEL 2

Hennissart, Martha 1929-
See Lathen, Emma
See also CA 85-88; CANR 64

Henry VIII 1491-1547 .... **LC 10**
See also DLB 132

Henry, O. ..... **SSC 5, 49; TCLC 1, 19; WLC**
See Porter, William Sydney
See also AAYA 41; AMWS 2; EXPS; RGAL 4; RGSF 2; SSFS 2, 18; TCWW 1, 2

Henry, Patrick 1736-1799 .... **LC 25**
See also LAIT 1

Henryson, Robert 1430(?)-1506(?) ..... **LC 20, 110; PC 65**
See also BRWS 7; DLB 146; RGEL 2

Henschke, Alfred
See Klabund

Henson, Lance 1944- .... **NNAL**
See also CA 146; DLB 175

Hentoff, Nat(han Irving) 1925- .... **CLC 26**
See also AAYA 4, 42; BYA 6; CA 1-4R; CAAS 6; CANR 5, 25, 77, 114; CLR 1, 52; INT CANR-25; JRDA; MAICYA 1, 2; SATA 42, 69, 133; SATA-Brief 27; WYA; YAW

Heppenstall, (John) Rayner 1911-1981 .... **CLC 10**
See also CA 1-4R; 103; CANR 29; CN 1, 2; CP 1, 2, 3; EWL 3

Heraclitus c. 540B.C.-c. 450B.C. ... **CMLC 22**
See also DLB 176

Herbert, Frank (Patrick) 1920-1986 .... **CLC 12, 23, 35, 44, 85**
See also AAYA 21; BPFB 2; BYA 4, 14; CA 53-56; 118; CANR 5, 43; CDALBS; CPW; DAM POP; DLB 8; INT CANR-5; LAIT 5; MTCW 1, 2; MTFW 2005; NFS 17; SATA 9, 37; SATA-Obit 47; SCFW 1, 2; SFW 4; YAW

Herbert, George 1593-1633 . **LC 24, 121; PC 4**
See also BRW 2; BRWR 2; CDBLB Before 1660; DAB; DAM POET; DLB 126; EXPP; RGEL 2; TEA; WP

Herbert, Zbigniew 1924-1998 ..... **CLC 9, 43; PC 50; TCLC 168**
See also CA 89-92; 169; CANR 36, 74; CD-WLB 4; CWW 2; DAM POET; DLB 232; EWL 3; MTCW 1; PFS 22

Herbst, Josephine (Frey) 1897-1969 .... **CLC 34**
See also CA 5-8R; 25-28R; DLB 9

Herder, Johann Gottfried von 1744-1803 .... **NCLC 8**
See also DLB 97; EW 4; TWA

Heredia, Jose Maria 1803-1839 .... **HLCS 2**
See also LAW

Hergesheimer, Joseph 1880-1954 ... **TCLC 11**
See also CA 109; 194; DLB 102, 9; RGAL 4

Herlihy, James Leo 1927-1993 .... **CLC 6**
See also CA 1-4R; 143; CAD; CANR 2; CN 1, 2, 3, 4, 5

Herman, William
See Bierce, Ambrose (Gwinett)

Hermogenes fl. c. 175- .... **CMLC 6**

Hernandez, Jose 1834-1886 .... **NCLC 17**
See also LAW; RGWL 2, 3; WLIT 1

Herodotus c. 484B.C.-c. 420B.C. .. **CMLC 17**
See also AW 1; CDWLB 1; DLB 176; RGWL 2, 3; TWA

Herrick, Robert 1591-1674 .... **LC 13; PC 9**
See also BRW 2; BRWC 2; DA; DAB; DAC; DAM MST, POP; DLB 126; EXPP; PFS 13; RGAL 4; RGEL 2; TEA; WP

Herring, Guilles
See Somerville, Edith Oenone

Herriot, James 1916-1995 .... **CLC 12**
See Wight, James Alfred
See also AAYA 1, 54; BPFB 2; CA 148; CANR 40; CLR 80; CPW; DAM POP; LAIT 3; MAICYA 2; MAICYAS 1; MTCW 2; SATA 86, 135; TEA; YAW

Herris, Violet
See Hunt, Violet

Herrmann, Dorothy 1941- .... **CLC 44**
See also CA 107

Herrmann, Taffy
See Herrmann, Dorothy

Hersey, John (Richard) 1914-1993 .... **CLC 1, 2, 7, 9, 40, 81, 97**
See also AAYA 29; BPFB 2; CA 17-20R; 140; CANR 33; CDALBS; CN 1, 2, 3, 4, 5; CPW; DAM POP; DLB 6, 185, 278, 299; MAL 5; MTCW 1, 2; MTFW 2005; SATA 25; SATA-Obit 76; TUS

Herzen, Aleksandr Ivanovich 1812-1870 .... **NCLC 10, 61**
See Herzen, Alexander

Herzen, Alexander
See Herzen, Aleksandr Ivanovich
See also DLB 277

Herzl, Theodor 1860-1904 .... **TCLC 36**
See also CA 168

Herzog, Werner 1942- .... **CLC 16**
See also CA 89-92

Hesiod c. 8th cent. B.C.- .... **CMLC 5**
See also AW 1; DLB 176; RGWL 2, 3

Hesse, Hermann 1877-1962 ... **CLC 1, 2, 3, 6, 11, 17, 25, 69; SSC 9, 49; TCLC 148; WLC**
See also AAYA 43; BPFB 2; CA 17-18; CAP 2; CDWLB 2; DA; DA3; DAB; DAC; DAM MST, NOV; DLB 66; EW 9; EWL 3; EXPN; LAIT 1; MTCW 1, 2; MTFW 2005; NFS 6, 15; RGWL 2, 3; SATA 50; TWA

Hewes, Cady
See De Voto, Bernard (Augustine)

Heyen, William 1940- .... **CLC 13, 18**
See also CA 33-36R; 220; CAAE 220; CAAS 9; CANR 98; CP 3, 4, 5, 6, 7; DLB 5

Heyerdahl, Thor 1914-2002 .... **CLC 26**
See also CA 5-8R; 207; CANR 5, 22, 66, 73; LAIT 4; MTCW 1, 2; MTFW 2005; SATA 2, 52

Heym, Georg (Theodor Franz Arthur)
1887-1912 .... **TCLC 9**
See also CA 106; 181

Heym, Stefan 1913-2001 .... **CLC 41**
See also CA 9-12R; 203; CANR 4; CWW 2; DLB 69; EWL 3

Heyse, Paul (Johann Ludwig von)
1830-1914 .... **TCLC 8**
See also CA 104; 209; DLB 129

Heyward, (Edwin) DuBose
1885-1940 .... **HR 1:2; TCLC 59**
See also CA 108; 157; DLB 7, 9, 45, 249; MAL 5; SATA 21

Heywood, John 1497(?)-1580(?) .... **LC 65**
See also DLB 136; RGEL 2

Heywood, Thomas 1573(?)-1641 .... **LC 111**
See also DAM DRAM; DLB 62; LMFS 1; RGEL 2; TEA

Hibbert, Eleanor Alice Burford
1906-1993 .... **CLC 7**
See Holt, Victoria
See also BEST 90:4; CA 17-20R; 140; CANR 9, 28, 59; CMW 4; CPW; DAM POP; MTCW 2; MTFW 2005; RHW; SATA 2; SATA-Obit 74

Hichens, Robert (Smythe)
1864-1950 .... **TCLC 64**
See also CA 162; DLB 153; HGG; RHW; SUFW

Higgins, Aidan 1927- .... **SSC 68**
See also CA 9-12R; CANR 70, 115; CN 1, 2, 3, 4, 5, 6, 7; DLB 14

Higgins, George V(incent)
1939-1999 .... **CLC 4, 7, 10, 18**
See also BPFB 2; CA 77-80; 186; CAAS 5; CANR 17, 51, 89, 96; CMW 4; CN 2, 3, 4, 5, 6; DLB 2; DLBY 1981, 1998; INT CANR-17; MSW; MTCW 1

Higginson, Thomas Wentworth
1823-1911 .... **TCLC 36**
See also CA 162; DLB 1, 64, 243

Higgonet, Margaret ed. .... **CLC 65**

Highet, Helen
See MacInnes, Helen (Clark)

Highsmith, (Mary) Patricia
1921-1995 .... **CLC 2, 4, 14, 42, 102**
See Morgan, Claire
See also AAYA 48; BRWS 5; CA 1-4R; 147; CANR 1, 20, 48, 62, 108; CMW 4; CN 1, 2, 3, 4, 5; CPW; DA3; DAM NOV, POP; DLB 306; MSW; MTCW 1, 2; MTFW 2005

Highwater, Jamake (Mamake)
1942(?)-2001 .... **CLC 12**
See also AAYA 7; BPFB 2; BYA 4; CA 65-68; 199; CAAS 7; CANR 10, 34, 84; CLR 17; CWRI 5; DLB 52; DLBY 1985; JRDA; MAICYA 1, 2; SATA 32, 69; SATA-Brief 30

Highway, Tomson 1951- ...... **CLC 92; NNAL**
See also CA 151; CANR 75; CCA 1; CD 5, 6; CN 7; DAC; DAM MULT; DFS 2; MTCW 2

Hijuelos, Oscar 1951- .... **CLC 65; HLC 1**
See also AAYA 25; AMWS 8; BEST 90:1; CA 123; CANR 50, 75, 125; CPW; DA3; DAM MULT, POP; DLB 145; HW 1, 2; LLW; MAL 5; MTCW 2; MTFW 2005; NFS 17; RGAL 4; WLIT 1

Hikmet, Nazim 1902-1963 .... **CLC 40**
See Nizami of Ganja
See also CA 141; 93-96; EWL 3; WLIT 6

Hildegard von Bingen 1098-1179 . **CMLC 20**
See also DLB 148

Hildesheimer, Wolfgang 1916-1991 .. **CLC 49**
See also CA 101; 135; DLB 69, 124; EWL 3

Hill, Geoffrey (William) 1932- ...... **CLC 5, 8, 18, 45**
See also BRWS 5; CA 81-84; CANR 21, 89; CDBLB 1960 to Present; CP 1, 2, 3, 4, 5, 6, 7; DAM POET; DLB 40; EWL 3; MTCW 1; RGEL 2

Hill, George Roy 1921-2002 .... **CLC 26**
See also CA 110; 122; 213

Hill, John
See Koontz, Dean R.

Hill, Susan (Elizabeth) 1942- ...... **CLC 4, 113**
See also CA 33-36R; CANR 29, 69, 129; CN 2, 3, 4, 5, 6, 7; DAB; DAM MST, NOV; DLB 14, 139; HGG; MTCW 1; RHW

Hillard, Asa G. III .... **CLC 70**

Hillerman, Tony 1925- .... **CLC 62, 170**
See also AAYA 40; BEST 89:1; BPFB 2; CA 29-32R; CANR 21, 42, 65, 97, 134; CMW 4; CPW; DA3; DAM POP; DLB 206, 306; MAL 5; MSW; MTCW 2; MTFW 2005; RGAL 4; SATA 6; TCWW 2; YAW

Hillesum, Etty 1914-1943 .... **TCLC 49**
See also CA 137

Hilliard, Noel (Harvey) 1929-1996 ... **CLC 15**
See also CA 9-12R; CANR 7, 69; CN 1, 2, 3, 4, 5, 6

Hillis, Rick 1956- .... **CLC 66**
See also CA 134

Hilton, James 1900-1954 .... **TCLC 21**
See also CA 108; 169; DLB 34, 77; FANT; SATA 34

Hilton, Walter (?)-1396 .... **CMLC 58**
See also DLB 146; RGEL 2

Himes, Chester (Bomar) 1909-1984 .. **BLC 2; CLC 2, 4, 7, 18, 58, 108; TCLC 139**
See also AFAW 2; BPFB 2; BW 2; CA 25-28R; 114; CANR 22, 89; CMW 4; CN 1, 2, 3; DAM MULT; DLB 2, 76, 143, 226; EWL 3; MAL 5; MSW; MTCW 1, 2; MTFW 2005; RGAL 4

Himmelfarb, Gertrude 1922- .... **CLC 202**
See also CA 49-52; CANR 28, 66, 102

Hinde, Thomas .... **CLC 6, 11**
See Chitty, Thomas Willes
See also CN 1, 2, 3, 4, 5, 6; EWL 3

Hine, (William) Daryl 1936- .... **CLC 15**
See also CA 1-4R; CAAS 15; CANR 1, 20; CP 1, 2, 3, 4, 5, 6, 7; DLB 60

Hinkson, Katharine Tynan
See Tynan, Katharine

Hinojosa(-Smith), Rolando (R.)
1929- .... **HLC 1**
See Hinojosa-Smith, Rolando
See also CA 131; CAAS 16; CANR 62; DAM MULT; DLB 82; HW 1, 2; LLW; MTCW 2; MTFW 2005; RGAL 4

Hinton, S(usan) E(loise) 1950- .. **CLC 30, 111**
See also AAYA 2, 33; BPFB 2; BYA 2, 3; CA 81-84; CANR 32, 62, 92, 133;

CDALBS; CLR 3, 23; CPW; DA; DA3; DAB; DAC; DAM MST, NOV; JRDA; LAIT 5; MAICYA 1, 2; MTCW 1, 2; MTFW 2005 !**; NFS 5, 9, 15, 16; SATA 19, 58, 115, 160; WYA; YAW

Hippius, Zinaida (Nikolaevna) .... **TCLC 9**
See Gippius, Zinaida (Nikolaevna)
See also DLB 295; EWL 3

Hiraoka, Kimitake 1925-1970
See Mishima, Yukio
See also CA 97-100; 29-32R; DA3; DAM DRAM; GLL 1; MTCW 1, 2

Hirsch, E(ric) D(onald), Jr. 1928- ... **CLC 79**
See also CA 25-28R; CANR 27, 51; DLB 67; INT CANR-27; MTCW 1

Hirsch, Edward 1950- .... **CLC 31, 50**
See also CA 104; CANR 20, 42, 102; CP 7; DLB 120; PFS 22

Hitchcock, Alfred (Joseph)
1899-1980 .... **CLC 16**
See also AAYA 22; CA 159; 97-100; SATA 27; SATA-Obit 24

Hitchens, Christopher (Eric)
1949- .... **CLC 157**
See also CA 152; CANR 89

Hitler, Adolf 1889-1945 .... **TCLC 53**
See also CA 117; 147

Hoagland, Edward (Morley) 1932- .. **CLC 28**
See also ANW; CA 1-4R; CANR 2, 31, 57, 107; CN 1, 2, 3, 4, 5, 6, 7; DLB 6; SATA 51; TCWW 2

Hoban, Russell (Conwell) 1925- ... **CLC 7, 25**
See also BPFB 2; CA 5-8R; CANR 23, 37, 66, 114, 138; CLR 3, 69; CN 4, 5, 6, 7; CWRI 5; DAM NOV; DLB 52; FANT; MAICYA 1, 2; MTCW 1, 2; MTFW 2005; SATA 1, 40, 78, 136; SFW 4; SUFW 2; TCLE 1:1

Hobbes, Thomas 1588-1679 .... **LC 36**
See also DLB 151, 252, 281; RGEL 2

Hobbs, Perry
See Blackmur, R(ichard) P(almer)

Hobson, Laura Z(ametkin)
1900-1986 .... **CLC 7, 25**
See also BPFB 2; CA 17-20R; 118; CANR 55; CN 1, 2, 3, 4; DLB 28; SATA 52

Hoccleve, Thomas c. 1368-c. 1437 ...... **LC 75**
See also DLB 146; RGEL 2

Hoch, Edward D(entinger) 1930-
See Queen, Ellery
See also CA 29-32R; CANR 11, 27, 51, 97; CMW 4; DLB 306; SFW 4

Hochhuth, Rolf 1931- .... **CLC 4, 11, 18**
See also CA 5-8R; CANR 33, 75, 136; CWW 2; DAM DRAM; DLB 124; EWL 3; MTCW 1, 2; MTFW 2005

Hochman, Sandra 1936- .... **CLC 3, 8**
See also CA 5-8R; CP 1, 2, 3, 4; DLB 5

Hochwaelder, Fritz 1911-1986 .... **CLC 36**
See Hochwalder, Fritz
See also CA 29-32R; 120; CANR 42; DAM DRAM; MTCW 1; RGWL 3

Hochwalder, Fritz
See Hochwaelder, Fritz
See also EWL 3; RGWL 2

Hocking, Mary (Eunice) 1921- .... **CLC 13**
See also CA 101; CANR 18, 40

Hodgins, Jack 1938- .... **CLC 23**
See also CA 93-96; CN 4, 5, 6, 7; DLB 60

Hodgson, William Hope
1877(?)-1918 .... **TCLC 13**
See also CA 111; 164; CMW 4; DLB 70, 153, 156, 178; HGG; MTCW 2; SFW 4; SUFW 1

Hoeg, Peter 1957- .... **CLC 95, 156**
See also CA 151; CANR 75; CMW 4; DA3; DLB 214; EWL 3; MTCW 2; MTFW 2005; NFS 17; RGWL 3; SSFS 18

Hostos (y Bonilla), Eugenio Maria de
1839-1903 .... **TCLC 24**
See also CA 123; 131; HW 1

Houdini
See Lovecraft, H(oward) P(hillips)

Houellebecq, Michel 1958- .... **CLC 179**
See also CA 185; CANR 140; MTFW 2005

Hougan, Carolyn 1943- .... **CLC 34**
See also CA 139

Household, Geoffrey (Edward West)
1900-1988 .... **CLC 11**
See also CA 77-80; 126; CANR 58; CMW
4; CN 1, 2, 3, 4; DLB 87; SATA 14;
SATA-Obit 59

Housman, A(lfred) E(dward)
1859-1936 .... **PC 2, 43; TCLC 1, 10;**
WLCS
See also AAYA 66; BRW 6; CA 104; 125;
DA; DA3; DAB; DAC; DAM MST,
POET; DLB 19, 284; EWL 3; EXPP;
MTCW 1, 2; MTFW 2005; PAB; PFS 4,
7; RGEL 2; TEA; WP

Housman, Laurence 1865-1959 .... **TCLC 7**
See also CA 106; 155; DLB 10; FANT;
RGEL 2; SATA 25

Houston, Jeanne (Toyo) Wakatsuki
1934- .... **AAL**
See also AAYA 49; CA 103, 232; CAAE
232; CAAS 16; CANR 29, 123; LAIT 4;
SATA 78

Howard, Elizabeth Jane 1923- ..... **CLC 7, 29**
See also BRWS 11; CA 5-8R; CANR 8, 62,
146; CN 1, 2, 3, 4, 5, 6, 7

Howard, Maureen 1930- .... **CLC 5, 14, 46,**
151
See also CA 53-56; CANR 31, 75, 140; CN
4, 5, 6, 7; DLBY 1983; INT CANR-31;
MTCW 1, 2; MTFW 2005

Howard, Richard 1929- .... **CLC 7, 10, 47**
See also AITN 1; CA 85-88; CANR 25, 80;
CP 1, 2, 3, 4, 5, 6, 7; DLB 5; INT CANR-
25; MAL 5

Howard, Robert E(rvin)
1906-1936 .... **TCLC 8**
See also BPFB 2; BYA 5; CA 105; 157;
FANT; SUFW 1; TCWW 1, 2

Howard, Warren F.
See Pohl, Frederik

Howe, Fanny (Quincy) 1940- .... **CLC 47**
See also CA 117, 187; CAAE 187; CAAS
27; CANR 70, 116; CP 7; CWP; SATA-
Brief 52

Howe, Irving 1920-1993 .... **CLC 85**
See also AMWS 6; CA 9-12R; 141; CANR
21, 50; DLB 67; EWL 3; MAL 5; MTCW
1, 2; MTFW 2005

Howe, Julia Ward 1819-1910 .... **TCLC 21**
See also CA 117; 191; DLB 1, 189, 235;
FW

Howe, Susan 1937- .... **CLC 72, 152; PC 54**
See also AMWS 4; CA 160; CP 7; CWP;
DLB 120; FW; RGAL 4

Howe, Tina 1937- .... **CLC 48**
See also CA 109; CAD; CANR 125; CD 5,
6; CWD

Howell, James 1594(?)-1666 .... **LC 13**
See also DLB 151

Howells, W. D.
See Howells, William Dean

Howells, William D.
See Howells, William Dean

Howells, William Dean 1837-1920 ... **SSC 36;**
TCLC 7, 17, 41
See also AMW; CA 104; 134; CDALB
1865-1917; DLB 12, 64, 74, 79, 189;
LMFS 1; MAL 5; MTCW 2; RGAL 4;
TUS

Howes, Barbara 1914-1996 .... **CLC 15**
See also CA 9-12R; 151; CAAS 3; CANR
53; CP 1, 2, 3, 4; SATA 5; TCLE 1:1

Hrabal, Bohumil 1914-1997 ...... **CLC 13, 67;**
TCLC 155
See also CA 106; 156; CAAS 12; CANR
57; CWW 2; DLB 232; EWL 3; RGSF 2

Hrabanus Maurus 776(?)-856 .... **CMLC 78**
See also DLB 148

Hrotsvit of Gandersheim c. 935-c.
1000 .... **CMLC 29**
See also DLB 148

Hsi, Chu 1130-1200 .... **CMLC 42**

Hsun, Lu
See Lu Hsun

Hubbard, L(afayette) Ron(ald)
1911-1986 .... **CLC 43**
See also AAYA 64; CA 77-80; 118; CANR
52; CPW; DA3; DAM POP; FANT;
MTCW 2; MTFW 2005; SFW 4

Huch, Ricarda (Octavia)
1864-1947 .... **TCLC 13**
See Hugo, Richard
See also CA 111; 189; DLB 66; EWL 3

Huddle, David 1942- .... **CLC 49**
See also CA 57-60; CAAS 20; CANR 89;
DLB 130

Hudson, Jeffrey
See Crichton, (John) Michael

Hudson, W(illiam) H(enry)
1841-1922 .... **TCLC 29**
See also CA 115; 190; DLB 98, 153, 174;
RGEL 2; SATA 35

Hueffer, Ford Madox
See Ford, Ford Madox

Hughart, Barry 1934- .... **CLC 39**
See also CA 137; FANT; SFW 4; SUFW 2

Hughes, Colin
See Creasey, John

Hughes, David (John) 1930-2005 ..... **CLC 48**
See also CA 116; 129; 238; CN 4, 5, 6, 7;
DLB 14

Hughes, Edward James
See Hughes, Ted
See also DA3; DAM MST, POET

Hughes, (James Mercer) Langston
1902-1967 ..... **BLC 2; CLC 1, 5, 10, 15,**
35, 44, 108; DC 3; HR 1:2; PC 1, 53;
SSC 6, 90; WLC
See also AAYA 12; AFAW 1, 2; AMWR 1;
AMWS 1; BW 1, 3; CA 1-4R; 25-28R;
CANR 1, 34, 82; CDALB 1929-1941;
CLR 17; DA; DA3; DAB; DAC; DAM
DRAM, MST, MULT, POET; DFS 6, 18;
DLB 4, 7, 48, 51, 86, 228, 315; EWL 3;
EXPP; EXPS; JRDA; LAIT 3; LMFS 2;
MAICYA 1, 2; MAL 5; MTCW 1, 2;
MTFW 2005; NFS 21; PAB; PFS 1, 3, 6,
10, 15; RGAL 4; RGSF 2; SATA 4, 33;
SSFS 4, 7; TUS; WCH; WP; YAW

Hughes, Richard (Arthur Warren)
1900-1976 .... **CLC 1, 11**
See also CA 5-8R; 65-68; CANR 4; CN 1,
2; DAM NOV; DLB 15, 161; EWL 3;
MTCW 1; RGEL 2; SATA 8; SATA-Obit
25

Hughes, Ted 1930-1998 . **CLC 2, 4, 9, 14, 37,**
119; PC 7
See Hughes, Edward James
See also BRWC 2; BRWR 2; BRWS 1; CA
1-4R; 171; CANR 1, 33, 66, 108; CLR 3;
CP 1, 2, 3, 4, 5, 6; DAB; DAC; DLB 40,
161; EWL 3; EXPP; MAICYA 1, 2;
MTCW 1, 2; MTFW 2005; PAB; PFS 4,
19; RGEL 2; SATA 49; SATA-Brief 27;
SATA-Obit 107; TEA; YAW

Hugo, Richard
See Huch, Ricarda (Octavia)
See also MAL 5

Hugo, Richard F(ranklin)
1923-1982 .... **CLC 6, 18, 32; PC 68**
See also AMWS 6; CA 49-52; 108; CANR
3; CP 1, 2, 3; DAM POET; DLB 5, 206;
EWL 3; PFS 17; RGAL 4

Hugo, Victor (Marie) 1802-1885 .... **NCLC 3,**
10, 21, 161; PC 17; WLC
See also AAYA 28; DA; DA3; DAB; DAC;
DAM DRAM, MST, NOV, POET; DLB
119, 192, 217; EFS 2; EW 6; EXPN; GFL
1789 to the Present; LAIT 1, 2; NFS 5,
20; RGWL 2, 3; SATA 47; TWA

Huidobro, Vicente
See Huidobro Fernandez, Vicente Garcia
See also DLB 283; EWL 3; LAW

Huidobro Fernandez, Vicente Garcia
1893-1948 .... **TCLC 31**
See Huidobro, Vicente
See also CA 131; HW 1

Hulme, Keri 1947- .... **CLC 39, 130**
See also CA 125; CANR 69; CN 4, 5, 6, 7;
CP 7; CWP; EWL 3; FW; INT CA-125

Hulme, T(homas) E(rnest)
1883-1917 .... **TCLC 21**
See also BRWS 6; CA 117; 203; DLB 19

Humboldt, Wilhelm von
1767-1835 .... **NCLC 134**
See also DLB 90

Hume, David 1711-1776 .... **LC 7, 56**
See also BRWS 3; DLB 104, 252; LMFS 1;
TEA

Humphrey, William 1924-1997 .... **CLC 45**
See also AMWS 9; CA 77-80; 160; CANR
68; CN 1, 2, 3, 4, 5, 6; CSW; DLB 6, 212,
234, 278; TCWW 1, 2

Humphreys, Emyr Owen 1919- .... **CLC 47**
See also CA 5-8R; CANR 3, 24; CN 1, 2,
3, 4, 5, 6, 7; DLB 15

Humphreys, Josephine 1945- ..... **CLC 34, 57**
See also CA 121; 127; CANR 97; CSW;
DLB 292; INT CA-127

Huneker, James Gibbons
1860-1921 .... **TCLC 65**
See also CA 193; DLB 71; RGAL 4

Hungerford, Hesba Fay
See Brinsmead, H(esba) F(ay)

Hungerford, Pixie
See Brinsmead, H(esba) F(ay)

Hunt, E(verette) Howard, (Jr.)
1918- .... **CLC 3**
See also AITN 1; CA 45-48; CANR 2, 47,
103; CMW 4

Hunt, Francesca
See Holland, Isabelle (Christian)

Hunt, Howard
See Hunt, E(verette) Howard, (Jr.)

Hunt, Kyle
See Creasey, John

Hunt, (James Henry) Leigh
1784-1859 .... **NCLC 1, 70**
See also DAM POET; DLB 96, 110, 144;
RGEL 2; TEA

Hunt, Marsha 1946- .... **CLC 70**
See also BW 2, 3; CA 143; CANR 79

Hunt, Violet 1866(?)-1942 .... **TCLC 53**
See also CA 184; DLB 162, 197

Hunter, E. Waldo
See Sturgeon, Theodore (Hamilton)

Hunter, Evan 1926-2005 .... **CLC 11, 31**
See McBain, Ed
See also AAYA 39; BPFB 2; CA 5-8R; 241;
CANR 5, 38, 62, 97; CMW 4; CN 1, 2, 3,
4, 5, 6, 7; CPW; DAM POP; DLB 306;
DLBY 1982; INT CANR-5; MSW;
MTCW 1; SATA 25; SFW 4

Hunter, Kristin
See Lattany, Kristin (Elaine Eggleston)
Hunter
See also CN 1, 2, 3, 4, 5, 6

Isler, Alan (David) 1934- .... **CLC 91**
   See also CA 156; CANR 105
Ivan IV 1530-1584 .... **LC 17**
Ivanov, Vyacheslav Ivanovich
   1866-1949 .... **TCLC 33**
   See also CA 122; EWL 3
Ivask, Ivar Vidrik 1927-1992 .... **CLC 14**
   See also CA 37-40R; 139; CANR 24
Ives, Morgan
   See Bradley, Marion Zimmer
   See also GLL 1
Izumi Shikibu c. 973-c. 1034 .... **CMLC 33**
J. R. S.
   See Gogarty, Oliver St. John
Jabran, Kahlil
   See Gibran, Kahlil
Jabran, Khalil
   See Gibran, Kahlil
Jackson, Daniel
   See Wingrove, David (John)
Jackson, Helen Hunt 1830-1885 .... **NCLC 90**
   See also DLB 42, 47, 186, 189; RGAL 4
Jackson, Jesse 1908-1983 .... **CLC 12**
   See also BW 1; CA 25-28R; 109; CANR
   27; CLR 28; CWRI 5; MAICYA 1, 2;
   SATA 2, 29; SATA-Obit 48
Jackson, Laura (Riding) 1901-1991 .... **PC 44**
   See Riding, Laura
   See also CA 65-68; 135; CANR 28, 89;
   DLB 48
Jackson, Sam
   See Trumbo, Dalton
Jackson, Sara
   See Wingrove, David (John)
Jackson, Shirley 1919-1965 . **CLC 11, 60, 87;
   SSC 9, 39; WLC**
   See also AAYA 9; AMWS 9; BPFB 2; CA
   1-4R; 25-28R; CANR 4, 52; CDALB
   1941-1968; DA; DA3; DAC; DAM MST;
   DLB 6, 234; EXPS; HGG; LAIT 4; MAL
   5; MTCW 2; MTFW 2005; RGAL 4;
   RGSF 2; SATA 2; SSFS 1; SUFW 1, 2
Jacob, (Cyprien-)Max 1876-1944 .... **TCLC 6**
   See also CA 104; 193; DLB 258; EWL 3;
   GFL 1789 to the Present; GLL 2; RGWL
   2, 3
Jacobs, Harriet A(nn)
   1813(?)-1897 .... **NCLC 67, 162**
   See also AFAW 1, 2; DLB 239; FL 1:3; FW;
   LAIT 2; RGAL 4
Jacobs, Jim 1942- .... **CLC 12**
   See also CA 97-100; INT CA-97-100
Jacobs, W(illiam) W(ymark)
   1863-1943 .... **SSC 73; TCLC 22**
   See also CA 121; 167; DLB 135; EXPS;
   HGG; RGEL 2; RGSF 2; SSFS 2; SUFW
   1
Jacobsen, Jens Peter 1847-1885 .... **NCLC 34**
Jacobsen, Josephine (Winder)
   1908-2003 .... **CLC 48, 102; PC 62**
   See also CA 33-36R; 218; CAAS 18; CANR
   23, 48; CCA 1; CP 2, 3, 4, 5, 6, 7; DLB
   244; PFS 23; TCLE 1:1
Jacobson, Dan 1929- .... **CLC 4, 14**
   See also AFW; CA 1-4R; CANR 2, 25, 66;
   CN 1, 2, 3, 4, 5, 6, 7; DLB 14, 207, 225,
   319; EWL 3; MTCW 1; RGSF 2
Jacqueline
   See Carpentier (y Valmont), Alejo
Jacques de Vitry c. 1160-1240 ...... **CMLC 63**
   See also DLB 208
Jagger, Michael Philip
   See Jagger, Mick
Jagger, Mick 1943- .... **CLC 17**
   See also CA 239
Jahiz, al- c. 780-c. 869 .... **CMLC 25**
   See also DLB 311

Jakes, John (William) 1932- .... **CLC 29**
   See also AAYA 32; BEST 89:4; BPFB 2;
   CA 57-60, 214; CAAE 214; CANR 10,
   43, 66, 111, 142; CPW; CSW; DA3; DAM
   NOV, POP; DLB 278; DLBY 1983;
   FANT; INT CANR-10; MTCW 1, 2;
   MTFW 2005; RHW; SATA 62; SFW 4;
   TCWW 1, 2
James I 1394-1437 .... **LC 20**
   See also RGEL 2
James, Andrew
   See Kirkup, James
James, C(yril) L(ionel) R(obert)
   1901-1989 .... **BLCS; CLC 33**
   See also BW 2; CA 117; 125; 128; CANR
   62; CN 1, 2, 3, 4; DLB 125; MTCW 1
James, Daniel (Lewis) 1911-1988
   See Santiago, Danny
   See also CA 174; 125
James, Dynely
   See Mayne, William (James Carter)
James, Henry Sr. 1811-1882 .... **NCLC 53**
James, Henry 1843-1916 .... **SSC 8, 32, 47;
   TCLC 2, 11, 24, 40, 47, 64, 171; WLC**
   See also AMW; AMWC 1; AMWR 1; BPFB
   2; BRW 6; CA 104; 132; CDALB 1865-
   1917; DA; DA3; DAB; DAC; DAM MST,
   NOV; DLB 12, 71, 74, 189; DLBD 13;
   EWL 3; EXPS; GL 2; HGG; LAIT 2;
   MAL 5; MTCW 1, 2; MTFW 2005; NFS
   12, 16, 19; RGAL 4; RGEL 2; RGSF 2;
   SSFS 9; SUFW 1; TUS
James, M. R.
   See James, Montague (Rhodes)
   See also DLB 156, 201
James, Montague (Rhodes)
   1862-1936 .... **SSC 16; TCLC 6**
   See James, M. R.
   See also CA 104; 203; HGG; RGEL 2;
   RGSF 2; SUFW 1
James, P. D. .... **CLC 18, 46, 122**
   See White, Phyllis Dorothy James
   See also BEST 90:2; BPFB 2; BRWS 4;
   CDBLB 1960 to Present; CN 4, 5, 6; DLB
   87, 276; DLBD 17; MSW
James, Philip
   See Moorcock, Michael (John)
James, Samuel
   See Stephens, James
James, Seumas
   See Stephens, James
James, Stephen
   See Stephens, James
James, William 1842-1910 .... **TCLC 15, 32**
   See also AMW; CA 109; 193; DLB 270,
   284; MAL 5; NCFS 5; RGAL 4
Jameson, Anna 1794-1860 .... **NCLC 43**
   See also DLB 99, 166
Jameson, Fredric (R.) 1934- .... **CLC 142**
   See also CA 196; DLB 67; LMFS 2
James VI of Scotland 1566-1625 .... **LC 109**
   See also DLB 151, 172
Jami, Nur al-Din 'Abd al-Rahman
   1414-1492 .... **LC 9**
Jammes, Francis 1868-1938 .... **TCLC 75**
   See also CA 198; EWL 3; GFL 1789 to the
   Present
Jandl, Ernst 1925-2000 .... **CLC 34**
   See also CA 200; EWL 3
Janowitz, Tama 1957- .... **CLC 43, 145**
   See also CA 106; CANR 52, 89, 129; CN
   5, 6, 7; CPW; DAM POP; DLB 292;
   MTFW 2005
Japrisot, Sebastien 1931- .... **CLC 90**
   See Rossi, Jean-Baptiste
   See also CMW 4; NFS 18

Jarrell, Randall 1914-1965 .... **CLC 1, 2, 6, 9,
   13, 49; PC 41; TCLC 177**
   See also AMW; BYA 5; CA 5-8R; 25-28R;
   CABS 2; CANR 6, 34; CDALB 1941-
   1968; CLR 6; CWRI 5; DAM POET;
   DLB 48, 52; EWL 3; EXPP; MAICYA 1,
   2; MAL 5; MTCW 1, 2; PAB; PFS 2;
   RGAL 4; SATA 7
Jarry, Alfred 1873-1907 .... **SSC 20; TCLC 2,
   14, 147**
   See also CA 104; 153; DA3; DAM DRAM;
   DFS 8; DLB 192, 258; EW 9; EWL 3;
   GFL 1789 to the Present; RGWL 2, 3;
   TWA
Jarvis, E. K.
   See Ellison, Harlan (Jay)
Jawien, Andrzej
   See John Paul II, Pope
Jaynes, Roderick
   See Coen, Ethan
Jeake, Samuel, Jr.
   See Aiken, Conrad (Potter)
Jean Paul 1763-1825 .... **NCLC 7**
Jefferies, (John) Richard
   1848-1887 .... **NCLC 47**
   See also DLB 98, 141; RGEL 2; SATA 16;
   SFW 4
Jeffers, (John) Robinson 1887-1962 .. **CLC 2,
   3, 11, 15, 54; PC 17; WLC**
   See also AMWS 2; CA 85-88; CANR 35;
   CDALB 1917-1929; DA; DAC; DAM
   MST, POET; DLB 45, 212; EWL 3; MAL
   5; MTCW 1, 2; MTFW 2005; PAB; PFS
   3, 4; RGAL 4
Jefferson, Janet
   See Mencken, H(enry) L(ouis)
Jefferson, Thomas 1743-1826 . **NCLC 11, 103**
   See also AAYA 54; ANW; CDALB 1640-
   1865; DA3; DLB 31, 183; LAIT 1; RGAL
   4
Jeffrey, Francis 1773-1850 .... **NCLC 33**
   See Francis, Lord Jeffrey
Jelakowitch, Ivan
   See Heijermans, Herman
Jelinek, Elfriede 1946- .... **CLC 169**
   See also AAYA 68; CA 154; DLB 85; FW
Jellicoe, (Patricia) Ann 1927- .... **CLC 27**
   See also CA 85-88; CBD; CD 5, 6; CWD;
   CWRI 5; DLB 13, 233; FW
Jelloun, Tahar ben 1944- .... **CLC 180**
   See Ben Jelloun, Tahar
   See also CA 162; CANR 100
Jemyma
   See Holley, Marietta
Jen, Gish .... **AAL; CLC 70, 198**
   See Jen, Lillian
   See also AMWC 2; CN 7; DLB 312
Jen, Lillian 1955-
   See Jen, Gish
   See also CA 135; CANR 89, 130
Jenkins, (John) Robin 1912- .... **CLC 52**
   See also CA 1-4R; CANR 1, 135; CN 1, 2,
   3, 4, 5, 6, 7; DLB 14, 271
Jennings, Elizabeth (Joan)
   1926-2001 .... **CLC 5, 14, 131**
   See also BRWS 5; CA 61-64; 200; CAAS
   5; CANR 8, 39, 66, 127; CP 1, 2, 3, 4, 5,
   6, 7; CWP; DLB 27; EWL 3; MTCW 1;
   SATA 66
Jennings, Waylon 1937-2002 .... **CLC 21**
Jensen, Johannes V(ilhelm)
   1873-1950 .... **TCLC 41**
   See also CA 170; DLB 214; EWL 3; RGWL
   3
Jensen, Laura (Linnea) 1948- .... **CLC 37**
   See also CA 103
Jerome, Saint 345-420 .... **CMLC 30**
   See also RGWL 3

Kavanagh, Julie 1952- .... **CLC 119**
See also CA 163
Kavanagh, Patrick (Joseph)
1904-1967 .... **CLC 22; PC 33**
See also BRWS 7; CA 123; 25-28R; DLB
15, 20; EWL 3; MTCW 1; RGEL 2
Kawabata, Yasunari 1899-1972 ..... **CLC 2, 5,
9, 18, 107; SSC 17**
See Kawabata Yasunari
See also CA 93-96; 33-36R; CANR 88;
DAM MULT; MJW; MTCW 2; MTFW
2005; RGSF 2; RGWL 2, 3
Kawabata Yasunari
See Kawabata, Yasunari
See also DLB 180; EWL 3
Kaye, M(ary) M(argaret)
1908-2004 .... **CLC 28**
See also CA 89-92; 223; CANR 24, 60, 102,
142; MTCW 1, 2; MTFW 2005; RHW;
SATA 62; SATA-Obit 152
Kaye, Mollie
See Kaye, M(ary) M(argaret)
Kaye-Smith, Sheila 1887-1956 .... **TCLC 20**
See also CA 118; 203; DLB 36
Kaymor, Patrice Maguilene
See Senghor, Leopold Sedar
Kazakov, Iurii Pavlovich
See Kazakov, Yuri Pavlovich
See also DLB 302
Kazakov, Yuri Pavlovich 1927-1982 . **SSC 43**
See Kazakov, Iurii Pavlovich; Kazakov,
Yury
See also CA 5-8R; CANR 36; MTCW 1;
RGSF 2
Kazakov, Yury
See Kazakov, Yuri Pavlovich
See also EWL 3
Kazan, Elia 1909-2003 .... **CLC 6, 16, 63**
See also CA 21-24R; 220; CANR 32, 78
Kazantzakis, Nikos 1883(?)-1957 .... **TCLC 2,
5, 33**
See also BPFB 2; CA 105; 132; DA3; EW
9; EWL 3; MTCW 1, 2; MTFW 2005;
RGWL 2, 3
Kazin, Alfred 1915-1998 ..... **CLC 34, 38, 119**
See also AMWS 8; CA 1-4R; CAAS 7;
CANR 1, 45, 79; DLB 67; EWL 3
Keane, Mary Nesta (Skrine) 1904-1996
See Keane, Molly
See also CA 108; 114; 151; RHW
Keane, Molly .... **CLC 31**
See Keane, Mary Nesta (Skrine)
See also CN 5, 6; INT CA-114; TCLE 1:1
Keates, Jonathan 1946(?)- .... **CLC 34**
See also CA 163; CANR 126
Keaton, Buster 1895-1966 .... **CLC 20**
See also CA 194
Keats, John 1795-1821 ...... **NCLC 8, 73, 121;
PC 1; WLC**
See also AAYA 58; BRW 4; BRWR 1; CD-
BLB 1789-1832; DA; DA3; DAB; DAC;
DAM MST, POET; DLB 96, 110; EXPP;
LMFS 1; PAB; PFS 1, 2, 3, 9, 17; RGEL
2; TEA; WLIT 3; WP
Keble, John 1792-1866 .... **NCLC 87**
See also DLB 32, 55; RGEL 2
Keene, Donald 1922- .... **CLC 34**
See also CA 1-4R; CANR 5, 119
Keillor, Garrison .... **CLC 40, 115**
See Keillor, Gary (Edward)
See also AAYA 2, 62; BEST 89:3; BPFB 2;
DLBY 1987; EWL 3; SATA 58; TUS
Keillor, Gary (Edward) 1942-
See Keillor, Garrison
See also CA 111; 117; CANR 36, 59, 124;
CPW; DA3; DAM POP; MTCW 1, 2;
MTFW 2005
Keith, Carlos
See Lewton, Val

Keith, Michael
See Hubbard, L(afayette) Ron(ald)
Keller, Gottfried 1819-1890 .... **NCLC 2; SSC
26**
See also CDWLB 2; DLB 129; EW; RGSF
2; RGWL 2, 3
Keller, Nora Okja 1965- .... **CLC 109**
See also CA 187
Kellerman, Jonathan 1949- .... **CLC 44**
See also AAYA 35; BEST 90:1; CA 106;
CANR 29, 51; CMW 4; CPW; DA3;
DAM POP; INT CANR-29
Kelley, William Melvin 1937- .... **CLC 22**
See also BW 1; CA 77-80; CANR 27, 83;
CN 1, 2, 3, 4, 5, 6, 7; DLB 33; EWL 3
Kellogg, Marjorie 1922-2005 .... **CLC 2**
See also CA 81-84
Kellow, Kathleen
See Hibbert, Eleanor Alice Burford
Kelly, Lauren
See Oates, Joyce Carol
Kelly, M(ilton) T(errence) 1947- ...... **CLC 55**
See also CA 97-100; CAAS 22; CANR 19,
43, 84; CN 6
Kelly, Robert 1935- .... **SSC 50**
See also CA 17-20R; CAAS 19; CANR 47;
CP 1, 2, 3, 4, 5, 6, 7; DLB 5, 130, 165
Kelman, James 1946- .... **CLC 58, 86**
See also BRWS 5; CA 148; CANR 85, 130;
CN 5, 6, 7; DLB 194, 319; RGSF 2;
WLIT 4
Kemal, Yasar
See Kemal, Yashar
See also CWW 2; EWL 3; WLIT 6
Kemal, Yashar 1923(?)- .... **CLC 14, 29**
See also CA 89-92; CANR 44
Kemble, Fanny 1809-1893 .... **NCLC 18**
See also DLB 32
Kemelman, Harry 1908-1996 .... **CLC 2**
See also AITN 1; BPFB 2; CA 9-12R; 155;
CANR 6, 71; CMW 4; DLB 28
Kempe, Margery 1373(?)-1440(?) ... **LC 6, 56**
See also DLB 146; FL 1:1; RGEL 2
Kempis, Thomas a 1380-1471 .... **LC 11**
Kendall, Henry 1839-1882 .... **NCLC 12**
See also DLB 230
Keneally, Thomas (Michael) 1935- ... **CLC 5,
8, 10, 14, 19, 27, 43, 117**
See also BRWS 4; CA 85-88; CANR 10,
50, 74, 130; CN 1, 2, 3, 4, 5, 6, 7; CPW;
DA3; DAM NOV; DLB 289, 299; EWL
3; MTCW 1, 2; MTFW 2005; NFS 17;
RGEL 2; RHW
Kennedy, A(lison) L(ouise) 1965- ... **CLC 188**
See also CA 168, 213; CAAE 213; CANR
108; CD 5, 6; CN 6, 7; DLB 271; RGSF
2
Kennedy, Adrienne (Lita) 1931- .... **BLC 2;
CLC 66; DC 5**
See also AFAW 2; BW 2, 3; CA 103; CAAS
20; CABS 3; CAD; CANR 26, 53, 82;
CD 5, 6; DAM MULT; DFS 9; DLB 38;
FW; MAL 5
Kennedy, John Pendleton
1795-1870 .... **NCLC 2**
See also DLB 3, 248, 254; RGAL 4
Kennedy, Joseph Charles 1929-
See Kennedy, X. J.
See also CA 1-4R, 201; CAAE 201; CANR
4, 30, 40; CWRI 5; MAICYA 2; MAIC-
YAS 1; SATA 14, 86, 130; SATA-Essay
130
Kennedy, William (Joseph) 1928- ..... **CLC 6,
28, 34, 53**
See also AAYA 1; AMWS 7; BPFB 2; CA
85-88; CANR 14, 31, 76, 134; CN 4, 5, 6,
7; DA3; DAM NOV; DLB 143; DLBY
1985; EWL 3; INT CANR-31; MAL 5;
MTCW 1, 2; MTFW 2005; SATA 57

Kennedy, X. J. .... **CLC 8, 42**
See Kennedy, Joseph Charles
See also AMWS 15; CAAS 9; CLR 27; CP
1, 2, 3, 4, 5, 6, 7; DLB 5; SAAS 22
Kenny, Maurice (Francis) 1929- ..... **CLC 87;
NNAL**
See also CA 144; CAAS 22; CANR 143;
DAM MULT; DLB 175
Kent, Kelvin
See Kuttner, Henry
Kenton, Maxwell
See Southern, Terry
Kenyon, Jane 1947-1995 .... **PC 57**
See also AAYA 63; AMWS 7; CA 118; 148;
CANR 44, 69; CP 7; CWP; DLB 120;
PFS 9, 17; RGAL 4
Kenyon, Robert O.
See Kuttner, Henry
Kepler, Johannes 1571-1630 .... **LC 45**
Ker, Jill
See Conway, Jill K(er)
Kerkow, H. C.
See Lewton, Val
Kerouac, Jack 1922-1969 ...... **CLC 1, 2, 3, 5,
14, 29, 61; TCLC 117; WLC**
See Kerouac, Jean-Louis Lebris de
See also AAYA 25; AMWC 1; AMWS 3;
BG 3; BPFB 2; CDALB 1941-1968; CP
1; CPW; DLB 2, 16, 237; DLBD 3;
DLBY 1995; EWL 3; GLL 1; LATS 1:2;
LMFS 2; MAL 5; NFS 8; RGAL 4; TUS;
WP
Kerouac, Jean-Louis Lebris de 1922-1969
See Kerouac, Jack
See also AITN 1; CA 5-8R; 25-28R; CANR
26, 54, 95; DA; DA3; DAB; DAC; DAM
MST, NOV, POET; MTCW 1, 2;
MTFW 2005
Kerr, (Bridget) Jean (Collins)
1923(?)-2003 .... **CLC 22**
See also CA 5-8R; 212; CANR 7; INT
CANR-7
Kerr, M. E. .... **CLC 12, 35**
See Meaker, Marijane (Agnes)
See also AAYA 2, 23; BYA 1, 7, 8; CLR
29; SAAS 1; WYA
Kerr, Robert .... **CLC 55**
Kerrigan, (Thomas) Anthony 1918- .. **CLC 4,
6**
See also CA 49-52; CAAS 11; CANR 4
Kerry, Lois
See Duncan, Lois
Kesey, Ken (Elton) 1935-2001 ... **CLC 1, 3, 6,
11, 46, 64, 184; WLC**
See also AAYA 25; BG 1:3; BPFB 2; CA
1-4R; 204; CANR 22, 38, 66, 124;
CDALB 1968-1988; CN 1, 2, 3, 4, 5, 6,
7; CPW; DA; DA3; DAB; DAC; DAM
MST, NOV, POP; DLB 2, 16, 206; EWL
3; EXPN; LAIT 4; MAL 5; MTCW 1, 2;
MTFW 2005; NFS 2; RGAL 4; SATA 66;
SATA-Obit 131; TUS; YAW
Kesselring, Joseph (Otto)
1902-1967 .... **CLC 45**
See also CA 150; DAM DRAM, MST; DFS
20
Kessler, Jascha (Frederick) 1929- ...... **CLC 4**
See also CA 17-20R; CANR 8, 48, 111; CP
1
Kettelkamp, Larry (Dale) 1933- .... **CLC 12**
See also CA 29-32R; CANR 16; SAAS 3;
SATA 2
Key, Ellen (Karolina Sofia)
1849-1926 .... **TCLC 65**
See also DLB 259
Keyber, Conny
See Fielding, Henry

Kubrick, Stanley 1928-1999 .... **CLC 16; TCLC 112**
See also AAYA 30; CA 81-84; 177; CANR 33; DLB 26

Kumin, Maxine (Winokur) 1925- ..... **CLC 5, 13, 28, 164; PC 15**
See also AITN 2; AMWS 4; ANW; CA 1-4R; CAAS 8; CANR 1, 21, 69, 115, 140; CP 2, 3, 4, 5, 6, 7; CWP; DA3; DAM POET; DLB 5; EWL 3; EXPP; MTCW 1, 2; MTFW 2005; PAB; PFS 18; SATA 12

Kundera, Milan 1929- . **CLC 4, 9, 19, 32, 68, 115, 135; SSC 24**
See also AAYA 2, 62; BPFB 2; CA 85-88; CANR 19, 52, 74, 144; CDWLB 4; CWW 2; DA3; DAM NOV; DLB 232; EW 13; EWL 3; MTCW 1, 2; MTFW 2005; NFS 18; RGSF 2; RGWL 3; SSFS 10

Kunene, Mazisi (Raymond) 1930- ... **CLC 85**
See also BW 1, 3; CA 125; CANR 81; CP 1, 7; DLB 117

Kung, Hans .... **CLC 130**
See Kung, Hans

Kung, Hans 1928-
See Kung, Hans
See also CA 53-56; CANR 66, 134; MTCW 1, 2; MTFW 2005

Kunikida Doppo 1869(?)-1908
See Doppo, Kunikida
See also DLB 180; EWL 3

Kunitz, Stanley (Jasspon) 1905- .. **CLC 6, 11, 14, 148; PC 19**
See also AMWS 3; CA 41-44R; CANR 26, 57, 98; CP 1, 2, 3, 4, 5, 6, 7; DLB 48; INT CANR-26; MAL 5; MTCW 1, 2; MTFW 2005; PFS 11; RGAL 4

Kunze, Reiner 1933- .... **CLC 10**
See also CA 93-96; CWW 2; DLB 75; EWL 3

Kuprin, Aleksander Ivanovich 1870-1938 .... **TCLC 5**
See Kuprin, Aleksandr Ivanovich; Kuprin, Alexandr Ivanovich
See also CA 104; 182

Kuprin, Aleksandr Ivanovich
See Kuprin, Aleksander Ivanovich
See also DLB 295

Kuprin, Alexandr Ivanovich
See Kuprin, Aleksander Ivanovich
See also EWL 3

Kureishi, Hanif 1954- .. **CLC 64, 135; DC 26**
See also BRWS 11; CA 139; CANR 113; CBD; CD 5, 6; CN 6, 7; DLB 194, 245; GLL 2; IDFW 4; WLIT 4; WWE 1

Kurosawa, Akira 1910-1998 ..... **CLC 16, 119**
See also AAYA 11, 64; CA 101; 170; CANR 46; DAM MULT

Kushner, Tony 1956- .... **CLC 81, 203; DC 10**
See also AAYA 61; AMWS 9; CA 144; CAD; CANR 74, 130; CD 5, 6; DA3; DAM DRAM; DFS 5; DLB 228; EWL 3; GLL 1; LAIT 5; MAL 5; MTCW 2; MTFW 2005; RGAL 4; SATA 160

Kuttner, Henry 1915-1958 .... **TCLC 10**
See also CA 107; 157; DLB 8; FANT; SCFW 1, 2; SFW 4

Kutty, Madhavi
See Das, Kamala

Kuzma, Greg 1944- .... **CLC 7**
See also CA 33-36R; CANR 70

Kuzmin, Mikhail (Alekseevich) 1872(?)-1936 .... **TCLC 40**
See also CA 170; DLB 295; EWL 3

Kyd, Thomas 1558-1594 .. **DC 3; LC 22, 125**
See also BRW 1; DAM DRAM; DFS 21; DLB 62; IDTP; LMFS 1; RGEL 2; TEA; WLIT 3

Kyprianos, Iossif
See Samarakis, Antonis

L. S.
See Stephen, Sir Leslie

Laȝamon
See Layamon
See also DLB 146

Labe, Louise 1521-1566 .... **LC 120**

Labrunie, Gerard
See Nerval, Gerard de

La Bruyere, Jean de 1645-1696 .... **LC 17**
See also DLB 268; EW 3; GFL Beginnings to 1789

Lacan, Jacques (Marie Emile) 1901-1981 .... **CLC 75**
See also CA 121; 104; DLB 296; EWL 3; TWA

Laclos, Pierre-Ambroise Francois 1741-1803 .... **NCLC 4, 87**
See also DLB 313; EW 4; GFL Beginnings to 1789; RGWL 2, 3

Lacolere, Francois
See Aragon, Louis

La Colere, Francois
See Aragon, Louis

La Deshabilleuse
See Simenon, Georges (Jacques Christian)

Lady Gregory
See Gregory, Lady Isabella Augusta (Persse)

Lady of Quality, A
See Bagnold, Enid

La Fayette, Marie-(Madelaine Pioche de la Vergne) 1634-1693 .... **LC 2**
See Lafayette, Marie-Madeleine
See also GFL Beginnings to 1789; RGWL 2, 3

Lafayette, Marie-Madeleine
See La Fayette, Marie-(Madelaine Pioche de la Vergne)
See also DLB 268

Lafayette, Rene
See Hubbard, L(afayette) Ron(ald)

La Flesche, Francis 1857(?)-1932 ...... **NNAL**
See also CA 144; CANR 83; DLB 175

La Fontaine, Jean de 1621-1695 .... **LC 50**
See also DLB 268; EW 3; GFL Beginnings to 1789; MAICYA 1, 2; RGWL 2, 3; SATA 18

Laforet, Carmen 1921-2004 .... **CLC 219**
See also CWW 2; DLB 322; EWL 3

Laforgue, Jules 1860-1887 . **NCLC 5, 53; PC 14; SSC 20**
See also DLB 217; EW 7; GFL 1789 to the Present; RGWL 2, 3

Lagerkvist, Paer (Fabian) 1891-1974 ..... **CLC 7, 10, 13, 54; TCLC 144**
See Lagerkvist, Par
See also CA 85-88; 49-52; DA3; DAM DRAM, NOV; MTCW 1, 2; MTFW 2005; TWA

Lagerkvist, Par .... **SSC 12**
See Lagerkvist, Paer (Fabian)
See also DLB 259; EW 10; EWL 3; RGSF 2; RGWL 2, 3

Lagerloef, Selma (Ottiliana Lovisa) .... **TCLC 4, 36**
See Lagerlof, Selma (Ottiliana Lovisa)
See also CA 108; MTCW 2

Lagerlof, Selma (Ottiliana Lovisa) 1858-1940
See Lagerloef, Selma (Ottiliana Lovisa)
See also CA 188; CLR 7; DLB 259; RGWL 2, 3; SATA 15; SSFS 18

La Guma, (Justin) Alex(ander) 1925-1985 . **BLCS; CLC 19; TCLC 140**
See also AFW; BW 1, 3; CA 49-52; 118; CANR 25, 81; CDWLB 3; CN 1, 2, 3; CP 1; DAM NOV; DLB 117, 225; EWL 3; MTCW 1, 2; MTFW 2005; WLIT 2; WWE 1

Laidlaw, A. K.
See Grieve, C(hristopher) M(urray)

Lainez, Manuel Mujica
See Mujica Lainez, Manuel
See also HW 1

Laing, R(onald) D(avid) 1927-1989 . **CLC 95**
See also CA 107; 129; CANR 34; MTCW 1

Laishley, Alex
See Booth, Martin

Lamartine, Alphonse (Marie Louis Prat) de 1790-1869 .... **NCLC 11; PC 16**
See also DAM POET; DLB 217; GFL 1789 to the Present; RGWL 2, 3

Lamb, Charles 1775-1834 ..... **NCLC 10, 113; WLC**
See also BRW 4; CDBLB 1789-1832; DA; DAB; DAC; DAM MST; DLB 93, 107, 163; RGEL 2; SATA 17; TEA

Lamb, Lady Caroline 1785-1828 ... **NCLC 38**
See also DLB 116

Lamb, Mary Ann 1764-1847 .... **NCLC 125**
See also DLB 163; SATA 17

Lame Deer 1903(?)-1976 .... **NNAL**
See also CA 69-72

Lamming, George (William) 1927- ... **BLC 2; CLC 2, 4, 66, 144**
See also BW 2, 3; CA 85-88; CANR 26, 76; CDWLB 3; CN 1, 2, 3, 4, 5, 6, 7; CP 1; DAM MULT; DLB 125; EWL 3; MTCW 1, 2; MTFW 2005; NFS 15; RGEL 2

L'Amour, Louis (Dearborn) 1908-1988 .... **CLC 25, 55**
See also AAYA 16; AITN 2; BEST 89:2; BPFB 2; CA 1-4R; 125; CANR 3, 25, 40; CPW; DA3; DAM NOV, POP; DLB 206; DLBY 1980; MTCW 1, 2; MTFW 2005; RGAL 4; TCWW 1, 2

Lampedusa, Giuseppe (Tomasi) di .... **TCLC 13**
See Tomasi di Lampedusa, Giuseppe
See also CA 164; EW 11; MTCW 2; MTFW 2005; RGWL 2, 3

Lampman, Archibald 1861-1899 ... **NCLC 25**
See also DLB 92; RGEL 2; TWA

Lancaster, Bruce 1896-1963 .... **CLC 36**
See also CA 9-10; CANR 70; CAP 1; SATA 9

Lanchester, John 1962- .... **CLC 99**
See also CA 194; DLB 267

Landau, Mark Alexandrovich
See Aldanov, Mark (Alexandrovich)

Landau-Aldanov, Mark Alexandrovich
See Aldanov, Mark (Alexandrovich)

Landis, Jerry
See Simon, Paul (Frederick)

Landis, John 1950- .... **CLC 26**
See also CA 112; 122; CANR 128

Landolfi, Tommaso 1908-1979 .... **CLC 11, 49**
See also CA 127; 117; DLB 177; EWL 3

Landon, Letitia Elizabeth 1802-1838 .... **NCLC 15**
See also DLB 96

Landor, Walter Savage 1775-1864 .... **NCLC 14**
See also BRW 4; DLB 93, 107; RGEL 2

Landwirth, Heinz 1927-
See Lind, Jakov
See also CA 9-12R; CANR 7

Lane, Patrick 1939- .... **CLC 25**
See also CA 97-100; CANR 54; CP 3, 4, 5, 6, 7; DAM POET; DLB 53; INT CA-97-100

Lane, Rose Wilder 1887-1968 ...... **TCLC 177**
See also CA 102; CANR 63; SATA 28, 29; TCWW 2

Limonov, Eduard
See Limonov, Edward
See also DLB 317

Limonov, Edward 1944- .... CLC 67
See Limonov, Eduard
See also CA 137

Lin, Frank
See Atherton, Gertrude (Franklin Horn)

Lin, Yutang 1895-1976 .... TCLC 149
See also CA 45-48; 65-68; CANR 2; RGAL 4

Lincoln, Abraham 1809-1865 .... NCLC 18
See also LAIT 2

Lind, Jakov .... CLC 1, 2, 4, 27, 82
See Landwirth, Heinz
See also CAAS 4; DLB 299; EWL 3

Lindbergh, Anne (Spencer) Morrow
1906-2001 .... CLC 82
See also BPFB 2; CA 17-20R; 193; CANR
16, 73; DAM NOV; MTCW 1, 2; MTFW
2005; SATA 33; SATA-Obit 125; TUS

Lindsay, David 1878(?)-1945 .... TCLC 15
See also CA 113; 187; DLB 255; FANT;
SFW 4; SUFW 1

Lindsay, (Nicholas) Vachel
1879-1931 .... PC 23; TCLC 17; WLC
See also AMWS 1; CA 114; 135; CANR
79; CDALB 1865-1917; DA; DA3; DAC;
DAM MST, POET; DLB 54; EWL 3;
EXPP; MAL 5; RGAL 4; SATA 40; WP

Linke-Poot
See Doeblin, Alfred

Linney, Romulus 1930- .... CLC 51
See also CA 1-4R; CAD; CANR 40, 44,
79; CD 5, 6; CSW; RGAL 4

Linton, Eliza Lynn 1822-1898 .... NCLC 41
See also DLB 18

Li Po 701-763 .... CMLC 2; PC 29
See also PFS 20; WP

Lipsius, Justus 1547-1606 .... LC 16

Lipsyte, Robert (Michael) 1938- ..... CLC 21
See also AAYA 7, 45; CA 17-20R; CANR
8, 57; CLR 23, 76; DA; DAC; DAM
MST, NOV; JRDA; LAIT 5; MAICYA 1,
2; SATA 5, 68, 113, 161; WYA; YAW

Lish, Gordon (Jay) 1934- ... CLC 45; SSC 18
See also CA 113; 117; CANR 79; DLB 130;
INT CA-117

Lispector, Clarice 1925(?)-1977 .... CLC 43;
HLCS 2; SSC 34
See also CA 139; 116; CANR 71; CDWLB
3; DLB 113, 307; DNFS 1; EWL 3; FW;
HW 2; LAW; RGSF 2; RGWL 2, 3; WLIT
1

Littell, Robert 1935(?)- .... CLC 42
See also CA 109; 112; CANR 64, 115;
CMW 4

Little, Malcolm 1925-1965
See Malcolm X
See also BW 1, 3; CA 125; 111; CANR 82;
DA; DA3; DAB; DAC; DAM MST,
MULT; MTCW 1, 2; MTFW 2005

Littlewit, Humphrey Gent.
See Lovecraft, H(oward) P(hillips)

Litwos
See Sienkiewicz, Henryk (Adam Alexander
Pius)

Liu, E. 1857-1909 .... TCLC 15
See also CA 115; 190

Lively, Penelope 1933- .... CLC 32, 50
See also BPFB 2; CA 41-44R; CANR 29,
67, 79, 131; CLR 7; CN 5, 6, 7; CWRI 5;
DAM NOV; DLB 14, 161, 207; FANT;
JRDA; MAICYA 1, 2; MTCW 1, 2;
MTFW 2005; SATA 7, 60, 101, 164; TEA

Lively, Penelope Margaret
See Lively, Penelope

Livesay, Dorothy (Kathleen)
1909-1996 .... CLC 4, 15, 79
See also AITN 2; CA 25-28R; CAAS 8;
CANR 36, 67; CP 1, 2, 3, 4; DAC; DAM
MST, POET; DLB 68; FW; MTCW 1;
RGEL 2; TWA

Livy c. 59B.C.-c. 12 .... CMLC 11
See also AW 2; CDWLB 1; DLB 211;
RGWL 2, 3

Lizardi, Jose Joaquin Fernandez de
1776-1827 .... NCLC 30
See also LAW

Llewellyn, Richard
See Llewellyn Lloyd, Richard Dafydd Vivian
See also DLB 15

Llewellyn Lloyd, Richard Dafydd Vivian
1906-1983 .... CLC 7, 80
See Llewellyn, Richard
See also CA 53-56; 111; CANR 7, 71;
SATA 11; SATA-Obit 37

Llosa, (Jorge) Mario (Pedro) Vargas
See Vargas Llosa, (Jorge) Mario (Pedro)
See also RGWL 3

Llosa, Mario Vargas
See Vargas Llosa, (Jorge) Mario (Pedro)

Lloyd, Manda
See Mander, (Mary) Jane

Lloyd Webber, Andrew 1948-
See Webber, Andrew Lloyd
See also AAYA 1, 38; CA 116; 149; DAM
DRAM; SATA 56

Llull, Ramon c. 1235-c. 1316 .... CMLC 12

Lobb, Ebenezer
See Upward, Allen

Locke, Alain (Le Roy)
1886-1954 .... BLCS; HR 1:3; TCLC 43
See also AMWS 14; BW 1, 3; CA 106; 124;
CANR 79; DLB 51; LMFS 2; MAL 5;
RGAL 4

Locke, John 1632-1704 .... LC 7, 35
See also DLB 31, 101, 213, 252; RGEL 2;
WLIT 3

Locke-Elliott, Sumner
See Elliott, Sumner Locke

Lockhart, John Gibson 1794-1854 .. NCLC 6
See also DLB 110, 116, 144

Lockridge, Ross (Franklin), Jr.
1914-1948 .... TCLC 111
See also CA 108; 145; CANR 79; DLB 143;
DLBY 1980; MAL 5; RGAL 4; RHW

Lockwood, Robert
See Johnson, Robert

Lodge, David (John) 1935- ...... CLC 36, 141
See also BEST 90:1; BRWS 4; CA 17-20R;
CANR 19, 53, 92, 139; CN 1, 2, 3, 4, 5,
6, 7; CPW; DAM POP; DLB 14, 194;
EWL 3; INT CANR-19; MTCW 1, 2;
MTFW 2005

Lodge, Thomas 1558-1625 .... LC 41
See also DLB 172; RGEL 2

Loewinsohn, Ron(ald William)
1937- .... CLC 52
See also CA 25-28R; CANR 71; CP 1, 2, 3,
4

Logan, Jake
See Smith, Martin Cruz

Logan, John (Burton) 1923-1987 .... CLC 5
See also CA 77-80; 124; CANR 45; CP 1,
2, 3, 4; DLB 5

Lo Kuan-chung 1330(?)-1400(?) .... LC 12

Lombard, Nap
See Johnson, Pamela Hansford

Lombard, Peter 1100(?)-1160(?) ... CMLC 72

London, Jack 1876-1916 .. SSC 4, 49; TCLC
9, 15, 39; WLC
See London, John Griffith
See also AAYA 13; AITN 2; AMW; BPFB
2; BYA 4, 13; CDALB 1865-1917; DLB
8, 12, 78, 212; EWL 3; EXPS; LAIT 3;
MAL 5; NFS 8; RGAL 4; RGSF 2; SATA
18; SFW 4; SSFS 7; TCWW 1, 2; TUS;
WYA; YAW

London, John Griffith 1876-1916
See London, Jack
See also CA 110; 119; CANR 73; DA; DA3;
DAB; DAC; DAM MST, NOV; JRDA;
MAICYA 1, 2; MTCW 1, 2; MTFW 2005;
NFS 19

Long, Emmett
See Leonard, Elmore (John, Jr.)

Longbaugh, Harry
See Goldman, William (W.)

Longfellow, Henry Wadsworth
1807-1882 .... NCLC 2, 45, 101, 103; PC
30; WLCS
See also AMW; AMWR 2; CDALB 1640-
1865; CLR 99; DA; DA3; DAB; DAC;
DAM MST, POET; DLB 1, 59, 235;
EXPP; PAB; PFS 2, 7, 17; RGAL 4;
SATA 19; TUS; WP

Longinus c. 1st cent. - .... CMLC 27
See also AW 2; DLB 176

Longley, Michael 1939- .... CLC 29
See also BRWS 8; CA 102; CP 1, 2, 3, 4, 5,
6, 7; DLB 40

Longstreet, Augustus Baldwin
1790-1870 .... NCLC 159
See also DLB 3, 11, 74, 248; RGAL 4

Longus fl. c. 2nd cent. - .... CMLC 7

Longway, A. Hugh
See Lang, Andrew

Lonnbohm, Armas Eino Leopold 1878-1926
See Leino, Eino
See also CA 123

Lonnrot, Elias 1802-1884 .... NCLC 53
See also EFS 1

Lonsdale, Roger ed. .... CLC 65

Lopate, Phillip 1943- .... CLC 29
See also CA 97-100; CANR 88; DLBY
1980; INT CA-97-100

Lopez, Barry (Holstun) 1945- .... CLC 70
See also AAYA 9, 63; ANW; CA 65-68;
CANR 7, 23, 47, 68, 92; DLB 256, 275;
INT CANR-7, -23; MTCW 1; RGAL 4;
SATA 67

Lopez de Mendoza, Inigo
See Santillana, Inigo Lopez de Mendoza,
Marques de

Lopez Portillo (y Pacheco), Jose
1920-2004 .... CLC 46
See also CA 129; 224; HW 1

Lopez y Fuentes, Gregorio
1897(?)-1966 .... CLC 32
See also CA 131; EWL 3; HW 1

Lorca, Federico Garcia
See Garcia Lorca, Federico
See also DFS 4; EW 11; PFS 20; RGWL 2,
3; WP

Lord, Audre
See Lorde, Audre (Geraldine)
See also EWL 3

Lord, Bette Bao 1938- .... AAL; CLC 23
See also BEST 90:3; BPFB 2; CA 107;
CANR 41, 79; INT CA-107; SATA 58

Lord Auch
See Bataille, Georges

Lord Brooke
See Greville, Fulke

Lord Byron
See Byron, George Gordon (Noel)

Lorde, Audre (Geraldine)
1934-1992 .... BLC 2; CLC 18, 71; PC
12; TCLC 173
See Domini, Rey; Lord, Audre
See also AFAW 1, 2; BW 1, 3; CA 25-28R;
142; CANR 16, 26, 46, 82; CP 2, 3, 4;

DA3; DAM MULT, POET; DLB 41; FW; MAL 5; MTCW 1, 2; MTFW 2005; PFS 16; RGAL 4

Lord Houghton
See Milnes, Richard Monckton

Lord Jeffrey
See Jeffrey, Francis

Loreaux, Nichol .... CLC 65

Lorenzini, Carlo 1826-1890
See Collodi, Carlo
See also MAICYA 1, 2; SATA 29, 100

Lorenzo, Heberto Padilla
See Padilla (Lorenzo), Heberto

Loris
See Hofmannsthal, Hugo von

Loti, Pierre .... TCLC 11
See Viaud, (Louis Marie) Julien
See also DLB 123; GFL 1789 to the Present

Lou, Henri
See Andreas-Salome, Lou

Louie, David Wong 1954- .... CLC 70
See also CA 139; CANR 120

Louis, Adrian C. .... NNAL
See also CA 223

Louis, Father M.
See Merton, Thomas (James)

Louise, Heidi
See Erdrich, (Karen) Louise

Lovecraft, H(oward) P(hillips)
1890-1937 .... SSC 3, 52; TCLC 4, 22
See also AAYA 14; BPFB 2; CA 104; 133; CANR 106; DA3; DAM POP; HGG; MTCW 1, 2; MTFW 2005; RGAL 4; SCFW 1, 2; SFW 4; SUFW

Lovelace, Earl 1935- .... CLC 51
See also BW 2; CA 77-80; CANR 41, 72, 114; CD 5, 6; CDWLB 3; CN 1, 2, 3, 4, 5, 6, 7; DLB 125; EWL 3; MTCW 1

Lovelace, Richard 1618-1657 . LC 24; PC 69
See also BRW 2; DLB 131; EXPP; PAB; RGEL 2

Lowe, Pardee 1904- .... AAL

Lowell, Amy 1874-1925 ... PC 13; TCLC 1, 8
See also AAYA 57; AMW; CA 104; 151; DAM POET; DLB 54, 140; EWL 3; EXPP; LMFS 2; MAL 5; MAWW; MTCW 2; MTFW 2005; RGAL 4; TUS

Lowell, James Russell 1819-1891 ... NCLC 2, 90
See also AMWS 1; CDALB 1640-1865; DLB 1, 11, 64, 79, 189, 235; RGAL 4

Lowell, Robert (Traill Spence, Jr.)
1917-1977 ..... CLC 1, 2, 3, 4, 5, 8, 9, 11, 15, 37, 124; PC 3; WLC
See also AMW; AMWC 2; AMWR 2; CA 9-12R; 73-76; CABS 2; CAD; CANR 26, 60; CDALBS; CP 1, 2; DA; DA3; DAB; DAC; DAM MST, NOV; DLB 5, 169; EWL 3; MAL 5; MTCW 1, 2; MTFW 2005; PAB; PFS 6, 7; RGAL 4; WP

Lowenthal, Michael (Francis)
1969- .... CLC 119
See also CA 150; CANR 115

Lowndes, Marie Adelaide (Belloc)
1868-1947 .... TCLC 12
See also CA 107; CMW 4; DLB 70; RHW

Lowry, (Clarence) Malcolm
1909-1957 .... SSC 31; TCLC 6, 40
See also BPFB 2; BRWS 3; CA 105; 131; CANR 62, 105; CDBLB 1945-1960; DLB 15; EWL 3; MTCW 1, 2; MTFW 2005; RGAL 2

Lowry, Mina Gertrude 1882-1966
See Loy, Mina
See also CA 113

Loxsmith, John
See Brunner, John (Kilian Houston)

Loy, Mina .... CLC 28; PC 16
See Lowry, Mina Gertrude
See also DAM POET; DLB 4, 54; PFS 20

Loyson-Bridet
See Schwob, Marcel (Mayer Andre)

Lucan 39-65 .... CMLC 33
See also AW 2; DLB 211; EFS 2; RGWL 2, 3

Lucas, Craig 1951- .... CLC 64
See also CA 137; CAD; CANR 71, 109, 142; CD 5, 6; GLL 2; MTFW 2005

Lucas, E(dward) V(errall)
1868-1938 .... TCLC 73
See also CA 176; DLB 98, 149, 153; SATA 20

Lucas, George 1944- .... CLC 16
See also AAYA 1, 23; CA 77-80; CANR 30; SATA 56

Lucas, Hans
See Godard, Jean-Luc

Lucas, Victoria
See Plath, Sylvia

Lucian c. 125-c. 180 .... CMLC 32
See also AW 2; DLB 176; RGWL 2, 3

Lucilius c. 180 B.C.-c. 101-02
B.C. .... CMLC 82
See also DLB 211

Lucretius c. 94B.C.-c. 49B.C. .... CMLC 48
See also AW 2; CDWLB 1; DLB 211; EFS 2; RGWL 2, 3

Ludlam, Charles 1943-1987 .... CLC 46, 50
See also CA 85-88; 122; CAD; CANR 72, 86; DLB 266

Ludlum, Robert 1927-2001 .... CLC 22, 43
See also AAYA 10, 59; BEST 89:1, 90:3; BPFB 2; CA 33-36R; 195; CANR 25, 41, 68, 105, 131; CMW 4; CPW; DA3; DAM NOV, POP; DLBY 1982; MSW; MTCW 1, 2; MTFW 2005

Ludwig, Ken 1950- .... CLC 60
See also CA 195; CAD; CD 6

Ludwig, Otto 1813-1865 .... NCLC 4
See also DLB 129

Lugones, Leopoldo 1874-1938 .... HLCS 2; TCLC 15
See also CA 116; 131; CANR 104; DLB 283; EWL 3; HW 1; LAW

Lu Hsun .... SSC 20; TCLC 3
See Shu-Jen, Chou
See also EWL 3

Lukacs, George .... CLC 24
See Lukacs, Gyorgy (Szegeny von)

Lukacs, Gyorgy (Szegeny von) 1885-1971
See Lukacs, George
See also CA 101; 29-32R; CANR 62; CD-WLB 4; DLB 215, 242; EW 10; EWL 3; MTCW 1, 2

Luke, Peter (Ambrose Cyprian)
1919-1995 .... CLC 38
See also CA 81-84; 147; CANR 72; CBD; CD 5, 6; DLB 13

Lunar, Dennis
See Mungo, Raymond

Lurie, Alison 1926- ..... CLC 4, 5, 18, 39, 175
See also BPFB 2; CA 1-4R; CANR 2, 17, 50, 88; CN 1, 2, 3, 4, 5, 6, 7; DLB 2; MAL 5; MTCW 1; SATA 46, 112; TCLE 1:1

Lustig, Arnost 1926- .... CLC 56
See also AAYA 3; CA 69-72; CANR 47, 102; CWW 2; DLB 232, 299; EWL 3; SATA 56

Luther, Martin 1483-1546 .... LC 9, 37
See also CDWLB 2; DLB 179; EW 2; RGWL 2, 3

Luxemburg, Rosa 1870(?)-1919 ..... TCLC 63
See also CA 118

Luzi, Mario (Egidio Vincenzo)
1914-2005 .... CLC 13
See also CA 61-64; 236; CANR 9, 70; CWW 2; DLB 128; EWL 3

L'vov, Arkady .... CLC 59

Lydgate, John c. 1370-1450(?) .... LC 81
See also BRW 1; DLB 146; RGEL 2

Lyly, John 1554(?)-1606 .... DC 7; LC 41
See also BRW 1; DAM DRAM; DLB 62, 167; RGEL 2

L'Ymagier
See Gourmont, Remy(-Marie-Charles) de

Lynch, B. Suarez
See Borges, Jorge Luis

Lynch, David (Keith) 1946- ...... CLC 66, 162
See also AAYA 55; CA 124; 129; CANR 111

Lynch, James
See Andreyev, Leonid (Nikolaevich)

Lyndsay, Sir David 1485-1555 .... LC 20
See also RGEL 2

Lynn, Kenneth S(chuyler)
1923-2001 .... CLC 50
See also CA 1-4R; 196; CANR 3, 27, 65

Lynx
See West, Rebecca

Lyons, Marcus
See Blish, James (Benjamin)

Lyotard, Jean-Francois
1924-1998 .... TCLC 103
See also DLB 242; EWL 3

Lyre, Pinchbeck
See Sassoon, Siegfried (Lorraine)

Lytle, Andrew (Nelson) 1902-1995 ... CLC 22
See also CA 9-12R; 150; CANR 70; CN 1, 2, 3, 4, 5, 6; CSW; DLB 6; DLBY 1995; RGAL 4; RHW

Lyttelton, George 1709-1773 .... LC 10
See also RGEL 2

Lytton of Knebworth, Baron
See Bulwer-Lytton, Edward (George Earle Lytton)

Maas, Peter 1929-2001 .... CLC 29
See also CA 93-96; 201; INT CA-93-96; MTCW 2; MTFW 2005

Mac A'Ghobhainn, Iain
See Smith, Iain Crichton

Macaulay, Catherine 1731-1791 .... LC 64
See also DLB 104

Macaulay, (Emilie) Rose
1881(?)-1958 .... TCLC 7, 44
See also CA 104; DLB 36; EWL 3; RGEL 2; RHW

Macaulay, Thomas Babington
1800-1859 .... NCLC 42
See also BRW 4; CDBLB 1832-1890; DLB 32, 55; RGEL 2

MacBeth, George (Mann)
1932-1992 .... CLC 2, 5, 9
See also CA 25-28R; 136; CANR 61, 66; CP 1, 2, 3, 4; DLB 40; MTCW 1; PFS 8; SATA 4; SATA-Obit 70

MacCaig, Norman (Alexander)
1910-1996 .... CLC 36
See also BRWS 6; CA 9-12R; CANR 3, 34; CP 1, 2, 3, 4; DAB; DAM POET; DLB 27; EWL 3; RGEL 2

MacCarthy, Sir (Charles Otto) Desmond
1877-1952 .... TCLC 36
See also CA 167

MacDiarmid, Hugh .... CLC 2, 4, 11, 19, 63; PC 9
See Grieve, C(hristopher) M(urray)
See also CDBLB 1945-1960; CP 1, 2; DLB 20; EWL 3; RGEL 2

MacDonald, Anson
See Heinlein, Robert A(nson)

Macdonald, Cynthia 1928- .... **CLC 13, 19**
See also CA 49-52; CANR 4, 44, 146; DLB 105

MacDonald, George 1824-1905 .... **TCLC 9, 113**
See also AAYA 57; BYA 5; CA 106; 137; CANR 80; CLR 67; DLB 18, 163, 178; FANT; MAICYA 1, 2; RGEL 2; SATA 33, 100; SFW 4; SUFW; WCH

Macdonald, John
See Millar, Kenneth

MacDonald, John D(ann)
1916-1986 .... **CLC 3, 27, 44**
See also BPFB 2; CA 1-4R; 121; CANR 1, 19, 60; CMW 4; CPW; DAM NOV, POP; DLB 8, 306; DLBY 1986; MSW; MTCW 1, 2; MTFW 2005; SFW 4

Macdonald, John Ross
See Millar, Kenneth

Macdonald, Ross ..... **CLC 1, 2, 3, 14, 34, 41**
See Millar, Kenneth
See also AMWS 4; BPFB 2; CN 1, 2, 3; DLBD 6; MSW; RGAL 4

MacDougal, John
See Blish, James (Benjamin)

MacDougal, John
See Blish, James (Benjamin)

MacDowell, John
See Parks, Tim(othy Harold)

MacEwen, Gwendolyn (Margaret)
1941-1987 .... **CLC 13, 55**
See also CA 9-12R; 124; CANR 7, 22; CP 1, 2, 3, 4; DLB 53, 251; SATA 50; SATA-Obit 55

Macha, Karel Hynek 1810-1846 .... **NCLC 46**

Machado (y Ruiz), Antonio
1875-1939 .... **TCLC 3**
See also CA 104; 174; DLB 108; EW 9; EWL 3; HW 2; PFS 23; RGWL 2, 3

Machado de Assis, Joaquim Maria
1839-1908 .... **BLC 2; HLCS 2; SSC 24; TCLC 10**
See also CA 107; 153; CANR 91; DLB 307; LAW; RGSF 2; RGWL 2, 3; TWA; WLIT 1

Machaut, Guillaume de c.
1300-1377 .... **CMLC 64**
See also DLB 208

Machen, Arthur .... **SSC 20; TCLC 4**
See Jones, Arthur Llewellyn
See also CA 179; DLB 156, 178; RGEL 2; SUFW 1

Machiavelli, Niccolo 1469-1527 ... **DC 16; LC 8, 36; WLCS**
See also AAYA 58; DA; DAB; DAC; DAM MST; EW 2; LAIT 1; LMFS 1; NFS 9; RGWL 2, 3; TWA; WLIT 7

MacInnes, Colin 1914-1976 .... **CLC 4, 23**
See also CA 69-72; 65-68; CANR 21; CN 1, 2; DLB 14; MTCW 1, 2; RGEL 2; RHW

MacInnes, Helen (Clark)
1907-1985 .... **CLC 27, 39**
See also BPFB 2; CA 1-4R; 117; CANR 1, 28, 58; CMW 4; CN 1, 2; CPW; DAM POP; DLB 87; MSW; MTCW 1, 2; MTFW 2005; SATA 22; SATA-Obit 44

Mackay, Mary 1855-1924
See Corelli, Marie
See also CA 118; 177; FANT; RHW

Mackay, Shena 1944- .... **CLC 195**
See also CA 104; CANR 88, 139; DLB 231, 319; MTFW 2005

Mackenzie, Compton (Edward Montague)
1883-1972 .... **CLC 18; TCLC 116**
See also CA 21-22; 37-40R; CAP 2; CN 1; DLB 34, 100; RGEL 2

Mackenzie, Henry 1745-1831 .... **NCLC 41**
See also DLB 39; RGEL 2

Mackey, Nathaniel (Ernest) 1947- .... **PC 49**
See also CA 153; CANR 114; CP 7; DLB 169

MacKinnon, Catharine A. 1946- .... **CLC 181**
See also CA 128; 132; CANR 73, 140; FW; MTCW 2; MTFW 2005

Mackintosh, Elizabeth 1896(?)-1952
See Tey, Josephine
See also CA 110; CMW 4

MacLaren, James
See Grieve, C(hristopher) M(urray)

MacLaverty, Bernard 1942- .... **CLC 31**
See also CA 116; 118; CANR 43, 88; CN 5, 6, 7; DLB 267; INT CA-118; RGSF 2

MacLean, Alistair (Stuart)
1922(?)-1987 .... **CLC 3, 13, 50, 63**
See also CA 57-60; 121; CANR 28, 61; CMW 4; CP 2, 3, 4, 5, 6, 7; CPW; DAM POP; DLB 276; MTCW 1; SATA 23; SATA-Obit 50; TCWW 2

Maclean, Norman (Fitzroy)
1902-1990 .... **CLC 78; SSC 13**
See also AMWS 14; CA 102; 132; CANR 49; CPW; DAM POP; DLB 206; TCWW 2

MacLeish, Archibald 1892-1982 ... **CLC 3, 8, 14, 68; PC 47**
See also AMW; CA 9-12R; 106; CAD; CANR 33, 63; CDALBS; CP 1, 2; DAM POET; DFS 15; DLB 4, 7, 45; DLBY 1982; EWL 3; EXPP; MAL 5; MTCW 1, 2; MTFW 2005; PAB; PFS 5; RGAL 4; TUS

MacLennan, (John) Hugh
1907-1990 .... **CLC 2, 14, 92**
See also CA 5-8R; 142; CANR 33; CN 1, 2, 3, 4; DAC; DAM MST; DLB 68; EWL 3; MTCW 1, 2; MTFW 2005; RGEL 2; TWA

MacLeod, Alistair 1936- .. **CLC 56, 165; SSC 90**
See also CA 123; CCA 1; DAC; DAM MST; DLB 60; MTCW 2; MTFW 2005; RGSF 2; TCLE 1:2

Macleod, Fiona
See Sharp, William
See also RGEL 2; SUFW

MacNeice, (Frederick) Louis
1907-1963 .... **CLC 1, 4, 10, 53; PC 61**
See also BRW 7; CA 85-88; CANR 61; DAB; DAM POET; DLB 10, 20; EWL 3; MTCW 1, 2; MTFW 2005; RGEL 2

MacNeill, Dand
See Fraser, George MacDonald

Macpherson, James 1736-1796 .... **LC 29**
See Ossian
See also BRWS 8; DLB 109; RGEL 2

Macpherson, (Jean) Jay 1931- .... **CLC 14**
See also CA 5-8R; CANR 90; CP 1, 2, 3, 4, 5, 6, 7; CWP; DLB 53

Macrobius fl. 430- .... **CMLC 48**

MacShane, Frank 1927-1999 .... **CLC 39**
See also CA 9-12R; 186; CANR 3, 33; DLB 111

Macumber, Mari
See Sandoz, Mari(e Susette)

Madach, Imre 1823-1864 .... **NCLC 19**

Madden, (Jerry) David 1933- .... **CLC 5, 15**
See also CA 1-4R; CAAS 3; CANR 4, 45; CN 3, 4, 5, 6, 7; CSW; DLB 6; MTCW 1

Maddern, Al(an)
See Ellison, Harlan (Jay)

Madhubuti, Haki R. 1942- ... **BLC 2; CLC 6, 73; PC 5**
See Lee, Don L.
See also BW 2, 3; CA 73-76; CANR 24, 51, 73, 139; CP 5, 6, 7; CSW; DAM

MULT, POET; DLB 5, 41; DLBD 8; EWL 3; MAL 5; MTCW 2; MTFW 2005; RGAL 4

Madison, James 1751-1836 .... **NCLC 126**
See also DLB 37

Maepenn, Hugh
See Kuttner, Henry

Maepenn, K. H.
See Kuttner, Henry

Maeterlinck, Maurice 1862-1949 ..... **TCLC 3**
See also CA 104; 136; CANR 80; DAM DRAM; DLB 192; EW 8; EWL 3; GFL 1789 to the Present; LMFS 2; RGWL 2, 3; SATA 66; TWA

Maginn, William 1794-1842 .... **NCLC 8**
See also DLB 110, 159

Mahapatra, Jayanta 1928- .... **CLC 33**
See also CA 73-76; CAAS 9; CANR 15, 33, 66, 87; CP 4, 5, 6, 7; DAM MULT

Mahfouz, Naguib (Abdel Aziz Al-Sabilgi)
1911(?)- .... **CLC 153; SSC 66**
See Mahfuz, Najib (Abdel Aziz al-Sabilgi)
See also AAYA 49; BEST 89:2; CA 128; CANR 55, 101; DA3; DAM NOV; MTCW 1, 2; MTFW 2005; RGWL 2, 3; SSFS 9

Mahfuz, Najib (Abdel Aziz al-Sabilgi)
.... **CLC 52, 55**
See Mahfouz, Naguib (Abdel Aziz Al-Sabilgi)
See also AFW; CWW 2; DLBY 1988; EWL 3; RGSF 2; WLIT 6

Mahon, Derek 1941- .... **CLC 27; PC 60**
See also BRWS 6; CA 113; 128; CANR 88; CP 1, 2, 3, 4, 5, 6, 7; DLB 40; EWL 3

Maiakovskii, Vladimir
See Mayakovski, Vladimir (Vladimirovich)
See also IDTP; RGWL 2, 3

Mailer, Norman (Kingsley) 1923- . **CLC 1, 2, 3, 4, 5, 8, 11, 14, 28, 39, 74, 111**
See also AAYA 31; AITN 2; AMW; AMWC 2; AMWR 2; BPFB 2; CA 9-12R; CABS 1; CANR 28, 74, 77, 130; CDALB 1968-1988; CN 1, 2, 3, 4, 5, 6, 7; CPW; DA; DA3; DAB; DAC; DAM MST, NOV, POP; DLB 2, 16, 28, 185, 278; DLBD 3; DLBY 1980, 1983; EWL 3; MAL 5; MTCW 1, 2; MTFW 2005; NFS 10; RGAL 4; TUS

Maillet, Antonine 1929- .... **CLC 54, 118**
See also CA 115; 120; CANR 46, 74, 77, 134; CCA 1; CWW 2; DAC; DLB 60; INT CA-120; MTCW 2; MTFW 2005

Maimonides, Moses 1135-1204 ..... **CMLC 76**
See also DLB 115

Mais, Roger 1905-1955 .... **TCLC 8**
See also BW 1, 3; CA 105; 124; CANR 82; CDWLB 3; DLB 125; EWL 3; MTCW 1; RGEL 2

Maistre, Joseph 1753-1821 .... **NCLC 37**
See also GFL 1789 to the Present

Maitland, Frederic William
1850-1906 .... **TCLC 65**

Maitland, Sara (Louise) 1950- .... **CLC 49**
See also BRWS 11; CA 69-72; CANR 13, 59; DLB 271; FW

Major, Clarence 1936- ... **BLC 2; CLC 3, 19, 48**
See also AFAW 2; BW 2, 3; CA 21-24R; CAAS 6; CANR 13, 25, 53, 82; CN 3, 4, 5, 6, 7; CP 2, 3, 4, 5, 6, 7; CSW; DAM MULT; DLB 33; EWL 3; MAL 5; MSW

Major, Kevin (Gerald) 1949- .... **CLC 26**
See also AAYA 16; CA 97-100; CANR 21, 38, 112; CLR 11; DAC; DLB 60; INT CANR-21; JRDA; MAICYA 1, 2; MAIC-YAS 1; SATA 32, 82, 134; WYA; YAW

Maki, James
See Ozu, Yasujiro

Makine, Andrei 1957- .... **CLC 198**
See also CA 176; CANR 103; MTFW 2005

Malabaila, Damiano
See Levi, Primo

Malamud, Bernard 1914-1986 .. **CLC 1, 2, 3,**
5, 8, 9, 11, 18, 27, 44, 78, 85; SSC 15;
TCLC 129; WLC
See also AAYA 16; AMWS 1; BPFB 2;
BYA 15; CA 5-8R; 118; CABS 1; CANR
28, 62, 114; CDALB 1941-1968; CN 1, 2,
3, 4; CPW; DA; DA3; DAB; DAC; DAM
MST, NOV, POP; DLB 2, 28, 152; DLBY
1980, 1986; EWL 3; EXPS; LAIT 4;
LATS 1:1; MAL 5; MTCW 1, 2; MTFW
2005; NFS 4, 9; RGAL 4; RGSF 2; SSFS
8, 13, 16; TUS

Malan, Herman
See Bosman, Herman Charles; Bosman,
Herman Charles

Malaparte, Curzio 1898-1957 .... **TCLC 52**
See also DLB 264

Malcolm, Dan
See Silverberg, Robert

Malcolm, Janet 1934- .... **CLC 201**
See also CA 123; CANR 89; NCFS 1

Malcolm X .... **BLC 2; CLC 82, 117; WLCS**
See Little, Malcolm
See also LAIT 5; NCFS 3

Malherbe, Francois de 1555-1628 .... **LC 5**
See also GFL Beginnings to 1789

Mallarme, Stephane 1842-1898 ...... **NCLC 4,**
41; PC 4
See also DAM POET; DLB 217; EW 7;
GFL 1789 to the Present; LMFS 2; RGWL
2, 3; TWA

Mallet-Joris, Francoise 1930- .... **CLC 11**
See also CA 65-68; CANR 17; CWW 2;
DLB 83; EWL 3; GFL 1789 to the Present

Malley, Ern
See McAuley, James Phillip

Mallon, Thomas 1951- .... **CLC 172**
See also CA 110; CANR 29, 57, 92

Mallowan, Agatha Christie
See Christie, Agatha (Mary Clarissa)

Maloff, Saul 1922- .... **CLC 5**
See also CA 33-36R

Malone, Louis
See MacNeice, (Frederick) Louis

Malone, Michael (Christopher)
1942- .... **CLC 43**
See also CA 77-80; CANR 14, 32, 57, 114

Malory, Sir Thomas 1410(?)-1471(?) . **LC 11,**
88; WLCS
See also BRW 1; BRWR 2; CDBLB Before
1660; DA; DAB; DAC; DAM MST; DLB
146; EFS 2; RGEL 2; SATA 59; SATA-
Brief 33; TEA; WLIT 3

Malouf, (George Joseph) David
1934- .... **CLC 28, 86**
See also CA 124; CANR 50, 76; CN 3, 4,
5, 6, 7; CP 1, 3, 4, 5, 6, 7; DLB 289; EWL
3; MTCW 2; MTFW 2005

Malraux, (Georges-)Andre
1901-1976 .... **CLC 1, 4, 9, 13, 15, 57**
See also BPFB 2; CA 21-22; 69-72; CANR
34, 58; CAP 2; DA3; DAM NOV; DLB
72; EW 12; EWL 3; GFL 1789 to the
Present; MTCW 1, 2; MTFW 2005;
RGWL 2, 3; TWA

Malthus, Thomas Robert
1766-1834 .... **NCLC 145**
See also DLB 107, 158; RGEL 2

Malzberg, Barry N(athaniel) 1939- ... **CLC 7**
See also CA 61-64; CAAS 4; CANR 16;
CMW 4; DLB 8; SFW 4

Mamet, David (Alan) 1947- .. **CLC 9, 15, 34,**
46, 91, 166; DC 4, 24
See also AAYA 3, 60; AMWS 14; CA 81-
84; CABS 3; CAD; CANR 15, 41, 67, 72,

129; CD 5, 6; DA3; DAM DRAM; DFS
2, 3, 6, 12, 15; DLB 7; EWL 3; IDFW 4;
MAL 5; MTCW 1, 2; MTFW 2005;
RGAL 4

Mamoulian, Rouben (Zachary)
1897-1987 .... **CLC 16**
See also CA 25-28R; 124; CANR 85

Mandelshtam, Osip
See Mandelstam, Osip (Emilievich)
See also EW 10; EWL 3; RGWL 2, 3

Mandelstam, Osip (Emilievich)
1891(?)-1943(?) .... **PC 14; TCLC 2, 6**
See Mandelshtam, Osip
See also CA 104; 150; MTCW 2; TWA

Mander, (Mary) Jane 1877-1949 ... **TCLC 31**
See also CA 162; RGEL 2

Mandeville, Bernard 1670-1733 .... **LC 82**
See also DLB 101

Mandeville, Sir John fl. 1350- ...... **CMLC 19**
See also DLB 146

Mandiargues, Andre Pieyre de .... **CLC 41**
See Pieyre de Mandiargues, Andre
See also DLB 83

Mandrake, Ethel Belle
See Thurman, Wallace (Henry)

Mangan, James Clarence
1803-1849 .... **NCLC 27**
See also RGEL 2

Maniere, J.-E.
See Giraudoux, Jean(-Hippolyte)

Mankiewicz, Herman (Jacob)
1897-1953 .... **TCLC 85**
See also CA 120; 169; DLB 26; IDFW 3, 4

Manley, (Mary) Delariviere
1672(?)-1724 .... **LC 1, 42**
See also DLB 39, 80; RGEL 2

Mann, Abel
See Creasey, John

Mann, Emily 1952- .... **DC 7**
See also CA 130; CAD; CANR 55; CD 5,
6; CWD; DLB 266

Mann, (Luiz) Heinrich 1871-1950 ... **TCLC 9**
See also CA 106; 164, 181; DLB 66, 118;
EW 8; EWL 3; RGWL 2, 3

Mann, (Paul) Thomas 1875-1955 . **SSC 5, 80,**
82; TCLC 2, 8, 14, 21, 35, 44, 60, 168;
WLC
See also BPFB 2; CA 104; 128; CANR 133;
CDWLB 2; DA; DA3; DAB; DAC; DAM
MST, NOV; DLB 66; EW 9; EWL 3; GLL
1; LATS 1:1; LMFS 1; MTCW 1, 2;
MTFW 2005; NFS 17; RGSF 2; RGWL
2, 3; SSFS 4, 9; TWA

Mannheim, Karl 1893-1947 .... **TCLC 65**
See also CA 204

Manning, David
See Faust, Frederick (Schiller)

Manning, Frederic 1882-1935 .... **TCLC 25**
See also CA 124; 216; DLB 260

Manning, Olivia 1915-1980 .... **CLC 5, 19**
See also CA 5-8R; 101; CANR 29; CN 1,
2; EWL 3; FW; MTCW 1; RGEL 2

Mano, D. Keith 1942- .... **CLC 2, 10**
See also CA 25-28R; CAAS 6; CANR 26,
57; DLB 6

Mansfield, Katherine .... **SSC 9, 23, 38, 81;**
TCLC 2, 8, 39, 164; WLC
See Beauchamp, Kathleen Mansfield
See also BPFB 2; BRW 7; DAB; DLB 162;
EWL 3; EXPS; FW; GLL 1; RGEL 2;
RGSF 2; SSFS 2, 8, 10, 11; WWE 1

Manso, Peter 1940- .... **CLC 39**
See also CA 29-32R; CANR 44

Mantecon, Juan Jimenez
See Jimenez (Mantecon), Juan Ramon

Mantel, Hilary (Mary) 1952- .... **CLC 144**
See also CA 125; CANR 54, 101; CN 5, 6,
7; DLB 271; RHW

Manton, Peter
See Creasey, John

Man Without a Spleen, A
See Chekhov, Anton (Pavlovich)

Manzano, Juan Franciso
1797(?)-1854 .... **NCLC 155**

Manzoni, Alessandro 1785-1873 ... **NCLC 29,**
98
See also EW 5; RGWL 2, 3; TWA; WLIT 7

Map, Walter 1140-1209 .... **CMLC 32**

Mapu, Abraham (ben Jekutiel)
1808-1867 .... **NCLC 18**

Mara, Sally
See Queneau, Raymond

Maracle, Lee 1950- .... **NNAL**
See also CA 149

Marat, Jean Paul 1743-1793 .... **LC 10**

Marcel, Gabriel Honore 1889-1973 . **CLC 15**
See also CA 102; 45-48; EWL 3; MTCW 1,
2

March, William .... **TCLC 96**
See Campbell, William Edward March
See also CA 216; DLB 9, 86, 316; MAL 5

Marchbanks, Samuel
See Davies, (William) Robertson
See also CCA 1

Marchi, Giacomo
See Bassani, Giorgio

Marcus Aurelius
See Aurelius, Marcus
See also AW 2

Marguerite
See de Navarre, Marguerite

Marguerite d'Angouleme
See de Navarre, Marguerite
See also GFL Beginnings to 1789

Marguerite de Navarre
See de Navarre, Marguerite
See also RGWL 2, 3

Margulies, Donald 1954- .... **CLC 76**
See also AAYA 57; CA 200; CD 6; DFS 13;
DLB 228

Marie de France c. 12th cent. - ..... **CMLC 8;**
PC 22
See also DLB 208; FW; RGWL 2, 3

Marie de l'Incarnation 1599-1672 ...... **LC 10**

Marier, Captain Victor
See Griffith, D(avid Lewelyn) W(ark)

Mariner, Scott
See Pohl, Frederik

Marinetti, Filippo Tommaso
1876-1944 .... **TCLC 10**
See also CA 107; DLB 114, 264; EW 9;
EWL 3; WLIT 7

Marivaux, Pierre Carlet de Chamblain de
1688-1763 .... **DC 7; LC 4, 123**
See also DLB 314; GFL Beginnings to
1789; RGWL 2, 3; TWA

Markandaya, Kamala .... **CLC 8, 38**
See Taylor, Kamala (Purnaiya)
See also BYA 13; CN 1, 2, 3, 4, 5, 6, 7;
EWL 3

Markfield, Wallace (Arthur)
1926-2002 .... **CLC 8**
See also CA 69-72; 208; CAAS 3; CN 1, 2,
3, 4, 5, 6, 7; DLB 2, 28; DLBY 2002

Markham, Edwin 1852-1940 .... **TCLC 47**
See also CA 160; DLB 54, 186; MAL 5;
RGAL 4

Markham, Robert
See Amis, Kingsley (William)

Markoosie .... **NNAL**
See Patsauq, Markoosie
See also CLR 23; DAM MULT

Marks, J.
See Highwater, Jamake (Mamake)

Marks, J
See Highwater, Jamake (Mamake)

Marks-Highwater, J
    See Highwater, Jamake (Mamake)
Marks-Highwater, J.
    See Highwater, Jamake (Mamake)
Markson, David M(errill) 1927- .... **CLC 67**
    See also CA 49-52; CANR 1, 91; CN 5, 6
Marlatt, Daphne (Buckle) 1942- .... **CLC 168**
    See also CA 25-28R; CANR 17, 39; CN 6,
    7; CP 4, 5, 6, 7; CWP; DLB 60; FW
Marley, Bob .... **CLC 17**
    See Marley, Robert Nesta
Marley, Robert Nesta 1945-1981
    See Marley, Bob
    See also CA 107; 103
Marlowe, Christopher 1564-1593 . **DC 1; LC
    22, 47, 117; PC 57; WLC**
    See also BRW 1; BRWR 1; CDBLB Before
    1660; DA; DA3; DAB; DAC; DAM
    DRAM, MST; DFS 1, 5, 13, 21; DLB 62;
    EXPP; LMFS 1; PFS 22; RGEL 2; TEA;
    WLIT 3
Marlowe, Stephen 1928- .... **CLC 70**
    See Queen, Ellery
    See also CA 13-16R; CANR 6, 55; CMW
    4; SFW 4
Marmion, Shakerley 1603-1639 .... **LC 89**
    See also DLB 58; RGEL 2
Marmontel, Jean-Francois 1723-1799 .. **LC 2**
    See also DLB 314
Maron, Monika 1941- .... **CLC 165**
    See also CA 201
Marquand, John P(hillips)
    1893-1960 .... **CLC 2, 10**
    See also AMW; BPFB 2; CA 85-88; CANR
    73; CMW 4; DLB 9, 102; EWL 3; MAL
    5; MTCW 2; RGAL 4
Marques, Rene 1919-1979 .. **CLC 96; HLC 2**
    See also CA 97-100; 85-88; CANR 78;
    DAM MULT; DLB 305; EWL 3; HW 1,
    2; LAW; RGSF 2
Marquez, Gabriel (Jose) Garcia
    See Garcia Marquez, Gabriel (Jose)
Marquis, Don(ald Robert Perry)
    1878-1937 .... **TCLC 7**
    See also CA 104; 166; DLB 11, 25; MAL
    5; RGAL 4
Marquis de Sade
    See Sade, Donatien Alphonse Francois
Marric, J. J.
    See Creasey, John
    See also MSW
Marryat, Frederick 1792-1848 .... **NCLC 3**
    See also DLB 21, 163; RGEL 2; WCH
Marsden, James
    See Creasey, John
Marsh, Edward 1872-1953 .... **TCLC 99**
Marsh, (Edith) Ngaio 1895-1982 .. **CLC 7, 53**
    See also CA 9-12R; CANR 6, 58; CMW 4;
    CN 1, 2, 3; CPW; DAM POP; DLB 77;
    MSW; MTCW 1, 2; RGEL 2; TEA
Marshall, Allen
    See Westlake, Donald E(dwin)
Marshall, Garry 1934- .... **CLC 17**
    See also AAYA 3; CA 111; SATA 60
Marshall, Paule 1929- .. **BLC 3; CLC 27, 72;
    SSC 3**
    See also AFAW 1, 2; AMWS 11; BPFB 2;
    BW 2, 3; CA 77-80; CANR 25, 73, 129;
    CN 1, 2, 3, 4, 5, 6, 7; DA3; DAM MULT;
    DLB 33, 157, 227; EWL 3; LATS 1:2;
    MAL 5; MTCW 1, 2; MTFW 2005;
    RGAL 4; SSFS 15
Marshallik
    See Zangwill, Israel
Marsten, Richard
    See Hunter, Evan
Marston, John 1576-1634 .... **LC 33**
    See also BRW 2; DAM DRAM; DLB 58,
    172; RGEL 2

Martel, Yann 1963- .... **CLC 192**
    See also AAYA 67; CA 146; CANR 114;
    MTFW 2005
Martens, Adolphe-Adhemar
    See Ghelderode, Michel de
Martha, Henry
    See Harris, Mark
Marti, Jose
    See Marti (y Perez), Jose (Julian)
    See also DLB 290
Marti (y Perez), Jose (Julian)
    1853-1895 .... **HLC 2; NCLC 63**
    See Marti, Jose
    See also DAM MULT; HW 2; LAW; RGWL
    2, 3; WLIT 1
Martial c. 40-c. 104 .... **CMLC 35; PC 10**
    See also AW 2; CDWLB 1; DLB 211;
    RGWL 2, 3
Martin, Ken
    See Hubbard, L(afayette) Ron(ald)
Martin, Richard
    See Creasey, John
Martin, Steve 1945- .... **CLC 30, 217**
    See also AAYA 53; CA 97-100; CANR 30,
    100, 140; DFS 19; MTCW 1; MTFW
    2005
Martin, Valerie 1948- .... **CLC 89**
    See also BEST 90:2; CA 85-88; CANR 49,
    89
Martin, Violet Florence 1862-1915 .. **SSC 56;
    TCLC 51**
Martin, Webber
    See Silverberg, Robert
Martindale, Patrick Victor
    See White, Patrick (Victor Martindale)
Martin du Gard, Roger
    1881-1958 .... **TCLC 24**
    See also CA 118; CANR 94; DLB 65; EWL
    3; GFL 1789 to the Present; RGWL 2, 3
Martineau, Harriet 1802-1876 ...... **NCLC 26,
    137**
    See also DLB 21, 55, 159, 163, 166, 190;
    FW; RGEL 2; YABC 2
Martines, Julia
    See O'Faolain, Julia
Martinez, Enrique Gonzalez
    See Gonzalez Martinez, Enrique
Martinez, Jacinto Benavente y
    See Benavente (y Martinez), Jacinto
Martinez de la Rosa, Francisco de Paula
    1787-1862 .... **NCLC 102**
    See also TWA
Martinez Ruiz, Jose 1873-1967
    See Azorin; Ruiz, Jose Martinez
    See also CA 93-96; HW 1
Martinez Sierra, Gregorio
    1881-1947 .... **TCLC 6**
    See also CA 115; EWL 3
Martinez Sierra, Maria (de la O'LeJarraga)
    1874-1974 .... **TCLC 6**
    See also CA 115; EWL 3
Martinsen, Martin
    See Follett, Ken(neth Martin)
Martinson, Harry (Edmund)
    1904-1978 .... **CLC 14**
    See also CA 77-80; CANR 34, 130; DLB
    259; EWL 3
Martyn, Edward 1859-1923 .... **TCLC 131**
    See also CA 179; DLB 10; RGEL 2
Marut, Ret
    See Traven, B.
Marut, Robert
    See Traven, B.
Marvell, Andrew 1621-1678 .... **LC 4, 43; PC
    10; WLC**
    See also BRW 2; BRWR 2; CDBLB 1660-
    1789; DA; DAB; DAC; DAM MST;
    POET; DLB 131; EXPP; PFS 5; RGEL 2;
    TEA; WP

Marx, Karl (Heinrich)
    1818-1883 .... **NCLC 17, 114**
    See also DLB 129; LATS 1:1; TWA
Masaoka, Shiki -1902 .... **TCLC 18**
    See Masaoka, Tsunenori
    See also RGWL 3
Masaoka, Tsunenori 1867-1902
    See Masaoka, Shiki
    See also CA 117; 191; TWA
Masefield, John (Edward)
    1878-1967 .... **CLC 11, 47**
    See also CA 19-20; 25-28R; CANR 33;
    CAP 2; CDBLB 1890-1914; DAM POET;
    DLB 10, 19, 153, 160; EWL 3; EXPP;
    FANT; MTCW 1, 2; PFS 5; RGEL 2;
    SATA 19
Maso, Carole (?)- .... **CLC 44**
    See also CA 170; CN 7; GLL 2; RGAL 4
Mason, Bobbie Ann 1940- ... **CLC 28, 43, 82,
    154; SSC 4**
    See also AAYA 5, 42; AMWS 8; BPFB 2;
    CA 53-56; CANR 11, 31, 58, 83, 125;
    CDALBS; CN 5, 6, 7; CSW; DA3; DLB
    173; DLBY 1987; EWL 3; EXPS; INT
    CANR-31; MAL 5; MTCW 1, 2; MTFW
    2005; NFS 4; RGAL 4; RGSF 2; SSFS 3,
    8, 20; TCLE 1:2; YAW
Mason, Ernst
    See Pohl, Frederik
Mason, Hunni B.
    See Sternheim, (William Adolf) Carl
Mason, Lee W.
    See Malzberg, Barry N(athaniel)
Mason, Nick 1945- .... **CLC 35**
Mason, Tally
    See Derleth, August (William)
Mass, Anna .... **CLC 59**
Mass, William
    See Gibson, William
Massinger, Philip 1583-1640 .... **LC 70**
    See also BRWS 11; DLB 58; RGEL 2
Master Lao
    See Lao Tzu
Masters, Edgar Lee 1868-1950 ...... **PC 1, 36;
    TCLC 2, 25; WLCS**
    See also AMWS 1; CA 104; 133; CDALB
    1865-1917; DA; DAC; DAM MST,
    POET; DLB 54; EWL 3; EXPP; MAL 5;
    MTCW 1, 2; MTFW 2005; RGAL 4;
    TUS; WP
Masters, Hilary 1928- .... **CLC 48**
    See also CA 25-28R; 217; CAAE 217;
    CANR 13, 47, 97; CN 6, 7; DLB 244
Mastrosimone, William 1947- .... **CLC 36**
    See also CA 186; CAD; CD 5, 6
Mathe, Albert
    See Camus, Albert
Mather, Cotton 1663-1728 .... **LC 38**
    See also AMWS 2; CDALB 1640-1865;
    DLB 24, 30, 140; RGAL 4; TUS
Mather, Increase 1639-1723 .... **LC 38**
    See also DLB 24
Matheson, Richard (Burton) 1926- .. **CLC 37**
    See also AAYA 31; CA 97-100; CANR 88,
    99; DLB 8, 44; HGG; INT CA-97-100;
    SCFW 1, 2; SFW 4; SUFW 2
Mathews, Harry (Burchell) 1930- ..... **CLC 6,
    52**
    See also CA 21-24R; CAAS 6; CANR 18,
    40, 98; CN 5, 6, 7
Mathews, John Joseph 1894-1979 .. **CLC 84;
    NNAL**
    See also CA 19-20; 142; CANR 45; CAP 2;
    DAM MULT; DLB 175; TCWW 1, 2
Mathias, Roland (Glyn) 1915- .... **CLC 45**
    See also CA 97-100; CANR 19, 41; CP 1,
    2, 3, 4, 5, 6, 7; DLB 27

Matsuo Basho 1644(?)-1694 ...... **LC 62; PC 3**
See Basho, Matsuo
See also DAM POET; PFS 2, 7, 18

Mattheson, Rodney
See Creasey, John

Matthews, (James) Brander
1852-1929 .... **TCLC 95**
See also CA 181; DLB 71, 78; DLBD 13

Matthews, Greg 1949- .... **CLC 45**
See also CA 135

Matthews, William (Procter III)
1942-1997 .... **CLC 40**
See also AMWS 9; CA 29-32R; 162; CAAS
18; CANR 12, 57; CP 2, 3, 4; DLB 5

Matthias, John (Edward) 1941- .... **CLC 9**
See also CA 33-36R; CANR 56; CP 4, 5, 6,
7

Matthiessen, F(rancis) O(tto)
1902-1950 .... **TCLC 100**
See also CA 185; DLB 63; MAL 5

Matthiessen, Peter 1927- ... **CLC 5, 7, 11, 32,**
64
See also AAYA 6, 40; AMWS 5; ANW;
BEST 90:4; BPFB 2; CA 9-12R; CANR
21, 50, 73, 100, 138; CN 1, 2, 3, 4, 5, 6,
7; DA3; DAM NOV; DLB 6, 173, 275;
MAL 5; MTCW 1, 2; MTFW 2005; SATA
27

Maturin, Charles Robert
1780(?)-1824 .... **NCLC 6**
See also BRWS 8; DLB 178; GL 3; HGG;
LMFS 1; RGEL 2; SUFW

Matute (Ausejo), Ana Maria 1925- .. **CLC 11**
See also CA 89-92; CANR 129; CWW 2;
DLB 322; EWL 3; MTCW 1; RGSF 2

Maugham, W. S.
See Maugham, W(illiam) Somerset

Maugham, W(illiam) Somerset
1874-1965 .. **CLC 1, 11, 15, 67, 93; SSC**
8; WLC
See also AAYA 55; BPFB 2; BRW 6; CA
5-8R; 25-28R; CANR 40, 127; CDBLB
1914-1945; CMW 4; DA; DA3; DAB;
DAC; DAM DRAM, MST, NOV; DFS
22; DLB 10, 36, 77, 100, 162, 195; EWL
3; LAIT 3; MTCW 1, 2; MTFW 2005;
RGEL 2; RGSF 2; SATA 54; SSFS 17

Maugham, William Somerset
See Maugham, W(illiam) Somerset

Maupassant, (Henri Rene Albert) Guy de
1850-1893 . **NCLC 1, 42, 83; SSC 1, 64;**
WLC
See also BYA 14; DA; DA3; DAB; DAC;
DAM MST; DLB 123; EW 7; EXPS; GFL
1789 to the Present; LAIT 2; LMFS 1;
RGSF 2; RGWL 2, 3; SSFS 4, 21; SUFW;
TWA

Maupin, Armistead (Jones, Jr.)
1944- .... **CLC 95**
See also CA 125; 130; CANR 58, 101;
CPW; DA3; DAM POP; DLB 278; GLL
1; INT CA-130; MTCW 2; MTFW 2005

Maurhut, Richard
See Traven, B.

Mauriac, Claude 1914-1996 .... **CLC 9**
See also CA 89-92; 152; CWW 2; DLB 83;
EWL 3; GFL 1789 to the Present

Mauriac, Francois (Charles)
1885-1970 .... **CLC 4, 9, 56; SSC 24**
See also CA 25-28; CAP 2; DLB 65; EW
10; EWL 3; GFL 1789 to the Present;
MTCW 1, 2; MTFW 2005; RGWL 2, 3;
TWA

Mavor, Osborne Henry 1888-1951
See Bridie, James
See also CA 104

Maxwell, William (Keepers, Jr.)
1908-2000 .... **CLC 19**
See also AMWS 8; CA 93-96; 189; CANR
54, 95; CN 1, 2, 3, 4, 5, 6, 7; DLB 218,
278; DLBY 1980; INT CA-93-96; SATA-
Obit 128

May, Elaine 1932- .... **CLC 16**
See also CA 124; 142; CAD; CWD; DLB
44

Mayakovski, Vladimir (Vladimirovich)
1893-1930 .... **TCLC 4, 18**
See Maiakovskii, Vladimir; Mayakovsky,
Vladimir
See also CA 104; 158; EWL 3; MTCW 2;
MTFW 2005; SFW 4; TWA

Mayakovsky, Vladimir
See Mayakovski, Vladimir (Vladimirovich)
See also EW 11; WP

Mayhew, Henry 1812-1887 .... **NCLC 31**
See also DLB 18, 55, 190

Mayle, Peter 1939(?)- .... **CLC 89**
See also CA 139; CANR 64, 109

Maynard, Joyce 1953- .... **CLC 23**
See also CA 111; 129; CANR 64

Mayne, William (James Carter)
1928- .... **CLC 12**
See also AAYA 20; CA 9-12R; CANR 37,
80, 100; CLR 25; FANT; JRDA; MAI-
CYA 1, 2; MAICYAS 1; SAAS 11; SATA
6, 68, 122; SUFW 2; YAW

Mayo, Jim
See L'Amour, Louis (Dearborn)

Maysles, Albert 1926- .... **CLC 16**
See also CA 29-32R

Maysles, David 1932-1987 .... **CLC 16**
See also CA 191

Mazer, Norma Fox 1931- .... **CLC 26**
See also AAYA 5, 36; BYA 1, 8; CA 69-72;
CANR 12, 32, 66, 129; CLR 23; JRDA;
MAICYA 1, 2; SAAS 1; SATA 24, 67,
105; WYA; YAW

Mazzini, Guiseppe 1805-1872 .... **NCLC 34**

McAlmon, Robert (Menzies)
1895-1956 .... **TCLC 97**
See also CA 107; 168; DLB 4, 45; DLBD
15; GLL 1

McAuley, James Phillip 1917-1976 .. **CLC 45**
See also CA 97-100; CP 1, 2; DLB 260;
RGEL 2

McBain, Ed
See Hunter, Evan
See also MSW

McBrien, William (Augustine)
1930- .... **CLC 44**
See also CA 107; CANR 90

McCabe, Patrick 1955- .... **CLC 133**
See also BRWS 9; CA 130; CANR 50, 90;
CN 6, 7; DLB 194

McCaffrey, Anne 1926- .... **CLC 17**
See also AAYA 6, 34; AITN 2; BEST 89:2;
BPFB 2; BYA 5; CA 25-28R, 227; CAAE
227; CANR 15, 35, 55, 96; CLR 49;
CPW; DA3; DAM NOV, POP; DLB 8;
JRDA; MAICYA 1, 2; MTCW 1, 2;
MTFW 2005; SAAS 11; SATA 8, 70, 116,
152; SATA-Essay 152; SFW 4; SUFW 2;
WYA; YAW

McCaffrey, Anne Inez
See McCaffrey, Anne

McCall, Nathan 1955(?)- .... **CLC 86**
See also AAYA 59; BW 3; CA 146; CANR
88

McCann, Arthur
See Campbell, John W(ood, Jr.)

McCann, Edson
See Pohl, Frederik

McCarthy, Charles, Jr. 1933-
See McCarthy, Cormac
See also CANR 42, 69, 101; CPW; CSW;
DA3; DAM POP; MTCW 2; MTFW 2005

McCarthy, Cormac ...... **CLC 4, 57, 101, 204**
See McCarthy, Charles, Jr.
See also AAYA 41; AMWS 8; BPFB 2; CA
13-16R; CANR 10; CN 6, 7; DLB 6, 143,
256; EWL 3; LATS 1:2; MAL 5; TCLE
1:2; TCWW 2

McCarthy, Mary (Therese)
1912-1989 .. **CLC 1, 3, 5, 14, 24, 39, 59;**
SSC 24
See also AMW; BPFB 2; CA 5-8R; 129;
CANR 16, 50, 64; CN 1, 2, 3, 4; DA3;
DLB 2; DLBY 1981; EWL 3; FW; INT
CANR-16; MAL 5; MAWW; MTCW 1,
2; MTFW 2005; RGAL 4; TUS

McCartney, (James) Paul 1942- . **CLC 12, 35**
See also CA 146; CANR 111

McCauley, Stephen (D.) 1955- .... **CLC 50**
See also CA 141

McClaren, Peter .... **CLC 70**

McClure, Michael (Thomas) 1932- ... **CLC 6,**
10
See also BG 1:3; CA 21-24R; CAD; CANR
17, 46, 77, 131; CD 5, 6; CP 1, 2, 3, 4, 5,
6, 7; DLB 16; WP

McCorkle, Jill (Collins) 1958- .... **CLC 51**
See also CA 121; CANR 113; CSW; DLB
234; DLBY 1987

McCourt, Frank 1930- .... **CLC 109**
See also AAYA 61; AMWS 12; CA 157;
CANR 97, 138; MTFW 2005; NCFS 1

McCourt, James 1941- .... **CLC 5**
See also CA 57-60; CANR 98

McCourt, Malachy 1931- .... **CLC 119**
See also SATA 126

McCoy, Horace (Stanley)
1897-1955 .... **TCLC 28**
See also AMWS 13; CA 108; 155; CMW 4;
DLB 9

McCrae, John 1872-1918 .... **TCLC 12**
See also CA 109; DLB 92; PFS 5

McCreigh, James
See Pohl, Frederik

McCullers, (Lula) Carson (Smith)
1917-1967 .... **CLC 1, 4, 10, 12, 48, 100;**
SSC 9, 24; TCLC 155; WLC
See also AAYA 21; AMW; AMWC 2; BPFB
2; CA 5-8R; 25-28R; CABS 1, 3; CANR
18, 132; CDALB 1941-1968; DA; DA3;
DAB; DAC; DAM MST, NOV; DFS 5,
18; DLB 2, 7, 173, 228; EWL 3; EXPS;
FW; GLL 1; LAIT 3, 4; MAL 5; MAWW;
MTCW 1, 2; MTFW 2005; NFS 6, 13;
RGAL 4; RGSF 2; SATA 27; SSFS 5;
TUS; YAW

McCulloch, John Tyler
See Burroughs, Edgar Rice

McCullough, Colleen 1937- ...... **CLC 27, 107**
See also AAYA 36; BPFB 2; CA 81-84;
CANR 17, 46, 67, 98, 139; CPW; DA3;
DAM NOV, POP; MTCW 1, 2; MTFW
2005; RHW

McCunn, Ruthanne Lum 1946- .... **AAL**
See also CA 119; CANR 43, 96; DLB 312;
LAIT 2; SATA 63

McDermott, Alice 1953- .... **CLC 90**
See also CA 109; CANR 40, 90, 126; CN
7; DLB 292; MTFW 2005

McElroy, Joseph (Prince) 1930- ... **CLC 5, 47**
See also CA 17-20R; CN 3, 4, 5, 6, 7

McEwan, Ian (Russell) 1948- .... **CLC 13, 66,**
169
See also BEST 90:4; BRWS 4; CA 61-64;
CANR 14, 41, 69, 87, 132; CN 3, 4, 5, 6,
7; DAM NOV; DLB 14, 194, 319; HGG;
MTCW 1, 2; MTFW 2005; RGSF 2;
SUFW 2; TEA

McFadden, David 1940- .... **CLC 48**
See also CA 104; CP 1, 2, 3, 4, 5, 6, 7; DLB 60; INT CA-104

McFarland, Dennis 1950- .... **CLC 65**
See also CA 165; CANR 110

McGahern, John 1934- ... **CLC 5, 9, 48, 156; SSC 17**
See also CA 17-20R; CANR 29, 68, 113; CN 1, 2, 3, 4, 5, 6, 7; DLB 14, 231, 319; MTCW 1

McGinley, Patrick (Anthony) 1937- . **CLC 41**
See also CA 120; 127; CANR 56; INT CA-127

McGinley, Phyllis 1905-1978 .... **CLC 14**
See also CA 9-12R; 77-80; CANR 19; CP 1, 2; CWRI 5; DLB 11, 48; MAL 5; PFS 9, 13; SATA 2, 44; SATA-Obit 24

McGinniss, Joe 1942- .... **CLC 32**
See also AITN 2; BEST 89:2; CA 25-28R; CANR 26, 70; CPW; DLB 185; INT CANR-26

McGivern, Maureen Daly
See Daly, Maureen

McGrath, Patrick 1950- .... **CLC 55**
See also CA 136; CANR 65; CN 5, 6, 7; DLB 231; HGG; SUFW 2

McGrath, Thomas (Matthew)
1916-1990 .... **CLC 28, 59**
See also AMWS 10; CA 9-12R; 132; CANR 6, 33, 95; CP 1, 2, 3, 4; DAM POET; MAL 5; MTCW 1; SATA 41; SATA-Obit 66

McGuane, Thomas (Francis III)
1939- .... **CLC 3, 7, 18, 45, 127**
See also AITN 2; BPFB 2; CA 49-52; CANR 5, 24, 49, 94; CN 2, 3, 4, 5, 6, 7; DLB 2, 212; DLBY 1980; EWL 3; INT CANR-24; MAL 5; MTCW 1; MTFW 2005; TCWW 1, 2

McGuckian, Medbh 1950- .... **CLC 48, 174; PC 27**
See also BRWS 5; CA 143; CP 4, 5, 6, 7; CWP; DAM POET; DLB 40

McHale, Tom 1942(?)-1982 .... **CLC 3, 5**
See also AITN 1; CA 77-80; 106; CN 1, 2, 3

McHugh, Heather 1948- .... **PC 61**
See also CA 69-72; CANR 11, 28, 55, 92; CP 4, 5, 6, 7; CWP

McIlvanney, William 1936- .... **CLC 42**
See also CA 25-28R; CANR 61; CMW 4; DLB 14, 207

McIlwraith, Maureen Mollie Hunter
See Hunter, Mollie
See also SATA 2

McInerney, Jay 1955- .... **CLC 34, 112**
See also AAYA 18; BPFB 2; CA 116; 123; CANR 45, 68, 116; CN 5, 6, 7; CPW; DA3; DAM POP; DLB 292; INT CA-123; MAL 5; MTCW 2; MTFW 2005

McIntyre, Vonda N(eel) 1948- .... **CLC 18**
See also CA 81-84; CANR 17, 34, 69; MTCW 1; SFW 4; YAW

McKay, Claude .... **BLC 3; HR 1:3; PC 2; TCLC 7, 41; WLC**
See McKay, Festus Claudius
See also AFAW 1, 2; AMWS 10; DAB; DLB 4, 45, 51, 117; EWL 3; EXPP; GLL 2; LAIT 3; LMFS 2; MAL 5; PAB; PFS 4; RGAL 4; WP

McKay, Festus Claudius 1889-1948
See McKay, Claude
See also BW 1, 3; CA 104; 124; CANR 73; DA; DAC; DAM MST, MULT, NOV, POET; MTCW 1, 2; MTFW 2005; TUS

McKuen, Rod 1933- .... **CLC 1, 3**
See also AITN 1; CA 41-44R; CANR 40; CP 1

McLoughlin, R. B.
See Mencken, H(enry) L(ouis)

McLuhan, (Herbert) Marshall
1911-1980 .... **CLC 37, 83**
See also CA 9-12R; 102; CANR 12, 34, 61; DLB 88; INT CANR-12; MTCW 1, 2; MTFW 2005

McManus, Declan Patrick Aloysius
See Costello, Elvis

McMillan, Terry (L.) 1951- . **BLCS; CLC 50, 61, 112**
See also AAYA 21; AMWS 13; BPFB 2; BW 2, 3; CA 140; CANR 60, 104, 131; CN 7; CPW; DA3; DAM MULT, NOV, POP; MAL 5; MTCW 2; MTFW 2005; RGAL 4; YAW

McMurtry, Larry 1936- .... **CLC 2, 3, 7, 11, 27, 44, 127**
See also AAYA 15; AITN 2; AMWS 5; BEST 89:2; BPFB 2; CA 5-8R; CANR 19, 43, 64, 103; CDALB 1968-1988; CN 2, 3, 4, 5, 6, 7; CPW; CSW; DA3; DAM NOV, POP; DLB 2, 143, 256; DLBY 1980, 1987; EWL 3; MAL 5; MTCW 1, 2; MTFW 2005; RGAL 4; TCWW 1, 2

McNally, T. M. 1961- .... **CLC 82**

McNally, Terrence 1939- ... **CLC 4, 7, 41, 91; DC 27**
See also AAYA 62; AMWS 13; CA 45-48; CAD; CANR 2, 56, 116; CD 5, 6; DA3; DAM DRAM; DFS 16, 19; DLB 7, 249; EWL 3; GLL 1; MTCW 2; MTFW 2005

McNamer, Deirdre 1950- .... **CLC 70**

McNeal, Tom .... **CLC 119**

McNeile, Herman Cyril 1888-1937
See Sapper
See also CA 184; CMW 4; DLB 77

McNickle, (William) D'Arcy
1904-1977 .... **CLC 89; NNAL**
See also CA 9-12R; 85-88; CANR 5, 45; DAM MULT; DLB 175, 212; RGAL 4; SATA-Obit 22; TCWW 1, 2

McPhee, John (Angus) 1931- .... **CLC 36**
See also AAYA 61; AMWS 3; ANW; BEST 90:1; CA 65-68; CANR 20, 46, 64, 69, 121; CPW; DLB 185, 275; MTCW 1, 2; MTFW 2005; TUS

McPherson, James Alan 1943- . **BLCS; CLC 19, 77**
See also BW 1, 3; CA 25-28R; CAAS 17; CANR 24, 74, 140; CN 3, 4, 5, 6; CSW; DLB 38, 244; EWL 3; MTCW 1, 2; MTFW 2005; RGAL 4; RGSF 2

McPherson, William (Alexander)
1933- .... **CLC 34**
See also CA 69-72; CANR 28; INT CANR-28

McTaggart, J. McT. Ellis
See McTaggart, John McTaggart Ellis

McTaggart, John McTaggart Ellis
1866-1925 .... **TCLC 105**
See also CA 120; DLB 262

Mead, George Herbert 1863-1931 . **TCLC 89**
See also CA 212; DLB 270

Mead, Margaret 1901-1978 .... **CLC 37**
See also AITN 1; CA 1-4R; 81-84; CANR 4; DA3; FW; MTCW 1, 2; SATA-Obit 20

Meaker, Marijane (Agnes) 1927-
See Kerr, M. E.
See also CA 107; CANR 37, 63, 145; INT CA-107; JRDA; MAICYA 1, 2; MAICYAS 1; MTCW 1; SATA 20, 61, 99, 160; SATA-Essay 111; YAW

Medoff, Mark (Howard) 1940- .... **CLC 6, 23**
See also AITN 1; CA 53-56; CAD; CANR 5; CD 5, 6; DAM DRAM; DFS 4; DLB 7; INT CANR-5

Medvedev, P. N.
See Bakhtin, Mikhail Mikhailovich

Meged, Aharon
See Megged, Aharon

Meged, Aron
See Megged, Aharon

Megged, Aharon 1920- .... **CLC 9**
See also CA 49-52; CAAS 13; CANR 1, 140; EWL 3

Mehta, Deepa 1950- .... **CLC 208**

Mehta, Gita 1943- .... **CLC 179**
See also CA 225; CN 7; DNFS 2

Mehta, Ved (Parkash) 1934- .... **CLC 37**
See also CA 1-4R; 212; CAAE 212; CANR 2, 23, 69; MTCW 1; MTFW 2005

Melanchthon, Philipp 1497-1560 .... **LC 90**
See also DLB 179

Melanter
See Blackmore, R(ichard) D(oddridge)

Meleager c. 140B.C.-c. 70B.C. ...... **CMLC 53**

Melies, Georges 1861-1938 .... **TCLC 81**

Melikow, Loris
See Hofmannsthal, Hugo von

Melmoth, Sebastian
See Wilde, Oscar (Fingal O'Flahertie Wills)

Melo Neto, Joao Cabral de
See Cabral de Melo Neto, Joao
See also CWW 2; EWL 3

Meltzer, Milton 1915- .... **CLC 26**
See also AAYA 8, 45; BYA 2, 6; CA 13-16R; CANR 38, 92, 107; CLR 13; DLB 61; JRDA; MAICYA 1, 2; SAAS 1; SATA 1, 50, 80, 128; SATA-Essay 124; WYA; YAW

Melville, Herman 1819-1891 ..... **NCLC 3, 12, 29, 45, 49, 91, 93, 123, 157; SSC 1, 17, 46; WLC**
See also AAYA 25; AMW; AMWR 1; CDALB 1640-1865; DA; DA3; DAB; DAC; DAM MST, NOV; DLB 3, 74, 250, 254; EXPN; EXPS; GL 3; LAIT 1, 2; NFS 7, 9; RGAL 4; RGSF 2; SATA 59; SSFS 3; TUS

Members, Mark
See Powell, Anthony (Dymoke)

Membreno, Alejandro .... **CLC 59**

Menand, Louis 1952- .... **CLC 208**
See also CA 200

Menander c. 342B.C.-c. 293B.C. .... **CMLC 9, 51; DC 3**
See also AW 1; CDWLB 1; DAM DRAM; DLB 176; LMFS 1; RGWL 2, 3

Menchu, Rigoberta 1959- .. **CLC 160; HLCS 2**
See also CA 175; CANR 135; DNFS 1; WLIT 1

Mencken, H(enry) L(ouis)
1880-1956 .... **TCLC 13**
See also AMW; CA 105; 125; CDALB 1917-1929; DLB 11, 29, 63, 137, 222; EWL 3; MAL 5; MTCW 1, 2; MTFW 2005; NCFS 4; RGAL 4; TUS

Mendelsohn, Jane 1965- .... **CLC 99**
See also CA 154; CANR 94

Mendoza, Inigo Lopez de
See Santillana, Inigo Lopez de Mendoza, Marques de

Menton, Francisco de
See Chin, Frank (Chew, Jr.)

Mercer, David 1928-1980 .... **CLC 5**
See also CA 9-12R; 102; CANR 23; CBD; DAM DRAM; DLB 13, 310; MTCW 1; RGEL 2

Merchant, Paul
See Ellison, Harlan (Jay)

Meredith, George 1828-1909 .. **PC 60; TCLC 17, 43**
See also CA 117; 153; CANR 80; CDBLB 1832-1890; DAM POET; DLB 18, 35, 57, 159; RGEL 2; TEA

Meredith, William (Morris) 1919- .... **CLC 4, 13, 22, 55; PC 28**
See also CA 9-12R; CAAS 14; CANR 6, 40, 129; CP 1, 2, 3, 4, 5, 6, 7; DAM POET; DLB 5; MAL 5

Merezhkovsky, Dmitrii Sergeevich
See Merezhkovsky, Dmitry Sergeyevich
See also DLB 295

Merezhkovsky, Dmitry Sergeevich
See Merezhkovsky, Dmitry Sergeyevich
See also EWL 3

Merezhkovsky, Dmitry Sergeyevich
1865-1941 .... **TCLC 29**
See Merezhkovsky, Dmitrii Sergeevich;
Merezhkovsky, Dmitry Sergeevich
See also CA 169

Merimee, Prosper 1803-1870 ... **NCLC 6, 65; SSC 7, 77**
See also DLB 119, 192; EW 6; EXPS; GFL 1789 to the Present; RGSF 2; RGWL 2, 3; SSFS 8; SUFW

Merkin, Daphne 1954- .... **CLC 44**
See also CA 123

Merleau-Ponty, Maurice
1908-1961 .... **TCLC 156**
See also CA 114; 89-92; DLB 296; GFL 1789 to the Present

Merlin, Arthur
See Blish, James (Benjamin)

Mernissi, Fatima 1940- .... **CLC 171**
See also CA 152; FW

Merrill, James (Ingram) 1926-1995 .. **CLC 2, 3, 6, 8, 13, 18, 34, 91; PC 28; TCLC 173**
See also AMWS 3; CA 13-16R; 147; CANR 10, 49, 63, 108; CP 1, 2, 3, 4; DA3; DAM POET; DLB 5, 165; DLBY 1985; EWL 3; INT CANR-10; MAL 5; MTCW 1, 2; MTFW 2005; PAB; PFS 23; RGAL 4

Merriman, Alex
See Silverberg, Robert

Merriman, Brian 1747-1805 .... **NCLC 70**

Merritt, E. B.
See Waddington, Miriam

Merton, Thomas (James)
1915-1968 . **CLC 1, 3, 11, 34, 83; PC 10**
See also AAYA 61; AMWS 8; CA 5-8R; 25-28R; CANR 22, 53, 111, 131; DA3; DLB 48; DLBY 1981; MAL 5; MTCW 1, 2; MTFW 2005

Merwin, W(illiam) S(tanley) 1927- ... **CLC 1, 2, 3, 5, 8, 13, 18, 45, 88; PC 45**
See also AMWS 3; CA 13-16R; CANR 15, 51, 112, 140; CP 1, 2, 3, 4, 5, 6, 7; DA3; DAM POET; DLB 5, 169; EWL 3; INT CANR-15; MAL 5; MTCW 1, 2; MTFW 2005; PAB; PFS 5, 15; RGAL 4

Metastasio, Pietro 1698-1782 .... **LC 115**
See also RGWL 2, 3

Metcalf, John 1938- .... **CLC 37; SSC 43**
See also CA 113; CN 4, 5, 6, 7; DLB 60; RGSF 2; TWA

Metcalf, Suzanne
See Baum, L(yman) Frank

Mew, Charlotte (Mary) 1870-1928 .. **TCLC 8**
See also CA 105; 189; DLB 19, 135; RGEL 2

Mewshaw, Michael 1943- .... **CLC 9**
See also CA 53-56; CANR 7, 47; DLBY 1980

Meyer, Conrad Ferdinand
1825-1898 .... **NCLC 81; SSC 30**
See also DLB 129; EW; RGWL 2, 3

Meyer, Gustav 1868-1932
See Meyrink, Gustav
See also CA 117; 190

Meyer, June
See Jordan, June (Meyer)

Meyer, Lynn
See Slavitt, David R(ytman)

Meyers, Jeffrey 1939- .... **CLC 39**
See also CA 73-76; 186; CAAE 186; CANR 54, 102; DLB 111

Meynell, Alice (Christina Gertrude Thompson) 1847-1922 .... **TCLC 6**
See also CA 104; 177; DLB 19, 98; RGEL 2

Meyrink, Gustav .... **TCLC 21**
See Meyer, Gustav
See also DLB 81; EWL 3

Michaels, Leonard 1933-2003 ..... **CLC 6, 25; SSC 16**
See also CA 61-64; 216; CANR 21, 62, 119; CN 3, 45, 6, 7; DLB 130; MTCW 1; TCLE 1:2

Michaux, Henri 1899-1984 .... **CLC 8, 19**
See also CA 85-88; 114; DLB 258; EWL 3; GFL 1789 to the Present; RGWL 2, 3

Micheaux, Oscar (Devereaux)
1884-1951 .... **TCLC 76**
See also BW 3; CA 174; DLB 50; TCWW 2

Michelangelo 1475-1564 .... **LC 12**
See also AAYA 43

Michelet, Jules 1798-1874 .... **NCLC 31**
See also EW 5; GFL 1789 to the Present

Michels, Robert 1876-1936 .... **TCLC 88**
See also CA 212

Michener, James A(lbert)
1907(?)-1997 .. **CLC 1, 5, 11, 29, 60, 109**
See also AAYA 27; AITN 1; BEST 90:1; BPFB 2; CA 5-8R; 161; CANR 21, 45, 68; CN 1, 2, 3, 4, 5, 6; CPW; DA3; DAM NOV, POP; DLB 6; MAL 5; MTCW 1, 2; MTFW 2005; RHW; TCWW 1, 2

Mickiewicz, Adam 1798-1855 . **NCLC 3, 101; PC 38**
See also EW 5; RGWL 2, 3

Middleton, (John) Christopher
1926- .... **CLC 13**
See also CA 13-16R; CANR 29, 54, 117; CP 1, 2, 3, 4, 5, 6, 7; DLB 40

Middleton, Richard (Barham)
1882-1911 .... **TCLC 56**
See also CA 187; DLB 156; HGG

Middleton, Stanley 1919- .... **CLC 7, 38**
See also CA 25-28R; CAAS 23; CANR 21, 46, 81; CN 1, 2, 3, 4, 5, 6, 7; DLB 14

Middleton, Thomas 1580-1627 ...... **DC 5; LC 33, 123**
See also BRW 2; DAM DRAM, MST; DFS 18, 22; DLB 58; RGEL 2

Migueis, Jose Rodrigues 1901-1980 . **CLC 10**
See also DLB 287

Mikszath, Kalman 1847-1910 .... **TCLC 31**
See also CA 170

Miles, Jack .... **CLC 100**
See also CA 200

Miles, John Russiano
See Miles, Jack

Miles, Josephine (Louise)
1911-1985 .... **CLC 1, 2, 14, 34, 39**
See also CA 1-4R; 116; CANR 2, 55; CP 1, 2, 3, 4; DAM POET; DLB 48; MAL 5; TCLE 1:2

Militant
See Sandburg, Carl (August)

Mill, Harriet (Hardy) Taylor
1807-1858 .... **NCLC 102**
See also FW

Mill, John Stuart 1806-1873 .... **NCLC 11, 58**
See also CDBLB 1832-1890; DLB 55, 190, 262; FW 1; RGEL 2; TEA

Millar, Kenneth 1915-1983 .... **CLC 14**
See Macdonald, Ross
See also CA 9-12R; 110; CANR 16, 63, 107; CMW 4; CPW; DA3; DAM POP;

DLB 2, 226; DLBD 6; DLBY 1983; MTCW 1, 2; MTFW 2005

Millay, E. Vincent
See Millay, Edna St. Vincent

Millay, Edna St. Vincent 1892-1950 ..... **PC 6, 61; TCLC 4, 49, 169; WLCS**
See Boyd, Nancy
See also AMW; CA 104; 130; CDALB 1917-1929; DA; DA3; DAB; DAC; DAM MST, POET; DLB 45, 249; EWL 3; EXPP; FL 1:6; MAL 5; MAWW; MTCW 1, 2; MTFW 2005; PAB; PFS 3, 17; RGAL 4; TUS; WP

Miller, Arthur 1915-2005 ..... **CLC 1, 2, 6, 10, 15, 26, 47, 78, 179; DC 1; WLC**
See also AAYA 15; AITN 1; AMW; AMWC 1; CA 1-4R; 236; CABS 3; CAD; CANR 2, 30, 54, 76, 132; CD 5, 6; CDALB 1941-1968; DA; DA3; DAB; DAC; DAM DRAM, MST; DFS 1, 3, 8; DLB 7, 266; EWL 3; LAIT 1, 4; LATS 1:2; MAL 5; MTCW 1, 2; MTFW 2005; RGAL 4; TUS; WYAS 1

Miller, Henry (Valentine)
1891-1980 .... **CLC 1, 2, 4, 9, 14, 43, 84; WLC**
See also AMW; BPFB 2; CA 9-12R; 97-100; CANR 33, 64; CDALB 1929-1941; CN 1, 2; DA; DA3; DAB; DAC; DAM MST, NOV; DLB 4, 9; DLBY 1980; EWL 3; MAL 5; MTCW 1, 2; MTFW 2005; RGAL 4; TUS

Miller, Hugh 1802-1856 .... **NCLC 143**
See also DLB 190

Miller, Jason 1939(?)-2001 .... **CLC 2**
See also AITN 1; CA 73-76; 197; CAD; CANR 130; DFS 12; DLB 7

Miller, Sue 1943- .... **CLC 44**
See also AMWS 12; BEST 90:3; CA 139; CANR 59, 91, 128; DA3; DAM POP; DLB 143

Miller, Walter M(ichael, Jr.)
1923-1996 .... **CLC 4, 30**
See also BPFB 2; CA 85-88; CANR 108; DLB 8; SCFW 1, 2; SFW 4

Millett, Kate 1934- .... **CLC 67**
See also AITN 1; CA 73-76; CANR 32, 53, 76, 110; DA3; DLB 246; FW; GLL 1; MTCW 1, 2; MTFW 2005

Millhauser, Steven (Lewis) 1943- .... **CLC 21, 54, 109; SSC 57**
See also CA 110; 111; CANR 63, 114, 133; CN 6, 7; DA3; DLB 2; FANT; INT CA-111; MAL 5; MTCW 2; MTFW 2005

Millin, Sarah Gertrude 1889-1968 ... **CLC 49**
See also CA 102; 93-96; DLB 225; EWL 3

Milne, A(lan) A(lexander)
1882-1956 .... **TCLC 6, 88**
See also BRWS 5; CA 104; 133; CLR 1, 26; CMW 4; CWRI 5; DA3; DAB; DAC; DAM MST; DLB 10, 77, 100, 160; FANT; MAICYA 1, 2; MTCW 1, 2; MTFW 2005; RGEL 2; SATA 100; WCH; YABC 1

Milner, Ron(ald) 1938-2004 ..... **BLC 3; CLC 56**
See also AITN 1; BW 1; CA 73-76; 230; CAD; CANR 24, 81; CD 5, 6; DAM MULT; DLB 38; MAL 5; MTCW 1

Milnes, Richard Monckton
1809-1885 .... **NCLC 61**
See also DLB 32, 184

Milosz, Czeslaw 1911-2004 .... **CLC 5, 11, 22, 31, 56, 82; PC 8; WLCS**
See also AAYA 62; CA 81-84; 230; CANR 23, 51, 91, 126; CDWLB 4; CWW 2; DA3; DAM MST, POET; DLB 215; EW 13; EWL 3; MTCW 1, 2; MTFW 2005; PFS 16; RGWL 2, 3

Oe, Kenzaburo 1935- .. **CLC 10, 36, 86, 187; SSC 20**
See Oe Kenzaburo
See also CA 97-100; CANR 36, 50, 74, 126; DA3; DAM NOV; DLB 182; DLBY 1994; LATS 1:2; MJW; MTCW 1, 2; MTFW 2005; RGSF 2; RGWL 2, 3

Oe Kenzaburo
See Oe, Kenzaburo
See also CWW 2; EWL 3

O'Faolain, Julia 1932- .... **CLC 6, 19, 47, 108**
See also CA 81-84; CAAS 2; CANR 12, 61; CN 2, 3, 4, 5, 6, 7; DLB 14, 231, 319; FW; MTCW 1; RHW

O'Faolain, Sean 1900-1991 ...... **CLC 1, 7, 14, 32, 70; SSC 13; TCLC 143**
See also CA 61-64; 134; CANR 12, 66; CN 1, 2, 3, 4; DLB 15, 162; MTCW 1, 2; MTFW 2005; RGEL 2; RGSF 2

O'Flaherty, Liam 1896-1984 .... **CLC 5, 34; SSC 6**
See also CA 101; 113; CANR 35; CN 1, 2, 3; DLB 36, 162; DLBY 1984; MTCW 1, 2; MTFW 2005; RGEL 2; RGSF 2; SSFS 5, 20

Ogai
See Mori Ogai
See also MJW

Ogilvy, Gavin
See Barrie, J(ames) M(atthew)

O'Grady, Standish (James)
1846-1928 .... **TCLC 5**
See also CA 104; 157

O'Grady, Timothy 1951- .... **CLC 59**
See also CA 138

O'Hara, Frank 1926-1966 .... **CLC 2, 5, 13, 78; PC 45**
See also CA 9-12R; 25-28R; CANR 33; DA3; DAM POET; DLB 5, 16, 193; EWL 3; MAL 5; MTCW 1, 2; MTFW 2005; PFS 8, 12; RGAL 4; WP

O'Hara, John (Henry) 1905-1970 . **CLC 1, 2, 3, 6, 11, 42; SSC 15**
See also AMW; BPFB 3; CA 5-8R; 25-28R; CANR 31, 60; CDALB 1929-1941; DAM NOV; DLB 9, 86; DLBD 2; EWL 3; MAL 5; MTCW 1, 2; MTFW 2005; NFS 11; RGAL 4; RGSF 2

O Hehir, Diana 1922- .... **CLC 41**
See also CA 93-96

Ohiyesa
See Eastman, Charles A(lexander)

Okada, John 1923-1971 .... **AAL**
See also BYA 14; CA 212; DLB 312

Okigbo, Christopher (Ifenayichukwu)
1932-1967 .. **BLC 3; CLC 25, 84; PC 7; TCLC 171**
See also AFW; BW 1, 3; CA 77-80; CANR 74; CDWLB 3; DAM MULT, POET; DLB 125; EWL 3; MTCW 1, 2; MTFW 2005; RGEL 2

Okri, Ben 1959- .... **CLC 87**
See also AFW; BRWS 5; BW 2, 3; CA 130; 138; CANR 65, 128; CN 5, 6, 7; DLB 157, 231, 319; EWL 3; INT CA-138; MTCW 1; MTFW 2005; RGSF 2; SSFS 20; WLIT 2; WWE 1

Olds, Sharon 1942- .. **CLC 32, 39, 85; PC 22**
See also AMWS 10; CA 101; CANR 18, 41, 66, 98, 135; CP 7; CPW; CWP; DAM POET; DLB 120; MAL 5; MTCW 2; MTFW 2005; PFS 17

Oldstyle, Jonathan
See Irving, Washington

Olesha, Iurii
See Olesha, Yuri (Karlovich)
See also RGWL 2

Olesha, Iurii Karlovich
See Olesha, Yuri (Karlovich)
See also DLB 272

Olesha, Yuri (Karlovich) 1899-1960 . **CLC 8; SSC 69; TCLC 136**
See Olesha, Iurii; Olesha, Iurii Karlovich; Olesha, Yury Karlovich
See also CA 85-88; EW 11; RGWL 3

Olesha, Yury Karlovich
See Olesha, Yuri (Karlovich)
See also EWL 3

Oliphant, Mrs.
See Oliphant, Margaret (Oliphant Wilson)
See also SUFW

Oliphant, Laurence 1829(?)-1888 .. **NCLC 47**
See also DLB 18, 166

Oliphant, Margaret (Oliphant Wilson)
1828-1897 .... **NCLC 11, 61; SSC 25**
See Oliphant, Mrs.
See also BRWS 10; DLB 18, 159, 190; HGG; RGEL 2; RGSF 2

Oliver, Mary 1935- .... **CLC 19, 34, 98**
See also AMWS 7; CA 21-24R; CANR 9, 43, 84, 92, 138; CP 4, 5, 6, 7; CWP; DLB 5, 193; EWL 3; MTFW 2005; PFS 15

Olivier, Laurence (Kerr) 1907-1989 . **CLC 20**
See also CA 111; 150; 129

Olsen, Tillie 1912- ... **CLC 4, 13, 114; SSC 11**
See also AAYA 51; AMWS 13; BYA 11; CA 1-4R; CANR 1, 43, 74, 132; CDALBS; CN 2, 3, 4, 5, 6, 7; DA; DA3; DAB; DAC; DAM MST; DLB 28, 206; DLBY 1980; EWL 3; EXPS; FW; MAL 5; MTCW 1, 2; MTFW 2005; RGAL 4; RGSF 2; SSFS 1; TCLE 1:2; TCWW 2; TUS

Olson, Charles (John) 1910-1970 .. **CLC 1, 2, 5, 6, 9, 11, 29; PC 19**
See also AMWS 2; CA 13-16; 25-28R; CABS 2; CANR 35, 61; CAP 1; CP 1; DAM POET; DLB 5, 16, 193; EWL 3; MAL 5; MTCW 1, 2; RGAL 4; WP

Olson, Toby 1937- .... **CLC 28**
See also CA 65-68; CANR 9, 31, 84; CP 3, 4, 5, 6, 7

Olyesha, Yuri
See Olesha, Yuri (Karlovich)

Olympiodorus of Thebes c. 375-c.
430 .... **CMLC 59**

Omar Khayyam
See Khayyam, Omar
See also RGWL 2, 3

Ondaatje, (Philip) Michael 1943- .... **CLC 14, 29, 51, 76, 180; PC 28**
See also AAYA 66; CA 77-80; CANR 42, 74, 109, 133; CN 5, 6, 7; CP 1, 2, 3, 4, 5, 6, 7; DA3; DAB; DAC; DAM MST; DLB 60; EWL 3; LATS 1:2; LMFS 2; MTCW 2; MTFW 2005; PFS 8, 19; TCLE 1:2; TWA; WWE 1

Oneal, Elizabeth 1934-
See Oneal, Zibby
See also CA 106; CANR 28, 84; MAICYA 1, 2; SATA 30, 82; YAW

Oneal, Zibby .... **CLC 30**
See Oneal, Elizabeth
See also AAYA 5, 41; BYA 13; CLR 13; JRDA; WYA

O'Neill, Eugene (Gladstone)
1888-1953 ... **DC 20; TCLC 1, 6, 27, 49; WLC**
See also AAYA 54; AITN 1; AMW; AMWC 1; CA 110; 132; CAD; CANR 131; CDALB 1929-1941; DA; DA3; DAB; DAC; DAM DRAM, MST; DFS 2, 4, 5, 6, 9, 11, 12, 16, 20; DLB 7; EWL 3; LAIT 3; LMFS 2; MAL 5; MTCW 1, 2; MTFW 2005; RGAL 4; TUS

Onetti, Juan Carlos 1909-1994 ... **CLC 7, 10; HLCS 2; SSC 23; TCLC 131**
See also CA 85-88; 145; CANR 32, 63; CD-WLB 3; CWW 2; DAM MULT, NOV;

DLB 113; EWL 3; HW 1, 2; LAW; MTCW 1, 2; MTFW 2005; RGSF 2

O Nuallain, Brian 1911-1966
See O'Brien, Flann
See also CA 21-22; 25-28R; CAP 2; DLB 231; FANT; TEA

Ophuls, Max 1902-1957 .... **TCLC 79**
See also CA 113

Opie, Amelia 1769-1853 .... **NCLC 65**
See also DLB 116, 159; RGEL 2

Oppen, George 1908-1984 ..... **CLC 7, 13, 34; PC 35; TCLC 107**
See also CA 13-16R; 113; CANR 8, 82; CP 1, 2, 3; DLB 5, 165

Oppenheim, E(dward) Phillips
1866-1946 .... **TCLC 45**
See also CA 111; 202; CMW 4; DLB 70

Opuls, Max
See Ophuls, Max

Orage, A(lfred) R(ichard)
1873-1934 .... **TCLC 157**
See also CA 122

Origen c. 185-c. 254 .... **CMLC 19**

Orlovitz, Gil 1918-1973 .... **CLC 22**
See also CA 77-80; 45-48; CN 1; CP 1, 2; DLB 2, 5

O'Rourke, P(atrick) J(ake) 1947- .. **CLC 209**
See also CA 77-80; CANR 13, 41, 67, 111; CPW; DAM POP; DLB 185

Orris
See Ingelow, Jean

Ortega y Gasset, Jose 1883-1955 ...... **HLC 2; TCLC 9**
See also CA 106; 130; DAM MULT; EW 9; EWL 3; HW 1, 2; MTCW 1, 2; MTFW 2005

Ortese, Anna Maria 1914-1998 .... **CLC 89**
See also DLB 177; EWL 3

Ortiz, Simon J(oseph) 1941- ... **CLC 45, 208; NNAL; PC 17**
See also AMWS 4; CA 134; CANR 69, 118; CP 3, 4, 5, 6, 7; DAM MULT, POET; DLB 120, 175, 256; EXPP; MAL 5; PFS 4, 16; RGAL 4; TCWW 2

Orton, Joe ...... **CLC 4, 13, 43; DC 3; TCLC 157**
See Orton, John Kingsley
See also BRWS 5; CBD; CDBLB 1960 to Present; DFS 3, 6; DLB 13, 310; GLL 1; RGEL 2; TEA; WLIT 4

Orton, John Kingsley 1933-1967
See Orton, Joe
See also CA 85-88; CANR 35, 66; DAM DRAM; MTCW 1, 2; MTFW 2005

Orwell, George ...... **SSC 68; TCLC 2, 6, 15, 31, 51, 128, 129; WLC**
See Blair, Eric (Arthur)
See also BPFB 3; BRW 7; BYA 5; CDBLB 1945-1960; CLR 68; DAB; DLB 15, 98, 195, 255; EWL 3; EXPN; LAIT 4, 5; LATS 1:1; NFS 3, 7; RGEL 2; SCFW 1, 2; SFW 4; SSFS 4; TEA; WLIT 4; YAW

Osborne, David
See Silverberg, Robert

Osborne, George
See Silverberg, Robert

Osborne, John (James) 1929-1994 .... **CLC 1, 2, 5, 11, 45; TCLC 153; WLC**
See also BRWS 1; CA 13-16R; 147; CANR 21, 56; CBD; CDBLB 1945-1960; DA; DAB; DAC; DAM DRAM, MST; DFS 4, 19; DLB 13; EWL 3; MTCW 1, 2; MTFW 2005; RGEL 2

Osborne, Lawrence 1958- .... **CLC 50**
See also CA 189

Osbourne, Lloyd 1868-1947 .... **TCLC 93**

Osgood, Frances Sargent
1811-1850 .... **NCLC 141**
See also DLB 250

Oshima, Nagisa 1932- .... **CLC 20**
See also CA 116; 121; CANR 78

Oskison, John Milton
1874-1947 .... **NNAL; TCLC 35**
See also CA 144; CANR 84; DAM MULT;
DLB 175

Ossian c. 3rd cent. - .... **CMLC 28**
See Macpherson, James

Ossoli, Sarah Margaret (Fuller)
1810-1850 .... **NCLC 5, 50**
See Fuller, Margaret; Fuller, Sarah Margaret
See also CDALB 1640-1865; FW; LMFS 1;
SATA 25

Ostriker, Alicia (Suskin) 1937- .... **CLC 132**
See also CA 25-28R; CAAS 24; CANR 10,
30, 62, 99; CWP; DLB 120; EXPP; PFS
19

Ostrovsky, Aleksandr Nikolaevich
See Ostrovsky, Alexander
See also DLB 277

Ostrovsky, Alexander 1823-1886 .. **NCLC 30,
57**
See Ostrovsky, Aleksandr Nikolaevich

Otero, Blas de 1916-1979 .... **CLC 11**
See also CA 89-92; DLB 134; EWL 3

O'Trigger, Sir Lucius
See Horne, Richard Henry Hengist

Otto, Rudolf 1869-1937 .... **TCLC 85**

Otto, Whitney 1955- .... **CLC 70**
See also CA 140; CANR 120

Otway, Thomas 1652-1685 ... **DC 24; LC 106**
See also DAM DRAM; DLB 80; RGEL 2

Ouida .... **TCLC 43**
See De la Ramee, Marie Louise (Ouida)
See also DLB 18, 156; RGEL 2

Ouologuem, Yambo 1940- .... **CLC 146**
See also CA 111; 176

Ousmane, Sembene 1923- ... **BLC 3; CLC 66**
See Sembene, Ousmane
See also BW 1, 3; CA 117; 125; CANR 81;
CWW 2; MTCW 1

Ovid 43B.C.-17 .... **CMLC 7; PC 2**
See also AW 2; CDWLB 1; DA3; DAM
POET; DLB 211; PFS 22; RGWL 2, 3;
WP

Owen, Hugh
See Faust, Frederick (Schiller)

Owen, Wilfred (Edward Salter)
1893-1918 ... **PC 19; TCLC 5, 27; WLC**
See also BRW 6; CA 104; 141; CDBLB
1914-1945; DA; DAB; DAC; DAM MST;
POET; DLB 20; EWL 3; EXPP; MTCW
2; MTFW 2005; PFS 10; RGEL 2; WLIT
4

Owens, Louis (Dean) 1948-2002 .... **NNAL**
See also CA 137; 179; 207; CAAE 179;
CAAS 24; CANR 71

Owens, Rochelle 1936- .... **CLC 8**
See also CA 17-20R; CAAS 2; CAD;
CANR 39; CD 5, 6; CP 1, 2, 3, 4, 5, 6, 7;
CWD; CWP

Oz, Amos 1939- ...... **CLC 5, 8, 11, 27, 33, 54;
SSC 66**
See also CA 53-56; CANR 27, 47, 65, 113,
138; CWW 2; DAM NOV; EWL 3;
MTCW 1, 2; MTFW 2005; RGSF 2;
RGWL 3; WLIT 6

Ozick, Cynthia 1928- .... **CLC 3, 7, 28, 62,
155; SSC 15, 60**
See also AMWS 5; BEST 90:1; CA 17-20R;
CANR 23, 58, 116; CN 3, 4, 5, 6, 7;
CPW; DA3; DAM NOV, POP; DLB 28,
152, 299; DLBY 1982; EWL 3; EXPS;
INT CANR-23; MAL 5; MTCW 1, 2;
MTFW 2005; RGAL 4; RGSF 2; SSFS 3,
12

Ozu, Yasujiro 1903-1963 .... **CLC 16**
See also CA 112

Pabst, G. W. 1885-1967 .... **TCLC 127**

Pacheco, C.
See Pessoa, Fernando (Antonio Nogueira)

Pacheco, Jose Emilio 1939- .... **HLC 2**
See also CA 111; 131; CANR 65; CWW 2;
DAM MULT; DLB 290; EWL 3; HW 1,
2; RGSF 2

Pa Chin .... **CLC 18**
See Li Fei-kan
See also EWL 3

Pack, Robert 1929- .... **CLC 13**
See also CA 1-4R; CANR 3, 44, 82; CP 1,
2, 3, 4, 5, 6, 7; DLB 5; SATA 118

Padgett, Lewis
See Kuttner, Henry

Padilla (Lorenzo), Heberto
1932-2000 .... **CLC 38**
See also AITN 1; CA 123; 131; 189; CWW
2; EWL 3; HW 1

Page, James Patrick 1944-
See Page, Jimmy
See also CA 204

Page, Jimmy 1944- .... **CLC 12**
See Page, James Patrick

Page, Louise 1955- .... **CLC 40**
See also CA 140; CANR 76; CBD; CD 5,
6; CWD; DLB 233

Page, P(atricia) K(athleen) 1916- ...... **CLC 7,
18; PC 12**
See Cape, Judith
See also CA 53-56; CANR 4, 22, 65; CP 1,
2, 3, 4, 5, 6, 7; DAC; DAM MST; DLB
68; MTCW 1; RGEL 2

Page, Stanton
See Fuller, Henry Blake

Page, Stanton
See Fuller, Henry Blake

Page, Thomas Nelson 1853-1922 .... **SSC 23**
See also CA 118; 177; DLB 12, 78; DLBD
13; RGAL 4

Pagels, Elaine Hiesey 1943- .... **CLC 104**
See also CA 45-48; CANR 2, 24, 51; FW;
NCFS 4

Paget, Violet 1856-1935
See Lee, Vernon
See also CA 104; 166; GLL 1; HGG

Paget-Lowe, Henry
See Lovecraft, H(oward) P(hillips)

Paglia, Camille (Anna) 1947- .... **CLC 68**
See also CA 140; CANR 72, 139; CPW;
FW; GLL 2; MTCW 2; MTFW 2005

Paige, Richard
See Koontz, Dean R.

Paine, Thomas 1737-1809 .... **NCLC 62**
See also AMWS 1; CDALB 1640-1865;
DLB 31, 43, 73, 158; LAIT 1; RGAL 4;
RGEL 2; TUS

Pakenham, Antonia
See Fraser, Antonia (Pakenham)

Palamas, Costis
See Palamas, Kostes

Palamas, Kostes 1859-1943 .... **TCLC 5**
See Palamas, Kostis
See also CA 105; 190; RGWL 2, 3

Palamas, Kostis
See Palamas, Kostes
See also EWL 3

Palazzeschi, Aldo 1885-1974 .... **CLC 11**
See also CA 89-92; 53-56; DLB 114, 264;
EWL 3

Pales Matos, Luis 1898-1959 .... **HLCS 2**
See Pales Matos, Luis
See also DLB 290; HW 1; LAW

Paley, Grace 1922- .. **CLC 4, 6, 37, 140; SSC
8**
See also AMWS 6; CA 25-28R; CANR 13,
46, 74, 118; CN 2, 3, 4, 5, 6, 7; CPW;
DA3; DAM POP; DLB 28, 218; EWL 3;
EXPS; FW; INT CANR-13; MAL 5;

MAWW; MTCW 1, 2; MTFW 2005;
RGAL 4; RGSF 2; SSFS 3, 20

Palin, Michael (Edward) 1943- .... **CLC 21**
See Monty Python
See also CA 107; CANR 35, 109; SATA 67

Palliser, Charles 1947- .... **CLC 65**
See also CA 136; CANR 76; CN 5, 6, 7

Palma, Ricardo 1833-1919 .... **TCLC 29**
See also CA 168; LAW

Pamuk, Orhan 1952- .... **CLC 185**
See also CA 142; CANR 75, 127; CWW 2;
WLIT 6

Pancake, Breece Dexter 1952-1979
See Pancake, Breece D'J
See also CA 123; 109

Pancake, Breece D'J .... **CLC 29; SSC 61**
See Pancake, Breece Dexter
See also DLB 130

Panchenko, Nikolai .... **CLC 59**

Pankhurst, Emmeline (Goulden)
1858-1928 .... **TCLC 100**
See also CA 116; FW

Panko, Rudy
See Gogol, Nikolai (Vasilyevich)

Papadiamantis, Alexandros
1851-1911 .... **TCLC 29**
See also CA 168; EWL 3

Papadiamantopoulos, Johannes 1856-1910
See Moreas, Jean
See also CA 117

Papini, Giovanni 1881-1956 .... **TCLC 22**
See also CA 121; 180; DLB 264

Paracelsus 1493-1541 .... **LC 14**
See also DLB 179

Parasol, Peter
See Stevens, Wallace

Pardo Bazan, Emilia 1851-1921 .... **SSC 30**
See also EWL 3; FW; RGSF 2; RGWL 2, 3

Pareto, Vilfredo 1848-1923 .... **TCLC 69**
See also CA 175

Paretsky, Sara 1947- .... **CLC 135**
See also AAYA 30; BEST 90:3; CA 125;
129; CANR 59, 95; CMW 4; CPW; DA3;
DAM POP; DLB 306; INT CA-129;
MSW; RGAL 4

Parfenie, Maria
See Codrescu, Andrei

Parini, Jay (Lee) 1948- .... **CLC 54, 133**
See also CA 97-100, 229; CAAE 229;
CAAS 16; CANR 32, 87

Park, Jordan
See Kornbluth, C(yril) M.; Pohl, Frederik

Park, Robert E(zra) 1864-1944 ..... **TCLC 73**
See also CA 122; 165

Parker, Bert
See Ellison, Harlan (Jay)

Parker, Dorothy (Rothschild)
1893-1967 . **CLC 15, 68; PC 28; SSC 2;
TCLC 143**
See also AMWS 9; CA 19-20; 25-28R; CAP
2; DA3; DAM POET; DLB 11, 45, 86;
EXPP; FW; MAL 5; MAWW; MTCW 1,
2; MTFW 2005; PFS 18; RGAL 4; RGSF
2; TUS

Parker, Robert B(rown) 1932- .... **CLC 27**
See also AAYA 28; BEST 89:4; BPFB 3;
CA 49-52; CANR 1, 26, 52, 89, 128;
CMW 4; CPW; DAM NOV, POP; DLB
306; INT CANR-26; MSW; MTCW 1;
MTFW 2005

Parkin, Frank 1940- .... **CLC 43**
See also CA 147

Parkman, Francis, Jr. 1823-1893 .. **NCLC 12**
See also AMWS 2; DLB 1, 30, 183, 186,
235; RGAL 4

Pepys, Samuel 1633-1703 ... **LC 11, 58; WLC**
See also BRW 2; CDBLB 1660-1789; DA; DA3; DAB; DAC; DAM MST; DLB 101, 213; NCFS 4; RGEL 2; TEA; WLIT 3

Percy, Thomas 1729-1811 .... **NCLC 95**
See also DLB 104

Percy, Walker 1916-1990 .... **CLC 2, 3, 6, 8, 14, 18, 47, 65**
See also AMWS 3; BPFB 3; CA 1-4R; 131; CANR 1, 23, 64; CN 1, 2, 3, 4; CPW; CSW; DA3; DAM NOV, POP; DLB 2; DLBY 1980, 1990; EWL 3; MAL 5; MTCW 1, 2; MTFW 2005; RGAL 4; TUS

Percy, William Alexander 1885-1942 .... **TCLC 84**
See also CA 163; MTCW 2

Perec, Georges 1936-1982 .... **CLC 56, 116**
See also CA 141; DLB 83, 299; EWL 3; GFL 1789 to the Present; RGWL 3

Pereda (y Sanchez de Porrua), Jose Maria de 1833-1906 .... **TCLC 16**
See also CA 117

Pereda y Porrua, Jose Maria de
See Pereda (y Sanchez de Porrua), Jose Maria de

Peregoy, George Weems
See Mencken, H(enry) L(ouis)

Perelman, S(idney) J(oseph) 1904-1979 .. **CLC 3, 5, 9, 15, 23, 44, 49; SSC 32**
See also AITN 1, 2; BPFB 3; CA 73-76; 89-92; CANR 18; DAM DRAM; DLB 11, 44; MTCW 1, 2; MTFW 2005; RGAL 4

Peret, Benjamin 1899-1959 .... **PC 33; TCLC 20**
See also CA 117; 186; GFL 1789 to the Present

Peretz, Isaac Leib
See Peretz, Isaac Loeb
See also CA 201

Peretz, Isaac Loeb 1851(?)-1915 ...... **SSC 26; TCLC 16**
See Peretz, Isaac Leib
See also CA 109

Peretz, Yitzkhok Leibush
See Peretz, Isaac Loeb

Perez Galdos, Benito 1843-1920 ..... **HLCS 2; TCLC 27**
See Galdos, Benito Perez
See also CA 125; 153; EWL 3; HW 1; RGWL 2, 3

Peri Rossi, Cristina 1941- .. **CLC 156; HLCS 2**
See also CA 131; CANR 59, 81; CWW 2; DLB 145, 290; EWL 3; HW 1, 2

Perlata
See Peret, Benjamin

Perloff, Marjorie G(abrielle) 1931- .... **CLC 137**
See also CA 57-60; CANR 7, 22, 49, 104

Perrault, Charles 1628-1703 .... **LC 2, 56**
See also BYA 4; CLR 79; DLB 268; GFL Beginnings to 1789; MAICYA 1, 2; RGWL 2, 3; SATA 25; WCH

Perry, Anne 1938- .... **CLC 126**
See also CA 101; CANR 22, 50, 84; CMW 4; CN 6, 7; CPW; DLB 276

Perry, Brighton
See Sherwood, Robert E(mmet)

Perse, St.-John
See Leger, (Marie-Rene Auguste) Alexis Saint-Leger

Perse, Saint-John
See Leger, (Marie-Rene Auguste) Alexis Saint-Leger
See also DLB 258; RGWL 3

Persius 34-62 .... **CMLC 74**
See also AW 2; DLB 211; RGWL 2, 3

Perutz, Leo(pold) 1882-1957 .... **TCLC 60**
See also CA 147; DLB 81

Peseenz, Tulio F.
See Lopez y Fuentes, Gregorio

Pesetsky, Bette 1932- .... **CLC 28**
See also CA 133; DLB 130

Peshkov, Alexei Maximovich 1868-1936
See Gorky, Maxim
See also CA 105; 141; CANR 83; DA; DAC; DAM DRAM, MST, NOV; MTCW 2; MTFW 2005

Pessoa, Fernando (Antonio Nogueira) 1888-1935 ..... **HLC 2; PC 20; TCLC 27**
See also CA 125; 183; DAM MULT; DLB 287; EW 10; EWL 3; RGWL 2, 3; WP

Peterkin, Julia Mood 1880-1961 ...... **CLC 31**
See also CA 102; DLB 9

Peters, Joan K(aren) 1945- .... **CLC 39**
See also CA 158; CANR 109

Peters, Robert L(ouis) 1924- .... **CLC 7**
See also CA 13-16R; CAAS 8; CP 1, 7; DLB 105

Petofi, Sandor 1823-1849 .... **NCLC 21**
See also RGWL 2, 3

Petrakis, Harry Mark 1923- .... **CLC 3**
See also CA 9-12R; CANR 4, 30, 85; CN 1, 2, 3, 4, 5, 6, 7

Petrarch 1304-1374 .... **CMLC 20; PC 8**
See also DA3; DAM POET; EW 2; LMFS 1; RGWL 2, 3; WLIT 7

Petronius c. 20-66 .... **CMLC 34**
See also AW 2; CDWLB 1; DLB 211; RGWL 2, 3

Petrov, Evgeny .... **TCLC 21**
See Kataev, Evgeny Petrovich

Petry, Ann (Lane) 1908-1997 .. **CLC 1, 7, 18; TCLC 112**
See also AFAW 1, 2; BPFB 3; BW 1, 3; BYA 2; CA 5-8R; 157; CAAS 6; CANR 4, 46; CLR 12; CN 1, 2, 3, 4, 5, 6; DLB 76; EWL 3; JRDA; LAIT 1; MAICYA 1, 2; MAICYAS 1; MTCW 1; RGAL 4; SATA 5; SATA-Obit 94; TUS

Petursson, Halligrimur 1614-1674 .... **LC 8**

Peychinovich
See Vazov, Ivan (Minchov)

Phaedrus c. 15B.C.-c. 50 .... **CMLC 25**
See also DLB 211

Phelps (Ward), Elizabeth Stuart
See Phelps, Elizabeth Stuart
See also FW

Phelps, Elizabeth Stuart 1844-1911 .... **TCLC 113**
See Phelps (Ward), Elizabeth Stuart
See also DLB 74

Philips, Katherine 1632-1664 . **LC 30; PC 40**
See also DLB 131; RGEL 2

Philipson, Morris H. 1926- .... **CLC 53**
See also CA 1-4R; CANR 4

Phillips, Caryl 1958- .... **BLCS; CLC 96**
See also BRWS 5; BW 2; CA 141; CANR 63, 104, 140; CBD; CD 5, 6; CN 5, 6, 7; DA3; DAM MULT; DLB 157; EWL 3; MTCW 2; MTFW 2005; WLIT 4; WWE 1

Phillips, David Graham 1867-1911 .... **TCLC 44**
See also CA 108; 176; DLB 9, 12, 303; RGAL 4

Phillips, Jack
See Sandburg, Carl (August)

Phillips, Jayne Anne 1952- .... **CLC 15, 33, 139; SSC 16**
See also AAYA 57; BPFB 3; CA 101; CANR 24, 50, 96; CN 4, 5, 6, 7; CSW; DLBY 1980; INT CANR-24; MTCW 1, 2; MTFW 2005; RGAL 4; RGSF 2; SSFS 4

Phillips, Richard
See Dick, Philip K(indred)

Phillips, Robert (Schaeffer) 1938- .... **CLC 28**
See also CA 17-20R; CAAS 13; CANR 8; DLB 105

Phillips, Ward
See Lovecraft, H(oward) P(hillips)

Philostratus, Flavius c. 179-c. 244 .... **CMLC 62**

Piccolo, Lucio 1901-1969 .... **CLC 13**
See also CA 97-100; DLB 114; EWL 3

Pickthall, Marjorie L(owry) C(hristie) 1883-1922 .... **TCLC 21**
See also CA 107; DLB 92

Pico della Mirandola, Giovanni 1463-1494 .... **LC 15**
See also LMFS 1

Piercy, Marge 1936- .... **CLC 3, 6, 14, 18, 27, 62, 128; PC 29**
See also BPFB 3; CA 21-24R, 187; CAAE 187; CAAS 1; CANR 13, 43, 66, 111; CN 3, 4, 5, 6, 7; CP 1, 2, 3, 4, 5, 6, 7; CWP; DLB 120, 227; EXPP; FW; MAL 5; MTCW 1, 2; MTFW 2005; PFS 9, 22; SFW 4

Piers, Robert
See Anthony, Piers

Pieyre de Mandiargues, Andre 1909-1991
See Mandiargues, Andre Pieyre de
See also CA 103; 136; CANR 22, 82; EWL 3; GFL 1789 to the Present

Pilnyak, Boris 1894-1938 . **SSC 48; TCLC 23**
See Vogau, Boris Andreyevich
See also EWL 3

Pinchback, Eugene
See Toomer, Jean

Pincherle, Alberto 1907-1990 ...... **CLC 11, 18**
See Moravia, Alberto
See also CA 25-28R; 132; CANR 33, 63, 142; DAM NOV; MTCW 1; MTFW 2005

Pinckney, Darryl 1953- .... **CLC 76**
See also BW 2, 3; CA 143; CANR 79

Pindar 518(?)B.C.-438(?)B.C. .... **CMLC 12; PC 19**
See also AW 1; CDWLB 1; DLB 176; RGWL 2

Pineda, Cecile 1942- .... **CLC 39**
See also CA 118; DLB 209

Pinero, Arthur Wing 1855-1934 .... **TCLC 32**
See also CA 110; 153; DAM DRAM; DLB 10; RGEL 2

Pinero, Miguel (Antonio Gomez) 1946-1988 .... **CLC 4, 55**
See also CA 61-64; 125; CAD; CANR 29, 90; DLB 266; HW 1; LLW

Pinget, Robert 1919-1997 .... **CLC 7, 13, 37**
See also CA 85-88; 160; CWW 2; DLB 83; EWL 3; GFL 1789 to the Present

Pink Floyd
See Barrett, (Roger) Syd; Gilmour, David; Mason, Nick; Waters, Roger; Wright, Rick

Pinkney, Edward 1802-1828 .... **NCLC 31**
See also DLB 248

Pinkwater, D. Manus
See Pinkwater, Daniel Manus

Pinkwater, Daniel
See Pinkwater, Daniel Manus

Pinkwater, Daniel M.
See Pinkwater, Daniel Manus

Pinkwater, Daniel Manus 1941- .... **CLC 35**
See also AAYA 1, 46; BYA 9; CA 29-32R; CANR 12, 38, 89, 143; CLR 4; CSW; FANT; JRDA; MAICYA 1, 2; SAAS 3; SATA 8, 46, 76, 114, 158; SFW 4; YAW

Pinkwater, Manus
See Pinkwater, Daniel Manus

Pinsky, Robert 1940- .... **CLC 9, 19, 38, 94, 121, 216; PC 27**
See also AMWS 6; CA 29-32R; CAAS 4; CANR 58, 97, 138; CP 3, 4, 5, 6, 7; DA3; DAM POET; DLBY 1982, 1998; MAL 5; MTCW 2; MTFW 2005; PFS 18; RGAL 4; TCLE 1:2

Pinta, Harold
See Pinter, Harold

Pinter, Harold 1930- .. **CLC 1, 3, 6, 9, 11, 15, 27, 58, 73, 199; DC 15; WLC**
See also BRWR 1; BRWS 1; CA 5-8R; CANR 33, 65, 112, 145; CBD; CD 5, 6; CDBLB 1960 to Present; CP 1; DA; DA3; DAB; DAC; DAM DRAM, MST; DFS 3, 5, 7, 14; DLB 13, 310; EWL 3; IDFW 3, 4; LMFS 2; MTCW 1, 2; MTFW 2005; RGEL 2; TEA

Piozzi, Hester Lynch (Thrale)
1741-1821 .... **NCLC 57**
See also DLB 104, 142

Pirandello, Luigi 1867-1936 .. **DC 5; SSC 22; TCLC 4, 29, 172; WLC**
See also CA 104; 153; CANR 103; DA; DA3; DAB; DAC; DAM DRAM, MST; DFS 4, 9; DLB 264; EW 8; EWL 3; MTCW 2; MTFW 2005; RGSF 2; RGWL 2, 3; WLIT 7

Pirsig, Robert M(aynard) 1928- ... **CLC 4, 6, 73**
See also CA 53-56; CANR 42, 74; CPW 1; DA3; DAM POP; MTCW 1, 2; MTFW 2005; SATA 39

Pisarev, Dmitrii Ivanovich
See Pisarev, Dmitry Ivanovich
See also DLB 277

Pisarev, Dmitry Ivanovich
1840-1868 .... **NCLC 25**
See also Pisarev, Dmitrii Ivanovich

Pix, Mary (Griffith) 1666-1709 .... **LC 8**
See also DLB 80

Pixerecourt, (Rene Charles) Guilbert de
1773-1844 .... **NCLC 39**
See also DLB 192; GFL 1789 to the Present

Plaatje, Sol(omon) T(shekisho)
1878-1932 .... **BLCS; TCLC 73**
See also BW 2, 3; CA 141; CANR 79; DLB 125, 225

Plaidy, Jean
See Hibbert, Eleanor Alice Burford

Planche, James Robinson
1796-1880 .... **NCLC 42**
See also RGEL 2

Plant, Robert 1948- .... **CLC 12**

Plante, David (Robert) 1940- . **CLC 7, 23, 38**
See also CA 37-40R; CANR 12, 36, 58, 82; CN 2, 3, 4, 5, 6, 7; DAM NOV; DLBY 1983; INT CANR-12; MTCW 1

Plath, Sylvia 1932-1963 ..... **CLC 1, 2, 3, 5, 9, 11, 14, 17, 50, 51, 62, 111; PC 1, 37; WLC**
See also AAYA 13; AMWR 2; AMWS 1; BPFB 3; CA 19-20; CANR 34, 101; CAP 2; CDALB 1941-1968; DA; DA3; DAB; DAC; DAM MST, POET; DLB 5, 6, 152; EWL 3; EXPN; EXPP; FL 1:6; FW; LAIT 4; MAL 5; MAWW; MTCW 1, 2; MTFW 2005; NFS 1; PAB; PFS 1, 15; RGAL 4; SATA 96; TUS; WP; YAW

Plato c. 428B.C.-347B.C. .... **CMLC 8, 75; WLCS**
See also AW 1; CDWLB 1; DA; DA3; DAB; DAC; DAM MST; DLB 176; LAIT 1; LATS 1:1; RGWL 2, 3

Platonov, Andrei
See Klimentov, Andrei Platonovich

Platonov, Andrei Platonovich
See Klimentov, Andrei Platonovich
See also DLB 272

Platonov, Andrey Platonovich
See Klimentov, Andrei Platonovich
See also EWL 3

Platt, Kin 1911- .... **CLC 26**
See also AAYA 11; CA 17-20R; CANR 11; JRDA; SAAS 17; SATA 21, 86; WYA

Plautus c. 254B.C.-c. 184B.C. ...... **CMLC 24; DC 6**
See also AW 1; CDWLB 1; DLB 211; RGWL 2, 3

Plick et Plock
See Simenon, Georges (Jacques Christian)

Plieksans, Janis
See Rainis, Janis

Plimpton, George (Ames)
1927-2003 .... **CLC 36**
See also AITN 1; CA 21-24R; 224; CANR 32, 70, 103, 133; DLB 185, 241; MTCW 1, 2; MTFW 2005; SATA 10; SATA-Obit 150

Pliny the Elder c. 23-79 .... **CMLC 23**
See also DLB 211

Pliny the Younger c. 61-c. 112 ...... **CMLC 62**
See also AW 2; DLB 211

Plomer, William Charles Franklin
1903-1973 .... **CLC 4, 8**
See also AFW; BRWS 11; CA 21-22; CANR 34; CAP 2; CN 1; CP 1, 2; DLB 20, 162, 191, 225; EWL 3; MTCW 1; RGEL 2; RGSF 2; SATA 24

Plotinus 204-270 .... **CMLC 46**
See also CDWLB 1; DLB 176

Plowman, Piers
See Kavanagh, Patrick (Joseph)

Plum, J.
See Wodehouse, P(elham) G(renville)

Plumly, Stanley (Ross) 1939- .... **CLC 33**
See also CA 108; 110; CANR 97; CP 3, 4, 5, 6, 7; DLB 5, 193; INT CA-110

Plumpe, Friedrich Wilhelm
1888-1931 .... **TCLC 53**
See also CA 112

Plutarch c. 46-c. 120 .... **CMLC 60**
See also AW 2; CDWLB 1; DLB 176; RGWL 2, 3; TWA

Po Chu-i 772-846 .... **CMLC 24**

Podhoretz, Norman 1930- .... **CLC 189**
See also AMWS 8; CA 9-12R; CANR 7, 78, 135

Poe, Edgar Allan 1809-1849 ..... **NCLC 1, 16, 55, 78, 94, 97, 117; PC 1, 54; SSC 1, 22, 34, 35, 54, 88; WLC**
See also AAYA 14; AMW; AMWC 1; AMWR 2; BPFB 3; BYA 5, 11; CDALB 1640-1865; CMW 4; DA; DA3; DAB; DAC; DAM MST, POET; DLB 3, 59, 73, 74, 248, 254; EXPP; EXPS; GL 3; HGG; LAIT 2; LATS 1:1; LMFS 1; MSW; PAB; PFS 1, 3, 9; RGAL 4; RGSF 2; SATA 23; SCFW 1, 2; SFW 4; SSFS 2, 4, 7, 8, 16; SUFW; TUS; WP; WYA

Poet of Titchfield Street, The
See Pound, Ezra (Weston Loomis)

Poggio Bracciolini, Gian Francesco
1380-1459 .... **LC 125**

Pohl, Frederik 1919- .... **CLC 18; SSC 25**
See also AAYA 24; CA 61-64, 188; CAAE 188; CAAS 1; CANR 11, 37, 81, 140; CN 1, 2, 3, 4, 5, 6; DLB 8; INT CANR-11; MTCW 1, 2; MTFW 2005; SATA 24; SCFW 1, 2; SFW 4

Poirier, Louis 1910-
See Gracq, Julien
See also CA 122; 126; CANR 141

Poitier, Sidney 1927- .... **CLC 26**
See also AAYA 60; BW 1; CA 117; CANR 94

Pokagon, Simon 1830-1899 .... **NNAL**
See also DAM MULT

Polanski, Roman 1933- .... **CLC 16, 178**
See also CA 77-80

Poliakoff, Stephen 1952- .... **CLC 38**
See also CA 106; CANR 116; CBD; CD 5, 6; DLB 13

Police, The
See Copeland, Stewart (Armstrong); Summers, Andrew James

Polidori, John William 1795-1821 . **NCLC 51**
See also DLB 116; HGG

Poliziano, Angelo 1454-1494 .... **LC 120**
See also WLIT 7

Pollitt, Katha 1949- .... **CLC 28, 122**
See also CA 120; 122; CANR 66, 108; MTCW 1, 2; MTFW 2005

Pollock, (Mary) Sharon 1936- .... **CLC 50**
See also CA 141; CANR 132; CD 5; CWD; DAC; DAM DRAM, MST; DFS 3; DLB 60; FW

Pollock, Sharon 1936- .... **DC 20**
See also CD 6

Polo, Marco 1254-1324 .... **CMLC 15**
See also WLIT 7

Polonsky, Abraham (Lincoln)
1910-1999 .... **CLC 92**
See also CA 104; 187; DLB 26; INT CA-104

Polybius c. 200B.C.-c. 118B.C. ...... **CMLC 17**
See also AW 1; DLB 176; RGWL 2, 3

Pomerance, Bernard 1940- .... **CLC 13**
See also CA 101; CAD; CANR 49, 134; CD 5, 6; DAM DRAM; DFS 9; LAIT 2

Ponge, Francis 1899-1988 .... **CLC 6, 18**
See also CA 85-88; 126; CANR 40, 86; DAM POET; DLBY 2002; EWL 3; GFL 1789 to the Present; RGWL 2, 3

Poniatowska, Elena 1933- . **CLC 140; HLC 2**
See also CA 101; CANR 32, 66, 107; CDWLB 3; CWW 2; DAM MULT; DLB 113; EWL 3; HW 1, 2; LAWS 1; WLIT 1

Pontoppidan, Henrik 1857-1943 .... **TCLC 29**
See also CA 170; DLB 300

Ponty, Maurice Merleau
See Merleau-Ponty, Maurice

Poole, Josephine .... **CLC 17**
See Helyar, Jane Penelope Josephine
See also SAAS 2; SATA 5

Popa, Vasko 1922-1991 . **CLC 19; TCLC 167**
See also CA 112; 148; CDWLB 4; DLB 181; EWL 3; RGWL 2, 3

Pope, Alexander 1688-1744 ...... **LC 3, 58, 60, 64; PC 26; WLC**
See also BRW 3; BRWC 1; BRWR 1; CDBLB 1660-1789; DA; DA3; DAB; DAC; DAM MST, POET; DLB 95, 101, 213; EXPP; PAB; PFS 12; RGEL 2; WLIT 3; WP

Popov, Evgenii Anatol'evich
See Popov, Yevgeny
See also DLB 285

Popov, Yevgeny .... **CLC 59**
See Popov, Evgenii Anatol'evich

Poquelin, Jean-Baptiste
See Moliere

Porete, Marguerite (?)-1310 .... **CMLC 73**
See also DLB 208

Porphyry c. 233-c. 305 .... **CMLC 71**

Porter, Connie (Rose) 1959(?)- .... **CLC 70**
See also AAYA 65; BW 2, 3; CA 142; CANR 90, 109; SATA 81, 129

Porter, Gene(va Grace) Stratton .. **TCLC 21**
See Stratton-Porter, Gene(va Grace)
See also BPFB 3; CA 112; CWRI 5; RHW

Porter, Katherine Anne 1890-1980 ... **CLC 1, 3, 7, 10, 13, 15, 27, 101; SSC 4, 31, 43**
See also AAYA 42; AITN 2; AMW; BPFB 3; CA 1-4R; 101; CANR 1, 65; CDALBS; CN 1, 2; DA; DA3; DAB; DAC; DAM MST, NOV; DLB 4, 9, 102; DLBD 12;

DLBY 1980; EWL 3; EXPS; LAIT 3; MAL 5; MAWW; MTCW 1, 2; MTFW 2005; NFS 14; RGAL 4; RGSF 2; SATA 39; SATA-Obit 23; SSFS 1, 8, 11, 16; TCWW 2; TUS

Porter, Peter (Neville Frederick)
1929- .... **CLC 5, 13, 33**
See also CA 85-88; CP 1, 2, 3, 4, 5, 6, 7; DLB 40, 289; WWE 1

Porter, William Sydney 1862-1910
See Henry, O.
See also CA 104; 131; CDALB 1865-1917; DA; DA3; DAB; DAC; DAM MST; DLB 12, 78, 79; MAL 5; MTCW 1, 2; MTFW 2005; TUS; YABC 2

Portillo (y Pacheco), Jose Lopez
See Lopez Portillo (y Pacheco), Jose

Portillo Trambley, Estela 1927-1998 .. **HLC 2**
See Trambley, Estela Portillo
See also CANR 32; DAM MULT; DLB 209; HW 1

Posey, Alexander (Lawrence)
1873-1908 .... **NNAL**
See also CA 144; CANR 80; DAM MULT; DLB 175

Posse, Abel .... **CLC 70**

Post, Melville Davisson
1869-1930 .... **TCLC 39**
See also CA 110; 202; CMW 4

Potok, Chaim 1929-2002 ... **CLC 2, 7, 14, 26, 112**
See also AAYA 15, 50; AITN 1, 2; BPFB 3; BYA 1; CA 17-20R; 208; CANR 19, 35, 64, 98; CLR 92; CN 4, 5, 6; DA3; DAM NOV; DLB 28, 152; EXPN; INT CANR-19; LAIT 4; MTCW 1, 2; MTFW 2005; NFS 4; SATA 33, 106; SATA-Obit 134; TUS; YAW

Potok, Herbert Harold -2002
See Potok, Chaim

Potok, Herman Harold
See Potok, Chaim

Potter, Dennis (Christopher George)
1935-1994 .... **CLC 58, 86, 123**
See also BRWS 10; CA 107; 145; CANR 33, 61; CBD; DLB 233; MTCW 1

Pound, Ezra (Weston Loomis)
1885-1972 .. **CLC 1, 2, 3, 4, 5, 7, 10, 13, 18, 34, 48, 50, 112; PC 4; WLC**
See also AAYA 47; AMW; AMWR 1; CA 5-8R; 37-40R; CANR 40; CDALB 1917-1929; CP 1; DA; DA3; DAB; DAC; DAM MST, POET; DLB 4, 45, 63; DLBD 15; EFS 2; EWL 3; EXPP; LMFS 2; MAL 5; MTCW 1, 2; MTFW 2005; PAB; PFS 2, 8, 16; RGAL 4; TUS; WP

Povod, Reinaldo 1959-1994 .... **CLC 44**
See also CA 136; 146; CANR 83

Powell, Adam Clayton, Jr.
1908-1972 .... **BLC 3; CLC 89**
See also BW 1, 3; CA 102; 33-36R; CANR 86; DAM MULT

Powell, Anthony (Dymoke)
1905-2000 .... **CLC 1, 3, 7, 9, 10, 31**
See also BRW 7; CA 1-4R; 189; CANR 1, 32, 62, 107; CDBLB 1945-1960; CN 1, 2, 3, 4, 5, 6; DLB 15; EWL 3; MTCW 1, 2; MTFW 2005; RGEL 2; TEA

Powell, Dawn 1896(?)-1965 .... **CLC 66**
See also CA 5-8R; CANR 121; DLBY 1997

Powell, Padgett 1952- .... **CLC 34**
See also CA 126; CANR 63, 101; CSW; DLB 234; DLBY 01

Powell, (Oval) Talmage 1920-2000
See Queen, Ellery
See also CA 5-8R; CANR 2, 80

Power, Susan 1961- .... **CLC 91**
See also BYA 14; CA 160; CANR 135; NFS 11

Powers, J(ames) F(arl) 1917-1999 ..... **CLC 1, 4, 8, 57; SSC 4**
See also CA 1-4R; 181; CANR 2, 61; CN 1, 2, 3, 4, 5, 6; DLB 130; MTCW 1; RGAL 4; RGSF 2

Powers, John J(ames) 1945-
See Powers, John R.
See also CA 69-72

Powers, John R. .... **CLC 66**
See Powers, John J(ames)

Powers, Richard (S.) 1957- .... **CLC 93**
See also AMWS 9; BPFB 3; CA 148; CANR 80; CN 6, 7; MTFW 2005; TCLE 1:2

Pownall, David 1938- .... **CLC 10**
See also CA 89-92, 180; CAAS 18; CANR 49, 101; CBD; CD 5, 6; CN 4, 5, 6, 7; DLB 14

Powys, John Cowper 1872-1963 ... **CLC 7, 9, 15, 46, 125**
See also CA 85-88; CANR 106; DLB 15, 255; EWL 3; FANT; MTCW 1; MTFW 2005; RGEL 2; SUFW

Powys, T(heodore) F(rancis)
1875-1953 .... **TCLC 9**
See also BRWS 8; CA 106; 189; DLB 36, 162; EWL 3; FANT; RGEL 2; SUFW

Pozzo, Modesta
See Fonte, Moderata

Prado (Calvo), Pedro 1886-1952 ... **TCLC 75**
See also CA 131; DLB 283; HW 1; LAW

Prager, Emily 1952- .... **CLC 56**
See also CA 204

Pratchett, Terry 1948- .... **CLC 197**
See also AAYA 19, 54; BPFB 3; CA 143; CANR 87, 126; CLR 64; CN 6, 7; CPW; CWRI 5; FANT; MTFW 2005; SATA 82, 139; SFW 4; SUFW 2

Pratolini, Vasco 1913-1991 .... **TCLC 124**
See also CA 211; DLB 177; EWL 3; RGWL 2, 3

Pratt, E(dwin) J(ohn) 1883(?)-1964 . **CLC 19**
See also CA 141; 93-96; CANR 77; DAC; DAM POET; DLB 92; EWL 3; RGEL 2; TWA

Premchand .... **TCLC 21**
See Srivastava, Dhanpat Rai
See also EWL 3

Prescott, William Hickling
1796-1859 .... **NCLC 163**
See also DLB 1, 30, 59, 235

Preseren, France 1800-1849 .... **NCLC 127**
See also CDWLB 4; DLB 147

Preussler, Otfried 1923- .... **CLC 17**
See also CA 77-80; SATA 24

Prevert, Jacques (Henri Marie)
1900-1977 .... **CLC 15**
See also CA 77-80; 69-72; CANR 29, 61; DLB 258; EWL 3; GFL 1789 to the Present; IDFW 3, 4; MTCW 1; RGWL 2, 3; SATA-Obit 30

Prevost, (Antoine Francois)
1697-1763 .... **LC 1**
See also DLB 314; EW 4; GFL Beginnings to 1789; RGWL 2, 3

Price, (Edward) Reynolds 1933- ... **CLC 3, 6, 13, 43, 50, 63, 212; SSC 22**
See also AMWS 6; CA 1-4R; CANR 1, 37, 57, 87, 128; CN 1, 2, 3, 4, 5, 6, 7; CSW; DAM NOV; DLB 2, 218, 278; EWL 3; INT CANR-37; MAL 5; MTCW 2005; NFS 18

Price, Richard 1949- .... **CLC 6, 12**
See also CA 49-52; CANR 3; CN 7; DLBY 1981

Prichard, Katharine Susannah
1883-1969 .... **CLC 46**
See also CA 11-12; CANR 33; CAP 1; DLB 260; MTCW 1; RGEL 2; RGSF 2; SATA 66

Priestley, J(ohn) B(oynton)
1894-1984 .... **CLC 2, 5, 9, 34**
See also BRW 7; CA 9-12R; 113; CANR 33; CDBLB 1914-1945; CN 1, 2, 3; DA3; DAM DRAM, NOV; DLB 10, 34, 77, 100, 139; DLBY 1984; EWL 3; MTCW 1, 2; MTFW 2005; RGEL 2; SFW 4

Prince 1958- .... **CLC 35**
See also CA 213

Prince, F(rank) T(empleton)
1912-2003 .... **CLC 22**
See also CA 101; 219; CANR 43, 79; CP 1, 2, 3, 4, 5, 6, 7; DLB 20

Prince Kropotkin
See Kropotkin, Peter (Aleksieevich)

Prior, Matthew 1664-1721 .... **LC 4**
See also DLB 95; RGEL 2

Prishvin, Mikhail 1873-1954 .... **TCLC 75**
See Prishvin, Mikhail Mikhailovich

Prishvin, Mikhail Mikhailovich
See Prishvin, Mikhail
See also DLB 272; EWL 3

Pritchard, William H(arrison)
1932- .... **CLC 34**
See also CA 65-68; CANR 23, 95; DLB 111

Pritchett, V(ictor) S(awdon)
1900-1997 ... **CLC 5, 13, 15, 41; SSC 14**
See also BPFB 3; BRWS 3; CA 61-64; 157; CANR 31, 63; CN 1, 2, 3, 4, 5, 6; DA3; DAM NOV; DLB 15, 139; EWL 3; MTCW 1, 2; MTFW 2005; RGEL 2; RGSF 2; TEA

Private 19022
See Manning, Frederic

Probst, Mark 1925- .... **CLC 59**
See also CA 130

Procaccino, Michael
See Cristofer, Michael

Proclus c. 412-485 .... **CMLC 81**

Prokosch, Frederic 1908-1989 ...... **CLC 4, 48**
See also CA 73-76; 128; CANR 82; CN 1, 2, 3, 4; CP 1, 2, 3, 4; DLB 48; MTCW 2

Propertius, Sextus c. 50B.C.-c. 16B.C. .... **CMLC 32**
See also AW 2; CDWLB 1; DLB 211; RGWL 2, 3

Prophet, The
See Dreiser, Theodore (Herman Albert)

Prose, Francine 1947- .... **CLC 45**
See also CA 109; 112; CANR 46, 95, 132; DLB 234; MTFW 2005; SATA 101, 149

Proudhon
See Cunha, Euclides (Rodrigues Pimenta) da

Proulx, Annie
See Proulx, E. Annie

Proulx, E. Annie 1935- .... **CLC 81, 158**
See also AMWS 7; BPFB 3; CA 145; CANR 65, 110; CN 6, 7; CPW 1; DA3; DAM POP; MAL 5; MTCW 2; MTFW 2005; SSFS 18

Proulx, Edna Annie
See Proulx, E. Annie

Proust, (Valentin-Louis-George-Eugene) Marcel 1871-1922 ..... **SSC 75; TCLC 7, 13, 33; WLC**
See also AAYA 58; BPFB 3; CA 104; 120; CANR 110; DA; DA3; DAB; DAC; DAM MST, NOV; DLB 65; EW 8; EWL 3; GFL 1789 to the Present; MTCW 1, 2; MTFW 2005; RGWL 2, 3; TWA

Prowler, Harley
See Masters, Edgar Lee

Ralegh, Sir Walter
See Raleigh, Sir Walter
See also BRW 1; RGEL 2; WP

Raleigh, Richard
See Lovecraft, H(oward) P(hillips)

Raleigh, Sir Walter 1554(?)-1618 .... **LC 31, 39; PC 31**
See Ralegh, Sir Walter
See also CDBLB Before 1660; DLB 172; EXPP; PFS 14; TEA

Rallentando, H. P.
See Sayers, Dorothy L(eigh)

Ramal, Walter
See de la Mare, Walter (John)

Ramana Maharshi 1879-1950 .... **TCLC 84**

Ramoacn y Cajal, Santiago 1852-1934 .... **TCLC 93**

Ramon, Juan
See Jimenez (Mantecon), Juan Ramon

Ramos, Graciliano 1892-1953 .... **TCLC 32**
See also CA 167; DLB 307; EWL 3; HW 2; LAW; WLIT 1

Rampersad, Arnold 1941- .... **CLC 44**
See also BW 2, 3; CA 127; 133; CANR 81; DLB 111; INT CA-133

Rampling, Anne
See Rice, Anne
See also GLL 2

Ramsay, Allan 1686(?)-1758 .... **LC 29**
See also DLB 95; RGEL 2

Ramsay, Jay
See Campbell, (John) Ramsey

Ramuz, Charles-Ferdinand 1878-1947 .... **TCLC 33**
See also CA 165; EWL 3

Rand, Ayn 1905-1982 ...... **CLC 3, 30, 44, 79; WLC**
See also AAYA 10; AMWS 4; BPFB 3; BYA 12; CA 13-16R; 105; CANR 27, 73; CDALBS; CN 1, 2, 3; CPW; DA; DA3; DAC; DAM MST, NOV, POP; DLB 227, 279; MTCW 1, 2; MTFW 2005; NFS 10, 16; RGAL 4; SFW 4; TUS; YAW

Randall, Dudley (Felker) 1914-2000 . **BLC 3; CLC 1, 135**
See also BW 1, 3; CA 25-28R; 189; CANR 23, 82; CP 1, 2, 3, 4; DAM MULT; DLB 41; PFS 5

Randall, Robert
See Silverberg, Robert

Ranger, Ken
See Creasey, John

Rank, Otto 1884-1939 .... **TCLC 115**

Ransom, John Crowe 1888-1974 .. **CLC 2, 4, 5, 11, 24; PC 61**
See also AMW; CA 5-8R; 49-52; CANR 6, 34; CDALBS; CP 1, 2; DA3; DAM POET; DLB 45, 63; EWL 3; EXPP; MAL 5; MTCW 1, 2; MTFW 2005; RGAL 4; TUS

Rao, Raja 1909- .... **CLC 25, 56**
See also CA 73-76; CANR 51; CN 1, 2, 3, 4, 5, 6; DAM NOV; EWL 3; MTCW 1, 2; MTFW 2005; RGEL 2; RGSF 2

Raphael, Frederic (Michael) 1931- ... **CLC 2, 14**
See also CA 1-4R; CANR 1, 86; CN 1, 2, 3, 4, 5, 6, 7; DLB 14, 319; TCLE 1:2

Ratcliffe, James P.
See Mencken, H(enry) L(ouis)

Rathbone, Julian 1935- .... **CLC 41**
See also CA 101; CANR 34, 73

Rattigan, Terence (Mervyn) 1911-1977 .... **CLC 7; DC 18**
See also BRWS 7; CA 85-88; 73-76; CBD; CDBLB 1945-1960; DAM DRAM; DFS 8; DLB 13; IDFW 3, 4; MTCW 1, 2; MTFW 2005; RGEL 2

Ratushinskaya, Irina 1954- .... **CLC 54**
See also CA 129; CANR 68; CWW 2

Raven, Simon (Arthur Noel) 1927-2001 .... **CLC 14**
See also CA 81-84; 197; CANR 86; CN 1, 2, 3, 4, 5, 6; DLB 271

Ravenna, Michael
See Welty, Eudora (Alice)

Rawley, Callman 1903-2004
See Rakosi, Carl
See also CA 21-24R; 228; CANR 12, 32, 91

Rawlings, Marjorie Kinnan 1896-1953 .... **TCLC 4**
See also AAYA 20; AMWS 10; ANW; BPFB 3; BYA 3; CA 104; 137; CANR 74; CLR 63; DLB 9, 22, 102; DLBD 17; JRDA; MAICYA 1, 2; MAL 5; SATA 100; WCH; YABC 1; YAW

Ray, Satyajit 1921-1992 .... **CLC 16, 76**
See also CA 114; 137; DAM MULT

Read, Herbert Edward 1893-1968 ..... **CLC 4**
See also BRW 6; CA 85-88; 25-28R; DLB 20, 149; EWL 3; PAB; RGEL 2

Read, Piers Paul 1941- .... **CLC 4, 10, 25**
See also CA 21-24R; CANR 38, 86; CN 2, 3, 4, 5, 6, 7; DLB 14; SATA 21

Reade, Charles 1814-1884 .... **NCLC 2, 74**
See also DLB 21; RGEL 2

Reade, Hamish
See Gray, Simon (James Holliday)

Reading, Peter 1946- .... **CLC 47**
See also BRWS 8; CA 103; CANR 46, 96; CP 7; DLB 40

Reaney, James 1926- .... **CLC 13**
See also CA 41-44R; CAAS 15; CANR 42; CD 5, 6; CP 1, 2, 3, 4, 5, 6, 7; DAC; DAM MST; DLB 68; RGEL 2; SATA 43

Rebreanu, Liviu 1885-1944 .... **TCLC 28**
See also CA 165; DLB 220; EWL 3

Rechy, John (Francisco) 1934- ...... **CLC 1, 7, 14, 18, 107; HLC 2**
See also CA 5-8R, 195; CAAE 195; CAAS 4; CANR 6, 32, 64; CN 1, 2, 3, 4, 5, 6, 7; DAM MULT; DLB 122, 278; DLBY 1982; HW 1, 2; INT CANR-6; LLW; MAL 5; RGAL 4

Redcam, Tom 1870-1933 .... **TCLC 25**

Reddin, Keith 1956- .... **CLC 67**
See also CAD; CD 6

Redgrove, Peter (William) 1932-2003 .... **CLC 6, 41**
See also BRWS 6; CA 1-4R; 217; CANR 3, 39, 77; CP 1, 2, 3, 4, 5, 6, 7; DLB 40; TCLE 1:2

Redmon, Anne .... **CLC 22**
See Nightingale, Anne Redmon
See also DLBY 1986

Reed, Eliot
See Ambler, Eric

Reed, Ishmael (Scott) 1938- . **BLC 3; CLC 2, 3, 5, 6, 13, 32, 60, 174; PC 68**
See also AFAW 1, 2; AMWS 10; BPFB 3; BW 2, 3; CA 21-24R; CANR 25, 48, 74, 128; CN 1, 2, 3, 4, 5, 6, 7; CP 1, 2, 3, 4, 5, 6, 7; CSW; DA3; DAM MULT; DLB 2, 5, 33, 169, 227; DLBD 8; EWL 3; LMFS 2; MAL 5; MSW; MTCW 1, 2; MTFW 2005; PFS 6; RGAL 4; TCWW 2

Reed, John (Silas) 1887-1920 .... **TCLC 9**
See also CA 106; 195; MAL 5; TUS

Reed, Lou .... **CLC 21**
See Firbank, Louis

Reese, Lizette Woodworth 1856-1935 . **PC 29**
See also CA 180; DLB 54

Reeve, Clara 1729-1807 .... **NCLC 19**
See also DLB 39; RGEL 2

Reich, Wilhelm 1897-1957 .... **TCLC 57**
See also CA 199

Reid, Christopher (John) 1949- .... **CLC 33**
See also CA 140; CANR 89; CP 4, 5, 6, 7; DLB 40; EWL 3

Reid, Desmond
See Moorcock, Michael (John)

Reid Banks, Lynne 1929-
See Banks, Lynne Reid
See also AAYA 49; CA 1-4R; CANR 6, 22, 38, 87; CLR 24; CN 1, 2, 3, 7; JRDA; MAICYA 1, 2; SATA 22, 75, 111, 165; YAW

Reilly, William K.
See Creasey, John

Reiner, Max
See Caldwell, (Janet Miriam) Taylor (Holland)

Reis, Ricardo
See Pessoa, Fernando (Antonio Nogueira)

Reizenstein, Elmer Leopold
See Rice, Elmer (Leopold)
See also EWL 3

Remarque, Erich Maria 1898-1970 . **CLC 21**
See also AAYA 27; BPFB 3; CA 77-80; 29-32R; CDWLB 2; DA; DA3; DAB; DAC; DAM MST, NOV; DLB 56; EWL 3; EXPN; LAIT 3; MTCW 1, 2; MTFW 2005; NFS 4; RGWL 2, 3

Remington, Frederic S(ackrider) 1861-1909 .... **TCLC 89**
See also CA 108; 169; DLB 12, 186, 188; SATA 41; TCWW 2

Remizov, A.
See Remizov, Aleksei (Mikhailovich)

Remizov, A. M.
See Remizov, Aleksei (Mikhailovich)

Remizov, Aleksei (Mikhailovich) 1877-1957 .... **TCLC 27**
See Remizov, Alexey Mikhaylovich
See also CA 125; 133; DLB 295

Remizov, Alexey Mikhaylovich
See Remizov, Aleksei (Mikhailovich)
See also EWL 3

Renan, Joseph Ernest 1823-1892 . **NCLC 26, 145**
See also GFL 1789 to the Present

Renard, Jules(-Pierre) 1864-1910 .. **TCLC 17**
See also CA 117; 202; GFL 1789 to the Present

Renault, Mary .... **CLC 3, 11, 17**
See Challans, Mary
See also BPFB 3; BYA 2; CN 1, 2, 3; DLBY 1983; EWL 3; GLL 1; LAIT 1; RGEL 2; RHW

Rendell, Ruth (Barbara) 1930- .. **CLC 28, 48**
See Vine, Barbara
See also BPFB 3; BRWS 9; CA 109; CANR 32, 52, 74, 127; CN 5, 6, 7; CPW; DAM POP; DLB 87, 276; INT CANR-32; MSW; MTCW 1, 2; MTFW 2005

Renoir, Jean 1894-1979 .... **CLC 20**
See also CA 129; 85-88

Resnais, Alain 1922- .... **CLC 16**

Revard, Carter (Curtis) 1931- .... **NNAL**
See also CA 144; CANR 81; PFS 5

Reverdy, Pierre 1889-1960 .... **CLC 53**
See also CA 97-100; 89-92; DLB 258; EWL 3; GFL 1789 to the Present

Rexroth, Kenneth 1905-1982 .... **CLC 1, 2, 6, 11, 22, 49, 112; PC 20**
See also BG 1:3; CA 5-8R; 107; CANR 14, 34, 63; CDALB 1941-1968; CP 1, 2, 3; DAM POET; DLB 16, 48, 165, 212; DLBY 1982; EWL 3; INT CANR-14; MAL 5; MTCW 1, 2; MTFW 2005; RGAL 4

Reyes, Alfonso 1889-1959 .... **HLCS 2; TCLC 33**
See also CA 131; EWL 3; HW 1; LAW

Robbins, Tom .... **CLC 9, 32, 64**
See Robbins, Thomas Eugene
See also AAYA 32; AMWS 10; BEST 90:3;
BPFB 3; CN 3, 4, 5, 6, 7; DLBY 1980

Robbins, Trina 1938- .... **CLC 21**
See also AAYA 61; CA 128

Roberts, Charles G(eorge) D(ouglas)
1860-1943 .... **TCLC 8**
See also CA 105; 188; CLR 33; CWRI 5;
DLB 92; RGEL 2; RGSF 2; SATA 88;
SATA-Brief 29

Roberts, Elizabeth Madox
1886-1941 .... **TCLC 68**
See also CA 111; 166; CLR 5;
DLB 9, 54, 102; RGAL 4; RHW; SATA
33; SATA-Brief 27; TCWW 2; WCH

Roberts, Kate 1891-1985 .... **CLC 15**
See also CA 107; 116; DLB 319

Roberts, Keith (John Kingston)
1935-2000 .... **CLC 14**
See also BRWS 10; CA 25-28R; CANR 46;
DLB 261; SFW 4

Roberts, Kenneth (Lewis)
1885-1957 .... **TCLC 23**
See also CA 109; 199; DLB 9; MAL 5;
RGAL 4; RHW

Roberts, Michele (Brigitte) 1949- .... **CLC 48, 178**
See also CA 115; CANR 58, 120; CN 6, 7;
DLB 231; FW

Robertson, Ellis
See Ellison, Harlan (Jay); Silverberg, Robert

Robertson, Thomas William
1829-1871 .... **NCLC 35**
See Robertson, Tom
See also DAM DRAM

Robertson, Tom
See Robertson, Thomas William
See also RGEL 2

Robeson, Kenneth
See Dent, Lester

Robinson, Edwin Arlington
1869-1935 .... **PC 1, 35; TCLC 5, 101**
See also AMW; CA 104; 133; CDALB
1865-1917; DA; DAC; DAM MST,
POET; DLB 54; EWL 3; EXPP; MAL 5;
MTCW 1, 2; MTFW 2005; PAB; PFS 4;
RGAL 4; WP

Robinson, Henry Crabb
1775-1867 .... **NCLC 15**
See also DLB 107

Robinson, Jill 1936- .... **CLC 10**
See also CA 102; CANR 120; INT CA-102

Robinson, Kim Stanley 1952- .... **CLC 34**
See also AAYA 26; CA 126; CANR 113,
139; CN 6, 7; MTFW 2005; SATA 109;
SCFW 2; SFW 4

Robinson, Lloyd
See Silverberg, Robert

Robinson, Marilynne 1944- ...... **CLC 25, 180**
See also CA 116; CANR 80, 140; CN 4, 5,
6, 7; DLB 206; MTFW 2005

Robinson, Mary 1758-1800 .... **NCLC 142**
See also DLB 158; FW

Robinson, Smokey .... **CLC 21**
See Robinson, William, Jr.

Robinson, William, Jr. 1940-
See Robinson, Smokey
See also CA 116

Robison, Mary 1949- .... **CLC 42, 98**
See also CA 113; 116; CANR 87; CN 4, 5,
6, 7; DLB 130; INT CA-116; RGSF 2

Roches, Catherine des 1542-1587 ...... **LC 117**

Rochester
See Wilmot, John
See also RGEL 2

Rod, Edouard 1857-1910 .... **TCLC 52**

Roddenberry, Eugene Wesley 1921-1991
See Roddenberry, Gene
See also CA 110; 135; CANR 37; SATA 45;
SATA-Obit 69

Roddenberry, Gene .... **CLC 17**
See Roddenberry, Eugene Wesley
See also AAYA 5; SATA-Obit 69

Rodgers, Mary 1931- .... **CLC 12**
See also BYA 5; CA 49-52; CANR 8, 55,
90; CLR 20; CWRI 5; INT CANR-8;
JRDA; MAICYA 1, 2; SATA 8, 130

Rodgers, W(illiam) R(obert)
1909-1969 .... **CLC 7**
See also CA 85-88; DLB 20; RGEL 2

Rodman, Eric
See Silverberg, Robert

Rodman, Howard 1920(?)-1985 .... **CLC 65**
See also CA 118

Rodman, Maia
See Wojciechowska, Maia (Teresa)

Rodo, Jose Enrique 1871(?)-1917 .... **HLCS 2**
See also CA 178; EWL 3; HW 2; LAW

Rodolph, Utto
See Ouologuem, Yambo

Rodriguez, Claudio 1934-1999 .... **CLC 10**
See also CA 188; DLB 134

Rodriguez, Richard 1944- .... **CLC 155; HLC 2**
See also AMWS 14; CA 110; CANR 66,
116; DAM MULT; DLB 82, 256; HW 1,
2; LAIT 5; LLW; MTFW 2005; NCFS 3;
WLIT 1

Roelvaag, O(le) E(dvart) 1876-1931
See Rolvaag, O(le) E(dvart)
See also CA 117; 171

Roethke, Theodore (Huebner)
1908-1963 .... **CLC 1, 3, 8, 11, 19, 46, 101; PC 15**
See also AMW; CA 81-84; CABS 2;
CDALB 1941-1968; DA3; DAM POET;
DLB 5, 206; EWL 3; EXPP; MAL 5;
MTCW 1, 2; PAB; PFS 3; RGAL 4; WP

Rogers, Carl R(ansom)
1902-1987 .... **TCLC 125**
See also CA 1-4R; 121; CANR 1, 18;
MTCW 1

Rogers, Samuel 1763-1855 .... **NCLC 69**
See also DLB 93; RGEL 2

Rogers, Thomas Hunton 1927- .... **CLC 57**
See also CA 89-92; INT CA-89-92

Rogers, Will(iam Penn Adair)
1879-1935 .... **NNAL; TCLC 8, 71**
See also CA 105; 144; DA3; DAM MULT;
DLB 11; MTCW 2

Rogin, Gilbert 1929- .... **CLC 18**
See also CA 65-68; CANR 15

Rohan, Koda
See Koda Shigeyuki

Rohlfs, Anna Katharine Green
See Green, Anna Katharine

Rohmer, Eric .... **CLC 16**
See Scherer, Jean-Marie Maurice

Rohmer, Sax .... **TCLC 28**
See Ward, Arthur Henry Sarsfield
See also DLB 70; MSW; SUFW

Roiphe, Anne (Richardson) 1935- .. **CLC 3, 9**
See also CA 89-92; CANR 45, 73, 138;
DLBY 1980; INT CA-89-92

Rojas, Fernando de 1475-1541 ... **HLCS 1, 2; LC 23**
See also DLB 286; RGWL 2, 3

Rojas, Gonzalo 1917- .... **HLCS 2**
See also CA 178; HW 2; LAWS 1

Roland (de la Platiere), Marie-Jeanne
1754-1793 .... **LC 98**
See also DLB 314

Rolfe, Frederick (William Serafino Austin Lewis Mary) 1860-1913 .... **TCLC 12**
See Al Siddik
See also CA 107; 210; DLB 34, 156; RGEL 2

Rolland, Romain 1866-1944 .... **TCLC 23**
See also CA 118; 197; DLB 65, 284; EWL 3; GFL 1789 to the Present; RGWL 2, 3

Rolle, Richard c. 1300-c. 1349 ...... **CMLC 21**
See also DLB 146; LMFS 1; RGEL 2

Rolvaag, O(le) E(dvart) .... **TCLC 17**
See Roelvaag, O(le) E(dvart)
See also DLB 9, 212; MAL 5; NFS 5;
RGAL 4

Romain Arnaud, Saint
See Aragon, Louis

Romains, Jules 1885-1972 .... **CLC 7**
See also CA 85-88; CANR 34; DLB 65,
321; EWL 3; GFL 1789 to the Present;
MTCW 1

Romero, Jose Ruben 1890-1952 .... **TCLC 14**
See also CA 114; 131; EWL 3; HW 1; LAW

Ronsard, Pierre de 1524-1585 . **LC 6, 54; PC 11**
See also EW 2; GFL Beginnings to 1789;
RGWL 2, 3; TWA

Rooke, Leon 1934- .... **CLC 25, 34**
See also CA 25-28R; CANR 23, 53; CCA
1; CPW; DAM POP

Roosevelt, Franklin Delano
1882-1945 .... **TCLC 93**
See also CA 116; 173; LAIT 3

Roosevelt, Theodore 1858-1919 ..... **TCLC 69**
See also CA 115; 170; DLB 47, 186, 275

Roper, William 1498-1578 .... **LC 10**

Roquelaure, A. N.
See Rice, Anne

Rosa, Joao Guimaraes 1908-1967 ... **CLC 23; HLCS 1**
See Guimaraes Rosa, Joao
See also CA 89-92; DLB 113, 307; EWL 3;
WLIT 1

Rose, Wendy 1948- . **CLC 85; NNAL; PC 13**
See also CA 53-56; CANR 5, 51; CWP;
DAM MULT; DLB 175; PFS 13; RGAL
4; SATA 12

Rosen, R. D.
See Rosen, Richard (Dean)

Rosen, Richard (Dean) 1949- .... **CLC 39**
See also CA 77-80; CANR 62, 120; CMW
4; INT CANR-30

Rosenberg, Isaac 1890-1918 .... **TCLC 12**
See also BRW 6; CA 107; 188; DLB 20,
216; EWL 3; PAB; RGEL 2

Rosenblatt, Joe .... **CLC 15**
See Rosenblatt, Joseph
See also CP 3, 4, 5, 6, 7

Rosenblatt, Joseph 1933-
See Rosenblatt, Joe
See also CA 89-92; CP 1, 2; INT CA-89-92

Rosenfeld, Samuel
See Tzara, Tristan

Rosenstock, Sami
See Tzara, Tristan

Rosenstock, Samuel
See Tzara, Tristan

Rosenthal, M(acha) L(ouis)
1917-1996 .... **CLC 28**
See also CA 1-4R; 152; CAAS 6; CANR 4,
51; CP 1, 2, 3, 4; DLB 5; SATA 59

Ross, Barnaby
See Dannay, Frederic

Ross, Bernard L.
See Follett, Ken(neth Martin)

Ross, J. H.
See Lawrence, T(homas) E(dward)

Ross, John Hume
See Lawrence, T(homas) E(dward)

Ryga, George 1932-1987 .... **CLC 14**
See also CA 101; 124; CANR 43, 90; CCA 1; DAC; DAM MST; DLB 60

S. H.
See Hartmann, Sadakichi

S. S.
See Sassoon, Siegfried (Lorraine)

Sa'adawi, al- Nawal
See El Saadawi, Nawal
See also AFW; EWL 3

Saadawi, Nawal El
See El Saadawi, Nawal
See also WLIT 2

Saba, Umberto 1883-1957 .... **TCLC 33**
See also CA 144; CANR 79; DLB 114; EWL 3; RGWL 2, 3

Sabatini, Rafael 1875-1950 .... **TCLC 47**
See also BPFB 3; CA 162; RHW

Sabato, Ernesto (R.) 1911- .... **CLC 10, 23; HLC 2**
See also CA 97-100; CANR 32, 65; CDWLB 3; CWW 2; DAM MULT; DLB 145; EWL 3; HW 1, 2; LAW; MTCW 1, 2; MTFW 2005

Sa-Carneiro, Mario de 1890-1916 . **TCLC 83**
See also DLB 287; EWL 3

Sacastru, Martin
See Bioy Casares, Adolfo
See also CWW 2

Sacher-Masoch, Leopold von
1836(?)-1895 .... **NCLC 31**

Sachs, Hans 1494-1576 .... **LC 95**
See also CDWLB 2; DLB 179; RGWL 2, 3

Sachs, Marilyn 1927- .... **CLC 35**
See also AAYA 2; BYA 6; CA 17-20R; CANR 13, 47; CLR 2; JRDA; MAICYA 1, 2; SAAS 2; SATA 3, 68, 164; SATA-Essay 110; WYA; YAW

Sachs, Marilyn Stickle
See Sachs, Marilyn

Sachs, Nelly 1891-1970 .... **CLC 14, 98**
See also CA 17-18; 25-28R; CANR 87; CAP 2; EWL 3; MTCW 2; MTFW 2005; PFS 20; RGWL 2, 3

Sackler, Howard (Oliver)
1929-1982 .... **CLC 14**
See also CA 61-64; 108; CAD; CANR 30; DFS 15; DLB 7

Sacks, Oliver (Wolf) 1933- .... **CLC 67, 202**
See also CA 53-56; CANR 28, 50, 76; CPW; DA3; INT CANR-28; MTCW 1, 2; MTFW 2005

Sackville, Thomas 1536-1608 .... **LC 98**
See also DAM DRAM; DLB 62, 132; RGEL 2

Sadakichi
See Hartmann, Sadakichi

Sa'dawi, Nawal al-
See El Saadawi, Nawal
See also CWW 2

Sade, Donatien Alphonse Francois
1740-1814 .... **NCLC 3, 47**
See also DLB 314; EW 4; GFL Beginnings to 1789; RGWL 2, 3

Sade, Marquis de
See Sade, Donatien Alphonse Francois

Sadoff, Ira 1945- .... **CLC 9**
See also CA 53-56; CANR 5, 21, 109; DLB 120

Saetone
See Camus, Albert

Safire, William 1929- .... **CLC 10**
See also CA 17-20R; CANR 31, 54, 91

Sagan, Carl (Edward) 1934-1996 .... **CLC 30, 112**
See also AAYA 2, 62; CA 25-28R; 155; CANR 11, 36, 74; CPW; DA3; MTCW 1, 2; MTFW 2005; SATA 58; SATA-Obit 94

Sagan, Francoise .... **CLC 3, 6, 9, 17, 36**
See Quoirez, Francoise
See also CWW 2; DLB 83; EWL 3; GFL 1789 to the Present; MTCW 2

Sahgal, Nayantara (Pandit) 1927- .... **CLC 41**
See also CA 9-12R; CANR 11, 88; CN 1, 2, 3, 4, 5, 6, 7

Said, Edward W. 1935-2003 .... **CLC 123**
See also CA 21-24R; 220; CANR 45, 74, 107, 131; DLB 67; MTCW 2; MTFW 2005

Saint, H(arry) F. 1941- .... **CLC 50**
See also CA 127

St. Aubin de Teran, Lisa 1953-
See Teran, Lisa St. Aubin de
See also CA 118; 126; CN 6, 7; INT CA-126

Saint Birgitta of Sweden c.
1303-1373 .... **CMLC 24**

Saint Gregory of Nazianzus
329-389 .... **CMLC 82**

Sainte-Beuve, Charles Augustin
1804-1869 .... **NCLC 5**
See also DLB 217; EW 6; GFL 1789 to the Present

Saint-Exupery, Antoine (Jean Baptiste Marie Roger) de 1900-1944 .... **TCLC 2, 56, 169; WLC**
See also AAYA 63; BPFB 3; BYA 3; CA 108; 132; CLR 10; DA3; DAM NOV; DLB 72; EW 12; EWL 3; GFL 1789 to the Present; LAIT 3; MAICYA 1, 2; MTCW 1, 2; MTFW 2005; RGWL 2, 3; SATA 20; TWA

St. John, David
See Hunt, E(verette) Howard, (Jr.)

St. John, J. Hector
See Crevecoeur, Michel Guillaume Jean de

Saint-John Perse
See Leger, (Marie-Rene Auguste) Alexis Saint-Leger
See also EW 10; EWL 3; GFL 1789 to the Present; RGWL 2

Saintsbury, George (Edward Bateman)
1845-1933 .... **TCLC 31**
See also CA 160; DLB 57, 149

Sait Faik .... **TCLC 23**
See Abasiyanik, Sait Faik

Saki .... **SSC 12; TCLC 3**
See Munro, H(ector) H(ugh)
See also BRWS 6; BYA 11; LAIT 2; RGEL 2; SSFS 1; SUFW

Sala, George Augustus 1828-1895 . **NCLC 46**

Saladin 1138-1193 .... **CMLC 38**

Salama, Hannu 1936- .... **CLC 18**
See also EWL 3

Salamanca, J(ack) R(ichard) 1922- .. **CLC 4, 15**
See also CA 25-28R, 193; CAAE 193

Salas, Floyd Francis 1931- .... **HLC 2**
See also CA 119; CAAS 27; CANR 44, 75, 93; DAM MULT; DLB 82; HW 1, 2; MTCW 2; MTFW 2005

Sale, J. Kirkpatrick
See Sale, Kirkpatrick

Sale, Kirkpatrick 1937- .... **CLC 68**
See also CA 13-16R; CANR 10

Salinas, Luis Omar 1937- ... **CLC 90; HLC 2**
See also AMWS 13; CA 131; CANR 81; DAM MULT; DLB 82; HW 1, 2

Salinas (y Serrano), Pedro
1891(?)-1951 .... **TCLC 17**
See also CA 117; DLB 134; EWL 3

Salinger, J(erome) D(avid) 1919- .. **CLC 1, 3, 8, 12, 55, 56, 138; SSC 2, 28, 65; WLC**
See also AAYA 2, 36; AMW; AMWC 1; BPFB 3; CA 5-8R; CANR 39, 129; CDALB 1941-1968; CLR 18; CN 1, 2, 3, 4, 5, 6, 7; CPW 1; DA; DA3; DAB; DAC;

DAM MST, NOV, POP; DLB 2, 102, 173; EWL 3; EXPN; LAIT 4; MAICYA 1, 2; MAL 5; MTCW 1, 2; MTFW 2005; NFS 1; RGAL 4; RGSF 2; SATA 67; SSFS 17; TUS; WYA; YAW

Salisbury, John
See Caute, (John) David

Sallust c. 86B.C.-35B.C. .... **CMLC 68**
See also AW 2; CDWLB 1; DLB 211; RGWL 2, 3

Salter, James 1925- .. **CLC 7, 52, 59; SSC 58**
See also AMWS 9; CA 73-76; CANR 107; DLB 130

Saltus, Edgar (Everton) 1855-1921 . **TCLC 8**
See also CA 105; DLB 202; RGAL 4

Saltykov, Mikhail Evgrafovich
1826-1889 .... **NCLC 16**
See also DLB 238:

Saltykov-Shchedrin, N.
See Saltykov, Mikhail Evgrafovich

Samarakis, Andonis
See Samarakis, Antonis
See also EWL 3

Samarakis, Antonis 1919-2003 .... **CLC 5**
See Samarakis, Andonis
See also CA 25-28R; 224; CAAS 16; CANR 36

Sanchez, Florencio 1875-1910 .... **TCLC 37**
See also CA 153; DLB 305; EWL 3; HW 1; LAW

Sanchez, Luis Rafael 1936- .... **CLC 23**
See also CA 128; DLB 305; EWL 3; HW 1; WLIT 1

Sanchez, Sonia 1934- .... **BLC 3; CLC 5, 116, 215; PC 9**
See also BW 2, 3; CA 33-36R; CANR 24, 49, 74, 115; CLR 18; CP 2, 3, 4, 5, 6, 7; CSW; CWP; DA3; DAM MULT; DLB 41; DLBD 8; EWL 3; MAICYA 1, 2; MAL 5; MTCW 1, 2; MTFW 2005; SATA 22, 136; WP

Sancho, Ignatius 1729-1780 .... **LC 84**

Sand, George 1804-1876 ..... **NCLC 2, 42, 57; WLC**
See also DA; DA3; DAB; DAC; DAM MST, NOV; DLB 119, 192; EW 6; FL 1:3; FW; GFL 1789 to the Present; RGWL 2, 3; TWA

Sandburg, Carl (August) 1878-1967 . **CLC 1, 4, 10, 15, 35; PC 2, 41; WLC**
See also AAYA 24; AMW; BYA 1, 3; CA 5-8R; 25-28R; CANR 35; CDALB 1865-1917; CLR 67; DA; DA3; DAB; DAC; DAM MST, POET; DLB 17, 54, 284; EWL 3; EXPP; LAIT 2; MAICYA 1, 2; MAL 5; MTCW 1, 2; MTFW 2005; PAB; PFS 3, 6, 12; RGAL 4; SATA 8; TUS; WCH; WP; WYA

Sandburg, Charles
See Sandburg, Carl (August)

Sandburg, Charles A.
See Sandburg, Carl (August)

Sanders, (James) Ed(ward) 1939- .... **CLC 53**
See Sanders, Edward
See also BG 1:3; CA 13-16R; CAAS 21; CANR 13, 44, 78; CP 1, 2, 3, 4, 5, 6, 7; DAM POET; DLB 16, 244

Sanders, Edward
See Sanders, (James) Ed(ward)
See also DLB 244

Sanders, Lawrence 1920-1998 .... **CLC 41**
See also BEST 89:4; BPFB 3; CA 81-84; 165; CANR 33, 62; CMW 4; CPW; DA3; DAM POP; MTCW 1

Sanders, Noah
See Blount, Roy (Alton), Jr.

Sanders, Winston P.
See Anderson, Poul (William)

Schoenberg, Arnold Franz Walter
 1874-1951 .... **TCLC 75**
 See also CA 109; 188
Schonberg, Arnold
 See Schoenberg, Arnold Franz Walter
Schopenhauer, Arthur 1788-1860 . **NCLC 51, 157**
 See also DLB 90; EW 5
Schor, Sandra (M.) 1932(?)-1990 ..... **CLC 65**
 See also CA 132
Schorer, Mark 1908-1977 .... **CLC 9**
 See also CA 5-8R; 73-76; CANR 7; CN 1, 2; DLB 103
Schrader, Paul (Joseph) 1946- . **CLC 26, 212**
 See also CA 37-40R; CANR 41; DLB 44
Schreber, Daniel 1842-1911 .... **TCLC 123**
Schreiner, Olive (Emilie Albertina)
 1855-1920 .... **TCLC 9**
 See also AFW; BRWS 2; CA 105; 154; DLB 18, 156, 190, 225; EWL 3; FW; RGEL 2; TWA; WLIT 2; WWE 1
Schulberg, Budd (Wilson) 1914- .. **CLC 7, 48**
 See also BPFB 3; CA 25-28R; CANR 19, 87; CN 1, 2, 3, 4, 5, 6, 7; DLB 6, 26, 28; DLBY 1981, 2001; MAL 5
Schulman, Arnold
 See Trumbo, Dalton
Schulz, Bruno 1892-1942 .. **SSC 13; TCLC 5, 51**
 See also CA 115; 123; CANR 86; CDWLB 4; DLB 215; EWL 3; MTCW 2; MTFW 2005; RGSF 2; RGWL 2, 3
Schulz, Charles M. 1922-2000 .... **CLC 12**
 See also AAYA 39; CA 9-12R; 187; CANR 6, 132; INT CANR-6; MTFW 2005; SATA 10; SATA-Obit 118
Schulz, Charles Monroe
 See Schulz, Charles M.
Schumacher, E(rnst) F(riedrich)
 1911-1977 .... **CLC 80**
 See also CA 81-84; 73-76; CANR 34, 85
Schumann, Robert 1810-1856 ...... **NCLC 143**
Schuyler, George Samuel 1895-1977 . **HR 1:3**
 See also BW 2; CA 81-84; 73-76; CANR 42; DLB 29, 51
Schuyler, James Marcus 1923-1991 .. **CLC 5, 23**
 See also CA 101; 134; CP 1, 2, 3, 4; DAM POET; DLB 5, 169; EWL 3; INT CA-101; MAL 5; WP
Schwartz, Delmore (David)
 1913-1966 ... **CLC 2, 4, 10, 45, 87; PC 8**
 See also AMWS 2; CA 17-18; 25-28R; CANR 35; CAP 2; DLB 28, 48; EWL 3; MAL 5; MTCW 1, 2; MTFW 2005; PAB; RGAL 4; TUS
Schwartz, Ernst
 See Ozu, Yasujiro
Schwartz, John Burnham 1965- .... **CLC 59**
 See also CA 132; CANR 116
Schwartz, Lynne Sharon 1939- .... **CLC 31**
 See also CA 103; CANR 44, 89; DLB 218; MTCW 2; MTFW 2005
Schwartz, Muriel A.
 See Eliot, T(homas) S(tearns)
Schwarz-Bart, Andre 1928- .... **CLC 2, 4**
 See also CA 89-92; CANR 109; DLB 299
Schwarz-Bart, Simone 1938- . **BLCS; CLC 7**
 See also BW 2; CA 97-100; CANR 117; EWL 3
Schwerner, Armand 1927-1999 .... **PC 42**
 See also CA 9-12R; 179; CANR 50, 85; CP 2, 3, 4; DLB 165
Schwitters, Kurt (Hermann Edward Karl Julius) 1887-1948 .... **TCLC 95**
 See also CA 158

Schwob, Marcel (Mayer Andre)
 1867-1905 .... **TCLC 20**
 See also CA 117; 168; DLB 123; GFL 1789 to the Present
Sciascia, Leonardo 1921-1989 .. **CLC 8, 9, 41**
 See also CA 85-88; 130; CANR 35; DLB 177; EWL 3; MTCW 1; RGWL 2, 3
Scoppettone, Sandra 1936- .... **CLC 26**
 See Early, Jack
 See also AAYA 11, 65; BYA 8; CA 5-8R; CANR 41, 73; GLL 1; MAICYA 2; MAI-CYAS 1; SATA 9, 92; WYA; YAW
Scorsese, Martin 1942- .... **CLC 20, 89, 207**
 See also AAYA 38; CA 110; 114; CANR 46, 85
Scotland, Jay
 See Jakes, John (William)
Scott, Duncan Campbell
 1862-1947 .... **TCLC 6**
 See also CA 104; 153; DAC; DLB 92; RGEL 2
Scott, Evelyn 1893-1963 .... **CLC 43**
 See also CA 104; 112; CANR 64; DLB 9, 48; RHW
Scott, F(rancis) R(eginald)
 1899-1985 .... **CLC 22**
 See also CA 101; 114; CANR 87; CP 1, 2, 3, 4; DLB 88; INT CA-101; RGEL 2
Scott, Frank
 See Scott, F(rancis) R(eginald)
Scott, Joan .... **CLC 65**
Scott, Joanna 1960- .... **CLC 50**
 See also CA 126; CANR 53, 92
Scott, Paul (Mark) 1920-1978 ...... **CLC 9, 60**
 See also BRWS 1; CA 81-84; 77-80; CANR 33; CN 1, 2; DLB 14, 207; EWL 3; MTCW 1; RGEL 2; RHW; WWE 1
Scott, Ridley 1937- .... **CLC 183**
 See also AAYA 13, 43
Scott, Sarah 1723-1795 .... **LC 44**
 See also DLB 39
Scott, Sir Walter 1771-1832 .... **NCLC 15, 69, 110; PC 13; SSC 32; WLC**
 See also AAYA 22; BRW 4; BYA 2; CD-BLB 1789-1832; DA; DAB; DAC; DAM MST, NOV, POET; DLB 93, 107, 116, 144, 159; GL 3; HGG; LAIT 1; RGEL 2; RGSF 2; SSFS 10; SUFW 1; TEA; WLIT 3; YABC 2
Scribe, (Augustin) Eugene 1791-1861 . **DC 5; NCLC 16**
 See also DAM DRAM; DLB 192; GFL 1789 to the Present; RGWL 2, 3
Scrum, R.
 See Crumb, R(obert)
Scudery, Georges de 1601-1667 .... **LC 75**
 See also GFL Beginnings to 1789
Scudery, Madeleine de 1607-1701 .. **LC 2, 58**
 See also DLB 268; GFL Beginnings to 1789
Scum
 See Crumb, R(obert)
Scumbag, Little Bobby
 See Crumb, R(obert)
Seabrook, John
 See Hubbard, L(afayette) Ron(ald)
Seacole, Mary Jane Grant
 1805-1881 .... **NCLC 147**
 See also DLB 166
Sealy, I(rwin) Allan 1951- .... **CLC 55**
 See also CA 136; CN 6, 7
Search, Alexander
 See Pessoa, Fernando (Antonio Nogueira)
Sebald, W(infried) G(eorg)
 1944-2001 .... **CLC 194**
 See also BRWS 8; CA 159; 202; CANR 98; MTFW 2005
Sebastian, Lee
 See Silverberg, Robert

Sebastian Owl
 See Thompson, Hunter S(tockton)
Sebestyen, Igen
 See Sebestyen, Ouida
Sebestyen, Ouida 1924- .... **CLC 30**
 See also AAYA 8; BYA 7; CA 107; CANR 40, 114; CLR 17; JRDA; MAICYA 1, 2; SAAS 10; SATA 39, 140; WYA; YAW
Sebold, Alice 1963(?)- .... **CLC 193**
 See also AAYA 56; CA 203; MTFW 2005
Second Duke of Buckingham
 See Villiers, George
Secundus, H. Scriblerus
 See Fielding, Henry
Sedges, John
 See Buck, Pearl S(ydenstricker)
Sedgwick, Catharine Maria
 1789-1867 .... **NCLC 19, 98**
 See also DLB 1, 74, 183, 239, 243, 254; FL 1:3; RGAL 4
Seelye, John (Douglas) 1931- .... **CLC 7**
 See also CA 97-100; CANR 70; INT CA-97-100; TCWW 1, 2
Seferiades, Giorgos Stylianou 1900-1971
 See Seferis, George
 See also CA 5-8R; 33-36R; CANR 5, 36; MTCW 1
Seferis, George .... **CLC 5, 11; PC 66**
 See Seferiades, Giorgos Stylianou
 See also EW 12; EWL 3; RGWL 2, 3
Segal, Erich (Wolf) 1937- .... **CLC 3, 10**
 See also BEST 89:1; BPFB 3; CA 25-28R; CANR 20, 36, 65, 113; CPW; DAM POP; DLBY 1986; INT CANR-20; MTCW 1
Seger, Bob 1945- .... **CLC 35**
Seghers, Anna .... **CLC 7**
 See Radvanyi, Netty
 See also CDWLB 2; DLB 69; EWL 3
Seidel, Frederick (Lewis) 1936- .... **CLC 18**
 See also CA 13-16R; CANR 8, 99; CP 1, 2, 3, 4, 5, 6, 7; DLBY 1984
Seifert, Jaroslav 1901-1986 . **CLC 34, 44, 93; PC 47**
 See also CA 127; CDWLB 4; DLB 215; EWL 3; MTCW 1, 2
Sei Shonagon c. 966-1017(?) .... **CMLC 6**
Sejour, Victor 1817-1874 .... **DC 10**
 See also DLB 50
Sejour Marcou et Ferrand, Juan Victor
 See Sejour, Victor
Selby, Hubert, Jr. 1928-2004 ..... **CLC 1, 2, 4, 8; SSC 20**
 See also CA 13-16R; 226; CANR 33, 85; CN 1, 2, 3, 4, 5, 6, 7; DLB 2, 227; MAL 5
Selzer, Richard 1928- .... **CLC 74**
 See also CA 65-68; CANR 14, 106
Sembene, Ousmane
 See Ousmane, Sembene
 See also AFW; EWL 3; WLIT 2
Senancour, Etienne Pivert de
 1770-1846 .... **NCLC 16**
 See also DLB 119; GFL 1789 to the Present
Sender, Ramon (Jose) 1902-1982 ...... **CLC 8; HLC 2; TCLC 136**
 See also CA 5-8R; 105; CANR 8; DAM MULT; DLB 322; EWL 3; HW 1; MTCW 1; RGWL 2, 3
Seneca, Lucius Annaeus c. 4B.C.-c. 65 .... **CMLC 6; DC 5**
 See also AW 2; CDWLB 1; DAM DRAM; DLB 211; RGWL 2, 3; TWA
Senghor, Leopold Sedar 1906-2001 ... **BLC 3; CLC 54, 130; PC 25**
 See also AFW; BW 2; CA 116; 125; 203; CANR 47, 74, 134; CWW 2; DAM MULT, POET; DNFS 2; EWL 3; GFL 1789 to the Present; MTCW 1, 2; MTFW 2005; TWA

Smith, Iain Crichton 1928-1998 .... **CLC 64**
See also BRWS 9; CA 21-24R; 171; CN 1, 2, 3, 4, 5, 6; CP 1, 2, 3, 4; DLB 40, 139, 319; RGSF 2

Smith, John 1580(?)-1631 .... **LC 9**
See also DLB 24, 30; TUS

Smith, Johnston
See Crane, Stephen (Townley)

Smith, Joseph, Jr. 1805-1844 .... **NCLC 53**

Smith, Lee 1944- .... **CLC 25, 73**
See also CA 114; 119; CANR 46, 118; CN 7; CSW; DLB 143; DLBY 1983; EWL 3; INT CA-119; RGAL 4

Smith, Martin
See Smith, Martin Cruz

Smith, Martin Cruz 1942- .. **CLC 25; NNAL**
See also BEST 89:4; BPFB 3; CA 85-88; CANR 6, 23, 43, 65, 119; CMW 4; CPW; DAM MULT, POP; HGG; INT CANR-23; MTCW 2; MTFW 2005; RGAL 4

Smith, Patti 1946- .... **CLC 12**
See also CA 93-96; CANR 63

Smith, Pauline (Urmson)
1882-1959 .... **TCLC 25**
See also DLB 225; EWL 3

Smith, Rosamond
See Oates, Joyce Carol

Smith, Sheila Kaye
See Kaye-Smith, Sheila

Smith, Stevie .... **CLC 3, 8, 25, 44; PC 12**
See Smith, Florence Margaret
See also BRWS 2; CP 1; DLB 20; EWL 3; PAB; PFS 3; RGEL 2

Smith, Wilbur (Addison) 1933- .... **CLC 33**
See also CA 13-16R; CANR 7, 46, 66, 134; CPW; MTCW 1, 2; MTFW 2005

Smith, William Jay 1918- .... **CLC 6**
See also AMWS 13; CA 5-8R; CANR 44, 106; CP 1, 2, 3, 4, 5, 6, 7; CSW; CWRI 5; DLB 5; MAICYA 1, 2; SAAS 22; SATA 2, 68, 154; SATA-Essay 154; TCLE 1:2

Smith, Woodrow Wilson
See Kuttner, Henry

Smith, Zadie 1976- .... **CLC 158**
See also AAYA 50; CA 193; MTFW 2005

Smolenskin, Peretz 1842-1885 .... **NCLC 30**

Smollett, Tobias (George) 1721-1771 ... **LC 2, 46**
See also BRW 3; CDBLB 1660-1789; DLB 39, 104; RGEL 2; TEA

Snodgrass, W(illiam) D(e Witt)
1926- .... **CLC 2, 6, 10, 18, 68**
See also AMWS 6; CA 1-4R; CANR 6, 36, 65, 85; CP 1, 2, 3, 4, 5, 6, 7; DAM POET; DLB 5; MAL 5; MTCW 1, 2; MTFW 2005; RGAL 4; TCLE 1:2

Snorri Sturluson 1179-1241 .... **CMLC 56**
See also RGWL 2, 3

Snow, C(harles) P(ercy) 1905-1980 ... **CLC 1, 4, 6, 9, 13, 19**
See also BRW 7; CA 5-8R; 101; CANR 28; CDBLB 1945-1960; CN 1, 2; DAM NOV; DLB 15, 77; DLBD 17; EWL 3; MTCW 1, 2; MTFW 2005; RGEL 2; TEA

Snow, Frances Compton
See Adams, Henry (Brooks)

Snyder, Gary (Sherman) 1930- . **CLC 1, 2, 5, 9, 32, 120; PC 21**
See also AMWS 8; ANW; BG 1:3; CA 17-20R; CANR 30, 60, 125; CP 1, 2, 3, 4, 5, 6, 7; DA3; DAM POET; DLB 5, 16, 165, 212, 237, 275; EWL 3; MAL 5; MTCW 2; MTFW 2005; PFS 9, 19; RGAL 4; WP

Snyder, Zilpha Keatley 1927- .... **CLC 17**
See also AAYA 15; BYA 1; CA 9-12R; CANR 38; CLR 31; JRDA; MAICYA 1, 2; SAAS 2; SATA 1, 28, 75, 110, 163; SATA-Essay 112, 163; YAW

Soares, Bernardo
See Pessoa, Fernando (Antonio Nogueira)

Sobh, A.
See Shamlu, Ahmad

Sobh, Alef
See Shamlu, Ahmad

Sobol, Joshua 1939- .... **CLC 60**
See Sobol, Yehoshua
See also CA 200

Sobol, Yehoshua 1939-
See Sobol, Joshua
See also CWW 2

Socrates 470B.C.-399B.C. .... **CMLC 27**

Soderberg, Hjalmar 1869-1941 ...... **TCLC 39**
See also DLB 259; EWL 3; RGSF 2

Soderbergh, Steven 1963- .... **CLC 154**
See also AAYA 43

Sodergran, Edith (Irene) 1892-1923
See Soedergran, Edith (Irene)
See also CA 202; DLB 259; EW 11; EWL 3; RGWL 2, 3

Soedergran, Edith (Irene)
1892-1923 .... **TCLC 31**
See Sodergran, Edith (Irene)

Softly, Edgar
See Lovecraft, H(oward) P(hillips)

Softly, Edward
See Lovecraft, H(oward) P(hillips)

Sokolov, Alexander V(sevolodovich) 1943-
See Sokolov, Sasha
See also CA 73-76

Sokolov, Raymond 1941- .... **CLC 7**
See also CA 85-88

Sokolov, Sasha .... **CLC 59**
See Sokolov, Alexander V(sevolodovich)
See also CWW 2; DLB 285; EWL 3; RGWL 2, 3

Solo, Jay
See Ellison, Harlan (Jay)

Sologub, Fyodor .... **TCLC 9**
See Teternikov, Fyodor Kuzmich
See also EWL 3

Solomons, Ikey Esquir
See Thackeray, William Makepeace

Solomos, Dionysios 1798-1857 .... **NCLC 15**

Solwoska, Mara
See French, Marilyn

Solzhenitsyn, Aleksandr I(sayevich)
1918- .. **CLC 1, 2, 4, 7, 9, 10, 18, 26, 34, 78, 134; SSC 32; WLC**
See Solzhenitsyn, Aleksandr Isaevich
See also AAYA 49; AITN 1; BPFB 3; CA 69-72; CANR 40, 65, 116; DA; DA3; DAB; DAC; DAM MST, NOV; DLB 302; EW 13; EXPS; LAIT 4; MTCW 1, 2; MTFW 2005; NFS 6; RGSF 2; RGWL 2, 3; SSFS 9; TWA

Solzhenitsyn, Aleksandr Isaevich
See Solzhenitsyn, Aleksandr I(sayevich)
See also CWW 2; EWL 3

Somers, Jane
See Lessing, Doris (May)

Somerville, Edith Oenone
1858-1949 .... **SSC 56; TCLC 51**
See also CA 196; DLB 135; RGEL 2; RGSF 2

Somerville & Ross
See Martin, Violet Florence; Somerville, Edith Oenone

Sommer, Scott 1951- .... **CLC 25**
See also CA 106

Sommers, Christina Hoff 1950- ...... **CLC 197**
See also CA 153; CANR 95

Sondheim, Stephen (Joshua) 1930- . **CLC 30, 39, 147; DC 22**
See also AAYA 11, 66; CA 103; CANR 47, 67, 125; DAM DRAM; LAIT 4

Sone, Monica 1919- .... **AAL**
See also DLB 312

Song, Cathy 1955- .... **AAL; PC 21**
See also CA 154; CANR 118; CWP; DLB 169, 312; EXPP; FW; PFS 5

Sontag, Susan 1933-2004 ... **CLC 1, 2, 10, 13, 31, 105, 195**
See also AMWS 3; CA 17-20R; 234; CANR 25, 51, 74, 97; CN 1, 2, 3, 4, 5, 6, 7; CPW; DA3; DAM POP; DLB 2; EWL 3; MAL 5; MAWW; MTCW 1, 2; MTFW 2005; RGAL 4; RHW; SSFS 10

Sophocles 496(?)B.C.-406(?)B.C. .... **CMLC 2, 47, 51; DC 1; WLCS**
See also AW 1; CDWLB 1; DA; DA3; DAB; DAC; DAM DRAM, MST; DFS 1, 4, 8; DLB 176; LAIT 1; LATS 1:1; LMFS 1; RGWL 2, 3; TWA

Sordello 1189-1269 .... **CMLC 15**

Sorel, Georges 1847-1922 .... **TCLC 91**
See also CA 118; 188

Sorel, Julia
See Drexler, Rosalyn

Sorokin, Vladimir .... **CLC 59**
See Sorokin, Vladimir Georgievich

Sorokin, Vladimir Georgievich
See Sorokin, Vladimir
See also DLB 285

Sorrentino, Gilbert 1929- .. **CLC 3, 7, 14, 22, 40**
See also CA 77-80; CANR 14, 33, 115; CN 3, 4, 5, 6, 7; CP 1, 2, 3, 4, 5, 6, 7; DLB 5, 173; DLBY 1980; INT CANR-14

Soseki
See Natsume, Soseki
See also MJW

Soto, Gary 1952- ... **CLC 32, 80; HLC 2; PC 28**
See also AAYA 10, 37; BYA 11; CA 119; 125; CANR 50, 74, 107; CLR 38; CP 4, 5, 6, 7; DAM MULT; DLB 82; EWL 3; EXPP; HW 1, 2; INT CA-125; JRDA; LLW; MAICYA 2; MAICYAS 1; MAL 5; MTCW 2; MTFW 2005; PFS 7; RGAL 4; SATA 80, 120; WYA; YAW

Soupault, Philippe 1897-1990 .... **CLC 68**
See also CA 116; 147; 131; EWL 3; GFL 1789 to the Present; LMFS 2

Souster, (Holmes) Raymond 1921- .... **CLC 5, 14**
See also CA 13-16R; CAAS 14; CANR 13, 29, 53; CP 1, 2, 3, 4, 5, 6, 7; DA3; DAC; DAM POET; DLB 88; RGEL 2; SATA 63

Southern, Terry 1924(?)-1995 .... **CLC 7**
See also AMWS 11; BPFB 3; CA 1-4R; 150; CANR 1, 55, 107; CN 1, 2, 3, 4, 5, 6; DLB 2; IDFW 3, 4

Southerne, Thomas 1660-1746 .... **LC 99**
See also DLB 80; RGEL 2

Southey, Robert 1774-1843 .... **NCLC 8, 97**
See also BRW 4; DLB 93, 107, 142; RGEL 2; SATA 54

Southwell, Robert 1561(?)-1595 .... **LC 108**
See also DLB 167; RGEL 2; TEA

Southworth, Emma Dorothy Eliza Nevitte
1819-1899 .... **NCLC 26**
See also DLB 239

Souza, Ernest
See Scott, Evelyn

Soyinka, Wole 1934- .. **BLC 3; CLC 3, 5, 14, 36, 44, 179; DC 2; WLC**
See also AFW; BW 2, 3; CA 13-16R; CANR 27, 39, 82, 136; CD 5, 6; CDWLB 3; CN 6, 7; CP 1, 2, 3, 4, 5, 6 ,7; DA; DA3; DAB; DAC; DAM DRAM, MST, MULT; DFS 10; DLB 125; EWL 3; MTCW 1, 2; MTFW 2005; RGEL 2; TWA; WLIT 2; WWE 1

Spackman, W(illiam) M(ode)
1905-1990 .... **CLC 46**
See also CA 81-84; 132

Stephen, Adeline Virginia
See Woolf, (Adeline) Virginia

Stephen, Sir Leslie 1832-1904 .... **TCLC 23**
See also BRW 5; CA 123; DLB 57, 144, 190

Stephen, Sir Leslie
See Stephen, Sir Leslie

Stephen, Virginia
See Woolf, (Adeline) Virginia

Stephens, James 1882(?)-1950 .... **SSC 50; TCLC 4**
See also CA 104; 192; DLB 19, 153, 162; EWL 3; FANT; RGEL 2; SUFW

Stephens, Reed
See Donaldson, Stephen R(eeder)

Stephenson, Neal 1959- .... **CLC 220**
See also AAYA 38; CA 122; CANR 88, 138; CN 7; MTCW 2005; SFW 4

Steptoe, Lydia
See Barnes, Djuna
See also GLL 1

Sterchi, Beat 1949- .... **CLC 65**
See also CA 203

Sterling, Brett
See Bradbury, Ray (Douglas); Hamilton, Edmond

Sterling, Bruce 1954- .... **CLC 72**
See also CA 119; CANR 44, 135; CN 7; MTFW 2005; SCFW 2; SFW 4

Sterling, George 1869-1926 .... **TCLC 20**
See also CA 117; 165; DLB 54

Stern, Gerald 1925- .... **CLC 40, 100**
See also AMWS 9; CA 81-84; CANR 28, 94; CP 3, 4, 5, 6, 7; DLB 105; RGAL 4

Stern, Richard (Gustave) 1928- ... **CLC 4, 39**
See also CA 1-4R; CANR 1, 25, 52, 120; CN 1, 2, 3, 4, 5, 6, 7; DLB 218; DLBY 1987; INT CANR-25

Sternberg, Josef von 1894-1969 .... **CLC 20**
See also CA 81-84

Sterne, Laurence 1713-1768 .... **LC 2, 48; WLC**
See also BRW 3; BRWC 1; CDBLB 1660-1789; DA; DAB; DAC; DAM MST, NOV; DLB 39; RGEL 2; TEA

Sternheim, (William Adolf) Carl
1878-1942 .... **TCLC 8**
See also CA 105; 193; DLB 56, 118; EWL 3; IDTP; RGWL 2, 3

Stevens, Margaret Dean
See Aldrich, Bess Streeter

Stevens, Mark 1951- .... **CLC 34**
See also CA 122

Stevens, Wallace 1879-1955 . **PC 6; TCLC 3, 12, 45; WLC**
See also AMW; AMWR 1; CA 104; 124; CDALB 1929-1941; DA; DA3; DAB; DAC; DAM MST, POET; DLB 54; EWL 3; EXPP; MAL 5; MTCW 1, 2; PAB; PFS 13, 16; RGAL 4; TUS; WP

Stevenson, Anne (Katharine) 1933- .. **CLC 7, 33**
See also BRWS 6; CA 17-20R; CAAS 9; CANR 9, 33, 123; CP 3, 4, 5, 6, 7; CWP; DLB 40; MTCW 1; RHW

Stevenson, Robert Louis (Balfour)
1850-1894 ...... **NCLC 5, 14, 63; SSC 11, 51; WLC**
See also AAYA 24; BPFB 3; BRW 5; BRWC 1; BRWR 1; BYA 1, 2, 4, 13; CD-BLB 1890-1914; CLR 10, 11; DA; DA3; DAB; DAC; DAM MST, NOV; DLB 18, 57, 141, 156, 174; DLBD 13; GL 3; HGG; JRDA; LAIT 1, 3; MAICYA 1, 2; NFS 11, 20; RGEL 2; RGSF 2; SATA 100; SUFW; TEA; WCH; WLIT 4; WYA; YABC 2; YAW

Stewart, J(ohn) I(nnes) M(ackintosh)
1906-1994 .... **CLC 7, 14, 32**
See Innes, Michael
See also CA 85-88; 147; CAAS 3; CANR 47; CMW 4; CN 1, 2, 3, 4, 5; MTCW 1, 2

Stewart, Mary (Florence Elinor)
1916- .... **CLC 7, 35, 117**
See also AAYA 29; BPFB 3; CA 1-4R; CANR 1, 59, 130; CMW 4; CPW; DAB; FANT; RHW; SATA 12; YAW

Stewart, Mary Rainbow
See Stewart, Mary (Florence Elinor)

Stifle, June
See Campbell, Maria

Stifter, Adalbert 1805-1868 .. **NCLC 41; SSC 28**
See also CDWLB 2; DLB 133; RGSF 2; RGWL 2, 3

Still, James 1906-2001 .... **CLC 49**
See also CA 65-68; 195; CAAS 17; CANR 10, 26; CSW; DLB 9; DLBY 01; SATA 29; SATA-Obit 127

Sting 1951-
See Sumner, Gordon Matthew
See also CA 167

Stirling, Arthur
See Sinclair, Upton (Beall)

Stitt, Milan 1941- .... **CLC 29**
See also CA 69-72

Stockton, Francis Richard 1834-1902
See Stockton, Frank R.
See also AAYA 68; CA 108; 137; MAICYA 1, 2; SATA 44; SFW 4

Stockton, Frank R. .... **TCLC 47**
See Stockton, Francis Richard
See also BYA 4, 13; DLB 42, 74; DLBD 13; EXPS; SATA-Brief 32; SSFS 3; SUFW; WCH

Stoddard, Charles
See Kuttner, Henry

Stoker, Abraham 1847-1912
See Stoker, Bram
See also CA 105; 150; DA; DA3; DAC; DAM MST, NOV; HGG; MTFW 2005; SATA 29

Stoker, Bram . **SSC 62; TCLC 8, 144; WLC**
See Stoker, Abraham
See also AAYA 23; BPFB 3; BRWS 3; BYA 5; CDBLB 1890-1914; DAB; DLB 304; GL 3; LATS 1:1; NFS 18; RGEL 2; SUFW; TEA; WLIT 4

Stolz, Mary (Slattery) 1920- .... **CLC 12**
See also AAYA 8; AITN 1; CA 5-8R; CANR 13, 41, 112; JRDA; MAICYA 1, 2; SAAS 3; SATA 10, 71, 133; YAW

Stone, Irving 1903-1989 .... **CLC 7**
See also AITN 1; BPFB 3; CA 1-4R; 129; CAAS 3; CANR 1, 23; CN 1, 2, 3, 4; CPW; DA3; DAM POP; INT CANR-23; MTCW 1, 2; MTFW 2005; RHW; SATA 3; SATA-Obit 64

Stone, Oliver (William) 1946- .... **CLC 73**
See also AAYA 15; 64; CA 110; CANR 55, 125

Stone, Robert (Anthony) 1937- ... **CLC 5, 23, 42, 175**
See also AMWS 5; BPFB 3; CA 85-88; CANR 23, 66, 95; CN 4, 5, 6, 7; DLB 152; EWL 3; INT CANR-23; MAL 5; MTCW 1; MTFW 2005

Stone, Ruth 1915- .... **PC 53**
See also CA 45-48; CANR 2, 91; CP 7; CSW; DLB 105; PFS 19

Stone, Zachary
See Follett, Ken(neth Martin)

Stoppard, Tom 1937- ... **CLC 1, 3, 4, 5, 8, 15, 29, 34, 63, 91; DC 6; WLC**
See also AAYA 63; BRWC 1; BRWR 2; BRWS 1; CA 81-84; CANR 39, 67, 125; CBD; CD 5, 6; CDBLB 1960 to Present; DA; DA3; DAB; DAC; DAM DRAM, MST; DFS 2, 5, 8, 11, 13, 16; DLB 13, 233; DLBY 1985; EWL 3; LATS 1:2; MTCW 1, 2; MTFW 2005; RGEL 2; TEA; WLIT 4

Storey, David (Malcolm) 1933- . **CLC 2, 4, 5, 8**
See also BRWS 1; CA 81-84; CANR 36; CBD; CD 5, 6; CN 1, 2, 3, 4, 5, 6; DAM DRAM; DLB 13, 14, 207, 245; EWL 3; MTCW 1; RGEL 2

Storm, Hyemeyohsts 1935- ... **CLC 3; NNAL**
See also CA 81-84; CANR 45; DAM MULT

Storm, (Hans) Theodor (Woldsen)
1817-1888 .... **NCLC 1; SSC 27**
See also CDWLB 2; DLB 129; EW; RGSF 2; RGWL 2, 3

Storni, Alfonsina 1892-1938 . **HLC 2; PC 33; TCLC 5**
See also CA 104; 131; DAM MULT; DLB 283; HW 1; LAW

Stoughton, William 1631-1701 .... **LC 38**
See also DLB 24

Stout, Rex (Todhunter) 1886-1975 ..... **CLC 3**
See also AITN 2; BPFB 3; CA 61-64; CANR 71; CMW 4; CN 2; DLB 306; MSW; RGAL 4

Stow, (Julian) Randolph 1935- ... **CLC 23, 48**
See also CA 13-16R; CANR 33; CN 1, 2, 3, 4, 5, 6, 7; CP 1, 2, 3, 4; DLB 260; MTCW 1; RGEL 2

Stowe, Harriet (Elizabeth) Beecher
1811-1896 .... **NCLC 3, 50, 133; WLC**
See also AAYA 53; AMWS 1; CDALB 1865-1917; DA; DA3; DAB; DAC; DAM MST, NOV; DLB 1, 12, 42, 74, 189, 239, 243; EXPN; FL 1:3; JRDA; LAIT 2; MAICYA 1, 2; NFS 6; RGAL 4; TUS; YABC 1

Strabo c. 64B.C.-c. 25 .... **CMLC 37**
See also DLB 176

Strachey, (Giles) Lytton
1880-1932 .... **TCLC 12**
See also BRWS 2; CA 110; 178; DLB 149; DLBD 10; EWL 3; MTCW 2; NCFS 4

Stramm, August 1874-1915 .... **PC 50**
See also CA 195; EWL 3

Strand, Mark 1934- .. **CLC 6, 18, 41, 71; PC 63**
See also AMWS 4; CA 21-24R; CANR 40, 65, 100; CP 1, 2, 3, 4, 5, 6, 7; DAM POET; DLB 5; EWL 3; MAL 5; PAB; PFS 9, 18; RGAL 4; SATA 41; TCLE 1:2

Stratton-Porter, Gene(va Grace) 1863-1924
See Porter, Gene(va Grace) Stratton
See also ANW; CA 137; CLR 87; DLB 221; DLBD 14; MAICYA 1, 2; SATA 15

Straub, Peter (Francis) 1943- ... **CLC 28, 107**
See also BEST 89:1; BPFB 3; CA 85-88; CANR 28, 65, 109; CPW; DAM POP; DLBY 1984; HGG; MTCW 1, 2; MTFW 2005; SUFW 2

Strauss, Botho 1944- .... **CLC 22**
See also CA 157; CWW 2; DLB 124

Strauss, Leo 1899-1973 .... **TCLC 141**
See also CA 101; 45-48; CANR 122

Streatfeild, (Mary) Noel
1897(?)-1986 .... **CLC 21**
See also CA 81-84; 120; CANR 31; CLR 17, 83; CWRI 5; DLB 160; MAICYA 1, 2; SATA 20; SATA-Obit 48

Stribling, T(homas) S(igismund)
1881-1965 .... **CLC 23**
See also CA 189; 107; CMW 4; DLB 9; RGAL 4

Tevis, Walter 1928-1984 .... **CLC 42**
 See also CA 113; SFW 4

Tey, Josephine .... **TCLC 14**
 See Mackintosh, Elizabeth
 See also DLB 77; MSW

Thackeray, William Makepeace
 1811-1863 .... **NCLC 5, 14, 22, 43; WLC**
 See also BRW 5; BRWC 2; CDBLB 1832-
 1890; DA; DA3; DAB; DAC; DAM MST,
 NOV; DLB 21, 55, 159, 163; NFS 13;
 RGEL 2; SATA 23; TEA; WLIT 3

Thakura, Ravindranatha
 See Tagore, Rabindranath

Thames, C. H.
 See Marlowe, Stephen

Tharoor, Shashi 1956- .... **CLC 70**
 See also CA 141; CANR 91; CN 6, 7

Thelwall, John 1764-1834 .... **NCLC 162**
 See also DLB 93, 158

Thelwell, Michael Miles 1939- .... **CLC 22**
 See also BW 2; CA 101

Theobald, Lewis, Jr.
 See Lovecraft, H(oward) P(hillips)

Theocritus c. 310B.C.- .... **CMLC 45**
 See also AW 1; DLB 176; RGWL 2, 3

Theodorescu, Ion N. 1880-1967
 See Arghezi, Tudor
 See also CA 116

Theriault, Yves 1915-1983 .... **CLC 79**
 See also CA 102; CCA 1; DAC; DAM
 MST; DLB 88; EWL 3

Theroux, Alexander (Louis) 1939- .... **CLC 2,
 25**
 See also CA 85-88; CANR 20, 63; CN 4, 5,
 6, 7

Theroux, Paul (Edward) 1941- ..... **CLC 5, 8,
 11, 15, 28, 46**
 See also AAYA 28; AMWS 8; BEST 89:4;
 BPFB 3; CA 33-36R; CANR 20, 45, 74,
 133; CDALBS; CN 1, 2, 3, 4, 5, 6, 7; CP
 1; CPW 1; DA3; DAM POP; DLB 2, 218;
 EWL 3; HGG; MAL 5; MTCW 1, 2;
 MTFW 2005; RGAL 4; SATA 44, 109;
 TUS

Thesen, Sharon 1946- .... **CLC 56**
 See also CA 163; CANR 125; CP 7; CWP

Thespis fl. 6th cent. B.C.- .... **CMLC 51**
 See also LMFS 1

Thevenin, Denis
 See Duhamel, Georges

Thibault, Jacques Anatole Francois
 1844-1924
 See France, Anatole
 See also CA 106; 127; DA3; DAM NOV;
 MTCW 1, 2; TWA

Thiele, Colin (Milton) 1920- .... **CLC 17**
 See also CA 29-32R; CANR 12, 28, 53,
 105; CLR 27; CP 1, 2; DLB 289; MAI-
 CYA 1, 2; SAAS 2; SATA 14, 72, 125;
 YAW

Thistlethwaite, Bel
 See Wetherald, Agnes Ethelwyn

Thomas, Audrey (Callahan) 1935- .... **CLC 7,
 13, 37, 107; SSC 20**
 See also AITN 2; CA 21-24R, 237; CAAE
 237; CAAS 19; CANR 36, 58; CN 2, 3,
 4, 5, 6, 7; DLB 60; MTCW 1; RGSF 2

Thomas, Augustus 1857-1934 .... **TCLC 97**
 See also MAL 5

Thomas, D(onald) M(ichael) 1935- . **CLC 13,
 22, 31, 132**
 See also BPFB 3; BRWS 4; CA 61-64;
 CAAS 11; CANR 17, 45, 75; CDBLB
 1960 to Present; CN 4, 5, 6, 7; CP 1, 2, 3,
 4, 5, 6, 7; DA3; DLB 40, 207, 299; HGG;
 INT CANR-17; MTCW 1, 2; MTFW
 2005; SFW 4

Thomas, Dylan (Marlais) 1914-1953 .... **PC 2,
 52; SSC 3, 44; TCLC 1, 8, 45, 105;
 WLC**
 See also AAYA 45; BRWS 1; CA 104; 120;
 CANR 65; CDBLB 1945-1960; DA; DA3;
 DAB; DAC; DAM DRAM, MST, POET;
 DLB 13, 20, 139; EWL 3; EXPP; LAIT
 3; MTCW 1, 2; MTFW 2005; PAB; PFS
 1, 3, 8; RGEL 2; RGSF 2; SATA 60; TEA;
 WLIT 4; WP

Thomas, (Philip) Edward 1878-1917 . **PC 53;
 TCLC 10**
 See also BRW 6; BRWS 3; CA 106; 153;
 DAM POET; DLB 19, 98, 156, 216; EWL
 3; PAB; RGEL 2

Thomas, Joyce Carol 1938- .... **CLC 35**
 See also AAYA 12, 54; BW 2, 3; CA 113;
 116; CANR 48, 114, 135; CLR 19; DLB
 33; INT CA-116; JRDA; MAICYA 1, 2;
 MTCW 1, 2; MTFW 2005; SAAS 7;
 SATA 40, 78, 123, 137; SATA-Essay 137;
 WYA; YAW

Thomas, Lewis 1913-1993 .... **CLC 35**
 See also ANW; CA 85-88; 143; CANR 38,
 60; DLB 275; MTCW 1, 2

Thomas, M. Carey 1857-1935 .... **TCLC 89**
 See also FW

Thomas, Paul
 See Mann, (Paul) Thomas

Thomas, Piri 1928- .... **CLC 17; HLCS 2**
 See also CA 73-76; HW 1; LLW

Thomas, R(onald) S(tuart)
 1913-2000 .... **CLC 6, 13, 48**
 See also CA 89-92; 189; CAAS 4; CANR
 30; CDBLB 1960 to Present; CP 1, 2, 3,
 4, 5, 6, 7; DAB; DAM POET; DLB 27;
 EWL 3; MTCW 1; RGEL 2

Thomas, Ross (Elmore) 1926-1995 .. **CLC 39**
 See also CA 33-36R; 150; CANR 22, 63;
 CMW 4

Thompson, Francis (Joseph)
 1859-1907 .... **TCLC 4**
 See also BRW 5; CA 104; 189; CDBLB
 1890-1914; DLB 19; RGEL 2; TEA

Thompson, Francis Clegg
 See Mencken, H(enry) L(ouis)

Thompson, Hunter S(tockton)
 1937(?)-2005 .... **CLC 9, 17, 40, 104**
 See also AAYA 45; BEST 89:1; BPFB 3;
 CA 17-20R; 236; CANR 23, 46, 74, 77,
 111, 133; CPW; CSW; DA3; DAM POP;
 DLB 185; MTCW 1, 2; MTFW 2005;
 TUS

Thompson, James Myers
 See Thompson, Jim (Myers)

Thompson, Jim (Myers)
 1906-1977(?) .... **CLC 69**
 See also BPFB 3; CA 140; CMW 4; CPW;
 DLB 226; MSW

Thompson, Judith (Clare Francesca)
 1954- .... **CLC 39**
 See also CA 143; CD 5, 6; CWD; DFS 22

Thomson, James 1700-1748 .... **LC 16, 29, 40**
 See also BRWS 3; DAM POET; DLB 95;
 RGEL 2

Thomson, James 1834-1882 .... **NCLC 18**
 See also DAM POET; DLB 35; RGEL 2

Thoreau, Henry David 1817-1862 .. **NCLC 7,
 21, 61, 138; PC 30; WLC**
 See also AAYA 42; AMW; ANW; BYA 3;
 CDALB 1640-1865; DA; DA3; DAB;
 DAC; DAM MST; DLB 1, 183, 223, 270,
 298; LAIT 2; LMFS 1; NCFS 3; RGAL
 4; TUS

Thorndike, E. L.
 See Thorndike, Edward L(ee)

Thorndike, Edward L(ee)
 1874-1949 .... **TCLC 107**
 See also CA 121

Thornton, Hall
 See Silverberg, Robert

Thorpe, Adam 1956- .... **CLC 176**
 See also CA 129; CANR 92; DLB 231

Thubron, Colin (Gerald Dryden)
 1939- .... **CLC 163**
 See also CA 25-28R; CANR 12, 29, 59, 95;
 CN 5, 6, 7; DLB 204, 231

Thucydides c. 455B.C.-c. 395B.C. . **CMLC 17**
 See also AW 1; DLB 176; RGWL 2, 3

Thumboo, Edwin Nadason 1933- .... **PC 30**
 See also CA 194; CP 1

Thurber, James (Grover)
 1894-1961 .. **CLC 5, 11, 25, 125; SSC 1,
 47**
 See also AAYA 56; AMWS 1; BPFB 3;
 BYA 5; CA 73-76; CANR 17, 39; CDALB
 1929-1941; CWRI 5; DA; DA3; DAB;
 DAC; DAM DRAM, MST, NOV; DLB 4,
 11, 22, 102; EWL 3; EXPS; FANT; LAIT
 3; MAICYA 1, 2; MAL 5; MTCW 1, 2;
 MTFW 2005; RGAL 4; RGSF 2; SATA
 13; SSFS 1, 10, 19; SUFW; TUS

Thurman, Wallace (Henry)
 1902-1934 ..... **BLC 3; HR 1:3; TCLC 6**
 See also BW 1, 3; CA 104; 124; CANR 81;
 DAM MULT; DLB 51

Tibullus c. 54B.C.-c. 18B.C. .... **CMLC 36**
 See also AW 2; DLB 211; RGWL 2, 3

Ticheburn, Cheviot
 See Ainsworth, William Harrison

Tieck, (Johann) Ludwig
 1773-1853 .... **NCLC 5, 46; SSC 31**
 See also CDWLB 2; DLB 90; EW 5; IDTP;
 RGSF 2; RGWL 2, 3; SUFW

Tiger, Derry
 See Ellison, Harlan (Jay)

Tilghman, Christopher 1946- .... **CLC 65**
 See also CA 159; CANR 135; CSW; DLB
 244

Tillich, Paul (Johannes)
 1886-1965 .... **CLC 131**
 See also CA 5-8R; 25-28R; CANR 33;
 MTCW 1, 2

Tillinghast, Richard (Williford)
 1940- .... **CLC 29**
 See also CA 29-32R; CAAS 23; CANR 26,
 51, 96; CP 2, 3, 4, 5, 6, 7; CSW

Timrod, Henry 1828-1867 .... **NCLC 25**
 See also DLB 3, 248; RGAL 4

Tindall, Gillian (Elizabeth) 1938- ...... **CLC 7**
 See also CA 21-24R; CANR 11, 65, 107;
 CN 1, 2, 3, 4, 5, 6, 7

Tiptree, James, Jr. .... **CLC 48, 50**
 See Sheldon, Alice Hastings Bradley
 See also DLB 8; SCFW 1, 2; SFW 4

Tirone Smith, Mary-Ann 1944- .... **CLC 39**
 See also CA 118; 136; CANR 113; SATA
 143

Tirso de Molina 1580(?)-1648 .... **DC 13;
 HLCS 2; LC 73**
 See also RGWL 2, 3

Titmarsh, Michael Angelo
 See Thackeray, William Makepeace

**Tocqueville, Alexis (Charles Henri Maurice
 Clerel Comte) de** 1805-1859 .. **NCLC 7,
 63**
 See also EW 6; GFL 1789 to the Present;
 TWA

Toer, Pramoedya Ananta 1925- ...... **CLC 186**
 See also CA 197; RGWL 3

Toffler, Alvin 1928- .... **CLC 168**
 See also CA 13-16R; CANR 15, 46, 67;
 CPW; DAM POP; MTCW 1, 2

Toibin, Colm 1955- .... **CLC 162**
 See also CA 142; CANR 81; CN 7; DLB
 271

Tolkien, J(ohn) R(onald) R(euel)
1892-1973 .... **CLC 1, 2, 3, 8, 12, 38; TCLC 137; WLC**
See also AAYA 10; AITN 1; BPFB 3; BRWC 2; BRWS 2; CA 17-18; 45-48; CANR 36, 134; CAP 2; CDBLB 1914-1945; CLR 56; CN 1; CPW 1; CWRI 5; DA; DA3; DAB; DAC; DAM MST, NOV, POP; DLB 15, 160, 255; EFS 2; EWL 3; FANT; JRDA; LAIT 1; LATS 1:2; LMFS 2; MAICYA 1, 2; MTCW 1, 2; MTFW 2005; NFS 8; RGEL 2; SATA 2, 32, 100; SATA-Obit 24; SFW 4; SUFW; TEA; WCH; WYA; YAW

Toller, Ernst 1893-1939 .... **TCLC 10**
See also CA 107; 186; DLB 124; EWL 3; RGWL 2, 3

Tolson, M. B.
See Tolson, Melvin B(eaunorus)

Tolson, Melvin B(eaunorus)
1898(?)-1966 .... **BLC 3; CLC 36, 105**
See also AFAW 1, 2; BW 1, 3; CA 124; 89-92; CANR 80; DAM MULT, POET; DLB 48, 76; MAL 5; RGAL 4

Tolstoi, Aleksei Nikolaevich
See Tolstoy, Alexey Nikolaevich

Tolstoi, Lev
See Tolstoy, Leo (Nikolaevich)
See also RGSF 2; RGWL 2, 3

Tolstoy, Aleksei Nikolaevich
See Tolstoy, Alexey Nikolaevich
See also DLB 272

Tolstoy, Alexey Nikolaevich
1882-1945 .... **TCLC 18**
See Tolstoy, Aleksei Nikolaevich
See also CA 107; 158; EWL 3; SFW 4

Tolstoy, Leo (Nikolaevich)
1828-1910 . **SSC 9, 30, 45, 54; TCLC 4, 11, 17, 28, 44, 79, 173; WLC**
See Tolstoi, Lev
See also AAYA 56; CA 104; 123; DA; DA3; DAB; DAC; DAM MST, NOV; DLB 238; EFS 2; EW 7; EXPS; IDTP; LAIT 2; LATS 1:1; LMFS 1; NFS 10; SATA 26; SSFS 5; TWA

Tolstoy, Count Leo
See Tolstoy, Leo (Nikolaevich)

Tomalin, Claire 1933- .... **CLC 166**
See also CA 89-92; CANR 52, 88; DLB 155

Tomasi di Lampedusa, Giuseppe 1896-1957
See Lampedusa, Giuseppe (Tomasi) di
See also CA 111; DLB 177; EWL 3; WLIT 7

Tomlin, Lily .... **CLC 17**
See Tomlin, Mary Jean

Tomlin, Mary Jean 1939(?)-
See Tomlin, Lily
See also CA 117

Tomline, F. Latour
See Gilbert, W(illiam) S(chwenck)

Tomlinson, (Alfred) Charles 1927- .... **CLC 2, 4, 6, 13, 45; PC 17**
See also CA 5-8R; CANR 33; CP 1, 2, 3, 4, 5, 6, 7; DAM POET; DLB 40; TCLE 1:2

Tomlinson, H(enry) M(ajor)
1873-1958 .... **TCLC 71**
See also CA 118; 161; DLB 36, 100, 195

Tonna, Charlotte Elizabeth
1790-1846 .... **NCLC 135**
See also DLB 163

Tonson, Jacob fl. 1655(?)-1736 .... **LC 86**
See also DLB 170

Toole, John Kennedy 1937-1969 ..... **CLC 19, 64**
See also BPFB 3; CA 104; DLBY 1981; MTCW 2; MTFW 2005

Toomer, Eugene
See Toomer, Jean

Toomer, Eugene Pinchback
See Toomer, Jean

Toomer, Jean 1894-1967 .. **BLC 3; CLC 1, 4, 13, 22; HR 1:3; PC 7; SSC 1, 45; TCLC 172; WLCS**
See also AFAW 1, 2; AMWS 3, 9; BW 1; CA 85-88; CDALB 1917-1929; DA3; DAM MULT; DLB 45, 51; EWL 3; EXPP; EXPS; LMFS 2; MAL 5; MTCW 1, 2; MTFW 2005; NFS 11; RGAL 4; RGSF 2; SSFS 5

Toomer, Nathan Jean
See Toomer, Jean

Toomer, Nathan Pinchback
See Toomer, Jean

Torley, Luke
See Blish, James (Benjamin)

Tornimparte, Alessandra
See Ginzburg, Natalia

Torre, Raoul della
See Mencken, H(enry) L(ouis)

Torrence, Ridgely 1874-1950 .... **TCLC 97**
See also DLB 54, 249; MAL 5

Torrey, E(dwin) Fuller 1937- .... **CLC 34**
See also CA 119; CANR 71

Torsvan, Ben Traven
See Traven, B.

Torsvan, Benno Traven
See Traven, B.

Torsvan, Berick Traven
See Traven, B.

Torsvan, Berwick Traven
See Traven, B.

Torsvan, Bruno Traven
See Traven, B.

Torsvan, Traven
See Traven, B.

Tourneur, Cyril 1575(?)-1626 .... **LC 66**
See also BRW 2; DAM DRAM; DLB 58; RGEL 2

Tournier, Michel (Edouard) 1924- .... **CLC 6, 23, 36, 95; SSC 88**
See also CA 49-52; CANR 3, 36, 74; CWW 2; DLB 83; EWL 3; GFL 1789 to the Present; MTCW 1, 2; SATA 23

Tournimparte, Alessandra
See Ginzburg, Natalia

Towers, Ivar
See Kornbluth, C(yril) M.

Towne, Robert (Burton) 1936(?)- ..... **CLC 87**
See also CA 108; DLB 44; IDFW 3, 4

Townsend, Sue .... **CLC 61**
See Townsend, Susan Lilian
See also AAYA 28; CA 119; 127; CANR 65, 107; CBD; CD 5, 6; CPW; CWD; DAB; DAC; DAM MST; DLB 271; INT CA-127; SATA 55, 93; SATA-Brief 48; YAW

Townsend, Susan Lilian 1946-
See Townsend, Sue

Townshend, Pete
See Townshend, Peter (Dennis Blandford)

Townshend, Peter (Dennis Blandford)
1945- .... **CLC 17, 42**
See also CA 107

Tozzi, Federigo 1883-1920 .... **TCLC 31**
See also CA 160; CANR 110; DLB 264; EWL 3; WLIT 7

Tracy, Don(ald Fiske) 1905-1970(?)
See Queen, Ellery
See also CA 1-4R; 176; CANR 2

Trafford, F. G.
See Riddell, Charlotte

Traherne, Thomas 1637(?)-1674 .. **LC 99; PC 70**
See also BRW 2; BRWS 11; DLB 131; PAB; RGEL 2

Traill, Catharine Parr 1802-1899 .. **NCLC 31**
See also DLB 99

Trakl, Georg 1887-1914 .... **PC 20; TCLC 5**
See also CA 104; 165; EW 10; EWL 3; LMFS 2; MTCW 2; RGWL 2, 3

Trambley, Estela Portillo .... **TCLC 163**
See Portillo Trambley, Estela
See also CA 77-80; RGAL 4

Tranquilli, Secondino
See Silone, Ignazio

Transtroemer, Tomas Gosta
See Transtromer, Tomas (Goesta)

Transtromer, Tomas (Gosta)
See Transtromer, Tomas (Goesta)
See also CWW 2

Transtromer, Tomas (Goesta)
1931- .... **CLC 52, 65**
See Transtromer, Tomas (Gosta)
See also CA 117; 129; CAAS 17; CANR 115; DAM POET; DLB 257; EWL 3; PFS 21

Transtromer, Tomas Gosta
See Transtromer, Tomas (Goesta)

Traven, B. 1882(?)-1969 .... **CLC 8, 11**
See also CA 19-20; 25-28R; CAP 2; DLB 9, 56; EWL 3; MTCW 1; RGAL 4

Trediakovsky, Vasilii Kirillovich
1703-1769 .... **LC 68**
See also DLB 150

Treitel, Jonathan 1959- .... **CLC 70**
See also CA 210; DLB 267

Trelawny, Edward John
1792-1881 .... **NCLC 85**
See also DLB 110, 116, 144

Tremain, Rose 1943- .... **CLC 42**
See also CA 97-100; CANR 44, 95; CN 4, 5, 6, 7; DLB 14, 271; RGSF 2; RHW

Tremblay, Michel 1942- .... **CLC 29, 102**
See also CA 116; 128; CCA 1; CWW 2; DAC; DAM MST; DLB 60; EWL 3; GLL 1; MTCW 1, 2; MTFW 2005

Trevanian .... **CLC 29**
See Whitaker, Rod(ney)

Trevor, Glen
See Hilton, James

Trevor, William .. **CLC 7, 9, 14, 25, 71, 116; SSC 21, 58**
See Cox, William Trevor
See also BRWS 4; CBD; CD 5, 6; CN 1, 2, 3, 4, 5, 6, 7; DLB 14, 139; EWL 3; LATS 1:2; RGEL 2; RGSF 2; SSFS 10; TCLE 1:2

Trifonov, Iurii (Valentinovich)
See Trifonov, Yuri (Valentinovich)
See also DLB 302; RGWL 2, 3

Trifonov, Yuri (Valentinovich)
1925-1981 .... **CLC 45**
See Trifonov, Iurii (Valentinovich); Trifonov, Yury Valentinovich
See also CA 126; 103; MTCW 1

Trifonov, Yury Valentinovich
See Trifonov, Yuri (Valentinovich)
See also EWL 3

Trilling, Diana (Rubin) 1905-1996 . **CLC 129**
See also CA 5-8R; 154; CANR 10, 46; INT CANR-10; MTCW 1, 2

Trilling, Lionel 1905-1975 ..... **CLC 9, 11, 24; SSC 75**
See also AMWS 3; CA 9-12R; 61-64; CANR 10, 105; CN 1, 2; DLB 28, 63; EWL 3; INT CANR-10; MAL 5; MTCW 1, 2; RGAL 4; TUS

Trimball, W. H.
See Mencken, H(enry) L(ouis)

Tristan
See Gomez de la Serna, Ramon

Tristram
See Housman, A(lfred) E(dward)

Usk, Thomas (?)-1388 .... **CMLC 76**
　　See also DLB 146

Ustinov, Peter (Alexander)
　　1921-2004 .... **CLC 1**
　　See also AITN 1; CA 13-16R; 225; CANR
　　25, 51; CBD; CD 5, 6; DLB 13; MTCW
　　2

U Tam'si, Gerald Felix Tchicaya
　　See Tchicaya, Gerald Felix

U Tam'si, Tchicaya
　　See Tchicaya, Gerald Felix

Vachss, Andrew (Henry) 1942- .... **CLC 106**
　　See also CA 118, 214; CAAE 214; CANR
　　44, 95; CMW 4

Vachss, Andrew H.
　　See Vachss, Andrew (Henry)

Vaculik, Ludvik 1926- .... **CLC 7**
　　See also CA 53-56; CANR 72; CWW 2;
　　DLB 232; EWL 3

Vaihinger, Hans 1852-1933 .... **TCLC 71**
　　See also CA 116; 166

Valdez, Luis (Miguel) 1940- ..... **CLC 84; DC
　　10; HLC 2**
　　See also CA 101; CAD; CANR 32, 81; CD
　　5, 6; DAM MULT; DFS 5; DLB 122;
　　EWL 3; HW 1; LAIT 4; LLW

Valenzuela, Luisa 1938- .... **CLC 31, 104;
　　HLCS 2; SSC 14, 82**
　　See also CA 101; CANR 32, 65, 123; CD-
　　WLB 3; CWW 2; DAM MULT; DLB 113;
　　EWL 3; FW; HW 1, 2; LAW; RGSF 2;
　　RGWL 3

Valera y Alcala-Galiano, Juan
　　1824-1905 .... **TCLC 10**
　　See also CA 106

Valerius Maximus fl. 20- .... **CMLC 64**
　　See also DLB 211

Valery, (Ambroise) Paul (Toussaint Jules)
　　1871-1945 .... **PC 9; TCLC 4, 15**
　　See also CA 104; 122; DA3; DAM POET;
　　DLB 258; EW 8; EWL 3; GFL 1789 to
　　the Present; MTCW 1, 2; MTFW 2005;
　　RGWL 2, 3; TWA

Valle-Inclan, Ramon (Maria) del
　　1866-1936 .... **HLC 2; TCLC 5**
　　See del Valle-Inclan, Ramon (Maria)
　　See also CA 106; 153; CANR 80; DAM
　　MULT; DLB 134; EW 8; EWL 3; HW 2;
　　RGSF 2; RGWL 2, 3

Vallejo, Antonio Buero
　　See Buero Vallejo, Antonio

Vallejo, Cesar (Abraham)
　　1892-1938 .... **HLC 2; TCLC 3, 56**
　　See also CA 105; 153; DAM MULT; DLB
　　290; EWL 3; HW 1; LAW; RGWL 2, 3

Valles, Jules 1832-1885 .... **NCLC 71**
　　See also DLB 123; GFL 1789 to the Present

Vallette, Marguerite Eymery
　　1860-1953 .... **TCLC 67**
　　See Rachilde
　　See also CA 182; DLB 123, 192

Valle Y Pena, Ramon del
　　See Valle-Inclan, Ramon (Maria) del

Van Ash, Cay 1918-1994 .... **CLC 34**
　　See also CA 220

Vanbrugh, Sir John 1664-1726 .... **LC 21**
　　See also BRW 2; DAM DRAM; DLB 80;
　　IDTP; RGEL 2

Van Campen, Karl
　　See Campbell, John W(ood, Jr.)

Vance, Gerald
　　See Silverberg, Robert

Vance, Jack .... **CLC 35**
　　See Vance, John Holbrook
　　See also DLB 8; FANT; SCFW 1, 2; SFW
　　4; SUFW 1, 2

Vance, John Holbrook 1916-
　　See Queen, Ellery; Vance, Jack
　　See also CA 29-32R; CANR 17, 65; CMW
　　4; MTCW 1

**Van Den Bogarde, Derek Jules Gaspard
　　Ulric Niven** 1921-1999 .... **CLC 14**
　　See Bogarde, Dirk
　　See also CA 77-80; 179

Vandenburgh, Jane .... **CLC 59**
　　See also CA 168

Vanderhaeghe, Guy 1951- .... **CLC 41**
　　See also BPFB 3; CA 113; CANR 72, 145;
　　CN 7

van der Post, Laurens (Jan)
　　1906-1996 .... **CLC 5**
　　See also AFW; CA 5-8R; 155; CANR 35;
　　CN 1, 2, 3, 4, 5, 6; DLB 204; RGEL 2

van de Wetering, Janwillem 1931- ... **CLC 47**
　　See also CA 49-52; CANR 4, 62, 90; CMW
　　4

Van Dine, S. S. .... **TCLC 23**
　　See Wright, Willard Huntington
　　See also DLB 306; MSW

Van Doren, Carl (Clinton)
　　1885-1950 .... **TCLC 18**
　　See also CA 111; 168

Van Doren, Mark 1894-1972 .... **CLC 6, 10**
　　See also CA 1-4R; 37-40R; CANR 3; CN
　　1; CP 1; DLB 45, 284; MAL 5; MTCW
　　1, 2; RGAL 4

Van Druten, John (William)
　　1901-1957 .... **TCLC 2**
　　See also CA 104; 161; DLB 10; MAL 5;
　　RGAL 4

Van Duyn, Mona (Jane) 1921-2004 .. **CLC 3,
　　7, 63, 116**
　　See also CA 9-12R; 234; CANR 7, 38, 60,
　　116; CP 1, 2, 3, 4, 5, 6, 7; CWP; DAM
　　POET; DLB 5; MAL 5; MTFW 2005;
　　PFS 20

Van Dyne, Edith
　　See Baum, L(yman) Frank

van Itallie, Jean-Claude 1936- .... **CLC 3**
　　See also CA 45-48; CAAS 2; CAD; CANR
　　1, 48; CD 5, 6; DLB 7

Van Loot, Cornelius Obenchain
　　See Roberts, Kenneth (Lewis)

van Ostaijen, Paul 1896-1928 .... **TCLC 33**
　　See also CA 163

Van Peebles, Melvin 1932- .... **CLC 2, 20**
　　See also BW 2, 3; CA 85-88; CANR 27,
　　67, 82; DAM MULT

van Schendel, Arthur(-Francois-Emile)
　　1874-1946 .... **TCLC 56**
　　See also EWL 3

Vansittart, Peter 1920- .... **CLC 42**
　　See also CA 1-4R; CANR 3, 49, 90; CN 4,
　　5, 6, 7; RHW

Van Vechten, Carl 1880-1964 ... **CLC 33; HR
　　1:3**
　　See also AMWS 2; CA 183; 89-92; DLB 4,
　　9, 51; RGAL 4

van Vogt, A(lfred) E(lton) 1912-2000 . **CLC 1**
　　See also BPFB 3; BYA 13, 14; CA 21-24R;
　　190; CANR 28; DLB 8, 251; SATA 14;
　　SATA-Obit 124; SCFW 1, 2; SFW 4

Vara, Madeleine
　　See Jackson, Laura (Riding)

Varda, Agnes 1928- .... **CLC 16**
　　See also CA 116; 122

Vargas Llosa, (Jorge) Mario (Pedro)
　　1936- .... **CLC 3, 6, 9, 10, 15, 31, 42, 85,
　　181; HLC 2**
　　See Llosa, (Jorge) Mario (Pedro) Vargas
　　See also BPFB 3; CA 73-76; CANR 18, 32,
　　42, 67, 116, 140; CDWLB 3; CWW 2;
　　DA; DA3; DAB; DAC; DAM MST,
　　MULT, NOV; DLB 145; DNFS 2; EWL
　　3; HW 1, 2; LAIT 5; LATS 1:2; LAW;

LAWS 1; MTCW 1, 2; MTFW 2005;
　　RGWL 2; SSFS 14; TWA; WLIT 1

Varnhagen von Ense, Rahel
　　1771-1833 .... **NCLC 130**
　　See also DLB 90

Vasari, Giorgio 1511-1574 .... **LC 114**

Vasiliu, George
　　See Bacovia, George

Vasiliu, Gheorghe
　　See Bacovia, George
　　See also CA 123; 189

Vassa, Gustavus
　　See Equiano, Olaudah

Vassilikos, Vassilis 1933- .... **CLC 4, 8**
　　See also CA 81-84; CANR 75; EWL 3

Vaughan, Henry 1621-1695 .... **LC 27**
　　See also BRW 2; DLB 131; PAB; RGEL 2

Vaughn, Stephanie .... **CLC 62**

Vazov, Ivan (Minchov) 1850-1921 . **TCLC 25**
　　See also CA 121; 167; CDWLB 4; DLB
　　147

Veblen, Thorstein B(unde)
　　1857-1929 .... **TCLC 31**
　　See also AMWS 1; CA 115; 165; DLB 246;
　　MAL 5

Vega, Lope de 1562-1635 ... **HLCS 2; LC 23,
　　119**
　　See also EW 2; RGWL 2, 3

Vendler, Helen (Hennessy) 1933- ... **CLC 138**
　　See also CA 41-44R; CANR 25, 72, 136;
　　MTCW 1, 2; MTFW 2005

Venison, Alfred
　　See Pound, Ezra (Weston Loomis)

Ventsel, Elena Sergeevna 1907-2002
　　See Grekova, I.
　　See also CA 154

Verdi, Marie de
　　See Mencken, H(enry) L(ouis)

Verdu, Matilde
　　See Cela, Camilo Jose

Verga, Giovanni (Carmelo)
　　1840-1922 .... **SSC 21, 87; TCLC 3**
　　See also CA 104; 123; CANR 101; EW 7;
　　EWL 3; RGSF 2; RGWL 2, 3; WLIT 7

Vergil 70B.C.-19B.C. ... **CMLC 9, 40; PC 12;
　　WLCS**
　　See Virgil
　　See also AW 2; DA; DA3; DAB; DAC;
　　DAM MST, POET; EFS 1; LMFS 1

Vergil, Polydore c. 1470-1555 .... **LC 108**
　　See also DLB 132

Verhaeren, Emile (Adolphe Gustave)
　　1855-1916 .... **TCLC 12**
　　See also CA 109; EWL 3; GFL 1789 to the
　　Present

Verlaine, Paul (Marie) 1844-1896 .. **NCLC 2,
　　51; PC 2, 32**
　　See also DAM POET; DLB 217; EW 7;
　　GFL 1789 to the Present; LMFS 2; RGWL
　　2, 3; TWA

Verne, Jules (Gabriel) 1828-1905 ... **TCLC 6,
　　52**
　　See also AAYA 16; BYA 4; CA 110; 131;
　　CLR 88; DA3; DLB 123; GFL 1789 to
　　the Present; JRDA; LAIT 2; LMFS 2;
　　MAICYA 1, 2; MTFW 2005; RGWL 2, 3;
　　SATA 21; SCFW 1, 2; SFW 4; TWA;
　　WCH

Verus, Marcus Annius
　　See Aurelius, Marcus

Very, Jones 1813-1880 .... **NCLC 9**
　　See also DLB 1, 243; RGAL 4

Vesaas, Tarjei 1897-1970 .... **CLC 48**
　　See also CA 190; 29-32R; DLB 297; EW
　　11; EWL 3; RGWL 3

Vialis, Gaston
　　See Simenon, Georges (Jacques Christian)

3, 4, 5; CP 1, 2, 3, 4; DLB 15, 27, 139, 155; EWL 3; MTCW 1, 2; MTFW 2005

Wajda, Andrzej 1926- .... **CLC 16, 219**
See also CA 102

Wakefield, Dan 1932- .... **CLC 7**
See also CA 21-24R, 211; CAAE 211; CAAS 7; CN 4, 5, 6, 7

Wakefield, Herbert Russell
1888-1965 .... **TCLC 120**
See also CA 5-8R; CANR 77; HGG; SUFW

Wakoski, Diane 1937- ...... **CLC 2, 4, 7, 9, 11, 40; PC 15**
See also CA 13-16R, 216; CAAE 216; CAAS 1; CANR 9, 60, 106; CP 1, 2, 3, 4, 5, 6, 7; CWP; DAM POET; DLB 5; INT CANR-9; MAL 5; MTCW 2; MTFW 2005

Wakoski-Sherbell, Diane
See Wakoski, Diane

Walcott, Derek (Alton) 1930- ... **BLC 3; CLC 2, 4, 9, 14, 25, 42, 67, 76, 160; DC 7; PC 46**
See also BW 2; CA 89-92; CANR 26, 47, 75, 80, 130; CBD; CD 5, 6; CDWLB 3; CP 1, 2, 3, 4, 5, 6, 7; DA3; DAB; DAC; DAM MST, MULT, POET; DLB 117; DLBY 1981; DNFS 1; EFS 1; EWL 3; LMFS 2; MTCW 1, 2; MTFW 2005; PFS 6; RGEL 2; TWA; WWE 1

Waldman, Anne (Lesley) 1945- .... **CLC 7**
See also BG 1:3; CA 37-40R; CAAS 17; CANR 34, 69, 116; CP 1, 2, 3, 4, 5, 6, 7; CWP; DLB 16

Waldo, E. Hunter
See Sturgeon, Theodore (Hamilton)

Waldo, Edward Hamilton
See Sturgeon, Theodore (Hamilton)

Walker, Alice (Malsenior) 1944- .... **BLC 3; CLC 5, 6, 9, 19, 27, 46, 58, 103, 167; PC 30; SSC 5; WLCS**
See also AAYA 3, 33; AFAW 1, 2; AMWS 3; BEST 89:4; BPFB 3; BW 2, 3; CA 37-40R; CANR 9, 27, 49, 66, 82, 131; CDALB 1968-1988; CN 4, 5, 6, 7; CPW; CSW; DA; DA3; DAB; DAC; DAM MST, MULT, NOV, POET, POP; DLB 6, 33, 143; EWL 3; EXPN; EXPS; FL 1:6; FW; INT CANR-27; LAIT 3; MAL 5; MAWW; MTCW 1, 2; MTFW 2005; NFS 5; RGAL 4; RGSF 2; SATA 31; SSFS 2, 11; TUS; YAW

Walker, David Harry 1911-1992 ...... **CLC 14**
See also CA 1-4R; 137; CANR 1; CN 1, 2; CWRI 5; SATA 8; SATA-Obit 71

Walker, Edward Joseph 1934-2004
See Walker, Ted
See also CA 21-24R; 226; CANR 12, 28, 53

Walker, George F(rederick) 1947- .. **CLC 44, 61**
See also CA 103; CANR 21, 43, 59; CD 5, 6; DAB; DAC; DAM MST; DLB 60

Walker, Joseph A. 1935-2003 .... **CLC 19**
See also BW 1, 3; CA 89-92; CAD; CANR 26, 143; CD 5, 6; DAM DRAM, MST; DFS 12; DLB 38

Walker, Margaret (Abigail)
1915-1998 .... **BLC; CLC 1, 6; PC 20; TCLC 129**
See also AFAW 1, 2; BW 2, 3; CA 73-76; 172; CANR 26, 54, 76, 136; CN 1, 2, 3, 4, 5, 6; CP 1, 2, 3, 4; CSW; DAM MULT; DLB 76, 152; EXPP; FW; MAL 5; MTCW 1, 2; MTFW 2005; RGAL 4; RHW

Walker, Ted .... **CLC 13**
See Walker, Edward Joseph
See also CP 1, 2, 3, 4, 5, 6, 7; DLB 40

Wallace, David Foster 1962- ... **CLC 50, 114; SSC 68**
See also AAYA 50; AMWS 10; CA 132; CANR 59, 133; CN 7; DA3; MTCW 2; MTFW 2005

Wallace, Dexter
See Masters, Edgar Lee

Wallace, (Richard Horatio) Edgar
1875-1932 .... **TCLC 57**
See also CA 115; 218; CMW 4; DLB 70; MSW; RGEL 2

Wallace, Irving 1916-1990 .... **CLC 7, 13**
See also AITN 1; BPFB 3; CA 1-4R; 132; CAAS 1; CANR 1, 27; CPW; DAM NOV, POP; INT CANR-27; MTCW 1, 2

Wallant, Edward Lewis 1926-1962 ... **CLC 5, 10**
See also CA 1-4R; CANR 22; DLB 2, 28, 143, 299; EWL 3; MAL 5; MTCW 1, 2; RGAL 4

Wallas, Graham 1858-1932 .... **TCLC 91**

Waller, Edmund 1606-1687 .... **LC 86**
See also BRW 2; DAM POET; DLB 126; PAB; RGEL 2

Walley, Byron
See Card, Orson Scott

Walpole, Horace 1717-1797 .... **LC 2, 49**
See also BRW 3; DLB 39, 104, 213; GL 3; HGG; LMFS 1; RGEL 2; SUFW 1; TEA

Walpole, Hugh (Seymour)
1884-1941 .... **TCLC 5**
See also CA 104; 165; DLB 34; HGG; MTCW 2; RGEL 2; RHW

Walrond, Eric (Derwent) 1898-1966 . **HR 1:3**
See also BW 1; CA 125; DLB 51

Walser, Martin 1927- .... **CLC 27, 183**
See also CA 57-60; CANR 8, 46, 145; CWW 2; DLB 75, 124; EWL 3

Walser, Robert 1878-1956 ..... **SSC 20; TCLC 18**
See also CA 118; 165; CANR 100; DLB 66; EWL 3

Walsh, Gillian Paton
See Paton Walsh, Gillian

Walsh, Jill Paton .... **CLC 35**
See Paton Walsh, Gillian
See also CLR 2, 65; WYA

Walter, Villiam Christian
See Andersen, Hans Christian

Walters, Anna L(ee) 1946- .... **NNAL**
See also CA 73-76

Walther von der Vogelweide c.
1170-1228 .... **CMLC 56**

Walton, Izaak 1593-1683 .... **LC 72**
See also BRW 2; CDBLB Before 1660; DLB 151, 213; RGEL 2

Wambaugh, Joseph (Aloysius), Jr.
1937- .... **CLC 3, 18**
See also AITN 1; BEST 89:3; BPFB 3; CA 33-36R; CANR 42, 65, 115; CMW 4; CPW 1; DA3; DAM NOV, POP; DLB 6; DLBY 1983; MSW; MTCW 1, 2

Wang Wei 699(?)-761(?) .... **PC 18**
See also TWA

Warburton, William 1698-1779 .... **LC 97**
See also DLB 104

Ward, Arthur Henry Sarsfield 1883-1959
See Rohmer, Sax
See also CA 108; 173; CMW 4; HGG

Ward, Douglas Turner 1930- .... **CLC 19**
See also BW 1; CA 81-84; CAD; CANR 27; CD 5, 6; DLB 7, 38

Ward, E. D.
See Lucas, E(dward) V(errall)

Ward, Mrs. Humphry 1851-1920
See Ward, Mary Augusta
See also RGEL 2

Ward, Mary Augusta 1851-1920 ... **TCLC 55**
See Ward, Mrs. Humphry
See also DLB 18

Ward, Nathaniel 1578(?)-1652 .... **LC 114**
See also DLB 24

Ward, Peter
See Faust, Frederick (Schiller)

Warhol, Andy 1928(?)-1987 .... **CLC 20**
See also AAYA 12; BEST 89:4; CA 89-92; 121; CANR 34

Warner, Francis (Robert le Plastrier)
1937- .... **CLC 14**
See also CA 53-56; CANR 11; CP 1, 2, 3, 4

Warner, Marina 1946- .... **CLC 59**
See also CA 65-68; CANR 21, 55, 118; CN 5, 6, 7; DLB 194; MTFW 2005

Warner, Rex (Ernest) 1905-1986 ...... **CLC 45**
See also CA 89-92; 119; CN 1, 2, 3, 4; CP 1, 2, 3, 4; DLB 15; RGEL 2; RHW

Warner, Susan (Bogert)
1819-1885 .... **NCLC 31, 146**
See also DLB 3, 42, 239, 250, 254

Warner, Sylvia (Constance) Ashton
See Ashton-Warner, Sylvia (Constance)

Warner, Sylvia Townsend
1893-1978 .. **CLC 7, 19; SSC 23; TCLC 131**
See also BRWS 7; CA 61-64; 77-80; CANR 16, 60, 104; CN 1, 2; DLB 34, 139; EWL 3; FANT; FW; MTCW 1, 2; RGEL 2; RGSF 2; RHW

Warren, Mercy Otis 1728-1814 ..... **NCLC 13**
See also DLB 31, 200; RGAL 4; TUS

Warren, Robert Penn 1905-1989 .. **CLC 1, 4, 6, 8, 10, 13, 18, 39, 53, 59; PC 37; SSC 4, 58; WLC**
See also AITN 1; AMW; AMWC 2; BPFB 3; BYA 1; CA 13-16R; 129; CANR 10, 47; CDALB 1968-1988; CN 1, 2, 3, 4; CP 1, 2, 3, 4; DA; DA3; DAB; DAC; DAM MST, NOV, POET; DLB 2, 48, 152, 320; DLBY 1980, 1989; EWL 3; INT CANR-10; MAL 5; MTCW 1, 2; MTFW 2005; NFS 13; RGAL 4; RGSF 2; RHW; SATA 46; SATA-Obit 63; SSFS 8; TUS

Warrigal, Jack
See Furphy, Joseph

Warshofsky, Isaac
See Singer, Isaac Bashevis

Warton, Joseph 1722-1800 .... **NCLC 118**
See also DLB 104, 109; RGEL 2

Warton, Thomas 1728-1790 .... **LC 15, 82**
See also DAM POET; DLB 104, 109; RGEL 2

Waruk, Kona
See Harris, (Theodore) Wilson

Warung, Price .... **TCLC 45**
See Astley, William
See also DLB 230; RGEL 2

Warwick, Jarvis
See Garner, Hugh
See also CCA 1

Washington, Alex
See Harris, Mark

Washington, Booker T(aliaferro)
1856-1915 .... **BLC 3; TCLC 10**
See also BW 1; CA 114; 125; DA3; DAM MULT; LAIT 2; RGAL 4; SATA 28

Washington, George 1732-1799 .... **LC 25**
See also DLB 31

Wassermann, (Karl) Jakob
1873-1934 .... **TCLC 6**
See also CA 104; 163; DLB 66; EWL 3

Wasserstein, Wendy 1950-2006 . **CLC 32, 59, 90, 183; DC 4**
See also AMWS 15; CA 121; 129; CABS 3; CAD; CANR 53, 75, 128; CD 5, 6; CWD; DA3; DAM DRAM; DFS 5, 17;

West, C. P.
See Wodehouse, P(elham) G(renville)

West, Cornel (Ronald) 1953- .... **BLCS; CLC 134**
See also CA 144; CANR 91; DLB 246

West, Delno C(loyde), Jr. 1936- .... **CLC 70**
See also CA 57-60

West, Dorothy 1907-1998 ...... **HR 1:3; TCLC 108**
See also BW 2; CA 143; 169; DLB 76

West, (Mary) Jessamyn 1902-1984 ... **CLC 7, 17**
See also CA 9-12R; 112; CANR 27; CN 1, 2, 3; DLB 6; DLBY 1984; MTCW 1, 2; RGAL 4; RHW; SATA-Obit 37; TCWW 2; TUS; YAW

West, Morris L(anglo) 1916-1999 ..... **CLC 6, 33**
See also BPFB 3; CA 5-8R; 187; CANR 24, 49, 64; CN 1, 2, 3, 4, 5, 6; CPW; DLB 289; MTCW 1, 2; MTFW 2005

West, Nathanael 1903-1940 .. **SSC 16; TCLC 1, 14, 44**
See also AMW; AMWR 2; BPFB 3; CA 104; 125; CDALB 1929-1941; DA3; DLB 4, 9, 28; EWL 3; MAL 5; MTCW 1, 2; MTFW 2005; NFS 16; RGAL 4; TUS

West, Owen
See Koontz, Dean R.

West, Paul 1930- .... **CLC 7, 14, 96**
See also CA 13-16R; CAAS 7; CANR 22, 53, 76, 89, 136; CN 1, 2, 3, 4, 5, 6, 7; DLB 14; INT CANR-22; MTCW 2; MTFW 2005

West, Rebecca 1892-1983 ... **CLC 7, 9, 31, 50**
See also BPFB 3; BRWS 3; CA 5-8R; 109; CANR 19; CN 1, 2, 3; DLB 36; DLBY 1983; EWL 3; FW; MTCW 1, 2; MTFW 2005; NCFS 4; RGEL 2; TEA

Westall, Robert (Atkinson) 1929-1993 .... **CLC 17**
See also AAYA 12; BYA 2, 6, 7, 8, 9, 15; CA 69-72; 141; CANR 18, 68; CLR 13; FANT; JRDA; MAICYA 1, 2; MAICYAS 1; SAAS 2; SATA 23, 69; SATA-Obit 75; WYA; YAW

Westermarck, Edward 1862-1939 . **TCLC 87**

Westlake, Donald E(dwin) 1933- . **CLC 7, 33**
See also BPFB 3; CA 17-20R; CAAS 13; CANR 16, 44, 65, 94, 137; CMW 4; CPW; DAM POP; INT CANR-16; MSW; MTCW 2; MTFW 2005

Westmacott, Mary
See Christie, Agatha (Mary Clarissa)

Weston, Allen
See Norton, Andre

Wetcheek, J. L.
See Feuchtwanger, Lion

Wetering, Janwillem van de
See van de Wetering, Janwillem

Wetherald, Agnes Ethelwyn 1857-1940 .... **TCLC 81**
See also CA 202; DLB 99

Wetherell, Elizabeth
See Warner, Susan (Bogert)

Whale, James 1889-1957 .... **TCLC 63**

Whalen, Philip (Glenn) 1923-2002 .... **CLC 6, 29**
See also BG 1:3; CA 9-12R; 209; CANR 5, 39; CP 1, 2, 3, 4, 5, 6, 7; DLB 16; WP

Wharton, Edith (Newbold Jones) 1862-1937 ... **SSC 6, 84; TCLC 3, 9, 27, 53, 129, 149; WLC**
See also AAYA 25; AMW; AMWC 2; AMWR 1; BPFB 3; CA 104; 132; CDALB 1865-1917; DA; DA3; DAB; DAC; DAM MST, NOV; DLB 4, 9, 12, 78, 189; DLBD 13; EWL 3; EXPS; FL 1:6; GL 3; HGG; LAIT 2, 3; LATS 1:1; MAL 5; MAWW;

MTCW 1, 2; MTFW 2005; NFS 5, 11, 15, 20; RGAL 4; RGSF 2; RHW; SSFS 6, 7; SUFW; TUS

Wharton, James
See Mencken, H(enry) L(ouis)

Wharton, William (a pseudonym) 1925- .... **CLC 18, 37**
See also CA 93-96; CN 4, 5, 6, 7; DLBY 1980; INT CA-93-96

Wheatley (Peters), Phillis 1753(?)-1784 .. **BLC 3; LC 3, 50; PC 3; WLC**
See also AFAW 1, 2; CDALB 1640-1865; DA; DA3; DAC; DAM MST, MULT, POET; DLB 31, 50; EXPP; FL 1:1; PFS 13; RGAL 4

Wheelock, John Hall 1886-1978 .... **CLC 14**
See also CA 13-16R; 77-80; CANR 14; CP 1, 2; DLB 45; MAL 5

Whim-Wham
See Curnow, (Thomas) Allen (Monro)

White, Babington
See Braddon, Mary Elizabeth

White, E(lwyn) B(rooks) 1899-1985 .... **CLC 10, 34, 39**
See also AAYA 62; AITN 2; AMWS 1; CA 13-16R; 116; CANR 16, 37; CDALBS; CLR 1, 21; CPW; DA3; DAM POP; DLB 11, 22; EWL 3; FANT; MAICYA 1, 2; MAL 5; MTCW 1, 2; MTFW 2005; NCFS 5; RGAL 4; SATA 2, 29, 100; SATA-Obit 44; TUS

White, Edmund (Valentine III) 1940- .... **CLC 27, 110**
See also CA 45-48; CANR 3, 19, 36, 62, 107, 133; CN 5, 6, 7; DA3; DAM POP; DLB 227; MTCW 1, 2; MTFW 2005

White, Hayden V. 1928- .... **CLC 148**
See also CA 128; CANR 135; DLB 246

White, Patrick (Victor Martindale) 1912-1990 ...... **CLC 3, 4, 5, 7, 9, 18, 65, 69; SSC 39, TCLC 176**
See also BRWS 1; CA 81-84; 132; CANR 43; CN 1, 2, 3, 4; DLB 260; EWL 3; MTCW 1; RGEL 2; RGSF 2; RHW; TWA; WWE 1

White, Phyllis Dorothy James 1920-
See James, P. D.
See also CA 21-24R; CANR 17, 43, 65, 112; CMW 4; CN 7; CPW; DA3; DAM POP; MTCW 1, 2; MTFW 2005; TEA

White, T(erence) H(anbury) 1906-1964 .... **CLC 30**
See also AAYA 22; BPFB 3; BYA 4, 5; CA 73-76; CANR 37; DLB 160; FANT; JRDA; LAIT 1; MAICYA 1, 2; RGEL 2; SATA 12; SUFW 1; YAW

White, Terence de Vere 1912-1994 ... **CLC 49**
See also CA 49-52; 145; CANR 3

White, Walter
See White, Walter F(rancis)

White, Walter F(rancis) 1893-1955 ... **BLC 3; HR 1:3; TCLC 15**
See also BW 1; CA 115; 124; DAM MULT; DLB 51

White, William Hale 1831-1913
See Rutherford, Mark
See also CA 121; 189

Whitehead, Alfred North 1861-1947 .... **TCLC 97**
See also CA 117; 165; DLB 100, 262

Whitehead, E(dward) A(nthony) 1933- .... **CLC 5**
See Whitehead, Ted
See also CA 65-68; CANR 58, 118; CBD; CD 5; DLB 310

Whitehead, Ted
See Whitehead, E(dward) A(nthony)
See also CD 6

Whiteman, Roberta J. Hill 1947- ...... **NNAL**
See also CA 146

Whitemore, Hugh (John) 1936- .... **CLC 37**
See also CA 132; CANR 77; CBD; CD 5, 6; INT CA-132

Whitman, Sarah Helen (Power) 1803-1878 .... **NCLC 19**
See also DLB 1, 243

Whitman, Walt(er) 1819-1892 .. **NCLC 4, 31, 81; PC 3; WLC**
See also AAYA 42; AMW; AMWR 1; CDALB 1640-1865; DA; DA3; DAB; DAC; DAM MST, POET; DLB 3, 64, 224, 250; EXPP; LAIT 2; LMFS 1; PAB; PFS 2, 3, 13, 22; RGAL 4; SATA 20; TUS; WP; WYAS 1

Whitney, Phyllis A(yame) 1903- .... **CLC 42**
See also AAYA 36; AITN 2; BEST 90:3; CA 1-4R; CANR 3, 25, 38, 60; CLR 59; CMW 4; CPW; DA3; DAM POP; JRDA; MAICYA 1, 2; MTCW 2; RHW; SATA 1, 30; YAW

Whittemore, (Edward) Reed, Jr. 1919- .... **CLC 4**
See also CA 9-12R; 219; CAAE 219; CAAS 8; CANR 4, 119; CP 1, 2, 3, 4, 5, 6, 7; DLB 5; MAL 5

Whittier, John Greenleaf 1807-1892 .... **NCLC 8, 59**
See also AMWS 1; DLB 1, 243; RGAL 4

Whittlebot, Hernia
See Coward, Noel (Peirce)

Wicker, Thomas Grey 1926-
See Wicker, Tom
See also CA 65-68; CANR 21, 46, 141

Wicker, Tom .... **CLC 7**
See Wicker, Thomas Grey

Wideman, John Edgar 1941- ... **BLC 3; CLC 5, 34, 36, 67, 122; SSC 62**
See also AFAW 1, 2; AMWS 10; BPFB 4; BW 2, 3; CA 85-88; CANR 14, 42, 67, 109, 140; CN 4, 5, 6, 7; DAM MULT; DLB 33, 143; MAL 5; MTCW 2; MTFW 2005; RGAL 4; RGSF 2; SSFS 6, 12; TCLE 1:2

Wiebe, Rudy (Henry) 1934- .. **CLC 6, 11, 14, 138**
See also CA 37-40R; CANR 42, 67, 123; CN 1, 2, 3, 4, 5, 6, 7; DAC; DAM MST; DLB 60; RHW; SATA 156

Wieland, Christoph Martin 1733-1813 .... **NCLC 17**
See also DLB 97; EW 4; LMFS 1; RGWL 2, 3

Wiene, Robert 1881-1938 .... **TCLC 56**

Wieners, John 1934- .... **CLC 7**
See also BG 1:3; CA 13-16R; CP 1, 2, 3, 4, 5, 6, 7; DLB 16; WP

Wiesel, Elie(zer) 1928- .... **CLC 3, 5, 11, 37, 165; WLCS**
See also AAYA 7, 54; AITN 1; CA 5-8R; CAAS 4; CANR 8, 40, 65, 125; CDALBS; CWW 2; DA; DA3; DAB; DAC; DAM MST, NOV; DLB 83, 299; DLBY 1987; EWL 3; INT CANR-8; LAIT 4; MTCW 1, 2; MTFW 2005; NCFS 4; NFS 4; RGWL 3; SATA 56; YAW

Wiggins, Marianne 1947- .... **CLC 57**
See also BEST 89:3; CA 130; CANR 60, 139; CN 7

Wigglesworth, Michael 1631-1705 .... **LC 106**
See also DLB 24; RGAL 4

Wiggs, Susan .... **CLC 70**
See also CA 201

Wight, James Alfred 1916-1995
See Herriot, James
See also CA 77-80; SATA 55; SATA-Brief 44

Wilson, Sloan 1920-2003 .... **CLC 32**
See also CA 1-4R; 216; CANR 1, 44; CN 1, 2, 3, 4, 5, 6

Wilson, Snoo 1948- .... **CLC 33**
See also CA 69-72; CBD; CD 5, 6

Wilson, William S(mith) 1932- .... **CLC 49**
See also CA 81-84

Wilson, (Thomas) Woodrow
1856-1924 .... **TCLC 79**
See also CA 166; DLB 47

Wilson and Warnke eds. .... **CLC 65**

Winchilsea, Anne (Kingsmill) Finch
1661-1720
See Finch, Anne
See also RGEL 2

Windham, Basil
See Wodehouse, P(elham) G(renville)

Wingrove, David (John) 1954- .... **CLC 68**
See also CA 133; SFW 4

Winnemucca, Sarah 1844-1891 .... **NCLC 79; NNAL**
See also DAM MULT; DLB 175; RGAL 4

Winstanley, Gerrard 1609-1676 .... **LC 52**

Wintergreen, Jane
See Duncan, Sara Jeannette

Winters, Arthur Yvor
See Winters, Yvor

Winters, Janet Lewis .... **CLC 41**
See Lewis, Janet
See also DLBY 1987

Winters, Yvor 1900-1968 .... **CLC 4, 8, 32**
See also AMWS 2; CA 11-12; 25-28R; CAP 1; DLB 48; EWL 3; MAL 5; MTCW 1; RGAL 4

Winterson, Jeanette 1959- .... **CLC 64, 158**
See also BRWS 4; CA 136; CANR 58, 116; CN 5, 6, 7; CPW; DA3; DAM POP; DLB 207, 261; FANT; FW; GLL 1; MTCW 2; MTFW 2005; RHW

Winthrop, John 1588-1649 .... **LC 31, 107**
See also DLB 24, 30

Wirth, Louis 1897-1952 .... **TCLC 92**
See also CA 210

Wiseman, Frederick 1930- .... **CLC 20**
See also CA 159

Wister, Owen 1860-1938 .... **TCLC 21**
See also BPFB 3; CA 108; 162; DLB 9, 78, 186; RGAL 4; SATA 62; TCWW 1, 2

Wither, George 1588-1667 .... **LC 96**
See also DLB 121; RGEL 2

Witkacy
See Witkiewicz, Stanislaw Ignacy

Witkiewicz, Stanislaw Ignacy
1885-1939 .... **TCLC 8**
See also CA 105; 162; CDWLB 4; DLB 215; EW 10; EWL 3; RGWL 2, 3; SFW 4

Wittgenstein, Ludwig (Josef Johann)
1889-1951 .... **TCLC 59**
See also CA 113; 164; DLB 262; MTCW 2

Wittig, Monique 1935-2003 .... **CLC 22**
See also CA 116; 135; 212; CANR 143; CWW 2; DLB 83; EWL 3; FW; GLL 1

Wittlin, Jozef 1896-1976 .... **CLC 25**
See also CA 49-52; 65-68; CANR 3; EWL 3

Wodehouse, P(elham) G(renville)
1881-1975 . **CLC 1, 2, 5, 10, 22; SSC 2; TCLC 108**
See also AAYA 65; AITN 2; BRWS 3; CA 45-48; 57-60; CANR 3, 33; CDBLB 1914-1945; CN 1, 2; CPW 1; DA3; DAB; DAC; DAM NOV; DLB 34, 162; EWL 3; MTCW 1, 2; MTFW 2005; RGEL 2; RGSF 2; SATA 22; SSFS 10

Woiwode, L.
See Woiwode, Larry (Alfred)

Woiwode, Larry (Alfred) 1941- ... **CLC 6, 10**
See also CA 73-76; CANR 16, 94; CN 3, 4, 5, 6, 7; DLB 6; INT CANR-16

Wojciechowska, Maia (Teresa)
1927-2002 .... **CLC 26**
See also AAYA 8, 46; BYA 3; CA 9-12R; 183; 209; CAAE 183; CANR 4, 41; CLR 1; JRDA; MAICYA 1, 2; SAAS 1; SATA 1, 28, 83; SATA-Essay 104; SATA-Obit 134; YAW

Wojtyla, Karol (Jozef)
See John Paul II, Pope

Wojtyla, Karol (Josef)
See John Paul II, Pope

Wolf, Christa 1929- .... **CLC 14, 29, 58, 150**
See also CA 85-88; CANR 45, 123; CD-WLB 2; CWW 2; DLB 75; EWL 3; FW; MTCW 1; RGWL 2, 3; SSFS 14

Wolf, Naomi 1962- .... **CLC 157**
See also CA 141; CANR 110; FW; MTFW 2005

Wolfe, Gene 1931- .... **CLC 25**
See also AAYA 35; CA 57-60; CAAS 9; CANR 6, 32, 60; CPW; DAM POP; DLB 8; FANT; MTCW 2; MTFW 2005; SATA 118, 165; SCFW 2; SFW 4; SUFW 2

Wolfe, Gene Rodman
See Wolfe, Gene

Wolfe, George C. 1954- .... **BLCS; CLC 49**
See also CA 149; CAD; CD 5, 6

Wolfe, Thomas (Clayton)
1900-1938 ...... **SSC 33; TCLC 4, 13, 29, 61; WLC**
See also AMW; BPFB 3; CA 104; 132; CANR 102; CDALB 1929-1941; DA; DA3; DAB; DAC; DAM MST, NOV; DLB 9, 102, 229; DLBD 2, 16; DLBY 1985, 1997; EWL 3; MAL 5; MTCW 1, 2; NFS 18; RGAL 4; SSFS 18; TUS

Wolfe, Thomas Kennerly, Jr.
1931- .... **CLC 147**
See Wolfe, Tom
See also CA 13-16R; CANR 9, 33, 70, 104; DA3; DAM POP; DLB 185; EWL 3; INT CANR-9; MTCW 1, 2; MTFW 2005; TUS

Wolfe, Tom .... **CLC 1, 2, 9, 15, 35, 51**
See Wolfe, Thomas Kennerly, Jr.
See also AAYA 8, 67; AITN 2; AMWS 3; BEST 89:1; BPFB 3; CN 5, 6, 7; CPW; CSW; DLB 152; LAIT 5; RGAL 4

Wolff, Geoffrey (Ansell) 1937- .... **CLC 41**
See also CA 29-32R; CANR 29, 43, 78

Wolff, Sonia
See Levitin, Sonia (Wolff)

Wolff, Tobias (Jonathan Ansell)
1945- .... **CLC 39, 64, 172; SSC 63**
See also AAYA 16; AMWS 7; BEST 90:2; BYA 12; CA 114; 117; CAAS 22; CANR 54, 76, 96; CN 5, 6, 7; CSW; DA3; DLB 130; EWL 3; INT CA-117; MTCW 2; MTFW 2005; RGAL 4; RGSF 2; SSFS 4, 11

Wolfram von Eschenbach c. 1170-c.
1220 .... **CMLC 5**
See Eschenbach, Wolfram von
See also CDWLB 2; DLB 138; EW 1; RGWL 2

Wolitzer, Hilma 1930- .... **CLC 17**
See also CA 65-68; CANR 18, 40; INT CANR-18; SATA 31; YAW

Wollstonecraft, Mary 1759-1797 .... **LC 5, 50, 90**
See also BRWS 3; CDBLB 1789-1832; DLB 39, 104, 158, 252; FL 1:1; FW; LAIT 1; RGEL 2; TEA; WLIT 3

Wonder, Stevie .... **CLC 12**
See Morris, Steveland Judkins

Wong, Jade Snow 1922- .... **CLC 17**
See also CA 109; CANR 91; SATA 112

Woodberry, George Edward
1855-1930 .... **TCLC 73**
See also CA 165; DLB 71, 103

Woodcott, Keith
See Brunner, John (Kilian Houston)

Woodruff, Robert W.
See Mencken, H(enry) L(ouis)

Woolf, (Adeline) Virginia 1882-1941 .. **SSC 7, 79; TCLC 1, 5, 20, 43, 56, 101, 123, 128; WLC**
See also AAYA 44; BPFB 3; BRW 7; BRWC 2; BRWR 1; CA 104; 130; CANR 64, 132; CDBLB 1914-1945; DA; DA3; DAB; DAC; DAM MST, NOV; DLB 36, 100, 162; DLBD 10; EWL 3; EXPS; FL 1:6; FW; LAIT 3; LATS 1:1; LMFS 2; MTCW 1, 2; MTFW 2005; NCFS 2; NFS 8, 12; RGEL 2; RGSF 2; SSFS 4, 12; TEA; WLIT 4

Woollcott, Alexander (Humphreys)
1887-1943 .... **TCLC 5**
See also CA 105; 161; DLB 29

Woolrich, Cornell .... **CLC 77**
See Hopley-Woolrich, Cornell George
See also MSW

Woolson, Constance Fenimore
1840-1894 .... **NCLC 82; SSC 90**
See also DLB 12, 74, 189, 221; RGAL 4

Wordsworth, Dorothy 1771-1855 . **NCLC 25, 138**
See also DLB 107

Wordsworth, William 1770-1850 .. **NCLC 12, 38, 111; PC 4, 67; WLC**
See also BRW 4; BRWC 1; CDBLB 1789-1832; DA; DA3; DAB; DAC; DAM MST, POET; DLB 93, 107; EXPP; LATS 1:1; LMFS 1; PAB; PFS 2; RGEL 2; TEA; WLIT 3; WP

Wotton, Sir Henry 1568-1639 .... **LC 68**
See also DLB 121; RGEL 2

Wouk, Herman 1915- .... **CLC 1, 9, 38**
See also BPFB 2, 3; CA 5-8R; CANR 6, 33, 67, 146; CDALBS; CN 1, 2, 3, 4, 5, 6; CPW; DA3; DAM NOV, POP; DLBY 1982; INT CANR-6; LAIT 4; MAL 5; MTCW 1, 2; MTFW 2005; NFS 7; TUS

Wright, Charles (Penzel, Jr.) 1935- .. **CLC 6, 13, 28, 119, 146**
See also AMWS 5; CA 29-32R; CAAS 7; CANR 23, 36, 62, 88, 135; CP 3, 4, 5, 6, 7; DLB 165; DLBY 1982; EWL 3; MTCW 1, 2; MTFW 2005; PFS 10

Wright, Charles Stevenson 1932- ..... **BLC 3; CLC 49**
See also BW 1; CA 9-12R; CANR 26; CN 1, 2, 3, 4, 5, 6, 7; DAM MULT, POET; DLB 33

Wright, Frances 1795-1852 .... **NCLC 74**
See also DLB 73

Wright, Frank Lloyd 1867-1959 .... **TCLC 95**
See also AAYA 33; CA 174

Wright, Jack R.
See Harris, Mark

Wright, James (Arlington)
1927-1980 .... **CLC 3, 5, 10, 28; PC 36**
See also AITN 2; AMWS 3; CA 49-52; 97-100; CANR 4, 34, 64; CDALBS; CP 1, 2; DAM POET; DLB 5, 169; EWL 3; EXPP; MAL 5; MTCW 1, 2; MTFW 2005; PFS 7, 8; RGAL 4; TUS; WP

Wright, Judith (Arundell)
1915-2000 .... **CLC 11, 53; PC 14**
See also CA 13-16R; 188; CANR 31, 76, 93; CP 1, 2, 3, 4, 5, 6, 7; CWP; DLB 260; EWL 3; MTCW 1, 2; MTFW 2005; PFS 8; RGEL 2; SATA 14; SATA-Obit 121

Wright, L(aurali) R. 1939- .... **CLC 44**
See also CA 138; CMW 4

Wright, Richard (Nathaniel)
1908-1960 ... **BLC 3; CLC 1, 3, 4, 9, 14, 21, 48, 74; SSC 2; TCLC 136; WLC**
See also AAYA 5, 42; AFAW 1, 2; AMW; BPFB 3; BW 1; BYA 2; CA 108; CANR

Zelazny, Roger (Joseph) 1937-1995 . **CLC 21**
See also AAYA 7, 68; BPFB 3; CA 21-24R;
148; CANR 26, 60; CN 6; DLB 8; FANT;
MTCW 1, 2; MTFW 2005; SATA 57;
SATA-Brief 39; SCFW 1, 2; SFW 4;
SUFW 1, 2

Zhang Ailing
See Chang, Eileen
See also CWW 2; RGSF 2

Zhdanov, Andrei Alexandrovich
1896-1948 .... **TCLC 18**
See also CA 117; 167

Zhukovsky, Vasilii Andreevich
See Zhukovsky, Vasily (Andreevich)
See also DLB 205

Zhukovsky, Vasily (Andreevich)
1783-1852 .... **NCLC 35**
See also Zhukovsky, Vasilii Andreevich

Ziegenhagen, Eric .... **CLC 55**

Zimmer, Jill Schary
See Robinson, Jill

Zimmerman, Robert
See Dylan, Bob

Zindel, Paul 1936-2003 ...... **CLC 6, 26; DC 5**
See also AAYA 2, 37; BYA 2, 3, 8, 11, 14;
CA 73-76; 213; CAD; CANR 31, 65, 108;
CD 5, 6; CDALBS; CLR 3, 45, 85; DA;

DA3; DAB; DAC; DAM DRAM, MST,
NOV; DFS 12; DLB 7, 52; JRDA; LAIT
5; MAICYA 1, 2; MTCW 1, 2; MTFW
2005; NFS 14; SATA 16, 58, 102; SATA-
Obit 142; WYA; YAW

Zinn, Howard 1922- .... **CLC 199**
See also CA 1-4R; CANR 2, 33, 90

Zinov'Ev, A. A.
See Zinoviev, Alexander (Aleksandrovich)

Zinov'ev, Aleksandr (Aleksandrovich)
See Zinoviev, Alexander (Aleksandrovich)
See also DLB 302

Zinoviev, Alexander (Aleksandrovich)
1922- .... **CLC 19**
See Zinov'ev, Aleksandr (Aleksandrovich)
See also CA 116; 133; CAAS 10

Zizek, Slavoj 1949- .... **CLC 188**
See also CA 201; MTFW 2005

Zoilus
See Lovecraft, H(oward) P(hillips)

Zola, Emile (Edouard Charles Antoine)
1840-1902 ...... **TCLC 1, 6, 21, 41; WLC**
See also CA 104; 138; DA; DA3; DAB;
DAC; DAM MST, NOV; DLB 123; EW
7; GFL 1789 to the Present; IDTP; LMFS
1, 2; RGWL 2; TWA

Zoline, Pamela 1941- .... **CLC 62**
See also CA 161; SFW 4

Zoroaster 628(?)B.C.-551(?)B.C. ... **CMLC 40**

Zorrilla y Moral, Jose 1817-1893 .... **NCLC 6**

Zoshchenko, Mikhail (Mikhailovich)
1895-1958 .... **SSC 15; TCLC 15**
See also CA 115; 160; EWL 3; RGSF 2;
RGWL 3

Zuckmayer, Carl 1896-1977 .... **CLC 18**
See also CA 69-72; DLB 56, 124; EWL 3;
RGWL 2, 3

Zuk, Georges
See Skelton, Robin
See also CCA 1

Zukofsky, Louis 1904-1978 ... **CLC 1, 2, 4, 7,
11, 18; PC 11**
See also AMWS 3; CA 9-12R; 77-80;
CANR 39; CP 1, 2; DAM POET; DLB 5,
165; EWL 3; MAL 5; MTCW 1; RGAL 4

Zweig, Paul 1935-1984 .... **CLC 34, 42**
See also CA 85-88; 113

Zweig, Stefan 1881-1942 .... **TCLC 17**
See also CA 112; 170; DLB 81, 118; EWL
3

Zwingli, Huldreich 1484-1531 .... **LC 37**
See also DLB 179

Literary Criticism Series
Cumulative Topic Index

This index lists all topic entries in Thompson Gale's *Children's Literature Review* (CLR), *Classical and Medieval Literature Criticism* (CMLC), *Contemporary Literary Criticism* (CLC), *Drama Criticism* (DC), *Literature Criticism from 1400 to 1800* (LC), *Nineteenth-Century Literature Criticism* (NCLC), *Short Story Criticism* (SSC), and *Twentieth-Century Literary Criticism* (TCLC). The index also lists topic entries in the Gale Critical Companion Collection, which includes the following publications: *The Beat Generation* (BG), *Feminism in Literature* (FL), *Gothic Literature* (GL), and *Harlem Renaissance* (HR).

CLC Cumulative Nationality Index

Nationality Index

Nationality Index

CLC-221 Title Index

ISBN 0-7876-7991-7

9 780787 679910

90000